THE NEW INTERNATIONAL
GREEK TESTAMENT COMMENTARY

Editors
I. Howard Marshall
and
W. Ward Gasque

THE GOSPEL OF LUKE

The New International Greek Testament Commentary

THE GOSPEL OF
LUKE

A Commentary on the Greek Text

by

I. HOWARD MARSHALL

Reader in New Testament Exegesis
University of Aberdeen

EXETER
THE PATERNOSTER PRESS
1978

ISBN:
Casebound: 0 85364 195 1
Study Edition: 0 85364 203 6

Copyright © 1978 The Paternoster Press Ltd

Second Impression, January 1979

AUSTRALIA:
*Emu Book Agencies Pty., Ltd.,
63, Berry St., Granville, 2142, N.S.W.*

SOUTH AFRICA:
*Oxford University Press,
P.O. Box 1141, Cape Town*

*Typeset by Input Typesetting Ltd
and Printed in Great Britain for The Paternoster Press,
Paternoster House, 3 Mount Radford Crescent, Exeter, Devon
by Redwood Burn Limited, Trowbridge & Esher*

Almighty God, who calledst Luke the Physician,
whose praise is in the Gospel,
to be an Evangelist, and Physician of the soul;
May it please thee, that,
by the wholesome medicines of the doctrine delivered by him,
all the diseases of our souls may be healed;
through the merits of thy Son
Jesus Christ our Lord.
Amen.

(Collect for St. Luke's Day)

CONTENTS

FOREWORD

The present volume is intended to be the first of a series of commentaries which will be published jointly by The Paternoster Press, Exeter, England, and Wm. B. Eerdmans Publishing Company, Grand Rapids, USA, under the title of *The New International Greek Testament Commentary*.

While there have been many series of commentaries on the English text of the New Testament in recent years, it is a long time since any attempt has been made to cater particularly for the needs of students of the Greek text. It is true that at the present time there is something of a decline in the study of Greek in many traditional theological institutions, but there has been a welcome growth in study of the New Testament in its original language in the newer evangelical schools, especially in North America and the Third World. It is hoped that this series will demonstrate the value of studying the Greek New Testament and help towards the revival of such study.

The purpose of the series is to cater for the needs of students who want something less technical than a full-scale critical commentary. At the same time, the commentaries are intended to interact with modern scholarship and to make their own scholarly contribution to the study of the New Testament. There has been a wealth of detailed study of the New Testament in articles and monographs in recent years, and the series is meant to harvest the results of this research in a more easily accessible form. The commentaries will thus include adequate, but not exhaustive, bibliographies. They will attempt to treat all important problems of history and exegesis and interpretation which may arise.

One of the gains of recent scholarship has been the recognition of the primarily theological character of the books of the New Testament. This series will, therefore, attempt to provide a theological understanding of the text, based on historical-critical-linguistic exegesis. It will not, however, attempt to apply and expound the text for modern readers, although it is hoped that the exegesis will give some indication of the way in which the text should be expounded.

Within the limits set by the use of the English language, the series aims to be international in character; the contributors, however, have been chosen not primarily in order to achieve a spread between different countries but above all because of their specialized qualifications for their particular tasks.

The supreme aim of this series is to serve those who are engaged in the ministry of the Word of God and thus to glorify his name. Our prayer is that it may be found helpful in this task.

I. Howard Marshall
W. Ward Gasque

PREFACE

After the lapse of over forty years there is some justification for a new commentary on the Greek text of Luke which will take into account the progress in scholarship since the appearance of the commentaries of J. M. Creed in 1930 and H. K. Luce in 1933. The latter of these was intended to be an elementary introduction to the Gospel, but still repays study. Creed's commentary was an important contribution to Lucan study. It provided a valuable summary of the religious-historical and form-critical approaches to the Gospel, while avoiding the more speculative conclusions of some adherents of these two schools. But it had two related weaknesses. First, it offered scanty comment on those parts of the Gospel which were based on Mark. Creed made no attempt to assess the significance of Luke's rewriting of Mark and thus to gauge his own importance as an Evangelist. Second, Luke was not regarded as a theologian in his own right. Creed's comments on the theological significance of the Gospel were decidedly thin, a fact which is not surprising in view of his own comment: 'There is no sufficient reason to suppose . . . that the writer wished to commend a particular theological attitude' (Creed, lxxi). Nevertheless, the student will still turn to Creed's work with profit; his comments, though brief, are often full of insight.

Creed wrote before the development of tradition criticism and redaction criticism. A modern commentator must inevitably make use of these critical methods, and the present commentary attempts to assess and elucidate the Gospel in the light of these new aids to its study. It can indeed be argued that the time is not yet ripe for a definitive commentary on Luke. It is perhaps still too early to assess the results of the revolution in Lucan studies which has been proceeding during the last quarter of a century. Nevertheless, there is great need for a commentary which will at least provide some sort of guide to the present state of scholarship, and in particular the needs of students of the Greek text cry out to be met.

The purpose of this commentary, therefore, is to help students, although I fear that in many places they may feel that it has expanded beyond the appropriate limits. I have attempted to provide the tools needed for study of the Gospel, to indicate the state of contemporary research and to offer some contribution to the understanding of the Gospel.

Nowadays the scope of a commentary is so vast that no one individual can compass it all. I am particularly conscious of the shortcomings of this work which arise from my own ignorance and the sheer impossibility of familiarity with all that has been written on the Gospel. One omission in particular should be mentioned. In order not to expand the commentary beyond measure I have deliberately refrained from offering an exposition of the text as Holy Scripture with a message for the contemporary world, although I believe that exegesis must lead to exposition. Since, however, the commentary attempts throughout to bring out the theological message of Luke the Evangelist, I hope that the reader will find that he gains the information which he needs in order to interpret and expound the text for today. It is my hope that, although this commentary has been written as a tool for scholarly study, it will nevertheless lay a foundation for understanding the Gospel of Luke as part of the Word of God.

In a work such as this an author incurs many debts. I must express my appreciation once again for the lectures and seminars conducted by Professor J. Jeremias in Göttingen in 1959–60 from which I gained much insight into the methods of Gospel study; some of the opinions expressed in the following pages can be traced back to his teaching. Above all, however, I owe much to the monumental work of Professor Heinz Schürmann; his commentary on the first nine chapters of Luke and his other Lucan studies dwarf all other contemporary attempts to interpret the Gospel, and all students of Luke look forward eagerly to the completion of his vast enterprise. My thanks are also due to Dr K. Junack of the Münster Institut für neutestamentliche Textforschung who kindly made available to me a list of the changes in the third edition of *The Greek New Testament* in advance of publication. Various parts of the manuscript were read by Dr R. T. France, Dr J. E. Rosscup, Dr P. Ellingworth, and Messrs. D. Burdett, W. S. Henderson and W. B. Hunter, and I have profited from their comments. I am also grateful to the staff of The Paternoster Press for their care with a difficult piece of work, to the Rev. Norman Hillyer for help with the proofs, and to Dr and Mrs. Colin Brown for compiling the indexes. The responsibility for omissions and inaccuracies is of course my own.

The writing of this commentary has occupied a good deal of my time and attention while serving as a member of the Department of New Testament Exegesis in the University of Aberdeen; my thanks are due to Professor R. S. Barbour, and to his predecessor Professor A. M. Hunter, for providing me with such congenial conditions for its composition.

At an earlier stage in the work I found it helpful to crystallize my views on the theology of Luke by writing what is in effect an introduction to the commentary: *Luke: Historian and Theologian.* The dedication to my wife in that first part of my work is now extended to this second, and major, part of the enterprise.

I. Howard Marshall.

ABBREVIATIONS AND BIBLIOGRAPHY

1. *Books of the Bible*

Gn., Ex., Lv., Nu., Dt., Jos., Jdg., Ru., 1, 2 Sa., 1, 2 Ki., 1, 2 Ch., Ezr., Ne. (LXX: 2 Esd.), Est., Jb., Ps. (Pss.), Pr., Ec., Ct., Is., Je., La., Ezk., Dn., Ho., Joel, Am., Ob., Jon., Mi., Na., Hab., Zp., Hg., Zc., Mal.

Mt., Mk., Lk., Jn., Acts, Rom., 1, 2 Cor., Gal., Eph., Phil., Col., 1, 2 Thes., 1, 2 Tim., Tit., Phm., Heb., Jas., 1, 2 Pet., 1, 2, 3 Jn., Jude, Rev.

References to the OT are to the chapter and verse divisions in English usage; where necessary, references to the LXX (especially in Pss.) are added in brackets; references to the Hebrew text are indicated by MT.

2. *Other Ancient Sources*

Apocrypha: 4 Ez., Tob., Jdt., Wis., Sir., Bar., Sus., 1, 2 Mac.

Pseudepigrapha: Jub., Arist., 1, 2, 3 En., T.XII, Sib., Ass. Moses, 2, 3, Bar., Ps. Sol.

Dead Sea Scrolls: the conventional sigla are used.

Rabbinic writings: the conventional sigla are used.

Other ancient sources: the conventional sigla are used.

3. *Textual and other Symbols*

The text cited in this commentary is that of *The Greek New Testament* (3rd edition, United Bible Societies, London, 1975).

The textual symbols employed are as in K. Aland, *Synopsis Quattuor Evangeliorum* (Stuttgart, 1964), with the following alterations:

f1	Family 1 (Lake)
f13	Family 13 (Ferrar)
TR	Textus Receptus
t	the *text* of a modern edition where the *margin* (mg) differs.
par.	is parallel to
diff.	differs from

The citation of a modern edition in brackets indicates that in this edition the word or phrase in question is bracketed.

The symbol Q is used for material common to Mt. and Lk., thought by many scholars to be based on a common documentary source (or sources) other than Mk.

The symbol L is used for material in Lk. 3–24 which has no parallels in Mk. or Mt. and is thought by some scholars to come from a documentary source (or sources).

An asterisk * after a Greek word or list of references signifies that all the occurrences of the word in Lk. are listed (in some cases, all the occurrences in Acts are similarly noted). A double asterisk ** indicates that all the occurrences of a word in the NT are cited.

An asterisk * after an author's name signifies that the work cited is listed in the bibliography at the end of the introduction to the relevant section of the commentary.

Where a bibliographical reference is given without an asterisk, the work cited is listed in the following sets of abbreviations.

4. Reference Works

AG	W. F. Arndt and F. W. Gingrich, *A Greek-English Lexicon of the New Testament and Other Early Christian Literature*, Cambridge, 1957
AP	R. H. Charles (ed.), *The Apocrypha and Pseudepigrapha of the Old Testament in English*, Oxford, 1913
ASTI	*Annual of the Swedish Theological Institute*
AV	*Authorised (King James') Version*
BA	*Biblical Archaeologist*
Barclay	W. Barclay, *The New Testament: A New Translation*, London, I, 1968
BC	F. J. Foakes-Jackson and K. Lake, *The Beginnings of Christianity*, London, I–V, 1920–33
BD	F. Blass and A. Debrunner, *A Greek Grammar of the New Testament* (translated by R. W. Funk), Cambridge, 1961
BFBS	G. D. Kilpatrick (ed.), *Η ΚΑΙΝΗ ΔΙΑΘΗΚΗ*, British & Foreign Bible Society, London, 1958
BG	W. Bousset und H. Gressmann, *Die Religion des Judentums im späthellenistischen Zeitalter*, Tübingen, 1966⁴
Bib.	*Biblica*
BJRL	*Bulletin of the John Rylands Library*
BZ	*Biblische Zeitschrift*
CBQ	*Catholic Biblical Quarterly*
Diglot	*Luke: A Greek-English Diglot for the Use of Translators* (British and Foreign Bible Society, London, 1962; this work incorporates the projected 3rd edition of the BFBS text of the Greek New Testament prepared by G. D. Kilpatrick)
Ditt. Syl.	W. Dittenberger, *Sylloge inscriptionum Graecarum*, Leipzig, 1915–24
EQ	*Evangelical Quarterly*
Ev.T	*Evangelische Theologie*
Exp.T	*Expository Times*
HTR	*Harvard Theological Review*
Jastrow, Dictionary	M. Jastrow, *A Dictionary of the Targumim*, London, 1903
JB	*Jerusalem Bible*
JBL	*Journal of Biblical Literature*
JJS	*Journal of Jewish Studies*
JMH	D. G. Miller and D. Y. Hadidian, *Jesus and Man's Hope*, Pittsburgh, I, 1970; II, 1971
JRS	*Journal of Roman Studies*
JTS	*Journal of Theological Studies* (ns: new series)
KB	L. Köhler and W. Baumgartner, *Lexicon in Veteris Testamenti Libros*, Stuttgart, 1958²
LSJ	H. G. Liddell and R. Scott, *A Greek-English Lexicon*, (revised by H. S. Jones and R. Mackenzie), Oxford, 1940
MH	J. H. Moulton, W. F. Howard and N. Turner, *Grammar of New Testament Greek*, Edinburgh, I, 1906; II, 1929; III, 1963; IV, 1976

MM	J. H. Moulton and G. Milligan, *The Vocabulary of the Greek New Testament*, London, 1914–1929
NBC	D. Guthrie (*et al.*), *The New Bible Commentary Revised*, London, 1970
NBD	J. D. Douglas (*et al.*), *The New Bible Dictionary*, London 1962
NEB	*New English Bible*
NIDNTT	C. Brown (ed.), *The New International Dictionary of New Testament Theology*, Exeter, 1975–78
NIV	New International Version
Nov.T	Novum Testamentum
NRT	Nouvelle Revue Théologique
NTA	New Testament Abstracts
NTA I, II	E. Hennecke, *New Testament Apocrypha* (translated by R. M. Wilson, *et al.*), London, 1963, 1965
NTS	*New Testament Studies*
OCD	M. Cary (*et al.*), *The Oxford Classical Dictionary*, Oxford, 1949
PC	M. Black (ed.), *Peake's Commentary*, Edinburgh, 1962
PW	Pauly-Wissowa, *Real-Encyclopädie*, Stuttgart, 1894–
RB	*Revue Biblique*
RHPR	*Revue d'histoire et de philosophie religieuses*
RIDA	*Revue internationale des Droites de l'Antiquité*
RQ	*Revue de Qumran*
RSV	*Revised Standard Version*
RV	*Revised Version*
SB	H. L. Strack und P. Billerbeck, *Kommentar zum Neuen Testament aus Talmud und Midrasch*, München, 1956[3]
SJT	*Scottish Journal of Theology*
SLA	L. E. Keck and J. L. Martyn (ed.), *Studies in Luke-Acts*, Nashville, 1966
ST	*Studia Theologica*
Synopsis	K. Aland, *Synopsis Quattuor Evangeliorum*, Stuttgart, 1964 (cited as giving the text of E. Nestle–K. Aland, *Novum Testamentum Graece*, Stuttgart, 1963[25])
TDNT	G. Kittel and G. Friedrich (ed.), *Theological Dictionary of the New Testament* (translated by G. W. Bromiley), Grand Rapids, 1964–76
TEV	*Today's English Version* (1966 edition)
THAT	E. Jenni und C. Westermann, *Theologisches Handwörterbuch zum Alten Testament*, München, 1971–76
Tisch.	C. Tischendorf, *Novum Testamentum Graece*, Leipzig, 1869–72[8]
TLZ	*Theologische Literaturzeitung*
TNT	*Translator's New Testament*
TR	*Theologische Rundschau*
TU	*Texte und Untersuchungen*
Tyn.B	*Tyndale Bulletin*
TZ	*Theologische Zeitschrift*
UBS	*The Greek New Testament* (3rd edition), United Bible Societies, London, 1976)
WH	B. F. Westcott and F. J. A. Hort, *The New Testament in Greek*, London, 1881
WH App.	*Ibid. Appendix*
ZNW	*Zeitschrift für die Neutestamentliche Wissenschaft*
ZRGG	*Zeitschrift für Religions- und Geistesgeschichte*
ZTK	*Zeitschrift für Theologie und Kirche*

5. *Commentaries and other Works*

Abel	F. M. Abel, *Géographie de la Palestine*, Paris, 1933–38
Alford	H. Alford, *The Greek Testament*, London, I, 1863[5]
Arndt	W. F. Arndt, *The Gospel according to St Luke*, St Louis, 1956
Aune	D. Aune (ed.), *Studies in New Testament and Early Christian Literature: Essays in Honour of A. P. Wikgren*, Leiden, 1972

Bailey	J. A. Bailey, *The Traditions Common to the Gospels of Luke and John*, Leiden, 1963
K. E. Bailey	K. E. Bailey, *Poet and Peasant*, Grand Rapids, 1976
Balmforth	H. Balmforth, *The Gospel according to St Luke* (Clarendon Bible), Oxford, 1930
Baltensweiler	H. Baltensweiler (ed.), *Neotestamentica et Patristica* (für O. Cullmann), Leiden, 1962
Balz	H. Balz und S. Schulz, *Das Wort und die Wörter* (für G. Friedrich), Stuttgart, 1973
Bammel	E. Bammel (ed.), *The Trial of Jesus*, London, 1970
Banks	R. J. Banks (ed.), *Reconciliation and Hope* (for L. Morris), Exeter, 1974
Barrett	C. K. Barrett, *The Holy Spirit and the Gospel Tradition*, London, 1947
Bartsch	H. W. Bartsch, *Wachet aber zu jeder Zeit*, Hamburg, 1963
Beasley-Murray	G. R. Beasley-Murray, *Jesus and the Future*, London, 1954
Beasley-Murray, Commentary	G. R. Beasley-Murray, *A Commentary on Mark Thirteen*, London, 1957
Benoit, Exégèse	P. Benoit, *Exégèse et Théologie*, Paris, I, 1961; II, 1961; III, 1968
Benoit, Passion	P. Benoit, *The Passion and Resurrection of Jesus Christ*, London, 1969
H.-D. Betz	H.-D. Betz (*et al.*), *Neues Testament und Christliche Existenz* (für H. Braun), Tubingen, 1973
O. Betz	O. Betz (*et al.*), *Abraham unser Vater* (für O. Michel), Leiden, 1963
O. Betz, Jesus	O. Betz, *What do we know about Jesus?* London, 1968
Beyer	K. Beyer, *Semitische Syntax im Neuen Testament*, Göttingen, I:1, 1962
Black	M. Black, *An Aramaic Approach to the Gospels and Acts*, Oxford, 1967[3]
Blaiklock	E. M. Blaiklock, *St Luke*, in *The Daily Commentary* (Scripture Union), London, III, 1974
Blinzler	J. Blinzler, *Der Prozess Jesu*, Regensburg, 1969[4]
Blinzler, Aufsätze	J. Blinzler (*et al.*), *Neutestamentliche Aufsätze* (für J. Schmid), Regensburg, 1963
Böcher	O. Böcher (*et al.*) *Verborum Veritas* (für G. Stählin), Wuppertal, 1970
Bornhäuser	K. Bornhäuser, *Studien zur Sondergut des Lukas*, Gütersloh, 1934
Bornhäuser, Death	K. Bornhäuser, *The Death and Resurrection of Jesus Christ*, Bangalore, 1958
Borsch	F. H. Borsch, *The Son of Man in Myth and History*, London, 1967
Bouwmann	G. Bouwmann, *Das Dritte Evangelium*, Düsseldorf, 1968
Braun, Qumran	H. Braun, *Qumran und das Neue Testament*, Tübingen, 1966.
Braun, Radikalismus	H. Braun, *Spätjüdisch-häretischer und frühchristlicher Radikalismus*, Tübingen, 1957.
Brown, John	R. E. Brown, *The Gospel according to John*, London, I–II, 1971
Brown, Apostasy	S. Brown, *Apostasy and Perseverance in the Theology of Luke*, Rome, 1969
Browning	W. R. F. Browning, *St Luke*, London, 1960
Bruce	F. F. Bruce, *The Acts of the Apostles*, London, 1951
Bultmann	R. Bultmann, *Die Geschichte der synoptischen Tradition*, Göttingen, 1958[4] (Erg.: *Ergänzungsheft*)
Burger	C. Burger, *Jesus als Davidssohn*, Göttingen, 1970
Cadbury	H. J. Cadbury, *The Style and Literary Method of Luke*, Cambridge, Mass., I–II, 1920
Caird	G. B. Caird, *St Luke* (Pelican Gospel Commentaries), Harmondsworth, 1963

Catchpole	D. R. Catchpole, *The Trial of Jesus*, Leiden, 1971
Christ	F. Christ, *Jesus Sophia*, Zürich, 1970
Conzelmann	H. Conzelmann, *Die Mitte der Zeit*, Tübingen, 1964[5]
Cranfield	C. E. B. Cranfield, *St Mark*, Cambridge, 1963[2]
Creed	J. M. Creed, *St Luke* (Macmillan), London, 1930
Cullmann	O. Cullmann, *The Christology of the New Testament*, London, 1959
Dalman	G. Dalman, *The Words of Jesus*, Edinburgh, 1909
Dalman, Sites	G. Dalman, *Sacred Sites and Ways*, London, 1935
Danker	F. W. Danker, *Jesus and the New Age*, St Louis, 1972
Daube	D. Daube, *The New Testament and Rabbinic Judaism*, London, 1956
Dauer	A. Dauer, *Die Passionsgeschichte im Johannesevangelium*, München, 1972
Dautzenberg	G. Dautzenberg, *Sein Leben bewahren*, München, 1966
Davies	W. D. Davies, *The Setting of the Sermon on the Mount*, Cambridge, 1964
Degenhardt	H. Degenhardt, *Lukas – Evangelist der Armen*, Stuttgart, 1966
Deissmann	A. Deissmann, *Light from the Ancient East*, London, 1927
Delling	G. Delling, *Studien zum Neuen Testament und zum hellenistischen Judentum*, Göttingen, 1970
Derrett	J. D. M. Derrett, *Law in the New Testament*, London, 1970
Descamps	A. Descamps (*et al.*), *Mélanges bibliques* (... au R. P. Béda Rigaux), Gembloux, 1970
Dibelius	M. Dibelius, *Die Formgeschichte der Evangelien*, Tübingen, 1971[6]
Dibelius, Botschaft	M. Dibelius, *Botschaft und Geschichte*, Tübingen, I, 1953
Dibelius Studies	M. Dibelius, *Studies in the Acts of the Apostles*, London, 1956
Dietrich	W. Dietrich, *Das Petrusbild der lukanischen Schriften*, Stuttgart, 1972
Dinkler	E. Dinkler (ed.), *Zeit und Geschichte* (für R. Bultmann), Tübingen, 1964
Dodd	C. H. Dodd, *Historical Tradition in the Fourth Gospel*, Cambridge, 1963
Dodd, Parables	C. H. Dodd, *The Parables of the Kingdom*, London, 1961[2]
Dormeyer	D. Dormeyer, *Die Passion Jesu als Verhaltensmodell*, Münster, 1974
Drury	J. Drury, *Luke* (J. B. Phillips' Commentaries), London, 1973
Drury, Tradition	J. Drury, *Tradition and Design in Luke's Gospel*, London, 1976
Dupont	J. Dupont, *Les Béatitudes*, Paris, I, 1969; II, 1969; III, 1973
Dupont, Jésus	J. Dupont (*et al.*), *Jésus aux origines de la christologie*, Gembloux, 1975
Easton	B. S. Easton, *The Gospel according to St Luke*, Edinburgh, 1926
Ellis	E. E. Ellis, *The Gospel of Luke* (New Century Bible), London, 1974[2]
Ellis, Jesus	E. E. Ellis and E. Grässer (ed.), *Jesus und Paulus* (für W. G. Kümmel), Göttingen, 1975
Ellis, Neotestamentica	E. E. Ellis and M. Wilcox (ed.), *Neotestamentica et Semitica* (for M. Black), Edinburgh, 1969
Eltester	W. Eltester (ed.), *Judentum–Urchristentum–Kirche* (für J. Jeremias), Berlin, 1964[2]
Eltester and Kettler	W. Eltester and F. H. Kettler, *Apophoreta* (für E. Haenchen), Berlin, 1964
Epp	E. J. Epp, *The Theological Tendency of Codex Bezae Cantabrigiensis in Acts*, Cambridge, 1966
Findlay	J. A. Findlay, 'Luke', in *The Abingdon Bible Commentary*, Nashville/New York, 1929, 1022–1059
Finegan	J. Finegan, *The Archaeology of the New Testament*, Princeton, 1964
Finegan, Handbook	J. Finegan, *Handbook of Biblical Chronology*, Princeton, 1964

Finegan,
  Überlieferung   J. Finegan, *Die Überlieferung der Leidens- und Auferstehungsgeschichte Jesu*, Giessen, 1934
Fitzmyer   J. A. Fitzmyer, *Essays on the Semitic Background of the New Testament*, London, 1971
Flender   H. Flender, *St. Luke Theologian of Redemptive History*, London, 1967
France   R. T. France, *Jesus and the Old Testament*, London, 1971
Franklin   E. Franklin, *Christ the Lord*, London, 1975
Fuller   R. H. Fuller, *Foundations of New Testament Christology*, London, 1965
Gärtner   B. Gärtner, *The Temple and the Community in Qumran and the New Testament*, Cambridge, 1965
Gasque   W. W. Gasque and R. P. Martin (ed.), *Apostolic History and the Gospel* (for F. F. Bruce), Exeter, 1970
Gaston   L. Gaston, *No Stone on Another*, Leiden, 1970
Geiger   R. Geiger, *Die Lukanischen Endzeitreden*, Bern/Frankfurt, 1973
Geldenhuys   N. Geldenhuys, *Commentary on the Gospel of Luke* (New London Commentary), London, 1950
Gilmour   S. M. Gilmour, 'Luke', in *The Interpreter's Bible*, Nashville, VIII, 1952
Gnilka   J. Gnilka, *Die Verstockung Israels*, München, 1961
Gnilka,
  Neues Testament J. Gnilka, *Neues Testament und Kirche* (für R. Schnackenburg), Freiburg, 1974
Godet   F. Godet, *Commentary on the Gospel of Luke*, Edinburgh, 1879
Goppelt   L. Goppelt, *Theologie des Neuen Testaments*, Göttingen, I, 1975
Grass   H. Grass, *Ostergeschehen und Osterberichte*, Göttingen, 1964[3]
Grässer   E. Grässer, *Das Problem der Parusieverzögerung in den synoptischen Evangelien und in der Apostelgeschichte*, Berlin, 1957
Grundmann   W. Grundmann, *Das Evangelium nach Lukas* (Theologischer Handkommentar zum NT), Berlin, 1966[3]
Gundry   R.H. Gundry, *The Use of the Old Testament in St. Matthew's Gospel*, Leiden, 1967
Haenchen   E. Haenchen, *Die Apostelgeschichte*, Göttingen, 1961[13]
Hahn   F. Hahn, *Christologische Hoheitstitel*, Göttingen, 1964[2]
Hahn,
  Mission   F. Hahn, *Mission in the New Testament*, London, 1965
Hamerton-Kelly   R. G. Hamerton-Kelly, *Pre-Existence, Wisdom and the Son of Man*, Cambridge, 1973
Hare   D. R. A. Hare, *The Theme of Jewish Persecution of Christians in the Gospel according to St Matthew*, Cambridge, 1967
Harnack   A. Harnack, *The Sayings of Jesus*, London, 1908
Hartman   L. Hartman, *Prophecy Interpreted*, Lund, 1966
Harvey   A. E. Harvey, *The New English Bible: Companion to the New Testament*, Oxford/Cambridge, 1970
Hasler   V. Hasler, *Amen*, Zürich/Stuttgart, 1969
Hastings   A. Hastings, *Prophet and Witness in Jerusalem*, London, 1958
Hauck   F. Hauck, *Das Evangelium des Lukas* (Theologischer Handkommentar zum NT), Leipzig, 1934
Hawkins   J. C. Hawkins, *Horae Synopticae*, Oxford, 1909
Hengel   M. Hengel, *Nachfolge und Charisma*, Berlin, 1968
Higgins   A. J. B. Higgins, *Jesus and the Son of Man*, London, 1964
Hill   D. Hill, *The Gospel of Matthew*, London, 1972
Hoehner   H. Hoehner, *Herod Antipas*, Cambridge, 1972
Hoffmann   P. Hoffmann, *Studien zur Theologie der Logienquelle*, Münster, 1972
Hoffmann,
  Orientierung   P. Hoffmann (*et al.*), *Orientierung an Jesus* (für J. Schmid), Freiburg, 1973
Holtz   T. Holtz, *Untersuchungen über die alttestamentliche Zitate bei Lukas*, Berlin, 1968
Hooker   M. D. Hooker, *Jesus and the Servant*, London, 1959

Hooker,	
Son of Man	M. D. Hooker, *The Son of Man in Mark*, London, 1967
Jeremias,	
Tradition	G. Jeremias (*et al.*), *Tradition und Glaube* (für K. G. Kuhn), Göttingen, 1971
Jeremias,	
Abba	J. Jeremias, *Abba*, Göttingen, 1966
Jeremias,	
Jerusalem	J. Jeremias, *Jerusalem in the Time of Jesus*, London, 1969
Jeremias,	
Parables	J. Jeremias, *The Parables of Jesus*, London, 1963[2]
Jeremias,	
Promise	J. Jeremias, *Jesus' Promise to the Nations*, London, 1958
Jeremias,	
Theology	J. Jeremias, *New Testament Theology*, London, I, 1971
Jeremias,	
Words	J. Jeremias, *The Eucharistic Words of Jesus*, London, 1966[2]
Jüngel	E. Jüngel, *Paulus und Jesus*, Tübingen, 1964[2]
Kaestli	J.-D. Kaestli, *L'eschatologie dans l'oeuvre de Luc*, Geneva, 1970
Käsemann,	
Essays	E. Käsemann, *Essays on New Testament Themes*, London, 1964
Käsemann,	
Questions	E. Käsemann, *New Testament Questions of Today*, London, 1969
Kertelge	K. Kertelge, *Die Wunder Jesu im Markusevangelium*, München, 1970
Kilpatrick	G. D. Kilpatrick, 'The Greek New Testament Text of Today and the *Textus Receptus*', in H. Anderson and W. Barclay (ed.), *The New Testament in Historical and Contemporary Perspective*, Oxford, 1965, 189–208
Klein	G. Klein, *Rekonstruktion und Interpretation*, München, 1969
Klostermann	E. Klostermann, *Das Lukasevangelium* (Handkommentar zum NT), Tübingen, 1929[2]
Knox	W. L. Knox, *The Sources of the Synoptic Gospels*, Cambridge, I, 1953; II, 1957
Kopp	C. Kopp, *The Holy Places of the Gospels*, Freiburg/Edinburgh, 1963
Kümmel	W. G. Kümmel, *Promise and Fulfilment*, London, 1957
Kümmel,	
Heilsgeschehen	W. G. Kümmel, *Heilsgeschehen und Geschichte*, Marburg, 1965
Ladd	G. E. Ladd, *Jesus and the Kingdom*, London, 1966
Lagrange	M.–J. Lagrange, *Evangile selon St Luc* (Etudes bibliques), Paris, 1941[5]
Lambrecht	J. Lambrecht, *Die Redaktion der Markus-Apokalypse*, Rome, 1967
Lampe	G. W. H. Lampe, 'Luke', in *Peake's Commentary*, London, 1962, 820–843
Lane	W. L. Lane, *Commentary on the Gospel of Mark*, Grand Rapids/London, 1974
Laurentin	R. Laurentin, *Structure et Théologie de Luc I–II*, Paris, 1957
Laurentin,	
Jésus	R. Laurentin, *Jésus au Temple*, Paris, 1966
Leaney	A. R. C. Leaney, *The Gospel according to St Luke* (Black's NT Commentaries), London, 1958
Légasse	S. Légasse, *Jésus et l'Enfant*, Paris, 1969
Lindars	B. Lindars, *New Testament Apologetic*, London, 1961
Linnemann	E. Linnemann, *Parables of Jesus*, London, 1966
Linnemann,	
Studien	E. Linnemann, *Studien zur Passionsgeschichte*, Göttingen, 1970
Lohfink	G. Lohfink, *Die Himmelfahrt Jesu*, München, 1971
Lohmeyer	E. Lohmeyer, *Das Evangelium des Markus*, Göttingen, 1959[15]
Loisy	A. Loisy, *L'évangile selon Luc*, Paris, 1924; Frankfurt, 1971
Lövestam	E. Lövestam, *Spiritual Wakefulness in the New Testament*, Lund, 1963

Luce   H. K. Luce, *The Gospel according to S. Luke* (Cambridge Greek Testament), Cambridge, 1933
Lührmann   D. Lührmann, *Die Redaktion der Logienquelle,* Neukirchen, 1969
Machen   J. G. Machen, *The Virgin Birth of Christ,* London, 1932[2]
Manson,
  Sayings   T. W. Manson, *The Sayings of Jesus,* London, 1949
Manson,
  Teaching   T. W. Manson, *The Teaching of Jesus,* Cambridge, 1935[2]
Manson   W. Manson, *The Gospel of Luke* (Moffatt NT Commentary), London, 1930
Marshall   I. H. Marshall, *Luke: Historian and Theologian,* Exeter, 1970
Metzger   B. M. Metzger, *A Textual Commentary on the Greek New Testament,* London, 1971
Miyoshi   M. Miyoshi, *Der Anfang des Reiseberichts Lk. 9:51–10:24,* Rome, 1974
Moore   G. F. Moore, *Judaism,* Cambridge, Mass., I–III, 1927–30
Morris   L. Morris, *Luke* (Tyndale NT Commentaries), London, 1974
Moule   C. F. D. Moule, *An Idiom-Book of New Testament Greek,* Cambridge, 1953
Neirynck   F. Neirynck (ed.), *L'évangile de Luc,* Gembloux, 1973
Nineham   D. E. Nineham, *Saint Mark,* Harmondsworth, 1963
Nineham,
  Studies   D. E. Nineham (ed.), *Studies in the Gospels,* Oxford, 1955
Ott   W. Ott, *Gebet und Heil,* München, 1965
Otto   R. Otto, *The Kingdom of God and the Son of Man,* London, 1938
Patsch   H. Patsch, *Abendmahl und historischer Jesus,* Stuttgart, 1972
Percy   E. Percy, *Die Botschaft Jesu,* Lund, 1953
Perrin   N. Perrin, *Rediscovering the Teaching of Jesus,* London, 1967
Pesch,
  Fischfang   R. Pesch, *Der reiche Fischfang,* Düsseldorf, 1969
Pesch,
  Jesus   R. Pesch and R. Schnackenburg, *Jesus und der Menschensohn* (für A. Vögtle), Freiburg, 1975
Pesch,
  Naherwartungen R. Pesch, *Naherwartungen,* Düsseldorf, 1968
Pesch,
  Taten   R. Pesch, *Jesu ureigene Taten?,* Freiburg, 1970
Plummer   A. Plummer, *St Luke* (International Critical Commentary), Edinburgh, 1922[5]
de la Potterie I. de la Potterie (ed.), *De Jésus aux Evangiles,* Gembloux, 1967
Rehkopf   F. Rehkopf, *Die lukanische Sonderquelle,* Tübingen, 1959
Reicke   B. Reicke, *Neutestamentliche Zeitgeschichte,* Berlin, 1965
Reicke,
  Diakonie   B. Reicke, *Diakonie, Festfreude und Zelos,* Uppsala, 1951
Reiling   J. Reiling and J. L. Swellengrebel, *A. Translator's Handbook on the Gospel of Luke,* Leiden, 1971
Rengstorf   K. H. Rengstorf, *Das Evangelium nach Lukas* (Das NT Deutsch), Göttingen, 1937
Rese   M. Rese, *Alttestamentliche Motive in der Christologie des Lukas,* Gütersloh, 1969
Rigaux   B. Rigaux, *Témoignage de l'Evangile de Luc,* Bruges, 1970
Roloff,
  Apostolat   J. Roloff, *Apostolat–Verkündigung–Kirche,* Gütersloh, 1965
Roloff,
  Kerygma   J. Roloff, *Das Kerygma und der irdische Jesus,* Göttingen, 1970
Sabbe   M. Sabbe (ed.), *L'Evangile selon Marc,* Gembloux, 1974
Sahlin   H. Sahlin, *Der Messias und das Gottesvolk,* Uppsala, 1945
Schenk   W. Schenk, *Der Passionsbericht nach Markus,* Gütersloh, 1974
Schenke   L. Schenke, *Studien zur Passionsgeschichte des Markus,* Würzburg, 1971

Schlatter	A. Schlatter, *Das Evangelium des Lukas*, Stuttgart, 1960²
Schlatter, *Matthäus*	A Schlatter, *Der Evangelist Matthäus*, Stuttgart, 1959⁵
Schmid	J. Schmid, *Das Evangelium nach Lukas* (Regensburger NT), Regensburg, 1960⁴
Schmid, *Mark*	J. Schmid, *The Gospel according to Mark*, Cork, 1968
Schmid, *Studien*	J. Schmid (*et al.*), Synoptische Studien (für A. Wikenhauser), München, 1953
Schnackenburg	R. Schnackenburg, *God's Rule and Kingdom*, London, 1963
Schneider	G. Schneider, *Verleugnung, Verpottung und Verhör Jesu nach Lukas 22, 54–71*, München, 1969
Schniewind, *Markus*	J. Schniewind, *Das Evangelium nach Markus*, Göttingen, 1958⁸
Schniewind, *Matthäus*	J. Schniewind, *Das Evangelium nach Matthäus*, Göttingen, 1950⁵
Schramm	T. Schramm, *Der Markus–Stoff bei Lukas*, Cambridge, 1971
Schürer	E. Schürer, *The Jewish People in the Time of Jesus Christ*, Edinburgh, 1885–1891
Schürer, *History*	E. Schürer, *The History of the Jewish People in the Age of Jesus Christ* (revised and edited by G. Vermes and F. Millar), Edinburgh, I, 1973
Schürmann	H. Schürmann, *Das Lukasevangelium* (Herders theologischer Kommentar zum NT), Freiburg, I, 1969
Schürmann, *Abschiedsrede*	H. Schürmann, *Jesu Abschiedsrede*, Münster, 1957
Schürmann, *Einsetzungsbericht*	H. Schürmann, *Der Einsetzungsbericht*, Münster, 1955
Schürmann, *Paschamahlbericht*	H. Schürmann, *Der Paschamahlbericht*, Münster, 1953
Schürmann, *Untersuchungen*	H. Schürmann, *Traditionsgeschichtliche Untersuchungen*, Düsseldorf, 1968
Schürmann, *Ursprung*	H. Schürmann, *Ursprung und Gestalt*, Düsseldorf, 1970
Schütz	F. Schütz, *Der leidende Christus*, Stuttgart, 1969
Schulz	S. Schulz, *Q – Die Spruchquelle der Evangelisten*, Zürich, 1972
Schweizer, *Markus*	E. Schweizer, *Das Evangelium nach Markus*, Göttingen, 1968
Schweizer, *Matthäus*	E. Schweizer, *Das Evangelium nach Matthäus*, Göttingen, 1973
Scobie	C. H. Scobie, *John the Baptist*, London, 1964
Sherwin-White	A. N. Sherwin-White, *Roman Society and Roman Law in the New Testament*, Oxford, 1963
Smith	M. Smith, *Tannaitic Parallels to the Gospels*, Philadelphia, 1968²
Spicq	C. Spicq, *Agapé dans le nouveau testament*, Paris, I, 1958, II, III, 1959
Stauffer	E. Stauffer, *Jesus and his Story*, London, 1960
Steck	O. H. Steck, *Israel und das gewaltsame Geschick der Propheten*, Neukirchen, 1967
Stonehouse	N. B. Stonehouse, *The Witness of Luke to Christ*, London, 1951
Streeter	B. H. Streeter, *The Four Gospels*, London, 1936⁵
Strobel	A. Strobel, *Untersuchungen zum eschatologischen Verzögerungsproblem*, Leiden, 1961
Stuhlmacher	P. Stuhlmacher, *Das paulinische Evangelium 1: Vorgeschichte*, Göttingen, 1968
Stuhlmueller	C. Stuhlmueller, 'The Gospel according to Luke', in *The Jerome*

	Bible Commentary, London, 1968, 115–164
Suggs	M. J. Suggs, *Wisdom, Christology and Law in Matthew's Gospel*, Cambridge, Mass., 1970
Talbert	C. H. Talbert, *Literary Patterns, Theological Themes and the Genre of Luke-Acts*, Missoula, 1974
Tasker	R. V. G. Tasker, *The Greek New Testament*, London, 1964
Taylor	V. Taylor, *The Gospel according to St Mark*, London, 1953
Taylor, *Behind*	V. Taylor, *Behind the Third Gospel*, Oxford, 1926
Taylor, *Passion*	V. Taylor, *The Passion Narrative of St Luke*, Cambridge, 1972
Taylor, *Sacrifice*	V. Taylor, *Jesus and His Sacrifice*, London, 1937
Thompson	G. H. P. Thompson, *St Luke* (New Clarendon Bible), Oxford, 1972
Tinsley	E. J. Tinsley, *The Gospel according to Luke* (Cambridge Bible Commentary), Cambridge, 1965
Tödt	H. E. Tödt, *The Son of Man in the Synoptic Tradition*, London, 1965
Torrey	C. C. Torrey, *The Four Gospels*, London, no date
Turner	N. Turner, *Grammatical Insights into the New Testament*, Edinburgh, 1965
van Iersel	B. M. F. van Iersel, *Der 'Sohn' in den synoptischen Jesusworten*, Leiden, 1964[2]
van Unnik	W. C. van Unnik, *Sparsa Collecta*, Leiden, I, 1973
Vermes	G. Vermes, *Jesus the Jew*, London, 1973
Vielhauer	P. Vielhauer, *Aufsätze zum Neuen Testament*, München, 1965
Vögtle	A. Vögtle, *Das Evangelium und die Evangelien*, Düsseldorf, 1971
Voss	G. Voss, *Die Christologie der lukanischen Schriften in Grundzügen*, Paris, 1965
Weinreich	O. Weinreich, *Antike Heilungswunder*, Giessen, 1909
Weiser	A. Weiser, *Die Knechtsgleichnisse der synoptischen Evangelien*, München, 1971
Weiss	B. Weiss, *Die Evangelien des Markus und Lukas* (Meyer: Kritisch-exegetischer Kommentar über das NT), Göttingen, 1885
J. Weiss	J. Weiss (und W. Bousset), *Die Schriften des Neuen Testaments*, Göttingen, I, 1917
Wellhausen	J. Wellhausen, *Das Evangelium Lucae*, Berlin, 1904
Wellhausen, *Einleitung*	J. Wellhausen, *Einleitung in die drei ersten Evangelien*, Berlin, 1911[2]
Wellhausen, *Markus*	J. Wellhausen, *Das Evangelium Marci*, Berlin, 1909[2]
Wellhausen, *Matthäus*	J. Wellhausen, *Das Evangelium Matthaei*, Berlin, 1904
Wilcox	M. Wilcox, *The Semitisms of Acts*, Oxford, 1965
Wilkinson	W. Wilkinson, *Good News in Luke*, London, 1974
Wilson	S. G. Wilson, *The Gentiles and the Gentile Mission in Luke-Acts*, Cambridge, 1973
Wink	W. Wink, *John the Baptist in the Gospel Tradition*, Cambridge, 1968
Winter	P. Winter, *On the Trial of Jesus*, Berlin, 1974[2]
Wrege	H.-J. Wrege, *Die Überlieferungsgeschichte der Bergpredigt*, Tübingen, 1968
Zahn	T. Zahn, *Das Evangelium des Lucas*, Leipzig, 1913[2]
Zerwick	M. Zerwick, *Biblical Greek*, Rome, 1963
Zmijewski	J. Zmijewski, *Die Eschatologiereden des Lukas-Evang.*, Bonn, 1972
ADDENDA	
Brown, *Birth*	R. E. Brown, *The Birth of the Messiah*, London, 1977
Egelkraut	H. L. Egelkraut, *Jesus' Mission to Jerusalem*, Frankfurt/Bern, 1976
Ernst	J. Ernst, *Das Evangelium nach Lukas*, Regensburg, 1977
Schneider, *Evang.*	G. Schneider, *Das Evangelium nach Lukas*, Gütersloh/Würzburg, 1977

INTRODUCTION TO THE COMMENTARY

With the notable exception of R. Bultmann's commentary on the Gospel of John, most biblical commentaries are prefaced by an introduction, sometimes of considerable length, in which general matters relating to the text which is about to be interpreted in detail are discussed. Since the present commentary on the Gospel of Luke lacks such an introduction, some justification for this omission requires to be offered. First, the Gospel of Luke is part of a two-volume work, and it is difficult to write a completely satisfactory or comprehensive introduction to one half of the whole work. Questions of authorship, date and purpose cannot be adequately handled without taking the Acts into detailed consideration, and on some of these points it offers more information than is provided by the Gospel. Second, in so far as an introduction to the Gospel can be written, an excellent piece of work has been done by E. E. Ellis in his important commentary, and I am not capable of writing a better one. Third, I have already provided a general interpretation of Luke-Acts in my book *Luke: Historian and Theologian* (Exeter, 1970), and this may be regarded as furnishing a separate introduction to the commentary. The further study involved in the completion of the commentary (which was begun before the book) has not led me to alter my basic understanding of Luke in any vital points.

Instead of an introduction to the Gospel of Luke, therefore, what is offered here is a brief introduction to the commentary.

The Text of Luke

The text on which this commentary is based is that of the third edition of *The Greek New Testament* (which is intended to be identical with that of the twenty-sixth edition of Nestle-Aland). The textual notes are based on the evidence cited in K. Aland's *Synopsis Quattuor Evangeliorum* with supplementation from *The Greek New Testament*, B. M. Metzger's *A*

Textual Commentary on the Greek New Testament, and other sources. I have attempted to discuss briefly most of the significant variants, especially where the text of *The Greek New Testament* differs from that of the other editions commonly used in the English-speaking world. In particular, I have often referred to the variant readings in *A Greek-English Diglot for the use of Translators;* the fascicule containing Luke has an eclectic text prepared by G. D. Kilpatrick which differs in many points of detail from texts in the Westcott and Hort tradition, often returning to readings found in the *Textus Receptus.* While I am not persuaded that an eclectic method always produces the right results and believe that it underestimates the importance of the Egyptian textual tradition, many of the variants adopted by Kilpatrick deserve careful consideration.

Language and Syntax

In his commentary on the Greek text of *The Acts of the Apostles* F. F. Bruce observed that 'The elementary character of many of the grammatical notes arises out of experience in the lecture room' (vii). The linguistic knowledge of students is scarcely any better a quarter of a century later, nor is it easy for students to find help on linguistic matters other than by tediously working through the indices of the standard grammars. I have therefore attempted to provide fairly full information on the meanings of the Greek words used by Luke (with particular indebtedness to the lexical information provided in the English translation of W. Bauer's lexicon), and to show which words—and constructions are of frequent occurrence in Lk. and hence may be characteristic of his style. The older works of J. C. Hawkins, B. S. Easton and H. J. Cadbury are still of basic importance in this area, together with the more recent investigations of H. Schürmann, F. Rehkopf and others who have attempted source analysis of particular sections in Lk. Considerable reference has also been made to the grammatical and syntactical information in the standard grammars of New Testament Greek; these books remain the best commentaries on problems peculiar to the *Greek* text of the NT.

The Sources of the Gospel

The commentary took as its point of departure the two-document solution of the synoptic problem, and its detailed preparation has confirmed that solution in broad outline. Although several alternative theories are being canvassed today, it would have been out of place to discuss them in detail throughout the commentary.

The view that Luke used Mk. substantially as we have it seems to me to be beyond reasonable doubt.

The position with regard to the 'Q' material is not so clear. The view that Luke drew this material from Mt. (Drury, *Tradition*, 120–173) comes to grief on those passages where Luke preserves a more primitive form of the common tradition. Various recent investigations of Q (such as those by D. Lührmann and S. Schulz) have claimed that Matthew and Luke used a virtually identical common source for those sections which they both include, differences in wording being entirely due to their redactional activity. But the simplest solution is not necessarily the right one. The existence of passages where it is difficult to account satisfactorily for all the differences between Mt. and Lk. in this way favours the view that the two Evangelists used varying recensions of Q (see pp. 245, 466, 493). This means that we must be cautious in drawing conclusions about Luke's redactional activity from his use of Q material.

Similar caution is needed with regard to material peculiar to Lk. The passages peculiar to Lk. are clearly not homogeneous. But there is material which has probably been drawn from one or two particular cycles of tradition. This is true of the birth stories, some of the teaching of Jesus and some stories about him, the Last Supper narrative, and possibly some parts of the passion and resurrection narrative. The existence of a connected 'L' source, containing most of this material, has not been confirmed by my investigations, although this is a matter that demands a fuller study than is possible on the present occasion. Some scholars, such as H. Schürmann, would attribute some of this material peculiar to Lk. to the Q tradition, and there are places where this is an attractive hypothesis. The view that Q contained *only* material found in both Mt. and Lk. is quite arbitrary and indeed improbable in view of the way in which the two Evangelists have individually omitted sections from Mk., but attempts to recognise this additional material are inevitably speculative. In some places a number of scholars suspect that the material peculiar to Luke is his own creation, since it displays his particular theological interests. This theory has been advanced particularly in respect of the birth stories, some of the parables, and passages where Luke has divergent accounts of incidents and teaching in Mk. But the general fidelity of Luke to his sources Mk. and Q, where these can be certainly identified, makes one sceptical of suggestions that he created material in the Gospel on any large scale. It is much more plausible that Luke's own attitudes were in considerable measure formed by the traditions which he inherited; for all his individuality he gives the impression of reflecting the outlook of a particular Christian community. Thus Luke's universalism and his attitude to wealth and poverty were probably the attitudes of his church. It is possible that we should identify this church as the church in Antioch with which Luke is connected by a respectable tradition; here the gospel was preached to non-Jews, and here there was concern for the poor and needy. At the same time, however, much of Luke's special material clearly has a Palestinian basis, and we should not narrowly limit the influences upon Luke to those of any one Christian community.

Tradition and Redaction

It is manifestly the task of a commentator on the Gospels in the present
scholarly situation to take up two connected issues. One of these is to
uncover the theological interests of the author. In a sense this is a return
to the pre-critical type of commenting which assumed that the object of
interest was the text itself. The rise of critical scholarship and the quest
of the historical Jesus led to a shift of emphasis in which attention was
directed to the isolation and reconstruction of the sources of the
Gospels, and there was a danger of regarding the Evangelist's own contribution to his Gospel in the shaping and ordering of his material as being like an outer skin which could safely be peeled off the onion. More
recently it has been seen that tradition, source and redaction critical
methods can lead to an enhanced appreciation of the text as the work of
an author with his own theological outlook and purpose. The primary
purpose of the present commentary is thus to carry out an exegesis of
the text as it was written by Luke so that the message of his Gospel for
his readers may stand out clearly and in its distinctiveness over against
the other Gospels. This is, therefore, a 'theological' commentary, and the
fact that it is based on the Greek text and deals at length with linguistic
matters should not obscure this intention; on the contrary, it is only by
meticulous analysis of the Greek text that the author's theological intention can be objectively determined.

To comment on the Gospel at this level is a big enough task in itself. But a commentary on one of the Gospels cannot stop at this point.
It must also enquire into the character of the tradition handled by the
author, and above all it must raise the question of the historical origin of
the tradition in the ministry of Jesus. The student wants to know
something of the relationship between Jesus and Luke's portrait of him.
To discuss all these questions adequately would turn one fairly large
volume into several large volumes and would defeat the purpose of attempting to provide a reasonably manageable companion to the study of
Lk. Thus, since Luke is so often dependent on Mk., a full treatment of
historical and traditional matters would require a detailed consideration
of the traditions used by Mark. Since a commentator on Lk. can hardly
be expected to incapsulate a commentary on Mk. in his own commentary, it must suffice to summarise, often very inadequately, the present
state of research on Marcan problems and to state positions briefly and
without detailed justification. Where Luke is dependent on Q and other
material, the commentator on Lk. has more scope and can be expected
to handle the issues more fully. But here again he enters upon disputed
territory, since the problems raised by Q and Luke's other sources are
only beginning to be tackled in detail by scholars and few persons will
wish to rush in with definitive conclusions. It may, therefore, seem rash
to attempt any kind of historical appraisal of the origins of the traditions
recorded in Lk. at the present time, and some readers may well feel that I

have by-passed traditio-historical investigation at various points.

Nevertheless, it is important to observe that in many cases the reasons often giving for ascribing the origins of traditions to the early church rather than to Jesus himself are both speculative and unconvincing, and that the case for finding the origins of most of the Gospel tradition in the activity and teaching of Jesus is stronger than is sometimes allowed. I am not persuaded that the nature of the tradition is such that sayings ascribed to Jesus in the Gospels should be regarded as sayings of other Jews or as creations by the early church unless evidence to the contrary is forthcoming; on the contrary, where there is no positive evidence that a saying must have originated in Judaism or in the early church, it is wiser to reckon with its origin in the ministry of Jesus. It is clear that the basic tradition of the sayings of Jesus was *modified* both in the tradition and by the Evangelists in order to re-express its significance for new situations; it is by no means obvious that this basic tradition was *created* by the early church. Similarly, it is unlikely that the stories about Jesus and the narrative settings for his teaching are products of the church's *Sitz im Leben*. The fact that such material was found to be congenial for use in the church's situation is no proof that it was created for this purpose. To some scholars this attitude of basic acceptance of the traditions regarding Jesus as having a historical basis may seem to be pure assumption and to fail to reckon with the obvious *Tendenz* to be found in the traditions. I believe, however, that it is justified by a study of the traditions as a whole. If this approach to the traditions offers a coherent and self-consistent picture of the ministry and teaching of Jesus, as I believe it does, this fact gives strong justification for the method which has been employed.

Authorship and Date

If the Gospel rests on sound tradition faithfully recorded, the name of its author is of secondary importance. The Gospel itself is anonymous and contains no information which would enable us to identify its author, although one may draw some conclusions regarding his milieu and situation. That he wrote for an urban church community in the Hellenistic world is fairly certain. From the latter half of the second century onwards the clear and consistent verdict of early church writers is that he was Luke, the 'beloved physician' and the companion of Paul. It is sometimes claimed that this tradition is simply an intelligent deduction from the NT evidence that Acts was written by a companion of Paul, who is most likely to have been Luke; consequently, it is argued, the tradition has no independent value. But the argument is stronger than this. The tradition in question may date back to the first half of the second century (Bruce, 4–8), and it is unequivocal in singling out Luke from among several possible candidates among Paul's companions during the period covered by the 'we' sections in Acts. There is never any suggestion of a rival candidate for the honour of writing the Gospel. Attempts have been made to strengthen the argument for authorship by a physician by finding examples of medical phraseology in Luke-Acts; these are too few to be made the basis of an argument, but there is perhaps just sufficient evidence to corroborate a view more firmly based on other considerations.

The traditional view of authorship faces two main difficulties. One is based on the evidence of Acts, where, it is claimed, the picture of Paul is too far removed from historical reality to be the work of a companion of the apostle. This point lies beyond the scope of a commentary on the Gospel, but reference may be made to *Luke: Historian and Theologian* where reasons are given for disputing the point (see further Ellis, 42–52). The other point is that Luke is said to give the impression of writing at a time when the early church had settled down into its 'early catholic' period; consequently he belonged to the post-Pauline period. But again the argument fails to convince. The two characteristics of the 'early catholic' period are held to be the decline of hope in the imminence of the parousia and the consequent development of an institutional Christianity. But, so far as the first is concerned, the postulate that the first Christians expected the parousia almost hourly and that only at a later date did they adjust to its delay is unwarranted. On the most probable reading of the evidence Jesus himself allowed for an interval before the parousia. If the first Christians did expect it to happen very soon (another assumption which requires to be tested), the evidence is quite clear that at an early point they recognised that it would not necessarily happen immediately. This is obviously the case with Paul who reckoned at first that he might belong to the company of those caught up to be with the Lord at the parousia but increasingly came to recognise that his own death might well precede the parousia. This means that, if there was any crisis caused by the 'delay' of the parousia, it had already taken place in the Pauline period. Luke himself clearly allows for the possibility of an imminent parousia (12:35–40; 17:20–37; 18:8; 21:5–36). It is not possible to date the Gospel by this criterion. As for the suggestion that Luke represents an institutionalised form of Christianity in which the church has become a *Heilsanstalt,* mistress of the word and sacraments and the distributor of salvation, it is sufficient to compare Luke with other, genuinely early catholic writings, to see that this characterisation is completely inapt (see further I. H. Marshall, ' "Early Catholicism" in the New Testament', in R. N. Longenecker and M. C. Tenney, (ed.), *New Dimensions in New Testament Study,* Grand Rapids, 1974, 217–231). In short, the best hypothesis is still that the Gospel was composed by Luke.

As for the date of composition, this is closely bound up with the dates of Mk. and Acts. There are two serious possibilities, a date in the early sixties or a date in the later decades of the first century. The latter is the view most commonly held, with AD 80 being suggested as a round figure. This date presupposes that Luke was not dependent on the writings of Josephus (*c.* AD 93) but that he did write after the fall of Jerusalem. While the possibility of *vaticinia ante eventum* is not to be ruled out, it may well be the case that the comparatively frequent and more precise references to the fall of Jerusalem in Lk., although based on genuine prophecy by Jesus, reflect a knowledge of and an interest in a recent event. On the other hand, the complete lack of interest in the fall of Jerusalem in Acts and the way in which that book ends its story before the death of Paul are strong indications of a date before AD 70. On the whole a date not far off AD 70 appears to satisfy all requirements.

The place of composition is uncertain. Early tradition connected Luke with Achaia, but has nothing positive in its favour. Luke's use of Mk. may indicate a connection with Rome, but his use of Q possibly brings him into a Syrian environment. Some slight evidence in favour of Antioch was noted earlier. Another possibility is Caesarea (H. Klein, 'Zur Frage nach dem Abfassungsort der Lukasschriften', Ev.T 32, 1972, 467–477). If we knew who Theophilus was, the situation might be much clearer, but his whereabouts are as obscure as those of Luke himself.

The Purpose of the Gospel

We are fortunate in that Luke has given us his own statement of intention at the beginning of the Gospel. He was concerned to write a Gospel, i.e. a presentation of the ministry of Jesus in its saving significance, but to do so in the context of a two-part work which would go on to present the story of the early church, thus demonstrating how the message of the gospel spread, in accordance with prophecy and God's command, to the ends of the earth. He wrote for people at some remove from the ministry of Jesus, both in geography and in time, and his task was to provide them with such an account of the story of Jesus as would enable them to see that the story with which they had already become partially acquainted was a reliable basis for their faith. Thus his work was probably intended for members of the church, but it could at the same time be used evangelistically, and its outward form (in the manner of a historical and literary work) strongly suggests that such a wider audience was in view.

Luke has therefore written the story of Jesus in a connected form, covering his life from his birth to his ascension. Of all the Evangelists he is the most conscious of writing as a historian, yet throughout his work the history is the vehicle of theological interpretation in which the significance of Jesus is expressed. He presents the story of Jesus as being the fulfilment of prophecy and indeed as being determined throughout by the will of God revealed in prophecy. The ministry is the period of fulfilment in which God's promises of salvation are realised. The keynotes sounded at the outset are the ideas of salvation and good news. The teaching, healings and acts of compassion shown by Jesus are all parts of the proclamation of good news, and the message of Jesus is finely summed up in the saying, 'The Son of man is come to seek and to save that which was lost'. Luke particularly stresses how this salvation is for all who are poor and needy and the total impact of the Gospel is to show the 'wideness in God's mercy'. Those who respond to the message of Jesus receive the blessings of the kingdom of God, and they are called to a strenuous life of self-denial and perseverance as they wait for the parousia of the Son of man. Luke underlines the call of Jesus to whole-hearted discipleship, especially over against the temptation to acquire riches and to settle down into the life of the world.

The message of Jesus is directed to Israel, especially to the needy people despised by official Judaism, and Jesus' task is to call the people of God back to him and to enlarge that people (although there are only faint adumbrations of the Gentile mission in the Gospel). But it was his lot from the very beginning to be rejected by many in Israel, particularly among the rulers, while the common people on the whole heard him gladly. The note of conflict sounds throughout the Gospel and reaches its climax in the passion of Jesus. But already before this Jesus had uttered his condemnation of the hypocritical religion found among many of the Pharisees and of the worship at the temple. So in the end he was condemned by the Jews, but God raised him from the dead to be a Prince and a Saviour.

Such, in briefest compass, is the story. So short a summary cannot do justice to the wealth of detail, nor can it note the individual marks of Luke's distinctiveness over against his sources and what his companion Evangelists made of them. Only the detailed study of the Gospel itself can reveal the scope of Luke's achievement in retelling the story of Jesus, and this the reader is now invited to undertake.

COMMENTARY

I

PREFACE

1:1–4

UNLIKE the other Evangelists, Luke begins his Gospel with a brief preface such as one would find in the work of a contemporary secular writer. For Jewish and Hellenistic parallels see H. J. Cadbury, BC II, 489–510. The Prologue to Ecclesiasticus is noteworthy for the way in which, like Luke, it justifies the author's writing of a fresh book alongside existing works on the same topic. More striking is Josephus, *Contra Apionem,* a work written in two parts ('books') with a preface to the whole work at the beginning of Book 1 and a brief recapitulation at the beginning of Book 2: 'In my history of our *Antiquities,* most excellent Epaphroditus, I have, I think, made sufficiently clear ... the extreme antiquity of our Jewish race ... Since, however, I observe that a considerable number of persons ... discredit the statements in my history ..., I consider it my duty to devote a brief treatise to all these points ... to instruct all who desire to know the truth concerning the antiquity of our race. As witnesses to my statements I propose to call the writers who, in the estimation of the Greeks, are the most trustworthy authorities on antiquity as a whole' (Jos. Ap. 1:1–4). 'In the first volume of this work, my esteemed Epaphroditus, I demonstrated the antiquity of our race ... I shall now proceed to refute the rest of the authors who have attacked us' (Jos. Ap. 2:1f.). These quotations, which offer significant parallels in other respects, suggest that Luke's prologue is meant to cover both parts of his two-volume work (Zahn, 50; *contra* Schürmann, I, 4, who is, however, correct in claiming that the content of the prologue refers primarily to the Gospel).

The preface is written in excellent Greek with a most carefully wrought sentence structure, and stands in contrast to the style adopted in the following narrative. It claims a place for the Gospel as a work of literature, worthy of an educated audience. Although the book is addressed to one reader, Theophilus, he is evidently Luke's literary patron, and although it must remain doubtful whether the Gospel was in fact meant 'for the book market' (Dibelius, *Studies*, 135; but see the cautious study of Vögtle, 31–42), it was meant to circulate widely. Luke has adopted the literary conventions of the time, but the resulting work is an expression of his own personality and purpose. We should not, therefore, interpret his statements in too conventional a manner, as if what he said was dictated purely by the style and vocabulary of his literary models. He was concerned to hand on tradition rather than to be a *littérateur*.

By writing in this fashion, then, Luke was claiming a place for Christianity on the stage of world history. How far his predecessors had made such claims we do not know, but the likelihood is that earlier Christian literature was produced for church purposes. Luke also had in mind the non-Christian world.

He justified his work by reference to the precedent of earlier, similar writings, to the trustworthy nature of his sources, and to his own qualifications to produce an orderly narrative based on careful research. He shows no disparagement of his predecessors; rather he felt that their example justified his own attempt to write a Gospel intended for the particular situation which he addressed. He does not question their accuracy, for they, like he, had received the tradition handed down by eyewitnesses of the events.

Luke's purpose was to give an historical account which would form the basis for a sound Christian faith on the part of those who had already been instructed, perhaps imperfectly and incompletely, in the story of Jesus. Throughout the preface there is a stress on the historical accuracy of the material presented. It has been argued that the preface is concerned to show that the career of Jesus was a series of divine acts rather than to affirm the factual certainty of those acts (U. Luck, 'Kerygma, Tradition und Geschichte bei Lukas', ZTK 57, 1960, 51–66). This thesis is correct in what it affirms, but wrong in what it denies. It is clear from Lk. 7:21 and Acts 1:3 that Luke was concerned with the historical reliability of his material (cf. H. Strathmann, TDNT IV, 492). It may be that the existence of gnosticizing or docetic teaching which minimized the importance of the historical Jesus played a part in shaping his aim.

Luke does not name himself in the preface; he is content to be seen as a member of the church which he serves, like the servants of the Word before him.

See further H. J. Cadbury, BC II, 489–510; Stonehouse, 24–45; G. Klein, 'Lukas i.1–4 als theologisches Programm', in Dinkler, 193–216; Schürmann, *Untersuchungen*, 251–271; Vögtle, 31–42; I. I. du Plessis, 'Once more: the purpose of Luke's prologue (Lk I 1–4)', Nov.T 16, 1974, 259–271; W. C. van Unnik, 'Remarks on the Purpose of Luke's Historical Writing (Luke 1, 1–4)', in van Unnik, I, 6–15; id. 'Once More St Luke's Prologue', *Neotestamentica* 7, 1973, 7–26; G. Schneider, 'Zur Bedeutung von Καθεξῆς im lukanischen Doppelwerk', ZNW 68, 1977, 128–131.

(1) The preface is composed of one long, periodic sentence, each of whose two parts contains three matching phrases (cf. Acts 15:24f.): The

stately opening conjunction ἐπειδήπερ** (here only in the Greek Bible; Jos. Bel. 1:17) is a Classical word meaning ' "inasmuch as" ' with reference to a fact already well known' (BD 456³). It is causal rather than concessive: Luke is using the work of previous writers positively to justify his own venture rather than stating that he is writing despite their efforts which were, after all, the indispensable sources for his own work. His predecessors were 'many' (πολλοί). This word was used frequently at the beginning of speeches and documents in a formal manner and need not be taken too literally (Acts 24:2; Heb. 1:1; in Acts 24:10 it refers to a few years). Luke's stress was not on the number of his predecessors but on the legitimacy of his claims to be associated with them (J. B. Bauer, 'ΠΟΛΛΟΙ Luke 1:1', Nov.T 4, 1960, 263–266). They will have included Mark and the compilers of collections of sayings of Jesus and other material. To describe their work as an 'attempt' is no disparagement of it. ἐπιχειρέω (Acts 9:29; 19:13**) does not indicate success or failure (MM 250f.), but points to the difficulty of the task, which was also felt by Luke (κἀμοί, 1:3). ἀνατάσσομαι** is 'to draw up, compile', perhaps to draw up an orderly account in writing in contrast to oral tradition (G. Delling, TDNT VIII, 32f.). In the use of διήγησις** ('narrative') Schürmann, I, 7f., sees a possible echo of Hab. 1:5 LXX: 'For I am working a work in your days that you will not believe unless someone tells (ἐκδιηγῆται) it'; thus the prophetic promise of a narrative of God's mighty deeds is being fulfilled. But would Luke's readers have been able to appreciate such an allusion? The meaning of the verb πληροφορέω*, used to describe the events (πρᾶγμα*; Acts 5:4*) recorded by Luke and his predecessors is 'to bring to full measure' (Col. 4:12; 2 Tim. 4:5, 17) or 'to convince fully (Rom. 4:21; 14:5;**; cf. πληροφορία, Col. 2:2; 1 Thes. 1:5; Heb. 6:11; 10:22**). The latter meaning is seen in the rendering 'things most surely believed' (AV; RV mg), but is inappropriate here. The thought is of events brought to completion, namely the events leading to salvation; the passive form suggests that these are divine acts which God himself promised and has now fully brought to pass, and the use of the perfect indicates that they are seen as a finished series in past time (G. Klein, 198). ἐν ἡμῖν will then refer to the members of the church in whose midst these events took place and among whom they retain their lasting, saving significance and power. (This means that ἡμῖν in 1:2 has a narrower reference to Luke and his contemporaries who were dependent on eyewitnesses for their knowledge of the earthly life of Jesus, but, pace Klein, there is no difficulty about such a shift in meaning.)

(2) Luke now provides the basis (καθώς, 'according as'; Lk. 17x; Mt. 3x; Mk. 8x) for the reliability of the information on which the narrative about Jesus rests. It has been 'handed down' as tradition (παραδίδωμι; the use of the Classical second aorist form, παρέδοσαν, instead of the more common first aorist, παρέδωκαν, adds to the literary refinement of the sentence). The verb is a technical term for the handing

down of material, whether orally or in writing, as authoritative teaching (Mk. 7:13; Acts 6:14; 1 Cor. 11:2, 23; 15:3; 2 Pet. 2:21; Jude 3; F. Büchsel, TDNT II, 169–173; O. Cullmann, *The Early Church*, 1956, 59–99; B. Gerhardsson, *Memory and Manuscript*, Uppsala, 1961; K. Wegenast, *Das Verständnis der Tradition bei Paulus und in den Deuteropaulinen*, Neukirchen, 1962). Those who handed this tradition down had been acquainted with the facts from the beginning of the ministry of Jesus (cf. Acts 1:22; 10:37). They were 'eyewitnesses' (αὐτόπτης**) who could not but speak of what they had seen and heard (Acts 4:20). They thus became 'servants of the word', a striking phrase conveying the thought of the centrality of the gospel message and of the way in which men are its servants; the use of ὑπηρέτης (4:20*; cf. Acts 26:16; 1 Cor. 4:1; ἡ διακονία τοῦ λόγου, Acts 6:4) emphasises that they 'were not propagandists for their own views of what happened with Jesus but had unreservedly put their persons and work in the service of Jesus' cause' (K. H. Rengstorf, TDNT VIII, 543; cf. 530–544). λόγος thus signifies the Christian message, unchanging in its central emphasis, but variable in its form and detailed exposition; here the record of the acts and teaching of Jesus is meant (cf. Acts 10:36–43), but Luke also uses the word for Jesus' own message (5:1; 8:11–21; 11:28). A. Feuillet suggests that 'word' is almost hypostatized here so that it can be seen and that the usage here is related to that in 1 Jn. 1:1f. (' "Témoins oculaires et serviteurs de la parole" (Lc i 2b)', Nov.T 15, 1973, 241–259). The syntax demands that the eyewitnesses and servants are one group of people (G. Kittel, TDNT IV, 115; W. Michaelis, TDNT V, 348). They are to be identified with the apostles, although not exclusively with the Twelve (*pace* Schürmann, I, 9). Since Luke distinguishes himself and his contemporaries from them, it follows that the content of their testimony was primarily the story of Jesus rather than of the early church, and also that Luke distinguishes between the writers of the Gospels and the apostolic eyewitnesses on whose testimony they were dependent.

(3) Having described the situation before he commenced his work, Luke now joins himself (κἀμοί) to the 'many' of 1:1 and records his own decision (δοκέω; in this sense: Acts 15:22, 25, 28) to record what had happened in view of his own qualifications to do so (cf. Lagrange, 5). παρακολουθέω literally means 'to follow, accompany' (Mk. 16:17). H. J. Cadbury (BC II, 501f.) has argued that the verb must mean 'to observe' here (cf. 1 Tim. 4:6; 2 Tim. 3:10**), and hence that Luke is here (falsely) claiming eyewitness authority for his work. But his claim that the word *cannot* mean 'to investigate' is not compelling, and this is the better meaning here (cf. AG s.v.). Luke means that he has thoroughly investigated all the facts (πᾶσιν) in the light of the available evidence. This claim is qualified by two adverbs. ἄνωθεν* (Acts 26:5*) can mean 'from the beginning' or simply 'for a long time'. It may refer, therefore, to the scope of Luke's investigation (stretching back beyond the 'beginning' of

Jesus' ministry (1:2) to the birth stories: Schürmann, I, 11), but more
probably it refers to Luke's lengthy researches (Lagrange, 5f). ἀκριβῶς*
(Acts 18:25f.; 23:15, 20; 24:22*) should certainly also be taken with
παρηκολουθηκότι (and not with γράψαι); it refers to the care with which
the research was undertaken. Luke was then ready to write his book,
describing the events καθεξῆς, i.e. 'in order, one thing after another'
(Acts 11:4; 18:23) or 'as follows', 'the following' (8:1; Acts 3:24**). The
latter meaning is inappropriate here (*pace* Cadbury, BC II, 504f.). With
the former meaning the adverb may be taken to imply chronological exactitude or simply an orderly and lucid narrative. Luke's actual
procedure may seem to rule out the idea of chronological exactitude, but
although he is not interested in assigning precise dates and places to the
events he records he is broadly chronological in his treatment (cf.
Schürmann, I, 12f.; and earlier commentators). F. Mussner ('Καθεξῆς
im Lukasprolog', in Ellis, *Jesus*, 253–255) adopts the meaning 'in order,
i.e. without omitting anything'. M. Völkel ('Exegetische Erwägungen
zum Verständnis des Begriffs καθεξῆς im Lukanischen Prolog', NTS 20,
1973–74, 289–299) argues that the word implies the continuity of items
within a logical whole, so that Luke's aim is to show that the story of
Jesus, taken as a whole, makes sense and is therefore worthy of belief.
G. Schneider* suggests that the continuity of events in a salvation-
historical scheme of promise and fulfilment is meant. κράτιστος is used
simply as a polite form of address (Jos., Vita 430; Ap. 1:1), such as
might be used in addressing some highly placed person (Acts 23:26;
24:3; 26:25**). Although older commentators deduced that Theophilus
was a Roman provincial governor, since the adjective was the appropriate courtesy title for a Roman *eques* (Geldenhuys, 53), nothing
can be deduced from it as to his precise standing. Nevertheless, his position as Luke's literary patron, who would perhaps assist in the
'publication' of the Gospel (Hauck, 17), may indicate his superior social
position. Theophilus cannot be identified with any other known person
(see the intriguing historical romance in Streeter, 535–539). The tradition that he came from Antioch (Ps.-Clem. Recog. 10:71; see Zahn 57 n.
41) is as strong or weak as Luke's own link with that city. Despite the
symbolical possibilities of Θεόφιλος, it remains probable that it is the
name of a real, but unknown, person.

(4) Whether Theophilus was already a Christian depends partly on
the meaning of κατηχέω; it may mean 'to report, inform' or 'to instruct'
(cf. Acts 18:25; 21:21, 24; Rom. 2:18; 1 Cor. 14:19; Gal. 6:6**). It is
possible that Theophilus had learned about Jesus by hearsay (Zahn,
58f.; H. W. Beyer, TDNT III, 638–640), but more probable that he
had received formal Christian instruction. Although the rigorous
catechumenate of a later age is unlikely in the early church, new converts were doubtless given careful training in the faith, and this Gospel
itself contains material for such training (cf. especially Schürmann, I, 13,
15). At the same time Luke will have included in his intended audience

those who had a minimal or defective knowledge of Christianity; he had an apologetic and evangelistic purpose, to present Jesus in such a way that any reader might accept him as Messiah, Lord and Saviour.

ἀσφάλεια signifies 'firmness' (Acts 5:23); 'safety, security' (1 Thes. 5:3**); 'certainty, reliability' (cf. Acts 2:36; 21:34; 22:30; 25:26; also 2 Pet. 1:16, 19). λόγοι refers to the various pieces of instruction which Theophilus has already received. The compressed construction with relative attraction and inclusion of the antecedent in the relative clause can be expanded as ἐπιγνῷς περὶ τῶν λόγων οὓς κατηχήθης τὴν ἀσφάλειαν or ἐπιγνῷς τῶν λόγων περὶ ὧν κατηχήθης τὴν ἀσφάλειαν. The former expansion is perhaps the more likely (BD 294[5]). By his method of presentation Luke wishes to show to Theophilus that reliable information was contained in the accounts which he had already received (van Unnik*). There may be a polemical reference to heretics who disputed the truth of the message, as it had been told to them. If many accounts of Jesus were circulating, Luke may have wished to enable his readers to sift out what was reliable from what was doubtful.

II
THE BIRTH AND CHILDHOOD OF JESUS

1:5 – 2:52

AS a prologue to the ministry of Jesus Luke relates the story of his birth, showing how he was born as the Son of God and destined to bring salvation to the people. The narrative is interwoven with that of the birth of his forerunner who was to prepare the people for the coming of the Lord. The parallelism in structure between the two accounts (Laurentin, 32f.; Wink, 59) shows that John and Jesus were not regarded as rivals, but each had his proper place in the unfolding of the divine scheme of salvation. They are placed side by side but in such a way that the superior place of Jesus is evident. John is the 'type' who finds fulfilment in the 'antitype' Jesus and is surpassed by him. It is unlikely that he is regarded as a priestly Messiah alongside the royal Messiah; his role is rather that of a prophet (Laurentin, 110–116).

Throughout the narrative there is a wealth of allusion to OT parallels and prophecies which demonstrates both that God's acts then were entirely consonant with his earlier dealings with his people and also that they fulfilled his earlier promises regarding the coming of the Messiah. The story itself is filled with the signs of God's intervention to accomplish his purposes through the activity of angelic messengers, the wonderful conceptions of both John and Jesus, and other supernatural phenomena.

This combination of features raises in an acute form at the very outset the nature of the 'reliability' to which Luke referred in 1:4. Can stories so laden with interpretation be historical, and can the miraculous events be taken literally? Moreover, while mythological parallels can be adduced for several elements in the stories, they have no independent historical attestation in other early Christian literature (the independent account in Mt. 1–2 is very different in detail).

The problems raised by these considerations are difficult, even for those who are unwilling to rule out the possibility of the supernatural from the outset. It must be granted that the narratives in their present form are the work of a mind (or minds) steeped in the OT and consciously making use of that knowledge, so that some of the details in them are due to the desire to mould the story in the light of the OT. Moreover, the hymns attributed to some of the principal actors are unlikely to have been spontaneous compositions, but serve, like the speeches in ancient histories, to express the significance of the moment in appropriate language. The narrative as a whole has been moulded into a unitary composition and has a careful dramatic form. It is not surprising that it has been characterised as 'legend', in the sense that it is not based on history, and does not purport to convey it, but rather has the edifying purpose of indicating the religious status of John and Jesus (Hauck, 25f.). Again, it has been described as 'midrash', a term used to describe a literature based on exposition of the OT. In an attempt to bring some precision into an area bedevilled by loose terminology, Schürmann (I, 21–24) has characterised the style as akin to that of Jewish haggadic literature: the narrative presents the divine origin of Jesus by means of a typological understanding of the OT and the use of apocalyptic imagery. But Schürmann is careful to insist that Luke was making use of traditions and not writing off the cuff. Similarly, Ellis, 9, speaks of 'interpretative alterations' rather than the creation of events.

Such interpretation of the basic events may have been carried out by Luke or by the authors of the sources which he may have used. But did he have any sources?

Certainly the vocabulary and style of the narrative show considerable traces of his hand, and the theology is closely integrated with that of the rest of his work (H. H. Oliver*; P. S. Minear*; Conzelmann's claims to the contrary (9 n. 2, 160) are unconvincing). One could argue that Luke's literary ability was equal to the composition of these narratives.

However, the narratives betray a Semitic background to a degree unparalleled elsewhere in Lk.-Acts. The whole atmosphere of the story is Palestinian. The language too is strongly Semitic, although the significance of this is disputed (R. Laurentin, Bib. 35, 1956, 449–456). 1. It may be explained as the result of the conscious adoption of Septuagintal style by Luke himself (Dalman, 39f.; N. Turner*; P. Benoit*; M. D. Goulder and M. C. Sanderson*). 2. The narrative may reflect an Aramaic source (Plummer, 7; Black, 151–156). 3. It may rest on a Hebrew source (Sahlin; P. Winter*; Scobie, 50–52; Laurentin, 12f.).

We can probably dismiss the second of these views, since there is little if any material that demands a specifically Aramaic background. With regard to the first, it must be admitted that the style of the whole section is Lucan, and that he often adopts a Septuagintal style (E. Plümacher, *Lukas als hellenistischer Schriftsteller*, Göttingen, 1972). The question is whether this is a sufficient explanation. a. There is a greater degree of Hebraic style in Lk. 1–2 than elsewhere in his writings.

It is not obvious why Luke should have regarded it as especially appropriate in this section. b. P. Winter has argued that some of the linguistic phenomena are not explicable in terms of use of the LXX by a practised Greek writer (cf. 1:17, 37; 2:34). c. It should be recognised that different parts of the narrative may show different linguistic characteristics. Thus the case for postulating Hebrew originals for the canticles is very strong (R. A. Aytoun*; J. Wragg*). The situation with regard to the narrative is not so clear; certainly Sahlin found that most of it could be turned into Hebrew without undue difficulty, although his case for a full-scale Hebrew source (whose original wording can be restored by textual emendation) is not convincing.

These considerations suggest that Luke has made use of some material, especially the canticles, which was originally composed in Hebrew, although it may well have reached him in a Greek form. But the problem of unravelling the history of the tradition may well defy solution. The following appear to be the main types of solution.

1. The view that Luke himself created the narrative without documentary sources, but in dependence on oral material, still finds supporters, despite the linguistic and other evidence adduced above (Klostermann, ad loc.; P. Benoit* (at least for the story of John); M. D. Goulder and M. C. Sanderson*).

2. Sahlin argues that there was a proto-Lucan document extending from 1:5 to 3:7a in Hebrew, and from 3:7b to Acts 1:15 in Aramaic; it contained the birth narrative as a continuous story, but various additions and alterations in order were made by Luke.

3. In various forms many scholars posit that the birth narratives have been composed on the basis of material from more than one independent source. Particularly influential has been the view of D. Völter* that 1:5–80 is based on a source emanating from followers of John the Baptist; originally it recounted two announcements of John's birth, one to his father and one to his mother, the latter having been replaced in the Gospel by the story of the annunciation which was modelled upon it. On this view, the Magnificat was originally placed on the lips of Elizabeth. The rest of the story is Christian legend.

Bultmann, 320–328, similarly held that 1:5–25, 57–66, was a Baptist legend, to which the originally independent hymns were added. The legend of the annunciation was independent, 1:34–37 being an addition by Luke himself. But 1:39–45 (which ignores 1:34–37) is a device to link together the two stories, and appears to be pre-Lucan, thus suggesting that the combination of the two stories antedated Luke. The narratives in 2:1–20, 22–40 and 41–52 were originally independent of one another and of the annunciation story; the link of the birth of Jesus with the census was made by Luke himself.

A very similar analysis was offered by M. Dibelius* (summarised in Dibelius, 120–124): 1:5–25, 57–66 is a Baptist legend. The story of the annunciation forms a second legend, which originally contained the motif of the virgin birth (*contra* Bultmann), but omitted any reference to Joseph. A third legend is that of the shepherds in 2:1–19. These were joined together by Luke who added the two hymns and the linking scene in 1:39–56. A fourth legend is contained in 2:22–38, which contains older elements, but has been heavily worked over.

4. In a number of publications, which the author was unable to synthesise in book form before his death, P. Winter* made an elaborate analysis of the birth narrative. Following Völter he argued for a Baptist source (B), originally in Hebrew, containing most of 1:5–80 and including an angelic announcement of John's birth to Elizabeth. This has been most heavily edited in 1:26–38, 39–46a, 56. Second, a source close to Jesus' family and strongly attached to the temple produced a Temple source (T), probably in Hebrew (possibly Aramaic), which contained the material in 2:22–39, 41–51a. Third, a so-called Nazarene adapter (N) combined these two sources, making the annunciation to Elizabeth refer to Mary and Jesus, and composing 2:4–21 as a counterpart to the story of John's birth. The adapter was a Palestinian Jew who probably worked in Hebrew or 'a sort of Hebrew-Aramaic mixture'. As for the hymnic material, the Magnificat and Benedictus were Maccabean war hymns used by the author of B (who himself composed 1:76–79). Lk. 2:14 is a fragment from a Hebrew messianic psalm, while 2:29–32 and 34b–35 are fragments of Christian hymns used by N. Luke's modifications were minor, except for the inclusion of 2:1–3.

5. A somewhat different analysis is offered by Leaney, 20–27, who finds two sources. The first, centred on Mary and the virginal conception, and possibly containing no reference to Nazareth or Joseph, comprised 1:5–45, 57–66, 80, 56; 2:21; ? 1:46–55. The second, centred on Jesus, knows nothing of signs before his birth but attests his messiahship to Mary and Joseph after his birth; it comprised 2:1–20; ? 1:46–55; 2:22–38; 1:68–79 (i.e. the Benedictus is attributed, with Sahlin, to Anna); 2:39–40; ? 2:41–52. This second source is probably earlier.

6. Schürmann, I, 140–145, holds that there was a unified Jewish-Christian Baptist narrative (1:5–25, 57–67, (68–75), 76–79, (80)), to which were added the parallel construction 1:26–38 and the linking narrative 1:39–56. But the stories about Jesus (1:26–38, 39–56; 2:1–20 (21); 2:22–38 (39f.) and 2:41–51 (52)) do not seem to have had any original connection with one another. The annunciation story in its present form was modelled on the Baptist story and linked with it; if an earlier form lay behind it, it can no longer be reconstructed. There may be a traditional link between 2:1–7 and 2:22–39. These stories come from Jewish Christian circles, and it is hard to date them, although the annunication story appears to be later than the Baptist story. The stories were probably put together in Palestine, and show little Hellenistic influence.

At the end of his investigation Schürmann has to confess that the tradition history of Lk. 1–2 is still wrapped in darkness. It appears most probable that Luke had sources at his disposal, and that these came from Palestinian Jewish Christian circles which had links with the family of Jesus. The view that these sources were independent of one another is not entirely convincing. But beyond this it is difficult to go, and we must be content to keep an open mind on the problem of Luke's sources and hence on the historicity of the events recorded in them.

See A. Harnack, *Luke the Physician*, London, 1907; D. Völter, *Die evangelische Erzählung von der Geburt und Kindheit Jesu kritisch untersucht*, Strassbourg, 1911; R. A. Aytoun, 'The Ten Lucan Hymns of the Nativity in their Original Language', JTS 18, 1917, 274–288; V. Taylor, *The Historical Evidence for the Virgin Birth*, Oxford, 1920; E. Norden, *Die Geburt des Kindes*, Berlin, 1924; K. Bornhäuser, *Die Geburts- und Kindheitsgeschichte Jesu*, Gütersloh, 1930; Machen; M. Dibelius, 'Jungfrauensohn und Krippenkind' (Heidelberg, 1932), cited from *Botschaft*, I, 1–78; Bultmann, 320–328; G. Erdmann, *Die Vorgeschichte des Lukas- und Matthäusevangeliums und Vergils vierte Ekloge*, Göttingen, 1932; M. S. Enslin, 'The Christian Stories of the Nativity', JBL 59, 1940, 317–338; Sahlin; P. Winter, 'Some Observations on the Language in the Birth and Infancy Stories of the Third Gospel', NTS 1, 1954–55, 111–121; id. 'On Luke and Lucan Sources', ZNW 47, 1956, 217–242; id. 'The Proto-Source of Luke 1', Nov.T 1, 1956, 184–199; N. Turner, 'The Relation of Luke 1 and 2 to Hebraic Sources and to the Rest of Luke-Acts', NTS 2, 1955–56, 100–109; P. Benoit, 'L'enfance de Jean-Baptiste selon Luc 1' (NTS 3, 1956–57, 169–194), cited from *Exégèse*, III, 165–196; R. Laurentin, 'Traces d'allusions étymologiques en Luc I–II', Bib. 37, 1956, 435–456; 38, 1957, 1–23; Laurentin (with bibliography); M. D. Goulder and M. C. Sanderson, 'St Luke's Genesis', JTS ns 8, 1957, 12–30; R. M. Wilson, 'Some Recent Studies in the Lucan Infancy Narratives', TU, 73, 1959, 235–253; H. H. Oliver, 'The Lucan Birth Stories and the Purpose of Luke-Acts', NTS 10, 1963–64, 202–226; P. S. Minear, 'Luke's Use of the Birth Stories', SLA 111–130; W. B. Tatum, 'The Epoch of Israel: Luke I–II and the Theological Plan of Luke-Acts', NTS 13, 1966–67, 184–195; J. Wragg, 'St Luke's Nativity Narrative with Special Reference to the Canticles in the Light of the Jewish and Early Christian Background', unpublished Ph.D. Thesis, Manchester, 1965; J. McHugh, *The Mother of Jesus in the New Testament*, London, 1975; R. E. Brown, 'Luke's Method in the Annunciation Narratives', in J. W. Flanagan and A. W. Robinson (ed.), *No Famine in the Land*, Missoula, 1975, 179–194.

a. The Prophecy of John's Birth (1:5–25)

The narrative begins with the announcements of the births of John and Jesus, so that the divine promises (1:5–56) can be seen to come to their fulfilment (1:57 – 2:52). The stories are deliberately parallel in form. Both show how the saving events were initiated by the action of God; in both the divine revelation about the birth and future role of the children is made by Gabriel, and in both a confirmatory sign is given as an earnest of the miracle to follow. The two stories are tied together by the facts that the confirmatory sign for Mary is the birth of her cousin Elizabeth's child and that the greatness ascribed to John is an indication of the superior greatness that will be ascribed to Jesus.

The story follows familiar OT patterns. The situation of Zechariah and Elizabeth resembles most closely that of the aged Abraham and Sarah, but it also echoes the situations of Jacob and Rachel (1:25), of Samson's parents, and of Samuel's parents. John himself is described in a way reminiscent of Samson and Samuel, but his role is specifically that of a second Elijah whose task is to prepare for God's visitation of his

people; there is no direct mention of the coming Messiah, but the term
'Lord' (1:15, 17) would convey the thought of 'Christ the Lord' (2:11) to
Christian readers. The greatness of the herald of this mighty event is
foreshadowed by his wondrous birth which indicates that God has a rich
destiny for him.

The accurate Palestinian background and the lack of Christian
colouring are important features in determining the origin of the story.
There is nothing here that demands its composition outside Palestine.
The supernatural motifs in the story have their closest parallels in the
OT and are related in deliberately reminiscent language. It has,
therefore, been suggested that the story arose in a Baptist sect which
flourished after John's death. It produced a story which, in its original
form, attributed high rank to John without recognising Jesus as the
Messiah or John as his forerunner; it may even have regarded John himself as the Messiah (cf. 1:17 note; so Bultmann, 320f.; Dibelius,
Botschaft I, 8; and other scholars listed by Wink, 60 n. 1). In its
developed form this view is very doubtful. It is not possible to uncover
with any certainty an original form of the story in which John is given a
position independent of Jesus, and certainly not one in which he himself
was regarded as the Messiah. The existence of a Baptist sect which made
such claims for John is also doubtful. It is more probable that some,
possibly the most prominent, members of John's circle became followers
of Jesus and amalgamated their traditions with those of the Christian
group which they entered (Wink, 71f.). If, however, there is a historical
basis for the kinship of Elizabeth and Mary, the stories of John and
Jesus may well have belonged together from the beginning. In any case it
seems unlikely that the two annunciation stories, so similar in construction and atmosphere, existed separately in their developed forms.

There is nothing improbable in the view that Zechariah and
Elizabeth had a child comparatively late in life, and that this event was
seen in the light of similar events in the OT. Nor is it improbable that
Zechariah may have suffered a stroke at the time. The historical
problem is whether the narrative incorporating these events is meant to
be taken literally or as a piece of symbolism indicating the importance of
the child to be born. Schürmann's suggestion (I, 32) that the device of
the angel is used to symbolise how the OT cult is broken through from
another world is artificial. If, however, the angel is not to be taken
literally, the narrative as a whole becomes devoid of historical basis
(beyond the birth of John to a previously childless couple).

The problem is, therefore, whether the coming of Jesus from God
and his return at the resurrection (together with associated events) were
literally surrounded by angelic appearances or had a significance which
the Evangelists could not expound without the use of motifs that are
symbolical rather than literal. So far as the exposition of the passage is
concerned, the outcome of this debate is not important; the *meaning*
of the passage is the same whether it be literal or symbolical. It is a

different matter for the historian who is concerned to discover what really happened, and who wants to know whether the significance of John was indicated by a supernatural intervention or by means of the symbolism employed by an inspired narrator. Two extremes must be avoided. There is the extreme which insists on taking literally what was never meant to be taken literally and fails to do justice to the literary character of the Gospels. There is also the extreme which sees so little history in the Gospels that there remain no grounds for ascribing to Jesus (rather than to anybody else or perhaps to nobody) the significance which the Evangelists attached to his historical existence. Despite Lewis Carroll, it is impossible to have the Cheshire cat's grin without the Cheshire cat as its bearer. The middle ground is adopted by those who insist that the several biblical narratives must be examined on their merits. Nor should the possibility be ignored that in a world which believed in supernatural phenomena it was appropriate for God to act in such a way in order to lead men to belief in him; it is intellectual snobbery for twentieth-century western man to claim that God should reveal himself in every age only in the way that he thinks is proper for his own age. If this point is granted, it still remains the case that the historicity of the present narrative cannot be positively established, since the origin and transmission of the tradition is obscure. Equally, however, the possibility of a historical basis to the narrative cannot be denied, since we have no historical knowledge that contradicts it. We must content ourselves with the cautious conclusion that a narrator, steeped in the OT, has brought out the theological significance of the birth of John; different readers will vary in their judgment to what extent supernatural elements were present in the events surrounding his birth.

See the bibliography to 1:5 – 2:52; Machen, 210–223; Wink, 58–82.

(5) Luke's style changes abruptly from that of the preface to one strongly reminiscent of the LXX; for the form of the present verse cf. Jdg. 13:2. ἐγένετο means 'there was' (4:36; Jn. 1:6). ἐν ταῖς ἡμέραις is a favourite phrase in Lk. (1:7, 18; 4:25; 17:26, 28; Acts 5:37; 13:41; see also 1:39 and note). Ἡρῴδης is here 'Herod the Great', ruler of Judaea 40–5/4 BC, and correctly described as 'king' (cf. 9:7 note; the omission of the article before a genitive is frequent in Lk.). Ἰουδαία is used in its wide sense (4:44; 6:17; 7:17; 23:5; Acts 1:8; et al.) and not in the narrow sense of the southern part of the country around Jerusalem as distinct from Samaria and Galilee (so 1:65; 2:4; 3:1; 5:17; 21:21; Acts 9:31; Zahn, 61 n. 50).

The name 'Zechariah' is frequent in the OT and means 'Yahweh remembers'. On the assumption that the story originally existed in a Hebrew form some commentators have seen a deliberate symbolical significance in the names of the characters in Lk. 1–2 (R. Laurentin, Bib. 37, 1956, 435–456; 38, 1957, 1–23). But it is doubtful whether Luke was conscious of such significance, and in any case most Jewish names had some pious significance which would be appropriate in a story such as this one. The use of ὀνόματι before the name is Lucan (Hawkins, 44).

The Jewish priesthood was divided into 24 courses, each composed of 4–9 families (1 Ch. 24:1–19; 2 Ch. 8:14). Apart from the three great festivals, they performed their duties for two separate weeks each year (details in Jeremias, *Jerusalem,* 198–207). The course of 'Αβιά** ('Yahweh is father') was eighth in the list in 1 Ch. 24:10. A late rabbinic source ascribes an evil reputation to the course of Abia (Eleazar ben Kalir's elegy, *c.* AD 730, in SB II, 68; so Grundmann, 49), but it is doubtful whether this notion goes back to the first century.

Priests were expected to marry virgins of Israelite birth (Lv. 21:7, 14), but to marry the daughter of a priest was preferable (SB II, 68–71; Jeremias, *Jerusalem,* 213–221). Such was Zechariah's wife; the phrase 'daughter of Aaron' corresponds to the rabbinic 'daughter of a priest' and is analogous to 'son of Aaron' (K. G. Kuhn, TDNT I, 4).

Unfortunately for the etymologizers the meaning of 'Ελισάβετ (or 'Ελεισάβετ) is not certain. The Hebrew equivalent 'ᵉlîšeḇaʿ is variously interpreted as 'my God has sworn' (Schürmann, I, 30 n. 18), 'God is my fortune' (J. H. Hertz, 'An Explanation of Bathsheba, Beersheba, Elisheba', Exp.T 45, 1933–34, 142; cf. 'My God is fortune, fulness', KB s.v.) or 'God is perfection' (Schmid, 35). The name was that of Aaron's wife (Ex. 6:23), but the coincidence that Joseph's wife bears the name of Aaron's sister (1:27; Ex. 15:20) is no reason for suspecting invention.

John thus came of priestly stock. This does not link him with the Qumran sect, since Zechariah belonged to the Jerusalem priesthood and served in the temple (cf. 1:80 note). Nor is there any indication that John was given a priestly ancestry to fit him to fulfil the role of Elijah who was regarded in Jewish tradition as of priestly descent and destined to be the messianic high priest (cf. J. Jeremias, TDNT II, 928–941).

(6) Luke stresses the piety of Zechariah and Elizabeth (cf. Acts 10:2) and shows that it gains its reward from God. They were δίκαιοι (1:17; 2:25; *et al.*) a word which in combination with ἐναντίον τοῦ θεοῦ implies a religious rather than a purely ethical character, seen in obedience to God's commands and going beyond a merely external, legal righteousness (cf. G. Schrenk, TDNT II, 189). ἀμφότερος is Lucan (5:7; 6:39; 7:42; Acts 3x; rest of NT, 6x). ἐναντίον is used in the same way in 24:19 (cf. 20:26; Acts 7:10; 8:32**; the v.l. ἐνώπιον (A D W Θ pl; TR; *Diglot*) is supported by the phraseology in Acts 4:19, but is probably due to substitution of the more common word (Lk.-Acts, 35x). It should undoubtedly be linked with δίκαιοι (as in Gn. 7:1), and not with πορευόμενοι (*pace* Grundmann, 49).

πορεύομαι in an ethical sense occurs here only in the Gospels, but is common elsewhere (Acts 9:31; 14:16; 1 Pet. 4:3; 2 Pet. 2:10; 3:3; Jude 11, 16, 18). Although found in Classical Greek, the usage here reflects the language of the OT (1 Ki. 8:61) and Judaism (e.g. T. Reub. 1:6; 4:1; see F. Hauck and S. Schulz, TDNT VI, 566–578, especially 571). Paul and John prefer to use περιπατέω. The combination of ἐντολή (15:29; 18:20; 23:56*; Acts 17:15) and δικαίωμα* is found in the LXX (Gn. 26:5; Dt. 4:40; et al.). ὁ κύριος is used for God some 25x in Lk. 1–2, thereafter less frequently; it is thus used in the NT mainly in contexts influenced by the OT (W. Foerster, TDNT III, 1086f.).

Finally, the couple are said to be 'blameless' (ἄμεμπτος* is here used almost adverbially). The ideal is again that of OT piety (Gn. 17:1; cf. Acts 23:1; 24:16), and the point is to show that the childlessness of the couple was not the result of sin (as in Lv. 20:20f.; 2 Sa. 6:23; Je. 22:30; 36:30) but 'in order that the works of God might be revealed' in them (Jn. 9:3).

The phraseology is that of the LXX, especially in its descriptions of Abraham and Solomon. But there is no direct quotation from the LXX, and the impression gained (which will be substantiated throughout Lk. 1–2) is that of an author whose mind is saturated with the language of the LXX and draws on it almost unconsciously as well as making conscious use of typological patterns based on the lives of particular characters.

(7) The introductory καί may be adversative, contrasting the lack of divine blessing on the couple with their godly lives. To be childless was a great reproach (1:25) and possibly a sign of divine punishment; to have children was a sign of blessing (Gn. 1:28; Pss. 127, 128). Zechariah and Elizabeth had, however, presumably given up hope of this blessing, since not only was the latter barren, like Rebekah and Rachel, but also both were now old, like Abraham and Sarah. καθότι has its Hellenistic meaning 'because' (19:9; Acts 2:24; 17:31; it is also used with its Classical meaning 'as, to the degree that' in Acts 2:45; 4:35**). The phrase προβεβηκότες ἐν ταῖς ἡμέραις αὐτῶν ἦσαν is based on OT language (cf. G. Delling, TDNT II, 950 n. 42). For προβαίνω (1:18; 2:36; Mt. 4:21; Mk. 1:19**) see especially Gn. 18:11; the use of the periphrastic form is frequent in Lk. The use of ἐν ταῖς ἡμέραις αὐτῶν (1:18; 2:36) instead of a simple genitive or dative (as in Gn. 18:11; Jos. 23:1; et al.) is unparalleled and has been cited as proof of literal translation from a Hebrew text (Sahlin, 72), but it may simply be due to Luke's fondness for ἐν (ταῖς) ἡμέραις (Benoit, Exégèse III, 170).

A late rabbinic comment observes that whenever Scripture says that someone had no child, later one was born to her (Gn. R 38 (23c) (c. AD 300), in SB II, 71). So here the implied parallelism with Abraham and Sarah and other OT couples prepares the reader for the possibility of a miracle.

(8) The action begins while Zechariah's course is engaged in its semi-annual round of duty in the temple. ἱερατεύω**, 'to perform priestly service', is frequent in the LXX. τάξις*, 'fixed order, succession', refers to the rota for duty (1 Ch. 24:19). ἔναντι,'opposite' (Acts 7:10 v.l.; 8:21**), is used of the temple service in Ex. 28:29.

Luke frequently begins a sentence with ἐγένετο δέ or καὶ ἐγένετο, corresponding to Hebrew *way^ehî*. (There is no corresponding idiom in Aramaic). The verb is 'meaningless' (BD 472³) and is best left untranslated (*pace* Beyer, I:1, 61f.). The construction used varies: 1. it is followed by another verb in the indicative (as here; Lk., 21x; Acts, 0x). 2. It is followed by καί and a verb in the indicative (Lk., 12x; Acts, 0x; cf. Dietrich, 26–28, who regards this construction as pre-Lucan). 3. It is followed by the infinitive (Lk., 5x; Acts, 17x). The first two of these constructions are Hebraising; the third has been assimilated to Greek idiom. See the tabulations in Plummer, 45; Creed, 9; Hawkins, 37f.; Schramm, 94f. Often the phrase is followed by an ἐν phrase, which gives the circumstances of the following action, as here, and corresponds to Hebrew idiom (Beyer, I:1, 29–62). The use of ἐν τῷ with the infinitive in this way is characteristic of Luke and rare outside Lk.-Acts (Hawkins, 40).

(9) The daily ritual at the temple included the offering of the morning and evening sacrifices; in both cases a burnt offering was made with various accompaniments. Before the morning sacrifice and after the evening sacrifice incense was offered on the altar of incense which was inside the shrine. The various daily duties were apportioned to the priests by lot. In view of the large number of priests (some 18,000), no priest was permitted to offer incense more than once in his lifetime; sometimes the high priest officiated (details in Tamid; SB II, 71–75; Schürer, II:1, 284–297). κατὰ τὸ ἔθος should be taken with ἔλαχε, not with 1:8 (*pace* Diglot). ἔθος can be used of a cultic ordinance (2:42) as well as of a habit (22:39*). λαγχάνω is 'to obtain (by lot)' (Acts 1:17; 2 Pet. 1:1); hence (as here) 'to be appointed (by lot)'; also 'to cast lots' (Jn. 19:24**). Usually it takes an accusative or simple infinitive; the use of τοῦ with the infinitive (1 Sa. 14:47 v.l.) is unusual and reflects Luke's liking for this construction (Hawkins, 48). θυμιάω** is 'to make an incense offering' (Ex. 30:1–9). εἰσελθών is a pendant nominative participle linked to θυμιᾶσαι, and has a pluperfect sense – 'having previously entered'. ναός (1:21f.; 23:45*; Acts 17:24; 19:24*) is the sanctuary, comprising the holy place and the holy of holies, as opposed to τὸ ἱερόν, the whole complex of temple buildings (2:27; *et al.*).

(10) While Zechariah was performing his duty inside the temple, the crowd of people who regularly gathered to share as spectators in the daily sacrifices were waiting outside. Their presence, and the parallelism with Dn. 9:21, suggest that the time of the evening offering (about 3.0 pm) is meant (cf. Acts 3:1). The mention of the people prepares for 1:21f.

The offering of incense was symbolic of prayer (Ps. 141:2; Rev. 5:8; 8:3f.; Philo, Her. 199). According to Tg. Ct. 4:16 (SB II, 79), the people prayed during the offering: 'May the merciful God enter the holy place and accept with favour the offering of his people'. Luke delights to draw attention to the importance of prayer (προσεύχομαι: Lk., 19x; Acts, 16x), especially at moments of divine revelation (3:21; 9:28; cf. 22:43; Acts 9:40; 10:9f., 30f.; 13:2; 22:17). πλῆθος, 'crowd', is frequent in Lk. (8x) and Acts (16x) but rare in the other Gospels. λαός, 'people', is also frequent (Lk., 36x; Acts, 48x) and often indicates the Jewish nation as such (2:32; 21:23; cf. H. Strathmann and R. Meyer, TDNT IV, 29–57). The positioning of ἦν within the genitival phrase is odd.

(11) The altar of incense (θυσιαστήριον, 11:51*) stood in the centre of the holy place (Yoma 33b, in SB II, 79; Schürer II:1, 281f.; J. Behm, TDNT III, 182f.). Zechariah's task was to place incense on the heated altar and then prostrate himself in prayer (Tamid 6:3). It was presumably at this point that he had a vision of an angel standing beside the altar. The passive form ὤφθη is used frequently with the sense 'to appear', usually but not exclusively (Acts 7:26) of the advent of heavenly visitors and the risen Lord. It denotes a real appearance rather than a dream (W. Michaelis, TDNT V, 350–361; K. H. Rengstorf, *Die Auferstehung Jesu*, Witten, 1960⁴, 117–127). Angels appear frequently in the birth stories and elsewhere in the Gospels (4:10; 22:43; 24:23; cf. 24:4). The angel of the Lord figures in the birth stories (2:9; Mt. 1:20, 24; 2:13, 19) and in Acts (5:19; 8:26; 12:7, 23). In the OT 'his significance is to be an express instrument of the particular relationship of grace which Yahweh has with Israel' (G. von Rad, W. Grundmann and G. Kittel, TDNT I, 74–87, especially 77); he appears to childless women in Gn. 16:10f.; Jdg. 13:3–21.

Appearances of God or of an angel in the temple are recorded in 1 Sa. 3; Is. 6, but the closest parallel is the story of John Hyrcanus who heard a heavenly voice while he was alone in the temple burning incense as high priest (Jos. Ant. 13:282f.; Sota 33a; other, late examples in SB II, 77–79; R. Meyer, *Der Prophet aus Galiläa*, Leipzig, 1940, 61, 147 n. 109). A remoter parallel is the experience of Heliodorus in the temple (2 Mac. 3:22ff.). The reference to the right side (ἐκ δεξιῶν, sc. μερῶν) may allude to its significance as the side of favour, honour and luck (cf. Mk. 16:5) and indicate that the angel brings good news.

(12) The motif of fear is common in accounts of supernatural appearances. For φόβος see 1:65; 2:9; 5:26; 7:16; 8:37; 21:26*, and for the present motif see 1:29f.; 5:8–10; 9:34; Jdg. 6:22f.; 13:6, 22; 2 Sa. 6:9; Is. 6:5; Dn. 8:16f.; 10:10f; Tob. 12:16; Mt. 28:2; Mk. 16:5; Acts 2:43; 5:5, 11; 19:17; Rev. 1:17; *et al.* (cf. H. Balz and G. Wanke, TDNT IX, 189–219, especially 209f.). There are parallels throughout this section with Dn. 9–10 (Schürmann, I, 32 n. 41), but this does not necessarily make the motif merely a literary one; it is frequent in literature precisely because men do fear in the face of the supernatural and the unknown. ταράσσω, 'to unsettle' (Acts 15:24; 17:8, 13*), is used here in the stronger sense 'to terrify' (24:38*; Mk. 6:50; cf. Lk. 1:29). ἐπιπίπτω (15:20*; Acts, 6x) is often used of fear falling on a person (Acts 19:17; Rev. 11:11; Gn. 15:12; Jos. 2:9; Dn. 4:2 LXX; 10:7 LXX; *et al.*).

(13) The use of εἶπεν/εἶπον is Lucan (Schürmann, *Paschamahlbericht*, 4f.); the latter is read here by D it; *Diglot* (cf. 1:34,

38), but although scribes may have had a propensity to substitute δέ for καί, the external evidence here is weak. The combination of a verb of saying with πρός rather than the more usual simple dative is also frequent in Lk. (98x; Acts, 56x; rest of NT, 30x; Rehkopf, 54f.; Schürmann, ibid.; cf. Plummer, lxii).

The angel's message to Zechariah (1:13–17) is poetic in style, although a precise analysis of it is impossible; for attempts to turn it and other poetic elements in Lk. 1–2 into Hebrew verse see R. A. Aytoun, JTS 18, 1917, 274–288; Sahlin. The message is addressed to the situation, and cannot represent a hymn used in the early church. The opening words μὴ φοβοῦ are the almost stereotyped reply of a heavenly visitor or divine Figure when appearing to the fearful recipient of a revelation (1:30; 2:10; Acts 18:9; 27:24; cf. Mt. 1:20; 28:5, 10; Rev. 1:17), and are used by Jesus in similar situations of self-revelation (5:10; 8:50 par. Mk. 5:36; Mk. 6:50; Mt. 17:7). The formula is frequent in the OT (Gn. 15:1; 26:24; Dn. 10:12, 19; cf. Is. 41:10, 13f.) and elsewhere (Homer, Iliad 24:171), and is almost an indicator of the divine presence.

Zechariah is not to fear because the angel brings him good news, namely that his petition has been heard. δέησις (2:37; 5:33*) stands in contrast to the more general term προσεύχομαι used of the people (1:10). εἰσακούω is 'to hear (prayer)', Acts 10:31; Mt. 6:7; Heb. 5:7 ('to obey', 1 Cor. 14:21**). For the whole phrase cf. Dn. 10:12 LXX; Sir. 51:11. The answer to the prayer is bound up with the birth of a son to Zechariah, but it is not certain what he was praying for. Many scholars think that he was praying specifically for a son (cf. 1 Sa. 1:10, 17; Protev. Jac. 4; Schürmann, I, 32f.; Danker, 7). But it is doubtful whether he and his wife felt that it was still worth praying for a son (1:18), and if the angel is referring to Zechariah's prayer in the holy place, he is unlikely to have been praying for a personal request at that time. Prayer for salvation for Israel was associated with the evening sacrifice (Dn. 9:20), and so Zechariah may have been praying for the coming of the Messiah and the era of salvation (cf. 2:25; 24:21; so, many scholars). It is just possible that the reference is to Zechariah's personal prayer on other occasions (Schürmann, ibid.). Whatever be the case, Zechariah was to be involved personally in the era of salvation as the father of a son who would be under God's special care and play his part in the dawn of salvation.

καλέσεις is a future indicative, equivalent to an imperative (1:31; Mt. 1:21; cf. BD 362). Since it was normally the father's privilege to choose the son's name (1:62f.), the fact that God commanded Zechariah to call him by a particular name indicated his unique position (Gn. 16:11; 17:19; 1 Ki. 13:2; Is. 7:14; 49:1). Ἰωάννης (Hebrew yôhānān; Aramaic yûhannān) was a common name, meaning 'The Lord has been gracious' (SB II, 79). A link between 'your prayer has been heard' and the meaning of 'John' would not be intelligible in Greek.

(14) The note of joy sounds throughout Lk.-Acts, and the three

words employed to express it here are favourites of Luke (χαρά, 2:10;
8:13; 10:17; 15:7, 10; 24:41, 52*; Acts, 4x; χαίρω, 1:28; 6:23; 10:20;
13:17; 15:5, 32; 19:6, 37; 22:5; 23:8*; Acts 7x; cf. H. Conzelmann,
TDNT IX, 359–372, especially 367f.; ἀγαλλίασις, 'rejoicing', 1:44; Acts
2:46; 11:28 v.l.; Heb. 1:9; Jude 24;** cf. ἀγαλλιάω, 1:47 note). The root
ἀγαλλια- particularly indicates the joy and happiness that arise from the
experience of God's saving action (Ps. 51:12 (50:10); R. Bultmann,
TDNT I, 19–21). Zechariah's joy will be occasioned not merely by the
birth of his son as such but above all by the work of his son in preparing
the people for the coming of the Lord. It will, therefore, be shared by the
people. πολλοί literally means 'many' and stands in contrast to σοι here.
Often, however, it conveys the Hebrew 'inclusive' sense of 'all' (contrasted with 'few') rather than the Greek 'exclusive' sense of 'many' (contrasted with 'all'). J. Jeremias (TDNT VI, 536–545, especially 541; cf.
Hauck, 20) finds this sense here, the word being equivalent to πᾶς ὁ λαός
in 2:10. But this may push the meaning too far, since the meaning is
hardly 'all' in 1:16. Schürmann, I, 33, probably also presses the meaning
too much when he claims that Luke is asking the reader whether he
belongs to the 'many' or not. γένεσις* will mean the 'coming' of John
rather than simply his birth.

(15) The reason why John's coming will spell joy is now given in a
description of his status and task. In the eyes of the Lord, i.e. in his estimation (ἐνώπιον, 22x; Acts, 13x; rest of the Gospels, 1 x), he will be
great. τοῦ is read before κυρίου by B D W al; TR; (UBS) and omitted
by A al; Diglot; cf. 1:76; on the whole Luke prefers to omit the article
(1:11, 17 et al.). μέγας by itself does not indicate any precise status, such
as that of a prophet (but so G. Friedrich, TDNT VI, 837, citing Acts
5:36D; 8:9). It receives closer definition from what follows, as in 1:32
where Jesus' greatness consists in his divine sonship. John's greatness
(7:28) is due to his personal dedication and divine empowering for his
task. σίκερα** transliterates Hebrew šēkār, as in the LXX; it refers to
strong drink or intoxicating liquor not made from grapes (Easton, 5).
Abstinence from wine and strong drink was demanded from priests
while on duty (Lv. 10:4; so here, Schlatter, 154). It was also a mark of
the Nazirite, and hence it has often been concluded that John was to be a
Nazirite (SB II, 80–88). But this is doubtful. The Nazirite vow also included abstinence from shaving the head and from defilement by a dead
body. A person might be a Nazirite from birth like Samson (Jdg. 13:4f.)
or for a specific period terminated by special sacrifices (Nu. 6:1–21).
None of these specific details, still less the actual title, is used with
references to John. The description is closer to that of Samuel (1 Sa.
1:11 LXX) who may have been a Nazirite, but it is safest to conclude
that John is simply described as an ascetic (cf. 7:33; G. B. Gray, 'The
Nazirite', JTS 1, 1900, 201–211; Lagrange, 16). He was dedicated to
God's service as a prophet (Zahn, 68). His abstinence may be linked
with his reception of the Spirit (Eph. 5:18; Leaney, 38).

Positively, John was to be filled with the Spirit. The activity of the Spirit is stressed in the birth narrative (1:35, 41, 67; 2:25, 26, 27) and throughout the Gospel (3:16, 22; 4:1, 14, 18; 10:21; 11:13; 12:10, 12) and Acts (H. von Baer, *Der Heilige Geist in den Lukasschriften*, Stuttgart, 1926; E. Schweizer, TDNT VI, 404–415). In the birth narrative the emphasis is on prophetic inspiration heralding the arrival of the new era. πίμπλημι is almost exclusively Lucan; it is used of filling, especially with the Spirit (1:41, 67; Acts 2:4; 4:8, 31; 9:17; 13:9), but also with fear, anger, *et al.* (4:28; 5:7, 26; 6:11); it can mean 'to fulfil' (1:23, 57; 2:6, 21, 22; 21:22*); cf. πλήρης, 4:1; 5:12; πληρόω, 1:20; *et al.*; G. Delling, TDNT VI, 128–131.

In John's case the gift of God was present with him from his mother's womb. κοιλία is the 'belly' or internal organs, especially the 'stomach' (15:16); following LXX usage it is often used for the 'womb' (1:41, 42, 44; 2:21; 11:27; 23:29*; J. Behm, TDNT III, 786–789). For the phraseology here cf. Jdg. 13:5, 7; 16:17; Pss. 22:9f.; (21:10f.); 71:6 (70:6); Is. 49:1, 5; Je. 1:5; Sir. 49:7; 1QH 9:29–31; Mt. 19:12; Acts 3:2; 14:8; Gal. 1:15. The language expresses divine choice and care of a person from his very birth, but here in connection with 1:41–44 a prenatal sanctification of John is implied; even before he was born, the hand of God was on him to prepare him for his work (Lagrange, 17). Thus in the strongest possible way the divine choice of John for his crucial task is stressed.

(16) This task is a prophetic one towards Israel. ἐπιστρέφω can be used transitively, 'to convert' someone (1:17; Acts 26:18; Jas. 5:19f.; cf. Mal. 2:6; Sir. 48:10), or intransitively of someone turning, returning or being converted (2:39; *et al.*). It became a technical term for Christian conversion (Acts 9:35; *et al.*; 2 Cor. 3:16; 1 Thes. 1:9; 1 Pet. 2:25; G. Bertram, TDNT VII, 722–729). Essentially it conveys the idea of turning from idolatry and sin to love and serve God. In Mal. 2:6 it is the task of the true priest to turn many from iniquity; this function appears to have been ascribed to Elijah (Mal. 2:7; 3:1; 4:5f.) and hence to John.

(17) The unnecessary use of αὐτός in the phrase καὶ αὐτός to pick up an existing subject is frequent in Lk. and may be a Hebraism (Hawkins, 41f.; Schürmann, *Paschamahlbericht*, 100; W. Michaelis, 'Das unbetonte καὶ αὐτός bei Lukas', ST 4, 1950, 86–93; Schramm, 98; it is not clear whether the construction is Lucan or pre-Lucan). The reading προελεύσεται is almost certainly correct; προσελεύσεται is read by B* C L f13, but does not give a good sense in the context and is a simple scribal error (cf. the same confusion in Acts 12:13; 20:5, 13; Metzger, 129). προέρχομαι, 'to go before' (22:47*; Acts 12:10; 20:5, 13*) expresses the thought of John as the forerunner preparing the way for the Lord (1:76; 7:27 par. Mt. 11:10; Mk. 1:2; Jn. 3:28). αὐτοῦ must refer to God (Mal. 3:1) who can be thought of as appearing on the earth (T. Sim. 6:5–8), but the pronoun could be regarded by Christian readers

as referring to the coming of God in Jesus. The lack of direct reference to Jesus here has led to the suggestion that originally John himself was regarded as a messianic figure whose coming would precede that of God himself; if so, this prophecy would have come from Baptist circles which did not recognize Jesus as the Messiah (see 3:15 note). But this supposition is unlikely and unnecessary, since the wording can be fully explained in terms of close dependence on Mal. 3:1, where no messianic function is in view.

John is not directly identified with Elijah (cf. Mt. 11:14; Mk. 9:13; Jn. 1:21), but is simply to be inspired by the same spiritual power as Elijah (cf. 2 Ki. 2:9–15; Wink, 42–45). The link of πνεῦμα and δύναμις is common (1:35; 4:14; cf. 24:49; Acts 1:8; 10:38; 1QH 7:6f.). The spelling Ἠλίου (from Ἠλίας) is uncertain, some MSS having the indeclinable form Ἠλεία (BD 38; 39³; 55ˡᵃ). The hope of Elijah's return goes back to Mal. 4:5; cf. Sir. 48:10; 2 Esd. 6:26f. Expectations were complicated by the hopes of the coming of a prophet like Moses (Dt. 18:15), and the strands of expectation are difficult to unravel (see SB I, 597; IV:2, 779–798; J. Jeremias, TDNT II, 928–941; G. Friedrich et al., TDNT VI, 781–861; Marshall, 124–128). See further 4:25f.; 9:8, 19, 30, 33, 54 v.l.*

Two infinitive phrases express the character of John's task, the second being loosely attached to the first. The latter sums up the effects of his work as preparing a people ready for the Lord (cf. Sir. 48:10b, καὶ καταστῆσαι φυλὰς Ἰακώβ; Wis. 7:27; Jos. Ap. 2:188). For ἑτοιμάζω (14x) see especially 1:76; 2:31; 3:4; and for κατασκευάζω see Lk. 7:27 par. Mt. 11:10 par. Mk. 1:2; cf. Mal. 3:1 (not LXX).

The preceding phrase is difficult. The first part, ἐπιστρέψαι καρδίας πατέρων ἐπὶ τέκνα, is close to Mal. 4:5 LXX (3:24 MT), ἀποκαταστήσει καρδίαν πατρὸς πρὸς υἱόν, and to Sir. 48:10b, ἐπιστρέψαι καρδίαν πατρὸς πρὸς υἱόν, but it is not a precise quotation of either passage. The plural forms πατέρων and τέκνα follow the MT; the choice of τέκνον rather than υἱός (LXX) may be to avoid confusion with 1:16. It has been argued either that Luke gives an independent translation of the MT (Schlatter, 158; P. Winter, NTS 1, 1954–55, 114f.), or that he has followed the Greek text of Sir. (cf. Benoit, Exégèse, III, 170f.). In view of Luke's freedom in handling the OT no definite verdict is possible, but the probability that a non-LXX text has been used is supported by other evidence in Lk. 1–2.

The second part of the phrase, καὶ ἀπειθεῖς ἐν φρονήσει δικαίων, has no known OT source (unless Schürmann, I, 35 n. 59, is right to see a free paraphrase of Mal. 4:5b LXX). The verb ἐπιστρέψαι should be supplied, and ἐν must mean 'into' or 'into a state of' (MH III, 257; cf. BD 218). This would give the meaning: 'and to turn the disobedient into the way of thinking of the righteous' (G. Bertram, TDNT IX, 233). Alternatively, we may take the phrase closely with what precedes, so that ἀπειθεῖς is a nearer definition of τέκνα and ἐν is instrumental: 'to turn the hearts of the fathers to the sons and disobedient by the thinking of the righteous' (cf. Schlatter, 158).

The meaning of the whole is doubtful: 1. The text in Mal. refers to the restoration of good family relationships: fathers and sons are reconciled to one another and neighbours to one another, and so together they seek God. Such may be the meaning here also (Lagrange, 18f.; Hauck, 21; contrast 12:51–53). 2. We may identify the fathers with the righteous and the sons with the disobedient: the disobedient sons are to undergo a change of life which causes their righteous fathers to be filled with new affection for them (Schlatter, ibid.). 3. Or we may identify the fathers with the disobedient and the sons with the righteous. Then the point will be that not only will the youth follow righteousness but also John will succeed in bringing the older generation to share the outlook of their sons (Zahn, 70f.; Grundmann, 52). 4. The 'fathers' will receive 'children's hearts' and thus turn from disobedience to righteousness (Sahlin, 83; Leaney, 80; Stuhlmueller, 121). Of these views, 4. departs considerably from the original meaning of Mal. 4:5. Since we have no reason to suppose that fathers or sons were any more wicked than each other – the evidences adduced by Schlatter and Grundmann tend to cancel each other out – views 2. and 3. lose support. Since Mal. 4:5 is clearly in the author's mind, view 1. remains the most probable: the people who are prepared for their God are those who have learned to live in peace and righteousness with one another.

(18) Faced by this astounding message, Zechariah responds like Abraham with a request for a confirmation of the promise (Gn. 15:8). He cannot believe the promise, for he and his wife are both old. In the OT God himself offered signs to his people (Ex. 3:12; Is. 7:11), and they could request them without being rebuked for doing so (Jdg. 6:36ff.; cf. 13:8ff.; 1 Sa. 10:2, 2 Ki. 20:8). We should not, therefore, regard Zechariah's request simply as a sign of lack of faith, or his dumbness simply as a punishment for unbelief (see especially Rengstorf, 21). These elements are certainly present (1:20), but in fact a sign is given, and it serves the deeper purpose of concealing the wonder of what was to happen until the due time.

(19) The angel's reply itself constitutes a confirmation of his prophecy. He names himself as Gabriel, and thus as one authorised to speak on behalf of God, especially with regard to the end-time (Zahn, 72). His name is a transliteration of gabrî'el, 'man of God', and is that of one of the angels (four or seven) who stand in God's presence as his special servants (1:26**; Dn. 8:16; 9:21; 1 En. 9:1; 10:9; 20:7; 40:9; 54:6; Apoc. Moses 40:1; 2 En. 21:3, 5; 24:1; Tg. Jerus. I, on Gn. 37:15 and Ex. 24:10; Tg. Ps. 137:7). In earlier literature he is a shadowy figure, but later rabbis discussed his activities in detail (SB II, 89–97; BG 325–328). παρίσταμαι is used of standing in someone's presence (19:24), and hence of waiting on him (cf. Job 1:6; 2:1; Dn. 7:10, 13; 2 Ch. 18:18 v.l.; Zc. 6:5; Tob. 12:15 v.l.; of heavenly beings). Here Gabriel's task is

to proclaim good news; εὐαγγελίζομαι bears this sense throughout Lk.-Acts (2:10; 3:18; 4:18, 43; 7:22; 8:1; 9:6; 16:16; 20:1*; Acts, 15x; Mt. 11:5; et al.; Marshall, 123f.; contra Conzelmann, 17, 206f. See further G. Friedrich, TDNT II, 707–721).

(20) To the confirmation of the angelic message given in the name and commission of the messenger is added a sign which is both a punishment for unbelief and a means of preserving the content of the revelation to Zechariah from the people at large. καὶ ἰδού is frequent in Lk. and Mt., and is a septuagintal phrase (BD 4²; 442⁷); Schürmann, Paschamahlbericht, 93). σιωπάω usually means 'to be silent' (19:40*; Acts 18:9*), but here 'to lose the ability to speak' (4 Mac. 10:18), as the following phrase makes clear (for the redundancy cf. Acts 13:11). The dumbness following a divine revelation in Dn. 10:15 LXX was due to shock; in Ezk. 3:26; 24:27 it served as a sign, and in 2 Mac. 3:29 as a judgment. ἄχρι, 'until', is Lucan (4:13; 17:27; 21:24; Acts, 15x), as is the relative attraction (1:4); it is an abbreviation for ἄχρι τῆς ἡμέρας ἐν ᾗ (BD 294). ἀνθ' ὧν means 'in return for which', hence 'because' (12:3; 19:44; Acts 12:23; 2 Thes. 2:10**). The relative οἵτινες is probably a simple relative, since Luke uses ὅς and ὅστις interchangeably (BD 293), but Creed, 12, suggested the nuance, 'Thou hast not believed my words, which nevertheless (deserved credence, for they) shall receive their due fulfilment.' πληρόω is 'to fulfil' (4:21; 24:44), also 'to complete, fill' (2:40; et al.). εἰς is often equivalent to ἐν in Hellenistic Greek (13:9; 18:5; BD 206¹).

(21) The scene shifts to the crowd waiting outside (προσδοκάω, 3:15; 7:19f.; 8:40; 12:46*; Acts, 4x). They expected Zechariah to reappear and give them the Aaronic blessing (Nu. 6:24–26; Tamid 7:2; Protev. Jac. 24:1f.). Normally the priest remained inside the temple for a short time: 'He prayed a short prayer. But he did not prolong his prayer lest he put Israel in terror' (Yoma 5:1). When he failed to appear, they were surprised at his delay. The plural form ἐθαύμαζον with ὁ λαός is ad sensum. For the use of ἐν see Is. 61:6; Sir. 11:21; 1 En. 25:1 Gk. χρονίζω is 'to delay' (12:45; Mt. 24:48; 25:5; Heb. 10:37**).

(22) When Zechariah finally appeared, unable to speak, the crowds drew the conclusion (ἐπιγινώσκω ὅτι is Lucan, 7:37; 23:7; Acts, 6x) that he had seen a vision and was suffering from shock (1:20 note; SB II, 77–79). He could only make signs by nodding (διανεύω**) and remained (διαμένω, 22:28*) mute: κωφός can mean 'dumb' (11:14) or 'deaf' (7:22) or both (Philo, Spec. 4:197f.). The third meaning is supported by the fact that Zechariah is regarded as deaf, as well as dumb, in 1:62 (see, however, Zahn, 110f.).

(23) Only when his term of duty was concluded could Zechariah return home. ὡς is Lucan (Hawkins, 49f.); for πίμπλημι, see 1:15. λειτουργία, 'service', was used in Classical Greek of service performed by wealthy citizens to the state, and in the LXX of religious and priestly service rendered to God (H. Strathmann and R. Meyer, TDNT IV,

215–231; cf. λειτουργέω, Acts 13:2). Zechariah lived outside Jerusalem in the hill-country (1:39), and would normally stay there, probably following a secular occupation, when not engaged in his priestly duties.

(24) As Hannah conceived a son after her visit to the tabernacle (1 Sa. 1:19f.), so now on the return of her husband from the temple Elizabeth conceives a son in fulfilment of God's promise. She then hid herself for five months. περικρύβω** is a Hellenistic formation from the aorist (ἐκρύβην) of κρύπτω. λέγουσα means that she thought, i.e. said (to herself), as follows.

(25) The opening ὅτι may be *recitativum* (i.e. introducing direct speech) or mean 'because' as the first word of Elizabeth's statement (P. Winter, '*Hoti*-recitativum in Lk. 1:25, 61; 2:23', HTR 48, 1955, 213–216). Elizabeth interprets her pregnancy as being due to the gracious act of God. ἐφοράω (Acts 4:29**) is a variant for ἐπισκέπτομαι, 'to visit', and refers to God's action in removing the barrenness which was regarded as a severe reproach by Jewish women (Gn. 16:4; 30:1; Dt. 28:18; 1 Sa. 1:6; 2 Sa. 6:23; SB II, 98). Like Rachel (Gn. 30:23) she praises the God who removes barrenness (Ps. 113:9). She does not seem to know yet of her son's destiny (Sahlin, 96f.). Her motive in hiding her pregnancy may have been: 1. to avoid further reproach from incredulous neighbours during the period when it would not be obvious (Plummer, 19); 2. to engage in grateful prayer (Easton, 7); 3. to follow her husband's example in not spreading the news of God's act (Grundmann, 53). Since Luke wished to ensure that the revelation of the pregnancy was first made to Mary six months later (1:26, 36, 56), the delay is probably a literary device (Klostermann, 11; Schürmann, I, 38), but this is not incompatible with the attribution to Elizabeth of one of the motives suggested (of which 1. is the most likely). Thus the 'divine timetable' in the unfolding history of salvation is maintained.

b. The Prophecy of Jesus' Birth (1:26–38)

The story of the announcement of the birth of Jesus is told in a manner very similar to that of the preceding narrative, but the interest centres on the mother of the child. Mary, a girl betrothed to a descendant of David, is informed of God's choice of her to bear a child named Jesus who will be called the Son of the Most High and will reign over Israel as the Davidic Messiah. His birth will be due to the influence of the Holy Spirit upon Mary, so that her child will indeed be God's Son. The fact that Mary's cousin Elizabeth has already conceived a child by supernatural means will act as confirmation to Mary of the angelic message.

The forms of the two narratives are so similar that it cannot be doubted that they have been consciously arranged to bring out the parallelism between them (A. George, 'Le parallèle entre Jean-Baptiste et Jésus en Lc 1–2', in Descamps, 147–171). Most scholars hold that the present story has been modelled on that of John (see the list in Wink, 60 n. 1; Schürmann, I, 59), but the opposite view, that the story of John was modelled (by Luke) on that of Jesus, is defended by Benoit, *Exégèse*, III, 193–196. Since, however, the story of John displays a greater dependence on OT types, it is unlikely that it was modelled on that of Jesus. On the other hand, the story of the annunciation of Jesus displays such a wealth of individual features that it cannot be regarded simply as an imitation of the story about John, and it is, therefore, best to postulate mutual dependence between the two stories (Wink, 71f.). Accordingly, the origin of the present narrative cannot be settled simply by consideration of its form.

The story itself is of such a character that it must be based upon information ultimately supplied by Mary herself, or be a theological construction, or be a combination of the two. Although the whole pericope has been regarded as a Lucan composition (Burger, 132–135), it is more probable that some tradition lies behind it. If the link with the story of John is secondary, vs. 36f. will be an addition to the original form. Many scholars have argued that vs. 34f. are an interpolation (by Luke or an earlier hand), introducing the motif of the virgin birth into an older story (A. Harnack*; V. Taylor*; Bultmann, 321f.; Luce, 88f.). The integrity of the narrative was maintained by Machen, 119–168, but more recently it has been argued that the christology in vs. 34f. differs from that in vs. 31–33: Luke is said to have combined two separate traditions, using v. 34 as a literary joint and himself creating v. 35 on the basis of a traditional motif (G. Schneider*; cf. J. Gewiess*).

Since the motif of the virgin birth is pre-Lucan (see note at end of this section), the narrative is based on tradition, and since this motif is present in the earlier part of the narrative (1:27, 31), one reason for regarding vs. 34f. as an addition disappears. Since, further, it is questionable whether there is a christological difference between vs. 31–33 and 34f., the other main reason for suspecting that two traditions have been linked loses its force. It is less easy to be certain about the significance of v. 34 as a literary device. On the whole, it is probable that the narrative should be regarded as a unity, but it shows signs of theological shaping.

See bibliography for 1:5 – 2:52, especially A. Harnack, V. Taylor, E. Norden, M. Dibelius, J. McHugh. Machen, 119–168, 280–379; S. Lyonnet, 'Χαῖρε κεχαριτωμένη', Bib. 20, 1939, 131–141; Barrett, 5–24; G. Delling, TDNT V, 826–837; J. P. Audet, 'L'annonce à Marie', RB 63, 1956, 346–374; E. Schweizer, H. Kleinknecht (*et al.*), TDNT VI, 332–451, especially 339–343, 402; J. B. Bauer, 'Monstra te esse matrem, Virgo singularis', *Münchener Theologische Zeitschrift* 9, 1958, 124–135 (as summarised in NTA 3, 1958–59, no. 367); id. 'Philologische Bemerkungen zu Lk. 1, 34', Bib. 45, 1964, 535–540; M. Zerwick, ' "... quoniam virum non cognosco" Lc 1:34', *Verbum Domini* 37, 1959, 212–224, 276–288 (summarised in NTA 4, 1959–60, no. 667); O. Michel und O. Betz, 'Von Gott gezeugt', in W. Eltester (*et al.*), *Judentum, Urchristentum, Kirche* (für J. Jeremias), Berlin, 1960, 3–23; E. Brunner-Traut, 'Die Geburtsgeschichte der Evangelien im Lichte ägyptologischer Forschungen', ZRGG 12, 1960, 97–111; J. Gewiess, 'Die Marienfrage Lk. 1.34', BZ 5, 1961, 221–254; A. Strobel, 'Der Gruss an Maria (Lc 1:28)', ZNW 53, 1962, 86–110; Voss, 62–83; P. Benoit, 'L'annonciation', in

Exégèse, III, 197–215; E. Schweizer (*et al.*), TDNT VIII, 334–397, especially 376f., 381f.; G. Schneider, 'Lk. 1, 34.35 als redaktionelle Einheit', BZ 15, 1971, 255–259.; Vermes, 213–222.

(26) The reference to the sixth month of Elizabeth's pregnancy (cf. 1:36) and the employment of the same heavenly messenger (1:19) link the story of the annunciation to that of John's conception. (The similar story of Gabriel announcing the birth of R. Ishmael (Beth ha-Midrash 2:65, in SB II, 98f.) is late and irrelevant (Grundmann, 55 n.)). Modern versions rightly translate πόλις as 'town', rather than 'city'; Luke uses it frequently, and even of villages. The description τῆς Γαλιλαίας (4:31) is added for the benefit of non-Palestinian readers who would probably never have heard of so insignificant a village as Nazareth (2:4, 39, 51; 4:16*; Acts 10:38*). The name is variously spelled, modern editors preferring Ναζαρέθ (see P. Winter, ' "Nazareth" and "Jerusalem" in Luke chs. 1 and 2', NTS 3, 1956–57, 136–142). The site of Nazareth in the Galilean hills has long been known, but only recently has inscriptional evidence of its identity been found (Finegan, 27–33).

(27) παρθένος (1:27b*; Acts 21:9*; Mt. 1:23; *et al.*) means a young, unmarried girl, and carries the implication of virginity. In view of 1:34 this implication is undoubtedly present here, a view which is strengthened by the probable allusions to Is. 7:14 here and in v. 31. In the LXX the sense of virginity in the word is strong (G. Delling*). This fits in with the fact that Mary was still merely betrothed to Joseph (μνηστεύω, 2:5; Mt. 1:18**). Betrothal could take place as early as 12 years old and usually lasted for about a year (SB II, 373–375, 393–398). Although it was regarded as equally binding as marriage, the girl having the same legal position as a wife, it was not normal for intercourse to take place during this period (SB I, 45–47; II, 393; Jeremias, *Jerusalem*, 364–367). We do not know how old Mary was; she was not yet living with Joseph, but he is mentioned at this stage because of his Davidic descent which is important for what follows. It has been argued that originally there was no mention of him here, and that Mary is regarded as a descendant of David (Dibelius, *Botschaft*, I, 13f.; Hauck, 24; Voss, 68), but this is improbable.

Luke uses ἀνήρ much more frequently than the other Evangelists (27x; Acts, 100x; Mt., 8x; Mk., 4x; Jn., 8x); they make greater use of ἄνθρωπος (Lk., 95x; Acts, 46x; Mt., 112x; Mk., 56x; Jn., 60x). ἀνήρ is used specifically of a husband, but here simply for 'man' (cf. 6:6/8). The name Ἰωσήφ (2:4, 16; 3:23; 4:22; also 3:24, 30*) means 'May he (God) add (sons) '; it is used here as part of the historical tradition rather than because of its adventitious symbolical value.

οἶκος, 'house', often means 'household, family' in Lk. (1:33, 69; 2:4; *et al.*; Hawkins, 44). David's descendants are here regarded as one large family or household (1:69; 2:4; 1 Sa. 20:16; 1 Ki. 12:19; 13:2; O. Michel, TDNT V, 129f.). Had the phrase been meant to refer to Mary, it would have had to be differently constructed. It is meant to show how Jesus was the 'son of David' through Joseph as his legal 'father' (3:23;

Mt. 1:16). It does not, therefore, contradict the fact of the virgin birth (*contra* Luce, 87). Nevertheless, Origen and others have held that the phrase was meant to refer to Mary, whose Davidic descent is asserted in Protev. Jac. 10:1; Ign. Eph. 18:2, Justin, Dial. 43, 45, 100, 120.

Μαριάμ (also spelled Μαρία, 1:41; 2:19; Μαριάμ(μ)η in Jos.; cf. BD 53³; MH II, 144f.) was a common name, the equivalent of *miryam* (Ex. 15:20f.) and said to mean 'exalted one' (possible etymologies in Lagrange, 27f.).

(28) Gabriel is pictured as appearing to Mary indoors (εἰσελθών). His greeting falls into three parts. The opening Χαῖρε is the normal form of address in the NT and in Greek usage. In a Jewish context it will represent šᵉlām (Schmid, 41), or possibly Aramaic ḥaday (H. Gressmann, in Klostermann, 13). A. Strobel* argues that it was specifically a morning greeting. Roman Catholic commentators especially have seen more in the word, and have linked it with Zp. 3:14; Zc. 9:9 (cf. La. 4:21; Joel 2:21) where the daughter of Zion is bidden to rejoice at the coming of salvation (S. Lyonnet*). On this basis Mary can then be identified as the daughter of Zion (Sahlin, 183–185; Laurentin, 64–71, 148–161). Schürmann, I, 43f., argues that no Greek reader would have understood the familiar greeting in such a way, and that further echoes of the OT passage in question would be expected (see also H. Conzelmann, TDNT IX, 367). It is just possible that the use of χαίρω in the LXX of these passages has influenced the present verse, and the continuation in Zc. 9:9 ('Your king is coming to you'; cf. Mt. 21:5, Jn. 12:15) is certainly relevant here. But a typological identification of Mary with the daughter of Zion is nowhere explicit, and it would tend to distract attention from the coming Messiah to the mother.

χαριτόω is 'to bestow favour upon', 'to bless' (Eph. 1:6**; cf. Sir. 18:17). The participle indicates that Mary has been especially favoured by God in that he has already chosen her to be the mother of the Messiah (1:30). There is no suggestion of any particular worthiness on the part of Mary herself (1:30 note). The Vulgate rendering, *gratia plena,* is open to misinterpretation by suggesting that grace is a substance with which one may be filled, and hence that Mary is a bestower of grace. S. Lyonnet* saw a connection between this verse and Jdg. 5:24 where Jael is described as 'most blessed' (εὐλογηθείη; cf. Ps. 45:2 (44:3); Dn. 9:23), but this is far fetched. (The addition of εὐλογημένη σὺ ἐν γυναιξίν at the end of the verse in many MSS is based on 1:42; Metzger, 129).

The greeting conveys the message ὁ κύριος μετὰ σοῦ. This is an OT greeting (Jdg. 6:12; Ru. 2:14), meant as a statement rather than a wish (ἐστίν is to be supplied). It prepares the recipient for divine service with the assurance 'The Lord will help you' (H. Gressmann). It does not, therefore, indicate the moment of conception (as in Sib. 8:459–472, in NTA II, 740), a thought excluded by the future tenses in 1:35.

(29) Gabriel's message was strange and perplexing, and Mary's

response paves the way for its elucidation. (This does not, however, mean that we have simply a literary device, since it would have been easier to omit v. 28 altogether). διαταράσσω**, 'to perplex, confuse', is a literary variant for ταράσσω (1:12); probably fear is implied (cf. v. 30). So Mary began to ponder (διαλογίζομαι, imperfect; 3:15; 5:21f.; 12:17; 20:14*) what sort of greeting she had heard. ποταπός, 'of what kind' (7:39*), is Hellenistic for ποδαπός. Luke uses the optative frequently: 1. It is used, as here, in an indirect question after a governing verb in the past tense, and corresponds to the indicative in direct speech (3:15; 8:9; 18:36; 22:23; Acts 17:11; 21:33; 25:20). 2. It is used with ἄν, corresponding to a potential optative or deliberative subjunctive in direct speech (1:62; 6:11; 9:46; 15:26; Acts 15:24; et al.; in some cases the MSS vary over the inclusion or exclusion of ἄν). 3. It is found in wishes (1:38; 20:16). Other NT writers scarcely use the optative. See BD 384–386; MH III, 118–133.

It is sometimes said that Mary's surprise was because it was not customary for a man to give a greeting (ἀσπασμός, 1:41, 44; 11:43; 20:46*) to a Jewish woman. But the rabbinic evidence is late and scanty (SB II, 99), and Mary's wonder was occasioned more by the character of a greeting which addressed her in such exalted terms, and implied that, like the great men of OT times, she was chosen to serve God and to be empowered by him (W. C. van Unnik, 'Dominus Vobiscum: The Background of a Liturgical Formula', in A. J. B. Higgins (ed.), New Testament Essays, Manchester, 1959, 270–305).

(30) Gabriel's reply is similar in form to 1:13–17 and has a poetic character; it fills out the message in v. 28. For μὴ φοβοῦ, see 1:13. εὑρίσκω χάριν is equivalent to the common OT phrase māsā' hēn (Gn. 6:8; Jdg. 6:17; 1 Sa. 1:18; 2 Sa. 15:25), and signifies the free gracious choice of God who favours particular men and women; the stress is on God's choice rather than human acceptability. On χάρις (2:40, 52; 4:22; 6:32–34; 17:9*; not in Mt. or Mk.) see H. Conzelmann, TDNT IX, 372–402, especially 392f.

(31) The wording of the annunciation closely resembles Gn. 16:11f., καὶ εἶπεν αὐτῇ ὁ ἄγγελος Κυρίου, Ἰδοὺ ἐν γαστρὶ ἔχεις καὶ τέξῃ υἱόν, καὶ καλέσεις τὸ ὄνομα αὐτοῦ Ἰσμαήλ ... οὗτος ἔσται ... (cf. Jdg. 13:5), but it also reflects Is. 7:14, ἰδοὺ ἡ παρθένος ἐν γαστρὶ λήμψεται καὶ τέξεται υἱόν, καὶ καλέσεις τὸ ὄνομα αὐτοῦ Ἐμμανουήλ. The text has been adapted to the present context, ἡ παρθένος having been shifted to v. 27. The annunciation is regarded as the fulfilment of Is. 7:14. The phrase συλλήμψῃ ἐν γαστρί is a conflation of Isaiah's phrase ἐν γαστρὶ λαμβάνειν and the more usual LXX usage of συλλαμβάνειν absolutely; cf. 1:24. Sahlin, 104–113, argues that συλλαμβάνω means 'to be pregnant' rather than 'to conceive', so that the angel is telling Mary that she is already pregnant (cf. Gn. 16:11; Jdg. 13:3–7). But the change of tense from Gn. 16:11 and the unlikelihood of Mary having become pregnant during her period of betrothal speak against this view. Mary is not told precisely

when she would conceive her son (but see 1:34 note).

As in the case of John, the child's name is given by God. The fact that the mother is to confer the name may possibly be an indication that the child will have no human father (Schürmann, I, 46f.), but in view of Gn. 16:11 the point cannot be pressed. The name Ἰησοῦς corresponds to Hebrew yᵉhôšua' or yešûa', and was a common Jewish name up to the beginning of the second century AD; thereafter both Jews and Christians ceased to call their children by it. Its meaning, 'Yahweh saves', was seen to be deeply significant (Mt. 1:21), and although Luke does not expressly draw attention to it, it is hard to believe that he was not aware of it (2:11; on the name see SB I, 63f.; W. Foerster, TDNT III, 284–293; Jeremias, *Theology*, I, 1 n.).

(32) The child's greatness (cf. 1:15) is to be seen in the lofty title that will be assigned to him; the passive form (κληθήσεται) indicates, as often, divine action (Jeremias, *Theology*, I, 9–14). But the title is more than a name; it indicates the true being of the person so called. The title is equivalent to the more common 'Son of God'.

ὁ ὕψιστος is a title for God found frequently in the LXX, where it is equivalent to 'ēl 'elyôn (Gn. 14:8), and in Jewish literature (AP II, 850), from whence it was taken over in the NT (1:35, 76; 6:35; 8:28 par. Mk. 5:7; Acts 7:48; 16:17; Heb. 7:13 see G. Bertram, TDNT VIII, 614–620). The title is frequently said to be Hellenistic (Hauck, 24; Schürmann, I, 48 n. 57), but, while it is true that the title was used for Greek deities, it had a Semitic background; the Hebrew equivalent occurs half a dozen times in the Dead Sea Scrolls (1QS 4:22f.; *et al.*). The phrase 'son(s) of the Most High' is found in Est. 16:16 LXX; Ps. 82:6 (81:6); Dn. 3:93 LXX (παῖδες); Sir. 4:10; and the singular form 'son of the Most High' has now been attested in Aramaic in 4Q 243 (4Q ps Dan Aᵃ) 2:1 (J. A. Fitzmyer, 'The Contribution of Qumran Aramaic to the Study of the New Testament', NTS 20, 1973–74, 382–407, especially 391–394; there are several parallels of language between this text and Lk. 1:32–35, but it is too early to assess their significance, beyond making the obvious point that they confirm the Palestinian character of the language and thought here).

The context suggests that we are to think of a title given to the Messiah. In 2 Sa. 7:14 (cf. Pss. 2:7; 88:26f.; 4QFlor. 1:10f.) the father-son relationship is used to express the divine care extended to David's son and his corresponding obligation of obedience to God. It is often thought that we have here a description of a human Messiah standing in an adoptive relationship to God, and that this stands in contrast with the idea of a 'metaphysical' sonship found in v. 5. If so, the two verses represent two divergent christological conceptions which have been joined together secondarily (Schürmann, I, 49). Other explanations, however, are possible. E. Schweizer (TDNT VIII, 376f., 381f.) thinks that in the present verse we have a Lucan formulation, intended to contrast Jesus with John who is merely the 'prophet of the Most High'

(1:76). In fact, there is reason to suppose that more than a merely adoptive relationship is being set forth. The mention of divine sonship *before* Davidic messiahship suggests that the latter is grounded in the former and should be interpreted in terms of it. The clear allusion to Is. 7:14 in v. 31 also suggests that something more than adoption is in mind. Clearly Luke himself intended 35 to be an elucidation of v. 32 in view of the common use of ὑψίστου. In christological content vs. 32 and 35 stand close together; the concept of divine sonship, stemming from OT royal ideology, has undergone a transformation of meaning. The use of ὕψιστος may well be Lucan in view of the usage elsewhere, and it may be that he has adopted this term to avoid a possible misunderstanding of 'Son of God' in terms of pagan concepts or to give a contrast with 1:76.

The status of Mary's son is now developed in terms of accession to the throne of David his father. The use of κύριος ὁ θεός without a genitive following (as in 1:16) is unusual (cf. Acts 3:22 v.l.). For ὁ θρόνος Δαυίδ see Acts 2:30; 2 Sa. 3:10; 7:13, 16; Is. 9:7 (cf. Ps. 89:3f.; 132:11f.; Is. 16:5 and also Ps. 45:6, cited in Heb. 1:8; O. Schmitz, TDNT III, 160–167; E. Lohse, TDNT VIII, 478–488; Burger). The use of πατήρ indicates that the child will be the royal messiah inasmuch as he is descended from David – hence the significance of the earlier reference to Joseph's descent.

(33) The messianic nature of the child's rule over Israel is confirmed by the prophecy that it will be eternal. The thought is based on Is. 9:7 (cf. Mi. 4:7). βασιλεύω with ἐπί (instead of a simple genitive) imitates Hebrew *mālak 'al* (BD 177; the verb is rare in the Gospels: Mt. 2:22; Lk. 19:14, 27). ὁ οἶκος Ἰακώβ is a synonym for Israel (Ex. 19:3; Is. 2:5; *et al.*) εἰς τοὺς αἰῶνας is a less common synonym for εἰς τὸν αἰῶνα (1:55), both meaning 'for ever' (H. Sasse, TDNT I, 197–208, especially 198–200). The eternity of the rule of David's line is taught in 2 Sa. 7:13, 16; Is. 9:7; Ps. 89:3f., 28f.; 132:11f.; cf. Mi. 4:7 Dn. 7:14; 2 Bar. 73. In the OT the thought is sometimes of a continuing line of kings (1 Ki. 8:25; Ps. 132:12), but here the Messiah himself is to reign for ever. The present verse says nothing about the commencement of the reign. There is nothing to suggest that the thought is of the parousia (Hahn, 247f.; Schürmann, I, 49: *contra* E. Lohse, TDNT VIII, 485 n. 47). The Jewish hope was of a kingdom in this world, but by NT times this was taking on transcendental features, described in terms of everlastingness and the return of paradise upon earth. The early church clearly associated the reign of Jesus with his resurrection and exaltation and linked this with the Davidic promises (Acts 2:30–36). This will have been Luke's understanding of the matter, but he is also conscious that the kingdom of God could be said to have arrived in the ministry of Jesus, so that the exaltation was the open recognition of One who had already acted in his earthly life with kingly power as the representative of God.

(34) Just as Zechariah asked for some explanation of how the angelic promise could be true in virtue of his and his wife's age (1:18), so

now Mary asks how the angelic promise will come true in view of her circumstances. (This parallelism alone is sufficient to justify rejection of the poorly attested variant Ἰδοὺ ἡ δούλη κυρίου· γένοιτό μοι κατὰ τὸ ῥῆμά σου. It is found only in b (cf. the omission of v. 38 by b e), but nevertheless was accepted by Streeter, 267f.; H. Vogels, 'Zur Textgeschichte von Lc. 1, 34ff.', ZNW 43, 1951–52, 256–260). Mary's perplexity arises from the fact that (ἐπεί*; Acts, 0x) she has no sexual relationship with any man. For γινώσκω in this sense see (of a man) Mt. 1:25; Gn. 4:1, 17; 1 Sa. 1:19; et al.; and (of a woman) Gn. 19:8; Jdg. 11:39; 21:12. The tense is strange, since the verb is normally used of the actual act of intercourse. It must mean 'I do not have a husband with whom I have sexual relationships'. Many Roman Catholic scholars have argued that the phrase expresses a vow of virginity: 'I have resolved not to know a man' (Laurentin, 176–188; Stuhlmueller, 122f. – listing earlier supporters). It is impossible to see how the text can yield this meaning. The evidence from parallels cited by Laurentin is irrelevant. It refers purely to chastity outside marriage, refusal to contract a second marriage (Jdt. 16:22), abstention from intercourse in special circumstances, and the practice of the Therapeutae. Easton, 9, commented: 'No writer with a knowledge of Jewish psychology could have thought of a vow of virginity on the part of a betrothed Palestinian maiden'; the rejoinder that Mary constitutes a special case (Benoit, Exégèse, III, 205) will convince only those who have other reasons for adopting this interpretation of the text.

Mary's question is puzzling, since, if the promised child is to be a descendant of David, she is already betrothed to a member of the house of David and can expect to marry him in the near future and bear his child. 1. It may be that Mary is thinking of an immediate conception and asks how this can be possible since she does not yet (οὐ equivalent to οὔπω) know a husband (Ellis, 71; Thompson, 53f.; and earlier scholars). J. B. Bauer* has strengthened this view by noting that in 1:31 ἰδοὺ συλλήμψῃ may translate Hebrew hinnāk hārāh, which would refer to the imminent future; he further suggests that ἄνδρα should be translated 'my husband', so that Mary is asking how she can bear a son of Davidic descent before marriage to her intended husband. 2. Vermes, 218–222, argues that παρθένος refers to a girl who has not yet attained to puberty ('Who is accounted a bethulah? She that has never yet suffered a flow, even though she was married', Nid. 1:4; cf. t. Nid. 1:6; p. Nid. 49a). Such a girl might conceive while still a 'virgin' in respect of menstruation, i.e. at the time of her first ovulation. Vermes argues that this was the case with respect to Mary, who cohabited with Joseph while still a 'virgin' in this sense. The present verse will then mean 'How can this be for I have not yet begun to menstruate? Should I nevertheless marry in spite of seeming not yet ready?' This situation could then have been misunderstood by the early church in terms of virginity with respect to sexual intercourse. But this hypothesis gives an impossible meaning to the present verse; it clashes with Mt. 1:25; and it depends on a possible meaning of virgin which would have been unintelligible to Greek readers. 3. If Mary realised that a virginal conception was intended, she could have been asking how this was possible without her having a normal sexual relationship with a husband (Geldenhuys, 80; Morris, 73). On this view, Mary must have understood the allusion to Is. 7:14 in v. 31 to imply a virgin birth. But it is doubtful whether an ordinary Jewish reader would have understood Is. 7:14 in this sense; more probably it would have been taken to mean that a young woman who was as yet unmarried would shortly marry and bear a son (G. Delling, TDNT V, 883). The Christian understanding of the verse was surely made in the light of the event or as a result of a revelation. 4. J.-P. Audet* similarly suggests that Mary is asking how it is possible for her to have a child and yet fulfil the prophecy of virginity; he argues that ἐπεί should be taken elliptically (BD 360²; 456³), giving the sense 'Comment cela se fera-t-il, puisque, alors (dans ce cas) je ne dois pas point connaître d'homme?' But grammatically this is far from easy. 5. Many recent writers, finding it impossible to make the question historically and psychologically credible on the lips of Mary, have concluded that it is a literary device by Luke to prepare the way for the announcement of the Spirit's activity in the next verse (cf. 1:24; J. Gewiess*; Schürmann, I, 49–52; G. Schneider*). On this view the question serves to emphasise that the child will have no human father.

A decision between these alternatives is not easy. The issue has been clouded by the fact that the information in v. 27 about Joseph's Davidic descent is provided for the reader and cannot be assumed to have been immediately present in Mary's mind. Again, a literary device is strictly unnecessary, since v. 35 could follow straight on from v. 33 (or v. 31) with a linking γάρ. Certainly the question serves to introduce the angelic explanation, and, since the scene makes no pretence to being a verbatim account of what happened, it is possible that the question should be regarded as part of Luke's retelling of the event.

(35) In conjunction with v. 34 the angel's statement indicates that the child is to be conceived without human agency. The Holy Spirit, here equated in poetic parallelism with the power of God (1:17 note; W. Grundmann, TDNT II, 300), is to be the agent, as is appropriate in the new creation (Ps. 104:30; cf. Mt. 1:18, 20; Ellis, 74). ἐπέρχομαι, 'to come upon' (11:22; 21:26; Acts 1:8; 8:24; 13:40; 14:19; Eph. 2:7; Jas. 5:1**), is used of the Pentecost event (Acts 1:8); behind the phrase here may lie Is. 32:15 v.l. (ἕως ἂν ἐπέλθῃ ἐφ' ὑμᾶς πνεῦμα ἀφ' ὑψηλοῦ). This background makes it unlikely that the word is used as a euphemism for sexual intercourse, a usage which in any case is not elsewhere attested (J. Schneider, TDNT II, 680f.). ἐπισκιάζω is 'to cover' (9:34 par. Mk. 9:7; par. Mt. 17:5) or 'to overshadow' (Acts 5:15**). It is used of God's presence resting on the tabernacle in the cloud (Ex. 40:35 (29)) and metaphorically protecting his people (Pss. 91:4 (90:4); 140:7 (139:8)).

God's powerful presence will rest upon Mary, so that she will bear a child who will be the Son of God. Nothing is said regarding how this will happen, and in particular there is no suggestion of divine begetting (Creed, 20). Daube's attempt (27–36) to find a background in Ru. 3:9 founders on the lack of any verbal link. Sahlin, 123–139, broadens the discussion by reference to other passages where *šākan* expresses the idea of divine protection; see further S. Schulz, TDNT VII, 399f.

διό, 'wherefore', introduces the result (7:7*; Acts, 8x; with καί, as here, Acts 10:29; 24:26). τὸ γεννώμενον is 'the child', neuter by analogy with τέκνον (BD 138¹); the present participle has a future reference (cf. 13:23; 22:19, 20, 21; BD 339²; Jeremias, *Words*, 178f.; Black, 131f.). The addition ἐκ σοῦ (C* Θ *al* it syᵖ Irˡᵃᵗ Ad (Epiph)) was probably made to achieve symmetry with the earlier part of the verse (WH App. 52; Metzger, 129f.). The child will be called, i.e. shall be (as in 1:32) ἅγιος, 'holy' (4:34 par. Mk. 1:24; Jn. 6:69; Acts 3:14; 4:27, 30; 1 Jn. 2:20; Rev. 3:7; cf. Jn. 10:36). Here the sense is 'divine' (Ps. 89: 5, 7) or 'Gottgehörig' (Grundmann, 58), rather than that the first-born is holy to Yahweh (2:23; Ex. 13:12), or that the child, like Samson, is dedicated to God (Jdg. 13:7 v.l.), or that the child is free from the slur of illegitimacy (cf. perhaps 1 Cor. 7:14). There may be the thought that, as the One begotten by the Holy Spirit, the child will be holy as the bearer of the Spirit (O. Procksch, TDNT I, 101; cf. Schürmann, I, 53f.). The description culminates in the phrase υἱὸς θεοῦ, here undoubtedly in its full sense of one begotten by God.

The syntax is disputed. 1. 'The child shall be called holy, the Son of God' (RV; RSV; NEB mg; TNT; Leaney, 83; detailed defence in Schürmann, I, 54f.). 2. 'The holy child shall be called the Son of God' (RV mg; NEB; TEV; NIV; Barclay; Lagrange, 35f.; Hauck, 25). But καλέομαι usually follows the predicate. 3. Sahlin 129–136, argues that υἱὸς θεοῦ should be omitted as superfluous. (He also argues that behind γεννώμενον lies Hebrew *nôṣēr*, and that Jesus was originally portrayed here as a Nazirite; cf. 2:22–24; 4:34; E. Schweizer, TDNT VIII, 376f. But, if this motif is present, it is better found in the use of ἅγιος, as in Jdg. 13:7 v.l.)

(36) Without being asked for confirmation of the prophecy, the angel proceeds to supply it (for καὶ ἰδού, cf. 1:20, 31). συγγενίς** is a rare form for συγγενής, 'a female relative', not necessarily a cousin. Mary's relationship to Elizabeth suggests that she too may have been of priestly descent (1:5). The fact of her pregnancy, now in its sixth month, is to be a sign to Mary that God can do the impossible. γήρει is an Ionian dative from γῆρας**, 'old age'. καὶ οὗτος is Lucan (Hawkins, 42), as is καλούμενος with a name or description (ibid.) Black, 53, 100, finds Aramaic influence in καὶ αὐτή (casus pendens; cf. 8:14f.; 12:10, 48; 13:4; 21:6; 23:50f.) and the use of αὐτῇ (proleptic pronoun; cf. 10:7).

(37) The angel explains how it has been possible for the barren Elizabeth to become pregnant, and hence how it will also be possible for

Mary to conceive her son: God is at work, and nothing is impossible for him. The wording is based on Gn. 18:14, μὴ ἀδυνατεῖ παρὰ τῷ θεῷ ῥῆμα; (hᵃyippāle' mēyhwh dābār), but the thought is a common one (Job 10:13 LXX par. 42:2; Je. 32:27; Zc. 8:6; Mt. 19:6 par. Mk. 10:27 par. Lk. 18:27). οὐ ... πᾶς is a Semitic expression, meaning οὐδείς (Acts 10:14; et al.; BD 302¹). ἀδυνατέω is 'to be impossible' (Mt. 17:20**). The MSS vary between παρὰ τοῦ θεοῦ (אᴺ* B D L W) and παρὰ τῷ θεῷ (A C Θ pl; TR). The better-attested genitive is closer to the meaning of the Hebrew (cf. Je. 32:17 MT; Schlatter, 166), and is used as evidence for a Hebrew original in Lk. 1–2 by P. Winter, NTS 1, 1954–55, 115f. It is also possible that Luke was using a non-LXX text (Schürmann, I, 57 n. 116). ῥῆμα (19x; Acts, 14x) may mean 'word' or occasionally 'thing' (cf. Hebrew dābār). Hence we may translate 'nothing will be impossible for God', or 'no word from God will be powerless' (Grundmann, 54; similarly, NEB t; Tasker, 417, claims that this sense of ῥῆμα is required if we adopt the genitive case. But the meaning of the preposition is sufficiently flexible to allow either case to stand with the generally accepted translation). Schürmann, I, 57, thinks that the verse is meant to defend the virgin birth not just to Mary but to critics in Luke's day who said that it was impossible.

(38) The scene closes with Mary's humble acceptance of the will of God. δούλη (1:48; Acts 2:18 (LXX)**) and its masc. equivalent are forms used by men in addressing their superiors, especially by righteous men addressing God (1 Sa. 1:11; 25:41; 2 Sa. 9:6; 2 Ki. 4:16; K. H. Rengstorf, TDNT II, 268, 273). κυρίου can be used without the article since it is tantamount to a proper name. γένοιτό μοι ..., a wish expressed by the optative (1:29 note), is based on Gn. 21:1; 30:34 LXX; cf. Lk. 2:29. Luke often notes the arrival and departure of heavenly beings (2:17; Acts 10:7). Nothing is said about the fulfilment of the angelic promise; we are left to infer from Mary's willingness to obey God that the miraculous conception by the Spirit (not by the angel) ensued.

The narrative of the annunciation contains various linked motifs: 1. The promise of the coming of the Davidic Messiah and the establishment of his eternal reign. 2. The promise of the birth of a child who will be called 'the Son of God' as a result of the coming of the Spirit upon Mary. 3. The fulfilment of the prophecy in Is. 7:14, seen as the birth of a child to a virgin who has not known a husband. Each of these motifs is expressed in OT terminology, and we have not observed any linguistic features which demanded other sources. In particular, motifs 1. and 2. are thoroughly in line with OT thought, and, if the motif of the virgin birth be bracketed off, the idea of God acting to assist in the normal process of birth is a familiar one; the case of John, where the parents were previously barren and the child is marked out for a special destiny, falls within this pattern, and the way in which this motif is used in close parallelism with the story of the birth of Jesus indicates that we are moving in this circle of ideas. It has, indeed, often been thought that originally the story of the birth of Jesus was a story of how God assisted at the birth of the child of Mary and Joseph; see Vermes, 218–22, for a recent form of this theory. But in its present form the action of God in the story is not that of working through a natural process but is a new, creative act of a supernatural character. There is no parallel to this in the OT, unless Is. 7:14 was originally understood in this way. In any case, Luke's language remains that of the OT. Even if this is so, however, we have still to seek the origin of the ideas thus expressed.

The motif of the virgin birth is not a Lucan invention. The same ideas are present in the independent narrative in Mt. 1–2; here too the birth of Jesus is seen as a fulfilment of Is. 7:14 and takes place by the Holy Spirit without the intervention of Joseph (Mt. 1:18–25). Although there is no other clear evidence of the tradition of the virgin birth in the NT (but a number of hints which are consistent with the tradition, e.g. Mk. 6:3), it can be safely assumed that the story is older than the Gospels. The silence of the NT writers may be due to the intimate character of the story which, if true, can have come only from the close family circle of Jesus.

Discussion of the issue is often bedevilled by the assumption that we are dealing with a theologoumenon rather than a historical fact, and hence by the assumption tht there *must* be some *religionsgeschichtlich* parallel which will explain the origin of the idea. Whatever be the historical basis, however, we need to enquire concerning the background to the terminology in which it has been expressed. A wide variety of comparative material has been examined from this point of view. It can be safely said that derivation of the idea direct from pagan sources can be ruled out. It is unlikely in the extreme that the early church would have gone direct to pagan material in order to explain the birth of Jesus, and in any case the general character of the pagan parallels is such that there is no real link with the restrained and delicate narratives in the Gospels.

It remains possible, however, that ideas ultimately of pagan derivation have been mediated to the church through Hellenistic Judaism, and some form of this theory is popular today.

In Egyptian thought the Pharaoh was regarded as the son of a god in a literal sense; the birth of each successive Pharaoh was attributed to the fertilisation of his mother by the god Amon who appeared to her in the form of the reigning king. It must be noted, however, that there does not appear to be any especial stress here on the virginity of the mother (although this appears to be assumed; cf. G. Delling, TDNT V, 829), and that the birth is due to an act of intercourse by the god in human form.

A somewhat different idea is found in the myth of the sacred bull Apis: 'This Apis, or Epaphus, is the calf of a cow incapable of conceiving another offspring; and the Egyptians say, that lightning descends upon the cow from heaven, and that from thence it brings forth Apis' (Herodotus 3:28). In later sources the birth was attributed to a ray of light from the moon (Plutarch, Isis et Osiris 43 (II, 368c); cf. Quaest. Conviv. VIII, 1 (II, 717–718)). This story was known to the Greeks, as the quotation from Herodotus indicates, and it was used by Aeschylus, Suppliants, where Io bears Epaphus as the son of life-begetting Zeus through his touch and breath upon her (cf. H. Kleinknecht, TDNT VI, 341f.). There is, however, as Kleinknecht emphasises, no connection between this isolated Greek story of the conception of a child by the breath of Zeus and the NT account of the birth of Jesus by the Spirit of God.

Stories involving the intercourse of divine beings with earthly women were common enough in the ancient world. Plato was said to be the child of Perictione by Apollo (Diogenes Laertius 3:2; Origen, Contra Celsum, 1:37). Plutarch rejected the idea of intercourse between a god and a woman, but suggested that on Egyptian analogy it was possible for a god to beget a child in some more refined manner: 'The Egyptians assert it to be possible for the spirit of God to approach a woman and engender certain beginnings of generation' (Plutarch, Numa, 4:4–6 (I, 62); cf. Quaest. Conviv. VIII, 1 (II, 717–718)). This would appear to be the nearest approach to the NT concept. (For a possible rabbinic parallel, see Daube, 5–9, but he does not name his source.)

In the writings of Philo, who lived in Egypt, stress is laid on a spiritual ideal of virginity according to which the pure soul abstains from intercourse with the world, but God sows in it the seeds of virtue. Philo expounds this idea by means of an allegorical interpretation of the stories of the wives of the patriarchs. 'Man and woman, male and female of the human race, in the course of nature come together to hold intercourse for the procreation of children. But virtues whose offspring are so many and so perfect may not have to do with mortal man, yet if they receive not seed of generation from another they will never of themselves conceive. Who then is he that sows in them the good seed save the Father of all, that is God unbegotten and begetter of all things? . . . For he (Moses) shows us Sarah conceiving at the time when God visited her in her solitude (Gen. xxi. 1), but when she brings forth it is not to the Author of her visitation, but to him who seeks to win wisdom, whose name is Abraham . . . The union of human beings that is made for the procreation of children, turns virgins into women. But when God begins to consort with the soul, He makes what before was a woman into a virgin again, for He takes away the degenerate and emasculate passions which unmanned it and plants instead the native growth of unpolluted virtues' (Philo, Cher. 43–52; cf. Spec. II, 30; L.A. III, 217–219; Deus 3–5). Here Philo is clearly allegorizing, and he does not suggest that the wives of the patriarchs actually bore physical children apart from intercourse with their husbands. One might, however, ask whether the idea of virgin women becoming pregnant by divine agency existed for Philo independently of its allegorical application to women in the OT: i.e. what moved Philo to allegorize Genesis in this particular way? (Dibelius, *Botschaft,* I, 29–34). In his otherwise full discussion of Philo, Machen (297–312) fails to deal with the question in this form, and thus appears to sidestep the question in the way in which it had already been raised by F. C. Conybeare (306). It seems probable that Philo may have been influenced here by Egyptian ideas of divine begetting, as described above. He is thus a witness to the continuing existence of these ideas, but there is no reason whatever to suppose that he accepted such myths literally or applied them literally to the women in the OT (E. Schweizer, TDNT VI, 402 n. 446).

Such, then, are the parallels. Do they in fact show that 'the Egyptian story is not only a parallel or analogy but the beginning and origin of the miracle of the birth of Jesus' (E. Brunner-Traut*, 105)? What has been shown is that: 1. Ideas of the fertilisation of human women by divine beings, usually in human form, were not uncommon in the ancient world. 2. Occasionally the thought of a divine 'spiritual' influence leading to conception is found. 3. The birth of rulers and great men was attributed to divine agency, so that they too were in some sense divine. That these are at least rough parallels to the conception of Jesus by the virgin Mary through the Holy Spirit is not to be denied. But one can find rough or close parallels to almost every detail in the story of Jesus in the ancient world, and their existence is not necessarily a proof that they are the origin of the story of Jesus (or vice versa). In the present case the details of the annunciation story are expressed in OT terms and framed in so characteristically Jewish a manner that the pagan parallels are extremely remote (cf. Vögtle, 45); nor have we found any Jewish evidence which would show how the pagan ideas could have been assimilated into Jewish thought, since the material from Philo is insufficient to prove that such myths were ever applied literally to any figures in Jewish thought (and certainly not to the Messiah). At most it might be claimed that the birth of Jesus has been narrated in terms comparable to those used to describe the birth of the Pharaohs and other great men, such language being influenced by the general popular environment of the early church but altogether free of pagan elements and expressed in a Jewish-Christian manner in terms of the creative activity of the Spirit of God.

The language used to describe the birth of Jesus is thus similar to that used elsewhere in the NT. Even when heavenly explanations are given by the voice of God or of angels (e.g. at the baptism), the language used is human and biblical, the ideas utilised being drawn from OT tradition. Existing human imagery is used to explain the significance of what is happening, since otherwise communication would be impossible.

From a literary point of view it is clear that the narrative as a whole bears the stamp of Lucan editing. But it is also clear that the ideas expressed are unlikely to have originated with Luke himself, although they would have been congenial to his outlook. It is probable that traditional material has been utilised, and the question is whether this tradition simply represents the church's attempt to express the significance of Jesus by means of a haggadic narrative, or whether a historical event lies beneath the symbolism. An answer to this question depends partly on whether the birth narrative presupposes the development of the church's christology (see Hahn, 304–308). But the concept fits in with the filial consciousness of the historical Jesus and with his consciousness of the presence of the Spirit. It appears to be independent of the general trend of christological development in the early church.

A further problem is the fact that the story does not seem to have influenced early Christian thinking about Jesus (cf. Vögtle, 43–54); this would suggest that the story was not known because it was created only at a late date. Luke, however, expressly states that there was a 'birth secret' (2:19, 51), and in any case it is unlikely that what was known only to a comparatively small group of people would have been widely remembered and had an influence some thirty years later. The objection, therefore, is not decisive.

The form of the narrative is obviously not a crucial factor as regards its historicity. Those who are prepared to accept the possibility of angelic visitations will see no difficulty in a story couched in such terms. Those who deny the possibility will declare the story to be imaginative. But there is perhaps a third possibility. In this narrative the writer is striving to express the ineffable in human terms. It is not surprising if human language breaks down under the strain and recourse must be had to the language of symbolism. The writer has used terms drawn from the biblical tradition to describe a secret and mysterious event. It remains possible that this language, while mythological in colouring, bears witness to some real event which cannot be described in literal terms and which remains veiled in mystery. Historical and literary investigation can take us thus far and no further.

From the historical point of view acceptance of the virgin birth is not unreasonable, granted the possibility of the incarnation. The alternative is that Jesus was begotten by Joseph or some other man. None of the references to Joseph as his parent demands any other interpretation than that Joseph was his legal father. It remains possible that some misunderstanding about his birth led to the suggestion that Joseph was not his father (e.g. the shift in the meaning of 'virgin' suggested by Vermes), but there is no clear evidence to support this view. The evidence that Jesus was a bastard is found in Jewish polemic, and as such is worthless. It is possible, however, that the slander goes back to an early date (Mk. 6:3; E. Stauffer, *Jesus and his Story*, London, 1960, 23–35; see, however, H. K. McArthur, ' "Son of Mary" ', Nov.T 15, 1973, 38–58), in which case it may be evidence that there was known to be something unusual about the birth of Jesus.

Modern theologians debate whether the doctrine of the virgin birth is an acceptable concept. Although this is often denied (E. Brunner, *The*

Mediator, London, 1934, 322–327; W. Pannenberg, *Jesus–God and Man*, London, 1968, 141–150), there is a good case that it is theologically necessary (K. Barth, *Church Dogmatics*, Edinburgh, 1956, I:2, 172–202).

The story of the annunciation gives us Luke's view, based on tradition, of how the birth of Jesus is to be understood. It shrouds the event in mystery, but it makes clear the fundamental fact: the son of Mary is the Son of God, the promised Messiah.

See further Creed, 13–16; Grundmann, 59–61; Schürmann, I, 58–64.

c. Mary's Visit to Elizabeth (1:39–56)

In obedience to the implicit command from Gabriel Mary goes to visit Elizabeth and stays until the birth of her child, thus seeing the fulfilment of the promised sign. Further confirmation of the angel's promise is given by Elizabeth herself under the inspiration of the Spirit, and even the child in her womb indicates its joy. Here is the beginning of John's witness to Jesus. Mary's response to this is expressed in the first of the 'hymns' in this story, known as the Magnificat. She gives thanks to God for the mercy which he has shown to her personally, and which corresponds with his practice of helping and vindicating the poor and needy, while at the same time bringing their proud, rich oppressors to nought; all this corresponds further with the covenant which he made with the ancestors of the Jewish race to show them mercy for evermore. In this way the birth of the Messiah is seen to fit into the general pattern of God's purpose with regard to Israel, and indeed to be the decisive act in that history. Throughout the section there rings out the note of joy at the beginning of the fulfilment of God's promises.

From a dramatic point of view the narrative serves to bind together the stories of John and Jesus, which would otherwise be parallel but independent. It has been regarded as a Lucan composition (Dibelius, *Botschaft*, I, 13f.), but this is improbable in view of the style and the Palestinian background (Schürmann, I, 69; cf. Bultmann, 322; Hauck, 27). It follows that the combination of the stories of John and Jesus was present in Luke's source. If, however, the stories of John and Jesus were originally independent, then this section must be regarded as a secondary link between them (Bultmann, 320). The story could certainly be detached from the narrative about John without loss. Historically, however, there is little to cause difficulty in it, and in general form and content it is of a piece with the surrounding narratives.

The hymn which forms part of the narrative poses two problems, the identity of the singer and the character of the song.

In place of Μαριάμ the reading *Elisabet* is found in a number of Latin sources in v. 46 (a b l* Iren[lat] lat MSS known to Origen Niceta; see UBS). The evidence for the variant is extremely weak. There is no Greek support for it, and the testimony of Irenaeus is divided (AH 3:10:2;

4:7:1). Although 'Elizabeth' is the harder reading, the external evidence seems decisive against it. Few have been willing to accept it (Klostermann, 17), but its existence has suggested that originally no name stood in the text (cf. 1 Sa. 2:1; so A. Harnack*); no MS, however, supports the omission and UBS retains the traditional reading (Metzger, 130f.).

Despite the weak textual evidence a number of scholars have argued that originally Elizabeth was regarded as the author of the hymn (A. Harnack*; Findlay, 1034; F. C. Burkitt*; Klostermann, 17; Creed, 22f.; J. G. Davies*; Drury, 30; Danker, 15): 1. Elizabeth, the childless woman, is a better antitype to Hannah (whose hymn is echoed here) than Mary. 2. For the same reason Elizabeth could speak more fittingly of her 'humiliation' than Mary (1:48; cf. 1 Sa. 1:11; Gn. 16:11; 29:32). 3. The hymn would give a parallel to the Benedictus spoken by John's father. 4. The mention of Mary in 1:56 implies a change of subject from the previous section. 5. The use of δούλη in 1:38 makes Mary an antitype of Hannah; its occurrence in 1:48 could have led to the hymn being wrongly attributed to Mary. 6. 'Elizabeth' is the harder reading, and the change to 'Mary' can be explained on doctrinal grounds as being due to increasing veneration for Mary.

These arguments are insufficient to give weight to a case which is already weak on textual grounds. 1. It is unlikely that Elizabeth would speak in her own favour after what she has said in 1:41–45. Hannah's hymn is the one suitable model in the OT for a woman's praise to God for the gift of a son, and hence it would be quite fitting on the lips of Mary. 2. ταπείνωσις can simply mean 'lowly state' and does not necessarily refer to childlessness. Other sentiments in the hymn (1:48b) would be exaggerated on the lips of Elizabeth. 3. Elizabeth's expression of thanks to God for her own son would come more fittingly at 1:25, and her present prophetic inspiration finds ample expression in 1:42–45. Admittedly, Bultmann, 323, would like to move the hymn to 1:25, but no evidence supports this conjecture. In fact the structure of the narrative requires that the hymn be assigned to Mary: it elaborates and underlines the first part of the scene, which is concerned with the annunciation and not with the birth of John. Some sort of reply to Elizabeth from Mary is appropriate (Ellis, 75). 4. The repetition of the name of the preceding subject in 1:56 is paralleled in OT style (Nu. 24:25; Dt. 32:44; 2 Sa. 2:1; et al.; Schmid, 53f.) and the style of the introduction favours Mary as subject (Schürmann, I, 73 n. 211). 5. J. G. Davies' argument has force only when the hymn has been plausibly assigned to Elizabeth on other grounds. 6. It would need only one scribe, convinced by the earlier arguments, to be responsible for the change to 'Elizabeth' in a small part of the textual tradition. The reverse change presupposes an early veneration of Mary which is unattested. The hymn should, then, be attributed to Mary (Harvey, 227f.).

As for its character, the hymn falls into the general pattern of Hebrew poetry with *parallelismus membrorum,* but no precise metric form has been established. The thought is Jewish in expression, and parallels from the OT can be easily cited. There are some parallels in style to the Qumran hymns, which are likewise messianic and nationalistic, but there are no close parallels (Braun, *Qumran*, I, 79, 85f.; A. J. G. Dreyer*). All that can be said is that the hymns come from the same Jewish milieu. This makes it unlikely that the Magnificat and the other hymns are Luke's own composition (A. Harnack*; G. Erdmann*), and suggests that they stem from Hebrew originals. H. Gunkel* argued that they were Jewish eschatological hymns adapted to their present use (e.g. by the addition of the personal allusions in 1:48, 49; similarly, Bultmann, 322f.). This view was refined by P. Winter* who suggested a more precise Maccabean war situation for them. Similarly, J. Wragg* claims that they are independent compositions, possibly centuries earlier, with some slight adaptations; the Magnificat takes up themes from Ru. 1:20; 2:10.

The background of the hymns is doubtless to be sought in Jewish poetry, and elements from older compositions may well have been used, but we have no means of distinguishing between tradition and redaction. One can with Gunkel omit the personal allusions in order to obtain eschatological community hymns, but Schürmann, I, 71, notes that the combination of personal thanksgiving and praise for eschatological acts already begun is perfectly normal.

The sentiments tend to be Jewish rather than characteristically Christian, and particularistic rather than universal (a fact which confirms that Luke is not the author). The hymns have been ascribed to Baptist circles (Bultmann, 322f.; see later on the Benedictus), but there is nothing specifically Baptist in them. The lack of Christian colouring suggests that the present hymn fits no situation better than that of Mary herself (Machen, 75–101; Schürmann, I, 78f.), although this does not necessarily mean that Mary herself composed the hymn at the precise occasion in the text.

See F. C. Burkitt, 'Who spoke the Magnificat?', JTS 7, 1905–06, 220–227; H. Gunkel, 'Die Lieder in der Kindheitsgeschichte Jesu bei Lukas', in K. Holl (*et al.*), *Festgabe für A. von Harnack*, Tübingen, 1921, 43–60; A. Harnack, *Studien zur Geschichte des NT und der alten Kirche*, Berlin, 1931, I, 62–85; G. Erdmann, *Die Vorgeschichte des Lukas- und Matthäusevangeliums und Vergils vierte Ekloge*, Göttingen, 1932, 31–33; Machen, 75–101; P. Winter, 'Magnificat and Benedictus – Maccabean Psalms?', BJRL 37, 1954, 328–347; A. J. G. Dreyer, *An Examination of the Possible Relation between Luke's Infancy Narratives and the Qumran Hodayot*, Amsterdam, 1962; J. G. Davies, 'The Ascription of the Magnificat to Mary', JTS ns 15, 1964, 307f.; Laurentin, 79–86; J. Wragg (see 1:5–2:52 note); D. R. Jones, 'The Background and Character of the Lukan Psalms', JTS ns 19, 1968, 19–50; R. C. Tannehill, 'The Magnificat as Poem', JBL 93, 1974, 263–275. F. Gryglewicz, 'Die Herkunft der Hymnen des Kindheitsevangeliums des Lukas', NTS 21, 1974–75, 265–273.

(39) The use of the introductory participle ἀναστάς is characteristic of Luke and corresponds to LXX usage (Hawkins, 35f.). The time reference is vague (ἐν ταῖς ἡμέραις ταύταις; 6:12; 23:7; 24:18*; Acts 1:15*; cf. Lk. 2:1), but from 1:56f. it follows that Mary went to

Elizabeth directly after the annunciation and before her marriage to Joseph.

ὀρεινή (1:65**; sc. χώρα), 'hilly, mountainous', is used of Judaea, following traditional practice (Jos. 20:7; 21:11; Jos. Ant. 12:7; Bel. 4:451), although it was hardly more hilly than Galilee. The journey was about 80–100 miles from Nazareth and would take about 3-4 days. Mary's haste (σπουδή*) reflects her obedience to the angelic message.

The meaning of πόλις 'Ιούδα is uncertain. 'Ιούδας (BD 53, 55) here means the tribe or territory of Judah (2 Sa. 2:1; 2 Ch. 23:2; Mt. 2:6). It has been argued that πόλις is here a mistranslation of the ambiguous word mᵉḏînah, which can also mean 'province' (cf. 1:26; 2:3; C. C. Torrey, 'Medina and πόλις and Luke 1, 39', HTR 17, 1924, 83–91; cf. Jeremias, Jerusalem, 206 n. 189; Black, 12). According to Black the 'province' was Palestine itself, but, if so, mistranslation should not be suspected here, since Mary was already in Palestine. Since the Hebrew word mᵉḏînah clearly means 'province, country', it is unlikely to have been mistranslated. The confusion could arise only in Aramaic, and it is doubtful whether Luke was dependent on an Aramaic source at this point. On the whole it is more likely that the wording reflects 2 Sa. 2:1, or possibly that Luke has omitted the name of the town from his source (Hauck, 27). Guesses at the identity of the town include Jutta (Jos. 15:55; 21:16), about 5 miles S. of Hebron in Edomite territory (B. Weiss, 284; Zahn, 94–96) and Ain Karim, 5 miles from Jerusalem; the latter has been the traditional site since the sixth century (Finegan, 3–5).

(40–41) The oriental greeting was an extended affair, 'a ceremonial act whose significance lay in the content of the message' (Ellis, 76). But here the important thing is not the content of the greeting but the person who made it. Even before Elizabeth herself could respond to Mary's words, the child in her womb leapt with joy (σκιρτάω, 1:46; 6:23**). Although it is said that an emotional experience of the mother can cause a movement of the foetus (Ellis, 76), it is more likely that a miraculous expression of the emotion of the unborn child is meant than that Elizabeth simply saw her own joy reflected in the unconscious movement of her child. Although it is not clear that the narrator of Gn. 25:22 thought of conscious movements of the twins in Rebekah's womb, the rabbis so interpreted the text, and there was also a tradition that the unborn children sang a song at the Exodus (SB II, 100f.; cf. Od. Sol. 28:2; Callimachus 4:162ff.). To jump for joy was of course a familiar enough idea (2 Sa. 6:16; Mal. 4:2; et al.; G. Fitzer, TDNT VII, 401f.). Is it coincidental that in Gn. 25: 22 the thought of the elder child serving the younger is expressed (Hauck, 28)?

If the child can do no more than jump for joy, his mother gives verbal expression to the significance of the scene, and for this purpose she receives prophetic inspiration from the Holy Spirit (cf. 1:15, 67). She is thus 'able to know the past and see what is hidden without anyone telling her' (G. Friedrich, TDNT VI, 835); she knows what has happened to Mary.

(42) To cry with a loud voice (ἀναφωνέω**; κραυγή*, 'shout') may be a formal mark of inspired utterance (Mk. 9:24 (Lohmeyer, 188); Jn. 1:15; 7:28, 37; Rom. 8:15; 9:27; Gal. 4:6) or of joyful praise (1 Ch. 16:4f.; Ps. 66:1; Is. 40:9) or simply of public proclamation. Here the first two senses are present (O. Betz, TDNT IX, 303 n. 7). Elizabeth's speech is couched in elevated prose. She addresses Mary as one who is 'blessed'.

εὐλογέω (1:64; 2:28, 34; 6:28; 9:16; 13:35; 19:38; 24:30, 50, 51, 53*) can mean 'to pray for God's blessing upon somebody' (Dt. 28:3f.) or 'to give thanks to God' (cf. the use of εὐλογητός, 1:68). The participle (13:35; 19:38; Mt. 25:34) is thus similar in meaning to μακάριος (1:45; cf. H. W. Beyer, TDNT II, 754–764, especially 762). The addition ἐν γυναιξίν shows that the participle is being used in a comparative or superlative sense: 'you are the most blessed among women' (cf. Ct. 1:8; BD 245³). The phrase is reminiscent of Jdg. 5:24 (Jael); Jdt. 13:18; cf. Lk. 11:27. As Schürmann, I, 68, remarks, this high evaluation of Mary depends entirely upon her Son, who is also declared blessed by Elizabeth in the same breath. ὁ καρπὸς τῆς κοιλίας is a traditional phrase (cf. Gn. 30:2; Dt. 28:4; La. 2:20; Acts 2:30; lQpHab. 6:11f.). Laurentin, 81f., detects a parallel with Jdt. 13:18, so that Mary's child here corresponds to 'the Lord God' there, but this may be no more than coincidental.

(43) Elizabeth's question indicates her unworthiness that the mother of the Messiah should visit her: what has *she* done to deserve this honour? After πόθεν (literally, 'whence', 13:25, 27; 20:7*; here, 'how, why') supply γέγονεν. ἵνα introduces an explanatory noun clause; the infinitive is the more appropriate construction when the epexegetical phrase refers to an actual fact (BD 394).

Jesus is described as κύριος (1:76; 2:11; 7:13, 19; 10:1, 39, 41; 11:39; 12:42; 13:15; 17:5f.; 18:6; 19:8, 31, 34; 20:42, 44; 22:61; 24:3, 34; cf. 1:15 (and note) for the use of the title for God). The use of κύριος in narrative to refer to Jesus is distinctive of Luke. Here ὁ κύριός μου (Ps. 110:1; Sir. 51:10; Jn. 20:28) may reflect 2 Sa. 24:21 where Araunah expresses to David his unworthiness of a royal visit (Danker, 14); Laurentin, 79–81, finds a parallel here to the sojourn of the ark of the Lord in the house of Obed-edom for three months (2 Sa. 6:2–11). The title may refer to the status of Jesus as the Messiah (20:41–44) and prefigure the position of Jesus over against John (cf. 7:19). There is no necessary contradiction between the attitude of Elizabeth and that of John in 7:19, since John's doubts were not so much about whether Jesus was the Messiah as about whether he was really fulfilling the kind of messianic role that John envisaged for him.

(44) Elizabeth explains that she knew that Mary was to be the mother of the Messiah by the joyous movements of her unborn child in response to Mary's greeting (cf. 1:41; Jn. 3:29f.). For ἰδοὺ γάρ cf. 1:48;

2:10; 6:23; 17:21b; Acts 9:11; 2 Cor. 7:11**. The use of φωνή with γίνομαι is Lucan (3:22; 9:35, 36; Acts, 4x; Hawkins, 49). The theme of ἀγαλλίασις is taken up from 1:14.

(45) Finally, Elizabeth pronounces a further blessing upon Mary for believing God's word to her. For μακάριος cf. 6:20 note; the use of the third person reflects OT style. Luke may have intended a contrast with 1:20 in the reference to Mary's faith. The ὅτι clause may express the reason why Mary is blessed – because what she believed will certainly come true (RV; Grundmann, 62); or it may give the content of what she believed. The analogy of Acts 27:25 favours the second interpretation (so most translations; Schürmann, I, 69, n. 187), which surely includes the former: 'Blessed is she who believed that God will fulfil his word (because he will fulfil it)'. τελείωσις is 'fulfilment' ('perfection', Heb. 7:11**; G. Delling, TDNT VIII, 84–86), and παρὰ κυρίου indicates the ultimate source of what was said by the angel.

(46) Mary's reply (see introductory note) begins by praising God. μεγαλύνω, 'to make great', hence 'to praise' (1:58*; Acts 5:13; 10:46; 19:17*) corresponds to Hebrew giddēl or higdîl (Pss. 34:4 MT; 69:31 MT). ἡ ψυχή μου is a periphrasis for 'I' (Ps. 35:9).

(47) The thought of 1:46b is repeated in poetic parallelism. ἀγαλλιάω (more commonly deponent) is a Hellenistic form from ἀγάλλω, 'to rejoice' (10:21*; Acts 2:26; 16:34*; cf. 1:14 note). The change to the aorist may reflect a Hebrew 'waw consecutive' construction, whereby a verb which normally refers to the past can take on a present value after a participle with that value (P. Joüon, cited by Zerwick, 260; Black, 128–130, finds the influence of an Aramaic stative perfect). πνεῦμα is often used in parallelism to ψυχή (Job 12:10; Is. 26:9; et al.). The phrase 'God my Saviour' is familiar in the LXX, where it represents the Hebrew 'God of my salvation' (Pss. 24:5 (23:5); 25:5 (24:5); Mi. 7:7; Hab. 3:18; Sir. 51:1; G. Fohrer, TDNT VII, 1012f.). The nearest OT parallels to the couplet as a whole are Hab. 3:18; Ps. 35:9 (34:9); 1 Sa. 2:1 (cf. Ps. Sol. 3:7; 17:3).

(48) As is usual in this kind of hymn (H. Gunkel*, 47f.), the expression of praise is followed by a statement giving the grounds for it. God has looked graciously at the lowly state of his servant. ἐπιβλέπω is often used of loving care (1 Sa. 1:11; 9:16; Lk. 9:38*; Jas. 2:3). ταπείνωσις means 'humble state' rather than 'humiliation' (Acts 8:33; Phil. 3:21; Jas. 1:10**; cf. 1:52 below). It need not refer to childlessness (1 Sa. 1:11) but expresses the humble state of Mary in the eyes of the world (W. Grundmann, TDNT VIII, 21), and perhaps also her humble attitude towards God (Schürmann, I, 73f.). Thus God is beginning his eschatological exaltation of the lowly, for from now on the name of Mary will be known to all generations and they will speak of her rich blessing by God. ἀπὸ τοῦ νῦν is Lucan (5:10; 12:52; 22:18, 69*; Acts 18:6*; Hawkins, 36) and refers to the time from 1:42 onwards. μακαρίζω, 'to bless' (Jas. 5:11**), reflects the sentiment expressed by

Leah (Gn. 30:13). The combination of motifs from 1 Sa. 1:11 and Gn. 30:13 expresses the new status of Mary (cf. 11:27).

Although it has been argued that the verse is an addition to the hymn to make it apply to the circumstances of Mary (Hauck, 29; Bultmann, 322), there are good grounds for regarding it as an integral part of the composition. Schürmann, I, 74, 77f., even suggests that the personal sentiments form the basis of the hymn, to which the more general elements in vs. 51–55 have been added (see also D. R. Jones*, 21–23).

(49) The hymn proceeds with a more general account of the reasons why future generations will pronounce Mary blessed. The mighty One has done great things for her: the thought answers to the promise in 1:37. For δυνατός, cf. 14:31; 18:27; 24:19*; it is a description of God in Ps. 24:8; Zp. 3:17; et al. For the general thought cf. Dt. 10:21; Pss. 71:19; 126:2f.

The second part of the verse is added loosely, possibly in imitation of Hebrew style; the relative pronoun οὗ would be better here and in 1:50a (BD 442⁶). The holiness which is here ascribed to God's name (11:2; Pss. 99:3; 103:1; 111:9; Is. 57:15) refers more to his exalted state than to his moral attributes; compare how ἅγιος is paralleled by φοβερός in Ps. 111:9 (110:9) (Klostermann, 20). The stress is thus on the might which God exerts in the cause of righteousness and mercy; his holiness is demonstrated in triumph over his enemies (Ps. 99:1–3).

(50) But the thought of God's might is qualified by that of his ἔλεος shown to his people. (Ps. 103:17 (102:17)). ἔλεος (1:54, 58, 72, 78; 10:37*) normally conveys the ideas of compassion and mercy to the unfortunate. From its use in the LXX to translate ḥesed it takes on the nuance of an attitude arising from a mutual relationship, 'faithfulness'. R. Bultmann renders it well here as 'gracious faithfulness' (TDNT II, 477–485, especially 483; but see also H. J. Stoebe, THAT I, 600–621). It is the attitude shown by God in respect of his covenant (1:72) to those who fear and worship him (Ex. 20:6). The thought of fearing God is frequent in Lk. (12:5; 18:2, 4; 23:40; Acts 10:2, 22, 35; 13:16, 26; Hawkins, 49; H. R. Balz, TDNT IX, 212f.). It expresses in OT language the proper response to the covenant mercy of God. εἰς γενεὰς καὶ γενεάς is a Hebraism for 'to many generations' (the LXX uses the form εἰς γενεὰν καὶ γενεάν; Ps. 49:11 (48:12); cf. 89:1 (90:1); but see T. Levi 18:8).

(51) From the initial personal note (vs. 46–49) the hymn now moves to the thought, adumbrated in v. 50, that God's dealings with Mary are in keeping with his general attitude to his people. A problem is caused by the use of the aorist in vs. 51–54 to refer to God's mighty acts of salvation. It could conceivably refer to what God has done in OT times, but this is not very likely in the context. If the hymn reflects the later faith of the church, it could be a means of looking back to the coming of Jesus (Wink, 66). A gnomic use to express a general truth is

improbable since this use was rare in Hellenistic Greek. Schmid, 55, suggests that the use represents the Hebrew iterative perfect, expressing what God always does. Perhaps it represents a 'prophetic' perfect (Hauck, 29) or refers to the events still future which had already begun to take place at the time of the hymn, and so could be regarded as partly realised (Klostermann, 20; Schürmann, I, 75). What God has now begun to do, and Mary regards prophetically as having already come to fruition, is described in terms of what God actually did in OT times, as expressed in Israel's praise in the OT.

Thus the kind of power which God showed at the Exodus is now demonstrated in the birth of the Messiah (Pss. 89:13 (88:11); 118:16 (117:15); Ex. 6:1, 6; Dt. 3:24; H. Schlier, TDNT I, 639f.). κράτος* ποιέω is equivalent to Hebrew 'āśāh ḥayil (rendered in the LXX by ποιέω δύναμιν). For βραχίων, 'arm', cf. Jn. 12:38; Acts 13:17**.

But salvation also implies judgment, and so God is also said to scatter his enemies (Nu. 10:35; Pss. 68:1; 89:10). For διασκορπίζω see 15:13; 16:1; Acts 5:37*; O. Michel, TDNT VII, 418–422. ὑπερήφανος, 'haughty', is a typical word to describe them, expressing the idea of pride and self-confidence over against God (Rom. 1:30; 2 Tim. 3:2; Jas. 4:6; 1 Pet. 5:5**; Ps. 88:11 LXX; Pr. 3:34; Is. 13:11; Ps. Sol. 17:8; cf. SB II, 101–106; G. Bertram, TDNT VIII, 525–529). διάνοια, 'thought, mind' (10:27*), is used in a dative of reference (Ps. 76:5 (75:6)); the use of the singular form where English idiom uses the plural is not uncommon (8:12, 15; et al.; MH III, 23).

(52) The proud are now described as the mighty and the rich (v. 53), and contrasted with the humble and needy. δυνάστης is a 'ruler' or 'court official' (Acts 8:27), and καθαιρέω, 'to remove' (usually of things rather than people in the LXX) is common in Lk. (12:18; 23:53; Acts 13:19, 29; 19:27; rest of NT, 3x). The language reflects Job 12:19; Jdt. 9:3; Sir. 10:14; cf. 1 En. 46:5. The overthrow of rulers who do not obey God's will is a sign of his power at work in history, and is here ascribed to the agency of the Messiah (C. Schneider, TDNT III, 411f.).

By contrast God exalts the humble (cf. v. 48). For ταπεινός*, cf. 3:5; R. Leivestad, 'ΤΑΠΕΙΝΟΣ-ΤΑΠΕΙΝΟΦΡΩΝ', Nov.T 8, 1966, 36–47; and for ὑψόω 10:15; 14:11; 18:34*; Acts 2:33; 5:31; 13:17*; G. Bertram, TDNT VIII, 606–613. For the thought, cf. 1 Sa. 2:7f.; Sir. 10:14; Pss. 75:7; 107:40f.; 113:7f.; 147:6; but it is of course not confined to Judaism, but expresses the universal longing of minorities under oppression (Euripides, Troades, 612f.; Xenophon, Hel. 6:4:23).

(53) From political relationships (v. 52) the thought moves chiastically to social position. The hungry are to be satisfied with the blessings that God provides (6:21; 11:13), while the rich are given nothing but deprived of what they already have (12:21). πεινάω (4:2; 6:3, 21, 25*) goes beyond mere physical hunger and expresses want generally. For ἐμπίμπλημι, 'to satisfy', cf. 6:25; Jn. 6:12; Acts 14:17 (also Rom. 15:24**). πλουτέω is 'to be rich' (12:21*). ἐξαποστέλλω, 'to

send away', is Lucan (20:10, 11; 24:49; Acts, 7x; Gal., 2x**), and with κενός the phrase is paralleled in 20:10f. par. Mk. 12:3.

It would be easy to over-spiritualise the meaning of these verses and ignore their literal interpretation. Schürmann, I, 76, rightly notes how the coming of the kingdom of God should bring about a political and social revolution, bringing the ordinary life of mankind into line with the will of God.

(54) Finally, God's action is seen to be in fulfilment of his covenant with Israel. Israel is his παῖς, 'servant' (Is. 41:8f.; 42:1; 44: 21; cf. 49:3; Je. 26:27f.), whom he has promised to help (ἀντιλαμβάνομαι Is. 41:9; 42:1; cf. 9:6; Acts 20:35; 1 Tim. 6:2**). The loosely added infinitive μνησθῆναι ('to remember', 1:72; 16:25; 23:42; 24:6, 8*; Acts 10:31; 11:16*) gives the sense, 'and he remembered' (BD 391⁴). The phrase (cf. Ps. 98:3) expresses the cause rather than the result of God's action, for his remembering is effective and leads to action (Grundmann, 66; cf. O. Michel, TDNT IV, 676; D. R. Jones*, 27).

(55) God's action is in accordance with his promises (Mi. 7:20; Lk. 1:73). The syntax is not clear: 1. τῷ 'Αβραάμ as the indirect object of μνησθῆναι ἐλέους, v. 55a being parenthetical (RV; NEB; JB; TEV; TNT; NIV; Barclay; so Mi. 7:20). 2. τῷ 'Αβραάμ in loose apposition to πρὸς τοὺς πατέρας ἡμῶν (cf. Bar. 2:34 and (for the change of construction) Bar. 1:11; Schürmann, I, 77 n. 252). 3. τῷ 'Αβραάμ as dative of interest with ἐλάλησεν ('as he spoke to our fathers in favour of Abraham'; Zerwick, 55). The first of these views remains the best, since otherwise εἰς τὸν αἰῶνα is awkwardly placed. For the thought cf. 2 Sa. 22:51. Abraham appears frequently in Lk. (15x; Acts, 7x; N. A. Dahl, 'The Story of Abraham in Luke-Acts', SLA 139–158). He is the spiritual father of Israel (1:73; 3:8; 16:24), and the latter are his 'seed', i.e. 'offspring' (σπέρμα, 20:28; Acts 3:25; 7:5f.; 13:23); here the thought appears to be confined to those who are spiritually his children (evil-doers have been removed from the people, 1:51–53), but there is as yet no trace of a universalism embracing the gentiles.

(56) The mention of Mary's name is necessary after the lengthy hymn as a literary device to indicate that the narrative is being resumed. She remains with Elizabeth for three months, the remaining time of her pregnancy. σύν is frequent in Lk. (23x; Acts, 52x; Mt., 4x; Mk., 6x; Jn., 3x). Luke uses both ὡς (B al) and ὡσεί (A C Θ pm; TR; Diglot; Schürmann, I, 80 n. 278) with numerals to impart an air of indefiniteness. Although Mary was probably present at the birth of John, Luke rounds off this section of the story, which concerns her particularly, by describing her return home before going on to the story of John's birth (cf. 3:18–20/21f.). ὑποστρέφω is frequent in Lk. 21x; Acts, 11x; not in the other Gospels). The reference to Mary's home indicates that she is not yet regarded as married to Joseph (1:27).

d. The Birth of John (1:57–80)

With the birth of John we come to the fulfilment of the promises of God which have occupied the first half of the birth narrative. The parallelism between the promises of the births of John and Jesus is continued in the accounts of their actual births and the acclamations that followed them. The narrative emphasises the way in which God fulfils his promises and brings joy to his people. The details about the naming of the child again indicate how he is destined for a significant career in the service of God. But the narrative is concerned at the same time to point forward to the birth of Jesus; the hymn which forms its culmination designates John as the prophet who will go before the coming of the Lord, and speaks of the redemption and salvation which God is preparing for his people in the house of David.

The general character of the narrative is similar to that in the rest of Lk. 1. If the Benedictus (1:67–79) is separated off, the remaining prose section could have formed the original continuation of 1:5–25, since it does not presuppose 1:26–56. It is possible, therefore, that originally there existed a self-contained story of the birth of John. So far as this part of the story is concerned, John is not presented in messianic terms. The story, therefore, can have come from Baptist or Christian circles; we have already seen that it is unlikely to have been a creation by Luke. But the neat division of the birth narratives into separate scenes is a literary device and not necessarily a sign of independent sources, and it is doubtful whether the narrative about John can be successfully prised from its present setting in the story of Jesus.

The link with the story of Jesus in the present part of the story is supplied by the Benedictus. Its general style is so similar to that of the Magnificat that it must have come from the same milieu, and it is improbable that either hymn is a Lucan imitation of the other (*pace* G. Erdmann*, 31f.). The hymn has been analysed as a unitary composition with a chiastic structure (A. Vanhoye*), but this analysis, which may contain elements of truth, does nothing to explain the progression of thought in the hymn. In particular there is a break at vs. 75/76, so that the hymn divides into two parts. The first part is a *berakah* or blessing. God is the object of praise because he has redeemed his people and brought about salvation (in accordance with his promises), namely salvation from their enemies, consisting in keeping faith with the fathers and remembering his covenant and oath to deliver his people and enable them to serve him. The second part is a *genethliakon,* i.e. a hymn in honour of a child at his birth. John is told that he will be a prophet, for his task will be to go before the Lord and to prepare his way, to give knowledge of salvation to his people through his mercy by which light will come to shine on those in darkness and guide them. In both parts of the hymn the phrases are very loosely attached to one another, and the case that the hymn is not an original Greek composition is strong.

The difference in style between the two parts of the hymn raises the question of its unity. Some scholars have detected differences in thought between the two sections. Hauck, 31, suggests that in the first part there are merely Jewish messianic ideas, but in the second part there is the specifically Christian doctrine of the forgiveness of sins. Schürmann, I, 88–90, adds that the first part of the hymn is complete in itself, and that it speaks of an earthly Messiah, whereas the second part (which alone contains the prophecy announced in 1:67) is concerned with a heavenly being who descends from above. Considerations such as these have led to various theories of composition. 1. Vs. 76–79 are an addition to the hymn in vs. 68–75. A Jewish or Baptist hymn has thus been Christianised (H. Gunkel*) or the hymn has been made to apply to John by his followers who thus expressed their messianic veneration for him (Vielhauer, 28–46; cf. P. Winter, ZNW 47, 1956, 239 n. 41). J. Gnilka* holds that the hymn consists of a messianic psalm joined to a hymn for the birth of John; the composition of the latter (and of the hymn as a whole), however, is to be ascribed to a Jewish-Christian circle whose piety is reflected in the Testaments of the Twelve Patriarchs. 2. Vs. 76 or 76f. are an addition to an early Christian hymn by Luke (Benoit, Exégèse, III, 184–189). 3. The original nucleus is vs. 67, 76–79, which has been expanded by the insertion of the hymn in vs. 68–75, which itself is of Christian origin (Schürmann, ibid.). 4. Vs. 76f., 79b form part of the Baptist story; it has been expanded to give a Christian reference by vs. 78, 79a, and the messianic hymn in vs. 68–75 has been prefixed (Hahn, 246f., 372–374).

The weakest of these views is that of Benoit, since it leaves a hiatus between vs. 75 and 77 or 78. While the hymn reflects two different kinds of Jewish verse, the arguments for separating the two parts from one another are not convincing. The wording of v. 75 need not mark a full conclusion to a psalm (see Pss. 90:14; 128:5; P. Benoit, ibid. 186), and the change of style in v. 76 is perfectly possible in a unitary composition (Daube, 201). The connection of thought is also lucid: having spoken in general terms of the messianic salvation which has begun to dawn, Zechariah goes on to speak of the particular role which his son will play in its dawning. The exegesis below will show that v. 78 refers to Jesus and not to John, and hence there is no reason to assume that a hymn in praise of John the Messiah has been Christianised (cf. Wink, 65–68). It is most probable that the hymn is a unitary composition (though possibly taking up motifs of contemporary Jewish hymns) and that it refers to the births of both John and Jesus.

See H. Gunkel; G. Erdmann; P. Winter; D. R. Jones (as in 1:39–56 note); P. Vielhauer, 'Das Benediktus des Zacharias (Lk. 1, 68–79)', ZTK 49, 1952, 255-272, cited from Vielhauer, 28–46; J. Gnilka, 'Der Hymnus des Zacharias', BZ 6, 1962, 215–238; A. Vanhoye, 'Structure du "Benedictus"', NTS 12, 1965–66, 382–389.

(57) The description of John's birth is similar in form to Gn. 25:24

with typical Lucan variation in the use of χρόνος for the LXX form αἱ ἡμέραι.

(58) Just as the shepherds later shared in the joy at the birth of Jesus, so Elizabeth's neighbours (περίοικος**) and relatives (συγγενής, 2:44; 14:12; 21:16*) now appear in the story. μεγαλύνω (1:46) is used here as in Gn. 19:19; 1 Sa. 12:24; Ps. 126:2f. (125:2f.) of God's activity in manifesting his mercy. συγχαίρω means 'to rejoice with' (15:6, 9; 1 Cor. 12:26; 13:6; Phil. 2:17f.**), but here may have the sense 'to congratulate'; for the motif, see Gn. 21:6.

(59) The intended parallelism with the story of Jesus continues with the account of the circumcision of the child (2:21). This was regularly carried out, as here, on the eighth day after birth (Acts 7:8; Phil. 3:5; Gn. 17:12; 21:4; Lv. 12:3; Shabb. 19:5; SB IV:1, 23–40; R. Meyer, TDNT VI, 72–84). It was performed by the head of the house, but sometimes by a woman (1 Mac. 1:60). The neighbours and relatives join in the ceremony (cf. Ru. 4:17), as at a modern christening. They wished to name the child Zechariah after his father (ἐκάλουν is probably a conative imperfect, BD 326). It was more usual to call a child after his grandfather (Creed, 24), but there are sufficient examples of use of the father's name to make the proposal here entirely credible (Tob. 1:9; Jos. Vita 1; Ant. 14:10; 20:197; Bel. 4:160; 5:534; SB II, 107f.). What is unusual is the association of name-giving with circumcision, which is otherwise unattested in contemporary Judaism. The earliest Jewish example of name-giving in connection with circumcision dates from the eighth century (Pirqe R. Eliezer 48 (27c), in SB II, 107). However, the giving of a name some days after birth was certainly a Hellenistic custom (Macrobius, Saturnalia, 1:16:36), and it is quite possible that this influence was being felt in Palestine. (Hauck, 31). καλέω normally takes a double accusative, and the use of ἐπί here is unusual (1 Esd. 5:38; 2 Esd. 17:63; Sir. 36:12).

Attempts have been made to find an Elijah symbolism in the incident based on the use of a chair called the throne of Elijah at circumcision; it may have been hoped that the child being circumcised would turn out to be the returning Elijah (Daube, 21f.; Ellis, 78). But there is no hint of this in the text.

(60) Elizabeth replies to the statement implied in v. 59 with a firm 'No' (οὐχὶ ἀλλά; 12:51; 13:3, 5; 16:30*). Luke leaves the question unanswered as to how to she knew that the child's name was to be John. There is no need to suppose that an independent revelation had been given to her (Creed, 24f.), and that this part of the story has been lost. It is more likely that Zechariah had communicated the angelic message to her – 'a hundred times over' (Godet, 108).

(61–62) But the neighbours refuse to accept the word of a mere woman, especially when she went against custom by choosing a name that was not in use in the family (συγγένεια, Acts 7:3, 14**), and they appeal to the deaf and dumb father by means of signs (1:22 note; cf.

Gittin 5:7). The formulation of the question is Lucan; he often introduces an indirect question by τό (9:46; 19:48; 22:2, 4, 23, 24; Acts 4:21;
22:30; Rom. 8:26; 1 Thes. 4:1; Hawkins, 47). The equivalent in direct
speech would be τί ἂν θέλοις (cf. 1:29 note).

(63) Zechariah requests a small wooden writing tablet, and on its
wax-coated surface writes 'John *is* his name' in a manner that brooks no
argument; the name has already been given. πινακίδιον** is the
diminutive of πίναξ (11:39), 'platter' (SB II, 108–110). The use of λέγων
with a verb of writing has Classical parallels (Thucydides, 6:54), but it
may be equivalent to Hebrew l'ēmôr (2 Sa. 11:15; 2 Ki. 10:6; 1 Mac.
11:57); it arises from the ancient habit of speaking aloud while writing or
reading (BD 420²; cf. 5:21 note). The neighbours' surprise is at the
firmness of Zechariah's statement, or at his confirmation of the unusual
name for his son, or perhaps at his agreement with his wife (since he
would not have heard her speaking, and the neighbours may have imagined that they had not conferred on the matter).

(64) Immediately Zechariah regains the use of his speech and his
first words are of praise to God. παραχρῆμα is Lucan (10x; Acts, 6x; rest
of NT, 2x). ἡ γλῶσσα is loosely attached to the preceding part of the
sentence, and the verb ἀνοίγω is not really appropriate (zeugma); D
adds ἐλύθη to ease the construction. For εὐλογέω of praising God, cf.
2:28; 24:53. It has been suggested that the Benedictus should follow at
this point (Schmid, 58), and Sahlin, 159–171, would insert the
Magnificat in his hypothetical Proto-Luke here. But Luke first of all
closes the present scene, with its effects upon the neighbours, and then
directs attention to the future task of John in the Benedictus, thus both
answering the question of the neighbours (1:66) and pointing directly
forward to the coming of Jesus (Schürmann, I, 84).

(65) The effect of Zechariah's miraculous recovery of his faculties
on top of all that has already happened is to produce fear, i.e. numinous
awe in the presence of divine activity, among the neighbours (cf. 1:12;
5:26; 21:26). ἐγένετο ἐπί is a Lucan construction (3:2; 4:25, 36; 23:44;
24:22; Hawkins, 36). The order ἐπὶ πάντας φόβος ... is for emphasis
(BD 472²); the more normal order φόβος ἐπὶ πάντας ... is adopted by
Diglot on flimsy textual grounds. For some time afterwards (imperfect!)
the events (1:38 note) were discussed in the locality. For διαλαλέω cf.
6:11**. B. Weiss, 292, found here Luke's source for the story.

(66) Those who heard the story 'treasured it in their hearts' (JB;
for the use of τίθημι cf. 9:44; Acts 19:21; for καρδία cf. 2:19, 51; and
for the whole phrase cf. 21:14; Acts 5:4; 1 Sa. 21:12; Wilcox, 62f.). People asked, 'What will become of a child like this?' For τί used of a person, see Acts 13:25; Jn. 21:21; 1 Jn. 3:2; BD 299². ἄρα is used to express inference (8:25; 12:42; 22:23; Acts 12:18). It is disputed whether
the following phrase, καὶ γὰρ χείρ ... belongs to the direct speech (Barclay; Zahn, 113; Schürmann, I, 83 n. 21) or is a comment by the
narrator (most translations; Klostermann, 24; Lagrange, 57). In favour

of the former view is the close connection expressed by καὶ γάρ (6:32, 33: 7:8; 11:4; 22:37, 59; Acts 19:40*), but against it is the tense of ἦν (the verb is omitted by D it sy⁵). It is better to take the phrase as a comment by the narrator expressing the thought which lay behind the people's question (Metzger, 131). The phraseology is based on the OT and gives a fitting conclusion to the scene (Ex. 13:3; 14:8; 15:6; Is. 26:11; cf. Acts 4:28, 30; 11:21; 13:11).

(67) Zechariah's praise of God is an appendix to the story, but its final position makes it carry the theological weight of the narrative. Like his son (1:15), Zechariah is filled with the inspiring power of the Spirit, so that what follows has the character of prophecy. The use of προφητεύω need not be confined to prediction, although this element is present. The praise of God can also be inspired by the Spirit (cf. 1 Cor. 14:26). What we have here is initially a psalm of praise giving a divinely inspired commentary on the significance of the events which have begun to take place (cf. G. Friedrich, TDNT VI, 835).

(68) The hymn begins with the stereotyped use of εὐλογητός (see 1:42 note) with the name of God (1 Sa. 25:32; 1 Ki. 1:48; Ps. 41:13 (40:14); 1QM 14:4; 1QH 5:20; 10:14; Shemoneh Esreh; et al.). κύριος is omitted by p⁴ W it sy⁵ sa Cypr; Diglot. It could be argued that the longer phrase is an assimilation to the LXX formula (Pss. 40:14 LXX; 105:48 LXX), but it has superior MS evidence, and the omission is easily explained as a scribal oversight (Metzger, 131). For ὁ θεὸς τοῦ Ἰσραήλ cf. Acts 13:17. The title reflects the Jewish outlook of the hymn, which does not take the gentiles into account.

The traditional formulation continues with the use of ὅτι (cf. 1:48, 49) to indicate the reason for praising God. ἐπισκέπτομαι is used of God 'visiting' men in the sense that he comes to bless and save them (1:78; 7:16*; Acts 15:14; Heb. 2:6; cf. Gn. 21:1; Ex. 3:16; Ru. 1:6; Pss. 8:4 (8:5); 106:4 (105:4)). The thought of divine judgment (Je. 44:13; 1QS 4:6, 11f.) is absent here. The verb is applied here to the action of God, but in 1:78 to his action in the Messiah (cf. 19:44; H. W. Beyer, TDNT II, 599–608, especially 605). As in 1:51ff., the question of the time-reference of the verb arises. The reference is undoubtedly to the saving work of God which has already begun with the birth of John and the conception of Messiah; but the content of the verbs indicates that Zechariah is looking forward to the redemption which is not yet accomplished but could be said to be 'as good as accomplished' now that the divine train of events has been set in motion.

The rather general idea of 'visitation' is made more concrete in terms of λύτρωσις, 'redemption' (2:38; Heb. 9:12**; cf. λυτρόω, 24:21*; ἀπολύτρωσις, 21:28*). The use here of ποιέω is unusual; ἀποστέλλω is used in Ps. 110:9 LXX). The background of this concept is to be seen in the OT thought of God setting his people free by his mighty act at the Exodus, which was then applied typologically to subsequent acts of deliverance. The language here is general, and the precise character of

the deliverance remains uncertain (F. Büchsel, TDNT IV, 328–356, especially 335, 351; further literature in I. H. Marshall, 'The Development
of the Concept of Redemption in the New Testament', in Banks,
153–168).

(69) The means of redemption is that God has brought onto the
stage of history (ἐγείρω, cf. Acts 13:22) a 'horn of salvation', i.e. 'a
mighty Saviour'. κέρας, 'horn', suggests the strength of a fighting
animal. It is used in Ps. 132:17 of a successor to David, but the language
here reflects Ps. 18:2 (see further 1 Sa. 2:1, 10; Dn. 7:7f.; 1 En. 90:9;
Shemoneh Esreh, 15; Rev. 5:6; 12:3; et al.; W. Foerster, TDNT III,
669–671). The reference to the house (1:27 note) of David his servant
(Acts 4:25; Did. 9:2; Shemoneh Esreh, 18; SB IV:1, 213; J. Jeremias,
TDNT V, 700) identifies the horn as the Messiah. The article is inserted
before οἴκῳ (A Θ pm; TR; Diglot) and παιδός (A C Θ pl; TR; Diglot).
Since there is nothing to link John himself with the house of David, the
reference here cannot be to John himself; rather Zechariah is pictured as
knowing of the conception of the Messiah by Mary (Lagrange, 59). The
view that the hymn as a whole reflects a messianic veneration of John is
thus exposed to strong objection (Wink, 68).

(70) What God has begun to do is what he had promised through
the prophets (cf. 1:55). The language is strongly Lucan. For διὰ
στόματος see Acts 1:16; 3:18, 21; 4:25; 15:7. The insertion of a considerable amount of qualification between the article and the noun (τῶν
... προφητῶν) is also Lucan (Hawkins, 50), and has led to scribal
corrections (Diglot inserts τῶν after ἁγίων with A C Θ pl; TR; see
Metzger, 132). ἀπ᾿ αἰῶνος is used hyperbolically, 'from early times' (cf.
Acts 3:21; 15:18**; Gn. 6:4; Tob. 4:12; et al.) The combination ἅγιοι
προφῆται is found in Acts 3:21; 2 Pet. 3:2; Wis. 11:1; cf. Eph. 3:5. The
language has a liturgical sound (Wilcox, 74–76), and it is closely
paralleled in Acts 3:21. Hence the verse may be a Lucan insertion into
the hymn (J. Gnilka*, 220; Hahn, 247 n. 1; Schürmann, I, 87), which
has led to the awkward connection with v. 71. On the other hand, if A.
Vanhoye's* analysis is correct, the verse is integral to the chiastic pattern (matching v. 76); its omission brings the two occurrences of
σωτηρία in vs. 69 and 71 rather close together. It is, therefore, more
likely that Luke has reworded an existing phrase. The verse may allude
to 2 Sa. 7:12–16.

(71) There follows a very loosely attached description of the salvation resulting from God's action, σωτηρίαν being in apposition to the
content of vs. 68f. The language, drawn from Ps. 106:10 (105;10) (cf. 2
Sa. 22:18; Ps. 18:17 (17:18)), suggests political deliverance, which is of
course not to be excluded from the Christian concept of salvation and
formed part of contemporary Jewish hopes (1QM 14:4–10; 18:6–11;
Ps. Sol. 17:23–27; Shemoneh Esreh, 7, 10, 12). But the language is formal, no particular enemies are specified, and the thought is of those 'who
now prevent us from serving God "without fear" ' (W. Foerster, TDNT

II, 813); political need and spiritual need are closely linked.

(72) The syntax is again loose, the infinitive construction probably expressing the purpose or result of God's action. By bringing salvation to his people he shows that he is keeping his promises to the fathers. ποιῆσαι ἔλεος μετά reflects Hebrew ʿāśāh ḥeseḏ ʿim (Gn. 24:12; Jdg. 1:24; 8:35; 1 Sa. 20:8; 2 Sa. 3:8; cf. Lk. 10:37; Acts 24:17; BD 206³; Wilcox, 84f.). If ἔλεος is translated as 'mercy', the thought must be of the 'mercy promised to our fathers' (RSV; cf. Barclay), rather than of showing mercy to them (as most translations). But the phrase surely means 'to keep faith with', ἔλεος expressing the idea of loyal behaviour in accordance with the covenant rather than mercy (1:50 note; Hauck, 33). Perhaps the fathers are thought of as alive and waiting (Easton, 18). The second part of the verse reflects Ps. 106:45 (105:45) (cf. Ex. 2:24; 6:5; Ps. 105:8). It speaks of the covenant as God's promise to his people (διαθήκη, 22:20*; Acts 3:25, 7:8*; cf. Lk. 22:29). Its solemnity is indicated by ἅγιος (Dn. 11:28, 30; 1 Mac. 1:15, 63).

(73) The covenant is further defined as God's oath. ὅρκον has been attracted from a genitive of apposition (το διαθήκης) to the case of the relative pronoun (20:17; Acts 10:36; BD 295). For the phraseology see Gn. 26:3; Je. 11:5; Ps. 105:9, and for the concept see J. Schneider, TDNT V, 176–185, 457–462. The promise made to Abraham (Gn. 22:16ff.; 26:3; cf. Ps. 105:9–11) is now understood in spiritual terms.

(74) The content of God's promise was to grant to his people the possibility of serving him without fear of persecution by their enemies. Luke is fond of τοῦ with the infinitive (1:77, 79; 2:21, 24, 27; 4:10; 5:7; 8:5; 9:51; 10:19; 12:42; 17:1; 21:22; 22:6, 31; 24:16, 25, 29; 45*; Acts, 17x; together with other examples which lack the idea of purpose; see Hawkins, 48; Schürmann, Paschamahlbericht, 12f.; Abschiedsrede, 104f.; BD 400). For δίδωμι followed by an infinitive cf. 8:10; Acts 2:4; 4:29; et al. For ἀφόβως cf. 1 Cor. 16:10; Phil. 1:14; Jude 12**. Before ἐχθρῶν the article is inserted by A C Θ pl; TR; Diglot; and it is followed by ἡμῶν in A C D Θ pm lat; TR; Diglot; these are probably secondary expansions (Metzger, 132). ῥύομαι is 'to deliver, rescue' (Mt. 6:13; 27:43; et al.), and the use may reflect Ps. 17:1 LXX (W. Kasch, TDNT VI, 1002). The dative of the participle would be better than the accusative (BD 410). λατρεύω is often used of priestly service in the OT, but came to have a more general meaning (2:37; 4:8*; Acts 7:7, 42; 24:14; 26:7; 27:23*; Rom. 1:9; Phil. 3:3; Heb. 12:28; H. Strathmann, TDNT IV, 58–65). For the hope expressed, cf. 1:71; Ps. Sol. 17:31, 50f.

(75) Such service will be characterised by holiness and righteousness. For ὁσιότης, see Eph. 4:24**; F. Hauck, TDNT V, 489–493, and for the combination with righteousness (1:6) see Wis. 9:3; Eph. 4:24. The two words may express duty to God and man respectively (Philo, Abr. 208). The stereotyped phrase 'all our days' is used as a closing formula in Pss. 16:11; 18:51; et al., and expresses the eternal nature of God's salvation and the corresponding human response. For the

Hellenistic use of the dative of time (where an accusative would be expected), see 8:29; Acts 13:20; Rom. 16:25; BD 201; MH III, 243.

(76) The style of the hymn now changes (cf. Is. 63:10–19; Mt.
5:10f.) as Zechariah begins to indicate the relation of his son to the saving acts of God. The child will be called – i.e. God will make him (1:35)
– a prophet of the Most High. This title is used in T. Levi 8:15 of the
anointed king, but nothing so sublime is intended by the phrase in its
present context, where it stands in conscious contrast to the title used in
1:32 for Jesus. As in 1:13f., the giving of the title is followed by the
reason for its use. John will act as a prophet by going before
(προπορεύομαι, Acts 7:40**) the Lord to prepare his ways. This description is based on Is. 40:3, which is used elsewhere in the NT to characterise John's activity 3:4–6 par. Mk. 1:2f. par. Mt. 3:3; Lk. 7:27 par.
Mt. 11:10). The same idea is taken up by Mal. 3:1 (possibly in dependence on Is. 40:3f.) and applied to the messenger who prepares the coming of the Lord, i.e. the Elijah figure of Mal. 4:5f. The Qumran community saw the prophecy fulfilled in their own activity (1QS 8:13f.;
9:19f.), and here it is applied to John (cf. 1:17; Acts 13:24). For Christian readers κυρίου would presumably refer to Jesus; the mention of God
in v. 78 need not mean that κυρίου refers to God here. It is not clear,
however, whether Zechariah was thinking of the Messiah here (as
Elizabeth did, 1:43) or of God (so Vielhauer, 40). J. Gnilka*, 235f.,
notes that κύριος means the Messiah in T. Levi 2:11 (cf. 4:4; T. Sim.
6:5), but this usage may be Christian.

(77) The use of τοῦ with the infinitive δοῦναι may indicate that it is
dependent upon the preceding infinitive (cf. 1:79; Acts 26:18; BD 400⁶),
but it makes better sense if the clause is taken as epexegetic of, or
parallel to, the preceding one (Zerwick, 385; Schürmann, I, 91, n. 67).
The way of the Lord is prepared by giving his people (1:68) the
knowledge of salvation. The compound phrase γνῶσις σωτηρίας is unparalleled, but the coupling of abstract nouns in this way was not
without precedent (D. R. Jones*, 36). The knowledge described is not
something imparted theoretically, but refers to the inward appropriation
or experience of salvation as the result of a divine gift (1QS 11:15f.; cf.
R. Bultmann, TDNT I, 706; J. Gnilka*, 234). The words ἐν ἀφέσει
ἁμαρτιῶν αὐτῶν should not be linked with δοῦναι (so Creed, 26), but
with σωτηρίας, indicating that the salvation envisaged consists in the
forgiveness of sins. It is regarded as a present experience (B. H.
Throckmorton, 'Σώζειν, σωτηρία in Luke-Acts', TU 112, 515–526). The
phraseology is reminiscent of the apostolic preaching in Acts 4:10–12;
5:31f.; 13:38; but there is no mention in the present context of baptism
(Acts 13:24); John's baptism, however, was 'for the forgiveness of sins'
(3:3), and hence his activity is accurately described here. Thus Je. 31:34
with its promise of knowledge of God and forgiveness is fulfilled.

(78) The connection of the next phrase is again loose; it has been
linked to προπορεύσῃ, σωτηρίας or ἄφεσιν. But the attempt to determine

a precise connection is fruitless, since the whole action is ultimately to be traced to the mercy of God in sending John to lead his people to salvation and forgiveness. For the rather odd use of διά to express the means of salvation cf. διὰ τῆς χάριτος, Acts 15:11; Gal. 1:15; in both cases the reference is to the merciful or gracious action of God. σπλάγχνα* (always plural in the NT) is literally the 'inward parts' of man or animal (Acts 1:18), but the word came to be used of the 'seat of feeling' in a man, especially the locus of compassion (Pr. 12:10; Sir. 30:7; T. Levi 4:4; T. Zeb. 7:3; 8:2; T. Naph. 4:5; H. Köster, TDNT VII, 548–559). The combination with the genitive of quality (cf. Col. 3:12) is found in T. Zeb. 7:3; 8:2, and reflects the Hebrew construction found in 1QS 1:22; cf. 2:1. Whereas earlier ἔλεος referred more to the covenant-loyalty of God to his people (1:50, 58, 72), here the phraseology reflects rather rahᵃmîm, and signifies that God's action is motivated by loving compassion.

As a result of this compassion there is promised a divine visitation. ἐν indicates attendant circumstances. The MSS vary between ἐπισκέψεται (p⁴ ℵ* B W Θ pc syˢᵖ sa bo) and ἐπεσκέψατο (A C D f1 f13 pl latt Cyr; TR). Most scholars regard the aorist as being due to assimilation to v. 68 (but see P. Benoit, Exégèse III, 186; D. R. Jones*, 38) and accept the better attested future, which fits in with the tense in v. 76 (Metzger, 132). The use of the future tense does not by itself settle the question whether the subject of the verb is to be identified with John or Jesus as the person through whom God graciously visits his people (cf. Vielhauer, 38), but the sentence structure, loose though it is, would be odd if the subject of this clause were to be identified with the 'prophet of the Most High'.

ἀνατολή originally meant the 'rising' of a heavenly body, hence the area of sunrise, 'the east' (13:29; Mt. 2:1; et al.); it can also mean 'growing', hence the 'shoot' of a plant. The meaning here is debated. 1. In the LXX it is used to translate ṣemah, 'branch, shoot' (Je. 23:5; 33:15 (40:15 LXX); Zc. 3:8; 6:12; cf. Is. 4:2 ᾿ΑΣΘ; G. Bertram, TDNT VIII, 605 n. 29), a word which came to be used as a messianic title (cf. SB II, 113; A. Jacoby, ῾᾿Ανατολὴ ἐξ ὕψους᾿, ZNW 20, 1921, 205–214). The corresponding verb ἀνατέλλω can also be used of the rise of the Messiah (Ezk. 29:21). But this meaning is not very suitable here, since the ἀνατολή comes from above and gives light. 2. The word can be used by metonymy for 'the rising sun' (see the inscription cited by H. Schlier, TDNT I, 353 n. 2; cf. the use of ἀνατελεῖ ... ἥλιος, Mal. 4:2 LXX). 3. The word can refer to the rising of a star, and hence perhaps to a star itself. The verb ἀνατέλλω is used of the star which arises from Jacob (Nu. 24:17) and which was interpreted messianically (CD 7:18f.; 1QM 11:6; 4QTest. 12; T. Levi 18:3; T. Jud. 24:1; cf. Braun, Qumran, I, 82; J. Gnilka*, 227–232). Although the noun itself is not attested in this concrete sense, the parallel case cited above (under 2.) suggests that ἀνατολή could refer to the star (H. Schlier, TDNT I, 352f.). This substantive use

may have been reinforced by the way in which ἀνατολή could mean
'shoot'. The double meaning of the word (a phenomenon also found with
the corresponding Syriac noun and with the Aramaic verb; J. Gnilka*,
228f.) allowed it to be applied to both the shoot and the star, so that in
effect two messianic images are brought together here (so Justin, Trypho
100:4; 106:4; 121:2; 126:1; cf. Philo, Conf. 60–63; Schürmann, I, 92;
Danker, 20). The imagery is thus that of the Davidic Messiah, the Shoot
from Jesse (Is. 11:1ff.) and the star from Jacob (Nu. 24:17) who is to
visit men from on high, i.e. from the dwelling place of God (2 Sa. 22:17;
et al.). Most translations follow interpretation 2. and use 'dawn' or 'sun'
to convey the sense.

(79) The connection of thought is again uncertain. It has been
assumed above that ἐπιφᾶναι describes the task of the ἀνατολή; if so the
second infinitive τοῦ κατευθῦναι should be taken as epexegetic of the first
(Schürmann, I, 92). Vielhauer, 35f., regards vs. 78–79a as a parenthesis,
so that v. 79 as a whole continues the description of John's task, but
ἐπιφᾶναι is most naturally linked in sense with v. 78b. ἐπιφαίνω is 'to
show oneself, appear' (of the shining of stars, Acts 27:20; cf. Tit. 2:11;
3:4**; R. Bultmann and D. Lührmann, TDNT IX, 1–10). For God giving light see Dt. 33:2; Ps. 118:27. The phraseology here reflects Ps.
107:10; Is. 42:7 and especially Is. 9:2 (9:1 MT). The closest parallel is to
be found in the non-LXX rendering of Is. 8:23 – 9:1 MT in Mt. 4:15f.
where the use of ἀνατέλλω (LXX: λάμπω) gives a significant link with
the present passage and suggests the existence of an exegetical tradition
(C. H. Dodd, According to the Scriptures, London, 1952, 80).

The idea of guiding those in darkness follows on naturally. For
κατευθύνω cf. 1 Thes. 3:11; 2 Thes. 3:5**. The 'way of peace' may
reflect Is. 59:8 (cited in Rom. 3:17); cf. Is. 9:6. Peace is closely
associated with salvation (2:14; et al.)

(80) The narrative about John is concluded before the author turns
to the birth of Jesus. The boy's childhood is described on the pattern of 1
Sa. 2:21. He undergoes normal physical growth to maturity (αὐξάνω,
2:40; 13:19*; Gn. 21:8, 20; Jdg. 13:24; 1 Sa. 2:26) and becomes strong
in spirit (κραταιόω, 2:40; 1 Cor. 16:13; Eph. 3:16**; cf. Ps. 26:14
LXX). The reference is to his human personality, but there may be a
suggestion that such growth was due to the hand of God (E. Schweizer,
TDNT VI, 415).

The plural ἔρημοι (5:16; 8:29) is a Septuagintalism (Gn. 21:20; BD
263). John's life is quiet and secret until the time for his public appearing. There is possibly the thought of the wilderness as the place of God's
presence (Schürmann, I, 94). The traditional area is Ain el-Ma'mud-
iyyeh, 4 miles west of Hebron, where there is a sixth-century church
beside a spring (Finegan, 13). But already in the nineteenth century
John was being linked with the Essenes in the Jordan area (a view rejected by Godet, 117f.), and in recent years it has been argued that he grew
up near Qumran, and even that he was a member of the community

there (A. S. Geyser, 'The Youth of John the Baptist', Nov.T 1, 1956, 70–75; J. A. T. Robinson, *Twelve New Testament Studies*, 1962, 11–27). There are a number of parallels between the thought and activity of John and those of the Qumran community, such as their eschatological expectation, use of Is. 40:3 and ritual washings, which may be held to point in this direction. The case, however, remains speculative, and there are some opposing factors, especially the fact that John's family was associated with the temple at Jerusalem (1:5; see especially Braun, *Qumran*, I, 83; II, 1–21). On the whole, therefore, it is improbable that John was a member of the community, although he will almost certainly have known of its existence and may well have been influenced by its views.

We are thus left uninformed about the activity of John before the time of his commissioning. ἡμέρα is a Hebraism for χρόνος (BD 165). ἀνάδειξις** is 'commissioning, installation' (Sir. 43:6; cf. ἀναδείκνυμι, Lk. 10:1; Acts 1:24**; H. Schlier, TDNT II, 31). The verse points forward to John's prophetic call in 3:2 (Sahlin, 178–182). Schlier thinks that the public 'manifestation' of John after his secluded life in the wilderness is meant. πρὸς τὸν Ἰσραήλ refers to John's public appearance before Israel or is perhaps pregnant: '(to go as a prophet) to Israel'. So John withdraws from the scene (cf. Danker, 21) while Jesus appears.

e. The Birth of Jesus (2:1–20)

The double promise of the births of John and Jesus and the description of the fulfilment of the first promise lead the reader to expect a description of the birth of Jesus; and just as the promise of the birth of Jesus formed a superior antitype to the promise of the birth of John, so the birth of Jesus is presented in a scene which is parallel to the earlier one but goes beyond it. There the birth was greeted by prophecy from the child's father, but here there is an angelic accompaniment and a heavenly proclamation of the significance of the new-born child. There is, however, the same note of wonder and praise to God on the part of those privileged to share in the joy of the birth.

In two important respects the story of the birth of Jesus is differentiated from that of John. First, it is given a setting in world history by the reference to the census which brought Mary and Joseph to Bethlehem. It is the first hint of the cosmic significance of the birth and foreshadows the universalism disclosed in 2:32. Second, the birth of Jesus takes place in lowly circumstances, a fact indicated by the use of the manger and the presence of the shepherds who represent the humble, possibly even the despised people of the land. The twin motifs of the rejection of Jesus by the world and of God's acceptance of ordinary humble and needy folk, to whom he chooses to reveal his salvation, thus come to expression in the story at the outset, and remain of decisive significance throughout the Gospel.

The hypothesis that the story rests on a pre-Christian legend, refashioned to apply to Jesus (H. Gressmann*), has been sufficiently criticised by Bultmann, 323–325, and Machen, 348–358. Recent study tends to regard the narrative as a creation on the analogy of the story of the birth of John (P. Winter; see 1:5 – 2:52 note) or as an independent Christian legend. (Those who take these views allow that pre-Christian legendary material has been incorporated; cf. Schürmann, I, 118 n. 164). In particular, it is often asserted that the narrative is quite separate from the stories in Lk. 1. It is of a different character and does not presuppose what has already been told. There is no mention of the supernatural conception of Jesus, and Mary appears to be ignorant of any previous announcement regarding the destiny of her child. Hellenistic motifs have been traced, both in the wording of the angelic messages and in the presence of the shepherds (who have been linked with Egyptian mythology or with Mithraism).

These points are not as forceful as they may seem at first sight. It is true that there is no reference back to the annunciation or to the supernatural conception of Jesus, but this is no proof that the narratives were originally separate; it merely allows for them to be separated if there are other good grounds for so doing (see on 2:19). The alleged Hellenistic motifs are no more than superficial colouring, and the story basically shows the same Palestinian Jewish traits as the earlier narrative. More weight attaches to the verdict that the rounded, complete form of the present story indicates that it was originally told in isolation from the others, but this appearance may be due simply to the way in which Luke has grouped the material and framed the story. It is more likely that the story comes from the same Christian circles as the narratives in Lk. 1, and that its apparent independence is due to the schematic way in which the whole narrative has been presented in a series of separate scenes. The story was probably already linked to the rest of the narrative before it reached Luke, and his hand was restricted to the stylistic revision to which he has subjected so much of his source material.

See E. Nestle, 'Die Hirten von Bethlehem', ZNW 7, 1906, 257–259; H. Gressmann, *Das Weihnachtsevangelium auf Ursprung und Geschichte untersucht*, Göttingen, 1914; C.-H. Hunzinger, 'Neues Licht auf Lc 2, 14, ἄνθρωποι εὐδοκίας', ZNW 44, 1952, 85–90; P. Winter, 'Lukanische Miszellen', ZNW 49, 1958, 65–77; D. Flusser, 'Sanctus und Gloria', in O. Betz, 129–152; Vögtle; 54–57; J. D. M. Derrett, 'The Manger: Ritual Law and Soteriology', *Theology* 74, 1971, 566–571; id. 'The Manger at Bethlehem', TU 112, 1973, 86–94; G. Schwarz, 'Der Lobgesang der Engel (Lukas 2, 14)', BZ 15, 1971, 260–264; C. Westermann, 'Alttestamentliche Elemente in Lukas 2, 1–20', in G. Jeremias (*et al.*), *Tradition und Glaube* (für K. G. Kuhn), Göttingen, 1971, 317–327; W. C. van Unnik, 'Die rechte Bedeutung des Wortes Treffen, Lukas II 19', in van Unnik, I, 72–91.

(1) The story begins with the action of the Roman Emperor in holding a census, as a result of which Mary and Joseph found themselves in Bethlehem. The census thus serves an important function in the development of the story, but at the same time it serves to place the birth

of Jesus in the context of world history and to show that the fiat of an earthly ruler can be utilised in the will of God to bring his more important purposes to fruition. The reference gives a date for the birth, but it is so vague that it cannot have been Luke's intention to give a precise chronological datum. It may well be that he had already composed 3:1ff., and there he does provide a precise date for the beginning of the public ministry of John; he may not have been able to date Jesus' birth precisely, since he has to content himself with saying that Jesus was 'about' thirty years old when he was baptised (H. U. Instinsky – see 2:3 note).

The introductory phrase ἐν ταῖς ἡμέραις ἐκείναις (4:2; Acts 2:18, 41; 9:37; cf. Lk. 5:35; 9:36; 21:23) refers back to the period before 1:80; cf. 1:5. δόγμα is here used of an imperial decree, corresponding to Latin *placitum, decretum* (Acts 17:7; Heb. 11:23 v.l.; of an ecclesiastical decree, Acts 16:4; cf. Eph. 2:15; Col. 2:14**; G. Kittel, TDNT II, 230–232). For the use of ἐξέρχομαι, cf. Dn. 2:13 Θ; the aorist is equivalent to a pluperfect. Καῖσαρ (3:1; 20:22, 24f.; 23:2*) may be meant as a proper name (so AG s.v.) or as a title, in accordance with later practice (Schürmann, I, 99). Likewise Αὐγοῦστος**, a Latin term usually translated into Greek as Σεβαστός (Acts 25:21, 25) may be a title, but is here a proper name. It was bestowed on Octavian (emperor, 31 BC – AD 14) by the Roman senate in 27 BC, and was used by subsequent emperors, but in his case it was a name (Bruce, 436).

The decree was concerned with an enrolment, such as preceded the collecting of taxes. ἀπογράφομαι, 'to register, record' (2:3, 5; Heb. 12:23**), is used in the papyri of official listing in registers for taxation (MM s.v.). In the light of 2:5 the form here and in 2:3 is middle and signifies 'to get oneself registered' (BD 317). The verb used for the actual payment of the taxes was ἀποτιμάω. οἰκουμένη (4:5; 21:26*) is 'the inhabited (world)', from οἰκέω, 'to dwell'. It was used of the Roman Empire which was exaggeratedly regarded as equal to the whole world (cf. O. Michel, TDNT V, 157 n. 1). Sahlin, 190, adopts a suggestion by C. C. Torrey that a Semitic expression meaning 'the whole land', sc. Palestine, has been misunderstood; but the phrase may rather be due to Lucan editing (Schürmann, I, 99 n. 7). On the census see 2:3 note.

(2) As the text stands, with a demonstrative not followed by the article, the most obvious translation is: 'This was the first census while Quirinius was governor of Syria' (BD 292). Some MSS insert ἡ, which eases the construction (so A C W *pl*; TR; *Diglot*) and gives: 'This census was the first . . .' ἀπογραφή (Acts 5:37**) is a 'list, inventory', hence also the activity of producing a list. The presence of πρώτη constitutes a problem, and Lagrange, 68, rightly asks why Luke included the word. 1. It may be intended to contrast this census with the previous census-less time, and/or 2. with future censuses. In both cases, the force is: 'This was the first census (and it took place) while Quirinius was governor of Syria'. Luke seems to know of only one census during this period (Acts

5:37, 'the census'). 3. πρῶτος has been taken as equivalent to πρότερος with a genitive of comparison: 'This census took place *before* Quirinius was governor' (cf. Jn. 5:36; 1 Cor. 1:25; so Lagrange, 66–68; MH III, 32). 4. The adjective might refer to 'the beginning of the census' (made before its completion by Quirinius; cf. Hdt. 7:92; Thuc. 1:55; 2:22; Zerwick, 152). 5. A variant of the preceding view is the suggestion that the phrase is a translation of Latin *descriptio prima,* the technical term for an enrolment prior to taxation (E. Stauffer*, see 2:3 note).

These different translations reflect the historical difficulty created by the mention of Quirinius as governor. ἡγεμονεύω (3:1**), 'to lead, command', is a general term used particularly of imperial legates and also of imperial prefects. (When writing of senatorial provinces governed by proconsuls, Luke correctly uses the noun ἀνθύπατος, Acts 13:7f., 12; 18:12; 19:38**.) Συρία (4:27*) was made into a Roman imperial province in 64 BC with Antioch as its capital; until AD 70 it included Judaea which had its own separate (and frequently changed) forms of administration (see 3:1). Κυρήνιος** is the Greek equivalent for Latin *Quirinius.* After holding a military command against the Marmaridae (in N. Africa?), Publius Sulpicius Quirinius became consul in 12 BC. At some point during the next 12 years he subjugated the Homonadenses, a race of brigands on the south border of Galatia. He acted as guide and supervisor of the young prince Gaius Caesar in Armenia, AD 3–4, and he was legate of Syria, AD 6–9; he died in AD 21 (Tacitus, Annals, 3:48; Strabo 12:6:5; E. Groag, PW 7A, 1931, 822–843; Schürer, *History,* I, 258f., 381f., 399–427; R. Syme, OCD 754f.; F. F. Bruce, NBD 1069). His census-taking activity is illustrated by the Lapis Venetus (CIL 3 Suppl. Nr. 6687): '*Iussu Quirini censum egi Apamenae civitatis millium hominum civium cxvll. Idem missu Quirini adversus Ituraeos in Libano monte castellum eorum cepi.*' For another example of Roman census activity, illustrating the language of the present verse, cf. P. Oxy. 181:3: ἀπογράφομαι κ(ατὰ) τὰ κελευσθέντα ὑπὸ Οὐαληφίου Πρόκλου τοῦ ἡγεμόνος.

(3) In consequence of the decree 'all' (sc. who were away from home) journeyed to their own cities. But the meaning is not clear. Was one's 'own city' determined by birth, ancestry, the holding of property or normal residence? In 2:39 Nazareth is said to be Mary and Joseph's own town. Sahlin, 199, argues that πόλις is a mistranslation for 'province' (cf. 1:26, 39). For ἑαυτοῦ (אc B D W *pc* lat syp sa bo), many MSS have ἰδίαν (so TR *Diglot*), which Klostermann, 32, strangely regards as an attempt to soften the difficulty.

Luke's description of the census and the date which he assigns to it have led to long and inconclusive debate; see Schürer, *History,* I, 399–427 (substantially repeating the earlier discussion in Schürer, I:2, 105–143); W. M. Ramsay, *Was Christ born at Bethlehem?* London, 1898; id. *The Bearing of Recent Discovery on the Trustworthiness of the*

New Testament, London, 1915, 238–300; Zahn, 129–135, 751–755; Machen, 239–243; R. Syme, 'Galatia and Pamphilia under Augustus', *Klio* 27, 1934, 122–148; T. Corbishley, 'Quirinius and the Census', *Klio* 29, 1936, 81–93; H. Braunert, 'Der Römische Provinzialzensus und der Schätzungsbericht des Lukas-Evangeliums', *Historia* 6, 1957, 192–214; H. U. Instinsky, *Das Jahr der Geburt Christi,* München, 1957; E. Stauffer, *Jerusalem und Rom,* Bern, 1957, 133f.; id. *Jesus and his Story,* London, 1960, 27–36; id. 'Die Dauer des Census Augusti', TU 77, 1961, 9–34; Sherwin-White, 162–171; Reicke, 79f., 100f.; G. Ogg, 'The Quirinius Question Today', Exp.T 79, 1967–68, 231–236; A. Schalit, *König Herodes,* Berlin, 1969, 265–278; H. R. Moehring, 'The Census in Luke as an Apologetic Device', in Aune, 144–160; C. F. Evans, 'Tertullian's References to Sentius Saturninus and the Lukan Census', JTS ns 24, 1973, 24–39; D. J. Hayles, 'The Roman Census and Jesus' Birth', *Buried History,* 9, 1973, 113–132; 10, 1974, 16–31; P. W. Barnett, 'ἀπογραφή and ἀπογράφεσθαι in Luke 2:1–5', Exp.T 85, 1973–74, 377–380; F. F. Bruce in A. R. Millard (ed.) *Documents of New Testament Times* (forthcoming).

(References to the above bibliography are indicated by ** in what follows).

The problems which surround Luke's statement are as follows:

1. The existence of a census covering the whole Roman Empire is said not to be attested by any other evidence. There is certainly no trace of any decree by Augustus requiring the assessment of the whole empire.

Augustus, however, did reform the administration of the whole empire, and new provinces were fitted into the pattern. After the conquest of Egypt (30 BC) it is 'practically certain' that a census was held in 10–9 BC (F. F. Bruce, NBD, 203; cf. Res Gestae 2:8), and that this was repeated every 14 years. About the same time a census, which took 40 years to complete, was commenced in Gaul. This latter census was a *prima descriptio,* a kind of 'Domesday Book' reckoning, to list for the first time all who were liable to taxation and what their resources were.

A similar act was carried out in Palestine on the banishment of Archelaus by Quirinius (Jos. Ant. 17:355; 18:1f.; 20:102; Bel. 2:117f.; 7:253). A further census by Quirinius in Apamea in Syria is attested by an inscription (2:2 note). Such a census would have taken some time to complete.

Behind such acts there will have been an edict from the emperor, used by the governor to justify his action to the people (Sherwin-White, 168f.), or the governor's edict may have been popularly regarded as stemming from the emperor himself (H. Braunert**, 201f.). In any case, Luke's statement can be regarded as a sufficiently accurate description of the emperor's intention that the whole empire should pay taxes. Schürer, *History,* I, 411, admits that in the time of Augustus censuses were held in many provinces, and Sherwin-White, 168, affirms more strongly that 'a census or taxation-assessment of the whole provincial empire (excluding client kingdoms) was certainly accomplished for the first time in history under Augustus'.

2. Judaea, however, was such a client kingdom during the reign of Herod, and therefore it was impossible for a census to be held within his domain. Would not a census be more likely in any case when his kingdom was made into a province?

Three possibilities have been suggested: a. A local census made by Herod himself may have been confused with a (later) general census by Quirinius (A. Schalit*). b. Relations between Augustus and Herod grew so strained towards the end of his reign that Augustus began to treat him as a vassal instead of a friend, and required all Judaea to take a vow of allegiance to both Herod and himself during the governorship of Saturninus (Jos. Ant. 16:290; 17:42). P. W. Barnett** has suggested that the purpose of the enrolment in Lk. 2:1f. was not taxation but the taking of the oath. c. These bad relations between Herod and Augustus may have led to Roman interference in taxation. E. Stauffer, *Jesus and his Story*,** 31–33, notes that Herod was permitted to mint only copper money, and contrasts his position with that of the Nabataean kings in Petra who were allowed to mint silver money, but were nevertheless under Roman fiscal control. When Archelaus succeeded Herod, the Romans were able to impose various changes in tribute (Jos. Ant. 17:319f.; Bel. 2:96f.). Appeal has also been made to the case of the Clitae, a tribe subject to the Cappadocian ruler Archelaus who conducted a census on the Roman model among them (Tacitus, Annals, 6:41), but this does not appear to have been a direct Roman action. The cases cited by Stauffer (including Apamea) are better evidence for Roman interference in taxation.

3. The requirement that each person should go to his own native place to be enrolled was contrary to Roman custom (which based tax on residence rather than ancestry) and would also be impractical.

Persons, however, with property in another district than the one where they resided had to go there to be registered (Ulpian 50:4:2; Schürer, *History*, I, 403 n. 15; E. Stauffer, op. cit. 35). A decree of C. Vibius Maximus, dated in AD 104, required absentees to return to their home towns for a census in Egypt (P. Lond. 904, 20f.; cited in Creed, 33). There is good reason to suppose that a similar procedure was followed in Palestine (cf. H. Braunert**, 201f.).

Although Luke does not make it clear, it must be presumed that Joseph had some property in Bethlehem. It is unlikely that everybody would have been compelled to return to their ancestral homes, but in view of Joseph's Davidic descent, which is more important for his story, Luke has stressed this aspect of the matter. As for the procedure being impractical, H. Braunert**, 205–208, notes that in a rural population most people do continue to live in the same place, and thus reside in the area to which they belong. In any case, with the custom of pilgrimage to Jerusalem, the Jews were used to travelling up and down their land.

From Galilee to Jerusalem would take about three days. B. Reicke, 79, observes that it is improbable that an inhabitant of Galilee would have had to travel to Judaea to be taxed after Herod's death when his kingdom had been divided up.

4. The presence of Mary with Joseph is strange, since only the head of the family needed to appear.

While this objection would be true of a census of Roman citizens in Italy, it does not apply to the present situation. In Syria women of 12 years and upwards were liable to a poll tax (Ulpian, 50:15:3; Schürer, *History*, I, 403 n. 12), and hence they may well have been required to appear personally at an enrolment which determined who was to pay taxes.

5. These considerations show that the character of the census described by Luke is far from impossible, and hence many recent writers are prepared to admit that Luke's description of a census reflects historical reality. The major difficulty that remains is the date. According to Lk. 1:5 and Mt. 1–2 Jesus was born during the reign of Herod the Great (ob. 4 BC), but Quirinius was governor of Syria after his death in AD 6–9. Josephus refers to the census carried out at this time, and describes the riots which accompanied it under Judas the Galilean (cf. Acts 5:37). Josephus' narrative gives the impression that this was the first Roman census in the country. Hence it has been concluded that Luke has wrongly associated the birth of Jesus which took place *before* Herod's death with the census which in fact happened some ten years *later*. (The contrary suggestion by Sherwin-White, 168f., that Jesus was in fact born at the time of the census, but Luke was misled into dating his birth before the death of Herod by synchronising it with the birth of John, is much less probable; it comes to grief on the later chronology of the life of Jesus). Reicke, 79, and A. Schalit** have taken up the earlier suggestion of Bleek and Schleiermacher that Luke may have confused a local census on the Roman pattern conducted by Herod himself with the later one held by Quirinius. H. Braunert**, 212–214, observes that the rise of Zealotism can be traced back into Herod's time (or immediately afterwards), although it was popularly associated with the rebellion against the census, and finds here a parallel to our problem. A Christian zealot group, which saw Jesus as the Messiah of Israel, attempted to link both his birth and the rise of zealotism with the same historical event, namely the census of Quirinius, and thus post-dated them both. Luke's material came ultimately from this group which admired both the Zealots and Jesus, and it led to his mistake (so also Leaney, 44–48, with caution).

Attempts have been made to postulate an earlier census. Tertullian (Adv. Marcion 4:19) stated that the census was held by Sentius Saturninus, governor of Syria in 9–6 BC. On this basis it has even been argued that originally 'Saturninus' stood in Luke's text (Easton, 20), but this is a desperate claim in the absence of MS evidence. Nor is there any historical evidence for a census by Saturninus, unless he possibly began a process which was completed by Quirinius. The accuracy of Tertullian's information has been queried by C. F. Evans**.

A second type of solution depends on positing an earlier governorship by Quirinius. A famous inscription, the *Lapis Tiburtinus* (CIL XIV, 3613; Dessau ILS 918), discovered in AD 1764 reads: '(*bellum gessit cum gente homonadensium quae interfecerat amyntam r)egem qua redacta in pot(estatem imp. caesaris) augusti populique romani senatu(s dis immortalibus) supplicationes binas ob res prosp(ere ab eo gestas et) ipsi ornamenta triumph(alia decruit) pro consul asiam provinciam op(tinuit legatus pr. pr.) divi augusti (i)terum syriam et ph(oenicen optinuit)*' (T. Mommsen's restoration, with conjectural material in brackets, as cited by Schürer, I:1, 354 n.). W. M. Ramsay** took this inscription to refer to Quirinius and held that he must have been governor of Syria twice (*'iterum'*); he postulated that he was an additional military governor in 10–7 BC, alongside the civil governor Saturninus, in order to prosecute the war against the Homonadenses in the Taurus Mountains. It is debatable whether the inscription does refer to Quirinius (so F. F. Bruce, NBD, 1069) or to some other Roman (e.g. L. Calpurnius Piso; Schürer, *History*, I, 258); it is also doubtful whether '*iterum*' refers to being governor of the *same* province twice (but see the defence of this view by Sherwin-White, 163 n. 5 – he does not, however, identify the unknown officer with Quirinius). R. Syme* argued that to conduct the Homonadensian war Quirinius was probably governor of Galatia. This particular solution, therefore, is surrounded by difficulty.

Other suggestions of the same kind have been made. Godet, 126f., offered as one possible solution that Quirinius was quaestor alongside the governor P. Quinctilius Varus (7/6–4 BC), but an ex-consul would hardly occupy such a position. T. Corbishley** attempted to find room for him as governor in 11–8 BC between M. Titius (c. 10 BC) and Saturninus (?10/9 – ?7/6 BC). G. Ogg has raised the possibility that he was governor before M. Titius (PC, 728; NBD, 223); others, such as F. B. Marsh, *The Founding of the Roman Empire*, Austin, Texas, 1922, 311, have suggested 3–2 BC, but this is too late. These views, which take advantage of the uncertainty regarding the succession in Syria at this period, have not found much favour, but that of Ogg perhaps deserves consideration.

In some of these theories the suggestion is that Quirinius held some kind of extraordinary command alongside the regular governor of Syria (so W. M. Ramsay). This suggestion has been developed by E. Stauffer**, who claims that Quirinius was a 'Generalissimo of the East' from 12BC onwards after serving as consul. Earlier, Pompey, Mark Antony and M. Vipsanius Agrippa had held commands of this nature. Now, it is claimed, Quirinius held this roving commission, being in sole charge of Syria at first, then along with Saturninus and Varus. Then C. Caesar was named as *Orienti praepositus* and was in the entourage of Quirinius;

when he died in AD 4 Quirinius again took charge, until he was replaced by Germanicus in AD 17. It was thus possible for Quirinius to institute a census during the reign of Herod. As has been indicated above, the process of enrolment would take a considerable length of time. Luke records the beginning of the operation, Josephus (whose accuracy should not be over-estimated) records the closing stages when the actual imposition of the tax led to riots. (This is a better suggestion than that of H. U. Instinsky**, 31–42, that there may have been *two* separate censuses). The validity of this suggestion depends upon the hypothesis of Quirinius's extraordinary command in the East.

In attempting to come to a conclusion on this matter, it seems certain that Luke intended to record an enrolment for the purposes of taxation on the Roman style which took place during the reign of Herod. He regarded this enrolment as resulting from the general policy of Augustus regarding taxation. It is not impossible that this enrolment was carried out by Quirinius acting in a special capacity before the death of Herod, but this theory remains speculative. It is also not impossible that Luke has recorded the first stages of an enrolment begun by another governor of Syria and completed by Quirinius, although the impression we get from Josephus is of a new action being commenced in AD 6. Historically, the solution least open to difficulty is that Herod was forced to carry out some kind of enrolment in his own realm under Roman pressure, perhaps in association with the oath of loyalty (Hauck, 37), and that this was regarded by Luke as part of the general fiscal measures of Augustus. This leaves the problem of the mention of Quirinius. Either Quirinius is to be thought of as exercising a broad command in the East before the death of Herod, so that the census could be attributed to his influence (and so as to point a link with his own later census in AD 6) or Luke means that it took place before his governorship. The form of the sentence is in any case odd, since it is hard to see why πρῶτος was introduced without any object of comparison, and it may be that πρῶτος should be understood as a comparative with the meaning 'before'. Luke does write loose sentences on occasion, and this may well be an example of such. No solution is free from difficulty, and the problem can hardly be solved without the discovery of fresh evidence.

(4) Joseph is portrayed as a law-abiding citizen – perhaps in deliberate contrast to the Zealots and other rebels against Rome – who in response to the imperial edict makes his way up from the comparatively low-lying countryside of Galilee to the hill-country of Judaea (ἀναβαίνω, as in 2:42; contrast καταβαίνω, 2:51; δὲ καί, 'and/but also', is a Lucan phrase (Hawkins, 37) which makes Joseph one of a larger group of people who obeyed the edict). He appears without introduction, a sign that this narrative belongs with the annunciation story, or that Luke has skilfully joined two independent stories. From Mt. 2:22 Bethlehem might appear to be his normal residence. Here his connection

is due to his belonging to the family and clan of David. διὰ τό with infinitive is Lucan (6:48; 8:6; 9:7; 11:8; 18:5; 19:11; 23:8*; Acts, 8x), as
is the use of εἶναι after a preposition and the article (2:6; 5:12; 9:18;
11:1, 8; 19:11*; Acts, 3x; Hawkins, 39). οἶκος and πατρία (Acts 3:25;
Eph. 3:15**) are probably synonymous (but see G. Schrenk, TDNT V,
1016f.). It is doubtful whether this family connection is sufficient to explain why Joseph had to go to Bethlehem, and he may also have had
property there.

   In the OT the 'city of David' is the hill of Zion in Jerusalem (2 Sa.
5:7, 9; et al.), but in the NT the description is applied to Bethlehem
(2:11); Burger, 136, claims that the appellation is due to Luke and is
erroneous; cf., however, Jn. 7:42. Bethlehem was about 4½ miles from
Jerusalem and 90 miles from Nazareth. Its name was popularly taken to
mean 'house of bread'. (The suggestion that it means 'house of (the god)
Lakhmu' (Schürmann, I, 102 n. 30) is to be rejected (D. F. Payne, NBD,
144)). But the significance lies not in its name but in its being the place
where David was brought up and where, according to Mi. 5:2 (cf. SB I,
82f.) the Messiah would be born. Thus the attentive reader is prepared
for the birth of a child to a descendant of David in the city of David.

   (5) Joseph was accompanied by Mary; σὺν Μαριάμ goes with the
preceding clause as a whole, rather than simply with ἀπογράψασθαι
(contra Klostermann, 35). She was living with him as his wife, although
the marriage had not yet been consummated (Mt. 1:25). This would appear to be the significance of ἐμνηστευμένη (cf. Lk. 1:27), since it is unlikely that she would have accompanied Joseph had she been merely
betrothed to him. But the text is uncertain: 1. ἐμνηστευμένη αὐτῷ (א B*
(C) D W (f1) syᵖ sa bo (Eus)) is generally accepted in modern editions
(cf. Schmid, 65; Machen, 123–125; Dibelius, Botschaft, I, 54f.). 2.
γυναικὶ αὐτοῦ (it syˢ) is accepted by Zahn, 128; Easton, 22; Klostermann, 35; Creed, 33; Schürmann, I, 103 n. 17). 3. μεμνηστευμένη αὐτῷ
γυναικί ((A) Θ f13 pl lat; TR). This reading is generally dismissed as a
conflation of variants 1. and 2., but it is important as providing indirect
attestation for 2. Moreover, 1. could be a modification of the text in the
light of 1:27. Hence 2. has attracted considerable support as the lectio
difficilior. Acceptance of it makes it easier to claim that 2:1–20 is a
story originally independent of Lk. 1 and making no reference to the
virgin birth. On the other hand, its textual attestation is extremely weak
– it does not occur as such in any Greek MS – and Luke does not
elsewhere speak of Mary as the γυνή of Joseph. J. Jeremias has
suggested (verbally) that syˢ, which supports it, shows Ebionite tendencies (i.e. suggesting that Jesus was the natural son of Mary and Joseph;
cf. Mt. 1:16, 21, 25 in syˢ); and Machen argues that 2. may have arisen
out of a desire to avoid apparent contradiction with Mt. 1:20, 24. On the
whole, the balance of probability favours 1.

   If this text is accepted, then the addition that Mary was pregnant
(ἔγκυος**) clearly implies the virgin conception of Jesus (Rengstorf, 37).

The fact that Mary journeyed with Joseph at what was (in the light of what followed) an advanced state of pregnancy has been a problem to some commentators (Luce, 98), so much so that some have explained her safe journey as miraculous. The point did not worry Luke, and one may wonder whether people in the ancient world were as much concerned over such medical risks as they would be today.

(6) On their arrival at Bethlehem (not earlier, as in Protev. Jac. 17:3; cf. Gn. 35:16ff.), the period of Mary's pregnancy was completed (cf. 1:23 note; 1:57; Gn. 25:24); αἱ ἡμέραι τοῦ τεκεῖν αὐτήν means 'the days to be fulfilled before the birth took place' (cf. 9:51).

(7) Mary's son is described as her 'first-born' (πρωτότοκος; Rom. 8:29; Col. 1:15, 18; Heb. 1:6; 11:28; 12:23; Rev. 1:5**; not to be confused with πρωτοτόκος, 'bearing one's first-born'; cf. W. Michaelis TDNT VI, 871–881). In contrast with μονογενής (7:12), the word *allows* that Mary had later children, but need not *demand* this (J.-B. Frey, 'La signification du terme πρωτότοκος d'après un inscription juive', Bib. 11, 1930, 373–390). The question whether in fact Jesus was Mary's only child cannot be discussed here (J. Blinzler, *Die Brüder und Schwester Jesu*, Stuttgart, 1967, gives the Roman Catholic interpretation). But if the word is not meant (1.) to contrast Jesus with Mary's later children (so Zahn, 136f.), the question arises why it is introduced here at all. 2. It may stress that Mary had no previous children – but why did this need to be said? 3. More probably it prepares for the narrative of the dedication of Jesus as the first-born in 2:22–24 (cf. Ex. 13:12; 34:19). 4. Hence it may stress the status of Jesus as the first-born who is to inherit the kingdom and thus be the Messiah (cf. 2 Ki. 3:27; 2 Ch. 21:3; J. Blinzler, op. cit. 56–61; Schürmann, I, 104). But the connection between Messiahship and being *Mary's* first-born is not obvious; hence a combination of views 1. and 3. is best.

Luke describes in detail how the child was cared for at birth, since this is significant for the directions to be given later to the shepherds. σπαργανόω (2:12**) is 'to wrap up in σπάργανα, i.e. swaddling clothes'; these were strips of cloth like bandages, wrapped around young infants to keep their limbs straight (Ezk. 16:4; Wis. 7:4; Dalman, *Sites*, 42). A child so wrapped would be recognised as newly born.

The child was laid down in a manger. ἀνακλίνω also means 'to recline for a meal' (12:37; 13:29*). φάτνη (2:12, 16; 13:15**) is a 'manger', i.e. a feeding trough for animals (T. Job 40:6). It is unlikely that here it means a 'stable' (as in Aelian, cited by AG s.v.) or a 'stall' or 'feeding place' under the open sky (see H. J. Cadbury, 'Lexical Notes on Luke-Acts III, Luke's Interest in Lodging', JBL 45, 1926, 317–319; 'Lexical Notes on Luke-Acts V, Luke and the Horse-Doctors', JBL 52, 1933, 61f.). See Creed, 34; M. Hengel, TDNT IX, 49–55. The midrashic features associated with the word by J. D. M. Derrett* appear to be the product of a lively imagination, and it is hard to believe that they would have occurred to Luke or his readers. There is no mention of the presence of the animals which normally used the manger; these found their way into the Christmas story from Is. 1:3; Hab. 3:2 LXX. The point is rather that at his birth Jesus had to be content with the habitation of animals because there was no room for him in human society (9:58). κατάλυμα, 'lodging', can be used of a guest-room (22:11; Mk. 14:14**), so that the reference may be to a room rather than to an inn (πανδοχεῖον, 10:34**), and to a room in a private house rather than to a room in an inn (Findlay, 1034; P. Benoit, ' "Non erat eis locus in diversorio" (Lc 2,7) ', in Descamps, 173–186). It has even been suggested that Bethlehem may not have had an inn for travellers. In any case no private room was available for the birth (Harvey, 231), and Mary and her child were deprived of normal comfort (see Schürmann, I, 105f.).

Are these details due to midrashic exegesis of the OT? There is a reference to the use of swaddling clothes at the birth of the Messiah in Ekah Rabbah 1:51 (Sahlin, 207; cf. j. Ber. 2:4 in SB I, 83). Mention of the manger could be due to the shepherd motif, which in turn can have arisen from the association of Bethlehem and David with shepherds; the 'tower of the flock' to which the kingdom would come (Mi. 4:8) was associated with the Messiah. Tg. J I on Gn. 35:21 speaks of 'the tower of Eder (i.e. flocks) from which King Messiah will be revealed at the end of days' (cf. Tg. Mi. 4:8; E. Nestle*; Sahlin, 208–211). But this explanation is unsatisfactory, since there is no hint of these associations in the story (J. Jeremias, TDNT VI, 490f.), and there is no suggestion of the manger or stable in the Jewish material.

A tradition which can be traced back to the second century located the birth of Jesus in a cave (Protev. Jac. 18f.; Justin, Trypho, 78:4; Origen, Contra Celsum, 1:15). Constantine erected a basilica at Bethlehem over a cave, and this has been excavated under the present Church of the Nativity. Jerome and Paulinus of Nola both mention the desecration of a cave in Bethlehem by the erection of a shrine for Adonis during the reign of either Hadrian or Decius; this probably implies desecration of a site sacred to Christians in the second or third century. Hence Jeremias (ibid.) and Finegan, 22f., claim that the identification of a cave at Bethlehem with the birthplace of Jesus is early. This tradition is not dependent on the NT, which knows nothing of a cave. Hengel, however, claims that it was originally separate from the manger story, since in Protev. Jac. the manger appears only later in the story as a hiding place for the young child from Herod. But caves were sometimes used to provide accommodation for animals, and houses were built near them, so that they might be used for this purpose. It is thus possible that the two traditions are complementary (Grundmann, 80f.), and hence that the tradition of the manger has a historical basis rather than a midrashic one; one cannot claim more than possibility for this suggestion (Dalman, *Sites*, 38–45), but it is a tempting one.

(8) The introduction of the shepherds (ποιμήν, 2:15, 18, 20*) can well be historical. J. Jeremias holds that they were the owners of the cave

in which Jesus was born, and that they had a firm place in the local tradition of his birth (TDNT VI, 491). This is possible, since the shepherds knew where to find the manger; the hypothesis would be supported if we read ἐν τῇ φάτνῃ in 2:12 with TR; *Diglot*, but the external evidence for inclusion of the article is too weak. On the assumption that the shepherds are legendary, various attempts have been made to explain their presence in the story: 1. The story was originally that of the discovery of a foundling by shepherds (H. Gressmann**; *contra* Bultmann, 324). 2. Shepherds represent the ideal, paradisical world in Hellenistic bucolic poetry (Creed, 34); but there is no trace of Hellenistic ideas of this kind in the story. 3. God's grace is revealed to a group of people held in low regard (e.g. as thieves) by the Jews. But the evidence for this view is late (SB II, 113f.), and in general shepherds receive honourable mention in the NT (Schürmann, I, 108f.). Nevertheless, the motif that God reveals the birth of the Saviour to ordinary, lowly people is undoubtedly present. 4. An allusion to the task of David as a shepherd (1 Sa. 16:11; Schürmann, I, 108) is unlikely, since it should be the child who is a shepherd, not the witnesses of his birth. 5. We have already discussed the suggestion that would link the manger with a shepherd motif based on the association of David and Bethlehem with shepherds. One might claim that shepherds were the appropriate people to be found in the vicinity of Bethlehem as witnesses of the birth of Jesus, but this fact speaks rather for the historicity of the story, since it implies that shepherds were likely to be found at hand.

The 'same area' refers to the area around Bethlehem. (There is no indication that Jesus was born in the open, near where the shepherds were; see 2:15f.). ἀγραυλέω**, literally 'to make one's ἀγρός one's αὐλή', is 'to be out of doors'. φυλάσσω (8:29; 11:21, 28; 12:15; 18:21*) takes a cognate accusative. Usually such an accusative has an attribute (2:9), except where it does not simply substantivise the verbal idea (BD 153³). Here τῆς νυκτός may be attached to the accusative with an attributive function (cf. Mk. 6:48). The verse describes the normal behaviour of shepherds who kept their flocks in the open and therefore had to mount a watch at night (each shepherd taking his turn on a rota) to guard against thieves and wild animals. Flocks were kept outside in this way from April to November (SB II, 114–116) and occasionally in suitable locations during the winter (cf. Morris, 84). The traditional scene of the revelation to the shepherds near Bethlehem is sheltered and could perhaps have been used in winter for flocks, but there is nothing in the narrative to indicate the time of year (Lagrange, 73), and the celebration of Christmas in winter in the northern hemisphere finds no support here, although it is not rendered impossible.

(9) The night may have seemed an appropriate time to Luke for a divine revelation (Drury, 37; cf. G. Delling, TDNT IV, 1123–1126). καὶ ἰδού is read by A D Θ f1 f13 *pl*; TR; *Diglot*; but, if original, it is hard to see why ἰδού was omitted (Metzger, 132). The angel of the Lord (1:11)

may well be Gabriel (1:19, 26). There is no indication that a separate tradition is being used (*contra* Schürmann, I, 109 n. 99), nor is it necessary to regard the angel of the Lord and the chorus of angels (2:13) as belonging to two separate traditions (2:13 note). The verb ἐφίστημι, 'to stand near, approach', is Lucan (2:38; 4:39; 10:40; 20:1; 21:34; 24:4; Acts, 11x; 1 Thes. 5:3; 2 Tim. 4:2, 6**); it may perhaps convey the sense of a sudden appearance (AG s.v.). The appearance of the angel is accompanied by the blazing glory which marks the presence of the divine (cf. 9:34; Acts 12:7; Ezk. 1). For δόξα in this sense cf. Acts 7:55; Tit. 2:13; Rev. 15:8; 21:23; *et al.*; also Lk. 9:26, 31f.; 21:27. This usage, derived from the LXX, is quite different from the Classical sense of 'opinion' (Ex. 16:10; 24:16; 40:34f.; Ezk. 1:28; 3:12, 23; *et al.*; G. von Rad and G. Kittel, TDNT II, 232–253, especially 248f.; for the association of deity with light see also A. Oepke, TDNT IV, 16–28; H. Conzelmann, TDNT IX, 319f.). Some authorities omit κυρίου after δόξα (D pc it; θεοῦ is a weakly attested variant) and this reading is adopted by Sahlin, 212, and (with hesitation) by Schürmann, I, 109 n. 97; cf. 9:31. περιλάμπω (Acts 21:13**) is 'to shine around'. The inevitable effect of such a heavenly visitation is fear (1:12f.); for the cognate accusative, see Schürmann, *Paschamahlbericht*, 5–7.

(10) The angelic message is a command not to fear followed by a reason (1:13, 30); the situation calls rather for joy since the angel brings good news (1:19 note) of an event that signals great joy (χαρά (1:14) is used concretely). Correspondingly with its joyful nature (ἥτις, as rendered by Kostermann, 37), this will be for all the people (πᾶς ὁ λαός is Lucan: 3:21; 7:29; 8:47; 9:13; 18:43; 19:48; 20:6, 45; 21:38; 24:19;* cf. 1:10; 2:31; Acts, 6x). The 'people' means Israel rather than the gentiles (Wilson, 34f.), but it is just possible that a wider reference is beginning to creep in, since the message echoes Hellenistic announcements affecting the whole world. To see the outlook of a Jewish Christian community expecting the conversion of Israel before the parousia is unwarranted (*pace* Schürmann, I, 110 n. 105).

The announcement is in rhythmic prose, and finds an interesting parallel in a statement about the birth of Augustus: ἦρξεν δὲ τῷ κόσμῳ τῶν δι' αὐτὸν εὐαγγελι(ῶν ἡ γενέθλιος) τοῦ θεοῦ . . . (Ditt. Syl. 458). This shows that such language was in common currency rather than that the present statement was necessarily contrived in opposition to imperial claims.

(11) The ὅτι clause expresses both the content of the good news and the reason for great joy. A birth has taken place which will benefit the shepherds and all who hear the news (ὑμῖν is dative of advantage). σήμερον is literally 'today' since the reference is clearly to the actual birth of Jesus, rather than metaphorically to the era of salvation now inaugurated (Sahlin, 214; Ellis, 80). The term σωτήρ, already applied to God (1:47), is comparatively rare and late in the NT (Jn. 4:42; Acts 5:31; 13:23; Eph. 5:23; Phil. 3:20; 2 Tim. 1:10; Tit. 1:4; 2:13; 3:6; 2

Pet. 1:1, 11; 2:20; 3:2, 18; 1 Jn. 4:14). The background is the OT concept of God as Saviour; he now acts to save men through Jesus. The
term was also applied to the Roman emperor and other Hellenistic
rulers, and was employed in the mystery religions and the cult of
Asclepius (G. Fohrer and W. Foerster, TDNT VII, 1003–1021; F.
Stolz, THAT I, 785–790). The origins of the language here can be
satisfactorily explained in terms of the Jewish background (W. Foerster,
TDNT VII, 1015), but Luke may well have expected his readers to see a
contrast with rival Hellenistic statements. Although the title is rare, the
thought of Jesus as Saviour pervades the NT and is fully expressed in
the birth story (1:69, 71, 77; Voss, 45–55).

The difficult phrase Χριστὸς κύριος may be translated 'Christ (and)
Lord' (cf. Acts 2:36; W. Grundmann, TDNT IX, 533 n. 276) or 'an
anointed Lord' (cf. 23:2). Many scholars think that there is a primitive
error in the text for Χριστὸς κυρίου, 'the Lord's anointed' (P. Winter*).
This reading has in fact some weak textual attestation (β r¹ sy ʰ ᵖᵃˡ Tat
Ephr). The problematic phrase is found in La. 4:20 LXX (where it is a
mistranslation) and Ps. Sol. 17:36 (cf. Ps. 88:52 LXX). The resemblance
of the variant reading to a Hebrew construct phrase without the article
supports its originality, as does its resemblance to the Lucan phrase in
2:26. On the other hand, the existing text gives a reasonable sense and
fits in with Lucan usage in 23:2. We should probably, therefore, retain
the text (Metzger, 132) and take it to mean that Jesus is 'the Messiah
(and) the Lord'. Behind it may lie the idea of a Saviour who is to be
regarded as the 'Messiah-Yahweh'; cf. the thought of the epiphany of the
Lord in T. Levi 2:11; see also T. Sim. 6:5; T. Levi 5:2 (Sahlin,
214–218; Marshall, 100f.). But the phrase could also represent a Lucan
elucidation of 'Messiah' for non-Jewish readers (Schürmann, I, 111f.; cf.
Laurentin, 127–130; W. Foerster, TDNT VII, 1015 n. 63). The mention
of the city of David fits the birth of the Messiah (Mi. 5:2).

Schürmann, I, 110 n. 107, notes a difference between the
christology here and in 1:26–38, in the earlier passage the (original) expectation of a future fulfilment, but here the sense of present fulfilment.
This difference is not, however, due to the use of two different traditions,
but to the change of perspective brought about by the actual birth of the
promised child.

(12) A sign of the truth of the message is now given. Although the
article τό is omitted before σημεῖον by B pc; Synopsis, it should be
retained, since it is a fixed part of the phraseology (Ex. 3:12; 1 Sa. 2:34;
14:10; 2 Ki. 19:29; 20:9; Is. 37:30; 38:7; 1 Sa. 10:1 LXX; K. H.
Rengstorf, TDNT VII, 231 n. 211). The formulation thus falls into line
with OT usage whereby God confirms what he is about to do by the
provision of a confirmatory sign. The purpose here is not only to identify
the child by indicating where he is to be found (cf. Mt. 2:9) but also in
this way to authenticate the messianic proclamation. The shepherds will
find an infant (βρέφος, 1:41) newly born and lying in a manger (καὶ

κείμενον is omitted by אּ D, probably by homoioteleuton; see also 2:8 note on the text). This is a paradoxical sign, since the promised Messiah is to be found in lowly conditions, but it brings the shepherds to the manger, so that they in turn act as a confirmatory sign to Mary.

(13) A second sign follows suddenly, i.e. immediately (ἐξαίφνης, 9:33; Acts 9:3; 22:6; Mk. 13:36**). The angel is joined by a great number of the host of heaven. στρατιά, 'host, army', is used to refer to a heavenly company in the LXX (1 Ki. 22:19; 2 Ch. 33:3, 5; Je. 8:2; 19:13; Zp. 1:5; 2 Esd. 19:6); the usual phrase is πλῆθος στρατιᾶς τοῦ οὐρανοῦ, which Luke may have adapted here. The phrase may refer to the stars, but it is clearly used of angels in 1 Ki. 22:19; 2 Esd. 19:6. αἰνέω, 'to praise' (2:20; 19:37; 24:53 v.l.; Acts 2:47; 3:8f.; Rom. 15:11; Rev. 19:5**) is used in the plural ad sensum (Mk. 9:15; BD 134[lb]) with στρατιᾶς; for the thought cf. Ps. 102:20f.; SB II, 117.

C. Westermann* argues that in this narrative there are two quite different concepts with different OT roots, namely the angel of the Lord and the heavenly attendants around God's throne; the manifestation of the latter is in effect a kind of theophany, whereas the angel of the Lord comes in an epiphany. In the present narrative vs. 13f. can easily be separated off; in v. 9 the element of heavenly glory which properly belongs to a theophany has been inserted in the description of the epiphany of the angel of the Lord, thus linking the two appearances together.

To assert that vs. 13f. *may* be separated off from the rest of the narrative, however, is not to prove that they *must* be. Luke saw no incompatibility between the two types of manifestation, and obviously thought of the earlier appearance of the angel to Zechariah as supernatural. The suggestion raises again the problem whether the angelic appearances are to be taken literally and historically or are essentially symbolical means of conveying a divine interpretation of historical events, drawn from different literary categories. In any case, the experience is regarded as visionary (since it will not have been seen by any other people in the neighbourhood), and it is not impossible that God should have revealed his message to the shepherds in the sort of way that fitted their expectations of how he would act.

(14) The angelic song is in effect a proclamation of the results of the birth of Jesus rather than a hymn of praise directly addressed to God. Older commentators saw in it a unit of three lines, based on the reading εὐδοκία (Θ f1 f13 pl sy[s p] bo Or[pt] Eus Epiph Cyr; TR; so AV). But the external evidence favours εὐδοκίας (אּ* A B* D W pc latt sa got Or[pt] Ir[lat] patr occ) and the internal evidence also supports this reading (WH App., 52–56; Metzger, 133). This means that the song is a couplet. The older interpretation is still favoured by D. Flusser*; for the modern view, see G. Schrenk, TDNT II, 747–750.

The first line ascribes δόξα (supply ἐστιν, Sahlin, 224f.) to God in heaven where he dwells (ἐν ὑψίστοις, 19:38; cf. 1:78). In 2:9 δόξα meant the bright appearance of glorious light, indicative of the presence of

God. Here the reference could be to the visible majesty of God, which is based ultimately on the graciousness of his character. The phrase will then be a recognition that glory and majesty belong to God, so that as a whole it forms an ascription of praise to him. Men and angels glorify God by recognising that he already possesses glory and worshipping him for it; in this sense they increase his glory. The word can thus also mean 'praise' (Schürmann, I, 114; C. Westermann*, 325 n. 17), but this is unlikely to be the primary meaning here, since it spoils the parallelism with the second line which also speaks of God's attributes and gifts (Grundmann, 84).

If the glory of God in heaven is revealed in the coming of his Son, the effect for men on earth is summed up in εἰρήνη (1:79). Here, however, more than the cessation of strife is meant, and the word is used to indicate the full sum of the blessings associated with the coming of the Messiah (Is. 9:5f.; Mi. 5:4). He brings a new situation of peace between God and men in which his blessings can be communicated to them; εἰρήνη is thus tantamount to σωτηρία (W. Foerster, TDNT II, 413; Grundmann, 84f.).

This gift is for ἄνθρωποι εὐδοκίας (ἐν is omitted in some authorities, but should be retained). εὐδοκία is 'will, good pleasure' (10:21 par. Mt. 11:26; cf. Pss. Sol. 3:4; 8:39; 16:12; 1 En. 1:8 Gk.; T. Levi 18:13; Shemoneh Esreh 17). It corresponds to Hebrew rāṣôn, used of the will of God (Pss. 51:18 (50:20); 89:17 (88:18); 106:4 (105:4)). Earlier scholars (G. Schrenk, ibid.) suspected that the unusual phrase here was the equivalent of 'anšē rāṣôn or bᵉnē rᵉṣônô or the corresponding Aramaic phrase. This guess has now been raised to virtual certainty by the attestation of such phrases at Qumran (1QH 4:32f.; 11:9; 4QAram Apoc; C.-H. Hunzinger*; further literature listed in Schürmann, I, 114 n. 143; C. Westermann*, 322 n. 12; cf. also Sir. 15:15; 39:18). The phrase means 'those upon whom God's will/favour rests', and expresses the thought of God's free choice of those whom he wills to favour and save. Hence the older translation 'men of goodwill' (homines bonae voluntatis, vg; cf. Zahn, 144–146; Lagrange, 76–78), unlikely on theological grounds with its suggestion of human merit, can be dropped from consideration.

The phraseology demonstrates decisively that a Semitic original must be postulated for the couplet; cf. Sahlin, 229f.; Black, 168; G. Schwarz*.

(15) Heaven is regarded as the dwelling place of God and the angels, to which they now return. οὐρανός is normally used by Luke in the singular form (31x; plural, 10:20; 12:33; 18:22; 21:26); both forms are used indifferently for the sky and heaven (G. von Rad and H. Traub, TDNT V, 497–536, especially 533). For οἱ ποιμένες, some MSS read καὶ οἱ ἄνθρωποι οἱ ποιμένες (A D f13 pm; TR; Diglot), a form which Easton, 24, regarded as 'eminently in Luke's style'. It could be a Hebraism with καί (for Hebrew wᵉ) in apodosis (Sahlin, 231f.). A con-

trast between the angels and the men left below on earth is possible
(Godet, 133). The preference of UBS for the shorter text rests on the external evidence (Metzger, 134). The wording of the shepherds' decision
to go to Bethlehem is Lucan in style. διέρχομαι is 'to go, go through'
(10x; Acts, 20x; rest of NT, 11x). ῥῆμα here means 'event' (1:37 note).
For τὸ γεγονός cf. 8:34–36; 24:12; Acts 4:21; 5:7; 13:12; Mk. 5:14**; 1
Sa. 4:16. γνωρίζω (2:17; Acts 2:38; 7:13**) is used especially of 'God's
declaration of his secret counsel of salvation' (R. Bultmann, TDNT I,
718). δή* is a particle of emphasis, especially with commands (cf.
Hebrew -nā'; Acts 6:13; 13:2; 15:36*; et al.).

(16) Like Mary (1:39) the shepherds go in haste; σπεύδω is Lucan
(19:5f.; Acts 20:16; 22:18; 2 Pet. 3:12**); for the use of the participle
see 1 Sa. 4:14, 16; Jos. Bel. 1:222. The search is rewarded by success,
ἀνευρίσκω (Acts 21:4**) implying that the object sought is actually
found. Note the use of τε (bracketed in Diglot; omitted by D). This is a
common connective particle in Lk.-Acts (12:45; 14:26; 15:2; 21:11a, b;
22:66; 23:12; 24:20; Acts, 140x; Mt., 3x; Mk., 0x; rest of NT, 55x). It
is used in conjunction with καί to mean 'both . . . and . . .' Normally it
follows the noun to which it refers (A. τε . . . καὶ B.), but precedes a noun
which has the article, as here. It may be followed, as here, by more than
one καί phrase (BD 443f.).

(17) It is not absolutely clear to whom the shepherds made known
the saying about the child. The wording 'this child' may imply that other
people were already present with Mary and Joseph and the child (cf.
Easton, 25), but the analogy of 1:66 may suggest that the shepherds
went and told other people in the neighbourhood. ῥῆμα here must mean
'saying', but Creed, 36, translated 'matter'.

(18) Three reactions to the event are described, those of the
hearers, of Mary (v. 19) and of the shepherds (v. 20). The hearers are
filled with wonder (1:63; cf. 1:21; 2:33). 'The astonishment . . . is a
means to prepare the ground for the fact that the story of Jesus has the
character of revelation' (G. Bertram, TDNT III, 39). There is no strong
external evidence for preferring ἐθαύμαζον (D; Diglot) to ἐθαύμασαν.
The Diglot reading reflects Kilpatrick's judgment (199) that scribes
tended to alter Hellenistic imperfects to Atticising aorists.

(19) Mary was able to take a deeper view of the situation, if δέ is
meant to express a contrast with the preceding verse. It is less natural to
suppose that the contrast is between the words of the shepherds and the
silence of Mary (pace Creed, 36). It is possible that the narrator intended
to separate Mary from the wonderers in v. 18 and to take into account
her earlier knowledge of her child's destiny (see, however, 2:33). The
MSS vary between Μαριάμ (A W pm; TR; UBS; Diglot) and Μαρία (‭א‬
B D al; Synopsis). συντηρέω is 'to protect', 'to hold or treasure up (in
one's memory)' (Mt. 9:17; Mk. 6:20**; cf. Sir. 39:2; Dn. 7:28; T. Levi
6:2; and for the thought see Gn. 37:11). συμβάλλω is frequent in Lk.: 'to
consider, ponder'; 'to converse' (Acts 4:15; 17:18); 'to meet' (14:31;

Acts 20:14); 'to help' (Acts 18:27**). The sense here is that Mary continued to think and ponder over the events as a whole so that she was able to discern their meaning (see van Unnik*, who shows that the verb means 'to get at the right meaning').

Earlier commentators held that the verse pointed to the source of Luke's story, namely Mary herself (2:51; Zahn, 147; Easton 25); Schürmann, I, 117, holds that the purpose of the verse is christological, to emphasise that a fulfilment of the promises made here was to be expected in the future. Neither interpretation excludes the other. The Lucan style of the verse has suggested that it is redactional and based on 2:51 (Dibelius, *Botschaft*, I, 54 n. 90; Hahn, 270); in fact its form and function are similar to those of 1:66.

(20) Finally, the shepherds depart, glorifying God. δοξάζω with θεόν as object is frequent in Luke (5:25f.; 7:16; 13:13; 17:15; 18:43; 23:47; cf. 4:15). οἷς is by relative attraction for ἅ. πᾶς ὅς/ὅσος is frequent in Lk. (12:8, 10, 48; 14:33; 18:12, 22; 19:37; 24:25; Mt. 22:10; Mk., 0x). Thus the coincidence of what they had heard from the angels with what they had seen led the shepherds to praise; by itself the birth of the child would have seemed to be a perfectly ordinary event. The motif of praise fittingly closes several pericopes in Lk. (especially 24:53).

f. The Presentation of Jesus in the Temple (2:21–40)

V. 21 relates briefly how Jesus was circumcised and named, the stress falling on the significant name which he was given before his conception. Prophecies regarding John's future had been made at his circumcision, but in the case of Jesus these took place later at the temple on the occasion of his presentation there (vs. 22–24). Thus the narrative leads up to the meeting of Simeon and Anna with Jesus and his parents in the temple, and again reference is made to the future rule of the child (vs. 25–35, 36–38). The child, duly circumcised, named and presented to God, is the fulfilment of the hopes of pious Israel, the redeemer of the people of God; nor is this all, for in the words of Simeon we have the clearest indication yet of the universal extent of the salvation to be brought by Jesus, together with the fact that, universal though the offer may be, there will be those who will reject it and come under judgment. But before all this will happen, the child must accompany his parents to their home, and there grow up to manhood (vs. 39f.).

The story is told throughout in a Palestinian setting. Apart from certain problems concerned with the presentation of Jesus (and due to the condensed nature of the narrative), the narrative contains the apparent miracle of Simeon and Anna being moved by divine inspiration to come into the temple at the right moment, to recognise the child and to prophesy about him. This point obviously affects the character of the story as a whole, since there would be no story left without it. Those who are prepared to accept the possibility of such events will find no essential difficulty in the story.

One may dismiss Bultmann's analysis (326f.) of the story into a series of ingenious motifs designed to get Jesus into the temple. The fact that Anna has nothing particular to say suggests to him that she is a doublet of Simeon. But on the contrary her rather otiose role is more likely to be an indication of historicity. Her presence provides the second of the two witnesses required to testify to the significance of Jesus (Dt. 19:15). A further difficulty has been seen in the wonder with which Mary and Joseph hear the prophecy of Simeon (v. 33): can this be compatible with their earlier knowledge of the birth and destiny of Jesus? But this motif, which may be held to suggest that originally this story was narrated in isolation from the earlier ones, is adequately explained by the fact that such wonder is a typical motif in miracle stories and similar events; in the present case, it is due to the fact that a stranger recognises the significance of the child. Finally, the fact that similar stories are told about other religious figures (e.g. Buddha) and heroes is no proof that the present story is an invention.

The historical difficulties in the story are thus not compelling. Those, however, who are unable to accept the possibility of the prophetic activity described here will have to explain the story as a legendary expression of the destiny of Jesus in the light of subsequent events (Hauck, 41). It is of course quite possible and indeed likely that such reflection has been incorporated in the narrative, even if it is in substance historical.

See P. Benoit, ' "Et toi-même, un glaive te transpercera l'âme" (Luc 2, 35) ' (originally in CBQ 25, 1963, 251–261), in *Exégèse*, III, 216–227; G. D. Kilpatrick, 'ΛΑΟΙ at Lk. 2:31 and Acts 4:25, 27', JTS ns 16, 1965, 127; D. R. Jones, JTS ns 19, 1968, 40–43.

(21) The verse is close in structure to v. 22 (cf. 1:23) and may be a Lucan formulation, linking the preceding and following narratives (Grundmann, 87; Sahlin's view, 239–242, that it is an insertion should be rejected). After eight days had elapsed (cf. 1:57, 59), Jesus was circumcised in the normal way. The articular infinitive τοῦ περιτεμεῖν has a consecutive sense (BD 400²). But the main emphasis is on the naming of the child. The introductory καί in the apodosis (cf. 2:28; 7:12; 11:34; 13:25) may simply imply 'in addition to being circumcised, he was also named', or may imitate Hebrew usage (BD 442⁷; Beyer, I:1, 69). The name bestowed is of course that which had previously been communicated by the angel. Thus the verse draws the parallel between John and Jesus (1:59f.), and also links this story to the annunciation.

(22) The story of the presentation of Jesus in the temple (2:22–24) is complicated by the fact that three distinct motifs underlie the story; these have been assimilated to one another so closely that it is difficult to disentangle them.

The first element is the purification of the mother of a child. The opening part of the verse is modelled on Lv. 12:6 which ordains what is to happen 'when the days of her purifying are completed, whether for a son or for a daughter'. After the birth of a son the mother was ceremonially unclean for 7 days until the circumcision, and then had to remain at home for a further 33 days; she then offered a sacrifice on the fortieth day at the Nicanor Gate on the east of the Court of Women (Lv. 12:1–8; SB II, 119f.). καθαρισμός (5:14* par. Mk. 1:44) is a late form for καθαρμός, 'cleansing'. The use of αὐτῶν is strange, since only the mother was unclean, and it is not clear whether Joseph or Jesus is included along with her. The MSS vary: αὐτῆς (76; cf. *Marie*, vg ᵐˢ) is supported by the ambiguous *eius* (it vg); the masculine form αὐτοῦ (D 2174* syˢ saᵐˢ) may be derived from it or may be due to transcriptional error (Metzger, 134). Other authorities omit the pronoun altogether (435 bo Irenˡᵃᵗ). It has been argued that αὐτῆς is the original text, altered because the scribe could not believe that Mary was impure; αὐτοῦ is an erroneous correction (referring to the child) and αὐτῶν is a conflation (cf. Easton, 26; Luce, 101; Hauck, 41). But it is improbable that scribes would transfer the impurity from Mary to Jesus, and the weighty external evidence stands against this view; the variants are attempts to ease a difficult text. Some interpret αὐτῶν in the light of the second half of the verse as Joseph and Mary (subjective genitive) whose duty it was to carry out the cleansing (cf. Godet, I, 136; Machen, 73). Others think that according to Greek ideas both mother and child are reckoned as unclean, but this is improbable in a Palestinian environment (see, however, 1:59 note). It is most likely that Luke has run together the cleansing of the mother and the offering of the child (see below) into one act (Schmid, 75; Schürmann, I, 121). The reality of the incarnation is seen in that it rendered Mary impure by Jewish standards (Danker, 30). The mention of the 'law of Moses' (2:39; Acts 22:12; 23:3; 24:14) underlines the thought of pious obedience which is present throughout the narrative (2:23, 24, 27; cf. 2:1–5).

Luke uses the two forms Ἱεροσόλυμα (13:22; 19:28; 23:7;* Acts, 23x) and Ἱερουσαλήμ (Lk., 26x; Acts, 39x). In the rest of the NT Ἱεροσόλυμα is found mostly in the Gospels (Mt., 11x; Mk., 10x; Jn., 12x; Gal. 1:17f.; 2:1**) and Ἱερουσαλήμ outside the Gospels (11x; Mt. 23:37 *bis* (Q)**). The former is a Hellenised, declinable form of the latter (BD 56¹), used mostly by non-Jews and also by Jews when addressing Greek readers, while the latter was used almost exclusively by Jewish writers and in the LXX. Plummer, 64, notes that the latter term is used when the reference is to the heavenly Jerusalem, and Hastings, 103–106, has followed up this point by suggesting that in general Luke used the latter (Jewish) form when he wished to stress the theological significance of Jerusalem. Schürmann, I, 121 n. 182, thinks that in the Gospel Luke was trying to write 'sacred prose' and so used the Hebrew form, but occasionally he slipped into using the Hellenised form, as in the present case. J. Jeremias ('ΙΕΡΟΥΣΑΛΗΜ/ΙΕΡΟΣΟΛΥΜΑ', ZNW 65, 1974, 273–276) demonstrates that Luke preferred the Hebrew form in the

Gospel, and that use of the Hellenistic form is due to failure to correct his sources consistently; he is less consistent in Acts, except in the opening chapters. See also E. Lohse, TDNT VII, 327f.; J. K. Elliott, 'Jerusalem in Acts and in the Gospels', NTS 23, 1976–77, 462–469.

The second element in the narrative is the offering of the child to the Lord in the temple. παρίστημι is frequently used in this transitive sense (e.g. Rom. 12:1; for the intransitive use see 1:19 note). The following verse shows that this offering was in accordance with the law requiring each first-born child (2:7) to be offered to God and a price paid for its redemption. Since, however, the child was brought to the temple, which was not necessary for the act of redemption, we should probably find a third element in the narrative, namely the offering of the child to God for his service, in the same way as Samuel was offered by his parents to God (1 Sa. 1:11, 22, 28; J. Weiss, 428; Schürmann, I, 122; Harvey, 232; Wilkinson, 15). Hence in the case of Jesus no redemption price was paid, for the child was not redeemed but rather consecrated to the service of God (B. Reicke, TDNT V, 840f.; *pace* Caird, 64; Morris, 87).

(23) In order to explain what was happening, Luke cites the relevant command in the law. For the formula καθὼς γέγραπται, see Acts 7:42; 15:15*; cf. Schürmann, I, 121 n. 177). The article is read before νόμῳ by D F; Diglot), but the external evidence favours omission. The citation is based on Ex. 13:2, 12, 15, but is not an exact quotation (Holtz, 82f.). διανοίγω, 'to open', happens to be a favourite word of Luke (24:31, 32, 45; Acts 7:56; 16:14; 17:3; Mk. 7:34**), but is here drawn from the LXX. μήτρα is 'womb' (Rom. 4:19**). The phrase ἅγιον ... κληθήσεται is repeated from 1:35 (the LXX uses ἁγιάζω).

The law (Ex. 13; 22:28f.; 34:19f.; Nu. 3:11–13, 40–51; 8:16–18; 18:15–18; Dt. 15:19f.; SB II, 120–123) required that the first-born of animals be offered in sacrifice to Yahweh. The choice of Levi as a sacred tribe was regarded as a substitute for the offering of the first-born of men, but at the same time a ransom price of 5 shekels was laid down. Although in Nu. 3:46f. this payment was made in the first instance only for the 273 Israelites in excess of the number of Levites, the payment had to be made subsequently for all first-born. It could be paid to a priest anywhere (M. Ex. 13:2 (22b)). The facts that the scene of the present incident is the temple, no ransom price is mentioned, and the child is present, show that Jesus is not here being redeemed but consecrated to the Lord.

(24) Finally, Luke reverts to the cleansing of the mother, which was effected by the sacrifice of a lamb with a young pigeon or turtledove as a burnt offering and a sin offering respectively (Lv. 12:6); Joseph and Mary, however, being poor, availed themselves of the concession to offer two doves or pigeons (Lv. 12:8; the wording is closer to Lv. 5:11 where the similar sacrifice for unwitting sin is described; cf. Lv. 14:22; Nu. 6:10). ζεῦγος (14:19**) is a 'pair', originally a 'yoke'.

τρυγών** is a 'turtle-dove'. νοσσός** is 'the young of a bird', and περιστερά (3:22*) 'pigeon, dove'.

(25) As the giving of John's name was followed by a prophetic statement combining praise to God and an indication of the child's destiny, so the naming and dedication of Jesus is followed by similar statements. καὶ ἰδού introduces a new event (5:12; 10:25; 13:11; 14:2; 19:2; et al.). The word order ἄνθρωπος ἦν (B) is inverted in TR; Diglot, with good external support to give a Semitic word order (Kilpatrick, 198). Black, 107, argues that here, as often elsewhere, ἄνθρωπος is a substitute for τις due to Aramaic influence, but this is unlikely in the present instance, since the word is taken up in the next clause.

Συμεών was a common Jewish name (Hebrew šim'ôn, Gn. 29:33; Lk. 3:30; Acts 13:1; 15:14; 2 Pet. 1:1; Rev. 7:7**; The form Σιμών (6:15) is much more common in the NT). He is described as δίκαιος (like Zechariah, 1:6) and εὐλαβής, 'devout' (Acts 2:5; 8:2; 22:12**) cf. εὐλάβεια, Heb. 5:7; 12:28**). The latter originally meant 'cautious' and hence 'careful in religious duties'; it is equivalent in meaning to εὐσεβής (Acts 10:2) which is a v.l. here. Although the word did not find favour as an expression for Christian piety, perhaps because of its negative tone, it is used here quite positively of a person who fulfilled the Jewish law (cf. R. Bultmann, TDNT II, 751–754).

It is a further mark of Simeon's Jewish piety that he was awaiting the comfort of Israel. προσδέχομαι is 'to await' (2:38; 23:51; Acts 23:21) or 'to receive, welcome' (12:36; 15:2*; Acts 24:15*). For the thought cf. Gn. 49:18; Ps. 119:166; Is. 25:9. παράκλησις, 'comfort, consolation' (6:24*; Acts 4:36; 9:31; 13:15; 15:31*), is used under the influence of Is. 40:1f. for the consolation brought about by the messianic era (Mt. 5:4; Is. 49:13; 57:18; 61:2; 2 Bar. 44:7; SB II, 124–126; O. Schmitz and G. Stählin, TDNT V, 773–799, especially 789f., 798). Simeon was thus one whose hopes would be fulfilled by the coming of the Messiah; he was now equipped to recognise the coming of the Messiah and to speak prophetically about it by the fact that the Holy Spirit was upon him. The word order πνεῦμα ἦν ἅγιον is perhaps for emphasis (Godet, I, 137; it is more conventional in D al; Diglot). For ἐπί used in this way see 4:18. The Spirit is here the inspirer of prophecy (SB II, 126–138; E. Schweizer, TDNT VI, 835f.).

(26) Simeon had already received an oracle that he would not die before seeing the Messiah. χρηματίζω has this sense in Mt. 2:12, 22; Acts 10:22; Heb. 8:5; 11:7. (It also means 'to bear a name', Acts 11:26; et al.; cf. B. Reicke, TDNT IX, 480–482). For the use of the passive of an intransitive verb see BD 312¹. 'To see death' is a phrase based on OT usage (Ps. 89:48; cf. 16:10; see Jn. 8:51; Acts 2:27; Heb. 11:5).

The combinations πρὶν ἤ ἄν, πρὶν ἤ, πρὶν ἄν and πρίν are all attested in the MSS here (along with ἕως ἄν) and elsewhere. In a sentence with a positive main clause, πρίν is constructed with the accusative and infinitive (22:61; Acts 2:20; 7:2; Mt. 1:18; Mt. 26:34 and 75 par. Mk.

14:30 and 72). If the main clause is negative, πρίν is used with the optative in historic sequence (Acts 25:16); in the present case, however, the
original subjunctive of the direct discourse is retained, as in Classical
usage; cf. BD 383³.

The phrase ὁ Χριστὸς κυρίου would normally require the article
with the dependent genitive, but it is omitted here on the analogy of the
Hebrew construction (1 Sa. 24:7 LXX). For this title see 9:20; 23:35;
Acts 3:18; 4:26 (Ps. 2:2); Rev. 11:15; 12:10. It follows that the consola-
tion of Israel is to be equated with the coming of the Messiah
(Grundmann, 90).

(27) Now the old man has reached the moment of fulfilment of
God's word, perhaps after years of waiting. Although ἐν τῷ πνεύματι has
been taken to mean 'in an ecstasy' (Rev. 1:10), the presence of the article
and the context suggest that he came into the temple by the guidance of
the Spirit (4:1). Consequently he was present when the parents of Jesus
brought him in to carry out the legal ceremony. Since the reader already
knows what was required, Luke does not stop to describe it, but can go
straight on to the element of interpretation provided by Simeon.

ἐν τῷ with the aorist infinitive gives the Hellenistic sense, 'when
they had brought...' (BD 404²). εἰσάγω, 'to bring in', is Lucan (14:21;
22:54; Acts, 6x; rest of NT, 2x). οἱ γονεῖς (omitted by 245 for dogmatic
reasons) is the natural term to use in this context for Mary and Joseph, if
resort was not to be had to an extended circumlocution; it is hyper-
critical to find here a tradition that did not know of the virgin birth. τοῦ
ποιῆσαι is an infinitive of purpose, dependent on the previous infinitive
(1:9 note; 1:77 note). ἐθίζω** is 'to accustom'; note the use of the
genitive after a perfect passive participle (Mt. 25:34; BD 229²).

(28) For καί introducing a main clause see 2:21 note. ἀγκάλη** is
used of the arm when bent so as to receive something (cf. the verb, 9:36).
εὐλογέω is here used of praising God (1:64), but in v. 34 of blessing people.

(29) Simeon's expression of praise and thanks to God takes the
form of a prayer which falls into three couplets, and thus has the most
obviously poetic form of any of the 'hymns' in the birth narrative. In
content it is similar to the Magnificat and Benedictus, and it is not impossible that it was used in Christian worship and private devotion at an
early stage.

The opening νῦν is given an emphatic position, indicating that the
era of salvation has come, and now Simeon is ready to die, having seen
the fulfilment of God's promise. ἀπολύω, 'to dismiss, send away', is used
euphemistically in the sense 'to let die' (cf. Gn. 15:2; Nu. 20:29; Tob.
3:6, 13; 2 Mac. 7:9; SB II, 138f.). The use of the present tense is
difficult. AG s.v. suggests that it is used modally: 'now mayest thou...'
(cf. the futuristic use of the present, BD 323). Black, 153, thinks that an
Aramaic participle should have been read as an imperative. More
probably, in enabling Simeon to see the Messiah, the Lord is already

carrying out part of the process of letting him die in peace; there is now nothing left which he must live to see (cf. Sahlin, 252–254). Simeon describes himself as a δοῦλος (1:38) and God as his δεσπότης. The former term expresses his life of righteousness (Ps. 27:9; 2 Ch. 6:23; Dn. 3:33, 44; Acts 4:29; K. H. Rengstorf, TDNT II, 273). The latter term is used of God in Acts 4:24; Rev. 6:10; and of Christ in 2 Pet. 2:1; Jude 4. It is much less common than κύριος, occurring only 13x in the LXX, but it is the appropriate correlative to δοῦλος, signifying a master of slaves (K. H. Rengstorf, TDNT II, 44–49). Having, then, seen the fulfilment of God's word, Simeon can die in peace (Gn. 15:15; cf. Gn. 46:30; Tob. 11:9; Pliny, Paneg. Trag. 22:3, 'alii se satis vixisse te viso, te recepto . . . praedicabant'). The thought, however, probably goes deeper. Simeon can entrust himself to death, knowing that life and immortality have been brought to light through the gospel (Schürmann, I, 125). He believes that God's word has been fulfilled without any outward sign, save that he saw a child at the time and place stated by God.

(30) The reason for Simeon's serene expectation is now stated. By the use of the phrase 'my eyes' (cf. Is. 52:10 MT; Lk. 10:23f.) he stresses the reality of his vision of God's salvation. σωτήριον, an adjective used as a noun (Tit. 2:11; cf. Bar. 4:24; CD 20:34), is 'the means of salvation, salvation itself' (Ps. 50:23 (49:23); Is. 56:1 LXX; Lk. 3:6 (Is. 40:5); Acts 28:28; Eph. 6:17). It is regarded as incorporated in the Saviour himself (cf. the use of φῶς below; 1 Clem. 36:1). For the phrase see also Is. 40:5; 52:10; Ps. 98:2; 1QH 5:12; 1QIsᵃ 51:5.

(31) This salvation has been prepared by God (cf. Ex. 23:20; 2 Sa. 7:24) in the presence of all peoples. Normally κατὰ πρόσωπον means 'face to face', but this sense is inappropriate here; for the present usage see Acts 3:13; 16:9 v.l.; BD 140; it is not necessarily a Septuagintalism (cf. AG s.v. πρόσωπον), and reflects Luke's liking for πρόσωπον, especially in prepositional phrases. Various scholars have thought that Luke is referring here to nothing more than a salvation which is to be seen, but not experienced, by the gentiles (J. Weiss, 429; Sahlin, 256; G. D. Kilpatrick*). It is true that the OT background passages refer to God's activity to save Israel in the sight of the nations (Ps. 98:1–3; Is. 52:10; Ezk. 29:27), but it is improbable that Luke would have seen this meaning in the present verse. The problem is complicated by the use of the plural λαοί (Acts 4:25, 27; Rom. 15:11; Rev. 7:9; et al.) G. D. Kilpatrick suggests that λαοί here refers to the Jews; it is so used in Acts 4:25, 27, and here it is equivalent to ἔθνη in Is. 52:10, Luke having made the alteration to avoid repetition of the same word in v. 32. But the use in Acts 4:25, 27 arises from the wording of Ps. 2:1f. when it is applied to a particular situation. Further, since Luke normally uses λαός to refer to Israel (e.g. Acts 26:17, 23) or to the new people of God, which includes the gentiles (Acts 15:14), it is more probable that his change of word here from Is. 52:10 LXX reflects a deliberate intention to show that the gentiles are included. Whether λαοί refers purely to the gentiles or is

meant to include both Jews and gentiles (Wilson, 36–38) is not clear. In any case, the use of Is. 40:3–5 in Lk. 3:4–6 to prove that 'all flesh will see the salvation of God' strongly suggests that the same thought is present here (Grundmann, 90; see further D. R. Jones*, 42; Schürmann, I, 125; R. Meyer and H. Strathmann, TDNT IV, 29–57).

(32) φῶς stands loosely in apposition to σωτήριον and refers to Jesus himself (Jn. 8:12). As light sent from God he is to be a means of revelation (ἀποκάλυψις*; cf. ἀποκαλύπτω, Is. 52:10) for the gentiles. εἰς expresses purpose, and the phrase is modelled on εἰς φῶς ἐθνῶν (Is. 49:6; cf. 42:6 v.l.; 60:3). In the interests of his theory that the original Hebrew source used by Luke had no universalistic outlook, Sahlin, 258–265, posits that an original 'ôr lᵉḡālûṯ gôîm, 'a light for the dispersion among the gentiles', was misunderstood as 'ôr lᵉḡallôṯ gôîm, 'a light for revelation for the gentiles', and he further argues that there was no Hebrew noun for 'revelation'. But the reconstruction is hypothetical, and Sahlin himself shows that a verb could be used instead of the non-existent noun; nor is it possible to explain away the universalistic sense of Is. 49:6; cf. I En. 48:4. G. D. Kilpatrick* claims that the phrase means 'a light that the gentiles may see', but Acts 13:47; 26:22f. show that something more than seeing is meant (Wilson, 37f.).

For Israel the coming of the Messiah spells glory (cf. Is. 46:13; 45:25). The gentiles will come to Israel as the place where God reveals his salvation, and Israel will share in the glory of the Messiah (Ps. Sol. 17:34f.). δόξαν may be in apposition to φῶς (so most commentators) or be parallel to ἀποκάλυψιν.

(33) Simeon's words lead to astonishment on the part of Joseph and Mary. The singular verb ἦν is used with a plural subject composed of two singular nouns (8:19; Acts 11:14; 16:31; BD 135¹). The natural, but loose, description of Joseph and Mary as the father and mother of Jesus caused offence to scribes and led to alterations (Metzger, 134; cf. 2:41, 43). Modern commentators too have deduced that the narrative originally did not presuppose the virgin birth or any previous revelations about the significance of Jesus to Mary and Joseph (Hauck, 43; Creed, 41f.). But wonder is a typical motif in stories of miracles and revelations, and the point should not be pressed (Zahn, 156; Sahlin, 267). Schürmann, I, 127, thinks that the phrase is a literary device to draw attention to the significance of Simeon's words. Here for the first time the significance of Jesus for the gentiles is revealed to his parents – and this is done by a stranger (Easton, 28; Ellis, 84).

(34) Having 'blessed' God for the coming of the child, Simeon now prays for God's blessing upon his parents in view of what lies ahead for them, and especially for Mary to whom he particularly addresses his words. (Or possibly he simply declares them to be blessed by God, i.e. fortunate in being chosen to be the parents of Jesus; cf. Schürmann, I, 127 n. 213.) The exclusion of Joseph from his statement is motivated (as far as the narrator is concerned) by the fact of the virgin birth and/or by

the likelihood that Joseph died before the crucifixion and so did not experience the same pangs of sorrow as Mary.

Jesus will have a double significance. First, Simeon takes up the
thought of the stone laid by God which is both a means of causing men
to fall and also the principal stone in the foundation of God's building, a
stone which one may safely trust (Is. 8:14; 28:16). This metaphor is of
considerable importance in NT theology (Rom. 9:33; 1 Pet. 2:6–8; Lk.
20:17f.; C. H. Dodd, *According to the Scriptures*, London, 1965,
41–43). The language reflects the MT rather than the LXX. κεῖμαι (Phil.
1:16; 1 Thes. 3:3; 1 Tim. 1:9), 'to lie, be destined', reflects the thought of
Is. 28:16. πτῶσις (Mt. 7:27**), 'falling, fall', may mean 'cause of falling',
and similarly with ἀνάστασις, 'rising' (La. 3:63; Zc. 3:8; also 'resurrection', Lk. 14:14; *et al.*). The allusion to rising does not fit in too well with
the metaphor (and is regarded as a gloss by Hauck, 44), but it reflects
the thought of Is. 28:16. But are we to think of one group of people who
fall and then rise – they 'will fall before they can rise to the promised
glory, will pass through the valley of humiliation before they can ascend
into the hill of the Lord' (Caird, 64)? Or are there two different groups of
people who fall and rise respectively (so most scholars; J. Jeremias,
TDNT VI, 541f., revising his earlier view in TDNT IV, 271f.). Jeremias
argues that πολλοί is to be taken comprehensively of the whole of Israel,
who either fall or rise and whose thoughts are thus revealed. But πολλοί
does not necessarily have this meaning, and the analysis of εἰς πτῶσιν
καὶ ἀνάστασιν πολλῶν into εἰς πτῶσιν πολλῶν καὶ ἀνάστασιν πολλῶν is
awkward. Moreover, if we take the reference to be to one group of people, we obtain a good antithetical parallel with the second εἰς phrase
which speaks of the rejection of the Messiah. On the whole, therefore,
the former view is preferable. In any case the reference is to the people of
Israel, since Simeon is thinking of Jesus' own ministry and its effects on
Mary.

Second, Simeon speaks of the negative aspect of Jesus' ministry.
He himself will be appointed as a sign (2:12) – the thought possibly being still governed by Is. 8:16–18 where signs and wonders are promised
by God in the shape of Isaiah and his children (so the MT; the LXX differs, thus giving proof that here Luke is not dependent upon it; cf. P.
Winter, NTS 1, 1954–55, 118f.). In himself, therefore, Jesus is the one
through whom God points to his salvation and offers proof of its reality.
But the sign is not accepted. ἀντιλέγω, 'to oppose, refuse' (20:27*), is
used to suggest that the sign is 'contradicted' or 'contested'; it is not
regarded as a real sign from God (K. H. Rengstorf, TDNT VII, 238f.),
and men set themselves in opposition to it (Schürmann, I, 128).

(35) The line of thought is interrupted by a parenthesis in v. 35a in
which the effect of the rejection of her Son upon Mary herself is stressed.
The style is Lucan (καὶ ... δέ (*si vera lectio; δέ* is omitted by B L W *pc*
lat Epiph; (UBS)); cf. Schürmann, *Abschiedsrede*, 65f.; διέρχομαι, 2:15;
et al.), and hence one may suspect an editorial addition (Creed, 42). W.

Michaelis, TDNT VI, 995 n. 17, however, argues that Luke himself always uses μάχαιρα (21:24; *et al.*) for 'sword', and not ῥομφαία (Rev. 1:16; *et al.*), but this argument is not compelling, for here both ῥομφαία and διέρχομαι are drawn from the LXX. The thought is of the anguish that Mary would share at the general rejection of her Son, culminating in the passion (Jn. 19:25–27). Origen wrongly interpreted the saying of Mary's doubts about Jesus. A closely similar statement, referring literally to warfare, is found in Sib. 3:316, but the language is in fact stereotyped and traditional (Ps. 37:15 (36:15); Ezk. 14:17). In view of the parallel with Ezk. 14:17, Black, 153–155, thinks that originally the saying was addressed to Israel and amends to: 'Through thee thyself, (O Israel), will the sword pass' (cf. Sahlin, 272–274). Others think that Mary is here being understood as representing Israel (Laurentin, 89f.; P. Benoit*).

Although P. Benoit argues that v. 35b follows on from v. 35a, the sword being regarded as an instrument of division in the community (cf. Heb. 4:12), most commentators link it with v. 34, so that it expresses the purpose of the child's coming. ὅπως is 'so that' (Acts 3:19; 15:17; Rom. 3:4); usually ἄν is omitted, contrary to Classical use (cf. 7:3; 10:2; 11:37; 16:26, 28; 24:20*). The stress is on the judgment inherent in the coming of Jesus, for διαλογισμός, 'thought, disputation', has on the whole a bad sense (5:22; 6:8; 9:46f.; 24:38; Mk. 7:21 par. Mt. 15:19; rest of NT, 6x; G. Schrenk, TDNT II, 96–98). πολλοί can mean 'many' or 'all', according to the view taken of v. 34. ἀποκαλύπτω, 'to reveal' (10:21f.; 12:2; 17:30*) is found in a similar sense in 1 Cor. 3:20 (cf. 14:25); it has a judicial nuance (A. Oepke, TDNT III, 590).

(36) The second witness is introduced with a surprising amount of detail. Ἄννα is the feminine form of Ἄννας and equivalent to Hebrew *ḥannāh* (1 Sa. 1:2). Φανουήλ is equivalent to *penû'el*, 'face of God' (1 Ch. 4:4; 8:25) and Ἀσήρ (Hebrew *'āšer*, 'good fortune') was one of the ten northern tribes (Rev. 7:6). As a προφῆτις (Rev. 2:20**) Anna possessed divine insight into things normally hidden from ordinary people, and hence was able to recognise who the child in the temple was and then to proclaim his significance to those who were interested (G. Friedrich, TDNT VI, 836). Stress is laid on her great age and on her single-minded devotion to God. πολλαῖς is redundant, perhaps to give a contrast with 1:7, 18. ἔτος, 'year' is frequent in Lk. (15x; Acts, 11x; Mt., 1x; Mk., 2x). παρθενία** is 'virginity'.

(37) After seven years of marriage she had become a widow (χήρα, 4:25f.; 7:12; 18:3, 5; 20:47; 21:2f.*; G. Stählin, TDNT IX, 440–465), and remained so for 84 years. It is less probable grammatically that the phrase means that she lived for a total of 84 years, *pace* Lagrange, 91; RSV; NEB t; JB; TNT t; NIV; Barclay. If the former view is accepted, and it is assumed that she was married at about 14 years, she would have been about as old as Judith (105 years, Jdt. 16:23) who likewise did not remarry after her husband's death and is presented as a figure of

honour for this reason (Jdt. 8:4–8; 16:22f.; cf. 1 Cor. 7:7f.; 1 Tim. 5:5, 19). In view of the case of Judith, there is nothing impossible about Anna's great age (see other examples in Zahn, 160 n. 91), but the way in which it is mentioned does not suggest that it has been consciously modelled on that of Judith.

Anna did not depart from the temple, but spent her time there in religious devotions. ἀφίσταμαι is frequent in Lk. with the intransitive sense 'to go away' (4:13; 8:13; 13:27; Acts, 5x; rest of NT, 4x; transitive, Acts 5:37**). It may be used with the genitive (1 Tim. 4:1), but is more commonly used with ἀπό (so here TR; *Diglot*). Fasting (νηστεία, Acts 14:23; 27:9; 2 Cor. 6:5; 11:27**; cf. νηστεύω, Jdt. 8:6; J. Behm, TDNT IV, 924–935) is often linked with prayer (cf. 5:33). For λατρεύω see 1:74 and especially Acts 26:7. The order 'night and day' corresponds to the Jewish time-reckoning which began the new day at sunset (18:7; Acts 9:24; 20:31; 26:7; *et al.*). Anna's way of life was thus similar to that of Judith (Jdt. 11:17; 2 Esd. 9:44) and was also found in the early church (1 Tim. 5:5). But the account of her staying in th temple should not be taken with prosaic literalness (cf. 24:53; *pace* Lagrange, 91), nor are we justified in thinking that she belonged to a special order of widows with religious duties at the temple (*pace* Hauck, 44; Ellis, 83; the material in SB II, 141, does not justify this supposition).

(38) The subject αὕτη is inserted after καί by TR (αὐτή, *Diglot*) probably through confusion with the following αὐτῇ (especially if this was originally written without accents; Alford, I, 460). αὐτῇ τῇ ὥρᾳ must mean 'at the same hour', αὐτός being used in a demonstrative sense (examples in AG s.v. αὐτός, 1h). Black, 108–112, however, argues that the phrase is an Aramaism with the sense 'in it, (namely) the moment', i.e. 'immediately, then'. The usage is frequent in Lk. (10:21; 12:12; 13:31; 20:19; 24:33; Acts 16:18; 22:13**; cf. Lk. 7:21; 13:1; 23:12; 24:13; Acts 16:33). ἀνθομολογέομαι** suggests the ideas of recognition, obedience and proclamation which occur in praise rendered publicly to God in return for his grace (O. Michel, TDNT V, 213; see, however, Sahlin, 285). Like the shepherds, Anna includes in her praise proclamation about him (sc. Jesus) to those who were looking for the redemption of Jerusalem (cf. 1:68; 2:25). The phraseology is based on Is. 52:9, and Jerusalem is used by synecdoche for Israel (on the text see Metzger, 135). λύτρωσις conveys the idea of divine deliverance which is to be brought about by Jesus, and is thus a messianic concept like 'comfort' in 2:25; cf. 24:21.

It has been suggested that the original source contained the words of Anna's prophecy. Sahlin, 286–288, 300–306, credits her with the Benedictus. This is unnecessary and conjectural.

(39) The note about the family's departure to Nazareth prepares the way for the following story (2:41–52); for the phraseology cf. Acts 13:29. Luke stresses their conscientious fulfilment of all that the law prescribed. For τελέω, 'to finish, complete', cf. 12:50; 18:31; 22:37; G.

Delling, TDNT VIII, 60. There is frequent confusion in the MSS between πᾶς and ἅπας (cf. ἅπαντα, A D Θ pm; TR; Diglot), and the usage is hard to define. Luke, who is particularly fond of ἅπας (about 21x in Lk.-Acts; rest of NT, about 11x), generally uses it after a consonant or for emphasis (see BD 275; MH III, 199; B. Reicke, TDNT V, 889). The use of the article with a prepositional phrase following is Lucan (8:15; 10:7; 19:42; 22:37; 24:19, 27, 35; Hawkins, 47). It is unnecessary to insert τήν before πόλιν with A Θ pl; TR; Diglot; the short form imitates the Hebrew construction of a noun with a pronominal suffix.

Luke says nothing about the visit to Egypt, which according to Mt. 2:13ff. preceded the settlement in Nazareth (cf. Lagrange, 91f.).

(40) The 'second conclusion' is parallel to 1:80 and is complemented by 2:52. During the first years of his life (before the age of 12) Jesus grows and above all is filled with wisdom. For the dative cf. Rom. 1:29; 2 Cor. 7:4; the variant σοφίας (אᵃ* A D Θ pl; TR; Diglot) assimilates to the more usual construction (Acts 2:28; 5:28; 13:52; et al.). A reference to the Spirit might have been expected (as in 1:80), but wisdom is singled out in view of the following narrative (Schmid, 79). Above all, God's favour (χάρις, 1:30; cf. 2:52) rests on Jesus. So he is superior to John in that from childhood onwards he possesses both wisdom and grace.

g. The Passover Visit of Jesus to the Temple (2:41–52)

The birth story comes to a climax with an account of an incident which took place when (by Jewish standards) Jesus was on the threshold of adult life. It illustrates the wisdom which he displayed in religious discussions even at this early age (2:40; R. Laurentin*, 135–141; Christ, 61), and links his interest in the temple with his consciousness of a filial relationship to God, so that ultimately the story serves to throw light on the character of Jesus as the Son of God. Hence a clear contrast is drawn between Jesus' earthly parents and his heavenly Father. The story concludes with a general note of his further growth until it was time for his adult ministry.

A story which tells of the unusual ability of a boy destined for a great future, or of the early insight of a future religious teacher, inevitably finds parallels in various cultures, even down to the detail of the boy being twelve years old. Bultmann, 327f., lists: Moses (Jos. Ant. 2:230; Philo, Mos. 1:21); Josephus (Jos. Vita 2); Cyrus (Herodotus 1:114f.); Alexander (Plutarch, Alex. 5); Apollonius (Philostratus, Vita Apoll. 1:7); Si Osiris; and Buddha. There is nothing surprising about such parallels; even today accounts of great men will devote attention to their precociousness (or lack of it!). Hence these parallels cannot be used to show that the story in Lk. is legendary, but only that the motif is a common one. Dibelius, 103–106, who is particularly insistent on the 'legendary' form of the narrative, emphasises that the form does not necessarily determine the historicity of the story. B. van Iersel* argues that vs. 44 and 47, which contain the most 'legendary' elements, are secondary features in a story of paradigmatic form whose chief point is the dissociation of Jesus from his earthly parents and his attachment to his heavenly Father; whether or not these verses are secondary (*contra* Schürmann, I, 134f.), van Iersel rightly sees that the story is not basically about a precocious Jesus.

In itself the story is a natural one, and does not include any supernatural features which might lead to sceptical estimates of its historicity. It portrays a growth in religious understanding such as might be expected in Jesus in view of his later life, and this understanding is complemented by his obedience to his parents. Both setting and contents are thoroughly Jewish.

It has been argued that the story betrays no knowledge of the virgin birth, and that the failure of Mary and Joseph to understand Jesus accords ill with the earlier narratives (2:19, 33). But this difficulty was not present to the mind of Luke, who has included v. 50. The surprise is a conventional feature, and is adequately explained by the way in which Jesus left them to stay behind in the temple; the picture is one of awe and fear as they wonder what their unusual child will do next. It is perhaps surprising that the parents should have travelled so far from Jerusalem without discovering their child was missing, and details about how Jesus fended for himself in Jerusalem are missing; but these features are due to concentration on the religous point of the story.

See E. R. Smothers, 'A Note on Luke II 49', HTR 45, 1952, 67–69; P. Winter, 'Lc 2, 49 and Targum Yerushalmi', ZNW 45, 1954, 145–179 (cf. ZNW 46, 1955, 140f.); Laurentin, 141–146, 168–173; id. *Jésus au Temple,* Paris, 1966; B. M. F. van Iersel, 'The Finding of Jesus in the Temple', Nov.T 4, 1960, 161–173; J. K. Elliott, 'Does Luke 2, 41–52 anticipate the Resurrection?' Exp.T 83, 1971–72, 87–89.

(41) Jesus' parents had the pious habit of going to Jerusalem annually for the feast of the passover. οἱ γονεῖς αὐτοῦ is altered in 1012 it for dogmatic reasons (cf. 2:33, 43). Passover was one of the three annual festivals which Jewish men were required to keep in Jerusalem, the others being Pentecost and Tabernacles; in practice only the Passover was strictly observed. By this time women also attended the feast (Ex. 23:14–17; 34:23f.; Dt. 16:16; 1 Sa. 1:7, 21; 2:19; Jos. Vita 2; SB II, 141f.; J. Jeremias, TDNT V, 896–904).

(42) At the age of 12 a boy was prepared for his entry to the religious community which took place when he was 13 (P. Aboth 5:21; SB II, 144–147; for 12 years as a significant age in religious development, see also Jos. Ant. 5:348; Ps.-Ign. Mag. 3, 2.4; Grundmann, 95). The story does not necessarily imply that this was Jesus' first visit to Jerusalem. The sentence is awkwardly expressed with a temporal clause, a lengthy genitive absolute phrase, and a temporal infinitive phrase

before the main verb. ἀναβαινόντων means 'on the occasion of their going up' (Creed, 45).

(43) The two feasts of Passover and Unleavened Bread occupied a total of seven days (Ex. 12:15; Lv. 23:8; Dt. 16:3), and pilgrims were required to stay at least two days (SB II, 147f.). Jesus' parents piously fulfilled the prescribed period. (This is implied by τελειόω, 13:32*; Acts 20:24*; cf. Jos. Ant. 3:201.) Jesus, however, stayed on even longer; ὑπομένω normally means 'to endure', here and Acts 17:14, 'to remain'. The description of him as a παῖς, 'boy', emphasises his youthfulness; Danker, 38, thinks that there is an allusion to the christological use of the word (cf. 1:54, 69; Acts 3:13, 26; 4:27, 30). His parents (again altered in some MSS; 2:41 note) did not realise that he was missing.

(44) They would have been travelling in a large caravan (συνοδία**) with other pilgrims, and a boy of his age might easily have been with relatives or friends. They therefore went for a whole day's journey (Gn. 31:23; Nu. 11:31; about 20–25 miles, Jos. Vita 52; Shabbath 5:2; SB II, 149), before they began to search for him among their relatives and their friends (γνωστός, 23:49*; Jn. 18:15f.; ἐν is repeated by TR; Diglot on weak MS authority). No doubt the search took place when they encamped at nightfall.

(45–46) When they could not find him (αὐτόν is added by A Θ pm; TR; Diglot, possibly influenced by v. 46), they returned to Jerusalem. Here they discovered him 'after three days', i.e. on the third day (Mk. 8:31; cf. Lk. 9:22). The first day would be that of the outward journey, the second that of the return to Jerusalem, and the third day that of the search for him. The three day period is so conventional that a prefiguring of the resurrection (R. Laurentin*, 101f.; J. K. Elliott*) is unlikely. Teaching by the rabbis may have taken place within the temple precincts or a neighbouring synagogue (Yoma 7:1; SB II, 150). The hearers sat on the ground, at the feet of the teachers who were themselves seated, on the analogy of synagogue practice (cf. SB I, 997 on Mt. 26:55 and II, 763–765 on Acts 22:3). Here only does Luke use διδάσκαλος for Jewish teachers; elsewhere he uses it for John (3:12) and Jesus (cf. K. H. Rengstorf, TDNT II, 148–159). For Jewish teachers (not Jesus) Luke uses νομοδιδάσκαλος (5:17), γραμματεύς (5:21; et al.) and νομικός (7:30; et al.). ἐν μέσῳ suggests a group of teachers; Easton, 32, thinks that Jesus went from teacher to teacher. Rabbinic teaching made considerable use of questions on the part of the pupils, out of which discussion could arise (SB II, 150f.). ἐπερωτάω is used almost exclusively of asking questions. (ἐρωτάω can also mean 'to make a request'.) H. Greeven, TDNT II, 687f., suggests that the word implies not just curiosity, but rather probing questions designed to elicit decisions; but the idea of critical encounter is not present here.

(47) Those who heard were astounded at Jesus' understanding and answers, i.e. his intelligent answers (hendiadys; BD 442[16]). ἐξίστημι is usually intransitive (8:56; Acts, 6x; also transitive, 'to astound', 24:22;*

Acts 8:9, 11). σύνεσις* is 'understanding' and ἀπόκρισις, 'answer' (20:26; Jn. 1:22; 19:9**). For the thought see Ps. 119:99f. and the story in t. Nidda 5:15 (646) (SB II, 151). Jesus appears as a pupil who astonishes his teachers by the understanding of the law apparent in his questions and answers to their counter-questions; there is no thought of his precociously teaching the experts (as in the Infancy Gospel of Thomas 19:2 (NTA I, 398f.) and the Arabic Infancy Gospel 50–53 (*Synopsis*, 18f.)).

(48) The unannounced change of subject has suggested that v. 47 may be an addition to the story (B. M. F. van Iersel*, 169f.), but it may simply be a case of loose syntax. Jesus' parents are amazed at the scene. ἐκπλήσσομαι (4:32; 9:43*; Acts 13:12*) may indicate fright or wonder, perhaps even joy in the present case (AG s.v.). Probably wonder at finding Jesus in the company of teachers in the temple is the dominant motif; for the first time the parents observe religious interest and insight on the part of Jesus, going beyond what a boy might have shown at this formal stage in his career. There is nothing here that conflicts with their earlier knowledge of his destiny. Mary's question is the natural one for a mother to ask in the circumstances. The reference to 'your father' is also perfectly in keeping (how else would she have referred to Joseph?), although again dogmatic alterations have been made by scribes. It may be significant that it is Mary and not Joseph who asks the question. The use of ὀδυνάομαι (16:24f.; Acts 20:38**), 'to sorrow, suffer torment', may perhaps indicate the first fulfilment of Simeon's prophecy (Grundmann, 96). καὶ λυπούμενοι is added by D it sy^c; *Diglot*, but the word is not Lucan and looks like an explanatory gloss. The imperfect ἐζητοῦμεν (A D C W Θ pl; TR; UBS; *Diglot*) is less vivid than the present ζητοῦμεν (ℵ* B 69; *Synopsis*). Schürmann, I, 135, claims that the feelings of Mary and Joseph are stressed by Luke in order to present a contrast with Jesus' expression of filial obedience to God.

(49) Jesus' first recorded words, uttered at a significant period in his life, set the tone for what follows in the Gospel (Schürmann, I, 136). With τί ὅτι supply γέγονεν (cf. Acts 5:4, 9; Jn. 14:22). The question is a gentle reproach, followed as it is by a further question (οὐκ ᾔδειτε . . .) to which Jesus expects the answer 'Yes'. His earthly parents should not have been anxiously seeking him, for they should have known where to find him. But the words of Jesus are difficult. His parents were bound to look for him when he was lost (for how would he have found his way back home?), and it was hardly right for a boy to leave his parents in this way without telling them what he was going to do. But these points are not taken up. Jesus' reply, though gentle in manner, suggests the establishment of a break between himself and his parents, although this will be modified in v. 51. There is thus a tension between the necessity felt by Jesus to enter into closer relationship with his Father and the obedience which he continued to render to his parents. The concept of necessity is frequent in Lk. (18x; Acts, 22x; Mt., 8x; Mk., 6x; W.

Grundmann, TDNT II, 21–25; Marshall, 106–111); it expresses a sense of divine compulsion, often seen in obedience to a scriptural command or prophecy, or the conformity of events to God's will. Here the necessity lies in the inherent relationship of Jesus to God which demanded obedience. ἐν τοῖς τοῦ πατρός μου can be taken in two ways: 1. 'in my Father's house' (RV and most translations; Klostermann, 47; Creed, 46; Black, 3; O. Michel, TDNT V, 122; AG s.v. ὁ, II.7; cf. BD 162⁸). See Est. 7:9; Job 18:19. 2. 'about my Father's business' (RV mg; JB; Leaney, 102f.). See 1 Cor. 7:33. The problem is discussed exhaustively by R. Laurentin*, 38–72. The first translation is perfectly possible linguistically and was accepted by the early church fathers (Lagrange, 95; E. R. Smothers*); it is also required by the context, since the point at issue is *where* Jesus is to be found. The temple is thus the 'house of God' (Jn. 2:16), and it is here that Jesus feels that he ought to be (cf. Heb. 3:6). This is why he absents himself from his earthly father's house, a contrast emphasised by the juxtaposition of vs. 48 and 49. The same point emerges later in the accounts of Jesus' relation to his parents (Mk. 3:31–35; Lk. 11:27f.; Jn. 2:4; cf. 7:3–10) and of the attitude he required from his disciples (9:59–62; 14:26; Mk. 10:29; Schürmann, I, 136).

The effect of the saying is to show that Jesus is indeed the Son of God, thus confirming 1:32, 35 (R. Laurentin*, 92). A personal relationship to God is expressed, a relationship such as might exist to some extent between an individual Israelite and God. P. Winter* has drawn attention to Frg. Tg. to Ex. 15:2 where infants claim that God is their father, with the implication that Jesus' words do not go beyond those of a pious Israelite. But the date of the phrase cited is uncertain (R. Laurentin*, 72–76) and the whole context suggests that a deeper significance is present. It is not simply the 'official' position of the Messiah, but a personal consciousness of God which finds expression both in worship and learning in the temple, and also in private communion with God. See Jeremias, *Abba*; van Iersel; G. Schrenk, TDNT V, 982–996; E. Schweizer, TDNT VIII, 366–378, 380–382; I. H. Marshall, 'The Divine Sonship of Jesus', *Interpretation* 21, 1967, 87–103.

(50) Two comments throw further light on v. 49. The first is that Mary and Joseph were unable to understand what Jesus had said (ἐλάλησεν is equivalent to a pluperfect, BD 347²). They are perplexed at the revelation of what divine Sonship implies, and for the moment they cannot take it in. There is a secret regarding Jesus' relation to the Father which not even they can fully understand (Lagrange, 97). Schürmann, I, 137, regards the verse as a way of saying to the reader, 'There is more in this than meets the eye'. See further R. Laurentin* for the history of the interpretation of the problem of Mary's apparent ignorance.

(51) The second comment is that this event was a temporary unveiling of Jesus' relationship with his Father; it remained a 'secret

epiphany', a momentary glimpse through a curtain into a private room. The episode is followed by Jesus' return to normal obedience to his parents on their return home. καταβαίνω is appropriate for the return from Jerusalem (10:30f.; Acts 8:15, 26; 24:1; 25:1f.; Mk. 3:22; cf. ἀναβαίνω, 2:4, 42; 18:10 note). Jesus is obedient to his parents (ὑποτάσσομαι, 10:17, 20*), since in general obedience to the Lord includes obedience to parents (Col. 3:20). Nevertheless, the incident has shown to Mary that Jesus' obedience to his parents lies within a more fundamental relationship to God. She treasures up in her heart all that has happened (διατηρέω, Acts 15:29** is a variant for συντηρέω, 2:19; cf. Gn. 37:11; Dn. 7:28; after ῥήματα, ταῦτα is added by ℵᶜ A C Θ pl lat syᶜ sa bo; TR; Diglot). As in 2:19 there may be an allusion to the source of the narrative (Easton, 33; Schmid, 83).

(52) The whole birth story closes with a note of Jesus' continued growth to manhood (2:40). προκόπτω, 'to progress, advance', has lost its original sense 'to make one's way forward by chopping away obstacles' (Rom. 13:12; Gal. 1:14; 2 Tim. 2:16; 3:9, 13**). G. Stählin, TDNT VI, 703–719, especially 713f., notes how ancient biographers emphasised the harmonious development of their subjects, and concludes that Luke has done so in Jewish terms here and in 1:80; 2:40. Thus he refers to the wisdom of Jesus (2:40), possibly with reference to Sir. 51:17. (The textual status of ἐν τῇ is uncertain, the MSS showing considerable confusion; UBS brackets the phrase (read by ℵ L pc) which may be a Hebraism). ἡλικία can mean 'physical stature' (19:3; Eph. 4:13) or 'age' (12:25 par. Mt. 6:27; Jn. 9:21, 23; Heb. 11:11). Here the thought is of the maturity associated with increasing age (J. Schneider, TDNT II, 941–943); the link between προκόπτω/προκοπή and ἡλικία was a common Hellenistic one (G. Stählin, TDNT VI, 712). Stählin holds that Luke had spiritual maturity especially in mind (cf. Eph. 3:16; 4:13 with Lk. 1: 80; 2:40). The final reference to favour (χάρις) with both God and man takes us back to the OT (1 Sa. 2:26; Pr. 3:4; Sir. 45:1; cf. P. Ab. 3:10; SB II, 152f.), although there is no direct parallel in the LXX. The intended picture is one of perfect development, the continuation of what has already been described in 2:40. When Jesus next appears, it will be as One ready to be consecrated to his task.

III
JOHN THE BAPTIST AND JESUS

3:1–4:13

ANY attempt to divide up the Gospel into whatever sections were in its author's mind is speculative, and there is no consensus of opinion on the matter. J. H. Davies* has argued that the prologue to Lk. consists of chs. 1–3 so that the major break comes at the end of ch. 3 rather than ch. 2. Schürmann, I, 146–148, divides up the main body of the Gospel to give: 3:1 – 4:44, The Beginning from Galilee; 5:1 – 19:27, Jesus' Public Ministry and Teaching in the Land of the Jews; 19:28 – 24:53, The Consummation in Jerusalem. Neither of these views is completely convincing. While Davies has shown the close connections between 1 and 2 – 3, he has not done justice to the clear break at the end of 2, and the difference in narrative style between 1 – 2 and 3. Although there are places where Luke makes extremely smooth transitions from one section to another, it is difficult to see grounds for a major break between 4 and 5, and Schürmann seems to have overplayed his hand in stressing the importance of the 'beginning' for Luke's account of the ministry.

We therefore prefer a simple, pragmatic approach which separates the prologue (1 – 2) from the rest of the story, and the preliminaries to the ministry from the ministry itself. Accordingly, the present section is regarded as terminating at 4:13. It covers the work of John in preparing for the ministry of Jesus, Jesus' own appointment to his ministry, and his testing by Satan. The material is mainly drawn from sources other than Mk.

See J. H. Davies, 'The Lucan Prologue (1–3)', TU 112, 1973, 78–85.

a. The Preaching of John (3:1–20)

Like the early Christian tradition (as reflected in Mk. and Q), Luke saw the real beginning of the gospel in the appearance of John the Baptist

(Acts 10:37). It is, therefore, fitting that the appearance of John rather than the birth of Jesus is given a precise date. Luke recounts his teaching at some length, laying emphasis on his appearance in fulfilment of OT prophecy and on his own prophetic role. Teaching peculiar to Luke brings out the nature of the repentance demanded by John. The account culminates in John's prophecy of the coming of the Messiah, and closes with a note about his imprisonment. His role in the baptism of Jesus, described in the next section, is thus played down.

The manner of presentation has suggested that Luke has deliberately separated John off from Jesus, so that he belongs to the old era rather than to the beginning of the new (Conzelmann, 12–21, 92–94, 103). It is better to see him as a bridge figure, belonging to both eras; his coming marks both the end of the old and the beginning of the new. His function is preparatory, but is essentially part of the new era. (Schürmann's estimate of his function in Lk. (I, 185–187) needs some correction; see Wink, 42–86; Marshall, 145–147.) Thus John preaches the gospel to the people by announcing to them the coming of the Messiah and by preparing them for his coming.

See A. Oepke, TDNT I, 529–546; W. F. Flemington, *The New Testament Doctrine of Baptism*, London, 1948, 3–24; H. Sahlin, *Studien zum dritten Kapitel des Lukasevangeliums*, Uppsala, 1949; G. R. Beasley-Murray, *Baptism in the New Testament*, London, 1962 (Exeter, 1972), 1–44; Scobie; Wink; J. D. G. Dunn, *Baptism in the Holy Spirit*, London, 1970; 8–22; H. Thyen, *Studien zur Sündenvergebung*, Göttingen, 1970, 131–145; E. Bammel, 'The Baptist in Early Christian Tradition', NTS 18, 1971–72, 95–128; Jeremias, *Theology*, I, 43–49; J. Becker, *Johannes der Täufer und Jesus von Nazareth*, Neukirchen, 1972; Hoffmann, 14–33; Schulz, 366–378; Goppelt, I, 83–93.

i. The Beginning of John's Ministry 3:1–6

The appearance of John is given an exact dating with an elaborate chronological synchronism reminiscent of Thucydides 2:2. Only the first phrase in v. 1 is necessary to fix the date; the remaining information is intended to give a rapid survey of the political situation at this crucial moment, and so to give the Christian gospel its setting in imperial and local history. John is presented in the manner of an OT prophet who commences to preach in the region of the Jordan, summoning his hearers to an act of repentance leading to forgiveness of sins. His work is seen as the fulfilment of Is. 40:3–5, which Luke quotes at length to show that nothing less than 'the salvation of God' is now being proclaimed.

The narrative is largely based on material in Q with some supplementation from Mk. (Schramm, 34–36; Schürmann, I, 161). Since Mk. and Q overlap here, it is impossible to distinguish the sources with any precision, but the use of Q (and not merely of Mk.) is highly likely. The opening chronological statement, however, is probably due to Luke himself.

See C. Cichorius, 'Chronologisches zum Leben Jesu', ZNW 22, 1923, 16–20; G. Ogg, *The Chronology of the Public Ministry of Jesus*, Cambridge, 1940, 170–201; Finegan, *Handbook*, 259–275; Hoehner, 307–312.

(1) The dating of John's appearance follows the manner of ancient historians (Thucydides 2:2; Polybius 1:3; Jos. Ant. 18:106) and also (in more general terms) of the OT prophetic books (Is. 1:1; Je. 1:1–3; *et al.*). Unfortunately the basic date, the fifteenth year of Tiberius is ambiguous: 1. Older scholars followed Ussher in regarding the reign of Tiberius as being reckoned from his co-regency with Augustus (AD 11/12), so that the date here is AD 25/26 or 26/27 (Godet, I, 166f.; W. M. Ramsay, *Was Christ born at Bethlehem?* 199–201, 221; Zahn, 182–188; cf. A. Strobel, as in 4:19 note). The advantage of this dating is that it does make Jesus about 30 years old if he was born in 4 BC. But this method of calculating is unprecedented (Ogg, 173–183; Hoehner, 308 n. 4). 2. Nearly all modern writers reckon from the death of Augustus on 19th August, AD 14. If the regnal years are counted inclusively from this date we arrive at AD 28/29, there being various minor differences among scholars regarding exactly when the fifteenth year would commence (details in Hoehner, 307–312). 3. In Syria it was normal to regard the first regnal year as extending from the date of accession to the first new year that followed it, i.e. to the following autumn; the succeeding regnal years were then full calendar years. The effect of this is to place the fifteenth year one year earlier, i.e. autumn 27 to autumn 28 (Lagrange, 99f.; C. Cichorius*; Caird, 71; Schürmann, I, 150). A date of AD 28 (plus or minus a few months) is thus probable, provided that Jesus' age of 30 years is not taken too literally. Tiberius remained in possession of his rule (ἡγεμονία**) until 16th March, AD 37; he is not mentioned by name elsewhere in the NT (but see 20:22–25; 23:2; Jn. 19:12, 15).

The rest of the information adds nothing to the chronology, but lists the rulers of the areas where Jesus worked and his influence was felt, in effect the former territories of Herod the Great. No governor of Syria is mentioned: Tiberius kept L. Aelius Lamia, the designated governor, in Rome AD 19–32 out of mistrust (Schürer, *History*, I, 261). Πόντιος (Acts 4:27; 1 Tim. 6:13**) Πιλᾶτος (13:1; 23:1–24, 52; Acts 3:13; 4:27; 13:28*) was prefect of Judaea (1:5 note) from AD 26 to AD 36–37 (Jeremias, *Jerusalem*, 195 n. 153 upholds the later date). ἡγεμονεύω (2:1) could be used of any sort of ruler. The v.l. ἐπιτροπεύοντος (D latt Eus^pt), which gives the correct technical term for the rule of a procurator, used to be regarded as a learned correction of the more general term by the western text. But an inscription discovered at Caesarea has shown that Pilate was not 'procurator' but 'praefectus'. Before the reign of Claudius Judaea was governed by a praefectus; from the reign of Claudius to AD 66 by a procurator, and from AD 70 by a legatus (Sherwin-White, 12). τετρααρχέω (*tris*)**, literally 'to be ruler of a fourth part', could be used of the ruler of a minor domain (cf. BD 124; Metzger, 400; AG s.v. τετράρχης). Herod is Herod Antipas, son of Herod the Great and Malthace, ruler of Galilee and Peraea from 4 BC until his deposition by Caligula in AD 39. Luke shows a particular interest in him (3:19; 8:3; 9:7, 9; 13:31; 23:7–15; Acts 4:27; 13:1*); see Hoehner, *passim*.

Philip, the son of Herod the Great and Cleopatra, was tetrarch of Ituraea and Trachonitis from 4 BC until his death in AD 33/34. This area lay N.E. of Galilee, with its capital at Caesarea Philippi. Little is said about Philip in the NT, but he was reckoned the best of the Herodian rulers. Ἰτουραία** is strictly an adjective (sc. χώρα), referring to territory along the Lebanon and Anti-Lebanon ranges. Τραχωνῖτις** (an adjective from τραχών, 'rocky ground, larva bed') indicates the Lejah, some 35 miles E. of Galilee.

Ἀβιληνή** is the territory around the city of Abila, N.W. of Damascus. In AD 37 it was given to Herod Agrippa I, and in AD 53 to Herod Agrippa II. H. S. Cronin ('Abilene, the Jewish Herods and St. Luke', JTS 18, 1916–17, 63–67) suggested that it was these later transfers which made it part of the 'holy land' and thus led to its mention here. (This is more likely than Harvey's view (234) that it had formed part of Herod the Great's kingdom.) Wellhausen, 4, held that the Λυσανίας** named here was an earlier ruler (Jos. Ant. 14:330; 15:92), so that Luke is guilty of an anachronism. The detailed notes in Creed, 307–309 and Schürer, *History,* I, 567–569, cite inscriptional evidence – already known to Godet, I, 168f., long before Wellhausen! – which makes it extremely probable that there was a second Lysanias during the reign of Tiberius.

(2) ἐπί with genitive means 'in the time of' (4:27; Acts 11:28; Mk. 2:26). ἀρχιερεύς is correctly used in the singular, despite the fact that two names follow, since there was only one high priest at the time; the v.l. ἀρχιερέων (TR; *Diglot* – on very weak textual authority) is to be rejected. Although Jews regarded the high priesthood as a life-office, the Roman administration changed the holders at will. Ἄννας (Jn. 18:13, 24; Acts 4:6**) held office from AD 6 to his deposition by Gratus in AD 15 (SB II, 568–571). He was succeeded by his son Eleazar (AD 16–17) and then by his son-in-law Καϊάφας (AD 18–37; Mt. 26:3, 57; Jn. 11:49; 18:13f., 24, 28; Acts 4:6**; Jeremias, *Jerusalem,* 195 n. 153). Thereafter four more of his sons held the high priesthood (Jos. Ant. 20:198). Clearly Annas continued to possess considerable power behind the scenes (Jn. 18:13–27), a fact which explains why Luke names him here and also calls him the high priest in Acts 4:6: the retired priest kept his title (Jeremias, *Jerusalem,* 157f.). Luke thus recognises that there was in fact one high priest in office, but shows his consciousness of the powerful position of the retired high priest; similarly, Jos. Vita 193 can refer to 'the high priests'. Schürmann, I, 149, 151, translates 'under Annas the high priest and Caiaphas', claiming that Luke regards the deposed Annas as being the real high priest (cf. Acts 4:6).

The scene thus set, Luke describes in a style typical of the call of the prophets how the word of God came to John (Je. 1:1; cf. 1:4, 11; Ho. 1:1; Joel 1:1; *et al.*). His description as the son of Zechariah both identifies him with the person described in ch. 1 and underlines the solemnity of the occasion. The use of υἱός is unnecessary in Greek idiom (BD 162¹) and may reflect Semitic usage. The phrase ἐν τῇ ἐρήμῳ is closely associated with John (1:80; 7:24 par. Mt. 11:7; Mt. 3:1 par. Mk. 1:4) and gives the link with Is. 40:3 cited below. Although the phrase has symbolic associations, there is no reason to suppose that it is not also geographical, but the precise area is unknown (cf. G. Kittel, TDNT II, 657–659).

(3) The area of John's activity is defined more precisely as the neighbourhood of the Jordan. περίχωρος, 'neighbouring', is used as a noun (sc. χώρα; 4:14, 37 par. Mk. 1:28; Lk. 7:17; 8:37; Acts 14:6; Mt. 3:5**. τήν is omitted by A B W al; Orᵖᵗ; and bracketed by UBS. The omission may be accidental). It can refer to land on both sides of a river (Gn. 13:10f.); see Jn. 1:28; 3:23 and 10:40 for John's activity on both banks. Luke does not suggest that the Jordan was not in the wilderness (pace Schürmann, I, 155), nor does he geographically distinguish the areas of activity of John and Jesus (against Conzelmann, 12–14, see Schürmann, I, 155 n. 53, 56).

The use of περίχωρος betrays the presence of Q material (cf. Mt. 3:5, where the word admittedly has a different sense by metonymy). But v. 3b is verbally identical with Mk. 1:4b and may well have been influenced by it, although Mk./Q overlap is possible. John is described as preaching (κηρύσσω; Acts 10:37), a word also used of Jesus (4:18f., 44; 8:1) and his followers (8:39; 9:2; 12:3; 24:47*); cf. προκηρύσσω, Acts 13:24**. Luke says little about the actual baptism carried out by John (but see 3:7, 16), and hence there is perhaps a greater stress on him as a preacher (as also in Q; Hoffmann, 19f.); for Luke he is essentially a prophet. Nevertheless, the content of John's preaching is his βάπτισμα (7:29; 12:50; 20:4*; Acts 1:22; et al.), so that what he proclaimed was the significance of his baptism and the need to submit to it. Baptism was regarded as an outward ritual signifying the washing away of sin. The mention of repentance shows that, like other Jewish ritual washings, it was understood as a symbolical action ineffective without the appropriate inward attitude (1QS 3:3–12). From 3:16 it is clear that it was also seen to be symbolic of the cleansing of men by the Holy Spirit. As a prophetic sign of what was to come, John's baptism was an effective anticipation of this future cleansing and forgiveness. The parallelism between baptism with water and the Spirit would be all the more probable if John's baptism was by affusion rather than immersion (Schürmann, I, 156; I. H. Marshall, 'The Meaning of the Verb "To Baptise" ', EQ 45, 1973, 130–140).

Since forgiveness was unthinkable without repentance, John summoned the people to express their repentance in baptism (E. Lohse, Märtyrer und Gottesknecht, Göttingen, 1955, 25–29). To some extent, however, baptism can be regarded as leading to repentance (Mt. 3:11; Lohmeyer, 14f.; J. Behm, TDNT IV, 1000f.), and for Luke repentance is a gift of God (Acts 5:31; 11:18). Nevertheless, repentance is an attitude to which men can be summoned (3:8). The concept is more prominent in Lk. than the other Gospels (μετάνοια, 3:8; 5:32; 15:7; 24:47*; Acts, 6x; Mk. 1:4; Mt. 3:8, 11; μετανοέω, Lk. 10:13; et al. – 9x; Acts, 5x; Mk., 2x; Mt., 5x). Luke stresses the stringency of God's demands and their moral aspects, but in so doing he has not altered the basic meaning of the concept (Marshall, 193–195; contra Conzelmann, 90–92, 213–215; see further J. Behm and E. Würthwein, TDNT IV, 975–1008).

Baptism leads to the forgiveness of sins (1:77). Schürmann, I, 159f., claims that for Luke this could only be a future forgiveness, since the gift of the Spirit remained future, and since John's baptism needed to be completed by faith in the coming One (Acts 19:4). This point should not be pressed too far. We may certainly think of a real anticipation of the messianic gift of forgiveness, regarded as the condition for the future reception of the Spirit; later in the church water baptism and Spirit baptism were so closely associated that forgiveness and the gift of the Spirit became one gift in normal circumstances (Acts 2:38). On the other hand, Matthew appears to avoid ascribing forgiveness to John's baptism altogether. The church had to reconcile the facts that forgiveness was associated with Christian baptism, and yet John had baptised men who confessed their sins so that they might escape judgment.

There is no room here to discuss the antecedents of John's baptism or its historical character, as compared with the account given by Lk. There is no reason to doubt the basic historicity of Luke's account. See the literature cited above.

(4) As in the other Gospels, John's activity is regarded as fulfilling OT prophecy. The introductory ὡς perhaps suggests that a prophecy here finds its deliberate fulfilment rather than that a general pattern is being followed (contrast καθώς, 2:23. See Acts 13:33 (Mk. 7:6); Schürmann, I, 154, n. 49). βίβλος is used of the individual books of the OT (20:42*; Acts 1:20; 7:42; Mk. 12:26), while βιβλίον (4:17–20) means the actual scroll. The addition of λέγοντος after προφήτου (A C Θ pm f q r¹ syᵖ boᵖᵗ; TR; Diglot) is due to assimilation to Mt. 3:3 (Alford, 466). All four Gospels give the citation from Isaiah. Only Luke quotes the whole of Is. 40:3–5 (cf. Holtz, 37–39), while Matthew and Mark quote one verse. All three have the same variations from the LXX in this verse: αὐτοῦ is substituted for τοῦ θεοῦ ἡμῶν, thus identifying the κύριος mentioned earlier as Jesus and not as God. John's preparation is thus the removal of the sins of the people before the coming of the Messiah. (The Qumran sect applied the verse to their task of studying the law in the wilderness, 1QS 8:13–15.) John is the one who shouts in the desert that men must prepare the way for the Lord (1:76) and make the paths (τρίβος, Mt. 3:3; Mk. 1:3**) straight for him – a poetic way of saying that the way of the Lord is made easier by having a people already repentant of their sins and prepared to meet him.

(5) The poetic imagery should not be over-pressed, but since Luke

could easily have omitted material not needed on the way to his desired
goal in the next verse it is probable that the verse has some metaphorical
significance (Lagrange, 105). Every valley (φάραγξ **) shall be filled up
and (every) hill (βουνός, 23:30 (LXX)**) shall be smoothed down; the
image is of the construction of a level road, easy for the traveller, across
the undulating desert. Luke may have seen significance in the use of
ταπεινόω to express the humbling of the proud (cf. 1:52; 14:11; 18:14*;
W. Grundmann, TDNT VIII, 16). σκολιός is 'crooked', also 'perverse'
(Acts 2:40; Phil. 2:15; 1 Pet. 2:18**), and τραχύς is 'rough' (Acts
27:29**). Such places will be made straight and smooth (λεῖος**; Pr.
2:20). The phrasing differs slightly from the LXX (e.g. the omission of
πάντα in agreement with MT). There may be a metaphorical significance
in the use of σκολιός to typify perverse men (Acts 2:40; G. Bertram,
TDNT VII, 406f.).

(6) The first part of Is. 40:5 is omitted (καὶ ἀποκαλυφθήσεται ἡ
δόξα τοῦ κυρίου; its absence from some MSS of LXX may be due to
assimilation to Lk.). Perhaps Luke did not regard it as being fulfilled in
the earthly ministry of Jesus, and, unlike John, did not see a revelation of
divine glory in him (cf. 24:26; Acts 3:13; Stuhlmueller, 127). But Luke
does include the statement that everybody (πᾶσα σάρξ, Acts 2:17 (LX-
X)) will see God's salvation; note that the word 'salvation' is absent
from the MT (Morris, 95). What had previously been seen and
recognised by Simeon (2:30) would become a universal experience
(Lagrange, 105f.). The same phrase is used with clear reference to the
Gentiles in Acts 28:28, and the meaning is doubtless the same here for
Luke (Wilson, 38f.). The extension of the quotation to make this point is
probably due to Luke rather than his source (pace Schürmann, I, 161).

ii. The Preaching of John 3:7–9

It is characteristic of Luke that he shows the greatest verbal agreement
with his sources when actually recording the words of his characters, especially of Jesus himself. The present section shows almost verbal identity with Mt. 3:7–10 in recording the words of John, only the introductory framework showing significant differences. Clearly one Gospel is
based on the other, or there is common dependence on a *Greek* source
here and elsewhere; the latter theory will be seen to be the more plausible, since in different places each Gospel appears to contain the more
original wording.

John here addresses people who assumed that baptism itself could
save them from the coming judgment without the evident fruits of repentance. Descent from Abraham is no prophylactic against judgment in
the absence of changed lives. Repentance is urgently needed, since the
axe is about to fall. Whereas vs. 7b–8a appear to be addressed to unrepentant Jews seeking baptism, v. 8b suggests that some of the audience

did not think that they needed baptism at all, unless the implication is that they thought that they could share the benefits of baptism without repentance by virtue of their Jewish descent.

The language is full of Semitisms, which speaks in favour of its Palestinian origin (Black, 144f.). Bultmann, 123, 134, claims that it was pure chance that it was attributed to John rather than Jesus, and states that it is in any case a Christian compilation; no evidence is given for these claims, and they can be rejected (Percy, 9; Wink, 19 n. 1). Schulz, 371f., adduces arguments that the passage belongs to the later, Hellenistic Jewish Christian section of Q, but he abstains from all discussion of whether authentic Johannine traditions (and Jesus traditions) were preserved by the so-called 'Q community'. It is necessary to distinguish between the use made of tradition in the early church and the possible origins of tradition in the actual teaching of John and Jesus. When this is done, it is quite possible that authentic tradition is to be found here, and indeed it is highly probable.

Schürmann, I, 181–183, argues that the passage shows traces of use in Christian pre-baptismal instruction: it is a call to those who repent to show the fruits of repentance. Behind this use in Q lies an oral stage at which the warning against making baptism a substitute for repentance was lacking, and the passage formed part of the mission preaching addressed to Jews who trusted in their Abrahamic descent and needed to be warned against judgment to come. Behind this oral tradition, however, lies the powerful personality of a prophet such as John himself; his disciples may well have brought traditions of what he said into the circle of Jesus' disciples before Easter. In criticism of this view it may be replied that an attack on mere ritualism would have been perfectly fitting in a Johannine setting, since at Qumran also it was necessary to stress the need for moral as well as outward cleansing. It is more likely that two different aspects of John's teaching are present, and that there is some tension due to their juxtaposition. In any case, however, the passage will have been used in Christian instruction and preaching, and Schürmann's suggestions in this regard are worthy of consideration.

See 3:1–20 note for literature.

(7) Luke often uses ἔλεγεν/ον to introduce statements (6:20; 9:23; 10:2; 12:54; 13:6; 14:7, 12; 16:1; 18:1); the imperfect precedes a statement of some length (BD 329) or perhaps indicates that this was what John habitually said (Godet, I, 175). Luke uses the singular of ὄχλος more often than the plural (sing., 22x; pl., 16x; Acts, sing., 15x; pl., 7x), while Mark and John overwhelmingly prefer the singular, and Matthew prefers the plural; no reason for the differences is discernible, and often the two forms are synonymous (5:1/3; 8:40/42). The plural, therefore, cannot be pressed to refer to successive groups of hearers. For Luke λαός (3:15) is similar in meaning to ὄχλος, and indicates that the crowds consist of God's people to whom the offer of salvation is being made.

Matthew has 'many of the Pharisees and Sadducees'; regarded as original by Rengstorf, 55; Ellis, 89 (contra Creed, 51; Schürmann, I, 163; Hoffmann, 16f.; Schulz, 366f.). While it may be argued that Luke was forced to generalise here before offering advice to particular groups of people in vs. 10–14 (an argument which loses force if the latter verses are also from Q), it is more important that elsewhere Matthew appears to have introduced the same identification (Mt. 16:1, 6, 11f.); he will have thought that the unrepentant were more likely to be found in these two groups of people. The use of ἐκπορεύομαι may reflect Mk. 1:5; for βαπτίζω see 3:12, 16, 21; 7:29f.; 11:38; 12:50*.

John's address to the people is deliberately harsh so as to awaken them to a sense of the realities of the situation. γέννημα (Mt. 3:7; 12:34; 23:33**) perhaps draws a contrast with what the Jews thought themselves to be, offspring of Abraham. ἔχιδνα is a 'viper' (Mt. 3:7; 12:34; 23:33; Acts 28:3**; Is. 30:6; 59:5 Job. 20:16; 1QH 2:28; 3:12, 17f.; SB I, 114f.). The offspring share the character of the parents, and this probably lies in the poisonous nature of the adder which is evil and destructive (Is. 11:8f.; 14:29; 30:6) rather than in its prudence in escaping from danger (cf. Mt. 10:16; Lagrange, 106). The phrase is akin to 'children of Satan' (Jn. 8:44), an association which is suggested by the familiar picture of Satan as a serpent (cf. 1QH 3:12, 17f.), but naturally the use of the plural here warns against pressing the point too far (W. Foerster, TDNT II, 815f.).

Just as adders flee before the approach of a bush fire, so the Jews are trying to escape from the judgment to come (Scobie, 60). ὑποδείκνυμι is usually 'to show, indicate' (6:47; 12:5; Acts 9:16; 20:35; Mt. 3:7**); it may perhaps also mean 'to warn' (AG). φεύγω (8:34; 21:21*) is also used of fleeing from divine wrath in Mt. 23:33; the use of ἀπό is Semitic (BD 149). The participle μέλλων means 'future' (Acts 24:25; cf. 1 Thes. 1:10), and ὀργή (21:23*) often signifies God's future expression of wrath at the judgment (Rom. 2:5; 5:9; Eph. 5:6; Col. 3:6; 1 Thes. 1:10; 5:9; Rev. 6:16f.; et al.; G. Stählin (et al.), TDNT V, 382–447). The question may mean: 1. 'Who warned you to flee from the wrath to come?' (Schürmann, I, 162, 164 n. 21). 2. 'Who has shown you how to flee from the wrath to come?' Stuhlmueller, 127, notes that ὑποδείκνυμι is a technical term for revealing something hidden, viz. an eschatological secret (cf. Sir. 48:25; Lk. 12:5). 3. 'Who has shown you how to flee from the wrath to come (merely by being baptised or by feigning conversion)?' The answer implied is 'Certainly not I, John' (H. Sahlin*, 30f.; G. Stählin, TDNT V, 444f.). This view is best. The question is rhetorical and indicates the sheer impossibility of escaping the coming total judgment, certainly not by any external, ex opere operato rite. John wanted the people to be baptised – but only if they were repentant.

(8) If John's hearers really want to escape, let them show the appropriate fruit. ποιέω, like Hebrew 'āśāh (Gn. 1:11f.), can be used of

producing fruit (3:9; 6:43; 8:8; 13:9; Mk. 4:32; *et al.*; Black, 138f.). καρπός often indicates the expression of a type of life in deeds, whether good or evil (Ps. 1:3; Je. 17:8; Acts 26:20). Matthew here has the singular form as in 3:9. Elsewhere Luke too uses the singular (6:43f. diff. Mt. 7:16–20; 20:10 diff. Mk. 12:2), and this must be balanced against the use of 'works befitting repentance' in Acts 26:20. It is more likely that the plural stood in his source here (*contra* most scholars). If so, the suggestion that in Q the original 'fruit' was simply repentance itself (Schürmann, I, 182; Hoffmann, 17f.) is ruled out – a theory that in any case is very doubtful in view of the OT and Jewish usage of the term (F. Hauck, TDNT III, 614–616). ἄξιος, 'worthy of', here means 'befitting' (cf. Acts 26:20).

The second part of the verse does not fit on very smoothly; Stählin (TDNT V, 436 n. 374) argues that it is an addition, disturbing the train of thought with v. 9 which again takes up the idea of trees that bear fruit. This view is preferable to that of Schürmann (see above). It is probable that two separate utterances of John have been combined here.

Luke's ἄρχομαι corresponds to Matthew's δοκέω ('to think, presume'). The latter is usually thought to be original in Q (Schürmann, I, 165 n. 25; Schlatter, 478; Schulz, 367). In favour it is noted that ἄρχομαι is frequent in Lk. (31x; Mt., 13x), and that elsewhere Matthew avoids δοκέω; δοκέω is also said to be closer to Semitic style. But J. H. Moulton claimed that δοκέω, 'to presume', is idiomatic Greek, and that Luke here represents the superfluous Aramaic verb šārî (MH I, 15). If so, Luke is here closer to the original – and incidentally not dependent on Mt. for his 'Q' material (Hauck, 50; Manson, *Sayings*, 40). λέγειν ἐν ἑαυτοῖς is also a Semitism, a circumlocution for the verb 'to think' (7:39, 49; 16:3; 18:4; Black, 302). πατήρ here means 'forefather'. The Jews held that since Abraham was God's friend, his descendants should be treated in the same way (Ps. Sol. 18:4). There may be the thought that Abraham's merits availed for his descendants (cf. Jn. 8:39; Rom. 4:12; also Lk. 13:16, 28; 16:22–30; 19:9; Gal. 4:22–31; Heb. 2:16; 6:13–20; SB I, 116–121; J. Jeremias, TDNT I, 8f.; W. D. Davies, *Paul and Rabbinic Judaism*, London, 1955², 270f.).

Like the Christian church, John attacked this sort of assumption. He did so indirectly by stating that since God can even turn the stones of the desert into his sons, Abrahamic descent does not count for anything: *all* are required to repent.

λέγω ὑμῖν is used to introduce an emphatic statement. It and similar locutions are frequent on the lips of Jesus, but are not peculiar to him (Rom. 11:13; Gal. 5:2; 1 Thes. 4:15). Schulz, 51, 57–61, argues that the phrase was originally used to introduce statements by Christian prophets, speaking in the name of the risen Lord, and later was used in a literary manner (as here) to couple statements together; the antithetic form here betrays the reflective polemic of a school rather than the direct statement of a prophet (cf. Hasler, 55). Such rigid and schematic form-critical arguments are quite out of touch with reality and far from convincing.

The use of ἐκ with ἐγείρω may be Semitic. The point is, not that the stones themselves are transformed into living people, but that they can bring forth living children as their progeny (Is. 51:1f.; J. Jeremias, TDNT IV, 270f.). λίθος is a stone of any kind. There may be a word-play in Aramaic between 'aḇnayyā', 'stones' and bᵉnayyā', 'sons' (Plummer, 90; Black, 145), but Jeremias (TDNT IV, 268) suggests that the Aramaic word kēp̄ā' ('rock') was more probably used here. The significance of the rocks is that they are lifeless, but there may well be an allusion to Is. 51:1f.: as God hewed Israel out of Abraham the rock, so he can produce children for himself even out of the stones in the wilderness (Plummer, 90). Possibly Luke saw a reference to the gentiles (Schürmann, I, 165 n. 31).

(9) John's message derived its urgency from the imminence of judgment. In addition to what had been said (δὲ καί diff. Mt.) John went on to state that already the axe (ἀξίνη, Mt. 3:10**) was poised at the root of the unfruitful trees. The passive form of the verb may signify that God is the active subject (SB I, 443; Jeremias, *Theology*, I, 10–14). The imagery (Is. 10:34; Sir. 6:3; 23:25; Wis. 4:3–5) is generally taken to be that of an axe ready to strike, but it may be that of a wedge already placed in position to split the wood when it is struck by a hammer (Lagrange, 108; H. Sahlin*, 36).

The final clause recurs in Mt. 7:19 on the lips of Jesus who can easily have echoed the phraseology of John. Good fruit is fruit befitting repentance; καλόν is omitted by p[4] a aur ff[2] vg[codd] Ir Or, but should probably be retained (Metzger, 135). It is normal for unfruitful trees to be cut down (13:7, 9) and for rotten wood to be burned, so that no allegorical significance need be sought. C. Maurer, TDNT VI, 988, finds the background to the passage in Mal. 4:1 where evil-doers are burned up root and branch. It is wrong, however, to regard the root as representing Israel collectively, since the use of the singular for the plural is a common Semitism (cf. 'the heart of the people' and similar phrases).

iii. The Ethical Teaching of John 3:10–14

John outlines the practical meaning of repentance in terms of love and justice for his hearers, including tax-collectors and soldiers.

Wellhausen, 5, denied that the teaching went back to John, pointing to the use of unique Greek expressions and the low moral content of the passage (contrast 6:29). Bultmann, 155, 159, likewise claimed that it is a late Hellenistic formation, neither Jewish nor primitive Christian, since it allows the possibility of a military career; in any case it is unlikely that soldiers would have gone to hear John. The section is a Lucan expansion of the traditional saying in v. 11 (cf. Hoffmann, 16 n. 5; E. Bammel*, 105).

There is, however, no more evidence of Lucan style in the passage than is usual in material which he has edited, and the use of non-Lucan expressions points to the use of source material (Schürmann, I, 169 n. 53). The Greek vocabulary does not suggest a late date, the morality is revolutionary (Danker, 46–48), and it is sheer supposition that soldiers would not have listened to John. It is, on the contrary, striking that John does not call people to give up professions regarded by the Pharisees as questionable, but to behave honestly in them (Harvey, 234). It is, then, probable that we have here the Baptist's teaching, shaped by catechetical use.

The section may come from Luke's special source material (Manson, *Sayings*, 253f.; Grundmann, 103) or be a piece of Q material omitted by Matthew (Schürmann, I, 169; H. Sahlin*, 37). Since Luke's special material contains no other traditions about John, the latter is more likely (cf. 7:29f. for similar material).

See 3:1–20 note for literature.

(10) For the use of the imperfect ἐπηρώτων see 3:7 note; cf. 3:14 and the equivalent use of the aorist in 3:12. The question of the crowds recurs in 10:25; 18:18 (par. Mk. 10:17); Jn. 6:28; Acts 2:37; 16:30; 22:10; in each case it is asked by persons seeking salvation or wishing to know God's will for their lives. It is not surprising that here and in vs. 12, 14 some authorities (D *al*) add ἵνα σωθῶμεν (Acts 16:30). Here the question is about the nature of true repentance.

(11) The question is perhaps asked despairingly (cf. 1 Sa. 10:2; H. Sahlin*, 37f.), but there is an answer. John gives two concrete instructions, whose nature is perhaps determined by the poverty of his audience. The χιτών (6:29; 9:3) was an under-garment worn over the bare body or over a linen vest (SB I, 343, 565f.) and beneath an outer coat (ἱμάτιον). A person might wear two under-garments for protection against cold on a journey, and Josephus tells how a messenger once wore two inner coats with a letter hidden inside the inner one (Ant. 17:136). The reference here may be to giving up one such inner garment or simply to sharing the spare contents of one's wardrobe with (it is implied) somebody who has none. μεταδίδωμι, 'to share' (Rom. 1:11; 12:8; Eph. 4:28; 1 Thes. 2:8**) is used of sharing both material possessions and the gospel; elsewhere in the Gospels the simple form is used (6:30), and it is possible that here there is influence from the vocabulary of the early church. Likewise the person who has food (βρῶμα, 9:13*; the plural may signify several items) should share with the person who has none. ὁμοίως is frequent in Lk. (11x; Mt., 3x; Mk., 2x) but absent from Acts.

John's answer falls within the sphere of Jewish ideas. The OT command to love one's neighbour (Lv. 19:18) found the same concrete expression as here in terms of the elementary, essential needs of the poor (Job 31:16–20; Is. 58:7; Ezk. 18:7; Tob. 1:17; 4:16). This is not the

same thing as the 'communism' of goods practised at Qumran (1QS
1:12), but reflects rather the Jewish idea of 'works of love' which go
beyond the 'works of the law' (SB IV:1, 559–610; W. Grundmann,
TDNT III, 545–548); the 'good fruit' of 3:9 is expounded in terms of
'good works', i.e. 'works of love'. Such works are the expression of
repentance or conversion, and not, as in rabbinic teaching, means of
securing merit in the sight of God, since the possibility of repentance is
due in the first place to God (3:3 note).

(12) Included in the crowds were even (καί – perhaps simply 'also')
tax-collectors (τελώνης see 5:27, 29f.; 7:29, 34; 15:1; 18:10f., 13*; cf.
19:2; SB I, 377–380; O. Michel, TDNT VIII, 88–105). These were tax-
farmers who had purchased for themselves the right to collect various indirect taxes, mainly customs or tolls; they employed subordinate
officials to carry out the work. The system abounded with abuses (cf. the
inscription from Palmyra which attempted to regularise the procedure,
in Creed, 52; O. Michel, TDNT VIII, 100). Consequently the collectors
were cordially hated and despised by their fellow-countrymen, and in addition their job made them ritually unclean. Such men, regarded as being
alienated from God by pious Jews, were welcomed by Jesus and also
found their way to John, while the more respectable religious people
failed to do so (7:29 par. Mt. 21:31f.). They addressed John as
διδάσκαλος (cf. ῥαββί, Jn. 3:26), a form of address frequently used by
non-disciples to Jesus in Lk. (7:40; et al.). They hardly thought of John
as a rabbi in the technical sense, but believed that he could expound the
will of God to them (K. H. Rengstorf, TDNT II, 152).

(13) Love must be worked out in terms of justice. Tax-collectors
are not necessarily to leave their jobs (since taxes must be collected), but
must refrain from making excess demands (cf. Sanh. 25b, in SB I, 378f.).
πράσσω, 'to do, accomplish' (22:23; 23:15, 41; Acts, 13x), is here 'to
collect (taxes, interest) ' (19:23*); the meaning is almost 'to extort' (see
19:8; and the use of παραπράσσω, as in the inscription cited by AG
705). παρά is 'beyond' (13:2, 4; 18:14; cf. ὑπέρ, 16:8). διατάσσω, 'to
command', is Lucan (8:55; 17:9f.*; Acts, 5x).

(14) The participle of στρατεύομαι* is used concretely to mean
'soldiers' (for the omission of the article see BD 413[1]). They were not
Roman soldiers, but the forces of Herod Antipas, stationed in Peraea
(possibly including non-Jews, like his father's army, Jos. Ant. 17:198f.),
or perhaps Jewish auxiliaries used in Judaea for police duties; they may
have been employed to assist the tax-collectors in their duties (Lagrange,
109f.; Jeremias, Theology, I, 48 n. 3). The form of their question may
convey the undertone, 'What shall we do – even we (καὶ ἡμεῖς) whose
calling is especially out of keeping with Jewish piety?' (Zahn, 194f.).

John tells them to avoid the sins of their profession. διασείω** is 'to
shake violently', hence 'to extort money by violence' or 'to intimidate';
cf. 3 Mac. 7:21. AG s.v. cite two papyrus references showing that the
verb was used of intimidation by soldiers and also in connection with

συκοφαντέω. This word, whose etymology is uncertain (Luce, 111, gives the traditional but unsubstantiated view), means 'to denounce', 'to cheat', 'to extort'. AG s.v. and C.-H. Hunzinger, TDNT VII, 759, suggest 'to oppress' here and 'to extort' in 19:8**. But the sense 'to rob by false accusation' (Creed, 53; Luce, 111; Grundmann, 104) should perhaps be preferred here to gain a contrast with διασείω; cf. Gn. 43:18; Pr. 14:31. This sense is further demanded by the following appeal to the soldiers to be satisfied with what they get. ὀψώνιον means 'provisions', hence 'ration-money' (1 Cor. 9:7; cf. Rom. 6:23; 2 Cor. 11:8**). The meaning 'provisions' rather than 'wages' is defended by C. C. Caragounis, 'ΟΨΩΝΙΟΝ: A Reconsideration of its Meaning', Nov.T 16, 1974, 35–57. Soldiers' remuneration was in fact low and the temptation to increase it by rapacious dealings was strong (H. W. Heidland, TDNT V, 591f.). The language used here is 'Hellenistic', but this arises naturally from the subject-matter and is hardly 'late'.

iv. The Coming of the Stronger One 3:15–17

John's message naturally raised the question of his authority and credentials: was it possible that he was the Messiah? His reply was to place himself in the position of a servant over against a stronger One who was to come after him and to contrast his own baptism of water with the baptism of the Holy Spirit and fire which would be carried out by his successor. His successor would bring about the great division among men, in view of which John was urging people to get ready by means of repentance.

The introduction to the sayings may be a Lucan editorial framework, created on the basis of the following sayings (Bultmann, 359, 386; Hoffmann, 16; Schulz, 368). Schürmann, I, 171, argues strongly that despite signs of Lucan redaction the essence of the introduction has been drawn from Q, on the grounds that the saying in vs. 16f. must have had some kind of introduction, and that the content of the saying implies that false hopes regarding the person of John were current; the language too shows signs of pre-Lucan origin. The introduction is absent from Mt., but it was less necessary if Matthew omitted the equivalent of vs. 10–14 and if the problem of John's being the Messiah was less acute for him.

The first part of John's statement is paralleled in Mk. 1:7f., but with the clauses arranged in two antithetic couplets; the order in Lk. (and Mt., i.e. in Q) which separates the parallel clauses about baptism is more likely to be original, and is paralleled in Jn. 1:26f. The vague character of the christology speaks against its being a Christian creation (pace Bultmann, 262), and the reference to the future baptism can also be from John himself (see below).

See 3:1–20 note for literature; J. D. G. Dunn, 'Spirit-and-Fire-Baptism', Nov.T 14, 1972, 81–92.

(15) The choice of the word λαός may reflect Luke's concept of the Jewish people as a religious body looking for the coming of the Messiah. While προσδοκάω can be used in an ordinary sense (1:21), it may suggest expectation of the eschatological denouement here (7:19f. par. Mt. 11:3; 2 Pet. 3:12–14). The combination of διαλογίζομαι with ἐν ταῖς καρδίαις αὐτῶν (5:22) is Semitic (cf. 3:8) and indicates a process of thought. μήποτε, 'whether perhaps', introduces an indirect question, the optative being used as in 1:29 (cf. BD 370³); for μήποτε in a direct question see Jn. 7:26, and for its use with the subjunctive in a clause expressing fear see 4:11; et al. The question whether John was the Messiah is also found in Jn. 1:20, 25; cf. Acts 13:25. Messianic expectations may well have surrounded the ministry of John, despite his own disclaimers (pace Klostermann, 54; H. Sahlin*, 43). What is more difficult to ascertain is whether such beliefs about him persisted after his death and into the period of the early church – and whether some passages in the NT may reflect expressions of such beliefs and polemic against them (1:17 note; 1:57–80 note). The existence of disciples of John who did not necessarily become Christians is attested in the Gospels (5:33; 7:18f; 11:1; Mk. 6:29; Jn. 3:25; but Acts 18:25 and 19:1–7 probably refer to Christians). There is no clear indication, however, that they held messianic beliefs concerning him. Such beliefs were expressed later (Ps.-Clem. Recog. 1:54, 60), but it is questionable whether one is entitled to work back from this basis and claim that passages in the NT are directed against a messianic veneration of John (but see Bultmann, 22, 177–179; 261f.; id. Das Evangelium des Johannes, Göttingen, 1959¹⁶, 4 n. 7; R. Schnackenburg, Das Johannesevangelium, Freiburg, 1965, I, 148–150). Traces of an attempt to correct excessive veneration of John may be seen most clearly in Jn., and the quantity of material concerning the relationship between John and Jesus preserved in the Synoptics probably indicates that the issue was a live one for their audiences. But there is no evidence that John made messianic claims for himself, and no clear evidence before the second century that such claims were made on his behalf. See the discussion in Wink.

For the nature of Jewish messianic expectations see above all W. Grundmann (et al.), TDNT IX, 493–580, especially 509–527. In the present passage the usage is no doubt influenced by the Christian content attached to the word, but the idea itself is pre-Christian; the expectation of an eschatological deliverer was not uncommon, although it is hard to define its precise form.

(16) John's reply is introduced in solemn terms. It is his 'official witness' to Jesus before all Israel (Schürmann, I, 170). The aorist middle of ἀποκρίνομαι is rare in comparison with the passive (23:9; Acts 3:12; Mt. 27:12; Mk. 14:61; Jn. 5:17, 19) and may be intended to give weight to what follows (Zerwick, 229).

John contrasts (μέν, par. Mt.) his own activity with that of the One who is to come. He baptises only with water (cf. 17:10; Rom. 3:28; Gal.

5:6; so J. Jeremias verbally). ὕδατι is brought forward for emphasis (diff. Mt.), and the absence of ἐν (par. Mk., diff. Mt.) may serve to indicate that the water is purely instrumental by contrast with ἐν πνεύματι below; H. Sahlin's* conjecture (45f.) that μέν should be emended to ἐν is quite unnecessary (cf. Acts 1:5; 11:16).

The next part of the saying follows the wording in Mk. (cf. Beyer, I:1, 205 n. 2). John awaits 'the stronger One' – the article suggests that a definite person is meant – who is to come; the phrase ὀπίσω μου is omitted, possibly as conveying a sense of inferiority (9:23; 14:27; cf. the explanation in Jn. 1:15). ὁ ἰσχυρός/ἰσχυρότερος does not appear to have been a significant 'messianic' title. In the OT there are prophecies of a strong man or men being overcome (Is. 49:25; cf. 53:12) which are taken up by Jesus when he speaks of himself as the stronger person who overcomes Satan (11:20–22). But here the contrast is between John and someone stronger than him. It is unlikely that God is meant (Grundmann, 105), since the comparison would be inept (Percy, 7); more might be said in favour of Elijah (J. A. T. Robinson, *Twelve New Testament Studies*, London, 1962, 25–82; but see Scobie, 75). But it is unlikely that a traditional title is being used; probably John is describing one who is stronger in view of his superior baptismal powers (cf. W. Grundmann, TDNT III, 399); if the wording in Mt. is more primitive at this point, there is no question of a 'title'. John goes on to speak of his great inferiority to the coming One. ἱκανός (cf. ἄξιος, Acts 13:25) is a favourite word of Luke, but is here traditional. ἱμάς is 'strap' (Mk. 1:7; Jn. 1:27; Acts 22:25**), and ὑπόδημα 'sandal' (10:4; 15:22; 22:35); the redundant αὐτοῦ is Semitic. Only non-Jewish slaves were required to perform this menial duty for their masters (M. Ex. 21:2 (82a); Keth. 96a, in SB I, 121; cf. IV:2, 712, 717f.). Instead of λύω, Matthew has βαστάζω which has the same force (AG s.v.).

The thought of baptism ἐν πνεύματι ἁγίῳ καὶ πυρί (par. Mt.; Mk., πνεύματι ἁγίῳ) has occasioned much discussion (J. D. G. Dunn, as in 3:1–20 note and 3:15–17 note, with bibliography). For Luke himself the fulfilment of John's prophecy was doubtless the event of Pentecost (Acts 1:5) which was also a fulfilment of the prophecy of the outpouring of the Spirit in Joel 2:28; on this view Spirit and fire should not be regarded as alternatives, signifying salvation or judgment (*pace* Schürmann, I, 174). But was this the original sense of the prophecy, and did John himself utter it? It has been argued: 1. There were disciples of John who had never heard of the Spirit (Acts 19:1–7). 2. In 3:17 the coming One is to separate the chaff from the wheat by means of wind (πνεῦμα) and burn the chaff. Hence the baptism foretold by John should be understood in terms of judgment rather than salvation, and in terms of the final judgment rather than the 'gracious judgment' of Pentecost. 3. It is doubtful whether John could have associated the Messiah with the gift of the Spirit. Those who are persuaded by these arguments suggest that the present verse is a Christian revision of an earlier form of words:

originally John referred only to baptism with fire, or to a baptism with wind and fire (i.e. omitting 'holy'), or perhaps to a baptism with the Holy Spirit ('and fire' being an addition in the light of Pentecost).

In fact, however, the way for John to speak of a baptism with the Holy Spirit and with fire had already been laid in Judaism, and he could well have taken the final, decisive step:

1. Acts 19:1–7 refers to people who claimed to be Christians, or whom Paul took to be Christians (K. Haacker, 'Einige Fälle von "Erlebter Rede" im Neuen Testament', Nov.T 12, 1970, 70–77). But in any case the passage means that the 'disciples' had not heard that the Spirit had now been given, rather than that they had never heard of the Spirit at all (Scobie, 73 n.). 2. V. 17 does not refer to the same activity as v. 16. It speaks of a separation between two groups and of the fate of the two groups after separation; this process can hardly be comprehended under the single term 'baptism'. 3. The term 'Holy Spirit' was known in OT and Jewish thought (Ps. 51:11; Is. 63:10f.; Ps. Sol. 17:42; 1QS 4:20; 8:16; CD 2:12). The coming of the Spirit in the last days is well attested in the OT (Is. 32:15; 44:3; Ezk. 18:31; 36:25–27; 37:14; 39:29; Joel 2:28f.; cf. 1QS 4:20f.). Of especial importance is the association of cleansing, judgment and fire in Is. 4:4. The contrast of water and the Spirit is familiar (Is. 44:3; Ezk. 36:25–27; 1QS 4:21), as is the association of the Spirit with fire (Joel 2:28–30; 1QS 4:13, 21). Judgment is also associated with fire (Is. 29:6; 31:9; Ezk. 38:22; Am. 7:4; Zp. 1:18; 3:8; Mal. 3:2; 4:1; Ps. Sol. 15:6f.; 1 En. 90:24–27; 1QS 2:8; 4:13; 1QpHab. 2:11–13) and with wind (Is. 40:24; 41:16; Je. 4:11f.; 23:19; 30:23; Ezk. 13:11–13; for wind and fire see Is. 29:6; 30:27f.; Ezk. 1:4; 4 Ez. 13:10, 27). Sometimes the wicked are plunged into a river of fire (Dn. 7:10; 4 Ez. 13:10f.; Sib. 3:54; 2:196–205, 252–254; 1QH 3:29–32). This evidence shows that in the first century the pouring out of the Spirit in the last days could be understood as a means of cleansing and salvation and/or as a means of fiery judgment. Less clearly attested is the association of the Messiah with the gift of the Spirit. He is certainly endowed with the Spirit (Is. 11:2; Ps. Sol. 17:42; 1 En. 49:3), but the evidence for his bestowal of the Spirit is in T. Levi 18:6–11; T. Jud. 24:2, passages which may well be Christian interpolations. J. D. G. Dunn (Nov.T, 14, 1972, 89–91) claims that it is just possible that the Qumran sect looked for the coming of an anointed One who would share his own endowment with the Spirit with God's people. John may have thought in similar terms. If so, the Spirit is to be seen as an agent of cleansing from sin – on the analogy of water baptism. But it is implied that those who fail to respond to John's teaching by repenting will face judgment. While, however, there is an undoubted element of judgment in baptism, it is difficult to take the word 'baptise' to mean simply 'to judge'. The parallelism between John and the coming One is surely synonymous rather than antithetical. Both men are saviours, and the contrast is between the limited efficacy of John's baptism as a symbol of Spirit baptism

and the full cleansing achieved by Spirit baptism itself. If this case is valid – and it cannot be more than a hypothesis – then Luke's understanding of baptism follows on from that of John. Some uncertainty must surround the words 'and fire', which may be due to the influence of the following verse.

(17) John's final comment on the stronger One is also introduced by οὗ. This should be taken with πτύον; αὐτοῦ will then go with χειρί rather than being a redundant Semitic pronoun after the relative conjunction (pace Black, 75). The picture is that of threshing. ἅλων (Mt. 3:12**) is the 'threshing floor' or the threshed grain (AG s.v.) which was taken to the threshing floor and there 'cleaned' (διακαθαίρω**; Matthew has the late form διακαθαρίζω**). The grain was tossed in the air with a shovel (πτύον, Mt. 3:12**), so that the wind could separate the wheat (σῖτος, 12:18; 16:17; 22:31*; Acts 27:38*) from the chaff (ἄχυρον, Mt. 3:12**), i.e. the mixture of husks and straw. The shovels were then used to carry away the grain to the barn (ἀποθήκη, 12:18, 24; Mt. 3:12; 6:26; 13:30**), while the chaff was burned (κατακαίω; cf. Mt. 13:30, 40; 1 Cor. 3:15). The use of 'unquenchable' (ἄσβεστος, Mt. 3:12; Mk. 9:43**) suggests that the parable has been influenced by the thought of eternal judgment and destruction (Job 20:26; Is. 34:10; 66:24; Jdt. 16:17; Mk. 9:43–48; Mt. 5:22; 13:42, 50; et al.). For the imagery of winnowing and harvest in relation to judgment see Pr. 20:28, 26; Je. 15:7; Is. 41:15f.; Ps. 1:4; Rev. 14:14–20. The distinctive feature here as against earlier usage is that the task of judgment is assigned to the stronger One rather than to God himself.

v. John's Imprisonment 3:18–20

The conclusion to the section indicates that John had other things to say in his good news to the people, but the stress lies on his stern words to Herod regarding his sins which led to John's arrest and imprisonment. John's story is thus concluded before that of Jesus' ministry begins; the presence of John when Jesus received the Spirit (3:21f.) is passed over in silence.

It has been argued that this was Luke's way of making a rigid distinction between the old era which concluded with John's ministry and the new era which began with Jesus' ministry (Conzelmann, 15; Schürmann, I, 183f.). It should be noted, however, that Conzelmann, 21f., also makes a significant division at 4:13/14 when the 'Satan-free' period of the ministry of Jesus begins. More probably, therefore, other considerations have affected Luke. He was able to conclude the story of John's baptism before beginning the story of Jesus' Spirit-filled ministry, thus achieving a more satisfactory literary structure. Also, his arrangement brings out the parallelism between John and Jesus: John's prophetic call, his ministry in fulfilment of Scripture, his preaching to all classes in society, his falling foul of Herod, and his ultimate fate all have

their counterparts in the career of Jesus (cf. Flender, 22). In particular
the shadow of the cross (2:35) falls over the ministry from the start.
Thus the parallelism begun in the birth stories continues in the main
narrative (G. Braumann, 'Das Mittel der Zeit', ZNW 54, 1963,
117–145, especially 124f.; Ellis, 91).

The paragraph is Luke's own composition, strongly Lucan in
language, and probably resting on Mk. 6:14–29 which Luke otherwise
passes over. Its brevity suggests that he presupposed a fuller knowledge
on the part of his readers, no doubt derived from current traditions.

(18) μὲν οὖν (here only in Lk.; Acts, 27x) summarises what has
gone before and prepares the way for a new contrasting theme (BD
451¹). ἕτερος had lost the sense of 'the other of two' and was used as a
synonym for ἄλλος (MH III, 197). For the linking of πολλά and ἕτερα
by καί see Acts 25:7; BD 442¹¹. Luke prefers ἕτερος to ἄλλος, in contrast to Mt. and Mk. παρακαλέω is 'to exhort' (7:4; 8:31f., 41; 15:28;
also, 'to comfort', 16:25*). On the meaning of εὐαγγελίζομαι see 1:19
note; K. Chamblin, 'Gospel and judgment in the preaching of John the
Baptist', Tyn.B 13, 1963, 7–15; id. 'John the Baptist and the Kingdom
of God', Tyn.B. 15, 1964, 10–16; Wink, 52f. John's summons to repentance is understood as a way of preaching the gospel, since it showed
men the coming way of salvation. Schürmann, I, 179, suggests that Joel
3:5b LXX has influenced Luke's wording; the prophecy of the
preaching of good news has begun to find its fulfilment.

(19) For τετραάρχης, see 9:7; Acts 13:1; Mt. 14:1** (for the spelling with double α see 3:1 note; Metzger, 400). John 'exhorted' the people, but he reproved Herod (ἐλέγχω*). After dismissing his first wife, the
daughter of the Arabian king Aretas, Herod had married Herodias, his
niece and the former wife of one of his brothers; some MSS add
Φιλίππου by assimilation to Mk. 6:17. The marriage, which took place
in AD 26, was unacceptable to Jewish sentiment, and John's boldness in
putting into words what many people felt made him into a dangerous opponent of the tetrarch. We are left to guess at the nature of his many
other evil deeds. περὶ πάντων is frequent in Lk.-Acts (7:18; 19:37;
24:14; Acts, 4x); the relative attraction is for an original περὶ πάντων
τῶν πονηρῶν ἃ ἐποίησεν ὁ Ἡρῴδης (cf. 1:4 note; BD 294⁵).

(20) But the climax – for the moment at least (cf. 13:31) – of
Herod's evil deeds came when he imprisoned John. προστίθημι, 'to add,
put to', also 'to give (in addition) ', is frequent in Lk.-Acts. In the LXX it
is often equivalent to Hebrew wayyōsēp, which is used with the infinitive
in the sense, 'to do another act of the same kind', 'to go on doing' (cf.
20:11f.; Acts 12:3; Mk. 14:25 D). It is also used with a finite verb
following, and this construction is reproduced in the LXX by the
participle of προστίθημι (Gn. 25:1; 38:5; Job 27:1; 36:1; cf. Lk.
19:11) or by the use of the finite verb (Jdg. 11:14; 2 Sa. 18:22). It is this
last construction which is probably used here, so that we have in fact a

Septuagintalism (cf. BD 419⁴; 435b; and especially MH III, 227). Peculiar to the present instance is the asyndeton (avoided by the insertion of καί in p⁷⁵ᵛⁱᵈ A C W Θ pl lat; TR; (UBS); Diglot; cf. BD 461²). The use of ἐπὶ πᾶσιν indicates that here we have not merely one more incident in the sequence, but the crowning instance. κατακλείω is 'to shut up' (Acts 26:10**). Diglot inserts τῇ before φυλακῇ with A C W Θ 118 131 209 al; TR; Lucan usage is ambiguous.

b. The Baptism of Jesus (3:21-22)

The traditional title given to this section is appropriate enough for the accounts in Mt. and Mk. In Lk., however, the actual baptism of Jesus is assigned to a subordinate place in the sentence construction (in Jn. it completely disappears), and the emphasis falls heavily upon the unique events which accompanied it – the descent of the Spirit from heaven and the voice declaring Jesus to be the Son of God. These points are common to the other narratives and are not especially Lucan. Luke, however, suggests that the baptism of Jesus took place after that of the people: it was the climax to the activity of John, and, after the Messiah had come, there was no place left for the ministry of the forerunner. All the Gospels place the reception of the Spirit by Jesus after his actual baptism with water. But this event is not the baptism with the Spirit prophesied by John, since the act is carried out on the stronger One and not by him, the symbolism of fire is replaced by that of the dove, and the gift is accompanied by a heavenly declaration; none of these features characterises Christian baptism. This event is different; it is the anointing of Jesus with the Spirit (4:18; Acts 4:27; 10:38), the attestation of his Sonship, and in effect his call to begin his ministry. It takes place in an atmosphere of prayer, i.e. the ideal situation for receiving a divine revelation.

The account shows clear signs of editing by Luke to bring out these points. It is close to Mk. 1:9-11. The slight agreements with Mt. against Mk. are insufficient in themselves to prove use of another source (G. O. Williams*). But the way in which the temptation narrative (Q) presupposes the divine sonship of Jesus makes it likely that some reference to the baptism followed the account of John's ministry in Q so as to give a link between John and Jesus; if so, the wording in Q must have been extremely close to that in Mk. (Schürmann, I, 197).

No significant voices are raised today against the historicity of Jesus' baptism by John (Bultmann, 263; E. Käsemann, New Testament Questions of Today, London, 1969, 112). But this does not settle the nature of the story as a whole. Bultmann, 263-270, categorised it as a 'legend', a story with miraculous features intended to serve an edifying purpose. It is not concerned with the significance of the baptism for

Jesus himself, but is a 'faith-legend', bringing out the significance of Jesus for Christians and providing a pattern for Christian baptism. As such, it comes from Hellenistic Jewish Christian circles. Similarly, Dibelius, 270–274, assigns the story to the 'myths', but admits that it is more of a 'legend'. He argues that Luke could not continue to regard the event as the 'adoption' of Jesus as the Son of God (which was the original thrust of the story), since he had already related the birth story; he therefore modified the account by stressing the bodily reality of the Spirit and by indicating the human piety of Jesus at prayer.

Against Dibelius, it must be said that Luke's alterations in the account are marginal, and do not suggest that he found the story incompatible with the birth story. The question then is whether at an earlier stage the narrative was intended to record an 'adoption' of Jesus as the Son of God. This is improbable. The descent of the Spirit is not understood as a divine 'begetting' of Jesus (Ps. 2:7) but rather as equipping him for his task. The hypothesis that the early church made the baptism into an act of adoption after previously regarding the resurrection in this manner is based upon the premiss that at first the life of Jesus was not understood in messianic terms; only later was it found necessary to read back a messianic character into it (Bultmann, 267). But in fact 'At no point is the literary or historical critic able to detect in any stratum of the synoptic material evidence that a Christological interpretation has been imposed upon an un-Christological history' (E. C. Hoskyns and F. N. Davey, *The Riddle of the New Testament,* 1931, 145). Once this presupposition is challenged, the case itself loses much of its weight. When the narrative can be fully understood on its own terms, it is doubtful whether we are entitled to press back to a conjectural earlier form and function by which we may hope to explain it more amply (cf. M. D. Hooker, 'On Using the Wrong Tool', *Theology* 75, 1972, 570–581).

If it be granted that the earthly life of Jesus was 'messianic' in some sense, it is credible that it was marked by an event similar to a prophetic call (though in many ways markedly different; note, however, the caution advocated by Vögtle, 335–342). The exegesis will show that there is nothing particularly Hellenistic about the account (*contra* Hahn, 340–346). The question then is whether the narrative reflects an account of Jesus' actual experience (which must have been handed down by him in esoteric teaching to his disciples) or represents the attempt of the early church to explain for Christians the significance of Jesus in terms of the calling with which his ministry must have begun. The problem is similar to that encountered earlier in the birth narratives where we have 'heavenly commentaries' on the significance of the story. The case that Jesus' ministry was preceded by some kind of 'call'-experience is strong (Jeremias, *Theology,* I, 55f.; Goppelt, I, 93), and the account may well express in concrete form the consciousness of divine calling with which he began his ministry; historical study can scarcely go beyond this possibility.

See W. F. Flemington, 25–29; H. Sahlin; G. R. Beasley-Murray, 45–67; Scobie; Wink; J. D. G. Dunn, 23–37; J. Becker – all as in 3:1–20 note; also Bultmann, 263–270; Dibelius, 270–274; G. O. Williams, 'The Baptism in Luke's Gospel', JTS 45, 1944, 31–38; Hahn, 340–346; Davies, 35–45; M. Sabbe, 'Le Baptême de Jésus', in de la Potterie, 184–211; Vögtle, 314–317, 335–342; E. Schweizer, TDNT VI, 400f.; id. TDNT VIII, 367f.; L. E. Keck, 'The Spirit and the Dove', NTS 17, 1970–71, 41–67; Jeremias, Theology, I, 49–56; Goppelt, I, 92f.

(21) The form of the sentence is cumbersome (cf. 2:42f.); the main clause has an ἐγένετο with infinitive construction (1:8 note) – in fact three coordinated infinitives are used – but before Luke reaches these he interposes an ἐν τῷ with infinitive phrase *and* a genitive absolute construction with two participles. The effect is to lay stress on the supernatural phenomena and to play down the importance of the attendant earthly circumstances. The event thus takes place after all (2:39 note) the people had been baptised (aorist infinitive, 2:27 note), i.e. 'all the people whom John did baptise' rather than all the people of Israel. Hence the present event is seen as the climax of John's work, although historically there was some overlap between the ministries of John and Jesus (Jn. 3:22ff.). Further, Luke's interest is in what happened *after* Jesus himself had been baptised and *while* he was at prayer. The aorist participle βαπτισθέντος may suggest that Jesus was baptised along with the people (BD 404²; cf. perhaps Jn. 1:33). Luke lays particular stress on Jesus at prayer (5:16; 6:12; 9:18, 28f.; 11:1; 22:41; 23:46; cf. Ott, 94–99). His prayer at baptism may be meant as an example for Christians to follow.

While Mark speaks of the heavens being rent (σχίζομαι; cf. Is. 63:19 MT; C. Maurer, TDNT VII, 962), both Luke and Matthew use ἀνοίγω (1:64), perhaps under the influence of Q; for the unusual augmented infinitive ἀνεῳχθῆναι cf. BD 66². For the motif see Is. 64:1; 19:11; Apoc. Jn. 47:30; H. Traub, TDNT V, 529f.; C. Maurer, TDNT VII, 962; W. C. van Unnik, 'Die "geöffneten Himmel" in der Offenbarungsvision des Apokryphons des Johannes', in W. Eltester (*et al.*), *Apophoreta* (für E. Haenchen), Berlin, 1964, 269–280. The opening of the heavens is an indication that divine revelation is about to take place. Many of the passages cited in this regard are apocalyptic (Davies, 36 n. 3), but the idea is rooted in OT prophecy. The significance is that after a period of apparent inactivity God himself comes down to act in power.

(22) Here the heavens open in order that the Spirit may descend (Is. 63:19 MT). The use of the full title 'Holy Spirit' (diff. Mk.) gives a link with v. 16. While Mark's absolute form τὸ πνεῦμα is not unheard of in Palestinian Judaism (as Dalman, 203 and Bultmann, 268, claimed), it is at least rare (1QS 4:6; E. Schweizer, TDNT VI, 400 n. 430; L. E. Keck*, 59f.). Luke's form represents a more probable Semitic phrase, and it is again just possible that there has been influence from Q (cf. Mt. πνεῦμα θεοῦ). The phrase σωματικῇ εἴδει stresses the reality of what was seen, whether by Jesus (Mk. 1:10) or by John (Jn. 1:32–34). σωματικός is 'bodily' (1 Tim. 4:8**; E. Schweizer, TDNT VII, 1059; cf. VI, 406), and εἶδος is 'form, outward appearance' (9:29; Jn. 5:37; G. Kittel,

TDNT II, 373–375). Compare the visible manifestations at Pentecost. It is probable that already in Mk. 1:10 the visible appearance of the Spirit is likened to a dove (2:24*), rather than that it is merely said to descend in the manner of a dove (H. Greeven, TDNT VI, 63–72, especially 67–69 with n. 59); this point is heightened by Luke.

But what is the significance of the dove? 1. H. Greeven argues that the imagery must have been immediately comprehensible to those who heard the story, and claims that the dove as a bird especially associated with the gods would be an obvious symbol for the Spirit. But the evidence for this association is non-Jewish, and this seriously weakens his case. 2. Rabbinic evidence likens the sound of the bath-qol to the cooing of a dove; the late Targum to Ct. 2:12 turns 'the voice of the turtle-dove' into 'the voice of the Spirit of salvation' (SB I, 123–125; cf. E. Schweizer, TDNT VI, 382 n. 360). This evidence, weak and late though it is, has been thought relevant to the present passage because here too a heavenly voice is present; the association, however, is doubtful, since the Spirit and the voice are in no way linked. 3. The rabbis interpreted the moving of the Spirit of God over the waters at creation (Gn. 1:2) in terms of a bird fluttering over its young, and in one version the bird in question is a dove (b. Hag. 15a). There is here no specific association of the dove with the Spirit; any bird will do to make the comparison. Nevertheless, the comparison with the *movement* of the dove has suggested to L. E. Keck* that the most plausible view of the present text is that an originally adverbial reference to the descent of the Spirit being like that of a dove has been misunderstood adjectivally in terms of the appearance of the Spirit (similarly, Jeremias, *Theology*, I, 52). If so, there was originally nothing more recondite in the story than a comparison with the gentle flight of a dove. Unfortunately, the rabbinic basis for this view is scanty, and it ignores the fact that Mk. 1:10 is most naturally interpreted of a visible descent of the Spirit so that 'like a dove' describes its appearance. 4. An allusion to Noah's dove (Gn. 8:8–12) 'gains in plausibility if John's baptism was intended to symbolise the coming flood of judgment . . ., so recalling the flood of Noah (cf. 1 Pet. 3: 20–21); for then the dove would signify the end of judgment and the beginning of a new era of grace' (J. D. G. Dunn*, 27 n. 13; cf. Bartsch, 51). Although this view has the most satisfactory OT basis, both Greeven and Keck dismiss it, especially in its somewhat fantastic developed forms, the latter regarding it as the fruit of later attempts to find symbolism in the dove, but hardly as the origin of the image. 5. Attempts to associate the dove with Israel (cf. Ho. 11:11) so that Jesus is linked to the new Israel (H. Sahlin, 103f.; Stuhlmueller, 129) scarcely need refutation. 6. Finally, some scholars attempt to explain away the dove altogether as the result of a misunderstanding.

None of the above explanations is entirely satisfactory. (For a full survey of the options, see L. E. Keck*.) It may be best to assume that the thought is of the Spirit gently descending upon the head of Jesus as a dove might descend, so that it looked like a dove. It is just possible that thoughts of the new creation brought about by the Spirit are in mind. We are not, however, told what the effect of the descent of the Spirit was; there is the same reticence here as in the annunciation story. The OT promise that God would put the Spirit upon his Servant is fulfilled (Is. 42:1); the Spirit rests upon the Branch (Is. 11:2; cf. 48:16; 61:1; Jewish evidence in E. Schweizer, TDNT VI, 384). Jesus is commissioned and equipped for his task. Such an act may be regarded as an anointing, appropriate for a kingly figure (E. Schweizer, TDNT VI, 400f.; VIII, 367f.; Borsch, 365–370). But it is not an act of adoption, still less of divine begetting, nor indeed the beginning of Jesus' messiahship (certainly not for Luke).

The gift of the Spirit was accompanied by a heavenly voice, identified by the content of the message as the voice of the Father (cf. Dt. 4:12). The rabbis taught that when the Holy Spirit ceased to speak through the prophets, God made use of the 'bath-qol', i.e. an echo, the idea being that men did not hear directly what God said in heaven, but only the echo caused by his voice. The bath-qol was consequently regarded as inferior to the voice of God through prophecy (SB I, 125–134). Various scholars have insisted that here, however, we do not have an inferior substitute for the voice of God, but his direct address to Jesus (Lohmeyer, 22; Hahn, 341). But it is unnecessary to bring in this distinction (L. E. Keck*, 61; J. D. G. Dunn*, 27). It is improbable that in NT times the voice of God was regarded as an inferior form of revelation to prophecy, and the derogatory view of the bath-qol is apparently later (see O. Betz, TDNT IX, 288–290, 298f.). The imagery is that employed with regard to Sinai where God spoke directly to the people (cf. Dn. 4:28; 2 Bar. 13:1), and the idea of the bath-qol is probably not present at all.

The wording of the heavenly message is identical with that in Mk. 1:11; Mt. 3:17 has essentially the same wording, but with the address in the second person turned into a proclamation in the third person. But the v.l. υἱός μου εἶ σύ, ἐγὼ σήμερον γεγέννηκά σε (Ps. 2:7 LXX; D a b c d ff² l r¹ Ju (C1) Or Meth Hil Aug) has received considerable modern support (Zahn, 199–203 Klostermann, ad. loc.; Hauck, 54f.; H. Sahlin*, 69–74; Leaney, 110f.; Grundmann, 107). In its favour may be argued: 1. If Luke was following a non-Marcan source (Q or some other source related to Mk.; cf. Jeremias, Theology, I, 49f.), this reading may represent the wording of that source. Grundmann claims that Q saw Jesus as the anointed high priest, and that Ps. 2:7 was understood to refer to him (cf. Heb. 1:5; 5:5; Midr. Ps. 2:2). 2. The reference to 'begetting' in Ps. 2:7 could have raised the suspicion of adoptionism, and led to the alteration of the text on doctrinal grounds. 3. The reading that was different from that in Mk. and Mt. is more likely to be original, and to have been assimilated to the synoptic parallels. Despite these arguments the reading is undoubtedly secondary (Schürmann, I, 193f.; Metzger, 136):

1. It is supported by only one Greek MS, and that an erratic one. Its other support is mainly western. 2. There are parallel examples of assimilation of the Alexandrian text to the LXX in the western text (see Acts 7:37; 13:33 (Ps. 2:8!); J. Jeremias, TDNT V, 701 n. 349). 3. Elsewhere in the NT Ps. 2:7 has been quoted without causing any dogmatic offence to later scribes (Acts 13:33). 4. There is no obvious reason why Luke should have followed the variant reading rather than the Marcan text. There is no suggestion of an act of begetting, and the stress for Luke is on the fact that Jesus (σύ emphatic) is here identified as the promised One.

The opening words are certainly reminiscent of Ps. 2:7, but the order has been changed to stress the fact that it is Jesus who is God's Son, rather than that the dignity of Sonship has been conferred on the person addressed (Lohmeyer, 23). The description of Jesus as ὁ υἱός μου will undoubtedly have been seen by Luke in terms of 1:35; cf. 2:49; the statement is thus the declaration of an existing status, not the conferral of a new dignity. But does this go beyond the original meaning of the saying? 1. J. Jeremias (TDNT V, 701f.; *Theology*, I, 53–55) has argued that υἱός has here replaced an original, ambiguous παῖς, which should have been understood to mean 'servant' rather than 'child, son'. If so, the saying as a whole is based on Is. 42:1; the substitution of υἱός, producing the verbal coincidence with Ps. 2:7, was a secondary, Hellenistic development. Against this view see I. H. Marshall, 'Son of God or Servant of Yahweh? – A Reconsideration of Mark I. 11', NTS 15, 1968–69, 326–336; Schürmann, I, 192 n. 31. 2. More commonly it is held that here Jesus is given the messianic title of 'Son' on the occasion of his 'institution into the office of the eschatological king' (E. Schweizer, TDNT VIII, 367f.). On this view, the understanding of Jesus as Messiah was primary, and it was only through the application of such 'messianic' verses as the present one that the title of Son came to be applied to Jesus, and only at a later stage that his sonship was understood in terms of a personal or metaphysical relationship to God. This view rests on the assumption that Jesus did not think of himself as being in any special sense the Son of God (or that such a consciousness was independent of the present christological development). But if, as Schweizer allows, 'he actually expressed and worked out more by his life and teaching than the titles themselves could ever say' (ibid. 366), there is no reason in principle why the titles themselves may not go back to the period of his earthly life. If the present saying is understood against the background of the filial consciousness of Jesus, it can contain more than a purely messianic element. 3. This claim is confirmed if we are right in seeing here also the influence of Gn. 22:2, 12, 16, where Isaac is described as ὁ υἱός σου ὁ ἀγαπητός. Isaac typology is found elsewhere in the NT, and it is applied to the baptismal story in T. Levi 18 (which probably contains Christian elements). If this parallel is justified, sonship is understood here in terms of personal relationship. It is, then, as the Son of God that Jesus is the

Messiah, rather than vice versa. So the saying probably contains more than a messianic element, and it leads beyond messiahship to that personal relationship to God which is basic for the self-understanding of Jesus.

ἀγαπητός (20:13*) is probably an attribute of υἱός rather than a separate title. It means 'beloved', but when applied to a son or daughter means 'only'. Its OT background is uncertain: 1. The Targum to Ps. 2:7 states: 'Thou art dear to me as a son to his father'. Hence the background may be found in the Jewish understanding of Ps. 2 (cf. E. Lövestam, *Son and Saviour*, Lund, 1961, 96). In Mt. 12:18 ἀγαπητός translates bāḥîr, 'elect', and in the Lucan form of the transfiguration story ἐκλελεγμένος replaces ἀγαπητός (9:35); in Jn. 1:34 ἐκλεκτός is a textual variant for υἱός. It is, therefore, possible that Is. 42:1 is the source of the expression here (J. Jeremias, ibid.). But the evidence is not compelling. Matthew's unusual translation of Is. 42:1 may be due to assimilation to the present text. In Lk. 9:35 ἐκλελεγμένος is due to Lucan assimilation to the LXX, and in Jn. 1:34 υἱός is probably the original text. A better source would be Is. 44:2, ἠγαπημένος. 3. Gn. 22:2, 12, 16 is clearly also a possible source. In any case, it is significant that the Greek word used is one which avoids any suggestion of election or adoption to sonship but rather stresses the unique relationship between Jesus as the only Son and God as his Father (W. Manson, 31f.).

The final phrase ἐν σοὶ εὐδόκησα expresses God's pleasure in his Son. εὐδοκέω, 'to be well pleased, take delight' (12:32*) is used in this sense in 2 Sa. 22:20; Pss. 44:3 (43:3); 149:4; 151:5 LXX; Is. 62:4; Hab. 2:4; Mal. 2:17; cf. Mt. 12:18 (citing a non-LXX form of Is. 42:1, where LXX has προσδέχομαι, but Θ has εὐδοκέω). The majority of scholars find an allusion to Is. 42:1 here, especially in view of the reference to the reception of the Spirit. E. Schweizer (TDNT VIII, 368) prefers to find the source in 2 Sa. 22:20 which speaks of God's deliverance of David 'because he delighted in me', thus stressing the motif of divine choice and adoption of the king. This seems less likely, since this passage can hardly be said to have exercise a great influence upon the NT. But it is known that Is. 42:1 was interpreted messianically in Judaism and linked with Ps. 2:7 (E. Lövestam, ibid. 95f.). We have, therefore, a combination of attributes belonging to the Messiah and the Servant, made in a way which is not unparalleled in Judaism: compare the way in which the Son of man in 1 Enoch displays the traits of the Messiah and the Servant of Yahweh. The significance will then be that God has appointed his Son to carry out the task of the Messiah, a task expressed in terms of the mission of the Servant (cf. G. Schrenk, TDNT II, 738–742). The aorist tense, εὐδόκησα, may reflect the influence of Is. 42:1 where a past decision is recorded, and indicate that a prior decision of God is now being revealed (Lane, 58); or it may be equivalent to a Hebrew stative perfect, expressing God's continuing delight in his Son (Black, 128f.). P. G. Bretscher, 'Exodus 4.22–23 and the Voice from Heaven', JBL 87, 1968,

301–312, has suggested the influence of the verses cited on the present saying; this allusion would strengthen the idea of serving the Father which is inherent in the idea of sonship. But the thought of Jesus incorporating Israel is not particularly obvious in the baptismal story.

c. The Genealogy of Jesus (3:23–38)

At this point there comes, rather surprisingly to the modern reader, a genealogy of Jesus. Ancient writers did not have the device of footnotes, which a modern writer might have utilised at this point. One might have expected a genealogy to have been included in the birth story, but if the first draft of the Gospel began at 3:1, as is suggested by advocates of the Proto-Luke hypothesis, then the inclusion of the genealogy at this point finds a suitable explanation: it occurs after the first mention of the name of Jesus (Streeter, 209). Whether this be the case or not, Luke allowed it to stand here in the final edition of the Gospel, and hence it may have a theological purpose at this point.

1. Various scholars have held that the presence of a genealogy of Jesus in the records is inconsistent with the tradition of the virgin birth; it is then argued that the genealogy represents an earlier stage in Christian thought before the development of the idea of the virgin birth (J. Weiss, 435; M. P. Johnson*, 238, holds that in Lk. 3–24 the tradition of the virgin birth is not taken into account, and the title of Son of God is understood in messianic terms). As we have seen, however, there is no inconsistency in Luke's mind between the account of the virgin birth and the naming of Joseph as one of the parents of Jesus. From the legal point of view, Joseph was the earthly father of Jesus, and there was no other way of reckoning his descent. There is no evidence that the compilers of the genealogies thought otherwise.

2. J. Jeremias (*Jerusalem*, 213–221, 275–302) has claimed that genealogical records were kept in the time of Jesus by both priestly and lay families (especially the former), and that such genealogies were not artificial constructions even if errors can be detected in them. The evidence has been re-examined by Johnson who admits that there was a serious concern for purity of descent but contests whether lay families in particular always had genealogical records at their disposal; some records were transmitted orally, and some developed on the basis of midrashic exegesis of biblical texts. These suggestions indicate that we may expect to find symbolical material in the biblical genealogies, but that the attempt to dismiss them out of hand as unhistorical is in no way justified. There is thus a case for raising the question of the historical value of the genealogy of Jesus.

3. At the very outset, however, the possibility of a historical record seems unlikely. The genealogy in Lk. differs very extensively from that in Mt. 1:1–17. It is recorded in the opposite direction, beginning from

Jesus and working backwards. It is considerably longer. Not only does it carry back the list beyond Abraham to Adam and then to God (giving a total of 78 names), but for the corresponding periods from Abraham to Jesus Luke has 57 names in comparison with only 41 in Mt. Finally, for the period from David to Jesus, the two lists are in almost total disagreement, coming together with certainty only in the names of Shealtiel and Zerubbabel, and even differing in the names given to Joseph's father. It is not surprising that the scribe of D replaced the list of names in Lk. with that given by Matthew. There is in fact no wholly satisfactory method of bringing the two lists into harmony with each other.

a. The theory of Annius of Viterbo (AD 1490) was that Matthew gives the genealogy of Joseph and Luke gives that of Mary (cf. Hauck, 51–58). On this view, Eli (3:23) was really the father of Mary, and v. 23 must be interpreted to mean either that Joseph was the son-in-law of Eli, or that Jesus was supposedly the son of Joseph but in reality the grandson of Eli (Geldenhuys, 151f.). Neither of these interpretations of the verse is at all plausible, and the theory does not fit in with 1:27 where the Davidic descent of *Joseph* is stressed.

b. The older solution of Africanus (Eusebius, HE 1:7) utilised the ideas of adoptive and physical descent, and employed the device of levirate marriage to harmonise the two genealogies. According to information which he claimed to have received from the descendants of James, the brother of Jesus, Africanus stated that Matthan (Mt. 1:15) married a certain Estha, by whom he had a son, Jacob; when Matthan died, his widow married Malchi (Lk. 3:24) and had a son Eli (Lk. 3:23; note that Africanus did not apparently know of Levi and Matthat who come between Malchi and Eli in Luke's list). The second of these two half-brothers, Eli, married, but died without issue; his half-brother Jacob took his wife in levirate marriage, so that his physical son, Joseph, was regarded as the legal son of Eli. Africanus admits that this theory is uncorroborated, but worthy of belief. It is not impossible (despite the criticisms made of it by G. Kuhn*, 225–228; E. L. Abel*, 203 n. 9), but it is improbable, especially if we accept the usual text of Lk.

c. The theory which has gained most support in modern times is that advanced by Lord A. Hervey* (cf. Machen, 202–209, 229–232; F. F. Bruce, NBD 458f.): Matthew gives the legal line of descent from David, stating who was the heir to the throne in each case, but Luke gives the actual descendants of David in the branch of the family to which Joseph belonged. The details of this theory vary in different authors. One method of harmonisation between the two lines of descent is to suppose that Jacob in Matthew's list was childless, and that Joseph, the physical son of Eli in Luke's list, was reckoned as his heir. Problems arise at the next stage backwards with regard to Matthat (Lk.) and Matthan (Mt.): were these one and the same person? (See Machen, 207–209, for a discussion of the different possibilities.) There are undoubted difficulties with this theory, but they may not be altogether incapable of solution. But solution depends upon conjecture, and there is no way of knowing whether the conjectures correspond to reality.

It is only right, therefore, to admit that the problem caused by the existence of the two genealogies is insoluble with the evidence presently at our disposal. To regard the lists, however, as merely literary constructions (M. P. Johnson*, 230; Schürmann, I, 200) is to go beyond the evidence.

4. Further problems arise within the Lucan genealogy itself.

a. G. Kuhn* noted that in 3:23–26 and 29–31 there are two roughly parallel lists of names:

1.	'Ιησοῦς	'Ιησοῦς
2.	'Ιωσήφ	
3.	'Ηλί	'Ελιεζέρ
4.		'Ιωρίμ
5.	Ματθάτ	Ματθάτ
6.	Λευί	Λευί
7.	Μελχί	Συμεών
8.	'Ιανναί	'Ιούδας
9.	'Ιωσήφ	'Ιωσήφ
10.	Ματταθίας	
11.	'Αμώς	
12.	Ναούμ	'Ιωνάμ
13.	'Εσλί	'Ελιακίμ
14.	Ναγγαί	Μελεά
15.	Μάαθ	Μεννά
16.	Ματταθίας	Ματταθά

The close correspondence between the names in pairs 1, 3, 5, 6, 9, 16, led Kuhn to conclude that the two lists were originally identical, and he suggested various emendations to make them correspond even more closely. He argued that the second list, which omits 'Ιωσήφ in the second place, is the more original and gives a genealogy of Mary, the daughter of 'Ηλί (or 'Ελιεζέρ). In the first list Joseph was inserted as the son-in-law of Mary's father. The corresponding list of names in Mt. was preserved in Joseph's family.

The effect of this analysis is to confirm that some historical material lies at the basis of Luke's list, but it has been muddled in transmission. However, there are various objections to it. Several of the proposed equations are unconvincing. Moreover, the fact that on the usual view we have repetitions of the same names at different points in the list is not really a difficulty, since there are plenty of examples of repetition of the same or similar names in Jewish families. Further, there is nothing elsewhere to suggest that Mary was a descendant of David. Finally, if the text of Lk. known to Africanus is sound, Ματθάτ and Λευί should be omitted from v. 24, and this seriously disturbs the alleged parallelism (Jeremias, *Jerusalem*, 297 n. 98).

b. A more serious difficulty is raised by Jeremias (ibid. 296) who observes that the names of the patriarchs Joseph, Judah, Simon and Levi appear among the descendants of David; we have, however, no evidence that the names of the patriarchs were used in Israel as personal names until after the exile. Hence this part of Luke's list is anachronistic. If, however, we can attach historical value to 1 Ch. 25:2 we have there the name 'Joseph' in the time of David, but most scholars would regard the names listed there as belonging to the Chronicler's own time.

Consequently, we cannot be sure that the genealogy in Lk. is accurate in detail. Since, however, the Jews of the time made use of midrashic techniques in the formulation of genealogies, it may be that Luke has followed the practice of his time, and should be judged by that practice rather than by modern standards.

5. What, then, is the theological purpose of the genealogy? The way in which the corresponding list in Matthew is framed shows that it was designed to show that Jesus was the offspring of David and *a fortiori* of Abraham. He thus appears as the Davidic Messiah, and also as the heir of the promises made to Abraham. It may be assumed that similar reasoning underlies the genealogy in Lk., although he has not drawn attention to the significance of Abraham and David in so obvious a way.

That this is so is clear from the structure of the genealogy. If the present text of Lk. is to be trusted, there are 77 names in the list from Jesus to Adam. These fall into 11 groups of 7, namely (in reverse order):

Adam	–	Enoch
Methuselah	–	Shelah
Eber	–	Abraham
Isaac	–	Admin
Aminadab	–	David
Nathan	–	Joseph
Judah	–	Joshua
Er	–	Salathiel
Zerubbabel	–	Mattathias
Maat	–	Joseph
Jannai	–	Jesus

When the names are grouped in this way, it will be observed that the significant names fall at the beginning or end of the groups. The arrangement can hardly be accidental. Luke, however, gives no hints of the presence of this arrangement.

Further, the fact that there are 11 groups suggests that the genealogy may reflect a division of world history into 11 'weeks', to be followed by the 12th 'week' of the messianic era (cf. 4 Ez. 14:11; SB IV:2, 986f.; Rengstorf, 61). But it is clear that this scheme was not in Luke's mind, since he presents the names in reverse order, and actually has 78 names (when that of God is included). It follows that Luke did not invent the genealogy, but took it over from a source (cf. Schürmann, I, 203; the possibility of a pre-Lucan significance is overlooked by Johnson, 231–233, when he rejects the idea).

We have, therefore, still to find the significance of the genealogy for Luke. Some have thought that the carrying back of the genealogy to God is a way of indicating that Jesus is the Son of God, so that the genealogy is anchored to 3:22 and 4:3, 9 (M. D. Johnson*, 235–239). But it is most unlikely that Luke thought of the divine sonship of Jesus in such a way. To regard all the names from Joseph to Adam as one gigantic parenthesis (B. Weiss, 301) misses the point of the genealogy, and to regard divine sonship as mediated to Jesus through his ancestors conflicts with the birth story. Hence the point of the genealogy is rather to show that Jesus has his place in the human race created by God. The fact that the genealogy is carried back to Adam, as the son of God, may perhaps point a contrast between this disobedient son of God and the obedient Son of God, Jesus. Hence the thought of Jesus as the Second Adam may be present (J. Weiss, 435; J. Jeremias, TDNT I, 141; Ellis, 93; the only real objection (out of those raised by M. D. Johnson*, 233–235) is that this thought does not play any part in Lucan theology elsewhere). At the same time, we may be sure that the carrying back of the genealogy to Adam is meant to stress the universal significance of Jesus for the whole of the human race, and not merely for the seed of Abraham.

An entirely different note is struck by Johnson, 240–252, when he comments on the way in which the lineage of Jesus passes through David's son, Nathan, instead of through the royal line. He draws attention to the equating of this Nathan with the prophet Nathan in a number of sources, most of them late, and claims that the intention is to present Jesus as a prophetic figure, in line with Luke's general emphasis on the prophetic function of Jesus (so, earlier, E. Nestle* and H. Sahlin*, 89). But while there is evidence that the offices of prophet and Messiah were being linked in the first century (E. L. Abel*), there is no evidence that Luke knew of this equation of Nathan, the son of David, with the prophet of the same name, and nothing in the context directs the reader's eye to the significance of this particular name. Another possibility is that the genealogy deliberately bypasses the kingly line passing through Solomon to Jehoiakim, of whom it was prophesied that no descendant of his would sit on the throne of David (Je. 36:30; cf. 22:30; H. Sahlin*, 90f.). H. Sahlin*, 89, also suggests that the number of priestly names in the genealogy may indicate a desire to show that Jesus was a priestly Messiah.

A. Hervey, *The Genealogies of our Lord and Saviour Jesus Christ*, London, 1853; E. Nestle, 'Salomo und Nathan in Mt 1 and Lc 3', ZNW 8, 1907, 72; G. Kuhn, 'Die Geschlechtsregister Jesu bei Lukas und Matthäus, nach ihrer Herkunft untersucht', ZNW 22, 1923, 206–228; Machen, 202–209, 229–232; Jeremias, *Jerusalem*, 213–221, 275–302; Hahn,

243–245; M. D. Johnson, *The Purpose of the Biblical Genealogies*, Cambridge, 1969; E. L. Abel, 'The Genealogies of Jesus Ο ΧΡΙΣΤΟΣ', NTS 20, 1973–74, 203–210.

(23) When he began his ministry Jesus was the 'right' age for his work, just as he could lay claim to the 'right' descent. The opening καὶ αὐτός ... Ἰησοῦς is probably meant as a solemn description: 'And he, namely Jesus'; the αὐτός is unemphatic, indeed unnecessary (1:17 and note), but Luke uses it to draw attention to Jesus (Schürmann, *Paschamahlbericht,* 100). ἀρχόμενος refers to the beginning of Jesus' ministry, a theme stressed by Luke (Acts 1:22; 10:37). The implication is that the ministry lasted for some time, certainly more than one year. The age of thirty (gen. of age) corresponds with that of David when he began to reign (2 Sa. 5:4; cf. Joseph, Gn. 41:46; the sons of Kohath, Nu. 4:3; Ezekiel, Ezk. 1:1), and hence may suggest that David is here seen as a type of Jesus. The use of ὡσεί (1:56 note; 9:14, 28; 22:41, 59; 23:44) suggests that in this case Luke is conscious of giving a round number. Zahn, 205f., took it as an exact number, and was thereby forced to give an impossible dating for the 15th year of Tiberius. Rabbinic tradition gave Jesus an age of 33–34 years (Sanh. 106b, in SB II, 155).

The phrase ὢν υἱός, ὡς ἐνομίζετο (or ὤν, ὡς ἐνομίζετο, υἱός A Θ *pm* lat; TR; *Diglot*) may mean that Luke was uncertain of the accuracy of the genealogy as a whole (Eusebius, QE 3:2; M. D. Johnson*, 230f.), or, more probably, that in reality Joseph was not the physical father of Jesus. ὡς ἐνομίζετο may have been added by Luke to his source in order to avoid possible misunderstanding in relation to chs. 1–2. νομίζω is Lucan (2:44*; Acts, 7x; rest of NT, 6x). H. Sahlin's* suggestion (76f.) that the phrase is a later interpolation is unwarranted.

The omission of the article before Ἰωσήφ led Godet, I, 198–201, (cf. Geldenhuys, 153f.) to the view that the whole phrase ὡς ... Ἰωσήφ was a parenthesis, so that Jesus was presented as the son of Eli (understood as his maternal grandfather). In fact, however, the τοῦ is, in each occurrence in the genealogy, not the article with the following noun; it stands in apposition with the preceding noun, so that the structure is: 'Jesus was the son ... of Joseph (who was) the (son) of Eli (who was) the (son) of ...'

Ἡλί is Hebrew ʿēlî (cf. 1 Sa. 1:3; 1 Ki. 2:27; *et al.*). The identification of the Miriam, daughter of Eli, in j. Hag. 2:77d, 50 (SB II, 155) with Mary, the mother of Jesus, so that Eli would be her father and the father-in-law of Joseph (cf. G. Kuhn*, 209 n.) is very conjectural, and is rejected by P. Billerbeck.

(24) Ματθάτ (3:29**) represents Hebrew *mattāṭ.* The name is similar to Ματταθά (3:31; 2 Esd. 10:33) and to Ματταθίας (3:25, 26). It also resembles Ματθάν (*mattān*; cf. 2 Ch. 23:17; Je. 45:1), which occupies the corresponding place in Matthew's list as the name of Joseph's grandfather (Mt. 1:15**); see the discussion above. It is not clear whether Λευί (3:29; 5:27, 29*; Hebrew *lēwî*) is an indeclinable form (BD 53¹) or a genitive form from Λευίς (BD 55ᵏ). This and the preceding

name were omitted from the text of Luke known to Africanus (see above) and possibly also from Irenaeus, whose list contained only 72 names (AH 3:32:3); but the omission may have been due to the apparent dittography with v. 29 (Schürmann, I, 203 n. 119). Μελχί (*malkî*, possibly an abbreviation for *malkiyyâ*, G. Kuhn*, 211) also occurs at 3:28**. 'Iανναί** is found here only, and 'Iωσήφ recurs at 3:30.

(25) Ματταθίας (3:26**), i.e. *mattityâ*, was a common name (2 Esd. 10:43; 18:4; 1 Ch. 9:31; 16:5; 1 Mac. 2:1, 14; *et al.*; Ep. Arist. 47; Jos., *passim*). 'Αμώς may represent '*āmôn*, the name of the king (2 Ki. 21:18). '*āmôs*, the father of Isaiah (2 Ki. 19:2) or '*āmôs*, the prophet. In Mt. 1:10** it is the name of the king. G. Kuhn's* suggestion (211) that in Lk. the name is a corruption of Simeon (*šim'ôn*) is unconvincing. For Ναούμ** (*nahûm*) cf. Na. 1:1. 'Εσλί** is otherwise unattested; the nearest equivalent is '*ªsalyāhû* (2 Ki. 22:3; 'Εσσελίας, LXX). For Ναγγαί** cf. Νάγαι (*nōgah*), 1 Ch. 3:7.

(26) Μαάθ is the equivalent of *mahat* (1 Ch. 6:35 (20); 2 Ch. 29:12; 31:13); in view of this OT usage G. Kuhn's conjecture that the word is a transliteration of *mē'et*, 'from', used to indicate a genealogical relationship, is unnecessary and unconvincing. For Ματταθίας, see 2:25. Σεμεΐν** is *šim'î* (Ex. 6:17; *et al.*) or *š°ma'yâ* (1 Ch. 5:4). 'Iωσήχ** is otherwise unattested. 'Iωδά** may equal *y°hûdâ* (1 Esd. 5:56 (58)) or *yôyādā'* (2 Esd. 22:10f.); the name is similar to 'Αβιούδ in Mt. 1:13 (*hôdaywāhû*, 1 Ch. 3:24 LXXᴬ, 'Ωδουιά).

(27) 'Iωανάν** is at first sight equivalent to *yôhānān* (BD 53²; 2 Esd. 10:6; 2 Ch. 23:1; *et al.*). But the Hebrew name has the same meaning as *h°nanyâ* ('Ανανιά, 1 Ch. 3:19), the divine name being used as prefix and suffix respectively (cf. 2 Ch. 21:7/22:1). The name could then be that of one of Zerubbabel's sons. In between this name and Zerubbabel, however, stands 'Ρησά**. This could be a proper name (*risyā'*, i.e. 'Ρασειά, 1 Ch. 7:39; cf. SB II, 156), but, since no son of Zerubbabel with this name is otherwise known, many scholars argue that the word is a transcription of Aramaic *rē'šâ*, 'prince', which originally stood in apposition to the name of Zerubbabel. If this conjecture is correct, then Luke was using at this point an originally Aramaic list which was not dependent on the LXX; it would also follow that the list was originally in reverse order, so that the title would follow the name of its bearer.

Ζοροβαβέλ (*z°rubbābel*) also occurs in Mt. 1:12f.** as the name of the leader of the Jewish exiles on their return to Jerusalem. His father's name is given here as Σαλαθιήλ (Mt. 1:12**; i.e. *š°altî'el*), in agreement with 1 Ch. 3:19 LXX; Ezr. 3:2; Ne. 12:1; Hg. 1:1. In 1 Ch. 3:19 MT, however, his father is called Pedaiah. Since Shealtiel and Pedaiah were brothers (1 Ch. 3:17f.), levirate marriage may well explain the anomaly (Machen, 206; cf. W. Rudolph, *Chronikbucher*, Tübingen, 1955, 29).

A further problem arises with Shealtiel's father, named here as Νηρί** (i.e. *nēr*), but in the OT as Jeconiah, the king of Israel (1 Ch. 3:17; cf. Mt. 1:12). Taking Je. 22:30 to imply that Jeconiah was childless, Plummer, 104, argued that he adopted as his heir the son of Neri who was descended through Nathan from David. Other scholars follow Eusebius QE 3:2 (cited by M. D. Johnson*, 243f.) in claiming that because of the curse on Jeconiah the line of the Messiah was deliberately traced so as to by-pass him. Jeremias, *Jerusalem*, 295f., suggests that the author of Chronicles caused the discrepancy by attempting to depict the restorer of the temple after the exile as the grandson of the last reigning king. Any of these conjectures may be correct.

(28) The list now proceeds through a set of names unknown in the OT back to David via his son Nathan. G. Kuhn*, 214f., argues that the first few names are a corruption of the names in 1 Ch. 3:17f. (cf. Schürmann, I, 201 n. 95), but this is improbable, especially since it is unlikely that the genealogy was based on 1 Ch. (Zahn, 218; Jeremias, *Jerusalem*, 295).

For Μελχί see v. 24. 'Αδδί** (with several variant spellings) is found in the LXX for 'iddô (1 Ch. 6:21). Κωσάμ** is not attested in the LXX. For 'Ελμαδάμ** cf. 'Ελμωδάμ (Gn. 10:26 LXX for 'almôdad). Ἤρ** ('ēr) is not uncommon (Gn. 38:3; 1 Ch. 2:3; 4:21).

(29) On the list of names commencing with 'Ιησοῦς see the introductory comments on the theory that this is a parallel list to vs. 23ff.

'Ελιεζέρ** corresponds to 'ĕlî'ezer (Gn. 15:2; Ex. 18:4). 'Ιωρίμ** may be the same as 'Ιωρείμ (2 Esd. 10:18). For Ματθάτ and Λευί see v. 24. See the introductory comments on the use of patriarchal names at this point.

(30) For Συμεών see 2:25, and for 'Ιούδα see 1:39. For 'Ιωνάμ** cf. 'Ιωνάν (yᵉhôhānān, 1 Ch. 26:3), and for 'Ελιακίμ (Mt. 1:13**) see 2 Ki. 18:18; et al. ('elyāqîm).

(31) Μελεά** is otherwise unattested. The same is true of Μεννά** (but see SB II, 156, for a possible equivalent). It is omitted by A, and may be a dittography of the previous name (Schlatter, 218; Jeremias, *Jerusalem*, 296 n. 97), but omission would disturb the numerical scheme. For Ματταθά** (mattaṭâ) see 3:24 note. Ναθάμ** v.l. Ναθάν, as in LXX) is nāṯān, a son of David (2 Sa. 5:14; 1 Ch. 3:5; 14:4; cf. Zc. 12:12. So the line reaches Δαυίδ (dāwiḏ), the king.

(32) From David to Abraham the genealogy is parallel to Mt. 1:2–6 with but slight differences. Matthew follows 1 Ch. 2:1–15, but Luke uses other sources, and possibly uses the MT rather than the LXX (G. Kuhn*, 217f.). See Ru. 4:18–22.

'Ιεσσαί is the same form as in LXX for yišay (Mt. 1:5f.; Acts 13:22; Rom. 15:12**; Ru. 4:22; 1 Ch. 2:12f.). 'Ιωβήδ (Mt. 1:5**, i.e. 'ôḇēḏ) is a v.l. in 1 Ch. 2:12, where the better text has 'Ωβήδ. In Lk. the variants 'Ιωβήλ, 'Ωβήδ and 'Ωβήλ are attested; confusion of final δ and λ would be easy. It is surprising that Mt. agrees with Lk. here against the LXX. Βόος** is bō'az (Ru. 4:21; 1 Ch. 2:11f.); Mt. 1:5 has Βόες. Σαλά (3:35**) is for śalmā'/śalmôn. This form of the name is used for the patriarch šelaḥ in Gn. 10:24; 11:13–15; 1 Ch. 1:18, 24; but for the present name the LXX has Σαλμάν (Ru. 4:20f.) or Σαλμών (1 Ch. 2:11; Mt. 1:4f.). Both of these forms appear as textual variants in Lk., but Σαλά has the best attestation. Metzger, 136, observes that it may be based on a Syriac tradition, since the corresponding form is found in Ru. 4:20f. syᵖ. Ναασσών is naḥšôn (Mt. 1:4**; Ex. 6:23; Nu. 1:7; Ru. 4:20; 1 Ch. 2:10f.).

(33) The text of the next three names is very uncertain, and UBS prints what Metzger, 136, can describe only as 'the least unsatisfactory form of text'. Ἀμιναδάβ ('ammînāḏāḇ) is found in Mt. 1:4**; Ex. 6:23; Nu. 1:7; 1 Ch. 2:10; Ru. 4:19f. It is omitted by B syˢ; G. Kuhn*, 217 n. 2 and Jeremias, Jerusalem, 293, explain it as a scribal addition by someone who did not realise that the following name was an abbreviation for this one, but Kuhn's suggestion that ʿdmyn and myndb were confused seems unlikely. The form, Ἀδμίν** is unattested in the LXX. Ἀρνί**, also unattested in the LXX, must correspond to Ἀράμ, i.e. rām (Mt. 1:3f.; 1 Ch. 2:9f.; Ἀρράν, Ru. 4:19). The variation in Lk. is due to textual corruption at some point. For Ἑσρώμ cf. Mt. 1:3**. The forms Ἑσρώμ and Ἑσρών for heṣrôn are found in Ru. 4:18f.; 1 Ch. 2:5, 9. Φάρες, i.e. pereṣ, is found in Mt. 1:3**; Gn. 38:29; Ru; 4:18; 1 Ch. 2:4f. For Ἰούδα cf. v. 30; Mt. 1:2f.

(34–38) Ἰακώβ (yaʿᵃqōḇ), Ἰσαάκ (yiṣḥāq) and Ἀβραάμ ('aḇrāhām) complete the parallelism with Mt. 1:2. The rest of the genealogy has no parallel in Mt., and gives a list of names found in Gn. 11:10–26; cf. 5:1–32; 1 Ch. 1:1–26. Θάρα** (teraḥ), Ναχώρ** (nāḥôr), Σερούχ** (śᵉrûḡ), Ῥαγαύ** (rᵉʿû), Φάλεκ** (peleḡ), Ἕβερ (ʿēber), Σαλά (3:32; šelaḥ), Καϊνάμ (3:37**), Ἀρφαξάδ** ('arpakśaḏ) and Σήμ** (šēm) are found in Gn. 11:10–26 (1 Ch. 1:17, 24–26) with the same spellings. The name Καϊνάμ is found only in the LXX, with no equivalent in the MT (it is omitted by p⁷⁵ ᵛⁱᵈ D); its presence shows that for this part of the genealogy Luke was using the LXX. The final set of names, Νώε (17:26f.; nōaḥ), Λάμεχ** (lemek), Μαθουσαλά** (mᵉṯûšelaḥ), Ἑνώχ (Heb. 11:5; Jude 14**; hᵃnôk), Ἰάρετ** (yered), Μαλελεήλ** (maḥᵃ lalʾēl), Καϊνάμ (3:36; qênān), Ἑνώς** (ʾᵉnôš), Σήθ** (šēṯ) and Ἀδάμ* ('āḏām) are derived from Gn. 5:1–32 (cf. 1 Ch. 1:1–4) with minor spelling differences; contrast Jos. Ant. 1:78f., where they are turned into declinable forms. On the significance of τοῦ θεοῦ (cf. Gn. 5:1) see introductory comments.

d. The Temptation of Jesus (4:1–13)

The twin themes in the story of the baptism of Jesus are taken up in the story of his temptation, so that there is no doubt that this narrative was derived from a source in which the baptism and temptation stood together. On the one hand, the story demonstrates how the Spirit, who had come upon Jesus, guided and empowered him in his new task; on the other hand, it shows how Jesus, as the Son of God, was obedient to God. The new factor in the situation is the devil, who attempts to deflect Jesus from obedience to God and hence from the fulfilment of the messianic task laid upon him by God. The temptation proves fruitless, so that at the end of it Jesus is able to enter Galilee in the power of the Spirit and to commence a task which includes the release of the devil's captives (4:18; cf. 13:16). Thus at the outset of his ministry Jesus is depicted as overcoming the evil one who stands in opposition to the work of the kingdom of God (11:19f).

These are the main points in the story as seen by Luke. We may be certain that the story was also told for its exemplary features in order to encourage Christians facing temptation and to indicate to them how to recognise and overcome it. They are to note that in each case Jesus replies to temptation with a quotation from Scripture, thereby indicating that the life of the man of God must follow certain clear principles expressive of God's will which have already been revealed in the OT. It has been argued that this reduces the story to the level of a rabbinic *Streitgespräch* in which Jesus overcomes the devil by a superior knowledge of Scripture (cf. Bultmann, 271–275), but the point is rather that Jesus is obedient to God's will in Scripture (H. Seesemann, TDNT VI, 23–36, especially 34–36 and n. 68), and not that he wins by superior dialectical skill.

The choice of texts used by Jesus is significant. They come from Dt. 8:3; 6:13, 16, passages which relate to Israel in the wilderness (4:1!), tempting God and being tested by him, and which occur in the context of the *Shema*, the authoritative claim by God upon Israel's worship and loyalty. The temptation of Jesus – and of his followers – is to be seen as antitypical of the experience of Israel. But where Israel fell, Jesus shows the way to victory (G. H. P. Thompson*; B. Gerhardsson*; France, 50–53).

The brief general account of temptation in Mk. 1:12f. has influenced Luke (Schramm, 36), but it is clear that his main source was Q. He agrees with Matthew in recording three acts of temptation, but with the second and third in reverse order, so that in Mt. the command to worship the devil comes last. Various late MSS altered the order in Lk. to conform to that in Mt., thereby suggesting that scribes regarded Matthew's order as original (Metzger, 137). In favour of Matthew's order it may be argued: 1. The command to Satan to depart comes more appropriately in the last temptation. (But did Luke omit the words when he transposed the order, or did Matthew introduce them?) 2. Luke may have transposed Matthew's geographical order (wilderness – Jerusalem – wilderness) in order to get rid of a change of scene (wilderness – ? wilderness – Jerusalem) and to obtain a climax at the temple in Jerusalem. Victory in Jerusalem foreshadows the final triumph of Jesus (J. Dupont*, 63–66). 3. Luke's order makes the devil, twice worsted by Jesus' citation of Scripture, appeal to Scripture himself. 4. It also puts the quotations from Dt. 6:13 and 16 into their scriptural order. 5. Matthew's order puts together the two 'Son of God' temptations, which surely were originally a pair. These arguments have convinced many commentators of the originality of Matthew's order (Lagrange, 130; Creed, 63; A. Feuillet*, 613–616; J. Dupont*, 33; Schulz, 177). The originality of Luke's order is supported by Manson, *Sayings*, 42f.; Findlay, 1036; Schürmann, I, 218, all of whom claim that Matthew has rearranged the order to gain a dramatic climax, and to lay stress on the mountain of temptation over against the mountain where Jesus displayed his omnipotence to the disciples (Mt. 28:16–20). But it is more probable that Luke wished to lay stress on the conclusion of the temptations in the temple (Grundmann, 113), and that he is responsible for the change in order.

The first and third temptations (in Luke's order) stand together over against the third in view of their use of the 'Son of God' motif; this might suggest that they have been transmitted independently. On the other hand, the unified background of all three temptations in Dt. and possibly in Jewish understanding of the Shema (B. Gerhardsson*) argues strongly in favour of a unified construction (J. Dupont*, 79–88). This consideration makes it unlikely that we have three separate traditions of one original temptation story (*pace* Jeremias, *Theology*, I, 71). It is also improbable that we have a development in Q from the brief narrative in Mk. 1:12f.

Since two of the temptations are concerned with Jesus as the Son of God and one of them (if not two) with the use of miraculous powers, it is possible that the narrative reflects a Hellenistic concept of the Son of God, since the Jewish idea of the Messiah was not associated with the performance of miracles (Bultmann, 275; cf. Hahn, 175f., 303). It can then be argued that the purpose of the narrative was to play down the idea of the Son of God as a miracle-working 'divine man' (Schulz, 182, 187). On this view, the narrative was created in the Hellenistic community. Earlier forms of the theory of 'community creation' have been summarised and criticised by J. Dupont*, 92–104. This more recent form of the theory is also open to objection. If Jesus was in fact a worker of miracles, or thought himself to be such, the existence of a discussion regarding his use of miracles need not be ascribed to a later, non-Palestinian stage of christological reflection. The narrative is about a Jesus who worked miracles, not about Jewish or Hellenistic ideas of the Messiah. Moreover, the narrative displays such a strong combination of Jewish features that it is impossible to assume that it went through a preliminary Hellenistic stage before receiving its present Jewish form. In particular, the objection that the use of the LXX here (and elsewhere in the Gospels) betrays a Hellenistic origin should be forgotten once and for all; the evidence implies nothing more than that when the story was told in Greek the narrator made use of the current Greek translation of the OT (Schürmann, I, 219 n. 248; see especially France). Finally, it must be insisted that it is one thing to show how a narrative was used in the early church, and quite another thing to claim that because it was used for a particular purpose in the church, it must have been created by the church without any historical basis.

Jesus certainly took for granted the reality of Satan and spoke about him, sometimes in a poetic manner (10:18). It is, therefore, possible that he described his inward experience of temptation in dramatic form, as here. But, while a brief fragment couched in the first person and describing how he was carried by the Spirit to Mt. Tabor may be cited in this connection (Gospel of the Hebrews, NTA I, 164), this is no doubt secondary and should not be used as evidence for a first-person account by Jesus. More important is the fact that Jesus underwent temptation on other occasions, and that the temptations described here reflect the experience of one who was tempted to prove the reality of his calling by signs and to adjust his ideas of his calling to those of his contemporaries. Throughout his ministry he was engaged in conflict with the forces of evil. It is by no means impossible that he communicated something of his inner experience to his disciples, and indeed highly likely that he did so. It is also probable that at the outset of his work he had to face up to the question of the nature of his vocation. The theory that the account of the temptation rests on a historical experience of Jesus fits in with what we know otherwise of his ministry and remains the most satisfying explanation of it (J. Dupont*, 104–126). It has often been argued that the narrative shows Jesus being tempted to be a political Messiah. This interpretation does not do full justice to the narrative which is much more concerned with the personal relation of obedience between Jesus and his Father and thus reflects the attitude of Jesus himself rather than of the early church about him. Behind the story lies the experience of Jesus, although the formulation of it will owe something to the early church.

See A. Feuillet, 'Le récit lucanien de la tentation (Lc 4, 1–13)', Bib. 40, 1959, 613–631; G. H. P. Thompson, 'Called – Proved – Obedient', JTS ns 11, 1960, 1–12; N. Hyldahl, 'Die Versuchung auf der Zinne des Tempels', ST 15, 1961, 113–127; B. Gerhardsson, The Testing of God's Son, Lund, 1966; J. Dupont, Die Versuchungen Jesu in der Wüste, Stuttgart, 1969; Jeremias, Theology, I, 68–75; Schulz, 177–190; P. Pokorný, 'The Temptation Stories and their Intention', NTS 20, 1973–74, 115–127. W. Wilkens, 'Die Versuchungsgeschichte Luk. 4, 1–13 und die Komposition des Evangeliums', TZ 30, 1974, 262–272.

(1) The opening verse is designed to link the temptation story with that of the baptism after the interposition of the genealogy and reflects Lucan terminology. The use of Ἰησοῦς without the article could be due to Luke's source (Rehkopf, 52), but this is not a necessary inference (cf. 2:52; 5:8; 8:41; 9:50; 22:48, 52; 23:28). From the baptism onwards Jesus is continually filled with the Spirit; for the use of πλήρης (5:12*) cf. Acts 6:3, 5; 7:55; 11:24 (see 1:15 note). Since the same phraseology is used of disciples in Acts, it is going too far to say that Jesus is 'the Lord of the πνεῦμα' (E. Schweizer, TDNT VI, 404f.). Nevertheless, Luke's choice of language does bring out more clearly than in Mt. or Mk. that

the Spirit is not an external, compulsive force upon Jesus but an inward inspiration. Thus equipped he returns from the Jordan; since, however, Luke does not tell us from where Jesus had come to the Jordan (contrast Mk. 1:9), ὑποστρέφω should be given the weaker sense 'to depart'. ἄγω is more appropriate for a person being led by the Spirit than Mk., ἐκβάλλω; cf. Mt., ἀνάγω, which suggests a common origin in Q. ἐν τῷ πνεύματι is 'under the impulse of the Spirit' (2:27) rather than 'in an ecstatic condition'. The role of the Spirit is primarily guidance, but there is no reason to exclude the thought of his powerful inspiration which (for Luke) enabled Jesus to overcome the tempter. The phrase ἐν τῇ ἐρήμῳ (diff. Mt. and Mk., εἰς) may give a clearer allusion to Dt. 8:2, where Israel was led in the wilderness by God in order to be tested.

(2) The verb πειράζω is used to express the experience of Jesus: cf. 11:16* and the use of πειρασμός (4:13; 8:13; 11:4; 22:28, 40, 46*; H. Seesemann, TDNT VI, 23–36; B. Gerhardsson*, 25–35). The verb means 'to test someone', and it is used in the OT both of God testing men in order to assess the reality of their faith and obedience (Gn. 22:1–19) and also of men testing God, usually because they doubt his goodness and power (Ex. 17:2). Especially during the wilderness period God tested the faithfulness of his people (Ex. 16:4; 20:20; Dt. 8:2; 13:2ff.; cf. Jdg. 2:22; 3:4; 2 Ch. 32: 31), and the people fell into sin by testing God (Nu. 14:22; Pss. 95:8ff.; 106:14; cf. Is. 7:12). The reference to the duration of the temptation – ἡμέρας τεσσεράκοντα – may be meant to give a further allusion to the wilderness period of 40 years of testing (Ps. 95:10; Dt. 8:2 MT); if so, a period of days is regarded as the appropriate counterpart for a single man to a period of years for a nation (B. Gerhardsson*, 41f.; cf., however, G. Kittel, TDNT II, 658, who sees more apposite parallels in the forty-day fasts of Moses, Ex. 34:28; Dt. 9:9, 18, and Elijah, 1 Ki. 19:5, 8). None of these passages, however, speaks of a period of human temptation by God or the devil, and so the typology should not be pressed too closely at this point.

Whereas in the OT it is God who tests Israel, here it is the devil, although the mention of leading by the Spirit shows that the devil's role falls within the purpose of God. What is intended by the devil as a means of defeating Jesus (cf. Schürmann, I, 208) becomes in the purpose of God the occasion of *his* defeat. The idea of testing by Satan had already developed in the OT (2 Sa. 24:1/2 Ch. 21:1; cf. Gn. 3:1–19; Job) and was taken further in Judaism (Jub. 17:15f.; 48:2; full references in W. Foerster, TDNT II, 72–81, especially 76; TDNT VII, 151–165, especially 152–156, adds the Qumran material). The term διάβολος (4:3, 6, 13; 8:12*) is used here by both Luke and Matthew in preference to Σατανᾶς, Mk. 1:13; both Q and Luke (cf. 8:12 diff. Mk.) prefer this name, but Luke can take over Σατανᾶς from Mk. and his special source (10:18; 11:18; 13:16; 22:3, 31*; Acts 5:3; 26:18*). Both Mark and Luke indicate that Jesus was tempted throughout the forty-day period, but the three recorded temptations come only at the end of the period. It is unnecessary to find any discrepancy between the statements, but in view of v. 26 Ellis, 93, is incorrect in stating that the three specific temptations may have fallen within the general period. Nor is it necessary, with Schürmann, I, 208, to read into the forty days a period of *demonic* activity before the devil himself comes on the scene. In view of v. 4 we should rather accept G. Kittel's suggestion (TDNT II, 658) that the forty days were for Jesus an intended period of communion with God accompanied by fasting; it was this communion which the devil sought to destroy.

Luke admittedly does not use the verb νηστεύω (Mt. 4:2) which he has elsewhere for a religious practice of fasting (5:33–35; 18:12; Acts 13:2f.), but follows the wording of Ex. 34:28; Dt. 9:9, describing the reception of the tables of the law by Moses. This may be an intentional piece of Lucan typology, since the rest of the sentence reflects his style. For ἐν ταῖς ἡμέραις ἐκείναις cf. 1:5 and 2:1 notes. συντελέω (4:13; Acts 21:27), is 'to complete'; the genitive absolute suggests Lucan redaction. It is stretching the point to suggest that Jesus was miraculously free from the pangs of hunger during the forty days (Schürmann, I, 208); the point is rather that when hunger was its height there came the temptation from the devil.

(3) Instead of δέ (B D L 33 latt sa bo) the connective καί is read by TR; *Diglot* (1:13 note; 4:9 and frequently). Matthew brings out the nature of the devil's statement by calling him ὁ πειράζων (1 Thes. 3:5), but Luke probably follows Q in using ὁ διάβολος. The temptation appeals to Jesus' status as God's Son, able to call on God's power; note the emphasis on τοῦ θεοῦ. Let him command (εἰπέ, cf. 10:40) the stone lying here at his feet (οὗτος) to become a loaf of bread. Matthew has the plural (cf. 3:8) which may be original. 1. The saying has been interpreted as a temptation to perform one of the signs expected in the messianic age in order to win the people over to his side: let Jesus repeat the miracle of the manna in the wilderness (Ex. 16; Manson, *Sayings,* 43f.). It can then be argued that this temptation is to be connected with the feeding of the five thousand (Jn. 6:31f.) and reflects the temptation to become king experienced by Jesus on that occasion (R. E. Brown, 'Incidents that are units in the Synoptic Gospels but dispersed in St. John', CBQ 23, 1961, 143–160, especially 152–155). But this view is certainly wrong. There are no onlookers (B. Gerhardsson*, 32), and the suggestion of producing *one* loaf is linked to Jesus' own hunger. Nothing suggests an allusion to the manna. Only in Ps.-Clem. Hom. 2:32 is the miracle turned into a messianic wonder performed by Simon Magus (Schürmann, I, 209; Schulz, 185 n. 84). 2. A second possibility is that the devil is attempting to cast doubt on Jesus' possession of the miraculous powers which would confirm for him the reality of his divine sonship (Ellis, 94). Jesus' answer, however, is not concerned with this point. 3. The third view remains the most likely, namely that Jesus is being tempted to use his power as Son of God for his own ends instead of being obedient to the

Father (Creed, 62; Schürmann, I, 209). It is suggested that Sonship can be expressed in independent authority rather than in filial obedience. Behind the temptation lies the desire to turn Jesus aside from the fulfilment of his messianic task by striking at his relationship to the Father. That this is the correct view of the temptation is confirmed by Jesus' reply.

(4) The wording ἀπεκρίθη πρὸς αὐτόν, diff. Mt. ἀποκριθεὶς εἶπεν, is probably original, since Luke himself prefers the wording in Mt. elsewhere. Jesus' reply expresses what stands written (γέγραπται, 2:23) as the abiding command of God in the OT. The ὅτι recitativum (diff. Mt.) is probably original here, since normally Luke avoids it (J. Dupont* 50 n. 30). The wording of the quotation from Dt. 8:3a is identical with the LXX; cf. Wis. 16:26; Jn. 4:34. In many MSS the quotation is completed by the inclusion of Dt. 8:3b, as in Mt. 4:4, but the evidence for omission is decisive (א B L W 1241 sy^s sa bo; Metzger, 137). Schürmann, I, 210 n. 164 argues from the reminiscence of the wording in 4:22 that the whole verse was in Q, but Luke omitted it because he disliked the attribution of the preservation of life to the word of God rather than to God himself; it is perhaps more likely that Matthew completed the quotation from the LXX (Holtz, 61). The point of the reply is usually taken to be simply that human life does not depend primarily upon physical food; it is more important to obey the word of God, even if obedience involves physical hunger. Schürmann, I, 210, however, takes the point to be that Jesus trusted the miraculous power of God which had already been able to sustain him during the absence of physical food, and therefore was prepared to continue to obey him. This view reads rather too much into the text. In any case what matters ultimately is the steadfast opposition to temptation which leads to a firm, tested character (Rom. 5:3).

(5) καί is original, diff. Mt. πάλιν (one of his favourite words). Now the devil leads Jesus (contrast v. 1) up to a high place. ἀνάγω (Mt. 4:1) may be original, diff. Mt. παραλαμβάνω (but see J. Dupont*, 51f.). It is unnecessary to suppose that Luke is thinking of physical levitation into the air (Easton, 46) instead of ascent of a mountain. He may have omitted mention of the mountain because he saw that it must be metaphorical (there is no literal mountain from which one may see the whole world), less probably because he regarded mountains as places of revelation. At this point the visionary nature of Jesus' experience is especially evident. Like a prospective seller, the devil points out all the kingdoms of the world in a brief moment. For the motif see Dt. 34:1–4; 3:27; 2 Bar. 76:3; B. Gerhardsson*, 62–64; and also Rev. 21:10; Bultmann, 274 n. ἔδειξεν replaces a historic present (Mt.), and οἰκουμένη (2:1) is probably secondary to Mt. κόσμος. στιγμή** is 'moment', and the whole phrase is probably Lucan.

(6) The words of the devil are reproduced more fully in Lk. than in Mt. It is a moot point whether Luke has expanded them (J. Dupont*,

53–56; Schulz, 180f.) or Matthew abbreviated them (Schürmann, I, 211). The basic thought is unaffected. The devil offers to Jesus the authority represented by all these kingdoms together with the glory that would accrue to their ruler. The phrase καὶ τὴν δόξαν αὐτῶν is awkwardly placed, with no antecedent in the preceding words of the devil, and will have been transferred here from the earlier position reflected in Mt. 4:8. The language is expressive of the authority given to the Messiah in Ps. 2:8 and to the Son of man in Dn. 7:14 (cf. Mt. 28:18). The reference is in contemporary terms at least to the Roman world (cf. 2:1); it is not clear how far Luke thought of territories outside its borders. Whereas in the OT this realm and authority lie in the hands of God, here the devil claims that it has been given to him and that consequently he has the right of disposal (cf. Mk. 16:14 W; Jn. 12:31; 14:30; 16:11; 1 Jn. 5:19; Rev. 13:2). Ultimately, however, the devil's claim was not true, nor was his word to be trusted.

(7) Nevertheless, he promises that all may belong to Jesus (for the genitive with ἔσται, cf. 18:16) on condition that he offers worship to him (προσκυνέω, 4:7; 24:52*; the use of ἐνώπιον is a Hebraism for the simple dative, BD 187²; cf. Rev. 3:9; 15:4). The temptation is thus to give the devil what belongs properly to God alone (H. Greeven, TDNT VI, 758–766, especially 763f.), not to follow the (devilish) path of being a political Messiah, which is not so much as hinted at in the context; it is again a temptation to act in a way inconsistent with the relation of the Son to the Father, although the word Son obviously could not be used in such a temptation.

(8) Luke's introductory formula καὶ ἀποκριθεὶς . . . εἶπεν αὐτῷ (cf. 4:12) differs from Mt. τότε λέγει . . . It is not clear whether Luke (Schulz, 181) or Matthew (J. Dupont*, 55) is closer to Q. The order ὁ Ἰησοῦς εἶπεν αὐτῷ is varied in the MSS (cf. Diglot). Luke does not have the phrase ὕπαγε, Σατανᾶ, found in Mt., which suggests the successful conclusion of the series of temptations and which is probably original (Schulz, 181). Again the devil is refuted with an appeal to Scripture, Dt. 6:13 LXX with slight variations. Both Gospels have προσκυνέω diff. LXX φοβέομαι, no doubt by assimilation to v. 7 (but Holtz, 62f., argues that here Q follows LXXᴬ). Both Gospels insert μόνῳ to bring out the full meaning of the original, and Luke alters the word order slightly. For λατρεύω see 1:74; 2:37. God alone is to be worshipped, so that there can be no question of the Son of God offering worship and service to the devil, even for such an apparently great reward.

(9) For the third temptation the devil leads Jesus to Jerusalem. Luke has ἄγω, diff. Mt. παραλαμβάνω (cf. 4:5 note). Matthew's phrase ἡ ἁγία πόλις (Mt. 27:53) is secondary. The devil stood Jesus (αὐτόν, added by A D W Θ pm lat; TR; Diglot, possibly by assimilation to Mt.) on a lofty part of the temple. πτερύγιον (Mt. 4:5**) is a diminutive of πτέρυξ, 'wing'. 1. It is usually taken to refer to the royal colonnade of the temple on the south side of the outer court. This overlooked a deep ravine and

was high enough to cause giddiness (Jos. Ant. 15:411f.). 2. Another suggestion is 'the lintel or superstructure of a gate of the temple' (J. Jeremias, 'Die "Zinne" des Tempels (Mt. 4, 5; Lk. 4, 9) ', *Zeitschrift des Deutschen Palästina-Vereins,* 59, 1936, 195–208). This may have been in the form of a balcony (cf. Grundmann, 116). 3. B. Gerhardsson*, 59, thinks that the name is deliberately used to give a contrast with the 'wings' of God in Ps. 91:4, but this is far-fetched. According to Eusebius, HE 2:23:11 the Jews stood James the Just on the 'wing' of the temple, and threw him down in order to murder him. A rabbinic tradition prophesied that the Messiah would reveal himself on the roof of the temple (Pes. R 36 (162a), in SB I, 151); but it is improbable that this has anything to do with the present story since 'there is no hint that the Messiah was expected to prove his title by leaping from the roof' (Manson, *Sayings,* 44). The claim of Simon Magus to be able to fly through the air (Ps.-Clem. Rec. 3:47; cf. Acts of Peter 32 (NTA II, 315f.)) is probably based on the present passage, and does not indicate that there was a tradition that the Messiah would act in such a way.

(10–11) The significance of the command is seen only when 'the tempter, twice repulsed with scripture texts, tries a text himself' (Manson, ibid.). The quotation is from Ps. 91:11f. (90:11f.), retaining the phrase τοῦ διαφυλάξαι σε (omitted in Mt.) and omitting the words ἐν ταῖς ὁδοῖς σου (which are unnecessary in the present context); the second half of the quotation is introduced rather unnecessarily by καὶ ὅτι, perhaps to draw attention to the immediately following phrase or to indicate that there is a gap in the quotation (Holtz, 57f.). The psalmist expresses his confidence that God will protect him from all kinds of danger. He has commanded his angels to care for him, especially to prevent him from stumbling upon a stony path or from being attacked by wild animals (Ps. 91:13; cf. Lk. 10:19). For ἐντέλλομαι*, see Acts 1:2; 13:47; *et al.*; διαφυλάσσω** occurs here only. Note that there does not appear to have been a messianic interpretation of the Psalm in Judaism. A promise addressed to the godly in general, however, applies *a fortiori* to the Son of God. The temptation is, therefore, to prove the truth of God's promise by putting it to the test – something which the godly man does not need to do because he has faith in God, and which is thus a sign of lack of faith. There is no suggestion that Jesus is being tempted to be an 'apocalyptic' Messiah by a spectacular demonstration of power, since there is no mention of any spectators. Nor is it likely that the devil was enticing Jesus to commit suicide on the (devil's) assumption that God would not keep his promise (Grundmann, 117). N. Hyldahl* thinks that Jesus was being tempted to submit voluntarily to the punishment for blasphemy (being thrown off the pinnacle of the temple).

(12) Again it is not clear whether Luke's introduction (as in v. 8) is secondary to Mt. ἔφη (Schürmann, *Abschiedsrede,* 27f.) or vice versa, probably the former. Jesus' reply is again a quotation, this time introduced by εἴρηται (cf. 2:24), probably a change for stylistic reasons (J.

Dupont*, 58f.). The wording follows Dt. 6:16 LXX (cf. Is. 7:12). On the analogy of the preceding quotations it is to be understood as a command to be obeyed by Jesus, and not as a command to Satan not to tempt the 'Lord God', i.e. Jesus. Jesus is not to follow the example of ungodly Israel in faithlessly putting God to the test. Again, therefore, it is the filial relationship of trust in the Father which is the object of the devil's attack.

(13) But each attack has failed. The devil has carried out fully (συντελέω, 4:2) every kind of temptation (πᾶς), and departs (ἀφίσταμαι, 2:37, diff. Mt. ἀφίημι) – but only until an opportune moment (Acts 13:11). Satan reappears in Luke's narrative at 22:3 in order to instigate the passion of Jesus, and Conzelmann, 22, has especially taken up the view of older commentators (J. Weiss, 436; Klostermann, 61; cf. Wellhausen, 7) that there is a gap in the activities of Satan until temptation sets in again at 22:3; thus there is a 'Satan-free' period during the ministry of Jesus. But Satan does not reappear to tempt *Jesus* at 22:3, and there are clear signs of his activity during the intervening period (cf. Marshall, 87f.). The valid inference from the evidence is that Luke sees the ministry of Jesus as a period of victory over Satan and the demons, following on from this initial repulse (cf. Schürmann, I, 214, 216f. – although he is perhaps inclined to follow Conzelmann too closely). That this view was not a Lucan innovation but can also be traced in Mk. has been argued by E. Best, *The Temptation and the Passion*, Cambridge, 1965.

Luke has no reference to the ministry of the angels to Jesus after the temptation (Mk. 1:13; Mt. 4:11). Jesus alone stands forth as the victor.

IV

THE MINISTRY IN GALILEE

4:14 – 9:50

NOW that the preliminaries are over, the ministry of Jesus begins with his return to Galilee from the wilderness and his ministry in the synagogue. Both source criticism and the content of 9:51 suggest that at that point a new stage in the Gospel begins, and hence we regard the present section as running to 9:50 and dealing primarily (but not exclusively) with Jesus' work in Galilee (see 4:44). In particular, it seems best to regard 4:14–44 as the beginning of this section rather than the conclusion of the previous one, but it must be remembered that Luke's sections tend to flow into one another, and that some of his paragraphs have a bridging function. The theme of the section as a whole is the ministry of Jesus before he set his face to journey to Jerusalem and face his passion. It is the story of a travelling ministry in which Jesus preaches and performs mighty works, wins disciples and rouses opposition, and in broad outline it follows the pattern set in Mk., although much of its distinctive character is due to the incorporation of material from other sources.

a. The Good News of the Kingdom (4:14 – 5:11)

The opening paragraphs are largely concerned with the teaching of Jesus (4:14f., 16–30, 31f., 42–44; 5:1–3) and with the response that it evoked (5:1–11); much of this is peculiar to Lk. and represents his own elaboration of traditions peculiar to this Gospel. It is interspersed with material describing the mighty works of Jesus that occurred in the Marcan tradition at this point. Like Mt. and Mk., Luke stresses at the outset the fact and character of the message proclaimed by Jesus in word and deed.

i. Introductory Summary 4:14–15

This short section which brings Jesus to Galilee and tells of his successful début as a teacher corresponds in content to Mk. 1:14f. and Mt. 4:12–17. For the moment Jesus is the centre of acclamation and interest, although the picture will soon be modified by the story of what happened at Nazareth.

The considerable difference in wording from Mk. and the contacts with Mt. have led H. Schürmann* to the hypothesis that behind Lk. and Mt. may be traced an independent account of the beginning of the ministry of Jesus, stemming from a tradition parallel to that in Mk. Since, as we have already seen, the Q material contained reference to the preaching of John and to the temptation of Jesus, there is some likelihood that it continued with some reference to the beginning of the ministry of Jesus. Schürmann's case has been strongly criticised by J. Delobel* who has argued that the linguistic data can be satisfactorily explained in terms of free redaction of Mk. 1:14f. We face here a problem which will recur elsewhere in the Gospel, the question of how to decide whether material similar to that in Mk. but differently presented is based on parallel source material or is due to Lucan redaction of Mk. Where the arguments are evenly balanced the presence of non-Lucan linguistic phenomena will be significant, although it is hard to be certain what a stylist like Luke could and could not write.

See H. Schürmann, 'Der "Bericht vom Anfang", Ein Rekonstruktionsversuch auf Grund von Lk. 4, 14–16' (originally in TU 87, 1964, 242–258), in Schürmann, *Untersuchungen*, 69–80; J. Delobel, 'La rédaction de Lc., IV, 14–16a et le "Bericht vom Anfang" ', in Neirynck, 203–223.

(14) Luke himself has clearly edited his source here. Having already mentioned the arrest of John (Mk. 1:14a), he had no need to refer to it here. He contents himself with describing the return of Jesus to Galilee (ὑποστρέφω, diff. Mk. ἔρχομαι is Lucan; cf. Mt. ἀναχωρέω). He adds the distinctive feature that Jesus was now equipped with the power of the Spirit (cf. Rom. 15:29). The association of the Spirit with power (cf. 1:17) is not infrequent in Lk. (24:49) and Acts (1:8; 10:38; cf. Rom. 15:13). The power of the Spirit is linked especially with the apostolic witness, and hence here the primary reference is presumably to the authority of Jesus to teach. But the thought of power to do mighty works may be present; the second part of the verse may imply that the power of Jesus was manifest in some visible manner, since it led to the spread of his fame. The theme is developed in v. 18 where the OT promise lying behind the gift of the Spirit is cited. Schürmann, I, 224, draws attention to the motif of power in Mk. 1:27, and suggests that the present verse originally introduced a story similar to that in Mk. 1:21–28; but this is less likely, since the key word δύναμις is absent from Mk. 1:27 (diff. Lk. 4:36!).

The second part of the verse has no parallel in Mk. at this point, but there is a similar statement in Mt. 4:23–25 par. Mk. 1:28 (Matthew omits Mk. 1:21–28) and a partial parallel in Mt. 9:26 which comes at the point where Matthew has omitted the story of the rejection at Nazareth (Mk. 6:1–6; cf. Mt. 13:54–58). These features may suggest that a source other than Mk. is being used here. The statement is such as might follow the account of a mighty work (cf. Mk. 1:28). Luke's audience will have known about such activities from the apostolic preaching (Acts 10:38; cf. Lk. 4:23) and hence will have been able to understand the previous part of the verse as a reference to mighty works. For φήμη, 'report', cf. Mt. 9:26** (J. Delobel*, 212, thinks the use was inspired by διαφημίζω, Mk. 1:45). For ἐξέρχομαι see 2:1; 7:17; Mk. 1:28. Aramaic influence (Black, 135f.) need not be postulated (cf. Rom. 10:18 LXX; 1 Cor. 14:36; 1 Thes. 1:8). κατά with genitive of place (accompanied by ὅλος) has a Lucan appearance (23:5; Acts 9:31, 42; 10:37), but may rest on a source (cf. Mt. 9:26; Mk. 1:39). The περίχωρος (3:3) will be the area within Galilee around the town (Capernaum, 4:23) where Jesus was at work.

(15) διδάσκω is frequently used to indicate the work of Jesus in all the Gospels and has much the same meaning as κηρύσσω (Mk. 1:14; J. J. Vincent, 'Didactic Kerygma in the Synoptic Gospels', SJT 10, 1957, 262–273; K. H. Rengstorf, TDNT II, 135–165). A peripatetic ministry round the synagogues is implied. The use of αὐτῶν with ἐν ταῖς συναγωγαῖς (cf. Mk. 1:39 par. Mt. 4:23; 13:54) is slightly odd. It is the phrase which a Christian (especially a gentile Christian) would use with respect to the Jews, but there is no antecedent here. We should think ad sensum of the inhabitants of Galilee (cf. 23:51; Acts 8:5; BD 282¹); possibly the phrase has come from an earlier, fuller narrative. Luke says nothing here about the content of the message of Jesus; this will become apparent in the following narrative. It is enough here to show that he taught in the power of the Spirit and aroused the praise of men. Elsewhere in Lk. δοξάζω is used of glorifying God, not men (2:20). The motif may be intended as a foil to the rejection of Jesus at Nazareth, and it is parallel to the initial success of the early church in its preaching (Acts 2:47; Schürmann, I, 223).

ii. Jesus teaches at Nazareth 4:16–30

Although the preceding summary of his ministry tells how Jesus was praised in the synagogues of Galilee, the present story, which is meant to serve, at least to some extent, as an illustration of his ministry, is an account of rejection. The significance of the contrast is all the greater if Luke has deliberately brought forward the story to this point: in Mk. (6:1–6; cf. Mt. 13:53–58) a similar story appears at a considerably later stage, and internal features in the present story (4:23) suggest that it is not in its original position. The narrative is placed here, then, for its programmatic significance, and it contains many of the main themes of Lk.-Acts *in nuce*.

The story begins by emphasising that the ministry of Jesus is to be seen as a fulfilment of the OT, both in the direct fulfilment of Is. 61:1f. and as the typological counterpart to the stories of Elijah and Elisha. Jesus' ministry is thus 'eschatological' in the sense that 'this day' the Scriptures have come to fulfilment and the last days have begun. The era of salvation has arrived; it is the year of the Lord's favour, characterised by the preaching of good news to the needy and the performance of mighty works. Above all, the fulfilment of Scripture is to be found in the person of Jesus himself, who has been anointed with the Spirit and appears as the eschatological prophet – a figure who is to be identified with the Messiah and the Servant of Yahweh. It is through his word that forgiveness comes to men.

Jesus' message is brought first of all to the people of his home town. But when Jesus goes on to speak by implication of the preaching of the gospel and the performance of mighty works among the gentiles, Nazareth begins to take on the symbolical meaning of the Jewish nation. So the narrative takes on a more than literal significance; it becomes a paradigm not merely of the ministry of Jesus but also of the mission of the church (B. Reicke*, 51–53). For the story shows how the words of grace spoken by Jesus met with rejection from his own people (cf. Jn. 1:11). They cried out for confirmatory signs to be done in their midst, since they could not believe the bare words of the son of Joseph – he could hardly be a real prophet. Jesus answered their unbelief with the threat of departure to other people who would (it is implied) be more responsive. God's plan would find fulfilment in the extension of God's mission to the gentiles. This was more than the people of Nazareth could bear; they were filled with anger and would have done away with Jesus, but he escaped unharmed from their midst. There may well be here a symbolic prophecy of the coming passion and resurrection of Jesus, events which are kept before the reader's mind throughout the Gospel (Schütz, *passim*).

The weight of theological meaning which may be found in the story at once raises the question how far the narrative has been the subject of interpretation by the author in order to bring out its deeper significance. This question becomes all the more pressing when the relation of this narrative to the simpler one in Mk. 6:1–6 is considered. In the latter, Jesus visits Nazareth with his disciples and preaches on the Sabbath (though *what* he said is unrecorded); the people are amazed at his wisdom and mighty works, but cannot bring themselves to accept this evidence, since Jesus is merely the local carpenter. So Jesus comments on the lack of honour received by a prophet in his home, is unable to do any mighty works and is surprised by their lack of faith. The difficulties in this narrative have been brought out by E. Grässer*, but there is no need to be as sceptical as he is about its historicity. Whatever the historical basis to the incident, Mark and Luke have brought out its significance in different ways. (The view of Lane, 201 n. 2, that *two* different visits are recorded in the Gospels is most unlikely.)

For many scholars the present narrative is due to Lucan redaction of Mk. 6:1–6, perhaps with the aid of some material drawn from tradition. Thus Bultmann, 31, 122, 134, claims that 4:25–27 is a secondary creation from the anti-Jewish polemic of the gentile church which Luke has placed in a scene created on the basis of Mk.; for this theory he offers no evidence. Similar views are suggested by Dibelius, 106–108; R. C. Tannehill* and W. Eltester*.

Luce, 121, laid stress on the break between 4:22a and 22b, where acceptance and rejection of Jesus stand in uneasy juxtaposition, and posited that two incidents have been combined, 4:16–22a being peculiar to Lk., and 4:22b–30 being based on Mk. (cf. Lagrange, 146–148). The possibility that *three* incidents are combined here (4:16–22a, 22b–24, 25–30) is raised by Stuhlmueller, 131f., but on the whole he favours the view that vs. 25–30 are a Lucan theological addition.

Greater stress is laid on use of non-Marcan traditions by Leaney, 50–54, who thinks that vs. 16–22a, 23a, 25–30 rest on non-Marcan material. H. Schürmann* (cf. Schürmann, I, 241–244) holds that vs. 17–21 and 25–27 are additions to the original story as compared with Mk.; they were not, however, added by Luke since they show signs of pre-Lucan composition. It follows that the narrative is not the product of redaction of Mk. by Luke (cf. Schramm, 37), a conclusion confirmed by an examination of the parallel sections in the two accounts. Schürmann is inclined to allot the original narrative to Q rather than to Luke's special source, since it shows links with other Q material. This earlier form of the story in Lk. was not derived from Mk. since in various places it gives the impression of being more primitive; at the same time, however, it also represents a secondary form of the tradition, the new material showing the sort of use of Scripture found in synagogue homilies. Schmid, 110, adopts what is perhaps the least radical analysis. Accepting the view of B. Violet** and Jeremias, *Promise*, 44f., that there is no break in the middle of v. 22, he claims that only v. 24 need be regarded as an insertion from Mk. into Luke's narrative. If the attempt of C. Perrot* to find a background to the use of the OT in the Jewish lectionary system could be regarded as successful, this would strengthen the arguments of Schürmann and Schmid for the unity of the narrative at a pre-Lucan stage, but this approach remains problematical (L. C. Crockett*, 1966; D. Hill*, 172–177).

The variety of analyses offered shows that there is no simple solution to the problems of the narrative. Let us examine it again point by point: 1. It is certain that Luke knew Mk. 6:1–6 and regarded this narrative as a substitute for it, but there is no evidence that he has used it as a source here (so rightly Schramm, 37). 2. The opening proclamation of Jesus can be regarded as authentic, since it coheres with other examples of his teaching inspired by Is. 61:1f. It may well have been spoken by him as his typical 'synagogue sermon' in a variety of places, and could have been spoken in Nazareth. Although Mark does not tell us what Jesus said in Nazareth, he must have said *something*, and it is not unlikely that Mark has omitted the details, as he often does. It is true that here the issue is one of christology, whereas in Mk. it is one of the wisdom and signs performed by Jesus, but these are not incompatible. The wisdom is that manifested by the prophet, and Mark (or his source) has abbreviated the incident while nevertheless retaining awareness of the fact that it was as a prophet that Jesus appeared (Mk. 6:4). An expression of a prophetic call is to be expected at the outset of a prophetic ministry. 3. We accept the view that there is no break at v. 22, such as would justify the assumption that two narratives (or accounts of two separate incidents) have been combined. 4. But the awkwardness of the transition and the difference in wording from Mk. suggest that the narrative may have been elaborated at this point; the wording of the people's response to Jesus is better preserved in Mk. 5. Similarly, the reply of Jesus is probably preserved more accurately in Mk. Luke's wording has been altered to fit the new position of the scene (4:23) and has a more literary flavour. The addition in vs. 25–27 fits in closely with the theme of Jesus as prophet, but its universalistic tone is strange at this early point in the ministry of Jesus and hence it may well be from another context. It can certainly be authentic teaching of Jesus. 6. There is some tension between the murderous threat with which the story concludes (vs. 28–30) and the milder conclusion in Mk. 6:5f. The Lucan motif has parallels elsewhere (Jn. 8:59; 10:39) and is in itself quite plausible: Jesus is threatened with the fate of a false prophet. But how is this to be reconciled with Mark's picture of Jesus performing some acts of healing at the end of his visit? (To place the miracles earlier in the visit (Mk. 6:2) causes tension with v. 23.) Why again should Mark have suppressed the threat of murder? But perhaps the force of these objections should not be pressed too far. It is difficult to see why anyone should have invented the conclusion of Luke's story, and it is more probable that Mark's tradition has abbreviated the story.

See B. Violet, 'Zum rechten Verständnis der Nazareth-Perikope', ZNW 37, 1938, 251–271; Jeremias, *Promise*, 44f.; A. Finkel, 'Jesus' Sermon at Nazareth (Luk 4, 16–30)', in O. Betz, 106–115; H. Anderson, 'Broadening Horizons: The Rejection at Nazareth Perikope of Lk 4, 16–30 in Light of Recent Critical Trends', *Interpretation* 18, 1964, 259–275; Hahn, 394–396; Flender, 150–157; Voss, 156–160; L. C. Crockett, 'Luke iv 16–30 and the Jewish Lectionary Cycle: A Word of Caution', JJS 17, 1966, 13–46; id. 'Luke 4, 25–27 and Jewish-Gentile Relations in Luke-Acts', JBL 88, 1969, 177–183; Rese, 143–154; H. Schürmann, 'Zur Traditionsgeschichte der Nazareth-Perikope Lk 4, 16–30', in Descamps, 187–205; Marshall, 118–128; D. Hill, 'The Rejection of Jesus at Nazareth (Luke IV:16–30)', Nov.T 13, 1971, 161–180; E. Grässer, 'Jesus in Nazareth (Mc 6:1–6a)' (originally published in English in NTS 16, 1969–70, 1–23), in W. Eltester (ed.), *Jesus in Nazareth*, Berlin, 1972, 1–37; A. Strobel, 'Die Ausrufung des Jobeljahres in der Nazareth-predigt Jesu: zur apokalyptischen Tradition Lc 4, 16–30', in ibid. 38–50; R. C. Tannehill, 'The Mission of Jesus according to Luke iv 16–30', in ibid. 51–75; W. Eltester, 'Israel im lukanischen Werk und die Nazareth-perikope', in ibid. 76–147; C. Perrot, 'Luc 4, 16–30 et la lecture biblique de l'ancienne synagogue', in *Revue des*

Sciences Religieuses, 47, 1973, 324–340; B. Reicke, 'Jesus in Nazareth – Lk 4, 14–30', in Balz, 47–55; J. A. Sanders, 'From Isaiah 61 to Luke 4', in J. Neusner (ed.), *Christianity, Judaism and other Greco-Roman Cults: Studies for Morton Smith at Sixty,* Leiden, 1975, Pt I, 75–106.

(16) The opening of the story resembles Mk. 6:1f., but without any signs of literary dependence. Schürmann, I, 227, understands the opening καὶ ἦλθεν against the background of 4:18, 43 and 3:16, so that Jesus 'comes' into the world and to Nazareth in particular at the command of the Father who sent him. This reads too much into a verse which rather gives an example – but a supremely important one – of the activity of Jesus described in 4:14f. The form Ναζαρά is found elsewhere only in Mt. 4:13**, a passage which may contain the remnant of a tradition of Jesus' activity in Nazareth before he settled in Capernaum (Lk. 4:31); i.e. the unusual form of the name may reflect a common, non-Marcan tradition. Streeter, 206f., regarded this mention of Nazareth as the cue to Luke to insert the present narrative here; Schürmann, I, 227f., uses it as evidence that the narrative itself occurred in Q at this early point.

The brief clause 'where he was brought up' reminds the reader of 2:39–51 and prepares for the reaction in v. 22. οὖ, 'where', is Lucan (5x; Acts, 9x). τρέφω (12:24; 23:29*; Acts 12:20*) is 'to nourish', here 'to bring up a child' (cf. ἀνατρέφω, Acts 7:20f.; 22:3). Jesus' visit to the synagogue probably reflected his normal custom since childhood (κατὰ τὸ εἰωθὸς αὐτῷ), but the parallel expression in Acts 17:2 suggests that here the reference is rather to his regular use of the synagogue for teaching (4:15). ἡ ἡμέρα τῶν σαββάτων (Acts 13:14; 16:13) is equivalent to ἡ ἡμέρα τοῦ σαββάτου (13:14, 16; 14:5); the use of the plural of σάββατον for the singular is well-attested (AG s.v.). Here Jesus stood up on the platform to read the Scriptures.

The present passage is the oldest known account of a synagogue service (Acts 13:14f.; Schürer, II:2, 52–89; SB IV:1, 154–171; W. Schrage, TDNT VII, 798–841 (disappointing on details of worship); P. Billerbeck, 'Ein Synagogengottesdienst in Jesu Tagen', ZNW 55, 1965, 143–161). After private prayer on entry to the building by the worshippers there was a public confession of the Jewish faith in the Shema (Dt. 6:4–9; 11:13–21), followed by prayers, including the Tephillah and the Shemoneh Esreh. Then came the centre of the worship, the reading of the Scriptures. A passage from the Pentateuch was read, according to a fixed scheme of lections, by several members of the congregation in turn, with an Aramaic paraphrase. There was also a lesson from the prophets; in later times this too was according to a fixed lectionary, but it is a matter of dispute whether this system existed in the first century, and, if so, what form it took (L. Morris, *The New Testament and the Jewish Lectionaries,* London, 1964, 11–34; L. C. Crockett* (1966); C. Perrot*). It is safest to assume that there was at least some freedom of choice of prophetic reading in the first century. Following the readings was a prayer, and then came a sermon, if there was somebody competent present to give one (Acts 13:15). Finally the Qaddish prayer was recited. The readers for the day were appointed before the service began. Schürmann, I, 227, argues that this was the first time that Jesus had stood up to read in the synagogue – hence the air of expectation – and that he did so on his own initiative, contrary to the custom. Neither point is sufficiently well-grounded. Possibly Jesus had informally requested permission to read before the service began, and Luke has not gone into the details of the arrangement.

(17) ἐπιδίδωμι simply means 'to hand over' (11:11f.; 24:30, 42; Acts 15:30; 27:15; Mt. 7:9f.**). The meaning 'to hand over in addition' (LSJ s.v.) would imply that Jesus read from the Pentateuch and then from the prophets, but this is less likely. It is to be assumed that Jesus was handed the particular book which he requested. Since Luke elsewhere uses βίβλος (3:4), the choice of βιβλίον (4:20*) in this passage may be due to his source. The word means a 'scroll', similar to those found at Qumran, in this case containing the prophecy of Isaiah. (The inversion of τοῦ προφήτου Ἡσαΐου in TR; Diglot is improbable in view of the external evidence; Lucan usage is indecisive). ἀναπτύσσω**, 'to unroll', is the appropriate verb to use (cf. πτύσσω, (4:20**), 'to fold up, roll up'), and is attested by ℵ D Θ f1 f13 pl latt; TR; the v.l. ἀνοίξας, though well-attested (A B L W pc; Synopsis; Diglot), may be due to scribes more familiar with codices than scrolls (Metzger, 137). The suggestion that the scroll opened by chance at the appropriate place (Wellhausen, 9) is alien to the sense of εὗρεν and to the stress on the initiative of Jesus. The pluperfect ἦν γεγραμμένον (4:16; 5:1, 17; BD 352) suggests 'where it stood in writing'; it corresponds to a perfect tense in non-historic sequence.

(18) The quotation, also found independently in Barn. 14:9, was already used at Qumran with reference to the work of the Teacher of Righteousness (1QH 18:14; Braun, Qumran, I, 87) and also in the Melchizedek document (11QMelch 6–9). It is taken from Is. 61:1f. LXX with certain changes (Holtz, 39–41): 1. UBS omits ἰάσασθαι τοὺς συντετριμμένους τὴν καρδίαν, a phrase read by A Θ f1 pm f (vg) syᵖ boᵖᵗ Ir (Hipp); TR. It is perhaps easier to explain the longer text as due to assimilation to the LXX (cf. 4:4); Holtz, 40, suggests that the phrase was absent from Luke's copy of the LXX. Or possibly Luke wished to reserve ἰάομαι for cases of physical healing. But it is possible that the phrase originally stood in Luke (Schürmann, I, 229 n. 58; Grundmann, 118; B. Reicke*, 48f.). The words would give a basis for the 'physician' saying in v. 23, and they may be alluded to in 5:17. B. Reicke argues that when the phrase is retained the quotation consists of four couplets. 2. The phrase ἀποστεῖλαι τεθραυσμένους ἐν ἀφέσει comes from Is. 58:6 LXX. Most scholars argue that such an insertion could not have been made in the actual course of a synagogue reading, and that hence the addition is due to Christian exegetical activity, possibly in order to introduce the concept of forgiveness. C. Perrot*, 332f., sees a possible link between the two passages in Jewish liturgical reading, and B. Reicke*,

49, holds that Jesus could well have acted in an unusual way in virtue of his prophetic authority. 3. In v. 19 κηρῦξαι replaces LXX καλέσαι; the familiar Christian technical term has been used. 4. The final phrase in the LXX καὶ ἡμέραν ἀνταποδόσεως, which refers to divine vengeance on the nations, has been omitted, perhaps deliberately so as to stress the grace of God (Jeremias, *Promise*, 38).

The punctuation is disputed. Most editors place a stop after πτωχοῖς so that εὐαγγελίσασθαι is dependent on ἔχρισεν (UBS). Others put a stop after με, so that εὐαγγελίσασθαι is dependent on ἀπέσταλκεν (NEB; JB; E. Nestle, 'Luc 4, 18:19', ZNW 2, 1901, 153–157; 'Zu Luc 4, 18.19', ibid. 8, 1907, 77f.; Schürmann, I, 230; B. Reicke*, 48). The latter punctuation agrees with that of the MT and LXX, and fits in with Luke's interpretation of the quotation in 4:43; it is to be preferred.

In its original context the prophecy may refer to the self-consciousness of the prophet that he is called to make known the good news of God's intervention to help his people, expressed in a variety of metaphors. But since the passage uses a language and style reminiscent of the earlier Servant passages it may have been interpreted in terms of the Servant of Yahweh. F. F. Bruce, *This is That*, Exeter, 1969, 90, suggests that Is. 61 itself may be 'the earliest interpretation of the Servant'. Whether or not the identification was made in Judaism, the similarity to the Servant passages was probably evident to the early church, and possibly even to Jesus himself (cf. C. H. Dodd, *According to the Scriptures*, London, 1952, 94). Some such connection was made at Qumran; in 11QMelch Is. 52:7 and 61:1f. are linked together (M. de Jonge and A. S. van der Woude, '11Q Melchizedek and the New Testament', NTS 12, 1965–66, 301–326).

In Lk. the point is not the identification of the speaker as a messianic figure, but rather that the functions of this OT figure are now fulfilled in Jesus who has been anointed with the Spirit for this purpose. The Spirit is upon Jesus (3:22; cf. 1:35; 2:25; Acts 1:8; *et al.*) now that God has anointed him (χρίω, Acts 4:27; 10:38; Heb. 1:9; cf. 2 Cor. 1:21**). In Is. 61 the anointing is clearly that of a prophet (cf. 1 Ki. 19:16; CD 2:12; 6:1; 1QM 11:7), and in view of 4:23 the same motif should be seen here, although Schürmann, I, 229, thinks that Luke himself reinterpreted his source in terms of a 'messianic', i.e. kingly, anointing. Ultimately, the concepts of the eschatological prophet and the Messiah merge (Marshall, 125–128).

The anointed prophet is sent to proclaim good news (1:19; and especially 4:43; 9:48; 10:16) to the poor. These are the people who are most in need of divine help and who wait upon God to hear his word (6:20 note). The following infinitival phrases bring out more fully through various metaphors the significance of the preaching. First, if the longer text is read, the message brings healing (ἰάομαι, 5:17 and frequently) to those who are broken-hearted (συντρίβω, 9:39; Mt. 12:20; Pss. 34:18 (33:19); 51:17 (50:19); 147:3 (146:3); Is. 61:1). Note the link with the beatitudes (Mt. 5:3f.). Second, there is the announcement of release to prisoners of war. For κηρύσσω see 3:3 and especially 8:1. For αἰχμάλωτος** cf. Rom. 16:7; Col. 4:10; Phm. 23. In normal Christian use ἄφεσις (4:10b) means 'forgiveness', and it is possible that the Christian reader should hear this undertone in the word (R. Bultmann, TDNT I, 511). Third, there is recovery of sight (ἀνάβλεψις**) for the blind (7:22; Is. 42:7). Here the reference is probably metaphorical, even if Christian readers would recognise the mighty works as physical symbols of spiritual salvation. Note that the LXX differs here from the MT ('release to the prisoners'; cf. France, 252f.). The fourth phrase is from Is. 58:6. ἀποστεῖλαι ... ἐν ἀφέσει is a circumlocution for 'to set free', and θραύω** is 'to break, bruise'. The insertion adds nothing to the sense, and it is hard to see why it was made (Holtz, 39–41), unless perhaps we are to stress the idea of forgiveness in ἄφεσις.

(19) Finally, the prophet announces the year 'acceptable' (δεκτός, 4:24; Acts 10:35; 2 Cor. 6:2; Phil. 4:18**) to the Lord, i.e. 'the year of the Lord's favour' (MT), the year which God has graciously appointed in order to show his salvation (cf. εὐδοκία, 2:14). Concretely, the allusion is to the 'year of jubilee', the year of liberation among men appointed by Yahweh (Lv. 25) and now made symbolic of his own saving acts. It was held every fifty years, and during it the fields lay fallow, persons returned to their own homes, debts were relinquished and slaves set free. A. Strobel* (also, id. Kerygma und Apokalyptik, Göttingen, 1967, 105–111) argues that behind Jesus' quotation lay the historical fact of a jubilee year in which he returned to his home (Lv. 25:10). It can be calculated that AD 26–27 was a jubilee year (cf. 3:1 note). Thus Jesus' citation took account of the actual jubilee year in which his ministry began and from which it gained a background of eschatological expectancy (cf. J. D. Yoder, The Politics of Jesus, Grand Rapids, 1972). Attractive as this suggestion is, it is hard to fit it into the chronology of the ministry.

(20) After the reading, Jesus rolls up the scroll and hands it back to the synagogue attendant. ὑπηρέτης (cf. Mt. 5:25) is generally regarded as the equivalent of ḥazzān (SB IV:1, 147–149; but see K. H. Rengstorf, TDNT VIII, 530–544, who doubts this identification). Jesus then sits down, a phrase which might simply mean that he resumes his seat in the congregation, but here no doubt refers to taking up the posture of a teacher (Mt. 26:55; SB I, 997; IV:1, 185; C. Schneider, TDNT III, 443. A standing position was sometimes adopted (Acts 13:16; Philo, Spec. 2:62), possibly under Greek influence). The scene is described in detail, not merely for the benefit of non-Jewish readers, but to enable the reader to sense the tense expectancy as everybody present looked intently at Jesus. πάντων is stressed by its position (especially if it is separated from οἱ ὀφθαλμοί by inversion as in D Θ pm lat; TR; Diglot – but the external evidence is weak). ἀτενίζω is Lucan (22:56; Acts, 10x; 2 Cor. 3:7, 13**).

(21) ἤρξατο may be simply a case of Semitic redundant usage, es-

pecially if what follows is to be regarded as a summary of the sermon rather than its opening words. It could simply refer to the transition from reading to preaching (cf. Plummer, 123; B. Reicke*, 49). But surely what follows is the arresting opening of a sermon, so that the use of the verb is justified. Perhaps too Luke wishes to stress that these are the opening words of Jesus' public ministry (cf. Acts 10:36f.; Schürmann, I, 231). A. Finkel* thinks that Jesus went on to pronounce the beatitudes, but this is more than speculative. σήμερον is emphatic. It refers primarily to the actual day on which Jesus spoke as being the day when prophecy began to be fulfilled (cf. 2:11), but this original 'today' has become part of the era of fulfilment, the 'year of the Lord's favour' which has now come and remains present (2 Cor. 6:2). Hence this 'today' does not refer only to the past, so that salvation belongs to the past and not to the present (Conzelmann, 30f.; but see Schürmann, I, 233 and n. 79). The 'today' of Jesus is still addressed to all readers of the Gospel and assures them that the era of salvation is present (cf. E. Fuchs, TDNT VII, 269–275). The particular Scripture quoted (αὕτη) has been fulfilled in that what it foretold has come to pass (1:20 note). The perfect tense (πεπλήρωται) is almost equivalent to a present (A. Debrunner, in TDNT V, 554 n. 108; cf. BD 341). The phraseology is close to Mk. 1:15, but whereas the stress there is on the imminence of the kingdom, here it is on the coming of Jesus himself. This led Wellhausen, 9f., to object that the message of Jesus, which was about the kingdom of God, has here been changed into a proclamation about himself. The objection fails to recognise how closely the person of Jesus and the kingdom are linked (cf. B. Gärtner, 'The Person of Jesus and the Kingdom of God', Theology Today, 27, 1970, 32–43). In any case, it is the teaching of Jesus which is here emphasised. The fulfilment of the Scripture takes place as the audience listens to the message (ἐν τοῖς ὠσὶν ὑμῶν; cf. Lagrange, 140; F. Horst, TDNT V, 543–559; the clause does not mean, 'This Scripture which is still ringing in your ears has been fulfilled', pace Klostermann, 63).

(22) μαρτυρέω, 'to bear witness to', can be taken in the sense 'to praise', with a dative of advantage (Acts 13:22; 14:3; 15:8; 22:5; Gal. 4:15; Col. 4:13), or in the sense 'to bear witness against', i.e. 'to condemn' (Mt. 23:31; cf. Sus. 41; Jn. 7:7; 18:23). The former meaning is adopted here by most commentators (including H. Strathmann, TDNT IV, 474–514, especially 496). It is open to the objection that it produces an awkward transition between the people's praise of Jesus in v. 22a, and the indignant surprise which follows in v. 22b and leads to mounting hostility in the rest of the story. This awkwardness is avoided if we adopt the latter sense ('sie machten ihm Vorwürfe'; B. Violet*; Jeremias, Promise, 44f.; Grundmann, 121). While Lucan usage favours the former translation, there are signs that the present narrative is dependent on a source, in which case Luke may have taken over an unusual meaning for the word. The parallel narrative in Mk. suggests that the attitude at

Nazareth was one of uniform hostility. Again, it is hard to credit Luke with an awkward transition in the middle of the verse. The alternative is to suppose that the people's initial favourable response was swiftly followed by recollection that he was merely Joseph's son and hence a reaction against him. This is perfectly possible, and on either view there is no need to find a seam in the narrative at this point.

A similar ambiguity affects θαυμάζω which can express both admiration (7:9) and opposition (Jn. 7:15; cf. Lk. 11:38). For the latter sense see G. Bertram, TDNT III, 38. The reaction was due to Jesus' λόγοι τῆς χάριτος. This could simply refer to 'gracious, pleasing words' (Ps. 44:3 LXX; Col. 4:6; Zahn, 239; Creed, 67), but is more likely to signify 'words filled with divine grace' (Acts 14:3; 20:24, 32); Flender, 153f., and H. Conzelmann, TDNT IX, 392 n. 153, think that Luke is consciously playing on both senses of the word, the people of Nazareth failing to see through the pleasing words to the message of salvation contained in them. The use of ἐκπορευομένοις ἐκ τοῦ στόματος αὐτοῦ is reminiscent of Dt. 8:3 LXX (cf. Lk. 4:4 v.l.!), and may suggest that Luke saw Jesus' words as divine words, bringing life and salvation (Schürmann, I, 234f.). If so, the point may be that Jesus' words were purely gracious; he omitted reference to the vengeance of God (Is. 61:2; Jeremias, *Promise,* 45, following K. Bornhäuser). Schürmann, I, 235 n. 95, dismisses this suggestion as fanciful historicising, but the references to gentiles later in the story and similar phenomena on other occasions (7:22f.) indicate that the hypothesis is well founded. What is doubtful is simply whether the people of Nazareth would have appreciated a point that was clear enough to Luke (and to Jesus). Grundmann, 121f., suggests that the people did not like the implication that they belonged to the poor and needy to whom the gospel was addressed. But the basic difficulty was that it was Jesus who was saying this. Rhetorically they asked, 'Is not this fellow Joseph's son?' (The καί will be adversative if θαυμάζω is interpreted in a favourable sense). The words move from surprise to indignation and hostility. They do not stand in opposition to the virgin birth (*pace* Luce, 121), since the reader knows that the description is inadequate. υἱὸς Ἰωσήφ (without the article) reflects Semitic usage (contrast Jn. 6:42). In Mk. 6:3 there is no mention of Joseph and Jesus is 'the carpenter, the son of Mary'. Schürmann, I, 236, claims that Luke's form is more primitive, and that Mark may reflect a church formulation in the light of the virgin birth. On the other hand, Mark's form may reflect Jewish polemic against Jesus as the illegitimate son of Mary (E. Stauffer, 'Jeschu ben Mirjam', in Ellis, *Neotestamentica,* 119–128; *contra* H. K. McArthur, 'Son of Mary', Nov.T 15, 1973, 38–58). If so, Mark may have preserved the original saying, which is a studied insult rather than merely a criticism of a 'local lad' for putting on airs and claiming to be a prophet. Such a strong rejection of Jesus is needed to account for the force of his reply.

(23) πάντως is 'certainly' (Acts 21:22; 28:4; Paul, 5x**) or

'perhaps' (H. J. Cadbury, 'Lexical Notes on Luke-Acts. I', JBL 44, 1925, 214–227, especially 223–227). The future ἐρεῖτε probably means 'You will go on to say to me' (cf. 11:30). It has been argued that according to Luke's account the mighty deeds at Capernaum *follow* this incident, and therefore here Jesus is prophesying what the people of Nazareth will say in the future (Wellhausen, 10); alternatively, Luke has changed the tense when he moved the story from an original position in his source after an account of Jesus' ministry in Capernaum (Grundmann, 122). But the first explanation is adequate, since mighty deeds elsewhere were implied in 4:14f. (B. Reicke*, 48). παραβολή is used as an equivalent to Hebrew *māšāl*, 'proverb' (1 Sa. 10:12; *et al.*; F. Hauck, TDNT V, 744–761, especially 747–749). For λέγω with a direct object see 5:36; ἡ παραβολὴ αὕτη is a Lucan phrase. The proverb itself has several parallels: 'Physician, heal your own limp' (Gn. R 23 (15c), in SB II, 156); ἄλλων ἰατρὸς αὐτὸς ἕλκεσιν βρύων (Euripides, Frg. 1071); 'A doctor who cures other people and is himself ill' (Arabic proverb, Bultmann, 112 n.). Cf. especially οὐδὲ ἰατρὸς ποιεῖ θεραπείας εἰς τοὺς γεινώσκοντας αὐτόν (P. Oxy. 1:6; G. Thomas 31). It has been argued that this form of the saying fits the situation better than the form in Lk. (Bultmann, 30f.), but more probably it is an adaptation of the saying in Lk. to bring out its meaning (Creed, 68). ἑαυτόν is a parabolic reference to Jesus' home town (πατρίς, Mk. 6:1). The people of Nazareth have heard – possibly with scepticism (Morris, 107) – of all that Jesus has done elsewhere; let him now do the same at home. ὅσος has the weak sense 'whatever'. ἀκούω takes an accusative and participle construction (BD 416). εἰς is used Hellenistically for ἐν (BD 205). For Καφαρναούμ see 4:31; 7:1; 10:15*. The mention of actions by Jesus seems unmotivated in Lk. and perhaps presupposes the kind of comment made in Mk. 6:2. Two accusations may be present: 1. Jesus should bring the same blessings to his own people as he has brought to Capernaum. There is jealousy of a rival town. 2. Jesus should provide signs to attest the verbal claims which he has made. Having heard Jesus speak, the people expect that he will now go on to do mighty works, but in fact since his words have not met with faith Jesus cannot go on to perform signs. He will not perform signs to satisfy human jealousy or lack of faith. Rather, he sees a further proverb fulfilled in Nazareth.

(24) The Hebrew word ἀμήν occurs only 6x in Lk. (12:37; 18:17, 29; 21:32; 23:43; J. C. O'Neill, 'The Six Amen Sayings in Luke', JTS ns 10, 1959, 1–9). Elsewhere Luke does not take it over from his sources and substitutes other phrases (ἀληθῶς, 9:27 (Mk. 9:1); 12:44 (Mt. 24:47); 21:3 (Mk. 12:43); γάρ, 22:18 (Mk. 14:25); ναί, 11:51 (Mt. 23:36); no equivalent, 10:12 (Mt. 10:15); 10:24 (Mt. 13:17)). H. Schlier, TDNT I, 335–338, and J. Jeremias, *Abba*, 145–152 (*The Prayers of Jesus,* London, 1967, 112–115) have argued that the use of the word to introduce an authoritative utterance (as distinct from the normal Jewish use, to confirm what has already been said) represents

one of Jesus' characteristic and authentic forms of speech. This argument remains cogent despite the criticisms made by V. Hasler, *Amen,* Zürich, 1969, and K. Berger, *Die Amen-Worte Jesu,* Berlin, 1970 (Jeremias, *Theology,* I, 36 n. 2); see also J. Strugnell, ' "Amen I say unto you" in the Sayings of Jesus and in Early Christian Literature', HTR 67, 1974, 177–190.

The form of the saying is different from that in the parallels. Jesus says that no prophet is accepted in his native place: δεκτός is used here of welcome and acceptance by men (contrast 4:19; Acts 10:35). It is proverbial that a great man is often regarded with suspicion and even rejection among his own people. (Dio Chrysostom 30 (47), 6: πᾶσι τοῖς φιλοσόφοις χαλεπὸς ἐν τῇ πατρίδι ὁ βίος; Philostratus, Vita Apoll. 1:354:12: ἡ πατρὶς ἀγνοεῖ; but there do not appear to be any Jewish parallels, SB I, 678). The form in P. Oxy. 1:6 (G. Thomas 31) is close to Lk. and is probably dependent on it: οὐκ ἔστιν δεκτὸς προφήτης ἐν τῇ πα(τ)ρίδι αὐτ(o)ῦ (Schürmann, *Untersuchungen,* 229f.); for the view that Thomas has the original form see Schramm, 37 n. 2; R. M. Wilson, *Studies in the Gospel of Thomas,* London, 1960, 60f. A similar form of the saying is found in Jn. 4:44 (Dodd, 239f.). Yet another form appears in Mk. 6:4 with a double negative and expansion at the end. Mark's expansion is probable secondary, and in any case omission of any reference to Jesus' family enables the saying to be understood in terms of Jesus' homeland as well as literally of his home town. The use of ἀμήν and the existence of the Johannine parallel show that Luke is not here dependent on Mk., but he may have edited the saying (δεκτός may be Lucan).

(25) What is to happen with regard to Nazareth, namely that Jesus will leave it and bring the gospel to those outside his home town, finds a parallel in the way in which Elijah and Elisha brought help to the gentiles rather than to the needy people of Israel – and a further parallel in the way in which Jesus, rejected by his own people, will bring the gospel to the gentiles (in the mission of the church). To be sure, the OT does not say that the action of the prophets was a conscious turning away from Israel to the gentiles. But in the case of Elijah the land was under divine judgment for turning to Baal, and so it is not surprising that God showed mercy to Elijah (and hence to the widow) outside Israel. The interpretation of the period of drought as $3\frac{1}{2}$ years, a figure suggestive of divine retribution, confirms this interpretation.

The force of the illustrations, however, is not crystal clear. 1. The point may be that the people of Nazareth should not make exclusive claims upon Jesus (v. 23): he has work to do elsewhere. 2. Because Nazareth has refused him (v. 24), Jesus has been sent (like Elijah) elsewhere. 3. Although Nazareth has rejected him, other places have accepted him, just as Elijah and Elisha found acceptance outside Israel. L. C. Crockett* (1969) has gone further and seen here a model of Jewish/gentile relations in the church. The difficulty of establishing the exact force of the verses raises some doubt as to whether they originally belong to the story, and they perhaps stem from an originally independent saying of Jesus.

ἐπ' ἀληθείας (20:21; 22:59; Acts 4:27; 10:34; Mk. 12:14, 32) may here be a substitute for an original ἀμήν, laying stress on the following saying. (If so, this would confirm the genuineness of the saying, but also suggest that originally it did not follow v. 24.) After ὑμῖν many MSS add ὅτι (so *Diglot*). For allusions to the Elijah and Elisha stories in the Gospels see Wink, 44; J. Jeremias, TDNT II, 928–941. Although the typology is particularly prominent in Lk., it is based on Jesus' own usage (cf. France, 48). Grundmann, 123, sees a 'fulfilment' of the typology in 7:11–17 and 17:12–19; Luke passes over the closer parallel to vs. 25f. in Mk. 7:24–30.

The passives ἐκλείσθη and ἐπέμφθη (v. 26) refer to God's action. For ἐπί with accusative of a period of time see 18:4; Acts, 9x (contrast 10:35). The 3½ year period of famine appears in Jas. 5:7 (cf. Rev. 11:2, 6), but in 1 Ki. 18:1 the period is simply 3 years. 1. We may simply have a round number (half of the round number 7) for a long time (SB III, 760f.). J. Jeremias, TDNT II, 934, thinks that a distinct Palestinian tradition is reflected. 2. The longer period here may be due to inclusion of the period from the latter rain in April to the former rain in October in the final year of the famine (E. F. F. Bishop, 'Three and a Half Years', Exp.T 61, 1949–50, 126f.; Ellis, 98). 3. A period of 3½ years is symbolic of persecution and distress (Dn. 7:25; 12:7; Rev. 11:2f.; 12:6, 14; 13:5; Jos. Bel. 1:32), and this symbolism may have been incorporated here (Schürmann, I, 238 n. 122). λιμός can mean 'hunger' (15:17) or 'famine' (15:14; 21:11; Acts 7:11; 11:28; it is usually masc. (2 Ki. 6:25), but fem. in 15:14; Acts 11:28). γῆ will mean 'land' rather than 'world' (SB II, 156).

(26) The construction πρός οὐδεμίαν ... εἰ μή may be exceptive ('to none of them ... except to one of them') or adversative ('to none of them ... but to somebody else'); here the latter sense is required (Rev. 21:27; Gal. 1:19 is ambiguous). The wording may reflect Aramaic *lâ* ... *'ellâ*, with εἰ μή equivalent to ἀλλά (Gn. 1:7; 1 Cor. 7:17; BD 448⁸), but it is also found in Classical Greek (Black, 114). Σάρεπτα** is Zarephath, between Tyre and Sidon (1 Ki. 17:9; Jos. Ant. 8:320); the adjective Σιδώνιος (Acts 12:20**; sc. χώρα) brings out the heathen character of the place (cf. 10:13). The phrase γυνὴ χήρα is from 1 Ki. 17:9f. LXX; hence there is not the slightest need for Wellhausen's conjecture (10f.) that Aramaic *'rmy'*, 'Syrian', has been misread as *'rml'*, 'widow', especially since the pagan setting has already been expressed by Luke.

(27) The story of Naaman (2 Ki. 5) is told in a similar pattern. That he alone was cured, despite the fact of other lepers in Israel, could be deduced from 2 Ki. 7:3. For λεπρός (7:22; 17:12) see 5:12 note. Ἐλισαῖος** is named here only in the NT.

(28) The effect of Jesus' words – vs. 23f. would be sufficient – was to fill the audience with rage as they listened (present participle!); for θυμός* (Acts 19:28*) see F. Büchsel, TDNT III, 167f. The reaction is similar to that in Mk. 6:3 (σκανδαλίζομαι), admittedly before Jesus' final words to them; it is the culmination of their resentment against a prophet whose words they failed to appreciate and who did nothing to justify his claims (cf. Dt. 13:2ff.).

(29) So they rose up from their places in the synagogue to attack Jesus; ἀνίσταμαι is especially used of hostile action (Acts 6:9; 7:54, 57). They forced Jesus outside the town (ἐκβάλλω, Acts 7:58; Lv. 24:14) and took him up to a brow (ὀφρῦς**) of the hill on which the town was built with the intention of throwing him down (κατακρημνίζω**; ὥστε is used of unfulfilled purpose, 9:52; 10:20; BD 390; 391³). The act envisaged is not a formal execution but lynch law – and on the Sabbath at that. It may have been intended to stone Jesus (cf. Jn. 8:59; Acts 7:54ff.; Sanh. 6; J. Blinzler, 'The Jewish Punishment of Stoning in the New Testament Period', in Bammel, 147–161). Since the attempt did not succeed, it is hard to guess what was intended. The geography is not clear. Nazareth was not built on top of a hill, but on the side of a valley. B. Reicke*, 51, stresses that ὀφρύος is anarthrous and means a cliff near the village; there were in fact suitable cliffs in the neighbourhood (Grundmann, 123).

(30) But Jesus passed through the midst of the crowd and went his way (Jn. 7:30; 8:59; 10:39). It is not clear whether a miraculous escape is meant. The Johannine parallels (cf. P. Eger. 2:30f.) express the point that his hour had not yet come. Schürmann, I, 240, finds a fulfilment of Ps. 91:11–13, and various commentators see an anticipation of the passion and resurrection. The shadow of rejection hangs over the ministry of Jesus from the outset.

iii. Jesus' Work at Capernaum 4:31–44

From the point of view of source criticism a new section of Lk. begins here, based on Mk. 1:21–39. Luke has already covered the material in Mk. 1:1–15 with the aid of other sources. He replaces the account of the call of the disciples in Mk. 1:16–20 with the narrative in 5:1–11, but leaves this story over until he has first given us information about the ministry of Jesus; the preaching of the good news precedes the call of the disciples to share in the task. The content of the present section is determined by the story in Mk. After an introductory comment on the teaching of Jesus in the synagogue (4:31f.) there follow the stories of the exorcism of a demoniac in the synagogue (4:33–37) and of the healing of Peter's mother-in-law (4:38f.). What is evidently meant to be an account of a typical day in the ministry of Jesus closes with a general account of healings in the evening (4:40f.); next morning Jesus departs for a wider sphere of work (4:42–44) – he is not tied to Capernaum any more than he is to Nazareth. Thus the opening account of Jesus' teaching (4:16–30) is matched by a description of his mighty works, but these too are placed in the context of preaching and teaching; they bear testimony to him as the Holy One of God, the Son of God and the Messiah.

(a) Teaching in the Synagogue 4:31–32

The account of the mighty works is set against a background of authoritative teaching, so that Jesus' teaching and mighty works are seen to reflect the same prophetic authority. This framework is variously regarded as an integral part of the following miracle story (Taylor, 171) or as a Marcan transition (Bultmann, 223; Schweizer, *Markus,* 26).

(31) κατέρχομαι (9:37; Acts, 13x; Jas. 3:15**; diff. Mk. εἰσπορεύομαι) is the appropriate word to use for a descent from Nazareth in the hills (over 1200 ft. high) to the lakeside (686 ft. below sea level). Capernaum is described as a πόλις τῆς Γαλιλαίας (diff. Mk.), an elucidation for Luke's readers which maintains the theme announced in 4:14; contrast 4:44. In Mt. 4:13–16 Jesus' ministry there is regarded as the fulfilment of prophecy, but there is no hint of this in Lk. Schürmann, I, 246f., would assign the mention of Galilee to the use of Q and place this verse in its original setting before the visit to Nazareth; but the evidence is weak, and Lucan redaction is a more probable explanation of the phrase (Schramm, 86).

Jesus' activity is characterised as teaching (4:15; periphrastic imperfect, as in Mk. 1:22). It is debatable whether the reference is to a period of teaching over some time or to the particular occasion when Jesus was interrupted by the demoniac. Decision depends on whether ἐν τοῖς σάββασιν refers to several Sabbaths (Easton, 54; Schürmann, I, 246 n. 175) or to one (Klostermann, 66; Luce, 123; Dietrich, 19 n. 7). The parallel in Mk. is no doubt meant as a singular (Taylor, 172). Luke nowhere uses τὰ σάββατα with a definitely plural meaning (possibly 6:2); he can use the plural with a singular meaning in the phrase ἡ ἡμέρα τῶν σαββάτων (4:16). But he often alters Mark's plural to a singular (6:1, 7, 9) and generally prefers the singular. A similar problem arises in 13:10, where teaching is followed by a mighty work; here the plural may be due to a source, and probably the meaning is singular. On the whole, the singular meaning is more likely here.

(32) ἐκπλήσσομαι (2:48 note) indicates amazement; the subject is to be supplied from the preceding αὐτούς (v. 31). The reaction to Jesus' teaching is the same as that to his mighty works (9:43). For the use of λόγος to describe his message see Mk. 2:2 and Lk. 5:1 note. The use of the word here allows Luke to avoid Mark's threefold repetition of the διδασκ- stem; by a further use in 4:36 he brings together the preaching and the wonder-working command of Jesus. Both are uttered ἐν ἐξουσίᾳ

(an associative dative, BD 198²); cf. 4:6. In view of the connection with δύναμις (4:36) we are justified in tracing the authority of Jesus to his possession of the Spirit (4:14; Barrett, 69–93; Schürmann, I, 246).

(b) The Exorcism of a Demoniac 4:33–37

Against the background of Jesus' authoritative teaching Luke presents the story of his exorcism of a demon in the synagogue. It is characterised by the claim of the demon to know who Jesus is, and by the remarkable impression which the exorcism makes upon the spectators and indeed upon the whole neighbourhood – an effect which is fitting in the case of the first recorded mighty act of Jesus. Schürmann, I, 251, notes that it is appropriate that Jesus' first mighty work should be an exorcism in view of his earlier conflict with Satan.

The narrative in Mk. has the form of a miracle story, but with considerable detail and colour (Bultmann, 223f.; corrected by Dibelius, 40, 51f.; Taylor, 171). Many scholars think that Mark has deliberately placed the exorcism in a context of teaching in order to avoid any overemphasis on Jesus as being primarily a worker of miracles (see R. P. Martin, *Mark: Evangelist and Theologian*, Exeter, 1972, 136–138, 214f.).

The question of the historicity of Jesus' mighty works cannot be discussed here. There is an increasing tendency to accept the historicity of at least some of the stories (e.g. Schweizer, *Markus,* 28; Jeremias, *Theology,* I, 85–92; Goppelt, I, 189–195: *contra* E. and M.-L. Keller, *Miracles in Dispute*, London, 1969), although they are often given a psychological explanation. It must suffice here to state our position, namely that the category of the miraculous is not to be rejected out of hand; if we accept the reality of the resurrection of Jesus, the possibility that he worked miracles becomes highly credible, and it is from this standpoint that the historicity of each individual story must be assessed.

See Kertelge, 50–60.

(33) Throughout the narrative Luke follows Mk. closely, cuts down his prolixity and improves his style. Thus he deletes εὐθύς (so already in 4:31, and frequently), and also αὐτῶν after συναγωγῇ (contrast 4:15). Since he uses ἐν πνεύματι for possession of the Spirit of God (2:27; 4:1, 14) he substitutes ἔχων here (8:27; 13:11; Acts 8:7; 16:16). For πνεῦμα ἀκάθαρτον he substitutes the unparalleled πνεῦμα δαιμονίου ἀκαθάρτου. Here is is probably clarifying for Greek readers for whom πνεῦμα did not have the sense of 'evil' spirit which it could have in Judaism (W. Foerster, TDNT II, 9; cf. H. Kleinknecht, TDNT VI, 339). Schürmann, I, 247 n. 188, argues that for Luke the effect is due to a power produced by a demon rather than to the direct indwelling of a demon, but it is the demon who is expelled in v. 35. The retention of ἀκάθαρτον stresses that the δαιμόνιον is evil and prepares for the con-

trast with ἅγιος in v. 34. Faced by the Holy One, the man cries out loudly; for ἀνακράζω see 8:28; 23:18*; φωνῇ μεγάλῃ has been brought forward from Mk. 1:26 to associate it with the actual words of the man. Such a cry is a mark of spirit-possession (Lohmeyer, 36).

(34) The exclamation ἔα** may be an interjection expressing surprise or displeasure, found in Classical Greek (AG s.v.). It may have been regarded as an equivalent to wāy, 'alas' (Tg. Jdg. 11:35; Tg. Joel 1:15; SB II, 157). Alternatively, it may be the imperative of ἐάω, with the sense 'let (us) alone' (cf. 22:51; Schürmann, I, 247 n. 194). In the latter case it forms part of the demon's attempt to defend itself against Jesus. τί ἡμῖν καὶ σοί; literally means, 'What have we in common?', but in the LXX it translates a phrase which means, 'Why are you interfering with me?' (Jos. 22:24; Jdg. 11:12; 2 Sa. 16:10; 19:22; 1 Ki. 17:18; 2 Ki. 3:13; cf. Lk. 8:28 par. Mk. 5:7; Mt. 27:19; Jn. 2:4). It is rhetorical, implying, 'Do not meddle with me'. Jesus is addressed as Ναζαρηνός (24:19; Mk. 1:24; 10:47; 14:67; 16:6**). To Luke the adjective (like Ναζωραῖος, which he prefers; 18:37; Acts 2:22; et al.) probably meant 'of Nazareth' (cf. Acts 10:38). The evidence that in the tradition it meant 'Nazirite' is equivocal. 'Have you come to destroy us?' is a shout of defiance. The demon's claim to know who Jesus is may represent an attempt to gain power over him through knowledge of his name. Schürmann's understanding of the whole utterance as a piece of flattery, a polite request to Jesus to refrain from exorcism (I, 248), seems less likely. The address ὁ ἅγιος τοῦ θεοῦ suggests a contrast with the unclean demon, but its roots lie in the idea of Jesus as the Son of God (1:35), separated to his service (Jdg. 13:7; 16:17 with Nu. 6:5, 8).

(35) It suffices for Jesus to rebuke the demon with a command to be silent and to leave the man. For ἐπιτιμάω cf. 4:39, 41; 8:24; 9:42; et al.; φιμόω occurs only here in Lk. As the demon leaves the man, it throws him into the middle of the room. Mark speaks simply of it convulsing him (σπαράσσω; cf. Lk. 9:26 par. Mk. 9:26**). Despite its violent exit, the demon was unable to harm the man (βλάπτω, Mk. 16:18**). The cure was complete.

(36) The miracle story culminates in the reaction of the spectators. Luke replaces ἐθαμβήθησαν ἅπαντες with a characteristic periphrasis. θάμβος (5:9; Acts 3:10**) is wonder, perhaps mingled with fear. For Mk. συζητέω, which might suggest dissension among the audience, he substitutes συνλαλέω (9:30 par. Mk. 9:4 par. Mt. 17:3; Lk. 22:4; Acts 25:12**). The rest of Mark's sentence is made smoother. The word διδαχή, which is less appropriate for a command to a demon, is replaced by λόγος, which can mean 'command' (cf. 2 Sa. 1:4 for the phrase). ὅτι will then be elliptical: sc. '(We ask the question) because . . .' (BD 456²; cf. 8:25). With ἐξουσία Luke couples δύναμις (diff. Mk.), stressing the power which Jesus possessed by reason of his divine authority and which came to expression in the exercise of that authority.

(37) As a result of the miracle the fame of Jesus spread into the

surrounding area. Having already used ἐξέρχομαι in v. 36, Luke here substitutes ἐκπορεύομαι, no doubt for the sake of variety. Since Luke uses ἀκοή, 'report', to mean 'ear' (7:1*), he uses ἦχος, which may be either 'report' (masc.; Heb. 12:19), or 'sound, noise' (neut.; 21:25); cf. Acts 2:2**. The verse stresses the magnitude of the wonder performed by Jesus; the effect of the spread of the news will be seen in 4:40f.

(c) The Healing of Peter's Mother-in-Law 4:38–39

The second miracle story in this section follows the pattern of Mark's narrative (Mk. 1:29–31) fairly closely, but with considerable freedom in wording. Mark's story is best seen as the literary deposit of a personal experience, no doubt that of Peter himself, which has not been reduced to a stylised form (Roloff, *Kerygma*, 115f.). In Luke's editing the effect is to 'heighten the miraculous element and omit details which seemed of secondary importance, although, in reality, it is these which give the story its life-like character' (Taylor, 178).

For Luke the fact that the subject of the healing was a woman was certainly significant; we have here an excellent example of how his sources furnished him with the material which he needed to achieve his own deliberate theological emphasis without any manipulation or even creation of fresh material. Thus Jesus' concern for both men and women, for demoniacs and the sick, is brought out in this pair of narratives (4:33–37, 38f.). At most, Luke has underlined the parallelism between the narratives by the common use of ἐπιτιμάω.

There is no especial stress on the place of Peter, nor has the narrative undergone any essential alteration in view of the fact that it now precedes the account of Peter's call and may perhaps be regarded as forming a prelude to it.

See Kertelge, 60–62; Roloff, *Kerygma*, 115–117; Dietrich, 18–23.

(38) The setting of the story shows verisimilitude: Jesus and his companions would be going to Simon's home for the main meal of the Sabbath, served just after the synagogue service (cf. 14:1). By using ἀναστάς Luke avoids Mark's rather clumsy ἐξελθόντες ... ἦλθον. He retains the name of Simon, which is essential to the telling of the story and would in any case be familiar to most readers who had some hearsay knowledge of the story of Jesus, but he leaves out the names of the other three disciples found in Mk., since these are not important for the story and have not yet appeared in his narrative (cf. 5:1–11). There is no obvious reason why Luke has omitted the article with πενθερά ('mother-in-law', 12:53*) but included it with Σίμωνος, diff. Mk. Although the use of συνέχομαι may be due to Luke's predilection for the word (6x; Acts, 3x; Mt., 4:24; Mk., Ox), it is in fact the correct term to use for 'being afflicted' by illness (Plato, Gorg. 512a; Jos. Ant. 13:398; Mt. 4:24; Acts 28:8) and stresses the severity of the complaint (H. Koester, TDNT VII,

877–885). Opinions vary whether the use of μέγας to describe the fever is meant to heighten the miracle by means of a word of which Luke was fond or is a reflection of medical usage which distinguished between μέγας and σμικρός in this connection (Galen, cited by Creed, xx, 71); probably the latter view is correct, and is based on Luke's deduction from Mark's description of the disease. The use of ἐρωτάω brings out the implicit request for healing in Mark's use of λέγω, and suggests that the disciples already had faith in what Jesus could do as a result of the preceding incident.

(39) In Mk. Jesus approaches the woman and lifts her by the hand (cf. Lk. 8:54). Here he stands over her, since she is lying on a pallet on the ground; ἐφίστημι is Lucan (2:9; et al.), and for the use of ἐπάνω cf. 2 Sa. 1:9; Schlatter, 50. Then Jesus rebukes the fever, in the same way as he had rebuked the demon (4:35; cf. Mk. 4:39 of rebuking the sea). The use of the word stresses that both miracles are wrought by the *word* of Jesus (cf. 18:42; Acts 3:7). Whether it is also implied that the fever is held to be due to a demon (Klostermann, 67) is not so certain; Luke regarded physical maladies as springing ultimately from the influence of Satan (13:16), but nothing more than personification of the malady may be present.

The effect of the command is instantaneous and complete. Luke has inserted παραχρῆμα (1:64; et al.), which he often uses to replace Mark's εὐθύς (5:25; 8:44, 55; 18:43; 22:60). The use of ἀναστᾶσα diff. Mk. ἤγειρεν αὐτήν may emphasise the completeness of the cure (Schürmann, I, 252), which is finally attested, as in Mk., by the fact that the woman was able to help in the preparations for the meal. Her help may also be regarded as a mark of gratitude for her cure, although Luke follows Mk. in stating that she served the company generally (αὐτοῖς) and not simply Jesus (Mt. 8:15). It is unlikely that the use of διακονέω is meant to indicate that this is the appropriate form of Christian service for women; it simply indicates the normal domestic arrangement. Gilmour, 98, notes that women were forbidden to serve Jewish men at table.

(d) The Sick healed at Evening 4:40–41

The two examples of healing of individuals are followed by an account of many needy people being brought to Jesus for healing, no doubt as a result of the news of what he had already done. The story culminates in the confession of the demons that he was the Son of God (or the Christ), a testimony which Jesus wished to silence, but which was nevertheless true.

The material is again drawn from Mk. (1:32–34) with little change, except the avoidance of redundancy. Luke, however, uses the incident to indicate that Jesus healed by the laying on of hands (Mk. 1:31), and to clarify the statements of the demons. In its Marcan form the story is hardly a redactional formulation (Bultmann, 366), but an account of a particular incident, closely linked with the preceding and following sections (Dibelius, 41; Taylor, 180). Marcan redaction is, however, present in the wording of the narrative (Schweizer, *Markus,* 29).

(40) Luke abbreviates Mark's tautologous time-phrase (Jeremias, *Words,* 17f.) and thus avoids the use of ὀψία, a word which he apparently dislikes (Schramm, 88). His change to the present participle, 'while the sun was setting', may mean that he has missed the point of Mark's phrase, namely that the sick could be carried to Jesus only after the Sabbath had ended and 'work' was possible. It may be that he thought of the sick walking on their own legs (ἄγω, diff. Mk. φέρω); or did he think that they shared Jesus' attitude to the Sabbath in their enthusiasm to be healed? The demoniacs are not mentioned at this point, but separately in v. 41. For Mk. κακῶς ἔχω (Lk. 5:31; 7:2), Luke uses ἀσθενέω* (Mk. 6:56; Acts 9:37; 19:12; 20:35*), and he brings forward νόσοις ποικίλαις from Mk. 1:34. The whole of Mk. 1:33, which describes the crowds at the door of the house, is omitted as an unnecessary detail (cf. Mt. 8:16) – hardly because Luke did not wish to represent Jesus as permanently staying there (*pace* Schürmann, I, 251 n. 231). The use of εἷς ἕκαστος, 'each one' (6:44; 16:5*; Acts, 6x), diff. Mk. πολλοί, is not a heightening of the miracle: clearly πολλοί is equivalent to the earlier πάντες in Mk. 1:32 (J. Jeremias, TDNT VI, 541).

A new feature in Luke's version is that Jesus accomplished his cures by laying his hands on the sick (13:13; cf. 5:13; Mk. 5:23, 41; 6:5; 7:32; 8:23, 25); Luke has generalised what he knew to be a frequent practice of Jesus, possibly under the influence of Mk. 1:31. Healing by the laying on of hands was unknown in Judaism, except in 1QapGen 20, 21, 22, 29 (E. Lohse, TDNT IX, 428), but is found in Hellenistic accounts of miraculous healings (ibid. 425). This does not mean that the stories of Jesus healing in this way must have originated in Hellenistic circles outside Palestine. There is no good reason why Jesus should not have followed a practice known in the pagan world and which was in any case familiar in Judaism as a means of conveying divine blessing. The act was symbolic of the flow of divine power from Jesus to the person healed; it should not be regarded as magical.

(41) The bringing forward of the verb may accentuate Jesus' victory over the demons, but the form of the sentence almost makes the exorcisms incidental to the healings. ἐξέρχομαι (diff. Mk. ἐκβάλλω) is a quasi-passive, 'to be driven out'. The plural is read by ℵ C Θ *al* Or; *Diglot,* but elsewhere Luke uses the singular verb with δαιμόνια. The description of the demonic cries has been brought forward from Mk. 3:10–12; Luke uses κραυγάζω*, 'to shout', diff. Mk. κράζω (but the latter is read here by (ℵ*) B C K Θ *pm*; TR; (UBS)). εἴα is the imperfect of ἐάω, replacing Mk. ἤφιεν. The content of the demonic cry, 'You are the Son of God', is as in Mk. 3:11; cf. 5:7. It represents an attempt by the

demon to demonstrate superiority to the exorciser by knowledge of his name, or it may be a confession of the superior might of Jesus on the part of the defeated demons (Schürmann, I, 253). In any case, Christians would recognise it as a true insight into the person of Jesus, who is now fulfilling the proper function of the Son of God instead of yielding to Satanic temptation to misuse his position. Luke's elucidation of the title in terms of the Messiah does not mean that he has down-graded 'Son of God' to become merely an attribute of the Messiah; this is impossible in the light of 1:32–35. Rather the term 'Messiah' is seen to be applicable to a more-than-earthly figure, able to exorcise demons, and on a different level from political saviours. At the same time, Luke's purpose may be to indicate that 'Son of God' must not be understood in purely Hellenistic categories as a reference to a charismatic, semi-divine figure, but must be seen in the light of Jewish messianic expectation.

Luke has taken over from Mk. both the demonic confessions and the rebukes addressed by Jesus to them. Despite Jesus' attempts to silence them, at least some of the demoniacs confessed who Jesus was. If there was a 'messianic' or 'Son of God' secret, it could not remain a secret. For Luke, as for Mark, Jesus' Messiahship did not remain a secret during his lifetime; rather, Jesus did not wish his Messiahship to be made known by demoniacs. He did not wish the truth about himself to be made known by the opposition; men must recognise the finger of God in a more positive way. But unwelcome though the testimony was, it forms the climax to the series of mighty works recorded here.

(e) Departure from Capernaum 4:42–44

After the successful day's work the local people urge Jesus to stay with them – in marked contrast to the inhabitants of Nazareth. Jesus, however, must leave them also because he has been sent by God to proclaim the good news of the kingdom not merely to them but throughout the whole land of the Jews.

The passage is again based on Mk. (1:35–39). Although Bultmann, 167, regards it as redactional, it appears to be based on traditional material (Lohmeyer, 42). This impression would be confirmed if Schürmann, I, 256, is right in detecting traces of a parallel account in Q behind Lk. and Mt. 4:23–25, but the evidence for this is far from strong (J. Delobel, in Neirynck, 214 n. 38).

Luke has considerably edited the section. Instead of the disciples it is the crowds who pursue Jesus to his place of quiet retreat. Surprisingly, there is no mention of Jesus at prayer, but Luke brings out the theological undertones in Jesus' reply to the crowds. He indicates that Judaea and not simply Galilee was the scene of Jesus' widening ministry.

(42) γενομένης ἡμέρας (Acts 12:18; 16:35; 23:12; cf. Lk. 22:26; Acts 27:39) is a simplification of Mark's cumbrous time-phrase; the

night has ended, and at dawn Jesus goes out to a lonely place. The motif
of Jesus' prayer is kept over until 5:16. Perhaps Luke did not wish to tell
how Jesus was interrupted at prayer, or more probably he wished to
concentrate attention on the single point that Jesus' mission must em-
brace other towns (Creed, 72; Ott, 99). Since he has not yet related the
call of the disciples, he substitutes a vague reference to the crowds, and
he softens Mark's καταδιώκω**, 'to hunt out', to ἐπιζητέω, 'to seek'
(12:30*). The use of κατέχω, 'to hold back, hinder', is Lucan (8:15;
14:9*; Acts 27:40*; not in Mt. or Mk.), as is τοῦ with infinitive (1:9; et
al.); the imperfect is conative: 'They tried to keep him from leaving.'

(43) Since Jesus' reply is no longer addressed to the disciples, it has
to be altered from the first person plural to the singular form. The hortatory subjunctive ἄγωμεν is replaced by an expression of the divine imperative which underlies Jesus' mission (δεῖ, 2:49 note; με δεῖ is inverted
in B (D) W pc Mcion; Diglot, but Lucan usage varies too much to offer
any guidance). The nature of the mission in God's plan requires that the
kingdom be proclaimed far and wide. For κηρύσσω Luke has
εὐαγγελίζομαι, possibly under the influence of Mk. 1:15, from where also
he may have derived ἡ βασιλεία τοῦ θεοῦ. This is Luke's first reference
to this concept, which is frequently stated to be the theme of Jesus'
message (8:1; 9:2, 60; 16:16; Acts 8:12). See Conzelmann, 87–127; R.
Schnackenburg, God's Rule and Kingdom, 1963; G. E. Ladd, Jesus and
the Kingdom, 1966; Marshall, 128–136; M. Völkel, 'Zur Deutung des
"Reiches Gottes" bei Lukas', ZNW 65, 1974, 57–70; O. Merk, 'Das
Reich Gottes in den lukanischen Schriften', in Ellis, Jesus, 201–220. In
Lk. the kingdom of God is his activity in bringing salvation to men and
the sphere which is thereby created; God is active here and now in the
ministry of Jesus and will consummate his rule in the future. Conzelmann's claims that it is the message rather than the kingdom itself
which is present, and that the future consummation is so distant as to be
irrelevant to the present time, need to be corrected (E. E. Ellis, 'Present
and Future Eschatology in Luke', NTS 12, 1965–66, 27–41; id.
Eschatology in Luke, Philadelphia, 1972 (German version, ZTK 66,
1969, 387–402); Wilson, 59–87).

Mark's ἐξῆλθον is interpreted in terms of Jesus being sent by God
to accomplish his mission (4:18; 9:48; 10:16). Mark's phrase refers to
Jesus going out on his mission, and has been correctly interpreted.

(44) Luke follows Mk. even to the retention of the pregnant use of
εἰς to indicate going into and preaching in the synagogues. But he omits
the reference to Jesus' exorcisms, so that all the stress lies on the
preaching through which the good news of the kingdom comes to men.
In place of Γαλιλαίας (read, by assimilation to Mk., in A D Θ f13 pm
latt syᵖ boᵖᵗ; TR) he has Ἰουδαίας. This can hardly refer to the southern
district of Judaea, as distinct from Galilee (pace Conzelmann, 33–35); it
is improbable that a ministry in the south should be interpolated here (cf.
Jn. 2:13 – 3:36; Grundmann, 126). Schürmann, I, 256f., uses the verse

to justify his distinction between the beginning of the ministry in Galilee (3:1 – 4:44) and its main course in Judaea as a whole (5:1 – 19:27). He is right in seeing that Judaea here means Palestine as a whole *including* Galilee (1:5 note), but it is questionable whether so sharp a distinction should be drawn between the two parts of Jesus' ministry. Rather v. 43 indicates that Jesus' ministry is directed to the Jews as a whole; the point is theological rather than geographical.

iv. The Call of the Disciples 5:1–11

From the general account of Jesus' preaching activity Luke singles out one particular episode by the Lake of Gennesaret, and then lets the spotlight fall upon one particular group of hearers, Simon and his companions, who not only listened to his preaching, but also responded to his command to go and fish in an unpropitious situation. When their obedience resulted in a miraculous catch of fish, Simon was overwhelmed with a sense of the holiness of Jesus as the Lord. But Jesus summoned him to join him in a new task of 'catching' men, and Simon and his companions (including the sons of Zebedee) abandoned their previous way of life to join him in his mission.

The story concentrates attention on Simon, the later leader of the church, and on his call to mission, shared by his colleagues. It is parallel to the account of the call of the first four disciples, related in a highly economical manner in Mk. 1:16–20, and to the brief account of Jesus' preaching by the lakeside in Mk. 4:1f.; cf. 2:13; 3:7–9. The fact that Luke has omitted Mark's story of the call of the four fishermen shows clearly that he regarded this story as equivalent to it. It is impossible that Luke has created his story simply on the basis of what he read in Mk.; the facts that it occurs at a different position in the narrative and that its contents go well beyond Mk. prove this point. Nevertheless, it is clear that Luke knew Mark's account and that it has influenced his own telling of the story; parallelism with Mk. can be seen in vs. 1–3, 10f., and many scholars would claim that Luke has drawn on Mk. for most or all of the material in these verses (Schramm, 37–40; Pesch, *Fischfang*, 53–76); it is disputed merely whether v. 10b is based on Mk. (Pesch, *Fischfang*, 72–76) or on an independent tradition (Klein, 21–25). Where, however, Mark has simply related the basic fact that the proper response to the gospel of the kingdom is instant obedience to the call to discipleship, Luke's story shows that the call took place only after the fishermen had made the acquaintance of Jesus and experienced a revelation of his heavenly power.

There is a parallel to the part of the incident not recorded in Mk., namely the miraculous catch of fish, in Jn. 21:1–14. The two stories show a considerable amount of agreement in detail: after fishing all night, the disciples have caught nothing. Jesus commands them to let the nets down. They do so, and make an enormous catch. The effect on the nets is noted. Peter (in Jn., the beloved disciple) reacts to the miracle. Jesus is called Lord. The other fishermen present say nothing. The motif of following Jesus is present, and the catch of fish is symbolic of missionary success (Brown, *John*, II, 1090). The question of the relation between Lk. and Jn. at this point is complicated by difficulties in the Johannine narrative. Many scholars find that two narratives have been interwoven in Jn., an account of a resurrection appearance of Jesus at a meal and the story of a miraculous catch of fish. It is then argued that the two accounts of the miraculous catch are variant forms of the same tradition, and on the whole it is thought that Jn. 21 shows more secondary features than Lk. 5. The question is then whether the story originally referred to the pre- or post-resurrection period. While it is often argued that Luke has ante-dated a post-resurrection story (e.g. Creed, 73f.; Leaney, 54–57; Klein, 25–30), C. H. Dodd (Nineham, *Studies*, 9–35) has claimed that the story lacks the essential 'form' of a resurrection story and must be placed in the pre-resurrection period.

We can leave aside here the analysis of John's narrative, since there is no evidence that Luke was dependent upon it. The question is rather that of the relation between the traditions used by the two Evangelists. As already indicated, Luke's story did not reach him as a resurrection-story (cf. Dietrich, 55f.). While few scholars would allow that Luke has recorded a tradition separate from that incorporated in Jn. 21, there is no real evidence that forbids this possibility. There are other examples in the Gospels of pairs of similar but distinct incidents (cf. 7:36–50) where the parallel features have led to some modification of each narrative in the light of the other, and this may well have been the case here. Jn. 21:1–14 may be regarded as a story in which Jesus is recognised by the similarity of his command and its consequences to those in the earlier incident (although the narrator was unaware of this correspondence); when Brown, *John*, II, 1090f., asks how Peter could have gone through the same situation and much of the same dialogue again without recognising Jesus, he greatly over-estimates the amount of this 'common dialogue', which amounts to no more than Jesus' command to let down the nets. Rengstorf, 74, is correct in affirming that neither narrative is based on the other. Although Pesch, *Fischfang*, 126–130, denies that a historical incident lies behind Lk., his arguments by no means exclude this possibility. Granted that the narrative shows 'legendary' features in the prominence of Simon and the interest in him as a person, this in no way invalidates it as history, and it may well contain historical reminiscence (Dibelius, 108–111).

This brings us back to the relation of the miracle story to the story of the call of the disciples in Mk. 1:16–20. We have seen that the wording in Mk. has influenced Lk. What is not clear is whether Luke's independent tradition contained material corresponding to Mk. 1:16–20. While most scholars argue that Luke has constructed the introduction to the scene out of Marcan material, this is questioned by Dietrich, 25–38,

63–76, who notes various features in the Lucan narrative which are difficult to explain purely on the basis of Mk. as a source. The biggest question concerns v. 10b. Did a call to be a fisher of men figure in the story of the miraculous catch? While Klein, 32–43, asserts that such a saying was contained in the (post-resurrection) tradition behind Jn. 21:1–14, Pesch, *Fischfang,* 72–76, claims that the Lucan saying is based on redaction of Mk.; the latter has the better of the argument, but his case is not compelling. On the whole, it seems most probable that Luke has incorporated the miracle story in a framework based on Mk., and in so doing he may have replaced the original ending of the miracle story with Marcan material.

See L. Brun, 'Die Berufung der ersten Jünger Jesu in der evangelischen Tradition', *Symbolae Osloenses* 11, 1932, 35–54 (as summarised in Pesch, *Fischfang,* 21–24); G. Klein, 'Die Berufung des Petrus', in Klein, 11–48 (originally in ZNW 58, 1967, 1–39); Pesch, *Fischfang;* id. 'La rédaction lucanienne du logion des pêcheurs d'hommes (Lc., V, 10c)', in Neirynck, 225–244; Dietrich, 23–81.

(1) Luke portrays a situation similar to that in Mk. 3:7–9; 4:1, in which Jesus is standing by the shore of the lake, surrounded by a crowd to which he can speak only with difficulty on account of its size. The way in which the crowd disappears without trace halfway through the story suggests that Luke has linked together two separate incidents, using a typical scene in Jesus' ministry from Mk. to stress that the call of Simon took place after he had heard the word of Jesus. *Diglot* follows p [75] in reading καὶ ἐγένετο for ἐγένετο δέ, but the external evidence is too weak to justify the change. For the use of the ἐγένετο ... καί ... construction, see 1:8 note. The καὶ αὐτὸς ἦν ἑστώς ... clause is then to be regarded as a circumstantial clause before the real apodosis begins in v. 2 with καὶ εἶδεν (Black, 83; Beyer, I:1, 49; Schürmann, I, 267 n. 30). ἐπικεῖμαι (23:23*; Acts 27:20*; Dietrich, 33f.) describes the physical pressure of the crowd on Jesus to hear his teaching, here solemnly described as 'the word of God' (8:11, 21; 11:28). The phrase is used frequently in Acts for the apostolic message, thus bringing out the continuity between the teaching of Jesus and that of the church; here the phrase stresses the significance of the message to be heard by Simon. Luke always uses λίμνη as the correct term to refer to Galilee, in contrast to Matthew and Mark who loosely describe it as a θάλασσα (Lk. 8:22, 23, 33). Γεννησαρέτ (Mt. 14:34; Mk. 6:53**) usually means the land immediately south of Capernaum, but is also found in the form Γεννησάρ as a local name for the lake (Jos. Bel. 3:463, 506; cf. OT 'Chinnereth', Nu. 34:11): has Luke avoided the term 'Galilee' here in view of his earlier alteration in 4:44?

(2) The text is uncertain: δύο πλοῖα (p [75] ℵ[c] D Θ *pm* lat; TR); πλοιάρια δύο (4 a); πλοῖα (ℵ*); πλοῖα δύο (B W *pc*; *Diglot*); and δύο πλοιάρια (A C* *al* f; *Synopsis*). Schürmann, *Abschiedsrede,* 130, apparently accepts the positioning of δύο after the noun here as a mark of Lucan style, and also reads πλοιάρια (from Mk. 3:9; cf. Jn. 6:22–24;

21:8**), but the consequent reading πλοιάρια δύο has no significant external support. The uncertainty in the position of δύo may suggest that it is a gloss; in any case the argument from Lucan style is too weak to settle its position. The evidence for πλοιάρια is superior to that for πλοῖα; it is an open question whether an original πλοιάρια has been assimilated to the form used later in the story, or whether Luke used the same term throughout, but Jn. 21: 3, 6, 8 shows that both forms could be used side by side. On the whole, δύο πλοιάρια has the best claims to be original. The use of ἑστῶτα παρὰ τὴν λίμνην to describe the boats moored at the shore is slightly inelegant after its use in a different sense in v. 1 and may reflect use of a source (Dietrich, 29). ἁλιεύς, 'fisherman', occurs only in this story (Mt. 4:18f.; Mk. 1:16f.**; note the spelling, BD 29⁵). ἀποβαίνω is correct for 'to disembark' (Jn. 21:9). After the night's fishing the nets would be washed out and then hung up to dry; δίκτυον occurs only in this story and its parallels; for πλύνω see Rev. 7:14; 22:14**. In Mark's account James and John are described as repairing the nets, an activity which would be carried out at the same time as washing (but which would be less consistent with being immediately able to fish at Jesus' command). Simon and Andrew, however, are there described as casting their nets in the sea. Whereas in Lk., the men have just completed a nocturnal task with a seine or drag net in deep water, in Mk. they are using a casting net, which was operated during the daytime from the shore or by a person standing in shallow water, and which was used by poorer fishermen who did not have a boat (Lohmeyer, 32 n. 3). After a fruitless night's work, the fishermen might well try their luck with the casting net.

(3) Since the pressure of the crowd prevented Jesus from speaking to them from the shore, he seized the opportunity to use one of the boats as a pulpit. For ἐμβαίνω, 'to embark', cf. 8:22, 37; Mk. 4:1; Acts 21:6. For εἷς as an indefinite pronoun, equivalent to τις, see Black, 104–106. The mention of Simon as the owner of the boat prepares the way for the miracle. For the use of the possessive genitive with εἶναι see MH III, 231. ἐπανάγω is 'to put out to sea' (5:4), also 'to return'. In the boat Jesus adopts the sitting posture of a Jewish teacher (4:20). *Diglot* has ἐδίδασκεν before ἐκ τοῦ πλοίου (p⁴ ᵛⁱᵈ A C (W) Θ pl; TR), on the grounds that scribes altered the dominant word order (verb first; see Kilpatrick, 198), but this reading may be a simplification of the more difficult order (Alford, I, 482).

Luke presumably regarded the crowd as dispersing before the following miracle. It is hard to tell whether the story has been so condensed that it contains a number of apparent inconcinnities, or whether two or more sources have been joined together.

(4) When he had finished his teaching (cf. 11:1), Jesus commanded Simon, as the captain of the boat, to sail out into deep water (βάθος*); there the men were to lower the nets for a catch. For χαλάω, see 5:5; Mk. 2:5; Acts 9:25; 27:17, 30; 2 Cor. 11:33*. ἄγρα is 'catch' or 'act of

catching' (5:9**). The second command is in the plural, since the task would involve all aboard the boat. There is no mention here or later of Andrew (Mk. 1:16f.), although James and John are mentioned later. All the attention is concentrated on Simon.

(5) Simon addresses Jesus as ἐπιστάτης (8:24, diff. Mk. 4:38, διδάσκαλος; 8:45, diff. Mk. 5:31 (no equivalent); 9:33, diff. Mk. 9:5, ῥαββί; 9:49, diff. Mk. 9:38 διδάσκαλος; 17:13**). This word is used only by disciples or near-disciples. It replaces ῥαββί, which Luke avoids completely, and appears to be an equivalent for it (SB II, 157; A. Oepke, TDNT II, 622f.; cf. O. Glombitza, 'Die Titel διδάσκαλος und ἐπιστάτης für Jesus bei Lukas', ZNW 49, 1958, 275–278). It also replaces διδάσκαλος, which Luke allows to stand on the lips of non-disciples (7:40 note). While the use in Marcan sections is redactional, this does not mean that Luke has introduced it here and 17:13 without some basis in his sources. Here too it may reflect an original ῥαββί. Dietrich, 38–43, holds that it is used in the context of a group placing itself under a master, and thinks that it reflects a communal consciousness on the part of the disciples – but this would be due to Luke's assessment of their consciousness rather than to primitive source material. In any case, the word signifies an attitude of obedience, which is heightened by the fact that despite a fruitless and wearisome night's fishing trip Simon is prepared to lower the nets. κοπιάω is 'to toil wearisomely' (12:27*; Acts 20:35). διά with genitive is used of a period of time. ἐπί has the sense 'on the strength of' (cf. Stuhlmueller, 133). The paradox would be heightened for readers who knew that fishing in deep water was unlikely to produce a good catch during daytime.

(6) When the nets were lowered they enclosed (συγκλείω, Rom. 11:32; Gal. 3:22f.**) a great quantity of fish (cf. 6:17; 23:27; Acts 14:1; 17:4). See especially Jn. 21:6. In consequence, the nets were in danger of bursting – a detail meant to establish the size of the catch. For διαρρήσσω see 8:29; Acts 14:14; Mk. 14:63 par. Mt. 26:65**; διερρήσσετο is an imperfect with inceptive force (not aorist, pace Schürmann, I, 269 n. 48); the variant διερρήγνυτο may be due to Atticising tendencies.

(7) It is not clear whether the other boat is thought of as being still moored by the shore or already out at sea, but probably the former situation is envisaged. Simon's boat will have been not far from the shore, so that the men in it could easily beckon (κατανεύω**) to their colleagues to come and help them. μέτοχος is used of partners in business (elsewhere in the NT it has a theological sense; Heb. 1:9; 3:1, 14; 6:4; 12:8**). For the use of συλλαμβάνω cf. Phil. 4:3; in 5:9 (cf. 22:54) it means 'to catch' (cf. also 1:24, 'to conceive'). ἦλθαν has a first aorist ending. The amount of fish landed was so great that the boats were in danger of sinking (βυθίζω, 1 Tim. 6:9**; the present infinitive has an inceptive sense).

(8) As the story approaches its climax, Simon is given his full name

(Σίμων Πέτρος, Mt. 16:16; 2 Pet. 1:1; Jn., frequently). Elsewhere Luke uses the form 'Simon . . . called Peter' (6:14; Acts 10:5, 18, 32, 11:13), and retains Σίμων by itself in 5:10; 22:31; 24:34. The omission of Πέτρος here by D W f13 it sy^s is probably a simplification, but is accepted by Klostermann, 69, and J. K. Elliott, 'Κηφᾶς: Σίμων Πέτρος: ὁ Πέτρος: An Examination of New Testament Usage', Nov.T 14, 1972, 241–256, especially 245f.; the latter argues that the combination is otherwise unattested in Lk. and may have been due to the influence of Jn. 21:2, 3, 7, 11 (cf. Bailey, 14 who thinks that Luke's story comes from a Johannine Easter tradition, and that the full name is, therefore, original here). But it is questionable whether scribes would have made this connection and more probable that any influence between Jn. and Lk. took place during the growth of the traditions. The presence of the name here may simply lay stress on the person of Simon (Dietrich, 44f.) or reflect the consciousness that Simon's call and his naming by Jesus were connected (Grundmann, 128), or draw attention to the identity of Simon with Peter, the leader of the Twelve.

Simon's reaction is to fall at the knees of Jesus. Leaney, 122, would take 'Ιησοῦ as a dative and translate, 'he fell on his knees before Jesus', but this is improbable. Such humility is appropriate before a person addressed as κύριος, which here presumably has a deeper meaning than ἐπιστάτης and is not simply equivalent to 'Sir' (6:46 note). But no precise connotation (e.g. of divinity) can necessarily be attached to it. For the late position of the vocative see 9:61; 19:8, 18; Acts 26:7; BD 474^6. Before Jesus, Simon is conscious of his sinfulness, and therefore he bids Jesus to go away; both ἀνήρ and ἐξέρχομαι ἀπό may be Lucan, but ἁμαρτωλός is probably from his source (Schürmann, I, 270 n. 53).

Critics have objected that Simon could scarcely have fallen before Jesus' feet in a sinking boat, and that Jesus could not be expected to go away from a boat at sea; hence the scene must have taken place on the land (cf. Jn. 21). Pesch, *Fischfang*, 71f., 116f., argues that in the pre-Lucan form of the story (which did not include the motif of Jesus preaching from the boat) Jesus was not in the boat, and the disciples came to land (v. 11a, transferred from its original position at 5:7/8) before Simon fell at Jesus' feet. Luke himself is responsible for the difficulty by moving v. 11a to its present position when he joined the two narratives. This is perhaps the best solution of a difficulty which arises from taking Luke's ordering of the narrative too seriously. In any case, however, the difficulties of Luke's story can be exaggerated: the boat did not in fact sink, and Simon's command was metaphorical (cf. Grundmann, 128).

More important is the question whether the saying belongs to a post-resurrection scene, since (it is argued) Simon's confession presupposes a concrete sin, namely his denial of Jesus. But while ἁμαρτωλός is often used of persons guilty of open, scandalous behaviour (5:30; 19:7), it can be used also in a more general moral sense (13:2; 24:7). What

Simon expressed was the sense of unworthiness (Mt. 8:8; Job 42:5f.) and fear (Jdg. 6:22; 13:22; 1 Ki. 17:18; Is. 6:5) which men should feel in the presence of the divine (cf. 18:13; Dietrich, 49–51; Rengstorf, 74). The revelation of Jesus' divine power in this eipiphany sufficed to demonstrate to Simon that he was in the presence of the Holy One (cf. 4:34) and to make him aware of his own inadequacy. A post-resurrection setting is not required.

(9) Simon's reaction is further explained as being due to θάμβος (4:36), wonder combined with fear, perhaps containing recognition of the presence of the divine (Schürmann, I, 270). περιέχω is 'to seize' ('to stand', 1 Pet. 2:6**). The wonder was shared by his companions in the boat as they realised that the size of their catch had no rational explanation. ὧν (p⁷⁵ B D pc bo) is by relative attraction for οὕς; it may be a simplification for ᾗ (Synopsis; Diglot).

(10) ὁμοίως (3:11) is a Lucan connective. It has the effect of separating James and John from the companions of Simon in v. 9. The order of the names is the reverse of that attested elsewhere in Lk. and suggests use of a source; this could well be Mk. 1:19 (cf. 10:35). The impression is that Luke has added their names to a story in which they did not appear. This view is not without difficulty (see Dietrich, 63–76, who thinks that the use of κοινωνός* puts them in a different category from the μέτοχοι in v. 7). It may be that Luke regards them as being in the second boat, but it is also possible that they were not in the boat at all but were spectators from the shore (cf. Mk. 1:19f.). The difficulties again arise from the compression and joining of the narratives. Schürmann, I, 272f., thinks that they did not figure in the original miracle story, and that all references to the second boat are Lucan additions to the original form of the story (see, however, Pesch, Fischfang, 80f.).

Despite the mention of them, however, the interest is still centred on Simon, and in effect v. 10b links directly to v. 8. Jesus addresses him with the μὴ φοβοῦ that characterises epiphany scenes (1:13) and which here has the function of a declaration of forgiveness. Luke has not taken over δεῦτε ὀπίσω μου from Mk., but it has an equivalent in the narrative in v. 11. There follows a prophecy which has the effect of a command. Jesus will not in fact depart from the sinner but calls him into the close association of discipleship as he prophesies that from this point onwards he will begin a new life, taking not fish but men. ἀπὸ τοῦ νῦν is Lucan and stresses (like σήμερον) the new stage that begins in a man's life when he meets Jesus; to be sure, Simon's new activity does not begin in its full sense immediately, but already he is called to prepare for this task. ζωγρέω is 'to take alive' (2 Tim. 2:26**), and was used in the LXX for saving persons alive from danger (Nu. 31:15, 18; Dt. 20:16; et al.). Hengel, Nachfolge, 85–87, suggests that the Lucan and Marcan formulations here are translation-variants for ṣayyād, which can mean both 'to fish' and 'to hunt'. But the thought of hunting is not present here. Luke's wording appears rather to avoid the negative implications that

might be detected in 'fishing for men', and hence to be secondary to the
Marcan form (Pesch, *Fischfang*, 74f.; R. Pesch*). On the theme see W.
H. Wuellner, *The Meaning of 'Fishers of Men'*, Philadelphia, 1967.

(11) Although the command is addressed only to Simon in Lk.,
Luke retains the fact that it was in reality addressed to his companions
also. The subject is, however, left indeterminate, and it is not clear
whether only James and John are regarded as answering it. When they
have brought the boats to shore (κατάγω, Acts 27:3; 28:12), they leave
everything behind (5:28; 14:33; 18:22, 28; 21:3f.; cf. Acts 2:45; 4:34;
5:1ff.; Mk. 12:44; Mt. 13:44f.) and follow Jesus, i.e. become his disciples
(5:27f.; 9:23, 49, 57, 59, 61; 18:22, 28, 43; G. Kittel, TDNT I,
210–216). What is thus described summarily must have been a more
complex process, although it is not necessary to speculate that the huge
catch of fish was intended by Jesus to be a means of support for the
fishermen's dependants during their absence (Geldenhuys, 182). Luke
does not lay particular stress on the thought of giving up all to follow
Jesus (Mk. 1:18, 20): the accent is on v. 10 with its call to mission.

b. The Beginning of Controversy with the Pharisees
(5:12 – 6:11)

In this section Luke recounts six incidents, in all of which (except the
first) various actions by Jesus and his disciples lead to criticism from the
Pharisees. The motif of opposition to Jesus, which has already become
apparent earlier in the Gospel, thus continues here, but it is not
necessarily the main point in the section. The controversial element has
been taken over from Mk., where these incidents form parts of a series of
'conflict stories', but in Lk. there is somewhat more stress on the positive
aspects of Jesus' ministry which led to the opposition, the wonderful acts
of healing which he performed, the grace which he showed to sinners,
and the sheer newness and joy of the gospel.

Luke here takes up the thread of Mark's narrative again after the
insertion of the story of the call of the disciples, and reproduces the section Mk. 1:40 – 3:6 with characteristic editing. It is unlikely that any
other source has been used alongside Mk. (*pace* Schramm, 91–112), but
in places the influence of oral traditions, or rather variations in the narration of the incidents, may be seen.

i. The Healing of a Leper 5:12–16

The opening incident relates the healing of a leper by Jesus (cf.
17:11–19). It is told, following Mk., in the formal style of a miracle
story, but it has several important features. Primarily it testifies to the
blessings brought in a miraculous way by Jesus, and thus becomes a

testimony to the fulfilment of the promise of the messianic age in him: among the signs of that age listed in 7:22, 'lepers are cleansed', a comment all the more significant because, unlike the other parts of that verse, it has no obvious OT prophecy behind it. A leper was, however, healed by Elisha, and hence there may well be the thought present that Jesus is a prophet like Elisha (cf. Pesch, *Taten* 63f.). The healing of a leper is called a cleansing, following OT terminology, and hence the incident will have been seen in the church as a symbol of the spiritual cleansing from sin which can be effected by Jesus, and to which there is implicit reference in both the preceding and the following incidents. Finally, it is noteworthy that Jesus is here seen to observe the requirements of the OT law in a case where it was not only sensible but also necessary to do so for the sake of the man's future position in society; the story may thus serve as a foil to the following narratives in which the question of Jesus and the OT law is raised in a different fashion.

The story does not vary greatly from the account in Mk. Some difficulties in the narrative are removed, with the result that the picture of Jesus is slightly different. The command to silence is retained, but Luke is unwilling to attribute direct disobedience of it to the cured leper. The greatest changes in the narrative occur, as is usually the case, at the beginning and end, and the direct speech has suffered least change.

The historicity of the incident has been sharply attacked by Pesch, *Taten*, 78–80, on the grounds that the story follows the typical pattern of a miracle story, contains no identifiable historical features (such as details of the place or time), and can be accounted for in terms of a belief in Jesus as the eschatological prophet and the desire to present him in terms of a Hellenistic thaumaturge superior to Elisha; the distinctive features in the story are thus kerygmatic in origin, not historical.

Since Pesch admits that the question of the miraculous is not to be settled by what modern man is prepared to believe that Jesus could have done, and since he admits that the *possibility* of Jesus' cure of lepers cannot be excluded, the historical question is whether the present narrative withstands critical scrutiny. Pesch, *Taten*, 143f., insists that positive proof of historicity must be produced, but it is hard to see what evidence would satisfy him. In the nature of things it is not possible to adduce positive proof of historicity, but at least it can be said that there is no evidence which rules out historicity. Thus the fact that the story is told in a particular *form* is no proof that it is unhistorical (or historical). The lack of biographical details is due to the narrator's desire to centre attention on the healing and its significance, and cannot be used to prove that the incident never happened anywhere or at any particular time. And if Jesus did heal people, it would not be surprising if he acted in the manner of other healers of his time or if his actions were reported in similar terms; what is significant is the lack of magical elements and the stress on other features. Admittedly, the historian cannot tell exactly what happened: was it a miraculous cure or an example of 'overpowering therapy' on a psychogenous disease (Jeremias, *Theology*, I, 92)? But in the present case at least, there is good reason to believe that this is a historical example of the kind of healing which Jesus was known to have performed.

See Kertelge, 62–75; Schramm, 91–99; Pesch, *Taten*, 52–113.

(12) The opening words are Lucan in style and give a smooth transition from the preceding narrative, although in fact the placing of the incident is quite vague; Mt. 8:1 appears to link the story to the period immediately following the Sermon on the Mount. The use of forms of ἐν μιᾷ τῶν ... is Semitic (Schramm, 96f.; cf. 5:3 note), and the mention of πόλεις is to be understood in the light of 4:43. The use of ἰδού in narrative (here par. Mt., diff. Mk.) is frequent in Lk., and he often agrees with Mt. against Mk. in inserting it; it appears to be a sign of popular story-telling, and is hardly due to use of a special source alongside Mk. (as Schramm, 91f., cautiously claims; cf. Rehkopf, 34f.). Where Mark describes the man simply as λέπρος, Luke calls him ἀνὴρ (Lucan!) πλήρης λέπρας. The use of πλήρης in this sense is attested in medical writers, though not in connection with leprosy (Creed, 76). The phrase is due rather to Luke's fondness for πλήρης (4:1; Acts, 8x) coupled with the influence of the LXX (2 Ki. 7:15; Is. 1:15). Hence there is no reason to see here an attempt to heighten the miracle.

The term leprosy in the Bible does not mean the disease commonly so called today (Hansen's bacillus) but covered a wide variety of skin diseases, including some which were obviously regarded as highly contagious and incurable, while others were capable of cure (Schmid, *Mark*, 52f.). It is therefore impossible to say precisely what disease is meant in the present passage, and some scholars think that a disease of nervous origin may be meant. In any case, the plight of a person suspected of leprosy was grave. He was sequestered from normal society, and, if cured, could be restored to it only after examination by the priest and the offering of sacrifice (Lv. 13–14). To the rabbis the cure of a leper was as difficult as raising a person from the dead (SB IV: 2, 745–763; W. Michaelis, TDNT IV, 233f., is very brief). It is not surprising that such a person should break through the confines of his isolation when he had the opportunity of meeting one who had already a reputation as a healer. There may also be the thought that visitation with leprosy was the result of sin, and that it would be included in the diseases which would no longer afflict men in the messianic age (SB I, 593–596; IV: 2, 747–750). When the man saw Jesus (ἰδὼν δέ; the variant καὶ ἰδών is found in A C D W Θ pl TR; *Diglot*), he fell on his face before him (8:41; 17:16; Acts 5:10; 10:25). Luke avoids Mk.'s γονυπετέω here and at 18:18, but the explanation that he wished to avoid portraying the man touching Jesus (Schürmann, I, 276) seems improbable, since the verb means 'to fall on one's knees', not 'to grasp someone's knees'; it is more likely that he simply disliked the word and replaced it with a Septuagintalism (Gn. 17:3).

He begged for cleansing (δέομαι, diff. Mk. παρακαλέω, is frequent in Lk.). Both Matthew and Luke include the address κύριε, diff. Mk.; cf. 5:8. It is a respectful form of address, perhaps regarded as appropriate in addressing one who was known to have special powers from God (Vermes, 122f.). Since Luke rarely adds titles to his Marcan source, and here agrees with Mt. in the addition, there may be some influence from oral tradition here. The leper's request indicates that he believes in the ability of Jesus to help him; he will have heard of Jesus' earlier healing activity, but the fact that cleansing a leper was known to be difficult may indicate that he was prepared to be daring in his faith. He addresses Jesus with a polite request for cleansing.

(13) Luke (par. Mt.) omits Mk.'s σπλαγχνισθείς (v.l. ὀργισθείς); he avoids expressions of Jesus' emotions. He does not pass over the action of Jesus in stretching out his hand to heal the leper, a phrase which is reminiscent of the way in which God stretches out his hand to accomplish mighty acts (Ex. 6:6; 14:16; 15:12; Je. 17:5; Acts 4:30), and also of the action of Moses (Ex. 4:4; et al.; Pesch, Taten, 68); here it is all the more significant in that by this action Jesus breaks down the barrier between himself as an ordinary member of society and the unclean leper. In response to the man's request he says, 'Yes' (θέλω), but the phrase perhaps conveys something of the sovereign authority of the One who by his word and touch can overcome the power of disease (G. Schrenk, TDNT III, 48). At the command 'Be cleansed', the man is immediately (εὐθέως, preferred by Luke to Mark's εὐθύς; contrast 6:49) healed as the leprosy leaves him (cf. 4:39; but in the present case there is no indication that the disease is regarded like an exorcised demon).

(14) Luke omits Mk. 1:43 with its difficult use of ἐμβριμησάμενος, possibly again to avoid describing the emotions of Jesus, and passes straight on (with an unnecessary αὐτός) to recount Jesus' command to the man. παραγγέλλω is Lucan. Luke turns Mark's direct command into indirect speech, but is unable to keep this style up and relapses into direct speech almost immediately (cf. 16:8f.; Acts 1:4; 7:6f.; 14:21f.; 17:3; 23:22; 25:4f.; BD 470²). The man is to tell nobody what has happened, but to go (Luke prefers ἀπέρχομαι to ὑπάγω, but not in any exclusive fashion) and show himself to the priest for inspection, and offer the sacrifice prescribed by Moses for such occasions (Lv. 14:1–32). The prohibition to speak to anybody is psychologically understandable; the man would want in his excitement to tell what had happened immediately, but instead he is to go first of all to the priest to obtain his 'health clearance' and to offer thanksgiving to God. At the same time, Jesus may have wanted to avoid crowds coming after him simply in order to seek healing (5:16). The 'secrecy' command is thus historically realistic here, and there is no indication that Luke has seen any deeper theological significance in it. Further, although this instruction occupies the place in a miracle story where confirmation of the cure would be expected, this does not mean that it is unhistorical and has been invented

to serve this purpose (*pace* Pesch, *Taten*, 71–75). Ultimately, the cure of the man and its attestation by the priest was to serve εἰς μαρτύριον αὐτοῖς, i.e. to be evidence to the people of the messianic act of God in Jesus (Schürmann, I, 277).

(15) Luke omits Mark's explicit comment that the cured leper disobeyed Jesus' command – perhaps again due to his respect for the authority of Jesus. Rather he concentrates attention on the positive fact of the spread of the story (λόγος) concerning 'him' (probably Jesus is meant, rather than the leper). Similarly, Luke does not speak of Jesus being hampered by the spread of his reputation, but simply notes how great crowds came together to seek Jesus. ὄχλοι πολλοί is the plural of ὄχλος πολύς, 5:29; it should not be translated 'many crowds'. Luke stresses that they came to hear Jesus and to be healed from their illnesses (ἀσθένεια 8:2; 13:11f.*; Acts 28:9*; Mt. 8:17), thereby placing the preaching of Jesus above his healing ministry.

(16) The crowds who sought Jesus did not, however, find him. He had retired (ὑποχωρέω, 9:10**) to the wilderness and stayed there (the imperfect expresses duration, BD 253) in order to pray; cf. 3:21 note and 4:42 note. Thus where Mark suggests that Jesus went away simply to avoid the crowds, Luke has no doubt correctly seen the positive point that his purpose in seeking loneliness was in order to pray; cf. Mk. 1:35. No special reason for the prayer is apparent, but in the light of 4:42f. it may be seen that Jesus was unwilling to yield to the temptation to stay on in any given place after he had preached to the people lest he might become their popular idol or even their servant; the mainspring of his life was his communion with God, and in such communion he found both strength and guidance to avoid submitting to temptation.

ii. Jesus' Authority to forgive Sins 5:17–26

The earlier stories of Jesus' mighty acts have already posed the questions of who he is (4:22) and what was the nature of his authority (4:36). Now the revelation of Jesus' person and authority is carried a stage further in a story in which the focus of attention is not the mighty act as such, but the nature of the authority to which it draws attention. By healing a paralysed man – an event eloquent in itself of the saving power demonstrated by Jesus – Jesus claims corroboration for his authority to forgive sins, since performance of the visible act of healing should have given at least some degree of proof that he possessed authority for the spiritual, and hence invisible and unprovable, act of forgiveness. The claim to such authority raised the beginnings of opposition to Jesus on the part of the Pharisees who appear as the strict guardians of the Jewish religion, and whose presence is significantly noted at the beginning of the story (contrast Mk. 2:6); they rightly saw that Jesus was claiming the prerogative of God, a prerogative which Jesus was prepared to justify as legitimately belonging to him on the grounds of his claim to be the Son of man; hence the miracle of healing was meant not simply to prove the reality of the act of forgiveness, but also to corroborate Jesus' claim to be the Son of man.

The story is taken over with little change in substance from Mk., but with a considerable amount of minor verbal alteration, especially at the beginning of the story in view of Luke's reordering of the material. A good many of these changes are shared with Mt., but it is doubtful whether their character is such as to justify Schramm, 99–103, in claiming that Luke can here be using a variant tradition of the story alongside Mk.; the cautious formulation of this conclusion indicates that it is weakly based. There is little theological content in the changes, beyond the formulation of the response to the miracle in characteristically Lucan terms; even here there is no real change of substance.

The story in Mk. has been dissected by scholars since it has a complex form, compared with the usual type of 'controversy story'; the break in Mk. 2:10, the disappearance of the critical Pharisees from the enthusiastic crowd at the end of the story, and the possibility of theological reflection regarding the Son of man in the central dialogue – these points have combined to suggest that the story has suffered interpolation. Bultmann, 12–14, 227, defended the view that Mk. 2:5b–10 was a secondary addition to a simple miracle story (cf. I. Maisch*). But this section is unlikely ever to have circulated on its own. More recent critics have argued that the interpolation is unlikely to have been made without some point of contact in the original story, and therefore it is suggested with greater plausibility that v. 5b belonged to the original story and gave the impulse for the addition of vs. 6–10 (Hahn, 43 n. 1; Schürmann, I, 286; cf. Dibelius, 63–66). One may, however, question whether the middle section should be regarded as an interpolation at all. It is obvious that neither Matthew nor Luke found the break in Mk. 2:10 awkward, since both have preserved it. The fact that no reaction of the Pharisees to the miracle is mentioned may well be because the narrator wished to show how their original criticism was effectually silenced by the mighty act of Jesus; at the same time Mark has saved up his comments on their reaction to the end of the series of stories at 3:6 – it would perhaps have spoiled the effect in the individual stories if they had not culminated in the act or word of Jesus and the enthusiastic response of the people. In any case, it seems highly unlikely that a story could have introduced the apparently irrelevant words, 'Your sins are forgiven', without some kind of explanation. The original unity of the story is to be accepted (Hooker*; cf. Lane, 97, who takes up the suggestion that Mk. 2:10 is a Marcan addition to a unified story).

See Hooker, *Son of Man*, 81–93; Kertelge, 75–82; I. Maisch, *Die Heilung des Gelähmten*, Stuttgart, 1971; J. Gnilka, 'Das Elend vor dem Menschensohn (Mk. 2:1–12)', in Pesch, *Jesus*, 196–209.

(17) The action takes place ἐν μιᾷ τῶν ἡμερῶν (8:22; 20:1; cf. 5:12 note), a phrase which simply means 'one day', perhaps referring vaguely

to the general period of time within which the incident fell (cf. 4:43f.; Schürmann, I, 280f.; but this interpretation would require some kind of qualification of τῶν ἡμερῶν; more probably the phrase is simply a Lucan equivalent for Mk. δι' ἡμερῶν). Luke omits mention of the name of the place involved, viz. Capernaum. Schürmann, I, 281, suggests that Luke wants to convey the impression of a widening circle of influence; but this aim is secured by the second part of the verse describing the spread of Jesus' reputation, and Jesus is in fact still near Capernaum in 7:1. Since there is no reference to the crowds in the house at this point, v. 18 needs some explanation, which is not provided until v. 19. The attention is concentrated rather on the critical section of the audience. The Φαρισαῖοι are not mentioned in Mk. in this story, but they do appear in Mk. 2:16, and the use of the name is justified here, since most of the lawyers were members of the Pharisaic party. The Pharisees appear in the Gospels as the defenders of the traditions of the elders, in which the law of Moses received many petty refinements, and hence as defenders of strict Jewish orthodoxy over against Jesus; cf. R. Meyer and H. F. Weiss, TDNT IX, 11–48, J. Bowker, *Jesus and the Pharisees,* Cambridge, 1973. The term νομοδιδάσκαλος, 'teacher of the law' (Acts 5:34; 1 Tim. 1:7**; K. H. Rengstorf, TDNT II, 159), appears to be a Christian coinage 'designed to mark off Jewish from Christian teachers at the decisive point, namely, the absolutising of the νόμος' (Rengstorf). It is equivalent in meaning to γραμματεύς (5:21; *et al.*) and νομικός (7:30; *et al.*). Since most lawyers were Pharisees, the whole phrase here is to be interpreted as a hendiadys. The reading οἳ ἦσαν ἐληλυθότες implies that every village had its quota of Pharisees; this is the hardest and best attested text; it is simplified by the omission of οἳ in ℵ* 33 and by the replacement of οἳ by δέ in D d e syˢ (so NEB), so that it is the sick who have come from each village to be healed (Metzger, 138). The three areas from which the visitors came are to be found in Mk. 3:8 (cf. Lk. 6:17); cf. Mk. 3:22. Ἰουδαία is here used in its narrower sense. The mention of Jerusalem is perhaps a reminder to the reader of the coming fate of Jesus at the hands of official Judaism, and Luke may indeed be thinking of an official delegation to examine the claims of Jesus, but the text gives no definite support to this suggestion. As a final piece of preparation for the action of the story we are told that the power of God was with Jesus to enable him to heal the sick; κύριος when used without the article means God. The variants for αὐτόν in the MSS are due to scribes taking κυρίου to mean Jesus and the pronoun to be the object of ἰᾶσθαι (cf. Metzger, 138).

(18) Like Matthew, Luke indicates the beginning of the action with ἰδού. The use of ἄνδρες (replacing Mark's 'impersonal plural') is Lucan. Luke prefers the verb παραλύω (5:24; Acts 8:7; 9:33; Heb. 12:12**) to the rare form παραλυτικός, and he uses κλίνη, 'bed', par. Mt., and κλινίδιον, 5:19, 24, instead of Mk. κράβαττος; see further 5:25 note. The use of ζητέω with infinitive is Lucan, and the imperfect has a conative

sense. The second αὐτόν is read by B Θ pc sa bo; (UBS); Diglot; it may well have seemed redundant to scribes.

(19) Since the men were unable to find a way by which they might bring the paralytic in, they climbed up onto the roof. ποίας, sc. ὁδοῦ, is a local genitive (for the Classical dative; 19:4; BD 186¹); the insertion of διά by TR; Diglot with weak MS evidence is an awkward grammatical improvement, leading to three examples of διά in a row. The insertion of ἀναβαίνω is a Lucan clarification. δῶμα is 'roof' (12:3; 17:31*; Acts 10:9*). Luke envisages the roof as made of tiles (κέραμος**), while Mark is usually thought to imply one made of mud and wattle. Hence it is often argued that Luke has rewritten the story in terms of Hellenistic architecture (cf. 6:48; 21:29 and possibly 12:57–59 with notes). But Morris, 116f., notes correctly that Mark does not state what the roof was made of, and that tiled roofs were in use in Palestine by this date (J. L. Kelso, NBD, 544). καθίημι is 'to let down' (Acts 9:25; 10:11; 11:5**).

(20) The perseverance and ingenuity of the companions of the sick man are seen by Jesus as an indication of the presence of a faith which believes in his power to such an extent that it is prepared to go to the limit in order to reach him. The relation of faith to the miracles of Jesus is here indicated for the first time; cf. 7:9; 8:25, 48, 50; 17:19; 18:42. But the lesson is a deeper one here; instead of simply healing the man's body in response to his faith, Jesus pronounces the forgiveness of his sins (cf. 7:50), thereby demonstrating that the full salvation of men, both spiritual and physical, depends upon faith in the ability of Jesus to act with the authority and grace of God. For the link of forgiveness and healing cf. Ps. 103:5; O. Betz, Jesus, 62. At the same time, it is implied that a partial salvation is not what Jesus wishes to bestow. His ministry was centred on his teaching which called men to repent and believe in the Gospel, and to accept its spiritual blessings, and he did not wish to perform physical healings which could become incomplete ends in themselves, and thus fail to be seen as symbolic parts of a greater whole. It is open to question whether Jesus here implies that the man's paralysis was due to some special sin (cf. Jn. 5:14; contrast Lk. 13:1–5; Jn. 9:2) or simply thinks of the man's sharing in universal human sinfulness. The thought of the time certainly associated sin with physical punishment and illness (SB I, 495f.), and nothing is done here to correct that impression; on the contrary, Jesus' action would suggest that the sin which caused the illness needed to be dealt with before the cure could proceed. Jesus addresses the man (αὐτῇ, A W pm; TR; Diglot, is a clarification), as ἄνθρωπε, diff. Mk. τέκνον (cf. Mk. 10:24; Lk. 15:31; 16:25); the address may be equivalent to 'friend' (12:14) or express a degree of reproach (22:58, 60; Rom. 2:1, 3; 9:20. Jas. 2:20; AG s.v.). The perfect form ἀφέωνται, diff. Mk. ἀφίενται, a 'punctiliar present', expresses the abiding force of the forgiveness.

(21) The introductory ἤρξαντο is not pleonastic (pace Schramm,

103), but is a deliberate correction of Mark's periphrastic imperfect, the point being that only after Jesus' declaration did the scribes (γραμματεύς, J. Jeremias, TDNT I, 740–742) and the other Pharisees present begin to discuss what had happened. The use of λέγοντες need not imply speech (1:63; 12:17), especially since Mark makes it clear that they were thinking, rather than speaking (cf. Lk. 5:22). The unspoken thoughts attributed to the audience are obvious enough, and serve to introduce Jesus' reply. The second question logically precedes the first. Only God can forgive sin, for only the offended person can forgive the offender; he may, however, act through a prophet or other agent (2 Sa. 12:13). Hence the question arises whether Jesus has any authorisation to speak in this fashion, either by usurping the prerogative of God or in virtue of a prophetic gift. Since the Pharisees believed that prophecy had effectually ceased, although they do not in fact appear to have been completely certain on the matter (R. Meyer, TDNT VI, 816–825), the question whether Jesus was a prophet was a rhetorical one, and hence they put their own answer into the question: he is uttering blasphemies (plural, used of one saying, BD 142). The term 'blasphemy' is understood in the Mishnah to mean use of the Name of God (the Tetragrammaton; Sanh. 7:5), but the NT evidence indicates that the term was used more widely to indicate any 'violation of the power and majesty of God' (H. W. Beyer, TDNT I, 621–625; cf. SB I, 1008–1019 for evidence that the concept was narrowed by the Rabbis). The word order ἁμαρτίας ἀφεῖναι is inverted in ℵ A C W Θ pm Cyr; TR; Diglot (ἀφιέναι ἁμαρτίας), but this reflects assimilation to Mk. rather than an original Semitic word order.

(22) Jesus realised what they were thinking (cf. 2:35; 6:8; 9:47; 24:38); such knowledge could well be regarded as perfectly normal, but here it may be seen as part of Jesus' prophetic powers.

(23) He therefore challenged them with a counter-question. Which is easier (εὔκοπος, 16:17; 18:25), he asks, to say to anybody (by omitting τῷ παραλυτικῷ, diff. Mk., Luke generalises), 'Your sins are forgiven', or to say, 'Rise and walk'? The implication is that neither act is possible for a man, certainly not the former, which is God's prerogative; but since the latter too can only be done by the power of God (cf. 5:17b), it follows that the person who can do the latter is also authorised to do the former (Schürmann, I, 283). Strictly speaking, neither act is easier than the other, since both require divine power, but the latter could be regarded as more difficult in the sense that while anybody could declare sin to be forgiven without having to submit his act to some kind of proof it is impossible to claim to heal a person without producing tangible evidence.

(24) In order, however, that the scribes may know that the Son of man does have authority on earth to forgive sins, Jesus pronounces the healing word to the paralytic, and thus demonstrates his authority *a fortiori*. The wording follows Mk. except in minor details such as

avoidance of the historic present and avoidance of ὑπάγω. There is no
suggestion that Jesus would not have healed the man if it had not been
necessary to demonstrate his claims to the scribes. The verse does,
however, pose difficulties with its use of the term 'Son of man' (see especially Tödt, 126–130; Higgins, 26–28; C. Colpe, TDNT VIII,
400–477, especially 430f.; Borsch, 321f.; Vielhauer, 120–122; Hooker*;
I. H. Marshall, 'The Synoptic Son of Man Sayings in Recent Discussion', NTS 12, 1965–66, 327–351, especially 341.; Jeremias,
Theology, I, 257–276; Goppelt I, 226–253; Pesch, *Jesus*). 1. The usage
here is identical with that in Mk. There is no indication that Luke has
anywhere created fresh uses of the title 'Son of man', or that he has his
own distinctive theology of the title (C. Colpe, TDNT VIII, 457–459;
see, however, G. Schneider, ' "Der Menschensohn" in der lukanischen
Theologie', in Pesch, *Jesus*, 267–282). 2. The Son of man is not
associated with the dispensing of forgiveness in any pre-Christian
sources (Tödt, 129). Nevertheless, the traditional figure of the Son of
man is of one who has the right to act as heavenly judge and ruler, and
such a figure has implicitly the power to forgive. 3. The fact that Jesus
forgave sins, though somewhat scantily attested, is undoubtedly to be
accepted as historical (Schürmann, I, 284; Goppelt, I, 177–185). 4. In
the present saying 'Son of man' undoubtedly refers to Jesus himself, and
cannot be understood to refer to some other, apocalyptic figure. In our
opinion, the view that Jesus spoke in other sayings (e.g. 12:8f.) of
another Son of man (Tödt) is certainly to be rejected. Hence three
possibilities arise in the present instance. a. The saying is a creation of
the early church, perhaps intended to justify the church's own practice
of declaring forgiveness by appealing to the authority of its Founder
(Higgins). Cranfield, 100f., suggests that the clumsy construction of the
verse indicates that it is a Marcan comment to the reader, explaining the
significance of the healing miracle; cf. Mk. 2:28 and (without this title)
7:19. There is, however, no indication in the narrative that the 'you' in
this verse means the readers rather than Jesus' audience. The view that
this is a church saying should be accepted only if there are difficulties in
attributing the saying to Jesus himself. As has already been stated, there
is no real problem in the reference to forgiveness; it is the use of 'Son of
man' that seems difficult. b. This difficulty may be avoided by
postulating that the original Aramaic expression used here meant simply
'man', so that Jesus was saying 'Not only God may forgive, but man too
in Me, Jesus' (Colpe, TDNT VIII, 430); the ambiguous term was then
given a messianic sense by the early church (ibid. 441). The difficulty
with this suggestion is that the saying would then imply that man in
general could forgive sins, which is manifestly false. This difficulty is
avoided by the earlier view of Wellhausen (cited by Colpe, ibid. 431 n.
236) that Jesus means that he can forgive *although* he is a man. This is a
possible view of the saying, but it is not without problems, since it leaves
the charge of blasphemy unanswered; the question is not whether a man

can forgive sins, but whether this man has God's authorisation to do so (Hooker*, 83f.). Colpe's view rests Jesus' right to forgive on an unstated messianic claim. It is more likely that the saying stated Jesus' authorisation to forgive. c. This authorisation is stated if Jesus spoke of himself as the Son of man. In this case the point of the saying is that Jesus claims to be the Son of man, and claims that the Son of man has authority to forgive sins, not merely when acting as heavenly judge, but also here and now on earth. This claim is then justified by Jesus' healing act. This interpretation of the saying faces the general criticism that Jesus did not refer to himself as the Son of man active on earth during his ministry; elsewhere we have attempted to show that this criticism can be countered, and that Jesus used the phrase 'Son of man' to designate his authority both on earth and at the parousia, an authority which was not recognised but rather rejected by the Jews in general during his ministry; see further R. Maddox, 'The Function of the Son of Man according to the Synoptic Gospels', NTS 15, 1968–69, 45–74, who stresses how the theme of eschatological judgment runs through the whole body of Son of man sayings and finds that this saying fits neatly into the general picture. 5. Behind the usage of Son of man here by Jesus there lies the concept which is to be found in Dan. 7:13f., where the phrase is applied to a human figure (the phrase should be translated 'a man') who is nevertheless of heavenly origin and is given dominion on earth as the leader of the 'saints of the Most High'; the precise history of this figure both before and after his appearance in Daniel is so uncertain that no firm conclusions can be ventured here, but it seems probable that this figure was capable of being understood in messianic terms (cf. 1 Enoch) and that Jesus adopted it because it formed the most suitable basis for expressing his own self-understanding, a basis which underwent considerable alteration in the course of his use of it.

(25) The confirmation of Jesus' claims was provided by the way in which the paralytic was able to respond to Jesus' healing word. Luke notes that the healing was immediate, a fact which could be deduced from the general character of the healings reported in the Gospel tradition. Once again he avoids the use of κράβαττος, diff. Mk. (cf. 5:19, 24) by taking a phrase from Mk. 2:4, but he does use Mark's word in Acts 5:15; 9:33. Finally, Luke adds that the man praised God (17:15, 18), a fact which could be deduced from Mark's description of the action of the bystanders: if the spectators glorified God, how much more was the healed man likely to do so also.

(26) Instead of Mark's simple verb ἐξίσταμαι, to express the surprise of the spectators, Luke uses the periphrasis ἔκστασις ἔλαβεν ἅπαντας; ἔκστασις, 'amazement' (Mk. 5:42; 16:18; Acts 3:10), can also mean 'trance' (Acts 10:10; 11:5; 22:17); the use of λαμβάνω may be Semitic (Ex. 15:15; Wis. 11:12), but is also attested in Classical Greek. Luke also refers to the fear of the spectators, par. Mt., diff. Mk., but the evidence is hardly strong enough to confirm use of some common source

other than Mk. The comment of the crowd is rephrased: we have seen
unexpected things (παράδοξος**) today (perhaps with an echo of 4:21).
The story thus closes with the fear and praise of the spectators in face of
the supernatural authority of Jesus, a feature that is prominent in Lk.
(7:16; 13:17; 18:43; Acts 3:9; 8:8). Schürmann, I, 285, suggests that the
intention is to indicate to the reader how he too should react to the telling of the story and to his own experience of the forgiving grace of God.

iii. Jesus' Attitude to Sinners 5:27–32

A story in which the authority of Jesus to forgive sins has been
demonstrated is fittingly followed by the present narrative in which he is
shown welcoming sinners and (it is implied) bestowing upon them a
forgiveness expressed symbolically in fellowship at table. Unlike the
story in 5:1–11, the brief account of the call of Levi deals only incidentally with the nature of discipleship. Its main purpose is to show the kind
of people whom Jesus called and hence to justify his action; the
narrative culminates in the sayings of Jesus which justify his going after
sinners despite the criticisms of the scribes. No more than a doctor could
he be expected to keep his hands clean. His duty lay with the needy, and
those who thought themselves to be righteous were not his primary concern.

In his re-telling of the story, Luke has, however, taken the opportunity to bring out the fact that discipleship did mean for Levi the for-
saking of all in order to follow Jesus. This fact may appear to stand in
tension with the way in which Levi was able to hold a great feast in his
house for his business associates, but the meal is clearly meant to be a
means of introducing them to Jesus, and this motive is in no way inconsistent with his decision to give up his lucrative trade in order to become
a disciple. Luke also reformulates the question of the scribes so that it
deals with the behaviour of the disciples rather than with that of Jesus,
although it is Jesus who answers on their behalf; the Master bears the
responsibility for what his disciples do (cf. D. Daube, 'Responsibilities of
Master and Disciples in the Gospels', NTS 19, 1972–73, 1–15). Such a
change may indicate that the transmission of the story reflects a *Sitz im
Leben* in which the early church sought to defend its own associations
with the outcasts of Jewish society, perhaps even with gentile 'sinners'
(Gal. 2:15; cf. R. Pesch*, in Descamps, 82–84). Finally, Luke has added
the words 'to repentance' to the closing saying of Jesus, thus indicating
that the evangelistic invitation of Jesus includes a summons to repentance on the part of sinners; since, however, for Luke repentance itself is
a gift of God (Acts 5:31; 11:18; cf. 2 Tim. 2:25), the phrase should not
be regarded simply as a moralising addition.

The Marcan form of the story falls into two clear parts, the call of
Levi (Mk. 2:13f.) and the meal at his house (Mk. 2:15–17). It is widely

accepted that originally these were two separate narratives. If Mark is
here using a collection of 'conflict stories', then it is the story of the meal
which has a place in the collection for its own sake, and the story of the
call must have been attracted to that of the meal (Schürmann, I, 290). R.
Pesch*, 1968, 43–45, argues that the story of the call is a Marcan creation to introduce the story of the meal and clarify v. 17b by describing
how Jesus had called Levi to be a disciple; v. 13 is a redactional link, and
v. 14 was composed on the pattern of Mk. 1:16–20 by using the name of
Levi and drawing appropriate deductions regarding his call (cf.
Bultmann, 26f.; Schürmann, I, 289). But while Mk. 2:13 may be due to
Marcan redaction (it is significantly omitted by both Matthew and
Luke), there is much less reason to doubt the historicity and traditional
nature of v. 14. Had the event really happened, and the story been pared
down to bare essentials (as in the case of Mk. 1:16–20), it would have
taken the same form as it actually has here. The reference to the seaside
in Mk. 2:13 may rather suggest that Mark took the story from a brief
complex which included Mk. 1:16–20 and has repositioned it to serve as
an introduction to 2:15–17.

As for the meal scene itself, Bultmann, 16, claimed that Mk. 2:15f.
is an ideal scene created to give a setting for the saying in v. 17; he regarded v. 17b as a secondary elaboration of v. 17a and allowed that v. 17a
might be authentic (ibid. 96, 109, 166f.). Van Iersel* also separates the
brief *Streitgespräch* in Mk. 2:16–17a from v. 17b, and regards the
authenticity of v. 17a as contestable, while that of v. 17b is more
probable. R. Pesch*, in Descamps, 63–87, argues that the scene has a
historical kernel, which is not significantly different from its present
form, except that Mk. 2:17a is separated off as an isolated logion (which
may well be authentic). Schürmann, I, 292f., argues that in view of the
tension between v. 16 and v. 17 the latter was probably handed down as
an independent saying, in which case v. 17a must have been followed by
v. 17b or it would have had no point of application. The fact that v. 17a
has Hellenistic parallels is not an argument against its authenticity (*pace*
Schweizer, *Markus*, 34).

There are, in our opinion, no grounds for regarding vs. 17a and 17b
as other than authentic sayings of Jesus, and the reasons for separating
them from each other are unconvincing (see below). Nor is the tension
between the situation in v. 16 and the reply in v. 17 strong enough to
justify separation of the situation from the saying or to indicate that the
scene has been composed on the basis of the saying. As Taylor, 203,
rightly comments: 'A narrator whose invention was uncontrolled by the
tradition would hardly have left so many points open'.

See B. M. F. van Iersel, 'La vocation de Lévi (Mc., II, 13–17, Mt. IX, 9–13, Lc., V, 27–32)',
in de la Potterie, 212–232; R. Pesch, 'Levi-Matthäus (Mc 2:14/Mt 9:9; 10:3) ', ZNW 59, 1958,
40–56; id., 'Das Zöllnergastmahl (Mk 2, 15–17) ', in Descamps, 63–87; Stanton, 138–142.

(27) Luke abbreviates Mark's introduction to the story. He retains
the transition from the preceding scene set in the house with ἐξῆλθεν and

substitutes μετὰ ταῦτα for Mark's πάλιν; this change was necessary because Luke also omits the detail that Jesus went out παρὰ τὴν θάλασσαν, in accordance with his frequent practice. The detail that Jesus was teaching the crowds is probably due to Marcan editing, and both Luke and Matthew omit it as being irrelevant to the story; earlier Luke has indicated that the call of Jesus to discipleship presupposes the earlier preaching of the gospel to whose who are called (cf. 5:1–11). Instead, attention is concentrated on the man whom Jesus saw (θεάομαι, 7:24; 23:55*; Acts, 3x), a strong verb which suggests that Jesus singled out Levi particularly. Λευίς (5:29*) appears only in this story; Matthew substitures the name Μαθθαῖος (Mt. 9:9; cf. 10:3). He was a tax-collector (τελώνης, 3:12 note), seated according to the custom of his occupation at his office (τελώνιον, Mt. 9:9; Mk. 2:14**). The occupation described here is that of collecting customs dues on goods arriving in the kingdom of Herod Antipas, and Levi was probably a subordinate official engaged in the actual collection of the tolls for a tax-farmer. Jesus called him with the words ἀκολούθει μοι (cf. 9:23; 9:59; 18:22; Jn. 1:44), a command that was implicit in the earlier call of Simon and his colleagues, 5:11. Here too the call appears to be to a literal accompanying of Jesus on his travels, although not all disciples were called to do so.

(28) Levi arose from his seat and followed Jesus, but the ἀναστάς should perhaps be taken less literally, especially since the Lucan detail that he left everything (cf. 5:11) can hardly mean that he simply left his office there and then without some formal settling of his business. Luke's phrase rather stresses his decisive break with his old life (aorist participle) followed by his continuing life of discipleship (imperfect indicative).

(29) Luke remodels the text to indicate clearly that it was Levi who acted as host to Jesus; Mark's wording could be ambiguous to anybody who did not realise (what Mark takes for granted) that Jesus had no home of his own. He stresses that Levi made an occasion of the meal, providing a great feast (δοχή, 14:13**). Elsewhere meal scenes figure prominently in Lk. and were evidently important for the Evangelist (7:36–50; 9:10–17; 10:38–42; 11:37–54; 14:1–24; 19:1–10; 22:4–38; 24:29–32, 41–43). But here the important feature is the character of the great company present (the word order ὄχλος τελωνῶν πολύς in A al; TR; *Diglot* should perhaps be preferred; cf. Alford, I, 486). It consisted of tax-collectors and 'others' – Luke's substitute for Mk. ἁμαρτωλοί, i.e. persons regarded as sinful by the Pharisees because of their immoral lives or low occupations (cf. Barclay; 'people with whom no respectable Jew would have had anything to do'; J. Jeremias, 'Zöllner und Sünder', ZNW 30, 1931, 293–300). These people were sitting at table with them, i.e. with Jesus and Levi, so that Jesus was clearly disregarding the Pharisaic standards according to which such people were both sinful in themselves and ritually unclean because of their contact with gentiles.

(30) We are not told where or when the Pharisees attacked the

conduct of the disciples; they would not have been at the feast, and it must be assumed that the conversation took place afterwards. The attack is mounted by the Pharisees and the scribes who belonged to their party (cf. 5:17). γογγύζω is 'to grumble' (Mt. 20:11; Jn. 6:41, 43, 61; 7:32; 1 Cor. 10:10**; cf. γογγυσμός, Acts 6:1; διαγογγύζω, Lk. 15:2; 19:7**; K. H. Rengstorf, TDNT I, 728–737); it brings out the sense of Mark's account and may draw a parallel with the attitude of Israel to God in the wilderness (Grundmann, 132); but the allusion is perhaps too subtle to be convincing. As in Mk., the question is directed to the disciples, but here it concerns the disciples' own conduct. Luke replaces Mark's ὅτι (in the sense 'why?') with διὰ τί, and adds the words καὶ πίνετε, which accentuate the crime (cf. 5:33; 7:33f.). The term 'sinners' naturally includes the 'tax-collectors', but this seems an insufficient reason for regarding 'and sinners' as an addition to the original question, since the whole phrase can loosely mean 'tax-collectors and (other) sinners'.

(31) Jesus' reply (ἀποκριθείς, diff. Mk. ἀκούσας) is given on behalf of the disciples (possibly indirectly to the disciples rather than to the opponents themselves), and falls into two halves. The first half is the proverbial-sounding statement that it is not people who are well who need a doctor but people who are ill. ὑγιαίνω, 'to be healthy' (7:10; 15:27*), replaces Mark's ἰσχύω, thereby restoring the correct sense of the probable Aramaic original bᵉri'a, which can mean 'strong' or 'healthy' (Jeremias, Parables, 125 n. 42); κακῶς ἔχω is 'to be ill', 7:2*. The saying reflects the metaphor of healing in 4:23. It has parallels in Hellenistic sources (Stobaeus, Ecl. 3:13–43; cf. also Taylor, 206). These parallels, however, provide no good reason for disallowing the saying to Jesus; not only is there no good reason for denying its authenticity, but the formulation of the saying in which the sick, not the doctor, form the subject speaks in favour of it; Jesus is not directing attention to himself, but justifying his concern for the sick, and at the same time challenging his listeners to self-examination regarding their own sickness (R. Pesch*, in Descamps, 81f.).

(32) The second half of the reply elucidates the first. Using the figure of the host, Jesus represents himself as calling not the righteous but sinners. The 'righteous' here will be the Pharisees, as they thought themselves to be, but the question of whether they were actually righteous or not is not raised; the stress lies on the positive call to the sinners. Luke's change of tense, ἐλήλυθα, diff. Mk. ἦλθον, expresses more exactly that Jesus' mission was still in progress; the aorist tense has suggested to some commentators on Mk. that such a saying as the present one looks back on the ministry of Jesus as a completed whole, i.e. is not authentic (Bultmann, 167f.), but this is not a necessary conclusion, especially if the verb translates the Aramaic form 'ᵃṭā (bā) lᵉ (J. Jeremias, 'Die älteste Schicht der Menschensohn-Logien', ZNW 58, 1967, 159–172, especially 166f.). In the original Marcan form the verb καλέω

probably had the specific sense 'to invite', using the metaphor of a meal. This sense has been obscured in Lk. by the addition εἰς μετάνοιαν (Jeremias, *Parables*, 121; cf. the addition of πιστεύω in 8:12). Jesus' saying is thus applied to those who are sinners in God's eyes. Luke thus brings out an element which was integral to the teaching of Jesus (Mk. 1:15; cf. Lagrange, 170), although it is often expressed in other categories (cf. 3:3 note). The addition, however, does not demand Schürmann's conclusion, I, 291, that for Luke the story justifies the church's practice of fellowship with sinners, provided that they have undergone conversion: the whole point of the story is that Jesus was prepared to eat with sinners in order to lead them to repentance.

If the two parts of Jesus' reply are authentic, the question arises as to whether both belong to the present story. The second part of the saying fits into the story quite appropriately (R. Pesch*, in Descamps, 79–81). The first part has no direct relation to a meal scene, but this is no argument whatever against its forming an original part of the story; had it had a clear relation to the story, we would have been told by the same critics that it had been composed to fit it, or had been attracted to it by the common theme. R. Pesch (ibid. 74f.) argues: 1. it could have been transmitted as an isolated logion; 2. it does not directly answer the scribes' question; 3. it is unusual for a pronouncement story to have two concluding sayings; 4. the use of οὐ . . . ἀλλά . . . in this saying (exclusive sense) is different from that in v. 32 (dialectic sense, 'not so much . . . as . . .'). These arguments are unconvincing. If the first half of the saying was part of the original story, then the second half was present also to provide a commentary on it, since the view that there could not be two sayings at the end of the story is quite arbitrary; nor need οὐ . . . ἀλλά . . . be taken in two different senses (cf. above; even if two different senses are present, this is no argument whatever against the unity of the saying). We may conclude that the two parts of the saying could well have belonged together in its original form.

iv. Jesus' Attitude to Fasting 5:33–39

Fasting was a familiar practice in the time of Jesus. The Jewish nation fasted on the Day of Atonement (Lv. 16:29) and also on four days in memory of the destruction of Jerusalem (Zc. 7:3, 5; 8:19), although it is not certain that the latter were universally observed. Individuals might fast at other times for a variety of reasons, especially as a sign of religious zeal in the sight of God. The Pharisees developed the practice of fasting twice weekly on Mondays and Thursdays in intercession for the nation as a whole (Lk. 18:12; Did. 8:1; cf. SB IV:1, 77–114; J. Behm, TDNT IV, 924–935). From the present passage we learn that voluntary fasting was also practised by the followers of John, a custom which would fit in with their leader's known ascetic habits (Lk. 7:33).

Although Jesus was criticised by the Jews for not being abstemious, he nevertheless fasted during the temptation in the wilderness (4:2) and made a vow of abstinence at the last supper (22:16, 18). He gave advice on the importance of observing fasts secretly instead of in order to attract human attention (Mt. 6:16–18), in a saying which presupposes that his hearers engaged in voluntary fasts. In the early church there was fasting on special occasions of prayer (Acts 13:2f.; 14:23; cf. 9:9; 2 Cor. 11:27; but 2 Cor. 6:5 probably refers to involuntary deprivation of food). Otherwise there is no evidence for regular fasting in the earliest church.

Jesus had to face the question why his disciples did not fast and pray frequently like the disciples of John and the Pharisees, but instead ate and drank; similar questions or accusations were directed against his own conduct (7:34). His answer, couched as a rhetorical question, is that it would be equally unthinkable for those present at a wedding to fast during the festivities: joy, not fasting, is the appropriate attitude for the companions of Jesus. The present time is thus likened to a wedding, and the period of Jesus' ministry is seen in terms of the messianic banquet. But a period will come when the bridegroom has been taken away, and then it will be appropriate to fast, apparently as an expression of grief. To this basic statement is added a parable. One does not patch an old garment with a piece from a new one, otherwise the new is spoilt and in any case the patch will not fit properly on the old garment. Similarly, if new wine is put into old skins, they will burst and both wine and skins will be lost. The new way of life associated with the gospel cannot be linked up with the old way of Judaism (perhaps of John the Baptist) without causing their destruction; the new way of life must be allowed to develop without being fettered by the old ways. A final saying, evidently added on the catch-word principle by Luke, ironically comments on the attitude of the Pharisees who preferred the old wine of Judaism to the new wine of the gospel (for a different view, see Flender, 21).

Luke's account, as thus summarised, contains a number of differences from Mk. which must be attributed to Luke himself. He may possibly have been influenced by parallel, oral traditions (Schramm, 105–111; Roloff, *Kerygma*, 237 n. 119). V. 39 is an added saying with no logical connection with what has preceded. In Mk. the questioners of Jesus are not identified, but in Lk. they are perhaps to be equated with the Pharisees in the preceding incident (but see below). The accusation now contains a reference to prayer, which is not taken up in Jesus' reply. It is perhaps a pointer to 11:1, but more probably Luke is clarifying for his readers the circumstances in which fasting took place, namely as an accompaniment to prayer; later it will be apparent that God is so willing to answer prayer that there is no need for his people to engage in fasting to secure his favour. Luke has shortened the saying about the wedding to avoid repetitiousness. He describes the second part of Jesus' answer as a parable (vs. 36–39), but the use of δὲ καί indicates that the preceding saying (vs. 34f.) is also parabolic (cf. 6:39; 18:9). The wording of the saying about the patch is brought into closer parallelism with the saying about the wine by stressing that the new garment from which the patch is taken is spoilt in the process.

The Marcan narrative raises various problems. It is doubtful whether the scene follows on directly from the previous one, and probably it should be regarded as a separate tradition. The coupling of the followers of John and the Pharisees has been thought odd, but it corresponds to historical reality. Both groups did fast, and it is not surprising that Jesus' disciples should have been compared with them (cf. 7:33f.); if Jesus preached repentance (5:32), it could be asked why he did not expect his followers to show the generally accepted signs (Roloff, *Kerygma*, 236). The question presupposes that Jesus' disciples did not fast, but this is probable enough: Jesus' teaching elsewhere does not rule out fasting, but certainly does not require it.

While the authenticity of Mk. 2:19a is generally accepted (Bultmann, 17f.; Perrin 79f.), it is widely held that vs. 19b–20 are a secondary addition. A. Kee*, 1969, holds that the substance of vs. 19b–20 is already contained in v. 19a, so that the whole saying must be regarded as the church's attempt to justify its practice of fasting although, as it falsely believed (but see above), Jesus' disciples did not fast. But the view that the saying is meant to provide an aetiology for the church's practice of fasting is surrounded by numerous difficulties (Roloff, *Kerygma*, 223–234) and can be safely set aside: fasting was not a question that raised problems in the early church. More important are the facts that in vs. 19b–20 Jesus appears to be identified with the messianic bridegroom and that there is allegorical reference to his violent death. It can be argued, however, that 'bridegroom' was not a current messianic expression and that Jesus could have used it without a specifically messianic content being conveyed to his hearers (cf. J. B. Muddiman*, 277–279, but his attempt to derive the image from Joel 2:16 is less convincing). Further, if Jesus anticipated a violent death (H. Schürmann, 'Wie hat Jesus seinen Tod bestanden und verstanden?', in Hoffmann, *Orientierung*, 325–363), and if the present saying need not be placed near the beginning of his ministry, then it fits in coherently with his expectations regarding his own destiny and can be regarded as authentic (Taylor, 208–212; Cranfield, 107–111; cf. Schniewind, *Markus*, 28f.). Nevertheless, there must be some doubt about the placing of the saying in this context, since it shifts the attention from the joy which forbids fasting to the grief which would surround the death of Jesus and thus goes beyond the point at issue.

Although the sayings about the patch and the wine have been added to the wedding saying without any break (so Mk., diff. Lk.), they may well have been originally separate from it; a connection of theme in terms of the essentials for a wedding (good clothes and plenty of wine) (J. B. Muddiman*, 279) is artificial. The function of the sayings here is to provide the general principle which justifies the disciples in refraining from fasting. But their original setting is obscure, and hence their precise application is uncertain. Bultmann, 90, 102f., suggests that the wine saying may have been formed on the analogy of the patch saying (but why not by Jesus who often employed double sayings?); the two sayings are proverbial in tone, and the point appears to be the contrast between new and old. Cranfield, 113, lists five possible meanings along these lines. A. Kee*, 1970, thinks that the point is the danger of loss: the parables warn against ill-considered actions through which men may suffer loss, and thus warn men to be prudently prepared for the imminent coming of the kingdom; but this is to ignore the clear point of the parables which is one of contrast.

See K. Th. Schäfer, ' "... und dann werden sie fasten an jenem Tage" (Mk. 2, 20 und Parallelen) ', in Schmid, *Studien*, 124–147; Jeremias, *Parables*, 116–118; J. Dupont, 'Vin vieux, vin nouveau', CBQ 15, 1963, 286–304; F. G. Kremer, *Die Fastenansage Jesu Mk 2, 20 und Parallelen,* Bonn, 1965 (not accessible to me); Perrin, 77–82; A. Kee, 'The Question about Fasting', Nov.T 11, 1969, 161–173; id. 'The Old Coat and the New Wine', Nov.T 12, 1970, 13–21; Roloff, *Kerygma*, 223–237; F. Hahn, 'Die Bildworte vom neuen Flicken und vom jungen Wein', Ev.T 31, 1971, 357–375; J. B. Muddiman, 'Jesus and Fasting. Mark ii. 18–22', in Dupont, *Jesus*, 271–281; B. Reicke, 'Die Fastenfrage nach Luk. 5, 33–39', TZ 30, 1974, 321–328.

(33) In the context of the preceding narrative the introductory οἱ δέ should refer to 'the Pharisees and their scribes' (5:30). This is unlikely in view of the content of the following statement with its reference to 'the disciples of the Pharisees' in the third person. In Mk. the subject is probably indeterminate ('impersonal plural' construction), but Matthew has reworded the sentence to make the disciples of John the subject. It is probable that the subject is not defined in Lk., and that the present narrative should not be linked too closely with the preceding one.

For John's disciples see 7:18; 11:1; Mk. 6:29; Jn. 1:35, 37; 3:25 (K. H. Rengstorf, TDNT IV, 455–457). The reference to disciples of the Pharisees (Mt. 22:16) is strange, since not all Pharisees were rabbinic teachers. The phrase could have been formed by analogy with what precedes (Bultmann, 17 n.), but K. H. Rengstorf (TDNT IV, 440, 444) notes that the phrase 'the sons of the Pharisees' is attested (11:19 par. Mt. 12:27; cf. Acts 23:6), and that Jos. Ant. 9:106 uses the term 'disciple' where the OT (2 Ki. 9:1) has 'one of the sons of the prophets'; hence the phrase here is a possible one, especially when it is remembered that 'son of' was used to mean 'pupil of' (E. Schweizer, TDNT VIII, 365). The phrase will refer to those who accepted the ideals of the Pharisees, but the unusual language may indicate that it has been assimilated in form to the preceding phrase. On νηστεύω see introduction to this section. πυκνά is 'frequently', Acts 24:36; 1 Tim. 5:23**. The phrase δεήσεις (1:13; 2:37*) ποιέομαι (Phil. 1:4; 1 Tim. 2:1) is a Classical Greek type of formulation (cf. 13:22; Zerwick, 227). The reference in G. Thomas 104 to prayer and fasting is probably based on Lk. Luke's formulation shows that he has interpreted Mark's question in terms of the practice of the people mentioned, whereas Mark refers to one specific event as the occasion of the saying (Mk. 2:18a, omitted by

Luke). The reference to Jesus' own disciples eating and drinking strengthens the link with the preceding narrative and intensifies the accusation. The reference is to prayer in general rather than to petition as such (H. Greeven, TDNT II, 40f.).

(34) Jesus (A Θ *al*; TR; *Diglot* omit the name) replies with what has become in Lk. a reproach to the questioners for trying to compel men to fast (diff. Mk.); they are not to rob the disciples of their joy, any more than one should try to introduce fasting at a wedding. νυμφών can mean the hall in which a wedding is held (Mt. 22:10 v.l.) or the bridal chamber in which the marriage is consummated (Tob. 6:14, 17); for the use of υἱός cf. 1 Mac. 4:2; rabbinic parallels in J. Jeremias, TDNT IV, 1103 n. 40). The persons meant are not the two 'friends of the bridegroom' (Jn. 3:29) who had special duties in connection with the wedding, but the wedding guests whose task was to contribute to the general festivity and joy of the occasion; hence the former meaning of νυμφών is required here (Lohmeyer, 59 n. 4; cf. SB I, 500–517). For νηστεύω Matthew has πενθέω 'to mourn', which Jeremias regards as a return to the more probable meaning of the ambiguous Aramaic 'iṯ'annê 'to be sad', 'to fast'; it is more likely, however, that the original sense is 'to fast' in view of the situation in which the words were spoken, and that Matthew has paraphrased in order to indicate that fasting is a sign of mournfulness. The period in question is defined as 'while the bridegroom is with them'. It has been suggested that this simply means 'while the wedding is in progress' (Dodd, *Parables*, 87 n. 5), but there does not seem to be any concrete evidence for this reduction in meaning. Nor is it likely in the present context, for the point is that it is as foolish to expect the companions of Jesus to fast as it is to expect the companions of the bridegroom to fast. The question itself says nothing about what is going to happen after the wedding. The figure of the bridegroom was used in the OT and Judaism to represent Yahweh in relation to his people (Ho. 2:18, 21; Ezk. 16; Is. 54:5–8; 62:5; Je. 2:2; E. Stauffer, TDNT I, 653f.; J. Jeremias, TDNT IV, 1101f.), but was never applied to the Messiah. The early church would have had no difficulty in applying to Jesus descriptions which originally applied to God himself, and it does not seem impossible that he could do the same, since in other ways he claimed the life-giving power of God. If he understood himself as bringing the age of salvation, there would seem to be a place for himself as the bridegroom (Schürmann, I, 296; cf. Kümmel, *Promise*, 57 n. 123, 75–77). The usage here, however, may be purely metaphorical and not messianic.

(35) Luke omits Mk. 2:19b, as does Matthew, no doubt because it seemed redundant, and goes straight on to the period of contrast. A time will come when things will be different. The phraseology is stereotyped (1 Sa. 2:31; Am. 4:2; cf. Lk. 17:22; 19:43; 21:6; 23:29). Luke moves καί forward in the sentence, perhaps to avoid making ὅταν refer to ἡμέραι (cf. Easton, 71; BD 382³); καί joins the two halves of the sen-

tence. ἀπαίρω, 'to take away, remove', is found only in this saying. In Is. 53:8 it is said of the Servant that he is taken away (luqqaḥ; LXX: αἴρεται ... ἡ ζωὴ αὐτοῦ; cf. Acts 8:33; Jn. 10:18), and a reminiscence of this verse is found here by Taylor, 211; J. Jeremias, who earlier accepted this view ((with W. Zimmerli), *The Servant of God*, 1957, 98), has given it up (cf. its absence from TDNT V, 712). In the present case a vague echo of one word is hardly sufficient to establish a definite allusion. Nevertheless, the thought of a violent end to the wedding festivities can hardly be excluded, and the possibility of such an end is confirmed by 4 Ez. 10:1–4, where a woman (who represents Zion) says: 'But when my son entered his wedding-chamber, he fell down dead (cf. Tobit 6:13f.) ... I have made up my mind ... to stay here eating nothing and drinking nothing, and to continue my mourning and fasting unbroken until I die' (cited by Jeremias, *Theology*, I, 283 n.). Only such an event as this can explain why a period of fasting ensues after the wedding 'in those days' (diff. Mk. singular). The parable is thus carried through to the end, and is not pure allegory. But it refers clearly enough to the way in which Jesus was taken away from the disciples by death. The saying is usually inter- preted as a justification of the church's continued practice of fasting after Easter (e.g. Schürmann, I, 296f., holds that Luke distinguishes clearly between the time of Jesus and that of the absence of Jesus when the church fasted on the day of his death); but it seems more probable that the reference is to the mourning which followed his death before the church became aware of the resurrection and the fact of his continual spiritual presence with it (Jn. 16:16–24); all the indications are that the early church lived in a spirit of joy and experienced fellowship with the risen Lord as it celebrated the Lord's Supper; when fasting is mentioned in the life of the early church, it is as an accompaniment of prayer for guidance rather than as an expression of mourning for the absence of Jesus (cf. Schniewind, *Markus*, 28f.). While 17:22; 2 Cor. 5:6–8 and Phil. 1:23 suggest that the early church felt sorrow because the Lord was absent, it also rejoiced in its communion with him (Phil. 3:8; 1 Pet. 1:8).

(36) Unlike Mark, Luke inserts a transitional phrase (δὲ καί is Lucan (2:4; *et al.*), as is παραβολὴν λέγω, 4:23; 6:39; 12:16 (cf. 12:41); 13:6; 14:7; 15:3; 18:1, 9; 19:11; 20:9, 19; 21:29). Jesus makes his point with an obvious truism (cf. 5:37, 39; 8:16; 9:62; 16:13; Mk. 3:27 for this characteristic form of utterance). Where Mark speaks of using a patch (ἐπίβλημα, Mk. 2:21; Mt. 9:16**) of undressed cloth, Luke refers to the folly of cutting a piece off a new garment in order to patch an old one. For σχίζω, cf. 23:45; C. Maurer, TDNT VII, 959–964. Luke uses ἐπιβάλλω, par. Mt., diff. Mk. ἐπιράπτω**. εἰ μή has the force 'If (anybody does) not (follow this advice) '; γε is added, par. Mt. (cf. 10:6; 13:9; 14:32; the particle is Lucan). Failure to heed this advice will mean that the new material will tear the old, and the patch will not agree with the old garment. Instead of the future σχίσει, the present form is read

here (and συμφωνεῖ) by TR; *Diglot*, possibly by assimilation to the tense in Mk. and Mt. For συμφωνέω see Acts 5:9; 15:15; Mt. 18:19; 20:2, 13**; O. Betz, TDNT IX, 304–309; and for καινός (5:38; 22:20*) and παλαιός (5:37, 39*) see J. Behm, TDNT III, 447–450; H. Seesemann, TDNT V, 717–720. The wording here differs from Mk. where it is said that the patch will pull away from the old garment and make a worse tear in it. In Mk. there is no suggestion that the new is superior to the old, the awkward phrase τὸ καινὸν τοῦ παλαιοῦ perhaps being an addition to the original saying; the point is the incompatibility of the patch and the garment. Luke's form of the saying, amplified by analogy with the wine saying, makes two points: the new garment is ruined by the piece being cut from it, and the patch will not fit properly on the old garment. Jeremias, *Parables*, 29, claims that Luke has lost Mark's point, namely that the tear in the old garment is made worse. But it is questionable whether this was Mark's point. The real point is the incompatibility of the two pieces of cloth, and the contrast of new and old is implicit (cf. Jeremias, *Parables*, 117f., on the symbolism of the new garment). To take only part of Jesus' message is to spoil the whole of it, and even a part of it is incompatible with the old life of Judaism. Whereas in Mk. the deficiencies of Judaism cannot be mended simply by a Christian 'patch', in Lk. the emphasis is on the impossibility of trying to graft something Christian onto Judaism. As in Mk., so in Lk. the saying cannot be directly applied to the question of fasting by an allegorical treatment. The point is that the old and new ways cannot be combined.

(37) Luke follows Mk. more closely in the wine saying. It is concerned with putting fresh wine that is not yet completely fermented into old bottles made of skin. βάλλω is used in its weak sense (13:8, 19; 16:20; 21:1–4). νέος is 'new' in the sense of 'young, fresh', by contrast with καινός, 'new' in the sense of 'novel' (cf. 5:38, 39; 15:12f.; 22:26*; J. Behm, TDNT IV, 896–899). Fermenting wine will continue to swell and so burst the skins (ῥήγνυμι, 9:42*). The wine itself will be poured out and the skins will be destroyed; ἐκχύννω (11:50; 22:20*) is a Hellenistic form for ἐκχέω (Mt. 9:17).

(38) New wine must therefore be put into new skins. Luke uses the verbal adjective βλητέος**, the only NT example of this form (BD 65³), and omits the verb (Classical usage, BD 127⁴). The words καὶ ἀμφότεροι συντηροῦνται appear in A C D Θ pl lat syᵖ boᵖᵗ; TR, as a result of assimilation to Mt. (Metzger, 138).

The point of the saying is essentially the same as that of the previous saying in its Marcan form. The incompatibility of new wine and old skins means that any attempt to combine them leads to the destruction of both. (Since a patch is not 'destroyed' in the same way as wine, Luke had to introduce the idea of the garment from which the patch was taken in order to gain parallelism between the two sayings.) To attempt to contain the gospel within the bounds of Judaism will only destroy both. But the saying goes further and makes the positive point: the gospel is radically new (cf. F. Hahn*, 370) and must be allowed to express itself in its own way.

(39) This verse, peculiar to Lk., is omitted by D it Mcion Iren Eus, i.e. by predominantly western authorities. Its omission may be due to: 1. assimilation to the synoptic parallels (which may have known the saying, but omitted it because of its difficulty); 2. Marcion's dislike of the support which it appeared to give to the authority of the OT (Metzger, 138f.); 3. its objectionableness to scribes with encratite tendencies (Jeremias, *Words*, 148). Whatever explanation be accepted, its external attestation is strong, and the verse should be retained (*pace* Gilmour, 110). The verse expresses the viewpoint of those who are content with the old, because they think it is good, and make no effort to try the new. It is thus an ironical comment on the Jews who refused to taste the 'new wine' of the gospel which was not hallowed by age. The introductory καί is omitted by אᶜ B *pc*; (UBS), giving a harsh asyndeton. After παλαιόν the adverb εὐθέως is added by A Θ *pl* lat; TR; *Diglot*, but this is probably a clumsy attempt to heighten the saying. χρηστός, 'good' (6:35*), has been thought to represent a Semitic use of the positive form of the adjective with a comparative meaning (cf. the v.l. χρηστότερος, A C Θ *pl* lat; TR; Black 117). This may be the case, but the positive sense is sufficient here: 'He who drinks old wine does not compare old and new; he is content not to try the new' (Creed, 84; cf. Alford, I, 488). The thought is proverbial and has both Jewish and Hellenistic parallels (Sir. 9:10; P. Ab. 4:20; b. Ber. 51a; Plautus, Casina 5; H. Seesemann, TDNT V, 163); these parallels constitute no argument against its authenticity (*pace* Bultmann, 107).

v. Plucking Corn on the Sabbath 6:1–5

The last two conflict stories in this section are concerned with the attitude of Jesus and his disciples to the Sabbath (cf. 13:10–19; 14:1–6). The wording follows Mk. fairly closely, mainly with stylistic changes. When Jesus' disciples plucked ears of corn, ground them in their hands and ate them, while they accompanied him on a Sabbath walk through the fields, the Pharisees raised objections. In Mk. the objection is addressed to Jesus, but in Lk. to the disciples themselves, and Jesus steps in to defend them; thus the position of Jesus as the Master who is prepared to step forward to his disciples' defence is emphasised (cf. 5:27–32 note; D. Daube, NTS 19, 1972–73, 7f.). Jesus' response is in the form of a counter-question and cites the example of David who in a case of hunger took the shewbread and shared it between himself and his men, although only the priests were entitled to eat it. The implication is that David had the authority to act as he did, and that Jesus has the same right, but in a higher degree, to reinterpret the law (France, 46f.). This point is expressed more forcefully in Lk. (cf. Mt.) by the omission of Mk. 2:27, so that the statement that the Son of man is lord of the Sabbath stands in direct juxtaposition to the allusion to David.

The history of the tradition behind this story is disputed. Bultmann, 14f., 49, 87f., seizes on the accumulation of sayings of Jesus at the end of the story, and argues that Mk. 2:27f. must be separated off as originally independent; he then argues that the narrative form reflects the interests of the church, and claims that the story is a community formation dealing with the problems of the early church (represented by the disciples). The saying in Mk. 2:27 can be genuine, but 2:28 cannot have existed on its own but only as a comment on 2:27. Similar opinions are expressed by many subsequent writers, although some regard 2:28 as an originally independent logion (cf. Taylor, 214–220; E. Lohse*; id. TDNT VIII, 21–4; Schweizer, *Markus*, 38f.).

An alternative view is that the original unit was Mk. 2:23f., 27, to which was added the scriptural proof in vs. 25f. and the christological comment in v. 28 (Schürmann, I, 305; similarly, Hooker, *Son of Man*, 98, holds that vs. 27f. have a better claim to being words of Jesus, though isolated sayings, than the 'possibly intrusive section about David').

It should be noted first of all that the fact that (in the Marcan form) Jesus is taken to task about the conduct of his disciples is no indication that the scene is a 'community formation' dealing with the behaviour of the early church, since Roloff, *Kerygma*, 55f., and D. Daube have sufficiently demonstrated the plausibility of the master being called to account for his disciples' behaviour. Moreover, the trivial nature of the illegality committed by the disciples suggests that an actual incident forms the basis of the tradition rather than that the early church chose this particular example to serve as the basis of a conflict story.

The reply of Jesus falls into two parts, joined by καὶ ἔλεγεν αὐτοῖς. While this phrase may join additional sayings to an existing narrative, it is quite arbitrary to insist that this must always be the case, and that a pronouncement story can have only one saying at its climax (cf. Cranfield, 116f.). That further sayings can be added to such a story is of course clear from Matthew's treatment of it. There are no good reasons to deny the authenticity of Mk. 2:27 (cf. E. Lohse*, 84f.) and 2:28 (Roloff, *Kerygma*, 58–62). The authenticity of the appeal to David has been attacked on the grounds that the saying lacks any reference to the new situation brought about by the coming of Jesus and that it breathes the atmosphere of the type of scribal discussion which was current in the early church but was not used by Jesus himself (Schweizer, *Markus*, 39). Neither of these arguments is convincing. The former ignores the fact that, as both Matthew and Luke have seen, there is implicit in the appeal to David a typological argument on the basis that 'a greater than David is here' (France, 46f.). The latter flies in the face of Jesus' repeated appeals to Scripture (cf. Mk. 12:10, 26). Hence both sayings may well go back to Jesus himself, although this does not require us to assume that both originally belonged to the present narrative. But the situation cannot have been related without mention of some answer by Jesus – this at least may be held to be demanded by the 'rules' of form criticism. It seems probable that the reference to David originally belonged to the story, since there is no common point between rubbing ears of corn (this, and *not* the eating of them is the point at issue) and taking the shewbread, and hence it is unlikely that the two motifs were arbitrarily joined together. But Mk. 2:27 is equally fitting as a reply to the original question, and is indeed more appropriate since it refers directly to the Sabbath which does not figure in the David episode. It is, however, more likely to be an independent logion than the allusion to David, and hence if there has been an addition to the story it is more likely to be found here (Roloff, *Kerygma*, 58f.).

See E. Lohse, 'Jesu Worte über den Sabbat', in Eltester, 79–89; id. TDNT VII, 21–24; P. Benoit, 'Les épis arrachés (Mt 12, 1–8 et par)', in *Exégèse*, III, 228–242; Roloff, *Kerygma*, 52–62; Goppelt, I, 144–147; F. Neirynck, 'Jesus and the Sabbath. Some observations on Mark II, 27', in Dupont, *Jésus*, 227–270.

(1) Luke uses the singular form σάββατον, diff. Mk. σάββατα, following his preference for this form (15x; pl., 6x; but he leaves the plural form standing in v. 2, since he is less prone to alter direct speech). Many MSS add δευτεροπρώτῳ (A C D Θ f13 *pm* lat Epiph; TR; *Diglot;* cf. *sabbato mane*, e). The external evidence for omission is strong (p⁴ p⁷⁵ᵛⁱᵈ ℵ B W f1 *al* it syᵖ sa bo), while the evidence for inclusion is confined to western and byzantine authorities. The word itself is otherwise unattested, and most commentators think that it is better explained as a scribal gloss than as a *lectio difficilior*. 1. WH App. 58 and Metzger, 139, explain it as a combination of glosses: πρώτῳ was inserted by a scribe to give a contrast with ἑτέρῳ in 6:6; another scribe deleted it with a row of dots over it and inserted δευτέρῳ in view of 4:31; and a third scribe mistakenly combined the two glosses into one. 2. The word has been taken to mean 'a second (Sabbath) after a first one', and to refer to the second Sabbath after the feast of Unleavened Bread (Nisan 15), the first Sabbath being that which fell during the actual week of the feast; this would give a date between Nisan 22 and 30 (SB II, 158). The same result is obtained if the word is taken to mean 'both first and second', and to refer to the day which was the first Sabbath after the feast of Unleavened Bread and the second after the Passover. The corn would be ripe at this time (Schürmann, I, 302; cf. E. Vogt, 'Sabbatum "deuteroproton" in Lc. 6:1 et antiquum Kalendarium sacerdotale', Bib. 40, 1959, 102–105 (cited by E. Lohse, TDNT VII, 23 n. 183); other explanations in Leaney, 130). 3. Others take the word to refer to the second Sabbath of a series in Lk. itself, i.e. the second after 4:16 (4:31 being the first; E. Lohse, ibid.). But this is a solution born of despair.

διαπορεύομαι, 'to go, walk through' (13:22; 18:36; Acts 16:4; Rom. 15:24**) is Luke's substitute for Mk. παραπορεύομαι; he simplifies the sentence by omitting ἤρξαντο ὁδὸν ποιεῖν. τίλλω, 'to pluck, pick', occurs only in this story. The law permitted such gleaning in the fields (Dt. 23:26; SB I, 618f.). Luke (par. Mt.) adds that the disciples ate the ears of corn, and he alone notes how they rubbed them with their hands (ψώχω**, a very rare, possibly medical word, Leaney, 131). The MSS vary in linking τοὺς στάχυας with ἤσθιον (p⁴ p⁷⁵ᵛⁱᵈ B C pc) or with ἔτιλλον (Metzger, 139). The act of plucking could be regarded as part of harvesting, which was forbidden on the Sabbath (Shab. 7:2; SB I, 615–618). The preparation of food by rubbing corn was also forbidden, so much so that one was required to prepare a meal in advance for any traveller who might happen to arrive on the Sabbath (Peah 8:7).

(2) We are not told at what point the Pharisees commented on the action, and it is nonsensical to find in this a historical difficulty, since the details of the story have been pared away, and one can easily visualise gossip about the behaviour of the disciples reaching their ears (cf. 5:30). A number of them ask the disciples why they are breaking the Sabbath law. Luke has inserted τινές, diff. Mk. (cf. 13:31; 19:39), and he has them question the disciples rather than Jesus (cf. αὐτοῖς, added by A Θ pm; TR: Diglot, probably an explanatory addition). For τί, 'why?', cf. Black, 121–124. After ἔξεστιν many MSS insert ποιεῖν or ποιεῖν ἐν, but the shorter reading (p⁴ p⁷⁵ᵛⁱᵈ B (D) pc it) is to be preferred.

(3) As Luke's introductory formula emphasises, it is Jesus who answers for the disciples. For the use of the rhetorical question with an appeal to Scripture see Mk. 12:10, 26; Mt. 12:5; 19:4; 21:6. Instead of ὅτε (par. Mt., Mk.), ὁπότε**, 'when' (used of concrete events in the past), should perhaps be read with A Θ al; TR; Synopsis; Diglot. After οἱ μετ' αὐτοῦ the participle ὄντες is omitted by p⁴ ℵ B D W Θ f1 pm; (UBS), probably because it seemed otiose and was missing from the parallels. The ὅτε/ὁπότε clause is attached to what precedes if we read ὡς (v.l., πῶς, ℵᶜ Θ al, by assimilation to Mt., Mk.) at the beginning of v. 4; if we omit the conjunction with p⁴ B D; (UBS); Diglot, the clause must go with what follows. Since the use of ὡς is Lucan, it should probably be retained.

(4) The incident is that related in 1 Sa. 21:1–9. On his flight from Saul, David arrived by himself at the shrine at Nob, explained that he had followers with him at a secret place, and that he was on a mission for the king. He asked for five loaves of bread or whatever was available. The priest gave him the twelve loaves of shewbread (οἱ ἄρτοι τῆς προθέσεως, Lv. 24:5–9), which was normally eaten only by the priests, on condition that his men were ritually pure, which David assured him that they were. Luke omits the difficult reference to Abiathar found in Mk. He adds the participle λαβών, which reflects Semitic usage (cf. 9:16; 13:19, 21; 24:30, 43; Jeremias, Words, 175; ἔλαβε καί is read by A al Mcion; TR; Diglot). He has brought forward the phrase καὶ ἔδωκεν τοῖς μετ' αὐτοῦ; the addition of καί after ἔδωκεν in many MSS is probably secondary (Metzger, 140). This part of the story has caused difficulty, since David's story about being on a mission for Saul was false, and it

has been claimed that his reference to the young men with him was also an invention: in reality he was looking for food to sustain himself during his flight. But this inference remains hypothetical. The point of the story is unaffected, namely that David and his men ate what was illegal, since it was food only for priests. This is to be explained as an overriding of the law in view of human need. Cranfield, 115, attempts to avoid this conclusion: 'the fact that Scripture does not condemn David for his action shows that the rigidity with which the Pharisees interpreted the ritual law was not in accordance with scripture, and so was not a proper understanding of the Law itself'. But this suggestion conflicts with the express statement in the text that the action was illegal. Hence France, 46f., claims that the point is the authority possessed by David to reinterpret the law, an authority possessed to greater degree by Jesus. Jesus thus claims the right to reinterpret the OT law on the basis that already in the OT itself it was possible for David to override it. There would be a closer connection between the action of Jesus and that of David if the story presupposes the rabbinic interpretation which placed David's deed on the Sabbath (SB I, 618f.; Rengstorf, 80; E. Lohse, TDNT VII, 22); this hypothesis would be more compelling if there was some clear allusion in the text.

(5) Both Luke and Matthew omit Jesus' comment that the Sabbath was made for man, but it is doubtful whether we should follow Benoit* in concluding that it was missing from their copies of Mk. By omitting the verse, Luke is able to bring together the figures of David and the Son of man to show that Jesus acts as the antitype of David and authorises his followers to do likewise. In Mk. the statement about the Son of man is based on the relation of man as such to the Sabbath. Taylor, 219, sees the link as being that if the Sabbath exists for man's benefit, then man's representative, the Son of man, has authority over its use. This presupposes a connection between mankind and the Son of man which conflicts to some extent with the usual significance of the Son of man as a heavenly figure. However, explanations which take 'Son of man' to be tantamount to 'man' here are unsatisfactory. Rather we should interpret Mk. 2:27 along the lines of Mekhilta Ex. 31:14 (109b): 'The Sabbath is given over to you and not you to the Sabbath', a text which refers not to mankind in general but to Israel as God's people: the authority of the Son of man is then due to his position vis-à-vis Israel. Luke omits the intermediate step in the argument and retains the christological conclusion. It is possible that the early church framed the statement; Cranfield, 118, regards Mk. 2:28 as a Marcan comment for the reader. But this conclusion is improbable, once it is granted that Jesus could use 'Son of man' as a means of self-designation with reference to his earthly activity (Goppelt, I, 234). The case against the authenticity of the present text is summed up by C. Colpe, TDNT VIII, 452, but his one real argument is the linguistic difficulty of turning the saying back into Aramaic: he claims that the use of *mar* (or a similar phrase) would give Jesus an

authority comparable to that of God himself, but this is unlikely 'since it is the disciples who are lords rather than Jesus'. But surely the point of the saying is that here Jesus claims an authority tantamount to that of God with respect to the interpretation of the law. See Roloff, *Kerygma*, 59–62; Hooker, *Son of Man*, 93–102.

The word order τοῦ σαββάτου ὁ υἱὸς τοῦ ἀνθρώπου is attested by ℵ B W. It is preferable to ὁ υἱὸς τοῦ ἀνθρώπου καὶ τοῦ σαββάτου (TR; *Diglot*) which is an assimilation to Mk. (Metzger, 140); but the possibility of assimilation of the UBS text to Mt. should not be overlooked.

Verse 5 is transferred to follow v. 10 in D, and in its place there stands the well-known *agraphon*: 'On the same day he saw a man working on the sabbath and said to him, "Man, if you know what you are doing, you are blessed; but if you do not know, you are accursed and a transgressor of the law" ' (translation, as in Metzger, 140). It is universally agreed that this saying is in no sense part of the text of Lk.; it is a piece of floating tradition which has come to rest here. Its authenticity as a genuine pronouncement story about Jesus is defended by J. Jeremias, *Unknown Sayings of Jesus*, 1957, 49–54 (cf. Grundmann, 136), but on the whole scholars reject its authenticity (E. Lohse, TDNT VII, 23f.; Schürmann, I, 304 n. 29; Roloff, *Kerygma*, 87f.; cf. W. Käser, 'Exegetische Erwägungen zur Seligpreisung des Sabbatarbeiters Lk. 6, 5 D', ZTK 65, 1968, 414–430).

vi. Healing a Man with a Withered Hand on the Sabbath 6:6–11

The fact that Jesus as the Son of man is lord of the Sabbath is taken out of the realm of simple assertion (6:1–5) by the present story in which Jesus demonstrates his power to heal on the Sabbath and thereby confounds his opponents. Implicit in the story is the same reasoning as in 5:17–26 where the fact that Jesus has authority to utter pronouncements in the name of God is confirmed by his possession of authority to perform mighty works. The explicit point, however, is the argument of Jesus that it is lawful to do good on the Sabbath rather than evil, and hence to do what will benefit a man rather than by neglect lead to his destruction; it may be that in Mk. a contrast is being drawn between the purpose of Jesus to heal the sick man and the purpose of his opponents to accomplish his destruction (Taylor, 222), but this thought is absent from Lk. (cf. 6:11 diff. Mk. 3:6).

The alterations made by Luke to his source are insignificant, and contribute, as often, simply to the clarification and better styling of the narrative. Of the various narratives dealing with Jesus' attitude to the Sabbath this one has raised the fewest historical problems. E. Lohse*, 84, notes that even if the individual details be doubtful, the fact that Jesus came into conflict with the Jewish Sabbath regulations is beyond historical doubt, and that this story may come nearest to portraying a historical situation in the life of Jesus; the crucial saying of Jesus in 6:9 must be authentic (ibid. 85f.). On the relationship of the present narrative to 14:1–6 see the notes ad loc.

The narrative has the form of a conflict story in which the miraculous element is not the central feature, but rather the opposition to Jesus and the way in which he overcomes it (cf. 5:17–26). It is surprising that in the earlier case of healing in the synagogue on the Sabbath (4:31–37) nothing is said about the legitimacy of healing on the Sabbath (cf. Schweizer, *Markus*, 41). In the former case, however, we have the first recorded example of a healing by Jesus, in which case the surprise at the healing would no doubt overshadow any considerations regarding the day on which it happened. Moreover, there the action of Jesus was to some extent compelled by the disturbance created by the man's cries. It is understandable that at a later stage the upholders of Sabbath restrictions should note what had happened, and then proceed to take action by arranging for a test case. It may even be that the man had been deliberately brought into the synagogue in order to see what Jesus would do (Easton, 77). It need occasion no surprise that Jesus' opponents granted his ability to perform mighty works (Schweizer, *Markus*, 40); by this time his abilities were no doubt widely proclaimed, and the Pharisees did not doubt their reality so much as the source of their inspiration (11:5).

The final verse of the story is often attributed to Mark himself, since it forms a conclusion to the whole series of conflict stories (Bultmann, 9; Dibelius, 42), but Lohmeyer, 70, rightly notes that the point of this story is that the action of Jesus produces a hostile reaction to Jesus, and hence it is more likely that Mark has edited an existing conclusion to the story (cf. Roloff, *Kerygma*, 63–66); the story will have been placed last in the series precisely because of this climax. Since the early church did not face conflict with the Jews over Sabbath healings, the question of creation of the story by the early church does not arise (Schürmann, I, 309f.).

See E. Lohse, in Eltester, 79–89; Roloff, *Kerygma*, 63–66.

(6) The opening sentence is rephrased by Luke to bring out the parallelism with 6:1. He accordingly inserts ἐν ἑτέρῳ σαββάτῳ (A Θ al; TR; *Diglot* insert καί, strengthening the connection), no doubt correctly, since it is unlikely that Mark regarded this and the previous incident as taking place on the same day (*pace* Luce, 140). The synagogue is presumably the one in Capernaum (Mk. 1:21; 3:1), but there is no clear indication of place. Luke adds the detail that Jesus entered it in order to teach, a detail that could easily be deduced from the central place which Jesus occupies in the ensuing narrative. The description of the man with the paralysed hand is couched in the form of a Semitic circumstantial clause. Luke observes that it was the man's right hand which was afflicted (δέξιος; cf. 22:50 diff. Mk. 14:47; Mt. 5:29 diff. Mk. 9:47; Mt. 5:39

diff. Lk. 6:29), a detail which accentuates the handicap involved; whether the information is accurate or otherwise cannot be ascertained (Easton, 78). In place of the rare participle ἐξηραμμένος used by Mark, both Matthew and Luke have ξηρός, 'lifeless, shrunken' (6:8; 23:31; cf. Mk. 3:3). The exact nature of the complaint is not certain, but some form of muscular atrophy or paralysis is indicated; it could be some type of psychosomatic complaint (cf. Taylor, 221). There is a variant of the story in the Gospel of the Nazaraeans (NTA I, 147f.) in which the man is a plasterer, compelled to beg for his living.

(7) The scene is set for conflict by the presence of watchers who wait to see whether Jesus will heal on the Sabbath so that they may have grounds for an accusation (Luke inserts a favourite word, εὑρίσκω). The audience is not named at this point in Mk., but Luke has brought forward the mention of the Pharisees from Mk. 3:6 (cf. Lk. 5:17), and added a reference to the scribes as their normal companions in such legal disputes as the present one. The Pharisaic Sabbath law was clear enough: only in case of mortal illness was medical help permitted (Yoma 8:6: 'Whenever there is doubt whether life is in danger this overrides the Sabbath'); midwifery and circumcision were permissible (Shab. 18:3; 19:2; cf. SB I, 623–629; II, 533f.; E. Lohse, TDNT VII, 14f.).

(8) Luke adds the note that Jesus intuitively knew their thoughts (2:35): cf. 5:22; 9:47; 11:17. The clause is perhaps a substitute for Mk. 3:5 which refers to Jesus' grief at their hardness of heart (Creed, 85). It is thus with full knowledge of what is involved that Jesus accepts the unspoken challenge and takes the initiative by commanding the sick man to stand in the middle of the assembly; Luke adds the clarifying καὶ στῆθι and explicitly notes that Jesus' command was obeyed.

(9) Then Jesus poses his rhetorical question with ἐπερωτῶ ὑμᾶς εἰ (p⁴ ℵ B D W lat cop; τί, TR: Diglot, is a transcriptional error). Two sets of alternatives are put before the hearers. The first is between doing good (ἀγαθοποιέω, 6:33, 35; 1 Pet. 2:15, 20; 3:6, 17; 3 Jn. 11**; diff. Mk. ἀγαθὸν ποιέω) and doing evil (κακοποιέω; Mk. 3:4; 1 Pet. 3:17; 3 Jn. 11). The second is phrased more particularly in terms of saving life and destroying it; ψυχή here means 'person' rather than 'life', following the OT usage of nepeš (cf. Lv. 23:30; Nu. 35:11; Acts 2:41; et al.; Dautzenberg, 154–160). σῴζω means the saving of a person from death, not the saving of a soul from damnation. By his use of the former principle Jesus relates the institution of the Sabbath to the good purpose of God for men which lay behind it and hence to the principle of love for each other which ought to characterise their use of it. The contrast is not between doing good and doing nothing, a set of alternatives which would have enabled the Pharisees to justify refraining from healing the sick man, but between doing good and positively doing evil: to fail to do good is tantamount to doing harm. Thus to fail to heal is to do harm to the sufferer who must continue to suffer.

To the question in this form there is no answer, except the

affirmative one, which removes the Pharisees' objection to Jesus' action. Luke does not even bother to record with Mark that they remained silent. For this type of 'Socratic' interrogation, cf. Daube, 151–157.

(10) Likewise he omits reference to Jesus' anger and grief at their hardness of heart (reinserted by D Θ f13 *pm* it; cf. Metzger, 140). Jesus simply looks round challengingly at them all (περιβλέπομαι*, par. Mk.), and then symbolically wins the argument by commanding the man to stretch out his hand; the act of faith is rewarded by the cure (ἀποκαθίστημι*).

(11) The closing verse is completely rewritten by Luke. In Mk. the Pharisees plot with the otherwise almost completely unknown Herodians to destroy Jesus. Luke omits mention of the Herodians (cf. 20:20 diff. Mk. 12:13), although later he mentions Herod's own threats against Jesus (13:31), and he leaves the reaction of the Pharisees much more vague. Grundmann's suggestion, 135, that Jesus takes the initiative regarding his own death, is weakened in force by 13:31, but his further point that Luke knows of a friendly relationship between Jesus and at least some of the Pharisees may help to explain why Luke plays down their hostile reaction here. They are filled with 'senseless wrath' (ἄνοια, 2 Tim. 3:9**), and discuss (διαλαλέω, 1:65**) what they should do with Jesus (indirect question with ἄν and aorist optative, corresponding to a direct potential optative, BD 385[1]; 386[1]; cf. 1:29 note; Acts 5:24; 26:29). The impression given is that they are at their wits' end and do not know what to do. For the moment no further action is taken, and Jesus continues his task unhindered.

c. The Teaching of Jesus to his Disciples (6:12–49)

Having given us a sketch of the general character of the ministry of Jesus and depicted his relationship to his opponents, Luke proceeds to describe the relationship of Jesus to his disciples. First of all he narrates the call of the twelve apostles (6:12–16). Then he describes how Jesus came down from the mountain where he had chosen them, to be met by a large crowd drawn from all over the country who sought healing for their sick (6:17–19). In their presence he taught his disciples the implications of discipleship (6:20–49). The whole scene has been regarded as a counterpart to the scene at Sinai where Moses ascended the mountain to commune with God and receive his law, and then descended to bring the law to the people (Ex. 19; 32; 34; Ellis, 113); it has also been seen as a model for the life of the church in which the risen Lord speaks through his chosen apostles to the disciples and the world around (Schürmann, I, 311f.). The parallels, however, are not precise, and the evidence for the suggested symbolism should not be overpressed.

i. The Call of the Twelve 6:12-16

Luke inserts the Sermon on the Plain at a point in his narrative corresponding to Mk. 3:13a; it is significant that Matthew makes the same choice of position for the Sermon on the Mount. Mark, however, has no sermon at this point; the account of healings by the sea (Mk. 3:7-12) is followed by the appointment of the Twelve (Mk. 3:13-19). In order to gain an audience for the sermon, Luke has deliberately reversed the order of the two paragraphs in Mk. – thereby incidentally showing that his primary concern was not to relate events in their strict chronological order. On the whole Luke does not alter the order of the material which he takes over from Mk., except for good reasons, as in the present case (J. Jeremias, 'Perikopen-Umstellungen bei Lukas?', NTS 4, 1957-58, 115-119; reprinted in *Abba*, 93-97). The material in both paragraphs is thus based on Mk., but there are some indications that another source may have been used as well (Schramm, 113f.; Schürmann, I, 318f., 323). The evidence, however, is insufficient to allow any precise conclusions; Luke may have used an alternative list of the twelve apostles, and this may have been in Q, but the evidence is weak.

Luke has in any case followed Mk. in describing the appointment of the Twelve at this point, whereas Matthew has delayed listing their names until his account of their mission and the preparatory discourse (Mt. 10). In both Gospels, however, the sermon of Jesus is presented as instruction for disciples and the crowds, and we should not attempt to find subtle theological differences between the Evangelists in their varied placings of the list of the Twelve. The fact that Luke has followed Mk. in his order here, and that he regards the sermon as addressed to the disciples (with no further especial mention of the apostles) weakens the case for the church symbolism mentioned above.

The significant points in Luke's narrative are his indication of the importance of the occasion by the mention of Jesus' preparatory prayer, the stress on the choice of the Twelve, and the summing up of their task in terms of apostleship. It is clear that for Luke an important stage in the founding of the church is to be seen here, the choice of those from among the company of Jesus' companions from the beginning of his ministry who were to be in a special sense the witnesses to his resurrection and the messengers of the gospel.

See Dietrich, 82-94.

(12) Luke has completely rewritten Mark's introduction to the scene, retaining only the words εἰς τὸ ὄρος (cf. Mt. 5:1). The motif of prayer is not present at this point in Mk., but the association of prayer with mountains and the wilderness is common (Lk. 9:28; Jn. 4:20f.; Mk. 6:46; cf. W. Foerster, TDNT V, 475-487, who provides evidence for the idea of mountainous places being near to God); the motif may be drawn from Mk. 6:46 which Luke later omits. The time reference (cf. 1:39)

provides a vague, but closer link with the preceding narrative. ἐξέρχομαι (diff. Mk. ἀναβαίνω) indicates the idea of Jesus seeking solitude for prayer. διανυκτερεύω**, 'to pass the night' (Job 2:9), is used of an all-night vigil (cf. 22:39–46) and stresses the solemnity of the occasion. For the rare objective genitive formation προσευχῇ τοῦ θεοῦ, 'prayer to God', cf. Mk. 11:22; Wis. 16:28; Jos. Ant. 2:211. Thus the choice of the Twelve is made only after seeking God's guidance (Acts 13:2; 14:23; cf. 1:24–26); cf. Acts 1:2 where διὰ πνεύματος ἁγίου may qualify ἐξελέξατο (Haenchen, 108 n. 1). As the references show, the same pattern of choice was followed in the early church.

(13) The following day (Acts 27:39), Jesus summons (προσφωνέω, 7:32; 13:12; 23:20; Acts 21:40; 22:2; Mt. 11:16**) his disciples and out of their number appoints twelve. In Mk. Jesus calls 'those whom he wished' to him and appointed the Twelve; in both cases the picture is of the choice of a small group out of a larger number. It may be presumed that the others descended, leaving Jesus alone for some time with the Twelve (Schürmann, I, 313). The element of choice is brought out by the use of ἐκλέγομαι (9:35; 10:42; 14:7*; cf. especially Acts 1:2, 24; 6:5; 15:7, 22, 25), a word used in the LXX of God's choice of his servants (cf. Nu. 16:5, 7). The verb appears here as a participle, which leads to anacolouthon as there is no following main verb; to link the sentence to v. 17 (RV) is awkward, and it is better to treat the participle as equivalent to a finite verb.

The observation that Jesus named (ὀνομάζω, 6:14; Acts 19:13) them apostles corresponds to Mark's description of their task, which was that they might be with Jesus and that he might send them out (ἀποστέλλω) to preach and exorcise. It differentiates them from the wider group of disciples (Dietrich, 91f.). The meaning of the word is thus to be explained in terms of their function. (It is possible, however, that the phrase 'whom he named apostles' stood in Luke's copy of Mk.; cf. Metzger, 80.) Unlike the other Evangelists Luke frequently refers to the Twelve as apostles (9:10; 11:49; 17:5; 22:14; 24:10; cf. Mt. 10:2; Mk. 6:30; Jn. 13:16), but he alone (cf. Mk. 3:14 v.l.) claims that Jesus himself used this name. It is widely held that this is an anachronism, and that the title first came into use after Easter (Klostermann, 77; Creed, 88; Grundmann, 137). At the same time the limitation of the term 'apostles' to the Twelve is seen as a Lucan modification of a wider usage. There are three issues here which need to be carefully distinguished. 1. The historicity of the Twelve as a group chosen by the earthly Jesus. Although doubts have been raised on this score (cf. Vielhauer, 68–71), the arguments used are far from convincing (Schweizer, Markus, 71f.; Jeremias, Theology, I, 231–234). 2. The use of the term ἀπόστολος by Jesus. The classical defence is by K. H. Rengstorf (TDNT I, 398–447, especially 427–429) who has argued that the underlying Aramaic term (šᵉlîḥâ, 'one who is sent') need not have a technical, ecclesiastical sense, but denotes 'a fully accredited representative with a specific commission'. Although later writers have assailed this argument (W. Schmithals, *The Office of Apostle in the Early Church*, 1971; G. Klein, *Die Zwölf Apostel*, Göttingen, 1961; cf. Roloff, *Apostolat*, 138–168), it is by no means impossible that the idea was used by Jesus (C. K. Barrett, *The Signs of an Apostle*, 1970, 68), although there is no positive evidence for his use of the actual term. 3. The Lucan conception of apostleship. If the two preceding points be granted, then the question of Luke's restriction of the title to the Twelve is not relevant to the historicity of what is described here. Luke, however, has used the present passage and others to indicate the continuity between the earthly ministry of Jesus and the time of the church by means of the concept of apostleship. Roloff, *Apostolat*, 179, would translate 'whom he (later) called apostles'.

(14) The names of the Twelve now follow in the accusative case (in apposition to δώδεκα or ἀποστόλους). The order in Luke's list differs from that in Mk. by placing Andrew second (par. Mt.), by omitting Thaddaeus and by inserting at a later point Judas of James. The list also varies from that in Acts 1:13 so far as the order of the names is concerned. First in all the lists is Σίμων; Luke avoids Mark's clumsy construction regarding his name of change to Πέτρος by using a relative clause. Up to this point Luke has used the name Σίμων, except in 5:8 (Σίμων Πέτρος); from now on he calls him Πέτρος except at 22:31; 24:34 where he is following his sources (on the usage in Acts and generally see Schürmann, *Abschiedsrede*, 100–102). The new name is no doubt meant to attest the new position of Simon as the leader of the Twelve; he is the rock (Aramaic *kēpā'*, hence the alternative form of his name, Κηφᾶς; cf. O. Cullmann, *Peter, Disciple – Apostle – Martyr*, 1953; id. TDNT VI, 100–112). Second, 'Ανδρέας is named alongside his brother, although in Mk. and Acts 1:13 he is placed after the more important sons of Zebedee; he is not mentioned again by Luke (except in Acts 1:13), although he figures in Mk. 13:3; Jn. 1:41, 45; 6:8; 12:22.

Next come 'Ιάκωβος and 'Ιωάννης; there was no need (diff. Mk.) to include their family details (cf. 5:10) or their by-name, which Luke (like modern scholars) probably found inexplicable. James is named before John here; in Acts 1:13; 8:51; 9:28 where the order is reversed, it is because Peter is also mentioned, and John is regarded as forming a pair with him (Schürmann, I, 316, n. 37; cf. 22:8 diff. Mk.).

The names are not arranged specifically in pairs (diff. Mt., Acts 1:13), but we may well be meant to understand them in this manner. If so, Φίλιππος and Βαρθολομαῖος come next together; the former appears as a distinct personality in Jn. 1:43–48; 6:5–7; 12:21f.; 14:8f.; but the latter plays no distinctive role, unless perhaps he is identified with Philip's companion in Jn. 1, Nathanael. This is quite possible, since several persons in the list and elsewhere in the NT bore two names, but it must remain speculative.

(15) Ματθαῖος and Θωμᾶς are taken over from Mk. Neither of

them figures later in the Gospel. The name of Ἰάκωβος ὁ τοῦ Ἀλφαίου is abbreviated diff. Mk. by the omission of the two articles (cf. BD 260). The name of Θαδδαῖος is omitted, and that of Σίμων is brought forward. In Mk. he is described as Καναναῖος, a transliteration of Aramaic qan'ānā', 'zealot'; Luke has substituted the corresponding Gk. word Ζηλωτής (Acts 1:13**). The name was used for adherents of the Jewish extreme nationalist party who came to the fore during the war with Rome. The word can also be used non-technically to mean 'zealous' (Acts 21:20; 22:3; 1 Cor. 14:12; Gal. 1:14; Tit. 2:14; 1 Pet. 3:13; A. Stumpff, TDNT II, 882–888). It is unlikely that this is the meaning here. It is true that it has been argued that the technical sense would be an anachronism during the time of Jesus (F. J. F. Jackson and K. Lake, BC I, 421–425); if this is the case, then the description is meant to identify him as an erstwhile follower of the radical nationalist group which later became known as Zealots. See M. Hengel, *Die Zeloten*, Leiden, 1961, 72f.

(16) The name of Ἰούδας Ἰακώβου indicates a son or possibly a brother of James (Lagrange, 181; BD 162⁴), more probably the former. The name is attested in Jn. 14:22. Luke presumably equated him with Thaddaeus in Mark's list, but has moved the name to bring the two Judases together. The equation has been defended by J. Jeremias (*Theology*, I, 232f.; amending an earlier suggestion in *Jesus der Weltvollender*, Gütersloh, 1930, 71 n. 4); he notes that in the case of disciples whose names appear twice in the list they are given by-names (e.g. Simon Peter and Simon the Zealot): on this view Mark gives us the by-name of Judas, Θαδδαῖος (equivalent to Θεόδοτος, Aramaic taddai; the names are not identical in meaning, but similar in sound; cf. Saul/Paul).

Finally, there is Ἰούδας Ἰσκαριώθ. The spelling of the second part of his name varies considerably in the MSS, since copyists did not understand its significance, but the form in the text is supported by the weight of external evidence (Metzger, 26f.). 1. The traditional interpretation is 'man of Kerioth' (Jos. 15:25). The use of ʾîš in this way has been thought unlikely (Wellhausen, *Einleitung*, 28), but is in fact quite possible (Dalman, 51f.; Smith, 1f.). 2. A derivation from sicarius, 'assassin', has been suggested (Wellhausen; F. Schulthess, 'Zur Sprache der Evangelien', ZNW 21, 1922, 250–258; O. Cullmann, 'Der zwölfte Apostel', in *Vorträge und Aufsätze 1925–62,* Tübingen, 1966, 214–222). Cullmann argues that Judas the Zealot is a doublet of Judas Iscariot. Against this derivation see M. Hengel, op. cit. 49 n. 3. 3. The name may be derived from Aramaic šᵉqar, 'falsehood' with prosthetic aleph, i.e. 'the false one' (C. C. Torrey, 'The Name "Iscariot" ', HTR 36, 1943, 51–62; B. Gärtner, *Die rätselhaften Termini Nazoräer und Iskariot,* Lund, 1957, 37–68; Ellis, 110). This suggestion, which fits in with the NT tradition about the character of Judas, is perhaps the most plausible. The by-name will then sum up the comment that Judas became a traitor (προδότης, Acts 7:52; 2 Tim. 3:4**; καί is inserted before ἐγένετο by A D Θ *al*; TR; *Diglot*, by assimilation to Mk.). It emphasises Judas's unfaithfulness rather than simply the fact that he handed Jesus over to the Jewish leaders (Grundmann, 138). Again, therefore, we are reminded of the coming passion which casts its shadow over the whole of Jesus' ministry.

ii. The Assembling of the People 6:17–19

Luke now returns to the section which he had passed over, Mk. 3:7–12, and makes it the introduction to the Sermon on the Plain. In this way he indicates that there was a substantial crowd present to hear the sermon (cf. 7:1), and that it was not delivered solely to the Twelve. Although the wording is based on Mk., the scene is in fact differently described. In Mk. the crowds are beside the sea, and Jesus addresses them from a boat; here, however, the place of assembly is a level one at the foot of the mountain. The tradition followed by Matthew locates the sermon on the mountain. We must conclude that Luke has taken over from Mk. the details regarding the sort of people who were following Jesus, but has not been bound by his scenery. There may have been an introduction to the sermon in the Q material (Schürmann, I, 323), in which case Luke has combined the two traditions; a similar procedure has been adopted by Matthew. But the simple fact that the sermon was known to be associated with a mountain would be adequate to explain the procedure of the two Evangelists.

The details of the healing ministry are taken over from Mk. and modified. In Mk. the healings are recounted more for their own sake, but here they are a prelude to the sermon, since Luke could rightly assume that Jesus carried on his healing and preaching ministries together. He has, however, reduced the importance of the healing narrative in its own right, and stressed that the people came together not merely to be healed but also to hear Jesus.

(17) In view of his change of order, Luke has to alter the introduction to the section. Jesus comes down with his newly-appointed apostles from the seclusion of the mountain to where the people are. One may see a parallel with Moses who came down from Sinai to the people (Ex. 32:1, 7, 15; 34:29), but there is no stress on it. Jesus takes his stand on a level (πεδινός**) place. Luke envisages a place where the people could easily assemble in large numbers and where the sick could be brought (Leaney, 132). A suitable site, halfway up the hillside, has been identified near Capernaum (Findlay, 1037). There is no symbolic significance in the place (despite the fantastic suggestions by J. Mánek, 'On the Mount – on the Plain (Mt. V.1 – Lk. VI. 17) ', Nov.T 9, 1967, 124–131). The difficulty that Matthew places the sermon on a mountain may be met by arguing that Luke is using a different symbolical geography

(Schürmann, I, 320), namely that of Moses at the foot of Sinai, or by claiming that Luke's description may mean a level place among the mountains rather than at sea level. (The word πεδινός is used in the LXX for the Shephelah, the low-lying plain below the central mountain range in Palestine.) The same area might appear to be a plain or a mountain, depending on one's point of view (cf. W. M. Christie, *Palestine Calling,* 1939, 35; Geldenhuys, 209 n.).

Here Jesus is met by a great crowd of his disciples and a great multitude of the people; the words are left hanging, and a verb needs to be supplied (ἔστη or ἦν). There are thus three groups of people, the apostles, the wider group of Jesus' disciples who have already committed themselves to him (cf. 6:13; 19:37), and the still wider group of people who are not yet committed to him (cf. Acts 2:43-47; 5:12-16; 6:6-8). While Luke often uses the term μαθηταί to refer to the comparatively small group who accompanied Jesus on his travels (and whose composition need not have been constant), there is no reason to suppose that here the term is used proleptically and symbolically for the church (Schürmann, I, 320f.), still less that it prefigures its office-bearers (Degenhardt, 36-41). There is no reason why Luke should not have regarded the work of Jesus as having already led to the conversion of numerous people.

λαός here means the people of Israel, and the thought of the new people of God is hardly present (despite Schürmann's cautious formulation of this possibility). The people come from the whole of Judaea (πάσης, added by Luke); Luke thus abbreviates Mark's detailed description, and his phrase therefore includes Galilee, Idumaea and Transjordan. He retains mention, however, of Jerusalem (cf. 5:17) which as the capital city deserved separate notice – and perhaps too as the place of Jesus' passion; and he also retains mention of Tyre and Sidon (Luke adds ἡ παράλιος**, 'sea-coast'); the construction suggests that Jews from that area are meant, but Tyre and Sidon are so much a symbol of heathenism (10:13f.) that perhaps gentiles are meant.

(18) Whereas Mark states that the people came because they had heard (ἀκούοντες) all that Jesus did, Luke says that they came to hear (ἀκοῦσαι) him, thus pointing forward to the coming sermon and stressing the priority of the word over the mighty works. He adds the general remark that they came to be healed from their diseases. Special attention is directed to those who were troubled (ἐνοχλέω, Heb. 12:15**) by demons and healed by Jesus (cf. 8:2 for the same indication that demon possession is a form of illness). The detail is drawn from Mk., but Luke omits his detailed development of the incident in terms of confession of Jesus as the Son of God. The emphasis falls entirely on the gracious healing performed by Jesus which releases the needy from an intolerable burden.

(19) Whereas ὄχλος in v. 17 meant the disciples, here the word is used for the people in general who were present. They longed for healing, and strove to touch Jesus (cf. 8:44-47; Mk. 6:56; see also Acts 5:15;

19:11f.) in the belief that healing would come to them in the same way as when he stretched out his hand to touch the sick. Superstitious their belief may have been, but God accepted it, and his power went out from Jesus and healed them all (cf. 5:17). The final clause is Luke's theological explanation of the incident, based on 8:46.

Thus the gospel is already presented in deed and word to those from whom some response is later to be demanded (6:17–19, 20–23/27–45; Schürmann, I, 322).

iii. The Sermon on the Plain 6:20–49

The Sermon on the Plain is a shorter version of the Sermon on the Mount (Mt. 5–7). It is generally accepted that one basic piece of tradition underlies the two Sermons and that both Evangelists (and possibly their predecessors in the transmission of the material) have expanded it and modelled it in accord with their own purposes. A greater degree of freedom has been shown by Matthew.

Commentators are far from unanimous about the structure of the Sermon owing to the lack of clear breaks and to the variety of themes. Luke operates here, as elsewhere, with 'bridging passages', so that a verse or paragraph may be reckoned as both closing one section and introducing another. This is probably the case with 6:36.

1. The majority of commentators recognise a break at 6:38/39. If we combine this with the universally recognised break at 6:26/27, we obtain a basic three-fold division of the Sermon which can be variously evaluated. Following Heinrici, Klostermann, 77f., and Hauck, 82ff., suggest that we have a prophetic section (6:20–26), a paraenetic section (6:27–38) and a parabolical section (6:39–49). Ellis, 111, regards the same sections as dealing with the promises of the kingdom, the principles of the kingdom, and the meaning of discipleship respectively. Essentially the same structure is offered by Grundmann, 140, but he finds a break between teaching for the disciples in 6:20–38 and for the Twelve as leaders of the community in 6:39–49; this suggestion, however, does not do justice to 6:47–49 which is clearly meant for the disciples rather than their leaders.

2. A refinement of the same scheme is found in Schürmann, I, 324f.: 6:39–45 is seen as a warning against confusing the teaching of Jesus on love (6:27–38) with other views, rather than as a set of illustrations on the character of love, and 6:46–49 is a conclusion to the sermon as a whole.

3. Other commentators ignore the break at 6:38/39. The most important such analysis is that of Dupont, I, 200: Exordium (6:20–26). I. Love for one's enemies (6:27–36). II. Brotherly love (6:37–42). Conclusion: the necessity of works (6:43–49) (cf. Schmid, 132; UBS). The advantage of this view is that it does justice to the apparent similarity of theme in 6:37f. and 41f. Its disadvantage is that it has to regard 6:39f. as

a maladroit insertion (Dupont, I, 194). But the fact that these verses are not in Matthew's sermon but are found in two separate places (Mt. 15:14; 10:24f.) suggests that they were not inserted here by Luke without good reason.

Let us summarise the contents of the Sermon to see how it may best be analysed.

1. 6:20–26 forms a single section in two contrasting parts. It pronounces divine blessing and woe upon two kinds of people, the poor and oppressed who can look forward to their needs being satisfied by God, and the rich, popular men who will suffer divine judgment. The section thus challenges people as to what kind of life they intend to lead. It invites men to become disciples and comforts those who are already disciples.

2. In 6:27–35 the disciples are commanded to love their persecutors, to give freely to all in need and thus to obey the 'golden rule'. If they do this, they will enjoy a heavenly reward and will show a character like that of God himself. Let them be merciful like him (6:36).

3. But the thought of mercy belongs more closely with what follows: a command not to judge others, but to give freely and thus receive correspondingly from God (6:36–38).

4. The following sections are concerned with the kind of inward character which produces such outward behaviour. A person who is blind cannot guide another person nor correct his faults. Hence the disciples are not to judge other people, for they do not have the ability to do so, not even when they have been taught by Jesus (6:39–42).

5. A person of bad character cannot produce good deeds or words (6:43–45). This warning is applied to false teachers in Mt. 7, but here the thought is rather that the disciples cannot bring forth the good deeds and words that are required of them unless they themselves are good and have good treasure in their hearts.

6. This leads, finally, to an appeal to hear and do the words of Jesus (6:46–49). It is addressed to people who heard, but did not do, what Jesus said (6:46), and hence reckons with the presence of merely nominal followers among the disciples. The implication is that the previous verses contained a warning against nominal discipleship. This final section thus belongs closely with what precedes, so that 6:39–49 is to be seen as a single section of the Sermon, concerned with the personal character of the disciples.

From this analysis it will be clear that the thought proceeds more by association of ideas than by close-knit argument, and that the type of structure suggested by Hauck and Ellis best fits the development of thought. The Sermon develops its theme in a series of closely connected sections, using catchwords, so that there is a unity in the whole; the total emphasis is on the blessings promised to God's poor, oppressed people, the need for them to show love and mercy, and the need for a basic inward attitude of obedience to God.

If the question of structure is difficult, that of the sources and pre-history of the Sermon defies solution.

1. The most refined attempt at source-analysis is that of Schürmann, I, 385f. Two originally independent collections of sayings, 6:27–38 on love for neighbours and enemies, and 6:39–45 directed against the Pharisees, have been joined together and furnished with an introduction (6:20–26) and conclusion (6:46–49). Schürmann attempts to analyse the first of these collections into smaller groups of sayings. Essentially the same basic source was used by Matthew (Mt. 5:3f., 6, 11f., 39b–42, 44–48; 7:1–6, 12–18, 20f., 24–27), but he has added con-siderably to it.

2. Literary theories have been strongly criticised by Wrege, who claims that the differences between Mt. and Lk. cannot be explained in terms of their editing a common source, but demand the postulation of independent oral sources. This view stands poles apart from that of Schulz, who attempts to explain all the Q material in terms of Matthaean and Lucan redaction of one common written source.

3. Progress towards solving the problem depends upon detailed study of the individual pericopes which constitute the Sermon. From such study it appears that while many differences between the Gospels can be explained in terms of redaction by the Evangelists this is not an adequate explanation; serious consideration must be given to the possibility that the Q material was available to them in different recen-sions. Basic traditions may well have gone through several stages of transmission, both oral and written, before being incorporated in the Gospels. Only some such theory will explain why some Q material is presented in virtually identical wording by both Evangelists, while the rest appears in very different forms. (To some extent such differences may be due to varying translations of a common Aramaic source, but there is not a great deal of solid evidence for this hypothesis.) For this view see J. Weiss, 444; Manson, *Teaching*, 27f.; *Sayings,* 18f. G. Bornkamm, in RGG[3] II, 756; Hahn, 83 n. 4; W. G. Kümmel, *Introduction to the New Testament*, London, 1966, 54; Schweizer, *Matthäus*, 2f.

4. The theory that Luke drew his Q material from Mt. remains im-probable, despite M. D. Goulder, *Midrash and Lection in Matthew*, London, 1975; Drury, *Tradition*, 131–138.

See Manson, *Sayings,* 46–62; Percy, 40–108, 123–164; W. Grundmann, 'Die Bergpredigt nach der Lukasfassung', TU 73, 1959, 180–189; Davies; Wrege; Lührmann, 53–56; Dupont; Schürmann, I, 323–386.

(a) Two Kinds of Men 6:20–26

The Sermon begins with a contrast between two kinds of people or two general types of character. The first group are those who by all outward appearance are to be pitied, but in the eyes of Jesus they are blessed or happy because of what is promised to them. The description of them as being persecuted for the sake of the Son of man shows that the thought is not simply of those who are literally poor and needy, nor of all such poor people, but of those who are disciples of Jesus and hence occupy a pitiable position in the eyes of the world. Their present need will be met by God's provision in the future. The effect of the beatitudes is thus both to comfort men who suffer for being disciples and to invite men to become disciples and find that their needs are met by God. The second group consists of those who are materially well off and enjoy the world's favour. Jesus' expression of sorrow for their condition is not directed against prosperity in itself but against those who enjoy such prosperity, are satisfied with it, and do not look beyond the satisfaction of their own desires. In general, however, the followers of Jesus, like the godly people described in the Psalms and wisdom literature, are literally poor and down-trodden, whereas many of those who reject the gospel enjoy material plenty. Riches can keep men out of the kingdom of God, and disciples must be prepared for poverty by worldly standards.

The corresponding section in Mt. 5:3–12 contains 8 (or 9) beatitudes and no woes. In general there is more of an ethical emphasis in Mt.; while Luke's beatitudes describe what the disciples actually are, Matthew's stress more what they ought to be. This is clear both from the differences between the beatitudes which they have in common and also from the character of the beatitudes peculiar to Mt. Dupont has argued that a set of four beatitudes (those common to both Gospels) with an originally messianic sense were present in Q and that these have been developed and adapted by the two Evangelists. By his addition of the woes and various small modifications Luke has brought out the social concern inherent in the message of Jesus and has accented the contrast between suffering now and future reward. Matthew, however, by adding further beatitudes and making more extensive modifications has turned the beatitudes into a programme of Christian righteousness. We may cite Dupont's summary regarding the situation in Mt.: 'Le royaume ne s'y présente plus comme la réalisation des promesses messianiques (rédaction primitive) ou comme une juste compensation pour ceux qui n'ont aucune part au bonheur du monde présent (rédaction de Luc); il est une recompense pour ceux qui s'en seront rendus dignes par leurs dispositions intimes et par leur manière de vivre le message evangélique ... elles sont une invitation: soyez miséricordieux ... afin d'avoir part au royaume' (*Les Béatitudes*, Paris, 1954, 298f.).

It is generally agreed that a common core lies behind Mt. and Lk. at this point. On this view the 'extra' beatitudes in Mt. are due to the Evangelist or to the tradition which he utilised. Dupont, I, 299–342, claims that the woes are an addition by Luke (although he allows that they may be pre-Lucan). Schürmann, I, 339–341, however, has given reason to believe that the woes are pre-Lucan, and suggests that they were in the source used by Matthew; he agrees, however, that they represent an addition made by the early church in order to bring out the significance of the beatitudes for its own situation. Wrege, 5–27, claims that the two traditions in Mt. and Lk. are quite separate, the woes being an addition made in the Lucan strand of the tradition. So far as the beatitudes themselves are concerned, it is generally thought that the final beatitude has a different origin from the other three in view of its different form and content (Bultmann, 115; Schulz, 454f.).

It may be taken as certain that the woes were composed in connection with the beatitudes to which they so closely correspond. If so, it is unlikely that they stood in the source which contained the extra beatitudes found in Mt. (We accept the view that the expansion is pre-Matthaean, with G. Strecker*, 259; pace Dupont, I, 251–264.) But there are links in wording between the woes and other material in Mt. which make it fairly certain either that Matthew (or his source) knew the woes (Lagrange, 190), or that Luke knew various passages in Mt. which he does not reproduce. The former of these possibilities is to be preferred, and it implies that Matthew's source was dependent upon an earlier tradition which included both beatitudes and woes. We must, then, postulate two different forms of the tradition behind Mt. and Lk., and it is possible that these ultimately go back to two separate, but closely related traditions of the teaching of Jesus. An original bifurcation in the tradition may be the best solution to the question of the originality of the second and third person forms of address.

The relation of the fourth beatitude to the other three is discussed below; there is good reason for believing that it originally formed part of the same series. The authenticity of at least the first three beatitudes is generally accepted (Schulz, 78; Schweizer, *Matthäus*, 47f.). That of the fourth is contested, but without adequate reason. The case that the woes are a commentary on the beatitudes by the early church is stronger.

See the literature cited in 6:20–49 note; Steck, 20–27, 257–260, 283f.; K. Koch, *The Growth of the Biblical Tradition*, London, 1969; S. Agourides, 'La tradition des béatitudes chez Matthieu et Luc', in Descamps, 9–27; G. Strecker, 'Die Makarismen der Bergpredigt', NTS 17, 1970–71, 255–275; H. Frankemölle, 'Die Makarismen (Mt 5, 1–12; Lk 6, 20–23). Motive und Umfang der redaktionellen Komposition', BZ 15, 1971, 52–75; Schulz, 76–84, 452–457; G. Schwarz, 'Lukas 6, 22a, 23c, 26. Emendation, Rückübersetzung, Interpretation', ZNW 66, 1975, 269–274.

(20) The introduction to the Sermon is differently worded from that in Mt. 5:1f. Jesus lifts up his eyes (16:23; 18:13) and sees his disciples, whereas in Mt. he 'sees the crowds'. Luke's expression (ἐπαίρω τοὺς ὀφθαλμούς) indicates taking note of somebody or something (cf. Mt. 17:8; Jn. 4:35; 6:5), and suggests that what follows is especially meant for the disciples and arises from a consideration of their needs (Lagrange, 186). Although the disciples are the primary audience, the crowds are also present (6:17; 7:1), and 6:24–26 may be regarded as especially addressed to them (cf. 20:45). Similarly, in Mt. 5:1; 7:28 the disciples and the crowds are both regarded as present (the contradiction found by Jeremias, *Parables*, 42 n. 70, between these two verses in Mt. is

unlikely). The gesture may indicate that Jesus is regarded as standing (6:17) – like a prophet (Grundmann, 142) – but there is no reason why he should not then have seated himself (Mt. 5:1) in order to deliver his teaching. The imperfect ἔλεγεν is appropriate at the commencement of a lengthy discourse (3:7 note).

The word μακάριος is used to introduce all four beatitudes (cf. Dupont, II, 324–338; F. Hauck and G. Bertram, TDNT IV, 362–370). In Greek usage it was used to express the happy, untroubled state of the gods, and then more generally the happiness of the rich who are free from care. In the LXX it usually translates 'ašᵉrê, the construct plural of 'ešer, 'luck, happiness', and is found in the form 'O the happiness of . . .'. It is thus accompanied by a statement which gives the reason why the person named is to be praised as being happy. The happiness, however, is the result of a state of divinely given salvation, so that a statement of blessing is in effect 'prädikativer Heilsspruch', a statement predicating salvation (M. Soebe, THAT I, 257–260). The form is 'Fortunate is X because . . .' Hence the reference is to the religious joy of the person who has a share in salvation (F. Hauck, TDNT IV, 367).

It may be appropriate at this point to note that another word is also translated 'blessed' in the NT. εὐλογητός (1:68) and the corresponding verb εὐλογέω (1:42) are used to translate forms of bārak (cf. C. A. Keller and G. Wehmeier, THAT I, 353–376; H. W. Beyer, TDNT II, 754–765). This stem is used much more frequently; the verb expresses God's act of favour to men, shown in material or spiritual gifts to them, but it can also be used of men blessing God in the sense of praising him, while the adjectival form is applied to men who receive such gifts from God or to God as the giver of them. In the NT the corresponding words are used much more of praise being offered to God, but while μακάριος is rarely used of God, εὐλογητός is always so used. As applied to men, however, in the OT bārûk and ašᵉrê are synonyms, the latter tending to replace the former in course of time (C. A. Keller, THAT I, 356); the former is more a prayer for blessing, the latter a statement that someone is blessed.

Blessings pronounced with ašᵉrê are usually in the third person form but the second person is also found (Dt. 33:29; Is. 32:20; Ps. 128:2; Ec. 10:17; Mal. 3:12). It is a matter of great dispute whether the second person in Lk. or the third person in Mt. represents the original teaching of Jesus; in favour of Luke see Dibelius, 248; Manson, Sayings, 47; Percy, 82–84; Schweizer, Matthäus, 45; but most commentators favour Matthew (Bultmann, 114; Klostermann, 79; Wrege, 8; Schulz, 77 n. 128). Schürmann, I, 329, holds that Luke's source had the second person, but that Jesus used the third person. Strecker 257 n. 1, claims that no compelling arguments for either view have been offered, not even in Dupont's detailed defence of Matthew's form (I, 272–296). The debate of course concerns only the first three beatitudes; the second person form of the fourth in both Mt. and Lk. is clearly original. The question is whether Luke (or his source) has assimilated the first three beatitudes to the form of the fourth. Since woes and curses are usually in the second person (but not necessarily), it is probable that the second person stood in both woes and beatitudes in Luke's source. It seems probable to us that the direct address form in Lk. is much more likely with the brief series of three beatitudes preceding the fourth one than an abrupt change from the third person to the second. Further, whereas the third person form may suit better the wisdom type of sayings in the OT, the second person form is more appropriate in the prophetic teaching of Jesus with its promises of salvation (Bouwman, 33–36). But this conclusion can be no more than probable.

The persons declared by Jesus to be fortunate are οἱ πτωχοί, 'the poor' (4:18; Percy, 40–108; F. Hauck and E. Bammel, TDNT VI, 885–915; Dupont, II, 19–51). The Gk. word means 'one who is so poor as to have to beg', i.e. one who is completely destitute. In the LXX it is used as the equivalent of various words: 39x it translates 'ānî, 'a dependent', hence 'one who is poor' (from 'ānāh, 'to be afflicted'). 21x it translates dal, 'lowly, weak'; and 10x it translates 'ebyōn, 'poor man, beggar'. In Proverbs it also translates rāš, 'needy, famished'. The antonym is not 'āšîr, 'rich', but rāšā', 'violent'. It is important that especially in the Psalms the pious man who calls on God to help him describes himself as poor and needy. Because of his need, and because he is not a believer in violence, the poor man calls on God for help and receives it (Pss. 86:1; 12:5). Hence the term came to be a self-designation for pious, humiliated people (Ps. Sol. 10:7; 4QpPs. 37 1:8f.; 1QH 5:13f.).

It follows that in the message of Jesus the hopes of the poor and the promises of Yahweh to them find fulfilment through the One who has been anointed to bring good news to the poor (Is. 61:1; Lk. 4:18; cf. Is. 57:15; 66:2). This is one of the constant themes of the message of Jesus. It is in no sense a limitation of the promise of salvation to a specific circle of people. Hence the basis for E. Bammel's denial that this beatitude is an authentic saying of Jesus is removed (TDNT VI, 906; contra Bammel see Grundmann, 142 n. 18). At the same time, however, the saying is addressed to those who are literally poor, or who share the outlook of the poor. Paul knew that God had chosen the contemptible people of this world to be his people (1 Cor. 1:26ff.), and James (2:5) clearly cites this beatitude with reference to the literally poor; it was, therefore, Christian experience that in a real sense the gospel was addressed to the poor. Yet, as the sequel makes clear, it is not poverty as such which qualifies a person for salvation: the beatitudes are addressed to disciples, to those who are ready to be persecuted for the sake of the Son of man.

It follows also that poverty as such is not a state of happiness. The happiness is because of the promise made to the poor (for the use of ὅτι cf. 2 En. 58:2). Theirs is the kingdom of God (4:43 note). The phrase is the all-inclusive one for the salvation of God – the action which brings salvation and the sphere of salvation. Thus the meaning here is that the blessings of God's reign are given to the poor. The thought is undoubtedly spiritual – not that the poor will become rich instead of poor; a simple reversal of worldly position is not envisaged, although it is true that the deprived will enjoy plenty in the kingdom of God (16:19–31). Human need will be met by the fullness of divine salvation.

Both Matthew and Luke have the promise in the present form (ἐστίν), whereas the other beatitudes are in the future tense. The ἐστίν can represent a timeless construction in Aramaic, and therefore can be taken in a future sense. It is, however, significant that both Gospels preserve the present tense here alongside the ensuing future tenses. We are justified in concluding that the kingdom is so near that the disciples as good as experience it now, or that there is a sense in which they already experience it, even though the rewards associated with it belong primarily to the future. Already the kingdom of God belongs to the poor, and hence they can be sure that they will inherit the blessings associated with it. What is significant is that it is Jesus who has the authority to declare that the kingdom of God is near and to state who will enjoy its blessings – the poor *and they alone* (Jeremias, *Theology*, I, 116).

In the Matthaean form of the beatitude there is one significant alteration, the qualification ἐν πνεύματι attached to πτωχοί. Since the resulting phrase has Semitic antecedents (cf. 1QM 14:7), it is not necessarily an editorial expansion by Matthew, but may well go back to an earlier stage in the tradition. It brings out more forcefully the ethical and spiritual associations of poverty, and precludes the misunderstanding that might arise from the Lucan form. If Jesus gave the teaching reflected here more than once (as is highly probable), the variation in wording may go back to him.

(21) The association of hunger with poverty is obvious (Is. 32:6f.; 58:7, 10; Job 24:9f.; Tob. 4:16). πεινάω (cf. 1:53; L. Goppelt, TDNT VI, 12–22, especially 17–19) can refer to any kind of want, but here the thought of physical hunger is uppermost. In the OT, however, hunger can mean a desire for spiritual satisfaction (Is. 55:1; Am. 8:11; cf. Sir. 24:21), and this sense should not be excluded here: 'The hungry are men who both outwardly and inwardly are painfully deficient in the things essential to life as God meant it to be, and who, since they cannot help themselves, turn to God on the basis of his promise' (L. Goppelt, TDNT VI, 18). The promise in question is God's word in the OT (Is. 49:10, 13; 55:1f.; Je. 31:12, 25; Ezk. 36:29), which his people knew that he was capable of fulfilling (1 Sa. 2:5; Pss. 107:9, 36f.; 146:7). Although this is the condition of the disciples now (νῦν, possibly a Lucan addition; cf. Dupont, III, 100–109), in the future they will be filled with what they need. χορτάζω, 'to be filled, to feed' (9:17; 16:21; cf. Phil. 4:12) expresses the idea of satisfaction (Ps. 17:15). The passive form may indicate the thought that *God* will feed the hungry (Jeremias, *Theology*, I, 11). The underlying reference is probably to the 'messianic banquet', the

picture of the kingdom of God in terms of a great feast where men can have fellowship with God at his table (cf. 13:28f.; 22:16, 30). The imagery finds concrete expression in the picture of Lazarus, hungry on earth, but sitting in the bosom of Abraham at God's table (16:20–22).

The ethical emphasis again appears in Mt. where the disciples hunger and thirst for righteousness. The blessing promised in both versions is granted by God, and there is no mention of the Messiah; the idea is rather that God vindicates those who follow Jesus as disciples.

The third beatitude is a promise to those who mourn. κλαίω, 'to weep', is frequent in Lk. and expresses mourning and sorrow of all kinds (K. H. Rengstorf, TDNT III, 722–725); no restriction in meaning should therefore be sought (Matthew does not qualify the verb). Matthew has πενθέω, which is often used in parallel with κλαίω (6:25; Mk. 16:10; Jas. 4:9; Rev. 18:11, 15, 19) and is a more general word for mourning and grief; it may reflect the influence of Is. 61:2. But although the terms used are general, we should perhaps see the thought of sorrow with the world as it is, and possibly even of penitence for sin (R. Bultmann, TDNT VI, 40–43).

Those who weep now will laugh with joy when the cause of sorrow has been removed. The thought is again based on the OT, on the promise that God will turn sorrow into joy (Is. 60:20; 61:3; 66:10; Je. 31:13; Bar. 4:23; 5:1; Is. 35:10; 65:16–19; Ps. 126:2, 5f.); it is taken up in Rev. 7:17; 21:4. Mt. 5:4 uses παρακαλέω (cf. Lk. 6:24, παράκλησις), which gives a more direct reference to the promises in Is. 61:2f.; cf. Sir. 48:24. Luke has γελάω (6:25**; K. H. Rengstorf, TDNT I, 658–662). This word is used in the LXX as an expression of superiority and scorn, but here the use may reflect the more neutral sense of the word in the Hellenistic world (cf. Ps. 126:2; Jas. 4:9; Dupont, III, 65:69). Since γελάω must be original in 6:25, it is probable that the word has been inserted here in order to bring out the parallelism more clearly; if so, the reference to Is. 61:2f. preserved by Matthew is probably original, although he may have altered an original κλαίω to πενθέω (cf. G. Strecker*, 263 n. 1; it follows that Luke did not compose the corresponding woe on the basis of the beatitude but used a tradition which may have influenced Mt.).

(22) Luke has nothing corresponding to Mt. 5:10 (on which see Wrege, 26f.), and moves straight on to the detailed blessing on the disciples in various kinds of tribulation. The form of this beatitude is considerably expanded, the ὅτι clause of the earlier ones being replaced here by an ἰδοὺ γάρ clause. Although the form is different, there is no good reason for claiming that it was originally independent of them (with Schürmann, I, 335; Schulz, 454f.; and most scholars); Daube, 196–201, has shown that often the last member of a series is longer than the preceding ones (cf. Wrege, 20). It has been argued that the first three beatitudes are addressed more to an oppressed social class and promise future happiness, but this one is addressed to a particular group of

persecuted disciples and summons them to present happiness. But the contrast is here over-stressed; if the first three beatitudes are addressed to men as they now are, and invite them to discipleship with its accompanying blessings, the fourth warns of the fate that may overtake them and calls them to be joyful despite this additional burden in this world. There is nothing strange about these two thoughts being coupled together, and if the early church could couple them with no sense of incongruity, there is no reason why Jesus also could not have done so. It is of course arguable that persecution lay beyond the horizon of Jesus – a point made without any supporting arguments by Bultmann, 115 (though Tödt, 123, says that he has 'convincingly demonstrated' it!) – but it is much more probable that he foresaw persecution both for himself and for his disciples (Jeremias, *Theology*, I, 239f.; Schürmann, I, 336.)

The description of the treatment which the disciples may experience from time to time (ὅταν is indefinite) contains four elements, whereas Matthew has only three. The last elements in both lists are equivalent; Matthew's first element is the same as Luke's third (ὀνειδίζω). It is not clear whether μισέω or ἀφορίζω in Lk. is meant to be an equivalent to διώκω in Mt. The Matthaean version appears to be less Jewish in expression than the Lucan at this point; διώκω may be meant to elucidate an original ὀνειδίζω. The insertion of the subject οἱ ἄνθρωποι may be due to Luke (Wrege, 20 n. 4); it refers to the non-Christian world: 6:26; 9:44; 12:8.

μισέω is commonly used of the attitude of those who are opposed to the people of God (Is. 66:5; Lk. 1:71; 21:17 par. Mt. 24:9; Mk. 13:13 par. Mt. 10:22; Jn. 15:18f.; 17:14; 1 Jn. 3:13). It expresses the basic attitude which lies behind the concrete acts described in the second clause.

ἀφορίζω* is 'to separate', in the sense of excluding a person from one's company. Behind the usage may lie Is. 66:5 MT, in which case the reference is a general one to social ostracism. This view is preferable to that which finds here a definite allusion to the Jewish practice of the ban (*niddui*; C.-H. Hunzinger, unpublished dissertation, as reported by Hare, 49) or to the synagogue ban imposed by the use of the Birkath ha-Minim (Schürmann, I, 333). The former appears to have been used to maintain uniformity of outlook among the Pharisees themselves rather than to discipline the people in general (Hare, 49–53), while the latter is questionable on account of the late date of the institution (AD 85). The hypothesis of social ostracism (cf. 1QS 5:18) is more likely. Matthew's use of διώκω may paraphrase this, but it is not a case of generalising a particular act of excommunication into a general process of persecution (as Schürmann, I, 333 n. 50, claims).

ὀνειδίζω, 'to reproach', reappears in the clear echo of this saying in 1 Pet. 4:14; cf. Rom. 15:3; Heb. 11:26; Mk. 15:32. This verb also has been thought to refer to the Jewish ban (Hauck, 84), with the meaning 'to curse, ban' (C. Colpe, TDNT VIII, 449 n. 344), but the evidence for this interpretation is weak. It is more probable that the reference is to 'face-to-face insults' (Hare, 118). It has been suggested that the word was added as an interpretation of the following phrase; if so, this must have happened at an early stage, since the word also appears in Mt. 5:11 and 1 Pet. 4:14.

The final phrase ἐκβάλωσιν τὸ ὄνομα ὑμῶν ὡς πονηρόν is generally thought to be a literal translation of hôṣî' šēm rā' 'al, 'to publish an evil name concerning', i.e. 'to defame' (Dt. 22:19; Sotah 3:5); the Matthaean phrase εἴπωσιν πᾶν πονηρὸν καθ' ὑμῶν (cf. Lk. 6:26 for the positive formulation) is then a free translation of the same idiom (Wellhausen, 24; Black, 135f.). But Luke's phrase has a different force from the Hebrew phrase (cf. the use of ὑμῶν) while Matthew's phrase is nearer to Semitic idiom and therefore more likely to be original (Steck, 23; Schulz, 453 n. 373; it is more probable that Matthew has the Q form at this point than that he has altered Luke's expression here in the light of Lk. 6:26). The name which is meant may then be the 'reputation' of the disciples or the name of Christian (cf. Jas. 2:7; 1 Pet. 4:14; Creed, 91). The allusion is hardly to a curse pronounced in connection with exclusion from the synagogue (pace Schürmann, I, 333).

All this happens for the sake of the Son of man (diff. Mt. ἐμοῦ). It has been claimed that the tendency was to add 'Son of man' to sayings which did not originally contain it (J. Jeremias, 'Die älteste Schicht der Menschensohn-Logien', ZNW 58, 1967, 159–172); if so, this must have happened at a pre-Lucan stage (Steck, 24 n. 3), since Luke does not seem to have added the title himself at any point (Rehkopf, 56). C. Colpe, TDNT VIII, 443, takes the further step of claiming that 'for my sake' is also an addition to the original saying. On the other hand, Matthew is capable of dropping references to the Son of man (16:21), and hence the Lucan form may well be original (Schürmann, I, 334 n. 62; Schulz, 453 n. 77). The question of authenticity has already been raised, so far as Jesus' prediction of persecution for his followers is concerned. But is the reference to the Son of man here authentic? Higgins, 119–121, argues that the persecution is inflicted for loyalty to Jesus as the Son of man active on earth: 'Clearly, therefore, it is the church which is speaking, the church which believes that the Jesus for faith in whom persecution has broken out is the Son of man in heaven.' This thought of loyalty, however, is surely a sign of authenticity. For elsewhere the Son of man himself is a figure of rejection (9:58), and here it is stated that those who side with him will also be rejected. Higgins' argument holds only if the first use of the title 'Son of man' with reference to Jesus was by a church which identified its heavenly Lord with the Son of man in heaven; if, however, Jesus used the title to apply to himself during his ministry, as we have already claimed, then there is no reason why the present reference should not also be authentic. Of greater weight is the argument put forward by Colpe (TDNT VIII, 443 n. 308) that ἕνεκα phrases are in general additions to the tradition: cf. 17:33 with Mt.

10:39. But in 17:33 the omission is probably due to the context in which the saying is used; the objection cannot be sustained.

(23) In such circumstances of persecution the disciples are to be joyful. Where Matthew has present imperatives, Luke has aorist imperatives and the phrase ἐν ἐκείνῃ τῇ ἡμέρᾳ (no doubt a Lucan addition; cf. 10:12; 17:31, diff. Mt.); this suggests that Luke has in mind a definite point of time. A reference to the last day is unlikely (*pace* Steck, 24 n. 4). Schürmann, I, 334, holds that the day of exclusion from the synagogue is meant. Since, however, the language does not support this suggestion in v. 22, a more general reference to any day of persecution is probable. The less specific form χαίρετε is in fact found in some MSS of Luke and adopted by TR; *Diglot*; but it is probably due to assimilation to Mt. σκιρτάω, 1:41, 44**, is used of jumping for joy, and may refer to a men's dance (Jeremias, *Parables*, 130 n. 82). It may be a translation variant for ἀγαλλιάομαι in Mt. (Black, 158, 193), but the latter can also be due to the influence of Is. 61:20, a chapter which may be echoed throughout Matthew's version of the beatitudes (Schürmann, I, 336 n. 84). It is not clear whether Matthew or Luke is original here. For the thought of joy amid persecution cf. Acts 5:41; 16:25; 21:13f.; Rom. 5:3–5; Jas. 1:2; 1 Pet. 1:2, 6; 4:13 (W. Nauck, 'Freude im Leiden', ZNW 46, 1955, 68–80).

The reason for joy is introduced by ἰδοὺ γάρ (frequent in Lk.), diff. Mt. ὅτι. There is a great reward for the disciples in heaven. On μισθός see E. Würthwein and H. Preisker, TDNT IV, 695–728; Smith, 49–73. The thought is of God's vindication of his faithful servants; cf. 12:8f.; Mk. 8:38; but the reference found in the parallel passages to the part played by the Son of man upholding his followers is absent here.

The connection of thought with the final clause is not clear. 1. The disciples can know that they are bound to suffer because the same thing happened to God's servants, the prophets. 2. They may be sure of their heavenly reward because (it is implied) the prophets also were rewarded after their sufferings. 3. The fact that they are being persecuted proves that they are God's servants, since this is how his prophets were treated. The third of these possibilities is to be preferred, since it gives the best parallel with v. 26, and is also supported by 1 Pet. 4:14 and Rom. 8:36 (cf. Schniewind, *Matthäus*, 50). On the fate of the prophets cf. J. Jeremias, TDNT V, 714; G. Friedrich, TDNT VI, 834f.; Steck. Hare, 116f., argues that the whole clause is an addition to the saying, since it equates the disciples with the prophets (which, he argues, did not happen until pneumatic phenomena developed in the church), and it is a superfluous addition to the original beatitude. But the equation of the disciples with the prophets is not so close as to warrant this conclusion, and Hare's understanding of the point of the saying is faulty.

κατὰ τὰ αὐτά, 6:26; 17:30; cf. Acts 14:1, is probably Lucan; Matthew has οὕτως. The use of ποιέω, diff. Mt. διώκω, may be original, since Matthew can have altered the word under the influence of the preceding verse. The prophets are clearly those of OT times; a reference to Essene prophets (K. Schubert, in K. Stendahl, *The Scrolls and the New Testament*, London, 1958, 123f.) is most improbable. The final phrase οἱ πατέρες αὐτῶν (cf. 11:48) is paralleled in Mt. by a qualification of the prophets as τοὺς πρὸ ὑμῶν. The attempt has been made to derive these two phrases from a common Aramaic original: Wellhausen, 24, suggested that the expression *daq'damaihôn* ('which (were) before them') was misread by Matthew's source as *daq'damaikôn* ('which (were) before you'); although this view is accepted by Black, 191f., there are numerous difficulties surrounding it (Hare, 174f.; Wrege, 24 n. 2), and Wellhausen himself later withdrew it (*Einleitung*, 2nd edition, omits it). More probably we have an insertion by Luke to supply a subject for the verb; elsewhere he uses πατέρες in the sense of ancestors (Dupont, I, 246–249).

(24) A strong contrast to the preceding beatitudes is introduced by the use of πλήν. It is debated whether the use of this word is due to Luke (Schürmann, *Abschiedsrede*, 5–7; Ott, 33f.; Dupont, III, 30–34) or to his source (Delling, 220 n. 87; Rehkopf, 8–10; Jeremias, *Parables*, 155 n. 13). Luke uses πλήν 4x in Acts, always as a preposition, 'except' (8:1; 15:28; and 27:22 with gen.; 20:23* with ὅτι); this sense is not found in the Gospel. 2. As a conjunction meaning 'only, nevertheless, however, but', it is used 15x in Lk. (including 17:1 v.l.; Mt., 5x; Mk., 1x). Luke has it in common with Mt. in 10:14 par. Mt. 11:22; 17:1 (si v.l.) par. Mt. 18:7. He never adds it to Mk., except possibly at 22:21, 22, 42 (where it is a moot point whether he is influenced by another source). The occurrences in 6:35; 10:11, 20; 11:41; 12:31 (diff. Mt. 6:33); 13:33; 18:8; 19:27 and 23:28 are debatable. But the use of πλήν οὐαί in Mt. 18:7 indicates that the usage is traditional, and hence it may be pre-Lucan here. Dupont, III, 34f., argues that 6:24, 26 have a parallel in 11:41, 42, which suggests Lucan editing here. Even, however, if the conjunction is Lucan (which, on the whole, we doubt), this does not prove that the following woes have been added here by Luke; see Schürmann, I, 339f.

οὐαί means 'alas for', and introduces an expression of pity for those who stand under divine judgment. The 'woe' form is to be found in the OT (Is. 1:4f.; 5:8–23; 10:5ff.; 33:1; Am. 5:18; 6:1; Hab. 2:6ff.; E. Jenni, THAT I, 474–477); for the combination of woes with blessings see Is. 3:10f.; Ec. 10:16f.; Tob. 13:12, 14; 1 En. 5:7; 99; 2 En. 52; Ber. 61b; Yoma 87a; Sukka 56b (SB I, 663f.; Dupont I, 326–335). Woes are fairly common in the NT: Lk. 10:13 par. Mt. 11:21; Lk. 11:42–52 par. Mt. 23:13–29; Lk. 17:1 par. Mt. 18:7; Lk. 21:23 par. Mk. 13:17; Lk. 22:22 par. Mk. 14:21; 1 Cor. 9:16; Jude 11; Rev. 8:13; *et al.* The evidence suggests that this form of speech was used by Jesus himself.

The saying is addressed to the people to whom the woe applies by means of ὑμῖν. It is usually thought that this is a case of apostrophe, since the persons in question are not present, and 6:27 takes up the theme of the Sermon addressed to those who are present (ὑμῖν ... τοῖς ἀκούουσιν). If this is the case, it is hard to see why Luke has used the second person form (especially if the original beatitudes were in the third person). It is more likely that the words are addressed directly to persons in spiritual danger, who may well have been present to listen to Jesus (on this or on some other occasion); certainly this situation seems to be presupposed in 6:46–49.

The people thus addressed are the rich (1:53), and the reason why they are to be pitied is because they have already received their consolation. The verb ἀπέχω was used in receipts to indicate that the person had had full payment of a debt, and hence that he had no further claims on the debtor (cf. Mt. 6:2, 5, 16). The rich have thus received all that they are ever going to get. For παράκλησις cf. 2:25, and the use of the verb in Mt. 5:4. There will be no divine consolation for such people, for they have already received their consolation in the form of what money can give to them. Hence the deeper reason for the woe is seen. It is the fact that the rich have used their wealth to purchase their own comfort, and have not used their wealth to help the needy (cf. 16:19–31); not only so, but their attitude suggests that they have been satisfied with their wealth and saw no need to secure for themselves treasure in heaven by giving to the needy (cf. 12:21). These points are made clearer in the succeeding woes. Nothing is said of the fate of the rich; it is enough to tell them that they are deprived of any divine blessing for the future.

(25) Second, there is a woe addressed to those who are now sated with food (ἐμπεπλησμένοι, 1:53). The verb brings out the idea of the rich satisfaction which they have obtained – they are not only fed but also well fed. In the future they will endure the pangs of hunger (cf. 1:53). The woe has its OT parallel in Is. 65:13f. where hunger and thirst, shame and sorrow are prophesied for those who do not serve God; cf. also Jas. 4:9.

Third, Jesus addresses those who laugh now. The verb (cf. 6:21 note) is used in the LXX of an evil kind of laughter, which looks down on the fate of enemies and is in danger of becoming boastful and self-satisfied. This nuance, which goes beyond the sense of mere joyfulness, may well be present here. The implication is that Jesus is describing people who are self-satisfied and indifferent to the needs of others. The tables will be turned, and as a result of their future deprivation they will be reduced to weeping and mourning.

(26) The fourth woe describes people who enjoy a good reputation among men; for the construction cf. Ex. 22:28; Acts 23:5. The word order ὑμᾶς καλῶς is adopted by UBS on the basis of p⁷⁵ B (it is inverted in Synopsis; Diglot; the reading πάντες οἱ ἄνθρωποι is defended by Metzger, 141 – the omission of πάντες by D al sy^sp Mcion is probably due to assimilation to 6:22).

The second half of the saying is identical with 6:23b. with the substitution of ψευδοπροφήτης (Mt. 7:15; 24:11, 24 par. Mk. 13:22; Acts 13:6; et al.). The reference is to false prophets in OT times (2 Pet. 2:1) who led the people astray and enjoyed a good reputation among them (Is. 5:31; 30:10; Mi. 2:11; Je. 5:31; 14:14–16; 23:17ff.). Those who live in this way are accordingly ranked with the false prophets who have turned away from Yahweh and stand under his judgment. The saying may originally have been directed against the Pharisees. It is possible that Luke had in view the false teachers in the church of his own day (Schürmann, I, 338f.). But the evidence of James, who knew the woes (Jas. 4:4, 9; 5:1), suggests that they were directed to the rich, especially the opponents of the church, and to those in the church who were attracted to their way of life.

(b) Love and Mercy 6:27–38

In the introductory analysis of the Sermon it became evident that in this section, which forms the heart of the discourse, the theme is the love that must be shown by the disciples.

In the first subsection (6:27–31) the accent is on the showing of love to those who hate and persecute the disciples; they are to be prepared to give freely and to obey the 'golden rule'. A second subsection teaches that such love will gain a heavenly reward, and contrasts it with the mutual love shown by sinners (6:32–36). From the thought that such conduct is like that of God who is merciful there develops the command to avoid judging others and to give freely in order to receive freely from God (6:36–38). By this point the thought has moved from love of enemies to relationships of a more general character.

The first subsection (6:27–31) is parallel to Mt. 5:44, 39b, 40, 42; 7:12. Two different structures are apparent. In Lk. there is a set of balanced clauses, assembled to form a unity. In Mt. there is material cast in the form of two separate antitheses (on retaliation and love for enemies) and presented separately from the golden rule. Despite the closeness of wording, there is a significant change of metaphor in v. 29b from Mt. 5:40. If the same source directly underlies both Gospels, one or both Evangelists has considerably revised its order and contents. The majority of scholars hold that the more original form is to be found in Mt. (Bultmann, 100; Dupont, I, 189–204; Schulz, 120f.): Luke has run together material from two separate groups in Mt., but has probably preserved something like the original position of the golden rule. This is disputed by Schürmann, I, 345f., who thinks that the original order was more like that in Lk. There are, however, places where each Gospel seems to have the more primitive wording (Lk. 6:27f.; Mt. 5:40), and hence there are grounds for suspecting that a simple solution in terms of one common source is inadequate (Wrege, 75–94). Both Gospels show signs of systematising the traditions before them, and this makes it almost impossible to reconstruct a hypothetical original.

The same difficulty exists in the second subsection, 6:32–36, which is parallel to Mt. 5:46, 47, 44, 45, 48. In Lk. there are three parallel statements indicating that certain forms of behaviour go no further than the common practice even of sinners. These are followed by a threefold command to go beyond such minimal actions, so that disciples may have a heavenly reward and become like God. The form is logical and clear. In Mt. the general command to love is followed by the aim of becoming like God. Then come two statements about minimal behaviour and an appeal to go beyond this by being 'perfect' like God. Luke is more 'Hellenistic' than Mt. here, probably as a result of Lucan editing (van Unnik*).

In the third subsection, 6:36–38, the theme is that the person who shows mercy, does not judge others and gives freely will receive from God. If the teaching in vs. 32–35 is that living purely on the level of normal human 'sinful' relationships does not deserve any reward from God, here we have a command to go beyond this kind of behaviour and thus to receive what God has promised in return. This takes the teaching of the beatitudes and woes further. Those who have nothing in this world because they give freely will have a divine reward, but those who have plenty in this world because they have lived in worldly-wise fashion will find that their lack of mercy to others results in the same attitude being shown to them by God.

This section is paralleled in Mt. 5:48; 7:1, 2b. Luke has nothing corresponding to Mt. 7:2a, but this half-verse may be a revised form of the source material reflected in Lk. 6:37b; there is a further parallel in Mk. 4:24. It is probable that the section was originally one in Mt., but has been broken up by the insertion of Mt. 6. Matthew has nothing corresponding to Lk. 6:38a, but he may have omitted this because it disturbed the theme of judgment (Schürmann, I, 362–365; contra Schulz, 146f.)

See Manson, Sayings, 49–56; Percy, 148–163; Spicq, I, 98–116; Dupont, I, 189–204; Wrege, 75–94, 124–129; Schulz, 120–141, 146–149; W. C. van Unnik, 'Die Motivierung der Feindesliebe in Lukas vi 32–35' (originally in Nov.T 8, 1966, 284–300), in van Unnik, I, 111–126; D. Lührmann, 'Liebet eure Feinde (Lk. 6:27–36/Mt. 5:39–48)', ZTK 69, 1972, 412–438.

(27) After the sayings directed to outsiders, the sort of people who might become persecutors of the disciples (Jas. 2:6f.), the next section begins with a transitional ἀλλά and an indication that the audience is again the disciples. But in Mt. 5:44 (ἐγὼ δὲ λέγω ὑμῖν) almost identical wording is used to draw a contrast, not between audiences, but between speakers, the stress lying on what Jesus now says in antithesis to the men of old. The sense of the authority of Jesus is, to be sure, not entirely lacking in Lk. λέγω ὑμῖν, especially when prefixed by ἀμήν, conveys the sense of Jesus' authority. The word order ὑμῖν λέγω is Lucan (11:9; 12:22 v.l.; 16:9; Rom. 11:13; Rev. 2:24; Jeremias, Parables, 45 n. 80; Ott, 100). τοῖς ἀκούουσιν is often taken as an indication that Jesus has been apostrophising absent opponents in vs. 24–26, but this is not a necessary conclusion; ἀκούω can have the sense 'to hear and obey'

(Acts 28:28; Mt. 18:15f.; cf. Lk. 9:35; 16:29, 31). A different view is suggested by P. S. Minear, 'Jesus' Audiences according to Luke', Nov.T 16, 1974, 81–109, especially 103–109. He suggests that vs. 20–26 are addressed to the disciples, and vs. 27ff. to the uncommitted crowds who came to *hear* Jesus (6:17f.). (On this view the woes are warnings to the disciples about the danger of their becoming false prophets.)

There is no direct link in thought between vs. 24–26 and 27ff. One can, however, see a possible catchword link with the beatitudes by means of μισέω (v. 22), and this may suggest that Luke has preserved an original form of the tradition, rather than that he has remodelled something like the present form of Mt. 5:38–48 (Schürmann, I, 345f.). The question whether Matthew and Luke are here altering the same tradition will depend on whether Matthew himself is responsible for creating the antitheses in Mt. 5.

The introduction is followed by four balanced imperatives in asyndeton (BD 462²). The most general command comes first (par. Mt. 5:44a). ἀγαπάω (6:32, 35; 7:5, 42, 47; 10:27; 11:43; 16:13*; Acts, Ox; Mt., 8x; Mk., 5x) is concerned less with emotional affection than with willing service and the desire to do good to the other person, as is clear from the three following imperatives and the use of ἀγαθοποιέω in 6:35 (on the concept see Spicq, I, 98–155). ἐχθρός (1:71, 74; 6:35; 10:19; 19:27, 43; 20:43*; Acts 2:35; 13:10*; W. Foerster, TDNT II, 811–814) is used to describe a person who has hostile feelings towards me, i.e. in an active sense. Since it is natural for me to feel hostility to such a person, the word can also have a passive sense. The meaning here, however, is clearly the former. Whereas the natural impulse is to hate those who hate us (Mt. 5:43), the disciple is commanded to return love for hate. Persecutors are especially in mind, but the thought is clearly wider.

This clause reappears in v. 35 to give a basis for the promised reward in v. 36, whereas in Mt. 5:44f. the command and reward appear together. It is arguable that Luke has brought the command forward in order to provide a heading for the section and to enable him to work in the material on non-retaliation in Mt. 5:39–42 (J. Weiss, 446). But the detailed content of vs. 27f. goes beyond that of Mt. 5:44, and it is more probable that Luke is following a separate tradition, or that Matthew has abbreviated and reordered the material.

The second clause makes clear the meaning of the first, and may well be an elucidation for Hellenistic readers (van Unnik*). καλῶς ποιέω is 'to do good' (cf. εὖ ποιέω, Mt. 12:12; Mk. 14:7); usually it means 'to do well' (Acts 10:33; *et al.*), but here it has the same meaning as the more elegant ἀγαθοποιέω, 6:33, 35. μισέω gives a link to 6:22 (cf. 1:71).

(28) On εὐλογέω see 1:42 note. The thought of blessing persecutors is found in Rom. 12:14; 1 Cor. 4:12; 1 Pet. 3:9, but apparently has no Jewish antecedents. καταράομαι, 'to curse' (Rom. 12:14; Mk. 11:21; Mt. 25:41; Jas. 3:9**) may have been taken as a reference to the Jewish curse pronounced in connection with excommunication, but

Rom. 12:14 suggests that a more general sense is present (cf. F. Büchsel, TDNT I, 448–451).

Finally, intercession is to be made for those who insult the disciples. For the use of περί, diff. Mt. ὑπέρ, cf. Acts 12:5. ἐπηρεάζω, 'to molest, insult' (1 Pet. 3:16**) belongs to the vocabulary of persecution. Matthew has διώκω (cf. Mt. 5:11; Rom. 12:14; 1 Cor. 4:12), probably as a more general term drawn from the persecution vocabulary.

(29) Vs. 29f. correspond to Mt. 5:39b–42 and occur in Mt. in the context of the antithesis on retaliation. It is hard to tell whether the Lucan or Matthaean placing is original, most scholars preferring the latter (Bultmann, 100). The theme is different from that in vs. 27f., in that the point here is readiness not to claim one's personal rights and not to retaliate against hostile acts; the context of persecution is the same, but the thought broadens out in v. 30 to more general situations. The change to the second person singular has suggested that vs. 29f. were originally transmitted separately from the surrounding commands which have the plural form, but this is a weak argument; the singular form is more appropriate for commands relating to particular situations than the plural. Even so, it is possible that we have originally separate sayings here. Matthew includes a further command, about going the extra mile; Luke may have omitted this because it applied to the conditions of the Roman occupation in Palestine (23:26) and was less relevant to his readers.

τύπτω, 'to strike' (12:45; 18:13; 23:48; Acts, 5x; Mk. 15:9; Mt. 24:49; 27:30; 1 Cor. 8:12**), is used of a blow with the hand or fist. Matthew has ὅστις σε ῥαπίζει, which may be a translation variant, but τύπτω is a more refined word than ῥαπίζω, (Creed, 93). Thereby Luke misses a possible allusion to the demeanour of the Servant of Yahweh (ῥάπισμα, Is. 50:6; cf. Did. 1:4). The blow is delivered on the cheek (σιαγών, Mt. 5:39**), Matthew mentioning the right cheek, a blow on which was said to be especially insulting (SB I, 342, 532; Manson, Sayings, 51). If so, Luke may have omitted a detail that had no significance for a non-Jewish audience (G. Stählin, TDNT VIII, 260–269, especially 263). Schürmann, I, 347 n. 33, however, claims that δέξιος is a Matthaean addition (cf. Mt. 5:29f., diff. Mk.), and that one would expect the more insulting action to come as the climax of the saying. παρέχω, 'to offer', is Lucan, and may be a substitute for Mt., στρέφω.

In the second example Luke differs considerably from Matthew in that he pictures a robber who tries to take away (αἴρω, 6:30) an outer garment (ἱμάτιον), and who is to be offered the inner garment (χιτών) as well. Matthew pictures a lawsuit in which a man is sued (κρίνω) for his inner garment and allows his opponent to have his outer garment as well. The form in Mt. reflects Jewish custom with regard to debt, and the allusion is lost in Lk. (Ex. 22:25f.; Dt. 24:13; G. Kittel, *Die Probleme des palästinischen Spätjudentums und das Urchristentum,* Stuttgart, 1926, 32f.). The use of κωλύω with ἀπό is Semitic, but may be a Septuagintalism (Gn. 23:6). Here it may be pre-Lucan, since the repetition of the ἀπό phrase in v. 30 is unlikely to be due to Luke. Problems have been seen in the reverse order of the garments in Lk. as compared with Mt., but both orders make good sense in the context. In Lk. a man is naturally robbed of his outer garment first (Manson, *Sayings*, 51); in Mt. Jesus says that the outer garment (to which a creditor had no claim) must be given in addition to the inner garment. It is uncertain whether the more general form is due to Luke himself (Schulz, 122f.) or to his source (Wrege, 76f.), but the latter is more likely if Did. 1:4 and Justin Apol. 1:16:1 are not dependent on Lk.

(30) Luke has nothing corresponding to Mt. 5:41. He goes straight on to more general commands on giving; Schürmann, I, 349, holds that v. 30 was originally separate from v. 29, but his argument is not convincing.

The generalising παντί is probably due to Luke (cf. 5:28; 11:4) as is the use of δίδου, diff. Mt. δός (cf. 11:3). In the second part of the saying the differences from Mt. are greater. Matthew speaks of not refusing a person who wishes to borrow (δανίζω); this theme is taken up in v. 34, which suggests that it was present in Luke's source, but, if so, it is hard to see why Luke should have removed the thought here; moreover, the repetitiousness of v. 30 compared with v. 29 is hardly due to Luke (Wrege, 78). Hence the difference from Mt. may have arisen at a pre-Lucan stage (cf. Klostermann, 81). For Luke the picture is the same as in v. 29b: if somebody takes something from you by force, do not ask for it back (ἀπαιτέω, 12:20**). Disciples must give freely, even to those who have no legitimate claim upon them; there is no place for the claims of self over against generosity to others (cf. Ps. 37:21; Pr. 21:26). The spirit is that of the beatitudes. It goes without saying that the examples and even the principles given by Jesus are not to be taken over-literally. If v. 29b were so taken, 'the issue would be nudism, a sufficient indication that it is a certain spirit that is being commended to our notice – not a regulation to be slavishly carried out. But this fact does not entitle us to evade the demand, which is here put forward in an extreme case. What Jesus here says is seriously, even if not literally, meant; and his followers have the task of manifesting the spirit of the injunction in the varied situations which arise in actual life' (Manson, *Sayings*, 51).

(31) The set of commands is rounded off with the golden rule, postponed by Matthew to Mt. 7:12. There can be little doubt that it belongs to the present context, and has been saved up by Matthew to form the conclusion of the main part of his Sermon (Wrege, 132 n. 1; Schürmann, I, 350–352; Schulz, 121). The wording differs slightly from Mt. Luke's καί, diff. Mt. οὖν, is probably original. καθώς and ὅσα ἐάν could be translation variants for kᵉmā᾽ dᵉ (cf. Gn. 41:13/44:1 LXX; Manson, *Sayings*, 18f.), but both phrases are characteristic of their authors. Schürmann, I, 350 n. 55, suggests that Matthew is concerned more with 'what' is given, Luke with 'how' one behaves. Likewise, the

use of ὁμοίως, diff. Mt. οὕτως, shows that both Evangelists are using their favourite expressions. Many MSS add καὶ ὑμεῖς (TR; *Diglot*), by assimilation to Mt. (the shorter text is found in p⁷⁵ ᵛⁱᵈ B 700 it Ir Cl; cf. Metzger, 141).

The rule is a positive command that we should treat others as we would wish them to treat us. The negative form is well known in Jewish literature (Tob. 4:15; Tg. Jerus. I on Lv. 19:18; Philo (in Eusebius PE 8:7); Shab. 31a, in SB I, 459f.) and in pagan literature (Creed, 94); see further Acts 15:20, 29 D; Did. 1:2; G. Thomas 6. A combination of negative and positive forms is found in Arist. 207, and the positive form occurs in T. Naph. 1; 2 En. 61:1. For details, see A. Dihle, *Die Goldene Regel*, Göttingen, 1962. Jesus is, therefore, not saying something new here, but it is significant that he stresses the positive form of the rule. The negative form is merely a rule of prudence: do not hurt other people lest they retaliate. The positive form is not prudential but absolute: this is how you are to treat others (positively), regardless of how they treat you (Schürmann, I, 349f.; Harvey, 40f.). Jesus thus goes beyond the negative form, citing the rarer and more demanding form. The fact that the rule is found in Judaism in no way suggests that the present saying cannot have been uttered by Jesus (Schürmann, I, 351f.; *contra* Bultmann, 107f.).

(32) The next section takes up the thought of vs. 27f. by means of a contrast between loving one's enemies and loving (only) one's friends. This might suggest that vs. 29–31 have disturbed the original connection of thought. If so, it may be that the content of Mt. 5:45 has been transferred to the end of the section (v. 35b; but see below). In fact, however, vs. 32ff. carry on the thought of treating others positively expressed in the Golden Rule.

The temptation to disciples is to love those who will show them love in return, instead of loving those from whom they have little hope of being treated as they would hope to be treated (vs. 29f., 31). The use of the present indicative (ἀγαπᾶτε, diff. Mt., aorist subjunctive) generalises the thought. Van Unnik* has shown that the thought of doing good to others in the hope that they would do good in return was common enough in the ancient world (1 Mac. 11:33; Sir. 12:1ff.; t. Meg. 4:16 (Thompson, 115); Epictetus 2:14, 18; Hesiod, Works and Days, 352; Aristotle, Rhet. ad Alex. 1446; cf. Lk. 14:12–14). Such conduct is not wrong; the point is that it brings no χάρις (diff. Mt. μισθός). This word can mean the approbation or favour of a superior (cf. 17:9), here of God (cf. 1 Pet. 2:19f.; Klostermann, 81). If a person does a good act in hope of some return, he will get none; the person who does a good deed for which no credit can be expected receives a gracious, undeserved act of thanks from God. The word has probably been introduced as a Hellenistic equivalent to μισθός, possibly by Luke, although he retains μισθός in 6:35; cf. H. Conzelmann, TDNT IX, 392. In the second half of the saying Luke's καί is flat compared with Mt., οὐχὶ καί, and is probably editorial (Wrege, 90 n. 4). For ἁμαρτωλοί, Matthew has τελῶναι; a Jewish expression has been altered to one comprehensible to gentile readers, but this may well be due to Luke's source rather than his own editing (see Schürmann, I, 353 n. 79, who questions whether τελῶναι is not due to Jewish-Christian editing rather than to Jesus himself).

(33) The second statement is built on the same pattern as the first. The linking γάρ, attested by p⁷⁵ ℵ* B 700; (UBS); *Diglot*, is unnecessary, and has probably been added by error. The saying corresponds to Mt. 5:47 in position and form, but the content is significantly different. Since Mt. 5:47 is couched in thoroughly Jewish terms in terms of greeting one's brothers (cf. Lk. 10:4; 11:43; 20:46), it is possible that Luke has generalised for gentile readers. Luke's phrase takes up the thought of v. 27c (καλῶς ποιεῖτε), with ἀγαθοποιέω (cf. 6:9; and see 6:32 note on the currency of this idea in the Hellenistic world). He continues with the same rhetorical question as in v. 32, but Matthew has 'What do you more?' (cf. Mt. 5:20). ἁμαρτωλοί, diff. Mt. ἐθνικοί, is again a change for the benefit of gentile readers (contrast 12:30 par. Mt. 6:32).

(34) The third statement has no parallel in Mt., and does not link up with any earlier statement in Lk. It takes up the theme of Mt. 5:42 (diff. Lk. 6:30) which Luke himself is hardly likely to have known in this form, and hence it follows that v. 34 is not a Lucan creation (*pace* Bultmann, 100; Schulz, 130f.). If, however, vs. 29–31 are an addition to the original set of sayings, it follows that v. 34 is a (pre-Lucan) addition, or rather composition (Schürmann, I, 354). It may have been in Matthew's source, and omitted because of its difficulty.

δανίζω, 'to give a loan', middle, 'to accept a loan', occurs only here (cf. Mt. 5:42) and v. 35. As antecedent to παρ' ὧν supply τούτοις. The use of ἐλπίζω may be Lucan (23:8; 24:21*; Acts 24:26; 26:7*; Mt. 12:21 (LXX); Mk., Ox). The object of λαβεῖν is uncertain. The reference may be to 1. the recovery of the principal; 2. the payment of interest by the debtor; or 3. the reception of loans in exchange (cf. G. Stählin, TDNT III, 344f.). The parallel with the preceding verses strongly suggests that the third possibility is correct (although 6:30b might indicate the first possibility; but the two verses are not closely connected). A decision depends on what the parallel phrase ἵνα ἀπολάβωσιν τὰ ἴσα can mean (cf. also v. 35, μηδὲν ἀπελπίζοντες). The most obvious sense here would be the first (Lagrange, 194f.), but this is unlikely: men do not lend *in order* to recover the principal, but hope to gain interest also. Moreover, δανίζω is hardly the right word to use of what would in effect be a gift. It is more likely, then, that τὰ ἴσα refers not to 'the same amount of money as was lent' but to 'similar services in return'. (It is just possible that the interpretation here rejected is right, if we presuppose a Jewish situation in which loans to fellow-Jews were free from interest, and hence especially meritorious (Ex. 22:25; Lv. 25:35–37; Dt. 23:20f.; SB I, 346–353); but this view still falls foul of the ἵνα.)

(35) The thought of the three preceding statements is now summed

up positively in a conclusion introduced by a strongly adversative πλήν. The first half of the verse has been regarded as a redactional formulation to introduce the promise in the second half; this was necessary since Luke had brought forward the imperatives here to form an introduction to the whole section (Bultmann, 100, cf. 83). It could, however, be argued that the negative statements in vs. 32–34 required to be followed by a positive injunction, and that Matthew altered the order reflected in Lk. 6:32f., 35, in order to place the love command at the beginning of his section after 5:43 (Schürmann, I, 355). In favour of Luke's order is the fact that v. 36 follows on better from v. 35 than from v. 33 (as in Mt.).

The commands to love and do good are thus repeated. The command to lend is also repeated, and if v. 34 is an addition to the original wording, the same will be true here. The qualification μηδὲν ἀπελπίζοντες causes difficulty. ἀπελπίζω usually means 'to despair'; cf. the Latin rendering *nihil desperantes*; Is. 29:19; Jdt. 9:11; 1 Clem. 59:3. But this translation introduces an alien thought into the passage. Adoption of the reading μηδένα ἀπελπίζοντες, 'despairing of no man' (א W *pc* sy [sp]; Turner, 32–35), does not greatly help. The verb is found from the time of Chrysostom, however, with the meaning 'to hope for some return', and this sense should be adopted here, despite the lack of earlier attestation (Lagrange, 195–197; AG s.v.; Bultmann, TDNT II, 533f.). If the participle is to be taken with ἀγαθοποιεῖτε as well as δανίζετε, the thought of lending with a view to gaining interest is ruled out.

The three commands are equivalent to a condition: if you do these things, you will gain a reward, a plentiful one – from God; cf. Mt. 6:4, 6, 18 for the same thought with regard to religious acts. Although the clause is absent from Mt. at this point, the preservation of μισθός here by Luke and the presence of the same thought in Mt. 6 strongly suggest that the thought was present in his source at this point; Matthew will have omitted the clause when he re-ordered the material.

It is not clear whether the next clause is to be regarded as epexegetic of the thought of reward. If so, the promise of divine sonship is a reward for faithful service; those who love will enjoy God's fatherly love and care. The next clause, however, and v. 36 both suggest that the point is that the disciples will show themselves to be God's children by their imitation of his character. Probably this thought is primary, but the idea that those who show themselves to be God's sons will receive his fatherly blessing cannot be excluded.

Luke has ὕψιστος (1:32 note) diff. Mt. ὁ πατὴρ ὑμῶν. The latter phrase is generally regarded as original (G. Schrenk, TDNT V, 985f.; van Iersel, 96–99; Schulz, 128), and Luke's phrase may reflect the influence of Sir. 4:10, where the omission of the article, as here (*pace* the weakly attested variant τοῦ ὑψίστου in TR; *Diglot*), represents a Hebraism. But Matthew may have been influenced by the wording in Mt. 5:48 par. Lk. 6:36, and there is no obvious reason why Luke should have substituted ὕψιστος here. Either form could be original. Whereas in Mt. God is kind to both good and bad men, in Lk. his goodness is to those who will show no return. For χρηστός (5:39), see Ps. 34:8; 1 Pet. 2:3; Rom. 2:4; Mt. 11:30. ἀχάριστος (2 Tim. 3:2**) is ungrateful. Although Luke's language appears secondary, and his thought less Palestinian than in Mt., where the importance of rain for the farmer forms the background to the saying, the thought fits in more closely with the preceding stress on doing good to those from whom no return is expected, than does Matthew's description of God's goodness to all men alike. Probably Matthew is nearer to the original form.

(36) γίνεσθε (imperative) has the same force as ἔσεσθε in Mt. The disciples are commanded to be 'merciful' (οἰκτίρμων); Jas. 5:11**; R. Bultmann, TDNT V, 159–161), according to the pattern (καθώς. diff. Mt. ὡς) shown by God who is merciful; cf. Pss. 103:8; 111:4. The omission of καί by B al sa bo; (UBS); *Synopsis* is due to assimilation to Mt. The basis for behaviour found here is also attested in Judaism, 'As our Father is merciful in heaven, so be merciful on earth' (Tg. Jer. I on Lv. 22:28; SB II, 159; cf. M. Ex. 15:2; Siphre Dt. 11, 22; 49 (85a); SB I, 372f.; Black, 181). The mercy of God supplies both a pattern for his children to follow and a standard of comparison for them to attain. The concept is close in meaning to ἔλεος (cf. 1:50 note; 10:37), but stresses more the idea of sympathy and pity shown to the unfortunate and needy. That God is described here as Father fits in with the description of believers as his sons in 6:35; cf. 11:2, 13; 12:30, 32. The force of the word here is again that children are expected to show the character of their father. The Matthaean parallel has τέλειος instead of οἰκτίρμων; cf. Mt. 19:21. The word means 'perfect' in the sense that God is 'undivided' or 'unrestricted in his goodness', and so too 'the disciples of Jesus should be "total" in their love, bringing even their enemies within its compass' (G. Delling, TDNT VIII, 67–78, especially 74). The word may reflect Heb. *tāmîm* or *šālēm*. Opinions are divided on whether Mt. or Lk. represents the original wording here. In favour of Mt. is the possible play on words in Aramaic (Black, 138f.), and the fact that Luke's word could be a simplification of a difficult expression for Gentiles. In favour of Lk. is the link with χρηστός in 6:35 and with the thought of mercy in 6:37f.; there is an OT link, and it could be argued that Matthaean theology is reflected in his wording. On the whole, Luke would appear to be more original here (Schürmann, I, 360; Schulz, 130).

(37) The principle in 6:36 is now developed with two negative commands followed by two positive ones and a final comment. The disciples are not to judge; κρίνω can mean 'to come to a right decision' (7:43; 12:57), 'to rule' (22:30), and, as here, 'to condemn' (19:22*). In their own day-to-day conduct the disciples are forbidden to usurp the place of God in judging and condemning other people. The context would suggest that it is the attitude which fails to show mercy to the guilty which is here being attacked. It is not the use of discernment and

discrimination which is forbidden, but the attitude of censoriousness. The saying 'does not imply flabby indifference to the moral condition of others nor the blind renunciation of attempts at a true and serious appraisal of those with whom we have to live. What is unconditionally demanded is that such evaluations should be subject to the certainty that God's judgment falls also on those who judge, so that superiority, hardness and blindness to one's own faults are excluded, and a readiness to forgive and to intercede is safeguarded' (F. Büchsel, TDNT, III, 939). Those who follow this command will find that (καί expressing result, diff. Mt. ἵνα) they are not judged by God: the passive κριθῆτε refers, as often, to a divine action. The point is clearly not that such people will escape the judgment of God, but rather that on the day of judgment, they will be treated mercifully (cf. Mt. 5:7; Shab. 151b, in SB I, 203).

The same thought is expressed in the second command, in which καταδικάζω, 'to condemn' (Mt. 12:7, 37; Jas. 5:6**), elucidates the meaning of κρίνω. There is no precisely corresponding sentence in Mt., but there is a rough parallel in Mt. 7:2a, which appears to have been edited to give parallelism with Mt. 7:2b. If the Lucan form is original, it provides a transition to the next (positive) command (Wrege, 125).

The command which follows demands forgiveness, and promises divine forgiveness in return (for ἀπολύω in this sense, cf. Mt. 18:27). As Schürmann, I, 361 n. 127, emphasises, the command is concerned with forgiving someone who has actually committed an offence against us, not with declaring an innocent person to be not guilty; cf. Lk. 11:4; Mt. 18:35; 1 Cor. 13:5. The reference is to personal insults and injuries, and expresses the same principle of not standing on one's own rights but rather of showing love to other people even at the cost of one's own pride and position which was taught earlier in 6:27–36. Hence the saying does not refer to the abolition of law and its sanctions in society at large; such action would not in fact be an imitation of the character of God who upholds the moral law and judges transgressors.

(38) The fourth command goes beyond the situation of personal injuries and forgiveness to advocate freely giving to the needs of others and to promise that such giving will earn a divine reward; cf. 2 Cor. 9:6–8. Thereby the giver is assured that selfless action will ultimately be vindicated and shown to be the right kind of action, that of which God approves. But the primary thought here is of the sheer generosity which we should be prepared to show in return for the immense goodness of God. For he bestows 'good measure'; the picture is of a measuring jar which is well-filled; in Dt. R. 11 (207b) (SB II, 160) a good, i.e. full, measure is contrasted with a bad, i.e. partly filled, one. The corn is pressed down into the measure so that it will hold as much as possible (cf. Jeremias, Parables, 222 n. 67). πιέζω 'to press', is an Attic form for Koine πιάζω (BD 29²; 101). Next, the corn is shaken together to make it settle into every available space (σαλεύω, 6:48; 7:24; 21:26*), and finally more is poured out over it so that it overflows

(ὑπερεκχύννω**; cf. Joel 2:24). The asyndeton is removed by adding καί (bis) in A C Θ pm; TR; Diglot. This is the kind of measure that God gives: the third person plural δώσουσιν (cf. 12:20, 48; 16:9; 23:31; Rehkopf, 99) is a rabbinic periphrasis for the name of God (cf. CD 2:13; Braun, Qumran I, 88f.; SB II, 221 – note especially Sotah 1:7). The fold of the garment (κόλπος) was used as a pocket by both Jews and Greeks (cf. Is. 65:6f. (Grundmann, 150); Ps. 79:12; Je. 32:18). That a fairly large skirt is meant is indicated by SB II, 160; Schürmann, I, 363 n. 140. The imagery as a whole is so obviously Palestinian that the question of Lucan creation does not arise, despite the omission of anything corresponding from Mt. (pace Bultmann, 83; Schulz, 146f.).

The final clause gives a basis for the teaching by re-emphasising that men will receive from God according to the measure that they themselves have employed. The saying is paralleled in Mt. 7:2b, the wording of which exactly corresponds to Mk. 4:24b. The Marcan saying has the addition 'and more will be added to you', which Schürmann, I, 363, regards as equivalent in meaning to Lk. 6:38b with its emphasis on generous giving. If so, this means that Luke is not here incorporating a saying from Mk. but following a parallel tradition; faced by the doublet, Matthew has conformed the wording of his source to that of Mk. The text is simplified in many MSS (Metzger, 141) to avoid inclusion of the antecedent in the relative clause. Luke's use of ἀντιμετρέω**, 'to give a measure in return', may be due to his own editing (cf. Schlatter, 246). There is a close parallel in Sotah 1:7: 'With what measure a man metes it shall be measured to him again'; i.e. God's judgments closely fit men's crimes, and his rewards fit their good deeds. Here, however, the thought is more of God's generosity. K. Bornhäuser, Die Bergpredigt, Gütersloh, 1927, 187ff. (cited by K. Deissner, TDNT IV, 632–634) suggested that the thought was of God's two measures, one of goodness (or generosity) and one of justice: a man is judged by whichever measure he himself chooses to use. But the thought of 'measure for measure' is so common (SB I, 444–446) that this proverbial usage is sufficient to explain the wording here. The saying here may appear to speak in terms of strict retribution, but the thought is rather that human generosity is rewarded with divine generosity, not with a precisely equivalent gift from God.

(c) The Inward Character of Disciples 6:39–49

The third, and final, section of the Sermon deals with the kind of inward character which produces the type of behaviour outlined in the earlier sections. It has already become apparent that the selfless, loving sort of attitude and actions required of disciples finds a basis in the hope of future vindication and reward from God. It is now taught that disciples are in themselves blind until they are enlightened by their teacher, and therefore should not judge others (6:39–42), that the fruit of good deeds can be produced only by those who have undergone an inward change of heart (6:43–45), and that disciples must obey the teaching given here by Jesus and not be content with a merely nominal discipleship (6:46–49).

A different understanding of the section is defended by Schürmann, I, 365–379 (cf. Schürmann, *Untersuchungen,* 290–309); he argues that 6:39–45 is directed against false teachers (originally the Pharisees, then the false teachers of Luke's own time, Acts 20:29f.), and has the purpose of warning disciples against following any other way than that of Jesus. In favour of this view is the use to which the corresponding material is put in Mt.; cf. Mt. 15:14; 7:15–20. It is, however, hard to fit Lk. 6:41f. (Mt. 7:3–5) into this pattern, since it appears to be addressed directly to the disciples. Had Luke intended us to see a polemic against false teachers in this section, the clues would surely have been more obvious. Others (e.g. Rengstorf, 90; Grundmann, 152) think that this section is addressed especially to the leaders among the group of disciples (cf. 6:40).

It seems probable that the first part of the section (6:39–42) is included here by Luke (or his source) because of its relevance to the question of judging others, and that the opening sayings, 6:39f., have been included because they formed part of this unit; originally, however, in the pre-Lucan tradition they appear to have belonged to Jesus' instructions to the Twelve. The sayings appear in different contexts in Mt., as an attack on the Pharisees, addressed to the disciples, and in the instruction for the Twelve before their mission; this suggests that Matthew was using a tradition different from that of Luke at this point, and that the Lucan tradition may represent a secondary adaptation of these sayings.

See Schürmann, *Untersuchungen,* 290–309; Schulz, 472–474, 449–451, 146–149, 316–320, 427–430, 312–316.

(39–42) The above remarks indicate our understanding of the origin of 6:39–42, the first subsection in this part of the Sermon. The sayings on not judging one's brother, 6:41f., to which 6:39f. were joined in pre-Lucan tradition, perhaps by the common theme of blindness, have been added to 6:37ff. in virtue of the common theme of judging. The combination of 6:39 and 40 is pre-Lucan, since no clear reason for Luke's joining of the sayings can be found, but they may well have been originally independent.

(39) The opening connective phrase is Lucan (5:36 note), but may well be based on a source (cf. Schürmann, I, 367 and n. 164). The meaning is perhaps that Jesus told them *another* parable, i.e. alongside 6:38. The parable takes the form of a double rhetorical question, the first half expecting the answer 'No', the second half, 'Yes' (BD 427²); in Mt. 15:14 and G. Thomas, 34, the form is that of a conditional sentence, and is probably secondary. A blind man cannot show the way to another blind man (τυφλός, Mt. 15:14; Jn. 16:13; Acts 8:31; Rev. 7:17**; cf. Rom. 2:19f.). Both leader and led will fall (ἐμπίπτω, 10:36; Mt. 12:11; *et*

al.) into a pit (βόθυνος, Mt. 12:11; 15:14**; cf. Is. 24:18; Je. 31:44). The thought of the blind leading the blind is proverbial (cf. Plato, Rep. VIII, 554b; Philo, Virt. 7; further refs. in W. Schrage, *TDNT* VIII, 270–294, especially 275, 286). In Mt. 15:14 the saying is prefixed by a reference to the Pharisees as blind leaders of the blind and applied to the fate of them and their misled followers. It then fits in with a common criticism of Pharisaic Judaism as blind and ignorant of the will of God (Mt. 23:16, 24; Rom. 2:19). The saying is here a Matthaean insertion into Marcan material, and Schürmann, I, 369, finds links between the insertion and the present passage (Mt. 7:4, 19/15:13). It is hard to say whether the Matthaean form comes from an anti-Pharisaic tradition like that in Mt. 23, or has been remodelled by Matthew on the basis of Mt. 23. In any case, there is no trace of the anti-Pharisaic point here in Lk. The saying appears to be understood by Luke in connection with 6:37: the disciples are blind and therefore cannot lead others, or criticise them. It is doubtful whether this is the original meaning of the saying; it may have been included on the catchword principle in the context of 6:41f., in which case the original application must be a matter of guess-work (Bultmann, 103). Rengstorf's view (90) that a polemical saying against the Pharisees is here used to warn the disciples may be near the mark (cf. Jeremias, *Parables*, 41, 167; Schulz, 473f.).

(40) The connection of this saying with the previous one demonstrates that the latter is to be applied to the disciples. The first half of the saying is identical with Mt. 10:24a. In days before the widespread availability of books a pupil depended on his teacher's instruction (Morris, 133). Hence a disciple or pupil could not be above, i.e. superior to, his teacher in knowledge. The statement in Mt. is paralleled by a similar one about a slave and his master, which in turn is paralleled in Jn. 13:16; 15:20a (with the addition of a comparison between a person who is sent and the person who sends him). In Mt. 10:24f. and Jn. 15:20 the point is that the disciples will be treated no better than their master and can expect persecution. In Jn. 13:16 the saying is concerned with the humble example of Jesus which his disciples must follow. The point in Lk. is to be deduced from the second half of the saying. Everyone who has been made complete (καταρτίζω) will be like his teacher. The form in Mt., 'It is sufficient for the disciple that he should be like his teacher', is perhaps original, especially since καταρτίζω may be due to Luke or to church usage (cf. Manson, *Teaching*, 237–240; 14:27 note). The verb can be used of the mutual edification of members of the church (Gal. 6:1) or of their upbuilding by God (1 Cor. 1:10; 2 Cor. 13:11; 1 Thes. 3:10; Heb. 13:21; 1 Pet. 5:10) and hence denotes 'the ideal of the Christian generally' (G. Delling, *TDNT* I, 475f.). The point is not clear: 1. Only complete agreement with the one authoritative teacher gives the disciples the authority to be teachers in the church (Wellhausen, 25). 2. No pupil can see if his teacher is blind; the teaching that he gets will not make him any better than his teacher (Schmid, 138). 3. The disciples

must not behave differently from, or in a superior fashion to, Jesus – and he did not judge others (Jn. 8:11; J. Weiss, 447). 4. The best pupil does not go beyond his teacher, but simply repeats his teaching (according to Jewish ideas): hence the disciples should beware of false teachers who go beyond what Jesus said in the present Sermon (Schürmann, I, 368f.). Most commentators take v. 40b as antithetic to 40a; we would suggest that it is a case of synonymous parallelism, the force being 'a disciple is not superior to his teacher'. This interpretation brings the meaning close to Mt. 10:25. If so, the point of the saying in its present context is given in view 3. above; cf. Jn. 13:16 for a similar use of the saying. In this case, Luke's use of the saying is probably close to its original meaning as an isolated saying; he has, however, applied it especially to the leaders of the disciples.

(41) The saying is a parabolic piece of teaching, whose meaning is crystal clear, and indeed all the sharper for being expressed in this form. Judging others is completely excluded, since we can never make ourselves perfect. The wording throughout is extremely close to that in Mt.; Wrege, 129–131, claims that the close parallelism does not demand common use of a literary source, but it would be precarious to deny the possibility. The structure of the saying consists of two rhetorical questions followed by an application.

The opening connective δέ is omitted by p⁷⁵ 1424 pc; Diglot. Instead of the question form 'Why?', we might perhaps have expected 'How is it possible for you to see ... and not to see ...?' But the meaning is obvious enough. καρφός, 'speck, chip', and δοκός, 'beam of wood', occur only in this context; κατανοέω, 'to notice, observe', is characteristic of Luke, but here based on his source (cf. Mt. 7:3). The saying has a proverbial ring, the contrast between the splinter of wood and the beam being rabbinic (Hor 3b; SB I, 446f.); R. Tarphon (c. AD 100) is credited with saying, 'I should be surprised if there were anyone in this generation who would accept correction. If one says to a man, "Remove the spelk from your eye", he will reply, "Remove the beam from yours."' (Arakh 16 b, translated by Manson, Sayings, 58; cf. SB I, 446f.). Classical parallels (Plutarch, De curios. 515d; Horace, Sat. 1:3:25) are given in Creed, 97. The slight difference in wording from Mt. is due to Lucan improvement of the style.

(42) The second rhetorical question is added in asyndeton (on the omission of the connective ἤ in p⁷⁵ ℵ B pc e ff², diff. Mt., see Metzger, 141; it may be editorial in Mt.). The wording δύνασαι λέγειν is taken by Black, 254, as an idiomatic rendering of the Aramaic imperfect, literally translated in Mt. as ἐρεῖς, but it may simply be due to Lucan editing (cf. 20:36; 21:15 diff. Mk.; Wrege, 130f.). The use of the vocative ἀδελφέ, diff. Mt., sounds patronising. ἄφες is used in the sense 'please allow me'; sc. ἵνα (BD 364; cf. Mt. 27:49; Mk. 15:36). The use of αὐτός ... οὐ βλέπων diff. Mt. καὶ ἰδού is less vivid and probably due to Luke; for οὐ with a participle cf. Acts 7:5; 26:22; 28:17 (BD 430²).

The man who behaves in this way is a ὑποκριτής (12:56; 13:15; Mk. 7:6; Mt., 13x**; cf. Lk. 12:1; U. Wilckens, TDNT VIII, 559–570). He professes piety and righteousness, especially in censuring others, but other aspects of his behaviour conflict with this, and so he is guilty of inconsistency. His real character is impious; his 'righteous censure' of others is thus play-acting. Let such a person put his own fault right first of all, and then he will see clearly (διαβλέπω, Mt. 7:5; Mk. 8:25**) to correct his brother. ἐκβαλεῖν is placed after διαβλέψεις in TR; Diglot, by assimilation to Mt.

Such a saying could have been addressed originally to the Pharisees (Jeremias, Parables, 167; but his argument that the use of ὑποκριτής demands this audience is invalid; cf. Schürmann, I, 372). There is, however, no good reason to question the setting given in the Sermon, namely the disciples and any other hearers. The same kind of argument is used by Paul in Rom. 2:1–3 against the Jews, possibly a distant echo of the present passage.

(43–45) The second subsection, 6:43–45, teaches the general principle that a person of bad character cannot produce good deeds or words, and in its context stresses the need for the disciples to rid themselves of the speck in their own eyes before they can live lives of outward goodness. The same sayings are found in two places in Mt., 7:15–20 and 12:33–35. The sayings have been inserted in Mt. 12 in the context of the sin of speaking blasphemously against the Holy Spirit, and they indicate that such evil speaking arises from an evil heart. The teaching is here addressed to the Pharisees and serves as a warning to them (cf. Jeremias, Parables, 167), but it may have been used in instruction of the disciples as a warning against false teachers (cf. Schürmann, I, 376 n. 212; Wrege, 144f.). The sayings are used as warnings to the disciples against 'false prophets' in Mt. 7:16–20, cf. 21–23, in order to indicate how they are to be recognised. But it is not so obvious that this is the purpose in Lk. (cf. 6:44a diff. Mt. 7:16, 20), and it is more probable that the general principles in the sayings are here applied to the disciples themselves. It is not clear that the separate sayings originally belonged together, and therefore it is difficult to deduce what their original purpose was; see below for the individual sayings.

Schürmann, I, 375f., indicates how the differences between Mt. and Lk. may have arisen on the basis of a common source, essentially the same as the Lucan form of the sayings. Matthew has used Lk. 6:44a at 7:16a and 20 to provide a framework for his teaching about false prophets. He has then added Lk. 6:44b, and then Lk. 6:43 (with a negative form preceding it), in order to conclude with the threat of judgment in Mt. 7:19 par. Mt. 3:10b. The sayings have been further used in Mt. 12:33–35 in the Lucan order, except that Lk. 6:45a and b appear in reverse order to give a better connection with the insertion at Mt. 12:34a. The argument is broadly convincing, but there are some points which are not easily explained on this basis (especially the names of the plants and fruits), and which suggest that we should be at least cautious about explaining everything in terms of one common literary source (Wrege, 136–146).

The section consists of two parables about trees and their fruit, 6:43–44a, 44b, followed by an application.

(43) The opening γάρ forms a weak link with the preceding section and simply expresses continuation (AG s.v. 4.). The use of the periphrastic present form ἐστιν ... ποιοῦν, diff. Mt., is hardly due to Luke, and the use of ποιεῖ in Mt. 7:17 is a stylistic improvement; on the other hand the form in Mt. 12:33 also looks primitive, so that the hypothesis of one written source for all three passages runs into difficulties.

καλός (Mt. 12:33; cf. 7:17) appears to be equivalent in meaning to ἀγαθός (cf. 6:45; Mt. 7:18); it is not obvious at first sight whether the word refers to healthy trees, or to good-quality trees as compared with bad ones of the same species, or to useful trees as compared with useless ones. σαπρός usually means 'decayed, rotten', but it may also mean 'unusable, unfit, bad' (AG); cf. the use of πονηρός as a synonym, Mt. 7:17f. The word usage thus leaves it ambiguous what is meant, and the solution adopted by O. Bauernfeind (TDNT VII, 94–97, especially 97) is best: 'The bad fruits and trees are "useless", "of no value", irrespective of their biological condition.' It is probable that Luke was thinking of useless trees in view of the connection with 6:44b, but Mt. 12:33 (cf. 7:17–19) may perhaps be thinking of unhealthy trees. The emphasis in Mt. lies on the second half of the saying, the impossibility of bad trees bearing good fruit, and the same may be true here in Lk. in view of 6:44b.

(44) The first half of the verse gives confirmation of the preceding statement. ἕκαστος can mean 'each, every', but also 'each of two' (Jeremias, Parables, 167 n. 76). Hence the statement means that both good and bad trees are recognised as such by their fruit. The saying is closer to Mt. 12:33b than to Mt. 7:16a, 20a, where it is used as a criterion by which the disciples can recognise false prophets; here it is simply a general statement. In Jas. 3:10–12 the 'fruit' in question is the words of men, and the same application is made here in Lk. 6:45; elsewhere, however, fruit can refer to deeds (cf. 3:8f.). For the thought cf. Sir. 27:6, 'As the fruit of the tree reveals the skill of its grower, so the expression of a man's thought reveals his character' (NEB).

The second half of the saying is similar in form to Mt. 7:16b and Jas. 3:12, but the names of the plants and their fruits differ. In Lk. the statement is a simple negative: men do not pick edible fruit from weeds, (συλλέγω is 'to pick', Mt. 7:16; 13:28–48; τρυγάω is 'to gather ripe fruit', Rev. 14:18f.**). Matthew has a rhetorical question, which is probably more primitive, since it is confirmed by the slightly different wording in Jas. 3:12. As for the plants, Luke has ἄκανθα, any thorny plant, especially cammock (*ononis spinosa*); cf. 8:7, 14*; Barn. 7:11; and βάτος (masc. or fem.), 'thorn bush', probably 'bramble' (20:37; Mk. 12:36; Acts 7:30, 35**). For the fruit he has σῦκον, 'fig' (Mt. 7:16; Mk. 11:13; Jas. 3:12**) and σταφυλή, 'bunch of grapes' (Mt. 7:16; Rev. 14:18**). Matthew has τρίβολος, 'thistle' (Heb. 6:8**) in place of βάτος, and reverses the order of the fruit. James has a different set of trees, and refers to the impossibility of the fig tree producing olives or the vine producing figs, i.e. to the impossibility of one good tree producing fruit of a different kind. It is hard to determine the relative originality of Mt. and Lk. In favour of Lk. it has been argued that the fruit of the bramble resembles grapes at a distance, but in favour of Mt. it can be urged that the combination of thorns and grapes is biblical (Is. 5:2, 4). Creed, 98, suggested that Luke altered 'thistle' to 'bramble', since the idea of looking for fruit on a thistle seemed foolish to him; but this still leaves the folly of looking for figs on a thorn bush. A literary solution seems forced, and it is better to think of variant oral forms affected by proverbial combinations of words; grapes and figs form a pair as do thorns and thistles (cf. C.-H. Hunzinger, TDNT VII, 751–757, especially 753f.). The saying speaks not only of the folly of expecting to find fruit on weeds, but also probably of the deceptive nature of the weeds which grow as tall as bushes (Schürmann, I, 374) and produce what looks like edible fruit.

(45) The first part of the application of the preceding parables is parallel to Mt. 12:35. The article with ἄνθρωπος is generic: a good man brings forth (προφέρω (bis)**, diff. Mt. ἐκβάλλω) what is good (sing., diff. Mt. pl.) from his good treasury (θησαυρός, 12:33f.; 18:22), namely his heart; καρδία, omitted in Mt. has probably been added from the second half of the verse. The heart is thus the source of goodness – or evil: cf. Mk. 7:21. But what makes the heart good is 'standing in the position of divine sonship inaugurated by Jesus' (W. Gutbrod, TDNT IV, 1062) or obeying the word of Jesus, Lk. 6:46. Thus a man's words are determined by what his heart is full of (περίσσευμα, 'abundance', 'fullness'; Mt. 12:34; 2 Cor. 8:13f.; 'reminder', Mk. 8:8**). The saying thus originally refers to words rather than to deeds, and in context links up with the statements about uttering judgments and censures in 6:37–42. The thought, however, has now become more general, and refers to speech in general. The text of the verse in TR; *Diglot*, has numerous clarifying additions; these are probably secondary, since Luke himself avoids repetition (cf. 6:47f./49).

(46–49) The third and final subsection, 6:46–49, is an appeal to the hearers of the Sermon (cf. 6:18) to obey the commands which they have heard, and not be content to be mere hearers of the word; cf. Jas. 1:21–25; Lk. 8:21; Rom. 2:13; SB III, 84–88. The connection with the preceding section is an implicit one rather than a direct one: the good person is the man who obeys the words of Jesus. But the section forms a conclusion to the Sermon as a whole, and its main purpose is to stress the importance of obedience to what has been heard.

6:46 is paralleled in Mt. 7:21; the form of the latter text has probably been altered in view of the inclusion of Mt. 7:22f., which has its Lucan parallel at Lk. 13:25–27. It warns of the danger of calling Jesus 'Lord' but not obeying him. This contrast between confession and obedience is slightly different from that between hearing and doing which dominates the following parable, but it is doubtful whether this difference is sufficient to justify the conclusion that 6:46 and 6:47–49 were originally independent of each other (*pace* Schürmann, I, 380).

Although the parable of the two houses has the same general structure in both Gospels, the difference in wording is considerable. While some differences can be attributed to editorial activity (details in Schulz, 312–314), it is difficult to account for all the differences in this way, especially since no good reason for such thoroughgoing alteration is evident. The form in Lk. reflects a non-Palestinian situation, but at the same time its wording is more akin to Aramaic style than that in Mt. (J. Weiss, 447); hence we may need to postulate two different forms of the parable in the tradition (cf. Wrege, 152–155).

(46) The question form in Lk. is probably original, with τί, 'why', but καλέω looks like a stylistic improvement for λέγω (Black, 193). The people in question address Jesus as κύριε, κύριε. The double vocative form is frequent in Lk. (7:14; 8:24; 10:41; 13:34; 22:31; 23:21; Acts 9:4; 22:7; 26:14), but its originality here is guaranteed by the parallel in Mt. (cf. Schürmann, *Abschiedsrede*, 101). The doubled form is found in Gn. 22:11; 46:2; Ex. 3:4; 1 Sa. 3:10, and was quite common in Judaism (SB I, 943; II, 258). It simply strengthens the form of address in the manner determined by the context, here as a sign of greater honour. The use of κύριε (5:8 note) represents what might be said by disciples to a rabbi, and corresponds to Aram. *mārî* (Hahn, 81–86). Hahn finds it difficult to believe that Jesus himself could have spoken in this way with reference to entry into the kingdom of heaven (Mt. 7:21) and regards the address as one used in prayer to Jesus as the coming Lord of the church (Hahn, 97f.). This argument is quite unconvincing, especially when applied to the Lucan form of the saying. The teaching in the Sermon and elsewhere is of no value if the authority of a prophetic teacher does not lie behind it, and there is no good reason for denying Jesus' consciousness of such authority (Bultmann, 135; *pace* Schulz, 428f.). To be sure, the authority of Jesus over his disciples goes beyond that of a rabbinic teacher: 'He is for them, not the rabbi, διδάσκαλος, but their Lord' (K. H. Rengstorf, TDNT IV, 455). Already, therefore, during his ministry the address of κύριε was taking on a deeper significance than a mere honorific 'sir'. This element of authority may be seen in the way in which Jesus claims obedience for his commands (ἅ λέγω; for λέγω in

this sense cf. Mt. 21:31; Mk. 3:35 par. Lk. 8:21). Matthew has 'the will of my Father in heaven', but the originality of Luke's form seems to be guaranteed by the connection with 6:47 par. Mt. 7:24 with its stress on the words of Jesus (Creed, 98; cf. Bultmann, 122f., 135); see, however, Hahn, 97).

(47) The insertion of ἐρχόμενος πρός με, diff. Mt., may refer back to 6:18 and reflects other sayings in which Jesus summons men to come to him; cf. 14:26; Mt. 11:28; Jn. 5:40; 6:35, 37. But there does not appear to be any theological stress on the 'coming' here; coming is inadequate unless accompanied by obeying. The hanging nominative construction is awkward and may perhaps reflect an original Aramaic construction (cf. Schürmann, I, 383 n. 19), which Luke has altered by the insertion of ὑποδείκνυμι (cf. 12:5; Acts 20:35). Both Evangelists use their favourite terms (ὅμοιος; cf. 7:31f.; 13:18f.; Mt.: ὁμοιόω) to introduce the parable.

(48) Matthew characterises the two builders as φρόνιμος and μωρός, probably editorially. It is unlikely that Luke has altered ἀνήρ (Mt.) to ἄνθρωπος of his own accord. Where Matthew simply relates how the man built his house on a rock, Luke gives a more elaborate account of the care which he took. He dug out the foundations (σκάπτω, 13:8; 16:3**), going down deep (βαθύνω**; cf. BD 471² on the style), and laying a foundation (θεμέλιος; 14:29*). A Hellenistic house with a basement is perhaps meant (Jeremias, *Parables* 27 n. 9). Then there came a flood (πλήμμυρα, for the spelling πλήμυρα (*Diglot*) see MH II, 101). A near-by river burst upon the house (προσρήσσω, 6:49**) and flooded it. But it was unable to move it (6:38) because it had been well built (on the text, see Metzger, 142). The description varies from that in Mt. which describes a storm accompanied by swollen mountain torrents (cf. AG s.v. ποταμός; K. H. Rengstorf, TDNT VI, 603). The house does not fall because it is founded on the rock. The difference in detail does not affect the main point at issue; both forms of the parable advocate wisdom and diligence in building, and make the point that it is as foolish to hear the sayings of Jesus without obeying them as to build a house without taking care how it is built. The person who obeys Jesus will safely survive the crisis of divine judgment; cf. 17:26–37; 1 Cor. 3:11–15.

(49) The accent falls on the folly of the second man whose story forms the climax of the parable and the sermon. His story is recounted as briefly as possible in Lk., whereas Matthew conforms both parts of the story closely to each other. Luke omits mention of the sand which figures in Mt., and states that the house was built without a foundation – possibly thinking of a city setting rather than a rural one. When the river rose, the house immediately fell. εὐθύς, diff. Mt., is pre-Lucan; συνπίπτω**, diff. Mt. πίπτω, is due to Luke's fondness for συν- compounds. Great was its fall; Luke uses ῥῆγμα**, diff. Mt. πτῶσις (Lk. 2:34**), perhaps under the influence of προσρήσσω.

The parable has an ancestor in Ezk. 13:10–16, and what may well be a descendant in Aboth R. Nathan 24 (SB I, 469f.; Creed, 99f.) in which the importance of keeping the Torah is emphasised.

d. The Compassion of the Messiah (7:1–50)

From the teaching of Jesus to his disciples, Luke now turns – in dependence on his sources – to further detail regarding the self-revelation of Jesus to the people. The themes already announced as characterising his ministry are taken up and developed. The central section, 7:18–35, forms a kind of commentary on the surrounding incidents, and makes it plain that the deeds of Jesus are to be seen as the signs of the presence of the Coming One, to whom John the Baptist had looked forward. What God had promised to do in the last days was being fulfilled; John himself was fulfilling the role of the coming Elijah, and Jesus was making the messianic era a reality. Above all, the characteristic of this era was the gracious intervention of God in the life of his people, answering their needs both physical and spiritual. Yet, as in the programmatic scene at Nazareth (4:16–30), this gracious activity, directed especially to the sinful and despised people in Israel and even to gentiles, aroused suspicion and downright opposition from the Pharisees and their scribes.

These themes are manifestly present in the incidents preceding and following the 'commentary'. Jesus is seen as antitype to Elijah in raising the dead (7:11–17). He shows compassion to a gentile (7:1–10), to a widow (7:11–17), and to a sinful woman (7:36–50). And his gracious acts, though acknowledged by the crowds as evidence of a divine visitation (7:16), are regarded with suspicion by Simon the Pharisee (7:39).

The material for this section came exclusively from Luke's non-Marcan sources. 7:1–10 and 18–35 have parallels in Mt. 8:5–13 and 11:2–19 respectively, and may reasonable be assigned to a common tradition (or to variant forms of a common tradition), and it is probable that the Sermon, the healing of the centurion's servant, and the coming of the messengers from John the Baptist formed a continuous sequence in the source. To this narrative have been added the two stories peculiar to Luke in 7:11–17 and 7:36–50, the former as an example of raising the dead (7:22), and the latter as an example of Jesus' relationship to sinners (7:34).

See Schürmann, I, 442f.

i. The Healing of the Centurion's Servant 7:1–10

The theme of the opening section is the faith of a gentile centurion who recognised the authority which Jesus had to perform cures in the name of God. He displayed not only faith but also humility over against Jesus, considering himself unworthy to approach him personally. His action in sending a group of Jews to speak on his behalf to Jesus bears witness both to the reputation for piety which he had with them and also to their willingness to bring him into relationship with Jesus. His story is thus an example of the fact that God is willing to accept all men alike and that everyone who fears him and performs righteousness is acceptable to him (Acts 10:34f.). At the same time the story shows that the Jews had no compunctions about bringing such a man into contact with Jesus, and this example will have been relevant to the problem of Jewish Christians and gentiles in the early church (Schürmann, I, 396f.). Nevertheless, despite this commendation of Jews who adopted such an attitude, the story voices criticism of the general lack of faith which Jesus found among the Jews, and provides evidence for the condemnation uttered in 7:31–35. Matthew or his source saw the relevance of the sayings which are found in Lk. 13:28f., and included them at this point (Mt. 8:11f.). It may well be that they were present here in Matthew's version of Q (Schweizer, *Matthäus*, 137; cf. Lagrange, 208). Schlatter, 251, rightly notes that while the Jews point to the good works of the centurion, Jesus commends the faith which lies behind them as the thing that ultimately matters.

The parallel account in Mt. 8:5–13 is a mixture of similarities and differences. Both stories begin similarly with a transitional verse, concluding the Sermon and moving over to the present story; in Mt. this traditional connection has been broken by the insertion of the story of the cleansing of a leper between 7:28 and 8:5. Both stories agree fairly closely in the content of the dialogue between Jesus and the centurion (7:6b–9 par. Mt. 8:8–10), and both report the cure of the servant. Otherwise, there are considerable differences in narration. Since there was very little narrative in the Q material, it has been argued that only the dialogue was recorded in Q, each Evangelist filling out the story for himself (Manson, *Sayings*, 63). But the dialogue must originally have been transmitted in some kind of framework, or else it would be meaningless. Opinions differ on the origin of the peculiarly Lucan elements in the story. Many hold that Luke himself is responsible for the motif of the messengers (Dibelius, 44 n. 3; Schulz, 237f.). Others argue that Luke had a parallel account to provide the extra material in 7:2–6 (Schlatter, 251f.; Rengstorf, 93; Schramm, 40f.); or that Luke used an edited version of Q (Grundmann, 155); or that Matthew has severely abbreviated the common Q version (Schürmann, I, 395f.).

The problem is that in Mt. the centurion approaches Jesus personally with his request for help, while in Lk. he sends two groups of intermediaries, the second of which delivers his message in the first person singular form. Luke's version is thus more complicated, if not actually improbable: it is odd that having requested Jesus to come to his house, the centurion then attempts to dissuade him, and that as a result Jesus and the centurion never meet. The following points are relevant: 1.

Matthew has a well-known tendency to abbreviate his sources (Mt. 9:2, 18ff.; 11:2f.). It is at least as probable that he has abbreviated here as that Luke has creatively expanded the story. 2. The centurion's speech to Jesus sounds better on his own lips than if committed to memory by the messengers, and Jesus' praise of him would be more reasonable if he were present (Wellhausen, 27). Nevertheless, the procedure is perfectly credible. For messengers reciting a memorised message see 2 Ki. 19:20–34 (Schlatter, 252), and for gentiles approaching Jesus through intermediaries see Jn. 12:20ff.; cf. Acts 10 (Schürmann, I, 395). 3. The idea of an embassy could have been borrowed from 8:49 where a messenger comes to tell Jairus that his daughter has died. But it is worth noting that, since Matthew omits this detail, it could be argued there also that Luke has introduced a characteristic motif, were it not that Luke is known to be dependent on Mk. there. In the present case also Luke could be dependent on his source. In any case, the function of the messengers in the two stories is different. 4. A weightier point is that the expansion demonstrates the piety of the centurion (cf. Acts 10:2, 34f.) and provides an example of faith in Jesus without having seen him (cf. 1 Pet. 1:8; Naaman, 2 Ki. 5:10). This could well be due to Lucan redaction (J. Weiss, 448; Wilson, 31f.). But the fact that Jesus welcomes such a God-fearer perhaps reflects the concerns of the primitive church rather than of Luke himself, to whom the gentile mission was a reality (cf. Schürmann, I, 392). 5. The language of the 'insertion' is Lucan (Schulz, 238 n. 410). Moreover, the use of third person narrative in 7:2 instead of the incorporation of this information in the centurion's own request to Jesus (Mt. 8:6) could be a Lucan alteration, since the insertion prevented him from using the first person style at this point; elsewhere too it is Luke's habit to assemble basic information at the beginning of a story (5:17). On the other hand, there are some un-Lucan features in the style, and it can be argued that the inclusion of two sets of messengers is too awkward to be attributed to Luke (Schürmann, I, 395). The balance between these arguments is very even. The linguistic evidence slightly favours the case for Lucan insertion, but it is hard to see why Luke should have altered the story to such an extent without some basis in his sources. The view that Luke has combined two sources is improbable. It is more likely that the story appeared in different forms in two versions of Q, and/or that Matthew has abbreviated it, but the possibility of Lucan expansion cannot be excluded.

The view of Bultmann, 39, 354, that the present story is a variant of that in Mk. 7:24–31 is highly unlikely. There is a better case that the story of the nobleman's son in Jn. 4:46–54 is a development from this narrative (Brown, *John*, I, 192f.; for a more cautious appraisal see Dodd, 188–195).

See Manson, *Sayings*, 62–66; Schulz, 236–246; J. D. M. Derrett, 'Law in the New Testament: The Syro-Phoenician Woman and the Centurion of Capernaum', Nov.T 15, 1973, 161–186; R. T. France, 'Exegesis in Practice: Two Samples', in I. H. Marshall (ed.), *New*

Testament Interpretation, Exeter, 1977, 253–264; J. E. Goldingay, 'Expounding the New Testament', in ibid., 352–357.

(1) The opening verse forms a transition from the Sermon; its closeness in form to Mt. 7:28a; 8:5a, shows that it has been taken from a common source, but each Evangelist has modified it in his own way. ἐπειδή diff. Mt. ὅτε, here means 'after' (BD 455¹), but normally means 'since' (11:6; Acts 13:46; 14:12; 15:24; Paul, 5x**). πληρόω (1:20; *et al.*) means 'to finish a task', and stresses the significance of the Sermon as a decisive piece of teaching by Jesus; cf. 21:24; Acts 12:25; 13:25; 14:26; 19:21. Matthew uses τελέω in the same sense, here and at the conclusion of Jesus' other discourses; cf. Lk. 2:39; *et al.* πάντα τὰ ῥήματα αὐτοῦ, a Lucan phrase, corresponds to Mt. τοὺς λόγους τούτους. ἀκοή means 'ear' (Acts 17:20) or 'hearing' (Acts 28:26); cf. the similar phrase εἰς τὰ ὦτα 1:44; Acts 11:22. The second half of the verse is from Q but resembles Mk. 2:1 (which Luke omits at 5:17).

(2) In Matthew's version of the story, the centurion approaches Jesus and explains the plight of his servant. Here, however, Luke describes the situation before telling how the centurion sent messengers to Jesus to seek for help. For the opening genitive in a story, cf. 12:16. ἑκατοντάρχου will be the genitive of ἑκατοντάρχης (7:6; 23:47; Acts, 13x), diff. Mt. ἑκατόνταρχος (cf. AG s.vv.). It is the Greek equivalent to Mark's Latinism κεντυρίων (Mk. 15:39, 44f.). There were no Roman forces in Galilee before AD 44 (Sherwin-White, 123f.), and therefore the man must have been a member of Herod Antipas's soldiery who were organised on Roman lines; his nationality is not stated, but he was not a Jew (cf. 7:5, 9), nor is there any indication that he was a proselyte.

The sick man was his δοῦλος; cf. 7:3, 8, 10. Luke also uses παῖς (1:54; *et al.*) in 7:7, which must here mean 'servant'. The same word is used throughout in Mt. (8:6, 8, 13), and also in Jn. 4:51 (cf. 4:49), where, however, it means 'son'. Bultmann, 39 n. and Manson, *Sayings*, 64, suggest that an original παῖς, meaning 'son', has been misinterpreted by Luke to mean 'slave': cf. the distinction between παῖς and δοῦλος in 7:7f., and the fact that in a similar rabbinic story it was the son of Rabban Gamaliel who was ill (Ber. 34b). But the reasoning is inconclusive: the use of δοῦλος in 7:8 is natural in the context of a command being given, and the use of παῖς in 7:7 stresses the affection of the centurion for his slave. δοῦλος is, therefore, Luke's correct synonym for παῖς.

The slave was ill: κακῶς ἔχω (5:31) is not a Lucan phrase and probably comes from the source. He was at the point of death (cf. AG s.v. μέλλω), and was thus too ill to be brought to Jesus. The description is similar to that in Jn. 4:47, but according to Matthew the boy was paralysed and in great pain. Luke adds that he was ἔντιμος to his master, a word that here means 'honoured, respected' (14:8; Phil. 2:29), rather than 'precious, valuable' (1 Pet. 2:4, 5**), and indicates why the centurion was so concerned over him; Luke's own concern for the inferior members of society is perhaps also reflected.

(3) The change of subject is abrupt, but is prepared for by the position of ἑκατοντάρχου in the previous sentence. ἀκούω περί is a Lucan combination. πρεσβύτερος, 'elder' (literal use, 15:25), is used of Jewish elders, 9:22; 20:1; 22:52*. Elsewhere it refers to members of the Sanhedrin, but here to leaders in the local community who acted as the disciplinary body of the synagogue (G. Bornkamm, TDNT VI, 660f.; Schürer, II: 1, 150–154). The absence of the article suggests that not all of the group (usually seven in number) were sent. The addition τῶν Ἰουδαίων (cf. 23:3, 37, 38, 51) is natural in a story dealing with Jewish-gentile relationships and is probably intended by Luke to stress this aspect of the story (cf. W. Gutbrod, TDNT III, 376). The participle ἐρωτῶν expresses the centurion's purpose (cf. 7:6, 19; 10:25; MH III, 157) in asking for Jesus to come and cure the slave; διασῴζω, 'to cure' (Acts 27:43f.; 28:1, 4; Mt. 14:36; 'to bring safely through', Acts 23:24; 1 Pet. 3:20**), perhaps indicates the dangerous character of the illness (Schlatter, 252).

(4) The participle of παραγίνομαι, 'to come, arrive, be present' (Lucan), is used adverbially: 'and when they came, they besought…' The use of the imperfect of παρακαλέω (Mt. 8:5; v.l. ἠρώτων ℵ D f13 700 al; Diglot) in a continuous sense does not indicate that Jesus was unwilling to respond, but rather that the elders were willing to press his case eagerly (σπουδαίως), and perhaps that they felt that Jesus might consider it improper to help a gentile. ὅτι introduces direct speech (1:25 note). While ἄξιος (3:8) often expresses human unworthiness of divine grace (Acts 13:46), here it has no theological connotation, but simply refers to the public reputation of a man held in esteem by his fellows (cf. W. Foerster, TDNT I, 379f.). The construction of the adjective with the relative pronoun is a Latinism (dignus est qui . . ., BD 5³ᵇ, 379); with the future indicative παρέξῃ (6:29) the clause expresses result (cf. 7:27; 11:6; 1 Cor. 2:16; 4:17).

(5) Jews use the term ἔθνος to refer to themselves over against gentiles (23:2; Acts 10:22; et al.; Jn. 11:48–52; 18:35). The centurion is regarded as worthy of help from a Jewish prophet because of his loving attitude to the Jewish people. He showed this especially by building the (local) synagogue for them. The giving of contributions by gentiles towards the upkeep of synagogues is well attested: t. Meg. 3:5 (224) (SB IV:1, 142f.); cf. Creed, 101; W. Schrage, TDNT VII, 813f. That a gentile should have built the synagogue itself, however, is unusual. Possibly he was simply a large, or the main, benefactor. The opportunities for personal enrichment in the police force were good, even for an honest man (Easton, 95), and therefore the centurion could have had the means to give. The implication of the account for the early church is that, if even Jews thought such a man worthy of help from Jesus, Jewish Christians should see no barriers to the acceptance of similar people (cf. Acts 10:2) into the church (Schürmann, I, 392).

(6) Jesus' positive acceptance of the recommendation is seen in his

accompanying of the elders towards the centurion's house (cf. Acts 10:20). But the main point in the verse is what happened while he was on the way ἐπορεύετο, imperfect; MH III, 66): Jesus was by this time (ἤδη) not far from the house. μακράν in an adverbial sense is not uncommon in Lk.-Acts (15:20; Acts 2:39; 17:27; 22:21; rest of NT, 5x), and the litotes is characteristic of him (Acts, 11x; Haenchen, 70). The centurion sent a group of his friends with a message to be delivered to Jesus as if he himself were actually saying it. φίλος is a favourite word of Luke (Mt. 11:19 par. Lk. 7:34; Mk., 0x; Lk., 15x; Jn., 6x; G. Stählin, TDNT IX, 146–171, especially 159–164).

With the direct speech the material common to Mt. begins. Jesus is addressed as κύριος, the gentile equivalent for 'Rabbi' (cf. 5:8; 6:46 and notes). The request μὴ σκύλλου, 'do not trouble yourself', recurs in 8:49 par. Mk. 5:35 when Jairus' friends tell him not to trouble Jesus because his sick daughter has died. The only other use of the verb is Mt. 9:36**. Schramm, 42, regards the phrase as being based on Mk. 5:35, and designed to smooth the transition between the preceding piece of narrative (taken, on his view, from a special source) and the dialogue (taken from Q). This is probable enough, whatever view we take of the source problem. The centurion does not feel worthy (ἱκανός, 3:16; cf. ἄξιος, v. 4) that Jesus should come under his roof (στέγη, Mt. 8:8; Mk. 2:4**). The thought is hardly of ritual uncleanness but of unworthiness, like that felt by John the Baptist, before the authority of a teacher sent from God (K. H. Rengstorf, TDNT III, 294f.; cf. J. D. M. Derrett*, 176).

(7) The first part of the verse is peculiar to Lk. and would be out of place in Mt. where nothing is said about the centurion's embassy to Jesus; it is, therefore, commonly regarded as due to Lucan redaction (Schramm, 42; Schulz, 238f.; cautiously, Schürmann, I, 393 n. 26). The language is largely Lucan: διό (1:35); ἐμαυτόν (7:8* par. Mt. 8:9; Acts, 4x); ἀξιόω (Acts 15:38; 28:22*; cf. καταξιόω, 20:35; Acts 5:41; 2 Thes. 1:5**); ἔρχομαι πρός (Lk., 9x; Acts, 6x); and for the whole saying cf. Acts 26:2. The saying is parenthetic, and interrupts the connection between v. 6 and v. 7b. (it is omitted by D pc it syˢ). Its point is that if the centurion is not worthy to have Jesus in his house, it follows that he is not worthy to meet him outside it. Let Jesus therefore simply say the word, and the boy will be healed without the need for any personal contact. After ἀλλά Matthew adds μόνον (so also Mt. 12:4; 21:19; 24: 36 diff. Mk.). λόγῳ is a rather redundant dative of instrument (cf. AG, 478a, for a parallel from Phalaris). For healing by a word cf. Ps. 107:20; Mt. 8:16; G. Kittel, TDNT IV, 107. The use of a second imperative (softened to a fut. indic. in Mt. and some MSS of Lk.; Metzger, 142) is equivalent to a conditional sentence, and, although it is possible in Classical Greek (BD 442²), it may reflect a Hebrew or Aramaic construction. (Beyer, I:1, 252 n. 2).

(8) The centurion knows that Jesus can heal simply by a com-

mand, for he also (καὶ γὰρ ἐγώ) is a person who is under authority and can use his delegated authority to give orders that others must obey; so Jesus being under the authority of God can give orders to others. For ἐξουσία, cf. 4:6, 32, 36; 5:24. The participle τασσόμενος, diff. Mt. is found 4x in Acts (cf. Luke's fondness for διατάσσω and ὑποτάσσω) and is probably a Lucan addition; the combination with ὑπό is classical (AG 813b). The paratactical construction λέγω τούτῳ ... καὶ πορεύεται is equivalent to a conditional sentence. The force of the opening clause has been understood in various ways by commentators. Jeremias, *Promise* 30, n. 4, holds that the stress lies on the participle ἔχων (cf. 13:28; 23:34), giving the sense, 'Although I am a man under authority, I have soldiers under me, and if I say ...' The same concessive force is found by Schürmann, I, 393, who thinks that the centurion is contrasting his own position under authority with the position of Jesus who is not under authority. But this seems less likely than the view adopted above (for which cf. Tödt, 257), which fits in with a subordinationist christology shared by Luke with the early church generally. There is no need to suppose that an Aramaic original has been mistranslated here (as by Manson, *Sayings*, 65; Black, 158f.). An allusion to Jethro (Ex. 18:13–27; J. D. M. Derrett*, 161f.) is by no means obvious.

(9) When Jesus hears this deduction from the character of military discipline to the nature of his own authority under God, he expresses surprise at the centurion (θαυμάζω with acc. of person, 2 Thes. 1:10). The addition of ταῦτα and αὐτόν, diff. Mt., may be Lucan. It is less easy to be certain about the inclusion of στραφείς which is frequent in non-Marcan sections in Lk. (7:44; 9:55; 10:23; 14:25; 22:61; 23:28) but is not found in Acts; it may be pre-Lucan (Rehkopf, 97). The reference to the crowds, diff. Mt., may be original (cf. Mt. 8:1). To these Jewish witnesses Jesus declares solemnly (cf. Mt. ἀμήν, diff. Lk.; see Lk. 4:24 note) that he has not found so great faith (τοσοῦτος, 15:29*) in the power of God revealed in himself even in Israel among the very people who might be expected to believe in his power. Matthew states more simply that Jesus has not found such faith among anybody in Israel, which may be original.

There follows in Mt. a saying about the eschatological entry of the gentiles into the kingdom of God, which is found in Lk. at 13:28f. Matthew also includes a saying of Jesus assuring the centurion that the healing will take place according to his faith, but this is probably editorial (cf. Mt. 17:18 diff. Mk.).

(10) Instead, Luke simply notes, in accordance with his own form of the story, that the messengers returned home and found the slave well; on the text cf. Metzger, 142. The language (including ὑγιαίνω, 5:31; 15:27; Mt., 0x; Mk., 0x) suggests Lucan formulation.

The narrative describes a healing which takes place without any contact between Jesus and the patient, as in Mk. 7:24–29, where it is again a case of curing a gentile. Such cures were believed to be possible

by Jews at the time (cf. Ber. 34b, in SB II, 441), and hence it is not surprising that similar stories were related about Jesus. The historical
possibility of such healings raises the same questions as in the case of
Jesus' other healings, although it could be argued that accounts such as
the present one represent exaggerations of the kind of healings that Jesus
actually carried out. But on a human level psychological cures of this
kind are not to be ruled out (J. D. M. Derrett*, 184–186; cf. Schweizer,
Matthäus, 139), and on the level of faith there is no greater problem in
principle than there is with the other miracles of Jesus (see Rengstorf,
94f.).

ii. The Raising of the Widow's Son 7:11–17

This narrative, like the preceding one, provides the 'text' on which the
'commentary' regarding the person and work of Jesus in 7:18–35 is
based. Jesus raises from the dead the son of a widow, thereby
manifesting the kind of powers similar to those of Elijah and Elisha (1
Ki. 17:17–24; 2 Ki. 4:18–37) which led the people to conclude that he
was a prophet and that through his activity God was visiting his people;
at the same time the stress on the helplessness of the widow, deprived of
the support of both her husband and her son, draws attention to the
gracious compassion of Jesus in caring for those in distress. There is less
emphasis on the place of human faith in God, but the story demonstrates
how the mighty action of God in Jesus leads to the believing acceptance
of what has happened in praise and acknowledgement of his power. The
story thus provides evidence for the statement in 7:22 that the era of
fulfilment, in which 'the dead are raised', has arrived.

The narrative has the typical form of a miracle story; it has come
from Luke's special source material, since there is no reason to suppose
that it stood in Q, and has been included here because of its obvious
relevance to the general theme of the section. Bultmann, 230, claimed
that it was created in Hellenistic Jewish Christian circles. In favour of
this suggestion is the fact that several parallels can be cited from
Hellenistic miracle stories. Pliny, NH 26:15, relates how Asclepiades met
the funeral cortege of a man unknown to him, had him removed from
the pyre, and saved his life. Philostratus, Vita Apoll. 4:45, tells how a
young bride was thought to have died on the day of her wedding; the
prophet met the funeral procession, touched the dead girl, said
something secretly to her, and awakened her from her apparent death. In
this case Philostratus was sceptical whether a miracle had really taken
place (for a comparison of the two stories see G. Petzke*). For other
parallels see Artemidorus 4:82; Apuleius, Florida 19; IG IV 952. 27ff.
(Weinreich, 171–173), and for Jewish parallels see SB I, 560. These
parallels prove, or rather disprove, nothing as regards the historicity of
the present story, since the motif of raising the dead is a familiar and
widespread one. In fact, the story as a whole finds its closest parallels in
the OT, and the only feature that cannot be so paralleled is the funeral

procession setting, which is surely integral to the story. Schürmann's conclusion, I, 403–405, that the story belongs to the preaching of the Palestinian Jewish church is much more plausible than that of Bultmann. The question of Lucan editing is raised by Dibelius, 71f., who suggests that the emphasis on Jesus' compassion to the widow, 7:13, 15b, is due to Luke, but this is unlikely (Schürmann, I, 401), and Lucan activity is more probable merely at the beginning and end of the narrative.

See G. Petzke, 'Historität und Bedeutsamkeit von Wunderberichten', in H.-D. Betz, 367–385.

(11) The narrative begins with a familiar Lucan καὶ ἐγένετο construction (1:8 note; cf. 2:46). The incident is placed chronologically ἐν τῷ ἑξῆς. ἑξῆς, an adverb meaning 'next', occurs in the phrase τῇ ἑξῆς (sc. ἡμέρᾳ as in 9:37) Acts, 3x**; cf. Luke's fondness for καθεξῆς, 1:3; et al.). The masculine form here, ἐν τῷ ἑξῆς (sc. χρόνῳ), 'soon afterwards', is less precise; it is altered in many MSS to the feminine form, but this is a correction, since Luke does not elsewhere use ἐν with the feminine form (contrast 8:1; Metzger, 142f.), and the reading of 𝔭⁷⁵ A B Θ f1 al. is to be preferred. For ἐπορεύθη (𝔭⁷⁵ ℵ B W f13 pc) TR and Diglot have ἐπορεύετο (cf. Kilpatrick, 199, as in 2:18 note); here the imperfect could be due to assimilation to the following verb. On πόλις cf. 1:26 note. The name Ναΐν** occurs in Jos. Bel. 4:511, 517, for an Idumaean village E of Jordan. The place meant here, however, is to be identified with modern Nen in the Plain of Jezreel, 6 m. SSE of Nazareth on the N edge of Little Hermon (cf. Gn. R 98 (62a); SB II, 161). The only difficulty about the identification is the lack of a gate to the town, but the fact that none has so far been discovered may be due simply to the inadequate archaeological investigation of the site (Kopp, 236–241). It is, however, possible that Luke was describing the scene in terms appropriate to a Hellenistic audience or that the detail is a reminiscence of 1 Ki. 17:10, but these assumptions are not justified in the present state of our knowledge. On his entry to Nain Jesus was accompanied by his disciples: some MSS (A C Θ f1 f13 pm; TR; Diglot) add ἱκανοί, which is a Lucan word; but the expression (with the article) is odd, and may be due to assimilation to 7:12; on balance UBS rejected it (cf. Metzger, 143). The disciples and a crowd of other people form witnesses to what was about to happen, and the picture of Jesus being surrounded by a considerable group of people on his travels fits in with the evidence of the Gospel tradition generally.

(12) The language is again Lucan (ὡς (1:23) δέ (5:4); ἐγγίζω, 18x); cf. 19:41. πύλη is a town gate (J. Jeremias, TDNT VI, 921–928). Burials took place outside towns, and graves have been found to the SE of Nain (Abel, II, 394f.). The committal took place as soon as was practicable after death (Acts 5:1–11). ἐκκομίζω** is the technical term for carrying out a corpse to burial. The perf. participle τεθνηκώς is used like a noun, 'a dead man' (cf. Jn. 11:44). He is described as an only son, a detail found editorially elsewhere in Lk. (μονογενής, 8:42 and 9:38*, diff. Mk.),

but there is no proof that it did not belong to the original form of the story here. The sadness of the bereavement, thus accentuated, is further emphasised by the additional comment that the mother was a widow. The καὶ αὐτή clause (so UBS) represents an Aramaic circumstantial clause (5:1 note), but the form αὕτη should perhaps be read (BD 277³; 290¹; cf. 2:25f.; 8:41; 10:39; 19:2), in which case we may have a feature of Lucan style. The fact that the mother was a widow is reminiscent of 1 Ki. 17:10 (cf. Lk. 4:25f.). Grundmann's suggestion (159f., following Bornhäuser, 55–57), that the death of husband and son was a judgment of God upon some especial sin of the widow, has no basis in the text. The attendance of a crowd at the funeral is in keeping with Jewish custom, since it ranked as a work of love (SB IV:1, 578–592). Mourning was all the greater for an only child (Je. 6:26; Am. 8:10; Zc. 12:10; cf. on mourning customs SB I, 521–523, 1047–1051). The use of ἱκανός and σύν is Lucan.

(13) The one who sees the sad widow as he approaches the town and is shortly to demonstrate his power is fitly described as ὁ κύριος. We have already encountered the use of the word in the vocative to address Jesus (5:8 note), and also its use to refer to God (1:6; et al.). Luke, however, also uses it in narrative to refer to Jesus: 7:13, 19; 10:1, 39, 41; 11:39; 12:42; 13:15; ? 16:8; 17:5, 6; 18:6; 19:8a; 22:61a, b; ? 24:3, 34; cf. 19:31, 34 par. Mk. 11:3; Lk. 20:42b, 44 par. Mk. 12:36f. To these references should probably be added 1:43, ? 76; 2:11 as descriptions of Jesus. The use of the term reflects the designation of Jesus in the early church as the one exalted by God to be the Lord (Acts 2:36; Rom. 1:4; Phil. 2:11), and indicates that already during his earthly ministry Jesus was exercising the functions of the Lord (cf. 1 Cor. 7:10, 12, 25; 9:5, 14; Heb. 2:3; Jn. 4:1; 6:23; 11:2; 20:2, 13, cf. C. F. D. Moule, 'The Christology of Acts', SLA 159–185; Franklin, 49–55). What is not clear is whether the use of the title in Lk. is due to the Evangelist himself (Vielhauer, 154–156; Ott, 34–40) or at least in part to his source material (Hahn, 88–90; Creed, 103f.; Rehkopf, 95). The fact that the title is never certainly introduced by Luke into Marcan material (19:34 is a repetition of the existing use in 19:31 par. Mk. 11:3, and is not in narrative; 22:61 may be from a passion source; 24:3 occurs in a post-resurrection scene) may well be significant. On the other hand, several occurrences in the Q and special source material appear to be editorial (7:19; 10:1; 11:39; 12:42; 17:5f.), and the problem is whether Luke's usage was determined by some precedent in his source. This possibility is an open one, and therefore each occurrence must be examined on its own merits. See further I. de la Potterie, 'Le titre KYPIOΣ appliqué à Jésus dans l'Evangile de Luc', in Descamps, 117–146.

In the present case, the verse goes on to describe how Jesus felt compassion for the widow: σπλαγχνίζομαι occurs at 10:33; 15:20* (both cases in special source material), but Luke takes over none of the four occurrences in Mk. (Mk. 1:41; 6:34; cf. 8:2; 9:22) and does not use the word in Acts. It is probably, therefore, pre-Lucan (cf. 1:78). Again, the use of λέγω with the dative may well be pre-Lucan. The wording μὴ κλαῖε is also found in 8:52, where Luke has altered the Marcan text to conform with the present passage. This evidence suggests that Luke is here making use of a source, and that the verse should not be ascribed (with Dibelius, 71) to Luke's own desire to express emotion and draw attention to Jesus' care for women; on the contrary, this desire is characteristic of his source (cf. 7:36–50; 8:2f., weeping is a stock attribute of widows, G. Stählin, TDNT II, 450 n. 94). If, then, the verse is from Luke's source, the possibility that he found the title κύριος in the source gains in strength.

(14) The sense of anticipation is already apparent in the command not to weep over the dead man. It is heightened by the description of how Jesus approaches the bier; προσέρχομαι, when used of Jesus, may indicate the first step in a messianic action (J. Schneider, TDNT II, 683f.; cf. Mk. 1:31; Mt. 17:7; 28:18). Jesus ignores the ritual uncleanness of the dead body (Nu. 19:11, 16) in approaching the bier and touching it, apparently in order to halt the procession (Klostermann, 89; against Wellhausen, 28, who claimed that Jesus must have touched the corpse in order to revive it).

σορός** is a 'coffin' or 'bier' (i.e. some means of transporting a bier or corpse to the grave; cf. Herodotus 2:78). A closed coffin is impossible in view of 7:15, and did not conform to Jewish custom. The suggestion that Luke has conformed the narrative to Hellenistic custom (so even Schürmann, I, 401, n. 100) is to be rejected in view of 7:15, and the fact that σορός can be used of an open bier (cf. MM 581; Creed, 104). At the implied command of Jesus the bearers (βαστάζω, cf. Jn. 20:15) come to a stop (cf. 17:12; 18:40). Then Jesus utters his word; cf. Mk. 5:41; Jn. 11:43. As in Mk. 5:41 (diff. Lk.), he issues a command on his own authority: σοὶ λέγω, and orders the young man (νεάνισκος*) to arise (cf. 8:54, where the active form is used instead of the passive, cf. Mt. 17:7).

(15) The command is obeyed as the dead man sits up (ἀνακαθίζω, Acts 9:40** of Tabitha) and demonstrates that he is alive by beginning to speak (cf. 1 Ki. 17:22 LXX (not MT); Philostratus, Vita Apoll. 4:45). The comment that Jesus gave him to his mother (cf. 9:42 diff. Mk.; 1 Ki. 17:23 LXX verbatim; 2 Ki. 4:36) serves to remind the readers of the Elijah typology and also to indicate Jesus' concern for the widow.

(16) Fear (cf. 1:12 note; 5:26) is the natural reaction of men to a demonstration of unearthly power; but the recognition of the source of that power leads also to a glorifying of God (2:20; 5:25f.; Mk. 2:12). The people offer a 'choral comment' on the significance of the miracle as they praise God for raising up a great prophet among them. ἐγείρω means 'to arise' (Jn. 7:52; Acts 13:22), not 'to resurrect' a former prophet. The reaction is a natural one in view of the Elijah typology present in the miracle; cf. 4:24; 7:39; 9:8, 19; 24:19. The use of the term μέγας need not necessarily place Jesus on a level above that of John the

Baptist (1:15), but does indicate that he is a prophet who can do things beyond the capacity of most prophets. It is not clear whether the statement implies that he is *the* final prophet (so G. Friedrich, TDNT VI, 846); probably the statement on the lips of the crowds does not go so far as this, but taken in the context of Lucan christology as a whole a deeper meaning is to be seen in it. The second comment by the crowds draws attention to the fact that God has acted in the mighty work done by Jesus; for ἐπισκέπτομαι cf. 1:68; *et al.*; Ex. 4:31; Ru. 1:6. The language is that of Jewish expectation and is perfectly natural in a Jewish context.

(17) The narrative concludes like earlier ones (4:37, 14) with a reference to the spread of the story of what Jesus had done: ὁ λόγος οὖτος means 'the story of this incident'; for ἐξέρχομαι cf. 4:14. ἐν means 'in', and is not equivalent to εἰς (BD 218). The whole of Judaea (23:5; cf. 1:65; Acts 9:31; 10:37) includes Galilee. πᾶσα ἡ περίχωρος (3:3) must mean the areas immediately outside Judaea rather than the neighbourhood of Nain itself (though Schlatter, 253f. suggests that Nain may have been thought of as being outside Judaea in the territorial area of Scythopolis); Luke may have thought of news reaching John the Baptist at Machaerus, outside Judaea (Lagrange, 212).

iii. Jesus' Answer to John 7:18–23

The central section in the present chapter falls into three parts, 7:18–23, 24–28 and 29–35, each of which has to do with the relationship between John the Baptist and Jesus. The close similarity in wording and the common order of the material indicates that behind this passage and Mt. 11:2–19 there lies a common source (Q) in which the three parts already formed a unity (Bultmann, 349; Suggs, 36–38).

The first part has the structure of a pronouncement story, culminating in the reply of Jesus to the messengers of John. John's question whether Jesus is the One who was to come is answered by reference to the mighty works performed by Jesus, including the preaching of good news to the poor. In these events may be seen the fulfilment of Is. 35:5f., and the person who recognises the fulfilment will know that Jesus is the coming One, and will not be put off by his failure to live up to traditional – or Johannine – expectations.

Luke has expanded this common narrative with additions absent from Mt. He is fuller in his description of how John sent two disciples who repeated exactly what he had commanded them to ask Jesus. More important, he includes an account of Jesus' healings in the presence of the two messengers, and thereby underlines the reality of the evidence which was to be reported to John.

Bultmann, 22, 115, 135, regards the answer of Jesus as being originally an independent logion which was then used in the early church's discussion with the disciples of John regarding the messianic character of Jesus' miracles; the church's reply was to point to the way in which the miracles fulfilled OT prophecy. The saying itself originally expressed the eschatological consciousness characteristic of Jesus but not of Judaism, but it referred to his proclamation rather than to his person. Bultmann thus regards the setting as secondary but the saying as authentic. Kümmel, 109–111, claims, however, that the setting itself was authentic. The description of Jesus as the coming One is too vague to attribute to the early church, which had other christological terms to hand, and John's question contradicts the general tendency in the early church to make him a witness to Jesus. Moreover, Jesus' reply does not directly answer his question but refers to his own actions and message as fulfilment of the OT promises of the end-time.

The saying itself is closely related to 4:18f. with its description of the messianic era in terms of Is. 61. But the fact that we have two similar descriptions here, couched in OT language, does not mean that one has been derived from the other; the tendency is to regard 4:18f. as secondary (Stuhlmacher, 225–229), but both passages can well be original. Jeremias, *Theology*, I, 87, 103–105, defends the view that what was originally a description of the signs of the time of salvation has been reinterpreted as a list of the miracles of Jesus: a metaphorical description of the effects of proclaiming the good news has been taken literally as a reference to the mighty works of Jesus. But there is no evidence for this hypothetical earlier understanding of the saying, and it is better to see it as being from the outset an attempt to provide an OT background for the deeds of Jesus (Marshall, 121f.). Nor is there any sound reason to doubt its authenticity. The case against it is put by Stuhlmacher, 218–222; Pesch, *Taten*, 36–44. They argue that the saying presents Jesus as the eschatological prophet and gives a list of his miraculous works. Why this understanding of the saying should preclude its authenticity is not at all obvious. The view that Jesus himself understood his mission in terms of the eschatological prophet has much to be said for it (Fuller, 125–131). Bultmann's earlier suggestion that Is. 35:5f. may originally have been used by followers of John with reference to mighty works done by him faces the difficulty that John did no mighty works (Jn. 10:41; E. Bammel, 'John did no miracle', in C. F. D. Moule (ed.), *Miracles*, London, 1966², 179–202). For further objections, see Vögtle, 219–242; A. George*, 286–292.

As for the setting of the saying, this can hardly have been created out of the saying itself (cf. Pesch, *Taten*, 39f.). The setting presupposes that John had doubts whether Jesus was the coming One whom he had prophesied. This may seem strange after the clear witness attributed to John at the time of Jesus' baptism (Jn. 1), but is in fact by no means odd when it is remembered that John was in prison and saw no signs that Jesus was acting in might and power, perhaps especially in regard to setting him free from impending martyrdom. Hoffmann, 198–201, and Vögtle, 223–231, argue that John, who expected the coming of the eschatological judge, could not possibly have wondered whether Jesus was this figure; but this objection assumes that Jesus was *not* baptised by John – against all historical probability. It remains most likely that, even if the pericope reflects the church's discussions with followers of John, it rests on a historical situation.

See Kümmel, 109–111; Strobel, 265–277; Stuhlmacher, 218–225; Wink, 23f.; Luhrmann, 25f.; Pesch, *Taten*, 36–44; Vögtle, 219–242; Hoffman, 198–215; Schulz, 190–203; A. George, 'Paroles de Jésus sur ses miracles (Mt. 11, 5, 21; 12:27, 28 et par.) ', in Dupont, *Jésus*, 283–301.

(18) The narrative opens with reports reaching John about the ministry of Jesus. Luke appears to have recast the introduction. He omits mention of John being in prison, diff. Mt., but the way in which John is unable to have direct contact with Jesus fits in with this situation, and in any case Luke has already referred to John's imprisonment, 3:20. The use of ἀπαγγέλλω (a Lucan word, 11x; Acts, 16x) has probably been suggested by its occurrence in v. 22 (Q). For John's disciples bringing him news, cf. Jn. 3:26; they would have been able to visit him in prison without difficulty. They brought news about all that Jesus was doing; περὶ πάντων τούτων refers to the activity of Jesus in general and not merely to the Sermon (so Manson, *Sayings*, 66, with reference to Q); cf. Matthew's reference to τὰ ἔργα τοῦ χριστοῦ. In Luke's context it refers especially to the deeds of Jesus just reported in 7:1–17.

In Lk. John's message is delivered by two of his disciples. For the phraseology cf. Acts 23:23. προσκαλέομαι, 'to summon, call', is Lucan (15:26; 16:5; 18:16*; Acts, 9x; but it is curious that Luke takes over none of the 9 uses in Mk.). The sending of *two* disciples corresponds to frequent Jewish and early Christian practice (J. Jeremias, 'Paarweise Sendung im Neuen Testament', in *Abba*, 132–139). Loisy's view, 222, that Luke's δύο arose from misreading διὰ τῶν μαθητῶν (Mt. 11:2) in Q is followed by Bultmann, 345; cf. 10:1; 19:29; 22:8; 24:4. If Q did originally refer to an indefinite number of disciples, it is quite possible that Luke has hit on the probable number. The two men then constitute the necessary number of witnesses for the declaration of Jesus. Note that δύο τινάς means 'a certain two', whereas in Classical Greek τις with numerals means 'about'.

(19) The description of Jesus as κύριος (B f13 *al* a ff² vg sa bo ᵖᵗ), diff. Mt., is Lucan (7:13; Ott, 37f.); the v.l. Ἰησοῦν TR; *Diglot*, is secondary, despite fairly strong attestation (Metzger, 143). Although John may have his doubts about Jesus, Luke as the narrator has none; similarly Matthew states that John had heard about 'the works of the Messiah', and this agreement between the two Evangelists in substance raises the question whether something similar stood in Q.

The question raised by John is whether Jesus is to be identified with 'the Coming One' or somebody else is to be awaited to fulfil that role. For ἄλλος (Lk., 11x; Mt., 29x), Matthew has ἕτερος (Lk., 33x; Mt., 9x). ἕτερος strictly means 'a second person', but in NT Greek it is synonymous with ἄλλος (J. K. Elliott, 'The use of ἕτερος in the New Testament', ZNW 60, 1969, 140f.). Schürmann, I, 409 and n. 13, holds that Luke has used the more correct term 'another (from many)'.

The participle ἐρχόμενος may be equivalent to an Aramaic timeless expression and hence have a future meaning (Black, 131f.; Jeremias, *Words,* 178f.). In 3:16 John announced the coming of 'the stronger One'; cf. Mt. 3:11 (Jn. 1:25, 27) where he speaks of 'the one coming after me'. The present phrase may simply echo this earlier statement and mean that John is enquiring whether Jesus is the One who was to come after him. Two closely related questions arise, however. What function did John expect the coming One to perform, and was 'the coming One' some sort of title?

In Mk. 11:9 and Lk. 13:35 the phrase 'Blessed is he who comes in the name of the Lord' (Ps. 118:26) is quoted, probably in a messianic sense. For the idea of a future coming by a messianic figure cf. Hab. 2:3; Mal. 3:1; Dn. 7:13; Heb. 10:37; Rev. 1:4; SB IV:2, 858, 860. A reference to 'Elijah who is about to come' is found in Mt. 11:14. Again, Jn. 6:14 speaks of the prophet who is coming into the world, and 11:27 of 'the Messiah, the Son of God, who is coming into the world'. Cullmann, 26, Hahn, 393f., and G. Friedrich, TDNT VI, 847, hold that in the present passage Jesus is seen as the coming prophet who will bring in again the paradisial conditions of the wilderness period. It is doubtful whether such an expectation should be attributed to John, and more likely that we should see a vague messianic expectation (cf. J. Schneider, TDNT II, 670; C. Maurer, TDNT VI, 726). Strobel, 265–277, traces the influence of Hab. 2:3, and it is possible that early Christian tradition saw this text reflected in John's question. Although, however, it is unlikely that John's question refers to the coming of the eschatological prophet, it remains true that the answer to his question does bear some relation to this expectation; see below.

(20) Luke alone describes how the messengers fulfilled their commission and repeated John's question to Jesus; cf. 15:18, 21; 19:30–34 par. Mk. It is probable that Matthew has here abbreviated the narrative, following his habit (Schürmann, I, 410, n. 18; *contra* Hoffmann, 192f.; Schulz, 191). The language, however, shows signs of Lucan editing: παραγίνομαι; ἀνήρ. The noun βαπτιστής is found at 7:33; 9:19 (par. Mk. 8:28; Mt. 16:14); Mk. 6:25 (par. Mt. 14:8); Mt. 3:1; 11:11f.; 14:2; 17:13**. Luke uses it here and 7:33 diff. Mt., and Mt. 11:11f. uses it diff. Lk. It seems likely, therefore, that it occurred in Q somewhere in this section; probably Luke has brought it forward to the first appropriate point.

(21) Before the verbal reply of Jesus to the question Luke inserts an account of how he performed mighty works in the presence of the witnesses; thus they were indeed able to 'hear and see' what was going on. The verse, which shows signs of Lucan style, is generally regarded as a Lucan addition, since it is awkwardly introduced into the context. For similar summaries of healings cf. 4:40f.; 6:18f. Luke's concrete description sums up what was happening in a more general fashion.

The phrase ἐν ἐκείνῃ τῇ ὥρᾳ recurs at Acts 16:33; Luke prefers the form αὐτῇ τῇ ὥρᾳ (A D Θ pm lat; TR; Diglot), which Black, 109–11, accepts here as an Aramaism. θεραπεύω ἀπό is Lucan (5:15 note). μαστίξ is literally 'lash', hence 'disease' (Mk. 3:10; 5:29, 34; Acts 22:24; Heb. 11:36**). πνεύματα πονηρά is used at 8:2; 11:26 (par. Mt. 12:45); Acts 19:12–16, and may be Lucan. χαρίζομαι, 'to give freely', Acts 3:14; 25:11, 16; 27:24*; 'to forgive', Lk. 7:42f.*, is Lucan.

(22) The reply of Jesus to John is almost identical in Lk. and Mt. Luke omits ὁ Ἰησοῦς (cf. 7:24), which probably seemed unnecessary. The disciples of John are to go back to their master and inform him of what they have seen and heard. Matthew has the verbs in reverse order in the present tense (ἀκούετε καὶ βλέπετε). Luke's past tense refers directly to the events recorded in v. 21; the present tense probably stood in Q (cf. 10:23f. par. Mt. 13:16f.), and referred to the ministry of Jesus as a whole. The reversal of order is probably also due to Luke who thus makes Jesus refer first to the deeds which the disciples have just seen (cf. Roloff, Kerygma, 192–194). Before the actual message for John ὅτι is inserted by A D al lat TR; Diglot; its absence in the majority of MSS could be due to assimilation to Mt.

The message itself consists of six brief parallel clauses followed by a closing comment, which gives a poetic form in Aramaic (six two-beat lines and one three-beat line; Jeremias, Theology, I, 20f.). In Lk. there are two groups of three clauses joined by καί; Matthew joins all the clauses by καί, except the second and third. There is no obvious reason for the variation, but Luke shows the better Greek style (Hoffmann; 93).

For the healing of the blind, cf. 7:21; 18:35–43 (par. Mk. 10:46–52); Mk. 8:22–26; Mt. 9:27–31; 12:22; 21:14; see also Lk. 4:18; 14:13, 21. ἀναβλέπω is 'to recover sight' (18:41–43; cf. ἀνάβλεψις, 4:18); 'to look up' (9:16; 19:5; 21:1*). The healing of the lame (χωλός 14:13, 21) is recorded in Mt. 15:30f.; 21:14; Jn. 5:3; Acts 3:1–10; 8:7; 14:8–10; Luke probably thought of the healing of paralytics under this heading (Acts 8:7; cf. Lk. 5:17–26). The cleansing of lepers occurs in 5:12–16 (par. Mk. 1:40–45); 17:11–19 (cf. Mt. 10:8 and perhaps Mk. 14:3). κωφός (1:22) here means 'deaf'; cf. Mk. 7:31–37. Elsewhere it means 'dumb' and cures of such people are narrated in 11:14 (par. Mt. 12:22); Mt. 9:32–34; cf. Mk. 7:31–37 (a deaf mute) and Mt. 15:30 (ambiguous). The raising of the dead figures in 7:11–17; 8:40–56 (par. Mk. 5:21–43); Jn. 11. No specific incidents regarding preaching to the poor are attested, but for general references see 4:18; 6:20; 14:13, 21. For the passive use of εὐαγγελίζομαι cf. 2 Sa. 18:31; Joel 2:32; Heb. 4:26; it corresponds to Aramaic usage (Dalman, 102).

It may be noted that the list does not correspond exactly to the mighty works recorded in 7:21; it refers to the ministry of Jesus as a whole, and it is based on OT language. Behind the list lie: Is. 29:18f. ἀκούσονται ... κωφοὶ ... καὶ οἱ ... ὀφθαλμοὶ τυφλῶν ὄψονται, καὶ ἀγαλλιάσονται πτωχοὶ διὰ Κύριον; Is. 35:5f. τότε ἀνοιχθήσονται ὀφθαλμοὶ τυφλῶν, καὶ ὦτα κωφῶν ἀκούσονται. Τότε ἁλεῖται ὡς ἔλαφος χωλός, τρανὴ δὲ ἔσται γλῶσσα μογιλάλων; Is. 61:1 εὐαγγελίσασθαι πτωχοῖς ... τυφλοῖς ἀνάβλεψιν; Is. 26:19 ἀναστήσονται οἱ νεκροί; cf. Lk. 4:18. Only the cleansing of lepers is not mentioned in the Isaianic passages, but here we may perhaps see an Elisha typology (2 Ki. 5; cf. Lk. 4:27). The combination of OT allusions indicates that the future era of salvation has arrived, but this is especially linked with the function of Jesus as the eschatological prophet who announces the good news to the needy; but whereas the prophet in Is. 61 simply announces the blessings, Jesus actually brings them. The fact that the saying finds its climax in the preaching of the good news (cf. G. Friedrich, TDNT II, 718) indicates how John the Baptist may have been perplexed by the ministry of Jesus, since the action of bringing about final judgment is conspicuously absent.

(23) Hence arises the force of the concluding blessing (cf. 1:45; 6:20 and notes). It is couched in general terms – so that it applies to all of whom it may be true – but is meant to apply especially to John. The verb σκανδαλίζω means 'to cause to stumble' (17:2); passive, 'to be caused to stumble', hence intransitively 'to take offence', 'to fall away' (Mk. 4:17; 6:3; 9:42–47; 14:27, 29; et al.; G. Stählin, TDNT VII, 339–358, especially 350). The saying thus refers to the possibility of a person not accepting Jesus as 'the coming One' because he 'stumbles' at the kind of things done or left undone by Jesus, and thinks that he should have behaved differently. Stumbling is thus the opposite to believing in Jesus. The saying pronounces an eschatological verdict upon the people concerned; by their attitude to Jesus they will stand or fall at the last judgment. As applied to John the saying may perhaps refer to the possibility of his 'losing confidence' in Jesus (G. Stählin, ibid.; JB). This explains its negative form: blessed is the man who retains his faith in me and does not give it up. The saying is thus an invitation to John to consider the scriptural significance of Jesus' ministry, and hence to attain to a deeper, and lasting, faith in him. How John responded to the message is not related; the accent falls upon the claim of Jesus, which is addressed to all who hear it.

iv. Jesus' Witness About John 7:24–28

The second part of the section is placed after the departure of John's messengers, and contains a comment by Jesus on John addressed to the crowds. It is directly linked to the preceding conversation (7:24 par. Mt. 11:7), and there is no need to dispute the possible historical correctness of this connection, unless it is held to be impossible that the gospel tradition could correctly link successive events. The wording in Lk. and Mt. is almost identical and indicates the use of a common source.

Jesus' comment stresses the fact that John was indeed a prophet, a man of strength and conviction who deserved the attention of the people.

Indeed, he was more than a prophet, for he fulfilled the prophecy of Mal. 3:1 about the coming of God's messenger to prepare the way for the Messiah. By virtue of this task John ranked as the highest of men. Nevertheless, even the most insignificant member of the kingdom ranks above the messenger who prepared the way for it. There is something more important than following John: entry to the kingdom. Thus, implicitly, John is placed in a subordinate position to Jesus. (This point is made explicitly if we interpret μικρότερος in a comparative sense with reference to Jesus himself.)

A comment by Jesus on the significance of John is historically probable, and the saying in vs. 24–26 can safely be ascribed to him, especially in view of its positive evaluation of John. V. 27 is often regarded as an addition, springing from the exegetical activity of the early church; it is argued that Jesus did not cite Scripture in this formal manner and compare current events with the exact wording of prophetic passages (Schweizer, *Matthäus*, 168; cf. Bultmann, 178; Hahn, 374–376; Schulz, 232 n. 367). But v. 26b demands a continuation (Schürmann, I, 417), and the view that Jesus could not have cited Scripture in this way is baseless supposition (on the use here see France, 91f.; 155, 242f.). V. 28b is often regarded as an addition on the grounds that it represents a Christian denigration of John over against Jesus (especially if the verse is a direct reference to Jesus) and thus contradicts the earlier, positive estimate of John in the passage (Bultmann, 177f.). Since, however, v. 28a and v. 28b appear to be formulated in antithesis to each other, it can be argued that both stand or fall together (Lührmann, 27). There is, however, no reason to dispute the authenticity of v. 28a (Hahn, 375). The force of v. 28b is misunderstood if it is regarded as a denigration of John; its point is rather to stress to Jesus' hearers the significant decision that faces them (cf. 13:23f.; Jüngel, 174 n. 5), and in this sense it raises no historical difficulty. Indeed it can be argued that Jesus could hardly have praised John in such high terms as in v. 26 without qualifying his praise with reference to his own mission in relation to the kingdom of God (Schweizer, *Matthäus*, 170; cf. Schürmann, I, 418f.).

Matthew (11:12–15) includes here sayings which have a partial parallel in Lk. 16:16; they show signs of reformulation by Matthew, and it is difficult to see why Luke kept back 16:16 to its present context if he was not influenced by his source; it is likely, therefore, that these verses are a Matthaean insertion here (Bultmann, 22; Schürmann, I, 422), rather than that Luke omitted them at this point (Lührmann, 27f.). It is possible that different versions of Q lay before the Evangelists, but this is less likely in view of the close parallelism throughout the whole section.

See Lührmann, 26–29; Hoffman, 215–224; Schulz, 229–236.

(24) The punctuation and interpretation of the three sets of questions and answers is disputed: 1. With τί meaning 'what?', we have, 'What did you go out into the desert to see? A reed shaken by the wind?

...' 2. With τί meaning 'why?', we have, 'Why did you go out into the desert? To see a reed shaken by the wind? ...' (*Diglot*). 3. With τί equivalent to Hebrew *mah*, introducing a rhetorical question, we have, 'Did you perhaps go out into the desert to see a reed shaken by the wind? ...' (Beyer, I:1, 100 n. 7). It is probable that view 3. represents the original meaning of the passage, and it can be argued that it fits the wording of both Lk. and Mt. But this sense may have been lost in transmission of the sayings in Greek. If so, view 2. is required for Mt. in view of the word-order in the third question (Mt. 11:9 (so *Synopsis*, diff. UBS), diff. Lk. 7:26). The different word order in Lk. makes it probable that we should adopt view 1. here, unless view 3. is thought to represent Luke's understanding.

John worked in the wilderness where one might expect to see reeds growing (κάλαμος, cf. Mt. 12:20). The shaking of reeds in the wind was proverbial (1 Ki. 14:15; for σαλεύω cf. Lk. 6:38), and the metaphor suggests a wavering (Easton, 102) or easy-going person: 'Man should strive to be tender like the reed and not hard like the cedar' (Taan. 20a, in Manson, *Sayings*, 68). But the question expects a negative answer: John stood firm.

(25) One might expect to see reeds in the desert, but not persons clothed in soft raiment. μαλακός, 'soft', was used to describe clothes of fine material (Mt. 11:8; also of effeminate persons, 1 Cor. 6:9**). The addition ἱματίοις, diff. Mt., is unnecessary (AG s.v.). ἀμφιέννυμι, 'to clothe' (Mt. 6:30; 11:8**; cf. the late form ἀμφιάζω, Lk. 12:28 v.l.), is here constructed with ἐν (BD 159[1]). The point is the austerity and asceticism of John who wore a garment of camel hair. He did not wear the splendid apparel of those who lived in king's palaces and were subject to the royal beck and call. He saw the need for stern repentance in the light of God's coming judgment. The wording here differs from Mt. and is probably Lucan. The use of ὑπάρχω (a Lucan word) strongly suggests this (the v.l. διάγοντες D *al* Cl is probably a secondary intensification, Metzger, 143). ἱματισμός, 'clothing, apparel' (9:29; Acts 20:33; 1 Tim. 2:9; Jn. 19:24**), and ἔνδοξος, 'glorious' (13:17; 1 Cor. 4:10; Eph. 5:27**), are probably Lucan. τρυφή, 'luxury', 'indulgence' (2 Pet. 2:13**), brings out the significance of the clothes. βασίλειος, 'royal' (1 Pet. 2:9**), is used in the neuter to mean 'palace' (Herodotus 1:30), diff. Mt. οἱ οἶκοι τῶν βασιλέων, which may reflect a Semitic phrase (cf. 2 Sa. 11:8; 15:35; 1 Ki. 7:31) and is therefore probably original.

(26) Whereas the preceding rhetorical questions had a negative answer, the third one has a positive, but inadequate one. The kind of person who was not tossed about by any wind of doctrine and did not kowtow to royalty was indeed a prophet, as the people recognised; cf. 20:6 par. Mk. 11:32; Lk. 1:76. John may have disclaimed being *the* prophet (Jn. 1:25), but he was nonetheless a prophet. Jesus confirms this estimate by his ναὶ λέγω ὑμῖν. For ναί, 'yes', cf. 10:21 (par. Mt. 11:26); 11:51 (diff. Mt. ἀμήν); 12:5; Mk. 7:28; Mt. 5:37; *et al.*; the question arises

whether ναί here conceals an original ἀμήν, but this is unlikely since here Jesus confirms what has just been said, whereas ἀμήν usually points forward to the truth of what he is about to say. John is 'more' or 'greater' (περισσότερον, 12:4, 48; 20:47*) than a prophet. It is not clear whether περισσότερον should be regarded as masculine or neuter (for the latter see F. Hauck, TDNT VI, 62 n. 4; cf. Mt. 12:6; Lk. 11:31f.). But in what sense is he greater? The view of G. Friedrich (TDNT VI, 839f.) that he was the eschatological deliverer is obtained only by neglecting vs. 27 and 28b as additions to the original saying, and by assuming that Jesus thought of somebody other than himself as the eschatological deliverer. Manson, *Sayings*, 68–70, holds that John did more than a prophet: he actively prepared people for the coming crisis by baptism. Cullmann, 24, argues that John is here *the* eschatological prophet. This view fits in with v. 27, where John is seen as the messenger of the last days who is to be identified with Elijah. But this prophet must be clearly distinguished from 'the coming One' whom John himself expected, and from the eschatological prophet like Moses who is distinguished from Elijah and the Messiah in Jn. 1:21. It is true that in Jn. 1:21 John himself disclaims being Elijah, which is odd, if Jesus so identified him. It is probable that Jesus was correcting an earlier, historical remark of John, who thought of himself as merely a voice in the wilderness (cf. J. Jeremias, TDNT II, 936f.). (It is strange that the Fourth Evangelist allowed this disclaimer to stand in view of Jesus' comment. It may be, however, that John reflects the Christian tendency to see all of these eschatological expectations fulfilled in Jesus, and therefore he allows the Baptist's remark to stand. Something of this same attitude is visible in Lk., where a straight identification of John with Elijah is not to be found (contrast Mt. 11:14); John appears in the spirit of Elijah.)

(27) The way in which John is more than a prophet comes to expression in the citation in v. 27. The view that the verse is an interpolation into Luke's text (Manson, *Sayings*, 69f.) is to be rejected; certainly the fact that v. 28a is transposed to precede v. 27 in D (a) is no argument. The form of citation (οὗτος . . .) indicates that certain Scriptures find a personal fulfilment in John. The same quotation is also found in Mk. 1:2. The first part of the quotation agrees with Ex. 23:20 LXX: ἰδοὺ ἐγὼ ἀποστέλλω τὸν ἄγγελόν μου πρὸ προσώπου σου. Both Luke and Mark omit ἐγώ, diff. Mt. It is true that Luke dislikes pronominal subjects (Cadbury, II, 191ff.), but the agreement with Mk. here suggests that the addition is due to Matthew (cf. Holtz, 27). The second part of the quotation appears to be from Mal. 3:1, but it differs considerably from the LXX (ἰδοὺ ἐξαποστέλλω τὸν ἄγγελόν μου, καὶ ἐπιβλέψεται ὁδὸν πρὸ προσώπου μου) and is closer to the MT. It is probable that the two verses were conflated in a Semitic form (and also linked with Is. 40:3 in Mk. 1:2f.), since the common link is given in the MT (ûpinnâ; the LXX translates ûpānâ in Mal. 3:1), and the two verses were linked in Jewish usage (France, 242f.; SB I; 597; cf. Gundry, 11f.). Ex. 23:20 (cf. Gn. 24:7; Is.

45:1f.) refers to God sending his angel before the people of Israel to guard them on their way to the promised land. The reference is not to Moses (*pace* Caird, 113, who finds a fusion of the figures of Moses and Elijah here) but to the presence of God himself through his angel (cf. Ex. 14:19; 32:34; 33:2). As God went before his people at the Exodus, so he would also do again in the future. Mal. 3:1 takes up this expectation with its threefold promise of the coming of 'my messenger', 'the Lord whom you seek', and 'the messenger of the covenant'; these three expressions refer to the coming of one person (France, 91 n. 31) or at most of two, God and his messenger (E. Jenni, THAT I, 35), but not of three (i.e. including the Messiah). In Mal. 4:5f. this messenger is equated with Elijah (cf. Suggs, 45f.). The text accordingly refers to the coming of Elijah as the messenger who prepares the way for the people of God (Ex. 23:20) or for God himself (Mal. 3:1). But whereas in Mal. the messenger prepares the way for God (μου), in the present quotation it is for 'you' (σου). If the use of Ex. 23:20 is regarded as the decisive influence, then the messenger is preparing the way for the people of Israel, i.e. preparing them for the day of the Lord (Danker, 97). If, however, Mal. 3:1 is decisive, then what was affirmed with reference to Yahweh there is here affirmed with reference to Jesus; the coming of Jesus (as Messiah) replaces that of Yahweh (France, 155; Schürmann, I, 417), and hence John points beyond himself to Jesus.

(28) The pericope reaches its climax in a saying introduced by λέγω ὑμῖν; the addition of ἀμήν in Mt. is no doubt original, since Luke omits it (4:24 note; 7:9; *contra* Hoffmann, 194; on the text see Metzger, 143). Although the form of the statement about John is comparative (μείζων), the effect is superlative. Nobody is (ἐστίν, diff. Mt. ἐγήγερται) greater than John among men; the phrase γεννητὸς γυναικός simply means 'a man', with stress on his mortality (Job 11:3, 12; *et al.*; 3 En. 6:2; Gal. 4:4; cf. Black, 298; F. Büchsel, TDNT I, 672). Some MSS make John the greatest 'prophet', but this reading is probably secondary (Metzger, 143f.). The praise of John is as unstinted as in 1:15, but it is immediately qualified. It is not enough to respect John; it is more important to be a member of the kingdom of God. For the person who is least (μικρότερος, in superlative sense; cf. 9:48) in the kingdom of God is greater than John. The saying has often been thought to exclude John from the kingdom. This understanding of it would conflict with the principle in 13:28 (par. Mt. 8:11), and is hence unlikely in the mind of Jesus or of the early church. The point is probably directed to the hearers; just as a place in heaven is worth more than authority over the demons (10:17–20), so possession of a place in the kingdom is more important than being the greatest of the prophets. If so, the question whether John is in the kingdom or not is not raised. Alternatively, the saying may place the 'shift of the aeons' after the ministry of John, and thus indicate the supreme value of belonging to the new era that John himself prophesied (cf. G. Friedrich, TDNT VI, 840f.). Even so, however,

nothing is said as to the place of John in the ultimate consummation.

The view that the saying refers to Jesus as the one who is lesser, i.e. younger than John (F. Dibelius, 'Zwei Worte Jesu: II', ZNW 11, 1910, 190–192) or the disciple of John (Suggs, 67), has found favour among many recent scholars (Leaney, 57–59; Grundmann, 166; O. Michel, TDNT IV, 653; Cullmann, 32; Hoffmann, 220–224) but is quite improbable, especially in view of the word order in the sentence.

v. The Rejection of John and Jesus 7:29–35

The third part of the section contains Jesus' verdict on the men of 'this generation' who rejected both John and himself. They are like children unwilling to play with their mates; they do not find the ascetic John to their liking, and they bitterly criticise Jesus for mixing with frivolous people and joining in their revels (7:31–34). This doleful picture is qualified in two ways. Despite this frequent rejection of God's messengers, nevertheless God's wisdom is shown to be right by her children, i.e. those who respond both to John and to Jesus (7:35). It was in fact basically the leaders of the people – the Pharisees and lawyers – who had rejected John, while the common people, and especially the despised tax-collectors, had been baptised by him and accepted his message (7:29f.). Thus John and Jesus are placed again alongside each other, with no suggestion that John holds an inferior place.

Vs. 31–35 are clearly drawn from a common source, but Matthew has no parallel at this point to vs. 29f., although he has similar material at 21:31f. It is not clear whether these verses are meant to be part of Jesus' discourse in Lk., as they are in Mt. (JB; NEB mg; most commentators), or a parenthetical comment by the narrator (most translations; Creed, 108). It is possible that the material occurred at this point in Q and was omitted by Matthew because of its awkwardness and his desire to include other material; he then made use of it, or a similar tradition, in Mt. 21:31f. In its Lucan form the passage cannot be anything other than a comment by the narrator, possibly based on an tradition of a saying of Jesus (as in Mt.); the language suggests a considerable degree of Lucan editing, but traces of a Lucan stress on the ethical character of John's ministry (Hoffmann, 194–196) are less obvious. Since elsewhere there is evidence that Luke did not manage to submit his work to a final stylistic revision, it may be that the same cause is responsible for the untidy situation here. It appears that Luke has had to alter a saying, originally addressed to the Pharisees, into a statement about them in order to accommodate the material to its present context (7:24). If this is so, however, either Luke has introduced the saying from another context, or he has smoothed out a poor connection in Q.

The authenticity of vs. 31f. as the kernel of the section is undisputed (Bultmann, 177f., 186; Lührmann, 29). It has been argued, however, that originally the parable may have referred simply to the

people's reaction to Jesus himself; they did not like his call to repentance
or his summons to joy. If so, the application in vs. 33f. to John and Jesus
is secondary. In favour of this view it is argued that there is a certain discrepancy between the parable and its interpretation, that elsewhere
parables are presented without interpretation, and that the references to
the Son of man and wisdom reflect the outlook of the early church (cf.
Bultmann, 186; Schürmann, I, 423–426; Lührmann, 29f.; Hoffmann,
227–230; Schulz, 380f.). Now, so far as their content is concerned, there
is every likelihood that vs. 33f. are an authentic logion of Jesus, possibly
without the use of the phrase 'Son of man' (but see below). Moreover, if
the parable is taken as a parable and not as a detailed allegory, the 'explanation' fits it well enough, and it is by no means improbable that the
parable had an application from the beginning (cf. Schweizer, *Matthäus*,
168; Jeremias, *Parables*, 160–162). It is, therefore, more likely that the
sayings formed an original unity.

V. 35 will also form part of this sayings-group. In its Lucan form it
can hardly mean anything other than that the divine wisdom which sent
John and Jesus has been vindicated by its children, i.e. by those who
have responded to their message (v. 29). It has, however, been suggested
that wisdom's children were originally regarded as John and Jesus
(Suggs, 35), or that Jesus himself was originally identified with wisdom
(Christ, 73 – admittedly as a secondary part of the preceding interpretation). In this case, the verse would form part of the testimony to a
wisdom christology in Q which was bound up with the concept of the
Son of man. But while the fate of wisdom in the wisdom-tradition shows
notable parallels to that of Jesus, it is doubtful whether this passage goes
so far as to identify the messenger of wisdom with wisdom itself. In any
case, there would seem to be no difficulty about Jesus commenting on
his mission in terms of wisdom categories.

See A. Feuillet, 'Jésus et la Sagesse divine d'après les évangiles synoptiques', RB 62, 1955,
161–196; F. Mussner, 'Der nicht erkannte Kairos (Mt 11, 16–19 = Lk 7, 31–35)', Bib. 40,
1959, 599–612; Jeremias, *Parables*, 160–162; Lührmann, 29–31; Légasse, 289–317; Christ,
63–80; Suggs, 33–58; Hoffmann, 224–230; Schulz, 379–386.

(29) The opening verses set the scene for the comments by Jesus in
vs. 31–35, and show that despite the rejection of John and Jesus by the
religious leaders of the people, there were also those among the common
people who responded to them. πᾶς ὁ λαός is a Lucan phrase (2:10; *et
al.*; cf. especially 18:43), and refers back to the popular support enjoyed
by John, 3:21; the tax-collectors who responded to him (3:12) are especially singled out for mention, although grammatically (ἀκούσας,
singular) they are something of an after-thought. When they heard what
Jesus said (not what John said), they acknowledged God to be in the
right; for δικαιόω in this sense cf. 7:35 (par. Mt. 11:19); 10:29; 16:15;
18:14; Acts 13:39; Mt. 12:37; cf. 4 Ez. 10:16; Pss. Sol. 2:15; 3:5; *et al.*;
Ps. 51:4; Sir. 18:2 (G. Schrenk, TDNT II, 213f.; see also 1QH 9:9;
1QM 11:14). It is not clear whether the participle βαπτισθέντες means

that the people vindicated God by their submission to baptism or that they vindicated God because they had previously been baptised by John. The latter view is more probable: the people who heard Jesus praised God that he spoke highly of John because they had already been baptised by him. The phrase τὸ βάπτισμα 'Ιωάννου is Lucan (20:4 par. Mk. 11:30; Acts 1:22; 18:25; 19:3), but based on primitive usage, and does not necessarily imply a contrast with Christian baptism.

(30) A different position was adopted by the Pharisees (5:17 note) and the lawyers. νομικός is used as an equivalent to γραμματεύς (10:25; 11:45,46, 52, 53; 14:3; Mt. 22:35; Tit. 3:9, 13**; cf. 4 Mac. 5:4; W. Gutbrod, TDNT IV, 1088). It is probably from Luke's source ('proto-Luke', Rehkopf, 95; Q, Schürmann, I, 422 n. 96); see, however, G. D. Kilpatrick, 'Scribes, Lawyers and Lucan Origins', JTS ns 1, 1950, 56–60; and R. Leaney, 'ΝΟΜΙΚΟΣ in St Luke's Gospel', JTS ns 2, 1951, 166f., for the view that Luke himself introduced the term to the Gospel – but this does not explain why he retained γραμματεύς in Marcan passages.

Not having been baptised by John, the Pharisees and lawyers showed that they had rejected God's purpose. For ἀθετέω see 10:16*; Mk. 6:26; 7:9; Jn. 12:48; C. Maurer, TDNT VIII, 158f. βουλή, especially when qualified by τοῦ θεοῦ, is Lucan (23:51; Acts, 7x; 1 Cor. 4:5; Eph. 1:11; Heb. 6:17**); it refers especially to God's plan of salvation, and here the use stresses that the activity of John and Jesus was the outworking of a divine purpose (G. Schrenk, TDNT I, 633–636; Marshall, 103–115). The phrase εἰς ἑαυτούς is variously understood: 1. with βουλήν, 'God's plan for themselves' (Easton, 103; Schürmann, I, 422 n. 97); 2. as equivalent to an Aramaic ethic dative, strengthening the subject (Manson, Sayings, 70; Black, 103); 3. 'so far as it concerned themselves' (Creed, 108). This last view is best.

(31) The parable follows without any indication that direct speech is again being introduced (cf. 7:40/41; 19:25/26); the need is supplied in some inferior MSS. The double introduction (diff. Mt.) is also found in 13:18 and Mk. 4:30f., and is probably original (Bultmann, 186). Luke's use of οὖν is appropriate in his context, as Matthew's δέ is in his. ὁμοιόω, 'to make like' (Acts 14:11), hence 'to compare' (13:18, 20), is used to introduce parables in Mk. 4:30; Mt. 7:24; et al.; for ὅμοιος cf. 6:46 (J. Schneider, TDNT V, 186–189).

The phrase ἡ γενεὰ αὕτη is found in 11:29–32 (par. Mt. 12:39–42); 11:50f. (par. Mt. 23:35f.); 17:25; 21:32 (par. Mk. 13:30); Mk. 8:12, 38; a similar use is found in 9:41 (par. Mk. 9:19); 16:8. Behind it lies the usage in Dt. 32:5, 20; Jdg. 2:10; Pss. 78:8; 95:10; Je. 7:29, which suggests the faithlessness of Israel and its subjection to the wrath of God (cf. F. Büchsel, TDNT I, 662f.). The word is thus used to characterise the contemporaries of Jesus as sharing in the perversity of faithless Israel (cf. Acts 2:40; Phil. 2:15; Heb. 3:10; see further on 21:32 and Ellis, 246f.). According to Lührmann, 30f., 43 (cf. Schulz, 381) the use of the word γενεά reflects the interests of the redactor of the Q material; earlier material is directed against the Pharisees rather than Israel as a whole. This is hardly convincing. Luke has added τοὺς ἀνθρώπους diff. Mt. (similarly in 11:31 diff. Mt. 12:42), thus stressing the serious situation of *men* who behave no better than *children*.

(32) If taken literally, the opening formula ὅμοιοί εἰσιν likens the men of this generation to the children who reproach the others for not joining in their game. But the opening formula probably rests on an Aramaic basis which means 'It is with them as with . . .' and which compares two situations with each other (Jeremias, *Parables*, 100–103); this would allow a broader basis of comparison. The formulation παιδίοις τοῖς . . . (i.e. noun, article, attribute), diff. Mt. (omission of article) is Hellenistic and means 'children, namely the ones who . . .' (BD 270³); it is probably due to Luke (cf. 15:22; 18:9; 23:49; Acts 7:35; *et al.*). ἀγορά is the market place (11:43 (par. Mt. 23:7); 20:46* (par. Mk. 12:38)); the omission of the article is common in this kind of stereotyped formula (cf. 1 Cor. 11:18; MH III, 179). Luke has probably improved the style of his source diff. Mt. ἐν ταῖς ἀγοραῖς (*contra* Schürmann, I, 423 n. 114).

The picture is apparently of a group of children sitting down to make music while their companions perform more strenuous activities at their bidding (Jeremias, *Parables*, 161, following E. F. F. Bishop, *Jesus of Palestine,* London, 1955, 104; F. Mussner*, 599f.). They call out instructions to their playmates, and when these are not obeyed, they reproach them. First, the children played the flute (αὐλέω, Mt. 11:17; 1 Cor. 14:7**), probably offering merry music, suitable for a wedding (contrast the dirge in Mt. 9:23). But their companions would not dance (ὀρχέομαι, Mt. 11:17; Mk. 6:22 par. Mt. 14:6**). For the motif, cf. Herodotus 1:141; Aesop, Fables, 27. Second, the children sang a dirge (θρηνέω, Mt. 11:17; also 'to mourn', 23:27; Jn. 16:20**), but their companions refused to mourn. The use of κλαίω, diff. Mt. κόπτω, 'to beat the breast', could be a translation variant, but more probably Luke has avoided a Palestinian expression referring to passionate beating of the breast in favour of one more typical of Hellenistic custom. It is clear that in Mt. one group of children suggest two different games to their comrades (ἑτέροις) in turn. Luke's use of ἀλλήλοις has suggested that he is thinking of two groups of children reproaching each other, perhaps with alternative suggestions for games, since neither group will follow the other's choice (Jeremias, *Parables*, 161). More probably Luke has in mind the cross-talk between the children who suggest what to play and their companions who refuse to join in, but he quotes only the reproaches made by the first group (Schürmann, I, 424).

How is the parable to be interpreted? 1. The first group of children may be a picture for the messengers of God; just as the other children refuse to play, so the Jews refuse to respond to whatever kind of message they bring (Schürmann, I, 423f.). 2. The first group may be a picture of the Jews who tell the ascetic John to dance and the joyful

Jesus to mourn. Neither John nor Jesus will satisfy them (Jeremias, *Parables*, 160–162). 3. The point may be the more general one that just as some children refuse to play the games suggested to them, so the Jews reject all God's advances to them. On this view, the picture is a general one of children who will not play games, and no allegorical interpretation is to be looked for (cf. F. Mussner*, 600f.; Légasse, 298f; for the various possibilities see especially Lagrange, 223–225). The second of these interpretations gives the best sense, especially in relation to vs. 33f. The reproach in v. 32 must be one directed by the Jews against God's messengers, rather than the verdict of Jesus on the Jews. It is the Jews who are dissatisfied both with the ascetic John and the joyful Jesus (in that order, *pace* Schulz, 381). The metaphorical language hints at the intended application, although the details (e.g. playing at funerals) are not to be pressed allegorically.

(33) The parable is now given its application. If John would not dance at the whim of the Jews, neither would Jesus mourn. The use of the verb ἐλήλυθεν (cf. Mt. ἦλθεν) here and in v. 34 has been taken to express a verdict passed upon John and Jesus after the completion of their lives and ministries (Bultmann, 167f.; Vielhauer, 125–127; this is an unnecessary supposition, for which the evidence offered by Bultmann is (as he himself virtually admits) by no means compelling (cf. C. Colpe, TDNT VIII, 431 n. 238; Fuller, 127f.). It is hard to say whether the perfect or aorist is original here (contrast Mt. 17:12 diff. Mk. 9:13 and Lk. 5:32 diff. Mk. 2:17), but the alteration is more probably due to Luke. The inclusion of John's title, ὁ βαπτιστής, diff. Mt., may also be due to Luke (cf. 7:20), but it could have been dropped by Matthew (cf. Mt. 11:11f.). John neither ate bread nor drank wine. ἄρτος and οἶνος are included by Luke, diff. Mt., and are probably a (correct) addition (L. Goppelt, TDNT VI, 140; Schürmann, I, 426 n. 135), since John lived on locusts and wild honey (Mk. 1:6) and did not drink wine (Lk. 1:15). According to O. Böcher ('Ass Johannes der Täufer kein Brot (Luk. vii. 33)?', NTS 18, 1971–72, 90–92), John avoided meat and wine because they were unclean and brought men under demonic influences; he used harmless substitutes for them. On this view, the longer text in Lk. is to be preferred, but behind ἄρτος we should trace an original *leḥem* that means 'food' and here could mean 'meat'. This is a plausible explanation of Mk. 1:6; but it is doubtful whether Aramaic *leḥem* does mean 'meat', and it is more likely that the saying refers to abstinence from normal forms of food. The suggestion that Luke has expanded the text, perhaps under the influence of Dt. 29:5 and Lk. 1:15 is preferable (cf. Schlatter, 495f.). The form of the double negative is uncertain. Luke has μή . . . μήτε . . . which is so unusual (only two doubtful examples in LSJ) that it has been altered by scribes to μήτε . . . μήτε . . . (assimilation to Mt.) or to μή . . . μηδέ . . . (ℵ W *pc*; *Diglot*).

It is not surprising that people said that John had a demon, i.e. showed the madness associated with demon-possession. Luke has the direct form λέγετε, which assumes that the Jewish leaders are included in the audience, diff. Mt. λέγουσιν; it is debatable which form is original (Lk.: Hoffmann, 197; Mt.: Schulz, 380 n. 14). For δαιμόνιον ἔχει cf. 8:27; Jn. 7:20; 8:48, 49, 52; 10:20; if the phraseology is Hellenistic (Schulz, 381), this shows how far Hellenistic superstitions were at home in Palestine. It is not clear whether the people attributed John's asceticism to demon-possession or claimed that by his asceticism he laid himself open to demon-possession (cf. O. Böcher, *Das Neue Testament und die dämonischen Mächte,* Stuttgart, 1972, 10, 44f.). In any case they did not appreciate that he was a living parable of the need for stern repentance in face of the coming judgment; they missed their opportunity both with him and with Jesus (F. Mussner*, 612).

(34) Jesus places himself alongside John under the appellation 'the Son of man' (5:24 note). The use of the phrase has raised doubts about the authenticity of the saying as a whole (Tödt, 114–118; Hahn, 44; Vielhauer, 125–127), but apart from this there is no real reason to dispute it (so rightly, Higgins, 121–123). The saying places John and Jesus alongside each other, instead of subordinating John to Jesus, and the insulting description of Jesus is hardly likely to have been placed on his own lips by the early church. The casting of the saying in the form, 'The Son of man (*or* I) came . . .' is due to the parallelism with the preceding saying (Percy, 253), and the use of the participles rather than the infinitive with ἐλήλυθεν distinguishes the saying from similar sayings which are often (but wrongly) judged to be community formations. In contrast to John Jesus ate and drank, and even took part in feasts. So he was described as a glutton (φάγος, Mt. 11:19**, is a rare, late word) and a tippler (οἰνοπότης, Mt. 11:19**; Pr. 23:20; cf. 28:7). The description resembles that of the unruly son in Dt. 21:20 MT who is to be stoned; thus a proverbial expression for apostasy is being applied to Jesus. Not only so, but he also associated with persons regarded as apostates by Pharisaic standards (5:30; 15:1; 19:7). Once again the Jewish leaders failed to see the significance of the living parable in the One who brought to sinners the offer of divine forgiveness and friendship.

As for 'the Son of man': 1. It is possible that this phrase has been introduced into a saying that was originally couched in the first person (Higgins, 121–123). It has been argued that an Aramaic phrase meaning 'that son of man' and used as a periphrasis for 'I' has been misunderstood as a title (Manson, *Sayings,* 70f.; for a stronger linguistic justification of this view see Vermes, 182). 2. C. Colpe, TDNT VIII, 431f., has taken up the earlier suggestion (Bultmann, 166; Jeremias, *Parables,* 160 n. 37) that *bar 'enāš(â)* here originally meant 'a man'. For a. this is required by the parallelism with the following ἄνθρωπος; b. it links together the two men, John and Jesus, as messengers of divine wisdom; and c. the antithesis with John had to be stated in the third person. So the phrase means 'a man', but not 'any man'; it refers specifically to Jesus, but is not a title. The second and third of these arguments have little force. The question is whether Jesus spoke of himself simply as 'a man', and this is just possible. 3. But the early church understood the phrase as a 'title', and this raises the question whether Jesus used a term which might have seemed to be merely a simple self-reference to his hearers but which in reality conveyed a deeper meaning. As it stands, the saying contains the note of rejected authority which is characteristic of the Son of man sayings generally (Percy, 251–253; Tödt, 115f.). This is more likely than the view of Hoffmann, 148f., that the saying refers to rejection of the one who will come at the End as the Son of man. This self-understanding of Jesus makes good historical sense (cf. Kümmel, 46 n. 93; E. Schweizer, 'Der Menschensohn', ZNW 50, 1959, 185–209, especially 199f.; Borsch, 325f.). H. Schürmann, 'Beobachtungen zum Menschensohn-Titel in der Redequelle', in Pesch, *Jesus*, 124–147, argues that here and elsewhere the Son of man sayings are probably redactional additions to the Q material. This view ignores the evidence that the present saying appears to reflect the lifetime of Jesus himself, and in general falls short of proof.

(35) The sayings-unit culminates in the statement that despite the rejection of John and Jesus by the Jews, yet, wisdom is shown to be right by her children. καί has the sense 'and yet'. For δικαιόω see 7:29 (where the word has perhaps been introduced under the influence of this verse); the aorist is timeless (Jeremias, *Parables*, 162 n. 42; MH III, 73). σοφία can be a periphrasis for 'God' (cf. 11:49; Jeremias, ibid.). It could also be a name for the Messiah (Ellis, 120, following W. D. Davies, *Paul and Rabbinic Judaism*, London, 1955[2], 156, who regards the saying as a creation by the early church). But behind the saying lies rather the Jewish tradition concerning wisdom as a quasi-personal hypostasis in heaven, a divine agent expressing the mind of God, who preaches to men and longs to dwell among them but is rejected by them (G. Fohrer and U. Wilckens, TDNT VII, 465–526; Christ, 13–60, 156–163, gives a survey of the basic texts: Job 28; Pr. 1; 8; Sir. 1; 24; 11QPs[a]XVIII; Bar. 3f.; 1 En. 42 *et passim*; 4 Ez. 5; 2 Bar. 48; Wis. *passim*). In the present passage, however, there is little to suggest that wisdom is thought of as a personal being, and the thought is rather than the rightness of God's plan (βουλή, 7:30) is demonstrated by those who accept it (cf. A. Feuillet*, 167; Christ, 65). But the construction is uncertain. ἀπό can be taken in various senses: 1. 'from', i.e. 'on account of', 'in view of', reflecting Aramaic min qᵒdam (Jeremias, *Parables*, 162 n. 43). This sense fits the text of Mt. (ἔργων), where the works of wisdom (the signs of the time seen in the ministries of John and Jesus) are evidence that the moment of crisis is at hand. 2. 'apart from', 'over against', reflecting min: wisdom is justified over against/despite her children who have rejected her (M. Dibelius, cited by U. Wilckens, TDNT VII, 516 n. 353). 3. 'from', i.e. 'by', again reflecting min (cf. Is. 45:25 LXX; Mt. 16:21; Jas. 1:13; *et al.*; Schürmann, I, 427 n. 145). This third possibility fits Lk. best: the claims of wisdom are proved to be true by her children. The

reference will be to those who have accepted the message of wisdom's envoys, John and Jesus, in contrast to those who rejected them (cf. Pr. 8:32f.; Sir. 4:11; Lührmann, 29f.; Hoffman, 228f.). The view that John and Jesus are the τέκνα (Suggs, 35; so possibly U. Wilckens, ibid.) is improbable, and is ruled out for Lk. by the inclusion of πάντων, which suggests that the disciples of both John and Jesus are meant (Lagrange, 226). For disciples as children of their teacher see Mk. 2:5; 10:24; Lk. 8:48; Jn. 13:33; SB II, 559. Luke's use of τέκνα, diff. Mt. ἔργα, is probably original, the change in Mt. being linked to the use of ἔργα in Mt. 11:2 (Schürmann, I, 428; Suggs, 56–58; Christ, 63f.; it is less likely that Aramaic 'b d y' was differently vocalised as 'abdayyā' ('servants') and 'ᵃbādayyā' ('works'): so P. Lagarde, cited by G. Schrenk, TDNT II, 214 n. 13).

vi. The Woman who was a Sinner 7:36–50

The final story in the section provides an example of the way in which Jesus acted as the friend of sinners and drew upon himself the reproaches of fastidious Jews (7:34); if the tradition followed by Luke in 7:29f. originally contained a reference to prostitutes (Mt. 21:31f.), then the relevance of this story, which is probably about a prostitute, is all the greater (Schürmann, I, 423 n. 107; cf. Lagrange, 227; but the fact that Luke omits the key word weakens this hypothesis). It is possible that the source which Luke was using at this point had a series of references to women (cf. 7:11–17, 36–50; 8:2f.: Schürmann, I, 448), which fitted in most appropriately with Luke's Q material.

The story is used here as an illustration of the association of Jesus with sinners, but the main point in it is a slightly different one. The central feature in the story, as brought out in the parable of the two debtors, is the contrast between the love shown by the woman to Jesus and the lack of love shown by Simon the Pharisee, as evidenced by the varying measures of generosity shown by them to Jesus. From this varied display of gratitude is drawn the fact that the woman's many sins have been forgiven, and this is confirmed by Jesus with an explicit declaration of forgiveness.

At the same time the question of who Jesus is figures prominently. The Pharisee wonders whether he is a prophet, since surely he would have known and avoided the touch of a sinner. The company gathered together wonder what kind of a person it is who declares the forgiveness of sins. Neither question is answered directly, but the answers are implicit. It is precisely because he is a prophet with divine authority that Jesus receives sinners and forgives them.

From this analysis it is patent that a number of different motifs are present in the story. Others have been added by scholars looking for a *redaktionsgeschichtlich* explanation of it; Bouwmann, 152–154, holds that it is an attack on Christian 'Pharisees' who criticised the way in which travelling preachers were willing to receive hospitality from women who had been notorious sinners before their conversion, but this explanation narrows down the significance of the story very considerably and is purely imaginative. The question is rather whether the various motifs fit together harmoniously or are the result of a process of growth. There are three main problems, which are interlinked.

First, did the parable originally belong to the story? It has been argued that the parable does not quite fit the situation. The woman is forgiven by Jesus on the basis of her great love, whereas the parable introduces an element of comparison with the Pharisee, takes up the idea of showing hospitality, and makes the woman's loving action the result or proof of forgiveness rather than the ground for it.

Second, the ending of the story, which contains a declaration of forgiveness that is superfluous after v. 47, seems to be an addition, based on matter from Mk. (cf. Schramm, 43–45, who regards the use of Mk. as certain at this point).

Third, the story has a parallel in the narrative of the anointing at Bethany (Mk. 14:3–9; cf. Mt. 26:6–13; and Jn. 12:1–8). Luke omits this alternative story, but there are some contacts in wording between this story and the narratives in Mk. and Jn. which raise the question of the relationship between all three main accounts.

These factors have led to various attempts to reconstruct the history of the tradition:

1. Wellhausen, 31f., held that the basis of the pericope was a rewriting of the story of the anointing in Mk. 14. To this was added the parable in vs. 41–43 (and with it the related comment in v. 47) which reversed the point of the narrative from love leading to forgiveness to forgiveness attested by love. The closing verses, 48 and 49f., are additions to a story whose proper conclusion is found in v. 47.

Similarly, G. Braumann* holds that the story consisted originally of vs. 36–39, 44–46, 48f. The key to the story is v. 39: Jesus does not separate himself from sinners, but forgives them. V. 48 makes good sense on its own after vs. 44–46, and v. 49 is a suitable conclusion to the story (cf. Mk. 4:41). But the parable is an addition, which translates an original all/nothing theme (vs. 44–46) into a much/little one. With the parable came v. 47 as a link to the main story. Vs. 40 and 44 are Lucan additions, and v. 50 is taken from Christian baptismal preaching (cf. Mk. 16:16; 1 Pet. 3:21; Mk. 1:4).

2. Essentially the opposite view is taken by Bultmann, 19f., who regards the parable, vs. 41–43, with v. 47a, as the original nucleus, to which all the rest has been added (on the basis of Mk. 14) to form a scene for it. Originally, the woman's love was the basis for her forgiveness (hence v. 47b is secondary).

3. Others hold that the narrative and parable belonged together from the start. The original nucleus was vs. 36–43; to this was added vs. 44–47 (or vs. 44–46), thereby turning the parable into an allegory;

finally vs. 48f. were appended to emphasise Jesus' part in the act of absolution (Easton, ad loc.; Schürmann, I, 436, 440f.). Roloff, *Kerygma*, 161–163, however, holds that vs. 48f., belong to the original story. U. Wilckens* claims that the motif of anointing was added to the story from Mk. 14, and with it came the secondary interpretation of the woman's action in vs. 44–46 (cf. W. Manson, 84–86); he also argues that v. 50 belonged to the original form of the story or was added to it (on the analogy of its occurrence in miracle stories) at an earlier stage in oral transmission. It is a story of conversion, told in connection with baptismal instruction.

In attempting to decide between these various possibilities we may offer the following observations:

1. The fact that Luke has omitted the narrative in Mk. 14:1–9 at the corresponding point in his own Gospel is no proof that he regarded this story as identical with Mark's one. It simply indicates that he saw the similarity between the two narratives and avoided repetition. The two narratives deal with separate incidents and have different characters and purposes; it is unlikely that Luke has reworked Mk. 14:1–9 or that Luke's tradition and Mark's tradition ultimately refer to one and the same incident (cf. Brown, *John*, I, 449–452). Nevertheless, there are links between the two incidents. In Lk. the woman's action takes place in the house of Simon and includes an anointing with an alabaster jar of perfume. In Jn. the woman anoints the feet of Jesus and dries them with her hair. The simplest solution is that there has been some cross-influence between the various traditions (influence on Lk. from Mk. and influence on Jn. from Lk.), which would not be surprising in view of the general similarity of the two stories (cf. Dodd, 162–173). In this case, it becomes even more apparent that the narrative is originally quite separate from the anointing story in Mk. 14. If so, there is a case for regarding vs. 44–46 as a secondary addition; but, since there is nothing objectionable about vs. 44f., only v. 46 need be regarded as secondary. (Vs. 44f. are misunderstood if they are taken to suggest that the woman was trying to make up for Simon's lack of courtesy; it is Jesus who reinterprets her action.)

2. Luke saw the story as a unity. Hence in view of the clear meaning of the parable, supported by v. 47, Luke will have regarded the woman's love as the consequence, not the cause, of her forgiveness. The only reasons for questioning whether this was the original significance of the woman's act are the facts that a. no prior act of forgiveness has been recorded, and b. an explicit declaration of forgiveness comes at the end of the story. But it is clear that Luke himself did not regard v. 48 as contradicting v. 47, and at the end of the story the woman's forgiveness is declared to be on the grounds of her faith, not of her love. It must, then, be assumed that there had been some previous contact between Jesus and the woman, not recorded by Luke. Indeed, Zahn, 321, rightly claims that without some such previous contact the woman's conduct in the

present story is inexplicable. (In the same way, the story omits mention of Simon's initial lack of courtesy to Jesus until vs. 44–46.) It may be because of the lack of mention of this earlier contact that Luke has recorded the declarations of Jesus in vs. 48 and 50. Up until that point no response by Jesus *to the woman* has been recorded; Luke could not leave the woman as simply the object of a discussion between Jesus and the Pharisee, and so his story had to contain some saying addressed to her. The fact that vs. 48–50 may be an addition to the story does not affect the basic point at issue. The problem is whether the difficulty of assuming a previous contact between Jesus and the woman is greater than that of assuming that the original story had a different meaning from the present one. Since even Schürmann (I, 431f.) who claims that v. 47 refers to love followed by forgiveness has to admit that there was a previous meeting between Jesus and the woman, the fact of such a meeting causes no real difficulty. Moreover, if the story originally had another meaning, it is difficult to see how the parable of the two debtors can have formed part of the original story. But there is no good reason for accepting the views of either Wellhausen or Bultmann at this point. The inconcinnity between the story and the parable detected by G. Braumann* is quite inadequate as a reason for separation; and U. Wilckens*, 400–404, has shown satisfactorily that the story must lead to a response by Jesus to Simon, and that the parable itself must have had a story setting such as the present one if it was to have any point. It follows that the scene and the parable fit together in such a way that neither was handed down without the other.

3. It is possible that vs. 48–50 are at least in part an addition to the story, especially since they have close parallels in Marcan material. It has already been observed that the story probably closed with a saying of Jesus to the woman; it is not clear whether it did in fact do so, or whether this obvious lack was supplied in the tradition. On the whole, it seems probable that vs. 48f. belong to the pre-Lucan form of the story, with v. 49 supplying the 'choral ending' to the story. V. 50 may then be an addition, drawn from what Jesus was known to have said in cases of healing, to give Jesus the last word, and perhaps to make a story that was originally concerned simply to contrast a sinful woman and a Pharisee into being at the same time a description of Jesus as the friend of sinners, the One who forgives sin on the basis of faith and leads men and women into the peace of God. It remains possible, however, that this part of the story is due to Luke himself.

See Spicq, I, 120–137; G. Braumann, 'Die Schuldner und die Sünderin Lk VII, 36–50', NTS 10, 1963–64, 487–493; J. Delobel, 'L'onction par la pécheresse, La composition littéraire de Lc., VII, 36–50', ETL 42, 1966, 415–475 (not accessible to me); W. Henss, '*Das Verhältnis zwischen Diatessaron, christlicher Gnosis und 'Western-Text'*, Berlin, 1967 (early history of interpretation); H. Drexler, 'Die grosse Sünderin Lc 7, 36–50', ZNW 59, 1968, 159–173; Derrett, 266–278; Roloff, 161–163; U. Wilckens, 'Vergebung für die Sünderin (Lk 7, 36–50)', in Hoffmann, *Orientierung*, 394–424.

(36) The story begins with an invitation to Jesus to have a meal in

the house of a Pharisee. The unusual order of words (τις αὐτὸν τῶν Φαρισαίων) stresses the unusual nature of the invitation; see, however, 11:37 and 14:1 for similar situations. In the present context a meal after the synagogue service on the Sabbath is probable (Jeremias, *Parables*, 126; 11:37 note). The guests would recline on divans round the table (κατακλίνω, 9:14f.; 14:8; 24:10**; κατάκειμαι 5:29; Mk. 14:3, and ἀνάκειμαι Mt. 26:7; Jn. 12:2 express the same meaning). The setting is vague, and only the meal situation is common to the story of the anointing in Mk. 14:3; Jn. 12:1f. Jesus displayed no reticence in accepting the invitation; the fact that he was especially interested in despised people did not mean that he was uninterested in the more respectable members of society; they too needed the gospel.

(37) After the scene has been depicted, the real action begins with καὶ ἰδού. In the town there was a woman who was a sinner. (The text is uncertain; the UBS text (ἥτις ἦν) may have arisen by dittography from τις ἦν (700 pc sy; cf. 14:2; 10:25 for the same construction), and the other readings (including the transposition in TR; *Diglot*) may represent attempts to obviate the resulting confusion.) The description cannot mean that she was simply the wife of an irreligious person, i.e. one who disdained the Pharisaic rules of piety (Schlatter, 259), since the story is concerned with her sins. Probably a prostitute is meant (Jeremias, ibid.; Derrett, 266–278), but Zahn, 320f., argued that she was an adulteress. That such a person might be among the uninvited guests was not impossible (cf. 14:2f.; SB IV:2, 615), but it may well be that for a prostitute to dare to enter the Pharisee's house was particularly objectionable in the eyes of people in general – except for Jesus (Schürmann, I, 431).

When the woman knew that Jesus was in the house of the Pharisee she came bringing (κομίζω) a flask of perfume. ἀλάβαστρος (Mk. 14:3; Mt. 26:7**) denotes a long-necked bottle of alabaster or glass. μύρον, 'ointment, perfume' (7:38, 46; cf. Mk. 14:3–5; Jn. 12:3f.), can cover a number of substances. A similar phrase is found in the story of Jesus' anointing at Bethany, and it has been claimed that the detail has been taken over by Luke from Mk. But the phrase was a stereotyped one (cf. the references in AG, 33), and need not necessarily be traced to Mk. The problem is rather whether the whole motif of anointing has been taken over from the other story.

(38) The woman's intention may well have been to anoint the head of Jesus with the perfume, and the significance of the action may be partly that the perfume would have been bought with her immoral earnings (cf. Derrett*). But it would seem that her emotions got the better of her. It would be natural for her to stand behind Jesus, if he was reclining on a divan; consequently, when she spontaneously broke out weeping, her tears fell on Jesus' feet and wetted them (βρέχω, 7:44; cf. Ps. 6:7 LXX; of rain, 17:29*). In her anxiety to make up for this mishap, and forgetful of social proprieties, she let down her hair (cf. Jeremias, *Parables*, 126 n. 57) and wiped Jesus' feet dry (ἐκμάσσω, 7:44; Jn. 11:2; 12:3; 13:5).

Thereupon she kissed his feet. καταφιλέω (7:45; 15:20; Acts 20:37; Mk. 14:45 par. Mt. 26:49**) here denotes a sign of deep reverence, such as was paid to teachers (SB I, 995f.; cf. 1 Sa. 10:1), but it may also be an expression of gratitude (Sanh. 27b; SB I, 996). The kissing of the feet would express reverence, although it is unnecessary to press the point as far as does K. Weiss (TDNT VI, 624–631, especially 630) who claims that as the Divine One, who forgives sins, Jesus is far above men and only his feet stretch into the sinful world. Finally the woman anointed Jesus with the perfume (ἀλείφω, 7:46; Jn. 11:2; 12:3). From v. 46 it appears that the woman anointed Jesus' feet, an action which is unparalleled (except in Jn. 12:3), since this act of honour was normally bestowed on the head.

The whole account makes sense when we assume that the woman's original intention was interrupted by her overwhelming emotions. Her tears could be understood as expressive of repentance (Klostermann, 93) or of joy (Zahn, 322). The latter motive is to be regarded as uppermost (see above), although it is not impossible that elements of the former are also present: it is the forgiven sinner who knows the true meaning of sorrow for sin (cf. Calvin, *Institute*, III, 3; Schürmann, I, 432f.).

There is, however, the question whether the motif of anointing, as distinct from that of weeping and wiping the feet of Jesus, is secondary in the story and has been drawn from Mk. This element, however, is clearly prior to the section vs. 44–46, and it may be doubted whether it should be separated off from the basic narrative.

(39) The unspoken implication in the account of the woman's action is that Jesus suffered this to be done to him and acknowledged her gratitude. It was this that the Pharisee who had invited Jesus saw (cf. Mt. 26:8 diff. Mk.) and that led to his unspoken comment; for the redundant use of λέγων cf. 12:16; 20:2; Mt. 22:1; BD 101, and for ἐν ἑαυτῷ cf. 3:8. If this man (οὗτος in the emphatic position) were a prophet, he would know who this woman is, and what kind of woman she is, namely a sinner. The sentence expresses an unreal condition in present time, i.e. both clauses are regarded as untrue: Jesus does not know who the woman is, and therefore he cannot be a prophet. Behind the statement lie the two assumptions of the Pharisee, that a prophet would not allow himself to be touched by a sinful, and therefore unclean, woman, and that the mark of a prophet is clairvoyance (cf. G. Friedrich, TDNT VI, 844 and n. 400). These considerations would apply to any prophet; some MSS, however, (B Ξ 482) prefix ὁ (so *Diglot*; (*Synopsis*)), which would make Jesus *the* eschatological prophet (cf. Grundmann, 171). The reading is regarded as secondary by Zahn, 322 n. 22; G. Friedrich, TDNT VI, 842 n. 386, and Metzger, 144, and it looks as though it is an exegetical addition by a scribe in the light of such verses as Jn. 1:21; it is unlikely that a Pharisee would have wondered whether Jesus was more than an ordinary prophet.

(40) But the Pharisee's assumptions are both wrong. Jesus is able

to read his thoughts and reply to them, and also not only is Jesus willing to accept the touch of a sinful woman, but he even suggests that her action is more welcome to him than that of his host. This latter point receives all the emphasis and is brought out in the parable that now follows.

Jesus addresses his host as Simon, which is also the name of the leper in whose house the anointing story in Mk. 14:3 is placed. This name is so common in the NT (at least eight bearers of the name appear; cf. AG s.v.), that it is rash to assume that the name has travelled from one story to the other, especially when Simon the leper is unlikely to have been a Pharisee. 'If the records were largely destroyed, historians of a distant future might find it difficult to believe that Admiral Cunningham, General Cunningham and Air Vice-Marshal Conyngham commanded simultaneously in the eastern Mediterranean in the 'forties of this century' (Blaiklock, 192). The formula ἔχω with object and infinitive is frequent in Lk. (7:42; 12:4 (50); 14:14; Acts 4:14; 23:17, 18, 19; 25:26; 28:19; cf. Mt. 18:25) and may be due to him here. The separation of φημί from its subject is found in Acts 2:38 v.l.; 23:35; 25:5, 22; 26:25; but is obviated in some MSS (so TR; *Diglot*). The use of the historic present, normally edited away by Luke (8:49 note) may be a sign of pre-Lucan tradition (Jeremias, *Words*, 150). It is thus likely that the parable was joined to the preceding narrative in Luke's source (cf. Schürmann, *Abschiedsrede,* 97f.).

It is noteworthy that the Pharisee addresses Jesus as διδάσκαλε (cf. 2:46 note), a word which is equivalent to 'rabbi', and which expresses very considerable politeness on the part of the Pharisee. In Lk. Jesus is described (8:49 par. Mk. 5:35) or addressed as 'Teacher' frequently by non-disciples (9:38; 20:21, 38; 21:7; also 20:39 and possibly 10:25 par. Mk.; 7:40; 11:45; 12:13; 19:39). Jesus himself uses it in 22:11 par. Mk. 14:14, and the disciples use it in 21:7. Luke does not substitute it for other forms of address in his sources, but he substitutes ἐπιστάτης for it (5:5 note; cf. 8:24; 9:33, 49). The title is thus indicative of Jesus' appearance to non-disciples, and is ultimately inadequate as a description of him.

(41) The parable (which may well have an Aramaic basis, Black, 181–183) begins without any indication of the change of speaker (cf. 7:31). It concerns a money-lender (δανιστής**) who had two debtors (χρεοφειλέτης, 16:5**). They owed him 500 and 50 denarii respectively. For ὁ εἷς ... ὁ δὲ ἕτερος cf. 17:34f.; 18:10; the construction may be a Semitism (Black 108; cf. MH II, 438; BD 247). ὀφείλω is 'to owe' (11:4; 16:5, 7; 17:10*). The suggestion by G. Braumann*, 488 that the difference between forgiveness in the narrative and remission of debts in the parable is significant overlooks the closeness of the two concepts in Jewish thought (cf. Mt. 6:12 diff. Lk. 11:4). δηνάριον (10:35; 20:24*) is a transliteration of Latin *denarius*, a Roman coin roughly equal in purchasing power to an agricultural labourer's daily wage.

The story has nothing in common with the parable in Mt. 18:21–35 and the rabbinic parable in Abodah Zarah 4a (SB II, 163) beyond the mention of two debtors and the remission of debts – which was no doubt a popular theme.

(42) Instead it takes its own way. Neither debtor was able to repay his debt; the genitive absolute is used unnecessarily, as often in the NT (BD 423[1]), and ἀποδίδωμι often indicates the repayment of debts (10:35; 12:59; 19:8; cf. 20:25). To both of them (ἀμφότεροι is Lucan) he granted remission of their debts (χαρίζομαι, 7:21). The parable passes over the unusual nature of this act on the part of the creditor, and concentrates instead on the response of the forgiven debtors with a direct question to Simon (and the reader): which of the two will love him the more? Some MSS insert εἶπε at this point ((A) f13 33 pm; TR; *Diglot*); it helps to soften the question, but may for that very reason be an addition, though a skilful one (it is rejected by UBS, Metzger, 144). The verb ἀγαπάω expresses the reaction of the debtor *after* the remission of the debt, and hence includes the notion of gratitude; it may in fact have this as its primary meaning here, since there is no specific verb 'to thank' in Hebrew, Aramaic or Syriac; for this sense cf. Ps. 116:1 (114:1); Jos. Bel. 1:198 (H. G. Wood, 'The use of ἀγαπάω in Luke viii. 42, 47', Exp.T 66, 1954–55, 319f.; Jeremias, *Parables*, 126f.). Love is the way in which gratitude is expressed.

(43) Simon's reply takes the form, 'I suppose that (it will be the one) to whom he forgave the more'. ὑπολαμβάνω, here 'to assume' (Acts 2:15), has a variety of meanings: 'to take up' (Acts 1:9); 'to receive (as a guest)' (3 Jn. 8); 'to reply' (Lk. 10:30**), and appears to be Lucan. There is ellipse of the main clause in Simon's reply. His response has been understood as supercilious indifference (Plummer, 212), but this is unlikely; it is more probable that it expresses caution, since there could be circumstances (especially in rabbinic casuistry) when it might be wrong. Most probably, however, Simon realises that he has been caught in a trap; the answer reluctantly anticipates what follows, namely the criticism of Simon's own lack of gratitude to Jesus. But, however cautiously expressed, the answer is correct: ὀρθῶς, 'rightly', may be Lucan (10:28; 20:21 (diff. Mk.); Mk. 7:35**).

(44) The woman is again brought to the centre of the scene as Jesus turns Simon's attention to her (for στρέφω (7:9; *et al.*) with πρός cf. 10:23; 14:25; 22:61; 23:28); the command is put in the form of a question. In what follows the interrelationship of the three people concerned is stressed by the careful use of the pronouns, and three aspects of the woman's deed are contrasted with three expressions of hospitality that Simon had not shown to Jesus. It should be noted that Simon had not acted discourteously; he had been correct enough as a host, but had not performed any especial acts of hospitality that went beyond the mere demands of the situation (Schürmann, I, 435f.; Harvey, 244). The provision of water for guests to wash their feet after travel is attested in

patriarchal times (Gn. 18:4; 19:2; 24:32; 43:24), but is not attested in Jewish literature as normal provision for guests. (The Jewish references are concerned with the fact that slaves performed this task for their masters; SB I, 427f.; cf. Jn. 13.) Hence Simon was not necessarily omitting an essential duty, although, if Jesus had come to his house after a journey on foot, it might have been a suitable luxury to offer him (cf. L. Goppelt, TDNT VIII, 323f. and n. 63). The wording ὕδωρ μοι ἐπὶ πόδας is not especially difficult, but has been eased in some MSS (cf. ἐπὶ τοὺς πόδας μου, A pm; TR; Diglot). δίδωμι means 'to give', as in 7:45 and usually; not 'to put, place', following Semitic usage (cf. 12:51; Black, 133).

(45) In the second place, Simon had not offered his guest a kiss (φίλημα, 22:48) on arrival. The kiss was an accepted form of greeting (2 Sa. 15:5; SB I, 995f.), but does not appear to have been a normal act of hospitality to a guest; G. Stählin (TDNT IX, 138 n. 224) finds it necessary to suggest that Luke may here have Greek practice in mind. What Simon had failed to do, the woman had done ceaselessly (διαλείπω**) from the time that (ἀφ' ἧς, sc. ὥρας; cf. Acts 24:11; 2 Pet. 3:4) Jesus entered the house. The expression is hyperbolical (Schürmann, I, 436 n. 35); hence there is no need to suppose that behind εἰσῆλθον lies a mistranslation of Aramaic 'ᵉṭayiṭ, which should have been translated as a 3rd person feminine form; some MSS substituted εἰσῆλθεν to ease the apparent difficulty (cf. J. Jeremias, 'Lukas 7:45 εἰσῆλθον', ZNW 51, 1960, 131).

(46) Third, Simon had not anointed his guest with olive oil (ἔλαιον, 10:34; 16:6*) – a cheap substance in comparison with perfume. Here too it is questionable whether a normal act of courtesy is being described (cf. SB I, 986; Schürmann, I, 435 n. 34). A number of MSS omit τοὺς πόδας μου (D W 079 it) in the description of the woman's act, so that it could be taken as an account of the anointing of Jesus' head. This reading is followed by K. Weiss, ('Der westliche Text Lk. 7:46 und sein Wert', ZNW 46, 1955, 241–245) who argues that the reference to Jesus' feet is an interpolation from Jn. 12. This avoids the difficulty of the otherwise unattested custom of anointing the feet (though there is in fact some evidence for this, SB I, 427), but the textual attestation is weak. It is more probable that the text is correct, and that the humble action of the woman receives stress.

The way in which the Pharisee and the woman are contrasted in these verses so that the Pharisee appears as a 'lesser sinner' is no reason for supposing that they are an addition to the original story (as Schürmann, I, 436 suggests); the fact that elsewhere the Pharisees consider themselves to be 'righteous' in no way demands that Jesus cannot have spoken of them as sinners here. Moreover, Jesus does not state that the Pharisee's few sins have been forgiven and that he is showing gratitude for the fact; as we shall see, v. 47b is to be taken more generally.

(47) The phrase οὗ χάριν, 'wherefore', may express a reason or a goal, but is here naturally taken as pointing backwards to what has just been said. What follows has been taken in two ways. 1. The words λέγω σοι may be taken parenthetically, and the ὅτι clause taken as giving a reason, so that the sense is: 'Because of this conduct (I say) her many sins have been forgiven, namely because she loved much' (Wellhausen, 32; Creed 110f.; and most RC commentators, including Lagrange, 231f.; Spicq, I, 120–137; Schürmann, I, 436–438). 2. The words οὗ χάριν should be taken closely with λέγω σοι, and ὅτι understood to mean 'as is evidenced by the fact that': hence 'Because of this conduct I tell you (that) her many sins have been forgiven, as is evidenced by the fact that she loved much' (JB; Schlatter, 263f.; Caird, 114f.; Schmid, 148f.; Jeremias, *Parables*, 127; U. Wilckens*, 404–411). In favour of the former view one may cite 1 Pet. 4:8 (cf. Pr. 10:12; Jas. 5:20; 1 Clem. 49:5; Mt. 6:14f.; Sir. 17:22; Dan. 4:27), but it is doubtful whether the NT supports the view that love covers, i.e. atones for, sin. Again, the tenses of the verbs are said to favour this view, the aorist ἠγάπησεν pointing back to the prior act of love by the woman; Jeremias, indeed, has to claim that the underlying Aramaic 'stative perfect' had a present meaning (cf. Black, 129) in order to defend the second view. But the objection here is without force, and Jeremias's reply to it is unnecessary, since Jesus is looking back to the conduct already shown by the woman in need and described in vs. 44–46. The difficulty with the first view is that it is contrary to the context: vs. 41–43, 47b and 50 combine to make it impossible. Even Schürmann has to admit that a statement along the lines of the second interpretation is what we would expect after what has preceded, and that such a statement may originally have stood there before it was altered in the redaction. These admissions show the weakness of the first interpretation, especially when (as we shall see) there is no reason to find here an editing process which wished to show that love precedes forgiveness. As for the second view of the verse, the case that ὅτι can be taken in the required sense is firmly founded (cf. 1:22; 6:21; 13:2; Gal. 4:6; Moule, 147; Zerwick, 422; Turner, 37–40).

Note further that the passive form ἀφέωνται can mean 'God has forgiven'; cf. 5:20–24, and that πολλαί, with its emphatic position, can mean 'all of them' (J. Jeremias, TDNT VI, 536–545, especially 542) but is perhaps better taken to mean 'many as they are'.

The antithetical statement in the second part of the verse is couched in general terms (hence the present tenses), and is hence formal and theoretical. It does not necessarily imply that the Pharisee had already been forgiven by Jesus and shown an appropriately small amount of gratitude; for in the end all talk of greater or lesser amounts of gratitude is irrelevant, as the sinner comes to realise the magnitude of his own personal debt to the Saviour. Hence the saying ultimately asks those who have little love for Jesus whether they have realised the magnitude of their sin and their need for forgiveness; if so, the saying could be ironic (cf. H. Seesemann, TDNT V, 172).

(48) It comes as something of a surprise that Jesus now turns to the woman and says to her, 'Your sins have been forgiven'; the use of the perfect tense (as in 7:47) can be taken to refer to a past act, or (in view of the use in 5:20, 23) to a present act. What Jesus says about the woman in v. 47 he now says directly to her. The statement is thus a confirmation of what has already taken place, and brings to the woman the personal assurance of God's dealing with her through Jesus. It is possible that the saying has been introduced into the story in order to achieve this end; it is verbally identical with 5:20 (par. Mk. 2:6), and has perhaps been taken over from there. The statement is thus a substitute for an account of how the woman obtained forgiveness from Jesus before the present story began; this will remain true whether she had had a previous direct contact with Jesus (see above) or had simply been led to repentance and the beginning of new life through some indirect knowledge of Jesus and his message.

(49) The question of who Jesus is had already been raised in v. 39, with the implication that he was a prophet. Now the christological significance of the story is carried a step further. The people who were present at the meal as fellow-guests (συνανάκειμαι, 'to recline with', 14:10, 15; Mk. 2:15 par. Mt. 9:10; Mk. 6:22 par. Mt. 14:9**) began to say, 'Who is this who even forgives sins?' The statement is similar to that in 5:21 diff. Mk., and its formulation may be due to Luke. It is not answered; as in the previous narrative, the reader is left to provide the answer.

(50) Instead, Jesus again speaks to the woman and draws out the final lesson of the story. With words also found at 8:48 par. Mk. 5:34; 17:19; and 18:42 par. Mk. 10:52, he states that she has been 'saved' through her faith. In the other references the phrase refers at least primarily to the healing power of Jesus. Probably in 17:19 there is the thought of the fuller healing of the whole person brought about by personal trust in Jesus, and hence the formula can be used, as here, in a case where physical healing is not involved; cf. W. Foerster, TDNT VII, 990. It follows that the formula 'go in peace' (8:48 par. Mk. 5:34) takes on a deeper sense also. What was a customary farewell in Judaism, meaning 'May God's peace be yours' (cf. Jdg. 18:6; 1 Sa. 1:17; 2 Sa. 15:9; 1 Ki. 22:17; Acts 16:36; Jas. 2:16), takes on a fuller meaning when it is used in the context of the bringing of divine salvation to men in Jesus (W. Foerster, TDNT II, 413).

e. Jesus teaches in Parables (8:1–21)

After the long section of non-Marcan material in which he has described the teaching of Jesus and his compassionate ministry (6:12–49; 7:1–50), Luke now precedes to a further section of his Gospel in which a description of the teaching of Jesus is followed by an account of his mighty works (8:1–21, 22–56). In this pattern he is governed by the presentation in Mk., whose contents he now follows until 9:50 when the use of other sources again begins. In his use of Mk. Luke had reached Mk. 3:19. He omits Mk. 3:20–30 at this point, since there will be a similar narrative later (11:14–26; based on Q material), and he transfers Mk. 3:31–35 to conclude the section on parabolic teaching (8:19–21), so that it fits more appropriately into his pattern. But before taking up the thread of Mark's narrative Luke inserts a brief note which introduces Jesus' further ministry and his companions during it.

i. Travelling Arrangements 8:1–3

Just as on previous occasions Luke has indicated that Jesus had companions who heard what he had to say and were witnesses of his mighty deeds, so at the beginning of this new section we are reminded that the Twelve were with him; alongside them are named various women who also formed part of the travelling band. With these companions Jesus set about a further systematic campaign of evangelism in the countryside, with the accent on the spoken word (in view of what is to follow immediately in 8:4–18). It is clear that the purpose of the paragraph for Luke is to introduce this further period of ministry which includes travel by Jesus into Decapolis (and then, at a later point the mission of the Twelve and further journeys by Jesus). To this end Luke has used material which may have come from Q: cf. Mt. 9:35; 4:23 and 11:1, where material parallel to Lk. but not in Mk. occurs (Schürmann, I, 447f.). In this way, the direction of Jesus' ministry is seen to be motivated by his own missionary concern, rather than, as may be the case in Mk., by the need to take heed of Pharisaic opposition to his work in the synagogues (Caird, 115f.).

This explanation, however, does not account for the mention of the women in 8:2f. There can be no doubt that the motif is historical, for it is firmly fixed in the tradition (Mk. 15:40.; cf. Lk. 23:49, 55; 24:6, 10; Acts 1:14). Luke has no doubt included it because of his wish to show that those who were witnesses of the resurrection of Jesus were the women who had accompanied him from Galilee (23:55; Mk. 15:40f.) and who were thus qualified to act as witnesses (cf. Acts 1:21f.; 13:31). But the reason why he includes this note here is that it occurred in his source at this point. It is highly probable that the mention of the women who had been healed by Jesus came at the end of the section in Luke's source which dealt with Jesus' compassion to the widow of Nain and the woman who anointed his feet. In that context the paragraph may have served to show how those who had been healed by Jesus demonstrated their gratitude to him, and to suggest that Christian women too should perform hospitable duties in the church.

We may, then, have a combination of Q and L material at this point. Grundmann, 173, notes that the present section has a continuation at 9:51, where in the next piece of non-Marcan material the theme is again the missionary travels of Jesus. If the Q and L material was already joined together before it was united with Marcan material, then Luke has inserted the Marcan material here at a most suitable point.

(1) For the καὶ ἐγένετο construction see 1:8 note; for ἐν τῷ καθεξῆς see 1:3 note; 7:11 note. διοδεύω, 'to journey about', is Lucan (Acts 17:1**); it conveys the idea of a continuing wandering ministry (imperfect!), rather than a journey from one point to another. Schürmann, I, 445, finds here a pattern of missionary work intended to be followed by the early church; cf. 13:22 with Acts 16:4. κατά is used in a distributive sense, 'from town to town' (8:4; 9:6; 13:22; 21:11 (par. Mk. 13:8); Acts 2:46; et al.). The combination of towns and villages appears in Mt. 9:35, and may suggest a common source. The use of κηρύσσω and εὐαγγελίζομαι alongside each other gives a hendiadys: 'preaching the good news of', and corresponds to Matthew's phrase κηρύσσων τὸ εὐαγγέλιον (cf. Mk. 1:14). For the kingdom of God as the theme of the message cf. 4:43; 9:2; 16:16; Acts 8:12; Mt. 4:23; 9:35; it will appear almost immediately at 8:10. The presence of the Twelve with Jesus was announced in 6:13, but it is only now that Luke takes up the theme of Mk. 3:14 that they were to be with Jesus in preparation for their own task (Schürmann, I, 445).

(2) Along with the Twelve are mentioned the women; they appear on the same level as the men (Grundmann, 174). The syntax is loose, but the meaning is clear. They had been healed (θεραπεύω, 4:23; et al.; here pluperfect) from evil spirits (7:21) and diseases (5:15). Three receive special mention. First, there was Mary from Magdala (cf. 24:10; Mk. 15:40; 47 and 16:1 par. Mt. 27: 56, 61 and 28:1; Jn. 19:25; 20:1, 18; cf. Mk. 16:9). Μαγδαληνός denotes an inhabitant of Μαγδαλά, mod. Migdal, a town which lay about three miles from Tiberias on the W side of the Lake of Galilee; it is probably to be identified with the village of Tarichaea mentioned frequently by Josephus, and its name is to be derived from migdal (a watch tower) (Finegan, No. 54; Kopp, 190–197). Mary receives especial mention at the head of the list because of the firm tradition that she occupied a prominent place among the witnesses of the resurrection on Easter morning. She had also been cured of possession by seven demons, possibly recurrences of mental disorder (Findlay, 1040); the round number expresses the worst possible state of demonic disorder (cf. 11:26 par. Mt. 12:45; K. H. Rengstorf, TDNT II, 630f.). The verb ἐξέρχομαι is used to express the passive of ἐκβάλλω, a construction which is found in Koine Greek (MH III, 53, 292). The way in which Mary is introduced here makes it clear that neither Luke nor his source identified her with the sinful woman in the preceding story; demon possession and sinfulness are to be carefully distinguished.

(3) Second, there was Ἰωάννα (24:10**), Heb. yôḥānâ, (the fem.

equivalent of 'John'), the wife of an otherwise unknown Χουζᾶς (a Nabataean name; AG s.v.) who was an official of Herod Antipas; ἐπίτροπος can mean 'manager, foreman, steward' (Mt. 20:8); a 'guardian' (Gal. 4:2**); or a Roman 'procurator' (cf. the use of the verb, Lk. 3:1 D). The precise office of Chuza cannot be ascertained, but he may have been a high functionary in Herod's court (cf. Jos. Bel. 1:487; Lagrange, 235). It may be that the special knowledge of Herod and his court reflected in Lk. came through him; he and his wife are no doubt named as well-known personalities in the church and are evidence for the existence of Christian disciples among the aristocracy.

Third, there was Σουσάννα** (i.e. šûšannâ, 'lily'; cf. Sus. passim.), otherwise unknown. Along with many others (cf. Mk. 15:40f. where a similar undefined company is mentioned), they provided for the apostolic band out of their possessions. The alteration of αὐτοῖς to αὐτῷ in some MSS is a christological heightening (Metzger, 144). τὰ ὑπάρχοντα is a frequent phrase in Lk. The implication is that these women were of some substance (e.g. Joanna) and able to provide financially for the travelling preachers; so large a company of people could not travel around together as one group without some provision for their needs; when it was a case of missionaries travelling in pairs they could expect to be put up by local people. The use of the verb διακονέω (Mk. 15:41) to describe their provision of support may be influenced by the later use of the term in the church to describe Christian service, but this does not mean that the description is anachronistic (as Conzelmann, 41 n. 1, suggests). The place of women among the followers of Jesus was no doubt unusual (cf. Jn. 4:27) in Palestine, but this very fact speaks in favour of its historicity; the supposition that the early church brought Hellenistic influences to bear upon the Palestinian communities is highly unlikely.

ii. The Parable of the Sower 8:4–8

The section 8:4–18 is based on Mk. 4:1–25. In Mk. this is part of a longer section (4:1–34) on the parabolic teaching of Jesus, which is expanded by the inclusion of further parables in the corresponding section in Mt. 13. Luke, however, has abbreviated his Marcan material at this point. After presenting the parable of the sower, the general comment on the meaning of parables, and the explanation of the parable of the sower, he includes the following sayings (Mk. 4:21–25) which, in his view, refer to the way in which the teaching of Jesus is heard and understood by men; but he omits the other parables recorded in Mk. 4, so that all attention is concentrated on the parable of the sower and its significance. Then he includes the brief narrative of how Jesus' relatives visited him (8:19–21 par. Mk. 3:31–35); by holding it over to this point, Luke is able to use it as a final comment on the parable of the sower – stressing the importance of hearing and obeying the word of God. The section as a whole is thus concerned with the theme of hearing the word of God, and the accent has been shifted somewhat from where Mark places it. To be sure, the shift can be over-emphasised, for in Mk. also the parable of the sower is concerned with hearing the word, but there is certainly a shift from a chapter concerned with the teaching of Jesus in parables to a unified section dealing with hearing the word of God.

Luke's version of the parable is based on Mk.; a number of contacts with Mt. have led to the suspicion that Luke also had some other source or tradition at his disposal (Easton, 112; Schramm, 114–123). These contacts might well be dismissed as negligible, were it not that there is some evidence which suggests that the orthodox view that Matthew was dependent upon Mk. in the whole of this section may need revision (D. Wenham*). It is possible that Luke was influenced by oral traditions alongside the text of Mk.

The situation in which the parable was spoken is given in very general terms; having already used the seaside setting at 5:1f., Luke drops it here. The wording of the parable is shortened to about three-quarters of that in Mk., and after the introduction it falls into four pairs of lines. The wording is altered at various points, but curiously Luke's interpretation of the parable is based on Mark's wording rather than his own version.

The parable is addressed to the crowd (8:4, 8, cf. 9f.), but leads on to teaching for the disciples; Schürmann's complex observations on this point (I, 449f., 452) are over-ingenious. The ensuing interpretation makes clear that the parable is concerned with the way in which men hear the Word of God, and constitutes a summons to them to take care how they hear it (8:8). This is no doubt the meaning of the parable in Mk., and there is no evidence that Luke differs significantly from his source. Many commentators, however, argue that the parable is meant to encourage the disciples, who saw that the mission of Jesus was attended by little success; it teaches that, although much of the seed is sown in vain, nevertheless some will bring forth good fruit, even a hundred-fold, and from this fact they can take comfort; Schürmann, I, 454f., goes so far as to claim that for Luke the 'fruit' represents not simply the ethical effects of the word but rather the 'fruit' of men won for the kingdom in great numbers by the preaching of the word in the future (cf. Col. 1:6). It is likely that the parable could have been so interpreted and used in the early church, and Schürmann's view, which regards the harvest as still future, is preferable to the variant interpretation that the harvest was already 'realised' during the ministry of Jesus (Dodd, *Parables*, 135–137; Jeremias, *Parables*, 149–151). Nevertheless, it is more probable that this is a secondary application of a parable which is open to more than one interpretation.

See I. H. Marshall, *Eschatology and the Parables*, London, 1963; id. 'Tradition and Theology in Luke (Luke 8:5–15)', Tyn.B 20, 1969, 56–75; J. Dupont, 'La parable du semeur dans la version de Luc', in Eltester and Kettler, 97–108; W. C. Robinson Jr., 'On Preaching the

Word of God (Luke 8:4–21)', SLA 131–138; C. F. D. Moule, 'Mark 4:1–20 Yet Once More', in Ellis, *Neotestamentica*, 95–113; D. Wenham, 'The Synoptic Problem Revisited: Some New Suggestions about the Composition of Mark 4:1–34', Tyn.B 23, 1972, 3–38.

(4) The introduction to the parable differs from that in Mk., but the evidence hardly justifies Schramm's conclusion (117f.) that it is based on a parallel tradition rather than on Mk.; it appears to be a Lucan link between his special source (used in 8:1–3) and Mk. Luke begins with a double genitive absolute, as often, and replaces Mark's συνάγω (which Luke uses for gathering *things* together) by σύνειμι, 'to come together'; the verb, which occurs here only in the NT, should not be confused with σύνειμι, 'to be with', 9:18. Luke describes the crowd as πολύς, par. Mt., diff Mk. πλεῖστος; the same change could easily suggest itself to both Evangelists. The second genitive absolute phrase is epexegetic of the first. οἱ κατὰ πόλιν will refer to the people who have been influenced by the evangelistic journeys of Jesus in 8:1; ἐπιπορεύομαι** is 'to go, journey to'. The use of the present participles ('while a crowd was gathering . . ., Jesus spoke') may be significant. To people who are intent on coming to him and perhaps joining the group of disciples Jesus speaks a word of invitation that is simultaneously a warning: 'be careful how you hear, and do not become merely nominal or superficial followers of mine'. Since only one parable follows, Luke has the singular παραβολή, diff. Mk. and Mt. For the use of διά, cf. Acts 15:27, 32.

(5) Luke omits Mark's opening ἀκούετε (but cf. v. 8) and ἰδού. ὁ σπείρων is generic, 'a sower', but Luke and the early church rightly saw in the figure Jesus himself. For the use of τοῦ with the infinitive of purpose (par. Mt.) cf. 1:9. Luke alone adds the object τὸν σπόρον αὐτοῦ (σπόρος, 'seed', 8:11; Mk. 4:26f.; 2 Cor. 9:10**), thereby making explicit that the parable is about the seed, i.e. the word of God preached by Jesus. The use of ἐν τῷ with the infinitive to mean 'while' is not found in classical Greek (MH III, 145). Both Luke and Matthew omit ἐγένετο, diff. Mk., and add the subject of the infinitive. ὃ μέν must mean 'one portion' of the seed. It fell along the path (rather than on the path; cf. AG s.v. παρά, III 1 b; Schürmann, I, 453 n. 63); at the edge of a path, the ground would be hard and the seed would not sink into soft earth. Hence it could be trodden down (καταπατέω, 12:1; Mt. 5:13; 7:6; Heb. 10:29**) by passers-by, and eaten (κατεσθίω, 15:30; 20:47*) by the birds – Luke adds the stereotyped phrase τοῦ οὐρανοῦ (9:58 par. Mt. 8:20; Lk. 13:19 par. Mk. 4:32); Acts 10:12; 11:6; Mt. 6:26; Gn. 1:26; *et al.*); some MSS omit the phrase, perhaps because it seemed inappropriate with symbols of evil (Metzger, 144). In the interpretation of the parable (8:12) it would appear that the birds are symbolical of the devil, and no reference is made to the crushing of the seed under foot; the detail may be meant to reflect the contempt which the word suffers in the world (Heb. 10:29), and its presence in Lk. may be due to the influence of oral variants to Mark's version of the parable.

(6) Luke prefers ἕτερος to Mark's ἄλλος (cf. 8:7f.; 20:11 and see

3:18 note on the meaning). The second portion of seed fell (καταπίπτω, 'to fall', Acts 26:14; 28:6**, diff. Mk. πίπτω, possibly under the influence of the preceding κατα- compounds) upon rock (πέτρα, diff. Mk. πετρώδης); the explanation shows that rock lightly covered by soil is meant, so that the seedlings could make only limited growth. Although they started to grow (φύω, 8:8; Heb. 12:15**; cf. συνφύω, 8:7), they dried up (ξηραίνω*) and died, because the rocky ground held no moisture (ἰκμάς**). Luke's wording, possibly based on Je. 17:8 (cf. H. B. Swete, *St Mark,* 1898, 70), avoids Mark's slightly misleading statement that the seedling had no root (in reality, no developed root system), but nevertheless he follows Mk. in the interpretation (8:13).

(7) A third portion of seed fell into the midst (ἐν μέσῳ, diff. Mk.; cf. 2:46 note) of thorns, i.e. weeds. Their seeds had fallen into the same plot of land, and as the good seeds grew, so also (συνφύω**, diff. Mk. ἀναβαίνω, which Luke uses of moving upwards) did the thorns, and choked them; ἀποπνίγω, par. Mt., diff. Mk. συνπνίγω, also means 'to drown', 8:33**; Luke uses Mark's word in 8:14, 42, so his avoidance of it here may be due to an attempt not to have two συν- compounds in succession. Both Luke and Matthew omit the detail that the seeds bore no fruit, which is perhaps surprising in view of the stress on fruit-bearing in the final part of the parable; but Luke is abbreviating throughout.

(8) Finally, the fourth portion fell into good ground; ἀγαθός has the same meaning as καλός (so Mk. here, and Lk. 8:15). It grew up (8:6) and produced fruit (ποιέω, diff. Mk. δίδωμι; cf. 3:8) one hundred-fold (ἑκατονταπλασίων, Mk. 10:30**). Luke has omitted the other degrees of fruitfulness found in Mk., possibly to avoid a Gnostic interpretation (Leaney, 151) or the idea that there are different grades of Christians (Schürmann, I, 465; cf. Schramm, 121 n. 4, who regards the threefold classification in Mk. as due to the influence of church instruction warning converts to produce as much fruit as possible). He concentrates on the simple fact of the great fruitfulness produced by the word in good soil.

The parable is ended, but before Jesus concludes his address to the crowd, he cries out (φωνέω) – an emphatic word, diff. Mk. λέγω: 'Whoever has ears to hear, let him hear'. The phrase is repeated at 14:35, and occurs in some MSS at 12:21; 13:9; and 21:4. cf. Mk. 4:23; 7:16 v.l.; Mt. 11:15; 13:43; 25:29 v.l. It was obviously used several times by Jesus, and as a result has floated into the manuscript tradition at various points. It is clearly appropriate in the present context. By it the hearers are summoned to hear at a deeper level than mere sense perception, to take hold of the meaning of the parable, to apply it to themselves, and thus ultimately to hear the word of God which can save them (Ezk. 3:27).

iii. The Reason for speaking in Parables 8:9–10

After the parable there comes a scene in which the disciples ask Jesus about the meaning of what they have just heard, and the reply which he gives to them forms the central part of the present section of teaching. Jesus' answer falls into three parts, of which the second (8:11–15) is an exposition of the parable itself. First, there comes a statement about the reason for teaching in parables (8:9f.), and finally some further teaching on the importance of hearing Jesus' teaching in the right way (8:16–18).

In the present brief section Luke is still following Mk., but he abbreviates his source considerably; the setting is simplified, and the stress on the private nature of the conversation between Jesus and the disciples disappears. But the kernel of the dialogue remains. The disciples ask about the meaning of the parable. Jesus replies that the meaning is, or should be, open to them. They have been granted by God to know the mysteries of the kingdom; but for the others it happens in parables – mysterious sayings – so that they neither see nor understand the message. But whereas in Mk. the quotation from Is. 6:9f. is completed with a reference to the way in which the uncomprehending people are not forgiven, this point is absent in Lk., and has an equivalent in 8:12. Luke will quote Is. 6:9f. at length in Acts 28:26f. as Paul's final comment on the attitude of the Jews.

The saying is difficult and obscure in Mk., but its Palestinian character and difficulty speak in favour of its authenticity, although this is denied by many scholars.

See 8:4–8 note for bibliography; Gnilka, 119–129.

(9) Luke, like Matthew, omits Mark's opening clause referring to the change of scene, but both Evangelists envisage a private conversation between Jesus and the disciples; the crowds are quietly forgotten. ἐπερωτάω (diff. Mk. ἐρωτάω) is preferred by Luke when the meaning is 'to ask a question' (cf. 2:46 note). A redundant λέγοντες is found in A Θ pm f l q; TR; Diglot. Both Luke and Matthew simplify Mark's rather elaborate description of the questioners and simply have 'his disciples'. In Mk. the disciples ask about τὰς παραβολάς; Luke changes to the singular form, since only one parable has been recorded, and he formulates an indirect question (1:29 note). The question concerns the meaning of the parable. But Jesus interposes a general remark on the understanding of the parables before proceeding to answer the question directly.

(10) The wording of Jesus' answer has been altered from that in Mk. and agrees in a number of particulars with that in Mt., so that the conclusion is unavoidable that some common tradition has influenced them; there are some grounds for thinking that the form in Mt. and Lk. is more primitive than that in Mk. (cf. D. Wenham*, 24–31). Whatever be the case, we must interpret Luke's actual wording. The initial ὑμῖν is

emphatically placed to give a contrast with what follows. The verb which comes next (diff. Mk.) in the perfect passive tense (δέδοται) should be taken to mean 'God has given'. What he has given is knowledge of the mysteries of the kingdom of God. The insertion of γνῶναι (par. Mt., diff. Mk.) brings out what is implicit in Mk., since to be given a mystery really means to be given knowledge of it. μυστήριον*, 'mystery', incorporates the OT and Jewish idea of the secret plan of God; the word is used in the LXX to translate Aram. rāz (Dn. 2:18, 19, 27–30, 47; cf. 4:6) with reference to the dream of Nebuchadnezzar which Daniel was able to interpret, thanks to the help which he received from the God who reveals mysteries. The word came to be used of God's mysteries, which are unknown to men (Wis. 2:22), and is used in the NT of his plan of salvation, formerly hidden from men, but now revealed to Paul and the church (cf. G. Bornkamm, TDNT IV, 802–827). In Mk. the singular form refers to the secret of the kingdom of God, now revealed to men through Jesus; the plural in Lk. and Mt. will refer to the various elements in the teaching of Jesus about different aspects of the kingdom of God. These elements are expressed frequently, but not exclusively, in the parables, so that the parables constitute part of the 'mysteries' (G. Bornkamm, ibid. 817–819). Thus Luke's form of the saying stresses the element of knowledge involved in the apprehension of the message of Jesus through which the hidden kingship of God is revealed to men; a similar view is found in Mt. 13:19 where stress is laid on the need to hear and understand the word of the kingdom.

Over against the disciples stand 'the others'; λοιπός, 'remaining, other' (12:26; 18:9, 11; 24:9f.), is often used of non-disciples and non-believers (Acts 5:13; 1 Thes. 4:13; 5:6; et al.), and its use here by Luke (diff. Mark's more difficult phrase ἐκεῖνοι οἱ ἔξω) may reflect church usage; cf. especially the same contrast between 'the elect' and the others in Rom. 11:7; Eph. 2:3. There is no verb in this part of the sentence, and the intended construction is not absolutely clear. Mark has τὰ πάντα γίνεται: 'for those outside everything is in parables', and this appears to be the sense of Luke's wording. NEB offers 'the others have only parables'. The contrast is between possession of knowledge and lack of knowledge. What comes in parables is obscure. People hear the words, but do not perceive their meaning. This point is expressed by wording based on Is. 6:9f. The LXX here has the form βλέποντες βλέψετε καὶ οὐ μὴ ἴδητε (cf. MT reʾû rāʾô weʾal tēḏāʿû). The participle is equivalent to the Hebrew infinitive absolute and conveys the sense, 'You may look and look again, but you will never see'. In Mk. this saying has been worked into a clause (ἵνα βλέποντες βλέπωσιν καὶ μὴ ἴδωσιν), and this has been abbreviated by Luke with βλέποντες replacing βλέποντες βλέπωσιν καί, and βλέπωσιν replacing ἴδωσιν. Similar changes have been made in the second, parallel clause. Luke has retained the inverted order of the clauses found in Mk., and it is noteworthy that this same order (and the same abbreviated form) is found in Mt. The saying thus expresses what happens when the outsiders hear the parables; they hear, but do not understand. But was this the intention of Jesus? The introductory ἵνα normally expresses purpose, but this seems harsh to many. It is possible that ἵνα may express result (cf. AG s.v. II 2 for discussion of this possibility) or even cause (MH III, 102f.), but neither of these possibilities is clearly indicated here. The fact that there is a clear allusion to the OT here suggests that the meaning may be, 'so that (the Scripture is fulfilled which says that)...'; cf. Mt. 13:14. Certainly this must be part of the meaning, but perhaps we do not need to take the verse to be any more than 'a vigorous way of stating the inevitable' (C. F. D. Moule*, 100). By his method of teaching in parables Jesus not only invited his audiences to penetrate below the surface and find the real meaning; at the same time he allowed them the opportunity – which many of them took – of turning a blind eye and a deaf ear to the real point at issue.

It should be observed that the statement of Jesus corresponds very closely to the message of the parable of the sower. The parable has a double function. It makes the point that some people hear the message and fail to apprehend it fully, while others hear it and receive it with understanding and faith, but at the same time it is itself an example of this very fact, being couched in parabolic form. What is stated in parabolic form in 8:4–8 and addressed to the crowds as a summons to them to hear the message, is now stated openly to the disciples in 8:10 as a description of what takes place. Thus the present statement fits admirably into its context, and there is no need to regard it as a misapplication of a more general remark (as Jeremias, *Parables*, 13–18; similarly, F. Hauck, TDNT V, 757f.; F. Horst, TDNT V, 554f.); on the contrary, it is an appropriate exposition of the meaning of the parable of the sower.

iv. The Meaning of the Parable 8:11–15

Still following Mk. Luke goes on to give the specific meaning of the parable of the sower. Those who have been given divine insight into the mysteries of the kingdom are now given further teaching about this particular parable. The parable is seen to be allegorical, in that the various elements in it have corresponding features in the activity of preaching and hearing the word of God. Hearing the word must lead to the production of fruit, or else the hearing is in vain (Lagrange, 240). The theme, however, is a unified one; once the vital equation, 'The seed is the word of God', has been made, the essential lesson follows inescapably.

Opinion is sharply divided as to whether the explanation represents authentic teaching of Jesus, with the majority of scholars strongly denying the possibility; see especially Jeremias, *Parables*, 77–79. Two points should be distinguished. First, is the explanation given here consistent with the meaning of the parable as told by Jesus? We have already seen that this is the case, although the interpretation of the parable which we have offered is not accepted by all scholars. The point of the parable is, in our view, the importance of hearing and receiving the word of God, and the explanation elucidates the parable in this way. The difference between the parable and the interpretation is that the parable is addressed to the crowds and summons them to hear, while the explanation is addressed to the disciples and describes to them what happens when men hear the word; hence the explanation is more concerned with telling the disciples why preaching is sometimes a failure and sometimes a success. But this difference in stress is perfectly natural. A more serious question is whether Jesus utilised allegory in the kind of way presented here. But in fact the case against this possibility appears to consist largely of mere assertion that he could not, or would not, have done so (cf. I. H. Marshall,* 1963, 8–11).

Second, does this particular explanation stem from Jesus? This question has been discussed with especial reference to the Marcan account by Cranfield, 158–161, and C. F. D. Moule*, who both claim that there is nothing there which militates against an origin in the teaching of Jesus. In Lk., however, there are clear signs of editing of the Marcan account, showing that the early church did take the passage, rewrite it in terms of its own vocabulary, and adapt it in the light of its own situation; it cannot be excluded that the results of this process may already been seen in Mk., and hence that the detailed form of the explanation may represent a development from hints given by Jesus.

So far as the explanation in Lk. is concerned, there is stress on the fact that the seed represents the word of *God*; the Christian message, proclaimed by Jesus and the early church, is not merely the words of men (1 Thes. 2:13). Men are required to believe this word in order to be saved, and those who fail to believe or do not persist in belief are lost. These are distinctive Lucan emphases in the exposition of the parable, but it is important to observe that they are based on elements in the teaching of Jesus as a whole, and do not represent the intrusion of alien theological motifs (I. H. Marshall,* 1969, 63–73).

See 8:4–8 note for bibliography.

(11) Luke omits the introductory question in Mk. 4:13; its suggestion that the disciples were unable to understand the parable may have seemed disrespectful and the question could be omitted with no sense of loss. The opening ἔστιν must be paraphrased as 'it means', and αὕτη is predicative: 'The parable means this'. Luke omits mention of the sower, who plays no part in the interpretation, and has no real significance in Mk. and Mt. (although a christological interpretation is possible). The seed is said to represent the word of God; cf. 5:1 note for this description of the teaching of Jesus, and especially 8:21, diff. Mk., where Luke significantly describes the true brethren of Jesus as those who hear and do the word (Mk., will) of God. Implicitly, therefore, Luke identifies the

sower with Jesus, but leaves open an interpretation in terms of the
preaching of the early church.

(12) The sentence construction in Mk. is extremely involved, and
both Luke and Matthew attempt to simplify it. The phrase οἱ παρὰ τὴν
ὁδόν, 'the ones beside the road', refers to the seeds planted by the road,
and the masculine form may refer to the individual seeds or the persons
represented by them. Strictly speaking, it is the various types of ground
which represent the different groups of people, but with an understandable looseness the people are identified rather with the plants which
spring from the ground as a result of the sowing of the seed. In the first
example, however, it is the ground which is the object of interest. Just as
the seed was plucked from it before it could germinate, so the word is
snatched away by the devil. εἶτα, 'then' is probably drawn from Mk.
4:17 (cf. Mk. 8:25; not elsewhere in the Synoptics). There is no obvious
reason why Luke and Matthew have altered Mark's Σατανᾶς to
διάβολος and πονηρός respectively; cf. 4:2 note. For the linking of the
devil with birds, cf. Jub. 11:11 (Stuhlmueller, 139). Luke and Matthew
both insert a reference to the word finding its lodging place in the heart
(1:51 note) of man. The phrase is a natural periphrasis for Mk. εἰς
αὐτούς. Brown, Apostasy, 121, finds theological significance in the heart
as 'a morally neutral faculty' in Lk., but lands in self-contradiction when
he goes on to say that its 'goodness or wickedness is determined only by
what proceeds from it'. It is unlikely that Luke was conscious of a
theological nuance here. But he does go on to introduce a clause which
has no equivalent in Mk. at this point, and is probably his replacement
for Mk. 4:12b. By this shift, it is claimed, he has avoided the suggestion
that the responsibility for men not being saved is God's; it is the devil's
(J. Dupont*, 102; Schmid, 159; Schramm, 117); this suggestion reads
too much into the shift, since Luke has left Mk. 4:12a standing, and he
quotes the whole reference at Acts 28:26f. (cf. Dietrich, 128 n. 230).
Here and in 8:13 Luke adds πιστεύω to his source, thereby showing that
the message of Jesus must be heard with faith; the aorist participle indicates the initial act of faith, and the present tense in 8:13 indicates that
a continuing attitude is meant (pace Brown, Apostasy, 35–48). What
Luke intends by his use of the word is the same as 'hearing and doing
my words' (6:47); cf. Mk. 1:15. Those who so believe are saved; cf. Mk.
5:34; 10:52; Lk. 7:50; 8:48, 50; 17:19; 18:42; Acts 14:9; 15:11; 16:31;
Rom. 10:9; 1 Cor. 1:21; Eph. 2:8; Jas. 2:14; 5:15. The phraseology is
common in the early church, but it is firmly rooted in Mk., and Luke is
simply bringing out what is already in his sources, namely that physical
healing and spiritual salvation are dependent upon faith in Jesus (cf. 5:20
par. Mk. 2:5).

(13) As for the seeds or plants that grow on the rock, these represent people who receive the word with joy. For δέχομαι (diff. Mk.
λαμβάνω) with τὸν λόγον, cf. Acts 8:14; 11:1; 17:11; 1 Thes. 1:6; 2:13;
Jas. 1:21 (and see Schürmann, Paschamahlbericht, 25–28); here Luke is

using a stereotyped early church phrase. For χαρά cf. 1:14 note; 1 Thes. 1:6. Despite this initial enthusiasm, these people (οὗτοι: v.l. αὐτοί, B* pc; Diglot) have no ῥίζα (cf. 8:6 note); cf. Col. 2:7; Eph. 3:17. The word here should perhaps not be taken literally, but metaphorically. C. Maurer, TDNT VI, 985–990, especially 988, sees significance in Luke's omission of Mark's ἐν ἑαυτοῖς, and thinks that for Luke what matters is 'not man himself but his rooting in the soil outside'; i.e. it is not the strength of the root which is in mind but its function in supplying moisture (8:6) for the plant. Admittedly, Luke does not attempt to explain where the 'moisture' comes from. Such people believe (πιστεύω is added by Luke) only for a time (πρὸς καιρόν, 1 Cor. 7:5; diff. Mk. πρόσκαιρος), Then they fall away: for ἀφίστημι cf. 2:37. Luke dislikes σκανδαλίζομαι (and σκάνδαλον), and has substituted his own favourite expression (cf. Brown, Apostasy, 30f., but his conclusions from the evidence are unconvincing). Luke has also substituted πειρασμός (4:13 note) for Mark's θλῖψις ἢ διωγμὸς διὰ τὸν λόγον. Conzelmann, 90, claims that Luke has done this to avoid a term (θλῖψις) with eschatological associations, but in fact θλῖψις is no more or less eschatological than πειρασμός. Brown, ibid. 12–16, holds that Luke avoided terms which referred to the experience of believers, and substituted one which applies only to apostates; this too is unlikely, for it plays down the significance of 4:1–13 and misunderstands 22:28. It is more probable that Luke has substituted a term which brings out the significance of persecution as a means of tempting erstwhile believers away from their incipient faith.

(14) The style changes from that of the two preceding sentences. Luke uses a neuter form (representing a portion of seed) and employs a pendant nominative (1:36 note; cf. Mt.). The use of πίπτω is a variant for σπείρω and is taken from the parable (8:5). The persons who hear (sc. 'the word', omitted by Luke) are '(crowded together and) choked' (συμπνίγω, 8:42*) and do not 'bear fruit to maturity' (τελεσφορέω**, sc. καρπούς). This happens because they are overcome by various factors. The participle πορευόμενοι (diff. Mk. εἰσπορευόμεναι, referring to the entry of various lusts) can be taken with the ὑπό phrase to mean 'driven along by' (a virtual passive) or absolutely, 'as they go on their way' (JB; AG s.v.: cf. 2 Sa. 3:1), in which case the ὑπό phrase goes with συμπνίγονται. The first possible factor is μέριμνα ('anxiety, worry, care', 21:34*). Mark adds τοῦ αἰῶνος, 'of the present (sinful) age'. Since Luke has similar phrases in 16:8 and 20:34, it is surprising if he has dropped the phrase without trace here, and hence it is probable that τοῦ βίου should be taken with all three preceding nouns (RSV; JB; cf. 21:34). Second is 'wealth' (πλοῦτος*). Luke omits ἀπατή from Mk., perhaps because the thought is taken up in the following phrase. Perhaps also he wanted to stress that riches in themselves constitute a danger to faith. Third, Luke substitutes ἡδοναί (ἡδονή, 'pleasure, enjoyment', Tit. 3:3; Jas. 4:1, 3; 2 Pet. 2:13**) for Mark's difficult phrase αἱ περὶ τὰ λοιπὰ

ἐπιθυμίαι (cf. Tit. 3:3 for the link of ἡδονή and ἐπιθυμία); cf. G. Stählin, TDNT II, 909–926. Brown's view (ibid. 26) that Luke has altered Mark's meaning by substituting a word referring to external events (feasting and drinking; cf. 12:45; 17:27; 21:34) for one referring to inward passions is over-subtle.

(15) Finally, we have what was sown in the good ground (pendant nominative); it represents people who hear the word and hold fast to it (κατέχω is Lucan). It finds a lodging place in a noble and good heart. This phrase, peculiar to Luke, is found in Hellenistic sources (W. Grundmann, TDNT I, 11f.; III, 538–544), and may represent the deliberate use of an expression which conveys the Hellenistic ideal of an honourable character. But this is uncertain. The phrase had found its way into Hellenistic Judaism without any particular force (Tob. 5:14; 2 Mac. 15:12), and it is more likely that Luke has simply used a current form of words suggested by the description of the soil (ἀγαθός in the parable, diff. Mk.; καλός in the explanation). Such persons produce fruit (καρποφορέω, Mk. 4:28; cf. Rom. 7:4f.; Col. 1:6, 10) – here ethical in character (cf. 3:8) – provided, as Luke emphasises in one last telling phrase, that they maintain their faith with steadfastness (ὑπομονή, 21:19; F. Hauck, TDNT IV, 581–588, especially 586; Brown, ibid. 50; cf. Acts 14:22; 11:23; 13:43).

v. The Parable of the Lamp 8:16–18

The last part of the teaching of Jesus in this section is still addressed to the disciples, although in Mk. 4:21–32 the audience is again the crowds; for Luke the teaching here is meant for disciples in particular, and is closely linked to what precedes. The group of sayings – a parable in v. 16, a comment on it in v. 17, and a final admonition with an accompanying comment in v. 18 – is obviously drawn from Mk. 4:21–25. Luke has omitted Mk. 4:23, a command for attention which may have seemed unnecessary for disciples, especially since it repeats 8:8b, and he has also omitted Mk. 4:24b to which he has an earlier parallel at 6:38. The rest of the material has parallels in Luke's other sources (11:33; par. Mt. 5:15; 12:2 par. Mt. 10:26; and 19:26 par. Mt. 25:29), and the wording here has been influenced by these parallels (Schramm, 23–26).

The fact that there are parallels scattered throughout the Q material to the Marcan passage as a whole suggests that in Mk. we may have a secondary combination of originally separate sayings of Jesus handed down orally (Schürmann, I, 469); in view of the general character of Mk. 4 as a collection of teachings of Jesus, this theory is not unlikely. This makes it all the more difficult to determine the original meaning of the separate sayings.

V. 18 should probably be taken as the closing statement of the whole section 8:4–18. It takes up a proverbial sounding statement that the rich become increasingly rich and the poor increasingly poor, which is also applied to stewardship of blessings given by God in 19:26, and applies it to the way in which the disciples hear the word of God; those who pay heed to it will receive further spiritual insight, while those who fail to pay attention will be deprived even of the little they seem to have. The point is parallel to that in 8:10, and emphasises the need to listen to the parables with care. The meaning of the saying in Lk. is essentially the same as in Mk., but in Mk. the thought is more of the last judgment (cf. Mk. 4:24).

The preceding sayings in vs. 16f. are more difficult. The point of the parable of the lamp is simple enough: lamps are not meant to be hidden but to give light to those who enter the house. The comment in v. 17 is that nothing is hidden which will not be revealed and known. The future tense (contrast Mark's purpose clause) probably comes from the Q form of the saying, and is decisive for Luke's understanding of the parable. The parable may then refer to a future manifestation of what is now concealed by God, or to the need for the disciples to spread abroad the knowledge which they have secretly received from Jesus. The former interpretation is suggested by v. 17, but the latter is closer to the actual parable and fits in with the emphasis on bearing fruit in v. 15 On either view there is a contrast between the veiled revelation in the earthly ministry of Jesus and an open revelation in the future. For the Evangelists there is a contrast between the secrecy and the humility which characterised the ministry of Jesus, culminating in the cross, and the open declaration that Jesus was Lord and Christ made in the light of the resurrection. If, then, for the moment Jesus teaches the crowds in parables, one day he will be openly declared to them through the resurrection and the proclamation of the disciples.

The sayings are thus applied especially to the disciples and stress the need for them to make the message of Jesus plain, so that others may see the light (cf. Mt. 5:15), and therefore to pay great heed to how they themselves hear it. There is thus a shift in application as compared with Mk. where the missionary element is lacking; Luke has been influenced more by the Q form of the saying. See further on 11:33 and 12:2 where the same sayings are used in other contexts.

See J. Jeremias, 'Die Lampe unter dem Scheffel', in *Abba*, 99–102; J. Dupont, 'La Lampe sur le lampadaire dans l'évangile de saint Luc (VIII, 16; XI, 33)' in *Au service de la Parole de Dieu (Mélanges offerts à A. M. Charue)*, Gembloux, 1969, 43–59; Derrett, 189–207; G. Schneider, 'Das Bildwort von der Lampe', ZNW 61, 1970, 183–209; F. Hahn, 'Die Worte vom Licht Lk 11, 33–36', in Hoffmann, *Orientierung*, 107–138.

(16) Luke omits Mark's opening καὶ ἔλεγεν αὐτοῖς ὅτι, since he envisages Jesus as continuing his previous teaching to the disciples. In Mk. the parable is expressed in two rhetorical questions, and the lamp is the subject; there is no statement about the purpose of the lamp. Luke, however, follows the Q formulation (11:33; Mt. 5:15) which has a statement in which the lamp is the object, so that the emphasis falls more on the activity of the person who is responsible for lighting it. It is

impossible to decide whether the Marcan form with its double question is original (so cautiously Bultmann, 82, 91; F. Hahn*, 111f.) or the Q form (G. Schneider*, 190f., 197–199). The Marcan and Q forms probably represent two independent traditions (Wrege, 32f.), perhaps going back to two originally distinct sayings.

λύχνος is an oil lamp (11:33f., 36; 12:35; 15:8*) and λυχνία a lamp-stand (11:33*; W. Michaelis, TDNT IV, 324–327). ἅπτω, 'to kindle', is Lucan (11:33; 15:8; Acts 28:2**); Mt. 5:15 has καίω, which Luke uses elsewhere with the sense 'to be burning'. καλύπτω, 'to cover up, hide' (23:30*), is peculiar to Luke's version and probably added by him as a clarification. Luke's use of σκεῦος, 'vessel' (17:31*), instead of μόδιος (11:33 and parallels) reflects town rather than country usage (Schürmann, I, 466 n. 163) or a Lucan dislike of foreign words (Schramm, 24); in either case it represents a clarification. The description is of a patently foolish action (though the saying may originally have referred to the normal way of extinguishing a lamp to avoid fumes, Jeremias, *Parables*, 120f.). It would be even more foolish to hide the lamp underneath the bed. ὑποκάτω occurs here only in Lk.-Acts, and there is no obvious reason for a change from ὑπό in the parallels (cf. BD 12³; 215²). The bed occurs in Mk. which is probably Luke's source at this point. Instead of such folly, men place a lamp on a lampstand; Luke here has ἐπί with the genitive against all the parallels which have the accusative, which is odd in view of Luke's own preference for the accusative, but may be simply elegant variation. A final clause, absent from Mk., indicates the purpose of the lamp; there is a parallel in Mt. 5:15 which shows that Luke is here following Q, though it is not clear which form is original. In Mt. the lamp gives light to everybody in the house, but in Lk. it is those who enter the house (εἰσπορεύομαι, 11:33; 18:24; 19:30; 22:10) who see the light (φῶς, Lk. 11:33). The suggestion that Luke is secondary because he is describing a Hellenistic house with a vestibule (Jeremias, *Parables*, 27 n. 9) is weak, because in any sort of house the light shines on those who enter. More important is the question whether Luke himself has introduced the guests in order to allude to gentile converts entering the church, or simply anybody who comes into the circle of Jesus' followers. Since the clause is also present in 11:33, where a reference to gentiles is unlikely, and since the missionary element was already present in Q, it is probable that Luke has merely stressed an existing emphasis. In the present context there may be a slight emphasis on the responsibility of the outsiders to come in and see the light, but it would be unwise to press this.

(17) We now have a commentary on the parable in which its significance is indicated; the commentary is not an exact fit with the parable, since the idea of something originally hidden is not present in the parable, unless perhaps in the thought of the unkindled lamp which sheds no light until it is lit. The wording follows Mk. closely, but with a change from Mark's final clauses to relative clauses, and the inclusion of

the idea of knowledge, as in the Q parallel, 12:2 (cf. 8:10). The use of the future, therefore, is not due to Luke himself, but it fits his understanding of the saying better than the Marcan construction. The saying states in two parallel clauses that whatever is hidden or secret will be revealed and made known. κρυπτός, 'hidden', is taken from Mk. but also occurs in the second clause of the Q form. Luke has φανερὸν γενήσεται diff. Mk., possibly under the influence of the following ἐγένετο in Mk. ἀπόκρυφος, 'hidden' (Col. 2:3), is also from Mk. εἰς φανερὸν ἐλθεῖν means 'to come to light' (AG 860). The passives suggest that a divine act may be in view. In 12:2 the logion is applied to the unveiling of secrets on the day of judgment. Here the context refers to the disciples making known publicly what Jesus has told them secretly (cf. Mt. 10:26f.) and the principle appears to be applied to the present secrecy and future manifestation of the message of the kingdom.

(18) Again (cf. 8:16) Luke omits Mark's connective, and substitutes a summarising οὖν. Let the disciples take care (βλέπω, cf. 21:8 par. Mk. 13:5) how they hear; the use of πῶς, diff. Mk. τί, clarifies the meaning. For ἀκούω Black, 300, suggests the meaning 'to be instructed', 'to receive (traditional) teaching from'. The parables must be heard with care and attention. For if a person (ὃς ἄν generalises, diff. Mk. ὅς) has knowledge, he will be given (more) – by God, but if he has none – though he may deceive himself into thinking he has some (cf. Jn. 9:40f.) – even the false knowledge which he thinks he has (δοκέω, added by Luke) will be taken away from him. H. Hanse, TDNT II, 827, interprets the saying to mean that if the disciples have understood the teaching in such a way that they spread it further, they have truly received it and will do so more and more; this is to read the teaching of vs. 16f. into the verse and narrows the sense.

vi. Jesus' True Relatives 8:19–21

Luke omits Mk. 4:26–34 (for Mk. 4:30–32 cf. Lk. 13:18f.), no doubt because the section was not relevant to his present purpose of presenting Jesus' teaching on the importance of hearing the word of God aright. Instead he substitutes material which he has held over from an earlier point (Mk. 3:31–35) and which now fits in admirably to conclude the present section by indicating the results of response to the message of Jesus. The person who responds to that message by hearing therein the word of God and obeying it is regarded as a member of the family of Jesus; his situation is the same as that of the man who hears the words of Jesus in the Sermon on the Plain and does them (6:46–49). What is termed 'hearing and doing' here corresponds to faith in other parts of the NT. The lesson thus emphasised is due to Luke who has altered an original 'do the will of God' in Mk. 3:35 to the present phrase which brings out the link with 8:11, 15. Moreover, Luke has abbreviated Mk. at this point, leaving out the material which deals especially with Jesus' attitude to his own family. Thus the note of possible strife between the family and Jesus is removed, and the motive of the visit and its results are left obscure; the arrival of the family becomes simply the occasion for the saying of Jesus on which Luke wishes to lay emphasis. It is perhaps significant that the place of Jesus in the 'spiritual' family is not defined; in other words, the saying has not been subject to any christological reflection and development.

Luke's source here is patently Mk. (cf. Schramm, 123f.). The origin of Mark's story is not clear. Dibelius, 60, regarded Mk. 3:31–34 as the original scene, to which 3:35 was appended by the church (by Mark himself: J. D. Crossan*, 97f.). Bultmann, 29, however, argued that Mk. 3:35 was the original logion, around which the ideal scene in 3:31–34 was composed by the community: to be sure, for Bultmann (153f.) v. 35 is itself a community product. This view has been taken up by J. Lambrecht*, 249–251, who argues that it was Mark himself, rather than the community, who created the ideal scene in vs. 31–34 for the saying in v. 35, which is a Marcan form of the Q logion in Lk. 11:28.

Bultmann's arguments for his position have been shown to be weak and doctrinaire (Taylor, 245), and Lambrecht's position is no stronger. It is possible to argue in Dibelius's favour that v. 35 is an addition to the pronouncement story which finds its climax in v. 34, but this view rests on the doubtful principle that a pronouncement story must end with only one statement by Jesus, all else being added by the church for its own purposes. In any case, it remains more probable that Mark is using a story drawn from tradition, and that this tradition has a historical basis.

See J. D. Crossan, 'Mark and the Relatives of Jesus', Nov.T 15, 1973, 81–113; J. Lambrecht, 'The Relatives of Jesus in Mark', Nov.T 16, 1974, 241–258.

(19) The scene begins with the arrival of Jesus' mother and brothers. Luke uses a favourite word, παραγίνομαι, diff. Mk. ἔρχομαι, and sets it in the singular, according to the rule that when the verb stands first it agrees with the nearer subject (MH III, 313; BD 135; cf. 8:22; Acts 11:14). After μήτηρ Luke omits αὐτοῦ diff. Mk.; it is added in ℵ D al it; Diglot (which thus avoid a minor Mt.-Lk. agreement against Mk.). It is generally thought that the brothers of Jesus were the children of Mary and Joseph (2:7 note); Joseph does not appear in the Gospels after the infancy narratives; the most plausible explanation of this is that he was by now dead. In Luke's account the family is unable to come into contact with Jesus (συντυγχάνω**) because of the crowd which, according to Mk., was sitting around him. Like Matthew, Luke lays little stress on the presence of the crowd, a fact which is connected with his omission of Mk. 3:34 in which Jesus identifies his true relatives in general terms with the crowd. Nor does Luke state why the relatives visited Jesus; Mk. 3:20f. is left out, for Luke's interest at this point is not in the relatives themselves.

(20) The use of ἀπαγγέλλω, diff. Mk. λέγω, is Lucan. Bystanders tell Jesus that his mother and brothers (Luke omits mention of his

sisters, diff. Mk.) are standing (cf. Mk. 3:31) outside; the use of ἔξω is slightly strange, since Luke has omitted to state that Jesus was in a house (Mk. 3:20); it is unlikely that Luke uses the term symbolically of being outside the circle of disciples (*pace* Schürmann, I, 470). The relatives wished to see Jesus; ἰδεῖν is perhaps used with the sense 'to visit' (Acts 16:40; 1 Cor. 16:7; AG s.v.; the interpretation of Conzelmann, 41f., that they wanted to see miracles (cf. 9:9; 23:8) is false).

(21) Luke omits Mk. 3:33b–34 which may have seemed derogatory to the family of Jesus, and avoids the general remark of Jesus about his true relatives in favour of the particular point that his mother and brothers (so Mk. 3:34 rather than 35) are those who hear (om. Mark) the word of God (11:28; diff. Mk. τὸ θέλημα τοῦ θεοῦ) and do it (αὐτόν, read by TR; *Diglot,* is with poor authority is redundant). Thus Luke stresses the need to hear the message of Jesus and respond to it in order to enter his family.

f. A Group of Mighty Works (8:22–56)

The pattern of events in Lk. continues to be determined by that in Mk.; following his source Luke now presents a sequence of mighty works, three in number (the third being a double miracle), in which Jesus is revealed to his disciples as the possessor of divine power over the elements, demons and physical evil, including death itself. Thus to the witness of Jesus by word is added that by power, and the whole sequence prepares the way for the confession of Jesus as Messiah in 9:18–27. The emphasis, however, is not simply on the power of Jesus; the mighty works reveal his compassion and willingness to save in situations of human need.

i. The Master of the Storm 8:22–25

Luke's account of a stormy journey across the Sea of Galilee, during which Jesus stilled the elements by his simple command and thus posed the question of his identity for the disciples, is taken from Mk. with his usual abbreviation and stylistic improvement. The agreements in wording with Mt. against Mk. are hardly sufficient to justify the suspicion that another tradition was also used (*pace* Schramm, 124f.).

As a result of his insertion of 8:19–21 into his source, and perhaps also to give the impression that the following incidents took place on the same day, Luke has altered Mark's setting on the evening of the day of teaching in parables to a vague 'one day'. He stresses the way in which Jesus took the initiative in entering the boat (though this is not absent from Mk.; cf. 4:35), and brings forward the detail about his falling asleep to a more logical place before the rise of the storm. The approach of the disciples to Jesus for help is expressed more respectfully than in Mk.

Similarly, Jesus treats the disciples less reproachfully, and attributes their cries to a forgetful faith rather than to complete lack of faith.

These changes do not significantly alter the content of the story as recorded in Mk., and the same basic lessons shine through Luke's account. Jesus is seen as the lord of the elements; the power possessed by God in the OT is seen to be present in him (cf. Pss. 89:8f.; 93:3f.; 106:8f.; 107:23–30; Is. 51:9f.). Just as men prayed to God for deliverance from the perils of the sea, so the disciples turn to Jesus. The motif of Jesus lying asleep during the storm has its OT counterpart in the story of Jonah, but it seems unlikely that we are intended to find in Jonah a type of Jesus at this point; there are merely natural echoes of the story (cf. J. Jeremias, TDNT III, 408). Taylor, 275, cites stronger echoes of Virgil, Aeneid IV, 554, 560.

Conservative scholars find it possible to accept the account as substantially historical (Taylor, 272f.; Rengstorf, 108; Schürmann, I, 479; cf. Schweizer, 60f.). The Jewish parallel (j. Berach. 11:1 (Bultmann, 249f.); cited as j. Berach. 9, 13b, 22 in SB I, 452) is obviously based on the story of Jonah, and is late. There is nothing in the story itself to demand that it is an invention, and hence a verdict on its historicity depends on the reader's general understanding of the person of Jesus.

See Kertelge, 91–100.

(22) Luke dates the incident vaguely ἐν μιᾷ τῶν ἡμερῶν (5:17; 20:1, diff. Mk. ἐν ἐκείνῃ τῇ ἡμέρᾳ; cf. 5:12 note), thereby retaining the connection with the preceding section of teaching. In Mk. Jesus takes the initiative by suggesting the boat trip to the other side, and is then taken by the disciples in the boat; in Lk. he enters the boat along with the disciples and then suggests the trip. Luke and Matthew both use ἐμβαίνω, diff. Mk.; the difference is due to the fact that only in Mk. is the trip connected with the parable scene in which Jesus is already in the boat and does not need to embark afresh in it. The phrase εἰς πλοῖον without the article (diff. Mk. and Mt.) leaves open whose boat it was, but it is obviously the disciples' boat; did Luke wonder whether those who had left all to follow Jesus still had 'the boat' at their disposal? Since the story does not begin at the lakeside (8:4 diff. Mk. 4:1), Luke clarifies τὸ πέραν*, 'the other side', by adding τῆς λίμνης (cf. 5:1). The use of ἀνάγομαι, 'to put out to sea' (Acts, 13x), is Lucan.

(23) The disciples set sail at Jesus' command; πλέω, 'to sail' is Lucan (Acts, 4x; Rev. 18:17**). Meanwhile, he falls asleep (ἀφυπνόω**, originally 'to arouse'; the aorist is ingressive), and is not disturbed by the storm that arises. The lake is surrounded by steep mountains down which the wind is funnelled in sudden, strong squalls. καταβαίνω (2:51) can be used of rain and the like (Mt. 7:25, 27; Rev. 16:21); λαῖλαψ is a 'whirlwind, hurricane' (Mk. 4:37; 2 Pet. 2:17**). The verb συμπληρόω, 'to be swamped' (also 'to be fulfilled', 9:51; Acts 2:1**), is used loosely with a personal subject, just as it can be in English. As a result

the disciples were in danger (κινδυνεύω, Acts 19:27, 40; 1 Cor. 15:30**). Luke tells us merely the essentials and leaves out the colourful details about Jesus asleep on the cushion in the stern in Mk.; he thus loses the climax which is stressed in Mk., namely that Jesus continued sleeping undisturbed by the storm.

(24) As in Mt. (diff. Mk) the disciples approach Jesus; for similar coincidences in the use of προσέρχομαι see 8:44; 20:27 and 23:52 (in these other cases Mark has ἔρχομαι); the coincidence is fairly natural, perhaps due to a reverential use of the word in the later Gospels (cf. Schürmann, I, 475 n. 16), but this point should not be pressed. The disciples address Jesus as ἐπιστάτης (diff. Mk. διδάσκαλος; Mt. κύριος); the title expresses the relationship between Jesus and the disciples as being different from that between him and other men (5:5 note), and the doubling (6:46 note) here suggests the urgency of the request. Luke omits Mark's οὐ μέλει σοι ὅτι, which may have seemed derogatory; Matthew inserts the appeal σῶσον. The use of ἀπόλλυμι (4:34; et al.) may take on a broader meaning in the light of its frequent use later in the Gospel where it signifies spiritual as well as physical danger (e.g. 13:3, 5; 15:24, 32; 19:10), and thus allow for a broader exposition of the story in terms of the spiritual need of the church and its members (Schürmann, I, 475).

The role of Jesus over against the disciples is stressed by the introductory ὁ δέ, diff. Mk. καί. He wakens (διεγείρω, only in this verse in Lk.), and rebukes the wind (cf. 4:35) and wave (κλύδων, Jas. 1:6**). With Matthew Luke omits the words spoken to the elements; the possibility of understanding the narrative as an exorcism of the wind is thus reduced. The wind and waves cease their commotion (παύομαι, 5:4, diff. Mk. κοπάζω) and there is a calm (γαλήνη, Mk. 4:39; Mt. 8:26**).

(25) But the point of the story is not simply that Jesus could still the storm, but rather that the disciples should have trusted his power to help them. Luke omits Mark's rebuke of their timidity (Matthew omits the whole of Jesus' comments) and simply leaves the question, 'Where is your faith?' The difference from Mk.: 'Do you not yet have faith?' suggests that for Luke disciples are characterised by faith, even if it can become weak or evanescent on occasion, whereas for Mark they do not yet possess faith (Conzelmann, 42; Brown, Apostasy, 58f.). This suggestion is perhaps unfair to Mark, for his question surely implies that by now the disciples ought to have had faith. Such faith is in the power of God – but in that power as revealed in Jesus.

The effect of the whole event was to fill the disciples with fear in the presence of the supernatural and also with wonder (θαυμάζω, par. Mt., diff. Mk.); cf. 9:43; 11:14. The latter attitude arises out of reflection on the incident and its implications for their understanding of Jesus. The question which must have often come into their minds on earlier occasions now takes on concrete form and prepares the way for Peter's later confession: in view of all this (ἄρα, 1:66; 12:42; 22:23) who is Jesus? For the form of the question and the elliptical use of ὅτι see 4:36. What was asked there in view of Jesus' power over demons, is now asked again in view of his ability to command the winds and sea; note how the clause is rephrased with ἐπιτάσσω (diff. Mk.) on the analogy of 4:36; the final clause καὶ ὑπακούουσιν αὐτῷ is omitted by p⁷⁵ B 700 eth; (*Diglot*), but is required by the parallel with 4:36, and its loss can be explained in terms of homoioarcton with 8:26. The question is not answered, but the answer is implicit for the reader who knows his OT: what God did then, Jesus does now.

ii. The Gerasene Demoniac 8:26–39

Following Mk. Luke proceeds to narrate the second in this series of mighty works performed by Jesus; it is possible that the juxtaposition of the stories was seen to be significant in the light of the description of God as the One who stills 'the roaring of the seas, the roaring of their waves, the tumult of the peoples' (Ps. 65:7; E. Hoskyns and N. Davey, *The Riddle of the New Testament*, London, 1947, 69–71; Nineham, 152). The story takes place expressly in the Decapolis, a predominantly gentile area, and this suggests that we may see in it an anticipation of the future ministry of the church to the gentiles (cf. Acts 26:18, cited by Schürmann, I, 480). But the main point is the demonstration of the power of Jesus to deal with an especially severe case of demon possession; through Jesus God did great things for an unhappy victim (8:39). There was no need for Luke to make extensive alterations to his source in order to underline the message, but at various points his typical vocabulary and motifs are evident. He stresses the 'saving' of the man (8:36), and the fear induced in the spectators (8:37). He alone refers to the 'abyss' in connection with the exorcism of the demons (8:31). Otherwise he has merely improved the narrative stylistically (cf. R. Pesch*, 57–64).

Mark's narrative is by no means free from difficulty (Bultmann, 224f.; Dibelius, 84–87; Taylor, 277f.; Schweizer, *Markus*, 62f.; R. Pesch, 9–49):

1. There are some uneven features (cf. Mk. 5:2/6 and the flashback in 5:8) which may suggest that the narrative has undergone some development and expansion.

2. Various motifs in the story of the exorcism, especially the account of the destruction of the pigs and the associated conversation, are said to be legendary. Hence it has been suggested that an originally secular story has been transformed into a story about Jesus, or that a simple story of an exorcism performed by Jesus has been considerably elaborated. Such motifs as the outwitting of the demons and the punishment of gentiles for keeping unclean animals in the holy land have been detected in the story of the drowning of the swine. The immorality of destroying the innocent swine has even been held against Jesus.

The moral problem can be safely dismissed: one man is of greater value than many swine. Nor do the motifs of outwitting demons and punishing gentiles appear to have been present to Mark (or Luke), although they cannot be ruled out at earlier stages in the tradition. The arguments for various features being additions to the story are weightier, but they perhaps depend on too rigorous an application of the 'rules' of form criticism which prescribe the patterns that stories of exorcisms *must* follow. The biggest problem lies in the demonology presupposed in the story, which is so similar to that attested in popular superstitions of the time that it is difficult to believe that it corresponds to objective fact. It may well be that Jesus, while not sharing the man's superstitions, allowed the destruction of the swine in order to convince him that he was really free from the demons. Or we may have to reckon with the early church's use of legendary features to express the supreme power of Jesus, while not denying the reality of the demonic forces opposed to Jesus (cf. Schürmann, I, 487).

3. The conclusion of the story (Mk. 5:18–20) has been regarded as an addition relating the story to missionary work in the Decapolis and to the 'messianic secret'. The addition, if any, is pre-Marcan. But the arguments for addition are not strong, and again presuppose that a story cannot have had a somewhat complex structure of motifs from the outset.

See Kertelge, 101–110; R. Pesch, *Der Besessene von Gerasa*, Stuttgart, 1972 (with full bibliography).

(26) The story follows directly on from that of the stilling of the storm. The disciples 'sail down', i.e. towards the land (καταπλέω**, diff. Mk. ἔρχομαι), and reach the territory of the Γερασηνοί. A difficult textual problem arises here, since in all three Gospels the MSS offer different readings for the name of the inhabitants of the area (for the evidence see especially Metzger, 23f., cf. 84, 145). The evidence is briefly as follows:

Γερασηνῶν	Mt. 8:28							it vg sy^hm2	sa
	Mk. 5:1	ℵ*	B	D				it vg	sa
	Lk. 8:26	p^75	B	D				it vg	sa
Γαδαρηνῶν	Mt. 8:28	(ℵ*)	BC		Θ			sy^sph	
	Mk. 5:1	A	C	K		f13 pl		sy^ph	
	Lk. 8:26	A		K	W	f13 pl		sy^csph	
Γεργεσηνῶν	Mt. 8:28	ℵc	C^m	K	LW	f1f13 pl	sy^hml	bo
	Mk. 5:1	ℵc		L	Θf1		sy^shm	bo
	Lk. 8:26	ℵ		L	Θf1			bo

Γερασηνοί refers to the inhabitants of Gerasa, modern Jerash, some 30 m. SE of the Sea of Galilee. It is unlikely to have had territory reaching to the shore of the lake. (R. Pesch*, 18f., suggests that this name belongs to an original form of the story which did not contain the swine episode; other readings are due to the inclusion of the swine motif and the need to obtain a location by the sea; but if so, it is hard to see how the name of Gerasa persisted in the textual tradition). Γαδαρηνοί refers to the inhabitants of Gadara, modern Um Qeia, 5 m. SE of the lake. It possessed lands extending to the lake (cf. Jos. Vita 42) and its coins often bore a ship on them (Lohmeyer, 94). The incident may have taken place in this toparchy, known by the name of its administrative centre, and this caused difficulty for scribes who thought that the town was meant (Sherwin-White, 128 n. 3). As for Γεργεσηνοί, this probably refers to the site known as Khersa on the lakeside, in the vicinity of which are cliffs.

The solution of the textual problem must begin from Mk. Here the best attested reading is Γερασηνῶν, and Cranfield, 176, suggests that Mark wrote this with reference to a town on the lakeside. Later scribes mistook this for a reference to Gerasa, and attempted to correct an obvious error. The reading Γεργεσηνῶν appears to be due to the influence of Origen (in Joh. 6:41; cf. 10:12) who spoke of a lakeside town called Gergesa. Gadara was another guess. It appears that Γαδαρηνῶν is the original text in Mt. – perhaps Matthew was the author of this correction, which then found its way into MSS of Mk. As for Lk., the best attested form is Γερασηνῶν, as in Mk., and the MSS reflect the same confusion as in the other Gospels. The same textual problem arises in 8:37, with some slight differences in the testimony of the MSS. For the benefit of his non-Palestinian readers Luke adds (correctly) that the place is opposite Galilee (ἀντιπέρα** takes a genitive of separation). For the site see Finegan, 62.

(27) Although Luke often features unnecessary genitive absolutes, he here removes one from Mk. and replaces it correctly with a participial phrase in the dative. As Jesus disembarked onto the land, he was met by a man with demons: ὑπαντάω, 'to (come or go to) meet'; also 'to oppose', 14:31*. Luke substitutes ἀνήρ for ἄνθρωπος. He adds ἐκ τῆς πόλεως (cf. Mk. 5:14) to prepare for the later mention of the inhabitants. For ἔχων δαιμόνια cf. 4:33; Diglot follows many authorities in reading ὃς εἶχεν for ἔχων (p⁷⁵ ℵ B al). The man had been possessed for a long time (χρόνῳ ἱκανῷ), the textual variants ἐκ χρόνων ἱκανῶν καί and ἀπὸ χρόνων ἱκανῶν ὅς are less well attested, and Lucan usage favours the reading in UBS (cf. 3:16 note; 20:29; 23:8; Acts 8:11; 14:3; 27:9); for the use of the dative see MH III, 243f. The aorist ἐνεδύσατο is equivalent to a pluperfect, and the detail is deduced from Mk. 5:15; for the verb cf. 12:22; 15:22; 24:49*. The man did not stay at home, but lived among the tombs (μνῆμα, 23:53; 24:1*), an obvious place to expect to find demons. Luke passes over the other details of his madness at this point and brings them in later.

(28) When the man saw Jesus – Luke omits the detail of his running from a distance to him – he cried out, fell before him and shouted

at him. The following verse makes it clear that all this was a reaction to the command of Jesus that the demon should leave the man. The words of the man are repeated almost identically from Mk., and their opening resembles 4:34 (par. Mk. 1:24). Again there is the exclamation, 'Do not meddle with me', but this time Jesus is addressed as the Son of the most high God (1:32 note). The title has been taken over from the tradition utilised by Mark and expresses the sovereign majesty of Jesus over against the demons. Hence the demon beseeches him ($\delta\acute{\epsilon}o\mu\alpha\iota$ diff. Mk. $\acute{o}\rho\kappa\acute{\iota}\zeta\omega$ is weaker) not to torment him ($\beta\alpha\sigma\alpha\nu\acute{\iota}\zeta\omega$*).

(29) Luke retains Mark's method of developing the story by means of a 'flash-back' which explains why the demon-possessed man cried out in this way. He strengthens Mark's $\lambda\acute{\epsilon}\gamma\omega$ by substituting $\pi\alpha\rho\alpha\gamma\gamma\acute{\epsilon}\lambda\lambda\omega$ to express the command; the use of the imperfect (where an aorist might be expected, MH III, 65) is perhaps meant to indicate the unfulfilled or incomplete action of the verb. The use of an indirect command diff. Mk. is a stylistic improvement. Then Luke develops the flash-back by incorporating the details about the man's madness which he had earlier omitted (cf. Mk. 5:4f.; for similar changes in order cf. 8:42a, 46b, 51b, 55c; 9:14a, 34b, 48c). By this alteration Luke perhaps emphasises the compassionate reason why Jesus acted to exorcise the man from the demon (Schürmann, I, 483). The use of the plural in the phrase $\pi o\lambda\lambda o\tilde{\iota}\varsigma\chi\rho\acute{o}\nu o\iota\varsigma$ is Lucan (20:9; 23:8; Acts, 3x); it can mean either 'for a long time' (Hellenistic use of the dative for an accusative of time; 1:75 note) or 'on many occasions' (diff. Mk. $\pi o\lambda\lambda\acute{\alpha}\kappa\iota\varsigma$). $\sigma\upsilon\nu\alpha\rho\pi\acute{\alpha}\zeta\omega$ (Acts, 3x**) is 'to seize with violence'. The ancient world knew only one answer for such mad behaviour, restraint. The man used to be bound ($\delta\epsilon\sigma\mu\epsilon\acute{\upsilon}\omega$, Acts 22:4; Mt. 23:4**) – note the iterative imperfects – with hand chains ($\ddot{\alpha}\lambda\upsilon\sigma\iota\varsigma$, Acts 12:6f.; 21:33; 28:20) and fetters on his feet ($\pi\acute{\epsilon}\delta\eta$, Mk. 5:4**); the datives should be construed with the participle $\phi\upsilon\lambda\alpha\sigma\sigma\acute{o}\mu\epsilon\nu o\varsigma$. Time and again, however, the man burst the fetters; for $\delta\iota\alpha\rho\rho\acute{\eta}\sigma\sigma\omega$ (cf. 5:6 (diff. Mk. $\delta\iota\alpha\sigma\pi\acute{\alpha}\omega$); $\delta\epsilon\sigma\mu\acute{\alpha}$ is a neuter plural from the masculine $\delta\epsilon\sigma\mu\acute{o}\varsigma$, 13:16; Acts, 5x. Then the man was driven ($\acute{\epsilon}\lambda\alpha\acute{\upsilon}\nu\omega$, Mk. 6:48; Jn. 6:19; Jas. 3:4; 2 Pet. 2:17**) by ($\acute{\alpha}\pi\acute{o}$, 8:34) the demon into the desert (Luke uses the plural; cf. 1:80).

(30) The story continues after the 'interruption'. Jesus' reply to the demon's outburst (v. 28) is to ask its name. There is no indication that the purpose of learning the demon's name is to gain power over it, for the information is not used in this way. The man answered, $\Lambda\epsilon\gamma\iota\acute{\omega}\nu$, a Latin loan-word (*legio*) meaning a legion or regiment of soldiers (Mk. 5:9, 15; Mt. 26:53**). The word expresses the man's feeling of being inhabited by a multitude of evil spirits (H. Preisker, TDNT IV, 68f.); the continuation of the story in Mk. 5:13 indicates that some 2,000 spirits are envisaged, although a legion was normally about 5–6,000 strong. The grave of a man of the Fourteenth Legion has been discovered at Gadara (G. A. Smith, *The Historical Geography of the Holy Land*, London, 1925, 461). It has been suggested that the man may have had a

traumatic experience in childhood with the soldiery which led to his insanity. Jeremias, *Promise*, 30 n. 99, has claimed that in Aramaic *ligyônō'* could mean a soldier or a legion, and that it has been wrongly understood in Greek in the latter sense; hence developed the embellishment of the story with the detail about the 2,000 swine. But Jeremias' explanation of the use of the name 'soldier' is unconvincing, and his theory remains unlikely. The one feature in its favour is the oscillation between singular and plural in the narrative; up to this point (but see v. 27) Luke has spoken of one demon, as in Mk., but from now on the plural is used (Jeremias is wrong in claiming that Mark returns to the singular usage in 5:15). This is intelligible, however, since to outward appearance the man was possessed by one demonic power; moreover, the possibility of multiple possession is found in Lk. 8:2.

(31) Where Mark uses the singular form of the verb (quite correctly) to refer to a plurality of demons, Luke removes the possible ambiguity by substituting the plural. The demons have no desire that Jesus should command them (8:25) to depart into the 'abyss'; ἄβυσσος, 'abyss, depth, underworld' (Rom. 10:7; Rev. 9:1, 3, 11; 11:17; 17:8; 20:1, 3**) is here used of the place of imprisonment for evil powers; it figures in Hebrew cosmology as the 'watery deep' below the earth to which the seas are connected, and the idea of spirits being confined in it appears in apocalyptic (Jub. 5:6ff.; 1 En. 10; 18; cf. Jude 6; 2 Pet. 2:4). There is no need to see Hellenistic influence at this point (Schmid 162,); cf. J. Jeremias, TDNT I, 9f. The mention of the abyss replaces Mark's simple reference to the demons being sent out of the area, but appears to arise from Luke's understanding of v. 28 where the demons fear being tormented by Jesus. Matthew has the insertion 'before the time'. It would appear that Matthew thinks of the demons being submitted to punishment before the end of the world, and that Luke has included the place of such imprisonment and punishment in place of Mark's rather vague phrase.

(32) Luke follows closely Mark's description of the herd of swine grazing on the hillside. ἀγέλη is 'herd' (8:33; Mk. 5:11, 13; Mt. 8:30–32**); χοῖρος is 'swine' (8:33; 15:15f.). ἱκανός in the plural (diff. Mk. μέγας) means 'numerous'. βόσκω is 'to feed, tend' (8:34; 15:15; Jn. 21:15, 17), passive, 'to graze'. Swine were unclean animals; for a Jewish narrator it would be highly appropriate for demons to inhabit them. The demons requested Jesus to allow them to enter them; Luke's use of ἐπιτρέπω, diff. Mk. πέμπω, conforms to the use of the verb at the end of the verse.

(33) Thus when the demons left the man, they entered the swine (Luke clarifies Mk. slightly). The visible effect was that the herd rushed (ὁρμάω, Acts 7:57; 19:29) down from the bank (κρημνός, Mt. 8:32; Mk. 5:13**) into the lake (5:1 note) and were drowned (8:7 note). Thus it is clear that the man has been freed from the demons. But what is the further effect? According to O. Bauernfeind, *Die Worte der Dämonen*

im Markusevangelium, Stuttgart, 1927, 34–56, the demons deceive
Jesus by causing the loss of the swine, bringing Jesus into bad odour
with the herdsmen, and thus scoring a final victory. In the end, however,
Jesus wins, for, although he himself is forced to leave the area, he leaves
the healed man as a witness. This motif may have been present in the
story at some stage in its transmission, but it is certainly not indicated in
any of the Gospels, and must remain hypothetical. According to
Schürmann, I, 484f., the destruction of the swine shows that even after
leaving the man the demons are still active and can cause harm; they
have not been sent to the abyss, nor drowned, but they can continue
their evil course – admittedly now only by permission of Jesus. This
suggestion depends on whether water as such is an abode of demons; it
is, however, 'a demon-destroying force' (T. Sol. 5:11; 11:6, cited by J.
M. Hull, *Hellenistic Magic and the Synoptic Tradition,* London, 1974,
100). It remains more likely that the motif is that of the destruction of
the demons, who gained only a temporary respite from punishment by
entry into the swine.

(34) The sight (ἰδόντες, diff. Mk.) naturally terrified the herdsmen
who fled and announced what had happened in the city and the countryside. Luke has added τὸ γεγονός from the following verse. For the use
of ἀγρός cf. 9:12; 15:15 note. The use of εἰς with ἀπαγγέλλω is loose,
but intelligible; the doubling of the preposition is said to be Semitic
(Black, 114f.).

(35) The people (impersonal plural) came out to see what had happened; Luke's use of ἐξέρχομαι avoids Mark's repetition of the simple
form. He also substitutes his favourite word εὑρίσκω for Mk. θεωρέω.
Mark's extremely awkward description of the man as one who had been
possessed by demons is avoided by a more elegant paraphrase. He is
now clothed (ἱματίζω,. Mk. 5:15**) and sound in mind (σωφρονέω, Mk.
5:15; 2 Cor. 5:13; cf. Rom. 12:3; Tit. 2:6; 1 Pet. 4:7**; U. Luck, TDNT
VII, 1097–1104). To Mark's description that he was sitting (instead of
rushing wildly about), Luke adds that he was at the feet of Jesus; cf.
8:41 (par. Mk. 5:22); 7:38; 10:39; 17:16; Mt. 15:30; Jn. 11:32; Acts
5:2, 10; *et al.* The implication is that the man was listening to what Jesus
had to say; the position is that of a disciple. It is no wonder that at the
sight of this miraculous transformation the people were afraid.

(36) Their fear increased as they heard from the witnesses the
story of how the former demoniac had been healed. It is curious that
Luke here has ἀπαγγέλλω, 'to announce', diff. Mk. διηγέομαι, 'to
narrate', and vice versa in v. 39; it looks as though he prefers ἀπαγγέλλω
for secular announcement and διηγέομαι for Christian narration. The introduction of σῴζω (diff. Mark's colourless γίνομαι) stresses the healing
of the man, and no doubt also – for Luke and his readers – the spiritual
'saving' of the man. Luke omits the detail that the witnesses also told
about the swine.

(37) Luke makes clear the change of subject (diff. Mk.) with ἅπαν

τὸ πλῆθος (a Lucan phrase; 19:37; 23:1; Acts 25:24; cf. Lk. 1:10; Acts 15:12). For περίχωρος cf. 3:3; and for Γερασηνῶν (and the variant readings) see 8:26 note. The people give a peremptory command (ἠρώτησεν, aorist; MH III, 65) to Jesus to depart, because they are so afraid – a Lucan addition (for the language cf. 1:12 note and 4:38 note). It is not clear whether they fear further loss to themselves (Rengstorf, 110) or are simply overcome by fright at the supernatural (Schürmann, I, 486). In any case, Jesus accepts their rejection of himself; Luke significantly develops Mark's casual genitive absolute into a full statement. Jesus' ministry leads to rejection as well as acceptance.

(38) But the final note in the story is acceptance. The healed man (cf. 8:35 for the description) begged Jesus that he might stay with him; ἐδεῖτο (5:12 note) is used conatively. But Jesus dismissed him (ἀπολύω, diff. Mk. οὐκ ἀφίημι), with a task to perform.

(39) Let the man return to his home (ὑποστρέφω, diff. Mk. ὑπάγω) and there tell all that God had done for him. Luke has ὁ θεός, diff. Mark's ambiguous ὁ κύριος, and he omits Mark's awkward καὶ ἠλέησέν σε. So the man more than obeyed. He went through all the town (diff. Mk. ἐν τῇ Δεκαπόλει) preaching what Jesus had done for him: it was thus in Jesus that God had acted to cure him. The story is a paradigm of what conversion involves: the responsibility to evangelise.

iii. Jairus's Daughter and the Woman with a Haemorrhage
8:40–56

The final episode in this section of mighty works is formed by the interwoven pair of stories which demonstrate the power of Jesus over disease and death. There is no evidence for any source other than Mk. being used at this point (Schramm, 126f.), and Luke has made little significant change in his source; his alterations are almost entirely abbreviations and stylistic improvements.

The 'sandwich' construction of the two stories is noteworthy, but it is widely regarded as secondary. Many scholars attribute the device to Mark himself, since it recurs elsewhere in the Gospel (Schürmann, I, 492). Others regard it as pre-Marcan (Bultmann, 228–230; Dibelius, 220; Kertelge, 110). In both cases the insertion of one narrative within the other is seen as motivated by the desire to fill in time between the original request to Jesus from Jairus for help for his sick daughter and the arrival of news that the girl had died. No doubt the link can be explained in this way – and must be explained in this way on the postulate that only isolated stories were originally handed down in the tradition – but the link can equally well be historical (Taylor, 289; Cranfield, 182; Schmid, *Mark*, 114).

The significance of the double story stands out clearly. It is in substance the same as that of the other healing miracles already recorded. The power of Jesus is seen to extend not merely to the curing of disease but also to the raising of the dead, a point with which Luke's readers were already familiar, but which is now re-emphasised as, following Mk., Luke approaches the question of who Jesus is. The motif of the compassion of Jesus is present, and is perhaps stressed by Luke's note that it was Jairus's only daughter who was ill. This element is implicit in the story of the woman whose complaint would have rendered her ritually unclean. A third motif lies in the conjunction of the elements of divine power and human faith. The mighty works of Jesus were accomplished by a divine power which could be said to emanate from him, but what could easily be regarded in a superstitious fashion as something magical is lifted to a higher level by the insistence of Jesus on faith as the means of a cure both for the woman and for Jairus's daughter. Moreover, the cure wrought in this manner extends beyond healing of the body; for the woman it involved a personal confrontation with Jesus, and in the formula 'Your faith has saved you' we should detect a deeper significance than that of mere physical healing. A final motif lies in the command to conceal what had happened in the house of Jairus. This feature is absent in the story of the raising of the widow of Nain's son, which takes place publicly, and contrasts with the instruction of Jesus to the cured demoniac in 8:39. Luke has taken it over from Mk., where it stands under suspicion of being a Marcan addition in the interests of a 'secrecy' theory. Schürmann, I, 496, suggests that in the eyes of Luke the miracle at Nain had led to an inadequate appreciation of Jesus as merely a prophet; now that the people had closed their eyes to the truth the mystery of the kingdom must remain hidden from them. But this negative verdict on the acclamation in 7:16 is unjustified. It is more probable that Luke saw Jesus' command as motivated by the Jewish scorn expressed in v. 53: such people were not fit recipients for this revelation of his power. The command itself should not be regarded as historically impossible: so long as the parents said nothing, the scornful Jews could persist in believing that the girl had been merely asleep. It should be noted that the secrecy motif extends back beyond the present command to v. 51, and is integral to the present form of the story.

See Kertelge, 110–120.

(40) Luke has removed a number of the details found in Mark's introduction to the story and rewritten it in a less precise manner. For the opening ἐν δέ . . . (p⁷⁵ B f1 pc) the majority of MSS have ἐγένετο δὲ ἐν . . . (so Diglot; cf. 1:8 note; 8:42b v.l.; 10:38 v.l.). The use of this construction avoids an illogical genitive absolute in Mk. One would expect the aorist infinitive here (so most MSS) instead of the present form ὑποστρέφειν (p⁷⁵ ℵ B pc), which must be translated 'As Jesus was returning, the crowd welcomed him' (Diglot); but see MH III, 145, where it is noted that the distinction between aorist and present forms is not rigid. Luke introduces the fact that the crowd welcomed Jesus; ἀποδέχομαι (9:11*; Acts, 5x) suggests 'to receive with pleasure' (Easton, 126). The

fact that the same word is used of the church welcoming returning missionaries does not justify Schürmann's suggestion (I, 489) of a conscious parallel in Luke's mind. The people's longing to see Jesus (προσδοκάω) may have been due to the desire for healings to be performed (cf. Mk. 6:53–56; Schürmann, I, 489).

(41) The story proper begins, as often, with καὶ ἰδού; the section generally has a more Semitic flavour than Mk. thanks to Luke's septuagintalising style (J. Weiss, 454), and the influence of Luke on the phraseology is frequently to be observed. The name of ᾿Ιάϊρος (from Heb. yā'îr, 'he will enlighten', or perhaps ya'îr, 'he will arouse') is taken over from Mk.; the theory that originally the name stood only in Lk. and thence found its way into the text of Mk. (where it is found in all authorities except D it) was upheld by Bultmann, 230 and developed by H. J. Cadbury, HTR 16, 1923, 89 n.; it is accepted with caution by Taylor, 287, but the arguments of Metzger, 85f., show that it is not tenable. Luke describes him paratactically (cf. 2:37; 5:1; 7:12; BD 277³) as a ruler of the synagogue (ἄρχων τῆς συναγωγῆς, diff. Mk. ἀρχισυνάγωγος, which Luke retains at 8:49; 13:14; Acts 13:15; 18:8, 17). Mark's title refers to the official who had charge of the arrangements for the synagogue services; the ὑπηρέτης (Lk. 4:20) did the actual work. SB IV:1, 145, claims that Luke's expression is identical in meaning with Mark's – as 8:49 shows. There was also a board of leaders of the synagogue, three or seven in number, and Schweizer, Markus 65, suggests that Luke's expression refers to a member of this board. Inscriptions, however, show that one person could hold both offices, and this is an alternative, but less likely, explanation of Luke's usage (see Lagrange, 253; W. Schrage, TDNT VII, 844–847, especially 847 n. 26; F. F. Bruce, Acts, 261). In any case a person of considerable standing is indicated, but like another similar person (Mk. 10:17 diff. Lk.) he was prepared to surrender his dignity in his situation of need; he knelt at the feet of Jesus and besought him to come to his house; Luke has altered Mark's wording, using indirect speech, and dropping the request that Jesus would lay his hands on his daughter – perhaps because it was not fulfilled.

(42) In the same way, Luke turns what is part of the ruler's request in Mk. into an editorial comment. He drops Mark's diminutive θυγάτριον, which would be inappropriate of a girl of twelve, but retains the pathos in Mark's phrase by adding the description that she was his only daughter (μονογενής, 7:12; 9:38). The detail is perhaps a deduction from Mark's phrase 'my daughter', which could be taken to mean 'my (one and only) daughter'. Luke has also brought forward the detail that she was twelve years old from its awkward position in Mk. 5:42; the age was that at which marriage might take place (Schürmann, I, 490). For Luke's use of ὡς with numerals cf. 1:56; 3:23. The significant fact comes last: she (αὐτή; UBS; Diglot; αὕτη, Synopsis) was about to die. For the imperfect cf. Jos. Ant. 5:4; AG s.v. ἀποθνῄσκω: The expression

avoids Mark's vulgar ἐσχάτως ἔχω (cf. Phrynichus 368). The expression
of need is an adequate statement of what Jairus wants Jesus to do; he
omits Mark's request that Jesus will act to heal her and make her live,
but cf. 8:50. It is taken for granted that Jesus will heed the request, so
that Luke can move smoothly over to the second part of the story with
ἐν δὲ τῷ ὑπάγειν αὐτόν; the verb is rarely used by Luke (10:3; 12:58;
17:14; 19:30*; Acts 0x; cf. perhaps Mk. 5:34 as the source). The
crowds are so dense that they crush Jesus (συνπνίγω, 8:14, diff. Mk.
συνθλίβω) – thus delaying the journey to Jairus's house and also forming
the scene in which the woman with the haemorrhage could secretly approach Jesus for healing.

(43) Luke follows Mk. in his description of the woman who approached Jesus. She was suffering from a haemorrhage. The use of the
participle of εἰμί with ἐν 'has a Semitic ring' (Taylor, 290), but has a
parallel in Classical Greek (Sophocles, Ajax 271, cited by AG 224a).
ῥύσις, 'flowing, flow' (Mk. 5:25**), is used with αἵματος in the LXX (Lv.
15:25; 20:18) as well as in medical and other writers; a uterine
haemorrhage may be meant, which would make the woman religiously
unclean. It had lasted for twelve years; for the use of ἀπό with the
genitive (diff. Mk., accusative of duration) cf. 2:36; the use of the actual
length of time that had elapsed (rather than the point from which the
period began) is unusual, but has parallels in expressions of distance (BD
161¹). Luke abbreviates Mark's involved description of how the woman
had got worse despite paying out all she had on unsuccessful medical
care, and substitutes the simple statement that she had not been able to
be cured by anybody; the use of ἰσχύω (6:48; cf. Mk. 5:4) here is very
weak, since it was not a question of the woman's strength, but rather of
the doctors' ability. Some MSS add the phrase ἰατροῖς προσαναλώσασα
ὅλον τὸν βίον (ℵ A K L W Θ f1 f13 pl lat syᶜᵖ bo) which is sufficiently
different in wording from Mk. to suggest that it may be an original part
of Luke's text (RV; Diglot; (UBS); Klostermann, 102; (Schürmann I,
488, 490 n. 137)). προσαναλίσκω**, is 'to spend lavishly'; the phrase
ὅλος ὁ βίος is paralleled in Mk. 12:44 (diff. Lk. 21:4). The language
could be Lucan, and Metzger, 145, asks 'whether anyone except Luke
himself would rewrite Mark in this way'. On the other hand, there is
good external evidence for omission: p⁷⁵ B (D) syˢ sa, and this is followed
by RSV t; NEB t; JB t: A clear-cut decision is impossible.

(44) The next phrase is one in which Luke agrees closely with Mt.
against Mk. in their common wording and omission of phrases from Mk.
The omissions are not significant, since both writers are abbreviating
Mk., especially Matthew. Both have προσελθοῦσα diff. Mk. ἐλθοῦσα (cf.
8:24 note). The woman comes from behind (ὄπισθεν, 23:26) and touches
the κράσπεδον of Jesus' garment. The word can mean the 'hem, edge,
border' of a garment, or the 'tassel' which the Jew wore on the four cor-
ners of his outer garment (Nu. 15:38f.; Dt. 22:12; J. Schneider, TDNT
III, 904; SB IV:1, 277–292), here probably the latter. Mark does not

have the word here, but uses it at 6:56 par. Mt. 14:36; cf. Mt. 23:5. It is added to Mark's text by f1 *al*, and omitted from Luke's by D it Mcion (so *Diglot*); Easton, 129; Creed, 123, but these variants are plainly secondary. The common use of the word by Matthew and Luke may be due to the influence of Mk. 6:56 (Schürmann, I, 490 n. 138) or to oral tradition. There is certainly nothing to indicate that any other written source is being used. Luke passes over the expression of the woman's hope of being cured (diff. Mk. and Mt.), perhaps because he felt that it contained an element of superstition, and stresses that her touch brought instant healing (παραχρῆμα, diff. Mk. εὐθύς; 1:64 note). For Mark's ξηραίνω, he uses ἵστημι, which may be a change in the direction of technical medical phraseology (cf. αἷμα ἀπὸ μυκτήρων στῆσαι in a medical document, P. Oxy, 1088, 21 (I AD), and Cyranides, cited by AG 383a). Luke also substitutes ῥύσις for Mk. πηγή.

(45) The cure may appear to have been wrought by magical means; simply to touch the healer may lead to the automatic flow of involuntary healing power from him to the sufferer (J. M. Hull, *Hellenistic Magic and the Synoptic Tradition*, 109f.). But the story, as taken over by Luke, at once corrects this false impression in the mind of the reader by showing how Jesus corrected it in the mind of the woman. He himself was conscious of what was happening, and he brought the woman to see that it was her faith in God which led to the cure. So, reversing Mark's order of narration, Luke records the prompt response of Jesus with the question, 'Who touched me?' (τίς ὁ ἀψάμενός μου; diff. Mk. τίς μου ἥψατο τῶν ἱματίων; the change perhaps lays the stress on the act of touching rather than on the identity of the toucher). Luke records the fact that everybody denied doing so (ἀρνέομαι, 9:23; 12:9; 22:57). Whereas in Mk. the disciples address Jesus rather critically, in Lk. the speaker is identified with Peter (cf. 22:8; but contrast 22:46), and the statement is re-worded so that it becomes a dialogue between Peter and Jesus. After Πέτρός (p⁷⁵ B *al* syˢ ᶜ sa) most MSS add καὶ οἱ σὺν αὐτῷ (*Diglot*) or καὶ οἱ μετ' αὐτοῦ (TR), probably by assimilation (Metzger, 146), although the use of σύν could be Lucan (cf. 8:38, 51). Peter addresses Jesus as ἐπιστάτης (5:5 note). diff. Mk. He describes the crowds as constraining (συνέχω, 4:38) and pressing upon Jesus (ἀποθλίβω**, diff. Mk. συνθλίβω which Luke has already avoided in 8:42). Various MSS assimilate the text to that of Mk. at this point also, adding 'And you say, "Who touched me?" '. But Luke's equivalent for this statement is to be found in the next verse.

(46) Whereas in Mk. Jesus looks round to find who has touched him, in Lk. he repeats his statement that someone has touched him and adds in the form of a further statement what Mark had already given in narrative form: he had realised (ἔγνων, aorist) that power had gone forth from him; note the use of the perfect (MH III, 160f.). This makes it clear that Jesus is not to be thought of as involuntarily dispensing healing power (6:19) the power is that of God (5:17), and it is thought of as

flowing from Jesus to the healed person, but this happens in response to faith. Matthew makes the point clear by bringing the healing into direct relationship with the word of Jesus (Mt. 9:22). This shows that he was conscious of some embarrassment about the story, which Luke has dealt with more boldly; taking up a feature which could appear to reflect primitive superstition, he has shown that this can be understood in terms of divine power. Cf. W. Grundmann, TDNT II, 300–303.

(47) In Mk. the woman is full of fear and wonder at what has happened and confesses to Jesus who has touched him. In Lk. she realises that Jesus knows who she is; she cannot escape notice (λανθάνω, Mk. 7:24; Acts 26:26; *et al.*), and so she comes trembling (τρέμω, Mk. 5:33; 2 Pet. 2:10**), and falls before him (cf. 8:40). Her confession takes on a wider aspect as she recounts before all the people why she touched Jesus and how she was healed immediately; the language is heavily Lucan: διά with αἰτία, Acts 10:21; 22:24; 28:18, 20; ἐνώπιον with πᾶς, 14:10; Acts 6:5; 19:19; 27:35). This motif is not in Mk., although it is evident from Mk. that the conversation probably took place in public. The contrast between this open display of healing power and the secrecy in 8:56 is notable.

(48) The story has been brought to a climax with the personal contact between Jesus and the woman, without which her cure might have been no more than physical. Now it is possible for Jesus to assure her that it is her faith that has cured her; she can depart (πορεύομαι diff. Mk. ὑπάγω) in peace (7:50 note). The peace is God's peace, so that the woman's healing is brought into direct relationship with his blessing and not left to be understood as due to some magical power residing in Jesus.

(49) The main story is resumed with a neat link; ἔτι αὐτοῦ λαλοῦντος is taken from Mk., but the construction is frequent in Lk. (9:42 note). An incident which could have been regarded as an incentive to Jairus's faith in the power of Jesus to cure his daughter must now have seemed to be a fatal interruption, for at this point there arrives a messenger from the house of (παρά, diff. Mk. ἀπό) Jairus; Luke has altered Mark's plural to a singular, but here only retains the vivid historic present form of the verb from Mk. (cf. 7:40 note). The messenger addresses Jairus (the addition of αὐτῷ by many MSS (so *Diglot*) is an unnecessary clarification). The wording of the message is altered. Luke replaces Mark's aorist ('she has died') with a perfect ('she is dead'), and places the verb first in the statement for emphasis, so that the sad finality of the event is stressed. Luke also alters Mark's question τί ἔτι σκύλλεις to a command (cf. 8:24, 52): do not trouble the teacher any longer (μηκέτι* should be read with p⁷⁵ ℵ B D syʰ sa against the majority reading μή). For σκύλλω see 7:6.

(50) Mark's ambiguous παρακούω ('to overhear', 'to ignore') is altered to ἀκούω, and his clumsy τὸν λόγον λαλούμενον is dropped. When Jesus hears the message, he promptly acts to restore Jairus's flagging spirit. Jairus must not be afraid at the news that nothing can be

done. If he will only believe, the child will be cured. What was done for the woman (8:48) can be done for her also, provided that the father is willing to trust the power of God in Jesus. Schürmann, I, 493f., claims that faith is not here regarded as a precondition for the miracle, but rather the promise of the miracle gives grounds for hope and faith, but this interpretation seems less likely. Jairus has already been given evidence of Jesus' power, and now he is being summoned on the basis of that to a greater faith. The aorist form πίστευσον, diff. Mk. present imperative, may mean 'start to believe' (MH III, 75). For the use of σῴζω cf. Mk. 5:23 diff. Lk.

(51) In Mk. Jesus is said at this point to allow only his three closest disciples to accompany him on the rest of the journey to the house, and then later in Mk. 5:40 they accompany him into the house. Luke has condensed Mark's account, so that Jesus now reaches the house (Mk. 5:38) and allows nobody to enter (εἰσέρχομαι σύν, diff. Mk. 5:37 συνακολουθέω) except Peter, John and James, and the parents (cf. Mk. 5:40); note how Luke alters the order of the names to bring Peter and John together as a pair (9:28; Acts 1:13).

(52) As a result of the change in v. 51 it is not clear where the mourners are situated. In Mk. and Mt. they are inside the house and Jesus ejects them. Luke's narrative may appear to suggest that they were outside the house and Jesus forbade them to enter it, but it is more likely that he has the same picture as Mk., and it is the room where the child is lying to which he denies them access. Luke avoids Mark's 'impersonal' use of participles by giving a descriptive statement of how all were weeping and mourning; κόπτομαι (active, 'to cut', Mk. 11:8 par. Mt. 21:8) is 'to beat one's breast', hence 'to mourn', 23:27; Mt. 11:17 (diff. Lk. 7:32); 24:30; Rev. 1:7; 18:9**. It expresses the intensity of Jewish mourning (cf. SB I, 521–523). Jesus interrupts the mourning with a command (diff. Mark's weaker question): 'Don't go on weeping' (MH III, 76). The child, he says, has not died, but is sleeping. The use of the verb 'to sleep' as a euphemism for death is common enough (R. Bultmann, TDNT III, 14 n. 60; A. Oepke, TDNT III, 431–437; κοιμάω cf. 22:45) is more frequent than καθεύδω in this sense). Here, however, the point is the contrast between death and sleep; death is not final, for it is possible to be wakened from it. Thus death is reinterpreted from the point of view of God, which is different from that of men, and cannot be appreciated by them.

(53) So it is not surprising that Jesus' statement is ridiculed by the mourners (καταγελάω, only in this v. and parallels). They think that Jesus means ordinary sleep. But he has not seen the child; they have, and they know that she is dead. They refuse to allow that one known to possess prophetic powers and the gift of healing may be right in any sense.

(54) The scene has already been prepared (diff. Mk.) so that Luke is able to place in direct contrast to the unbelief of the mourners the

powerful act of Jesus. He takes the dead girl by the hand (κρατέω, 24:16, otherwise avoided by Luke in the Gospel) and calls to her – the choice of word (φωνέω, diff. Mk. λέγω) perhaps suggests that her spirit is distant and has to be summoned back to her body. The words of Jesus are recorded in Greek with ἡ παῖς replacing Mark's diminutive τὸ κοράσιον (cf. 8:42); Luke omits, as usual, Aramaic phrases. ἐγείρω can mean 'to arise from the dead' or 'to sit up'; here both senses are included, and the gesture of Jesus is to be understood as help to sit up rather than as a means of transfer of divine power; the healing is accomplished by summoning the spirit back to the body rather than by resuscitating the body (cf. Acts 9:41).

(55) That this is Luke's understanding of the miracle is made clear by his addition that the spirit of the girl returned (ἐπιστρέφω, 1:16). The πνεῦμα is regarded as surviving death and being separated from the body (cf. 23:46; Acts 7:59; Jub. 23:26–31; 1 En. 22:39:4ff.); it corresponds to ψυχή in Greek thought (cf. E. Sjöberg, TDNT VI, 376–380). But the expression here is drawn from the OT (1 Ki. 17:21), and serves not only to indicate what is happening, but also to suggest the parallel between the activity of Jesus and that of Elijah the prophet. As a result the girl immediately arose. Luke omits the detail that she was able to walk – as proof of her healing – and brings forward the instruction of Jesus that she should be given something to eat; for διατάσσω diff. Mk. διαστέλλω, cf. 3:13. Thus it is emphasised that she is not a 'spirit' (24:41–43), and has really been brought back to life (cf. Dibelius, 76 n. 1).

(56) By his alteration in order Luke is able to conclude with the reaction of the parents (Mark leaves the subject of ἐξέστησαν unnamed). They were astounded (ἐξίστημι, 2:47; 24:22*), a word Luke often uses for the reaction of men to the supernatural. Schürmann, I, 495f., claims that for Luke the parents did not come to a proper understanding of what was happening, and gives praise to God. But Luke is simply following his source; he does not suggest that Jesus' command in 8:50 was in vain; and a reaction of wonder is natural in the circumstances. The suggestion is over-ingenious.

The account closes with the direction to the parents not to relate what had happened to anybody (expressed in Lucan language on the basis of Mk.). For the significance of the command, see the introduction to the section.

g. Jesus and the Twelve (9:1–50)

In the previous main section the emphasis has been largely on the ministry of Jesus among the people, in the course of which he taught them and performed mighty works which demonstrated his divine power and compassion. Throughout this period the Twelve are to be thought of as accompanying Jesus and observing what he said and did. But from now onwards the emphasis falls increasingly upon the relationship of Jesus to the disciples and the teaching which he gave to them through which they were to come to some understanding of his person and work; his revelation to them was not fully understood at this stage, but its significance would become apparent to them later when he had been openly identified by God as Lord and Christ through the resurrection (cf. Acts 2:36).

Luke omits the narrative of Jesus' visit to Nazareth in Mk. 6:1–6, to which he has already given a parallel (4:16–30), the story of John's death in Mt. 6:17–29 (cf. Lk. 3:19f.) and the whole of Mk. 6:45 – 8:26 (see below). Otherwise, he follows Mk. closely, and by these omissions is able to build up a section whose uniting theme is the revelation of Jesus to the disciples. The opening pericope deals with the mission of the disciples and leads up to the revelation of Jesus' power in the feeding of the multitude (9:1–17). With this Luke juxtaposes the account of Peter's confession of Jesus, in which all the stress lies on the path of suffering which must be followed by Jesus and his disciples (9:18–27). There follows the transfiguration in which the same theme is emphasised: Jesus, who must suffer, is nevertheless the glorious, chosen Son of God, and his greatness is further demonstrated in the healing of the boy with the unclean spirit (9:28–36, 37–45). Finally, the way of humility is again put before the disciples (9:46–50). Thus two themes interact throughout the section, the revelation of Jesus as the mighty Son of God, who must nevertheless tread the path of suffering, and the call to the disciples to follow the way of their Lord, both in missionary service and in readiness for suffering and humiliation.

See E. E. Ellis, 'La composition de Luc 9 et les sources de sa christologie', in Dupont, *Jésus*, 193–200 (English version in G. F. Hawthorne (ed.), *Current Issues in Biblical and Patristic Interpretation*, Grand Rapids, 1975, 121–127).

i. The Mission of the Twelve 9:1–6

Luke begins by narrating how Jesus sent out the Twelve on an evangelistic mission, and then, between the accounts of their departure and return, he includes a brief interlude in which the reaction of Herod Antipas and the people to Jesus is recorded. Throughout he follows Mk., but at one or two points he appears to be influenced by the wording of the account of the sending out of a wider group of disciples in 10:1–12. The parallel passage in Mt. 10:1–14 likewise shows affinities both to Mk. 6:7–13 and to the material in Lk. 10:1–12. The generally accepted explanation of these facts – and there is no good reason to question it – is that there were two accounts of the sending out of disciples on mission, one in Mk. and one in the Q material. Luke has utilised these separately in chs. 9 and 10 respectively (but with some assimilation between them), but Matthew has conflated his two sources (cf. Schramm, 26–29). A more difficult question is whether the material in Mk. and Q ultimately goes back to one tradition or represents two separate mission discourses. On the whole the former theory is more probable in view of the close parallelism in structure between the two accounts (cf. Bultmann, 155f.; Hahn, *Mission*, 41–46).

The historicity of a mission by the disciples of Jesus has often been denied (Wellhausen, *Markus,* 44). F. W. Beare* claims that we have so little information about it as to make its importance extremely doubtful, and Hoffmann, 262f., says that it is a Marcan construction based on a tradition that the disciples shared the work of Jesus. Nevertheless, it has rightly been described as 'one of the best-attested facts in the life of Jesus' (Manson, *Sayings*, 73; cf. Schweizer, *Markus,* 71f.; Roloff, *Apostolat,* 150–152). The question of the historicity of the mission is to be distinguished from that of the historicity of the call of the Twelve; even if the latter is denied (see, however, 6:13 note), this need not involve denial of the former. If these two questions are separated, the problem then becomes that of the authenticity of the mission instructions given by Jesus; the comments below will show that this can be accepted without difficulty.

It is significant that Luke has included the narrative of the mission of the Twelve here and has not contented himself with the 'doublet' in ch. 10. Whether or not the material in Lk. 10 was associated with a mission by a wider group, Luke wished to record how the Twelve, who figure prominently in Acts as witnesses and missionaries, were already called by Jesus and experienced a prefigurement of their later ministry. At the same time the inclusion of the narrative at this point in the Gospel suggests that it is significant in the structure of the section as a whole. The Twelve experience the power and authority given to them by Jesus, and so are faced anew with the question of who Jesus is; at the same time the instructions they receive constitute the beginning of a call to the same life of poverty, dependence upon God and rejection by men as was lived by Jesus himself. Thus the narrative has acquired for Luke a significance beyond that which it has in Mk.

The heart of the narrative is the instructions for the missionaries contained in it. They are prefaced by a brief note about the empowering of the disciples and followed by an account of how they obeyed their command to preach and heal. But we are told nothing about the course of the mission, and the emphasis lies upon the teaching of Jesus. First, the disciples are (implicitly) commanded to make the theme of their preaching the kingdom of God (cf. 10:8, 11); in Mk. the theme is not stated, but we are told that they preached that men should repent (Mk. 6:12). Luke has stressed the positive activity of preaching the good news (9:6) of the kingdom, although he himself often emphasises repentance; the good news of the kingdom (cf. 4:16–21) precedes the call to repent.

Second, the disciples are commanded to travel with the minimum of equipment. They are to avoid the appearance of other missionaries in the Hellenistic world, who made a good thing out of their preaching. At the same time, their lack of material possessions indicates that they put their trust in God to sustain them on his work.

Third, when they enter a house to stay there, they are not to move around from one lodging to another, apparently looking for better conditions. As 10:7 makes clear, they are labourers worthy of what they receive, but this means that they are to be content with what they receive and not look for more.

Finally, if they get a hostile reception – 10:10 makes it clear that this is from a town as a whole rather than from a single house – they are to treat the inhabitants of the place in the same way as Jews treated gentiles, by making use of a symbolical act indicative of the lack of fellowship between the people of God and aliens.

These instructions give the impression of being meant for a particular time and place; a missionary enterprise in a restricted area of Palestine among Jews is indicated, and later on Jesus was to allude to what he had said to the disciples and indicate that a different reception would await them (22:35–38). It is plausible that the instructions were handed down in the church because they continued to be followed in the Palestinian mission. Their preservation by Mark and the other Evangelists indicates that the basic principles in them were regarded as of lasting value for the church.

See Hahn, *Mission*, 41–46; F. W. Beare, 'The Mission of the Disciples and the Mission Charge: Matthew 10 and Parallels', JBL 89, 1970, 1–13; Hoffmann, 245–248.

(1) The account begins with the summoning together of the Twelve: Luke uses συγκαλέω (15:6, 9; 23:13; Acts 5:21; 10:24; 28:17; Mk. 15:16**) diff. Mk. προσκαλέω. For Luke the action is necessitated by the brief separation noted in 8:51, since the verb implies the summoning of people who are not yet on the scene. The Twelve are characterised in some MSS as ἀποστόλους (ℵ C L Θ f13 *al* lat bo) or μαθητὰς αὐτοῦ (C³ *al* it), but the shorter text (p⁷⁵ A B D W *al* sy Mcion; TR) is to be followed. First (diff. Mk.) they were empowered for their task. The use of the aorist ἔδωκεν, diff. Mk. ἐδίδου, hardly implies that the gift was being made only for this one particular occasion, however likely that may be on general grounds (*pace* Schürmann, I, 500). To Mark's ἐξουσία, signifying authority, Luke adds δύναμις, spiritual power, such as enabled Jesus to heal (cf. 4:14, 36; 5:17; 6:19; 8:46; Acts 10:38). With such power and the authority to use it the disciples were able to overcome demons of all kinds (πάντα; Luke adds ἐπί by way of clarification of Mark's genitival phrase) and also to heal diseases; this last detail has probably been brought forward from Mk. 6:13, but the presence of the same detail in Mt. 10:1 also raises the question whether the Q narrative was the source for it (but against this there is no trace of it in Lk. 10).

(2) The concept of sending out (ἀποστέλλω) the Twelve is taken from Mk. (cf. Lk. 10:1): K. H. Rengstorf (TDNT I, 429) claims that this incident (rather than the earlier call) is their real appointment as apostles. Luke omits mention of their being sent out two by two (diff. Mk.),

and Schürmann, I, 500, suggests that he is emphasising their collegial function which becomes prominent later in Acts. But Matthew also has the same omission. Their task is twofold. First, they are to preach the kingdom of God; this detail is missing in Mk. (but cf. Mk. 3:14), and is probably drawn from Q (Mt. 10:7 par. Lk. 10:9, 11). Conzelmann, 105 n. 3, argues that Luke has substituted 'to preach the kingdom of God' for 'to preach that the kingdom of God has drawn near' (so Mark and Matthew), thereby avoiding the element of time in the original proclamation; but it is highly unlikely that any theological significance should be seen in the change of phraseology (cf. Marshall, 128–136). Second, the disciples are to heal (ἰάομαι 9:11, diff. Mt. θεραπεύω); many MSS (א A D L f1 al) add τοὺς ἀσθενεῖς, which is retained by UBS with brackets. The phrase is regarded as a scribal addition by Hoffmann, 246 n. 35, who claims that both it and the v.l. τοὺς ἀσθενοῦντας are expansions of the original short text (read by B syᶜˢMcion). Lucan style, however, favours the reading (Schürmann, I, 501 n. 16; Metzger, 146f.). The summary of the work of the disciples corresponds to that of Jesus himself (9:11).

(3) Mark does not have the full set of instructions for missionaries that we find in Q (cf. 10:2f.) but moves straight to the directions for travelling light. Luke has altered his verb of command (παραγγέλλω) with an indirect command following to a simple λέγω followed by direct imperatives (cf. Lk. 10:2–4; Mk. 6:9b). The disciples are to take nothing for the road (Luke's addition of the article with ὁδός may be due to Q, 10:4, or perhaps indicate that one particular journey is in mind). The instruction is developed with reference to five particular items. 1. A staff (ῥάβδος, 1 Cor. 4:21; Heb. 1:8; 9:4; 11:21; Rev. 2:27; et al.; C. Schneider, TDNT VI, 966–970) is forbidden. The reference is to a traveller's staff, needed on long journeys on foot. The prohibition may be because this, like the satchel, was a mark of the wandering preacher whom the disciples were not to resemble; the suggestion that the rabbinic rule that one must not walk on the temple hill with a staff, sandals or girdle (Ber. 9:5) has exerted an influence here (Manson, *Sayings,* 181) seems unlikely. In Mk., however, it is expressly stated that the disciples must take nothing except a staff. Although the staff is missing from Lk. 10:4, it is forbidden in Mt. 10:10, which suggests that Luke is following Q rather than deliberately altering Mk. Schürmann, I, 501 n. 19, suggests that Mark was allowing the disciples to carry a staff as a sign of their master's authority like Gehazi (2 Ki. 4:29), and that Luke failed to appreciate the allusion. But in Gehazi's case it was the *master's* staff that was used, not the disciple's, and in any case Luke is here altering Mk. in the light of Q. Another possibility is that Aramaic confusion lies behind the difference ('ellā', 'except', confused with wᵉlā', 'and not'; Black, 216f.; Beyer I:1, 109 n. 4); this is possible in terms of the history of the tradition behind Mk. and Q, but it is not perhaps very likely. It remains most probable that Q gives the original, rigorous instructions of Jesus

for a brief mission, whereas in Mk. we have an adaptation of the demands to fit in with the different, more harsh conditions of later missions over a wider area. 2. Luke has πήρα, 'bag', before ἄρτος, 'bread', diff. Mk. The πήρα is a bag for carrying provisions and other necessaries for a journey (10:4; 22:35f.; W. Michaelis, TDNT VI, 119–121) rather than a beggar's bag for collecting food. Its normal content would be 3. bread (cf. Jn. 6:9). 4. ἀργύριον, 'money' (19:15, 23; 22:5; originally 'silver', Acts 3:6; et al.), is more general than Mk. '(copper) money in your belt'; 10:4 has βαλλάντιον, 'purse'. 5. Finally, the disciples are forbidden two shirts (χιτών, 3:11). ἀνά is added by ℵ B C* F pc lat and bracketed in UBS; its use is distributive (cf. 9:14; 10:1; BD 204, 208¹) and it could be Lucan (Metzger, 147), with omission due to assimilation to the parallels. It is not clear what force should be attached to ἔχειν (an imperatival infinitive, BD 389): does it mean to wear two tunics at once (so Mk.; cf. Jos. Ant. 17:136) or to carry a spare one? Probably the latter is meant (cf. 3:11; Hoffmann, 247 n. 41).

Although the passage as a whole is described as a community formation by Bultmann, 155f., he offers no evidence for this assertion, beyond the observation that the risen Lord commanded the disciples to engage in mission. The view of Hahn, *Mission*, 46, has a better basis: this saying 'is radical in its nature and parallel to the words about following Jesus, which likewise demand the renunciation of private property; and thus it is entirely compatible with Jesus' attitude'.

(4) Those who go out on mission without resources are dependent on the goodwill of the community to which they go. Following Mk. Luke gives brief instructions regarding behaviour in the case of acceptance and then in case of rejection. The first command is slightly obscure in its present context. Mark's introduction by καὶ ἔλεγεν αὐτοῖς may indicate a lack of connection with the previous verse, and this is confirmed by Lk. 10:5–7 where fuller instructions about going to a house with the message of the gospel are given. Those who accept the message are expected to give a hospitable welcome to the missionaries. Luke's wording (εἰς ἣν ἄν diff. Mk. ὅπου ἐάν) is influenced by Q and is an improvement on Mk. When the disciples enter a house they are to remain there and to go out from there (diff. Mk., remain there, until they depart from there). This sounds tautologous. Mark's wording perhaps means that they are to stay in the one house until they leave the town in question. The point is the same as in Q: do not move around from house to house seeking better lodging, but be content with what is put before you; there must be no suggestion of making a good thing out of missionary work. This sense is probably meant by Luke, but ἐξέρχεσθε may refer not to leaving the town, but to going out from the house to do further evangelism in the town itself (Klostermann, 103). For the need to regulate the conduct of missionaries at a later stage cf. Did. 11:4f. Since this part of the saying, especially when seen in its fuller form in 10:5–7, appears to be an addition to a saying dealing with the preaching of the gospel in houses,

Hahn, *Mission*, 42, 46, regards it as a later expansion of the saying; see the comments later on this point.

(5) The second instruction is concerned with what to do if the inhabitants reject the message. Luke is apparently thinking of the reaction of a town as a whole (ἔξω/ἀπὸ τῆς πόλεως par. Mt., diff. Mk.), although at first sight the clause (ὅσοι ἄν) appears to refer to the inhabitants of houses: ὅσοι has no real antecedent (it refers vaguely to '(their) city'). δέχομαι is used of welcoming both the messengers and their message; in Mk. it is supplemented by μηδὲ ἀκούσωσιν ὑμῶν (apparently not in Q). As they leave the town (Mt. adds 'house'), they are to shake off (ἀποτινάσσω, Acts 28:5**. diff. Mk. ἐκτινάσσω; cf. Q ἀπομάσσω, Lk. 10:11) the dust (κονιορτός, 10:11; Mt. 10:14; Acts 13:51; 22:23**; so Q, diff. Mk. χοῦς) on their feet. Luke has the present imperative, diff. Mk., aorist, with no apparent change in meaning. The action of shaking off the dust of a gentile city from one's feet was practised by Jews; they removed what was ceremonially unclean before returning to their own land, lest they should defile it. Thus the practice implied that the place in question was heathen and that the Jew had no fellowship with it (BC V, 269–271; SB I, 571). When the Christian missionaries did the same to Jews (Acts 13:51; cf. 18:6), it was a symbolic piece of evidence (μαρτύριον, par. Mk.; cf. 5:14; 21:13) against (Luke adds ἐπί) them that they were no part of the true Israel; they had refused the message of the kingdom of God (cf. H. Strathmann, TDNT IV, 503). Manson, *Sayings*, 182, suggests that in the light of Ber. 9:5 the disciples are to cleanse themselves from defilement before proceeding on their sacred mission; but the parallel between entering the sacred precincts of the temple and going on a missionary journey is not obvious, and the text makes the action significant for the spectators rather than for the disciples themselves. There is no reason to doubt that the instruction goes back to Jesus himself (Hahn, *Mission*, 46; Schweizer, *Markus*, 72).

(6) In obedience to the instructions the disciples set out (ἐξέρχομαι), and made a tour (διέρχομαι, 2:15; cf. διοδεύω, 8:1) of the villages in the area; Grundmann, 185, claims that while Jesus visited the towns, the disciples' activity was confined to the villages; it is unlikely that the point should be pressed; Luke's language here may be reminiscent of Mk. 6:6b, and can correspond to the realities of the situation. In particular, it is unlikely that the activity of the Twelve should be regarded as different from that of the 70 (72) in 10:1. They preached the good news, i.e. the message of the kingdom, and healed (cf. the fuller description in Mk. 6:13) everywhere. πανταχοῦ may mean no more than 'everywhere they went', but Schürmann, I, 504, finds a hint of the fact that the gospel is for all men everywhere (Acts 17:30; 24:3; 28:22; cf. Mk. 1:28; 16:20; 1 Cor. 4:17).

ii. Herod's Question about Jesus 9:7–9

Between the account of the commissioning of the Twelve and the note about their return from their mission, Luke includes a brief section on the various opinions which were in the minds of the people about Jesus. Interest is centred on the reaction of Herod Antipas to the rumours that were circulating, and it is on his lips that the question 'Who then is this?' is placed. The question prepares the way for the account of the way in which Jesus asked the disciples about his role and proceeded to give them further instruction about his work in 9:19–27. At the same time, it looks forward to the further dealings of Herod with Jesus in 13:31ff. and 23:6–12; in due course Herod's wish to see Jesus was to be fulfilled, though not in the way that he expected. Luke has taken the narrative from Mk. 6:14–16, and in essentials it serves the same function of filling in the gap in the story of the mission of the Twelve and preparing for Peter's confession. But Luke has turned Herod's statement about Jesus into a question, thereby emphasising the inadequacy of the answers given at this stage. Moreover, he has dropped the lengthy narrative Mk. 6:17–29 in which the story of John's execution is given, and which serves in Mk. to cast a shadow over the future destiny of Jesus; Luke has already noted briefly how Herod imprisoned John (3:19f.), and felt no need to develop the story; at this point in his narrative he was omitting material from Mk., perhaps to make room for his non-Marcan material, and this story, which does not deal directly with Jesus, was an obvious candidate for sacrifice.

The brief narrative in its Marcan form could be an isolated one which Mark has inserted at this point for literary reasons. Nevertheless, it fits in at this point in the Gospel since from this point onwards Jesus avoids Galilee. That Herod knew about the activities of Jesus is to be seen in the independent tradition in Lk. 13:31ff. But, whereas Herod's hostility to Jesus appears more clearly in that episode, there is no evidence there that Jesus felt the need to avoid his territories. Even, however, if Jesus stood up to Herod's threats with boldness, he may still have judged it wise to keep out of his way, for the appointed place of his suffering was Jerusalem. The present incident, therefore, can be associated with 13:31ff., but is from a different tradition.

See Wink, 8–13.

(7) Luke agrees with Mt. in describing Herod (3:1, 19) as tetrarch (3:19 note) instead of as 'king', the popular designation that Mark allows him to bear. He heard about all that was happening; Luke likes to use participles of γίνομαι (4:23; 13:17; 24:18; cf. 8:34f., 56). Some MSS add ὑπ' αὐτοῦ (A C³ W Δ Θ Π fl *pm* syᵖ; TR; *Diglot*) to indicate that Jesus' activity is meant, but Luke may have in mind the spread in the fame of Jesus (cf. Mk. 6:14) caused by the mission of the Twelve and the growth of rumours about him. Along with the stories of what Jesus was doing

went the conjectures of the people as to who this strange person could be, and it was the various attempts to answer this question which caused Herod considerable perplexity (διαπορέω, 'to be perplexed', Acts 2:12; 5:24; 10:17**, perhaps reflecting ἀπορέω, Mk. 6:20). Luke substitutes an elegant διὰ τό with infinitive phrase for Mark's impersonal plural ἔλεγον (this should be regarded as the correct text in Mk., not ἔλεγεν; Metzger, 89). Three opinions are recorded as coming to Herod's notice: 1. John (Luke omits 'the Baptist') has risen from the dead. Luke has the aorist ἠγέρθη, diff. Mk. ἐγήγερται, and omits Mark's addition 'That is why these powers are at work in him'. The statement implies that by this time Herod had executed John (9:9; contrast 7:18ff.), and attests a popular belief that he had come to life again in a different guise. This is an odd belief, for although the Gospels state that Jesus began his ministry after the imprisonment of John (and Jn. 3:22–24 makes it begin earlier), and indeed that he was baptised by John, this statement implies that Jesus did not appear until after the death of John. Further, there are no contemporary analogies for the belief that a person could be resurrected and reincarnated in another person (Schürmann, I, 506f.). We have, therefore, a very ill-informed piece of popular superstition here, but there is no reason why such strange beliefs should not have existed.

(8) The second view (2.) was: Elijah has appeared. For φαίνω, 'to appear' (diff. Mk. εἰμί), cf. 24:11*; Mt. 1:20; et al. Since Elijah was regarded as being in heaven, this was the appropriate expression to describe his appearance: he had no need to be resurrected. The suggestion is that Jesus has taken on the role of Elijah who was expected to reappear as an 'eschatological prophet' and thus to herald the End (cf. J. Jeremias, TDNT II, 936). Again we are dealing with popular expectation, and hence there is no need to try to harmonise this statement with others in the NT about John or Jesus being identified with Elijah. 3. The third view was that one of the old prophets had arisen. The contrast is with the various people who appeared during this period and claimed to be new prophets; for such, see R. Meyer, *Der Prophet aus Galiläa*, Leipzig, 1940; summarised in TDNT VI, 812–828. A 'real' OT prophet, risen from the dead, is meant: ἀνίστημι is synonymous with ἐγείρω, and the change is due to no more than literary variation. Luke's wording, however, differs significantly from that in Mk. which has προφήτης ὡς εἷς τῶν προφητῶν which appears to mean 'a prophet (not like the other contemporary prophets, but a real one) like one of the (OT) prophets'. It is difficult to equate Luke's statement with this one, although Mk. 8:28 could be taken in Luke's sense, and Easton, 135, thinks that Luke has misunderstood Mk.; it is more likely that Luke has edited Mk. in the light of Mk. 8:28 and the analogy with the two preceding statements.

(9) Faced by these statements Herod (read ὁ Ἡρῴδης, B L Ξ Ψ f1 f13 700 *al*; so H. Greeven, NTS 6, 1959–60, 292–295) expresses his perplexity. He states categorically that he had beheaded John (ἀποκεφαλίζω, Mt. 14:10; Mk. 6:16, 28**); if so, who could this person

be about whom he heard such things (τοιοῦτος, 18:16*)? The implication is that John – and presumably the other persons suggested – could not rise from the dead, despite what people said, so that the puzzle of Jesus' identity remaine unsolved. Luke here differs again from Mk., where Herod agrees with the suggestion that John has been raised, and also from Mt., which attributes the words of the people in Mk. to Herod himself. Has Luke simply edited Mk., to show the inadequacy of the popular statements, or did he have some other tradition which indicated that Herod's opinions vacillated? In any case, Luke closes the incident with Herod's desire to see, i.e. 'get to know' (AG s.v. εἶδον) Jesus, a feeling prompted by curiosity or malice, not by faith.

iii. The Feeding of the Five Thousand 9:10–17

After the brief interlude in 9:7–9 the story is resumed with the return of the Twelve – now described as 'apostles' – to Jesus and their report about their mission. Jesus takes them away by themselves, no doubt for a period of refreshment and rest (a motif more clearly presented in Mk.), but large crowds follow them, so that Jesus himself has to continue the work of preaching and healing which is still needed despite the work of the apostles. At the end of the day the Twelve would have sent the crowds away to provide for their own food and lodging. They were not aware that they had any resources of their own with which to feed them. But Jesus was able to take their limited and totally inadequate resources and give them back to them in such a way that they were able to feed the crowds and have enough to spare. Thus the narrative in its Lucan form depicts the inadequacy of the disciples in contrast to the ability of Jesus to help the crowds. With his help the disciples could do what otherwise they could not do.

At the same time the incident poses again the question, 'Who is this?' In its context in Lk. it prepares for the confession scene which follows, and constitutes a decisive revelation of Jesus to the disciples. The miracle is one that is meant for the eyes of the disciples; no account of its effect on the crowds is given. The element of Jesus' concern for the crowds is not absent; indeed, it stands out by contrast with the unwillingness of the disciples, springing from their inability to act, but it is not emphasised so much as in Mk. (Mk. 6:34). But the stress on the OT background of the incident is there; what God did through Moses and Elisha in OT times, feeding the people with manna in the desert (Ex. 16; Nu. 11) and a hundred men with barley loaves and grain (2 Ki. 4:42–44), he now does again plenteously through Jesus. The question whether this is the prophet 'like Moses' and a prophet greater than Elisha is inevitably raised. What is not so clear is whether Luke saw in the narrative specifically messianic traits which led directly to the following christological confession. To the early church this may well have been the case. There is no avoiding the fact that the language used at the decisive point in the narrative is reminiscent of the Last Supper; the form of the 'words of institution' used at the Lord's Supper would be brought to mind as the story was told in the church, and hence it would inevitably be suggested to the hearers that the One who broke bread in this manner was the One who gave himself in death for many and who continued to be present with his disciples in the Lord's Supper. The story may also have suggested ideas of the feast to be celebrated in the kingdom of God, a motif which we know to have been familiar to Luke (14:15); the One who provides such an 'antepast of heaven' cannot be other than the Messiah. Hence, through associations such as these, Luke may be indicating to his readers that the feeding should be seen as providing the basis for the confession of Jesus as the Messiah.

Luke's narrative is closely dependent upon that of Mk.; there are one or two agreements with Mt. against Mk. which may go beyond mere coincidence, but they hardly testify to anything more than the existence of continuing oral traditions of a familiar story. The theological emphases of Luke as opposed to Mark have been noted above. The main difference lies in the enhanced christological stress; by contrast Mark dwells more on the significance of Jesus as the supplier of human needs, the giver of bread from heaven, the shepherd of the needy flock.

How far all these various theological motifs extend back to the original incident, it is hard to say. The problem is complicated by the presence of two feeding miracles in Mk., and by the existence of an independent Johannine account. It must suffice to note that behind the various accounts lies a tradition that Jesus appeased the hunger of a needy multitude with a small quantity of food that miraculously sufficed them; in this act the early church saw the supernatural power of Jesus to provide for human need and a picture of his spiritual help. Such stories were also told in the OT; it is not surprising that the early church believed that Jesus could do the same, but it would be surprising if they had come to this belief without some basis in the actual ministry of Jesus. If the precise details cannot be proved historically, it is equally impossible to deny on historical grounds that what the Gospels narrate took place in some sort of way.

See B. M. F. van Iersel, 'Die wunderbare Speisung und das Abendmahl in der synoptischen Tradition', Nov.T 7, 1964, 167–194; Kertelge, 129–139; I. de la Potterie, 'Le sens primitif de la multiplication des pains', in Dupont, *Jésus*, 303–329; full bibliography in Schürmann, I, 509.

(10) In the first part of the verse Luke reproduces the substance of Mk. 6:30 with his own stylistic variations (ὑποστρέφω diff. Mk. συνάγομαι; διηγέομαι diff. Mk. ἀπαγγέλλω; cf. 8:39 note). Like Mark he refers to the Twelve as ἀπόστολοι; cf. 6:13. This makes it clear that the title applies to those who carry out the functions of preaching the gospel and healing the sick as a result of a commission from Jesus himself; this preliminary definition of what it means to be an apostle must be kept in mind when the idea recurs later in Acts. For Luke the report of their activity is confined to what they did, but this may also include ὅσα

ἐδίδαξαν, a Marcan phrase which Luke has omitted, perhaps because ὅσα seemed an inappropriate term to use of teaching. There was in any case no need to report *what* they had taught, since they had presumably followed their instructions; what needed reporting was the extent of their work and the response to it, although neither Mark nor Luke has any information to give his readers about this.

Luke omits the material in Mk. 6:31 which refers to the disciples' need for rest and their inability to have it because of the crowds. He concentrates rather on the way in which Jesus takes the disciples aside (παραλαμβάνω, 9:28; 11:26; 17:34f.; 18:31*), so that they might be away from the crowds; the indications are that a time of private (κατ' ἰδίαν) conversation was intended, but this intention had to be postponed; however, the dramatic or literary effect of the comment may be to indicate that what did happen in the presence of the crowds was really meant for the disciples. The verb ὑποχωρέω (5:16**) suggests withdrawal or retreat. While this may have been simply from the crowds, Matthew (ἀναχωρέω, diff. Mk. ἀπέρχομαι; cf. Jn. 6:15) suggests that it may have been, at least partly, a strategic retreat from the sphere of influence of Herod Antipas. While the other Gospels describe the goal of Jesus as 'a desert place', Luke identifies it with 'a town called Bethsaida' (πόλιν καλουμένην Βηθσαϊδά, (p⁷⁵) ℵ¹ B L Ξ 33 pc). The MSS vary considerably here, many assimilating to Mk. 6:32 or to Lk. 9:12, or making the place into a village (Mk. 8:23, 26), whereas Luke regarded it as a town (10:10–13); thus we have: κώμην λεγομένην B. (D); τόπον ἔρημον (ℵ* ᵉᵗ² al syᶜ ⁽ᵖ⁾ boᵖᵗ); κώμην καλουμένην B. εἰς τόπον ἔρημον (Θ); τόπον ἔρημον πόλεως καλουμένης B. ((A) C W pm; TR; omitting ἔρημον, f1 700 (syˢ)). The indeclinable Βηθσαϊδά and Βηθσαϊδάν both occur in the MSS. Bethsaida was a 'new town' built by Herod Philip at the head of the lake (Jos. Ant. 18:28; Bel. 2:168). In Mk. 6:45 it is mentioned as the destination of the disciples after the feeding. Luke knew that the feeding took place in the wilderness; he names Bethsaida as the nearest well-known town, and also to prepare the way for its mention in 10:13 (Schmid, 165).

(11) Luke's description is less clear than Mark's as a result of abbreviation. Jesus is seen going with his disciples (Mk.) and is recognised by the crowds, who follow him (Luke has ὄχλος and ἀκολουθέω par. Mt. and Jn., diff. Mk.). The crowds were probably of local people, but J. Jeremias (TDNT V, 899) speculates that at the root of the story there lies 'a meeting between Jesus and a procession of Galilean pilgrims' to the Passover. Luke omits the details of how they reached the spot, and concentrates on how Jesus received them (ἀποδέχομαι, 8:40 note; Acts 28:20). He proceeded to give them a lengthy discourse (ἐλάλει, imperfect!) about the same theme as that of the Twelve during their mission, the kingdom of God (cf. 4:43; 8:1; Acts 1:3); at the same time he healed (ἰάομαι, again imperfect; cf. Mt. 14:11b) those who were in need of healing (χρείαν ἔχω, cf. 5:31; θεράπεια, 'healing' (Rev. 22:2); also, 'the

servants', Lk. 12:42**). Luke omits mention of Jesus' sympathy for the crowds, and also the detail that he saw them as sheep without a shepherd. His statement about healings may be meant to summarise the events in Mk. 6:53–56; 8:22–26 (Schürmann, I, 513).

(12) The time was now late in the day; κλίνω, 'to decline, be far spent', 24:29 (cf. Je. 6:4); also 'to lay down, bow', 9:58; 24:5. The period before the end of the Jewish day at sunset is meant; this was the usual time for an evening meal. There could be an allusion to the time of the Lord's Supper in the early church. Jesus was approached by the Twelve (diff. Mk. 'disciples') with a request which Luke has reworded. Jesus should send the crowd away so that they may go to the surrounding villages and hamlets (ἀγρός: cf. 8:34; 15:15 note). Here they could find lodging (καταλύω, 19:7; also, 'to destroy', 21:6*) – a detail which Luke alone mentions, and which gives some support to Jeremias's view that they were not local people – and also food (ἐπισιτισμός**). If the people stayed where they were, they would go roofless and hungry, for they were in a desert, i.e. uninhabited area. The indications are that they were further round the E side of the lake than Bethsaida, possibly in gentile territory (the Decapolis) where Jews might not be sure of a welcome.

(13) The disciples must have been considerably surprised by Jesus' rejoinder to their request, which Luke gives in wording taken over from Mk.: 'You give them something to eat'. The UBS text (with most MSS) has the same word order as Mk.; *Synopsis* follows the singular reading of B in placing ὑμεῖς emphatically at the end of the clause (so Schürmann, I, 514), but it is doubtful whether one should follow the authority of only one MS. In any case, the command is reminiscent of 2 Ki. 4:42 where Elisha's servant is told to place a small quantity of food before a large company of people. The allusion is one that the disciples would be unlikely to catch; but it prepares a reader who knows the OT thoroughly for what is to follow. As in the OT story, so here a conversation follows in which human inability to fulfil such a command is expressed, and the way is prepared for the divine provision of plenty. Luke has abbreviated the conversation and rearranged it: the disciples protest that their supply of food is ludicrously inadequate (Mk. 6:38b) unless they go and buy more (Mk. 6:37b). Luke's form of expression (οὐκ εἰσὶν ἡμῖν πλεῖον ἤ . . . (cf. Acts 4:17; 15:28; 24:4, 11; 25:6) is close to that in Mt. (οὐκ ἔχομεν ὧδε εἰ μή . . .). In Mk. the food is apparently what can be found among the crowd, but in Lk. the disciples speak of what they have; the difference in expression should not be pressed (e.g. to indicate that the church must feed the world from its own resources). The fish appear alongside the loaves as a relish like a modern sandwich filling; a typological reference to the delicacies of Egypt (Nu. 11:4f., 22) or to the fresh ears of grain in 2 Ki. 4:42 (Schürmann, I, 515) seems unlikely. The form εἰ μήτι (2 Cor. 13:5) with the subjunctive (rather than the expected indicative; cf. BD 376) means 'if we do not perhaps buy . . .'. For the

plural use in βρώματα cf. 3:11. Luke adds εἰς πάντα τὸν λαὸν τοῦτον, to stress the enormity of the need, and omits the reference to 200 denarii, perhaps because he knows (cf. Jn. 6:7) that it would be insufficient to purchase the food required.

(14) This point is emphasised by mention of the size of the crowd at this juncture (cf. Mk. 6:44; Mt. 14:21); Luke adds his favourite ὡσεί with numerals (3:23). Schürmann, I, 515, raises the question whether the number should be taken literally, and not rather as a hyperbolic means of expressing a very large number of people and hence the power of Jesus to supply great need. In view of the well-known inability of ancient writers to express large numbers accurately, this possibility should not be rejected out of hand. It may be that Luke is employing a common feature of ancient literary style; and in any case the fundamental principle of the miracle is not affected even by a substantial reduction in the number of people present. Jesus commands the disciples to make the people sit down. εἶπεν (diff. Mk. ἐπέταξεν) has often this sense (6:46). κατακλίνω is Lucan for ἀνακλίνω (cf. 7:36), and is also used at 24:30. κλισία**, 'a group of people eating together', is used here in an accusative of respect: 'so as to form groups'. ἀνὰ πεντήκοντα means 'of fifty each', with ἀνά distributive; the preceding ὡσεί is omitted by A W Θ f1 f13 pl latt; TR; and bracketed by UBS. The suggestion that in Mk. the text implies 50 ranks or rows each of 100 (Moule, 59f.) is not supported by Luke, unless κλισία means 'row' (an unattested meaning). A reference to Ex. 18:21, 25 (as in 1QS 2:21f.) or to the usual size of Christian house-groups (Schürmann, I, 516) is improbable.

(15) The disciples follow Jesus' command and cause the people to sit down. There may be a slight stress on the place of the disciples (contrast Mk.), but this should not be pressed. Luke is rather noting that the command of Jesus was obeyed by the people to whom it was addressed, although it must have seemed strange to them when they did not know from where the food for the crowd was to come.

(16) Like Mark, Luke does not note the change of subject by introducing the name of Jesus (diff. Jn. 6:11); it is self-evident who is meant. The language used to describe his action indicates the usual action of the host at a meal, taking the food, giving thanks for it, and distributing it; but the usual action, described in such detail, was undoubtedly of special significance for Christian readers who would be reminded of the closely similar wording of the institution of the Lord's Supper. The differences should not be overlooked. There is no Passover setting (diff. Jn. 6:4), and the persons fed are a crowd of people who were not necessarily disciples; whereas at the Last Supper the disciples were fed, here they are Jesus' helpers in feeding others. There was no multiplication of the food at the Last Supper, and, while bread was a common factor, fish cannot be equated with wine. Above all, there were no words of interpretation at the feeding miracle. These points warn us against any attempt to identify the two meals, as regards their basic character;

nevertheless, there are sufficient similarities between the two to make us ask how each is to be interpreted in the light of the other. The lesson of the present feeding is the ability of Jesus to satisfy the physical needs of the people – and to go on doing so in the future. In the Lord's Supper the stress is on spiritual food; John makes the link explicit by seeing in the feeding miracle a sign of the Lord's ability to provide spiritual food. This link is implicit in the Synoptic accounts in the use of eucharistic language, but that is as far as it goes. Luke, however, perhaps goes further than Matthew or Mark in that he records the meal at Emmaus and the breaking of bread by the early church, meals in which the church continued to eat bread in the presence of the risen Lord, and so to some extent this feeding miracle may be seen as a foreshadowing of the Lord's Supper in the church, although the decisive foreshadowing is of course the Last Supper itself.

For $\lambda\alpha\beta\acute{\omega}\nu$ as the initial act in the meal cf. 22:19; 24:30; 6:4 note. An element not found in the Last Supper narrative is that Jesus looked up to heaven in an attitude of prayer; cf. 18:13; Mk. 7:34; Jn. 11:41; this was a rare attitude among the Jews (SB I, 685; II, 246f.), found especially among the Essenes (Philo, Vita 66). The insertion of $\pi\rho\sigma\eta\acute{\upsilon}\xi\alpha\tau o$ $\kappa\alpha\acute{\iota}$ by D (a reading which appealed to Creed, 129) brings out the meaning. The prayer is natural in the circumstances, Jesus seeking the miraculous power of God for what is about to happen, whereas it is unnecessary in the context of the Last Supper. The use of $\varepsilon\grave{\upsilon}\lambda o\gamma\acute{\varepsilon}\omega$ (1:28) raises problems. It usually signifies the act of praising God for something, i.e., giving thanks; here, therefore, it can refer to the normal grace before a meal, and this appears to be the case in Mk. 6:41 where it is used without an object. However, here and also in Mk. 8:7; 1 Cor. 10:16, it has a material object, and the question arises whether the verb now means 'to bless' the food in the sense of consecrating it (Jeremias, Words, 175, with reference to the present verse) so that the miracle may take place (Schürmann, I, 517). This seems unlikely. Although the reading of D it sy$^{(s)c}$ Mcion, $\varepsilon\pi$' $\alpha\grave{\upsilon}\tau o\acute{\upsilon}\varsigma$, is unlikely to be original, it may well point in the direction of the correct interpretation, namely that $\alpha\grave{\upsilon}\tau o\acute{\upsilon}\varsigma$ is an accusative of respect. Further, Lk. 22:19 has $\varepsilon\grave{\upsilon}\chi\alpha\rho\iota\sigma\tau\acute{\eta}\sigma\alpha\varsigma$, diff. Mk. $\varepsilon\grave{\upsilon}\lambda o\gamma\acute{\eta}\sigma\alpha\varsigma$, which suggests that Luke was aware of the proper meaning of the word; he also uses $\varepsilon\grave{\upsilon}\lambda o\gamma\acute{\varepsilon}\omega$ in 24:30 with no apparent difference in meaning. It is, therefore, more probable that $\varepsilon\grave{\upsilon}\lambda o\gamma\acute{\varepsilon}\omega$ here refers to a prayer of thanks for the bread, rather than to a blessing or consecration of it; but Jesus' prayer of thanks will here be one of thanks for what God is able to do to the bread (cf. Jn. 11:41f.). The bringing forward of $\alpha\grave{\upsilon}\tau o\acute{\upsilon}\varsigma$ to follow the first of the three verbs (rather than the second, as in Mk.) may simply be stylistic; Matthew was conscious of the same difficulty in Mk. and has also altered the wording. Thereupon, Jesus broke the loaves and fish in pieces ($\kappa\alpha\tau\alpha\kappa\lambda\acute{\alpha}\omega$, Mk. 6:41**), an act which has a different significance here from that in the Last Supper; here it is a matter of miraculous increase, there of simple distribution. The im-

perfect ἐδίδου indicates the successive acts of distribution to the disciples, who then put the pieces in the hands of the crowd; for the aorist
παραθεῖναι, A D W *pm*; TR; *Diglot* have παρατιθέναι, which perhaps
fits better. Thus the disciples are able to do for the people what they
could not do by themselves. A number of commentators (Schürmann, I,
517f.) find here an allusion to the place of the leaders of the church in
providing for the needs of the members and of the outside world,
whether as servers at the Lord's Supper or more generally in the life of
the church. This idea is certainly present in general terms, but it is a
question how far it should be taken in terms of the service of church
leaders. Certainly in Jn. 6:9 the thought is that Jesus can take the offerings of ordinary people and use them richly in his service, and this
suggests that in the present narrative the thought is not so much of the
task of church leaders at the Lord's Supper as of the dedication of their
gifts by ordinary believers to the service of God.

(17) But the final emphasis falls not upon the role of the disciples
but upon the abundance of the provision. There was enough for the
crowds: Luke places πάντες in an emphatic position. The hungry are
filled (χορτάζω, 6:21). There is also provision to spare. Here Luke has
improved Mark's extremely clumsy statement in the light of Mk. 8:7; cf.
Mt. 14:20. He turns the clause into a passive statement. περισσεύω
means here 'to be left over', (Mt. 14:20; 15:37; cf. περίσσευμα, Mk. 8:8)
elsewhere 'to be abundant, plentiful' (12:15; 15:17; 21:4*). κλάσμα*,
'broken piece', is taken over from Mk. κόφινος* is a large basket, such as
was carried by soldiers for their equipment and rations (Jos. Bel. 3:95;
cf. AG). The motif of the left-overs appears in 2 Ki. 4:44. The twelve
baskets signify the great amount, and incidentally point to the activity of
the twelve disciples who did the work.

Nothing is said about the reaction of the crowd to what had happened (contrast Jn. 6:14). For the Synoptic tradition the emphasis is not
on the miracle (which is not described) but on the results, and the
audience is not the crowd but the disciples. The lesson is one for disciples: Who then is Jesus?

iv. Peter's Confession 9:18–20

The question, 'Who is Jesus?', which is raised by the preceding
narratives finds its answer in the closely connected paragraphs, 9:18–20,
21f., 23–27 and 28–36; thereafter, the new theme which has arisen in
the answer to the question continues to be elaborated in the following
narratives and sayings (9:37–50). We have separated these paragraphs
for the sake of easier exposition.

In this first part of the narrative Jesus is presented at prayer (diff.
Mk.) in the presence of his disciples; he puts to them a question
regarding the popular opinions held about himself which arouses the
same answers as had already been given in 9:8. Now, however, he asks

for the disciples' own answer, and receives Peter's word, spoken on behalf of all, that he is the Christ of God. The answer indicates what function or office the disciples believed that Jesus held in the light of his earlier teaching and activity. We are not told precisely what content they put into the notion, nor what it was about Jesus that led to this estimate of him: why, for example, did they feel that he fulfilled some other function than that of a prophet? What had they seen that the people had not seen? The answer would appear to lie in the way in which Jesus had revealed himself as the giver of life, especially in the raising of Jairus's daughter, and perhaps as the provider of the messianic banquet in the feeding of the multitude, events which were revelatory only to the disciples. They also had the insight to see more deeply into the other events and teaching than the crowds, and to realise that the person who brought the blessings of the new age must be more than a prophet. The disciples also stand over against Herod, who was left in his perplexity.

In expressing this point Luke follows closely the text of Mk. 8:27–29, although the setting is considerably altered; there is no mention of Caesarea Philippi, and the incident is placed in close conjunction with the feeding miracle by the omission of all that is contained in Mk. 6:45 – 8:26 (cf. Mt. 14:22–16:12; Jn. 6:16–66).

This omission is doubtless deliberate on Luke's part. There is no reason to suppose either that the present text of Lk. is defective (cf. Streeter, 174f., for a final refutation of this view) or that Luke was using a defective copy of Mk. (Schürmann, I, 527, provides evidence for Luke's knowledge of the omitted section.) The reasons for omission must accordingly be found in Luke's purpose. a. The omitted section is repetitious of earlier material and does not materially add to the presentation of Jesus as the Messiah. b. Luke had to make omissions from Mk. in order to accommodate his extra material within a convenient length of book. c. More positively, Luke wished to move straight from the feeding miracle (and the preceding incidents) to the christological confession which was aroused by it. d. It is possible that Luke knew of a tradition which joined together the feeding miracle and Peter's confession, as in Jn. 6 (J. Weiss, 456; Ellis, 139); note, however, that Jn. 6 retains the story of Jesus walking on the water. e. Possibly also Luke wished to maintain the unity of the scene in Galilee and to avoid Mark's description of Jesus' work in gentile territory.

The historical authenticity of the paragraph cannot be considered in isolation from that of the following paragraphs; the questions of the unity of the whole section (9:19–27) and also of the historicity of the individual sections arise. So far as the present section is concerned, the decisive question is whether Jesus asked his disciples who he was and received the answer recorded here.

1. According to Bultmann, 275–278, the whole section (Mk. 8:27–30) is a legend created by the early church in which its faith in the messiahship of Jesus is read back into his lifetime. Bultmann argues that

the fact that Jesus takes the initiative is a sign of a secondary narrative; in rabbinic discussions it is the pupils who ask the questions, not the teacher. Further, the opening part of the narrative shows Jesus asking the disciples about the opinions of the people, about which he must have been as well informed as they were.

Neither of these arguments carries conviction. One cannot argue from rabbinic practice to the practice of Jesus in this kind of way; had the initiative been taken by the disciples, one suspects that Bultmann would have claimed that the likeness of the narrative to rabbinic discussions was a sign of its artificiality. Hahn, 227 n. 3, claims that nearly all incidents in which Jesus takes the initiative are secondary on other grounds, but he fails to state what these 'other grounds' are. In the present case, the argument that Jesus would not have asked for information on a matter on which he was already informed is weak: the evident purpose of Jesus' question is to see whether the disciples are prepared to go beyond the crowd's estimates of his function.

2. Hahn, 226–230, and Fuller, 109, argue that the original pericope contained Mk. 8:29 followed by v. 33; i.e. Peter's confession of Jesus as Messiah was immediately followed by a rejection of it as a Satan-inspired temptation to follow a religious-nationalist ideal. The argument for this view is that Mk. 8:30 and 31f. can be regarded as a piece of Marcan redaction and a detachable passion prediction respectively. But this argument does not prove that vs. 30–32 were inserted into an originally existing unit which linked vs. 29 and 33; v. 33 could well have been originally linked to vs. 31f. Further, there is no evidence that the title of Messiah was ever rejected by Jesus, although it is clear that its associations rendered it inadequate. Nor is it probable that at any time in the early church the use of 'Messiah' was regarded as Satan-inspired, or that such an accusation could have been hurled against Peter in this connection.

3. Hence it remains possible and indeed most likely that the title was applied to Jesus by the disciples during his lifetime, and that he accepted it – admittedly with the corrections which are made in the next paragraph. It may be significant that the confession is not ascribed to Jesus himself, but above all it would be strange if the possibility of Jesus being regarded as the Messiah had not arisen in his lifetime. The application of the title to him by the Romans and by the early church is incomprehensible if there were not some grounds for this during his ministry. While, therefore, it can be argued that it is more probable that the ascription of the title to Jesus reflects the post-Easter confession of the church, it must be asserted that the post-Easter confession presupposes the raising of the messianic question before Easter, and that it is thus more likely that the church took over the pre-Easter confession of the disciples than that it created the present scene.

See E. Haenchen, 'Die Komposition von Mk. VIII 27 – IX 1 und Par.', Nov.T 6, 1963, 81–109; Hahn, 226–230; Horstmann, 8–31; W. Grundmann, TDNT IX, 529f.; Goppelt, I, 217–220.

(18) The opening of the scene is completely rewritten by Luke who abandons the setting in the neighbourhood of Caesarea Philippi on a journey. Luke begins with a familiar καὶ ἐγένετο ἐν τῷ . . . construction. He pictures Jesus as being at prayer (3:21; 6:12; 9:28), an attitude often associated with significant events in his ministry; Klostermann, 106, suggested that here Luke takes up Mk. 6:46, but if so he has completely altered the situation. The phrase κατὰ μόνας, sc. χώρας or ὁδούς, means 'alone, privately'; cf. Mk. 4:10 where the same phrase is applied to Jesus, although he is in fact with his disciples. Hence there is no difficulty about the statement here that the disciples were with him (σύνειμι, Acts 22:11**), and the reading συνήντησαν (B* pc f; Creed, 130) is unnecessary. Similarly, in 11:1 Jesus prays in the presence of the disciples. The prayer here is apparently for divine guidance before making the decisive revelation which is to follow. Jesus then takes the initiative by asking his disciples whom the crowds (diff. Mk. ἄνθρωποι) say that he is, i.e. what role does he fulfil.

(19) The answers (ἀποκριθέντες, diff. Mk. λέγοντες, which is redundant after εἶπαν) given by the disciples are the same as those in 9:7f. where they are narrated as the popular opinions which had come to the ears of Herod Antipas. The wording, however, follows Mk. with the abbreviated construction: (sc. οἱ μὲν λέγουσίν σε εἶναι) Ἰωάννην . . ., but in the third case a noun clause is used: Luke adds ἀνέστη, as in 9:8, perhaps preparing the way for the mention of resurrection in 9:22. The closeness of the wording to 9:7f. suggests that the same tradition may have been incorporated in both narratives (Bultmann, 329; contra Taylor, 376).

(20) The question of Jesus to the disciples implies the inadequacy of the popular estimation of himself as a prophet, or even as Elijah. (Luke avoids Mark's repetition of ἐπερωτάω by substituting λέγω.) The position of ὑμεῖς is emphatic, and brings out the contrast between the crowds and the disciples. Although the question is addressed to all, it is Peter who replies as their spokesman; Luke brings his name forward for emphasis (but TR and Diglot assimilate to Mk.). The confession in Mk. (par. Mt.; cf. Jn. 6:69) has the σὺ εἶ form, but Luke has assimilated the form to that of the preceding clauses (9:19, 20a). To the simple title ὁ χριστός Luke has added τοῦ θεοῦ; cf. Jn. 6:69: ὁ ἅγιος τοῦ θεοῦ. The title of Messiah is one that has already been applied to Jesus by the angels at his birth (2:11) and by the narrator (2:26), and it is regarded as being known to the demons (4:41); cf. 24:26, 46. It follows that the title is in Luke's eyes a correct one, even if its content needs to be filled out. This estimate of the title is confirmed by the addition τοῦ θεοῦ, emphasising that Jesus is the one anointed by God and thus appointed to his service (cf. 2:26; 23:35; Acts 3:18; 4:26). Moreover, the recurrence of the same form in 23:35 may link the title of Christ especially with the passion, the thought that is developed in 9:22 (cf. Dietrich, 96–103). To be sure, Luke has seen in the title more than Peter himself may have meant. For

the latter, it may have meant no more than 'the promised One', someone more than a prophet (Goppelt, I, 218).

v. The Reply of Jesus 9:21–22

In Mk. the confession of Peter is followed by a command to a silence and then comes the prediction of the passion as a fresh piece of teaching; the section concludes with Peter's rebuke of Jesus and Jesus' counter-rebuke of Peter. Luke, however, joins together the command to silence and the prediction of the passion very closely, so that the command to silence loses in importance. He also omits the rebuke by Peter, which is an understandable procedure if, for Luke, Peter's confession already contains an implicit reference to the passion. Thus Peter no longer appears in a bad light, and the omission enables Luke to link together more closely the prediction of Jesus' own suffering and his call to the disciples to take up the cross and follow him. The disciples are represented as those who are prepared to do this; they will not die (sc. possibly as martyrs) before they see the kingdom of God (9:27).

The main emphasis thus falls, as in Mk., on the fate of Jesus. As the Son of man, he stands under divine necessity to undergo great sufferings; specifically he is to be rejected by the members of the sanhedrin, the Jewish ruling body, and to be put to death. After three days, however, he will be raised from the dead.

The historicity of the tradition reproduced here is much disputed. Many scholars regard the command to silence as stemming from Mark himself in the interests of his 'messianic secret' theology. It is pointed out that Mark knows of no reply by Jesus in direct speech to Peter's confession (Bultmann, 276). But the prediction of the passion is a suitable reply. It is, however, not incredible that Jesus should have told the disciples to refrain from divulging this confession; not only could it be misunderstood in a nationalistic sense, but also it could lead to police action against Jesus (Taylor, 377). Hence the real question is whether it is more probable that the command is to be explained in terms of Mark's theological purpose (cf. Mk. 7:36; 9:9; *et al.*). The stereotyped nature of the commands speaks rather strongly in favour of this view, although it does not rule out the possibility that Mark was expressing something that had a certain historical basis in the attitude of Jesus himself (cf. Schmid, 156–159; J. D. G. Dunn, 'The Messianic Secret in Mark', Tyn.B 21, 1970, 92–117).

The prediction of the passion is likewise much disputed:

1. The original connection of the prediction with the confession of Messiahship is disputed. It is curious that a statement about Messiahship is followed by one about the Son of man. In Mk. there is a series of predictions about the passion of the Son of man (8:31; 9:31; 10:33) which gives the impression of being a series of insertions at appropriate points into the narrative. In other words, the connection appears to be

due to Mark himself. The existence of the difficulty is confirmed by the way in which Matthew drops the Son of man title at this point (Mt. 16:21). It remains possible, however, that the saying originally contained no title (C. Colpe, TDNT VIII, 443f.).

2. The attribution of the title 'Son of man' to Jesus is strongly contested, especially when (as here) it applies to himself and refers to suffering and resurrection. This point is of secondary importance, since it is possible to postulate an original form of the saying which lacked the title. There is, however, in our opinion a strong case that Jesus did use the title with respect to himself, and that it was used in contexts which expressed the humiliation and rejection of one who should have been recognised as God's authoritative agent (I. H. Marshall, in NTS 12, 1965–66, 348–350; cf. 5:24 note).

3. It has been argued that Jesus did not anticipate suffering and death for himself, but this point has been decisively refuted (J. Jeremias, TDNT V, 713f.; *Theology* I, 278–280; H. Schürmann*; cf. Patsch, 151–225).

4. If Jesus anticipated suffering and death, it is possible that the present saying reflects his own teaching on this theme, a verdict that is unaffected by the doubt concerning the original context of the saying and by the uncertainty whether it originally referred to the Son of man. The prophecies of the passion all stand under suspicion of being prophecies after the event, but the arguments brought forward to justify this suspicion cannot prove more than that they have been edited in the light of events by the church. It is possible that they contain original material. So far as Mk. 8:31 is concerned, recent study has shown that this saying is not a creation by Mark, but contains earlier material. There is considerable uncertainty regarding the interrelation of Mk. 8:31 and 9:31, some scholars arguing that 8:31 is prior to 9:31 (G. Strecker*, 30) and others arguing the opposite (Hahn, 46–53; C. Colpe, TDNT VIII, 444). Both sayings appear to contain primitive elements, and it is perhaps best not to attempt to derive one from the other. It is a more promising approach to note that two types of formulae appear to lie behind the prophecies. On the one hand, there is the form 'The Son of man must suffer and be rejected' (cf. Mk. 9:12; Lk. 17:25). On the other hand, there is a three-membered formula which refers to betrayal into the handؚ͟. ֡ men, death and resurrection – possibly developed from a simpler form which merely included the first member (Mk. 9:31; 14:41; Lk. 24:7). In their simplest forms these formulae are free from any precise details which might be regarded as additions in the light of the crucifixion. Lohmeyer, 164f., argued that the former type was older, (cf. J. Roloff*, 39 n. 3), while Jeremias, *Theology*, I, 281, defends the latter with its possible Aramaic word-play (cf. Patsch, 196f.; R. Pesch*, 176–178). The present saying may represent a coalescence of elements from these two types of saying. How far the details go back to Jesus himself it is difficult to say with certainty; it is certainly not impossible

that he looked beyond suffering to vindication and that this found expression in his prophecy.

See Hahn, 46–53; Higgins, 30–36; Tödt, 152–221; Borsch, 329–353; Hooker, *Son of Man*, 103–116; G. Strecker, 'Die Leidens- und Auferstehungsvoraussagen im Markusevangelium (Mk. 8, 31; 9, 31; 10, 32–34)', ZTK 64, 1967, 16–39; W. Popkes, *Christus Traditus*, Zürich, 1967, 154–169; Horstmann, 21–31; Jeremias, *Theology*, I, 276–286; Patsch, 185–197; J. Roloff, 'Anfänge der soteriologischen Deutung des Todes Jesu (Mk. x. 45 und Lk. xxii. 27)', NTS 19, 1972–73, 38–64; P. Hoffmann, 'Mk. 8, 31. Zur Herkunft und markinischen Rezeption einer alten Überlieferung', in Hoffmann, *Orientierung*, 170–204; H. Schürmann, 'Wie hat Jesus seinen Tod bestanden und verstanden?' in Hoffmann, *Orientierung*, 325–363 (reprinted in H. Schürmann, *Jesu ureigener Tod*, Freiburg, 1976, 16–25); Goppelt, I, 234–241; R. Pesch, 'Die Passion des Menschensohns', in Pesch, *Jesus*, 166–195.

(21) Luke has taken over ἐπιτιμάω from Mk. Usually it means 'to rebuke' (4:35), but here it means 'to charge, speak seriously', and refers forwards rather than backwards. The element of command is reinforced by the addition of παραγγέλλω (5:14; 8:56), after which Luke regularly has the infinitive construction. Instead of the personal form 'to speak about him', Luke has the neuter form 'to tell this (fact)', perhaps because he has in mind the complex of ideas associated with the title in Peter's confession (cf. Dietrich, 100). It is obvious that the command does not imply any repudiation of the confession; it is to be kept quiet not because it is false but because it is true (Hooker, *Son of Man*, 105), and because its content, which is now to be delineated, is beyond the understanding of the people.

(22) The prediction of the passion follows immediately and is closely connected to the command to silence by the participle εἰπών. The wording is almost identical with that in Mk., except in the final phrase. The prediction is concerned with ὁ υἱὸς τοῦ ἀνθρώπου (cf. 5:24; 6:5, 22; 7:34; 9:26, 58; *et al.*) Luke has taken over the title from Mk., where it is clearly synonymous with 'Messiah' but perhaps expresses more adequately the function of Jesus; it is any case the title which Jesus himself preferred to use. The passion predictions generally refer to the Son of man, but in Lk. 24:26, 46 it is the Christ who suffers. The verb δεῖ expresses the divine purpose which 'must' be fulfilled in the career of Jesus; cf. 2:49 note and, with reference to the passion, 13:33; 17:25; 22:37; 24:7, 26, 44; Acts 17:3. The verb may express an original future in Aramaic (Patsch, 193f.). The parallel passages 18:31; 24:46; Mk. 9:12; 14:21 indicate that for Luke and the early church this 'must' lay in the necessity to fulfil what was laid down in the Scriptures. Other forms of the prediction omit this reference: Mk. 9:31; 10:33. The temptation is to regard this third type of saying as primitive, and one can see an example of the addition of the 'Scripture' motif in 18:31 diff. Mk. 10:33. But there is no way of proving this point, and it remains probable that different forms of the prediction brought different motifs into play.

Four infinitives express the way of the Son of man. First, he must suffer many things. For πάσχω cf. 17:25; 22:15; 24:26, 46; Acts 1:3; 3:18; 17:3; Mk. 9:12; Heb. 2:18; 5:8; 9:26; 13:12; 1 Pet. 2:21, 23; 3:18

v.l.; 4:1, and for the combination with πολλά cf. 17:25; Mk. 9:12 (also Mk. 5:26; Mt. 27:19). The verb means 'to suffer', and it can be used of suffering in general or of death (for the latter cf. Tg. Pr. 26:10; Ass. Moses 3:11; Jos. Ant. 13:268, 403; D. Meyer, '*ΠΟΛΛΑ ΠΑΘΕΙΝ*', ZNW 55, 1964, 132). The usage is possible in Semitic, in the light of these references. The ultimate source may be Ps. 34:19 (R. Pesch*, 169); but there is no direct OT source (cf. Ps. 33:20); a reference to Is. 53:4, 11 (W. Michaelis, TDNT V, 915) is unlikely (Schütz, 28). The precise meaning here is uncertain. 1. The phrase may refer to sufferings preceding the rejection by the sanhedrin (E. Haenchen. 'Die Komposition von Mk VIII 27 – IX 1 Par', Nov.T 6, 1963, 88 n. 3). This seems unlikely, although Heb. 5:8 might be held to support an allusion to Jesus' sufferings in Gethsemane. 2. The phrase may refer to the whole of Jesus' final sufferings and death; it will then stand as a general summary before the next two phrases in the list. But the structure of the sentence is rather against this view. 3. Matthew has omitted the following verb, so that his text has 'to suffer many things from the elders . . .' This suggests that originally the two verbs πάσχω and ἀποδοκιμάζω were closely linked together as a pair, as is confirmed by Mk. 9:12; Lk. 17:25. (Lohmeyer, 164f.; W. Michaelis, TDNT V, 914f.; cf. Tödt, 161–170). Together they refer to Jesus rejection by the Jews and his persecution by them. The term is thus not a simple synonym for 'to die', as it later became. The use of πολλά indicates that there is a wider reference.

Second, the Son of man must be rejected. ἀποδοκιμάζω is 'to reject, declare useless'; 17:25; 20:17 par. Mk. 12:10; cf. Heb. 12:17; 1 Pet. 2:4, 7. An OT background in Ps. 118:22 is expressly given in 20:17 (cf. 1 Pet. 2:4, 7), and is probable here also (Lagrange, 267). But there is a complication: in Mk. 9:12 we have ἐξουδενέω, and in Acts 4:11 the Psalm is quoted with ἐξουθενέω. Now this verb may reflect Is. 53:3 (in the non-LXX translation found in Aquila, Symmachus and Theodotion), and hence the question arises whether ἀποδοκιμάζω also represents influence from Is. 53. It is possible that influence from Is. 53 is present in Mk. 9:12, but there is no evidence for this in Mk. 8:31 par. Lk. 9:22, especially in view of the ἀπό construction which names the persons responsible for the rejection. If so, this indicates that we are dealing with two separate or separately developed traditions.

Luke (par. Mt.) has ἀπό, diff. Mk. ὑπό, to indicate the agent; cf. 17:25 and contrast 1 Pet. 2:4. The three groups of people named constituted the sanhedrin. For πρεσβύτεροι see 7:3; 20:1; 22:52; for ἀρχιερεῖς see 3:2; 19:47; *et al.*; for γραμματεῖς see 5:21, 30; 6:7; *et al.* The three groups are listed together here (par. Mk. 8:31; Mt. 16:21); Mk. 11:27 par. Lk. 20:1; Mk. 14:43; 15:1; but sometimes only two of the three groups are named. Here Luke stresses the unity of the three groups by omitting the article with the second and third nouns, diff. Mk. It is noteworthy that in 9:43 par. Mk. 9:31 the present phrase is parallled by παραδίδοσθαι εἰς χεῖρας ἀνθρώπων. The vaguer phrase may be original, especially as it produces a word-play with ὁ υἱὸς τοῦ ἀνθρώπου. If two separate formulae are involved, it is possible that ἀποδοκιμάζω has replaced παραδίδωμι in the present combined form.

Third, the Son of man must be killed; ἀποκτανθῆναι is a late first aorist form for ἀποθανεῖν. For the usage cf. 18:33 par. Mk. 10:34; Mk. 9:31; Acts 3:15; *et al.* At a later stage the more precise verb σταυρόω found its way into the tradition (Mt. 20:19; cf. Lk. 24:6).

Fourth, he must be raised on the third day. There are two changes here from Mk. Where Mark has μετὰ τρεῖς ἡμέρας, Luke (par. Mt.) has the more precise τῇ τρίτῃ ἡμέρᾳ; cf. 13:32; 18:33 (diff. Mk.); 24:7, 21, 46. The two expressions can mean the same thing, but Mark's expression could also mean 'after a short time' and is thus ambigous. On the expression see G. Delling, TDNT VIII, 220. The verb ἐγείρω replaces Mk. ἀνίστημι. The aorist passive brings out more forcefully the idea that it is God who raises up Jesus, an idea which is already present in Mark's verb; the view that Mark's usage makes the resurrection into Jesus' own act is popular (Schürmann, I, 535f.), but does not stand up to examination (I. H. Marshall in Gasque, 101–103). The idea that Jesus would die and be resurrected, would not have been strange or inconceivable to disciples who knew of the raising of the widow's son and Jairus's daughter. Hence the difficulty of the saying lies in the facts that this could happen to the Son of man, and that it was a necessary, divinely ordained part of his source. The question whether the disciples understood the saying is not raised at this point (nor at 17:25), although at 9:44 and 18:34 this motif is present. The greater problem is whether Jesus could have anticipated death and resurrection in this way. It is a well-known observation that while the sequences death-resurrection and death-parousia both occur, we never find the sequence death-resurrection-parousia in an incontestably authentic statement of Jesus. Hence it has been argued that Jesus reckoned at most with a final triumph or vindication by God, expressed in vague terms, and that the early church spoke of this in the light of the event as his resurrection while still preserving the hope of a subsequent parousia. This view has much to be said for it, especially as the early church did see the vindication and exaltation of Jesus as taking place at his resurrection. But the exaltation of a dead man presupposes his resurrection, and consequently, there is no need to doubt that if Jesus looked forward to vindication he could also have looked forward to resurrection and spoken of it.

vi. Implications for the Disciples 9:23–27

Still following Mk. closely, Luke goes on to relate the consequences for the lives of the disciples when they follow the suffering Son of man. To all who would follow him – not merely the disciples who have already thrown in their lot with him – Jesus issues the summons to be willing to say 'No' to themselves and their own ambitions and to follow him, even to the point of daily readiness for martyrdom. This principle (v. 23) is given a grounding in v. 24: only through willingness to surrender one's life for Jesus will one really gain it, for the person who tries to preserve his life for himself will ultimately lose it. This point is repeated in v. 25 in question form: such loss is loss indeed, which not even the gaining of all that the world has to offer can offset. Then v. 26 makes it plain that saving and losing one's life is determined by one's attitude to Jesus now, for upon this attitude depends the attitude of the Son of man at the judgment. V. 27 follows rather loosely. The thought of possible martyrdom has already been introduced; now comes a promise to the disciples that they will see the kingly rule of God before they die, and so they receive confirmation that it is better to follow Jesus than to obey the claims of self.

The differences from Mk. here are largely due to omission, especially the complete omission of Mk. 8:37, which introduces a slightly different line cf thought which Luke does not take up here or later (cf. Mk. 10:45). One or two Marcan phrases are omitted without loss, but more significance attaches to the omission of ἐν δυνάμει in v. 27 diff. Mk. 9:1. Luke alters the introduction to the section to avoid Mark's change of scene.

Certain of the sayings have parallels in Q material. For 9:23 cf. 14:27 par. Mt. 10:38; for 9:24 cf. 17:33 par. Mt. 10:39; for 9:26 cf. 12:9 par. Mt. 10:33. This suggests that we have here a series of independent sayings of Jesus which have been brought together in the course of the tradition. Nevertheless, it is observable that there is a certain unity in at least some of the sayings: vs. 23–25 certainly form a unity, as is attested by the linking in Mt. 10:38f., but vs. 26 and 27 may be isolated sayings. The same unity of theme is to be found in Jn. 12:23–27 where the fate of Jesus and the fate of his disciples are placed alongside each other, and this suggests that the connection made here between the prediction of the passion and the call to discipleship is a historical one (cf. Schweizer, *Markus*, 99).

The historical problems which arise in the case of the individual sayings are sufficiently complex to demand that they be discussed in the exegesis.

See E. Dinkler, 'Jesu Wort vom Kreuztragen', in W. Eltester (*et al.*), *Neutestamentliche Studien für Rudolf Bultmann*, Berlin, 1954, 110–129; Grässer, 43; Hahn, 32–36; Higgins, 57–60; Tödt, 40–46; Vielhauer, 76–79, 101–107; A. Vögtle, 'Exegetische Erwägungen über das Wissen und Selbstbewusstsein Jesu', in Vögtle, 296–344, especially 325–328; E. E. Ellis, 'Present and Future Eschatology in Luke', NTS 12, 1965–66, 27–41, especially 30–35; I. H. Marshall, NTS 12, 1965–66, 327–351 (cf. 5:24 note); Dautzenberg, 51–67; Perrin, 16–20, 199–201; Hooker, 116–122; C. K. Barrett, 'I am not ashamed of the Gospel', in *New Testament Essays*, London, 1972, 116–143; Patsch, 119–123; W. G. Kümmel, 'Das Verhalten Jesu gegenüber und das Verhalten des Menschensohns', in Pesch, *Jesus*, 210–224.

(23) Luke's use of the imperfect ἔλεγεν, diff. Mk. εἶπεν, may indicate that he regards what follows as teaching that Jesus used to give, i.e. more than once, to the people, but it is perhaps more likely that the

imperfect is used to introduce a continuation of a discourse, 'he went on to say' (cf. BD 329). In the present case there is a break from what preceded, because Jesus now addresses all; what follows is no longer private teaching for the disciples but lays down the rules of discipleship for all who contemplate following Jesus. Mark achieves this point by indicating that Jesus called together the crowd, but Luke has avoided this change of scene. The saying speaks of the conditions, apparently three in number, for anybody who wishes to follow Jesus. The phrase ὀπίσω ... ἔρχεσθαι, with the present infinitive (diff. Mk.) expressing the continuing nature of the relationship, is a synonym for ἀκολουθεῖν. For ὀπίσω in this sense cf. Mk. 1:17–20; Lk. 14:27 par. Mt. 10:38; Jn. 12:19; cf. Lk. 21:8 of following false Messiahs. The phrase has an OT background in the possibilities of following false gods or Yahweh (Jdg. 2:12; Dt. 13:5; 1 Ki. 18:21; H. Seesemann, TDNT V, 289–292). But whereas in the OT the phrase is used of following, i.e. obeying, gods, in the teaching of Jesus it is taken more literally of those who follow Jesus as their Master, and in the case of the Twelve and others actually travel around the country with him.

Those who answer this call are required, first, to deny themselves. Luke's form ἀρνέομαι (8:45) appears to be equivalent in meaning to the compound ἀπαρνέομαι used in Mk.; cf. H. Schlier, TDNT I, 469–471. The idea of *self*-denial occurs only here in the NT (though cf. Tit. 2:12; 2 Tim. 2:13 has a different meaning); Bultmann, 173 n. 1 (with Erg. 25), argues that the expression has no Semitic equivalent and is a Greek substitute for μισεῖν τὴν ψυχήν. If so, the phrase may summarise the thought of 14:26 par. Mt. 10:37.

Second, the would-be disciple must take up his cross. (The omission of the phrase by D a 1 is a scribal error, Metzger, 147f.). The phrase αἴρω τὸν σταυρόν is used literally of carrying one's cross to the place of execution (Mk. 15:21; cf. the similar use with βαστάζω (Jn. 19:17; Lk. 14:27, diff. λαμβάνω, Mt. 10:38). Crucifixion was a common fate in first-century Palestine, and the use of the metaphor requires no elaborate explanation. Jesus calls his followers to be prepared for death by crucifixion. The saying is, however, from the first metaphorical, since it refers to the action of the already condemned man in bearing the *patibulum* of his cross to the place of execution. Let the disciples take up the position of the man who is already condemned to death. Hence the saying refers not so much to literal martyrdom as to the attitude of self-denial which regards its life in this world as *already finished*; it is the attitude of dying to self and sin which Paul demands (cf. Bultmann, 173; on the varied possibilities of interpretation see J. Schneider, TDNT VII, 577–579). Hence Luke's addition of the phrase καθ' ἡμέραν (a Lucan phrase, 11:3; 16:19; 19:47; 22:53; Acts, 8x; Mt. 26:55 par. Mk. 14:49) fits the sense correctly; the proposal by Turner, 31, to follow C D W *pm* it sy^s sa^pt; TR; in omitting the phrase because it consorts ill with the aorist imperative should be rejected on textual grounds (Metzger, 147f.).

Where Mark has in mind the initial act of self-renunciation, Luke stresses the need for a daily renewal of such an attitude. For the thought see also 1 Cor. 15:31; Rom. 8:36.

Reference should be made to the view of E. Dinkler* that the saying originally referred to eschatological marking with a *tau* or *chi* (T or X) as in Ezk. 9:4ff. But it is quite clear that the saying did not have this meaning for the Evangelists, and there is no proof that it was so understood at an earlier stage. Other scholars take the saying in its traditional meaning as an early Christian creation in the light of the actual death of Jesus (Creed, 194; Grässer, 43); but there is no necessary reference to Jesus' own death in it, although the early church would not be slow to interpret the saying in the light of it.

Finally, the disciples must follow Jesus; for ἀκολουθέω cf. 5:11. Since ἀκολουθέω is equivalent in meaning to ὀπίσω ἔρχομαι, the force must be 'and (in this way) follow me', unless we take the verb to mean 'to follow wholeheartedly' (Lagrange, 268). The point is that the disciple who takes up his cross is doing what Jesus does; he is following in the same way as his Master. This is brought out clearly in 14:27 par. Mt. 10:38, where bearing the cross and following Jesus are joined together as the two conditions for being a disciple.

There need be no doubt about the authenticity of the sentiments in this verse, although it may represent a summary of the sayings found in 14:26f. and the original wording can hardly be reconstructed. The use of the basic imagery appears to have been known in Judaism: 'Abraham took the wood and laid it on his son Isaac, like a man who carries a cross on his shoulder' (Gn. R 56 (36c), in SB I, 587).

(24) The second saying in this group of five is again taken almost verbatim from Mk. It places in opposition two types of men. First, there is the person who wishes to preserve (σῴζω) his life. The word ψυχή (1:46; 2:35; 6:9; *et al.*) can mean 'soul' or 'life', and often the two meanings run into each other. Here the meaning appears to be a person's 'real' life, or what he considers to be 'real'; it is the existence of a particular, individual being (cf. Dautzenberg, 51–67). A person who wishes to preserve his own way of life by avoiding self-denial or martyrdom will lose his life, i.e. at the final judgment, and will not enjoy it in the age to come (cf. Jn. 12:25). Second, there is the person who is prepared to lose his life, i.e. to be willing to give up what he considers valuable. Such a person will paradoxically preserve his life. Through the experience of loss he will come to save his life in a deeper sense. Such a loss, however, is undergone for a particular reason, namely for the sake of Jesus (ἕνεκεν ἐμοῦ), i.e. for the sake of loyalty to him. Mark adds the words καὶ τοῦ εὐαγγελίου; Luke's omission of them (cf. 18:29) has the effect of concentrating attention on personal loyalty to Jesus. The addition of οὗτος by Luke lays a certain accent on the person who is rewarded for such loyalty. The saying may refer to self-denial in general or to martyrdom; the former is more likely, but of course the extreme case is not to

be excluded from the general thought.

The paradoxical thought expressed in the saying is paralleled elsewhere (Tamid 66a; SB I, 587f.). There is no reason why Jesus should not have employed it to express his point. The parallel form in 17:33 par. Mt. 10:39 differs in wording and appears to be a translation variant (see note there); Luke does not have the qualification ἕνεκεν ἐμοῦ, diff. Mt., but this may be due to the new context in which he has placed the saying (cf. 6:22 note: though see C. Colpe, TDNT VIII, 443 n. 308). The context in 17:33 is one of martyrdom, but it seems doubtful whether this is original.

(25) The urgency of the command to choose between two ways of life in v. 24 is now stressed in the third saying of the series by a rhetorical question which points out the folly of gaining what the world has to offer while losing one's self or real life. Luke is following Mk., but he has altered the form of the question from an accusative and infinitive construction to a personal subject with the verb ὠφελέω, 'to help, aid, benefit, be of use to', which is now placed in the passive (par. Mt.). The thought is of material gain (κερδαίνω, 'to gain'; also 'to avoid something unpleasant', Acts 27:21*), complete and total. The man gains the whole of the κόσμος (11:50; 12:30*), here thought of as something valuable, but as a temptation to lead men away from God; there is also the suggestion of its transitory nature (cf. 1 Jn. 2:17; H. Sasse, TDNT III, 967–898, especially 888). The contrast is between gain and loss; ζημιόω 'to inflict injury or punishment', passive, 'to suffer loss, forfeit something', is used in Mk. (par. Mt.) with τὴν ψυχὴν αὐτοῦ as accusative of respect (cf. Phil. 3:8). Luke has paraphrased Mk. He has substituted ἑαυτόν for τὴν ψυχὴν αὐτοῦ, and he has introduced the participle ἀπολέσας. Thereby he has made it clear that the subject of this verse is the same as that of the preceding one; at the same time, however, he has slightly complicated the syntax, for ἑαυτόν must now serve both as a direct object and as an accusative of respect. This view assumes that the two participles are equivalent in meaning, so that ἀπολέσας· is used to elucidate ζημιωθείς. Schürmann, I, 546f., argues that the two participles have different meanings, the former referring to total loss, the latter to harm suffered by one who is eventually saved 'as through fire' (1 Cor. 3:15); this seems unlikely, since the contrast in the saying is between total gain of the world and total loss of what really matters.

In Mk. the saying goes closely with Mk. 8:37, where the point is that a man cannot give anything – not even the whole world – as an exchange for a life that stands under condemnation. The view that the sayings were originally independent (Bultmann, 86) rests on a failure to see the OT background (Ps. 49) of the sayings. Luke, however, has omitted v. 37. By doing so he has gained a better connection with the next (originally independent) saying; it may be also that the thought of a ransom for the soul was one which he did not wish to develop. But the suggestion that he could not interpret Mk. 8:37 with regard to eternal loss (Schürmann, I, 547) is unlikely. There is no reason to question the authenticity of the sayings (despite the general remarks of Bultmann, 105f.).

(26) In the fourth saying the element of loyalty to Jesus which appeared in vs. 23f. comes to fuller expression. The issue in the earlier verses was that of costly discipleship as the way to ultimate salvation. Now it is made clear why the choice between following and not following Jesus is so crucial. It is upon one's attitude to Jesus now that ultimate salvation depends; the point is put negatively: to refuse Jesus leads to rejection by the Son of man at the judgment. The saying is concerned with the possibility of being ashamed of Jesus. ἐπαισχύνομαι is found only in this saying in the Gospels, but the thought of being ashamed of the gospel occurs in Rom. 1:16 (cf. 2 Tim. 1:8, 12, 16), and it has been plausibly argued that the Pauline statement is closely related to this saying (C. K. Barrett*, 116–143). The implication of the word is probably that a situation of persecution is meant, and this is confirmed by the form of the saying in 12:8f. which refers to denying Christ. The saying speaks of being ashamed of με καὶ τοὺς ἐμοὺς λόγους. In both Lk. and Mk. some textual authorities omit λόγους, so that the meaning would be presumably 'me and my (followers)'; so (in Lk.) D it sy᷃ᶜ Orig; Diglot; NEB. But the omission here and in Mk. is unlikely to be original (Metzger, 99f.; C. K. Barrett*, 132–134), and the text undoubtedly refers to rejection of the message of Jesus. This element has been thought to be Marcan (since it is absent from the Q form), and derived from Mk. 13:31; cf. Mk. 8:35. This is debatable, since it is not clear why Mark should have altered the common possessive μου to the rare ἐμός used here (Mk. 8:38; 10:40*). Mark's form adds the phrase 'in this adulterous and sinful generation', which Luke has omitted, probably in order to generalise the saying. Luke then brings forward the antecedent of the opening relative clause for emphasis (τοῦτον, diff. Mk. αὐτόν). Such a person who is ashamed of Jesus will find that he experiences condign treatment from the Son of man. He will be ashamed of him, i.e. will refuse to own him; for this phrase used of Jesus cf. Heb. 2:11, and of God, cf. Heb. 11:16. The subject is the Son of man who appears as the decisive arbiter of human destiny. The decision is associated with the 'coming' of the Son of man. Reference to the coming of the Son of man is found in Mk. 13:26 (citing Dn. 7:13f.); 14:62; Mt. 10:23; 16:28 (diff. Mk. 9:1); 24:44 (par. Lk. 12:40); Mt. 25:31; Lk. 18:8. The thought, which is based on Dn. 7:13f., is a common one, and the OT allusion indicates that the idea is of a coming for judgment. It is appropriate that the one who comes as judge should be accompanied by glory (2:9), i.e. visible majesty. In Mk. it is the glory of his Father; Luke has altered the phrase to give 'his glory and (that) of the Father and (that) of the holy angels'. Thus the christology is heightened by ascribing to the Son of man his own glory. God is referred to as the Father; the addition of αὐτοῦ by D pc expresses the sense: the Son of man is understood to be

the Son of God. Where in Mk. the Son of man is accompanied by the holy angels, here he is accompanied by the glory of the angels (cf. 2:9); hence there is a triad of Son of man, Father and the angels. It is not clear whether the angels are thought of as being present; the point is rather that the Son of man comes with the glory associated with all three members of the triad.

The saying appears in a somewhat different form in 12:8f. par. Mt. 10:32f.; here it is the second part of a double expression, containing positive and negative statements. The most striking difference is the absence of the positive statement, with its promise of recognition by the Son of man, from the Marcan saying. If we are not dealing with two separate sayings, it is probable that Mark has omitted this part of the saying since it did not fit into his chain of thought, and it may be that he regarded 8:34 as a substitute for it (cf. Hooker, *Son of Man*, 118f.). Certain phrases in the present saying may be regarded as additions to the original form ('and my words', 'this ... generation', 'when he comes ...'). The difference between ἐπαισχύνομαι and ἀρνέομαι is of little importance, since variants could easily arise in the course of transmission. The most important point is the use of the term 'Son of man'. This is missing from Mt. 10:32f. (where it is replaced by 'I'), and it is also absent from Lk. 12:9 where a passive construction is used; but the use of 'Son of man' in Lk. 12:8 strongly suggests that it belongs to the original form of the double saying, and has been edited away in order to make the identity of Jesus and the Son of man clearer. It is just at this point, however, that the difficulty arises. The saying has been interpreted as distinguishing between Jesus and a separate Son of man, and its authenticity has been defended precisely because it would then reflect a christology different from that of the early church (Tödt, 55–60, following Bultmann, 117). This interpretation of the saying is most improbable (I. H. Marshall, NTS 12, 1965–66, 337–343), and it is much more likely that the saying contrasts the present lowly condition of Jesus – one of whom men might well be tempted to be ashamed – with his future glory as the Son of man – the one in whose hands is human destiny (Schnackenburg, 168–170; W. G. Kümmel*, 221–224). Other scholars, who accept some such interpretation of the saying, deny its authenticity (Vielhauer, 76–79, 101–107; Käsemann, *Questions,* 77f.) for reasons that are inadequate (I. H. Marshall, NTS 12, 1965–66, 343–345; Hooker, *Son of Man,* 116–122; Schweizer, *Markus,* 100f.).

(27) The group of sayings closes with what is meant to be a promise that some of those who face the possibility of martyrdom will have an experience of seeing the kingdom of God which will confirm their attachment to Jesus and their readiness to deny themselves as his disciples. Luke has joined the saying closely to what precedes by omitting Mark's καὶ ἔλεγεν αὐτοῖς, which may be an indication that originally the saying was an isolated logion; the use of δέ draws a contrast with the preceding verse, between the experience of those who are

ashamed of Jesus at the coming of the Son of man and the experience of others, i.e. the disciples, during their lifetime. The saying is particularly solemn, introduced as it is in Mk. by ἀμήν, which Luke has replaced by ἀληθῶς (4:24 note). Jesus' statement concerns 'some of those standing here'. Luke substitutes αὐτοῦ, 'here' (Acts 18:19; 21:4; 15:34 v.l.; Mt. 26:36**), for Mark's ὧδε, without any difference in sense, and improves the word order. It is not clear whether the 'certain people' are the disciples as opposed to the crowds who are present (Mk. 8:34), or some of the disciples as opposed to all the group. While one may be tempted to the latter view if the verse is seen as primarily referring to the transfiguration, it is more probable that the former view is right, so that the contrast is between those who accept and those who reject Jesus. These people, regarded as a particular group (οἵ, diff. Mk. οἵτινες) are promised that they will not die until they see the kingdom of God. The use of οὐ μή with the aorist subjunctive expresses a fairly emphatic negative statement, though not as emphatic as in Classical Greek (BD 365); it is a mark of the solemn utterance of Jesus (cf. MH I, 187–192). γεύομαι, 'to taste' (14:24*), here means 'to experience'; the use of the verb with θάνατον as the object is a stereotyped phrase (Jn. 8:52; Heb. 2:9; 4 Ez. 6:26; SB I, 751f.; J. Behm, TDNT I, 675–7) which brings out the bitter 'taste' of death, and perhaps refers especially to the pain of martyrdom. The saying does not imply that the persons concerned will not die; the similar phraseology in Jn. 8:51f. has a different meaning (namely that anybody who keeps the word of Jesus will not suffer eternal death), and it would be hazardous to see a connection with the present saying (cf. R. Schnackenburg, *Das Johannesevangelium,* Freiburg, 1971, II, 296 n. 1). On the contrary, they will see something *before* they die, namely the kingdom of God. In its Lucan form the reference must be to the presence of the kingdom of God as something that can be seen or experienced (since 'see' need not necessarily be taken literally); cf. Tg. Is. 53:10, 'They will see the kingdom of their Messiah' (SB I, 482). The same interpretation should probably be accepted for the saying in its Marcan form, where the sight is of 'the kingdom having come with power': the use of the perfect participle here indicates that the reference is not to experiencing the coming of the kingdom as an event but to seeing that it is already present. Now there are some Lucan texts which refer to the future appearance of the kingdom, but there is none which refers to the kingdom as '*coming*' in the distant future (unless 22:18 be taken in this sense; see 11:2; 17:20f.). The presence of the kingdom to which Luke is referring lies in the evidence of its power seen in the events of the resurrection and Pentecost. (cf. Rom. 14:17; 1 Cor. 4:20; Ellis, 141; Danker, 114f.). This is the significance of the saying in Mk., since for Mk. the conditions for the coming of the end have already been fulfilled (Mk. 9:13) and it is likely that he saw the decisive stage in the coming of the kingdom in the entry of Jesus to Jerusalem and the subsequent events (Mk. 11:10). It is true that Matthew has rewritten the saying in terms of seeing the coming of the Son of man (Mt. 16:28), but we should not be too hasty in seeing this as an interpretation in terms of the parousia – a view which is the more improbable the later the date of composition of Gospel in which it occurs; it is again more likely that Matthew was thinking of the coming of the Son of man as being fulfilled in one (or more) historical events (cf. R. V. G. Tasker, *St Matthew*, 1961, 108, 163, 223ff.; N. B. Stonehouse, *The Witness of Matthew and Mark to Christ*, 1944, 226ff.). It is, however, also possible that the saying was seen by the Evangelists as bearing some relation to the transfiguration, which can be regarded as a revelation of the kingdom of God in the person of Jesus; but this extension of meaning is secondary since the saying does not fit very neatly into this context; one does not speak of 'not dying' before seeing an event within the next few days, provided that there is no imminent threat of death; nor is a vision of the kingdom of God the most apt description of a vision of Jesus.

But while it is fairly clear that the Evangelists have understood the saying in terms of a kingdom which was present at the time when they wrote, the question arises whether the saying originally referred to the parousia. By many the saying is regarded as a prophecy of the imminence of the kingdom which was mistakenly made by Jesus (Kümmel, 25–29). By others it is regarded as providing for an interval before the parousia (not at once, but nevertheless within the lifetime of Jesus' contemporaries) and hence as a creation to deal with the problem of the delay of the parousia; while some who hold this view regard it as a creation of the early church (Grässer, 131–137), it is more popular now to regard it as a creation by Mark on the basis of 13:30 (A. Vögtle*, 325–328; Schürmann, I, 551f.; Perrin, 16–20, 199–201). On this view the saying refers to men who would not die, but see the kingdom coming (cf. 4 Ez. 6:25f.), and contains a threat of the imminence of the parousia. There are various difficulties in the way of this hypothesis. To begin with, it is not clear why Mark should have created a saying about the kingdom when the theme of the present section (and of Mk. 13) is the Son of man; the present saying has much more the appearance of an isolated logion which does not fit too neatly into its present context. Further, our earlier discussion has shown that a different understanding of the saying is probable for Mark himself. Third, the saying makes good sense on the lips of Jesus as a prophecy of the coming of the kingdom, which he saw to be associated with his own death and subsequent vindication. As regards the meaning of Mk. 13:30 see our comments below on Lk. 21:32. So far as the present text is concerned, a saying of Jesus about the coming of the kingdom has been misinterpreted in apocalyptic terms from the time of the early church down to the present day.

vii. The Transfiguration of Jesus 9:28–36

The story of the transfiguration is so closely coupled to the preceding scene that we are justified in seeking some intimate relationship between them in the minds of the Evangelists. The story is presented as a private scene in which Jesus' inmost circle of three disciples take part. At the top of a mountain, a place of seclusion suitable for a divine revelation, Jesus engaged in prayer (diff. Mk.) and his face and clothes underwent a transformation to give the impression of heavenly light and glory, such as might be associated with his heavenly exaltation or his appearance at the parousia. Along with him there appeared Moses and Elijah, two prominent OT figures, both of whom had unusual departures from this world, and both of whom were regarded as types of figures to appear at the end of the age. They appeared and spoke with Jesus about his impending 'exodus' in Jerusalem, a word which refers not simply to his death but also to his departure from the world, and perhaps to the way in which his departure would lead the way for his people out of the world and into heaven. But, just as the later predictions of the passion were hidden from the comprehension of the disciples (9:45; 18:34), so too on this occasion they failed to appreciate what was said because of sleepiness. When they awoke, it was only to see the glory of Jesus and his companions. It would seem that what was hid from the disciples was not so much the fact of Jesus' sufferings (already made known in 9:22) as the rationale and purpose of them; but the fact of the glory was revealed, though without their being able to understand how it fitted into the divine scheme; hence they thought perhaps of an immediate parousia rather than of the resurrection of Jesus. The vision was fleeting, and Peter wished to prolong it by providing tents for Jesus and his companions to stay in. The suggestion reflected the confusion in Peter's mind, and the remainder of the narrative is intended as corrective to it. A cloud, symbolical of the presence of God, covered the disciples and filled them with fear; the implication is that the divine revelation stands over against the theorisings of the disciples and bids them be silent in the presence of God. The heavenly voice from the cloud then affirmed that the Jesus whom they followed was none other than the Son of God, the One chosen by God to carry out his purpose (which includes suffering on the cross); obedience must be rendered to him, as the prophet promised by Moses. In confirmation of the voice, Jesus alone was seen as the one deserving of honour and obedience; his companions had gone, and he (it is implied) appeared again in his normal form. There was nothing more for the disciples to say in the aftermath of such an epiphany, nor did they share their experience with anybody else. It was purely an experience for the Three, but one which is now recorded for all readers of the Gospel, so that they too may have a foretaste of the heavenly glory of Jesus.

The above interpretation of the story has included the typically

Lucan features of a narrative which is based mainly on Mk. The main Lucan changes are: the dating of the incident eight days after the previous scene; Jesus at prayer; the change in Jesus' facial appearance (par. Mt.) and the mention of his glory; the conversation about his exodus; the sleep of the disciples; the association of fear with the coming of the cloud. There is a good case that for some of these alterations Luke may be dependent on other source material (Schramm, 136–139; Dietrich, 104–109; following many other scholars including Easton, 142–146; Rengstorf, 121f.; Grundmann, 191f.). It is hard to see why Luke himself should have altered Mark's dating of the incident, or to credit him with the ungainly style of v. 30 if he was not joining a couple of sources at this point. On the other hand, the case for Lucan editing of Mk., as presented by Schürmann, I, 559, 563, and F. Neirynck (cf. Neirynck, 173f.), is strong, since most of the additions and changes can be regarded as expressing Lucan motifs; if so, Luke has shown considerable freedom in inserting the prayer of Jesus, asking what Moses and Elijah were talking about and supplying an appropriate answer, and suggesting the cause of Peter's confusion. It may be best to assume that continuing oral traditions lie behind Luke's reworking of Mark's narrative, especially since some of his changes are shared by Matthew; a documentary source is very unlikely.

As for the nature of Mark's narrative, this is unique in the Gospel story. It is not a misplaced and reinterpreted resurrection story (as Bultmann, 278–281, and many others). It can, however, be interpreted as an anticipatory vision of the glory of Jesus at his resurrection or his parousia. Its christological content is complex, since it combines elements of Jesus as – most clearly – the Son of God and prophet like Moses, and – less directly – as the Son of man who appears in the manner of Yahweh at Mount Sinai. The suggestion that the Son of God motif was originally a Servant of Yahweh motif is unlikely. The incident itself is complex, and attempts have been made to remove various secondary elements or even to divide it into two strands, so that the metamorphosis of Jesus is regarded as a Hellenistic component joined to a Palestinian confession of Jesus as the Son or servant of God (Hahn, 334–340). This division is unnecessary, since both components are comprehensible within a Jewish setting. The event comprises three main items – the metamorphosis of Jesus, the appearance of the heavenly visitors, and the voice from the cloud. All are supernatural, and all have biblical parallels. Hence the narrative falls into the category described by Dibelius, 275f., as 'myth', and the question is whether we have to do with a supernatural event, described in biblical language, or simply an expression of the nature of Jesus employing mythical motifs cast into the form of a narrative. The former of these two possibilities is the more likely, since it is impossible to see how the narrative could have developed without some actual event to trigger off its formulation. But the nature of the event is such as to almost defy historical investigation.

See: G. H. Boobyer, *St Mark and the Transfiguration Story*, Edinburgh, 1942; H. Riesenfeld, *Jésus Transfiguré*, Copenhagen, 1947; A. M. Ramsey, *The Glory of God and the Transfiguration of Christ*, London, 1949; H. Baltensweiler, *Die Verklärung Jesu*, Zürich, 1959; H.-P. Müller, 'Die Verklärung Jesu', ZNW 51, 1960, 56–64; Hahn, 334–340; Horstmann, 72–103; M. Thrall, 'Elijah and Moses in Mark's account of the Transfiguration', NTS 16, 1969–70, 305–317; Dietrich, 104–116; W. Liefeld, 'Theological Motifs in the Transfiguration Narrative', in R. N. Longenecker and M. C. Tenney (ed.), *New Dimensions in New Testament Study*, Grand Rapids, 1974, 162–179; F. Neirynck, 'Minor Agreements Matthew-Luke in the Transfiguration Story', in Hoffmann, *Orientierung*, 253–266; J. M. Nützel, *Die Erklärungserzählung im Markusevangelium*, Würzburg, 1973, 289–299.

(28) The beginning of a fresh narrative is indicated by Luke's Ἐγένετο δέ ... [καί] ... construction (1:8 note; 5:1 note). καί is omitted by p⁴⁵ א* B H pc it syᵖ sa bo; (UBS); *Diglot*, but is Lucan and may be original. The phrase μετὰ τοὺς λόγους τούτους should be translated 'after these sayings', and serves to tie the incident closely to the conversation which has just preceded; the prophecy of the sufferings and of the glory of the Son of man is to be heard in close conjunction with the vision of the glory of Jesus after his 'exodus'. Wellhausen's translation (43), 'after these events' (Gn. 22:1; 1 Mac. 7:33), should be dropped from discussion, since no 'events' have been described in the immediately preceding context. Luke has substituted ὡσεὶ ἡμέραι ὀκτώ for Mark's 'six days', and thereby created a puzzle for commentators. For the grammatical anomaly see BD 144. In Ex. 24:16 the glory of Yahweh rests on Sinai for six days, and on the seventh day he calls to Moses out of the cloud. This reference is usually thought to lie behind Mark's statement, so that an OT 'type' is present in the story as a whole. But the function of the six days is different, and 'after six days' cannot mean 'on the seventh day', although it is just possible that Mark is thinking of an event on the seventh day (especially if it takes place by night at the close of the six days; cf. H. Baltensweiler*, 46–51). Since the OT typology is expressed clumsily, it may be that Luke has deliberately abandoned it (Danker, 115), and substituted a different phrase which also means 'on the seventh day' by inclusive reckoning (cf. Jn. 20:26; Creed, 134). Luke may be using a hellenistic form of reckoning based on an eight-day week by contrast with the Jewish seven-day week (Grundmann, 192). It is also possible that Luke's figure comes from a separate tradition (B. Weiss, 616). The addition of ὡσεί may indicate that he is conscious of giving an approximation to Mark's figure. The view that the eighth day as the day of the new creation is meant (Grundmann, 192; Ellis, 142, 275f.) should be rejected: Luke never uses this phrase, except here.

As Moses was accompanied by three companions (Ex. 24:1, 9), so Jesus is accompanied by his three closest disciples (cf. 8:51 for the alteration in the order of the names from Mk.). ἀναβαίνω is substituted for Mark's less suitable ἀναφέρω. The mountain (Luke omits ὑψηλόν, diff. Mk.) is the place of revelation; 6:12. Luke is not concerned about which mountain it was, and since he has no reference to Caesarea Philippi in the preceding incident, it is doubtful whether he was thinking of Hermon (the most likely identification in view of Mark's geography).

W. Liefeld*, 167 n. 27, supports Mt. Meron, NW of Galilee. The typology of Ex. 24:16 is probably present. Only Luke has the addition προσεύξασθαι (cf. 9:29; 3:21 note). Prayer is the appropriate posture for a divine revelation, although here the revelation is not to the One praying but to the accompanying disciples. The thought is rather that in prayer Jesus is caught up into the presence of God, and hence the disciples are able to see him transfigured in the divine realm. The motif is probably due to Luke himself, and its insertion is probably due to this suggested line of reasoning: if Jesus was transfigured, then it must have been through his reflecting the glory of God in whose presence he was while at prayer. The fact that Jesus was at prayer may suggest that the incident took place by night – although Luke knows that revelations of divine glory can take place at midday (Acts 22:6; 26:13).

(29) It is, then, during communion with God that Jesus is transfigured. Luke has dropped Mark's verb μεταμορφόω (on which see J. Behm, TDNT IV, 755–759), probably because it could be misunderstood in a Hellenistic sense (although this was not intended by Mark). The background is rather to be sought in the experience of Moses (Ex. 34:29f.), whose face shone because he had been speaking to Yahweh on Mount Sinai. The same motif is used by Paul in 2 Cor. 3:7, 13. See further Dn. 12:3; 4 Ez. 7:97; 1 En. 38:4; 104:2; 2 Bar. 51. Both Luke and Matthew speak of the change in Jesus' face; Matthew says that it shone like the sun (4 Ez. 7:97), Luke that the outward appearance (εἶδος, 3:22) of it became different – a colourless description, which is filled out in v. 32.

A second line of thought is associated with this Moses typology in the description of the change in Jesus' clothing (ἱματισμός, 7:25) to become white, flashing like lightning. White (λευκός) is the colour of heavenly and angelic garments (Acts 1:10; Mk. 16:5; Rev. 3:4f.; et al.). The description may simply mean that Jesus appeared in the garments appropriate to a heavenly being, or possibly that his glorified body shone through his clothes so that they appeared to share in the transformation (cf. W. Michaelis, TDNT IV, 241–250, especially 247f.). Mark's closer description of their whiteness as gleaming (στίλβω) is replaced by a stronger word; ἐξαστράπτω is 'to flash like lightning' (cf. 24:4; Mt. 28:3; Dn. 10:6; of angels) – a simile not uncommon in Lk. (10:18; 11:36; 17:24; Acts 9:3; 22:6). The rather banal Marcan simile of the fuller is dropped by Luke and Matthew. Whether this description is that of the hidden glory of Jesus while on earth (cf. 2 Ki. 6:17 for the idea) or of a proleptic vision of his future glory is perhaps an unreal question; for Luke the answer probably lies in the second alternative (W. Michaelis, ibid.). The picture may be that of the righteous one who has come through tribulation (Dn. 12:3; Rev. 3:5; Danker, 116).

(30) The 'action' begins with καὶ ἰδού, par. Mt. Luke alone describes Jesus' companions as ἄνδρες δύο (cf. v. 32), a phrase which may perhaps look forward to the resurrection and ascension scenes

(24:4; Acts 1:10) where two heavenly visitors again give a commentary on the proceedings, although these two sets of visitors are probably angels. If this allusion is correct, then the phrase here may be due to Luke rather than a source. But in both these cases, Luke may be dependent on special source material, and so Lucan redaction cannot be certainly affirmed here, especially since it is doubtful whether Luke would have introduced the phrase ἄνδρες δύο at the cost of the rather clumsy οἵτινες ἦσαν ... clause in which the names of the two visitors are added from Mk. They are Moses and Elijah (cf. 1:17), the names appearing in the usual chronological order, diff. Mk. In Mk. Elijah is the principal figure, and the ensuing discussion (Mk. 9:11–13) is concerned with him exclusively. Hence the question arises whether in an earlier stage of the story only Elijah was named. They appear in the story to talk with Jesus, though Mark does not reveal the subject of their conversation. The reason for their presence in the story is not clear, and many different answers have been given. See M. Thrall*, who suggests that Mark's purpose was to refute any idea that Jesus was merely on a level with them. Jesus is superior to them, and perhaps, therefore, they were meant to appear as witnesses to him; perhaps too at some stage the point was that Jesus is not to be identified with Moses or Elijah. This motif of witness may well be present in Luke, so that they appear as the representatives of the law and the prophets. At the same time, it is appropriate that the two men who had mysterious departures from this world and who were expected (either personally or in their counterparts) to appear again at the end of the world should be present in this scene of eschatological anticipation.

(31) Luke's description of the appearance of the two men goes beyond that of Mark. The participle ὀφθέντες, is probably based on Mk. (ὤφθη; cf. 1:11 for the use of the verb in regard to visionary appearances). The new feature is that the visitors appear ἐν δόξῃ, like Jesus himself (cf. 2:9 note). Thereby they are shown to be visitors from heaven. Luke then indicates the subject of their conversation with Jesus; for the use of the accusative in this way cf. 5:36. (See Black, 75f., but his theory of mistranslation is unnecessary.) It is Jesus' ἔξοδος, literally, 'departure'. The word is used of the 'departure *par excellence*', the Exodus from Egypt (Heb. 11:22), and euphemistically of death (Wis. 3:2; 7:6; cf. 2 Pet. 1:15, significantly in the context of an allusion to the transfiguration). But the precise force here is uncertain; it may refer to: 1. simply the death of Jesus (W. Michaelis, TDNT V, 107; Schürmann, I, 558); 2. the whole event of Jesus' death, resurrection and ascension as his departure to heaven (cf. 9:51; Zahn, 383); 3. the death of Jesus as an act of salvation, repeating the Exodus conducted by Moses (J. Mánek, 'The New Exodus in the Books of Luke', Nov.T 2, 1955, 8–23); 4. the whole life of Jesus as a 'way' which leads from his εἴσοδος (Acts 13:24) to its conclusion in Jerusalem. Although the accent is firmly on the death of Jesus, we should probably not exclude the thoughts of the

resurrection of Jesus (since for Luke cross and resurrection belong firmly together) and of the saving significance of the event (Ellis, 142). This event was to be fulfilled by Jesus in Jerusalem.

πληρόω (1:20 note) may refer either to Jesus fulfilling the OT predictions of his destiny (24:25–27) or to his completing the task which he had to do (Acts 12:25; 13:25; 14:26; G. Delling, TDNT VI, 297); the language favours the second view, since the object is not 'the Scriptures' but the actual event prophesied. Jerusalem is the place of both the passion and the resurrection. From now onwards this goal of Jesus' journeyings is constantly in view (9:51, 53; 13:33f.; 17:11; 18:31). The phrase ἦν ἤμελλεν ... is thus a Lucan explanation of the meaning of ἔξοδος for the readers. The whole verse may be regarded as Luke's substitute for the conversation in Mk. 9:11–13 which he omits.

(32) If the disciples were meant to hear the conversation and hence to receive heavenly confirmation of the destiny of Jesus in Jerusalem, they failed to do so. Up to this point they play no part in the scene (Dietrich, 110–112). Elsewhere, their incomprehension is attributed to a divinely caused lack of understanding, but here the cause is that Peter – singled out because of the leading role he is to play in the next verse – and his companions were weighed down with sleep. βαρέω 'to weigh down, burden', is used of sleep (Mt. 26:43) or of drunkenness (Lk. 21:34); Luke's language may reflect καταβαρέω, used in Mk. 14:40 of the sleepy disciples at Gethsemane, and the motif may be Luke's equivalent for Peter's failure to understand the prediction of the cross in Mk. 8:32f. (Schürmann, I, 559); sleep is less culpable than direct refusal to accept the word of Jesus, but leads to failure to understand (24:25). It follows that there were no witnesses to the conversation described by Luke, so that its content must have been later disclosed by Jesus or has been sympathetically supplied by the narrator. Nevertheless, the disciples did awake (διαγρηγορέω). The verb can also mean 'to remain awake', and this possibility deserves consideration, in which case the sense would be that although the disciples were extremely sleepy they nevertheless managed to stay awake. But the sense is unaffected; in either case, the disciples failed to take in the message about the 'exodus' and only saw the glory of Jesus and the fact that he was accompanied by the two men standing with him (συνίστημι*); the prophecy of glory in 9:26 is substantiated.

(33) In Mk. there is no mention of the departure of the heavenly companions of Jesus at this point; only after the cloud has enveloped them all do we find that Jesus alone remains. Luke's mention of their departure at this point is perhaps meant to suggest a motive for Peter's proposal to establish resting places for them. The present infinitive of διαχωρίζομαι** gives the sense 'while they were beginning to go away'. Peter addresses Jesus as ἐπιστάτα, diff. Mk., ῥαββί (cf. Mt. κύριε); cf. 5:5 note for this respectful title used by the disciples when addressing Jesus as a person of authority. (Dietrich, 114f., however, suggests that Luke

lets Peter use a title which is inadequate for a glorious figure (cf. 5:5, 8) and thus fits in with the inappropriate character of his suggestion to Jesus.) First, he makes a statement, 'It is good that we are here', which can be taken in two ways: 1. 'It is a good thing for us to be able to enjoy this experience (and so let us continue it)' (Schürmann, I, 560); 2. 'It is a good thing that we are here to be of service to you (by making booths)' (Easton, 144; W. Michaelis, TDNT VII, 379 n. 64). The first interpretation is much more likely, since there is no reason why the heavenly beings should want booths if it were not for the benefit of the disciples who wish to prolong the experience. The thought of serving the heavenly beings is not clearly expressed (although the rest of the story may contain a warning against worshipping them).

The idea of making the three booths is perhaps the most obscure in the whole story. σκηνή is originally a 'tent'; it is used in the LXX to translate 'ōhel, probably a pointed tent; sukkâ, a structure made of matting; and miškan, a dwelling (W. Michaelis, TDNT VII, 368–381). The term was particularly applied to the tabernacle, the movable place of worship erected in the wilderness, and also to the booths, made out of leafy branches, which the Israelites erected for use as shelters during the Feast of Tabernacles (Lv. 23:42f.; Ne. 8:14–17). 1. The idea that three tabernacles on the pattern of the wilderness tabernacle are meant is most improbable; the thought of giving to heavenly beings the kind of place of worship or dwelling reserved for Yahweh is hardly likely in the NT. 2. More weight might be attached to the theory that motifs from the Feast of Tabernacles play a part here (cf. H. Riesenfeld*; H. Baltensweiler*, 37–46; for a description of the feast see SB II, 774–812; C. N. Hillyer, 'First Peter and the Feast of Tabernacles', Tyn.B 21, 1970, 39–70). The feast celebrated the harvest; it looked back to Israel's journey through the wilderness; it celebrated the sovereignty of God; and it looked forward to the consummation when all the nations of the world would join with Israel in celebration of the festival (Zc. 14:16–21). Adopting this motif, Schürmann, I, 560, suggests that Peter regards the consummation as having come, and wishes that he and his companions may share the booth to be made for Jesus. This is most unlikely, and the arguments assembled by W. Michaelis (TDNT VI, 380) against this view are convincing. The booths ought to be for the disciples rather than for the heavenly visitors (unless the provision of booths for the disciples is taken for granted, Schweizer, Markus, 103). 3. The theory that the Jews thought of an eschatological tent for the Messiah does not seem to have any foundation. 4. In Lk. 16:9 there is a reference to eternal dwellings in the world to come (cf. Jn. 14:2). This may be linked with the thought that God has a dwelling in heaven (cf. Rev. 21:3). Hence the possibility arises that Peter wished to erect earthly counterparts to the heavenly dwelling places of the three visitors, so that they would have somewhere to stay on earth, and thus the glorious experience might be prolonged. For this idea cf. 1 En. 39:4–8; 41:2; 71:16; 2 En. 61:2;

Tanch. *'mwr* 9 (cited by A. Schlatter, *Der Evangelist Johannes*, Stuttgart, 1930, 292; cf. F. Hauck, TDNT IV, 579–581). This is the most probable explanation of the motif. If so, the fact that Peter did not know what he was saying means that he did not realise that the glorious scene had not come to stay; first of all there must occur the fulfilment of the 'exodus' of Jesus, and for the disciples continuing obedience to the Son of God (cf. Acts 1:6–8). Luke has omitted the element of fear which accounts for Peter's confusion in Mk.

(34) Both Luke and Matthew couple the next event closely with Peter's comment, Luke by adding ταῦτα δὲ αὐτοῦ λαλοῦντος, diff. Mk. (cf. 22:60; 24:36; Mt. 9:18; 12:46). The cloud (νεφέλη) which appears is a sign of the divine presence, as in Ex. 16:10; 19:9; 24:15–18; 33:9–11; *et al.* (cf. A. Oepke, TDNT IV, 902–910, especially 908f.). It serves to indicate that God is there, while at the same time hiding him from the sight of men. Clouds may also be a means of, or associated with, taking men up into heaven (Acts 1:9; Rev. 11:12; cf. the coming of the Son of man, Dn. 7:13; Mk. 13:26; 14:62; Rev. 1:7; 14:14–16; and the rapture of believers, 1 Thes. 4:17). Here the cloud is said to 'cover' them; ἐπισκιάζω (1:35), is used as in Ex. 40:29 (35) where the cloud of the divine presence rests upon the tabernacle and is associated with the divine glory which fills the tabernacle. But the closer parallel is with Ex. 24:15–18 where the cloud that covers the mountain appears to be the same as the glory of Yahweh. Here too Moses goes into the cloud and communes with God. Thus the tabernacles proposed by Peter become unnecessary: God's own dwelling place comes to earth and accommodates his people. But whom does the cloud cover? αὐτούς (par. Mt., diff. Mk. αὐτοῖς) can refer to Jesus and his companions and/or the three disciples. It is obvious that the former group is meant; the doubts concern the inclusion of the latter. In favour of the view that the cloud separated them from Jesus and his companions is the fact that the voice came from (ἐκ) the cloud; this seems in any case to be the view of Mark (A. Oepke, ibid.). On the other hand, Luke's statement that they were afraid as they entered the cloud can mean that the disciples were afraid as they themselves entered it, in which case he has reinterpreted Mk. (Schürmann, I, 561). But Luke's statement can equally well mean that the disciples were frightened as they saw the others (especially Jesus) disappear in the cloud, and there is no indication in the story that the disciples were to be taken into the presence of God.

(35) The disappearance of Jesus and the two men is followed by a voice out of the cloud; the voice is that of God, as at the baptism of Jesus, and the statement made is clearly intended to be an echo of what was said then. But whereas at the baptism the voice was addressed to Jesus and the message concerned him (so 3:22 par. Mk. 1:11; but diff. Mt. 3:17), here the statement is made in the third person, οὗτός ἐστιν . . ., and is addressed to the disciples. It is to them that the significance of the scene is to be revealed. Again Jesus is presented as the Son of God, in

language reminiscent of Ps. 2:7. Mark repeats the phrase ὁ
ἐκλελεγμένος. This at least is the reading of p⁴⁵ p⁷⁵ ℵ B L Ξ 892 1241;
the variant ὁ ἐκλεκτός is also found (Θ f1 1365); and one or other of
these readings is reflected in a aur ff² l syˢ ʰᵐᵍ sa bo arm; the rest of the
MSS have ὁ ἀγαπητός (as in Mk.), to which some add ἐν ᾧ εὐδόκησα,
(as in Mt.). There can be little doubt that ὁ ἐκλελεγμένος is the harder
text (Metzger, 148), so that Jesus is here described as the 'chosen One'.
The participle is unusual, and hence the change to ὁ ἐκλεκτός is understandable. The verb ἐκλέγω, corresponding for the most part to Heb.
bāḥar, is used frequently in the OT of God's choice of the people of
Israel, but also of particular individuals to fulfil particular tasks, such as
Aaron (Ps. 104:26) and the Servant (Is. 44:1f; 49:7); the adjective
ἐκλεκτός is used in the same way, of Moses (Ps. 106:23), David (Ps.
89:19), and the Servant (Is. 42:1). In 1 Enoch the term is applied to the
Son of man, a figure who is portrayed with messianic traits (1 En. 39:6;
40:5; 45:3f.; 49:2, 4; 51:3, 5; 52:6, 9; 55:4; 61:5, 8, 10; 62:1). In the
present case, the usage may reflect Is. 42:1, the passage which is usually
thought to have influenced the saying at the baptism of Jesus; if so, it is
possibly a translation variant for ἀγαπητός, both reflecting Heb. baḥir.
Luke has then assimilated his rendering to the LXX. But, although this
explanation contains an element of truth, it does not account for the fact
that Luke has carried through the change only here, and not in the story
of the baptism. Since Luke has the term ἐκλεκτός at 23:35, the suspicion
arises that he saw in it a word that applied particularly to God's choice
of his Son to tread the path of suffering that leads to glory: 'He is the
elect, not merely in or in spite of his passion, but in his appointment
thereto' (G. Schrenk, TDNT IV, 189; cf. 144–192). When we find that
Luke uses the concept of God's Servant (παῖς) in Acts (3:13, 26; 4:27,
30) with reference to the glorification of Jesus after his suffering, the
suspicion is increased that he saw in the Servant terminology a clear indication of suffering; by his assimilation of the present text to the LXX
form he has made the point clearer than it was in Mk. Like Mark, he
does not include the phrase ἐν σοὶ εὐδόκησα from the baptismal story
(diff. Mt.). Instead he gives the command αὐτοῦ ἀκούετε, i.e. 'obey him',
which reflects Dt. 18:15, and which may be meant implicitly to identify
Jesus with the prophet like Moses; but the accent lies rather on the call
to obedience than on the christological statement. What the disciples
have heard from Jesus – including especially his command to follow him
in the way of the cross – is confirmed by God and demands their
obedience. The placing of αὐτοῦ emphatically at the beginning of the
phrase (diff. Mk.) may draw a contrast between Jesus and other possible
authorities (such as Moses or Elijah, although it is doubtful whether Elijah (in himself or as a representative of the prophets) was really a live
option for the obedience of the disciples).

(36) Once again Luke closely binds the different stages in the
narrative together, this time by his καὶ ἐν τῷ ... phrase, which means

'after the voice had spoken' (aorist infinitive, BD 404²). Now only Jesus is to be 'found'; for the passive use of εὑρίσκω cf. 17:18; Acts 5:39; 8:40; *et al.* Luke's briefer phrasing, culminating in μόνος, brings out more forcefully the fact that Jesus alone remained with them. In Mk. the episode is followed by a command not to relate the incident to others until after the resurrection of the Son of man. Luke abbreviates by stating that the disciples were silent (σιγάω is Lucan; 18:39; 20:26; Acts 12:17; 15:12f.; Rom. 16:25; 1 Cor. 14:28, 30, 34**) and said nothing to anybody 'in those days', i.e. during the earthly lifetime of Jesus, concerning the things which they had seen; for the relative attraction (οὐδὲν ὧν for οὐδὲν τούτων ἅ) cf. BD 294⁴. The use of the perfect ἑώρακαν is odd. MH I, 144, argues that the form ἅ ἑωράκαμεν is found in this way in reported speech, which is virtually what we have here. Can it be an aoristic perfect (MH III, 70; BD 343³)? Or does it refer to the lasting effects of the vision (cf. Acts 22:15; 1 Cor. 9:1; BD 342²)? This last view seems best. Luke's change (diff. Mk. εἶδον) is probably deliberate and brings out the continued importance of an event which for the time being had to remain secret. Only later was its significance to become fully apparent.

viii. The Healing of a Boy with an Unclean Spirit 9:37–43a

Luke keeps to the order of Mark by following the account of the transfiguration with this story of the exorcism of an unclean spirit from a boy. The narrative is told in a simple and straightforward way – as is obvious when it is compared with the longer version in Mk. – and follows the normal course of a miracle story. In assessing its significance for Luke it is important to note the various omissions made by him at the beginning and the end of the story. At the beginning Luke has omitted details of the conversation in Mk. 9:11–13 in which Jesus speaks about the coming of Elijah (i.e. John the Baptist, as Mt. 17:13 correctly observes) and the suffering of the Son of man. This omission may be partly due to the difficulty of the conversation for his intended readers and also to Luke's own attitude to John the Baptist; at the same time Luke has already dealt with the approaching sufferings of Jesus in 9:31. But the positive effect of the omission is to bring the present story into closer connection with the transfiguration. It is the Jesus who has been transfigured who now appears to help men at the foot of the mountain; what the disciples cannot do, he can do. He appears like a visitor from another world who has to put up with the unbelief of men.

At the other end of the story Luke has omitted the teaching given to the disciples by Jesus about the need for faith in performing mighty works: contrast the way in which Matthew has developed this motif (Mt. 17:20). Thus the story is no longer, as in Mk., an example by which the disciples are taught about their own healing activity. All the stress falls on the authority of Jesus himself, and the narrative closes in typically

Lucan fashion (diff. Mk.) with the wonder of the crowds at the greatness
of God revealed in Jesus. There follows immediately the next incident in
which Jesus foretells the betrayal of the Son of man to his incom-
prehending disciples. Thus the lesson of the transfiguration – that the
gloriously revealed Son of God must suffer – is reinforced: the Son of
man who has power to heal must be betrayed by the unbelieving people
whom he would gladly help.

In general Luke has considerably abbreviated Mark's narrative,
and he has also altered the wording freely; but there are no major
changes of substance, except at the ending of the story where a
stereotyped feature of miracle stories has been added (9:43). The
evidence that Luke had access to another written source is very weak
(*pace* Schramm, 139f.).

The origins of the Marcan story are diversely estimated. Bultmann,
225f., held that two separate stories (roughly Mk. 9:14–20 and 21–27)
had been combined before Mk. Taylor, 395f., and Schweizer, *Markus*,
106, prefer the view that two separate versions of the same story have
been united. Recent scholars prefer to see one basic story which has
been considerably expanded in the process of transmission and by Mark
himself (Kertelge, 174–179; Roloff, *Kerygma*, 143–152; W. Schenk*). It
is interesting that the details which Luke has omitted are largely those
which many critics hold to be secondary in Mk., and this raises anew the
question whether Luke was influenced by a parallel tradition. In any
case the basis of the account is an exorcism story.

See W. Schenk, 'Tradition und Redaktion in der Epileptiker-Perikope Mk. 9:14–29', ZNW
63, 1972, 76–94.

(37) Luke's introduction uses elements from Mk. 9:9 and 13. He
has added a time note τῇ ἑξῆς ἡμέρᾳ. The variant διὰ τῆς ἡμέρας (Dit sy^s
^{c}; cf. τῆς ἡμέρας, p^{45}) perhaps reflects Jewish chronology in which the day
began at sunset (Schürmann, I, 569 n. 113). For ἑξῆς cf. 7:11 note. The
implication is that Luke regarded the transfiguration as taking place by
night (or as followed by sunset and the new Jewish day, Lagrange, 275).
So it is the next morning when Jesus and his three companions descend
from the mountain; Luke has altered the tense of the participle to the
aorist, since he describes what took place after the descent, whereas
Mark records a conversation during the descent. Here Jesus is met by a
large crowd; the other disciples are assumed to be with them (cf. 9:40).
For συναντάω cf. 9:18 v.l.

(38) As often the action begins with καὶ ἰδού (cf. v. 39). Luke substitutes his favourite ἀνήρ for Mk. εἷς; the man shouts (cf. 18:38; diff.
Mk.) to Jesus for help. He addresses him as διδάσκαλε (par. Mk.), but
the polite wording of his request (δέομαί σου; cf. 8:28) is Lucan style.
ἐπιβλέψαι may be aorist active infinitive (Acts 26:3; 2 Cor. 10:2) or
aorist middle imperative (cf. Acts 21:39; 2 Cor. 5:20; Gal. 4:12; cf. the
v.l. ἐπίβλεψον, D E W f1 *pm*; TR), probably the former. The verb can be
used of God, to express his watchful concern for men (1:48; Jos. Ant.

1:20; Grundmann, 194f.). Matthew expresses the same idea with ἐλεέω; cf. Mk. 9:22, σπλαγχνίζομαι. Luke alone adds the detail that the boy was the only son of his father (7:12; 8:42), which heightens the pathos; it may be a deduction from Mark's description of the father's great concern. The word order ἐστίν μοι (W Θ pl lat; TR; Diglot) is poorly attested.

(39) The description of the boy's condition appears in wording largely different from Mk. Mark has two accounts of the demon possession, 9: 18 and 22, cf. 20, and Luke has followed his own way in dealing with them. An (evil) spirit seizes the boy (λαμβάνω, diff. Mk. καταλαμβάνω) and subjects him to sudden attacks: Luke's ἐξαίφνης (2:13) brings out the sense of Mk. ὅπου ἐάν ... It cries out inarticulately (cf. Mk. 9:26), a detail which may explain why Luke has dropped Mark's description of the spirit as causing dumbness and deafness, although there is in fact no real contradiction involved. It rends the boy's body (σπαράσσω, Mk. 1:26; 9:26**) and causes him to foam at the mouth (ἀφρός**; cf. Mk. 9:18, ἀφρίζω). It will scarcely leave him alone while it continues to wear him out; μόλις is Lucan (Acts 14:18: 27:7, 8, 16; Rom. 5:7; 1 Pet. 4:18**); ἀποχωρέω (Acts 13:13; Mt. 7:23) is perhaps used as a virtual passive; συντρίβω is 'to wear out', 'to bruise', Mk. 5:4; et al. This detail is not found in Mk. who describes the frequency of the attacks over a long time (Mk. 9:21f.) rather than their persistency, but perhaps Luke has Mk. 9:26b in mind. The description corresponds to epilepsy (cf. Mt. 17:15).

(40) Just as Gehazi was impotent apart from the presence of his master (2 Ki. 4:31; Schürmann, I, 569 n. 123), so the disciples could not cure this especially hard case of demon possession without Jesus, despite the earnest petition of the father; Luke has δέομαι, diff. Mk. λέγω, to bring out the parallelism with the father's request to Jesus. Like Matthew he has δύναμαι, diff. Mk. ἰσχύω, which is used more fittingly of strength than ability.

(41) Jesus' reply is apparently addressed to the father (diff. Mk. αὐτοῖς, with reference to the crowd), but it seems to refer to the people present generally, to the father who lacks faith in the power of God in the disciples, and to the disciples who lack faith in God to perform mighty works through themselves. They are members of an unbelieving generation; for γενεά cf. 7:31; 11:29–32, 50f.; 17:25; 21:32; Acts 2:40; Phil. 2:15); for ἄπιστος cf. 12:46. The wording echoes Dt. 32:20, but the OT allusion is clearer when we take into account the addition καὶ διεστραμμένη (om. a e Mcion Tert; (Diglot)), par. Mt., diff. Mk., which is reminiscent of Dt. 32:5, 20; cf. Phil. 2:15; for διαστρέφω, 'to twist, pervert', cf. 23:2; Acts 13:8, 10; 20:30**. The phraseology thus reflects that of God when confronted by the faithless and disobedient generation in the wilderness. The addition, 'how long shall I be with you and put up with you?' may be reminiscent of Is. 46:4, but the point there is somewhat different. Here it is a case of impatience with the continued

lack of faith shown by the people. Dibelius, 278, regarded the saying as a mythical expression by a divine being, temporarily visiting the earth. It certainly fits into the context of the transfiguration. Over against the unbelief of men Jesus acts with authority and commands that the boy be brought to him; προσάγω is more appropriate of a person than Mk. φέρω. Both Luke and Matthew add ὧδε, diff. Mk.

(42) In place of Mark's parataxis Luke uses a neat (but illogical) genitive absolute with ἔτι (cf. 8:49 par. Mk.; and frequently). As in Mk. the boy is immediately attacked by the demon which dashes him to the ground (ῥήσσω, 5:37*) and convulses him (συνσπαράσσω, Mk. 9:20**); Luke uses δαιμόνιον, diff. Mk. here. At this point Mark describes the conversation between Jesus and the father in which the latter's plea for help is answered by a call for faith which leads in turn to the father's confession, 'I believe'. Luke, like Matthew, has omitted this, and thus concentrates attention on the healing power of Jesus, rather than on the lesson about faith which was obviously important for Mark. Jesus rebukes the unclean spirit (cf. 4:39; 8:24), and heals the boy (ἰάομαι; cf. Mt. θεραπεύω, diff. Mk.); then he returns him to his father; cf. 7:15, where the same compassionate gesture occurs.

(43a) The story ends with the astonishment of all present at the majesty of God. For ἐκπλήσσομαι, cf. 2:48; 4:32; Mk. 6:2; 7:3. μεγαλειότης, 'grandeur, majesty, sublimity', is found at Acts 19:27; 2 Pet. 1:16**; cf. the stress on the 'great' deeds of God at Acts 2:11 (on the word, see W. Grundmann, TDNT IV, 541f.). The incident is thus seen by Luke as a sign of the powerful, saving presence of God; cf. 7:16 and 5:25; 17:16, 18. What was visible only to the chosen three on the mountain is here visible to a greater number.

ix. Jesus Announces his Betrayal 9:43b-45

Following the healing of the epileptic boy, Mark records a private conversation with the disciples in a house on the need for faith to work such miracles; they then set out on a journey which takes them through Galilee secretly, and in the course of it Jesus gives them teaching about the passion of the Son of man. We have already seen how Luke omits the lesson on faith and concentrates attention on the figure of Jesus as the One in whom the majesty of God is revealed. Since Luke has not described the scene of the transfiguration, and in particular has not mentioned a location outside Galilee, he is also able to dispense with Mark's geographical detail in Mk. 9:30, and hence to append the prediction of the betrayal of Jesus directly to the healing story. In this way the path of suffering, as revealed to the disciples, is placed in direct contrast to the wonder of the crowd at the mighty works. But the prediction, which is given in the briefest terms (cf. 17:25), is incomprehensible to the disciples and they make no attempt to understand it. Luke brings out more clearly than Mk. the thought of a divine purpose being fulfilled in the veiling of the prediction from the disciples (cf. 18:34). The predictions are understood only later after the resurrection when the risen Lord shows from the Scriptures the necessity of his path through suffering to glory. There is thus a 'suffering secret' in Lk., corresponding to the so-called 'Messianic secret' in Mk. Luke's purpose is evidently to show that the way of Jesus was understood only in the light of the event and of the scriptural knowledge which the disciples acquired after Easter.

The wording of the pericope differs markedly from that in Mk., and has led to the suspicion that another source has been employed here alongside Mk. (Easton, 149; Schramm, 132f.); in particular it has been suggested that Luke here follows a different tradition of the passion prediction from Mk. (E. Schweizer, *Lordship and Discipleship*, 1960, 19 n. 2; cf. W. Popkes, as in 9:44 note, 158, 163; Patsch, 194); but the linguistic evidence by itself is not sufficient to support this. It remains significant, however, that the part of the prediction common to both Mk. and Lk. is precisely the part which is generally regarded as the most primitive in wording. There are thus some grounds for believing that Luke may have had access to oral traditions which reflected a more primitive form of the narrative than we find in Mk.

(43b) The context for Jesus' prediction is set in a genitive absolute construction which describes the wonder of all the people (cf. 9:23); for θαυμάζω cf. 1:21; the word may denote belief or unbelief (cf. 4:22 note), and here indicates the reaction of the crowds who have seen mighty acts but do not know anything about the deeper secrets of the kingdom which are to be revealed to the disciples. The phrase ἐπὶ πᾶσιν ... sums up the public ministry of Jesus to this point, and is not confined to the preceding incident.

(44) Jesus' announcement to the disciples regarding the passion is preceded by a demand for attention which serves to highlight the subsequent incomprehension which they showed. The phrase is a Hebraism, but has no precise equivalent in the LXX: for the use of τίθημι in this way cf. 21:14; Mal. 2:2 (but with καρδία), and for εἰς τὰ ὦτα cf. Ex. 17:14 (but with δίδωμι; cf. Je. 9:20). Hence the closest equivalent is Ex. 17:14 MT. It is not clear whether Luke is following a source which reflected a Hebrew phrase or whether he has produced a Septuagintal-sounding phrase. It is also debated whether τοὺς λόγους τούτους refers backwards to 'these things', in which case the thought is: 'strengthen your faith by recollecting the mighty acts which you have seen, for the Son of man is to be betrayed' (Lagrange, 279; Rengstorf, 124, takes λόγους to refer to the words of the crowds in praise of Jesus); alternatively, most scholars take 'these words' to be the immediately following prediction of the passion, with γάρ epexegetic (Schürmann, I, 573 n. 143), and this is on the whole more likely.

The actual prediction is brief. Again the subject is the Son of man (9:22 note). Both Luke and Matthew have a form of words in which μέλλω with the infinitive replaces Mark's simple present tense, and correctly reproduces the future sense of the underlying Aramaic participle (Jeremias, *Theology*, I, 281). The verb παραδίδωμι (1:2; 4:6) can be used of the 'handing over', i.e. betrayal, of Jesus by Judas (22:4; *et al.*); here, however, it is used in the passive of the action of God (cf. the force of 'it is necessary' and 'as it is written' in the other passion predictions) in handing over Jesus to death (cf. Rom. 4:25; 8:31f.; the usage is passed over in silence by F. Büchsel, TDNT II, 169–173; see W. Popkes, *Christus Traditus*, Zürich, 1967). εἰς χεῖρας is a non-Greek expression and represents Aramaic *lîdê* (J. Jeremias, TDNT V, 715), and the vague ἀνθρώπων can represent an Aramaic *bᵉnê 'ᵉnāšā'* which gives a play on words with *bar 'ᵉnāšā'* at the beginning of the saying (Jeremias, *Theology*, I, 282; TDNT V, 715). The statement says nothing about death or resurrection and is cryptic in meaning; it is not obvious why Luke should have abbreviated Mark's form so drastically, unless he is under the influence of a parallel tradition (cf. C. Colpe, TDNT VIII, 444, 457). In any case, the form of wording is independent of that in Mk. 8:31 and represents a second tradition of the passion prediction which in all probability reflects the teaching of Jesus himself (9:21f. note; Patsch, 196f.).

(45) Luke takes over Mark's statement that the disciples did not understand this saying; for ἀγνοέω cf. Acts 13:27; 17:23. He develops the thought independently. The saying was hidden from them; the use of παρακαλύπτω** with ἀπό is a Hebraism (Ezk. 22:26; cf. BD 155³), and the passive again indicates divine action; this is confirmed by the ἵνα clause which should be understood as expressive of purpose (E. Stauffer, TDNT III, 327 n. 43; cf. 8:10) rather than simply of result (so most commentators); perhaps we should classify it as 'intended result'. αἰσθάνομαι**, 'to understand', occurs here only (G. Delling, TDNT I, 187f.). Following Mk., Luke adds that the disciples were afraid to ask Jesus (ἐρωτῆσαι, diff. Mk. ἐπερωτῆσαι which is found in some MSS of Lk. and adopted by *Diglot*); was their fear that of hearing more explicitly something that they did not want to hear (Schürmann, I, 573)? If so, the disciples were a long way from obeying the command that followed the first prediction of the passion, 9:23–27.

x. Strife among the Disciples 9:46–48

Each of the three passion predictions in Mk. is followed by a section in which the inability of the disciples to comprehend the teaching of Jesus about self-sacrifice is illustrated by their worldly attitudes. In the case of the first prediction this is seen in the response of Peter (Mk. 8:32f.). In the remaining two the desire of the disciples for position and prestige emerges. Luke retains this motif in the present case, and indeed accentuates it. By removing Mark's geographical setting, in the same way as in 9:43, and abbreviating the beginning of the pericope, he has heightened the contrast between the prediction of the passion and the disciples' ignorance of what Jesus really meant. Jesus knows – apparently intuitively – the jealous thoughts of the disciples; he places a child in their midst, and then draws an object lesson. In Mk. the response of Jesus falls into two parts, Mk. 9:35 and 37, separated by the action with the child; Luke has combined the two statements into one in reverse order, so that what seemed to him to be the main lesson in Mk. now comes at the end as a climax. It is the one who is least in importance who is really the greatest. This principle is illustrated in the fact that Jesus regards the person who welcomes and pays attention to a child, commonly regarded in the ancient world as of no importance, as receiving Jesus, and thus receiving God himself.

The fact that Luke has altered Mark's order suggests that it is not entirely logical. Mark in fact contains two separate lessons at this point, and each has parallels elsewhere. To Mk. 9:35 corresponds Mk. 10:43f. par. Lk. 22:26; and to Mk. 9:37 corresponds Lk. 10:16 (cf. Mt. 10:40–42; Jn. 13:20). To the same set of motifs also belongs Mk. 10:13–16. It seems probable that two originally separate traditions have been linked together by Mark in a section (Mk. 9:33–50) which displays other signs of compilation; Luke has then tied them together more closely. Mk. 9:33f. forms a brief pronouncement story; the motif of the disciples' wrangling for positions of honour is well attested in different sources and is historically credible (cf. Lk. 14:8–10; Schmid, *Mark* 178), and the reply of Jesus is also so well attested as to leave no doubt of its authenticity, although the precise wording and significance may be uncertain. The saying about receiving a child in Mk. 9:37 belongs to a different circle of ideas in which the worth of children is emphasised (Mk. 9:42).

See Légasse, 17–36.

(46) Luke has dropped Mark's introduction with its reference to a house in Capernaum, since it is unnecessary in his scheme of thought. He also drops Mark's account of Jesus' question to the disciples about a dispute which they had had while on their journey, and replaces it by an editorial comment that a dispute had arisen among them. For διαλογισμός cf. 2:35 note; it corresponds here to Mk. διαλογίζομαι. The rest of the verse corresponds closely to the parallel account in 22:24 where Luke uses φιλονεικία**. For the form of the question, τὸ τίς ἄν..., cf. 1:62 note. The question concerns which of them was the greatest (μείζων used for a superlative), not who might be greater than the disciples as a group. The question is concerned with greatness in the sense of rank, position and prestige (cf. W. Grundmann, TDNT IV, 529–541, especially 531–533).

(47) In Mk. it is implicit that Jesus knows intuitively what the disciples refused to tell him about their dispute; Luke states it explicitly: Jesus

knows without being told what is still going on in their hearts, the contentious thoughts that are still present (cf. 5:22; 6:8). For εἰδώς (p⁷⁵ ℵ B 700 al sy sa), ἰδών (A C D W Γ Δ Θ f13 pm latt bo; TR) and γνούς (f1) appear as variants; εἰδώς has better early attestation, although it is difficult to see why it should have been altered if original (cf. Metzger, 24, 148). Luke omits the verbal reply of Jesus at this point (cf. v. 48b) and passes straight on to his action in taking a child. ἐπιλαμβάνομαι, 'to take hold of, grasp, catch', is Lucan (14:4; 20:20, 26; 23:26; with the acc., as here, Acts 9:27; 16:19; 18:17, instead of the more usual gen.), diff. Mk. λαμβάνω. Jesus makes the child stand beside himself, παρ' ἐαυτῷ, diff. Mk. ἐν μέσῳ αὐτῶν. The place beside Jesus suggests honour for the child, and the action replaces the description of Jesus' embracing the child which is found in Mk., a rather human trait which Luke omits (cf. 18:15–17 diff. Mk., and Luke's general avoidance of attributing human emotions to Jesus).

(48a) The action is followed by interpretation. It has been argued, to be sure, that it was the 'interpretation' which gave rise to the creation of the action (Bultmann, 65; Schweizer, *Markus*, 109; Schürmann, I, 577). Since, however, the other forms of the saying do not refer to children, we should have to assume that, first of all, the saying was adapted to refer to children for no apparent reason, and that then the scene was created to go with it. This seems less likely than the supposition that the scene and the saying belong together, although not necessarily in their present context.

The saying falls into two parts. The first part states: whoever receives this child in my name receives me. δέχομαι is used in the sense of welcoming and caring for a person (cf. W. Grundmann, TDNT II, 50–54), whereas in other forms of the saying the thought is more of showing faith and respect (cf. Schmid, *Mark*, 179). Luke has τοῦτο τὸ παιδίον, diff. Mk. ἐν τῶν τοιούτων παιδίων. The change is significant. Whereas in Mk. the saying is concerned with an attitude towards *children* and the reference to children is in general terms (cf. Mt. for an even clearer wording), in Luke the saying is concerned with the *disciples* and their attitude to the present situation in which a child is before them: *whichever of them* is prepared to receive a child will receive Jesus. (A different explanation of the change in wording is given by Schürmann, I, 576f., who identifies 'this child' with 'the one who is least' in v. 48b.) For the significance of children in the ancient world see A. Oepke, TDNT V, 639–652. Such recognition of children takes place 'on the basis of my name'. The phrase ἐπὶ τῷ ὀνόματί μου (Mk. 9:39; 13:6; Lk. 9:49 v.l.) has the meaning 'on the basis of' (H. Bietenhard, TDNT V, 277) and qualifies the action, not the recipient; elsewhere the phrase 'on/in my name' refers to the power to do mighty works that stems from Jesus, but here it suggests action on the basis of discipleship; it is because the audience are disciples of Jesus who has just symbolically received a child that they are to do the same. They act under his authority and according to his will (Schlatter, *Matthäus*, 546). At this point the saying takes a surprising turn. Instead of affirming the greatness of the person who is prepared to serve in this way, or of stating that he is like Jesus, Jesus states that to receive a child is to receive himself. This shows that the original point of the saying is concerned with the worth of the child, and that it affirms the importance of serving the child by saying that to do so is to serve Jesus himself. The thought is the same as in Mt. 25:35–40 where it is developed at length with regard to the needy and afflicted with whom Jesus identifies himself. Cf. also the idea that to serve a disciple is to render service to Jesus himself (Mk. 9:41). The present thought is not so much that of the 'Shaliach' (see below) as of an identification between Jesus and the little ones on the lines of Yahweh's close link with the needy in the OT (Schürmann, I, 576), although there is no precise parallel to this actual identification.

In the second part of the saying, however, the 'Shaliach' idea emerges. Jesus is the one who was sent by the Father (cf. 10:16; Jn. 12:44f.; 13:20; cf. 5:23). Hence to receive him is tantamount to receiving the Father. For this concept see especially K. H. Rengstorf, TDNT I, 414–420. The verb δέχομαι appears to have undergone a shift in meaning at this point, since it seems to refer more to obedient acceptance of Jesus as Lord than to charitable service performed to him. But this slight change of meaning is understandable, and does not necessarily imply that two different sayings have been joined together. It remains possible, however, that an original saying about caring for children has been enlarged by a clause from a separate 'Shaliach' saying. The clause has an implicit christological reference in that it shows that Jesus regarded himself as the messenger of God.

(48b) The saying in Mk. 9:35 is now used to form the climax of Jesus' statement. Although the formulation is parallel, the wording is quite different and reflects the influence of parallel traditions. Jesus says that the person who is least (μικρότερος, comparative for superlative; cf. 7:28) among all the disciples (ἐν ... ὑμῖν, par. 22:26) is either 'great' (Lagrange, 282; Schürmann, I, 577 n. 15) or 'the greatest' (μέγας, positive for superlative; 5:39; Zerwick, 146; cf. BD 245). But the connection of thought is obscure. 1. Leaney, 57–59, suggests that the clause refers concretely to Jesus himself as the 'junior' (7:28) in the group of disciples; thus it was appropriate for Jesus to use the child as a symbol for himself. The saying teaches the pre-eminence of Jesus over John the Baptist, and the original setting (the strife among the disciples) is slurred over. This interpretation reads a good deal into the text. 2. The more usual view is that Jesus is teaching that the person who is willing to take the lowest place is really great – such willingness being shown in caring for such despised members of society as children. This appears to be the point in Mk. 9:35–37. It would follow that there can be no question of 'greatness' among the disciples, since the person who is prepared to act as servant has abandoned all desire for greatness (unless, of course, he is serving purely out of a desire for greatness and thus hypocritically). 3. Schürmann, I, 576f., rightly notes that the clause is concerned not with *becoming* great by acting as a servant but with being great. He therefore argues that 'the least' is the child in the midst of the disciples; the child is 'great', and the disciples should forget their desire for pre-eminence and be content to serve the lowly who are truly great in the eyes of God. This gives a good connection of thought. It is hard to decide between views 2. and 3., both of which give in effect the same point, but the latter perhaps gives the clearer connection of thought.

xi. The Strange Exorcist 9:49–50

It is probable that the story of the stranger who cast out demons follows at this point in Mk. because of its catch-word connection ('the name') with the preceding pericope. The incident is tied more closely to the preceding one by Luke so that the common theme of 'welcoming' others is stressed. But it was probably an originally independent pericope. If the previous story concerned relationships within the group of disciples, this one deals with the attitude to outsiders. The case concerned a person who exorcised demons in the name of Jesus, but without belonging to the Twelve; the disciples would have forbidden him, but Jesus took a different attitude. Luke omits Mark's defence that a person who performs mighty works thanks to the name of Jesus is unlikely to speak ill of him. He passes straight on to the further statement that a person who is not against the disciples is on their side. Mk. 9:41, in which a promise of reward is made to those who care for the disciples, is omitted by Luke, perhaps since he is thinking of the attitude to be shown by the disciples rather than to them.

The historicity of the story is generally denied (Bultmann, 23f.; Schweizer, *Markus*, 110f.; Creed, 138f.) on the grounds that exorcism in the name of Jesus would be unlikely to be practised in his lifetime, and that the formulation in terms of 'following us' refers to membership of the church rather than to following Jesus; the early church was disturbed by exorcisms performed by outsiders (Acts 19:13). But the language shows possible Semitic poetical features (Black, 169–171). The narrative fits in with the disciples' consciousness of their authorisation from Jesus to perform exorcisms. Luce, 193f., observes that the early church would have been unlikely to tolerate freelancers who were independent of ecclesiastical authority. The fact that the problem of strange exorcists was present in the early church is no proof that the story must have arisen at that point. The background of the story lies rather in the appointment of the Twelve to mission, and their incredulity that one who had not been authorised in the same way should be doing the same work. It is thus a NT parallel to the situation in Nu. 11:24–30.

(49) Luke links the story closely to the preceding one with

ἀποκριθείς. John, as one of the leading members of the Twelve, intervenes with his story. Ἰωάννης is read by p⁴⁵ p⁷⁵ B C*ᵛⁱᵈ D W al; UBS; the article is inserted by rell; TR; Synopsis; Diglot, but is probably a scribal addition. After Luke's substitution of ἐπιστάτης for διδάσκαλος (5:5 note), the wording follows Mk. closely. A man had been seen casting out demons in the name of Jesus (cf. 9:48 note for the significance of the name). If the description ὅς οὐκ ἀκολουθεῖ ἡμῖν was in the text of Mk. used by Luke, he has omitted it as redundant before the next part of the sentence, but its textual status in Mk. is uncertain (it is accepted by Synopsis; Diglot; but rejected by UBS; cf. Metzger, 101; Black, 71). John and his companions had tried to prevent him (conative imperfect), because he did not follow μεθ' ἡμῶν, (diff. Mk. ἡμῖν), i.e. did not follow (Jesus) along with the Twelve; Luke has altered Mk. to avoid a possible misunderstanding.

(50) Jesus' reply is in proverbial form: they are not to prevent such a person, for, although he may not have been authorised by Jesus, a person who is not opposed to the disciples is on their side. The saying is couched in terms of belonging to 'you' rather than to 'us' (so Mk., and some MSS of Lk.). This suggests that Luke may be applying the saying more particularly to the church, in which case it is less likely that in its original Marcan form it was a church creation. The saying stands in a certain tension with 11:23, where the inverse statement is addressed to outsiders and warns them that neutrality is impossible: whoever has not taken the side of Jesus is against him (cf. Plummer, 259f.). For the two forms cf. Cicero, pro Ligario, 32. Nevertheless, even opponents of Jesus are to be treated without recriminations, as the next pericope will show.

V

PROGRESS TOWARDS JERUSALEM

9:51 – 19:10

A T the end of 9:50 Luke ceases to follow Mk.; he will rejoin Mark's story at 18:15 par. Mk. 10:13, but he omits the whole of Mk. 9:41 – 10:12. He has left out various sayings, some of which have parallels elsewhere in the Gospel (17:2 par. Mk. 9:42; 14:34f. par. Mk. 9:49f.), others of which might possibly have been open to misunderstanding (Mk. 9:43–48). There is a rough parallel to the intimation of Jesus' journey in Mk. 10:1 in Lk. 9:51, and the section on divorce, Mk. 10:2–12, is paralleled in Lk. 16:18. By these omissions Luke gains a smoother transition from the promise that the person who receives him receives God (9:48; cf. 9:50) to the contrasting story of the Samaritans who would not receive Jesus (9:52–56). Moreover, at other points where Luke leaves Mk. he omits material in this way.

We, therefore, start here a lengthy section (9:51 – 18:14) in which Luke is no longer using Mk. but follows his other sources, both material also in Mt. ('Q' material) and material peculiar to himself.

The basic structure is the same as in Mk. In Mk. 10:1–52 Jesus is on a journey from Galilee to Jerusalem. This same motif appears in Lk., but on a much greater scale. Further, just as the journey is the occasion of teaching given by Jesus in Mk., so in Lk. also the main content of the section is teaching given by Jesus, and there is little in the way of action and mighty works.

The fact that Luke here changes his main source is not necessarily an indication that a new, major section of the Gospel begins at this point, and the links between 9:48–50 and 52–56 have been noted above. Zahn, 337–455, regarded 8:1 – 11:13 as forming one continuous section, its theme being Jesus as the teacher of his disciples. In fact there are a number of thematic links between the two halves of Zahn's section (e.g. the sending out of the Twelve and the Seventy). Nevertheless, there is such a clear caesura at 9:51 that a new start at this point is probable. This is all the more the case if 9:51 is a Lucan composition. It will then correspond in intention with Mk. 10:1. Schürmann, I, 260f., it is true, regards 5:1 – 19:27 as forming one major section of the Gospel, but he subdivides it into two parts at 9:50/51.

There is also uncertainty over where the section ends. Our suggestion is that the terminus is at 19:10. There is a good case for concluding it at 19:27 just before the entry of Jesus to Jerusalem (19:28–46); but the parable of the pounds which occurs at 19:11–27 looks forward rather than backward, and so the break is perhaps more appropriate before it. The parable is really a bridge passage between the two sections of the Gospel at this point.

The whole section gives the impression at first sight of a journey from Galilee to Jerusalem, for we are constantly reminded of the fact: 9:51–56, 57; 10:1, 38; 11:53; 13:22, 33; 17:11; 18:31, 35; 19:1, (11, 28). This led many scholars to regard this as a 'travel section' or to find here a ministry of Jesus in Peraea. In fact, however, Jesus has been portrayed as a traveller from much earlier on in the Gospel (cf. 4:42; 8:1–3); what is different is that now Jerusalem comes into view as the goal of Jesus' movements. More importantly, it is now recognised that it is impossible to construct an itinerary that runs clearly through this section, although one or two scholars have suggested that one or more itineraries in Luke's source material have been obscured in the composition of the Gospel. (cf. G. Ogg* for the unlikely view that Luke used two independent accounts of the same journey). What is important is that Luke cannot have been consciously providing a geographical progress from Galilee to Jerusalem. The incidents are not tied to specific locations; if in 10:38–42 Jesus is on the outskirts of Jerusalem (assuming that the home of Mary and Martha was at Bethany, which is admittedly not stated by Luke), in 17:11 he is apparently still on the border between Galilee and Samaria, which in any case is strange after the incident in Samaria in 9:52–56. Consequently, it is unlikely that a journey as such is significant from Luke's point of view. It is probable that the journey motif was present in Luke's sources (cf. 8:1–3; 9:52–56 – pericopes which may have followed each other in Luke's source), and that he has taken over the idea because of its usefulness. It afforded him a useful framework for the material which he now includes in the Gospel, just as the meal table is also used to form a framework for teaching by Jesus. Above all, Luke is able to stress that Jerusalem is from now onwards the goal of Jesus; the dark hints adumbrated in 9:22, 31 and 44 are emphasised, and the coming passion throws its shadow over what precedes it, so that the whole of this section is to be seen in the context of the cross and resurrection of Jesus. Jesus is now conscious that he must suffer, and 'Jerusalem' becomes a symbol of this fact; the reader too is able to penetrate the symbolism, since he knows what lies ahead, although the original disciples remained in the dark.

It follows that the real importance of the section lies in the teaching given by Jesus. Here again, however, we land in difficulties, for the general themes of the section are hard to define, and it is even more difficult to find any kind of thread running through it. Attempts to establish a chiastic structure (M. D. Goulder*; K. E. Bailey*) are not possible without doing some violence to the text. There is an alternation between teaching directed mainly to the disciples of Jesus and teaching meant for the crowds and for his opponents. Here Luke differs from Mark, who gives mainly teaching for the disciples in the corresponding section. Within the section various smaller complexes of teaching may be discerned, with the emphasis on the disciples at first (9:51 – 10:24; 10:25 – 11:13) then on the opponents of Jesus (11:14–54), but thereafter clear divisions of audience are not possible. The difficulty of tracing a logical progression through the section may well be due to the nature of the material as it reached Luke. He was governed by what he found in his sources.

This raises the further question of the nature of the sources. We can distinguish between material paralleled in Mt. and peculiar to Lk., although in some cases it may be difficult to allocate material to one category or the other; Q may have contained material preserved by Luke but not by Matthew and vice versa. It is also not clear whether these sources had been combined with each other before Luke incorporated them in the Gospel. The fact that Luke has not used Mk. in this section (except in the most superficial manner) speaks strongly in favour of this possibility. In this case we have three stages in composition – the composition of the sources, the combining of the sources, and Luke's editing of the combined source – and the unravelling of such a process is likely to be extremely conjectural.

See C. C. McCown, 'The Geography of Luke's Central Section', JBL 57, 1938, 51–66; J. Blinzler, 'Die literarische Eigenart des sogenannten Reiseberichtes im Lukas-Evangelium', in Schmid, Studien, 20–52; J. Schneider, 'Zur Analyse des lukanischen Reiseberichtes', in Schmid, Studien, 207–229; Conzelmann, 53–66; C. F. Evans, 'The Central Section of St Luke's Gospel', in Nineham, Studies, 37–53; B. Reicke, 'Instruction and Discussion in the Travel Narrative', TU 73, 1959, 206–216; W. Grundmann, 'Fragen der Komposition des lukanischen "Reiseberichtes" ', ZNW 50, 1959, 252–270; W. C. Robinson, Jr., 'The Theological Context for interpreting Luke's Travel Narrative (9:51ff.) ', JBL 79, 1960, 20–31; J. H. Davies, 'The Purpose of the Central Section of St. Luke's Gospel', TU 87, 1963, 164–169; M. D. Goulder, 'The Chiastic Structure of the Lucan Journey', TU 87, 1963, 195–202; Bouwmann, 70–75; Marshall, 148–153; G. Ogg, 'The Central Section of the Gospel according to St Luke', NTS 18, 1971–72, 39–53; G. W. Trompf, 'La section médiane de l'évangile de Luc: l'organisation des documents', RHPR 53, 1973, 141–154; P. von der Osten-Sacken, 'Zur Christologie des lukanischen Reiseberichts', Ev.T 33, 1973, 476–496; Miyoshi; J. L. Resseguie, 'Interpretation of Luke's Central Section (Luke 9:51 – 19:44) since 1856', Studia Biblica et Theologica 5:2, Oct. 1975, 3–36; Drury, Tradition, 138–164; K. E. Bailey, 79–85.

a. The Duties and Privileges of Discipleship (9:51 – 10:24)

The first part of the new section is concerned with the disciples of Jesus who are accompanying him on his way to Jerusalem. Having already faced the question of their attitude to other people, they are now confronted by the hostility of a Samaritan village, which is an object lesson to them as Jesus indicates how such a situation is to be met (9:51–56). In a second incident the cost of discipleship is apparent; there must be absolute commitment to Jesus (9:57–62). These two sections form the prelude to the main core of the section, an account of the instructions given by Jesus to his disciples before mission. The narrative culminates in the successful return of the disciples and leads to Jesus' rejoicing at the revelation which has been given to the disciples and received by them (10:1–24). Thus the section develops the thought of the contrast between the disciples and the outside world, including the hostile and unrepentant, and the half-hearted. The absoluteness of the commitment of the disciples to Jesus is matched by the greatness of the divine power and revelation given to them. Duty and privilege go together.

The material in this section is partly drawn from Q. For 9:57–62 see Mt. 8:19–22; for 10:1–11 see Mt. 9:37–10:15; for 10:13–15 see Mt. 11:20–24; for 10:16 see Mt. 10:40; for 10:21f. see Mt. 11:25–27; and for 10:23f. see Mt. 13:16f. There is sufficient similarity in order between Mt. and Lk. here to suggest that they are following a common source which dealt with the mission of the disciples and the privileges which they enjoyed. This structure has been more clearly preserved by Luke.

i. Jesus and the Samaritan Village 9:51–56

The opening verse of the pericope sets the theme of the whole 'travel' section, and is probably to be ascribed to Luke himself. The appointed time of Jesus being 'taken up' has been fixed by God, and the days that lie before it are running out; therefore Jesus must face up to his fate and resolutely turn his eyes towards Jerusalem.

This theme continues in the story which follows. At the outset of the journey to Jerusalem there is opposition to Jesus, but he accepts it quietly and refuses to seek vengeance upon those who insult him. The story is thus significant for what it reveals of the spirit in which Jesus faced hostility, and is a foretaste of his passion, just as the rejection at Nazareth occupies a similar position at the beginning of the previous main section of ministry (Grundmann, 210). There is a rejection of the spirit of Elijah, although it is over-ingenious to suggest that there is polemic against an Elijah-like concept of the Messiah held in Baptist circles. The story is at the same time a lesson for the disciples when seen in the context of the preceding sections and of the following instructions for mission. In both ways it was relevant for the early church.

But the incident is concerned with Samaritans in particular and illustrates the typical hostility they showed towards Jews, a trait that is very different from that depicted in 10:30–37 and 17:11–19. The story forbids returning hostility with hostility, but does not go beyond this lesson; the implication, however, may well be that Samaritans who reject the gospel are to be treated in the same way as Jews. A positive injunction to preach the gospel to the Samaritans is lacking; this belongs to the period after Pentecost (Acts 8:4–25). The positive aspect of the ministry of Jesus is found only in what are usually thought to be scribal additions to 9:54f.

Since in what follows Jesus is still in Galilee, it is likely that the story is chronologically out of place if it belongs to Jesus' last journey to Jerusalem; if, however, Jesus visited Jerusalem as a pilgrim more than once, it could belong to an earlier journey. In any case, Luke has probably placed the narrative here for its programmatic significance.

The story has no parallel in Mt. It shares an interest in Samaria displayed elsewhere in Luke's special source material, and is probably to be ascribed to that source. It has certainly not been created by Luke but is a piece of tradition. It is hard to see why Bultmann, 24, should prefer to see reflected in it the experience of the church rather than of Jesus and his disciples.

Dibelius, 44f., felt that the colourless rebuke of the disciples at the end was not original, and that something more was originally present – as some later scribes also thought and attempted to supply the deficiency. The story was originally about two nameless disciples; when these were identified with James and John – perhaps because the narrative appeared to exemplify their character as 'sons of thunder' – the rebuke of Jesus was modified, so that not the rebuke by Jesus but the zeal shown by the disciples was stressed. But this is at most a minor theme of the story, and the stress is rather on the attitude of the Samaritans and how it should be met. Nevertheless, the way in which James and John are mentioned may be a sign that the names have been inserted.

The most odd feature to which Dibelius draws attention is the mention of the messengers who fulfil no real function in the story; they could be omitted without loss. But the mention of them seems so pointless that it is hard to believe that the messengers are a secondary addition to the story. It is more likely that an advance party was necessary if a large group of pilgrims was seeking accommodation for the night.

Flender, 33f., argues that Luke has made use of an old tradition contained in vs. 51b, 52b and 53ff., which was governed by the idea of political messiahship with Jesus understood as Elijah *redivivus*. Luke has removed the political accent by making it clear that Jerusalem is the place of Jesus' divine exaltation (v. 51a) and by associating the account with the sending out of disciples on mission (v. 52a). On this view, Luke has provided a preface to the story (v. 52a, c) in the light of Jesus' practice in 10:1, and the accent has shifted from christology to the character of the disciples' mission. This explanation makes good sense of the passage.

See J. M. Ross, 'The Rejected Words in Luke 9, 54–56', Exp.T 84, 1972–73, 85–88; G. Friedrich, 'Lk. 9, 51 und die Entrückungschristologie des Lukas', in Hoffmann, *Orientierung*, 48–77; Miyoshi, 6–32.

(51) For the use of ἐγένετο . . . καί . . . with a finite verb, cf. 5:1; the formulation is Lucan. συμπληρόω, 'to fulfil' (8:23; Acts 2:1**), is used of the coming of a time in fulfilment of a divine plan (cf. G. Delling, TDNT VI, 308f.). The use of the present infinitive with a plural noun indicates the completion of the period before the decisive event takes place, and should be translated 'While the days leading to his "taking up" were being fulfilled'. This is preferable to E. Lohse's view that the expression means 'When the time up to his exaltation had run its course', and that a perfect infinitive would have been more appropriate (TDNT VI, 50 n. 38; cf. Jos. Ant. 4:176): But in Acts 2:1 the meaning is 'while the day of Pentecost was being fulfilled'. Lohfink, 214, claims that Luke has misunderstood an OT idiom, but the expression seems perfectly possible. The period is that before the ἀνάλημψις** of Jesus. The noun, literally meaning 'taking up, receiving', can be used simply to mean 'death' (Ps. Sol. 4:20; so here Schmid, ad loc.; G. Friedrich*, 70–74), but the corresponding verb can be used both of death and of being taken up into heaven (Acts 1:2, 11, 22; Mk. 16:19; 1 Tim. 3:16). The primary reference here is probably to the death of Jesus, but it is hard to resist the impression that there is also an allusion to Jesus being 'taken up' or 'taken back' to God in the ascension, especially in view of the presence of Elijah typology in the context (9:54; cf. 2 Ki. 2:10f.; Plummer, 262); cf. the way in which ἔξοδος (9:31) is used allusively. See further G. Delling, TDNT IV, 7–9; Lohfink, 212–217. Some think that the journey of Jesus to Jerusalem is part of the ἀνάλημψις.

Since the time appointed by God was now come, Jesus himself resolved to go to Jerusalem. στηρίζω is 'to fix, establish' (16:26; 22:32*; Acts 18:23*; G. Harder, TDNT VII, 653–657); for the -σ- form of the aorist (p⁴⁵ B C L al) see BD 71; the -ξ- form is found in A D al; TR; and the imperfect is adopted by Diglot. The use of στηρίζω is slightly unusual. The whole phrase is usually said to be based on an LXX phrase which in turn translates Hebrew śîm pānîm 'el, 'to turn towards, against' (Ezk. 6:2; 13:17; Je. 3:12; 21:10; et al.) According to Harder, the Hebrew phrase means simply 'to plan', whereas the LXX phrase expresses 'the divine and prophetic turning to a place or person either to test or judge'; but to find the latter sense here is to read too much into the phrase, and it is more probable that the phrase is used here to stress Jesus' own decision to go to Jerusalem without being diverted from his intention (E. Lohse, TDNT VI, 776). There is a parallel in 2 Ki. 12:18 MT, which might be evidence of a pre-Lucan formulation here. The Hebrew here means 'to determine to do something', and this is the sense in Lk. rather than the 'to turn towards, against' meaning found in the prophets; cf. Dn. 11:17 Θ; Je. 51 (44):11f.; 2 Ch. 20:3. It follows that Luke has *not* misunderstood a Septuagintal phrase (so Dalman, 30f.), but follows a Hebrew idiom expressive of determination to do something. If so, the second half of the verse may be from a source used by Luke, and is not due to his free creation.

(52) The direct journey to Jerusalem lay through Samaria, and this was the regular route taken by pilgrims for Jerusalem; it was about three days' journey (Jos. Ant. 20:118 par. Bel. 2:232; Vita 269). It would appear that at this time Jews did not regard Samaritan food as unclean (Easton, 152). It is of course possible that the Jews carried enough food with them to last throughout the journey, but the present story appears to assume that Jews might lodge with Samaritans. Nevertheless, the general attitude between the two races was one of hostility, so that friendly overtures were likely to be rejected or at least received with suspicion and hostility (Jn. 4:9; cf. SB I, 538–560; Jeremias, *Jerusalem*, 352–358; J. Jeremias, TDNT VII, 88–94). Such was the experience of Jesus on this occasion. He had sent messengers on ahead of him in order to prepare for his coming. For ὡς (p⁴⁵ p⁷⁵ ℵ* B it; v.l. ὥστε (cf. 4:29)) with the infinitive see AG s.v. IV.3b; and for ἑτοιμάζω cf. 22:8. In view of the large entourage with Jesus (cf. 8:1–3) it is probable that he would not want to stop in a village without first making preparations for hospitality. The task of the messengers was apparently confined to this; there is no positive indication that they were to preach the gospel, but, even so, the principle of 10:16 would apply to them.

(53) But Jesus was unwelcome. The Samaritans would not receive him (contrast 9:48b); we are presumably to think of indirect rejection of him in the persons of the messengers, who then reported back on their experience. Persons travelling to Jerusalem were unwelcome. The phrase τὸ πρόσωπον . . . ἦν πορευόμενον is Semitic (2 Sa. 17:11 LXX; cf. Ex. 33:14 MT). Luke's usage is again criticised as inaccurate by Dalman, 31, on the grounds that the Hebrew phrase in 2 Sa. 17:11 means 'you yourself are going'; cf. Ex. 33:14, 'my presence will go with you'. But the phrase is perhaps indicative of determination (Lagrange, 285). It may be that Luke (or his source) has simply formulated on the basis of 9:51, and that the parallel with 2 Sa. 17:11 is coincidental; we may thus have an example of language that sounds Septuagintal but is not directly based on the Septuagint.

(54) The attitude of the Samaritans provoked a reaction from the disciples who were watching the interview: one would have expected ἀκούσαντες rather than ἰδόντες here. (After μαθηταί many MSS add αὐτόν; so *Diglot*; but the omission (p⁴⁵ p⁷⁵ ℵ B f1 *pc*) is likely to be original.) The naming of James and John is slightly awkward syntactically, and may be an addition. Wellhausen, 46, and others have suggested that the story is an explanation of how they came to be known as 'sons of thunder'. This is very improbable for the name 'Boanerges' is not used in the story, and it is unlikely that Jesus would have given his disciples a derogatory nickname; it is possible, however, that the two names were added to the story by some person who thought that it fitted this nickname. The request made to Jesus goes well beyond the instruction given to missionaries in 9:5, and in any case the issue here is not moral obstinacy and opposition to the gospel but inherited racial

prejudice against Jews (Easton, 153); this is not to be met by retaliation. But the disciples ask what the will of Jesus is. For θέλω with subjunctive (supply ἵνα) cf. 18:41 par. Mk. 10:51; Mt. 13:28; BD 366 ³; Plummer, 264. λέγω here means 'to command' (cf. 6:46). The wording of the suggested action alludes to 2 Ki. 1:10, 12, where Elijah states that if he is a man of God καταβήσεται πῦρ ἐκ τοῦ οὐρανοῦ καὶ καταφάγεταί σε. This threat against the messengers of Ahaziah was duly fulfilled, and served to establish that Elijah was indeed a man of God (cf. Rev. 11:5 for the same motif). For LXX κατεσθίω Luke has ἀναλίσκω, 'to consume' (Gal. 5:15**). The typology is made clearer by the addition in many MSS of ὡς καὶ ᾿Ηλίας ἐποίησεν (A C D W Θ f1 f13 pm it sy ᵖ bo ᵖᵗ Mcion); the evidence for omission is strong (p⁴⁵ p⁷⁵ ℵ B L Ξ 1241 1 sy ˢ sa bo; cf. Metzger, 148) and suggests that the phrase is an explanatory gloss. The saying raises the interesting question whether the disciples were speaking figuratively or believed that they had such power as a result of their association with Jesus (so Lagrange, 285).

(55) The use of στραφείς (7:9; et al.) seems to be conventional with rebukes (14:25; 22:61; 23:28). The wording is close to Mk. 8:33, which Luke omitted earlier. No saying of Jesus is recorded; the record of rebuke is sufficient. But the deficiency is made up by a number of MSS which make two additions: 1. καὶ εἶπεν, Οὐκ οἴδατε ποίου πνεύματός ἐστε (D d geo); 2. καὶ εἶπεν, Οὐκ οἴδατε οἵου πνεύματός ἐστε· ὁ γὰρ υἱὸς τοῦ ἀνθρώπου οὐκ ἦλθεν ψυχὰς ἀνθρώπων ἀπολέσαι ἀλλὰ σῶσαι (Θ f1 f13 al lat sy ᶜ ᵖ bo ᵖᵗ Mcion); there are considerable minor variations in the wording of the addition (see UBS apparatus). The additions are rejected by most editors and commentators on the grounds of poor attestation (Metzger, 148f.; WH App. 59f.), but accepted by *Diglot*; Zahn, 400–403, 765–768; J. M. Ross*. In favour of the addition: 1. The addition is as old as Marcion, and it is strange that he could make such an addition without his opponents commenting on it. 2. The story is odd if it does not culminate in a saying of Jesus. 3. The character of the addition is in accord with Lucan theology (cf. 19:10). There is admittedly nothing characteristic of Luke in the language (except perhaps the use of ψυχή in the plural (21:19; Acts, 8x), which is found elsewhere in the Synoptics only in Mt. 11:29). 4. The saying could have been offensive to later scribes because of its implied condemnation of Elijah. Against the addition: 1. The textual evidence is decidedly weak, and the considerable variation among the witnesses is typical of an interpolation (cf. Jn. 7:53 – 8:11). 2. It is easy to understand a scribe filling out a story that seemed to end abruptly. 3. The wording of the addition could be based on 19:10; Jn. 3:17. 4. It may be doubted whether later scribes would have found the implied condemnation of Elijah offensive. The Marcionite nature of the addition was defended by J. R. Harris, *Texts and Studies* II:1, 232. A number of scholars think that while the words are no part of Luke's text they reflect authentic tradition (Geldenhuys, 294; Dodd, 355 n.). There is a similar addition in Mt. 18:11, which suggests that the thought

in Lk. 19:10 was popular among scribes. But this does not explain the earlier part of the addition. Decision is difficult, and it may be safest to omit or bracket the words in face of the considerable doubt that surrounds them.

(56) It is not clear whether the next village to which Jesus and his disciples went (cf. 9:5; 10:10; Acts 13:51) was in Samaria (Klostermann, 112) or not; Otto, 18, argued that in view of this rebuff Jesus did not enter Samaria, but went along the Galilean side of the border into Peraea (cf. 17:11). But the geographical decision is in any case unimportant; what matters is that by this act Jesus and the disciples follow the principle of 'no retaliation'.

ii. Readiness for Discipleship 9:57–62

From the theme of opposition to Jesus Luke turns to his attitude to would-be disciples, three of whom express their willingness to follow him while he is on his way to Jerusalem but misunderstand the degree of self-sacrifice involved; to each of them Jesus indicates the stringent nature of discipleship. Those who would follow him wherever he goes must be ready to share the homeless lot of the Son of man, to place discipleship above the claims of family and duty, and to persevere to the end. The commitment required is absolute, and goes beyond that of a pupil to a rabbinic teacher (Hengel, *Nachfolge*, 3–17), or of an Elisha to Elijah.

A parallel to the first two encounters is found in Mt. 8:18–22 in almost identical wording. The suspicion that both Gospels are drawing on Q material is confirmed by the fact that the next piece of Q material in both of them is a missionary charge to the disciples (10:1ff. par. Mt. 9:37ff.). Lührmann, 58, notes that the preceding Q material – if we bracket off the section about John the Baptist and Jesus (7:18–35 par. Mt. 11:2–19) – is all concerned with discipleship (6:46–49; 7:1–10); hence it is probable that both Gospels here follow the order of Q, and that here Q contained material organised under the general theme of discipleship.

A problem is raised by the third encounter, 9:61f., which is not in Mt. It is a creation by Luke (Dibelius, 159 n. 1; Luhrmann, 58 n. 5; Schulz, 435 n. 239) or an addition from Luke's special source (Manson, *Sayings*, 72), or from Q, in which case it comes from a section omitted by Matthew (Hengel, *Nachfolge*, 4 n. 10) or from a recension of Q not known to Matthew (Hahn, 83 n. 4). Since this third encounter is so closely parallel to the second, it is hard to see why Luke should have invented it, and it is more likely that it stems from Q.

Bultmann, 27f., 58–60, argues that we have a succession of 'ideal' scenes here; the settings have been constructed to fit the sayings. But although the character of the questioner in the first encounter is different in Mt. and Lk., the pericope contains both the saying of the would-be disciple and the answer of Jesus, and there is no reason why the dialogue should not be an original unit of tradition. His claim to the contrary rests upon his erroneous understanding of the Son of man saying as an in-authentic wisdom saying. His objection to the historicity of the third encounter is that v. 61 sounds comical if taken as a description of real life. But the situation fits in with the stringency of Jesus' demands, and the whole point is that an apparently reasonable request meets with an apparently unreasonable answer. As for the second encounter, Bultmann has to admit that the reply of Jesus must have been handed down in the context of a concrete situation, but nevertheless claims – without any evidence – that here the meaning of discipleship has been expressed symbolically in a concrete scene.

O. Glombitza* thought that Luke added the third saying in order to have a series of three incidents in which Jesus is presented in prophetic, high priestly and messianic roles respectively. This interpretation is not obtained without some element of eisegesis.

S. Schulz, 434–442, notes that the two scenes (omitting the third) resemble the two calling scenes in Mk. 1:16–20 (cf. Mk. 2:13f.) in their brevity and terseness, but they betray later features in that the Marcan elements of calling despised fishers and tax-collectors in an epiphany scene are absent; the scenes are therefore late, 'ideal' creations by the Q community which reflect its rigorism in face of the imminent end which demands immediate and whole-hearted discipleship. There is no real connection with the historical Jesus. This reasoning is typical of Schulz's approach, according to which nearly all of the Q material is late and Hellenistic, the creation of a hypothetical Q community. The general view of tradition-history adopted here is fanciful and unrealistic, and ascribes to the community an outlook which there is no reason to deny to Jesus. Since there is nothing in the incidents which is incompatible with a historical origin in the ministry of Jesus, Schulz's verdict is to be rejected.

See H. G. Klemm, 'Das Wort von der Selbstbestattung der Toten', NTS 16, 1969–70, 60–75; O. Glombitza, 'Die christologische Aussage des Lukas in seiner Gestaltung der drei Nachfolgeworte Lukas ix 57–62', Nov.T 13, 1971, 14–23; Hengel, *Nachfolge, passim*; Schulz, 434–442; Miyoshi, 33–58.

(57) The setting in Lk. is different from that in Mt. where Jesus is approached by the would-be followers just before crossing the lake from Capernaum to Decapolis; it is probable that Matthew has inserted the incident at this point because it seemed appropriate. Similarly, Luke has included the incident here because it fitted appropriately into the general setting of discipleship taken from Q, but he has linked it with the thought of Jesus' journey to Jerusalem and with the preceding incident in which Jesus finds no welcome in Samaria, so that the first encounter offers a commentary on what has gone before (Klostermann, 112). The first speaker is not identified by Luke; in Mt. he is a γραμματεύς, which may well be correct (*contra* Hahn, 83f.; Schulz, 434). In Mt. he addresses

Jesus as διδάσκαλε, which may also be original; there is nothing corresponding in Lk., but at the end of the saying some MSS add the appellative κύριε (A C W Θ pm f q (b) syᵖ boᵖᵗ; TR; *Diglot*), which may possibly be Lucan (9:61; 19:8). The man is willing to follow Jesus literally where he goes (22:33). The thought is of belonging to the close group of disciples who accompanied Jesus on his travels rather than to the wider group who were not called to be with him in this way.

(58) But Jesus bids the man count the cost. As the Son of man he experiences rejection and homelessness, and (it is implied) his followers must be prepared for the same experience. ἀλώπηξ is 'fox' (13:32; Mt. 8:20**), and φωλεός 'den, lair, hole' (Mt. 8:20**). κατασκήνωσις is 'a place to live' (Mt. 8:20**; cf. κατασκηνόω 13:19), and may refer to a perch where a bird can settle for the night or to a nest where it may rear its young. A contrast is thus drawn between the homes enjoyed even by animals and the lack of home and rest for Jesus. An allusion to wisdom which could find no home among men and therefore returned to her place in heaven (1 En. 42:1f.; cf. 94:5; Grundmann, 204; Christ, 70; Hoffmann, 181f.; Hamerton-Kelly, 29) seems unjustified. Bultmann, 27, argued that a proverbial saying, true of man in general, had been secondarily applied to Jesus. But the parallels which he cites in favour of this do not prove the point (Homer Od. 18:13ff.; Plutarch, Tib. Gracchus 9, p. 828c); in any case the saying is not true of men in general. Vielhauer, *Aufsätze*, 24, argued against the saying that it was not true of Jesus, who often enjoyed the hospitality of others; but this does not affect the basic point that Jesus knew what rejection meant (Hengel, *Nachfolge*, 60), as the preceding incident testifies (9:51–56; cf. 4:16–30). The content of the saying is unobjectionable as a saying of Jesus. The real problem is the use of the term 'Son of man'. There can be no doubt that the early church understood this as a title for Jesus, and that in its present form it expresses the humiliation and rejection which must be suffered by One who is destined for authority and glory; if the Son of man must be humiliated in this way, how much more must this be true of his followers (Hoffmann, 149f.). It is hazardous to follow or trust such a leader (Sir. 36:26; Danker, 124f.). The question is whether Jesus could have used the title in this way. We have argued above that this is perfectly possible (5:24; 7:34 notes). Nevertheless, the possibility has been raised that the title has replaced an original use of 'man' in the saying: 'Even animals have dens, but a man such as I, Jesus, has nowhere to lay his head' (C. Colpe, TDNT VIII, 432f.); it is, however, hard to see why Jesus should have drawn a contrast between himself *as a man* and the animals, and so the proposal is unlikely. Alternatively, 'Son of man' has replaced a simple 'I' in the saying (Hoffmann, 182), but this is pure conjecture. See further H. Schürmann, in Pesch, *Jesus*, 132f., for the view that this saying is a secondary formation in the Q material; no real evidence is offered.

(59) In the second encounter Luke makes Jesus take the initiative

in summoning another man to follow him; the man makes an objection
and Jesus replies to it. The pattern in Mt. is different in that the initiative
is taken by the man, who is described as a disciple, and the two statements by Jesus are run together in his reply to the man. It seems
probable that the Matthaean form is original, and that Luke has shifted
Jesus' command 'Follow me' to the beginning of the scene, so that the
conversation begins less abruptly and Luke is able to add the command
to go and preach at the end of the reply of Jesus. If so, we have to
assume that in this conversation Jesus was calling one of his disciples in
the broad sense to join his group of closer companions. The man replies
to the invitation of Jesus by addressing him as κύριε, which is bracketed
by UBS in view of its absence from B* D *al* sy^s Origen (*Synopsis* and
Diglot omit it altogether). The evidence is finely balanced (Metzger,
149). The request is for permission to go away first of all and bury his
father. For θάπτω cf. 9:60; 16:22*. The word order ἀπελθόντι πρῶτον is
reversed in *Synopsis* following p⁴⁵ p⁷⁵ C *al*; TR. Burial of the dead was a
religious duty that took precedence over all others, including even study
of the Law. Priests, who were not normally allowed to touch dead
bodies, could do so in the case of relatives (Lv. 21:1–3). To assist in
burying a person who had no claims on one as a relative was a work of
love which carried great reward from God both in this life and in the
next world. It follows that the burial of a father was a religious duty of
the utmost importance (Gn. 50:5; Tob. 4:3; 6:15; SB I, 487–489; IV: 1,
578–592). To leave it undone was something scandalous to a Jew.
Elisha was permitted to return home to say farewell to his parents before
following Elijah (1 Ki. 19:20). The request to carry out an even more important duty was thus reasonable.

(60) It is against this background that the full rigour of Jesus' reply
is to be appreciated. The precise meaning of the first half of the statement has caused dispute. Some have found the saying so difficult that
resort has been had to mistranslation of a hypothetical Aramaic original
(Black, 207f.). But the meaning is simply 'Let the (spiritually) dead bury
the (physically) dead'; the use of 'dead' in a metaphorical sense was
known to Jews (SB I, 489; III, 165; Hengel, *Nachfolge*, 8) and gives a
good sense. Manson's suggestion (*Sayings*, 73; similarly H. G. Klemm*,
73) that we simply have a paradoxical way of saying 'That business
must look after itself' lacks evidence. The implications are important.
Those who do not follow Jesus are regarded as spiritually dead (cf.
15:24, 32; Jn. 5:25; Rom. 6:13; Eph. 2:1; 5:14). They have missed the
life associated with the kingdom. The metaphor, however, should not be
pressed in terms of the later Christian development. Second, the duty of
following Jesus is placed above the most stringent of human duties. See
Hengel, *Nachfolge*, 9–17 *et passim*, for a development of this point. It is
possible that the father was old and on the point of death, rather than
that he had already died, but in both cases Jesus' command is rigorous
and goes against both Jewish teaching and the ethic of the early church

(1 Tim. 5:8); the urgency of the task of preaching the gospel could not be clearer.

The second part of the statement is probably a Lucan addition, since it is absent from Mt. (although it may not have suited Matthew's context), and the motif is Lucan (4:43; Bultmann, 94, 353). It may have been added to provide a link with the next scene. But the motif may have been present in Mt. where the conversation is with a disciple. For διαγγέλλω, 'to proclaim far and wide', cf. Rom. 9:17 (also, 'to give notice of', Acts 21:26**). Conzelmann, 96, argues that the addition has shifted the emphasis of Jesus' statement from eschatology to mission; the urgency of repentance has given way to the urgency of evangelism (cf. H. G. Klemm*, 63f.). But this is not so. There is no indication in the sources that the only way to enter the kingdom was by literal following of Jesus; the conversation is concerned with accompanying Jesus to aid him in his work, and this means that preaching the gospel is the task envisaged.

(61) The third man may perhaps be regarded as asking for a lesser privilege than the second, merely to say farewell to those at home, and he could have quoted 1 Ki. 19:20f. in support of his wish. The wording is close to that in v. 59. ἀποτάσσομαι is 'to say farewell to' (Mk. 6:46; Acts 18:18, 21), hence also 'to renounce' (Lk. 14:33**).

(62) But the demands of Jesus are more stringent than those of Elijah. Jesus' reply to him (πρὸς αὐτόν, omitted by p⁴⁵ p⁷⁵ B; UBS) is proverbial in sound. ἄροτρον** is a 'plough'. The closest parallel is in Hesiod, Works and Days, 443, 'one who will attend to his work and drive a straight furrow and is past the age for gaping after his fellows, but will keep his mind on his work' (Loeb translation); cf. P. Ab. 3:7; AZ 5b in SB II, 165. A person who harks back to the past way of life (cf. Phil. 3:13; Heb. 12:1f.) is not fit (εὔθετός, 14:35; Heb. 6:7**) for the kingdom or its work (on the text see Metzger, 149).

iii. The Second Mission 10:1–16

Luke has already recorded how Jesus sent out the Twelve to preach and heal (9:1–6 par. Mk. 6:7–12). He is the only Evangelist to record a further mission by seventy(-two) other disciples. As in the case of the earlier account, the emphasis falls upon the instructions given by Jesus, and we hear nothing about the course of the campaign. This is not surprising, because the tradition was much more interested in what Jesus said and did than in what the disciples did when they were not in his company.

The sayings have parallels in Mt. 9:37f.; 10:7–16; 11:21–23; cf. 10:40. What is addressed to the Twelve in Mt. is here addressed to the Seventy(-two). Moreover, when Luke refers back to the instructions given to the Twelve in 22:35, the allusion is in fact to the wording of the present passage (10:4). Finally, Luke based his account of the mission of the Twelve on Mk. (with some influence from Q), but Matthew conflated material from Mk. with parallel material from Q; both the Marcan and Q material were probably based ultimately on the same tradition. These facts raise the question of the historicity of the present account. It can be argued that Luke regarded the accounts in his two sources, Mk. and Q, as references to two separate missions, whereas in reality there was only one. If the instructions given in Q were not specifically addressed to the Twelve, Luke could have regarded them as being addressed to a wider group of disciples. At the same time we must ask why Luke, who on the whole avoids 'doublets', has allowed these two very similar accounts to stand in his Gospel.

The framework for the sayings is provided by 10:1, 17–20. It has been argued that this framework is a Lucan creation, and that the section as a whole was designed by Luke to point forward to the future universal mission of the church (Hoffmann, 248–254; cf. Ott, 36; Schulz, 404). But the argument, which is largely linguistic, cannot prove more than that Luke has strongly edited the opening and conclusion of the section in accordance with his normal habit. Further, the sayings themselves contain hints that the original tradition had in mind mission work by a wider group of disciples than the Twelve (10:2) and even that the number 'seventy' was associated with the original tradition (10:3 note). It is unlikely that Luke simply invented the second mission in order to deal with the tension between the call of the Twelve by Jesus and the existence of a larger body of evangelists in the church (Hoffmann, 251 n. 62), and more probable that he was following his sources (Lagrange, 291f.). It seems likely that the mission sayings in Q were addressed to a wider group than merely the Twelve, and that Mark has narrowed their scope.

The function of the section for Luke has been explained by Flender, 22f., in terms of 'transcending parallelism': what happened in 9:1–6, 10, is repeated on a grander scale. Luke is able to show that the task of mission was not confined to the Twelve – a fact which is not unimportant for his conception of witness and apostleship. Although the content of the sayings is related to mission in Palestine, it is possible that Luke regarded this mission as prefiguring the church's mission to the gentiles (especially if Mt. 10:5f. was in his source and he has deliberately omitted it; cf. H. Schürmann*).

The task of determining the precise extent, order and wording of Luke's source is far from easy. The beginning and ending (10:2, 13–16) appear in almost identical form in Mt. and must be from Q. The same is true of 10:3, although it appears in a different position in Mt. The wording in 10:4–12 differs considerably from that in Mt., but is probably based on the same source; many of the differences are due to Matthew's conflation with Mk. and his own special source material, and the possibility that Matthew and Luke used different recensions of Q should also be borne in mind.

The section gives the impression of a set of isolated sayings brought together by their common theme. The opening saying deals with the need for more workers in view of the greatness of the harvest, and is appropriately placed before the mission discourse in Mt. Those who go out are warned about the dangers to which they will be exposed (10:3). Nevertheless, they are to go out without any equipment as a sign of their faith in God to supply their needs (10:4). Next come three sets of sayings with similar introductions (10:5–7, 8f., 10–12). The first deals with behaviour on entering a house. The disciples bring a greeting which may or may not be received. In the case of a favourable welcome, they may expect to receive hospitality in the house, and they are to regard this both as that which they deserve and as that with which they must be satisfied. Second, when they enter a town, they are to take what they are offered and to preach the message of the kingdom. But, third, if they are not received in any town, they are to warn the people by an acted parable that the kingdom of God is near and that they have excluded themselves from it and will come under judgment. Finally, in 10:13–16 we have a sad comment by Jesus on the cities which had refused the gospel despite the mighty wonders which he himself had performed, and then a comment that the way in which the disciples are treated is really directed towards himself.

See Manson, *Sayings*, 73–78; Hahn, *Mission*, 41–46; H. Schürmann, 'Mt 10, 5b–6 und die Vorgeschichte des synoptischen Aussendungsberichtes', in Schürmann, *Untersuchungen*, 137–149 (originally in Blinzler, *Aufsätze*, 270–282); Hoffmann, 236–334; Schulz, 404–419, 360–366; 457–459; Miyoshi, 59–94.

(1) The language of the introduction is strongly Lucan but appears to be based on tradition. For μετὰ δὲ ταῦτα ἀνέδειξεν ὁ κύριος there is the variant ἀπέδειξεν δέ (D it (Mcion)). Apparently under its influence *Diglot* brackets ὁ κύριος. Both verbs are Lucan: ἀναδείκνυμι is 'to commission' or 'to show forth' (Acts 1:24**; cf. Lk. 1:80), while ἀποδείκνυμι is 'to appoint' (1 Cor. 4:9; 2 Thes. 2:4), 'to attest, prove' (Acts 2:22; 25:7**). The external evidence favours the UBS text. Before ἑτέρους (p 75 B *pc* sy^{s p}) many MSS insert καί (so TR; *Diglot*; cf. Alford, 533; Lagrange, 293); this addition agrees with Lucan style (3:18; 4:43; 23:32; Acts 13:35) and could be original.

A major problem concerns the number of missionaries. The number ἑβδομήκοντα δύο is attested by p 75 B D 33 *pc* it vg sy ^{c s} sa bo ^{pt}, and adopted by RV mg; RSV mg; NEB; JB; NIV; *Synopsis*; (UBS); *Diglot*; Lagrange, 292f.; Creed, 144; Schmid, 183f.; K. Aland (in Metzger, 151). The alternative reading ἑβδομήκοντα is attested by ℵ A C L W Θ f1 f13 *pl* f q ?r¹ sy^p bo^{pt}, and adopted by RV; RSV; NEB mg; JB mg. The same variants occur in 10:17, where p 45 and 33 also support ἑβδομήκοντα. For discussion of the problem see B. M. Metzger, 'Seventy or Seventy-two Disciples?', NTS 5, 1958–59, 299–306 (summarised in Metzger, 150f.). 1. The external evidence is evenly balanced. But although B and ℵ are ranged against each other, B is supported by p 75 and D. The combination of Alexandrian, Western and Syriac evidence in favour of 72 is the stronger. 2. Transcriptional arguments are indecisive. Confusion with the following ἀνὰ δύο could operate in either direction. 3. While the number 70 appears in a variety of symbolical uses, the use of 72 is much less frequent. Hence intrinsic probability strongly favours 72. 4. The possible symbolism may furnish an explanation of both numbers. There were 70 elders of Israel (Ex. 24:1; Nu. 11:16f., 24f.); the attempt to obtain 72 by including Eldad and Medad (Nu. 11:26; Miyoshi, 61, 79) is forced. For other groups of 70 persons see Ex. 1:5; 15:27; Jdg. 9:2; 2 Ki. 10:1; Bel 10; there were 70 members of the sanhedrin, excluding the high priest. There were reckoned to be 70 nations in the world (Gn. 10; cf. 1 En. 89:59ff.; Tanchuma *tôl ᶜḏôṯ* 32b); the LXX of Gn. 10, however, lists 72 nations. There were 72 elders who prepared the LXX (Ep. Arist. 46–50). There were reckoned to be 72 princes and 72 languages in the world (3 En. 17:8; 18:2f.; 30:2). It has been suggested that Luke was alluding to some aspect of this symbolism, e.g. to the 70 elders of Israel (SB II, 166; Wilson, 45–47); but this particular suggestion does not adequately explain the number 72 in the textual tradition. Another view is that the translators of the LXX were in Luke's mind, and he altered an original 70 in the tradition to 72 (S. Jellicoe, 'St Luke and the Letter of Aristeas', JBL 80, 1961, 149–155). Most commentators, however, see a reference to the nations of the world, and find a foreshadowing of the later evangelism by the church in the world (K. H. Rengstorf, TDNT II, 634f.). This last suggestion gives a plausible solution of the textual problem. In 10:3 there is an implicit reference to the 70 nations of the world (see note). It is plausible that Luke, following Gn. 10 LXX (and/or possibly thinking of the missionary intent of the 72 translators of the LXX) wrote 72; later copyists, familiar either with the tradition behind 10:3 or with Gn. 10 MT, then altered the number back to the more familiar 70. If this reasoning is correct, it follows that the use of 72 (70) is not due to Lucan creation (Wellhausen, 48; Schulz, 404) but is derived from tradition. The understanding of the mission, described in strictly Palestinian terms, as prefiguring the gentile mission, was thus possible in the pre-Lucan tradition, and Luke has taken it over. He has not, however, developed it in any detail; indeed the fact that the disciples are sent out in pairs suggests that the idea of 72 (70) disciples going to 72 (70) nations is not taken up in the passage.

The task is to be carried out by 'others'. The contrast is hardly with the messengers in 9:52 (Easton, 156) or with the would-be disciples in 9:57–62, but with the Twelve (Klostermann, 114). They are sent out in pairs. The MSS vary between ἀνὰ δύο δύο (B Θ *al* Eus; (UBS)) and ἀνὰ δύο. For the use of ἀνά cf. 9:14 (the meaning in 9:3 is different). The (UBS) reading has parallels in the papyri and can be defended as Koine Greek (BD 248¹; cf. AG on both words). The purpose of the pairing (cf. Mk. 6:7) was not merely to provide mutual comfort and help, but also to give attested, binding testimony (J. Jeremias, 'Paarweise Sendung im Neuen Testament', in Jeremias, *Abba*, 132–139). This indicates that their task was mission, rather than the arranging of hospitality (9:52). There is a difficulty in that they are said to go before Jesus, perhaps like John the Baptist (7:27), into *every* town and place where he intended to go. But it is inconceivable that Jesus himself could follow up all the visits of 36 pairs of missionaries, nor is there any evidence that he did so. Is the reference to the spiritual coming of Jesus after the resurrection? This view is supported by the fact that the messengers were in fact to take the place of Jesus (10:16). If so, there appears to be an allusion (probably due to Luke) to the future mission of the church as well as to the present task of the disciples.

(2) After the introduction, the wording of the first saying is identical with that in Mt. 9:37f. with one minor alteration in word order (where Matthew is probably original, Hoffman, 263). In the first part of the saying there is a contrast between the size of the harvest and the number of labourers. θερισμός is 'harvest', i.e. 'the crop to be harvested' (Rev. 14:5) or 'the process (or time) of harvesting' (Mt. 13:30, 39; Mk. 4:29; Jn. 4:35). The background is that of the final gathering of God's people (Is. 27:12; Joel 3:13 LXX; F. Hauck, TDNT III, 132f.). Elsewhere it is carried out by the angels or the Son of man (Mt. 13:39; Rev. 14). Here, however, the task is entrusted to the disciples. Thus the eschatological gathering of God's people is regarded as taking place in the mission of the disciples. But this does not mean that the force of the saying lies simply in the nearness of the End (so Hoffmann, 289–293; Schulz, 411); the saying explicitly points to the greatness of the task (πολύς). In the eyes of the Evangelist it may look forward to the greatness of the world mission, especially since the OT image of harvest is applied to the judgment on the gentiles as well as to Israel, in which case the saying is understood in terms of grace rather than of judgment (cf. Lührmann, 60); but in its original context the reference may be purely to Israel. In the second part of the saying the consequence is drawn. The disciples must pray (δέομαι; Acts 8:22) to the lord of the harvest (i.e. God) that (ὅπως, expressing the content of the prayer, BD 392¹) he will send out workers into the harvest. βάλλω is used in its weak sense (6:42); Luke's word order (ἐργάτας ἐκβάλῃ (p⁷⁵ B D 0181 700 e)) is less Semitic than Matthew's; but many MSS offer the same order as Mt. (so TR; *Diglot*) with the present subjunctive form, ἐκβάλλῃ and this may be original, in which case the more elegant Greek is due not to Luke but to a scribe (Kilpatrick, 198). The saying is more a comment on the pressing situation than a charge to the missionaries themselves; but it is in fact missionaries themselves who are most conscious of the need for more workers, and it is quite appropriate that Jesus should wish for more workers than were available (Easton, 159). Hence Matthew's positioning of the saying before the mission discourse is better; it is an isolated saying which has been attracted here by the theme of

mission. There are good reasons for upholding its authenticity (Hahn, *Mission*, 40 n. 3).

(3) The next saying appears at a later stage in Mt., namely 10:16, and it could have been transferred there to provide an introduction for Mt. 10:17ff. If so, the opening word of dismissal, ὑπάγετε, is probably original and has been omitted by Matthew since it was less suitable in his long discourse (cf. Hoffmann, 257, 263f.; *contra* Schulz, 405); the same thought appears in Mt. 10:5f. Jesus (Mt. ἐγώ is emphatic) sends the disciples out like lambs in the midst of wolves. The application of ἀποστέλλω to the disciples is significant; here is the root of the concept of apostleship understood in terms of mission, possibly based ultimately on OT ideas (Steck, 229f.). Bultmann, 170, 176, regards the saying as an 'I-saying', stemming from the primitive church and giving the risen Lord's command to mission; he compares Mt. 23:34, which, he claims, is a citation turned into a saying by Jesus. Against this wholesale rejection of the 'I-sayings' as sayings of the earthly Jesus, see Jeremias, *Theology* I, 250–254.

Luke describes the disciples as 'lambs'. For ἀρήν**, Matthew has the more general word πρόβατον, 'sheep', which is more likely to be original (Hoffmann, 264; *contra* Schulz, 405). The wolf (λύκος) is often used in metaphor (Mt. 7:15; Jn. 10:12; Acts 20:29), and the defencelessness of the lamb against the wolf is illustrated by Homer, Il. 22:263; Is. 11:6; 65:25; Sir. 13:17; Epig. Gr. 1038, 38 (in AG 105); cf. J. Jeremias, TDNT I, 340; G. Bornkamm, TDNT IV, 308–311; H. Preisker and S. Schulz, TDNT VI, 689–692. Nevertheless, the fact that Jesus already knows about the dangers affords some comfort to the disciples (G. Bornkamm), and behind the saying there may lie the thought of divine protection mediated through Jesus (cf. 2 Clem. 5:2–4). A rabbinic conversation runs as follows: 'Hadrian said to R. Jehoshua (c. AD 90): There is something great about the sheep (Israel) that can persist among 70 wolves (the nations). He replied: Great is the Shepherd who delivers it and watches over it and destroys them (the wolves) before them (Israel)' (Tanchuma tôlᵉḏôṯ 32b, as translated in TDNT I, 340). The conversation, though over half a century later than Jesus, raises the question whether a current saying about Israel among the nations has been reapplied by Jesus to the true Israel, and whether Jesus saw himself in the role of the Shepherd of the flock of God, bringing protection to his disciples.

(4) After the commission and a warning about the dangers of the mission there follows a list of preparations to be made for the task (v. 4a). The striking thing is that the list is entirely negative in form, and mentions things that must not be taken. The list is shorter than that in 9:3, where Mk. has been utilised, but agrees in general tenor. There are three prohibitions introduced by μὴ βαστάζετε, diff. Mt. μὴ κτήσησθε. Since βαστάζω is fairly common in Lk., its uses here may be redactional, but the same could be true of Matthew's use of κτάομαι to refer to

seeking reward for missionary service; Schürmann, *Abschiedsrede*, 122, cf. 118f., suggests that Q may have used αἴρω (cf. 9:3, 22:36). For βαλλάντιον, 'purse' (12:33; 22:35f.**), Matthew has 'gold, silver or copper in your girdles'. The reference to the girdle may stem from Mk. 6:8, where copper is the only coinage listed. The use of a purse is less primitive than the custom of tying coins into the belt, and so the word may represent a re-writing for townspeople by Luke (K. H. Rengstorf, TDNT I, 525f.) or be a variant from Mark's word already found in Q (Schürmann, ibid.). For πήρα, a bag for provisions, see 9:3. ὑποδήματα, 'sandals' (3:16), par. Mt., are forbidden, but σανδάλια are allowed in Mk. 6:9 (cf. A. Oepke, TDNT V, 310–312). The discussion above (9:3 note) suggested that the more rigorous demand in Q is original. The significance of the prohibitions (cf. the possibilities listed by Schulz, 415 n. 84) is discussed at length by Hoffmann, 312–331, who finds that the disciples are here denied the normal equipment for a journey. Comparable restrictions were imposed by the Essenes (Jos. Bel. 2:124–127), but these were tolerable because Essene travellers could obtain hospitality and help from other members and groups of the sect. The disciples were to be a striking example of faith in God to supply their needs. Hoffmann finds the significance of Jesus' instruction to lie in the expression of poverty and peaceableness, i.e. the sort of character commended in the beatitudes. Schulz, 414f., argues that the radical rejection of possessions illustrates the pressing stringency of the final, apocalyptic mission to summon Israel to radical repentance. But where Hoffmann and Schulz attribute this ideal to the community which produced Q, we may ask whether the symbolism does not go back to Jesus himself. Later Jesus was to qualify this instruction (22:35f.).

In the second half of the verse a further prohibition is found, peculiar to Lk. There is no reason to ascribe it to Luke himself; it is not based on 2 Ki. 4:29 LXX, and is therefore not a Lucan Septuagintalism; κατὰ τὴν ὁδόν may, however, be a Lucan phrase (Acts 8:36; 25:3; 26:13). The view that it is from L depends on whether the surrounding sayings also come from L (Manson, *Sayings*, 73–78, 256f.), but this is doubtful. It is more probable that Matthew omitted the saying in his re-ordering of the Q material (cf. Schulz, 405). The saying forbids greeting people on the way. Oriental greetings (ἀσπάζομαι, 1:40*) were important, long and time-consuming (SB I, 380–385; H. Windisch, TDNT I, 496–502). The command to dispense with them is so unusual that it must be original (cf. Easton, 160). The reason lies in the need for urgency on the task of mission; there is an OT background in the similar command to Gehazi by Elisha (2 Ki. 4:29; Manson, *Sayings*, 257). The saying must be linked with the positive evaluation of greetings given in the house by the disciples (vs. 5f.). The outward formality of the greeting in the street was unimportant when the house greeting was filled with new content (Schlatter, 276f.); the omission of the normal practice would draw attention to the new element in the mission of the disciples.

(5) The construction suggests that the positive instruction which now follows is to be seen as a contrast to the preceding negative instruction. The saying extends to the following verse, and is concerned with the extending of a greeting to a household and its possible acceptance or rejection. It is followed by two verses (vs. 7–8) which are concerned with the attitude of the disciples to the hospitality which they may receive. The whole passage forms the first of the three sections into which this part of the discourse is divided in Lk. The content is closely paralleled in Mt. 10:12f., but the wording is surprisingly different. Hence Manson, *Sayings,* 74, concluded that vs. 4–7 were from L. But the structure is so similar that it is more likely that the same source is being used, and the differences can be explained in terms of (mostly) Matthaean alterations (Hoffmann, 272f.; Schulz, 405).

The saying is preceded in Mt. by an instruction (Mt. 10:11) that whenever the disciples enter a town or village they are to enquire who in it is worthy, and to remain there (i.e. in that person's house) until they leave the place. Part of this instruction appears in Mk. 6:10 and is probably taken from there; the thought of seeking out a worthy person (ἄξιος) appears to be Matthaean (cf. Mt. 10:37f.; 22:8). Hence the absence of a corresponding saying from Lk. at this point (contrast 9:4) is explained. On entering a house the disciples' first duty is to express a greeting. The introductory εἰς ἣν δ' ἄν is probably from Q (Mt. 10:11); for εἰσέλθητε οἰκίαν, TR and *Diglot* have οἰκίαν εἰσέρχησθε (A W Θ *pm*); the use of πρῶτον, diff. Mt., may be Lucan (cf. 12:1; 17:25; 21:9). For λέγετε Matthew has ἀσπάσασθε αὐτήν, and he omits the wording of the greeting. It is probable that the greeting stood in Q, for otherwise the mention of peace in v. 6 is rather abrupt, but Matthew's use of ἀσπάζομαι may derive from the source behind Lk. 10:4, or the original wording of Q may have been as in Mt. 10:12 v.l. A greeting on entering a house was normal practice (1:28f., 40f.), and the wording of the greeting is also normal (cf. 24:36; Jn. 20:19, 21, 26; SB I, 380f.; W. Foerster, TDNT II, 400–417, especially 408f., 411). It follows that the especial mention of the greeting in this context must convey some deeper sense; the word 'peace' is no longer an empty formality but refers to the peace which is associated with the coming of the salvation of God (Jn. 14:27; Acts 10:36). 'The greeting which they give on entering a house is not a wish. It is a gift which is either received or rejected as such' (W. Foerster, TDNT II, 413). The saying, however, is so brief and cryptic that the force inherent in it is far from obvious. οἶκος here means 'household'.

(6) Where Matthew continues his theme of the worthiness of the house, Luke speaks of the presence in it of a 'son of peace'. (On the text, ἐκεῖ ἤ (p⁷⁵ B *pc*) or ἤ ἐκεῖ (TR; *Diglot*) see Kilpatrick, 198, who claims that the word-order in TR is Semitic.) A 'son of peace' is an example of an idiom found in Classical and Hellenistic Greek but also frequent in Semitic (MM 649; F. W. Danker, 'The υἱός Phrases in the New

Testament', NTS 7, 1960–61, 94; E. Schweizer, TDNT VIII, 365). It can mean 1. a peaceable person; or 2. a man worthy of, destined for peace; cf. 'a son of the world to come', 'children of hell', 'sons of the resurrection' and similar expressions (20:36; cf. 16:8; SB I, 476–478; II, 166). This is undoubtedly the meaning here (Lagrange, 295; Manson, *Sayings*, 257). The saying does not refer to finding a house in which there are already disciples, but to offering salvation to those who are willing to receive it, as Matthew's use of ἄξιος indicates. Such a person will receive the blessing offered to him. ἐπαναπαήσομαι is the second future passive of ἐπαναπαύω, 'to rest, find rest' (Rom. 2:17**; Nu. 11:25; 2 Ki. 2:15). Matthew has the imperative ἐλθάτω. Luke expresses the alternative situation with εἰ δὲ μή γε (5:36), which has replaced the fuller expression reflected in Mt. If not received, the blessing will return to the disciples (ἐπιστρέφω, which is again perhaps original). The idea is not that the disciples get the blessing instead, but simply that the intended recipient forfeits it; its withdrawal is tantamount to a curse (H. Windisch, TDNT I, 496–502, especially 499). Behind the saying lie Semitic ideas of the power of the spoken word, now understood in terms of the efficacy of the proclamation of the gospel (cf. 1 Thes. 2:13).

(7) In the four clauses which make up this verse the theme shifts from the message of peace to the conduct of the missionaries and their right to subsistence. First, the disciples are commanded to stay ἐν αὐτῇ ... τῇ οἰκίᾳ. This should mean 'in the house itself', which does not give a good sense in the context. It is possible that αὐτός is used as a demonstrative, 'in that house' (cf. 10:21; MH I, 91), or that it translates an Aramaic proleptic pronoun, 'in it, namely the house' (Black, 72; Zerwick, 205). This instruction is repeated in the fourth clause: do not move about from house to house. (For μεταβαίνω cf. Acts 18:7; *et al.*) Whereas the first clause is paralleled in Mt. 10:11 and Mk. 6:10 par. Lk. 9:4, this clause is without parallels, and it is not clear whether it stood in Q (Schulz, 406), or was added by Luke to make the point clearer. In between the two clauses stand instructions about subsistence. First, there is the phrase commanding the disciples to eat what is set before them. The use of the form ἔσθω (so *Synopsis*; UBS has ἐσθίω; cf. 7:33f.; 22:30) may reflect tradition (Schürmann, *Abschiedsrede*, 49). τὰ παρ' αὐτῶν means 'what they have' or 'what is given by them' (BD 237²). The suggestion is that the disciples are entitled to their food and drink; in return for spiritual gifts they receive material help (Gal. 6:6). This is indicated by the following clause. The worker (cf. 10:2) deserves his μισθός, i.e. 'reward' or 'wage' (6:23). Matthew has the saying earlier in connection with the instructions not to take equipment for the journey, and has τροφή, 'nourishment, food' (cf. Did. 13:1f.), diff. μισθός (cf. 1 Ti. 5:18). It is probable that the position of the saying in Lk. is original (Hoffmann, 274). Matthew may have altered the wording to avoid the idea of this-worldly rewards (Hoffmann, ibid.), but it is quite possible

that he has preserved the primitive wording (cf. Dodd, 392 n.). What the disciples are promised is 'not opulence, but simply sustenance' (H. Preisker, TDNT IV, 698 n. 6). There is a certain tension in the verse between the stress on the promise of reward and the warning against seeking excessive reward, and this may suggest that the reward clause is an addition. There is also a possible tension with the preceding verse, since the implied command to evangelise the various houses, and the instruction not to go from house to house conflict with each other. The tension is accentuated if we accept Hoffmann's suggestion (297) that the eating and drinking is an act of table fellowship which seals the acceptance of the gospel by the household, for in this case presumably table fellowship should have taken place in each receptive household. We must assume that instructions given at greater length, and perhaps in independence of one another, have been condensed in the present passage.

(8) From the individual house Luke turns to the town in a verse that has no parallel in Mt. The opening forms a positive counterpart to the negative statement in 10:10, and it is hard to believe that the negative statement was not originally preceded by a positive one. Further, there is a partial parallel in Mt. 10:11. The question is whether Matthew has in effect combined two sets of sayings (about houses and towns) to give one, or whether Luke has expanded one set of sayings into two by creating this verse. Despite the arguments for the latter possibility by Hoffmann, 276–281, we are inclined to favour the former view (Schulz, 406). In particular, it seems doubtful whether Luke would have created the odd connection here between entering a town and eating what is provided there, especially since this involves a repetition of the thought in v. 7. The language here is Lucan: for παρατίθημι cf. 9:16; 11:6; 12:48; 23:46*; Acts, 4x. There is an echo of the verse in 1 Cor. 10:27 with reference to Christians eating food as guests in pagan households, and accepting what is put before them without raising scruples about the origin of the food. It is not clear whether the same thought is present here, but certainly this interpretation could have been attached to the words by Christians engaged on mission among gentiles (cf. Schlatter, 277; Rengstorf, 132).

(9) We come at last to the positive instructions regarding the content of missionary work. In Mt. 10:7f. these come earlier and form part of the initial commission to the disciples; here, however, they are placed in the context of work in the towns which are receptive to the messengers. Luke's positioning may reflect Q (Hoffmann, 274f.). The impression given is that in Lk. the activities now described confirm the people's acceptance of the missionaries, whereas Matthew regards them as part of the initial task of evangelism. But this point should not be pressed. More important perhaps is the way in which the command to heal the sick (ἀσθενεῖς diff. Mt. ἀσθενοῦντας may be Lucan) precedes the command to preach. This suggests that the healings are to be regarded as a sign of the presence of the kingdom (cf. 11:20; Schulz, 417).

Matthew has a longer list of signs, which are parallel to those of Jesus in
Mt. 11:5 par. Lk. 7:21f., and he appears to be responsible for the addition, in order to show that the activities of the missionaries are the same
as those of Jesus himself. The theological weight of the verse lies in the
content of the message. Luke introduces it with λέγετε, diff. Matthew's
more formal κηρύσσετε, and it is given in direct speech. On the phrase ἡ
βασιλεία τοῦ θεοῦ see 4:43 note. The verb ἐγγίζω is hard to translate. It
means 'to draw near', and this is its normal meaning in the LXX, but it
can also mean 'to arrive, reach' (Jon. 3:6). The problem is whether the
perfect form, 'to have drawn near', means that the subject has come into
a position of nearness or has fully arrived. The former translation is required in Rom. 13:12; Jas. 5:8 and 1 Pet. 4:7; the translation in Mt.
26:45, 46; Lk. 21:8, 20 is debatable, but certainly very close proximity is
meant. So far as the other tenses of the verb are concerned, both meanings are to be found; the line between approaching and arriving is
manifestly a thin one. The present phrase is also found in the summary
of the preaching of Jesus in Mk. 1:15, where it follows a statement that
'the time has been fulfilled'. There is also a parallel statement in Lk.
11:20 par. Mt. 12:28 with the phrase ἔφθασεν ἡ βασιλεία; here the
meaning is not in doubt, and the statement can only mean that the
kingdom of God has reached men. The fact that 11:20 includes the
words ἐφ' ὑμᾶς suggests that they formed part of the Q text here, despite
their omission by Matthew (Hoffmann, 275; contra Conzelmann, 98;
Grässer, 140f.; Schulz, 407). The question now is whether the meaning
of 11:20 determines the meaning here. Kümmel, Promise, 23f., denies
that this is so on the grounds that the same source (Q) is unlikely to have
translated one Aramaic word by two different Greek words. Even if this
is the case, the passages must be considered together. They make essentially the same point. In 11:20 the presence of the kingdom is attested by
the exorcisms and its power is available for the hearers, whereas here the
power of the kingdom has drawn near to those to whom it is being
preached and may be received by them if they respond to the message.
Attempts have been made to elucidate the texts by distinguishing between temporal and spatial nearness. In Mk. 1:15 the nearness is more
temporal, whereas here it is more spatial. But this distinction should not
be pressed. It is the presence of Jesus (or that of his commissioned disciples) which brings the kingdom near, and this presence is both temporal (it is here now, but it was not before), and spatial (it is near to
those who are reached by the mission). The kingdom of God is not
therefore a timeless reality (as has been argued with respect to Luke by
Conzelmann, 98f., 104–111), but it comes near to men in and through
Jesus and his disciples; the reference is not so much to the glorious
manifestation of the kingdom as to its saving power for men. See further
K. L. Schmidt, TDNT II, 330–332; J. Y. Campbell, 'The Kingdom of
God has come', Exp.T 48, 1936–37, 91f.; C. H. Dodd, 'The Kingdom of
God has come', ibid. 138–142; Black, 208–211; Cranfield, 67f.; N.

Perrin, *The Kingdom of God in the Teaching of Jesus*, 1963, 64–66; Schulz, 417f.

(10) In the third of the subsections of the discourse Jesus turns his attention to the town which does not receive the missionaries. Luke's formulation differs from that in Mt., which in turn is influenced by Mk. 6:11; Luke, therefore, may here be following Q. δέχομαι is used of welcoming the messengers and accepting their message; cf. the addition of ἀκούω in Mt. 10:14 par. Mk. 6:11. In this case the disciples are to go out. It is not clear whether this means out of the houses or the town as a whole; while Matthew offers both possibilities, Lk. 9:5 suggests that only the latter is meant here. πλατεῖα is a 'wide road, street' (13:26; 14:21; Acts 5:15). The phrase is probably Lucan, and suggests that Luke is thinking of an action done publicly so that the people can see it.

(11) The saying given here is meant to accompany an acted parable. Mt. 10:14 par. Mk. 6:14 (Lk. 9:5) simply commands the action. Hoffmann, 269f., follows Bultmann, 342, in regarding direct speech as a sign of lateness, and thinks that Luke has formulated in this way to gain parallelism with 10:5, 9. It is more probable that Luke follows Q here (at least in v. 11a; Schulz, 407), and Matthew follows Mk. κονιορτός, 'dust', (9:5) is probable derived from Q (Mt. 10:14 diff. Mk. 6:11). The description of the dust as being ἐκ τῆς πόλεως ὑμῶν may perhaps be from Q (cf. Mt. 10:14, where the word πόλις also occurs), but the whole phrase is so elegant (cf. the ἡμῖν / ὑμῶν contrast) that it may be Lucan. κολλάω, 'to cling, join oneself to', may be Lucan (15:15; Acts, 5x). After εἰς τοὺς πόδας (p⁴⁵ p⁷⁵ ℵ B D *pc* it, many MSS add ἡμῶν (A C K W Θ f1 f13 *pm* sy sa bo; *Diglot*); the whole phrase is omitted by *al* vg; TR. ἀπομάσσομαι**, 'to wipe off', may be due to Luke (cf. his use of ἐκμάσσω, 7:38); the present tense indicates that the saying accompanies the action. The final ὑμῖν is a dative of disadvantage and corresponds to εἰς μαρτύριον ἐπ' αὐτούς, 9:5 (cf. Mk. 6:11). It is lacking in Mt., and Hoffmann, 271f., argues that it was unnecessary in Q where a threat of judgment follows. In Lk. it is necessary because another clause intervenes before v. 12. In it the message of 10:9 is repeated without the phrase ἐφ' ὑμᾶς (so p⁴⁵ p⁷⁵ B D f1 *pc*; it is included by *rell*; TR; *Diglot*); the omission indicates that although the power of the kingdom is present, the town has lost its chance of receiving it – unless perhaps it repents even at this late hour (so Grundmann, 210). πλήν (6:24 note) may be drawn from tradition or may be Lucan; the use of γινώσκω may also be Lucan (Hoffmann, 272). Hence there is a possibility that Luke has added this part of the verse (Schulz, 407).

(12) There is no doubt that a saying contrasting the fate of a city which rejects the gospel with Sodom followed in Q at this point in view of the parallelism with Mt. 10:15. However, the wording in Lk. is close to that in the similar saying Mt. 11:24, and it appears that Luke has conflated the two sayings. He is thus able to pass over the introductory ἀμήν in Mt. 10:15 (see 4:24 note), and can also ignore the πλήν in Mt. 11:24

(has he used it in v. 11?). The fate of the people of Sodom (Gn. 19) had become proverbial (Is. 1:9f.); according to a rabbinic saying, 'the people of Sodom will not rise again' (Aboth R. Nathan 36; cf. Sanh. 10:3; SB I, 574; IV:2, 1188). Matthew has probably expanded a simple reference to Sodom to include Gomorrah also. ἀνεκτός, 'tolerable' (10:14; Mt. 10:15; 11:22, 24) is found only in this set of sayings. For ἡ ἡμέρα ἐκείνη (cf. 21:34; Mt. 7:22; Mk. 13:32; 2 Ti. 1:12, 18; 4:8) Matthew has ἡμέρα κρίσεως (Mt. 11:22, 24; 12:36; 2 Pet. 2:9; 3:7; 1 Jn. 4:17); here Luke has the original form (Hoffmann, 284). The point is that if there is no hope for Sodom, there is even less for a city which rejects the gospel.

(13) The verses which follow at this point form a soliloquy on the cities which rejected Jesus' own ministry, and they interrupt the sequence of thought with v. 16. It is unlikely, therefore, that they stand in their original context, and in Mt. 11:20–24 they occupy a position subsequent to the mission discourse, but in the same position relative to the next section of Q material, the thanksgiving of Jesus, Lk. 10:21–24, par. Mt. 11:25–27. It is probable that the sayings have been added to their present position; the problem is whether this has been done by Luke or had already taken place in Q. Manson, *Sayings* 76f., offers the suggestion that vs. 16 and 13–15 were reversed by Luke, so that v. 12 and vs. 13–15 were brought together; if so, then Mt. 11:20 may be derived from Q. The alternative view (Lührmann, 60–63; Hoffmann, 284f.) is that the order in Luke is that of Q; the woes were pronounced as part of the mission discourse (cf. λέγω ὑμῖν, Mt. 11:22, 24); Matthew has moved them to a different context, where they form part of a section on the opposition of Israel to Jesus, and he has formed v. 24 (on the pattern of Mt. 10:15) to serve as a conclusion; he also created v. 23b. The weakness of this view lies in its failure to account for the position of v. 16. Hence the view of Manson is preferable. Schulz's arguments (362f.) against the authenticity of the sayings (cf. Bultmann, 117f.; Lührmann, 63f.) are unconvincing.

V. 13 is almost identical in wording with Mt. 11:21 (except for ἐγενήθησαν, diff. Mt. ἐγένοντο; cf. Mt. 11:23). For οὐαί see 6:24 note; it is an expression of sorrow at the fate about to be described. Χοραζίν (Mt. 11:21**) is otherwise unknown (except perhaps in Men. 85a; SB I, 605), but is usually identified with mod. Kerazeh, 3 m. N of Tell Hum (Finegan, 57f.). This is the only indication that Jesus had visited it. For Bethsaida see 9:10. For Sidon see 4:26; 6:17. The two cities represent the pagan world, and Tyre especially was regarded as subject to divine judgment (Am. 1:9f.; Is. 23:1–18; Jer. 25:22; 47:4; Ezk. 26–28). Yet both of them would have repented of their sins if the mighty works done by Jesus had been done in them. δύναμις (4:14 note) is here a mighty deed wrought by the power of God; (cf. 19:37; Mk. 6:2; Acts 2:22; *et al.*).

σάκκος, 'sackcloth' (Rev. 6:12), was regarded as a sign of repentance or mourning (Mt. 11:21; Rev. 11:3**; cf. Is. 58:5; Dn. 9:3 LXX;

Jon. 3:6–8; Est. 4:2f.; 1 Mac. 3:47). The material was made out of goats' hair; cf. G. Stählin, TDNT VII, 56–64. σποδός, 'ashes' (Mt. 11:21**), were also a sign of mourning, often associated with sackcloth (cf. the references above). Ashes might be placed on the head (cf. Mt. 6:16) or the person sat among them (Job 2:8; Jon. 3:6; cf. SB IV:2, 103f.). Luke has καθήμενοι, which suggests the latter; if so the picture is of sitting on a penitential mat of sacking (Is. 58:5; Est. 4:3; Jos. Ant. 19:349); Matthew, who omits the participle, may be thinking of wearing sackcloth and covering the head with ashes (G. Stählin, ibid, 61f.).

(14) πλήν has adversative force: although the people of Tyre and Sidon did not have the opportunity to repent, nevertheless they will be treated more lightly at the judgment than the towns of Galilee. The point is not that Tyre and Sidon will be justified, but that Galilee will certainly be condemned. Luke omits λέγω ὑμῖν, perhaps because of his new positioning of the saying in the mission discourse, and to avoid an inconcinnity with the use of the phrase to address the disciples in v. 12. The phrase ἐν τῇ κρίσει (11:31f.), diff. Mt., is probably original (Schulz, 360f.).

(15) A second saying is addressed to the town of Capernaum (4:23) which had been especially the scene of Jesus' labours. The saying makes use of a typology drawn from the description of Babylon in Is. 14:13, 15. There the king of Babylon is described in terms of Lucifer as saying εἰς τὸν οὐρανὸν ἀναβήσομαι, to which God replies εἰς ᾅδην καταβήσῃ (cf. Ezk. 26:20; Ps. Sol. 1:5). The wording here is textually uncertain. UBS reads: μὴ ... ὑψωθήσῃ (p⁴⁵ p⁷⁵ ℵ B D pc it (syˢ ᶜ)); the alternative is ἡ ... ὑψωθεῖσα (A C W f1 f13 pl lat; TR; Diglot). The former text may be due to assimilation to Mt., but the latter could have arisen out of the loss of the initial μ by haplography with a consequent grammatical change. (See Metzger, 30f. on the same problem in Mt. 11:23.) The force of the question is, 'Do you really expect to be raised to heaven because I visited you?' (Percy, 113; cf. 13:26). ᾅδης, 'Sheol' (16:23; Mt. 11:23; 16:18; Acts 2:27, 31; Rev. 1:18; 6:8; 20:13f.**; J. Jeremias, TDNT I, 146–149), is regarded as spatially the opposite of heaven; whereas in the OT it was the place of the dead in general, in NT times it was increasingly regarded as a temporary place of punishment for the ungodly. Hence the thought is not merely of humiliation, but also perhaps of punishment. The text is again uncertain in both Lk. and Mt. Diglot reads καταβιβασθήσῃ (so most MSS; TR) from καταβιβάζω**, 'to bring down, drive down'; the alternative is καταβήσῃ (p⁷⁵ B D 579 syˢ ᶜ eth arm; Synopsis; UBS) from καταβαίνω (2:51; et al.). The readings in Mt. 11:23 are: καταβιβασθήσῃ (ℵ C Θ f1 f13 pl syᵖ bo; TR) and καταβήσῃ (B D W pc lat syˢ ᶜ sa; Iren; Synopsis; Diglot; UBS). In Mt. Metzger, 31, favours καταβήσῃ on the grounds of its early attestation, despite the fact that it could be due to assimilation to Is. 14:15 LXX; in his comment on the present passage (ibid. 151f.) he notes that the UBS committee again relied on external evidence, since transcriptional argu-

ments were inconclusive. But it is hard to see how the variants arose if both Gospels originally had the same verb.

This saying is followed in Mt. by a statement, parallel to that in vs. 13f. above, in which the fate of Capernaum is compared with that of Sodom. Has Matthew created this to produce a piece of poetic parallelism (Schulz, 361), or has Luke omitted it? Since Luke has already included a statement about Sodom in v. 12, it is plausible that he did not wish to repeat it here, and hence dropped the whole of Mt. 11:23b–24. On the other hand, the phrase μέχρι τῆς σήμερον may be Matthaean (cf. Mt. 28:15), and this strongly suggests that Matthew has had a part in the formulation of the saying, although it does not prove that he created it.

(16) The discourse is brought to an end with a saying which authorises the disciples to act in the name of Jesus, for the way in which they are treated by the people is in effect the people's response to Jesus and to God. The saying deals with both positive and negative responses. Hence ἀκούω is used here in the sense of hearing and accepting. The word may reflect Aramaic qabbēl, 'to receive, hear' (cf. Mt. δέχομαι;) and Mt. 10:14) or Luke may have used a word appropriate to the reception of preaching. The negative response is expressed by ἀθετέω (7:30; Jn. 12:48; 1 Thes. 4:8). To reject the messenger is to reject the message; but the point stressed here is that to reject the messenger is to reject the One who sent him (cf. Jn. 20:21), and in turn to reject God who sent Jesus. (For the concept, see SB II, 167; K. H. Rengstorf, TDNT I, 426.)

The same basic thought appears in a number of forms in the Gospels:

He who receives (δέχομαι, Mt. 10:40; 18:5 par. Mk. 9:37 par. Lk. 9:48)
accepts (λαμβάνω, Jn. 13:20)
hears (ἀκούω, Lk. 10:16)

you (Mt. 10:40; Lk. 10:16)
whomsoever I send (Jn. 13:20)
one such child (Mk. 9:37; cf. Mt. 18:5; Lk. 9:48)

receives (cf. variants above) me,

and whoever receives/accepts me receives/accepts the one who sent me (Mk. 9:37 parr; Jn. 13:20; cf. Jn. 12:44, 45).

And he who rejects you rejects me,

and he who rejects me rejects the one who sent me
(Lk. 10:16; cf. Jn. 5:23).

It is clear that one basic structural form underlies these various texts, and the question is which of the texts may be derived from one other. Dodd, 343–347, claims that we have several forms of an oral tradition. Bultmann, 152f., argues that both Luke and Matthew found a saying in the form of Lk. 10:16 at the end of the mission discourse in Q; Matthew substituted for this the separate tradition Mt. 10:40–42 (cf. Mk. 9:37). Hoffmann, 285f., argues, however, that Mt. 10:40 is the original form, and that Luke has rewritten it to give a parallel to the double fate of the message in 10:8f., 10f. (cf. Grundmann, 211). Against this view is the independent attestation of the negative form in Jn. 5:23 (cf. Jn. 15:23); cf. the use of ἀθετέω in Jn. 12:48. It is more probable that Luke here reproduces the Q form of a saying which existed orally in a variety of forms, no doubt because Jesus used the basic structure in various forms. At most Luke may have altered an original δέχομαι to ἀκούω but this is not certain: Mt. δέχομαι may be based on Mk. 9:37 (Schulz, 457). Bultmann's argument that this is a community creation depends on the probative force of a 'naturally', in which, we may justifiably claim, there is in fact no force.

iv. The Return of the Missionaries 10:17–20

We have already observed that our sources contain no account of the course of the mission undertaken by Jesus' disciples, although 9:49f. may date from this period. Luke proceeds straight from the closing saying of Jesus' discourse to an account of the return of the missionaries with their glad comment that they have been able to exorcise demons. But here too the interest lies principally in the sayings of Jesus; he expresses his sense of victory over Satan, and reaffirms the authority of the disciples; nevertheless, what matters in the end is their own certainty of salvation.

The source of this section is uncertain. Hoffmann, 248–254, regards it as a Lucan creation on the basis of some isolated sayings, and claims that it forms part of Luke's theology of mission; it speaks to the situation of his own time in which Christians could no longer perform mighty works but could rejoice that their names were written in heaven. The argument, however, proves no more than that Luke has edited existing material. There is more to be said for the view that this section comes from Q. For it is easy to see that Matthew, who has used the mission discourse in relation to a mission by the Twelve, would have no place for a return by the 72 disciples at this point. Schürmann, *Untersuchungen*, 146 n. 37, argues that traces of the influence of the present section can be seen in Mt. 7:21–23. Further, the inclusion of this section in Q gives a frame of reference for 'in that hour' (10:21) and for v. 18 which are otherwise left hanging in the air. The remaining possibility, that the section comes from Luke's special source, is improbable, since we have not found any other evidence for an account of the mission of the disciples in this material (*contra* Manson, *Sayings*, 74, 258f.).

Vs. 17 and 20 clearly belong together. V. 19 is related to the mission of the disciples, but v. 18 could have a more general meaning in a different context. A verdict will depend on the exegesis of the individual verses. The historicity of the section as a whole hangs on that of a mission by the disciples; see introduction to the previous section.

See Miyoshi, 95–119.

(17) On the text see 10:1 note: The language describing the joyful return of the disciples is Lucan (ὑποστρέφω, 1:56; *et al.*; χαρά, 1:14; *et al.*; see especially 24:52). The disciples comment with surprise on the way in which even the demons were subject to them when they acted in the name of Jesus (cf. Mt. 7:22; Lk. 9:49f.; Acts 19:13). The power to exorcise demons is not mentioned in ch. 10, but appears in the sending of the Twelve, 9:1 (cf. Mt. 10:8). It is possible that Luke omitted mention of it at the beginning of ch. 10 in view of the present saying. The use of the name of Jesus fits in with the idea of the disciples being sent with the authority of Jesus in 10:16. Miyoshi, 98f., holds that the verse was composed by Luke on the basis of 9:49 and 10:20.

(18) Jesus' reply is to be seen in its context as an expression of the significance of the power of his name over the demons. θεωρέω can be used of literal or mental perception; cf. 14:29; 21:6; 23:35, 48; 24:37, 39* for the former sense, and Jn. 4:19; 12:19; Acts 27:10 for the latter (cf. W. Michaelis, TDNT V, 345f.). The imperfect has been thought to represent a continuous (Creed, 147) or repeated experience, but K. G. Kuhn (in TDNT V, 346 n. 161) observes that there is only one Aramaic past tense that can lie behind the verb here. It is more likely that the imperfect is used because the aorist of θεωρέω was not in common use; generally a form of θεάομαι was used instead (BD 101). The important question is whether the saying refers to a vision (Creed, 147; Bultmann, 113, 174; Grundmann, 212) or is to be understood symbolically (Schmid, 187). In the former case, it is possible that the reference is to an experience in Christ's pre-existent life (cf. G. Kittel, TDNT IV, 130 n. 220). The latter view, however, is more probable. The use of the Jewish name Σατανᾶς (4:2 note) indicates that we are in the realm of Jewish tradition. πίπτω may be meant as a passive for βάλλω (Klostermann, 117), in which case the picture is of Satan being cast out from heaven; on the constative aorist participle, see MH I, 134. The expression ὡς ἀστραπήν (cf. 17:24 par. Mt. 24:27; Mt. 28:3; Rev. 4:5; *et al.* in 11:36 ἀστραπή means a beam of light) refers not so much to the brightness of lightning as to its sudden and swift fall from heaven to earth (W. Foerster, TDNT I, 505).

The saying is related to a Jewish tradition. In Rev. 12:7–10, 13 Michael fights and overcomes the dragon (Satan) in heaven, so that he is cast down to the earth where he pursues the woman who bore the male child. Behind the picture lies the myth of the fall of Lucifer from heaven

(Is. 14:12; cf. the allusion to this myth in Lk. 10:15). In Jn. 12:31 the ruler of this world is cast out. He is to be overcome (Rom. 16:20), bound and cast into the abyss, so that he is no more (Rev. 20:1–3, 10; cf. T. Levi 18:12; T. Jud. 25:3; T. Ash. 7:3; T. Dan 5:10f.; Ass. Moses 10:1; Jub. 23:29). This evidence suggests that the mythological idea of the fall and defeat of Satan is here being utilised by Jesus to express symbolically the significance of the exorcism of the demons. The exorcisms are a sign of the defeat of Satan (cf. Mk. 3:27). Thus the eschatological defeat of Satan is seen to take place in the ministry of Jesus and his disciples (cf. 11:20). There is no reason to suppose that an original eschatological saying has been reinterpreted in missionary terms (for this view see Hoffmann, 252); nor does the saying indicate that the missionaries are understood as pneumatic wonder-workers rather than preachers of the imminent End (ibid.). The disciples task was to preach *and* to heal, and there is no conflict between the two.

(19) A second saying refers directly to the authority (ἐξουσία, 9:1) which Jesus has given to his disciples (δέδωκα, rell; δίδωμι, A D Θ f13 pm; TR; *Diglot* seems less appropriate). πατέω is 'to tread upon' (21:24; Rev. 11:2; 14:20; 19:15**; G. Bertram and H. Seesemann, TDNT V, 940–945); ὄφις is 'serpent' (11:1 par. Mt. 7:10; cf. Mk. 16:18), and is used of Satan in 2 Cor. 11:3; Rev. 12:9, 14f.; 20:2; σκορπίος is 'scorpion' (11:12; Rev. 9:3, 5, 10**). The language is reminiscent of Ps. 90:13 LXX, ἐπ' ἀσπίδα καὶ βασιλίσκον ἐπιβήσῃ, καὶ καταπατήσεις λέοντα καὶ δράκοντα. The preceding verse is quoted in 4:10f. See also the rabbinic material in Miyoshi, 103–105. There is a notable parallel to the present verses (18 and 19) in T. Levi 18:12 where it is said of the coming priest, 'And Beliar shall be bound by him, and he shall give power to his children to tread upon the evil spirits'. (cf. T. Sim. 6:6; T. Zeb. 9:8). The evil spirits in this passage are here described in terms of serpents and scorpions. The promise reflects OT ideas; cf. Gn. 3:15; Is. 11:8. W. Foerster's view (TDNT V, 579) that the reference is to the end of the deadly conflict between man and nature and the beginning of the new creation (cf. Mk. 16:18) is out of place here. The enemy (ἐχθρός) is of course Satan himself (Mt. 13:39; T. Dan 6:3f. Apoc. Moses 2:4; 7:2; 25:4; 28:4; W. Foerster, TDNT II, 813f.). The final promise is that nothing will harm the disciples. οὐδέν may be the subject of the verb (G. Schrenk, TDNT I, 161) or an internal accusative (Klostermann, ad loc.; cf. Acts 25:10; Gal. 4:12; Phm. 18); ἀδικέω* is 'to injure, harm'. The promise is reminiscent of Mk. 16:18; cf. Lk. 21:18; Acts 28:3–6; it foreshadows the conditions of the apostolic age.

The verse is regarded as an intrusion, breaking the connection of thought between vs. 18 and 20, by Manson, *Sayings*, 258f. But in fact vs. 18 and 19 hang well together, and v. 20 offers a contrast to the thought contained in both of them. T. Levi 18:12 might be taken as showing the close connection of ideas between vs. 18 and 19, but it must stand under suspicion of Christian editing.

(20) Now comes the contrast (πλήν, cf. 6:24; 10:14). The saying should probably be interpreted in terms of Semitic idiom to mean, 'Do not rejoice primarily that..., but rather that...' (cf. 10:21; 12:4f.; 14:12f.; 23:28; Je. 7:22; Ho. 6:6; 1 Cor. 1:17; Mt. 10:20; Mk. 9:37; Jn. 7:16; Jn. 12:44; Zerwick, 445; detailed discussion in H. Kruse, ' "Dialektische Negation" als semitisches Idiom', *Vetus Testamentum* 4, 1954, 385–400). τὰ πνεύματα, when unqualified, means 'evil spirits' in a Jewish context (Dalman, 203). That the demons are subject to the disciples is not so important as the fact that their own names have been written in heaven. ἐγγράφω is 'to enrol, write' (2 Cor. 3:2f.); the passive form, coupled with ἐν τοῖς οὐρανοῖς, indicates that divine action is meant. The metaphor is that of listing names in a roll of citizens; here it is applied to the idea of the book of life (G. Schrenk, TDNT I, 769f.). The thought of heavenly books is widespread in Jewish sources (SB II, 169–176; III, 840; IV, 1037, 1041; G. Schrenk, TDNT I, 618–620). Here the reference is to the book of life, containing the registers of God's people (Ex. 32:32f.; Ps. 68:29; Dn. 12:1; 1 En. 47:3; 108:3; Jub. 19:9; 30:20ff.; 36:10; Phil. 4:3; Heb. 12:23; Rev. 3:5; 13:8; 17:8; 20:12, 15; 21:27; cf. the earthly lists of God's people in Ne. 7:5, 64; 12:22f.; Ps. 86:5–7; Ezk. 13:9). But why does Jesus say this? The saying has been interpreted as a warning against spiritual pride or as stressing the importance of individual salvation: Hoffmann, 253f., thinks that it prepares for the time in the church when the disciples would no longer be capable of the miraculous deeds of the earliest days. From the earliest days, however, the thought of individual salvation was important. The saying is paralleled in the teaching of Jesus by 13:23f. where the importance of being sure that one is saved is stressed.

v. Jesus' Thanksgiving to the Father 10:21–24

The close link between 10:21–24 and the preceding sections is to be seen in the time note in v. 21 and the mention of the disciples as the audience for 10:23f. A new section is signalised by the change of scene in 10:25. The present section is thus the culmination of the long passage on the duties and privileges of disciples which began at 9:51. In the first part of the section (10:21f.) Jesus addresses the Father in a prayerful expression of rejoicing and praise because it has been his will to reveal things hidden from the wise to the disciples; they have been privileged to see the signs of God's kingly power over Satan in the defeat of the demons. What has been revealed to the disciples, however, has come from the Father through the Son who possesses all power and knowledge and who alone can reveal the Father. In the second part of the section (10:23f.) Jesus pronounces a blessing upon the disciples because they have been able to see and hear what was not possible even to prophets and kings in an earlier age; the disciples are privileged to live in the era of divine revelation.

It seems doubtful that this section was originally a unity. The two sections appear in different contexts in Mt. (11:25–27; 13:16f.), and in Mt. the first section is followed by the 'great invitation' (Mt. 11:28–30). It appears most likely that Mt. 11:28–30 has been inserted here by the Evangelist and did not stand in Q (Bultmann, 171f.; Manson, *Sayings*, 185–187; Suggs, 77–81; Hoffmann, 104; *contra* Dibelius, 280 n. 1); U. Wilckens, TDNT VII, 516f.). In both Gospels the thanksgiving is closely associated with the woes on the Galilean cities, which formed part of, or closely followed, the missionary discourse. The blessing on the disciples has been inserted by Matthew into a Marcan context, and hence Luke may preserve the original setting in Q. Nevertheless, the themes are not quite the same. Although both sayings are concerned with the privileged position of the disciples, the former contrasts them with their contemporaries, the latter with their predecessors. The former deals with the revelation of divine wisdom and knowledge of the Father, the latter with the mighty works and preaching of Jesus as the signs of fulfilment. It is probable, therefore, that we have two originally separate sayings here.

The authenticity of the second saying (10:23f.) is generally admitted and needs no discussion (Bultmann, 114, 133; Hoffmann, 210; see, however, Schulz, 419–421, who assigns the 'apophthegm' to the later stage of Q and presumably denies its authenticity on general grounds but without any real basis in the saying itself).

The character and unity of the first saying (10:21f.) is much debated. It falls into two parts. V. 21b is cast in the form of a prayer and speaks of the revelation of 'these things' by the Father to the 'simple'; there is no mention of the place of Jesus in it. V. 22 is a declaration by Jesus which speaks of the authority given by the Father to the Son: there is complete mutual knowledge between the Father and Son, so that only the Son can reveal the Father to men. Bultmann, 171f., argued that the two sayings were originally separate, the first having an Aramaic background, while the second reflects Hellenistic mysticism. But while there are Hellenistic parallels to the second saying, these do not suffice to explain it fully, and it can be better understood against a Jewish background (cf. Hahn, 322–326). A different approach is taken by Hoffmann, 108f., who notes that the two sayings are parallel, but whereas the first saying speaks of revelation by the Father to the simple, the second speaks of revelation by the Son. The parallelism forbids the separate origin of the two sayings and the differences rule out their original unity; hence it must be concluded that the second saying was composed as a commentary on the first in order to remove its obscurity (cf. Schulz, 215). This suggestion magnifies the difference between the two sayings, and it is much more probable that the second saying represents a development of the thought in the first saying by the same author, especially since the same motifs in fact appear in both sayings. The fact that the two sayings are assigned to different form-critical categories will be found a difficulty only by those who impose a rigid schematisation on the Gospel tradition.

The background of the sayings has been increasingly recognised in recent years as lying in Jewish thinking about wisdom. Divine wisdom is entrusted with the secrets of God and reveals them to men; she is rejected by the mass of men, especially the wise, but is accepted by the poor and unlearned. The structure of the second saying is thoroughly Semitic, and the individual ideas find their closest parallels in Judaism, especially in the wisdom tradition. This same tradition appears elsewhere in the Q material. (See especially A. Feuillet*; Christ; Suggs.)

The rediscovery of the Jewish background of the saying reopens the question whether it goes back to Jesus himself. Whereas advocates of a Hellenistic origin naturally denied authenticity, the question has now become much more open. Authenticity is denied on the grounds of the disunity of the section, the use of Hellenistic Jewish ideas and the attribution of a 'Son' christology to Jesus. These grounds are not compelling. The section can be seen as a unity, and we cannot rule out the use of so-called 'Hellenistic' ideas by Jesus. The christology is of a piece with Jesus' recognition of God as his Father in a unique sense and acceptance of it as an authentic expression of his self-understanding helps to make better sense of the Gospel tradition as a whole (cf. A. Feuillet*; A. M. Hunter*; I. H. Marshall*; Christ, 93 (very cautiously); Jeremias, *Theology*, I, 56–59; *contra* Suggs, 71 n. 24; Hoffmann, 102–142; Schulz, 215).

See E. Norden, *Agnostos Theos* (1913), Darmstadt, 1956; W. Bousset, *Kyrios Christos*, Göttingen, 1921[2], 45–50; Bultmann, 171f.; Dibelius, 279–284; T. Arvedson, *Das Mysterium Christi*, Uppsala, 1937 (not accessible to me); A. Feuillet, 'Jésus et la Sagesse divine d'après les Evangiles synoptiques', RB 62, 1955, 161–196; P. Winter, 'Matthew xi. 27 and Luke x. 22 from the First to the Fifth Century', Nov.T 1, 1956, 112–148; A. M. Hunter, 'Crux Criticorum – Matt. xi. 25–30 – A Re-appraisal', NTS 8, 1961–62, 241–249; Hahn, 321–333; van Iersel, 146–161; J. M. Robinson, 'Die Hodajot-Formel in Gebet und Hymnus des Frühchristentums', in W. Eltester (*et al.*), *Apophoreta* (Festschrift für E. Haenchen), Berlin, 1964, 194–235; U. Wilckens, TDNT VII, 516f.; I. H. Marshall, 'The Divine Sonship of Jesus', *Interpretation* 21, 1967, 87–103; Jeremias, *Abba*, 47–54; id. *Theology* I, 56–61; E. Schweizer, TDNT VIII, 372f.; Légasse, 121–185; Christ, 81–99; Suggs, 71–97; Hoffmann, 102–142; Schulz, 213–228, 419–421; Miyoshi, 120–152.

(21) In both Mt. and Lk. the section begins with a temporal phrase, characteristic of each Evangelist; for Luke's ἐν αὐτῇ τῇ ὥρᾳ see 2:38 (cf. 12:12), for Matthew's ἐν ἐκείνῳ τῷ καιρῷ cf. Mt. 12:1; 14:1. It is hard to say which Evangelist reproduces the wording in Q, but the phrase is certainly based on Q and refers back to the occasion of whatever sayings preceded it in Q (10:13–15 or 10:17–20). For Luke it refers back to the revelation of divine power seen in the exorcism of demons by the disciples, but in Mt. it gives a strong contrast between the rejection of Jesus' message by the Galilean cities and the acceptance of his message as divine revelation by the disciples. The contrast expressed in the saying between the wise and the simple may perhaps favour Matthew's ordering of the sayings, but this is by no means conclusive.

Luke describes the feelings of Jesus with the verb ἀγαλλιάομαι (1:47*); the link of thought with χαίρω in 10:20 may be simply coincidental. Since the following phrase is probably Lucan, the same may be true of the verb, which in any case is lacking in Mt. at this point. Here the meaning is that Jesus was inspired with joy by the Spirit (Acts 13:52; R. Bultmann, TDNT I, 21). This interpretation depends on the solution to the textual problem surrounding the next phrase. The variants are:

1. ἐν τῷ πνεύματι τῷ ἁγίῳ (‫א‬ D al it; (UBS));
2. τῷ πνεύματι τῷ ἁγίῳ (p⁷⁵ B al; NEB, Synopsis);
3. ἐν τῷ πνεύματι (p⁴⁵ Cl; Diglot);
4. τῷ πνεύματι (A W f13 pm f q; TR).

Variant 4, which is weakly attested, is a simplification to avoid the strange expression 'rejoiced in the Holy Spirit'. Variant 3 might appear to be supported by Lucan usage (2:27; 4:1; Acts 19:21), but in the first two parallels the adjective ἅγιος is missing because the full phrase has just been used (2:25f.; 4:1), which is not the case here. The strongest external evidence favours variants 1 and 2, but it is not easy to decide whether ἐν should be included or not (Metzger, 152). The force is that Jesus is filled with joy and the Spirit before an inspired saying (E. Schweizer, TDNT VI, 405).

The saying which follows has the form of a thanksgiving psalm in which the speaker praises God because of something that he has done (J. M. Robinson*). A close parallel is given by 1QH 7:26: 'I give (Thee thanks, O Adonai), for Thou hast given me understanding of Thy truth and hast made me to know Thy marvellous Mysteries and Thy favours to (sinful) man (and) the abundance of Thy mercy toward the perverse heart.' The parallel shows similarity not only of form but also of content and helps to confirm that the thought of the present verse is fully explicable in Jewish terms (Jeremias, Theology I, 190). ἐξομολογέομαι, 'to confess', hence 'to praise', is common in the LXX (cf. especially Sir. 51:1), especially to render the hiphil of yāḏāh (O. Michel, TDNT V, 199–220; C. Westermann, THAT I, 674–682); cf. Rom. 14:11; 15:9; and ἀνθομολογέομαι, Lk. 2:38. Jesus addresses God first as πάτερ, corresponding to Aram. 'abbâ. While this form is found in Greek prayers (3 Macc. 6:3, 8), its use in a Palestinian context appears to be found uniquely in the prayers of Jesus and in the way in which he taught his disciples to pray. The Greek form reflects an Aramaic word used by small children as well as by adults, and expresses an intimate filial relationship with God, such as is developed in v. 22; it is a small step from addressing God as Father in this way to knowing oneself to be the Son of this Father. Alongside this intimate expression Jesus also uses the phrase κύριε τοῦ οὐρανοῦ καὶ τῆς γῆς (the last three words are omitted by p⁴⁵ Mcion; on this and other odd textual phenomena here see J. N. Birdsall in P. R. Ackroyd and C. F. Evans (ed.), The Cambridge History of the Bible, Cambridge, 1970, I, 331 f.). The expression is thoroughly Jewish; it is based on Gn. 14:19, 22, as understood in

Judaism (1QapGen 22:16; Tephilla (cited by Jeremias, *Theology*, I, 187f.); Tob. 7:17; cf. the rabbinic 'Lord of the world', SB II, 176). It is a relevant form of address in a saying which goes on to speak of the supremacy which has been bestowed by the Father on the Son.

It is possible that Jesus thanked God for hiding something from the wise; by so doing he puts all human arrogance in the wrong (A. Oepke, TDNT III, 973). Nevertheless, it is perhaps better to see here a saying in which the first clause is unstressed: 'I give thanks ... that although you have hidden ... you have nevertheless revealed...' (Creed, 148; cf. 10:20 for a related idiom). The compound ἀποκρύπτω, diff. Mt. κρύπτω, is perhaps chosen to give assonance with ἀποκαλύπτω; for ἀποκρύπτω cf. 1 Cor. 2:7; Eph. 3:9; Col. 1:26**; and for ἀποκαλύπτω cf. 2:35; 10:22; 12:2; 17:30* (A. Oepke, TDNT III, 957–978, 563–592). The thought is of the secrecy of God's plans and purposes which he reveals at his own appointed time to his chosen people. The content of his plan is indicated by a ταῦτα which lacks a clear antecedent. The reference was probably originally to the gospel of the kingdom, attested by the preaching and mighty works of Jesus (Grundmann, 215). What was happening remained obscure in its significance to one group of people, but to the disciples it constituted a revelation of God's saving action.

The former group are described as wise (σοφός*) and understanding (συνετός, Mt. 11:25; Acts 13:7; 1 Cor. 1:19**; cf. U. Wilckens and G. Fohrer, TDNT VII, 465–526, and H. Conzelmann, TDNT VII, 888–896). The latter group are described as νήπιοι*, 'infants', i.e. 'the childlike, innocent ones, unspoiled by learning with whom God is pleased' (AG s.v.; cf. G. Bertram, TDNT IV, 912–923). By means of this contrast the traditional Jewish estimate of the wise as the recipients of God's revelation (4 Ez. 12:35–38) is overturned. There is an implicit condemnation of the religious leaders of the community who despite their wisdom have failed to gain a true perception of God and his will. Jesus takes up the thought, for which there was some preparation in the Jewish wisdom tradition and at Qumran, that God addresses himself to the poor and simple who are prepared to listen to him because they have no wisdom of their own (cf. Sir. 3:19; Wis. 10:21; Bar. 3:9ff.; 1QS 11:6f.; 1QpHab 12:4; 1QH 2:8–10). The same line of thought is taken up by Paul (1 Cor. 1:18–31). Thus Jesus gives thanks not 'because "these things" are reserved for a portion of mankind but because they are revealed to those who humanly speaking could not have expected it' (H. Conzelmann, TDNT VII, 893 n. 46). He thus stands close to the Qumran sect (cf. Hoffmann, 113f.), but for Jesus the childlike and poor are not the meticulous performers of law and ritual but the needy and downtrodden who accept the gospel.

In the concluding part of the verse the nominative ὁ πατήρ is equivalent to a vocative (BD 147³). ναί (7:26) is an expression of agreement, giving the sense: 'Yes, O Father, (you have done this) because it was your will, and I agree with what you have done', or 'Yes, O Father,

(I praise you) that this was your will'. The variant οὐά, ὁ πατήρ, ὅτι ἔμπροσθέν σου εὐδοκία μοι ἐγένετο (Marcosian version, preserved by Irenaeus AH 1:13:2) is unlikely to be genuine (*contra* Grundmann, 217), but it may possibly reflect an Aramaic tradition with οὐά for Aramaic *wah* as an expression of joy (Black, 246). The word order ἐγένετο εὐδοκία (p⁴⁵ ℵ A D W Θ *pl*; TR; *Diglot*) may be original since the UBS reading could be due to assimilation to Mt. εὐδοκία (2:14) expresses the saving purpose of God, and the construction with ἔμπροσθεν reflects Aramaic usage (G. Schrenk, TDNT II, 745; Jeremias, *Theology*, I, 190 n. 7). The use of the corresponding verb in 1 Cor. 1:21 together with the general similarity of thought suggests that the saying was known to Paul (Jeremias, ibid.).

(22) At the beginning of the second part of the saying various MSS insert καὶ στραφεὶς πρὸς τοὺς μαθητὰς εἶπεν (A C* W Θ *al* it sy ᴾ bo ᵖᵗ; TR; NEB). Tasker, 420, claims that the phrase is necessary for the sense, and was omitted because of its similarity to 10:23. It is, however, unlikely that Luke would have been so repetitious, and the phrase was probably inserted by homoioarcton (Metzger, 152). The addition, however, correctly indicates the fact that although Jesus is engaged in prayer his words are directed to the disciples (Dibelius, 282).

There is an important textual problem concerning the verse as a whole. The text in the majority of witnesses has the order 'no one knows who is the son except the father, and who is the father except the son'. This order is reversed ('no one knows who is the father except the son, and who is the son except the father') by U N b Mcion Al Ath; a similar change is found in the text of Mt. (N X Justin and other fathers). The inversion of order was defended as original by Harnack (*The Sayings of Jesus*, 1908, 272–310; cf. Dibelius, 281 n. 1) and more recently by P. Winter*; cf. J. N. Birdsall, in *The Cambridge History of the Bible*, I, 337–339. From this variation in order, Harnack concluded that the text had been interpolated with the clause 'who is the son except the father'; the omission is attested in Lk. by 1216 1579 a. Although the patristic evidence for a variant reading is fairly strong in Mt., it is hopelessly weak in Lk. (neither Al nor Ath offers it consistently). Moreover, it is a methodological rule that the evidence of the fathers should not be preferred to the almost unanimous witness of the Greek MSS (especially when these include p⁴⁵ and p⁷⁵; B. M. Metzger, 'Patristic Evidence and the Textual Criticism of the New Testament', NTS 18, 1971–72, 379–400). Winter ignored J. Chapman's arguments against Harnack, which have lost none of their force ('Dr Harnack on Luke x. 22: No man knoweth the Son', JTS 10, 1908–9, 552–566). With the inverted order the connection with the last clause of the saying is difficult, if not impossible. It is more probable that the inverted order is due to early church theologians who wished to stress the unknowability of the Father (E. Schweizer, TDNT VIII, 372 n. 276). Chapman rightly pointed out that the element of paradox in the usual text is confirmed by Mt. 16:16f.;

436 THE DUTIES AND PRIVILEGES OF DISCIPLESHIP [10:22

Gal. 1:15, where the need for the Father to reveal the Son is stressed. See further the detailed study by Suggs, 71–77.

The saying falls into four lines, and its style is Semitic. This point may be regarded as settled by the researches of Jeremias (summed up in *Theology* I, 56–61; cf. *Abba*, 47–50). This means that a Hellenistic content is unlikely, and this is in fact confirmed by the exegesis.

The first clause states that all has been handed over to Jesus by the Father. (P. Winter*, 128, argues for the omission of μου after πατρός with D a c l vg sy^s Mcion Justin Iren.) The verb παραδίδωμι (1:2) can be used of the handing down of knowledge, especially of a tradition handed on from a teacher to a pupil (cf. Mk. 7:13; 1 Cor. 11:2, 23); it can also be used of the transfer of power or authority (4:6; cf. CH 1:32). The subject πάντα can also be understood in both senses. Since the context is undoubtedly one of knowledge and revelation, many scholars accept the former interpretation: 'My Father has given me a full revelation' (Jeremias, *Theology* I, 59; cf. Creed, 148; Grundmann, 217). A majority of scholars are impressed by the parallelism with Dn. 7:13f. and Mt. 28:18 (cf. Jn. 3:35; 13:3) and adopt the second interpretation (Lagrange, 307; Schniewind, *Matthäus*, 151; A. Feuillet*, 188f.; F. Büchsel, TDNT II, 171; W. Foerster, TDNT II, 568; G. Schrenk, TDNT V, 993 n. 289). On this view what is hidden from men is not the knowledge of the Son but the fact of his authority. Hoffmann, 120, claims that the statement is tautologous if what is revealed to the simple is merely the fact that the Son possesses all knowledge; but this assumes that the content of ταῦτα (v. 21) is the statement in v. 22. B. Reicke (TDNT V, 895) solved the deadlock by arguing that 'all power' includes knowledge as well. This is probably the best solution of the problem, since it is difficult to take πάντα by itself to mean 'all knowledge', and the Johannine usage points in the direction of authority. But the point of the saying is certainly that knowledge has been conferred on the Son; the clause must be understood in relation to what follows, and this refers to both the knowledge of the Son and his authority to reveal the Father.

The second and third clauses refer to the mutual knowledge of father and son. The formulation is determined by the fact that the Semitic languages lack a reciprocal pronoun (cf. Tob. 5:2 ℵ; Dalman, 283; Jeremias, *Theology* I, 57f.). Hence the meaning of the saying is to be found in the two clauses taken together, and it is misleading to expound them separately. (Failure to realise this point is the ultimate reason for the textual confusion.) The meaning is, then, 'Only a father and a son know each other'; from this follows the conclusion: 'Therefore, only the son can reveal the father'. Luke has the simple verb γινώσκω, diff. Mt. ἐπιγινώσκω; the two words are synonymous (A. Feuillet*, 169 n. 2), but Luke may have wished to avoid the possible element of 'getting to know' in ἐπιγινώσκω. Luke also has τίς ἐστιν ... clauses instead of the simple accusatives found in Mt.; here too his version is probably secondary (cf. 13:25; 22:60 and parr.).

The concept of knowledge here has Hellenistic parallels; cf. the magic formula, 'I know you, Hermes, and you know me. I am you, and you are me' (P. Lond. 122, 50) and Akhnaton's hymn to the Sun, 'No other knows thee save thy son, Akhnaton. Thou hast initiated him into thy plans and thy powers' (Bultmann, 172 n. 2). But in view of the Semitic style it is right to look for a Jewish background. This is furnished by the OT with its references to God's knowledge of man (2 Sa. 7:20; 1 Ki. 8:39; Ps. 139:1; Am. 3:2; Je. 1:5; 12:3) and to man's knowledge of God (Nu. 24:16; 1 Sa. 3:7; (1 Ki. 8:43); Pss. 36:10; (91:14); (Is. 52:6); Je. 9:24 (23 MT); 31:34; Ho. 2:20; 4:1; 6:6), as well as to mutual knowledge (Ex. 33:12f.); cf. Schniewind, *Matthäus*, 152; C. H. Dodd, *The Interpretation of the Fourth Gospel*, Cambridge, 1954, 151–169; W. Schottroff, THAT I, 682–701. It is noteworthy that OT statements about man's knowledge of God tend to be negative. Many scholars interpret God's knowledge of the Son here in terms of the note of election found in such passages as Am. 3:2; Je. 1:5, and thus find here 'election by the Father and acknowledgement by the Son' (E. Schweizer, TDNT VIII, 373). But to bring in the thought of election destroys the reciprocity of the relationship, since 'know' is now being used in two distinct senses, for the Son cannot be said to 'choose' the Father. It is, therefore, better to begin from the secular understanding of the verb in terms of mutual trust and insight (cf. Tob. 5:2; Wis. 2:13, 16 – but the latter text is hardly the main parallel to the passage, *pace* Suggs, 91f.). Jeremias, op. cit., has claimed that the nouns here should be taken generically of *any* son and *any* father and not understood as titles for Jesus and God. This generic understanding of the idea of knowledge is correct, and is preferable to the view developed by Hoffmann, 127–131, that there is an apocalyptic background to the saying, so that it speaks of knowledge of the Father's secret plan of salvation and of the Son's supreme place as the coming Son of man. But Jeremias's view needs correction at two points. First, it is probable that the thought of the closeness of wisdom to God stands in the background of the saying (Job 28:25–28; Pr. 8:22–30; Sir. 1:1–10; Bar. 3:27–38; Wis. 8:3f.; Christ, 89). Second, since Jesus refers to God as 'Father' in the first line of the saying, the 'secular' formula found in lines two and three must be understood to apply to him; if so, it follows that the term 'son' is being applied to Jesus himself. Jesus is thus described as the son of God, and it is not a far cry from this description to the development of a title. (Hoffmann's criticism of Jeremias (119f.) is thus partly justified, but does not require us to reject Jeremias's view.)

In the fourth clause Jesus teaches that knowledge of the Father is bestowed by the Son at his will; to the εὐδοκία of the Father (v. 21) corresponds the βούλομαι of the Son. For the link between knowledge of God and the ability to reveal him to other men see 1QS 4:22; 1QSb 4:24–27 (E. Schweizer, TDNT VIII, 373 n. 281; see further W. D. Davies, ' "Knowledge" in the Dead Sea Scrolls and in Matthew

11:25–30', HTR 46, 1953, 113–139). Here Jesus takes up the role of the Son of God, and claims to stand in an exclusive relationship to him and to be the sole mediator of knowledge of God to men. This relationship is adequately explained in terms of Jesus' consciousness of God as Father. The thought is still within the limits of the metaphor used in lines two and three, but for Christian readers 'a son' (generic) could only be understood as an allusion to the unique status of Jesus.

(23) The change from the prayer form in the previous saying is indicated by the introductory formula. Although it is lacking in Mt. (where, however, the context does not require it), and its language is partly Lucan (στραφείς, 7:9; et al.), it is based on Q, since the phrase κατ' ἰδίαν (9:10 par. Mk. 6:31) is not Lucan (cf. Schulz, 419).

The saying itself pronounces a blessing on, i.e. announces the fortunate state of, the people who see what the disciples see (Pss. Sol. 17:50; 18:7). For μακάριος cf. 1:45; 6:20–22; 7:23; 11:28. The personification of ὀφθαλμοί is common (2:30) and stresses the element of real, personal experience (cf. Job 19:27; 42:5) rather than sense-perception as such (W. Michaelis, TDNT V, 347). The accent lies both on the act of seeing (Mt., diff. Lk.) and on what is seen. What the disciples see are the signs of the era of salvation, the mighty works done by Jesus, the indications that the era of fulfilment has come (which men of the past were unable to see). Hence implicit in the saying is the need for true perception of the significance of what is happening – a nuance more clearly expressed by the saying in its Matthaean context (cf. Black, 70f.). The Lucan form of the saying differs from that in Mt. in two particulars. First, in Mt. the blessing is promised to the disciples themselves, whereas in Lk. it is more generally addressed to all who see what the disciples already see. Although Luke might be suspected of generalising here, it is more probable that the first half of the saying is parallel to the second, and that Matthew has altered the form of the saying to fit his context in which there is a contrast between those who do not understand and the disciples. Second, Matthew includes a phrase about hearing which corresponds to a similar phrase in the second part of the saying; here it is likely that Luke has abbreviated the saying, thereby losing the original parallelism of eyes and ears (Schürmann, *Paschamahlbericht*, 2; cf. Bultmann, 114; Kümmel, 112; W. Michaelis, ibid.; *contra* Schulz, 420). Hoffmann's suggestion (254) that Luke wished to stress the eye-witness function of the apostles is improbable, since the saying is about those who see what the apostles saw. By his abbreviation Luke has lost an important element in the saying, since the stress on *hearing* the words of Jesus is unique compared with Jewish expectations of the age of salvation which were in terms of seeing (W. Michaelis, ibid.). Luke, however, has in mind the mighty works which the disciples reported in 10:17.

(24) The element of eschatological fulfilment emerges clearly in the second part of the saying which contrasts the longings of men of the past with the experience of those who live in the present time. Luke has omit-

ted the introductory ἀμήν (diff. Mt.) as usual (4:24 note). The prophets are cited as examples of men who looked into the future and longed for the fulfilment of what God had revealed to them (1 Pet. 1:10–12). There may also be the suggestion that even the pious men of the past failed to enjoy the era of salvation. The significance of 'kings' alongside prophets is less obvious. Matthew has δίκαιοι, which suggests 'those who live by the word of the Lord which the prophets proclaim' (J. A. Ziesler, *The Meaning of Righteousness in Paul*, Cambridge, 1972, 139). But this appears to be a Matthaean simplification (cf. Mt. 10:41; 23:29; Manson, *Sayings*, 80). Luke's wording may reflect Is. 52:15; 60:3, where kings look forward to the era of salvation. Or possibly the thought is that even the most religious and the most important people failed to see what the ordinary, humble people can now see (K. L. Schmidt, TDNT I, 577). For θέλω, Matthew has ἐπιθυμέω with no apparent difference in meaning. In the final part of the saying Luke retains the mention of hearing, which for Jesus is as important as seeing in religious experience (cf. G. Kittel, TDNT I, 220). The point, however, is not merely hearing the word of God, which was common enough, but hearing the proclamation that the age of salvation has come (F. Horst, TDNT V, 553).

b. The Characteristics of Disciples (10:25 – 11:13)

The second main part in the major teaching section of Lk. deals with various aspects of the life of disciples. The three incidents which compose it are of different kinds, but all appear to contain this motif. In the first, Jesus is approached by a lawyer, who is not apparently a disciple but is at least friendly to him, and the conversation between them indicates that Jesus' followers must obey the two main commands in the law in order to inherit eternal life, with stress being laid in the story on the practical explication of the command to love one's neighbour (10:25–37). The second incident is a brief pronouncement story which provides something of a counterbalance to the emphasis on practical love in the first incident by stressing the need for disciples to attend to the teaching given by Jesus (10:38–42). The third incident is a piece of teaching by Jesus on prayer, given in response to a request for instruction by the disciples (11:1–13). Very roughly one may say that the three incidents handle the relation of the disciples to their neighbours, to Jesus, and to God respectively. Whether this structure is due to Luke himself depends on an answer to the source-critical question.

The kernels of the three incidents (10:29–37; 10:38–42; 11:5–8) are peculiar to Lk., but this does not necessarily indicate that they were absent from Q. The section 11:9–13 is closely parallel to Mt. 7:7–11, and may well be from Q, but the section on the Lord's Prayer (11:1–4) differs markedly from Mt. 6:9–13. The conversation between the lawyer and Jesus (10:25–28) has a doublet in Mk. 12:28–34; Matthew's version

of Mark's incident (Mt. 22:34–40) has one or two points of contact with
Lk. against Mk. which may be significant. It is difficult to frame a single
hypothesis which will cover these phenomena. Nevertheless, it seems
most probable that the present passage indicates that a fusion of so-
called Q and L material had taken place, and that the Q material used by
Luke underwent a certain amount of pre-Lucan recension which distinguishes it from that in Mt.

i. The Lawyer's Question 10:25–28

The story of the lawyer's question and the parable of the Good
Samaritan manifestly belong together in the mind of Luke; although the
latter appears to follow as a kind of appendix, it is integral to the
pericope and forms the climax. The two sections in fact fit perfectly
together, and it is difficult to imagine the parable without its present
setting to provide a context for it. Nevertheless, the story of the lawyer is
not simply an introduction to the parable. It has its own importance in
that it raises the question of the way in which a man may obtain eternal
life and answers it in thoroughly Jewish fashion by the citing of the two
commandments to love God and one's neighbour. If the latter commandment is developed in the ensuing parable, it is perhaps also true to
say that the former commandment receives some exposition in 10:38 –
11:13. The same stress on the two commandments is also found in Mk.
12:28–34; it was obviously regarded as a key element in the teaching of
Jesus, one which expressed his basic agreement with the fundamental
teaching of the OT and brought out the continuity between the law,
rightly understood, and his own teaching. Luke's emphasis elsewhere on
the value of traditional Jewish piety, nourished on the teaching of the
OT, here finds its justification. There is all the difference in the world between the loving service of God commended here and the salvation by
works of the law which Paul condemned.

The crucial problem in the narrative is its relationship to Mk.
12:28–34. In both stories there is a conversation between Jesus and a
lawyer in which the two chief commandments are cited. In Mk. it is
Jesus who offers this summary of the law, and if in Lk. it is the lawyer
who does so, the lawyer in Mk. echoes the words of Jesus with approval.
The question is whether Luke has drawn his narrative from Mk. There
are one or two small agreements in wording between Lk. and Mk. (apart
from what might be expected in any case in the narration of the same incident or broadly similar incidents), and Luke has omitted the narrative
at the corresponding point in his own Gospel (Lk. 20:39/40; cf. Mk.
12:28a, 34b). Hence it is incontestable that Luke knew Mark's form of
the story and regarded his own as an equivalent to it, although this does
not mean that he regarded the two incidents as identical. Further, a number of differences between Mk. and Lk. can be ascribed to Luke's redactional activity. Thus the question of the lawyer has been altered from the

more theoretical 'which is the first commandment of all?' to the more practical 'what shall I do to inherit eternal life?' (cf. Mk. 10:17), and this change could have led to the omission of the 'Hear, O Israel' formula; again, the linking of the incident to the following parable could have led to the reformulation and abbreviation of the end of the story. It is not surprising that many scholars regard Luke's story as a re-working of Mark's account (Klostermann, 118; Schmid, 190; Ellis, 158; B. Reicke*). There are, however, some unexplained factors on this hypothesis. First, there are a number of contacts between Mt. and Lk. (Schramm, 47 n. 4) which strongly suggest that Matthew knew a recension of the story also familiar to Luke. Second, these and some other features are hard to explain as being due to Lucan redaction of Mk.; cf. especially the phrase πῶς ἀναγινώσκεις and the wording of the second commandment. These two factors make it likely that Luke was following an independent version of the story which was also known to Matthew (cf. cautiously, Bultmann, 21). It is possible that this version was in Q (although Matthew might then have shown more influence from it), but we cannot be certain; for this possibility see Schürmann, *Unter-suchungen*, 280 n. 15; G. Sellin*, 20–23; Daube, 248, thinks·that the text of Lk. has been assimilated to Mt.

If, however, Luke's version of the story is not from Mk., is it an independent account of the same incident, or were there two similar incidents? It is certainly possible to regard the versions in all three Gospels as independent developments of the one basic story; opinions then vary as to whether the more primitive form is to be found in Lk. (J. Weiss, 463; Easton, 169f.) or in Mk. (Linnemann, 141–143). Over against this view stands the sturdy commonsense argument of T. W. Manson (*Sayings*, 259–261); cf. Lagrange, 309f.; Jeremias, *Parables*, 202), that 'great teachers constantly repeat themselves'. The sort of question raised by the lawyer was one that could arise frequently, especially since we know that it was asked in rabbinic circles; Manson makes the point that there is nothing surprisingly about the lawyer repeating what he already knew to be the answer of Jesus himself to the question in order to put his own counter-question regarding the scope of neighbourliness.

See 10:29–37 note for literature.

(25) The incident opens without details of time or place, but may have taken place in or near Jerusalem (Grundmann, 221). The story concerns a νομικός, 'lawyer', diff. Mk. γραμματεύς (cf. 7:30 note). Nowhere else does Luke make this alteration to Mark's wording; in 5:17 he uses νομοδιδάσκαλος diff. Mk. It is, therefore, unlikely that he is responsible for the alteration here, a supposition which is strengthened if the same word is read in Mt. here (νομικός, is, however, omitted in Mt. by f1 e sy[s] arm Or[lat]; *Diglot*; cf. Streeter, 320; G. D. Kilpatrick, 'Scribes, Lawyers and Lucan Origins', JTS ns 1, 1950, 56–60. But the textual evidence is too weak to support the omission, and insufficient attention is

paid to the possibility of influence on Mt. from oral tradition or perhaps
from Q). The lawyer rises up to question Jesus; for this rather vague use
of ἀνίστημι cf. Acts 6:9; 20:30. Luke has nothing corresponding to
Mark's link with the preceding controversies. He notes that the lawyer's
intention was to 'test' Jesus. For ἐκπειράζω, par. Mt. πειράζω, see 4:12
note. Bultmann, 54, argues that by this addition the original 'scholastic
dialogue' in Mk. is turned into a 'controversy dialogue', but this assumes
that Luke is editing Mk. The suggestion is that a recognised religious
authority is testing the unofficial teacher to see whether he gives the right
answers; we should probably not see here the motif of temptation or of
'testing the Lord' (cf. H. Seesemann, TDNT VI, 28, 35). Before λέγων
the conjunction καί is added by A C D W Θ f1 f13 pl lat; TR; Diglot;
but asyndeton with participles is not uncommon (BD 421).

Jesus is addressed as διδάσκαλε, par. Mt., diff. Mk. (cf. 18:18 par.
Mk. 10:17). The question which follows is exactly parallel to 18:18
(Luke's re-wording of Mk. 10:17; cf. Flender, 10), and is usually thought
to be drawn from that passage. But it may equally well belong to the
source used by Luke here, in which case Luke has assimilated the
wording of Mk. 10:17 to the form found here. There is nothing surprising in the question being asked on more than one occasion, since it was a
rabbinic theme: Rabbi Eliezer (c. AD 90) was asked by his pupils,
'Rabbi, teach us the ways of life so that by them we may attain to the life
of the future world' (b Ber. 28b; SB I, 808). The question is couched in
terms of 'doing' (cf. Jn. 6:28f.); it would be forced to see in the use of the
aorist participle the implication that one single action would be a sufficient qualification. In any case the answer (present imperative, 10:28)
indicates that a way of life is commended by Jesus. Nor does the question demand an answer in terms of 'salvation by works'. Just as in Jn.
6:28f. the 'work' required is faith, so here it is love, an inner disposition,
not an outward qualification. Similarly, in 18:18–23 alms-giving and discipleship are the 'qualifications' for eternal life. ζωή, 'life' (12:15; 16:25;
18:18, 30*), is tantamount to salvation. The thought is primarily of life
with God after death, which can be expressed by ζωή or (as here) by
ζωὴ αἰώνιος (R. Bultmann, TDNT II, 856 n. 197; cf. Dn. 12:2; 4 Mac.
15:3; Ps. Sol. 3:16; T. Ash. 5:2). κληρονομέω, 'to inherit' (18:18*; J.
Herrmann, and W. Foerster, TDNT III, 767–785, especially 780), can
be weakened to mean simply 'to obtain', but here has the idea of being
qualified now to receive a future blessing from God. The verb is often
linked with the concept of eternal life (Ps. Sol. 14:10; 1 En. 40:9; T. Job
18).

(26) Jesus replies with a counter-question which directs the lawyer
to the Old Testament. What is written there is decisive. But in this way
the theme is shifted from the teaching of Jesus himself to how the lawyer
understands the law, and it is his view which is tested by Jesus.
Grundmann, 222, observes that Jesus is interested in the written law, not
the oral tradition. The question πῶς ἀναγινώσκεις is one that reflects

Jewish methods of argumentation, although its precise force is debated. According to Jeremias (*Theology* I, 187) the question means 'How do you recite?', i.e. what is the law recited by the lawyer as part of his regular worship, and therefore the lawyer is forced to reply with the words of the 'Shema'. Daube, 433, and Derrett, 223f., prefer the meaning, 'How do you expound the law on this point?' (But the rabbinic basis for this interpretation, Abodah Zarah 2:5 (cf. SB I, 692f.), refers to different ways of vocalising an unpointed text.) Jeremias' view is preferable, although it is exposed to the difficulty that the lawyer recites more than the contents of the Shema. The Jewish form of the question, together with the contact with Mt. (ἐν τῷ νόμῳ), make it unlikely that the wording is due to Luke.

(27) The lawyer replies by citing Dt. 6:5 (from the Shema) and Lv. 19:18. The text and wording of the first citation are difficult. The LXX has: ἀγαπήσεις κύριον τὸν θεόν σου ἐξ ὅλης τῆς καρδίας (v.l. διανοίας) σου καὶ ἐξ ὅλης τῆς ψυχῆς σου καὶ ἐξ ὅλης τῆς δυνάμεώς σου. 1. The LXX has three phrases introduced uniformly by ἐξ. Mark uniformly has ἐξ (but with four phrases), and Matthew has ἐν, without textual variation. The text of Lk. is confused: one ἐξ followed by three uses of ἐν (p⁷⁵ ℵ B Ξ *pc; Synopsis*; UBS) or ἐν throughout (A C W Θ f13 *pl*; TR; *Diglot*). The former is the harder reading and transcriptionally more probable. Luke's divergence from Mk. and from the LXX suggests that he is following a non-Marcan version of the citation. 2. The inclusion of τῆς before καρδίας is doubtful (om. p⁷⁵ B Ξ 0124 *pc*; (UBS)); cf. 5:5. 3. Most curious of all is the divergence of all three Gospels from the LXX list of phrases. Mark's use of ἰσχύς, diff. LXX δύναμις, is explicable as a translation variant. The oddity is his inclusion of a fourth phrase with διάνοια, which appears to be an alternative to καρδία, included by an oversight. Matthew may be presumed to have restored the triple nature of the formula by omission of the last phrase in Mk. In Lk. the first three terms follow the LXX order, but διάνοια is added at the end; the omission of the phrase in D *pc* it; Mcion Al is probably a correction, and is hardly an indication that two versions of the text have been conflated (*contra* Leaney, 182). J. Jeremias, ('Die Muttersprache des Evangelisten Matthäus', ZNW 50, 1959, 270–274) suggests that Luke has here conformed the text in his independent source to that of Mk. by this addition at the end.

The command was rightly regarded as forming the heart of Jewish religion. It puts at the centre of religion a love for God, i.e. an undivided loyalty to him. The concept is central in Deuteronomic theology and may reflect diplomatic terminology in which it refers to the sincere loyalty of covenant partners to each other; it thus includes notes of faithfulness and obedience (W. L. Moran, 'The Ancient Near Eastern Background of the Love of God in Deuteronomy', CBQ 25, 1963, 77–87; E. Jenni, THAT I, 60–73). The prepositional phrases together indicate the totality of mind and will that must be brought to the worship of God. No clear distinctions can be made between the different aspects of human personality here listed. They were, however, differentiated in rabbinic theology (B. Gerhardsson, 'The Parable of the Sower and its Interpretation', NTS 14, 1967–68, 165–193, especially 167–169).

The second commandment, Lv. 19:18, appears as a separate citation in Mt. and Mk., but in Lk. it has been made into a part of the first by the omission of the verb. It commands that one love one's neighbour equally with oneself. The ensuing parable turns on the meaning of ὁ πλησίον. The phrase means 'one who is near', 'a neighbour' (10:29, 36; Acts 7:27), and was used in the LXX to translate rē'a, a person with whom one has something to do. The Jews interpreted this in terms of members of the same people and religious community, fellow-Jews (cf. Mt. 5:43–48). There was a tendency on the part of the Pharisees to exclude the ordinary people from the definition, and the Qumran community excluded those whom they termed 'the sons of darkness' (1QS 1:10; 9:21f.). In Lv. 19:34 (cf. Dt. 10:19) the same obligation of love is extended to the gēr, the resident alien, but Jewish usage excluded Samaritans and foreigners from this category. Cf. J. Fichtner and H. Greeven, TDNT VI, 311–318; SB I, 353–364; J. Bowman, 'The Parable of the Good Samaritan', Exp.T 59, 1947–48, 151–153, 248f. The Greek term admitted of a wider meaning, but in the present context the Jewish usage is decisive; this is how the lawyer could be expected to understand the phrase.

The combination of the two commandments is paralleled in T. Iss. 5:1f.; 7:5.; T. Dan 5:3, but is is impossible to be certain that these texts have not been subject to Christian influence. But tendencies to see Lv. 19:18 as a fundamental ethical ruling are to be found in rabbinic Judaism (H. Greeven, ibid. 316 n. 38). The linking of the two commandments may accordingly have taken place in Judaism (cf. Philo, Spec 2:63; Goppelt, 153), but it is doubtful whether we should go further than saying that Judaism had by this time provided an atmosphere in which the combination was natural, and it is best to suppose, with Greeven, that the 'strong emphasis on the unity of the two commandments seems to be particularly significant in Jesus'. If so, we must accept Manson's view that the lawyer was quoting Jesus' own words.

(28) Jesus replies by accepting the lawyer's statement. The use of ὀρθῶς (7:43) is probably Lucan. But Jesus improves the occasion by calling the lawyer to be sure to practise the commandments. The double imperative is equivalent to a condition: 'if you do this, you will live'; cf. Lv. 18:5; Gal. 3:12.

ii. The Good Samaritan 10:29–37

The story of the good Samaritan, as it is related in 10:30–35, is simple and conveys a clear lesson. It contrasts the lack of compassion shown by two members of the Jewish priesthood towards an unknown and unfortunate sufferer with the obedience to the law shown in practical compassion by – to Jewish eyes – the most unlikely of men, a Samaritan. The lesson is hardly the mere point that love appears in unlikely places; it is obvious that the Samaritan is presented as an example to be followed. (J. D. Crossan* has argued that the parable, taken on its own, is not primarily an example to follow but a means of showing that the coming of the kingdom of God demands the complete upturning of conventional opinions, such as the impossibility of a Jew bringing himself to talk of a *good* Samaritan. But this is quite unconvincing.)

The parable may be based to some extent on OT patterns (especially 2 Ch. 28:8–15; cf. Derrett, 208–227), but it stands on its own feet as a story. The familiar three-pattern found in folk-lore provides its framework.

In its present form the parable closes with a question by Jesus (v. 36) together with an answer (the only possible one) by the scribe (v. 37). Some such application of the parable is necessary, and must belong to its original form (Bultmann, 192). This means that the parable is concerned with the concept of the 'neighbour', and answers the question, 'What does it mean to behave like a neighbour?' But this question must have arisen in some such context as that which immediately precedes the parable, i.e. in answer to such a question as that in v. 29. The question now is whether the context provided by Luke was originally linked with the parable. The difficulties are: 1. The linking of 10:25–28 and 10:29–37 tends to downgrade the conversation with the lawyer, making it merely an introduction to a discussion of the meaning of 'neighbour'. 2. The link is contrived, for while the lawyer asks, 'To whom should I show love?' Jesus replies with an answer to the question 'Who showed love?' 3. If the context is dependent in part or whole on Mk. 12:28–34, it would appear to be redactional.

The first of these difficulties is purely subjective. The story in 10:25–28 stands in its own right as a summary of the way to eternal life; the parable may at first sight give the impression of being an appendix, but it has its own importance. In our comments on 10:25 – 11:13 we have suggested that for Luke the whole of 10:29 – 11:13 is in effect an exposition (in chiastic order) of the two commandments, so that it is untrue to say that for Luke the opening situation and conversation have been downgraded.

As regards the second difficulty, it is unlikely that anybody would have created v. 29 as a secondary link between the conversation and the parable, since the parable does not directly answer the question. 1. The effect of the parable is to state that enquiries regarding the meaning of 'neighbour' as the object of love are irrelevant and impossible; what matters is the subjective side of the relationship of neighbourliness. In other words, the effect of the parable is to demonstrate that the question asked in v. 29 is a false one; in fact the parable expounds the meaning of 'love' rather than of 'neighbour', and thus has a close link to Lv. 19:18. 2. G.

Sellin* claims that the scribe's question was not 'whom shall I love?' but rather 'who belongs to the concept of "neighbour"?', with 'neighbour' being understood in the sense of 'fellow-member of the covenant'; Jesus' answer is that any person is a 'neighbour' if he belongs to the circle of those who regard the law as valid and keep it. This was true of the Samaritan in the story; in other words, non-Jews can be 'neighbours', and Jews themselves (as typified by the priest and Levite) must take care that they too qualify as 'neighbours' by keeping the law. In this way the change from the objective (v. 29) to the subjective (v. 36) use of 'neighbour' is explained. On either explanation the unusual feature is the use of 'neighbour' in a subjective sense in v. 36, since in the OT the neighbour is consistently the object of an action, although we may see the development to the subjective aspect in Pr. (17:17; cf. 27:10). The first explanation is to be preferred; in the second explanation no real answer to v. 29 is given, and the parable comes dangerously near to teaching that one should love Samaritans *because* they keep the law.

The third difficulty raises the whole question of the origin of the parable. Creed, 151f., pointed to the polished literary style of the parable and claimed that in its present form it is an original Greek composition, although he thought it likely that several stages of composition could be traced behind it (cf. Drury, 120f.). More far-reaching is the claim made by M. D. Goulder* that in general the parables peculiar to Lk. display such an array of common features and such differences from the parables in Mk. and in Mt. that only one group (those in Mk.) can stem from Jesus, the other two groups being due to the respective Evangelists. This point has been developed with specific reference to the present parable by G. Sellin*. He claims that the parables beginning with 'a certain man' represent in general a late stage of composition in the evolution of the parabolic form. The present parable shows Lucan vocabulary and style. Its motifs are to be understood only against the background of Lucan theology in which the Samaritans as keepers of the law occupy a position between Israel and the gentiles and form the link between them in the spread of the gospel. Further, the parable belongs inextricably to its Lucan context; it is incomprehensible without vs. 36f. and 29, and the latter verse arises out of the situation in vs. 25–28; it follows that the whole section (vs. 25–37) is a Lucan redactional composition, and the possibility of a literary source for the parable cannot be entertained.

This suggestion stands contrary to what we otherwise know of Luke's faithfulness to his sources, which can be tested objectively by his use of Mk. It is undeniable that the parables peculiar to Lk. have a characteristic structure, but their Palestinian background suggests the effects of a distinct line of tradition rather than Lucan creation. The parable itself makes good sense apart from a background in Lucan theology, and its suitability to its context can be due to the context being substantially historical rather than to literary formation.

See J. Mann, 'Jesus and the Sadducean Priests, Luke 10:25–37', *Jewish Quarterly Review* ns 6, 1915, 415–422; Jeremias, *Parables*, 203–205; B. Gerhardsson, *The Good Samaritan – The Good Shepherd?* Lund, 1958; H. Binder, 'Das Gleichnis vom barmherzigen Samariter', TZ 15, 1959, 176–194; Derrett, 208–227 (reprint of 'Law in the New Testament: Fresh Light on the Parable of the Good Samaritan', NTS 11, 1964–65, 22–37); Linnemann, 51–58; M. D. Goulder, 'Characteristics of the Parables in the Several Gospels', JTS ns, 19, 1968, 51–69; J. D. Crossan, 'Parable and Example in the Teaching of Jesus', NTS 18, 1971–72, 285–307; B. Reicke, 'Der barmherzige Samariter', in Böcher, 103–109; G. Sellin, 'Lukas als Gleichniserzähler: Die Erzählung vom barmherzigen Samariter (Lk. 10, 25–37)', ZNW 65, 1974, 166–189; 66–1975, 19–60.

(29) The formulation of the introduction is probably Lucan with its use of δικαιόω (7:29). The lawyer is depicted as wishing to justify his earlier question and regain the initiative after the command which he has just received. He looks rather foolish having asked a question to which he himself has been forced to give the answer; Jesus has said in effect, 'You have no need to ask me the question about eternal life; as a lawyer you know the answer. All you have to do is to practise what you preach'. So he professes inability to practise the law until its meaning has been clarified. The commandment speaks about loving one's neighbour. But where are the limits of duty to be set? The question implies that there can be a non-neighbour (Derrett, 225). For the use of πλησίον without the article see BD 266.

(30) ὑπολαμβάνω (7:43) has the sense 'to answer', only here in the NT. Jesus' reply has the stereotyped ἄνθρωπός τις introduction (13:6; 15:11; 16:1, 19; 18:2; 19:12; *et al.*; cf. G. Sellin*, 175–189). The man is intentionally left undescribed; he can be any man, although a Jewish audience would naturally think of him as a Jew. One particular interpretation of the story regards the man as standing for Jesus himself who was rejected by the Jews but accepted by the Samaritans (H. Binder*). But this can be no more than a secondary interpretation by the early church, and does not fit in with the purpose of Jesus in telling the story. The man was travelling (κατέβαινεν – imperfect) from Jerusalem to Jericho along a road which descends some 3,300 ft in the course of 17 miles. It runs through desert and rocky country, well suited for brigands (Jos. Bel. 4:474; Strabo 16:2:41 describes how Pompey destroyed brigands here, and Jerome (in Jerem. 3:2) spoke of Arab robbers in his time). It is not surprising that on his journey the man encountered robbers. περιπίπτω is 'to fall in with, encounter (especially misfortunes)' (Acts 27:41; Jas. 1:2**; note the aorist).

λῃστής, 'robber, brigand' (10:36; 19:46; 22:52*; K. H. Rengstorf, TDNT IV, 257–262), may be used of zealots, but the identity of the bandits is irrelevant. The force of οἵ καί ... is disputed. Creed, 153, takes it to mean, 'who, as you would expect, ...', but Easton, 171, simply has, 'who besides robbing him ...' AG s.v. 6 state that it 'often gives greater independence to the following relative clause', but Haenchen, 108 n. 6, regards it as a Koine idiom with no particular force. The construction is in fact so common in the NT that Creed's use of it as evidence of 'idiomatic Greek' seems unjustified. The brigands stripped the man of his clothes (ἐκδύω*), and beat him (πληγή, 12:48; with ἐπιτίθημι, Acts 16:23). Then they went off, leaving him lying there, half-dead (ἡμιθανής**); a number of MSS add τυγχάνοντα (A C W Γ Δ Π f13 pm; TR; Diglot) with the sense 'to happen to be, find oneself' (cf. AG s.v. 'They left him for half-dead, as indeed he was'); the word is sufficiently characteristic of Luke (20:35*; Acts, 5x) to be possibly original here, but it could also have arisen as a marginal gloss on the following phrase (κατὰ συγκυρίαν).

(31) συγκυρία** is 'coincidence, chance'. The point is that the road was lonely, and a man might lie a long time before help arrived. The word perhaps emphasises also the exalted status of the bypasser as a priest. He would be returning from a period of duty in the temple to his home in the country (cf. 1:23), for Jericho was one of the principal country residences for priests (SB II, 66, 180). ὁδός is used here to mean a road (the only other NT example of this meaning is Acts 8:26; W. Michaelis, TDNT V, 66). The priest, however, passed by on the opposite side of the road (ἀντιπαρέρχομαι, 10:32**), without offering any help. His motives have been much discussed. The simplest is that he feared ambush by the robbers. It is also possible that the priest thought that the man was dead and was unwilling to defile himself by contact with a dead body (J. Mann*); according to Mann, the Pharisees held that a priest would not be defiled by touching a dead body when there was nobody else available to perform the burial, but the Sadducees stated that he would be defiled. The matter has been further discussed by Derrett, 211–217, who concludes that the priest was entitled to pass on for fear of defilement and its consequences, but could have found justification for defiling himself, had he so desired. Billerbeck, however, points out that the story is concerned with giving help to a living man, and that the possibility of the man being dead is not raised; hence it is the heartlessness of the priest which is at issue (SB II, 183). Similarly, Jeremias, Parables, 203f., is sceptical whether ritual considerations were involved. The most that we can say is that there may be an attack on the ritualism which prevents acts of love, just as in the case of Jesus' healings on the Sabbath, but the essential point is the attack on failure to show love, whatever the pretext.

(32) What happened in the case of the priest was repeated (ὁμοίως, 3:11; et al., is Lucan) with a Levite (Λευίτης, Jn. 1:19; Acts 4:36**; R. Meyer, TDNT IV, 239–241). In NT times the Levites were an order of cultic officials, inferior to the priests but nevertheless a privileged group in Jewish society. They were responsible for the liturgy in the temple and for policing it. After Λευίτης (p⁷⁵ א^c B L f1 pc) many authorities add γενόμενος (so TR; (UBS); Diglot), but some of these (p⁴⁵ D pc lat) omit ἐλθών. The longer form of the text with both participles is either redundant (and therefore shortened by copyists) or conflate (Metzger, 152f.). In favour of the longer text is the fact that γενόμενος κατά may be a Lucan expression (Acts 27:7; for the use of κατά with the sense

'towards, up to', cf. 10:33; AG s.v. IIb); moreover we get a good sense with the picture of the Levite reaching the spot, then actually going up close to the man to see him, but not stopping to help (cf. *Diglot*). After ἰδών the object αὐτόν is added by A D Γ Δ al lat; *Diglot*. It may be assumed that the same kind of motives for not helping were in the mind of the Levite as in the case of the priest; Derrett, 211, suggests that he might have felt less bound by ritual requirements than the priest.

(33) The contrast between the first two travellers and the third is stressed by the emphatic position of Σαμαρίτης at the beginning of the sentence. The audience may well have expected the third character in the story to be an Israelite layman, thereby giving an anti-clerical point to the story. Those scholars who have in fact suggested that in its original form the story had an Israelite and not a Samaritan merely betray their own pedantry and lack of insight. Jesus, however, deliberately speaks of a member of a community hated by the Jews; relations between them were especially bad at this time (cf. 9:52; Jeremias, *Parables*, 204). There was, of course, nothing strange about a Samaritan travelling in Jewish territory, just as Jews also journeyed through Samaria. ὁδεύω** is 'to be on a journey'. After ἰδών, αὐτόν is added by A C D W Θ f13 pl lat; TR; *Diglot*. Derrett, 217, notes that the Samaritan too might have been deterred from touching a possibly dead man by ritual considerations. But whatever his feelings, the point of the story is that he kept the law (B. Reicke*, 106f.), showed compassion (7:13) and did something to help the man.

(34) From this point onwards the story shows certain parallels with the account of how the Israelites set free their Judaean captives and took them from Samaria to Jericho, providing for their needs on the way with food and clothing, and transporting the sick on asses (2 Chr. 28:15). The Samaritan bandaged the wounds of the injured man; καταδέω** is 'to bind up' (Sir. 27:21); τραῦμα**, 'wound'. At the same time he poured on (ἐπιχέω**) olive oil (7:46) and wine. The use of these two healing agents (curiously denied by Wellhausen, 53) is well-attested (Shab. 14:2; 19:4; SB I, 428; cf. Theophrastus, Hist. Plant. 9:11:1); the further symbolic meanings found in the phrase by Derrett, 220f., may be possible, but I find it hard to believe that any audience could pick them up from the story, and feel that this approach is open to the kind of dangers which Jülicher saw in the older type of allegorisation.

After first-aid, the Samaritan mounted the man on his own steed to take him to an inn where he could care for him properly. ἐπιβιβάζω is Lucan (19:35; Acts 23:24**; cf. 2 Sa. 6:3; 1 Ki. 1:33). κτῆνος is a domesticated animal of any kind, including animals for riding or bearing burdens (Acts 23:24; cf. 1 Cor. 15:39; Rev. 18:13**). πανδοχεῖον** is an inn, and πανδοχεύς (10:35**) the inn-keeper. For ἐπιμελέομαι 'to take care of', cf. 10:35; 1 Tim. 3:5**.

(35) After resting for the night the Samaritan had to resume his journey the next day; for ἐπί with accusative of time cf. Acts 3:1; 4:5.

He therefore took steps to provide for further care for the injured man at the inn till he was fit to move elsewhere. Since the man had been stripped and left penniless, he had to make advance payment to the inn-keeper for him. Black's view (136) that ἐκβάλλω here means 'to expend' is excluded by the context; it is simply used in the weak sense 'to take out' (AG s.v. 3). If a day's board cost one twelfth of a denarius (Jeremias, *Parables*, 205; cf. *Jerusalem*, 123), the payment in advance was sufficient for several days, and it bound the inn-keeper to look after the man as long as was necessary. Any further expense (προσδαπανάω**) would be met by the Samaritan on his return journey by the same route. The phrase ἐν τῷ ἐπανέρχεσθαι means 'on my return journey' by contrast with ἐν τῷ ἐπανελθεῖν, 'after my return' (19:15; the verb is found only in these two places); cf. MH I, 249; BD 404². Derrett's discussion whether the Samaritan could hope to reclaim his payments from the injured man completely misses the point of the story. It would be possible for the early church to see in the Good Samaritan a picture of Jesus, and in his 'return' a symbol for the second advent (B. Gerhardsson*; B. Reicke*, 105f., thinks that the Samaritan's *activity* prefigures that of Jesus); but this was surely not the original meaning of the story, and the allegorising involved is unnatural.

(36) Now comes the application as Jesus asks the lawyer directly for his verdict. Which of the three men, do you think, behaved as a neighbour? The lawyer's original question has been deliberately altered, so that further argument is avoided. 'One cannot define one's neighbour; one can only be a neighbour' (H. Greeven, TDNT VI, 317).

(37) The lawyer can make only one reply. The phrase 'to show mercy to' is Semitic (1:72; SB II, 184), but the lawyer may have chosen it to avoid actually naming the despised Samaritan (Jeremias, *Parables*, 205); by his answer he shows that being neighbourly means showing mercy (Creed, 154). Implicitly, racial considerations are shown to be irrelevant. Jews were forbidden to receive works of love from non-Jews (SB IV:1, 537, 543f.); both the giving and receiving of mercy transcends national and racial barriers (cf. Grundmann, 224 n.). All that remains is that men should put this into effect. With authority Jesus commands the lawyer to go away and begin to follow the Samaritan's example; the command in v. 28 cannot be evaded.

iii. Serving Jesus 10:38–42

After the parable which elucidates the meaning of the second commandment comes a story which may be regarded as elucidating the first commandment (Grundmann, 225) and dealing with the duty of listening to Jesus as the teacher of the word of God (Klostermann, 122). This means that Luke has understood this story in a spiritual sense, a fact which should be borne in mind when dealing with the interpretation of vs. 41f.

Jesus commends Mary for choosing to listen to him and will not allow Martha to deprive her of the opportunity to do so; to hear his word is manifestly of primary importance. Martha, as the hostess, was distracted from listening by her preparations for a meal, and Jesus' lesson to her was that she had allowed her preparations to become too burdensome; she wished to honour him with an elaborate meal, but it was more important to listen to him (and therefore to be content with giving him a simpler meal). Thus the story is not meant to exalt the contemplative life above the life of action, but to indicate the proper way to serve Jesus; one serves him by listening to his word rather than by providing excessively for his needs (cf. Jn. 6:27). E. Laland* thinks that the story was used in the early church to give instructions to women entertaining travelling missionaries; they must show hospitality, but not to excess. For a Jewish audience it would be of great significance that a place was given to women by Jesus not simply to do domestic duties in the church but to listen and learn.

The story relates to two sisters, well known from Jn. 11; 12:1–8, who lived at Bethany near Jerusalem. If Luke was aware of this – and the extent of his common traditions with John makes this probable – he has omitted the name because he does not regard Jesus as being near Jerusalem at this point (cf. Schlatter, 289f.). The contacts with Johannine tradition indicate that the story is based on old tradition, but do not settle the question of its historicity. Bultmann, 33, 57f., 64, regards the story as an 'ideal scene', a biographical apophthegm, of Hellenistic origin; the story is a unitary composition, since the saying of Jesus could not have circulated on its own. He brings, however, no evidence for declaring the scene to be 'ideal', and one is more justified in accepting the verdict of Dibelius, 293, that it has a historical basis, even if it may have been modified in course of transmission (cf. Grundmann, 225f.).

See E. Laland, 'Die Martha-Maria Perikope Lukas 10, 38–42', ST 13, 1959, 70–85; A. Baker, 'One Thing Necessary', CBQ 27, 1965, 127–137; M. Augsten, 'Lukanische Miszelle', NTS 14, 1967–68, 581–583.

(38) The theme of Jesus as the traveller – who therefore needs hospitality – emerges in the opening words. For the simple $'Εν\ δὲ\ τῷ$ ... opening (p⁴⁵ p⁷⁵ $\aleph$ B pc) many witnesses offer $'Εγένετο\ δὲ\ ἐν\ τῷ$ ... (A C D W $Θ$ f1 f13 pl latt; TR; $Diglot$); cf. 17:11. Before $αὐτός$, $καί$ is inserted by much the same authorities. From Jn. 11:1; 12:1 we have information that the village was Bethany (Lk. 19:29). The name $Μάρθα$ is the Aramaic feminine of mar, 'mistress' (SB II, 184f.). She appears as the mistress of the household, and Easton, 173, suggests that she may have been a widow. For $ὑποδέχομαι$, 'to receive, welcome, entertain as a guest', cf. 19:6; Acts 17:7; Jas. 2:25. There is an obvious contrast with 9:53. The closing words of the verse are textually uncertain. UBS has $αὐτόν$ (p⁴⁵ p⁷⁵ B sa); $Synopsis$ has $αὐτὸν\ εἰς\ τὴν\ οἰκίαν$ (p³ $\aleph$ C* L $Ξ$ 33); and TR; $Diglot$: $αὐτὸν\ εἰς\ τὸν\ οἶκον\ αὐτῆς$ (A D W $Γ\ Δ\ Θ$ f1 f13 pl lat). Metzger, 153, supports the short text on the grounds that no reason for

the deletion of the phrase 'into her house' is discernible; the variant forms of this phrase suggest that it is an addition.

(39) ὅδε, 'this (person) ', here 'she', had become rare in Hellenistic Greek (Jas. 4:13), and survives in the NT mostly in the stereotyped τάδε λέγει (Acts 21:11; Rev. 7x**); even here it is used incorrectly for οὗτος by Classical standards as a result of LXX influence (BD 289). For the name Μαριάμ cf. 1:27 note. The textual status of the relative ἥ is insecure (om. p⁴⁵ p⁷⁵ ℵ* L pc; (UBS)). The characters of Martha and Mary here correspond to the portrayal in Jn. 12, where Martha is again the one who prepares the meal while Mary has time to give Jesus an extravagant anointing. παρακαθέζομαι** is 'to sit beside', and the position at the feet of a teacher (Acts 22:3; P Ab. 1:4) was typical of pupils; Mary's posture expresses zeal to learn (cf. K. Weiss, TDNT VI, 630), and it is significant that Jesus encourages a woman to learn from him, since the Jewish teachers were generally opposed to this (A. Oepke, TDNT I, 781f.). As a teacher Jesus is designated as κύριος (cf. 7:13 note); the use of the word may well be due to tradition, but it could be redactional (cf. Hahn, 89).

(40) The interest shifts back to Martha. The verb περισπάομαι** means in the passive 'to be pulled, dragged away', hence 'to become distracted, busy, overburdened', and is often constructed with περί, as here (AG s.v.). The implication is that Martha wished to hear Jesus but was prevented from doing so by the pressure of providing hospitality (Luce, 208). Paul's use of the adverb ἀπερισπάστως (1 Cor. 7:35) suggests a recurrence of the same motif. διακονία is household service, the preparing of meals and the like. Easton, 173, suggests the meaning 'halting in her work' for ἐπιστᾶσα (cf. LSJ s.v. B. IV., citing Plato, Symp. 172a). Perhaps she had already tried to secure Mary's help; now she called on Jesus to intervene. Was he not concerned (μέλει*; Acts 18:17) at her being left alone to do the work? Let him command (cf. 4:3) her sister to come to her help (συναντιλαμβάνομαι, Rom. 8:26**).

(41–42) Jesus' reply is couched in sympathetic terms, as the double vocative (cf. 6:46) indicates. Unfortunately, the precise wording is textually uncertain, there being no fewer than six variant forms of the text, nearly all of which have found support from scholars.
1. Μάρθα, Μαριάμ ...
    (it sy^s ; J. Weiss, 464f.);
2. Μάρθα, θορυβάζῃ· Μαριάμ ...
    (D; RV mg 1; NEB mg 2; Wellhausen, 54; Caird, 149f. (1. or 2.); A. Baker*);
3. Μάρθα, θορυβάζῃ περὶ πολλά· Μαριάμ ...
    ((Clem) Aug; Manson, Sayings, 264 (cf. μεριμνᾷς καὶ θορυβάζῃ ... c));
4. Μάρθα, μεριμνᾷς καὶ θορυβάζῃ περὶ πολλά, ἑνὸς ἐστιν χρεία· Μαριάμ ...
    (p⁴⁵ p⁷⁵ C W Θ pc vg sy^{c p} Basil (with τυρβάζῃ A pm; TR); TR; RV;

RSV; NEB; UBS; *Diglot*; Zahn, 439 n. 21; Schmid, 195f.);
5. *Μάρθα, μεριμνᾷς ... πολλά, ὀλίγων δέ ἐστιν χρεία· Μαριάμ ...*
　　(38 *al* sy[pal] arm geo; M. Augsten*);
6. *Μάρθα, μεριμνᾷς ... πολλά, ὀλίγων δέ ἐστιν χρεία ἤ ἑνός· Μαριάμ ...*
　　(p[3] ℵ B L fl 33 sy[h mg] bo; RV mg 2; RSV mg; NEB mg 1; Plummer,
292; Easton, 173f.; Leaney, 183).

We may at once explain *τυρβάζῃ* as a gloss on the rarer word
θορυβάζῃ (Metzger, 153). Although a number of scholars regard some
form of the shorter text (1. – 3.) as original, with the other forms being
due to scribal additions, it seems most unlikely that an originally simple
text could lead to such confusion. Variant 1. gives three proper names in
a row, which is scarcely credible in Lk. (Dibelius, 116 n.), and the
original text must surely have contained something to start off the
process of change. A. Baker* questions whether spiritualising glosses
were likely as early as the second century. So we are thrown back on the
longer text in some form as original, the western text being caused by
scribes applying drastic surgery to deal with the existing confusion. We
now have to deal with three possibilities: did Jesus speak of 'one thing',
'few things' or 'few or one'? Despite the excellent MSS support for the
combination (variant 6.) it is hard to give it a good sense: 'few dishes for
the meal – but really one would be enough', and therefore it is probably
a conflation. The question is then whether an original 'one thing', meant
spiritually, was understood to refer to 'one dish' and then softened to
'few' (Metzger, 153f.), or 'few things', meant to refer to food, was altered
to refer to the one spiritual goal (Augsten*). Although the latter reading
has poor external support, it is indirectly attested in the good MSS which
have the conflate reading, and is therefore not to be dismissed out of
hand. Moreover, the change from 'few' to 'one' is comprehensible;
scribes were perhaps more likely to think that Jesus would give teaching
not about practical hospitality but about the one spiritual goal (cf.
Dibelius, 115, who thinks like such a scribe). If 'one thing' is original, it
is difficult to see why it should ever be changed; the suggestion that
scribes misinterpreted it to mean 'one dish' is perhaps not very likely. On
the other hand, the stress on 'one thing' is biblical (18:22; Phil. 3:13),
and the external evidence is better. The transcriptional evidence,
therefore, is in favour of variant 5. ('few'), but the intrinsic and external
evidence for variant 4. ('one') is strong, and a final decision is difficult.

μεριμνάω is 'to be anxious, to be (unduly) concerned' (12:11, 22,
25, 26* (Mt. 6:25–34); cf. R. Bultmann, TDNT IV, 589–593). It often
expresses a worldly attitude which is due to unbelief and which can
divert a person's attention away from a proper concern for the things of
God (cf. 1 Cor. 7:32–35). The rare verb *θορυβάζω*** is 'to cause
trouble', hence the passive 'to be troubled, distracted'; the variant
τυρβάζω (adopted in TR; *Diglot*) has the same meaning. *περὶ πολλά*
clearly refers to the excessive preparations for a meal, but does not
necessarily indicate a number of dishes or courses.

(42) In fact, (if ἑνός is read) there is need of only one thing; the reference is undoubtedly spiritual with reference to the 'good portion' chosen by Mary. The implications are that Mary should be not deprived of it by helping Martha, and that Martha should so curtail her domestic cares that she too will be able to have the one thing that matters. Then χρεία refers to Martha's own personal need. If, however, ὀλίγων is read, then the sense is that there is need for only a few preparations for Jesus' meal, so that Mary does not have to be taken away from listening to Jesus in order to help Martha. There is then no positive lesson for Martha, but only a rebuke. This, together with the fact that Luke probably understood the saying in a spiritual sense, speaks strongly in favour of 'one' being original.

Martha should therefore follow the example of Mary and get her priorities right. For Mary has chosen the better part; for the positive adjective used as a comparative cf. 9:48 note; Zerwick, 146. For μερίς cf. Acts 8:21; 16:12; 2 Cor. 6:15; Col. 1:12. Here the good thing is to be understood as the teaching of Jesus, or perhaps the blessings of the kingdom to which it testified (cf. Ps. 16:5). This must not be taken away from her (Many MSS have ἀπ' αὐτῆς; so TR; *Diglot*) by Martha or anybody else; it is her inalienable right and possession, guaranteed by Jesus.

iv. The Lord's Prayer 11:1–4

The third part of the present section of teaching on the characteristics of disciples is concerned with the relationship of the disciples to God in prayer. Ott, 13–18, has shown that in Lk. prayer is treated as a main theme in the instruction of the disciples, whereas in Mt. teaching on prayer is not presented thematically (except, however, in Mt. 6:5–15) but is incidental to other themes. Here we have a piece of exhortation regarding prayer which Jeremias, *Abba*, 156f., has analysed as help for men who have to learn how to pray and need to be given encouragement that God will hear them; he argues further that the form of the passage as a whole developed in a gentile setting and was taken over by Luke.

The section may be analysed into a request for instruction on how to pray, followed by a pattern prayer (11:1, 2–4); then come a parable which speaks of the readiness of God to hear prayer (11:5–8), a statement on the certainty of God's answering prayer (11:9f.), and a final argument that God will answer prayer even more readily than a human father will respond to his children's requests (11:11–13).

The Lucan form of the Lord's Prayer differs considerably from the Matthaean form which at several points is fuller and has slight differences in wording. These differences have been ironed out in many MSS of Lk., but there is no doubt that the shorter, divergent text is original (Metzger, 154–156). The problems are whether Matthew and Luke have employed a common source here, and whether the two versions ultimately represent òne tradition or not. It is not difficult to see that the differences in wording between Lk. and Mt. can be largely explained in terms of editorial modifications, mostly on the part of Luke. It is, however, unlikely that Luke (or earlier tradents) would have omitted clauses from a prayer taught by Jesus, and the attempts of M. D. Goulder* and Ott, 112–123, to explain Luke's prayer as a redaction of the Matthaean and Q forms respectively are unconvincing. Hence the prayer existed, so far back as we can trace, in two forms (E. Lohmeyer*, 293), or else the longer form in Mt. is due to additions to the basic form attested by Luke (Jeremias, *Abba*, 160). The additions in Mt. can be explained in large measure as being due to his own outlook, but it is again unlikely that an individual Evangelist on his own initiative would alter a prayer used in church, and it is more probable that Matthew's form represents the prayer as used in his church. It follows that we do not have here simply two editorial modifications of the Q version of the prayer. More probably, Matthew has substituted the form of the prayer familiar to him for that which he found in Q. But did Luke's form come from Q, (with editorial modification)? Other variations from Q in the context (such as the inclusion of 11:5–8, peculiar to Lk., and the marked differences in wording between 11:11–13 and Mt. 7:9–11) have suggested that Luke is not here dependent on Q (Streeter, 277f.; Manson, *Sayings*, 265), but on the whole it is probable that Luke has drawn this section, including the prayer, from Q, or rather from a recension of Q which may have differed in wording from that used by Mt. (It may be that Matthew's form of the prayer had already been incorporated in the recension of Q used in his church and available to him.)

The prayer shows unmistakable signs of translation from a Semitic original, whether Aramaic (Black, 149–153; K. G. Kuhn*, 32f.; Jeremias, *Abba*, 160) or Hebrew (J. Carmignac*, 29–52, 396), and has a poetic structure in both of its forms (K. G. Kuhn*, 38f.; Wrege, 101, 105). Nevertheless, we appear to have variant forms of a Greek prayer in the Gospels, since the parallelism in wording is so close. Attempts to emend the text of the prayer, based on the assumption that Jesus followed OT poetic rules without deviation (G. Schwarz*), are unconvincing.

There are no grounds for reasonable doubt that the prayer goes back to Jesus himself. M. D. Goulder* assigns its composition to Matthew (from whose Gospel it was copied by Luke); his article has the merit of showing the links between the prayer and other aspects of the teaching of Jesus, but it fails to prove that Matthew composed the prayer on the basis of these parallels. The prayer sums up the teaching of Jesus in brief fashion, expressing the longing which the disciples should feel for the action of God in setting up his kingdom, their dependence upon him as Father for their daily needs, their new relationship of reconciliation with him and their fellow men, and their need of his power to preserve them from yielding to temptation.

See E. Lohmeyer, *The Lord's Prayer*, London, 1965 (E. Tr. of *Das Vater-Unser*, Göttingen, 1946); 95–113; J. Jeremias, 'Das Vater-Unser im Lichte der Neueren Forschung', in *Abba*, 152–171 (E. Tr.: *The Lord's Prayer*, Philadelphia, 1964; *The Prayers of Jesus*, London, 1967, 82–107); cf. *Theology* I, 193–203; W. Marchel, *Abba Père*, Rome, 1971; M. D. Goulder, 'The Composition of the Lord's Prayer', JTS ns 14, 1963, 32–45; Ott, 112–123; G. Schwarz, 'Matthäus VI. 9–13/Lukas XI. 2–4. Emendation und Rückübersetzung', NTS 15, 1968–69, 233–247; Wrege, 100–106; J. Carmignac, *Recherches sur le 'Notre Père'*, Paris, 1969; Schulz, 84–93; A. Vögtle, 'Der "eschatologische" Bezug der Wir-Bitten des Vaterunser', in Ellis, *Jesus*, 344–362.

(1) The introductory verse to the section gives the setting. The style shows several Lucan features: καὶ ἐγένετο ἐν τῷ . . . (1:8); ὡς (1:23); παύομαι (5:4); καθώς (1:2). These, however, are insufficient to prove Lucan creation of the setting (*pace* Schulz, 84 n. 185), and the reference to John's disciples, which adds nothing to the scene, is hardly due to Luke. Interest in John is shown by both Q and Luke's special source material (3:10–14), but also by Luke himself (5:33). The reference to Jesus being at prayer could be due to Luke (cf. 3:21; 9:18), but there is no reason why such a situation could not have been the historical setting for the question of the disciples. We have here the only request in the Gospels for Jesus to give teaching (cf. SB II, 186 for some formal parallels). Jeremias, 161, suggests that the disciples want a prayer that will be characteristic of their position as a community around Jesus, just as other Jewish groups, including the disciples of John, had their own distinctive prayers.

(2) Jesus' reply offers them a form of words to be used when they are engaged in prayer; Easton, 175, presses ὅταν to mean 'whenever', i.e. 'on all occasions of prayer'.

Luke's prayer begins with the address Πάτερ. This is the simple form used by Jesus in his own prayers (10:21 note) and there is fairly general agreement that it represents Aramaic *'abbâ*. If so, we have here the basis for the form of address used in prayer in the early church (Rom. 8:15; Gal. 4:6). Jewish prayers referred to God as Father, but the simple form is not attested in Palestinian usage in which God is addressed as 'our' or 'my' Father. Matthew has the fuller form 'Our Father in heaven', which corresponds to ordinary Jewish usage. W. Marchel*, 185–189, argues that Matthew's form is original, and that Luke has substituted a form used in gentile communities; he claims that it is unlikely that Jesus shared so intimate a form of address with his disciples, who would have considered it impious, and that, if Jesus had told them to pray in this way, it is unlikely that the longer form would have arisen subsequently (cf. J. Carmigmac*, 74–76). Further, Luke 11:13 is held to be a testimony to the longer form. These arguments are insufficient to overturn the generally accepted opinion. The use of the intimate form was the amazing new thing that Jesus wished to teach his disciples, initiating them into the same close relationship with the Father that he enjoyed, and it is improbable that the early Christian usage can be explained apart from a definite command by Jesus himself. The longer

form can well have arisen in Jewish circles under the persistent influence
of the Jewish liturgy. Finally, Lk. 11:13 may well be an isolated logion,
and its wording is in any case different from Mt. 6:9; 7:11. The force of
the term is to assure the disciples of God's loving care for them, so that
they can ask him for gifts with the certainty of being heard (cf. G.
Schrenk, TDNT V, 984f., 1002., 1006; E. Lohmeyer*, 32–62; J. Carmignac*, 55–69).

After the address come two sets of petitions. The first set, composed of two parallel requests, is concerned with the establishment of
God's purposes on a cosmic scale, while the second set, composed of
three petitions, is concerned with the personal needs of the disciples.
Thus the prayer begins with a theocentric attitude.

The first petition asks that God's name may be hallowed. God's
name is in effect his reputation among men, but it essentially stands for
God himself: men are to speak of him with appropriate reverence and
honour. This attitude is indicated by the verb ἁγιάζω (cf. 1 Pet. 3:15).
The roots of the thought lie in Is. 8:13; 29:23; Ezk. 36:23, but the
nearest parallel to the prayer of Jesus lies in the Jewish Qaddish prayer:
'Exalted and hallowed be his great name in the world which he created
according to his will' (translation as in Jeremias, *Theology* I, 198). The
passive form of the verb may be a circumlocution for naming God himself as the subject: the prayer is for God to act in such a way as to lead
to the hallowing of his name by men (O. Procksch, TDNT I, 111; H.
Bietenhard, TDNT V, 276; E. Lohmeyer*, 63–87). God is petitioned to
bring about a situation in which men will reverence and worship him instead of blaspheming him or sinning against him: the prayer thus has action by men as well as by God in view (J. Carmignac*, 83–85). Ultimately this is achieved at the final consummation, and some exegetes
think this alone is in view (Schulz, 89), but a broader reference may have
been present from the first (J. Carmignac*, 337–347). In any case, the
establishment of God's glory is the first theme of the prayer.

The second theme is closely related to it. The disciples are to pray
that God's kingdom may come. See 4:43 note, and for the hope of its
coming see Mk. 9:1 (diff. Lk. 9:27); Mk. 11:10 (diff. Lk. 19:38); Lk.
17:20; 22:18 and 10:9, 11 (Perrin, 57–59). The emphasis is on the
sovereignty of God, as the parallelism with the first petition indicates. At
the same time the phrase is used with particular reference to the blessings that come to men when God is acknowledged as king and his
beneficent rule is allowed full sway. God's rule means the end of Satan's
rule. The petition is, then, for God to act by setting up his rule. Jewish
language is again echoed. The Qaddish prayer cited above continues:
'May he let his kingdom rule in your lifetime and in your days and in the
lifetime of the whole house of Israel, speedily and soon'. Outwardly, the
two prayers are the same; the Christian prayer is distinguished by the
fact that those who pray it have been taught by Jesus that the kingdom
of God is at hand. They look forward to the consummation of the

promises of God (cf. E. Lohmeyer*, 88–110; Perrin, 160f.).

The exegesis above assumes the correctness of the generally accepted text of the prayer. But there is an important variant at this point. Marcion had in place of the two petitions the following text: ἐλθέτω τὸ πνεῦμά σου τὸ ἅγιον ἐφ' ἡμᾶς καὶ καθαρισάτω ἡμᾶς. ἐλθέτω ἡ βασιλεία σου (Tertullian, Adv. Mcion 4:26). A similar variant is also found in two late Gk. MSS and some Fathers: ἁγιασθήτω τὸ ὄνομά σου. ἐλθέτω τὸ πνεῦμά σου τὸ ἅγιον ἐφ' ἡμᾶς καὶ καθαρισάτω ἡμᾶς (162) 700 Greg ᴺʸˢˢ Max^tau . And what may be a reminiscence of this reading is found in D d: ἁγιασθήτω ὄνομά σου ἐφ' ἡμᾶς ἐλθέτω σου ἡ βασιλεία. The variant in 700 has attracted scholarly support throughout modern times (Harnack, 63f.; J. Weiss, 465; Streeter, 277; A. R. C. Leaney, 'The Lucan Text of the Lord's Prayer (Lk. 11, 2–4) ', Nov.T 1, 1956, 103–111; (cf. Leaney, 59–68); Grässer, 109–111; Ott, 112–120; R. Freudenberger, 'Zum Text der zweiten Vaterunserbitte', NTS 15, 1968–69, 419–432). In its favour it can be argued: 1. Although it is attested by only a handful of witnesses, these deserve respect because the tendency to assimilate the text to that of Matthew must have been strong. 2. The wording, especially with its stress on the Holy Spirit, is Lucan (cf. 11:13; Acts 4:31; 10:15; 11:8; 15:9). A prayer for the parousia is replaced by one more appropriate in a church for which the parousia is long delayed. 3. There are echoes of the wording in the early church (A. R. C. Leaney*, 106). 4. The wording would fit in well with the use of the prayer at baptism, or perhaps as an epiclesis at the Lord's Supper for holy worshippers. 5. The wording has an OT and Jewish background (cf. Pss. 51:11; 143:10; Wis. 9:17; 1QS 4:21; also Acts of Thomas 27 (NTA II, 457)). 6. A reference to the Holy Spirit is fitting in a prayer that stands in contrast to a Johannine prayer (11:1).

These arguments are insufficient to overturn the almost unanimous witness of the Greek MSS. A reading which is attested in only two late Greek MSS is highly unlikely to be original. Moreover, the witnesses to the variant show considerable differences among themselves; the oldest version in Marcion occupies a different place in the prayer as a whole. The apparent trace of the variant in D can be explained otherwise (E. Lohmeyer*, 258–261). It is more probable that the variant represents an early liturgical usage which has contaminated the text of Lk. (E. Lohmeyer*, 261–270; J. Carmignac*, 89–91).

Luke does not have the third petition found in Mt., 'Thy will be done', although many MSS assimilate the text to that of Mt.

(3) The second part of the prayer is concerned with the personal requests of the worshippers. The first petition is for ἄρτος (4:3), which should be taken in the broader sense of 'food' rather than simply 'bread' alone (7:33; Jn. 13:18; 2 Thes. 3:8, 12; AG s.v.; J. Behm, TDNT I, 477f.); hence it is improbable that the prayer is simply for the barest necessities of life which men need in the brief period before the imminent consummation (pace Schulz, 90f.).

In its Lucan formulation the prayer is that God will go on providing food day by day, whereas in Mt. the use of the aorist imperative instead of the present imperative (BD 377⁴) and of σήμερον make the petition apply specifically to the day in question. Since τὸ καθ' ἡμέραν is a Lucan phrase (19:47; Acts 17:11; cf. Ex. 16:4; cf. Lk. 9:23 diff. Mk.), the generalised form may be due to Luke himself, and may represent an attempt to elucidate the difficult word ἐπιούσιος.

This word is found for the first time in the present petition (Mt. 6:11**) and thereafter only in dependence upon it (e.g. Did. 8:2). Claims that the word has been found in a papyrus of the fifth century AD with the possible sense of 'daily ration' and in an inscription from Rhodes remain unsubstantiated (the papyrus has been lost, and the inscription has been misread: B. M. Metzger, 'How many times does "epiousios" occur outside the Lord's Prayer?' Exp.T 69, 1957–58, 52–54).

We are, therefore, thrown back on the evidence of etymology, ancient interpretations of the word, and possible Semitic equivalents. (See W. Foerster, TDNT II, 590–599; E. Lohmeyer*, 141–146; J. Carmignac*, 121–143, 214–220.) As a Greek word, ἐπιούσιος may mean: 1. 'necessary for existence' (derived from ἐπί + οὐσία; so Origen; cf. SB I, 420); 2. 'for the current day' (ἐπὶ τὴν οὖσαν (ἡμέραν); cf. the parallel form ἐφημέριος, for which it may be a Semitizing equivalent; BD 123 ⁹). 3. It may be connected with ἡ ἐπιοῦσα (ἡμέρα), 'the following day' (Acts 16:11), and thus refer to 'the coming day', i.e. 'Today' in a morning prayer and 'tomorrow' in an evening prayer (cf. the authorities cited by W. Foerster, TDNT II, 592 n. 16; J. Carmignac*, 134f.). 4. The word may be connected with ἐπιέναι (as in view 3.) but giving the sense 'Give us today the bread *that comes to it*', i.e. 'the bread *that we need* for today'.

J. Carmignac*, 122–128, shows that the early interpretations of the word varied between views 1. and 3., i.e. 'necessary, appropriate for our existence' and 'for the coming day'.

Jerome states: 'In the so-called Gospel according to the Hebrews in place of "supersubstantiali pane" (i.e. the Vulgate rendering) I found "mahar" which means "crastinum", so that the sense is "Give us today our bread for tomorrow, i.e. for the future" ' (In Mt. 6:11; cf. NTA I, 147). The Vulgate rendering would correspond to interpretation 1. and the Semitic phrase cited by Jerome corresponds to interpretation 3. Modern scholars have sought other possible Semitic equivalents. Thus Black, 203–207, argues that an Aramaic idiomatic phrase *yoma den wᵉ yomaḥra*, literally meaning 'today and tomorrow', and hence idiomatically 'day by day', has been literally translated into Greek. Luke's τὸ καθ' ἡμέραν gives the correct sense, but he has retained from Q the unnecessary ἐπιούσιος; Matthew preserves more clearly the mistranslation of the Aramaic. But there are difficulties about this suggestion: how did Luke manage to get the meaning of the Aramaic idiom correctly on the basis of a Greek source? If a text can be credibly interpreted without recourse to theories of mistranslation (as by Jeremias, *Abba*, 160, 165f.; J. Carmignac*, 215f.), a theory involving misunderstanding should not be accepted. Similar considerations apply to K. G. Kuhn's* reconstruction (35–37); it is difficult to see why the simply *lᵉ yômâ* which he postulates should have given rise to such misunderstandings.

We can now attempt to understand the phrase as a whole: 1. The sense 'the bread necessary for existence', 'the bread we need', has wide support (W. Foerster, TDNT II, 599; Grässer, 102; Schulz, 90f.). This view can be linked with the concept of the manna (which is probably present in the background) of which just the right amount was available for those who gathered it (Ex. 16:18; cf. Pr. 30:8). But the idea of the bare minimum necessary for existence before the consummation or parousia is more than the phrase contains. On this view, ἐπιούσιος is an expression of measure rather than of time. 2. Somewhat similar is the sense 'bread for the coming day', so that the prayer is for what we need to sustain us in the immediate future (J. Carmignac*, 214–221). Here again the thought is determined by the daily gathering of the manna. 3. A different view is espoused by E. Lohmeyer*, 134–159, and Jeremias, *Abba*, 165–167, who understand 'for the coming day' to mean 'for the age to come'. The petition is then to be understood in the sense 'Give us today the bread which we shall enjoy in the future in the kingdom of God', and 'bread' is to be understood not merely in terms of material sustenance but primarily (though not exclusively) in terms of spiritual food. (For discussion of the relation of the material and spiritual aspects see especially J. Carmignac*, 143–214.)

It is not possible to be dogmatic about the meaning of the word, since etymology is not necessarily a good guide to current usage. It can be assumed, however, that some unusual expression must have been present in Aramaic or Hebrew to justify the unusual Greek phrase, and that this will have been a phrase incorporating *māḥār* or a phrase on the lines of Pr. 30:8 (*leḥem huqqî*) rather than a phrase incorporating *yôm*. Carmignac's interpretation (2. above) is unlikely, since it gives a rather banal sense (cf. W. Foerster's objections, TDNT II, 595–597). A decision between interpretations 1. and 3. is difficult, but in fact they are not very different in meaning from each other. The food which God provides is food for body and soul; he gives men what they need and he gives them a foretaste of the rich provision available in the kingdom of God – and he does so each and every day in answer to their prayers. A. Vögtle*, 359, suggests that we are to ask God to provide us with food so that we need not be worried about it but can care about spiritual matters.

(4) The second petition is for forgiveness of sins. For ἀφίημι see 5:20. Luke's ἁμαρτία is a correct rendering of Aramaic *ḥôḇâ*, 'debt, sin', which is rendered more literally in Mt. as ὀφείλημα (Black, 140); the two words could be translation variants, but in view of the closeness of wording elsewhere in the prayer, it is more likely that Luke has

elucidated the Greek version of the prayer – a view confirmed by the presence of ὀφείλοντι in the next clause (Klostermann, 125). Luke thus nearly loses the idea of sin as debt (cf. 7:41–43; 13:4; Mt. 18:23–35). To sin is to come under obligation to God and hence to owe him restitution. Often debtors become slaves to their creditors. But Jesus speaks of the forgiveness of sinners and debtors without any restitution being offered by them to God (cf. F. Hauck, TDNT V, 559–566; F. C. Fensham, 'The Legal Background of Mt. VI. 12', Nov.T 4, 1960, 1f.). Such forgiveness is associated with the final judgment, which leads Schulz, 91f., to think that originally the imminent final judgment was in view here, but E. Lohmeyer*, 179, rightly argues that the petition here is robbed of its urgency if it is not given an immediate, present significance; it corresponds to the idea of present justification in Paul.

The petition has a 'condition' attached. God can be asked to forgive us because we too forgive everyone who is indebted to us. J. Carmignac*, 230–235, observes that the condition is attached to our *asking* God to forgive and not to his act in forgiving which is dependent purely on his grace. Luke's καὶ γάρ avoids the *quid pro quo* element that might be detected in Mt. ὡς καί. He also has the verb in the present tense, expressing a continual readiness to forgive, while Matthew's perfect form suggests a condition that must be fulfilled before we can ask God to act (cf. Sir. 28:1–7; Mt. 5:23f.; 6:14f.). In neither case, however, is there the thought of laying a good work before God. Rather it is emphasised that no obstacle must stand in the way of God's forgiveness, and the person praying is reminded of the prerequisite for his prayer to be heard (F. Hauck, TDNT V, 563). This point may have been clearer if the original Aramaic had a *perfectum coincidentiae*, 'as herewith we forgive our debtors' (Jeremias, *Theology*, I, 201). The insertion of παντί may be Lucan (cf. 6:30; Klostermann, 125), but Wrege, 78 n. 3, holds that the absence of the article speaks against Lucan style here. On the authenticity of the condition see A. Vögtle*, 345–347.

The whole prayer closes with a petition that God will not bring the disciples into πειρασμός (4:13). A reference to tempting or testing God (4:12; Ex. 17:7; Acts 5:9; 15:10; 1 Cor. 10:9; Heb. 3:9) is improbable, especially in view of Matthew's expansion. Even less likely is a reference to the final, great tribulation (Jeremias, *Abba*, 170; Schulz, 92); the absence of the article is decisive (J. Carmignac*, 340f.; cf. Grässer, 104). The word refers rather to inward temptations and seductions and to outward tribulations and trials which test faith (Sir. 2:1f.; Rom. 5:3–5; Jas. 1:13; Creed, 157); such tribulations are, however, to be seen as part of, or as foreshadowings of, the final tribulation (H. Seesemann, TDNT VI, 23–36, especially 30f.). While it is true that it is ultimately God who allows men to be tested in this way by Satan (cf. Job), the thought here is not simply of asking God in his mercy to preserve men from temptation. Following a suggestion by J. Heller, J. Carmignac*, 236–304, 437–445, has shown that 'to enter temptation' means not 'to be tempted' but 'to yield to temptation' (4QFlor 1:8), that the verb reflects a Hebrew causative, and that the negative qualifies the idea of entry, so that the thought is not 'do not cause us to succumb to temptation', but rather 'cause us not to succumb to temptation'. This sense fits in admirably with the additional clause in Mt.: in the midst of temptation and tribulation God will deliver his people from the power of evil.

v. The Friend at Midnight 11:5–8

The second part of the section on prayer is a parable peculiar to Lk. which is clearly meant to be an incentive to prayer. It is a story which illustrates how even when motives of neighbourliness are lacking a man will still respond to the request of someone in need. Hence there are two possible lessons in the parable. On the one hand, the parable is meant to depict the character of God by contrast with the unwilling householder. It is true that this lesson is not explicitly drawn in the text; the justification for it is to be found in the parallel parable of the unjust judge (18:1–8) in which the point is clearly made, and also in the appended teaching in 11:9–13, especially v. 13 where the comparison between men and God is clearly made. On the other hand, the parable can be seen as an encouragement to go on praying, despite the lack of an immediate answer. This is how the parable was interpreted in the Old Latin MS tradition (which adds at the beginning of v. 8: *et si ille perseveraverit pulsans*), and it fits in with Luke's explanation of the parable of the unjust judge in 18:1.

According to Jeremias, *Parables*, 105, 157–159, the former of these interpretations gives us the original sense of the parable, as told by Jesus, whereas the latter is a secondary interpretation by Luke or his source which has been imposed upon the parable by placing it in its present context (11:9–13). This distinction appears to be over-subtle and does not do justice to certain features of the text. The fact is that any encouragement to go on praying must necessarily be based on an assurance that God answers prayer. The point of the parable is clearly not: Go on praying because God will eventually respond to importunity; rather it is: Go on praying because God responds graciously to the needs of his children. This point is confirmed by 11:9–13 where the point stressed is the certainty of God's answer to prayer and the assurance that he will give good gifts to those who ask him. It is improbable, therefore, that Luke has lost the alleged original point of the parable. The question is rather whether he has detected in the parable an emphasis on importunity which was not originally present. This too is improbable. The situation in which a parable such as the present one is told is one in which men wonder whether it is worth praying to God because they do not get their prayers answered; Jesus' reply is that men can pray with confidence because God is gracious, like a friend (cf. G. Stählin, TDNT IX, 164); therefore, let them continue to pray. There is thus an element of importunity in the original lesson of the parable; this point may be traced elsewhere in the teaching of Jesus (see on 11:10), and hence is not unlikely in the present parable. Luke has not laid undue emphasis on the element of importunity in the parable; the two possible interpretations of the parable belong together as one whole. If the parable teaches that the character of God is such that men do not need to nag at him to obtain their requests, at the same time it is an encouragement to go on praying despite all contrary appearances because God is sure to answer. Persistent, rather than importunate prayer is the point.

Because of the similarity in structure with the parable of the unjust judge the question arises whether the two parables were originally transmitted as a pair (for examples of such see Jeremias, *Parables*, 90–94). Wellhausen, 56f., went so far as to claim that the two parables were variants of the same basic parable. (It is a curiosity of criticism that he held that 18:1–8 was older because of its eschatological reference, whereas Jülicher regarded 11:5–8 as older because of the lack of eschatological reference!) Ott, 25–29, 71f., argues that the two parables came from different traditions but were brought together in Luke's source; at this stage the original parable, 11:5–7, was assimilated to 18:2–7, by the addition of v. 8. The original force was: If nobody can imagine a friend who will refuse an inconvenient request, how much more will God answer your prayers? This was altered to give more stress on the need for persistence in prayer. Luke then separated the two parables and placed the present one here; by adding the closing exhortations he made it teach the lesson: Go on asking and you will receive. For Luke the stress lay not on the goodness of God, but rather on the duty of men. This reconstruction of the tradition-history is speculative, and is open to the objections made above.

There is no essential connection between the parable and the Lord's Prayer. The parable itself, however, must be about prayer, although it contains no application, and there is a catchword connection between 11:3 and 5 (ἄρτος). The present setting is thus appropriate, even if we cannot be sure that it is original. We do not know whether 11:2–4 and 5–8 are from the same source; the view that 11:5–8 stood in Luke's recension of Q (Schürmann, *Untersuchungen*, 119) is possible but lacks positive evidence (Ott, 92).

See Jeremias, *Parables*, 105, 157–159; Ott, 23–31, 71f., 99–102; K. E. Bailey, 119–123.

(5) The parable opens with the formula τίς ἐξ ὑμῶν which is found in 11:11; 12:25; 14:28; 15:4; 17:7 (cf. 14:31; 15:8) and is thus characteristic of Q and L material. The effect of it is to address the hearers personally and force them to decision on what is being told to them. Its force is roughly: 'Can anyone of you imagine that...?' and it establishes an incontrovertible fact of ordinary life as a basis for a spiritual lesson. The formula has no contemporary parallels (but see Is. 42:23; 50:10; Hg. 2:3) and hence it is to be regarded as in all probability

characteristic of Jesus himself (H. Greeven, cited by Jeremias, *Parables*, 103). The τίς is understood as the man who needs the bread and the φίλος as the man in bed by RSV; TEV; JB; TNT; NIV; Klostermann, 125, but vice versa by NEB; Barclay; Creed, 157; Jeremias, *Parables*, 158. Against the latter interpretation we may note that the change of subject with πορεύσεται is awkward, and that the emphatic κἀκεῖνος is also odd if it refers back to the original τίς. Moreover, the hearer is surely in the position of the petitioner rather than of God. These factors seem to weigh against Creed's argument from the parallels in the other parables (where, in any case, only one actor is involved, and the question concerns human spiritual attitudes). The sentence structure is awkward with its long string of paratactic verbs. It represents a Semitic conditional protasis with the apodosis introduced by κἀκεῖνος (v. 7) (cf. 11:11f.; 12:25, 42f.; 14:5, 28, 31; 15:4, 8; Beyer I:1, 287–293; cf. BD 442³). The whole thing forms a rhetorical question which runs to the end of v. 7 (cf. RSV).

The situation described is one in which demands are made upon a neighbour (cf. 10:36f.), here called a friend (7:6). The locating of the incident at midnight (μεσονύκτιον, Mk. 13:35; Acts 16:25; 20:7**; gen. of time) shows verisimilitude, since journeys were often undertaken by night in order to avoid the heat of the day (cf. Mt. 2:9; Plummer, 298). The change of mood to the subjunctive (εἴπῃ, vs. 5 and 7) is variously explained. In a deliberative or doubtful question either the subjunctive (23:31) or the future indicative (16:11f.) may be used. It is possible that the forms could be mixed in Koine Greek. Zerwick's explanation (297) in terms of the mood of the expected reply to the question seems improbable.

χρῆσον is the 1st aorist imperative of κίχρημι**, 'to lend'; the more common δανίζω is used for business loans on which interest is charged. Three loaves would be more than enough for one person (K. E. Bailey, 121f.). The situation is obviously one in which the shops are closed or (in the case of a small village) there are no shops, and the unexpected visitor has taken the household by surprise; it would be unthinkable not to provide him with hospitality.

(6) For ἐπειδή cf. 7:1; παραγίνομαι, 7:4. ἐξ ὁδοῦ is 'after a journey'. The use of the future indicative παραθήσω in the relative clause is Classical, when a sort of result is being expressed, but in Classical Greek ὅ τι would have been used (BD 379; cf. 7:4).

(7) κἀκεῖνος is Lucan (22:12; Acts 5:37; 15:11; 18:19) but may be dur to a source here (cf. 11:42 par. Mt. 23:23; 20:11 par. Mk. 12:4f.; Schürmann, *Paschamahlbericht*, 100). ἔσωθεν is 'within' (11:39f.*). The disturbed man omits the address 'friend', no doubt out of annoyance at being awakened (Manson, *Sayings*, 267). He does not mind giving the bread; it is the trouble of getting up to answer the door. κόπος is here 'trouble' (18:5; Mk. 14:6), elsewhere, 'toil, work'. The door has been closed 'long ago' (ἤδη; 14:17; Jn. 19:28); there would be a wooden or

iron bolt thrust through rings to keep it shut, and it might not be too easy to manipulate (cf. Ct. 5:4f.; Easton, 177). The house is a single-roomed peasant's cottage (Mt. 5:15) in which the whole family sleep together on a mat which serves as a bed (κοίτη*). οὐ δύναμαι is tantamount to 'I won't' (Manson, *Sayings*, 267).

(8) Jesus answers his own question (cf. 15:7, 10; 16:9; 18:8, 14). For the construction of εἰ καί with οὐ and the future indicative cf. BD 372²; 428¹. ἀναστάς comes rather awkwardly after the verb, although it refers to a preceding action. The two διά phrases are ambiguous. Does the first mean 'because the man in the house is a friend (active) of the man at the door' or 'because the man at the door is a friend (passive) of the man in the house'? The former is perhaps more likely (cf. G. Stählin, TDNT IX, 161), but it may be better to regard φίλος as expressing a mutual relationship. As for the second phrase, the interpretation depends on the meaning assigned to ἀναίδεια**, literally 'shamelessness'. This can mean the attitude of the man at the door, his 'sheer impudence' in coming at such an hour with his request, or less probably his 'unblushing persistence' in continuing to demand an answer (Ott, 29–31, 102; Leaney, 188; cf. Vulgate, cited above). It should be noted that the parable itself says nothing about persistence, but rather it deals with the unreasonableness of the request. However, the word may also refer to the attitude of the man in the house who does not want to have the shame of being known as a refuser of neighbourly requests, i.e. 'so as not to lose face' (A. Fridrichsen, cited by Jeremias, *Parables*, 158). The former view is supported by some late rabbinic parallels (Sanh. 105a; p Taan 2, 65b, 32; in SB I, 456) and also by Greek word usage (cf. AG s.v. ἀναιδεύομαι and ἀναιδής), but the latter view is also possible linguistically. The question is whether the lesson is concerned with the human attitude that gains a hearing from God or with the character of God himself. Decision is not easy, but I am inclined to prefer the latter alternative on the grounds that the parable is centred on the attitude of the man in bed and that v. 8 is offering a contrast to the attitude expressed in v. 7 (so also K. E. Bailey, 125–133). So the parable concludes with a phrase, 'as much as he needs' (χρῄζω, 12:30* par. Mt. 6:32), which may simply be literary variation, but more probably is meant to express the generosity of the householder (Rengstorf, 143).

vi. Encouragement to Pray 11:9–13

The final piece of instruction on prayer is composed of two sayings units. The first contains encouragement to make requests because they are sure to be answered (11:9f.). In the second unit an argument *a minori ad maius* proves from the practice of human fathers who give good rather than evil gifts to their sons that the heavenly Father will give the gift of the Spirit to those who ask him (11:11–13).

The two sayings units are each self-contained, and are unlikely to be composed of originally independent sayings (*contra* Bultmann, 90). The first of them refers to making requests from God (cf. the use of the passive) and contains three more or less synonymous expressions for prayer. It is preserved here with its original meaning as a saying encouraging the disciples to pray. The second unit also refers to the way in which God answers prayer, although here the point is not the certainty of an answer but the goodness of the gifts bestowed by God. Following A. T. Cadoux, Jeremias, *Parables*, 144f., claims that it was a saying addressed to the opponents of Jesus and vindicating the goodness of God in giving his gifts to the sinners whom they despised. This suggestion is interesting, but falls short of complete proof. If correct, it implies that originally the two sayings units were independent. Their present linking by means of the common theme expressed in the catch-word αἰτέω is in any case appropriate.

The two units are also to be found in Mt. 7:7–11 with almost identical wording. Was this passage, then, taken by Luke and Matthew from the same source? There is a significant difference in wording in 11:11f. par. Mt. 7:9f., which seems hardly explicable in terms of redaction by either Evangelist. Further, the context of the sayings in Mt. is quite different from that in Lk. In Lk. the sayings form part of a carefully wrought instruction on prayer, but in Mt. they appear in a context where it is notoriously difficult to trace any connection of thought, and the use made of the sayings appear to be quite different. (The connection in Mt. 7:6–11 is also to be seen in G. Thomas 92–94.) It is hard to understand how Matthew managed to get the sayings into such a strange context if originally they were transmitted in the context of teaching on prayer. The alternative is that Matthew found the sayings in their present catch-word connection (Mt. 7:6, 7–11) and that Luke or his source has dropped Mt. 7:6 and used the sayings for what was clearly their original purpose. It is unlikely that it was Luke himself who acted in this way; more probably it was his source in which so-called Q and L material had, to some extent at least, been amalgamated. It may, therefore, be best to assume that the wording here represents 'Q' material which has come to Luke in a different recension from that used by Matthew.

See Ott, 99–112; Schulz, 161–164; K. E. Bailey, 134–141.

(9) The saying begins with a transitional phrase: κἀγὼ ὑμῖν λέγω. For κἀγώ cf. 1:3. For ὑμῖν λέγω cf. 6:27 note. The phrase is not found in Mt. and it is not clear whether he has omitted it because it was unnecessary or Luke (or his source) has added it to give a connection with what precedes. It links the present sayings more appropriately to 11:5–8 than to 11:2–4, and so it may have been added at the same time as the parable (cf. Schulz, 161).

The first of the three parallel phrases is concerned with 'asking'. αἰτέω is regularly used of prayer (11:10, 13; Mt. 18:19; Mk. 11:24; Jn. 11:22; Eph. 3:20; *et al.*; G. Stählin, TDNT I, 191–193). That prayer is meant is confirmed by the use of δοθήσεται, where the passive means

'God will give' (Jeremias, *Theology* I, 11). For the thought cf. Jn. 16:24; 14:13f.; 15:7. It is not clear where the accent should be placed. The saying may mean, 'You must ask, in order to receive', 'You won't get anything unless you ask for it' (Lagrange, 326; Ott, 101; the accent falls on the first half), or 'If you ask, you can be sure that you will receive' (with the parataxis equivalent to a conditional sentence). The second sense is certainly present in the next verse, which gives the basis for this verse, and hence we should probably adopt the first sense, so that the saying is an invitation to pray, but not necessarily a command to be importunate in prayer (as Jeremias, *Parables*, 159f., understands it). (But the connection of thought might be: Since anybody who asks (anybody else) receives, you can be sure that if you ask God you will receive.)

The second phrase is about 'seeking'. The verb is commonly used of seeking for God (Dt. 4:29; Is. 65:1; 55:6; cf. Ex. 33:7; Ps. 104:4); to seek God's face is to pray (2 Sa. 21:1; Pss. 23:6; 26:8; Ho. 5:15), although this is not the background here (despite H. Greeven, TDNT II, 892f.). In the NT the verb is used of seeking after God (Acts 17:27) or seeking to enter the heavenly banquet (Lk. 13:24). The thought here is moulded by the OT language of seeking after God and finding him (Dt. 4:29; Is. 55:6; 65:1; cf. Rom. 10:20). The thought is of a calling to God by people who do not know whether he will listen to them, i.e. whether he is 'there' at all: the OT stresses that such 'seeking' is characterised by repentance and fear, since it is sin that has separated men from God (cf. G. Gerleman, THAT I, 333–336). The promise here is that God is waiting to be found by those who will seek after him (cf. Dt. 4:29; Is. 55:6; 65:1; Je. 29:13; cf. Pr. 8:17), and it is noteworthy that such seeking is paralleled by prayer in Je. 29:12f., and that to find God means that he will pour out his blessings upon his people (Je. 29:14).

The third phrase uses the picture of a man knocking at a closed door, manifestly in order to gain entry; for κρούω cf. 12:36; 13:25; G. Bertram, TDNT III, 954–957. In rabbinic usage the metaphor was used of prayer (Meg. 12b; SB I, 458f.). J. Jeremias, TDNT III, 178, thinks that the picture is of seeking admission to the heavenly, festal hall, but this is less appropriate. Hence the three phrases should all be taken as applying to prayer.

(10) We are now given the justification for the statements in v. 9. But the nature of the justification is not clear. Following K. H. Rengstorf, J. Jeremias, *Parables,* 159f., regards the first part of this verse as giving a piece of gnomic wisdom drawn from the experience of the beggar who knows that if he persists long enough in asking he will get what he wants by sheer pertinacity; how much more certain can men be that their pertinacity will gain gifts from God. The difficulty with this interpretation is that it stresses pertinacity, whereas there is nothing in the saying itself to indicate that this is meant by Jesus. Further, this interpretation stands by itself; there is apparently no comparable interpretation for the other two phrases. A second possibility (with which the first

can be combined) is to say that it is general human experience that people get what they want (cf. Ott, 104) – the saying 'envisages the normal case of knocking at a door . . . in the justifiable expectation that it will be opened' (G. Bertram, ibid. 955). This may generally be true of knocking at doors; I would hesitate to apply it to searching for lost objects. Therefore, it may be best, thirdly, to see in this verse an apodictic assertion of the certainty of God's willingness to respond (cf. Lagrange, 327; Schulz, 163f.). This is perhaps suggested for the first phrase by the Johannine parallels, and for the second phrase by the OT parallels. In this case, we have an authoritative statement on the part of Jesus which rests on his own personal relationship to God as the Father.

Jeremias, *Parables*, 111, regards the opening πᾶς as a generalising addition, but in any case it gives the sense correctly. For ἀνοιγήσεται (p⁴⁵ vid ℵ C L Θ f1 f13 *al*) there are the variants ἀνοίγεται (p⁷⁵ B D sy bo; *Diglot*) and ἀνοιχθήσεται (A E W *pm*; TR). The first aorist form is probably secondary. The choice between the future (which could be due to assimilation to v. 9 or to Mt. 7:8) and the present (which could be due to assimilation to the other verbs in v. 10) is difficult (Metzger, 156f.).

(11–12) The first sentence in the second group of sayings is very awkwardly expressed with anacolouthon at ἰχθύν; Matthew's different formulation of the same thought reflects a Semitic conditional sentence expressed paratactically with the apodosis in the form of a question (cf. Lk. 11:5–7; 12:42f.), and Luke's version appears to be an attempt to clarify the syntax. What is required is a conditional sentence: 'If any father among you is asked by his son for a fish, will he give him a serpent instead of a fish?' The difficulty arises from the opening τίς ἐξ ὑμῶν construction. Luke's δέ is probably original, diff. Mt. ἤ. Awkwardness is caused by the description τὸν πατέρα (diff. Mt. ἄνθρωπος) which looks like an insertion based on 11:13; it is so awkward and redundant (in view of the presence of υἱός) that it is hard to credit it to Luke. αἰτέω gives a catchword connection with the previous saying.

The second clause is introduced in Semitic style by καί (preserved in p⁴⁵ p⁷⁵ B sa *al*; UBS; *Diglot*; Metzger, 157). The phrase ἀντὶ ἰχθύος is absent from Mt.; it may be Lucan (Schulz, 162 n. 184), but since he uses ἀντί elsewhere only in the phrase ἀνθ᾽ ὧν, and since the repetition of ἰχθύς is unlikely from him (Wrege, 108 n. 2), it is more probably original. The serpent (ὄφις, 10:19*) resembles a fish in appearance, especially the eel or the scaleless *barbût* (*clarias macracanthus*); but an attempt to pass off the serpent as a *barbût* is ruled out by the fact that the latter was an unclean fish (Jeremias, *Parables*, 226). Ott, 104–106, suggests that the word refers to some sea-creature such as might be caught accidentally in a net (Mt. 13:47f.). But the general similarity between a fish and a serpent is sufficient to make the point. The postulated cruelty thus has the elements of refusing to give what is asked, deceiving the recipient into thinking that he is getting what he wants, and (if the reptile is alive) giving something positively harmful. The point is the contrast with God who gives *good* gifts.

In Mt. the fish/serpent is the second pair of objects, and it is preceded by bread/stone. The text of Lk. is assimilated to that of Mt. by the insertion (after υἱός) of ἄρτον μὴ λίθον ἐπιδώσει αὐτῷ ἢ (καὶ) ἰχθύν (א A C D L W Θ f1 f13 *pm* lat sy ᶜᵖ bo; TR). The shorter text in p ⁴⁵(p ⁷⁵) B *al* it syˢ sa is to be accepted (Metzger, 157). If so, each Gospel has two pairs of objects: Matthew has bread/stone; fish/serpent; and Luke has fish/serpent; egg/scorpion (ᾠόν**; σκορπίος, 10:19*). How has this difference arisen? 1. Originally there were three pairs in the common source, and each Evangelist has reproduced two of them (K. E. Bailey, 136f.). But if so, the coincidence in omission is odd. 2. Hirsch (cited by Grundmann, 235 n. 26) suggests that there was one pair in Q, and each Evangelist expanded the saying for liturgical reasons. 3. W. Foerster, TDNT V, 579f., suggests that the form in Mt. with its development from the useless stone to the harmful serpent is superior to that in Lk., since scorpions are not more harmful than snakes, and bread and fish constituted the staple Galilean diet. But scorpions were considered harmful, and eggs were also commonly eaten in Palestine, and no reason for the change is evident. 4. Ott, 109–112, holds that Luke altered the Q form preserved in Mt. in order to get two harmful gifts in contrast to the good gift of the Spirit; he regarded earthly gifts as harmful. The motive ascribed to Luke here is incredible, but the first part of the suggestion (replacement of harmless by harmful substitutes) is possible (Schulz, 162 n. 185), although a convincing motive is lacking. 5. The best explanation is that of Dodd, 337 n. who claims that divergence in different branches of an oral tradition is responsible for the difference (perhaps as a result of the motivation in 4.?).

(13) The conclusion is now drawn. πονηρός can be used of men (6:45) and their deeds (3:19). ὑπάρχοντες is probably Lucan, diff. Mt. ὄντες. The same phrase is used of the Pharisees in Mt. 12:34, and hence it has been argued that here too Jesus is addressing his opponents. This does not necessarily follow, since Jesus generally assumes the sinfulness of men (cf. G. Harder, TDNT VI, 554). For the thought cf. Heb. 12:7–10. For the *a minore* argument cf. Is. 49:15. The phrase ὁ ἐξ οὐρανοῦ (diff. Mt. ὑμῶν ὁ ἐν τοῖς οὐρανοῖς) is textually uncertain. It is supported by A B C D W Θ f1 f13 *pl* syˢ⁽ʰ⁾; TR. The possessive ὑμῶν has been added (it) as a result of assimilation to Mt. ἐξ οὐρανοῦ (without the article) appears in p⁷⁵ א L 33 *al* vg syᶜᵖ sa bo; *Diglot*, and ὁ οὐράνιος in p⁴⁵ 1. This last form may again be due to assimilation to Mt. The UBS text is to be preferred with the pregnant use of ἐξ, 'The Father who (gives gifts) from heaven' (BD 437; Jeremias, *Abba*, 40f.; cf. Metzger, 157f.). Matthew's form is generally regarded as original (Jeremias, ibid; van Iersel, 98f.; cf. G. Schrenk, TDNT V, 986), but if so, it is hard to see why the Lucan form developed from it; development in the opposite direction is more likely (Schulz, 162). The attribute characterises the

Father as dwelling in heaven, by contrast with the earthly fathers in the earlier part of the saying, and prepares for the idea of a spiritual gift. This gift is described as 'Holy Spirit' (πνεῦμα ἅγιον); some MSS assimilate to δόματα ἀγαθά in the earlier part of the verse and in the Matthaean parallel (Θ al (cf. Metzger, 158); there are other variants including πνεῦμα ἀγαθόν p⁴⁵ L pc aur vg; Grundmann, 235, suggests that possibly this is original). The 'good gifts' in Mt. should certainly be understood in a spiritual sense (Rom. 3:8; 10:15; Heb. 9:11; 10:1; cf. Lk. 1:53; Jeremias, *Parables*, 144f.), so that the meaning in Mt. and Lk. is very much the same. Most commentators regard Matthew as original here, with 'Holy Spirit' being due to Luke (Lagrange, 328; Klostermann, 126; Ellis, 164; Ott, 107–109; Schulz, 162). But this is not certain. Wrege, 108, claims that Luke does not add references to the Spirit being available before Easter for the disciples, and argues that the change arose earlier in liturgical usage. C. S. Rodd (see on 11:20) argues that Luke has no greater tendency than Mt. to introduce references to the Spirit. The form in Mt. could be a generalising one, made in order to assimilate the second part of the saying to the first. It is difficult to arrive at a certain verdict on the point.

The closing phrase τοῖς αἰτοῦσιν αὐτόν makes the link with 11:9–12. Jeremias, ibid, thinks that the change to the third person from the second, strengthens the case that Jesus is addressing his opponents and referring to how God gives his gifts not to them but to the despised sinners who call upon him. This implies that Matthew's reference to 'your' Father is mistaken, and the wording certainly does not demand this reconstruction of the situation; the phrase is surely meant to stress the need to ask God for what we need, and is a final summons to confident prayer.

c. Controversy with the Pharisees (11:14–54)

In the third main section of this division of the Gospel Jesus is presented in controversy with the Pharisees on a variety of topics. The material is divided into four sections of unequal length. In the first (11:14–26) the question at issue is the authority of Jesus: Jesus claims that his exorcisms are signs that the power of God is at work in him, and warns against the dangers of the evil spirits associated with the devil. The second, brief section (11:27f.) teaches the importance of hearing and obeying the word of God, as taught by himself. In the third section (11:29–36), Jesus replies to the request for a sign by claiming that the Son of man will be a sign to this generation in the same way as Jonah was to the people of Nineveh. The sayings on light which follow may be an exhortation to the hearers to respond to the light which they have in Jesus. Finally, in 11:37–54 we have a detailed criticism of the Pharisaic religion which concentrates on the secondary matters of the law, rejects the message of the prophets, and thus keeps men out of the kingdom of God.

It is clear that a variety of topics are handled in the section, but there is a basic unity of theme. The material is basically drawn from the Q tradition, where teaching against the Pharisees has been gathered together in one place, but related sayings have also been included. Matthew has separated off the woes against the Pharisees in order to use them at a later point in conjunction with similar material from Mk.

i. The Beelzebul Controversy 11:14–26

From the theme of the Holy Spirit given by the Father to those who ask for him the subject turns to that of the evil spirits who are under the control of Satan. The pericope opens with the account of the exorcism of a spirit causing dumbness; the event leads to a mixed response by the audience. While some were filled with wonder, others ascribed the exorcism to the power of Beelzebul, the ruler of demons (11:14f.). Yet others asked that Jesus would give them a sign from heaven (11:16). Jesus' reply consists of several sayings. First, he observes that Satan, i.e. Beelzebul, is unlikely to be responsible for exorcising his own agents, since this would imply a serious weakness in his rule (11:17f.). Second, for the Jews to ascribe Jesus' exorcisms to Satan is implicitly to ascribe exorcisms performed by themselves to the same agent (11:19). Third, the casting out of demons by the power of God – since no other agent comes into question – is a sign of the presence of the kingdom (11:20). For, fourth, the release of Satan's victims implies that their master has been overcome (11:21f.). There follows, fifth, a warning that those who do not side with Jesus are in fact on the side of evil (11:23). Finally, there is a general saying on the folly of exorcising demons without replacing them by something good; it is a warning to those who attempt exorcisms without proclaiming the message of the kingdom (11:24–26).

It is probable that several items of teaching have been gathered together in this section. This is confirmed by the fact that we have a parallel account of the main core of the section in Mk. 3:22–27. The linguistic phenomena suggest that Luke is here following an independent source, which has also been used by Matthew: Matthew, however, has conflated material from Mk. and Q, whereas Luke has essentially followed the account in Q, and Marcan influence is negligible. The literary problem is disputed, but this seems to be the most likely solution. On this view, the differences between Mk. and Q indicate that a basic common tradition has been amplified in different ways. Bultmann, 10f., argues that the Q form, with the opening miracle story is more primitive. The core of the account consists of vs. 14f. followed by the reply of Jesus in vs. 17f. (cf. Mk. 3:22–26). The remaining sayings are additions to this basic core. Essentially the same view is held by Schulz, 206, but Schweizer, *Matthäus*, 184f., holds that originally the accusation in vs. 14f. was followed by the reply in v. 19, since in both sayings Beelzebul figures, whereas in the intervening verses (17f.) the talk is of Satan; on this view v. 18b is an addition made to link the two traditions, and v. 20 is a secondary addition to v. 19. The loose nature of the discussion suggests that it reflects several occasions of controversy aroused by the exorcisms performed by Jesus, and, although any reconstruction of the history of the tradition must be speculative, Schweizer's view is to be preferred to that of Bultmann.

See L. Gaston, 'Beelzebul', TZ18, 1962, 247–255; S. Légasse, 'L'homme fort de Luc 11:21–22', Nov.T 5, 1962, 5–9; Lührmann, 32–43; Schulz, 203–213, 476–480.

(14) In both Lk. and Mt. the narrative opens with the account of an exorcism, which is absent from Mk. and must have been recorded in their common source. The wording, however, is very different, and a closer parallel is given by Mt. 9:32–34. It seems likely that the story in Mt. 9 gives the original Q form, and that the version in Mt. 12:22–24 is a doublet of this story which has been rewritten by Matthew. He has used the theme twice, once to illustrate the healing power of Jesus, and once to introduce the theme of the Pharisaic opposition to Jesus. The original Q wording is difficult to ascertain from this set of versions, but is probably close to Lk. (Schulz, 204).

The use of the periphrastic form ἦν ἐκβάλλων is slightly odd. It is probably meant to set the scene for the saying in v. 15. The characteristic conferred by the demon is ascribed to the demon itself (cf. Mk. 9:17) which is described as dumb (κωφός, 1:22 note; cf. SB IV:1, 501–535). Before κωφόν (p⁴⁵ p⁷⁵ ℵ A* B L fl (syᶜˢ) cop) various authorities insert καὶ αὐτὸ ἦν (A C W Θ f13 pm latt; TR (UBS)), which is Lucan in style but weakly attested (Metzger, 158). The second part of the verse is close to Mt. 9:33 with the use of ἐξέρχομαι as an equivalent to the passive of ἐκβάλλω. Luke alone has the ἐγένετο δέ ... (καὶ ἐγένετο ..., Diglot) construction (1:8 note).

(15) Luke leaves the critics of Jesus unnamed, as part of the crowd, whereas in Mt. they are identified with the Pharisees. In Mk. the reference is to scribes from Jerusalem. While many critics think that Luke is original here (Schulz, 204 n. 206), he may have altered the wording, since τις ἐκ is a favourite phrase of his, and also since he has a further group of speakers in the next verse. Grundmann, 237, suggests that Luke wishes to play down the hostility of the Pharisees for the moment in view of 11:37. Be this as it may, the charge against Jesus is that he casts out demons by Beelzebul the prince of demons. The name Beelzebul is found in the same context in Mk. 3:22 where Jesus is said to have 'Beelzebul' and to cast out demons by means of the prince of demons. Although it might be argued that the name of Beelzebul was absent from Q (cf. Mt. 9:34) and that Luke has conflated the Mk. and Q forms, this is improbable, because the name of Beelzebul was also used by Q elsewhere (11:19 par. Mt. 12:27; Mt. 10:25**), and it is unlikely that Matthew also made the same conflation independently. The spelling

of the word varies in the MSS. The form βεελζεβούλ (UBS; *Diglot*) is that found in most MSS, but *Synopsis* follows ℵ B in reading the abbreviated form βεεζεβούλ; the English form 'Beelzebub' comes from the Latin and is due to assimilation to 2 Ki. 1:2, 3, 6. The derivation of the name is disputed, and is in any case unimportant for the meaning of the text, since Beelzebul is simply a popular name for the prince of the demons. The name does not occur in Jewish literature, but appears to represent the same figure as Belial in the intertestamental literature. 'Beel-' is clearly equivalent to 'Baal', i.e. 'lord'. The second part of the word has been traced to 1. *z*ᵉ *bul*, 'house, high place, temple'(1 Ki. 8:13; Is. 63:15), giving 'lord of the house' (cf. Mt. 10:25 so L. Gaston*, with reference to Jesus' claim to be 'lord of the temple');´ 2. the name *z b l* found in a Ras Shamra text, where the word may be a proper name or mean 'prince' in the phrase *zbl b'l*; 3. Aramaic *d*ᵉ*bābā*, 'enmity', giving the meaning 'the enemy' (Tg. Nu. 10:35; Ct. R. 7:10). The form Baalzebub for the god of Ekron in 2 Ki. 1:2 is probably a derisive pun ('lord of the flies') on an original 'Baalzebul'. See W. Foerster, TDNT I, 605f.

(16) A second group of people is mentioned at this point. Their identity (ἕτεροι, 3:18) is again not clear. Their purpose was to test Jesus (πειράζω, 4:2; cf. 10:25 note), i.e. to ascertain whether he had the right credientials for his ministry. Exorcisms, it is implied, were inadequate as a proof of divine authorisation; what was needed was a sign from heaven, an unmistakable indication from God. There is no corresponding comment in Mt. or Mk. at this point, but there is a similar remark at Mk. 8:11 (Mt. 16:1). Luke's wording here corresponds to this Marcan text (Schramm, 46f.) rather than to the wording in Mt. 12:38 which introduces the saying about the sign of Jonah found in Lk. 11:29–32 par. Mt. 12:39–42. Luke intends the verse to prepare for this later saying, and he may have meant to suggest that the exorcisms performed by Jesus made a sign from heaven unnecessary.

(17) The introduction to the saying of Jesus is close to Mt. 12:25, but there are two slight changes. The inclusion of αὐτός is probably Lucan, and the emphatic position of αὐτῶν may also be due to him (cf. 11:19b). διανόημα**, 'thought', is probably original; Matthew shows a slight preference for ἐνθύμησις (9:4; cf. his use of the verb, 1:20; 9:4), which he perhaps associated with evil or incorrect thoughts.

The first part of Jesus' reply agrees closely with Mt. and is clear in meaning. A kingdom which is divided against itself becomes desolate. So, it is implied, if the kingdom of evil is divided, with Beelzebul taking sides against his subordinates, then his kingdom will not stand (11:18). διαμερίζω, 'to divide, separate', is Lucan (11:18; 12:52f.; 22:17; 23:34 (par. Mk. 15:24); Mt. 27:35; Jn. 19:24; Acts 2:3, 45**) for μερίζω (12:13). ἐφ' ἑαυτήν may follow Mk. 3:24 (Schramm, 46; Schulz, 205), but could be original in Q, since Matthew's καθ' ἑαυτῆς may be due to his liking for κατά with the genitive. ἐρημόω is 'to lay waste, depopulate'

(Mt. 12:25; Rev. 17:16; 18:17, 19**).

The second phrase is not clear: 'and house(hold) falls upon house(hold)'. There are three possibilities: 1. 'Every household divided against itself falls' (RV, NEB; JB; TEV; NIV; Creed, 160). This takes the saying in the same way as in Mt. and Mk. and gives a parallel to the preceding clause. 2. '(In time of civil strife) one house falls upon another' (RSV; Barclay; Wellhausen, 58; Lagrange, 330; Easton, 180). This can hardly refer literally to houses falling in ruins on each other (Klostermann, 127), but to one household attacking another; for this possible meaning of πίπτω see LSJ II, 1406f. 3. 'House after house collapses' (TNT; cf. Phil. 2:27). The second view gives the best sense grammatically; if it represents Luke's source, Matthew has here followed Mk., who has two parallel metaphors in place of the one in Q. The view that Luke has misunderstood and simplified his source (Schulz, 205; cf. Schürmann, *Paschamahlbericht*, 2) is improbable. See O. Michel, TDNT V, 132 n. 5, for parallels to the idea.

(18) From the general truth expressed in the previous verse the particular application is now drawn. The use of εἰ δὲ καί (diff. Mt., Mk. καὶ εἰ) may be Lucan style, but again the possibility that Matthew has assimilated to Mk. should not be discounted. The equivalence of Satan and Beelzebul is taken for granted; the fact that the equation is not made elsewhere is of no significance, since the title is not attested elsewhere, and since Satan had a rich variety of nomenclature. Here 'Satan' is used by metonymy for his kingdom (cf. 1 Cor. 12:12). Luke has only one conditional clause, whereas Mark (cf. Matthew) has two. The word ἐκβάλλω which occurs in Matthew's extra clause is also found in the second part of the verse in Lk., which has no parallel in Mt. or Mk. (unless we find one in Mk. 3:30). It looks as though Luke here follows Q, and Matthew has rewritten the verse in conformity with Mk. V. 18b follows so awkwardly that it is unlikely to be a Lucan addition (*pace* Bultmann, 353). It serves to round off the opening argument.

(19) The second argument accuses the Jews of inconsistency in ascribing Jesus' exorcisms to Beelzebul, and not doing so in the case of their sons' exorcisms; the two categories should surely stand together. υἱός is used here in the sense of 'adherent' or 'pupil' (1 Pet. 5:13; Heb. 12:5). Exorcisms were carried out by the contemporaries of Jesus: Acts 19:13f.; Jos. Ant. 8:45–48; SB IV:1, 527–535. Jesus here assumes the reality of such acts and that they were carried out by the power of God. This raises a problem in view of the next saying, in which Jesus claims that his exorcisms are signs of the arrival of the kingdom of God: ought not the same to be true of Jewish exorcisms (Bultmann, 12; B. Noack, *Satanas und Soteria*, Copenhagen, 1948, 28, 71)? The problem may be due to the fact that two originally unrelated sayings have been brought together (Creed, 160f., regards vs. 18b–19 as an addition; Kümmel, 105f., holds that v. 20 is an independent saying). Alternatively, Jesus may be claiming that the kingly rule of God is evident wherever the

power of God is demonstrated. In any case, in the present verse Jesus is making the point that the adherents of the critics will be their judges, since the accusation made against Jesus is implicitly directed against them also: Danker, 138, suggests that 'judges' means 'instructors', which is less likely. The reference is probably eschatological and suggests that God will uphold the exorcists who acted by his power against their critics. The point is the same as that made in the 'blasphemy against the Spirit' saying.

(20) The third statement which is made by Jesus does not stand in parallel with the preceding ones as an argument against the accusation of acting by the power of Beelzebul. It assumes that the accusation has been rejected, and states the consequence. If Jesus' exorcisms have been carried out by the power of God, then they constitute evidence that the kingdom of God has arrived. In its present position the verse states the alternative to v. 19. If Jesus does not cast out demons by Beelzebul, then the alternative is that he does so by the finger of God, and, if so, then the (correct) consequence which should be drawn is that the kingdom of God has appeared. The logical connection is sound enough, and does not justify the conclusion that we necessarily have two independent sayings here.

There is one significant difference from the wording in Mt. Luke has δακτύλος, 'finger' (11:46 par. Mt. 23:4; Lk. 16:24) where Matthew has πνεῦμα. The close verbal agreement in the rest of the verse indicates that one word must be a substitution for the other by the Evangelist or his source (if we are dealing with two recensions of the same source). The meaning is the same in both versions. For the phrase 'finger of God' see Ex. 8:19 (MT 15); Dt. 9:10 par. Ex. 31:18; Ps. 8:3; cf. Dn. 5:5; H. Schlier, TDNT II, 20f. More common is the 'hand of God' (Ex. 7:4f.; 9:3, 15; et al.). OT usage indicates that 'hand of God' and 'Spirit of God' were similar in meaning (1 Ch. 28: 12, 19; Ezk. 8:13a/b; R. G. Hamerton-Kelly, 'A note on Matthew xii. 28 par. Luke xi. 20', NTS 11, 1964–65, 165–167). Although the meaning is thus the same, both phrases indicating the action of God, the question remains whether Jesus himself here made one of his rare references to the Spirit in a verse which is generally recognised to be his authentic teaching. A majority of scholars hold that δακτύλος stood in Luke's source (Schulz, 205 n. 218). It is argued that Luke is fond of references to the Spirit, and would hardly remove one that already stood in his source; that Matthew may have been removing an anthropomorphism and assimilating the wording to Mt. 12:18, 31; that the Spirit is not known as an exorciser in Jewish sources (cf. SB IV:1, 532–535), but the 'finger of God' may be so attested (Deissmann, 309 n.5); and that 'finger' gives a direct allusion to the OT (Manson, Teaching, 82f.; F. Hauck, TDNT I, 528 n. 5; E. Schweizer, TDNT VI, 398; Ellis, 165; cf. Kümmel, 106 n. 3). On the other hand, it has been argued convincingly by C. S. Rodd ('Spirit or Finger', Exp.T 72, 1960–61, 157f.) that Luke has no greater predilection for adding references to the Spirit in the body of his Gospel than Matthew; cf. 20:42 par. Mt. 12:36. We need not, therefore be surprised if Luke has removed an original reference to the Spirit. There is no clear case where Matthew has added a reference to the Spirit to his source. However, he does use πνεῦμα θεοῦ in 3:16 diff. Mk. (Schulz, 205). The case for Matthaean alteration thus falls short of proof, but on the whole it remains more likely that this is the case, since no good reason for a change by Luke can be found.

It is difficult to know whether ἐγώ should be read in this clause with p⁷⁵ B f13 *al* ff² l q r¹; UBS; (*Synopsis*); *Diglot*; its inclusion could be due to assimilation to Mt. or to v. 19, and the fact that the word appears in a transposed position in D *pc* may support the theory of insertion. (The transposition, however, may be due to assimilation to the word order in v. 19.)

The force of the main clause is determined by the meaning to be assigned to ἔφθασεν. The verb means 'to come before, to precede', 1 Thes. 4:15; 'to have just arrived', hence 'to arrive, come'; cf. Rom. 9:31; 2 Cor. 10:14; Phil. 3:16; 1 Thes. 2:16; G. Fitzer, TDNT IX, 88–92. Dodd, *Parables*, 44, argued that the phrase implied the arrival of the kingdom, and regarded the text as important evidence for his theory of 'realised eschatology'. Similar interpretations are defended by BD 101; Kümmel, 105–109. But this view has been disputed. J. Y. Campbell, 'The Kingdom of God has come', Exp.T 48, 1936–37, 91–94, suggested that we have a 'timeless' aorist with a future meaning: 'The kingdom of God will be upon you immediately', or that the phrase means 'The kingdom of God has come close upon you'. Dodd's reply to this claim ('The Kingdom of God has come', Exp.T 48, 1936–37, 138–142) gets the better of the argument. The matter was taken further by K. W. Clark, ' "Realized Eschatology" ', JBL 59, 1940, 367–383, who argued that the verb means 'to draw near, even to the very point of contact', but no more. It is, however, splitting hairs to take this to mean that the kingdom has not arrived. What is of significance is surely the addition ἐφ' ὑμᾶς; the point is that the kingly and saving power of God has drawn near to the hearers and is there for them to grasp; and the proof that it is near to them is that its power has been evidenced in the lives of other people, namely in the exorcisms. See further Schulz, 209–211; T. Lorenzmeier, 'Zum Logion Mt. 12, 28; Lk. 11, 20', in H.-D. Betz, 289–304; E. Grässer, 'Zum Verständnis der Gottesherrschaft', ZNW 65, 1974, 3–26.

(21) The fourth part of Jesus' argument is the parable of the strong man. The wording differs considerably from that in Mk., which is followed by Matthew. There do not appear to be any contacts between Lk. and Mt. here. Hence the problem is whether Luke has followed a version in Q which Matthew decided not to use (Schürmann, *Paschamahlbericht*, 2) or has himself elaborated the Marcan parable (Klostermann; S. Légasse*; Lindars, 84f.; cf. Lührmann, 33). The latter

supposition is unlikely: both Luke and Matthew have the saying in 11:23, which is from Q (not Mk.) and whose position here can be accounted for only if both writers were following the order in Q (Schweizer, *Matthäus*, 185). It is unlike Luke to rewrite Mk. so extensively. It is by no means impossible that Matthew should prefer the version in Mk. to that in Q. There remains, however, the difficulty that the Lucan form with its allusions to the LXX gives the impression of being a later development of the simpler parable in Mk. Such development could, however, have taken place in Luke's source, or just possibly we have to do with two independent sayings of Jesus.

The form of the saying is parabolic. *ὁ ἰσχυρός* is therefore to be taken generically, 'a strong man'. *καθοπλίζω*** is 'to arm fully, to equip'. For *τὴν ἑαυτοῦ αὐλήν* p⁴⁵ D lat; *Diglot* have *τὴν αὐλὴν αὐτοῦ*, but the construction in the text is Lucan and has better MS support. *αὐλή* (22:55*) can be 'house' or 'palace' here (in 22:55*, 'courtyard'), probably the latter. *τὰ ὑπάρχοντα* (8:3) is Lucan and *ἐν εἰρήνῃ* is a Septuagintalism, 'out of danger' (AG).

(22) *ἐπάν* (11:34; Mt. 2:8**) introduces a future temporal clause, and may be Lucan. *ἰσχυρότερος* is generic, since we are still in the realm of the parabolic, and hence the addition of *ὁ* in A C W *pm*; TR; *Diglot*, which makes the identification with the Messiah explicit, is secondary. *ἐπέρχομαι* is here used in a hostile sense (contrast 1:35). Once the strong man has been overcome (*νικάω**), it is possible to strip him of his armour and his possessions. *πανοπλία* (Eph. 6:11, 13**) is a 'full set of armour'; although there is no corresponding word in Hebrew, the word is used in 2 Sa. 2:21 LXX and 4 Mac. 3:12A. Luke's use of it is no more Hellenistic than the LXX or Josephus (Bel. 2:649; *et al.*), but the word may be his own choice, perhaps under the influence of *καθοπλίζω* (S. Légasse*; cf. K. G. Kuhn, TDNT V, 300). There may be the thought of trust in human resources, which are weak compared with the power of God, in the use of *πείθω*; cf. Ps. 20:7 and references to trusting in riches, Ps. 49:6; Pr. 11:28. *σκῦλα*** (usually plural), originally the weapons of a defeated foe, and then 'booty, spoil' generally, is here used in the latter sense. In conjunction with *διαδίδωμι*, 'to distribute' (18:22; Acts 4:35; Jn. 6:11**), it may be an echo of Is. 49:24f. and 53:12, following the MT rather than the LXX (cf. J. Jeremias, TDNT V, 713; Lindars, 85).

How is the parable to be interpreted? The simple form in Mk. states that a person must first bind a strong man before he can plunder his house. The application is generally taken to be that Jesus' 'plundering' of Satan by releasing men from the control of his demons presupposes that he has overcome Satan (and hence cannot be casting out the demons by the power of Satan). It is not clear whether the victory over Satan is to be identified with the wilderness experience or with the still-future crucifixion and resurrection, or is deliberately left vague. The Lucan form has a fuller meaning. It emphasises that the goods of the strong man are safe so long as there is not a stronger man around. It also emphasises that victory over him leads not only to the capture of his weapons, so that henceforward he is helpless, but also to the distribution of what he amassed. Although a case has been made out that the stronger man represents God (Percy, 181–187), it is more likely that the reference – at least in the eyes of Luke and his source (cf. the context, 11:20, 23) – is to Jesus. If so, the Lucan form of the parable makes all the more explicit the new era which has been inaugurated by Jesus, with the contrast between the period of Satan's power and his weakness. Further, Luke's form stresses the blessings that accrue to others from the distribution of Satan's booty; it would be wrong to press the metaphor so that the booty represents the prisoners released from Satan (cf. 13:16; W. Grundmann, TDNT III, 397–402, especially 399–401), but the general idea remains unaffected. Finally, it is noteworthy that whereas Mark's picture is of burglary, Luke's is of battle, and has as its background the OT idea of God armed as a hero for battle against his enemies (Is. 59:16–18) and the Qumranic concept of the messianic war (cf. O. Betz, 'Jesu heiliger Krieg', Nov.T 2, 1957, 116–137). S. Légasse* claims that Luke has developed the story to show the victory of Jesus over riches and those who put their trust in them, but there is, as we have seen, no indication in the story that the strong man· trusts in riches. Rather, there may be the thought that what is selfishly amassed by Satan is redistributed by Jesus. Danker, 138–140, claims that in Lk. the strong man is Israel which does not realise the source of her peace (19:41–44) in God and is in danger of being overpowered by Satan. This interpretation fits in with the following verses 23, 24–26, which also deal with Israel, but it lacks a convincing basis in the text.

(23) The fifth element in the sayings complex is a statement which speaks of the impossibility of neutrality in the strife between Jesus and Satan which has been revealed in the previous sayings. To criticise Jesus is to be opposed to him. The saying is found with the same wording in Mt. 12:30, and is manifestly from Q; it corresponds in function to Mk. 3:28. It may originally have been a detached saying, but it fits so well into its context that this assumption is unnecessary. The first half of the saying is perfectly clear, and stands in paradoxical relation to 9:50; both statements are true in their respective contexts. The second half of the saying uses the metaphor of gathering a flock together (Easton, 181); a person who does not help in this task is helping the flock to scatter (σκορπίζω, Mt. 12:30; Jn. 10:12; 16:32; 2 Cor. 9:9**). The addition of με in ℵ Θ pc syˢ bo^pt supplies a transitive verb with an inappropriate object; it is a scribal blunder (Metzger, 158).

(24) The sixth and final part of Jesus' reply to his critics is the description of the man who loses one evil spirit only to find that seven worse ones accompany the original spirit back into him. The precise point of the saying is not clearly stated, and a decision on this matter is complicated by uncertainty regarding the positioning of the saying. The saying appears in almost identical wording in Mt. 12:43–45, but with the

addition of an application, 'so shall it be with this evil generation', which indicates that the saying is to be taken parabolically (cf. B. Noack, *Satanas und Soteria*, 65f.); Further, in Mt. the saying comes after the sayings about the sign of Jonah and the queen of the south (Mt. 12:38–42) which follow it in Lk. 11:29–32; both Gospels include other material in the same context. It is probable that the order in Lk. was that in Q, and that Matthew has moved the saying to what seemed to him to be a more appropriate position (Bultmann, 11; Lührmann, 34; Schulz, 476 n. 562), although it could be argued that Luke has put an originally detached saying in what seemed to him to be a more suitable context.

Luke appears to understand the saying literally, with direct reference to the situation of a person who has been exorcised of a demon (J. M. Hull, *Hellenistic Magic and the Synoptic Tradition*, 102). The unspoken point is then generally thought to be a warning against the danger of failing to prevent the re-entry of an exorcised demon by filling the empty 'house' with a new inhabitant. The problem is whether this point should not have been made more clearly in the saying itself.

There is another possibility. In its present context the saying appears to have the same kind of warning significance as it has in Mt. It may be a warning to those who exorcise demons without giving a positive substitute to their patients. Those who do not take the side of Jesus and commend his teaching are merely making matters worse, scattering instead of gathering. It is not sufficient to cast out demons if there is no acceptance of the kingdom whose presence is attested by the expulsion of the demons. So the saying may be a criticism of the Jews who practise exorcisms, but do not take the side of Jesus and thereby make the situation worse. Understood in this way, the saying forms the climax of Jesus' argument in which he carries the war into the enemy camp by asserting that those who refuse his message, as attested by the exorcisms, are creating a worse situation (cf. Lagrange, 333f.; Schulz, 479f.).

Luke has no connective with what precedes, diff. Mt. δέ. ὅταν simply means 'when', but the case described is a general one; similarly, τὸ ... πνεῦμα has generic force. For πνεῦμα as an evil spirit cf. 4:43, and for ἐξέρχομαι as a virtual passive cf. 11:14. ἄνυδρος (Mt. 12:43; 2 Pet. 2:17; Jude 12**) is 'waterless, dry'. In the OT demons are found in deserted cities (Is. 13:21; 34:14; Bar. 4:35; Rev. 18:2; cf. SB IV:1, 516); the point is perhaps not the dryness but the absence of men from such desert regions, so that the demon cannot find anywhere to rest (ἀνάπαυσις, used concretely). (Mk. 5:13 might suggest that demons prefer wet haunts, a superstition attested in very late Jewish sources (SB IV:1, 517f.), but more probably the water is a means of destroying them.) After εὑρίσκον some MSS add τότε (p⁷⁵ B Θ al b l sa bo), probably by assimilation to Mt. (Metzger, 158). Since τότε is a favourite word of Matthew, Luke probably has the original text of Q. But ὑποστρέφω is probably secondary compared with Mt. ἐπιστρέφω. The spirit regards the human body as a dwelling place (οἶκος). ὅθεν is 'from where' (Acts 14:26; 28:13; 'wherefore', Acts 26:19). The demon no doubt would *not* regard ἐξῆλθον as a virtual passive!

(25) In v. 24 εὑρίσκον has conditional force. The conditional sense continues in v. 25 expressed in paratactical style. The parable does not, therefore, mean that the spirit will necessarily find its former home vacant; it describes what will happen if this is the case. H. S. Nyberg, 'Zum grammatischen Verständnis von Matth. 12, 44f.', *Coniectanea Neotestamentica* 13, 1949, 1–11, regards v. 25 as a paratactic conditional protasis to v. 26. Beyer I:1, 281–286, is critical of this view, and claims that we have the story of a possible contingency told as if it had once happened; the intention is to convey a general truth, but the conditional character of the circumstances has become obscured. The demon finds its former dwelling swept clean and tidied. σαρόω is a late form for σαίρω (15:8; Mt. 12:44**). κοσμέω is 'to decorate' (21:5; Mt. 23:29; Rev. 21:19) or 'to put in order' (Mt. 25:7). Matthew's text includes the participle, σχολάζοντα, which is included in Lk. by B C f1 565 *al* f1 r¹ bo, but is probably due to assimilation to Mt. (Metzger, 158f.).

(26) If the house is unoccupied, the spirit now comes and brings with it (Mt. adds μεθ' ἑαυτοῦ) seven even worse spirits: note how Luke uses ἑπτά as a climax. The eight spirits together will be better able to resist exorcism (κατοικέω). J. M. Hull, op. cit. 103f., thinks that the eight form a unity as a multiform type of demon. So the man finishes up in a worse condition (2 Pet. 2:20).

The saying may be understood to some extent against the background of the idea of the two spirits or impulses which may inhabit a man (cf. 1QS 3:18 – 4:26); when the good impulse fails to gain admission, the way is open for further tyranny by evil. But the evil impulse is not quite the same concept as a host of demons, and the parallel should not be pressed, although it does point towards the nature of the positive action which the man has failed to take.

ii. True Blessedness 11:27–28

The brief dialogue which follows the discourse of Jesus has the form of a simple pronouncement story (Bultmann, 11). The point therefore lies in the saying of Jesus in which he commends those who hear and do the word of God. For Luke the word of God is the teaching of Jesus, so that the saying forms a suitable conclusion to the preceding discourse: Jesus' critics should receive and obey his sayings instead of attacking his mighty works. The saying by the woman has little positive importance in the present context (although Catholic scholars assess it more positively: Lagrange, 336, McHugh, 347). But the incident, which is to be regarded as a unity, is not necessarily in its original historical context, and when taken by itself it contrasts physical relationship with Jesus with spiritual relationship; cf. Mk. 3:31–35. Although Jewish parallels can be cited in which similar statements are made about the mother of the Messiah, this motif does not appear to be present here.

The incident does not appear in Mt., but both Mk. and Mt. have the story of the visit of Jesus' mother and brethren at the end of the Beelzebul controversy in the same position as the present narrative (Mk. 3:31–35; Mt. 12:46–50). Luke has already used this incident at 8:19–21. It seems probable that he therefore substituted this similar story for it here. The question then arises whether the present story was taken from Q (Schürmann, *Untersuchungen*, 231) or some other source or was created by Luke. There are no indications that Matthew knew this story, although it is possible that he simply omitted it in favour of the parallel in Mk. (cf. 11:21 note). Easton, 184, has observed how appropriately this story would have followed 10:38–42, which in his view is Luke's last extract from L; if so, it could be from L material. There is no strong reason for regarding it as a Lucan creation; the Lucanisms in it may simply be due to editorial revision.

Finally, there is the question whether the story is a doublet of the one in Mk. which has the same basic theme, a possibility raised by D. F. Strauss (in Bultmann, 30), and supported by Wellhausen, 59; Klostermann, 127f.; Easton, 184. Bultmann, however, has pointed out that the themes are not identical, for the transmutation of the idea of kinship in Mk. is not present in Lk., and that there is no literary connection between the narratives. This is the more probable verdict on the situation. There is no reason why Jesus should not have said substantially the same thing on two different occasions. It should be added that there is no good reason for supposing that the occasion is an imaginary one.

The incident appears in a secondary form in G. Thomas 79.

(27) The opening phraseology is typically Lucan; the similarity of the link to Mt. 12:46 is probably coincidental. For the use of ἐπαίρω (6:20) with φωνήν see Acts 2:14; 14:11; 22:22; cf. Lk. 17:13; Acts 4:24. The order of words τις φωνὴν γυνή is unusual (but cf. 18:18; Rom. 1:11); BD 473[1] suggests that the purpose is to put unemphatic words as near the beginning of the clause as possible. The order τις γυνὴ φωνήν is found in A C W Γ Δ Θ f1 *pl*; TR; *Diglot*. For the presence of the crowd cf. 11:14: Luke envisages one connected scene.

The woman's statement is similar in form to 1:45; 14:15. It forms an elaborate reference to the mother of Jesus. For κοιλία (1:15) in this sense cf. Gn. 49:25; P. Ab. 2:8. βαστάζω (7:14; *et al.*) occurs here only in the sense 'to bear (children)'; there does not appear to be any parallel to this meaning in the LXX or secular Greek. μαστός is 'breast' (23:29; Rev. 1:13**), and θηλάζω is 'to suck', 'to give suck' (21:23; par. Mt. 24:19 and Mk. 13:17; Mt. 21:16**). The whole saying simply means, 'Happy is the mother of such a son', or 'Such a mother must have been especially blessed by God'. But there may also be the implied thought, 'If only I could have had such a son' (Easton, 184). For parallels cf. 2 Bar.

54:10; Gn. R. 98 (62d); Hag. 49b (SB I, 663f.; II, 187). There is a similar saying about the mother of the Messiah in Pesiq. 149a (SB I, 161), but it would be sheer speculation to find in the present saying an implicit confession of Jesus as Messiah, since the point of the saying is quite different.

(28) For Jesus emphatically corrects the woman's statement with his μενοῦν**, 'nay, rather' (cf. μενοῦνγε, Rom. 9:20; et al.; BD 400⁴). For φυλάσσω in the sense of keeping God's word or law cf. 18:21 par. Mk. 10:20; Jn. 12:47; Acts 7:53; 21:24; Rom. 2:26; et al. For the general sentiment of the verse cf. 8:21 par. Mk. 3:34f.; Lk. 6:46–49 par. Mt. 7:24–27; Rom. 2:13; Jn. 13:17; 15:14; Jas. 1:22.

iii. The Sign of Jonah 11:29–32

Luke has already told us of a request from certain members of the crowd for a heavenly sign from Jesus. Jesus now replies to this request in the second main part of his answer to the criticisms brought against him. Having already mentioned the request, Luke has to reformulate the beginning of the paragraph by a fresh reference to the presence of the crowds. The saying itself appears to come from Q material, since there is a parallel to it in Mt. 12:38–42. There are two significant differences in the wording. In Mt. the meaning of the sign of Jonah is expressed more fully (12:40); while most scholars regard this as being due to a Matthaean addition, it has been argued by France, 80–82, that it stood in Q, in which case Luke has abbreviated his source. The order of the sayings about the queen of the south and the men of Nineveh is also reversed in Mt., and it seems likely that here Matthew has reversed the original sequence in order to bring the references to Jonah and the Ninevites together. The differences can accordingly be accounted for satisfactorily on the hypothesis of a single source.

There is also, however, a parallel saying in Mk. 8:11f. par. Mt. 16:1–4, which in its Marcan form denies that Jesus will give a sign at all and makes no reference to Jonah. The general assumption in recent studies is that we have to do with two traditions of one basic saying. A. Vögtle* adopts the view that the original saying is to be found in Lk. 11:29 which simply states that only the sign of Jonah will be given (cf. Schulz, 252). Mk. 8:12 (which gives the original wording, as is demonstrated by its Semitisms) represents an abbreviation of this saying: the sign of Jonah means 'no sign at all'; the sayings in Lk. 11:30 and Mt. 12:40 give different forms of an explanation of the saying found in Q, in which the parousia is the intended sign, and the resurrection is regarded as pointing towards it. A different explanation is offered by R. A. Edwards*, who holds that the Marcan form is original, and that the reference to the sign of Jonah in the Q parallel was created as a result of the juxtaposition of the Marcan saying with the double saying about the queen of the south and the men of Nineveh; this was supplemented by the saying in Lk. 11:30 par. Mt. 12:40 which has a form identified by Edwards as an 'eschatological correlative' (cf. Lk. 17:24, 26, 28, 30; Mt. 13:34f.; cf. Lk. 12:8, 39f.): thus for Q the sign is the assumption of Jesus, the preacher, to the right hand of God as the coming judge.

Edwards fails to justify his assumptions that the original 'no sign' saying and the double saying were juxtaposed in Q before the reference to the 'sign of Jonah' was inserted, and that this juxtaposition would have led to the creation of the phrase 'the sign of Jonah' and the following explanation of it. Further, his claim that the eschatological correlative construction does not stem from Jesus, and that the Son of man christology is later than Jesus is unjustified. His thesis is, therefore, to be rejected.

The original form of the tradition, then, probably included the reference to the sign of Jonah, and this has been omitted by Mark or the strand of tradition which reached him. Opinion is divided whether Mt. 12:40 or Lk. 11:30 represents the original form of the 'explanation' of the saying. Mt. 12:40 has been regarded as an expansion of a less explicit saying by a commentator (such as Matthew himself) who noted detailed correspondences between the career of Jesus and the OT, while Lk. 11:30 can be explained as an abbreviation of the fuller form in Mt. to avoid misunderstanding regarding the actual length of Jesus' period in the tomb. In either case, the sign will be the attestation of the preaching of Jesus by the resurrection or the parousia, seen as a divine vindication of his message.

The double saying about the queen of the south and the men of Nineveh is less problematic. The two statements contrast the success of two OT preachers to the gentiles with the way in which the Jews fail to appreciate the message of one who is superior to both wise man and prophet. The whole group of sayings may form an original unity (cf. Schweizer, *Matthäus*, 188–190), but it is also possible that the two sets of sayings were brought together by catchword links.

See J. Jeremias, TDNT III, 406–410; A. Vögtle, 'Der Spruch vom Jonaszeichen', in Vögtle, 103–136 (originally in Schmid, *Studien*, 230–277); K. H. Rengstorf, TDNT VII, 233–236; Higgins, 133–140; Tödt, 52–54, 211–214; Perrin, 191–195; C. Colpe, TDNT VIII, 449f.; Lührmann, 34–42; R. A. Edwards, *The Sign of Jonah in the Theology of the Evangelists and Q*, London, 1971; France, 43–45, 80–82; Schulz, 250–257; H. Schürmann, in Pesch, *Jesus*, 133–135.

(29) The request for a sign which is found in the parallel passages has already been recorded by Luke at v. 16 and so is omitted here. It is not clear whether the opening reference to the crowds is from Q (since Matthew's introductory reference to the Pharisees could be due to assimilation to Mk. 8:11) or is a new formulation by Luke, but the latter view is more probable (Manson, *Sayings*, 89).

ἐπαθροίζω**, 'to collect besides, in addition', is found here only but is probably Lucan (cf. 24:33; Acts 12:12; 19:25).

The opening words of Jesus differ from Mt. For γενεά cf. 1:48 and especially 7:31. Matthew speaks of 'an evil and adulterous generation' (cf. Mt. 16:4). Luke speaks of 'this generation' (par. Mk.) and predicates that it is evil. Since the temptation would have been to add αὕτη under the influence of the parallel passage, it is perhaps more probable that Luke has here added it, and also that he has omitted μοιχαλίς, which would not have been intelligible to gentile readers. The wickedness of the contemporaries of Jesus is seen in their demand for a sign, since it represents a refusal to hear and obey the word of God brought by Jesus. For ζητεῖ Matthew has ἐπιζητεῖ, but the linguistic evidence is insufficent to determine which word stood in the source; Luke may again have been influenced by Mk. On σημεῖον (2:12, 34; 11:16) see K. H. Rengstorf, TDNT VII, 200–261, especially 233f. Some kind of divine authentication of the message of Jesus is being sought. The exorcisms could be regarded as the work of Satan: something unequivocal is being demanded. Jesus' response to the request is that no sign will be given. This is expressed in stronger terms in Mk. in an ἀμήν saying with a Hebrew oath form. It is an absolute refusal to give such a sign. In Q, however, the saying continues with an addition, 'except for the sign of Jonah (Mt. adds, the prophet)', i.e. the sign which consists in Jonah (cf. Is. 8:18; 20:3; Ezk. 12:6). Now the wording in Mk. with its absolute negative represents a Hebrew oath form, which does not exist in Aramaic (MH II, 468f.). It appears, therefore, that at this point Mark's formulation may be secondary to that in Q which represents a normal Aramaic form of a qualified absolute negative (Mt. 15:24; Mk. 2:17; et al.; A. Kuschke, 'Das Idiom der "relativen Negation" im NT', ZNW 43, 1950–51, 263).

(30) In order to ascertain the nature of this sign, we must take v. 30 into consideration, since it offers us insight at least into Luke's understanding of the preceding verse. It states quite simply that in the same way as Jonah himself was a sign to the people of Nineveh so the Son of man will be a sign to this generation. The saying is parallel in form to Mt. 12:40. Where Luke has καθώς (1:2 and frequently; Mt., 3x), Matthew has ὥσπερ (Mt., 10x; Lk., 2x); if a source is being used, it is probable that Matthew has altered its wording. Luke's ἐγένετο will be original if Matthew has substituted ἦν in expanding the verse from Jon. 2:1, but this remains an open question. Before Ἰωνᾶς, ὁ is read by B pc; (Synopsis); it could be due to dittography, or alternatively be an elegant anaphoric use of the article lost in other MSS by haplography. The order τοῖς Νινευΐταις σημεῖον is inverted in p45 A D W Θ f1 f13 pl lat; TR; Diglot. The καί before ὁ υἱὸς τοῦ ἀνθρώπου (diff. Mt.) is probably original (12:8; 17:26; Mt. 17:11; Mk. 8:38). According to this saying, then, the Son of man will be a sign to this generation in the same way as Jonah was to the Ninevites. It can be assumed that for Luke the Son of man is Jesus. A difficulty for interpretation is caused by the future tense ἔσται. This has been traditionally understood as a real future, in which case it points forward to some event following the ministry of Jesus,

perhaps even to the parousia of the Son of man (cf. 17:24, 26, 28, 30; Mt. 13:40f.; R. A. Edwards*, 49–51). But it may also be understood as a logical future, parallel to δοθήσεται in v. 29 (Schulz, 256 n. 545). In v. 32 the comparison of Jesus with Jonah is in the present tense: a greater than Jonah *is* here. If we adopt this latter alternative, the sign may be regarded as the preaching of Jesus (Manson, *Sayings*, 90f.; Schulz, 255–257) or the person of Jesus himself as the One through whom God is at work (K. H. Rengstorf, TDNT VII, 233f.). But what the Jews are asking for is some divine accreditation of Jesus' message, and a reference to Jonah hardly conveys the point that the preaching is meant to be self-authenticating. The reference must be to the outstanding feature in the story of Jonah, which would at once spring to the mind of every reader, namely his miraculous deliverance from death (J. Jeremias, TDNT III, 409; Vögtle, 111–115). The fact that we have no record that Jonah spoke about this to the Ninevites is not a serious objection: it is the picture of Jonah in the mind of Jesus' contemporaries which is significant, and to them he was the person who preached in Nineveh after a miraculous intervention by God. The corresponding feature in the mission of Jesus will be his future vindication by God as the Son of man. It is true that in the case of Jesus this *follows* the preaching, rather than precedes it, as in the case of Jonah, but this is not a serious difficulty, especially if Luke is thinking of the preaching authorised by Jesus which followed his resurrection (cf. 24:47). That Luke interpreted the saying of the resurrection is confirmed by 16:30f.; Acts 1:3; 17:31 (cf. Lagrange, 337f.). To be sure, the Jews did not themselves see this sign, a point regarded by Vögtle, 120, as an objection to this interpretation, but then neither did the Ninevites witness the resuscitation of Jonah. The sign also remains one that may not be accepted as such, but this is of the nature of biblical signs. The alternative is to see a reference to the future coming of Jesus as the Son of man at the parousia (cf. 17:26; Bultmann, 124; Schniewind, *Matthäus*, 162; Higgins, 138; Tödt, 52–54; C. Colpe, TDNT VIII, 449f.). The difficulty with this view is that the sign comes too late to confirm belief in the message of Jesus (cf. Tödt, 53).

Matthew's interpretation was essentially the same as Luke's. Since it is difficult to see why Luke should have deleted a clear reference to the death and resurrection of Jesus from his source (unless he found the mention of three days and nights difficult) and produced a somewhat enigmatic statement, it is more probable that Matthew (or his tradition) expanded the saying to bring out the correspondence between the experience of Jonah and Jesus.

There is no great difficulty about attributing the basic statement in v. 29 to Jesus himself, especially in the light of v. 32. The detailed arguments adduced by Schulz, 253 n. 534, against the pericope as a whole rest on arbitrary and improbable assumptions, and they certainly do not affect the authenticity of v. 29. The Q form is primitive compared with that in Mk. 8:11; Mark may well have reckoned that a sign which did not occur during the ministry was no sign at all; possibly in line with his understanding of the 'messianic secret' he wished to underline the point that Jesus offered no hint of divine legitimation of himself to the Jews until the trial scene with its prophecy of divine vindication.

V. 30 is sufficiently enigmatic in content to be an original saying of Jesus. Its difficulty lies in the fact that it does not explain v. 29 in any tangible way, beyond making clear that it is the Son of man who is to be the sign to Israel. The saying implicitly identifies Jesus as the Son of man, but it does so in cryptic fashion. If Jesus did identify himself with the Son of man, there is no reason to deny the authenticity of this saying. It is much less likely that it was created to link vs. 29 and 31f. (*pace* Lührmann, 41) or as an expansion of v. 29 (C. Colpe, ibid). Schweizer, *Matthäus*, holds that the entire pericope vs. 29–32 may stem from Jesus, with v. 32 indicating how at the last judgment the men of Nineveh who accepted the sign of Jonah will confirm the sign of the Son of man to the unbelieving Israelites.

(31) Luke's ordering of the two sayings about the queen of the south and the men of Nineveh is to be preferred; he would not have altered the Matthaean order so as to separate the two references to Nineveh, unless by so doing he wished to get the climax of repentance in 32 as against merely hearing Solomon. For βασίλισσα, 'queen' cf. Mt. 12:42; Acts 8:27; Rev. 18:7**; νότος is 'south wind' (12:55; Acts 27:13; 28:13), hence 'south' (13:29; Rev. 21:13), and here 'south land' (Mt. 12:42**). The description appears to be a unique way of referring to the queen of Sheba (LXX Σαβά; cf. 1 Ki. 10:1–13; 2 Ch. 9:1–12), i.e. probably the Yemen in S. Arabia. The verb ἐγείρω may refer to being raised from the dead to appear at the last judgment. Following earlier scholars, J. Jeremias, TDNT III, 408 n. 15, and Black, 134, argue that ἐγείρω μετά is equivalent to *qûm 'im* i.e. 'to rise up in judgment with, to accuse', and that ἐν τῇ κρίσει has been added to make the meaning clear. This view gives a better sense to ἐν with τῇ κρίσει, and, although a literal reference to resurrection disappears, the imagery remains that of the last judgment and presupposes the resurrection of the men of the past to take part in it. After μετά Luke has τῶν ἀνδρῶν, diff. Mt., which may be intended to draw a contrast with the queen (feminine; Easton, 185). The addition is probably Lucan. κατακρίνω will mean 'to bring a charge' (*hayyēb*), rather than 'to pronounce judgment'. The queen came from the 'end' (πέρας, Mt. 12:42; Rom. 10:18; Heb. 6:16**) of the earth to hear Solomon (1 Ki. 10:4, 6f.) who was famed for his splendour (12:27) and his wisdom. How much more should men respond to Jesus, since here there is something 'more' than Solomon. The fact that πλεῖον appears in the neuter raises the question whether a simple contrast between Solomon and Jesus is meant. But the neuter can be used where the emphasis is less on the individual than on a general quality (MH III, 21), and this is the case here where it is the wisdom spoken by Solomon which is being contrasted with that uttered by Jesus. The saying

obviously does not identify Jesus with divine wisdom, but makes him the speaker of wisdom; only in the light of other sayings is he to be regarded as himself Wisdom (cf. Christ, 62). Our saying forms part of a series in which the claim of Jesus to be the fulfilment of the OT wisdom tradition is to be found.

(32) In the same way Jesus is the consummation of the OT series of prophets, and the second saying contributes to this picture by claiming that in him there is something greater than Jonah. In the actual saying ἀνίστημι is synonymous with ἐγείρω in v. 31. For the repentance of the Ninevites see Jon. 3:6–10; for the use of εἰς, 'at, because of' cf. BD 207¹. Both sayings thus contrast the appeal of the word of God to gentiles in OT times with the failure of Jesus' contemporaries to respond to the clearer revelation given by him (cf. 7:9).

iv. Light and Darkness 11:33–36

Before the new topic of the specific dangers of Pharisaism is introduced (11:37–54) Luke brings this controversial section to an end with a closing admonition on the need for those who hear Jesus to respond to his teaching instead of continuing in the darkness of ignorance. Jesus (or his message of the kingdom) is like a light which illuminates those who enter a house. There is nothing hidden about this light. Any lack of illumination is due to the recipient: if he has a sound eye, the light will enter his whole being, but if his eye is evil, no light will enter. Let Jesus' hearers, then, beware lest the light they think they have within them is really darkness. But if they are truly possessed by the light now, they will receive the illumination of the heavenly light of Jesus at the final judgment.

The two sayings which appear here have been taken from Q. The former (v. 33) has a doublet in 8:16 par. Mk. 4:21, where the lamp represents Jesus or his message and the thought is of the future missionary work of the disciples. The parallel in Mt. 5:15 is from the same source as the present form of the saying, and is applied to the need for disciples to let their light shine before men in Christian witness. The use of the saying in the present context is different. It is not clear whether the present saying was originally linked with the preceding section, 11:29–32 (cf. F. Hahn*, 132–134), but it is probable that Luke saw a connection. Wrege's suggestion (114) that the connection is that it is as foolish to hide a lamp as to ask for a sign from Jesus is artificial. The point is rather that God has given in Jesus a light which is not hidden (so that a sign would be needed to confirm his message) but which is sufficiently clear to give light to all (Lagrange, 339; Klostermann, 129; Easton, 185f.; Grundmann, 243).

The second saying (v. 34–36) has a partial parallel in Mt. 6:22f. which again suggests use of a common source (Q). The basis of the saying is the antithesis in v. 34b with the introduction in v. 34a. This appears to have been followed by an application in two antithetical parts, preserved in Mt. 6:23b (cf. Lk. 11:35) and Lk. 11:36 (F. Hahn*, 114–117). It is often thought that v. 36 is a Lucan addition to the saying (Schulz, 469), but it is much more probable that it is from Q and has been omitted by Matthew because of its obscurity or because of his rearrangement of the sayings (Manson, *Sayings*, 93f.; Wrege, 114; F. Hahn*, 114–117, 127–132). The point is that the entry of light to the 'body' depends on the eye which functions as a lamp. In Mt. 6:22f. the saying appears to be interpreted in terms of generous and avaricious attitudes, but here the thought is of reception of the light of the gospel; it is a call to self-examination and contains the promise of full illumination for those who respond to Jesus. V. 36 thus links vs. 34f. with v. 33 to give a thematic connection and a christological point. This connection is pre-Lucan, but it is not clear whether it goes back to Jesus himself; most scholars regard the application of the saying in vs. 35f. as a secondary elaboration.

See bibliography to 8:16–18; C. Edlund, *Das Auge der Einfalt*, Copenhagen, 1952; E. Sjöberg, 'Das Licht in dir (Zur Deutung von Matth. 6, 22f. Par.)', ST 5, 1952, 89–105; Schulz, 474–476, 468–470.

(33) Luke's wording of the parable is close to 8:16 but closer still to Mt. 5:15. It is hard to say whether the third person singular form is secondary as compared with the plural in Mt. 5:15 (cf. G. Schneider*, 184f.; Schulz, 474 n. 553; but see F. Hahn*, 111 n. 11). ἅπτω is Lucan (8:16 note). Luke has a new element in his use of κρύπτη**. This refers to a hidden, and hence dark place. This is often taken to refer to the cellar which would form part of a substantial Hellenistic house (Dodd, *Parables*, 106 n. 32) in contrast to the one-roomed Galilean peasant's cottage. This is doubtful, since a cellar is the very place where a light would be required – unless the point is that a light in the cellar offers no illumination in the main part of the house. The point is simply that the light is placed in a hidden location; the phrase may be a Lucan variant for ὑποκάτω κλίνης (8:16). Alternatively, the lamp may be placed under a measuring vessel. μόδιος (Mt. 5:15; Mk. 4:21**; diff. Lk. 8:16 σκεῦος) is a peck measure (8.75 litres), but the word can be used for any similar vessel (Jeremias, *Abba*, 101). This may have been used to extinguish the light, so that its fumes would not spread through the room (Jeremias, ibid., with rabbinic parallels; *pace* Derrett, 192 n. 3, whose reconstruction of the background in terms of the Hanukkah festival is not convincing). The phrase οὐδὲ ὑπὸ τὸν μόδιον, however, is textually uncertain in Lk., being omitted by p⁴⁵ p⁷⁵ L Ξ 0124 f1 700 *al* syˢ sa; (UBS); *Diglot*; NEB; it could be due to assimilation to the parallels, but the structure of Mk. 4:21 suggests that the original wording had two phrases, as here (of which Matthew has omitted one; cf. Metzger, 159). In place of φῶς, a number of authorities (p⁴⁵ A W 33 *pm*; TR; *Synopsis*; *Diglot*) have φέγγος (Mt. 24:29 par. Mk. 13:24**), 'light, radiance'; the UBS reading may be an assimilation to 8:16. For the significance of the parable, see

introduction. Its authenticity is indisputable (F. Hahn*, 112f.; *pace* Bultmann, 102, 107).

(34) In the second saying we have a different use and application of the term λύχνος. Here it is stated that light is given to the body by the eye which acts as a lamp to the interior in the sense that light enters the body by it; the eye is thought of as receiving light from outside the body (F. Hahn*, 126f.). The saying is not to be understood with crass literalness, since 'body' can mean the personality as a whole, especially in the phrase 'the whole body' in Aramaic (Manson, *Sayings*, 93, following G. Dalman). Two alternatives are presented. Matthew has preserved the parallelism better with ἐάν ... ἐάν ...; Luke is not over-fond of ἐάν (Mt., 66x; Mk., 39x; Lk., 29x; Acts, 11x) and has replaced it by ὅταν ... ἐπάν ... (cf. 11:22; *contra* Schulz, 468f.) ἁπλοῦς means 'simple, single, sincere'. It can thus mean 'generous' (Pr. 11:25; cf. Rom. 12:8). The corresponding Hebrew and Aramaic terms (*tāmîm* and *š ᵉlîl*) can mean 'healthy'. The meaning 'generous' fits the context in Mt. 6:22f., and corresponds to the antonym πονηρός which can mean 'malicious, grudging'. But, although this thought would have been congenial to Luke, there is no evidence of its presence here. We should probably take ἁπλοῦς as an over-literal translation of an Aramaic word, perhaps with a contrast to the idea of 'double vision'; the metaphorical sense of 'whole-hearted, single-minded' (T. Iss. 3:4; 4:6) is basic in the application (cf. O. Bauernfeind, TDNT I, 386; C. Edlund*, 19–79; Schulz, 470). If the eye is healthy and lets in light, i.e. if the person is single-mindedly receptive to the light of the gospel, then his whole being will be filled with light (φωτεινός, 'shining', 'illuminated'; 11:36; Mt. 6:22; 17:15**). πονηρός will then mean 'in poor condition, sick'; the sense 'grudging' (Mt. 6:23; cf. G. Harder, TDNT VI, 55f.) is probably too specific here (cf. W. Michaelis, TDNT V, 377). The thought is of refusal to receive the gospel.

(35) The application is now made. In Mt. 6:23b the saying functions as a warning, but in Lk. it has become an exhortation, introduced by σκοπέω 'to look out, to consider' (Rom. 6:17; 2 Cor. 4:18; Gal. 6:1; Phil. 2:4; 3:17**). μή with the indicative is interrogative and means 'whether'. The hearers are bidden to examine whether what they think to be light is really darkness (cf. Jn. 9:40f.). For the thought of light within a person see Pr. 20:27. Jeremias, *Parables*, 163, suggests that σκότος is a mistranslation of Aramaic *hᵃšāk* which can mean 'dark' as well as 'darkness', but this is unnecessary.

(36) This verse is peculiar to Lk., but it forms an antithesis to Mt. 6:23b; hence it is probable that Mt. 6:23b is original as compared with Lk. 11:35 and that Lk. 11:36 stems from Q. Its difficulty may have led to its omission by Matthew, and has caused confusion in the MS tradition. The verse takes up the alternative to v. 35, namely the situation when a person's whole being is full of light, without any dark patch. μέρος is 'part' (12:46; 15:12; 24:42*; cf. Acts 5:2). If the μὴ ἔχων ...

phrase is repetitious, the apodosis seems positively tautologous when it states that the body will be wholly light, just as when the light illuminates ($\phi\omega\tau\iota\zeta\omega$*) a person with its rays ($\dot{\alpha}\sigma\tau\rho\dot{\alpha}\pi\eta$, 10:18). 1. Manson, *Sayings*, 94, adopts the suggestion of mistranslation of an Aramaic original propounded by C. C. Torrey. The word *kōllā*, translated as an adjective ('whole') in the protasis, should be translated as a noun ('the whole', i.e. 'the world') in the apodosis and made the subject: 'If, however, your whole body is lighted up, with no part dark, then all about you will be light; just as the lamp lights you with its brightness'. Taken in this way, the verse refers to the light-giving quality of those who have been illuminated by Jesus and gives an equivalent to Mt. 5:14 (cf. G. Thomas 24). 2. The saying has been interpreted of people who have not seen Jesus and yet have light within themselves: 'When your body is completely light (through the "inner light"), then it is of itself just as light as when the lamp illuminates it with its brightness'. Those who do not have the good fortune to see the light (i.e. Jesus) can still be 'bright' provided that their inner light is in good order (J. Weiss, 467, with considerable hesitation). 3. 'If the heart is truly receptive of light, it will receive light from the true light when it shines, that is from Christ' (Is. 60:1; Creed, 164; cf. Zahn, 475f.; Schlatter, 517–519). F. Hahn*, 129–131, offers a variant of this view when he argues that the person who is illuminated now by the light which comes from Jesus (v. 33) will experience the full revelation of God's light at the consummation (cf. the use of $\ddot{\epsilon}\sigma\tau\alpha\iota$, a real future); the $\dot{\omega}\varsigma$ $\ddot{\delta}\tau\alpha\nu$ clause must also refer to the future). Since in v. 36a the body is already wholly light, the reference in v. 36b must be future, and Hahn's explanation gains in plausibility, although it must be confessed that the saying is so obscurely expressed that it is hard to be certain of its meaning.

v. The Hypocrisy of the Pharisees and Scribes 11:37–54

The preceding section was concerned with an attack made on Jesus and his reply to it. In the present section the starting point is again a criticism of Jesus, this time with regard to his failure to observe Pharisaic rules of religious cleanliness, but the reply of Jesus moves from the immediate point at issue to a full-scale attack on Pharisaic religion. It need not be doubted that the picture painted here is one of the dangers of Pharisaism, rather than a portrait of every single Pharisee. Nevertheless, the point is that any human form of religiosity, however virtuous in intention, can turn men away from God.

The attack is couched in the form of six woes, three directed to the Pharisees in general, and three to their scribes in particular, and their effect is cumulative. Jesus laments over the practices of the Pharisees which will bring them under divine judgment. He attacks the kind of religion which is concerned with outward purity but ignores inward greed and covetousness; if the Pharisees would only learn to free themselves from the latter by giving alms, the former element would take care of itself. The Pharisees were concerned with trivialities, and ignored the justice and love of God which should have been primary. They were filled with pride and self-importance as religious teachers. All of these were inward sins, with the result that the Pharisees were misleading the people who were not aware of their inner unfitness. Such accusations naturally affected the scribes who were of the Pharisaic persuasion, but they were also guilty on other counts as well (cf. H. F. Weiss, TDNT IX, 38). Their casuistry in the interpretation of the law made it difficult for men to keep. Like their fathers they were opposed to the prophets and refused to listen to their message. They fulfilled the prophecy regarding the slaying of prophets and apostles, and the price would be paid by this generation. Finally, they had effectively removed the key to true knowledge of God, and kept both themselves and others from entering into it. It is not surprising that after such a catalogue of criticisms the scribes and Pharisees had it in for Jesus.

Such is the content of the section as Luke has presented it. But the question of its origins is far from clear. There is a brief section in Mk. 12:38–40 which contains similar criticisms of the scribes for their pride, greed and hypocrisy; this passage is repeated in almost identical form in Lk. 20:46, but the present passage (see the verbal parallel in 11:43) is not based on it, and is drawn from Q (cf. Mt. 23:6). There is also a parallel in Mk. 7:1–9 on the question of ritual purity; Luke has omitted this section of Mk. as part of his 'great omission'. The problem is whether he himself has constructed the present introductory section on ritual purity (11:37f.) on the basis of Mk. 7 or has used another source which has not influenced Matthew. The former suggestion is unlikely, since there are no significant verbal correspondences. Now the saying in vs. 39–41 demands a setting and it is probable that Luke offers us the original one. Since Matthew has transferred the present discourse to a Marcan setting (Mt. 23) he had no need of the original Q setting. Similar considerations apply to 11:53f. This again could be a Lucan composition to close the section, but the presence of Lucanisms in it is not sufficient to prove this point, since Luke edits the openings and closings of sections rather thoroughly, and hence it may come from Q. Manson's view (*Sayings*, 94–96) that 11:37–41; 11:53 – 12:1 come from L is less likely.

Essentially the same teaching is found in Mt. 23, but the order and wording of the sayings is often very different. A comparison will be helpful:

Lk. 11		Mt. 23	
37f.	Introduction	–	
–		1–3	Introduction
39f.	Cleanliness (no 'Woe')		
		4	Burdens (no 'Woe')

Lk. 11		Mt. 23	
		5	Phylacteries
		6–7a	Pride (no 'Woe'; cf. Mk. 12:38f.)
		7b–12	Titles
		13	Key
		15	Proselytes
		16–22	Oaths
42	Tithes	23f.	Tithes
43	Pride		
		25f.	Cleanliness
44	Tombs	27f.	Tombs
45	Interjection		
46	Burdens		
47f.	Prophets	29–32	Prophets
		33	Vipers
49–51	Wisdom saying	34–36	Wisdom saying
	(13:34f.)	37–39	Lament
52	Key		
53f.	Conclusion		

Luke has an introductory saying (11:39f.; in 'woe' form in Mt.) followed by two sets of three woes. Matthew has an introductory section, which includes two of Luke's woes in non-'woe' form, followed by seven 'woe' sayings, two of which ('proselytes' and 'oaths') are not in Lk.

We know from his practice elsewhere that Matthew combines material from several sources and rearranges the order, whereas on the whole Luke does not conflate his sources or re-order his material. It is, therefore, unlikely that Matthew has preserved the original order here (*pace* Bultmann, 118–120). On the contrary, there is a good case that Luke has preserved something like the order in Q, and Matthew's changes can be understood in terms of his editorial activity (Schulz, 94 n. 5). Matthew begins with material from Mk., whose general structure is being followed at this point. It is clear that the similarity between Mk. 12:38f. and the corresponding Q saying on 'pride' (Lk. 11:43 par. Mt. 23:22) has led him to bring forward this saying. It can also be argued that he has brought forward the saying about 'burdens' (Lk. 11:46 par. Mt. 23:4) which fits in with his opening material (Mt. 23:3). In both cases he has removed the 'woe' form so as to accommodate the material in the opening statement. It is probable that the sayings about 'cleanliness' and 'tombs' (Lk. 11:39f. par. Mt. 23:25f.; Lk. 11:44 par. Mt. 23:27f.) have been brought together on a catchword principle ('tombs'). If Luke's introduction belongs to the source, then the 'cleanliness' saying must have stood at the beginning. The 'key' saying too (Lk. 11:52 par. Mt. 23:13) may also have been brought forward to link up with Mt. 23:15; its original position, however, is uncertain, since its placing in Lk. after the wisdom saying is odd. It is not clear whether the Q material contained seven sayings in 'woe' form, but this is possible if Lk. 11:39f. was originally in 'woe' form. Matthew has regained the number of seven woes by including other sayings from his special source material in this form. The division of the woes between the Pharisees and scribes in Lk. is probably original over against the stereotyped form given to all the woes in Mt. (Manson, *Sayings*, 96).

The differences in wording between the sayings are on occasion sufficiently great to suggest that different recensions of the material were available to the two Evangelists; if so, it is quite possible that the re-ordering of the material was also taking place at this stage.

Scholars tend to be sceptical about the amount of material in the section which can be traced back to Jesus himself (cf. Schweizer, *Matthäus*, 280). Some of the sayings reflect an attitude to Jewish legalism which is held to be more typical of rigid Jewish-Christian circles than of Jesus himself. So sceptical a verdict is unjustified. The basic criticisms of Pharisaism made here fit in with what we otherwise know of the attitude of Jesus himself. See the exegesis for further details.

The 'wisdom' saying in vs. 49–51 stands apart from the rest of the discourse; it probably formed the conclusion to it, as in Mt., but Luke has transferred the 'key' saying to the end to provide what he regarded as a more suitable conclusion; see below for fuller discussion of the critical problems.

See Manson, *Sayings*, 94–105, 227–240, 268–270; E. Haenchen, 'Matthäus 23', ZTK 48, 1951, 38–63; J. D. M. Derrett, ' "You build the Tombs of the Prophets" (Lk. 11, 47–51, Mt. 23, 29–31)', TU 103, 187–193; Lührmann, 43–48; Schulz, 94–114; J. Neusner, ' "First Cleanse the Inside" ', NTS 22, 1975–76, 486–495.

On vs. 49–51 see also Steck, 29–40, 50–53, 222–227; O. J. F. Seitz, 'The Commission of Prophets and "Apostles". A Re-examination of Mt. 23, 34 with Luke 11, 49', TU 103, 236–240; Christ, 120–135; Suggs, 13–29, 58–61; Hoffmann, 164–171; G. Klein, 'Die Verfolgung der Apostel. Lukas 11, 49', in Baltensweiler, 113–124; Schulz, 336–345.

(37) The scene is connected to what precedes by the ἐν τῷ construction (2:27 note). With the aorist infinitive we must translate: 'when he had finished speaking'; the subject αὐτόν is added in A *al; Diglot*; and αὐτὸν ταῦτα appears in Θ f1 *al*. Both readings look like attempts to clarify the text. The use of the historic present ἐρωτᾷ (ἠρώτα; TR; *Diglot*) may indicate that Luke is here using a source (cf. 11:45): for the usage with ὅπως cf. 7:3. After Φαρισαῖος the adjective τις is added by A C (D) Δ Θ *pm*; TR; *Diglot*. ἀριστάω is 'to eat', especially the first meal of the day (Jn. 21:12, 15**). Upper class Jews usually had two meals on weekdays, a light meal in mid-morning (ἄριστον), and a main meal in the late afternoon (δεῖπνον); a snack meal might also be taken before starting the day's work. Compare the Roman custom of having two meals, *prandium* and *cena*. Three meals were eaten on the Sabbath, the principal one being held about midday after the synagogue service (7:36; 14:1; cf. Jos. Vit. 279; Shabbath 16:2, SB I, 611–615; II, 202–206; IV:2, 611–639; Jeremias, *Words*, 44–46). The use of the word ἄριστον (v. 38; cf. 14:12) suggests, but does not demand that the earlier

meal of the day is meant. A Sabbath meal may well be meant. ἀναπίπτω is used especially of reclining at a meal (14:10; 17:7; 22:14; Mk. 6:40; 8:6 par. Mt. 15:35; Jn. 6:10; 13:12, 25; 21:20**; the word may be from Luke's source, Schürmann, *Paschamahlbericht*, 107f.). The meal setting may be from Luke's source (*contra* Ott. 36): the linguistic evidence shows merely that Luke has edited the opening verses of the scene, and there is no evidence that he has invented every meal setting in the Gospel.

(38) The Pharisee who invited him was astonished to see that Jesus did not follow the ritual practice of washing his hands before the meal (Mk. 7:2). Luke's use of βαπτίζω may just possibly be related to Mt. 23:26 diff. Lk. 11:41. For βαπτίζω in this sense cf. Mk. 7:4 and for the practice see Jn. 2:6 (cf. F. Hauck and R. Meyer, TDNT III, 413–426). The practice appears to have been a Pharisaic rule, and was not demanded by the OT law; Jesus and his disciples did not observe it, even in the house of a Pharisee. The motif is the same as in Mk. 7:1–5, but the wording and details are so different that literary dependence is unlikely.

(39) Jesus replies as ὁ κύριος (cf. 7:13; *et al.*). The saying is found in Mt. 23:25f. with considerable difference in wording and in the form of a 'woe'. Klostermann, 130, regards the 'woe' form as original; Luke avoids having Jesus begin the conversation with a woe directed against his host (Schulz, 95). This is possible, with νῦν as a Lucan replacement; νῦν is not found in this logical non-temporal sense elsewhere in Lk. but is so used in Acts 3:17; *et al.* ὑμεῖς will then be the remnant of an original ὑμῖν. But if Matthew has transferred the saying to a later point in the discourse, he may well have altered its form to suit its new position. The fact that Matthew too begins his chapter with a section not couched in 'woe' form may imply that he was aware of a similar structure in Q (cf. E. Haenchen*, 50). The criticism is that the Pharisees cleanse (i.e. ritually) the outside (ἔξωθεν, 11:40*) of a dish, but leave the inside untouched. πίναξ is 'platter, dish' (Mk. 6:25, 28 par. Mt. 14:8, 11**), and may be a literary correction for Mt. παροψίς**. For the cleansing of the interior and exterior of vessels see Kelim 25. The saying appears to presuppose a custom of washing only the outside of vessels and ignoring the inside. Since, however, the OT law required the cleansing of the latter (Lv. 11:33; 15:12; cf. Kelim 25), we must conclude that Jesus' words do not reflect a custom of cleansing merely the exterior of a vessel; rather he is suggesting that the Pharisaic ritual of *only* washing the outside of a man is as foolish as only washing the exterior of a dirty vessel. The vessel may be full of unclean things. For γέμω see Mt. 23:25, 27; cf. Rom. 3:14; Rev. 4:6; *et al.* ἁρπαγή, '(act of) robbery' (Heb. 10:34) can mean concretely 'what has been stolen' (so Mt. 23:25** according to AG) or abstractly 'greed, rapacity'. πονηρία, 'wickedness', may perhaps refer especially to 'envy, greed' (cf. Rom. 1:29: 'moral worthlessness as a result of avarice', G. Harder, TDNT VI, 565). In Mt. 23:25 the saying is metaphorical in form and speaks of vessels which are filled with the

proceeds of robbery and greed. The interpretation in Lk. depends on whether ὑμῶν (added, diff. Mt.) qualifies τὸ ἔσωθεν (so G. Harder, TDNT VI, 565 n. 18) or ἁρπαγῆς καὶ πονηρίας (SB II, 188). The former view, rightly adopted by most translations, implies that the application is inserted into the metaphor: the Pharisees may be ritually clean externally, but their hearts are filled with rapacity and greed. If the latter view is adopted, the metaphor is preserved throughout, and the point is that the vessels used by the Pharisees are full of the proceeds of their rapacity. Luke's version is probably secondary, but not confused (as L. Goppelt, TDNT VI, 149 n. 15, claims). Luke's πονηρία may also be secondary, diff. Mt. ἀκρασία, 'lack of self-control' (1 Cor. 7:5**). The whole accusation is paralleled by Ass. Moses 7:7–9, which may represent Essene criticism of the Pharisees. This confirms the fact that such criticism of the Pharisees was in the air, no doubt with good reason, and is an example of the fact that the existence of a Jewish parallel to a saying in the Gospels confirms rather than weakens its authenticity as a saying of Jesus.

(40) The address ἄφρων, 'foolish' (12:20*; cf. μωρός, Mt. 5:22; 23:17), perhaps corresponds to Mt. 23:26 τυφλός (which may be editorial; cf. Mt. 15:14; 23:16, 17, 19, 24). The word characterises the Pharisees as ungodly men in their false piety (G. Bertram, TDNT IX, 220–235, especially 230f.). The following clause, peculiar to Lk., stresses that the inside is as important as the outside. The sense is: 'Did not he (the potter or God) who made the outside also make the inside (and therefore you must cleanse both)?' (Plummer, 310; E. Haenchen*, 51 n.). An alternative interpretation is: 'He who has "done" (i.e. cleansed) the outside has not thereby dealt with the inside' (cf. 2 Sa. 19:25; Wellhausen, 61 (on the basis of the D text); Manson, Sayings, 269), but the position of οὐχ favours the first view, which gives perfectly good sense. Schulz, 96, holds that the wording is Lucan and that there was no reason for Matthew to omit the verse if it was in Q. But the saying could have been omitted by Matthew because it seemed obscure or unnecessary.

(41) The criticism is followed by a command. If men give alms, then everything will be clean. If the Pharisees overcome their rapacity, i.e. their inward uncleanness, then they will be fully clean, and ritual washing will presumably not be necessary. ἐλεημοσύνη is 'alms, charitable giving' (12:33; Acts, 8x; Mt. 6:2, 3, 4**; R. Bultmann, TDNT II, 485–487). It is simplest to take τὰ ἐνόντα, literally 'what is inside', as an accusative of respect: 'so far as what is inside is concerned, give alms'. N. Turner suggests that we have an adverbial accusative meaning 'inwardly', i.e. 'give alms from the heart' (MH III, 247). Another possibility is that we understand the reference as being literally to a vessel and translate as a direct object: 'Give the contents as alms'; Percy, 118 n. 3, holds that here the original sense of the whole saying, which was concerned purely with the inside and outside of a vessel, and

not with the heart of man, can still be detected. See further Moule, 34.

Matthew's wording is different: 'first cleanse the inside of the cup'. Wellhausen, 61, conjectured that Luke's version arose from a confusion of Aramaic *dakki* ('cleanse') with *zakki* ('give alms'); cf. F. Hauck, TDNT III, 425 n. 76. Black, 2, thinks that the mistranslation represents a wrong but deliberate reinterpretation of the saying. But in general Luke himself shows no signs of Aramaic influence, and any alteration is more likely to have taken place in pre-Lucan tradition. In any case, the Aramaic basis for this conjecture remains highly problematical: according to Moule, 186, the verb *zki* can mean both 'to give alms' and 'to cleanse morally', but it is doubtful whether it was current in Palestinian Aramaic. It may be simplest to see a deliberate interpretation by Luke or his source; cf. the similar case in 12:33 diff. Mt. 6:19. The second half of the verse also differs from Mt. Where Matthew speaks of the *outside* becoming clean, Luke has πάντα (or ἅπαντα, p⁷⁵ f13 pc; Diglot). In Lk. the application has again been incorporated in the parable. The verse as a whole could represent a reformulation of Mt. 23:26 (cf. Bultmann, 139), but the differences are such that Schlatter, 303–306, and Manson, *Sayings*, 268f., ascribe the two forms to different sources, while Schulz, 96f., holds that we have two separate redactional additions intended to show that Jesus abandoned Pharisaic ritual observances. But this last view is improbable. The evidence that Jesus dispensed with ritual washing is quite clear, and the context of the present saying is criticism for his failure to do so; the present saying, making use of the metaphor of cleansing vessels, is meant to be applied to men themselves and to claim that inner cleansing makes outward cleansing superfluous. Luke's form may well be an interpretation of the basic form attested in Mt. (Manson, *Sayings*, 269), but the application of the metaphor is inherent from the start.

(42) While Grundmann, 248, suggests that Luke has introduced vs. 42f. at this point and upset the original connection between vs. 39–41 and 44 which both deal with the theme of purity (cf. Mt. 23:25f., 27f.), it is more probable that Matthew has brought together sayings that he regarded as connected in theme. From ritual cleansing Luke turns to other trivial practices by the Pharisees. The opening ἀλλά (diff. Mt.) is editorial, drawing a contrast between what the Pharisees ought to do (v. 41) and their actual practice. Luke simply has τοῖς Φαρισαίοις in the dative (agreeing with the preceding ὑμῖν), but Matthew has the stereotyped vocative γραμματεῖς καὶ Φαρισαῖοι ὑποκριταί, which is no doubt secondary. ἀποδεκατόω is 'to give, collect a tithe' (Mt. 23:23; Heb. 7:5**; cf. ἀποδεκατεύω, 18:12**). The OT law required the payment of tithes of farm and garden produce (Dt. 14:22–29; 26:12–15; Lv. 27:30–33; Mal. 3:8–10), and rabbinic legislation filled out the details (Maaseroth; Maaser Sheni; cf. SB I, 932f.; II, 189; G. Bornkamm, TDNT IV, 65–67). Three herbs are specifically mentioned. ἡδύοσμον (Mt. 23:23**) is the garden-plant 'mint' (*mentha longifolia*, 'horse mint';

Aramaic *nînyâ*). πήγανον** is 'rue' (*ruta graveolens* or possibly *ruta chalepensis*, var. *latifolia*; *pēygam*), a plant about 3 ft. high with grey-green foliage and yellow flowers. λάχανον (Mt. 13:32 par Mk. 4:32; Rom. 14:2**) is a general word for 'edible garden herb, vegetable' (Hebrew *yārāq*). Problems arise concerning the relation of this list to that in Mt. and whether the various items were in fact tithed. Both Gospels have mint; there is no specific record that this was liable to tithe. For 'rue' Matthew has ἄνηθον, 'dill' (*anethum graveolens*; Hebrew *šebet*). The Aramaic words *šabbārâ*, 'rue', and *š^eḇeṭâ*, 'dill', are sufficiently alike for the possibility of confusion to have arisen (Black, 194, following E. Nestle). Dill was certainly tithed (Maaseroth 4:5), but there is a rabbinic statement that rue was not tithed (Shebiith 9:1; Schlatter, 519, however, suggests that the existence of this statement implies that there was doubt on the matter). Finally, for 'every vegetable' Matthew has κύμινον**, 'cummin' (*cuminum cyminum*; Hebrew *kammôn*), a herb producing seeds used as a condiment and liable to tithe (Demai 2:1).

Thus in Mt. we have a list of two and possibly three items which were tithed under rabbinic law. Luke lists one item which was said to be exempt from tithe and gives a generalising reference to vegetables. Manson, *Sayings*, 98, thinks that Matthew derived dill and cummin, which were liable to tithe, from M, but mint, which was not liable to tithe, from Q. The Q version, reflected in Lk., attacks the Pharisees for tithing mint and rue (the latter of which was not liable to tithe) and indeed every kind of vegetable (no doubt including some that were not liable to tithe) – i.e. for going beyond the law by paying tithes where none was required. D. Correns, 'Die Verzehntung der Raute. Lk. xi. 42 and M. Schebi ix.1', Nov.T 6, 1963, 110–112, argues that only the garden species of herbs were tithed, and that Luke's list refers to these. It is probably impossible to clear the matter up satisfactorily. The two lists probably reflect different recensions of Q (rather than M and Q traditions), and in both cases the Pharisees are attacked for meticulous observance of the law, certainly for going beyond the requirements of the OT and possibly for going beyond the oral law (although we cannot know for sure what was generally reckoned as liable to tithe in the first century).

Such meticulous legalism stands in contrast to the Pharisees' neglect of other things. παρέρχομαι is 'to pass by, neglect' (12:37; 15:29; 16:17 (par. Mt. 5:18); 17:7; 18:37; 21:32f. par. Mk. 13:30f.) diff. Mt. ἀφίημι (which is more Palestinian, according to Schlatter, 519). Matthew has τὰ βαρύτερα τοῦ νόμου, i.e. the more important commandments (G. Schrenk, TDNT I, 558). Both Gospels list κρίσις, 'justice, righteousness' (cf. Mt. 12:18, 20), here no doubt to be understood of social relationships (Easton, 189): the Pharisees are 'indifferent to the right of the poor' (F. Büchsel, TDNT III, 941f.). In view of the following phrase, Schulz, 100f., argues that Luke has misunderstood κρίσις to mean 'the judgment of God', but this is an impossible interpretation. In place of καὶ τὸ ἔλεος καὶ τὴν πίστιν Luke has καὶ τὴν ἀγάπην τοῦ θεοῦ. ἀγάπη* is rare in the teaching of Jesus (only Mt. 24:12) but the verb is common enough (6:27; *et al.*). The reference must be to love for God or to the kind of love demanded by God rather than to the love shown by God (*pace* Luce, 222). In the light of 10:37 and his reluctance to use ἀγάπη elsewhere (Acts, 0x), it is improbable that Luke has altered his source here (*pace* Schulz, 100). The change may be on the side of Matthew (cf. Mt. 9:13; 12:7) or due to variations in oral transmission.

The final clause is given almost identically in the two Gospels. The Pharisees ought to have carried out the latter duties while not neglecting the former. Luke has παρίημι, 'to neglect' (also 'to let fall at the side', Heb. 12:12**) diff. Mt. ἀφίημι, which is secondary. This statement appears to give surprising support to ritual observance, while admittedly placing it in a secondary position, and it is not remarkable that the clause is absent from D Mcion. Although the clause has been regarded as an assimilation to the text of Mt. (Klostermann, 131; Easton, 189; Luce, 222, Manson, *Sayings*, 98; Grundmann, 248), the external evidence and the vocabulary favour its originality in Lk. (Metzger, 159). Nor is the saying out of place in Lk., since elsewhere he upholds the OT law and expects that Jewish Christians will continue to observe it (cf. 16:17). Similarly, it is not surprising to find this attitude in Jewish-Christian material. What is odd is that this statement stands alongside what is evidently a criticism of the Pharisees for exaggerated observance of the tithing law, but it is possible that the OT principle of tithing (apart from scribal elaborations) is simply being upheld. More difficult is the question whether Jesus, who evidently broke with ritual cleansing, would have upheld the law in this way. But there is a difference between rejection of the oral tradition regarding cleansing and the upholding of the OT principle of tithing, which was meant to have a humanitarian purpose; Jesus certainly upheld the OT law, and hence it is doubtful whether we need to regard v. 42b as a Jewish-Christian addition to the original saying.

Luke does not have the following statement (Mt. 23:24) about straining out a gnat and swallowing a camel; it presumably did not stand in his source.

(43) This saying has a parallel in Mk. 12:38b–39, but the wording and especially the agreements with Mt. demonstrate clearly that it is not based on Mk. but follows a different tradition (Schulz, 104; *pace* Hoffmann, 170 n. 49). In Mt. the saying has been conflated with wording from Mk. and has lost the 'woe' form. The use of ἀγαπάω may give a catch-word connection with the preceding saying; Matthew has φιλέω, which Luke uses diff. Mk. θέλω in the doublet 20:46. The charge is directed against the scribes in Mk., but Luke regarded it as applying to them here also (11:45). They enjoyed sitting in the front seat in the synagogues (πρωτοκαθεδρία, sing., as in Mt., diff. Mk.; 20:46 par. Mk. 12:38 par. Mt. 23:6**; W. Michaelis, TDNT VI, 870f.); for the correctness of the accusation see the evidence in SB I, 915f. They also

desired respectful greetings in the streets, for it was a sign of respect to a superior if he was greeted first by another man (cf. H. Windisch, TDNT I, 498: SB I, 382). In Mt. Jesus goes on to criticise the Pharisees for seeking respectful titles, and to indicate that a different state of affairs must exist among the disciples; this material may be from a different source, since in the Q discourse Jesus is not addressing the disciples but the Pharisees, or else it has been adapted to a Christian audience. The present saying, however, in Lk. is from Q, and there is no reason to doubt its authenticity (for the thought cf. Ass. Moses 7:4).

(44) The opening formula omits the word 'Pharisees', possibly in order to prepare for the transition to the scribes in the next verse. The saying in Lk. likens the Pharisees to tombs ($\mu\nu\eta\mu\varepsilon\tilde{\imath}o\nu$ 11:47; 23:55; 24:2, 9, 12, 22, 24*; Acts 13:29*), contact with which produced religious pollution (Nu. 19:16). But it was not obvious that these tombs were tombs; they were $\check{\alpha}\delta\eta\lambda o\varsigma$, 'unseen' ('indistinct', 1 Cor. 14:8**), and hence men could walk over them without realising that they were being defiled. The $\kappa\alpha\acute{\imath}$ clause is equivalent to a relative clause. Before $\pi\varepsilon\rho\iota\pi\alpha\tauo\tilde{\upsilon}\nu\tau\varepsilon\varsigma$ the article $o\acute{\imath}$ is omitted by p^{75} A D W f1 f13 pm; TR; (UBS); Diglot. The omission could be due to haplography.

The saying appears in a very different and extended form in Mt. Whereas in Lk. the point is that the outwardly correct behaviour of the Pharisees conceals the fact that they are inwardly corrupt (cf. O. Michel, TDNT IV, 681), in Mt. they are like whitewashed tombs (following Jewish custom) so that they appear beautiful, i.e. righteous, but really are full of uncleanness. These two sayings may be thought contradictory (cf. Creed, 166): in Mt. the tombs are obviously tombs, but in Lk. they are disguised and hidden. In both cases, however, the point is that what looks all right on the outside is evil inside; in Lk. the criticism is that the Pharisees conceal their true nature, but Matthew stresses the element of outward show that is involved. The real purpose of the whitewash was to draw attention to the grave, lest people be defiled by it (SB I, 936f.), but Jesus stresses the incidental, beautifying effect of the whitewash. The Lucan form is simpler and more primitive; the Matthaean form draws out the point in greater detail with reference to a custom practised by some Jews in the spring time. Matthew's saying could be a development from the form in Lk. (Schulz, 105f.).

(45) Luke alone has this transitional verse which leads on to the woes directed specifically against the scribes. Luke likes such transitions (cf. 12:41; 13:23), and hence it is often claimed that he has created this one. This may be the case, but Manson, Sayings, 96, allows that the division between two groups of woes may have existed in Q; moreover, the language is consistent with a pre-Lucan comment: cf. the historic present $\lambda\acute{\varepsilon}\gamma\varepsilon\iota$. For $\nu o\mu\iota\kappa\acute{o}\varsigma$, another possibly pre-Lucan word, see 10:25. The lawyer must be presumed to be a member of the Pharisaic party, as indeed most lawyers were. He perceives that the activity of meticulously codifying the law stands under Jesus' condemnation as much as the

careful observance of it. ὑβρίζω is 'to insult' (also 'to mistreat', 18:32; Acts 14:5; Mt. 22:6; 1 Thes. 2:2**); G. Bertram, TDNT VIII, 305f., suggests that there is an element of the proud or mockingly ironic in the word.

(46) The following woe is specifically directed at the lawyers for creating harsh burdens for men to bear. The saying appears in Mt. 23: 4 without the 'woe' form and in the third person, doubtless because of its changed position. φορτίζω is 'to cause somebody to carry something' (Mt. 11:28**), diff. Mt. who uses a longer phrase. φορτίον is 'burden' (Acts 27:10; Mt. 11:30; 23:4; Gal. 6:5**), and δυσβάστακτος (Mt. 25:4 v.1.**) is 'hard to bear'; cf. Acts 15:10. Luke's rendering is less pictures-que and more literary than Matthew's (cf. Creed, 166; Schulz, 106f.), but the language is paralleled in Mt. 11:28–30.

But the real gravaman of the charge lies in the second part of the verse. The scribes do not touch (προσψαύω**, diff. Mt. κινέω) the bur-dens with one finger. This has been interpreted as: 1. The scribes es-caped the obligations of the laws which they imposed on others (SB I, 913f., offers clear parallels; Lagrange, 345; Creed, 167; Schulz, 107f.). 2. The scribes did not do anything to help those who broke down under the burden of the law (Easton, 190; Manson, Sayings, 100f.). The for-mer interpretation is clearly adopted by Matthew; it fits in with the stress on the Pharisees' hypocrisy; they preach, but do not practise (Mt. 23:3). It should probably be accepted. Yet the point earlier was that the scribes did keep the trivialities of the law, and this favours the second interpreta-tion. But the first interpretation should be accepted. Casuistry in framing laws can well be accompanied by skill in giving the impression of keep-ing them while avoiding their minute demands. And this reflects lack of love for the people who are forced to bear the yoke while the framers of the law themselves go scot-free (Braun, Radikalismus II, 93 n. 1).

(47) No specific audience is addressed in this woe; the audience is wider than the scribes. The accusation is that they build tombs for the prophets, while their fathers slew them. Hence the conclusion is drawn (v. 48) that they are testifying that they agreed with the attitude of their ancestors. The activity of building and revering the graves of dis-tinguished figures of the past was characteristic of Judaism at this time (cf. Acts 2:29f.; O. Michel, TDNT IV, 680f.; and especially J. Jeremias, Heiligengräber in der Umwelt Jesu, Göttingen, 1958). For οἱ δέ Diglot has καὶ οἱ (‭א‬* C* Mcion Epiph).

(48) The conclusion is drawn with ἄρα (Lucan, diff. Mt. ὥστε). The audience are μάρτυρες in that they bear approving witness to what their ancestors did. This point is clarified by the addition of συνευδοκέω, 'to agree with, approve of' (Acts 8:1; 22:20; Rom. 1:32; 1 Cor. 7:12f.**), which looks like a Lucan explanation of a difficult phrase. The final οἰκοδομεῖτε without an object is harsh and led to textual alterations (cf. Metzger, 159). One would normally regard the erection of a tomb as a sign of honour for the dead, but this cannot be the thought here. 1. The

saying may be bitterly ironic: 'Your fathers killed the prophets, and you make sure that they stay dead; you simply complete what your fathers did' (Manson, *Sayings*, 101; Schweizer, *Matthäus*, 284). 2. 'You are no better than your fathers who refused to hear the prophets and killed them. You, to be sure, build their tombs, but you are equally unwilling to hear them' (so most commentators; cf. O. Michel, TDNT IV, 681; Schulz, 109f.). On this view the outward piety of the Jews is implicitly contrasted with their real attitude to the word of God, as in v. 42. Steck, 280–283, sees the saying in the context of the Jewish concept of the violent death of the prophets (Ne. 9:26): he claims that the point lies in the boasting (Mt. 23:30) of the Jews who claim that by their honour of the prophets they are better than their fathers, and in this way avoid the real repentance that they should show in view of the continuing guilt of the Jewish people by obeying the words of the prophets (see, however, Hoffmann, 162–164).

The occurrence of the saying in very different wording in Mt. 23:29–32 raises considerable difficulty. First, Matthew speaks of building the tombs of the prophets and adorning the graves of the righteous. The righteous are absent in the later part of the saying; the extra word for tombs (τάφος) is Matthaean, and the combination of prophets and wise men is Matthaean (Mt. 10:41; 13:17 diff. Lk. 10:24). Hence it is probable that at this point the saying has been expanded by Matthew.

Second, Matthew has the words, 'and you say, if we had been there in the days of our fathers, we would not have shared with them in the blood of the prophets', to which Luke has no equivalent apart from the use of 'fathers'. Has Luke abbreviated the saying in order to make an easier transition from the statement in v. 47a to the ironic comment in v. 48 (Steck, 28f.), or has the saying been expanded by Matthew in order to underline the idea of hypocrisy (Hoffmann, 164)? The former is perhaps more likely.

Third, Mt. 23:31 differs in wording from Lk. 11:48. Matthew's μαρτυρεῖτε ἑαυτοῖς will be original, diff. Lk. μάρτυρές ἐστε, and συνευδοκεῖτε . . . will be an explanatory addition, replacing υἱοί ἐστε τῶν φονευσάντων . . . 'To be a son of' here implies kinship of character: 'Your action shows that you stand on the same side as your fathers'. C. C. Torrey (cf. Black, 12f.) thought that Luke's οἰκοδομεῖτε and Matthew's υἱοί ἐστε τῶν could both be based on the same Aramaic phrase 'twn bnyn 'twn, but this is not very likely, since the phrases are hardly parallel. The whole phrase ὅτι αὐτοί . . . in Lk. is tautologous, but for that very reason is unlikely to be Lucan.

Fourth, Luke has nothing corresponding to Mt. 23:32.

The differences taken as a whole are hard to explain in terms of literary redaction of a common source, and the hypothesis of differing oral traditions contributing to two recensions of the Q material again accounts better for some of the facts.

(49) The saying in vs. 49–51 stands apart from the woes by reason of its different style as a prophecy of judgment couched in wisdom terminology. In Mt. 23:34–36 it appears at the end of the woes and is followed by the Jerusalem saying which appears in Lk. 13:34f. Luke, however, has a further woe after the present passage. It seems most likely that it is Luke who has altered the order of the sayings in the present discourse in order to conclude with a statement specifically referring to the lawyers, and that originally the woes concluded with a consequent expression of judgment as in Is. 5:8–23, 24ff. It is also probable that the Jerusalem saying followed the present saying in Q in view of the implicit link between the death of Zechariah in 11:50 (by stoning, 2 Ch. 24:21) and the use of λιθοβολέω in 13:34 (Bultmann, 120; U. Wilckens, TDNT VII, 515; Lührmann, 48; *contra* Steck, 47f.; Schulz, 339 n. 131). Whether this collocation in Q reflects an earlier linking of the sayings is a more difficult problem. Since the tomb saying (vs. 47f.) is not applied to the scribes in particular, it could have formed part of an address to the unrepentant Jewish leaders in general. The difference in form is no argument against the original linking of the sayings. There was, so far as we know, no unwritten rule (or even unconscious feeling) among the Jews that a person who begins to speak in one particular 'form' of discourse is not allowed to change to another in midstream.

The opening διὰ τοῦτο gives a close link with the preceding woes and corresponds to *lāken* in Is. 5:24; Je. 23:2; *et al.* The force is: 'Because of your evil deeds, therefore judgment will come upon you', but this is obscured by the insertion of a quotation formula and repetition of the reason for the judgment. The sense is: 'Because of your attitude to the old prophets, wisdom has prophesied that (further) messengers will be sent to Israel, so that, when you have killed them, you in this generation may undergo the full judgment that Israel deserves'.

The saying is put on the lips of ἡ σοφία τοῦ θεοῦ who speaks in the first person; by the omission of this phrase the saying is in effect ascribed directly to Jesus in Mt. Although the phrase has been regarded as a Lucan insertion (Schlatter, 521; Kümmel, 80), it is much more probable that it is original and has been omitted by Matthew, perhaps so as to identify Jesus with wisdom (E. Haenchen*, 53; Steck, 29; Suggs, 14; Christ, 120f.; Schulz, 336 n. 96); admittedly the intended identification would be evident only to those readers who recognised the saying as a wisdom saying despite the absence of a reference to wisdom. On σοφία see 7:35 note. The use of the term here raises the two questions of the significance of the introductory phrase and the source of the following statement. For the phrase itself the following possibilities arise: 1. 'The Wisdom of God' is the name of a lost Jewish apocryphal book from which the following citation is drawn (Bultmann, 119; Grundmann, 249). It is, however, strange for the name of a book to be followed by εἶπεν, and we have no other knowledge of a book with this title. 2. The phrase may be a self-designation of Jesus (Tatian; so Geldenhuys, 346, but he also supports the next view (343)). But there is no explanation of Jesus' choice of this title, and the use of the aorist remains strange. An identification of Jesus with divine wisdom would be possible in a community formation, and this identification is, as we noted, made in Mt. 3. The phrase may mean 'God in his wisdom', i.e. it indicates a personalised attribute of God (Creed, 167; Manson, *Sayings*, 102; Danker, 146; Suggs, 18, thinks Luke so interpreted the phrase). This is less open to objection, but it remains unclear why this particular attribute of God has been linked to this saying. 4. The reference is to 'divine wisdom' (U. Wilckens, TDNT VII, 515; Steck, 224; Christ, 125f.; Suggs, 19f.; Schulz, 340). This fits in with the way in which wisdom is personified in the OT and Judaism; she is capable of speaking to men (e.g. Pr. 1:20–33; 8) and sends messengers to them (Wis. 7:27); Lk. 7:35).

This last view is probably the best, but acceptance of it still leaves unsettled the nature of the following saying: 1. It may be a citation from a Jewish apocryphal book (Suggs, 19f.). This view can be held independently of the view that the book was called 'The Wisdom of God'. If so, all trace of the book has disappeared. 2. A slightly different view is advanced by Steck, 51–53, who holds that the introductory formula does not introduce a citation but is a prophetic messenger formula, analogous to 'Thus says the Lord'. He claims that the basis of the saying (vs. 49f.) is a Jewish piece of tradition which has been taken up by Jesus or the early church, probably the latter (ibid. 280–289). 3. Hoffmann, 166–171, and Schulz, 341, deny that the saying had a pre-Christian history. While its background lies in the Deuteronomic motif of the violent fate of the prophets coupled with wisdom motifs, the saying itself was formulated in the early church and belongs to the later strands of Q. 4. Similarly, Ellis, 171–174, argues that a saying from Jesus' pre-resurrection ministry has been '*pesher*-ed' and given detailed application by a Christian prophet to the judgment on 'this generation' which culminated in the fall of Jerusalem (cf. E. E. Ellis, 'Luke xi. 49–51: An Oracle of a Christian Prophet?' Exp.T 74, 1962–63, 157f.). This view does not take sufficiently into account the Deuteronomistic and wisdom background of the saying. We should probably reckon with a more complex history of the saying. At its basis may lie a Jewish wisdom saying, although in the absence of a clear understanding of the situation in which such a saying can have arisen and been preserved, this suggestion must be offered with extreme caution. Such a saying can have been taken up by Jesus and re-used to express the judgment of God upon his contemporaries (cf. Christ, 131f., who rightly leaves this possibility open). It has, however, been also taken up by the early church who saw it being fulfilled in their own time and re-worded it accordingly (see especially Matthew's formulation).

The saying appears to express a statement by wisdom looking prophetically at the course of Jewish history. It is not, however, necessary to assume that the saying is uttered before the creation of the world (so Suggs, 14); wisdom could equally well be regarded as speaking at a given point in time when Jewish apostasy was becoming evident. For ἀποστελῶ, Matthew has ἐγὼ ἀποστέλλω, but his present tense is equivalent to a future; the use of ἐγώ identifies Jesus more closely with the figure whose words he has taken over. Luke's εἰς αὐτούς diff. Mt. πρὸς ὑμᾶς will be original, the latter giving a more direct application. Hence the saying could have referred originally to the Jews in pre-Christian times, but the church understood it to refer to (or at least to include) its contemporaries.

The identity of the messengers is obscure. Where Luke has 'prophets and apostles' Matthew has 'prophets and wise men and scribes'. In both Gospels προφῆται can be a reference to the OT prophets (11:47f.); this sense is demanded by v. 51 and also by the order 'prophets and apostles' in Lk., since Christian 'apostles and prophets' always appear in the reverse order (1 Cor. 12:28; Eph. 2:20; 3:5; 4:11). It is possible, however, that the early church saw here an allusion to Christian prophets, an identification that is made by Matthew. 1. Suggs, 22–24, raises the possibility that the original wisdom text referred only to prophets, the other names being Christian additions. 2. Luke's ἀπόστολοι has appeared to most scholars to be a Christian term (Bultmann, 119 n. 1; E. Haenchen*, 53); in this case it refers to Christian apostles alongside OT prophets, and Matthew's formulation in Jewish terms is primitive. 3. There is, however, a non-technical use of the participle ἀπεσταλμένοι in 13:34, and the term šᵉlûhîm could be used of God's emissaries in pre-Christian times (K. H. Rengstorf, TDNT I, 428; Steck, 30 n. 2; Seitz*; Suggs, 23f. (with hesitation); Christ, 122f.; Schulz, 336f.). Steck, however, argues that the term cannot refer to the prophets themselves, since the addition weakens the saying, and hence must refer to their successors in the wisdom tradition who shared their fate. This is perhaps over-subtle and ignores 1 Ki. 14:6 LXX (Seitz*). On this view, the early church would tend to see ἀπόστολοι as a reference to its own apostles. The wording in Matthew will then be a secondary expansion with reference to the messengers of God in a Jewish-Christian setting; for Christian scribes see Mt. 13:52. The use of σοφοί of Christian teachers is difficult, but the term was current in Judaism. It may be that Jewish terms are applied loosely to Christian teachers.

The case for Matthaean originality has been restated by G. Klein*, who holds that the introduction of ἀπόστολοι in a Christian sense is comprehensible as Lucan redaction of Matthew's phrase. He agrees with Steck that Luke would not have introduced the term to refer to pre-Christian messengers of God, but claims that for Luke the saying is intended to bring out the connection between the murder of the prophets in the past, which God allowed to go unpunished (Acts 14:16; 17:30), and the persecution of the apostles as the crowning act which brought about judgment. It is difficult to see why Matthew should have redacted the

Lucan wording, but it can be argued that Luke regarded γραμματεύς as a word with a bad sense, and would not have been willing to use it for a messenger of God; σοφός too (10:21*) has a negative sense in Q and Lk. Klein does not go into the question whether the Matthaean wording is itself explicable as the original wording in Q. Matthew appears to have understood the various names as applying to Christian preachers, but originally (if a Jewish tradition has been utilised) they must have referred to Jewish figures. On the whole, it seems probable that if a Jewish saying has been utilised, the Matthaean wording is original with a reference to Jewish emissaries of wisdom, both past and present; in Lk. the wording has been Christianised by a reference to the apostles. For the thought cf. 2 Ch. 24:19.

The second part of the prophecy refers to the slaying and persecution of some of these. For ἐξ αὐτῶν as a partitive cf. 21:16; Jn. 16:17; for διώκω cf. 17:23; 21:12*; Mt. 5:10–12; and for the use of the same language with reference to pre-Christian prophets and preachers see Acts 7:52 (a verse which could be regarded as supporting the interpretation of 'apostles' as pre-Christian figures here). The language in Mt. is more precise (cf. Mt. 10:17, 23), and looks like 'pesher' interpretation of the text to make the contemporary reference clearer. The placing of 'killing' before 'persecuting' is odd, but the second word will define the character of the first.

(50) Luke's ἵνα, diff. Mt. ὅπως, is probably original (Schulz, 337). The clause is dependent on ἀποστελῶ . . . (as in Mt.), rather than on ἡ σοφία εἶπεν. The purposive force of ἵνα is toned down by Manson, *Sayings*, 103, who argues that in Semitic idiom the result of an action can be described as if it were the purpose; contrast the view of E. Stauffer (TDNT III, 328 n. 46): 'Behind the strictly final ἵνα of Lk. 11:50 is a conception of the murder of the righteous common to the theology of martyrdom, namely, that by such murder the enemies of God fill up the measure of their sins and bring the judgment day upon themselves.' Danker, 145, notes the close parallel of thought in Wis. 19:4. ἐκζητέω is 'to seek out' (11:51*; Acts 15:17 (LXX)*), and is applied to seeking vengeance for someone's blood in 2 Sa. 4:11; Ps. 9:12 (9:13); Ezk. 33:6, 8). Matthew's phraseology here is secondary (Schulz, 337; *pace* Suggs, 15 n. 22), as also in the remainder of the verse. The reference to αἷμα is metaphorical for death. For πάντων τῶν προφητῶν Matthew has δίκαιον, perhaps to avoid the inconcinnity with the mention of Abel who was hardly a prophet. ἐκχέω (Mt. ἐκχύννω) is 'to shed (blood)' (Acts 22:20; Rom. 3:15; Rev. 16:6; cf. Lk. 22:20; also 'to pour out', Acts 2:17f.; *et al.*). καταβολή is 'foundation, beginning', always used in the NT with ἀπό or πρό to refer to the beginning of the world (except Heb. 11:11). The phrase is omitted by Matthew. Luke also has ἀπὸ τῆς γενεᾶς ταύτης, which corresponds in thought to Mt. ἐφ' ὑμᾶς. The phrase is demanded by the syntax of the sentence and hence is original (*pace* Steck 32 n. 1). The guilt of the entire Jewish people is thus visited upon this (last)

generation, since it shows no more sign of repentance than its predecessors (11:47f.). The thought is compressed, and it is not clear that the reference to this generation, typical of Jesus (7:31), goes back to a Jewish text.

(51) The reference to the sweep of history in v. 50 is clarified (v. 51a) with a third phrase rather awkwardly introduced with ἀπό. The explanation is widely regarded as a Christian gloss on the preceding clause (E. Haenchen*, 54; Steck, 223; cf. Hoffmann, 168). It should be noted, however, that it begins with Abel, who was not a prophet, and concludes with Zechariah, an OT prophet, and makes no reference to Jesus himself or the apostles. It is, therefore, hardly a Christian gloss, and appears to be an original part of the saying, or perhaps an explanation added by Jesus to an existing Jewish saying. Abel is named as the first of the martyrs (cf. Heb. 11:4; 12:24; 1 En. 22); his inclusion as a 'prophet' implies a very broad use of the term. The reference to Zechariah creates problems. So far as Lk. is concerned the obvious identification is with Zechariah, the son of Jehoiada, who was stoned in the court of the house of the Lord (2 Ch. 24:20–22; cf. Gospel of the Nazarenes 17 (NTA I, 149)). For τοῦ ἀπολομένου Matthew has ὃν ἐφονεύσατε (cf. Mt. 23:31). μεταξύ, 'in between' (16:26;*), takes a double genitive. The altar (θυσιαστήριον, 1:11) of burnt offering stood outside the inner shrine (οἶκος, diff. Mt. ναός, is original (Steck, 31 n. 8)). The detail fits the OT narrative which states that Zechariah stood above the people, and stresses the sanctity of the place which was defiled by the murder. It is of interest that the OT narrative includes the prophet's cry to God for vengeance. If the Books of Chronicles stood last in the OT canon of the time, then the reference is to the last murder of a prophet in the Scriptures. There is no doubt that Luke has rightly understood his source in this sense (Steck, 23–40). The problems arise when the parallel in Mt. is taken into account where Zechariah is described as the son of Barachias. This identification rests on a confusion of the son of Jehoiada with the writing prophet (Zc. 1:1) or on a tradition (otherwise unknown) that the latter Zechariah was also murdered; there is more to be said for the theory that the reference is to Zechariah the son of Bareis who was slain by zealots in the temple in AD 67 (Jos. Bel. 4:334–344), so that the whole gamut of Jewish prophet murders right up to the outbreak of the Jewish war is covered, and the fall of Jerusalem is seen as the divine vengeance (Steck, 37–40). The problem would then be whether the identifying phrase in Mt. was in Q and has been omitted by Luke, or is a Matthaean addition. Since we have found considerable evidence of Matthaean redaction in this section, the latter possibility is the more likely (Schulz, 338 n.120).

The section closes with Jesus' own confirmation of what has gone before, introduced by an ἀμήν formula, altered by Luke to ναί (pace Steck, 32; cf. 4:24 note). For the structure cf. 12:5; and 7:26; 10:21.

(52) Whereas in Mt. the saying against this generation forms the

climax of the chapter of woes, Luke returns at last to the scribes and sums up their activities in a final woe which he has probably moved to its present position for effect: in Mt. 23 it is the first saying couched in 'woe' form and thus occupies an emphatic position there. The scribes have taken away the key (κλείς, Mt. 16:19; Rev. 1:18; 3:7; 9:1; 20:1**) of knowledge (γνῶσις, 1:77). They thus prevent other people entering in, while they make no attempt to use the key themselves. The saying thus implicitly refers to the kingdom of God as a present reality. The wording differs in Mt. which speaks of shutting up (κλείω, Rev. 3:7f.; 21:25) the kingdom of heaven before men, and uses present tenses instead of aorists. Black, 129, 260, explains the differences in tense as being due to variant translations of the Aramaic perfect, which is tantamount to a present tense. Certainly it is hard to see why a Greek author should have changed the tense, unless Luke saw here a final verdict on what the scribes had done. The genitive τῆς γνώσεως may be one of apposition, 'the key that consists in knowledge' (Ps.-Clem. Hom. 3:18; 18:15; Ps.-Clem. Rec. 2:30, cited by J. Jeremias, TDNT III, 747f. (n. 40)), or it may be an objective genitive, 'the key that leads to knowledge', sc. of God or of salvation (Lagrange, 349). Although older scholars regarded the second possibility as showing signs of Hellenistic influence, it is in fact paralleled in 1QH 4:11, 'And they stopped the thirsty from drinking the liquor of knowledge', in a context which makes it clear that the Torah is meant (Thompson, 179). But we should probably not separate these two ideas from each other: in and by God's revelation he himself is known. The key consists of the knowledge of God and leads to the knowledge of God. Elsewhere the thought of knowledge plays no especial part in Lk. or in the Gospels generally; there is no development of gnostic ideas (such as might possibly be found in G. Thomas 39). Hence Luke's phraseology may be original despite the preference of most scholars for Matthew's wording (Schulz, 110 n. 123).

(53) The closing passage has no parallel in Mt., and would be inappropriate in his context. Although, therefore, it has Lucan features of language, it may be from Luke's source. It exhibits a curious textual history with significant variants for each major phrase. The variants are mostly in the western text (D it) with much conflation in TR.

κἀκεῖθεν, 'and from there', is probably Lucan (Mk. 9:30; Acts 8x**). For the opening phrase κἀκεῖθεν ... αὐτοῦ (p⁴⁵ ℵ B C bo) other authorities have λέγοντος δὲ αὐτοῦ ταῦτα πρὸς αὐτούς (A W pl latt sy; TR), or the same wording plus ἐνώπιον παντὸς τοῦ λαοῦ (D it syᵖ cur (Θ)). For the addition cf. 8:47; 12:1; Mt. 23:1, and for the alternative cf. 13:17. The alternative readings are less appropriate, since the plotting of the scribes and Pharisees is more likely to have taken place after Jesus had left them.

All texts have ἤρξαντο, but the subject varies. Most authorities have οἱ γραμματεῖς καὶ οἱ Φαρισαῖοι. The variants οἱ νομικοὶ καὶ οἱ Φαρισαῖοι (f1) and οἱ Φαρισαῖοι καὶ οἱ νομικοί (D it vg), along with the conflation οἱ γραμματεῖς καὶ οἱ Φαρισαῖοι καὶ οἱ νομικοί (Θ), are probably due to an attempt to assimilate to Luke's use of νομικός earlier in the passage: the change may reflect use of a source.

δεινῶς is 'fearfully, terribly' (Mt. 8:6**). The best attested verb is ἐνέχειν (sc. χόλον), 'to have a grudge against' (Mk. 6:19), 'to be very hostile' (cf. also Gal. 5:1**). The variant ἐπέχειν in C is probably a simple error; other MSS have ἔχειν (D it), substituting a more common phrase. The second infinitive ἀποστοματίζειν** is difficult. In Classical Greek the verb means 'to teach by dictation', 'to repeat from memory'; according to AG early commentators interpreted it as 'to catch someone in something he says', i.e. 'to watch his utterances closely'; on this view, v. 54 brings out the meaning. Others translate 'to question closely, interrogate' (cf. RSV: 'to provoke him to speak'). It is not surprising that the verb is replaced by συμβάλλειν, 'to quarrel, dispute' (D it sy ᶜˢ bo). In περὶ πλειόνων we have the comparative adjective used for the positive (cf. Jn. 13:27 and possibly Acts 17:21; Zerwick, 150).

(54) ἐνεδρεύω, 'to lie in wait for', is probably Lucan (Acts 23:21**). It is replaced by, or conflated with ζητοῦντες in many authorities, but is manifestly original. θηρεύω** is 'to hunt, catch'. Many authorities add ἵνα κατηγορήσωσιν αὐτόν, probably by assimilation to 6:7. Some substitute the phrase ἀφορμήν τινα λαβεῖν αὐτοῦ (D it sy ˢᶜ), 'to grasp an opportunity against him'. This again looks like western paraphrase. On the whole textual problem see G. D. Kilpatrick, 'Western Text and Original Text in the Gospels and Acts', JTS 44, 1943, 24–36, especially 33.

d. Readiness for the Coming Crisis (12:1 – 13:21)

The fourth main section in this division of the Gospel is concerned again principally with teaching for the disciples, although at the end of the section the crowds, who have been present throughout, become the principal object of Jesus' teaching. The opening part directs the attention of the disciples to the coming of judgment upon those who live hypocritically, concealing their true character from men. Disciples should not be afraid of men and conceal their allegiance to Jesus, but should boldly confess it with the aid of the help of the Spirit. Let them not be silent out of fear of men, but let them rather fear to offend against God, the mighty judge (12:1–12).

In the second section the theme changes to the way in which attachment to wealth can make men unfit for the day of judgment; by amassing earthly wealth they can become poor with regard to the things that ultimately matter (12:13–21).

If the disciples are afraid to have a proper sense of priorities, and are unwilling to escape from the rat-race for wealth, Jesus bids them have faith in their heavenly Father who will assuredly provide for the

needs of those who seek his kingdom. Let them, therefore, be prepared
to give away their earthly wealth and find a heavenly treasure in place of
it (12:22–34).

So their attitude is to be that of men whose minds are fixed on the
coming of the Son of man and who live their earthly lives in an appropriate fashion. At any time the crisis may come; let them live as those
who are always ready for the coming of the Master, so that they may
not be taken by surprise and be filled with shame or, worse still, be found
guilty of flagrant sin and suffer the penalty meted out to witting offenders (12:35–48).

To live in this way is not easy. For the mission of Jesus leads to
conflict and affliction as men range themselves for and against him, and
his opponents persecute his disciples. Nevertheless, all the signs of the
times point to the truth of what Jesus is saying: the crisis is at hand, and
it behoves men to settle their affairs while there is still time (12:49–59).

Some people imagine that because they pass through life unscathed
by suffering they are all right with God. But in fact all are sinners and all
need to repent, lest a worse judgment than mere physical suffering come
upon them. Let the people of Israel in particular take note: they have
been spared divine judgment for long enough, but one day the patience
of God with a recalcitrant people will be exhausted (13:1–9).

Over against the hypocritical attitude of the Jewish leaders and
their disbelief there stands the evidence of God's saving power
demonstrated in the cure of a crippled woman (13:10–17). Her healing is
one of the pointers to the presence of God's kingdom, tiny in its beginnings but destined to become great (13:18–21).

The outline demonstrates that while the section has a certain unity
of theme, there is some artificiality about the arrangement of the
material which suggests that several pieces of teaching have been
brought together by Luke and his predecessors. This is confirmed by the
fact that material from several sources has been brought together here.

i. Fearless Confession 12:1–12

The passage begins with a comment addressed to the disciples which
sums up the teaching of the previous section directed against the
Pharisees. Hypocrisy is ultimately futile, for the secret thoughts of men
will one day be revealed (12:1, 2f.). The connection of thought in Luke's
mind appears to be: disciples too may be tempted to conceal the real
allegiance of their hearts before men, but they should not fear what men
may do to them. Let them rather fear God who has the ultimate power
of life and death. They can be sure that he will remember and care for
them in the midst of persecution, just as he cares even for birds.
Whoever is faithful to Jesus before men will be upheld by the Son of man
before God, but whoever denies him will face ultimate rejection (12:4f.,

6f., 8f.). Similarly, anyone who sins against the Spirit will suffer condemnation, but the person who speaks against the Son of man will be forgiven. Hence, when the disciples face persecution and are tempted to forswear their allegiance, let them not be afraid, for the Holy Spirit will direct them what to say (12:10, 11f.).

The connection of thought is somewhat artificial, with several motifs intertwined. Alongside the thought of God's care for his people, which removes all need for them to worry (cf. 12:22–32), there is the thought of his stern judgment. Alongside warnings about failure to confess Jesus is the promise of the Spirit to help disciples under persecution. The initial warning against hypocrisy links to the preceding attack on the Pharisees.

V. 1 has a parallel in Mk. 8:14f., but there is one slight agreement with Mt. 16:6 diff. Mk., which supports the hypothesis that it is derived from Q and not from Mk.; if so, Matthew has lost its original context. Vs. 2–9 are paralleled in the mission discourse in Mt. 10:26b–33, a chapter which contains material from various sources. V. 10 has a Matthaean parallel in Mt. 12:31f., where it forms part of a passage, placed in a Marcan context, which conflates Marcan and Q material. Finally, vs. 11f. have parallels in Mt. 10:19f.; Mk. 13:11; Lk. 21:14f. The core of the section is thus the common unit of Q material in vs. 2–9. The fact that v. 10 occurs in a different context in Mt. strengthens the suspicion that it did not originally belong with vs. 8f., a saying with which it stands in tension, since v. 9 excludes the possibility of forgiveness for denial of Jesus while v. 10 allows forgiveness for speaking against the Son of man (i.e. Jesus – at least in the eyes of the compiler of Q, Matthew and Luke).

In the common unit, vs. 2–9, v. 3 conveys a different sense from Mt. 10:27, and this affects the force of v. 2. In Mt. (10:26f.) the sayings give a reason for missionaries not to be afraid of opposition, but in Lk. there is no mention of the opposition, and the sayings have been understood as a warning against hypocrisy. Some alterations of the wording to suit new contexts appear to have been made. Vs. 4–9 are substantially the same in both Gospels, but the strange differences in v. 6 diff. Mt. 10:29 are hard to explain redactionally. Although vs. 8f. introduce the new motif of the Son of man (so Lk., diff. Mt.), the thought is parallel to that in vs. 4f., and the connection may be original. Nevertheless, the strong contrast between vs. 4f. and 6f. is remarkable, and may imply compilation. Vs. 11f. occur earlier in Mt. 10 (vs. 19f.); in Lk. there is a good link with vs. 8f. and also with v. 22 (catchword μεριμνάω) which suggests that Luke may have preserved the original connections here and that Matthew has re-ordered the sayings. The wording of v. 12 diff. Mt. 10:20 is a puzzle and lends support to the idea that two different recensions of the Q material were used.

Luke's general theme is the need for fearless witness under persecution, while Matthew has placed the sayings in a context of mission, but these two contexts are closely related to each other. Luke appears to have preserved the Q context.

See Higgins, 57–60 (on vs. 8f.), 127–132 (on v. 10); Vielhauer, 76–79, 101–107 (on vs. 8f.); Tödt, 55–60, 89f., 339–344 (on vs. 8f.), 118–120, 312–318 (on v. 10); C. Colpe, TDNT VIII, 442f.; R. Schippers, 'The Son of Man in Matt, xii. 32 = Lk. xii. 10 compared with Mk. iii. 28', in TU 103, 231–235; E. Lövestam, *Spiritus Blasphemia*, Lund, 1968; Lührmann, 49–52; Wrege, 156–180 (on v. 10); I. H. Marshall, 'Uncomfortable Words VI. "Fear him who can destroy both soul and body in hell" (Mt. 10:28 RSV)', Exp.T 81, 1969–70, 276–280; id. *Kept by the Power of God*, Minneapolis, 1975², 76–82 (on v. 10); Schulz, 461–465 (on vs. 2f.), 157–161 (vs. 4–7), 66–76 (on vs. 8f.), 246–250 (on v. 10), 442–444 (on vs. 11f.); A. J. B. Higgins, ' "Menschensohn" oder "Ich" in Q: Lk. 12:8–9/Mt. 10:32–33?', in Pesch, *Jesus*, 117–123; H. Schürmann, in Pesch, *Jesus*, 135f., 136f.; W. G. Kümmel, 'Das Verhalten Jesu gegenüber und das Verhalten des Menschensohns', in Pesch, *Jesus*, 210–224.

(1) ἐν οἷς is 'meanwhile' (Acts 26:12**; cf. Acts 24:18). ἐπισυνάγω is 'to gather together' (13:34 par. Mt. 23:37; Lk. 17:37; Mk. 1:33; 13:27 par. Mt. 24:31**). The use in 13:34 suggests fairly conclusively that Luke employed the word here because of its occurrence in the passage of Q which he has held over to ch. 13, but which followed 11:51 in his source. The aorist participle gives the sense, 'when they ... had gathered'. The use of the article with μυριάδων suggests that 'the usual crowds' are meant (Klostermann, 133). μυριάς, literally 'ten thousand' (Acts 19:19), hence, as here, 'a very large number' (Acts 21:20; Heb. 12:22; Jude 14; Rev. 5:11; 9:16**). The implication is that the crowds have increased in size since 11:29. For ὥστε in this context cf. Mk. 2:2; 3:20; 4:1. Despite the presence of the crowds the following remarks are addressed to the disciples, and the crowds do not figure actively in the scene until v. 13. The situation is similar to that in the Sermon on the Plain and elsewhere (cf. 20:45) where teaching intended primarily for the disciples is given in the presence of the crowds who are thus taught what is involved in discipleship.

This situation is relevant for the meaning of πρῶτον. If construed as part of the preceding sentence it means that Jesus spoke first to the disciples before addressing the crowds (12:13; AG s.v.), or that he spoke primarily and especially to the disciples (Creed, 170); Klostermann, 133, claims that the word should be taken with the following clause, 'above all, beware...', since πρῶτον usually precedes the phrase it qualifies (10:5; *et al.*; So RVmg; JBmg). But the linguistic evidence favours the former construction (cf. 21:9; Acts 7:12, also 3:26; 13:46).

προσέχω can mean 'to care for, pay attention to' with a following dative; for the use with ἑαυτοῖς cf. 17:3; 21:34; Acts 5:35; 20:28**; it can also be used with ἀπό, 'to beware of' (Mt. 7:15; 10:17; 16:11, 12; Lk. 20:46), and the two constructions are here combined. The parallel use in Mt. 16:6 diff. Mk. 8:15, suggests that here Luke is following Q rather than Mk. (Schramm, 49 n. 1; cf. Schürmann, *Untersuchungen*, 123f.) ζύμη, 'leaven' (13:21 par. Mt. 13:33; Mt. 16:12; 1 Cor. 5:6; Gal. 5:9), is used metaphorically (Mk. 8:15; Mt. 16:6, 11; 1 Cor. 5:7f.**) of the pervasive influence of the thing signified (H. Windisch, TDNT II, 902–906, especially 906). The phrase τῶν Φαρισαίων, which follows rather awkwardly at the end of the sentence in p⁷⁵ B L 1241 e sa, is bought forward in p⁴⁵ *rell*; TR; *Diglot* (cf. Metzger, 159). The ἥτις . . . clause looks as though it may have been a clarifying addition, but it probably stood in Q, since otherwise the use of the link passage is hard to explain. ὑπόκρισις is 'hypocrisy' (Mk. 12:15; Mt. 23:28; Gal. 2:13; 1 Tim. 4:2; 1 Pet. 2:1**); see 6:42 note. The word sums up the preceding description of the Pharisees and scribes. The disciples are warned against being contaminated by the same kind of outlook. (U. Wilckens, TDNT VIII, 567 n. 45, however, thinks that Luke added the word and the phraseology of Mk. 8:15, because of the occurrence of 'hypocrites' in the Q version of the woes. This is unlikely because Mark does not provide the necessary equation between leaven and hypocrisy; Matthew was able to interpret it differently, Mt. 16:11f.)

(2) The saying opens with the statement of a general principle. The double negative form gives a strong positive affirmation. Since Luke likes συν- compounds, his use of συγκαλύπτω**, 'to cover (completely), conceal', is probably secondary to the simple form in Mt. In Mt. the saying follows a command not to be afraid of persecutors (which is probably a redactional link with the preceding sayings), and the force is not absolutely clear; the following verse suggests that a general principle is being applied to the esoteric teaching of Jesus which must be declared publicly by the disciples, so that the force is simply 'all secrets will inevitably come out'. A somewhat similar meaning is present in the doublet Lk. 8:17 par. Mk. 4:22. But in Lk. the saying is plainly applied to the future judgment, and the force appears to be that whatever is kept secret by men will be revealed and made known in the end; hypocrites will be unmasked. Bultmann, 99f., regards the saying as originally a secular proverb, but here it certainly applies to the Judgment (cf. Manson, *Sayings*, 106; Jeremias, *Parables*, 221 n. 66).

(3) The connective ἀνθ' ὧν may mean 'because' (1:20; or 'therefore' (Jdt. 9:3; BD 208¹); the latter is more likely here, so that the general rule is followed by its specific application to the disciples. The connective may be Lucan, but the fact that elsewhere he uses it in the former sense is an argument against this theory. ὅσος, diff. Mt., may be original, or reflect use of a different tradition. Luke refers to what people say in the dark, i.e. in secret, whereas Matthew refers to what Jesus says to the disciples secretly. The rather artificial use of light/darkness suggests a link with the similar pattern of sayings in Mk. 4:21f. (F. Hahn (as in 8:16–18 note), 120f.). The saying is applied in the present context to the Pharisees (G. Friedrich, TDNT III, 705). The second clause repeats the meaning in poetic parallelism. The phrase πρὸς τὸ οὖς can be used both of speaking and of hearing. ταμεῖεον, 'inner chamber' (12:24; Mt. 24:26; 6:6**), may also be spelled ταμιεῖον (the older form, found in *Synopsis*, but without MS authority). The reference to the housetops is proverbial in tone (cf. SB I, 580). In Lk. what is said secretly by men will be made known publicly; secrets will not remain hidden. In Mt.,

however, the disciples are commanded to proclaim openly what they have learned secretly; the gospel must be spread and made known. Which form of the saying is original? The Matthean form is defended at length by F. Horst, TDNT V, 553 (cf. 170). But the Lucan form can equally well claim originality (cf. Schweizer, *Matthäus*, 159). Both forms give a good sense with what follows. Luke has the better link with the immediately preceding verse, since the principle in v. 2 is better as a justification for the conclusion drawn in Lk. than for the imperative in Mt. It is possible that Matthew had a different form of the sayings with a different catechetical purpose (Schweizer, ibid.).

(4) The introductory transitional phrase shows that for Luke the previous sayings were concerned particularly with the Pharisees and their hypocrisy. The formula λέγω δὲ ὑμῖν is peculiar to Lk. (cf. 6:27; 12:5, 8), but may have stood in his source, since in Lk. Jesus is already addressing the disciples. The description of the disciples as φίλοι is found only here in the Synoptic Gospels (cf. Jn. 15:13–15) and is used to express the close relationship between Jesus and those who do his will and are entrusted with his secrets (Grundmann, 253). Although φίλος is a favourite word of Lk., it is usually based on his sources (cf. G. Stählin, TDNT IX, 163); *pace* Schulz, 157). The use of φοβέομαι with ἀπό (Mt. 10:28**) is Semitic. Luke uses ἀποκτέννω (UBS), diff. Mt. ἀποκτείνω. The contrast is between the ability to kill the body and thereafter being unable to do anything more; Matthew speaks of killing the soul, and this formulation is probably original since the language in Lk. may be editorial (ἔχω with the infinitive; cf. Schulz, 158): There is admittedly no obvious reason why Luke should have objected to the body/soul dualism which appears in 12:19–23; Acts 20:10. Perhaps he disliked the idea of killing the soul, since the soul survives death (16:19ff.; Acts 2:27; E. Schweizer; 646). The point in any case is that men can destroy only the body; they cannot touch the essential life of a man.

(5) The opening phrase, emphasising a solemn contrast, is again peculiar to Lk., and may be due to him (cf. the use of ὑποδείκνυμι 3:7 (par. Mt. 3:7); 6:47; Acts 9:16; 20:35**). Its function corresponds to that of μᾶλλον in Mt. The disciples are to fear the one who after killing has power to cast into Gehenna. The μετὰ τό phrase is lacking in Mt. and could be Lucan. Luke has ἔχω ἐξουσίαν diff. Mt. δύναμαι which brings out the thought of authority, rather than mere power, to act. ἐμβάλλω** is 'to throw into', diff. Mt. ἀπόλλυμι. Again there may be an attempt to avoid the idea of annihilation, but Matthew himself hardly took the word in this way. γέεννα* is the fiery place of final punishment in Jewish eschatology (cf. Mk. 9:43–47; J. Jeremias, TDNT I, 657f.). The one who has power to cast into Gehenna is God (cf. Mk. 9:45, 47; Jas. 4:12), and not the devil (as Grundmann, 253); the latter has power over death (Heb. 2:14), but the NT places the final authority over men in the hands of God. The verse closes with an emphatic repetition of the thought (cf. 11:51 and 7:26; 10:21; the parallels suggest that this is

original, and not a Lucan addition). See further I. H. Marshall*.

(6) If the preceding saying has emphasised the importance of a fear for God which enables disciples to overcome their fear of persecution from men, the present saying now offers them comfort by speaking of the fatherly concern of God for them. God cares even for birds that are sold cheaply for food. στρουθίον (12:7; Mt. 10:29, 31**) is a diminutive form of στρουθός, 'sparrow'. The word, however, here means any small bird used for food, since sparrows were not in fact eaten. Luke gives the rate of sale as five for two assaria: ἀσσάριον (Mt. 10:29**) was a Roman copper coin worth about 1/16 of a denarius. Matthew gives a rate of two birds for one assarion. There is no obvious reason for editorial alteration of the value here, and it is more probable that we have two forms of an oral tradition. Luke says that not one is neglected (ἐπιλανθάνομαι; cf. Heb. 6:10; 13:2, 16; also 'to forget', Mt. 16:5; Mk. 8:14; Phil. 3:13**) in the eyes of God. Matthew has 'fall to the ground without your Father'; the use of 'Father' is probably Matthaean, since it is unlikely that Luke would have altered it, but Creed, 171, and Manson, *Sayings*, 108, think that the rest of the saying is original, since it gives a link with the (falling) hairs of the head and has a rabbinic parallel: 'No bird perishes without God – how much less a man' (p. Shebi, 9, 38 d, 22; SB I, 582f.) Luke, however, regards the hair as not falling (21:18).

(7) The conjunction ἀλλὰ καί, diff. Mt. δὲ καί is possibly Lucan (16:21; 24:22*; Acts, 4x; Mt. 21:21). Matthew's phrasing gives a stronger contrast between the disciples and the birds. The reference to hair (cf. Mt. 5:36; Lk. 21:18; Acts 27:34) is proverbial: cf. 1 Sa. 14:45; 2 Sa. 14:11; 1 Ki. 1:52. For ἀριθμέω, 'to count', cf. Mt. 10:30; Rev. 7:9**; Matthew has the periphrastic form. The force of the saying is that God knows even the smallest detail about the disciples and is concerned for them; if the hairs of their heads are numbered, they have no need to be afraid of men, and they can be sure that they matter more to God than sparrows. Wellhausen argued that πολλῶν is a mistranslation of Aramaic sagî', which should have been rendered by πολλῷ (cf. 12:24 par. Mt. 6:26; Mt. 12:12). It would be strange, however, if the compiler of Q translated correctly in one place and incorrectly in another, and the point of the 'many' is to draw a contrast with the 'one' in the previous verse, so making the contrast all the stronger. διαφέρω does not need to be qualified by an adverb when expressing a comparison (1 Cor. 15:41; Gal. 4:1).

(8) In the preceding verses it has been made clear that the fate of men at the last judgment depends upon their attitude to Jesus here and now; vs. 4f. refer to the situation of persecution in which disciples may be tempted to dissemble their loyalty to Jesus out of fear of men. This thought is repeated in vs. 8f. in a double saying which contrasts earthly confession/denial of Jesus with confession/ denial of men in the presence of God. The second, negative part of the saying is paralleled at 9:26 in a somewhat different form; the Matthaean parallel here conflates elements

from Mk. and Q. The opening λέγω δὲ ὑμῖν is probably from Luke's source (cf. 12:4; diff. Mt. οὖν which is probably editorial); it might, however, be derived from Mk. 3:28 (par. Lk. 12:10), and have been brought forward to introduce the pair of sayings here, although this is less likely. ὁμολογέω, 'to confess', constructed with ἐν is equivalent to Hebrew *hôḏāh lᵉ* or Aramaic *'ôḏî bᵉ* with the meaning 'to acknowledge, declare allegiance to' (cf. O. Michel, TDNT V, 208 n. 27). The use of ἔμπροσθεν (5:19) stresses that a public acknowledgement is meant, and it may refer specifically to standing before a judge; the fact that the second part of the saying alludes to the heavenly court does not demand that a forensic situation be seen on the earthly level also, but it is not impossible that Jesus may have had this in mind. The main clause speaks of acknowledgement of those who are faithful to Jesus in the presence of the angels of God, diff. Mt. 'my Father in heaven'. The phrase is hardly a periphrasis for the name of God since God is named in it – unless we assume that τοῦ θεοῦ is an addition to the original phrase (Dalman, 157; Klostermann, 134); the reference is to God's heavenly court. The alternative phrase in Mt. may be based on Mk. 8:38 and is connected with his use of κἀγώ in place of ὁ υἱὸς τοῦ ἀνθρώπου.

This raises the question of the original subject of the main clause. In the negative form in v. 9 the main clause is expressed in the passive; this leads C. Colpe, TDNT VIII, 442, cf. 447, to the hypothesis that in the original saying, as spoken by Jesus, there was no reference to the Son of man; this is confirmed by the omission of the phrase 'Son of man' from the Matthaean version of the saying (cf. Lagrange, 355; Schweizer, *Matthäus*, 160). Hence the original Q form was roughly: 'Anyone who confesses me before men, him will men (one) confess before ... but whosoever denies me before men, he will also be denied before...' Colpe allows that perhaps Jesus spoke in the first person in the saying (12:8b); but in any case the title of Son of man was added to the saying by the church to express the role of Jesus at the final judgment. Colpe's argument has two consequences. First, the kernel of the saying can be defended all the more confidently as an authentic saying of Jesus, notwithstanding the claims of Vielhauer, 76–79, 101–107, to the contrary. Second, in its original form the saying does not make the apparent differentiation between Jesus and the Son of man which formed the starting point for the thesis that Jesus (or the earliest church) regarded the Son of man as an eschatological functionary who was not to be identified with himself. But Colpe's reconstruction remains hypothetical. It is possible that Matthew substituted 'I' in the saying for an original 'Son of man' to bring out more forcefully the eschatological role of Jesus (so most scholars; cf. Schulz, 68 n. 66). Further 'Son of man' must have stood in Luke's source, in view of the catchword connection with v. 10, and it is attested in Mk. 8:38; (but Matthew and Luke may have had different versions of Q at this point). It is thus more likely that 'Son of man' was present in the Q form of the saying, although this does not prove that it was present in the earliest form of the saying. The use of 'Son of man' raises the question whether: 1. Jesus spoke of himself as the future Son of man; or 2. Jesus spoke of a future Son of man whom he did not identify with himself; or 3. the introduction of 'Son of man' as a title for Jesus is due to the early church, which either created the saying as a whole or added the term to an existing saying. For these possibilities see 9:26 note and the literature cited there.

(9) The second part of the saying follows the pattern of the first, but is expressed more briefly with a participial construction: For ἀρνέομαι cf. 8:45. The verb is the antonym of 'to acknowledge' and corresponds to ἐπαισχύνομαι (9:26). The compound ἀπαρνέομαι (22:34, 61) has the same meaning, but the prefix may strengthen the force of the verb in this context to express the irrevocable nature of the final rejection of the person in the heavenly court. ἐνώπιον, a favourite Lucan word, replaces an original ἔμπροσθεν. The Son of man is not mentioned in this part of the saying (diff. 9:26), but the thought of denial by him is required by the parallel in v. 8. The passive construction may have been introduced by Luke in order to avoid a clash with the following verse which states that speaking against the Son of man is forgivable (Kümmel, 44f.; Vielhauer, 101f.). For the ascription of the same function to Jesus see 13:26f. par. Mt. 7:23.

It is not clear whether the saying as a whole has been introduced for the sake of the positive encouragement to confession and witness in v. 8 (cf. vs. 6f.) or for the sake of the warning against denial and apostasy in v. 9 (cf. vs. 4f.). Both thoughts may well be present. The saying brings out the vital significance of men's attitude to Jesus here and now in view of the coming judgment.

(10) The saying about forgiveness of sins has a parallel in Mk. 3:28f. There is a further parallel in Mt. 12:31f., where Matthew has conflated the Marcan form with the Q form represented by Lk. to give a double saying. In Mk. and Mt. the saying comes in the context of the Beelzebul controversy. It may stand in its original Q context in Lk. where it has a catchword connection ('Son of man') with the preceding saying and also ('Holy Spirit') with the following saying. It seems to have been an originally isolated saying since it stands in tension with the previous saying which announces final rejection for those who deny Jesus (i.e. the Son of man); it is perhaps to be regarded as a corrective of the previous saying (E. Lövestam*, 79). It is closely connected with the following saying: if the present saying warns against sin against the Spirit, the following saying assures disciples of the help of the Spirit in time of temptation.

The Q form lacks the ἀμὴν λέγω ὑμῖν introduction found in Mk. which may belong to the original form of the saying. Luke's formulation of the saying with πᾶς ὅς in the first part and a participle phrase in the second part is parallel to vs. 8f. Matthew's use of ὅς ἐάν may be influenced by Mk. 3:29. For the casus pendens (πᾶς ὅς, taken up by αὐτῷ)cf.

1:36 note. In the first part Luke has λέγω λόγον εἰς ... (diff. Mt. κατά), a phrase which is a Semitism meaning 'to curse' (Job 2:9) and is equivalent in meaning to Mk. βλασφημέω εἰς ... (cf. Acts 6:11/13; Black, 194f.) which may be regarded as a more elegant Greek rendering. The future tense ἐρεῖ may simply express an indefinite statement (cf. BD 380²; Mt. 10:32 diff. Mt. 10:33). The Son of man is Jesus. The future tense ἀφεθήσεται refers to the final judgment (cf. vs. 8f.). It would not need to be pointed out to a Jewish audience that the forgiveness promised here is not granted automatically but is conditional on the repentance of the person seeking it (E. Lövestam*, 58–61).

In the second part of the saying the construction with the participle gives a parallel to v. 9. Matthew has retained the original Q construction with ὅς δ' ἄν. (The noun phrase in Mt. 12:31b is due to assimilation to the first part of the verse.) Instead of λέγω κατά Luke uses βλασφημέω, probably under the influence of Mk. 3:29 (Schramm, 46f.; Schulz, 246f.), but it is possible that the word was in his recension of Q. βλασφημέω is 'to revile, defame' (22:65; 23:39*; Acts 13:45; 18:6; 19:37; 26:11*), and is used of speaking against God or his Spirit. Whereas in later Jewish usage blasphemy involved the clear use of the name of God (Sanh. 7:5), the NT reflects a less strict earlier usage; here the word refers to 'the conscious and wicked rejection of the saving power and grace of God towards man' (H. W. Beyer, TDNT I, 621–625, especially 624; cf. SB I, 1009f.; For the OT background see especially E. Lövestam*, 7–57). Such rejection of the saving power of God deprives a man of the possibility of divine forgiveness – a thought which may appear to be tautologous, but which has its point when directed to people who think that they can reject the particular way of salvation laid down by God and yet still enjoy his favour in the end.

The meaning of the saying and its relation to Mk. 3:28f. are far from clear. 1. Most commonly the saying is regarded as a post-Easter formulation which draws a contrast between sin committed during the ministry of Jesus, when men might speak ignorantly against the Son of man, and sin during the period of the early church, when it would be a witting sin to speak against the manifest work of the Spirit (A. Fridrichsen, as cited by Bultmann, 138 n. 1; O. Procksch, TDNT I, 104; E. Schweizer, TDNT VI, 397, 405; C. Colpe, TDNT VIII, 452f.; Tödt, 119; Wrege, 167f.; Schulz, 247–250). 2. Patristic interpretation saw in blasphemy against the Son of man the pre-baptismal sin of the heathen committed in ignorance, whereas blasphemy against the Spirit was a witting act of apostasy by the baptised and as such incapable of forgiveness (so Barrett, 105–17; Higgins, 130f.). 3. If spoken by Jesus, the saying could refer to the possibility of slander against himself as the 'Son of man', a phrase which could express his humiliation and hiddenness and was not necessarily recognisable as a title of dignity, whereas blasphemy against the Spirit of God was a culpable sin. 'It is excusable to a point to fail to recognize the dignity of the One who hides himself under the humble appearance of a man, but not to disparage works manifestly salutary which reveal the action of the Divine Spirit' (M.-J. Lagrange, *Evangile selon Saint Marc*, Paris, 1929, 76, as summarised by Taylor, 242; J. Weiss, 105).

None of these views is free from difficulty. There is no distinction of tenses in the saying to support view 1. (cf. Borsch, 328 n. 3), and it requires a good deal of reading into the text to discover the two periods of salvation-history which have been found in it. In the same way it is far from obvious that one part of the saying refers to sin committed by unconverted Jews and the other to sin committed by Christians. The real difficulty, however, with both views 1. and 2. is to find a situation in the early church in which blasphemy against the Son of man could be regarded as less culpable than blasphemy against the Spirit. R. Scroggs* attempts to find such a situation in a group of ecstatically minded Christians which over-emphasised the gifts of the Spirit even to the extent of exalting the Spirit over Jesus; but it is incredible that a saying from such a source should have come to be attributed to Jesus, and the existence of such a group remains problematical. The more 'Son of man' came to be understood as a title of dignity, the less likely is it that blasphemy against the Son of man could be placed on a lower level than blasphemy against the Spirit. Further, 'Son of man' does not seem to have been a confessional title in the early church; in all forms of the saying in 12:8 it is confession of *Jesus* which is confirmed by the Son of man.

As for view 3., it is inconceivable that this could have been the interpretation of the saying accepted by Luke for whom 'Son of man' was a title of dignity and not a cypher concealing the real identity of Jesus. A more basic problem is whether 'Son of man' could have been used by Jesus in a non-titular sense.

The Marcan form of the saying by contrast avoids these difficulties. All sin and blasphemy can be forgiven to the sons of men except blasphemy against the Spirit. Many scholars regard this form of the saying as original and hold that the Q form has been derived from it or from an Aramaic original with the same meaning as Mk. The original Aramaic form spoke of sins and blasphemies 'on the part of men' or 'against men', using *bar 'enaš(â)* as a generic or collective term. Mark understood the phrase in the former sense, while Q understood it in the latter sense and took *bar 'enaš(â)* to be a reference to the Son of man (Wellhausen, *Einleitung*, 67; ibid. *Matthäus*, 63; Bultmann, 138; Manson, *Sayings*, 109f.; Wrege, 164–167; C. Colpe, TDNT VIII, 442f.). The opposite view, that the Marcan form is secondary to the Q form is defended by Percy, 253–256; Higgins, 127–132; Tödt, 312–318, and Schulz, 247. Certainly Mark's form can be regarded as an attempt to ease the difficulty present in the Q saying in Greek, and certainly in other respects the Q saying is nearer to Semitic style than the Marcan saying. But neither of these arguments can be regarded as conclusive.

The best solution of the problem is to be found in the hypothesis of an ambiguous Aramaic original. Mark's 'sons of men' cannot have arisen except as an expansion of an original *bar ' ᵉnaš(â)* in a collective sense; it is not possible that his form of the saying arose out of a rewriting of the Greek Q saying. The same phrase was taken by Q to refer to speaking against the Son of man. It is quite credible that Jesus could tell his opponents that speaking against him was forgivable, while warning them that denial of the work of the Spirit was unforgivable. While this could have happened with the Aramaic understood in the Marcan form, it is perhaps more probable that a self-reference by Jesus using 'Son of man' as a self-designation was originally intended (cf. Percy, 255f.; R. Schippers*; Vermes, 182 with n. 77). Only in a saying of the earthly Jesus does 'Son of man' give an intelligible meaning. The saying is then to be regarded as addressed to opponents, while the preceding saying in vs. 8f. which warns against denial of Jesus must be understood as a warning to disciples against apostasy (cf. Schmid, 217). For Luke the emphasis falls on the second part of the statement, namely on the warning against blaspheming against the Spirit who is sent to help the disciples (Creed, 172). The tension between v. 8 and v. 10a may not have appeared so great to Luke. The significance of the saying in Q cannot be determined with certainty. In any case it cannot have been created at this stage; the wording demands an origin in the teaching of Jesus.

(11) The saying about speaking against the Holy Spirit is closely followed by one which promises the help of the Holy Spirit to teach the disciples what to say in situations of persecution when they are being tempted to deny their faith. They do not need to worry about what to say because the Spirit will provide them with the words. There is a similar saying in Mk. 13:11 which is paralleled in Mt. 10:19f. At the corresponding point in Luke's version of the apocalyptic discourse there is a third form of the saying which differs considerably in wording from the others, speaking of the wisdom given by Jesus with no reference to the Spirit (21:14f.). How these sayings are related to one other is uncertain. Both Lucan sayings show some signs of Lucan language, and it is curious that the present saying in a Q context resembles the Marcan saying more than does Lk. 21:14f. One possibility is that Luke has used the Marcan saying here, and then used a variant form of the saying in order to avoid repetition in Lk. 21. But there are two or three minor points of agreement between Lk. and Mt. which suggest that Matthew has conflated the Marcan saying with a Q form of the same saying, which was very similar to the Marcan form, and which Luke has used here (Schulz, 442). Then Lk. 21:14f. is either another form of the saying (from Luke's special source) or is due to his own editing of Mk. There are no linguistic contacts between Mt. 10:19f. and Lk. 21:14f. which would show that the latter saying was based on Q. Schürmann, *Untersuchungen*, 150–155, argues that the present saying formed a unity with Mt. 10:23 in Q and that this combination had a catch-word connection ('Son of man') with the preceding sayings.

The saying opens with a ὅταν clause, par. Mk. and Mt. (cf. also Mt. 10:23), indicating the confessional situation; Luke has δέ, par. Mt., diff. Mk. Since there has been no preceding indication of the nature of the situation, Luke has a reference to being brought before various courts (cf. Mk. 13:9 par. Mt. 10:17f.). Despite its absence from Mt. this will be from Q (Schulz, 442f.). The synagogues are the Jewish courts before which the disciples might have to answer for themselves. While the wording may reflect experience (W. Schrage, TDNT VII, 833), it probably reflects Jesus forebodings (Beasley-Murray, 193f.). The other two terms must refer to gentile courts. For ἀρχή, 'rule, authority', cf. 20:20 (diff. Mk.), where we also find ἐξουσία (4:6) in the same sense: the combination may therefore be Lucan (Ellis, 176), but the fact that it is singular and abstract in 20:20, whereas it is plural and concrete here, urges caution. The phrase was a current one in the early church in the singular (1 Cor. 15:24; Eph. 1:21; Col. 2:10) and the plural (Eph. 3:10; 6:12; Col. 1:16; Tit. 3:1). It may correspond to the rabbinic use of r^ešût with reference to the gentiles. Luke and Matthew agree in using μεριμνάω diff. Mk. προμεριμνάω** (cf. Lk. 21:12 προμελετάω) to describe the anxiety which the disciples were to avoid. The unusual combination πῶς ἤ τί is also found in both Lk. and Mt.; cf. the material parallel in 21:15. The textual status of the phrase is open to some doubt, since D it sy^{c p} sa^{pt} C1 Or read πῶς, and r¹ sy^s has τί; the reading of D is defended by Klostermann, 135, and Kilpatrick, 192, and is given some support by UBS. But the textual evidence is weak, and it looks as though copyists were trying to avoid a redundant expression, rather than that the whole Gk. MSS tradition (apart from D) has been assimilated to Mt. (Metzger, 159f.). Here, therefore, is a significant agreement between Lk. and Mt. which indicates that the Spirit gives guidance regarding both the general form of a speech and the actual content. Luke has ἀπολογέομαι here and in 21:14 (Acts 6x; Rom. 2:15; 2 Cor. 12:19**), 'to speak in one's defence', diff. Mk. and Mt. λαλέω (which is perhaps echoed in the closing ἤ τί εἴπητε). The whole expression is rather redundant, and suggests that Luke may be combining sources.

(12) The disciples need not be afraid because they will receive teaching (διδάσκω, cf. Jn. 14:26; 1 Cor. 2:13) what to say from the Spirit. The language has been modified by Luke. ἐν αὐτῇ τῇ ὥρᾳ may be Lucan (10:21; 13:21; cf. 2:38 note); for δεῖ cf. 2:49; The formulation of the phrase τὸ ἅγιον πνεῦμα may be due to Luke (contrast Mk. 13:11; Mt. 10:20). Since the corresponding saying in 21:15 has no reference to the Spirit, it has been claimed that the Spirit is a secondary insertion into the tradition (Barrett, 130ff.; for the contrary view see E. Schweizer, TDNT VI, 398 n. 414). But the reference to the Spirit here is likely to be primitive; it is improbable that a saying about the exalted Jesus giving wisdom to his followers would be weakened into one about God's gift of the Spirit. Schulz's view that the saying represents a late strand in Q for which the Spirit was no longer the possession of every believer (444) is

unjustified, since the saying in no way conflicts with the concept that every believer has the Spirit. The restraint of the saying is a mark of its primitive nature, and there is no good reason to deny it to Jesus. See G. R. Beasley-Murray, 'Jesus and the Spirit', in Descamps, 463–478, especially 473f.

ii. The Parable of the Rich Fool 12:13–21

Jesus' teaching to his disciples is interrupted by a question from one of the crowd which directs attention away from the theme of fearless confession to that of material possessions and their fair distribution. If in the earlier section the hypocrisy of the Pharisees introduced teaching for the disciples on avoiding hypocrisy and being fearless in confession, Jesus now uses the avarice of the crowd to introduce teaching for the disciples on trust in God and freedom from greed for material possessions (12:22–34).

Jesus is called upon to intervene in a dispute, but refuses to do so, not merely because he is not qualified to do so, but above all because he is opposed to the covetous desire which underlies the request for his arbitration. A disciple is one who has a true sense of values and recognises that real life is not measured in terms of possessions. It only needs God to take away the real life of a man (cf. 12:4f.), and at once it is apparent that ultimately his possessions are of no value to him. The man who is not rich in regard to God is indeed poor, no matter how big his bank balance. He is, therefore, in the last analysis a fool, a godless and hence a senseless man (cf. 11:40). He has, as he thought, prepared for his own comfort, but he has not prepared for his ultimate destiny. He heaped up treasure for himself, the implication being that if he had given up his wealth in alms he would have secured a lasting treasure for himself (v. 33).

The introduction is a brief pronouncement story or apophthegm (Bultmann, 21), but this is perhaps too formal a description of a simple request and reply. Bultmann argues that Luke joined the originally independent conversation to the parable by creating v. 15 as a bridge (cf. Schmid, 218), but there is no very good reason for separating the various parts of the section in this way (Manson, *Sayings,* 270f.). The fact that the introduction and the parable appear separately in G. Thomas 72 and 63 is not significant, since Thomas may well be dependent on Lk. (cf. Schürmann, *Untersuchungen,* 232f.).

The parable belongs to the 'a certain man . . .' variety which is peculiar to Lk. and which some critics tend to regard as being created by Luke (cf. M. Goulder and G. Sellin, as in 10:29–37 note). It does in fact show a number of features in common with the other parables peculiar to Lk. and Lucan features of style and language. Moreover, it fits neatly into its present context as an example of the negative attitude condemned in the surrounding teaching. It could be argued that Luke has composed it (and the introduction) as a suitable preface to the Q material in vs. 22ff.

This conclusion, however, is unjustified. Although the introduction and parable are not found in Mt., there is some evidence that they originally stood in Q (Easton, 201; Schürmann, *Untersuchungen*, 119f., 232f.). It is intelligible that Matthew omitted the passage when formulating the Sermon on the Mount, and there is some evidence that he knew the omitted passage (Mt. 6:19f., 25). If so, the case for Lucan composition falls to the ground. If, however, the material is not from Q, it is still improbable that it is a free Lucan composition.

See D. Daube, 'Inheritance in two Lukan Pericopes', *Zeitschrift der Savigny-Stiftung für Rechtsgeschichte*, rom. Abt. 72, 1955, 327ff.; Jeremias, 164f.; J. N. Birdsall, 'Luke XII, 16ff. and the Gospel of Thomas', JTS ns 13, 1962, 332–336; J. D. M. Derrett, 'The Rich Fool. A Parable of Jesus Concerning Inheritance', *Heythrop Journal*, 18, 1977, 131–151.

(13) The opening formulation εἶπεν δέ τις . . ., which uses an interruption from the audience to take the narrative further, may have been recast by Luke (cf. 11:27, 45). ἐκ τοῦ ὄχλου gives a link with the preceding scene (12:1). Jesus is addressed as a teacher (cf. 7:40), i.e. a rabbi, since he is being asked to act in this capacity. For λέγω with the force 'to command' cf. 6:46. The situation is that of a man whose elder brother refused to give him his share of their father's inheritance (κληρονομία, 20:14*). It was possible, and may even have been considered desirable, for the heirs to a property to live together and so keep it intact (cf. Ps. 133:1 and the practice alluded to in Jos. Bel. 2:122). In this case the younger brother apparently wanted to separate off his own share of the inheritance and be independent. Such disputes were settled by appeal to rabbis on the basis of the existing law (Nu. 27:1–11; Dt. 21:15ff.; B.B. 8f.; D. Daube*). The situation is thus typically Palestinian.

(14) For the use of ἄνθρωπε cf. 5:20; 22:58, 60 (all diff. Mk.). Jesus' reply reflects the phraseology in Ex. 2:14 par. Acts 7:27. Rhetorically he asks who has made him an arbiter in such matters. The implied answer is that he has no legal standing as a rabbi to do so, but at a deeper level it is suggested that he has a more important mission to fulfil (Ellis, 178). καθίστημι, 'to appoint', is fairly common in Lk. (12:42, 44 par. Mt. 24:45, 47; Acts, 5x). For κριτής cf. 11:19. μεριστής** is 'divider, arbitrator'. The MSS are confused here, but the UBS text, supported by p⁷⁵ ℵ B L f1 f13 *al*, is to be preferred to the variants which show assimiliation to Ex. 2:14 (Metzger, 160).

(15) Jesus proceeds to address the crowd with a warning against the covetousness which he has detected behind the man's request. For ὁράω, 'to beware', cf. Mk. 1:44; 8:15; Mt. 18:10; 24:6; and for φυλάσσομαι cf. 2 Thes. 3:3; 1 Jn. 5:21; T Jud. 18:2. πλεονεξία is 'greediness, covetousness' (Mk. 7:22; G. Delling, TDNT VI, 266–274). πᾶς must mean 'every kind of'. The syntax of the concluding clause is strange, and C. F. D. Moule ('H. W. Moule on Acts iv. 25', Exp.T 65,

1951-54, 220f.) suggests that two expressions have been combined: a. οὐκ ἐν τῷ περισσεύειν τινὶ ἡ ζωή and b. οὐκ ἐκ τῶν ὑπαρχόντων τινὶ ἡ ζωή. Such clumsiness suggests that Luke is not composing freely at this point. The meaning is in any case clear. The real life of a man is not dependent on the abundance (περισσεύω, 9:17), or perhaps superfluity (J. D. M. Derrett*, 135f.), of his possessions; hence avarice is dangerous, since it leads a person to direct his aim to the wrong things in life and to ignore what really matters, namely being rich towards God. The wording is not Lucan and is based on a source.

(16) The parable begins with a typical Lucan introduction (6:39). The opening phrase in the genitive may again be Lucan style (7:2; for the construction see BD 473[1]). Here the effect is to lay stress on the adjective πλούσιος (6:24); the view of F. Hauck and W. Kasch (TDNT VI, 328) that something more than mere possession of material goods is meant here lacks support. χώρα (2:8; et al.) here means 'estate, property' (Jas. 5:4; Jos. Ant. 11:249; 16:250), and εὐφορέω** is 'to bear good crops, yield well'. The man is thus rich at the outset of the story; contrast the pattern in Sir. 11:18f.; 1 En. 97:8–10.

(17) Soliloquy is not uncommon in Lk.: 12:45 (par. Mt. 24:48); 15:17–19; 16:3f.; 18:4f.; 20:13 (par. Mk. 12:6). For διαλογίζομαι (1:29; et al.) with ἐν ἑαυτῷ/ἑαυτοῖς see Mt. 16:7f.; 21:25; Mk. 2:8. For ἑαυτῷ B L* have αὐτῷ; cf. 12:21; 23:12; 24:12 for other possible examples. The αὐτός form was dying out in Hellenistic Greek, but there are probably some genuine cases of it in the NT; see BD 64[1]; Moule, 119. In the question τί ποιήσω (16:3; 20:13 diff. Mk. 12:6) it is uncertain whether the verb is future indicative or aorist subjunctive, since both are possible (BD 366). The rich man's problem is that he has no permanent stores for his grain (Jeremias, Parables, 165). He assumed that his wealth would last; his problem was simply where to keep it.

(18) For the expression of determination what to do cf. 16:4. The solution is to tear down (καθαιρέω, 1:52; et al.) the existing barns and build larger ones. These will then hold all the man's grain and goods. The text is attested by p[75c] B L f1 f13; πάντα τὰ γενήματά μου is read by ℵ* D it (sy[sc]), and πάντα τὰ γενήματά μου καὶ τὰ ἀγαθά μου by A W Θ pm vg; TR. Kilpatrick, 190f., 202f., adopts the third of these readings, noting that it is indirectly supported by the existence of the second reading (with loss by homoioteleuton), and attributes its alteration in the Egyptian text to an Atticistic dislike for γένημα (cf. Is. 65:21; Je. 8:13 LXX). Grundmann, 257 n. supports the second reading. WH II, 103, however, claim that the presence of γένημα is due to the influence of LXX phraseology. Kilpatrick's case is the more plausible. For γένημα, 'product, fruit, yield', cf. 22:18; 2 Cor. 9:10.

(19) For ψυχή in self-address cf. Pss. 41:6, 12: 42:5; Ps. Sol. 3:1. The phrase κείμενα ... πίε is omitted by D it (so Grundmann, 257f.), but this purely western omission is to be rejected, especially since the phrase is quite Lucan in style (Jeremias, Words, 149). Since the rich man has

plenty of resources stored away for the foreseeable future, he can afford to relax and enjoy his wealth. ἀναπαύομαι is 'to rest' (Mk. 6:31; 14:41; et al.). εὐφραίνομαι is 'to be glad, enjoy oneself, rejoice' (15:23f., 29, 32; 16:19*; Acts 2:26; 7:41*). Similar combinations of expressions are found in Ec. 8:15; Tob. 7:10 (par. 1 Cor. 15:32); Sir. 11:19 and in Greek literature (Euripides, Alcestis 788f.; Lucian, Navig. 25; and the epitaph of Sardanapalus ἔσθιε πίνε ὄχευε, cited by Creed, 173). The rich man is implicitly depicted as selfishly enjoying his riches without thought for his needy neighbours or concern about God (cf. 16:19–31).

(20) Such an attitude is folly in the eyes of God who now steps into the story and addresses the man directly as ἄφρων (cf. 11:40; Ps. 14:1). Such a way of life fails to reckon with the possibility of sudden and swift crisis. That very night – the phrase is emphatically placed – the rich man's life is demanded from him. For the third person plural as a periphrasis for God cf. 6:38; Grundmann, 258, however, argues that it is a periphrasis for the angel of death (cf. Heb. 2:14; SB I, 144–149), which is perhaps more likely, since God is here the speaker. The verb ἀπαιτέω may convey the idea of life as a loan which must be returned to God (Wis. 15:8); the reading αἰτοῦσιν (p⁷⁵ B al) is probably secondary (Metzger, 160). When death occurs, the goods so carefully stored up are no longer of any help; cf. Ps. 39:6 (38:7 LXX); Ec. 6:1f. There is no good reason for adopting Jeremias's interpretation that the parable refers to the coming of eschatological catastrophe rather than to the death of the individual. The same thought of the imminence of death is also present in the story of the rich man and Lazarus.

(21) The closing verse is omitted by D a b, probably by accident, the omission would produce an awkward transition from v. 20 to v. 22 (Metzger, 160f.; Jeremias, Words, 149). The comment brings out the latent meaning of the parable. The rich man gathered treasure (θησαυρίζω, Mt. 6:19f.) for himself (αὐτῷ, א B pc; ἑαυτῷ, rell; TR; Diglot), but failed to grow rich as regards God. He thus failed in the end even to gather wealth for himself. The phrase appears to mean the same as laying up treasure in heaven; Jeremias, Parables, 106, suggests that it means entrusting one's wealth to God. Jeremias (ibid.) is inclined to regard the rest of the verse as a moralising addition to the parable, changing it from an eschatological warning to a warning against the wrong use of riches. Creed, 173, sees it as a transition to the next section; but the thought of treasure in heaven is so far away (v. 33) that this is unlikely. The comment fits the message of the parable according to our interpretation of it, and can be original. Various late MSS add to the end of the verse the stereotyped phrase ταῦτα λέγων ἐφώνει ὁ ἔχων ὦτα ἀκούειν ἀκουέτω (cf. 8:8 and similar additions at 8:15; 13:9; 21:4; cf. Mt. 25:29, 30); it is due to lectionary usage and is not original, despite the presence of a similar addition in G. Thomas 63 (J. N. Birdsall*).

iii. Earthly Possessions and Heavenly Treasure 12:22–34

The present section of teaching addressed to the disciples is a positive contrast to the warning about the false regard for wealth in the preceding section. Disciples are not to be anxiously concerned about food and clothing. These are of less importance than the person himself. Nor is concern necessary: even birds who show no forethought for themselves are supplied by God, and the disciples matter more to him. In any case, the disciples cannot lengthen their lives by anxious care, and therefore they should not be anxious about other things over which they have no control. If God gives to flowers a glorious appearance beyond that of Solomon, he can be trusted to clothe the disciples as well. Let them not be anxious seekers after the things sought by other men; if they seek after God's kingdom, the other things they need will be provided for them. God has certainly promised them the kingdom. So let them sit lightly to material possessions and help the poor; let them seek heavenly treasure, which will not perish, and thereby set their affections in the right place.

The connection of thought is not absolutely logical, but we are not to expect this in the discourses of Jesus which are akin in this respect to some of the wisdom literature. It is therefore hard to say how far the passage consists of isolated sayings which have been put together to form a continuous discourse. The parallelism between vs. 24 and 27f. leads Bultmann, 84, to suggest that v. 25 is an addition, which Luke has fitted more neatly into the present context by the editorial bridge in v. 26 (cf. 119f.); with less reason v. 32 is regarded as a secondary creation by the church (Bultmann, 116). The problem is complicated by the relationship of the passage to the Matthaean parallel. Essentially the same material occurs with one inversion of order in Mt. 6:25–34, 19–21; the order in Lk. is original, since Luke is unlikely to have removed v. 34, which would give a good link with v. 21, away from the beginning of the passage, and v. 35 has a catchword link with v. 39. Moreover, Matthew has added other sayings at the beginning of the section (Mt. 6:22–24). The wording is fairly close throughout the section, but there are marked differences in vs. 24, 26, 29, 32 and 33. Some of these go well beyond what can be explained by editorial activity on the part of the two Evangelists (cf. Wrege, 109–113, 116–124), and suggest that we have two variant forms of the tradition before us; the theory that the Q material existed in more than one form receives further support from this passage.

In general the authenticity of the teaching of Jesus in this section is uncontested, although various individual sayings stand under some critical suspicion. The section as a whole is not a collection of proverbial sentiments; on the contrary it contains promises made by Jesus to the disciples as people who have made their supreme aim in life the attainment of the kingdom of God. The passage thus has an eschatological basis. In its warnings against striving for wealth it goes beyond Pharisaic

Judaism and stands nearer to Qumran (Braun, *Radikalismus* II, 77; Schulz, 144f.).

See R. Bultmann, TDNT IV, 591–593; W. Pesch, 'Zur Formgeschichte und Exegese von Lk. 12, 32', Bib. 41, 1960, 25–40; id. 'Zur Exegese von Mt. 6, 19–21 und Lk. 12, 33–34', Bib. 41, 1960, 356–378; Wrege, 116–124; Schulz, 149–157, 142–145.

(22) The redactional introduction directs the following teaching to those who have responded to the call of Jesus, i.e. his disciples. The αὐτοῦ is omitted by p⁴⁵ ᵛⁱᵈ p⁷⁵ B 1241 c e, but retained by *Diglot* and with brackets by *Synopsis*; UBS (Metzger, 161). The saying is introduced by διὰ τοῦτο which gives a good connection with the preceding section: in view of the folly of storing up material goods the disciples should refrain from similar concern. The same phrase gives a different connection in Mt. 6:25 with the preceding saying about serving mammon (If you want to have an undivided mind with which to serve God, do not be concerned about food, etc). Jesus forbids the attitude expressed by μεριμνάω. The verb usually means 'to take anxious thought'. Following earlier suggestions Jeremias, *Parables*, 214f., argues that the meaning is 'to put forth an effort', i.e. 'to strive after'; the verb is thus close in meaning to ζητέω (cf. 12:29 par. Mt. 6:33; 1 Cor. 12:25 with 10:33; 13:5). With this alternative understanding, however, the thought of *worried* effort is still present (v. 29); see further R. Bultmann, TDNT IV, 589–593 (with an excellent exposition of the present passage). The object of anxious concern is the provision of food in order to support life and of clothing in order to keep the body warm and alive. ψυχή and σῶμα accordingly stand in parallelism rather than in opposition to each other (E. Schweizer, TDNT VII, 1058); after ψυχή and σῶμα Matthew adds ὑμῶν which Luke has probably removed for stylistic reasons (Wrege, 117); various MSS restore it on both occasions in Lk.; it is retained after σώματι by *Diglot* and with brackets by *Synopsis* with B f13 *al* a sa bo, but omitted by UBS.

(23) The first reason for refraining from anxious striving for material things is that there is more to life than food and clothing. Life ultimately depends upon God and his word (4:4). Matthew has rhetorical questions here and in the parallels to vs. 24 and 28; Luke himself is probably responsible for the change of structure (Schürmann, *Abschiedsrede*, 11, 80f.; Wrege, 117). The neuter form πλεῖον indicates that life is a more important *thing* than food (τροφή*), and the body than clothing (ἔνδυμα*; Mt. 7x**). It is not clear whether the saying means that life is more important than food, or that there is more needed to support life than food. Probably the second thought is contained within the first: if life is more important than food, the disciples should be concerned about life as a whole and not merely about the material aspects of maintaining it.

(24) A second reason for refraining from anxiety is given: God will provide what is needed without the disciples striving for food, just as he cares for birds. The disciples are bidden to observe them and draw a

lesson from them. For κατανοέω cf. 6:41 (Q); Luke has it here and in
v. 27, whereas Matthew has ἐμβλέπω and καταμανθάνω**. No strong
editorial reasons for the difference can be established (Wrege, 117).
Luke has κόραξ**, 'crow'. Since the crow was an unclean bird (Lv.
11:15; Dt. 14:14), it is possible that Matthew wished to avoid the
reference and substituted the stereotyped phrase πετεινὰ τοῦ οὐρανοῦ
(Grundmann, 260). The specific mention that the birds do not work implies that it is assumed that men do work: Jesus is not advocating a lazy,
carefree attitude to life. The reading οὐ ... οὐδέ (UBS; Diglot), though
supported by the majority of MSS, may be an assimilation to Mt. and
οὔτε ... οὔτε ... (ℵ D al; Synopsis) should be preferred; The birds
neither sow nor reap (θερίζω, 19:21f. par. Mt. 25:24–26), and
correspondingly do not have a store-house (ταμεῖον, 12:3) – presumably
for seed – nor a barn (12:18). The wording differs in Mt. who omits
ταμεῖον (12:3 possibly Lucan) and uses συνάγω; since the latter word
has already occurred in 12:18 it may be that Luke has altered the phrasing for the sake of variety, but it is doubtful whether he would
deliberately remove the verbal link between the parable and this saying.
Here again, therefore, is evidence that we have two variant forms of the
tradition. The force of the following καί is 'and yet'. Luke has simply ὁ
θεός where Matthew has the full phrase 'your heavenly Father'. In view
of the usage in v. 32, this is strong evidence that Luke was not using Mt.
as his source (the view upheld at length by Schlatter, passim). For τρέφω
see 4:16. The conclusion is drawn by means of an a minori argument
(for the style see SB I, 582f.; II, 191); cf. 11:13; 12:28. If the disciples
are more important than birds (Luke has a statement, Matthew a
rhetorical question), (it is implied that) God will certainly provide for
them.

(25) Verses 25f. present what is in effect a third reason for refraining from anxious striving, namely that it is ineffective. The section is
widely regarded as an insertion which separates the two parallel statements in vs. 24 and 27f. (Bultmann, 84); the rhetorical τίς ἐξ ὑμῶν form
(11:5) is regarded as a mark of address to the crowds by Jeremias
(Parables, 171; cf. Wrege, 119), and the saying has been attached to its
present context by the catchword μεριμνάω. But this argument is not
convincing. The two parabolic sayings need not necessarily have stood
in direct connection with each other, especially since in Mt. they have
different introductions and in both Gospels they vary in structure.
Jeremias's proposed original setting for v. 25 as a warning in face of eschatological catastrophe is also unconvincing, and the introductory formula need not necessarily have been confined to discussions with opponents (cf. 11:5). The wording of the saying is ambiguous. ἡλικία (2:52
note) can mean 'age' or 'bodily stature'. πῆχυς is usually a measure of
length, 'cubit' (about 18 in.; 46 cm.; Jn. 21:8; Rev. 21:17), but could
possibly be used metaphorically as a measure of time, an 'hour' (cf.
πήχυιον ἐπὶ χρόνον, 'for only a cubit of time', Mimnermus 2, 3, cited by

AG 662). Although RV, NEB and Barclay opt for 'a cubit unto his stature' (so also Manson, *Sayings* 113; Danker, 151), the majority of commentators prefer 'a cubit to his span of life' (RSV; JB; TEV; NIV; J. Schneider, TDNT II 941–943). Since the cubit is regarded as the 'least' possible increase, a measure of length is unlikely; in regard to height an extra cubit would be positively unwelcome! For the application of a measure of length to a life-span see also Ps. 39:5. Manson's argument for the other view, that if you cannot make yourself grow by worrying, you cannot make corn grow either, is over-subtle. The saying is strengthened in Mt. by the addition of εἷς, 'even one', which Luke may have omitted as unnecessary (Wrege, 118 n. 3; *contra* Schulz, 150).

(26) The point of the previous saying is now drawn out in a verse that has no parallel in Mt. and may be Lucan (Schulz, 150). The disciples cannot make the slightest difference (ἐλάχιστος, 16:10; 19:17*) to the length of their lives: why, then, should they be anxious about other things which will not lengthen it (cf. Easton, 202)? The use of τὰ λοιπά is odd; it recurs in Mk. 4:19 and may possibly have been a technical term in the teaching of Jesus and the early church for worldly concerns, i.e. concerns other than the kingdom of God. Here, however, it may simply mean 'things like clothing'. In place of the verse Matthew has simply καὶ περὶ ἐνδύματος τί μεριμνᾶτε which provides a direct introduction to the next saying, and leaves the hearer to draw the lesson of the previous statement. Since ἔνδυμα is a favourite word of Matthew, it is also possible that he may have been responsible for the alteration here in order to produce a more connected flow of thought.

(27) For κατανοέω, repeated from v. 24, Matthew has καταμανθάνω, which may be original. κρίνον (Mt. 6:28**) is a flower; the identification is quite uncertain, and a general reference to Galilean flowers may be meant; Manson, *Sayings*, 112, follows Dalman in suggesting the purple anemone, which would contrast with the purple robes of Solomon. Matthew adds τοῦ ἀγροῦ, possibly to give a contrast with τοῦ οὐρανοῦ in Mt. 6:26. The description of what the flowers do is confused in the MSS. The best text in Mt. has πῶς αὐξάνουσιν· οὐ κοπιῶσιν οὐδὲ νήθουσιν, but a number of later MSS have the singular forms of the verbs which is grammatically more correct and may also be an assimilation to the Lucan text. In Lk. most MSS have πῶς αὐξάνει· οὐ κοπιᾷ οὐδὲ νήθει (p⁴⁵ p⁷⁵ ℵ A B W Θ f1 f13 vg syᵖ sa bo; TR). The variant πῶς οὔτε νήθει οὔτε ὑφαίνει is attested by D (a) syˢᶜ(Mcion) C1; *Synopsis*; *Diglot*; and a conflate reading is found in b ff²i l r¹. Although the UBS text could be an assimilation to Mt., the attestation for the variant reading is purely western; Metzger, 161, argues that the latter is a stylistic refinement introducing a reference to weaving (ὑφαίνω**) alongside that to spinning (νήθω Mt. 6:28**) in view of the following mention of Solomon's clothes. This seems over-subtle for a scribe, and the western reading deserves consideration, but for the fact that only one Greek MS supports it. With either text the flowers are regarded as

female with feminine occupations in contrast to the male birds (Grundmann, 261). For Solomon's glory see 2 Ch. 9:13ff. περιβάλλω is 'to clothe' (23:11; Acts 12:8), used intransitively in the middle voice. After ὑμῖν the conjunction ὅτι is inserted, par. Mt., by ℵ A D *pm* it C1; TR; Diglot.

(28) The wording of the application differs slightly from that in Mt., so that in Lk. there is a double contrast between ἐν ἀγρῷ and εἰς κλίβανον, and between σήμερον and αὔριον. For a brief period – 'today' – the flowers blossom in the field; only a day later they are thrown into the oven (κλίβανος, Mt. 6:30**) as fuel. For the transitoriness of plant life as a picture of human life see Job 8:12; 14:2; Ps. 37:2; 90:5f.; 103:15f.; Is. 37:27; 40:6–8; 1 Pet. 1:24; SB I, 438. The point, however, in the present reference is that despite the brief life-span of flowers, God nevertheless gloriously clothes them (ἀμφιέζω,** diff. Mt. 6:30 ἀμφιέννυμι; Lk. 7:25 par. Mt. 11:8**; there is no obvious reason for the difference). How much more, then, will he provide for the disciples, thereby making the weakness of their faith unjustifiable (ὀλιγόπιστος, Mt. 6:30; 8:26; 14:31; 16:8**; cf. Mt. 17:20; cf. the rabbinic phrase qᵉṭannē ᵃmānāh, SBI, 438f.).

(29) Luke and Matthew differ considerably at this point. In Mt. the verse forms a conclusion to what has preceded: in view of what has been said the disciples should not worry about food, drink or clothing. Luke's version draws the conclusion by comparing the disciples (καὶ ὑμεῖς) with the flowers (and birds). They should not seek (ζητέω, diff. Mt. μεριμνάω, thereby gaining a contrast with v. 31) what they are to eat and drink. There is no mention here of clothing, diff. Mt. Instead Luke adds a command καὶ μὴ μετεωρίζεσθε. The verb, which occurs here only in the NT, originally means 'to raise up', hence in the passive 'to be anxious, worried'. More commonly it means 'to be over-bearing, presumptuous', especially in the LXX (Ps. 130:1), but this meaning is less suitable here (K. Deissner, TDNT IV, 630f.), despite its adoption by vg (*et nolite in sublime tolli*) and Klostermann, 137. It is possible that Luke has added the verb when he substituted ζητέω for μεριμνάω in order to preserve the element of freedom from worry.

(30) The force of the conjunction γάρ appears to be: don't worry, for by doing so you become like the gentiles who seek after material things; unlike them you have no need to worry, for your Father knows your needs.

πάντα could qualify ταῦτα (as it must do in Mt. with his different word order) or ἔθνη, but Lucan usage favours the former (16:14; 18:21; 21:12, 36; 24:9). The phrase τὰ ἔθνη τοῦ κόσμου (diff. Mt.) is rabbinic (SB II, 191), and hardly likely to have been created by Luke (*pace* Schulz, 151). It describes pagans who do not trust in God and therefore have to worry about the means of life. In Lk. the emphatic position of ὑμῶν at the beginning of the next clause draws a contrast between the pagans and the disciples, whereas in Mt. the stress is more on the fact that God knows of their need, so that the preceding clause (Mt. 6:32a) is rendered parenthetical. Wrege's view (122) that Matthew is closer to the original here is subjective. Ott, 108f., claims that Luke's wording is meant to forbid prayer for material necessities (cf. 21:34–36), but this view has no basis in the text.

(31) Finally comes the positive command to the disciples that instead of seeking after material things they are to seek for the kingdom of God; if they do this (parataxis, equivalent to a condition, 10:28), the material things will be given to them in addition. The introductory πλήν, diff. Mt. δέ, is regarded by Wrege, 10 n. 4, as a sign of catechetical style; it is hard to say whether it is editorial (so Schürmann, *Abschiedsrede*, 6). The presence of πρῶτον in Mt., which weakens the contrast with the previous statements, may be due to Matthew (cf. 11:41 diff. Mt. 23:26). 'To seek the kingdom' can be variously understood: 1. to seek that God's rule may come, and to advance its coming rather than to care about material things. 2. to seek the (spiritual) blessings of the kingdom rather than material benefits. 3. to submit to God's rule (Grundmann, 262). 4. to pray the Lord's prayer. The addition of v. 32 suggests that for Luke the second interpretation should be adopted. For αὐτοῦ (א B D* *pc* a c cop) many MSS have τοῦ θεοῦ, which is probably a clarification (Metzger, 161). After ταῦτα Matthew has πάντα, diff. Lk., but the sense is not affected, since the πάντα in Lk. 12:30 controls the paragraph. In any case, as Bultmann has commented, while the full provision of material needs is the normal situation for the disciples, in view of Mt. 10:29–31 par. this cannot be pressed to mean that man's life is always secured by God. Rather his uncertainty need not cause anxiety (TDNT IV, 592).

(32) This verse has no parallel in Mt., where an entirely different ending to the section is to be found. The Lucan saying gives an assurance to disciples who pray for the kingdom. Outwardly they constitute a little 'flock', weak and helpless in face of danger (cf. Mt. 10:16); for this description cf. Acts 20:28f.; 1 Pet. 5:2f., and for the disciples as Jesus' flock see Mk. 6:34; 14:27; Mt. 10:6 par. 15:24; 25:32f.; Lk. 15:4–6; Mt. 18:12; Jn. 10:1–27; 21:16f.; Mt. 2:6. Such a group are liable to fear, and therefore they are commanded not to be afraid (1:13, 30; 5:10; cf. especially Gn. 50:21; 2 Sa. 9:7; Tob. 4:21). For it is the good pleasure (3:22) of the Father (6:36; 12:30) to give them (Mt. 21:43; Lk. 22:29) the blessings of the kingdom. Behind the saying may lie the imagery in Zc. 13:7 (cf. 11:7, 11; France, 208) and J. Jeremias (TDNT VI, 501 and n. 20) claims that the language displays Semitic features: the use of the nominative as vocative (BD 147³); the Aramaic wordplay on *mar'itha* and *ra'e* (Black, 168); and an echo of Dn. 7:27. If so, the saying is not a late community formation (so Bultmann, 116). It may, however, originally be an isolated saying, which promised the disciples a share in royal dominion (cf. Dn. 7:27), and which has become attached to its present context by the keywords 'kingdom' and 'Father'.

For the thought cf. Mk. 14:27f.; Lk. 22:29f. W. Pesch*, 25–40, holds that the saying was originally addressed to Jesus' disciples to prepare them for the disquiet caused by his death and the ensuing scattering and persecution: the small persecuted flock will become the glorified community in the future kingdom. Luke has then universalised its significance. The relation of the saying to Mt. 6:34 is not clear; neither Evangelist appears to be aware of the other's tradition at this point.

(33) The closing two verses of the section have a parallel in Mt. 6:19–21, but differ markedly in wording. Matthew's wording is more rhythmical and has a poetic parallelism which is missing from Lk. Opinions differ as to whether both Evangelists have drawn on the same source or have used different sources. Manson, *Sayings*, 114, 172f., suggests that Luke used Q while Matthew used M, but Grundmann, 262, and Schlatter, 311f., claim that Matthew used Q while Luke used L. None of these scholars offers evidence for his views. The parallelism between the two versions is so close that it is more probable that both depend ultimately on the same source. W. Pesch*, 356–378, strongly defends the view that a source, which has been preserved in essentially its original form in Mt., has been adapted by Luke to catechetical purposes and inserted at this point in the discourse. Wrege, 109–113, agrees that Luke's formulation is catechetical, but claims that the modification was due to Luke's (oral) source. The wording in Lk. does appear to be secondary to that in Mt., and the view that Luke received it in this form from his recension of Q seems most probable.

The Lucan form of the saying is dominated by positive imperatives, whereas in Mt. there is an elaborate contrast between laying up treasure on earth and in heaven (cf. 12:16–21), which is only indirectly present in Lk. Those who have placed their trust in God and their hopes on his kingdom can be commanded to have a new attitude to such earthly possessions as they have. Let them sell them (πωλέω, cf. 18:22; τὰ ὑπάρχοντα, cf. Mt. 19:21 diff. Lk. 18:22) and give (the proceeds as) alms; for the phraseology cf. 11:41, but Wrege, 111, notes that Luke himself prefers the verb ποιέω in this connection (Acts 9:36; 10:2; 24:17). This instruction appears to be an interpretation of Mt. 6:19, in line with Jewish teaching on the value of almsgiving (Tob. 4:8f.; 1 En. 38:2; 2 En. 50:5; SB I, 429–431). It could be due to Luke himself (cf. 11:41), but, as far as the linguistic evidence is concerned, it could be due to his source.

A second command follows: the disciples are to make for themselves (cf. 16:9 for the phrase ποιεῖν ἑαυτοῖς) purses that will not grow old (παλαιόω, Heb. 1:11; 8:13**). The following phrase indicates that this refers to receptacles for heavenly treasure: such purses will not perish and hence lose their contents. There is an implied contrast with earthly treasuries which are perishable and hence are a cause of anxiety to their owners. The θησαυρός is the content of the purses, put in apposition with the receptacle, or perhaps has the meaning 'treasury' (cf. 6:45;

Mt. 2:11; 13:52). Such a store will be unfailing (ἀνέκλειπτος, Wis. 7:14; 8:18; cf. the use of ἐκλείπω in Lk. 16:9). It cannot be attacked by a burglar (κλέπτης, 12:39) or the moth (σής, Mt. 6:19f.**). The moth is mentioned because one common form of wealth in ancient times was expensive clothing, or because the moth might attack the purse. Again there is the implied contrast with earthly treasure and its corruptibility, which is made explicitly in Mt. The significance of the metaphor is not clarified: what is treasure in heaven? Jewish writings indicate that almsgiving was a means of storing up a good deposit for the day of adversity (Tob. 4:7–11; Sir. 29:11f.); the person who practises righteousness treasures up life for himself with the Lord (Ps. Sol. 9:9). Similarly, in 16:9 the proper use of mammon makes friends for the disciples so that they may be received into the eternal dwellings. The suggestion is that the person who ceases to trust in material things and places his trust in God is promised spiritual blessing in heaven from God.

(34) If a person seeks such heavenly treasure, the implication is that his heart, i.e. his affections, is directed in the right way, whereas if a person piles up earthly treasure, the evidence shows that his affections are earthbound and hence his heart is not truly related to God. Hence the saying provides a motive for the preceding command, by showing that the person who continues to hold on to earthly wealth and does not fulfil the command in v. 33 is not really seeking after the kingdom of God. The two attitudes are mutually exclusive. The saying has parallels in pagan philosophy (Epictetus II, 22, 19; Sentences of Sextus, 136). Luke has the plural form of the personal pronoun, diff. Mt., which is grammatically better and indicates the universal application of the saying. Pesch argues that the original form of the saying was addressed to would-be disciples and that Matthew and Luke have variously applied it catechetically to disciples. Certainly Jesus addressed wealthy would-be disciples in similar terms (18:22), but there is no reason why he should not have addressed committed disciples in similar terms.

iv. The Coming of the Son of Man 12:35–48

Jesus' teaching to the disciples continues without any break (asyndeton at 12:34/35), but the theme switches from that of ceasing to be anxious about worldly possessions to that of being spiritually prepared for the coming of the Son of man (v. 40). Freed from worldly cares through trust in the fatherly care of God and hope in the coming of the kingdom, the disciples are not to let themselves be enticed by the temptations of the world to laziness, self-indulgence and self-assertion, but are to spend their time profitably and in readiness to serve the Son of man when he appears. This lesson is given by means of parabolic teaching. The opening parable likens the disciples to servants waiting expectantly for the return of their master at night and promises them a reward beyond human imagining in the picture of the master serving the servants

(12:35–38). It is followed by a warning against unreadiness, as typified by a householder who fears the coming of a burglar: the implication is that the coming of the Son of man has serious effects for those who are unready (12:39f.). A question by Peter elicits the fact that this teaching is meant particularly for the leaders of the disciples. They will be rewarded with further authority if they faithfully discharge their duties, but if they presume on the delay of the master they will be suddenly overtaken with judgment. In general, judgment is in proportion to a person's knowledge of the master's will, and those who have the greater responsibilities and privileges will face the sterner judgment (12:41–48).

The major part of the section is derived from Q: this is attested by the clear parallelism between 12:39f., 42–46 and Mt. 24:43–51. It is not certain whether the teaching in vs. 35–38 also stood in Q (which omits them from consideration). It shows similarities to Mk. 13:33–37 and Mt. 25:1–13, neither of which is paralleled in Lk. While Grundmann, 264, assigns it to L, Creed, 176, and Manson, *Sayings*, 115f., allocate it to Q. In favour of this latter view it can be argued that Matthew has omitted it in favour of the parable of the virgins and the parable of the talents, and that it disappeared as part of his editorial work in uniting Marcan and Q material at this point; it may also be the case that Mt. 24:42 is a remnant of this parable rather than simply a recasting of Mk. 13:35 (Schürmann, *Untersuchungen*, 124). V. 41 may be a Lucan clarification (Bultmann, 361; Ott, 36f.) or a part of Q which Matthew omitted (or due to a pre-Lucan redactor, Jeremias, *Parables*, 99 n. 389). Finally, vs. 47f. appear to be separate sayings added at this point by Luke or his source; there is no evidence that they belonged to Q.

The sayings envisage a situation in which the disciples are awaiting their absent master, the Son of man. At least for the early church the Son of man is to be identified with Jesus, and hence the passage refers to the period between the departure of Jesus at the ascension and his return as the Son of man. It envisages the disciples (or some of them, including Peter) as occupying positions of leadership and pastoral responsibility. The question is whether Jesus himself anticipated this situation and prepared the disciples for it.

Many scholars believe that this was not the case, and hence that whatever teaching of Jesus may lie behind this passage has been adapted and applied to the situation of the church. Jeremias, *Parables*, 48ff., argues that the parables reflect the delay of the parousia and a change of audience. Originally these parables were intended as warnings of impending disaster addressed to the crowds and the opponents of Jesus, urging them to repent before the eschatological disaster overtook them. The church reapplied them to the situation of its own members by means of christological allegorising, so that now they explain how disciples must live during the period of delay before the parousia. Sayings originally addressed evangelistically to the hearers of Jesus have been given a hortatory application to the members of the church. Similarly,

Weiser* holds that parables which were originally meant to announce the coming of the final kingdom of God quite unallegorically were treated allegorically by the early church in the light of the delay of the parousia.

Other scholars, such as Grässer, 84–95, and Schulz, 268–277, hold that the allegorical features belong to the basic form of the parables, and that therefore they are creations by the early church with little or no basis in the teaching of Jesus.

The weakness in the view of Jeremias is that it does not explain how Jesus came to produce parables which were so ideally suited for the later allegorical use made of them by the church. Weiser argues that the features of 'delay' in the parables spring from the parabolic imagery rather than from the need to give teaching about delay, but parables in which an element of 'delay' forms a constitutive part were surely originally composed with this in mind.

Common to both types of theory is the assumption that Jesus did not give teaching to his disciples (or anybody else) about the parousia of the Son of man, or at least about his own return as the Son of man. Further, he spoke in terms of the imminence of the End in a way that allowed for no 'delay'. Thus Weiser, 126–130, claims that it cannot be shown to a sufficient degree of certainty that Jesus did teach that he would return as the Son of man, and Grässer, 3–75, argues that Jesus' teaching was governed by the concept of the imminent End in a way that allowed for no delay or postponement.

This assumption, however, though widely held, is open to strong criticism. The preceding section of teaching in Lk. 12 presupposes the continuation of ordinary life for some time during which the disciples must live by faith in God. The present section is complementary to this earlier one and makes explicit the 'in-between' character of this period which is terminated by the coming of the Son of man. The view that Jesus expected the End to happen more or less immediately simply does not do justice to the facts (Kümmel, 54–64; I. H. Marshall*, 16–25). Further, the prediction of the coming of the Son of man is a firm part of the teaching of Jesus, although not all scholars would agree that he identified himself with the coming Son of man.

The parables here are couched in terms of the return of a master, but the stress is not so much on the idea of 'return' as on the coming of an event for which the disciples must be prepared. Since elsewhere Jesus taught that men's attitude to himself would be determinative of the attitude of the Son of man at the judgment, the idea of judgment by the Son of man in the present parables fits coherently into his teaching. The parables were open to the identification of Jesus with the Son of man, and they were open to understanding in terms of an interval before the coming of the Son of man, both of which motifs could be – and were – developed by the early church; for Luke's development of the ideas of watchfulness, service and faithfulness, see G. Schneider*. On the whole, it is most probable that they were originally addressed to the disciples to encourage them to live in the light of the parousia rather than that they were originally addressed to the crowds and opponents of Jesus.

See Grässer, 84–95; Strobel, 203–233; Jeremias, *Parables*, 48–63 and *passim*; I. H. Marshall, *Eschatology and the Parables*, London, 1973²; Lövestam, 78–107; Weiser, 161–225; Hoffmann, 43–50; Schulz, 268–271, 271–277; W. Harnisch, *Eschatologische Existenz*, Göttingen, 1973, 84–95; G. Schneider, *Parusiegleichnisse im Lukas-Evangelium*, Stuttgart, 1975.

(35) The passage opens with a twofold command to the disciples to be ready for service. The first picture used is that of girding up the loins. ὀσφύς is 'waist, loins' (Mk. 1:6; Mt. 3:4; Eph. 6:14; 1 Pet. 1:13; as locus of organs of reproduction, Acts 2:30; 7:5, 10**). περιζώννυμι is 'to gird', i.e. 'to put a girdle round' (12:37; 17:8; Eph. 6:14; Rev. 1:13; 5:6; cf. ἀναζώννυμι, 1 Pet. 1:13; A. Oepke, TDNT V, 302–308). The use of the perfect participle with the imperative of εἰμί gives the sense, 'be the kind of person who never needs to be told to gird up his loins because they are always girded up' (Turner, 41f.). Garments were worn loosely around the waist without a belt in the house; to tie them up with a belt was a sign of readiness for departure on a journey (Ex. 12:11; cf. Strobel, 209, n. 4, who finds a passover symbolism; see 17:20 note) or for activity and service (Philo, Sacr. 63). (*Diglot* has the inverted order αἱ ὀσφύες ὑμῶν, with little support.)

The second picture is that of lamps (λύχνος, 8:16) burning (καίω, 24:32) and thus providing light. It suggests readiness for activity during a period of darkness, and fits in with the imagery of wakefulness found in the following parable and elsewhere. It is therefore unlikely that the metaphor has been taken over from the parable in Mt. 25:1–13, which in any case uses the word λαμπάς. The disciples are thus to be watchful and ready for service (W. Michaelis, TDNT IV, 326), a thought which is developed in the parable immediately following. The picture perhaps suggests readiness for future service rather than active service now, but it would be wrong to press this point which is solely due to the nature of the imagery being employed. It is probable that 1 Pet. 1:13 represents an echo of this saying, as it was utilised in Christian paraenesis with the same stress on readiness for the parousia (*pace* E. Best, *1 Peter*, 1971, 53); cf. the use of the plural form in both verses. The verse is absent from Mt. and may be a Lucan introduction to the parables (Weiser, 161–164; G. Schneider*, 30–37; cf. Dodd, *Parables*, 121), but the evidence for Lucan composition is not compelling (Weiser 161 n. 2).

(36) The parable proper commences here; it is joined rather loosely to the preceding verse with καὶ ὑμεῖς, since a change of verb (ἐστέ) is really required. For ὅμοιος cf. 6:47–49; 7:31f. (par. Mt. 11:16); 13:18f., 21 (par. Mt. 13:31, 33). προσδέχομαι (2:25; *et al.*) could be Lucan, but some such word is essential for the story. The use of κύριος in a secular sense is common in the parables (cf. Mk. 13:35), but it could easily be understood to refer to Jesus or God. πότε can introduce an indirect ques-

tion, but here the clause is almost adverbial; the subjunctive expresses the uncertain time of his coming. Cf. Mk. 13:33, 35; Lk. 17:20; 21:7 for this eschatological expectation clause. ἀναλύω is 'to depart' (Phil. 1:23**), hence 'to return' (cf. Jos. Ant. 11:34). γάμος in the plural can mean 'wedding celebration' or 'banquet' (cf. Est. 2:18; 9:22; Lk. 14:8; the Aramaic mištutha has the same double meaning, Jeremias, *Parables*, 26). An allegorical reference to the messianic banquet is completely excluded, since this follows the parousia. The point is the uncertain length of a banquet (cf. Mt. 25:10 for a similar motif). There is no reason to follow Weiser's suggestion (166–168) that the phraseology here is due to Luke (cf. G. Schneider*, 34). The servants are to be ready in order that they may open the door (cf. Mt. 25:11) to the master as soon as (εὐθέως) he comes and knocks at the door; note the use of the genitive absolute a. without a substantive (which is permitted, if it is implicit, BD 423[6]; cf. Acts 21:10, 31; *et al.*), and b. illogically (BD 423[1]; cf. 14:29; 17:12; 22:10; *et al.*). In the present parable it is the master who stands outside and knocks at the door; contrast 13:25 and Mt. 25:11. The picture is reminiscent of Rev. 3:20, and Weiser, 167f., claims that the detail is due to Lucan redaction, which has added a further echo of Rev. 3:20 in v. 37b; if there is dependence, however, it is more probably the other way round, especially in view of the relative dates of Lk. and Rev.

(37) The parable proceeds with a benediction upon the servants who are awake and ready when the master comes; the same form appears in 12:43 par. Mt. 24:46 in almost identical pattern. The emphasis lies on the verb γρηγορέω, 'to be awake, alert', Mk. 13:34, 35, 37; Mt. 24:42f.; 25:13; Acts 20:31, which is common in early Christian paraenesis: 1 Cor. 16:13; Col. 4:2; 1 Thes. 5:6, 10; 1 Pet. 5:8; Rev. 3:2f.; 16:15 (in addition to the very scanty treatment by A. Oepke, TDNT II, 338f., see Lövestam. The opposite concept is expressed by καθεύδω (Mk. 13:36; Eph. 5:14; 1 Thes. 5:6f.). The verb expresses readiness for action, as opposed to sleep due to weariness, laziness or self-indulgence. The imagery is of the present world as a place of darkness and night in which one is tempted to sleep (Lövestam, 84–91).

The blessing is followed by an ἀμήν declaration which gives the reason for declaring such disciples blessed. The fact that Luke habitually omits ἀμήν when he finds it in his sources indicates that here he is using a source which he has not redacted (cf. 4:24 note), and that the saying is of special importance. The master will gird up his own clothes (cf. 12:35; Jn. 13:4); he will make the servants recline at table (ἀνακλίνω, 2:7; cf. 13:29*), and he will come (παρέρχομαι (cf. 17:7), used redundantly, in Semitic fashion) and serve them with a meal; for the use of διακονέω of Jesus cf. 22:26f.; Mk. 10:45; cf. Rom. 15:8. The imagery is Jewish, and there is no need to find influence from the Roman Saturnalia.

The authenticity of this statement is widely questioned. Weiser, 169–171, regards it as a Lucan addition, replacing some unknown phrase in Q. The one solid argument in favour of this view is the presence of Lucanisms, especially visible when the wording is compared with 17:8 (which Weiser, 109f., also regards as redactional). But the linguistic arguments do not affect the substance of the saying. Weiser argues that Lk. 17:7–10 is also from Q and that the tension between the two pictures, the master being served and the master serving, forbids both sayings being from the same source. This argument is fallacious, since he regards the vital verse 17:8 as being due to Lucan redaction; in any case it is uncertain whether 17:7–10 is from Q. But the tension is not intolerable, and is no argument against ascribing both pictures to the same author. But this author was not Luke; the Semitizing style suggests that the saying was in his source (Jeremias, *Parables*, 54 n. 18). Nevertheless, it is possible that the saying represents an allegorical addition to the parable in Luke's source (Jeremias, ibid.; cf. Klostermann, 139; Grässer, 89). It points to the activity of Jesus at the messianic banquet, and it may reflect the story of the incident in Jn. 13 where Jesus serves his disciples. It is wholly at variance with the normal behaviour of a master (17:7–10) and therefore must be allegorical. But it is difficult to see why Jesus should not have told a parable with a surprising twist in the middle, one which refers indirectly to his own position as the servant. This concept is so firmly anchored in the teaching and activity of Jesus that there is no reason to suspect that the early church has imported the idea here.

(38) Although the parable appears to have reached a climax, a second blessing now follows. This applies in the situation if (κἄν, equivalent to καὶ ἐάν, which is read by TR; *Diglot*) the master does not return during the first watch of the night but only during the second, or third watches. For φυλακή cf. 2:8; Mt. 24:43. The Jews divided the night into three watches, (SB I, 688–691), while the Romans had four watches (Mt. 14:25 par. Mk. 6:48; cf. Acts 12:4; and the names in Mk. 13:35). Luke here thus follows the Jewish system (*pace* Zahn, 506 n. 33; Lagrange, 367), and hence this verse is taken from his source. Servants who are prepared to stay awake until late in the night will be blessed. The same thought is present in Mk. 13:35, where the four Roman watches are mentioned. The verse reckons with a certain interval before the parousia, although it springs naturally enough from the imagery of the parable. The case for this verse being an addition to the original parable is stronger, but it should be remembered that such a warning is in line with the teaching of Jesus which allowed for a certain interval before the parousia.

The parable as a whole bears a close resemblance to Mk. 13:34–37, but has a more positive character of promise. The two parables may reflect one original parable, handed down in the two separate traditions, but this presupposes considerable freedom on the part of the tradition, and it is perhaps more likely that the tradition reflects different forms in which Jesus conveyed the same basic teaching.

(39) The second parable in the series is nothing more than a parabolic saying followed by an application. Where the tone of the previous parable was one of encouragement to faithful service with the promise of reward, this time there is a warning note to people who may not be ready for the coming of the Son of man. If the previous parable emphasised the possibility of delay in the coming of the master, this parable stresses the sudden and unexpected arrival of the burglar.

Luke's opening τοῦτο is probably secondary to Mt. ἐκεῖνο. For the use of γινώσκετε cf. 10:11. The saying has the form of an unfulfilled condition in past time, with the verb ᾔδει used as equivalent to an aorist (see, however, Zerwick, 317). οἰκοδεσπότης is a 'householder' (13:25; 14:21; 22:11* par. Mk. 14:14), responsible for the security of his own premises. For ὥρα Matthew has φυλακή. Jeremias, *Parables*, 48, suggests that ὥρα translates Aramaic ša‘ᵃthā, 'moment' (cf. Mt. 26:45; Mk. 14:41; 1 Cor. 4:11; Gal. 2:5). This would suggest that Luke has the original wording here, but it could also be that he has conformed the wording here to v. 40. Luke does not confine housebreaking to night-time. κλέπτης is generic, '*a* burglar', and ἔρχεται is equivalent to a future. For the metaphor cf. 1 Thes. 5:2, 4; 2 Pet. 3:10; Rev. 3:3; 16:15. In the apodosis, many MSS add ἐγρηγόρησεν ἄν καί; the words, which are omitted by p⁷⁵ ℵ* (D) e i syˢ ᶜ saᵖᵗ arm Mcion, are probably an assimilation to Mt. (Metzger, 161f.); in Mt. they are probably an editorial addition to stress the lesson in Mt. 24:42. For ἀφίημι, Matthew uses ἐάω (which is found 1x in Mt.; 2x in Lk. and 7x in Acts). The two terms are synonymous and could be translation variants (Jeremias, *Parables*, 48 n. 1), but this is unlikely in view of the otherwise close correspondence between the passages. Since no reason for change by either Evangelist can be seen, the differences may reflect different recensions of Q. διορύσσω is 'to break through' (Mt. 6:19f.; 24:43**), and suggests a burglar burrowing through a clay wall; Jeremias, ibid., takes up the suggestion of SB I, 967, that it is the less felicitous translation of Aramaic hᵃthar, which can also mean 'to break in' (without specifying the means or route). Luke has probably substituted οἶκος diff. Mt. οἰκία.

(40) The parable is applied to the audience of Jesus' disciples. Since they do not know when the Son of man will come, they must be constantly ready. Jeremias, op. cit. 48–51, argues at length that this is a reapplication of a parable originally intended to warn the crowds against the future eschatological catastrophe associated with the coming of the Son of man; the figure of the thief suggests the element of warning against judgment, but the disciples would be prepared for the event and would not need to be warned about an event that meant salvation for them and not judgment. But if the early church needed to warn its members about being unready for the parousia, there is no reason why Jesus should not have felt the same need, and hence we may interpret the ὑμεῖς here as referring to any of Jesus' hearers who might be tempted to ignore its imminence. The addition of διὰ τοῦτο in Mt. is probably secondary,

since it is typical of his style. ἕτοιμος is 'ready' (14:17; 22:33*). Luke's word order ᾗ ὥρᾳ οὐ δοκεῖτε is less Semitic than Mt. ᾗ οὐ δοκεῖτε ὥρᾳ, and hence secondary; the antecedent has been attracted into the relative clause. The reference to the coming of the Son of man has aroused critical suspicion. Vielhauer, 73f., and Schulz, 268 n. 12, regard the whole parable as a creation by the early church with reference to the delay of the parousia, but other scholars adopt a less radical conclusion. Jeremias, ibid. and G. Schneider*, 20–23, regard the reference to the Son of man as a Christian allegorical expansion of a parable which originally referred to the coming of the day of the Lord, but the personal imagery used in the parable does not encourage this conclusion, nor is a 'day' fittingly said to come at an 'hour' or 'moment'. Higgins' view (140f.; cf. Hahn, 38 n.) that the whole verse is a preacher's hortatory comment is less vulnerable. Similarly, C. Colpe, TDNT VIII, 451f., holds that the comment does not fit the parable (which he interprets in the manner of Jeremias), but regards it as an independent saying, possibly genuine or possibly a doublet of Mt. 24:37 or Lk. 17:30. W. Harnisch* holds that the parable teaches that one can be prepared for the burglar if one knows when he is coming; since the crisis comes unexpectedly, one cannot prepare beforehand and escape from it; the application, however, urges preparedness for an unexpected event, and therefore it must be secondary. Schulz, 269 n. 14, cites the conclusion of G. Strecker (*Der Weg der Gerechtigkeit*, Göttingen, 1966², 241): 'The saying does not imply the warning not to let oneself be surprised, but contains the admonition to draw the consequences from the fact that one will be taken unawares'. Hence the comment is not inappropriate despite the apparent tension. The argument that the stress on unexpectedness presupposes the delay of the parousia (Grässer, 93f.; Schulz, 269) is likewise unjustified (cf. Hoffmann, 47). In short, the arguments against the authenticity of the parable and the Son of man saying do not convince. An original reinterpretation is offered by R. Maddox, 'The Function of the Son of Man according to the Synoptic Gospels', NTS 15, 1968–69, 45–74, especially 51f.: in its Lucan context, as opposed to its eschatological setting in Mt., the saying refers to the coming of Jesus from Galilee to Jerusalem which is seen as judgment upon that city (cf. 13:1–5, 32–35; 19:10f.). The context makes this interpretation most unlikely. The use made of the parable in G. Thomas 21, 103, is so different that no conclusions can be drawn from its lack of eschatological application.

(41) In Mt. Jesus continues his discourse with the parable of the steward and the servants, but in Lk. there is an interruption at this point (41–42a) in which Peter raises a question. The interruption is regarded as an insertion by Luke by most scholars (Klostermann, 139; Ellis, 180, Ott, 36f.); Jeremias, *Parables*, 99, claims that while the verse is an addition, its style is that of Luke's source rather than of Luke himself. Manson, *Sayings*, 117, and, more strongly, C. F. D. Moule, *The Birth of the*

New Testament, 1962, 147–149, argue that it stood in Q, and Matthew dropped it because of its unintelligibility; otherwise the ἄρα in v. 42 is otiose. This view is confirmed by the language (κύριε, ὁ κύριος; possibly εἶπεν αὐτῷ, *si vera lectio*). The argument to the contrary is given in detail by Weiser, 216–219 (cf. Schulz, 271), who finds that the language is Lucan, and that the function of the verse is explained by a conscious relationship to Mk. 13:37. Possibly Luke has heavily edited a comment in his source. It would seem that in, any case the interruption is secondary, and is perhaps meant to explain the following ἄρα. For it is not clear which parable is meant by Peter, since two parables precede the saying; the question fits 12:35–38 rather than 12:39f., but it is possible that both parables are in mind (cf. 5:36; 15:3), since they hang closely together. Further, it is difficult to see what motivated Peter's question, and it looks more like a saying created in the light of the following parable and intended to make clear in advance its particular reference. If so, the saying contrasts 'us', the Twelve, with the crowds (G. Schneider*, 24). In its Lucan context, however, which extends into the age of the church, the reference must be to the disciples, especially to those with responsibilities of leadership.

(42) The opening narrative phrase is required after Peter's question, and is naturally missing from Mt. The opening statement of the parable is couched as a question, and conveys the sense, 'Who then is willing to be a faithful steward . . .?' It apparently invites the hearer to identify himself with the subject of the parable (Bultmann, 185; Grundmann, 267). But it is probable that the Greek formulation represents a Semitic idiom in which the question serves as a conditional protasis: 'If there is a steward . . ., he will be blessed when his master comes and finds him so doing' (11:5 note; Black, 118f.; Beyer, I; 1, 287–293; Weiser, 180–183). Cf. Dt. 20:5; Ps. 25:12; Mt. 7:9f.; Lk. 14:5 par. Mt. 12:11. The answer of Jesus then becomes an indirect reply to Peter's question: he answers Peter with a parabolic saying that is concerned with the situation of the servant who is placed in charge of other servants; thereby the general application of the earlier parables is not lost, but rather they are seen to apply especially, but not exclusively, to the Twelve and other leaders among the disciples. The force of the initial ἄρα is not clear; cf. v. 41 note. If v. 41 is not original, then it could be a means of drawing a consequence from the fact of the Son of man's sudden coming in v. 40; in view of this, a blessing attaches to the servant who is found acting faithfully when the master comes. Luke has οἰκονόμος, 'steward, bailiff' (16:1, 3, 8*), diff. Mt. δοῦλος, which is generally thought to be original in the parable (12:43; 45, 46, 47). Luke's change makes it all the more clear that it is the leaders of the church who are being addressed (cf. 1 Cor. 4:1f.; Tit. 1:7; 1 Pet. 4:10; also 1 Cor. 9:17; Eph. 3:2; Col. 1:25), but in fact the description of the servant's functions in both Gospels makes it clear that it is a *ben bayit*, a slave set over other slaves, who is meant (O. Michel, TDNT V, 149–151; SB II,

192). To be πιστός is the characteristic quality expected of a steward (1 Cor. 4:2). φρόνιμος, 'sensible, prudent, wise', is also a quality associated with stewards (16:8; cf. 1 Cor. 4:10; 10:15), but it can also indicate a quality required in disciples as they face the coming of the eschaton (Mt. 25:2, 4, 8f.); the addition of the second adjective to ὁ οἰκονόμος with the article (diff. Mt. καί) is unusual, since there is no particular emphasis (BD 269; MH III, 186f.). Weiser, 182, argues that the adjectives represent a secondary addition to the parable, since they come too early in the structure of the story; they describe the kind of conduct the steward should practise, rather than the qualities necessary for his appointment. The future tense καταστήσει (12:14) is no doubt to be understood allegorically of the appointment of leaders in the church after the departure of Jesus; the aorist in Mt. may perhaps refer back to the earlier choice of the Twelve as leaders. The element in itself is quite natural and fits into the context of the parable. θεραπεία (9:11) here means 'the servants', diff. Mt. οἰκετεία**, which is rare and late. For διδόναι (Mt. δοῦναι), Diglot has διαδιδόναι (11:22; 18:22). ἐν καιρῷ signifies 'at the right time' (cf. 20:10; Thucydides 4:59:3, cited by AG). Before σιτομέτριον the article τό is omitted by p⁷⁵ B D 69 pc, and bracketed by Synopsis; UBS; the noun σιτομέτριον** means 'measured allowance of food, ration', and is rare (for the verb cf. Gn. 47:12, 14). Mt. has τροφή, which gives a reminiscence of Ps. 103:27 LXX: δοῦναι τὴν τροφὴν αὐτοῖς εὔκαιρον. Creed, 177, and Weiser, 185, regard Luke as secondary here. The allegorical idea of providing spiritual nourishment for the church as the household of God is not present.

(43) The apodosis is now presented in the form of a blessing (cf. v. 37a), which has no religious flavour and thus fits into the parabolic framework (Weiser, 187f.). ἐκεῖνος almost has the sense 'that sort of servant'.

(44) The reason why the servant is pronounced 'happy' is given in a solemn statement introduced originally by ἀμήν (Mt.; Luke has altered the wording as he does often; contrast 12:37). The difficulty is that the reward promised does not seem essentially different from the task already given to the servant. It is impossible that v. 44 is meant as a repetition of v. 42, giving the sense: Whom will the Lord appoint on his return as his steward? Answer: a servant who is found doing his (subordinate) duties faithfully when he comes; that sort of servant will be appointed as steward. This interpretation would not fit in with the second part of the parable where the servant is clearly already in a position of authority before the master's return. The solution lies in the point made by Weiser, 219–222, that for Luke's audience in the Hellenistic church the term οἰκονόμος was suggestive of service and subordination and not of authority; the same is obviously true of δοῦλος. If so, the promise made here is one of authority: the servant is appointed to a position equal to that of his master. He moves from being temporarily in charge to being permanently in control of all his possessions (Findlay, 1046).

Similarly, the disciples receive treasure in heaven (cf. 16:11f.); they have authority in the new era (cf. 19:17).

(45) The same servant, however, (ἐκεῖνος) may act otherwise. As time goes past, he may think that his master is away for some time, and that he can take advantage of this to act as he please. λέγειν ἐν τῇ καρδίᾳ is Semitic for 'to think'. χρονίζω (1:21) is 'to take a long time' and has the same function of expressing the interval before the eschatological denouement in Mt. 25:5 (cf. Heb. 10:37, citing Hab. 2:3). It is, therefore, a term associated with the parousia (*pace* Weiser, 191). In itself the detail fits naturally into the story which presupposes an interval between the departure and return of the master. This interval is built into the parables of watchfulness. The problem is whether the parables have been created by the early church around this concept, or stem from Jesus, and, if the latter is the case, whether he was merely warning against the coming crisis or preparing his disciples for an interval without him. Could Jesus have used χρονίζω in this way? Bultmann, 125, holds that Jesus could have characterised the false security of his contemporaries like this: they could have felt that no final consummation was at hand, but Jesus warned them that the Son of man would come unexpectedly. In any case, the parable presupposes an interval before the Son of man comes, and this situation existed during the ministry of Jesus and in all probability he foresaw a further period of the same kind. It is, therefore, quite possible that this feature belonged to the parable as an original parable of Jesus addressed to disciples who might share in the feeling of their contemporaries. The early church would apply it to the continuing interval in their own day. As Grässer (113) himself admits, the imminent expectation of the parousia is present in the parable. While certainty is impossible, there is no compelling reason to deny the authenticity of the parable in substance, although the possibility of elaboration (in vs. 45ff.) cannot be dismissed out of hand. On the whole problem see further D. E. Aune, 'The Significance of the Delay of the Parousia for Early Christianity', in G. F. Hawthorne (*et al.*), *Current Issues in Biblical and Patristic Interpretation,* Grand Rapids, 1975, 87–109.

The use of ἄρχομαι is Semitic and redundant. τύπτω is the action of one who thinks that he can act as master and has a position of dominion (cf. G. Stählin, TDNT VIII, 264, but it is going too far to speak of disciples 'seeking to play the Lord'). For menservants (παῖς) and maidservants (παιδίσκη, 22:56) Matthew has σύνδουλος; Matthew emphasises the way in which the slave puts himself above his fellows, whereas Luke emphasises his superior situation (Creed, 177), and is probably original. For μεθύσκω*, 'to become intoxicated', Matthew has the phrase μετὰ τῶν μεθυόντων. The description of the servant's misdeeds is traditional (Ahikar 3:1f; 4:15; cf. Weiser, 194f. for further examples). The details are meant literally as part of the parable, but the example of the church at Corinth (1 Cor. 11:21; cf. 2 Pet. 2:13; Jude 12) shows that the parable could be applied fairly literally to the church; cf. B. Reicke,

Diakonie, Festfreude und Zelos, Uppsala, 1951, 234–240, for such a picture.

(46) The choice of the verb ἥκω to indicate the return of the master may reflect the terminology in Hab. 2:3, quoted in Heb. 10:37: ἥξει καὶ οὐ χρονίσει (cf. Lk. 13:35; 19:43; 2 Pet. 3:10; Rev. 2:25; 3:3; the verb is also used in Lk. 13:29; 15:27*; For the motif cf. Strobel, 203ff.). ἡμέρα and ὥρα stand in parallelism with each other, and form a stereotyped phrase (Job 38:23; Dn. 12:13; Mk. 13:32 par. Mt. 24:36; Mt. 25:13; Rev. 9:15); the phrase is one which was applied to the parousia (Weiser, 196–198). The relative pronoun ᾗ is differently constructed in its two occurrences. The first time it expresses a dative of relation or time, and the phrase ἔρχεσθαι αὐτόν should be supplied as the object of προσδοκᾷ. The second time it stands by relative attraction for ἥν as the object of γινώσκει (Weiser, 196). The servant's fate is expressed first of all by the unusual verb διχοτομέω (Mt. 24:51). It means 'to cut in pieces', and was used to signify execution by this drastic method (Apocalypse of Baruch 16, cited in AG). In the LXX it is used of cutting an offering in pieces (Ex. 29:17; cf. the noun, Gn. 15:11, 17; Lv. 1:8; Ezk. 24:4). Such a grisly fate was not unknown in the ancient world (Homer, Odyssey, 18:339; Herodotus 2:139; Sus. 55; Heb. 11:37; cf. Lk. 19:27; SB IV: 2, 737–739), and hence there is no difficulty about adopting this meaning here (H. Schlier, TDNT II, 225f.). The objections are that the treatment sounds exceptionally ferocious, but this is countered by the evidence cited, which shows that such an idea is found elsewhere in the teaching of Jesus; and that the next part of the verse may imply that the servant was still alive after the treatment. Hence various other interpretations have been offered. Lagrange, 370, and AG suggest that the meaning may be metaphorical, 'to punish with the utmost severity'. (The modern threat, 'I'll tan your hide,' is equally metaphorical!) Others suggest that an Aramaic phrase has been wrongly or misleadingly translated. Manson, *Sayings*, 118, suggested that Aramaic *nattaḥ*, 'to take away, separate', had been confused with Hebrew *nittaḥ*, 'to cut in pieces', but the linguistic basis is doubtful. Black, 256f., follows Torrey, in suggesting an Aramaic original *yᵉphallᵉginneh mᵉnatheh*, 'he will divide him his portion' (cf. syˢ), but it is difficult to see how this phrase ever got altered. Jeremias, *Parables*, 57 n. 31, argues that in an original *yᵉphallegh leh*, the *leh* was misunderstood as an accusative instead of a dative, the original sense being 'he will give him (blows)'; but the absence of a word for 'blows' makes this problematical. Finally and most convincingly, O. Betz ('The Dichotomized Servant and the End of Judas Iscariot', RQ 5, 1964, 43–58) suggests that we have an over-literal translation of the phrase 'he will be cut off (*niḵraṭ*)' – sc. 'from all the sons of light', as in 1QS 2:16. The phrase τὸ μέρος αὐτοῦ τίθημι μετά is Semitic and means 'to treat someone as' (Jeremias, *Parables*, 57 n. 31; J. Schneider, TDNT IV, 597 n. 19; cf. Ps. 49:19; SB I, 969). For the thought cf. 1QS 2:17. The

servant thus shares the fate of the 'unfaithful', and the clause should be regarded as epexegetic of the preceding clause, rather than as a description of a further punishment. For ἄπιστος Matthew has ὑποκριτής; it is hard to know which is original (cf. Weiser, 201f., who finally opts for the Lucan form). Both words may represent Aramaic *hnp'*, 'wicked, hypocrite'.

(47) Matthew concludes the parable with a warning about weeping and gnashing of teeth; the clause goes beyond the parabolic situation and envisages the final lot of the wicked (Mt. 8:12; 13:42, 50; 22:13; 25:30; Lk. 13:28). It is probable that the addition is due to Matthew, but it could be due to his source. In Lk. it is replaced by another saying (vs. 47–48a) which also appears to be an addition to the original parable since it has a different theme. Where the parable spoke of trustworthiness and untrustworthiness, this saying speaks of greater and lesser knowledge of the will of God. It could thus be appropriately directed to the Twelve and to church leaders who may be presumed to have greater knowledge (cf. Am. 3:2; Jas. 3:1). In v. 48b there is the thought of greater and less responsibility, which is again a somewhat different theme, and hence this saying is perhaps also to be regarded as independent.

In the former of the two sayings the picture of the servant-master relation is maintained. The introductory ἐκεῖνος may be meant as a connective (cf. 17:31; 20:18; 21:23; Acts 8:1; 12:1; 16:33). For θέλημα, 'will', cf. 22:42; 23:25*. The reading μὴ ἑτοιμάσας ἢ ποιήσας (p⁷⁵ ℵ B) is uncertain; the variants are ἑτοιμάσας μηδὲ ποιήσας (A Θ f1 *pl* f vg; TR) ἑτοιμάσας (L W f13 it sy); and ποιήσας (p⁴⁵ D 69 Mcion). Although the Egyptian text gives the appearance of conflation, it was probably its redundancy that led to the variants. πρός has the sense 'for, with a view to'. δέρω is 'to beat' (12:48; 20:10f. par. Mk. 12:3, 5; Lk. 22:63*). With πολλάς supply πληγάς (BD 154; 241⁶). O. Betz, op. cit. 48, traces the influence of Dt. 29:18–21 (cf. 1QS 2:11–17; Rev. 22:18f.) where the verb *māhāh* means 'to blot out', but the corresponding Aramaic verb means 'to beat'.

(48) The second part of the saying completes the familiar OT contrast between unwitting sins and witting sins (Nu. 15:30; Dt. 17:12; Ps. 19:13; 1QS 5:12; 7:3; 8:17, 22, 24; 9:1f.; CD 8:8; 10:3; BB 60b; SB II, 192). It is not clear whether any particular groups of people are being contrasted: church leaders and laity (Klostermann, 140; Creed, 178); scribes and the Jewish people (Jülicher); Jews and gentiles (Wellhausen, 69); it is safer to say that we have a general principle (cf. H. Seesemann, TDNT V, 173). The saying is regarded as authentic by Jeremias, *Parables*, 104, 166, but this is denied by Weiser, 222–224, who argues that the casuistic spirit is alien to Jesus and resembles that of the 'Sentences of Holy Law' created by the early church (cf. Braun, *Radikalismus*, II, 23–29, 80–83). It may be doubted whether these arguments carry conviction.

In the second part of the verse the theme is again that of responsibility. πάντι has been attracted to the case of the relative, and is taken
up by αὐτοῦ in the main clause (BD 295; 466³; cf. 1:36 note). A person
to whom much has been given (sc. by God) will be required to give
much; this thought is apparently repeated in the second half of the saying where the third person plural subject to παρέθεντο ('to entrust') is
God (6:38; 12:20; *et al.*). The force of περισσότερον may be that more
will be asked of the person to whom much is given than of the person to
whom little has been given (Creed, 178). There is no reason to deny this
saying to Jesus (cf. Weiser, 224). What is not clear is whether vs. 47f.
stood in Q or have been drawn from Luke's special source; there is no
compelling evidence either way.

v. The Coming Crisis 12:49-59

The connection of thought between the preceding section and this section is not at all clear. The matter is complicated by the fact that Luke's
use of sources here is also a puzzle, and hence we cannot tell what order
there may have been in any source that he was following. Nor is the line
of thought within the section obvious.

The first four verses form a unity (12:49-53). Jesus expresses a
longing for the fulfilment of certain events, the kindling of a fire and the
completion of his baptism. Nevertheless, these events do not lead to
peace but to division within households. The audience is still the disciples, and the sayings appear to suggest to them that a time of fulfilment
is at hand, the result of which, however, will be persecution; it is in that
situation that the summons to faithfulness in the preceding section takes
on especial relevance and stringency. Vs. 49f. are peculiar to Lk.; there
is a somewhat similar saying to v. 50a in Mk. 10:38b, which occurs in a
section omitted by Luke. Although H. Köster (TDNT VII, 885 n. 77)
thinks that Luke has reformulated the saying in Mk., V. Taylor finds no
reasonable doubt that the two sayings are independent (Taylor,
Sacrifice, 165). The Semitic nature of v. 49 rules out the possibility that
it is a Lucan creation (*pace* Schulz, 258), and it may well be that both
sayings come from Luke's special source material (Easton, 210), but it is
also possible that they were in Q and Matthew omitted them when forming his second major discourse by Jesus, in which the following verses
(12:51-53) have a parallel (Mt. 10:34-36). The verbal link between Lk.
12:49 and Mt. 10:34 (βάλλω) supports the second possibility (Manson,
Sayings, 120; Schürmann, *Untersuchungen*, 213; *contra* G. Klein*, 374
n. 4).

The second section (12:54-56) is addressed to the crowds, and is a
clear warning to them to discern the significance of the present time. The
saying will in any case have referred originally to the crisis which Jesus
saw as being caused by his ministry. Klein argues that in its Lucan context it refers to the new situation brought about by the death of Jesus:

the period of the church under persecution should be recognised as one of decision, and men should join themselves to the church. The saying is thus in effect a call for men to join the ranks of the faithful servants before it is too late. This saying has a parallel in the longer text of Mt. 16:2f. which is textually doubtful, and probably represents a floating piece of tradition (cf. Lk. 6:4 D; Mt. 20:28 D). The relation between the two traditions is uncertain; the view that the saying in Mt. is based on Lk. (D. Hill, *Matthew*, London, 1972, 257) is improbable; Klein, op. cit. 387, claims that the Lucan form is secondary to the Matthaean.

The third section (12:57–59) contains the parable of the defendant who must come to terms with his adversary, and is a strong summons to reach the point of decision before it is too late. This is then confirmed by the warnings in the following section. This passage is from Q, as the parallel in Mt. 5:25f. indicates, but the wording varies considerably.

The section as a whole is thus probably based on Q material in which the note of crisis sounded by Jesus in respect of the significance of his proclamation of the kingdom is stressed in terms of the division that will result as men take sides for or against him. The continuing validity of this teaching for the church is brought out by Luke's editing of the passage.

See G. Delling, 'Βάπτισμα βαπτισθῆναι' in Delling, 236–256 (originally in Nov.T 2, 1958, 92–115); T. A. Roberts, 'Some Comments on Matthew x. 34–36 and Luke xii. 51–53', Exp.T 69, 1957–58, 304–306; G. Klein, 'Die Prüfung der Zeit (Lukas 12, 54–56)', ZTK 61, 1964, 373–390; Schulz, 258–260, 421–424.

(49) Jesus' saying consists of two parallel expressions which correspond closely in form with each other (G. Delling, 246f.). The first half has the 'I came' form, which Bultmann, 167, regards as a reason for suspecting the authenticity of an otherwise unexceptionable statement (cf. Braun, *Radikalismus* II, 129 n. 3). But this sweeping verdict is unjustified, and is refuted by Grundmann, 269, who refers to similar statements by the Teacher of Righteousness (1QH); cf. Jeremias, *Theology* I, 293 n. 6. The phrase πῦρ βάλλειν is said to be a Semitism meaning 'to kindle fire' (Jeremias, *Parables*, 163 n. 56, but no evidence is cited), but it would appear to be tolerable Greek in a metaphorical saying (cf. Mt. 10:34; Jos., Ant. 1:98). τί must be taken in the sense 'How (much)'; this usage is more clearly Semitic (2 Sa. 6:20; Mt. 7:14; BD 299⁴; Black, 123, 275). Similarly θέλω εἰ, 'I wish that', is Semitic (Is. 9:5; Sir. 23:14; see, however, Herodotus 6:52; 9:44). ἀνάπτω is 'to kindle' (Jas. 3:5**). The whole clause thus means, 'How I wish that it was already kindled!', and there is no need to seek for a more recondite translation. But what is the significance of the fire? There are two main types of interpretation. According to the first, the fire represents the power of the Spirit (or the church) (Bultmann, 165, but he also proposes a quite improbable interpretation in terms of the Gnostic redeemer myth; Geldenhuys, 366f.; Grundmann, 270; Ellis, 182; cf. Taylor, *Sacrifice*, 165). There is, however, nothing in the context to support this interpretation, and

Grundmann concedes that it is not the original meaning of the saying but rather the interpretation placed upon it by Luke (cf. Acts 2:3). It is more probable that the saying in its present context should be understood with reference to judgment (cf. Acts 2:19; Rev. 8:5, 7; 20:9; so Schlatter, 316; Grässer, 190f.; F. Lang, TDNT VI, 944; Delling, 247–250; cf. Stuhlmueller, 146). But this process of judgment works by way of the separation of good from evil, and hence leads to the persecution of the righteous and division among men; fire is therefore taken to be a symbol of strife and division by Easton, 209; Klostermann, 140f.; Creed, 178; G. Klein*, 377. This interpretation fits in with 3:16 where the coming One is to baptise with the Spirit and with fire, the fire being expressive of the judgment that falls upon the wicked. At the same time, however, the fire also falls upon the righteous, and it may be right to see it as affecting both Jesus and his disciples who must submit to the baptism described in the next verse. Consequently, it may be possible to bring the two main interpretations together by identifying the fire as the Spirit 'who will mediate the "judging" message of the kingdom' (Ellis, 182).

(50) The second part of the saying is again concerned with Jesus; contrast the parallel saying in Mk. 10:38 where the centre of interest is the fate of the disciples. The verb βαπτίζω is here used without primary reference to the rite of baptism, but in the metaphorical sense of being overwhelmed by catastrophe; this use is not found in the LXX but is not uncommon in Hellenistic sources and in the later Greek versions of the OT (AG s.v.; A. Oepke, TDNT I, 538f.; Delling, 242–244). Cf. Pss. 42:7; 69:1f. The parallel image of the cup in Mk. 10:38 has the sense of submitting to divine judgment. Delling, 248, draws attention to Ps. 11:6 where the imagery is of God raining down fire upon the wicked and causing a scorching wind to be the content of their cup. If this verse lies in the background of the saying, it suggests that the verb βαπτίζω may have the sense of deluging someone from above with fire, and thus a closer link occurs between the two parts of the saying. Jesus himself then shares in the judgment which is to come upon the world. But the saying indicates that his baptism is the pre-condition for what is to follow; this is the probable force of the δέ. Hence the longing of Jesus is for his baptism to be accomplished.

συνέχω has the sense 'to be distressed' (8:37; 4:38; Phil. 1:23) or 'to be dominated by (a thought)' (Acts 18:5; 2 Cor. 5:14; H. Köster, TDNT VII, 877–885, especially, 884f.). For ἕως ὅτου, 'until', cf. 13:8; 22:16; Mt. 5:25. τελέω (2:39; cf. Jn. 19:28, 30) conveys the idea that the death envisaged by Jesus (for nothing else can be meant) is no mere fate or accident but a destiny to be fulfilled; cf. especially 13:32; 22:37 (Klein*, 377). The thought is thus 'How I am totally governed by this until it be finally accomplished!' (H. Köster, ibid. with C. Colpe, TDNT VIII, 444). H. Köster regards the saying as a Lucan reformulation of Mk. 10:38, since συνέχω appears to be a Lucan word, but this proves no more than that Luke has edited an existing saying which already went beyond the brief formulation in Mk. 10:38.

(51) The implications of the previous, enigmatic statements are now brought out. The general tone of Jesus' teaching may well have led people to think that his message was one of unqualified peace (cf. the earlier references in this Gospel alone: 7:50; 8:48; 10:5f.). For this use of δοκέω (1:3) cf. 13:2, 4. It is not clear whether the Matthaean parallel μὴ νομίσητε is secondary (cf. the similar structure in Mt. 5:17). παραγίνομαι is a favourite word of Luke (7:4; *et al.*) and may have displaced an original ἔρχομαι (Mt.) in the interests of literary variation from v. 49. (On Mt. 10:34 see R. Banks (as in 16:16f. note), 204–206.) The use of δίδωμι 'to put, place', is Semitic (15:22; Black, 133 n. 1); Matthew's use of the rougher βάλλω may be with a view to the second accusative μάχαιραν in his formulation. The saying may echo the promise in 2:14. But such peace cannot come without war preceding it. Luke's wording differs considerably from Matthew's. The question is answered with οὐχί (cf. 13:3, 5); for ἀλλ' ἤ, 'but rather', cf. 2 Cor. 1:13. διαμερισμός** is 'dissension, disunity', and links with the use of the verb in v. 53 (cf. Mi. 7:12). The Lucan form may be secondary to that in Mt. (Schürmann, *Paschamahlbericht*, 2; *contra* T. A. Roberts*). Matthew's form has a possible echo in Rev. 6:4. It is perhaps more likely that Matthew and Luke are following different sources at this point, since the linguistic links between 12:51 and 13:3, 5 are hardly likely to have been created by Luke (*pace* Schulz, 258). The changes may then have been due to Luke's source.

(52) The nature of the 'division' mentioned in the previous verse is now delineated. The verb (διαμερίζω, 11:17) is in the periphrastic future perfect tense (MH III, 89), but the sense appears to be durative: 'they will be in a state of division'. A state of affairs is envisaged, commencing from 'now', ἀπὸ τοῦ νῦν (1:48); in the light of 22:69 G. Klein*, 374, argues that the time-point indicated is the end of Jesus' life rather than some point within it (Zahn, 516; Grundmann, 271). In view of the similar prophecy in 22:35f. the former interpretation is possible. It is more likely, however, that the 'now' refers to the whole event of the coming of Jesus, which is seen as falling within the end-time (Schulz, 260). It is a situation in which there are five people in one house (ἐνὶ οἴκῳ; inverted order in *Diglot*), so that there is mutual enmity between two and three of them. The saying represents an interpretation of Mi. 7:6, which is quoted in the next verse. As that verse indicates, the enmity is between the older and younger generations (Jub. 23:19; Sotah 9:15; cf. SB I, 586; IV:2, 982). For enmity of the old against the young see 1 En. 100:2; for attacks by the young on the old see Jub. 23:16. See further Lk. 1:17, where the reconciliation of divided families is the task of the Messiah's forerunner, as in Mal. 4:5. The saying may be a secondary interpretation of v. 53, since it is absent from Mt. (Schulz, 258f.). It does not, however, make clear which generation is thought to be on the side

of Christ. On the syntax, a Semitic noun clause which can be misunderstood as a complete sentence, see Beyer, I:1, 237 n. 1.

(53) The verb διαμερισθήσονται may be attached to the preceding verse (*Synopsis*; NEB) or taken with the present verse (UBS; cf. the reading διαμερισθήσεται, TR; *Diglot*); the latter gives better sense. What follows is based on Mi. 7:6 υἱὸς ἀτιμάζει πατέρα, θυγάτηρ ἐπαναστήσεται ἐπὶ τὴν μητέρα αὐτῆς, νύμφη ἐπὶ τὴν πενθερὰν αὐτῆς, ἐχθροὶ ἀνδρὸς πάντες οἱ ἄνδρες οἱ ἐν τῷ οἴκῳ αὐτοῦ. Whereas in Mi. the hostility is in one direction – the young against the old – Luke, diff. Mt., makes it mutual, employing chiasmus to express the opposing factions. Luke uses ἐπί, as in Mi., but varies between the dative and accusative cases; Matthew uses κατά. For πενθερά cf. 4:38; αὐτῆς is added by ℵᶜ A Θ *pm* lat; TR; *Diglot*. νύμφη* is a 'bride', hence 'daughter-in-law' (a linguistic development in the LXX (J. Jeremias, TDNT IV, 1099). The picture is of a family of five – father, mother, daughter, son and son's wife; Grundmann's alternative suggestion, which replaces the son's wife by the daughter's mother-in-law (271 n. 7) is unlikely. For division in families caused by the gospel cf. 14:26; 17:34f.; Mk. 10:29f. Gundry, 78f., suggests that Luke's wording is more primitive, but conforms slightly to the LXX, while Matthew has assimilated to the MT and extended the quotation; Schulz; 259, however, holds that Matthew has preserved the Q wording.

(54) The saying about interpreting the time is addressed to the crowds (cf. 3:7; 13:14) as distinct from the disciples, and expresses the consequences of the revelation which Jesus has given to the disciples; for this structure cf. especially 9:21–27. Two types of weather warning are described. First, there is the appearance of a cloud in the west. Before νεφέλην the article τήν is inserted by p⁴⁵ D W Θ *pm*; TR; (UBS); *Diglot*. ἀνατέλλω is 'to rise' (Mt. 5:45; 13:6; Mk. 4:6; 16:2; Jas. 1:11; cf. 2 Pet. 1:19; Mt. 4:6; Heb. 7:14**). δυσμός is used in the plural to mean 'west' (13:29*). The sign heralds rain (ὄμβρος**, 'rain-storm, thunder-storm'). This agrees with conditions in Palestine (1 Ki. 18:44), or indeed any country with a western seaboard.

(55) Similarly, the blowing (πνέω*, Acts 27:40*) of the south or south-west wind (νότος, Acts 27:13; 28:13*; cf. Lk. 11:31; 13:29) signifies that there will be heat (καύσων, especially of the heat of the sun, Mt. 20:12; Jas. 1:11**; Is. 49:10); the reference is simply to the warm air brought from the south by wind that has travelled across the desert. Again this would apply to Palestine.

The variant tradition found in Mt. 16:2f. v.l. describes the red sky at night, promising good weather, and the red sky in the morning, threatening a storm. G. Klein*, 386f., argues that these signs would fit a wider area than those in Lk., but his reasons for preferring this form as original compared with that in Lk. are not convincing.

(56) The application is now made. The crowds are addressed as ὑποκριταί (6:42; 13:15*). They use their skill (cf. οἴδατε) to discern the

meaning of (δοκιμάζω; 12:56b; 14:19*) the appearance (πρόσωπον, Ps. 103 (104):30; Jas. 1:11) of the earth and heaven (γῆς ... οὐρανοῦ (‭א‬* A B); οὐρανοῦ ... γῆς, (p⁷⁵ ‭א‬ᶜ D L *pm* Mcion); the confusion probably arises from the strangeness of the mention of the earth in this context; Klostermann, 141, conjectures that it is not original). The wording of the rest of the verse is uncertain. The connective πλήν (instead of δέ) is attested by p⁴⁵ D 157 c e; *Diglot*, and is perhaps original, since scribes might regard it as awkward before the following πῶς (which is omitted by D it syˢᵉ Mcion). For οὐκ οἴδατε δοκιμάζειν (p⁷⁵ ‭א‬ B L Θ *pc* sa bo; UBS; Diglot) the shorter form οὐ δοκιμάζετε is offered by p⁴⁵ A D W Γ *pl* lat; TR; *Synopsis,* and is defended by G. Klein*, 379. But the longer text is to be preferred with Metzger, 162. The people are reproached for being unable (or, with the shorter reading, unwilling) to discern the meaning of the present time. The reference appears to be to the significance of the events associated with the ministry of Jesus (G. Delling, TDNT III, 459f.); these may be seen as pointing to the presence of salvation or to the advent of judgment, but in any case to the action of God which demands a decision from men. Many scholars see a reference to the political events signalling the approaching war with Rome or to the signs that the End itself was at hand (Jeremias, *Parables,* 162; Kümmel, 22). In accordance with his general view of the passage G. Klein*, 377–380, 385–390, argues that Luke has de-apocalypticised a saying which originally referred to apocalyptic signs of the imminent end, and has made it apply to the time of divisions after the death of Jesus, which men should recognise for what it is; then they should decide for or against the church. Such an interpretation is probable for Luke, but it does not necessitate the break between the original and Lucan meanings of the saying which Klein suggests. There is a continuity between the time of Jesus and the time of the church, in both of which the 'now' of salvation is present. The saying has a parallel in Mt. 16:3 v.l. which appears to be from a different tradition. The accusation of hypocrisy made at the beginning of the verse is fitting, for it indicates the contradiction between the ability to discern weather signs and the lack of ability to discern the signs of God's action; the implication is that people with intelligence enough to recognise the former should also be able to recognise the latter; if they fail to do so, it may be unwillingness rather than inability which is the cause. Hence the word is not a secondary addition; cf. U. Wilckens, TDNT VIII, 566f. and n. 41.

(57) The parable which closes the section has an introduction which is missing from the parallel in Mt. 5:25f. The introduction may have been omitted by Matthew in adapting the parable to a new context, but it is more commonly regarded as a transition created by Luke (Bultmann, 95, 185f.; Schulz, 421). The language hardly permits of a verdict. δὲ καί is Lucan (2:4; *et al.*) For ἀφ' ἑαυτῶν cf. 21:30 diff. Mk. κρίνω τὸ δίκαιον can mean 'to give a just judgment' (cf. Acts 4:19), but the sense here is rather 'to judge what is right' (cf. 2 Pet. 1:13; G.

Schrenk, TDNT II, 188). It is a question of discerning what it is fitting to do in the circumstances; hence κρίνω is close in meaning to δοκιμάζω here (G. Klein*, 384).

(58) The character of this appropriate action is described in a parable which puts the hearer in the situation of a person on his way (ὑπάγω, 8:42) with a legal adversary (ἀντίδικος, 18:3; Mt. 5:25) to appear before a magistrate (ἄρχων, 8:41). The case implied is probably that of a debtor who is being dragged before a court, and the language may suggest that a Hellenistic court is meant, since a Jewish dispute would have been settled by a scribe (12:13f.) acting as a judge. The sensible thing is to make a settlement out of court, i.e. on the way, and every effort should be made to accomplish this. δίδωμι ἐργασίαν, 'to take pains' is a Latinism (do operam; BD 5³ᵇ), probably due to Luke (for ἐργασία cf. Acts 16:16, 19; 19:24f.; Eph. 4:19**). ἀπαλλάσσω is 'to free, release' (Heb. 2:15), (middle) 'to depart' (Acts 19:12**). In the passive the verb can mean 'to be reconciled' (Plato, Leg. 915c), a sense supported here by the Matthaean parallel (ἴσθι εὐνοῶν); so NIV. Findlay, 1046, and G. Klein*, 383, argue that Luke has deliberately adopted the middle form: the result of the implied settlement is not that the two parties are reconciled to each other, but rather that the adversary goes away for good (perfect tense!). For Klein, the parable exhorts men to throw in their lot with the church and make a clean break with its opponents. A somewhat similar interpretation was upheld by Klostermann, 143, who identified the adversary as the devil. Klein's interpretation is unacceptable, since the point of the parable lies in the danger of falling under judgment rather than in getting rid of the adversary. The wording does not support Klein's view that the person who fails to settle up will be condemned to the company of his adversaries at the judgment.

The danger confronting the man is that his adversary will drag him by force (κατασύρω**) before the judge. The latter will commit him (σε παραδώσει is inverted by D pc; Diglot) to the 'bailiff', who will then throw him into the debtor's prison. πράκτωρ is generally taken to be the official in a Roman judicial system, whereas the ὑπηρέτης who appears in Mt. is the Jewish synagogue official (4:20) who saw to the imprisonment of debtors (C. Maurer, TDNT VI, 642; Jeremias, Parables, 27); a somewhat different interpretation is offered by AG 704 and K. H. Rengstorf (TDNT VIII, 539) who show that ὑπηρέτης was a term used in Hellenistic practice as well as Jewish to describe the court official who executed the sentence imposed by the court, while πράκτωρ had the more restricted sense of the official who dealt with debts and was in charge of the debtors' prison. This second view should undoubtedly be accepted. If so, it follows that the parable has not necessarily undergone secondary Hellenisation at the hands of Luke. After μήποτε the subjunctive is appropriate (κατασύρῃ), but Luke quickly alters to the future indicative (cf. 14:8, 10; BD 369³).

(59) Jesus' final statement begins with ἀμήν (Mt. diff. Lk.), and

stresses with an emphatic future negative (οὐ μή) that there is no escape from the prison until the last part of the debt has been repaid. λεπτόν (21:2; Mk. 12:42**) is a small copper coin, said to be equivalent to the Jewish pᵉrutah. Matthew has κοδράντης, Latin quadrans ($\frac{1}{4}$ of an *as*), said to be equal to two λεπτά (Mk. 12:42). Here, therefore, Luke is more likely to be original.

What is the meaning of the parable? Get matters right with your adversary before the judge sends you to prison. This may be taken to mean settling accounts with the devil (Klostermann) or with God (Schulz, 423f.) or with one's fellowmen before it is too late – too late either because death puts an end to the possibility (G. Klein*, 381) or because of the final nature of God's judgment. It may be wrong to try to press the details of the parable allegorically in order to get a clear interpretation of it. In Mt., however, it is clear that the parable is applied to the possibility of a person who has been wronged rising up at the last judgment to confront his opponent (Schniewind, *Matthäus*, 61f.). This may well be the original sense of the parable, although it has been generalised in Lk. to apply to readiness for the last judgment (cf. Kümmel, 56, who holds, however, that Matthew has turned the parable into a prudential, ethical maxim). Klein's particular application of the parable to the situation of division in 12:51–53 is artificial, and is unlikely to represent Luke's view of the connection.

vi. The Need for Repentance 13:1–9

The report of a tragedy in Jerusalem, thought by Jesus' hearers to be due to the especial sinfulness of those who had suffered in it, leads him to affirm that all of his hearers are equally in danger of divine judgment and to quote a further example from which the same point is repeated. This leads up to a parable indicating that, if Israel does not take the chance of repentance afforded to it by God's patience, the day of reckoning will duly arrive.

The section is peculiar to Lk. Bultmann, 21, regards vs. 1–5 as an apophthegm used to introduce the following parable, and claims that this apophthegm is probably a creation by the early church (ibid. 57). But the discussion of the background by J. Blinzler* indicates that the episode can well be historical. It is to be placed in Galilee, which is the most likely place where such a report as in v. 1 would have been brought to Jesus.

The lesson of the parable is different from that of the introduction. While the introduction speaks merely of the need for universal repentance, the parable indicates that mercy is available for those who repent in time. The connection of these complementary pieces of teaching can be historical. The parable has certain affinities with the story of the cursing of the fig-tree (Mk. 11:12–14) which Luke later omits; but there is no reason to believe that the parable and the story are variants of one basic motif.

See J. Blinzler, 'Die Niedermetzelung von Galiläer durch Pilatus', Nov.T 2, 1958, 24-49.

(1) ἐν αὐτῷ τῷ καιρῷ (2:38 note) serves to link with the preceding incident. πάρειμι* can mean 'to be present' (Acts 10:33), but may also mean 'to arrive' (Acts 10:21; 12:20; 17:6; 24:19*; Diodorus Siculus 17:8:2, cited by Creed, 180). The impression is that messengers have arrived from Jerusalem bringing news of the latest incident there (J. Blinzler*, 25); ἀπαγγέλλω has the sense 'to bring news of something fresh' (7:18; Gn. 26:32; Est. 6:2; 1 Mac. 14:21). The situation reported concerns certain Galileans – the number, unspecified, need have been no more than a couple (Easton, 213) – who had been offering sacrifice at the temple in Jerusalem. The occasion could have been Passover, the only time when the laity slaughtered their own animals (Jeremias, *Words*, 207 n. 4), and the incident involved the killing of the men while they were sacrificing. Thus Pilate could be said to mix (μίγνυμι, Mt. 27:34; Rev. 8:7; 15:2**) their blood with that of their sacrifices (cf. SB II, 193). The expression need not be taken literally, but could simply be a gruesome metaphor for the two events taking place simultaneously. A number of events to which allusion is possibly being made are discussed by J. Blinzler*, 32–37. These include: 1. the affair of the ensigns in Jos. Bel. 2:169–174; Ant. 18:55–59, but this took place in Caesarea in AD 26; 2. the tumults associated with the building of an aqueduct (Jos. Bel. 2: 175–177; Ant. 18:60–62), but this incident involved the murder of Judaeans with cudgels outside the temple; 3. an attack on some Samaritans (Jos. Ant. 18:85–87), but this took place in AD 36; 4. the slaughter of about 3,000 Jews offering Passover sacrifices by Archelaus in 4 BC (Jos. Bel. 2:8–13; Ant. 17:213–218). This incident, however, took place some thirty years earlier and was committed by a different ruler; moreover, the murder of 3,000 men would not bear comparison with an accident to 18. It is wisest to conclude that the event is not attested from secular sources. This, however, is no argument against its historicity, since Josephus' account of Pilate's career is very incomplete (cf. Philo, Leg. 299–305). Pilate would have been in Jerusalem at Passover time, and the Galileans had a reputation for rebelliousness. The suggestion that Zealots were involved (O. Cullmann, *The State in the NT*, London, 1957, 14) lacks proof.

(2) In general the Pharisees believed that calamity was a punishment for sin (cf. Job 4:7; 8:20; 22:4f.; Jn. 9:1f.; SB II, 193–197). It could, therefore, be argued that these men were greater sinners than other Galileans; ἁμαρτωλοί is almost used as an adjective (Zerwick, 145) and παρά (equivalent to Hebrew *min*) means 'beyond, than' (13:4; Jeremias, *Parables*, 141 n. 49; BD 236³). πάντας must mean 'all *other* Galileans' (cf. 3:20; 14:10). Note how the ὅτι clause gives evidence for the preceding statement (cf. 7:47); this may explain why the verb is in

the perfect tense, describing the state of affairs which led to the verdict of 'sinners'.

(3) Jesus emphatically negates his own question with οὐχί (12:51). Unless his hearers repent (10:13), i.e. of their sin in general, they will all be destroyed in the same way. This is hardly to be taken literally of a similar slaughter, although it could refer to the destruction of Jerusalem, which Jesus foresaw (cf. Creed, 181). More likely the reference is to the last judgment (1 En. 98:16; 99:9; 98:3; Lk. 9:24f.; 17:33; Jn. 3:16; *et al.*). The point is then that natural calamities afford no proof that those who suffer in them are any worse sinners than anybody else; far more important is the fact that all sinners face the judgment of God unless they repent.

(4) Jesus reinforces the point by adding a second example of his own. Eighteen men had been killed when a tower fell at Siloam. For δεκαοκτώ (13:11), the variant δέκα καὶ ὀκτώ is read by אᶜ A *al*; TR; *Diglot* (similarly at 13:11 by A L *al*; TR; *Diglot*), as in 13:16 (all MSS); scribes were more likely to be consistent than Luke who likes literary variation; cf. BD 63²; MH II, 171. πύργος, 'tower', can also mean 'farm building' (14:28; Mk. 12:1 par. Mt. 21:33**).

Σιλωάμ was the name of the reservoir associated with the water supply from Gihon to Jerusalem (Jn. 9:7, 11;** Is. 8:6); it lay near the junction of the S and E walls, and the tower may have been part of the fortifications in this area (cf. Jos. Bel. 5:145; so SB II, 197; Finegan, 114f.). Pilate built an aqueduct to improve the water supply, and it is also possible that the tower (and its collapse) had something to do with this building operation (Jos. Bel. 2:175; Ant. 18:60). Nothing is otherwise known of the disaster, an incident too trifling to figure in a history book. Nevertheless, there is a rabbinic statement that no building ever collapsed in Jerusalem (Aboth RN 35; SB II, 197), but this is unlikely to be reliable evidence against the statement here. The victims are described as ὀφειλεταί*, 'debtors' (Mt. 6:12; 18:24), which is a translation variant for 'sinners' (cf. 11:4 note), and indicates that the story has a Semitic background. For κατοικέω cf. 11:26. Luke frequently uses it with a direct accusative as here (Acts 1:19; 2:9, 14; 4:16; 9:32, 35; 19:10, 17); hence the addition of ἐν (א A W Δ Θ f13 *pm*; TR; *Diglot*) is unjustified.

(5) The punch-line is repeated from v.3. μετανοῆτε is read by 𝔭⁷⁵ אᶜ B W Δ *al;* TR; UBS; *Diglot*, the variant μετανοήσητε (*Synopsis*) being due to assimilation to v. 3 and to the preference of scribes for the aorist form. ὡσαύτως, 'likewise' (20:31; 22:20*), is a translation variant, or more probably a literary variant for ὁμοίως in v. 3; the latter is read here by 𝔭⁷⁵ A D W Δ Θ f13 *pm*; TR; *Diglot* (note that ὁμοίως is read in v. 3 by A W Δ *pm*; TR).

(6) The opening parabolic formula is Lucan, but elsewhere the order αὐτὴ ἡ παραβολή is always reversed (4:23; *et al.*). συκῆ (note the accent; MH II, 119f.) is a fig-tree (13:7; 21:29; Mk. 11:13, 20f. par. Mt.

21:19–21; Mk. 13:28 par. Mt. 24:32; Jn. 1:49, 51; Jas. 3:12; Rev. 6:13**; C.-H. Hunzinger, TDNT VII, 751–757, especially 755f.). In the parable its fruit is symbolical of the Jewish people, but the OT references (Ho. 9:10; Je. 8:13; 24:1–8; Mi. 7:1) hardly suggest that a standing symbol for Israel is being used. There is nothing strange about a fig-tree being planted (φυτεύω, 17:6, 28; 20:9 par. Mk. 12:1) in a vineyard (ἀμπελών, 20:9–16 par. Mk. 12:1–9); indeed the latter word is tantamount to 'fruit garden', since fruit trees of all kinds were regularly planted in vineyards (Dt. 22:9; 1 Ki. 5:5; 2 Ki. 18:31; Mi. 4:4; SB I, 873). The coincidence of language between ἦλθεν ζητῶν and the similar phrase in Mk. 11:13 is natural. The owner's expectations are disappointed; hence the tree in the parable must have been one that was already fit to bear fruit, not an immature one on which it would be foolish to seek for fruit.

(7) The owner discusses the situation with the vine-dresser or gardener (ἀμπελουργός**): although fig-trees bore fruit annually, this one had gone for three years without fruit. τρία ἔτη is a *nominativus pendens* (13:16; Mk. 8:2; BD 144), and 'three' is simply a round number. ἀφ' οὗ (sc. χρόνου) is 'since' (13:25; 24:21; Rev. 16:18; Rehkopf, 92). ἔρχομαι is to be translated as a perfect 'I have been coming' (BD 322). After ἔκκοψον the conjunction οὖν is added by p⁷⁵ A L Θ Ψ 070 f13 33 *pm* lat syˢ sa bo; (UBS); the external evidence is fairly equally divided (Metzger, 162). Although G. Stählin, TDNT III, 859, holds that ἐκκόπτω refers to punishment taking place within this aeon, the thought is of eternal perdition in Mt. 3:10; 7:19, and this may well be the point here too: unrepentant Israelites will be excluded from salvation (cf. Rom. 11:22; Mt. 21:43). For ἱνατί, 'why, for what reason', (sc. γένηται) cf. Acts 4:25; 7:26. καί expresses the thought, 'unfruitful itself, why should it also waste ground that could be put to fruitful use?'; the tree not only takes up space, but in fact exhausts the ground by taking nourishment from it (καταργέω; cf. G. Delling, TDNT I, 452). Is there a hint that another vine will be planted in its place?

(8) Thus far the parable has resembled a similar story of a palm tree which asked for a year's grace and was refused it. (Ahikar 8:35 (in AP II, 775); the story may be a later addition to the text.) (A further variant is found in Aboth RN 16 (6a) (SB IV:1, 474) where a field that had been manured still produced only 1 kor of grain.) Now the story takes a different turn with the successful intercession of the vine-dresser. Note the historic present λέγει, which suggests use of a tradition by Luke (Jeremias, *Parables*, 182f.; Rehkopf, 99). ἀφίημι is 'to leave alone' and ἕως ὅτου 'until' (22:16; cf. 15:8; 22:18). σκάπτω, 'to dig', is here used of loosening the soil around the roots (cf. Diodorus Siculus 5:41:6, cited in AG s.v.), and κόπριον** (neuter plural) is 'dung, manure' (cf. 14:35). For the treatment cf. Ho. 9:10; Is. 5:1–7; Joel 1:7; 1QH 8:20–26.

(9) Two possibilities lie open. The tree may bear fruit εἰς τὸ μέλλον,

i.e. 'for the future' (1 Tim. 6:19) or (sc. ἔτος) 'next year' (AG, citing P. Lond. 1231, 4). The protasis is not followed by an apodosis, giving aposiopesis, with the implication, ' (in that case,) well and good' (BD 454⁴; the construction is Classical). The construction is weakened in many MSS, which place εἰς τὸ μέλλον after εἰ δὲ μήγε (p⁴⁵ ᵛⁱᵈ A D W Θ f1 f13 pl latt sy; TR), and thus produce a poorer sense (Metzger, 162). For εἰ μήγε, 'otherwise' cf. 5:36; BD 439¹; the future indicative ἐκκόψεις expresses a polite imperative or granting of permission. The day of grace will come to an end, despite the intercession of the vine-dresser which could only be for a limited remission of judgment; Jeremias, Parables, 170f., suggests that the disciples may later have seen an allusion to the role of Jesus himself in the parable (cf. 22:31f.).

vii. The Healing of a Crippled Woman 13:10–17

The connection of thought at this point in the Gospel is far from clear. There appears to be a break at the end of 13:9, so that 13:10 might be regarded as the beginning of a new section. However, there is a more distinct break at 13:21/22, and it may be better to place the caesura there. If so, the present verses are to be regarded as forming the conclusion of the section which began in 12:1. The story of the healing of the woman with the bent back is then presented from two aspects. It is an illustration of the hypocritical attitude of the Jewish leaders which has already been castigated in 11:37–54. At the same time it exemplifies the saving power of God in delivering his people from the power of Satan, and thus provides the kind of sign that should have been recognised by the Jews. In such signs as this the power of the kingdom is to be seen; even though it may seem tiny and almost unrecognisable, it is the evidence that something tremendous is in progress, as the following pair of parables illustrates. Thus the section closes with a powerful stress on the saving work of Jesus.

The story is peculiar to Lk., and is an independent story with no necessary connection with the surrounding material. It is a healing story which leads into a conflict between the leader of the synagogue and Jesus and culminates in a pronouncement by Jesus. Bultmann, 10, 65, regarded it as a clumsy construction, based on the originally isolated saying in v. 15, in which the healing illogically precedes the debate, so that the shame of the opponents is not properly motivated: contrast the construction in 14:1–6 and Mk. 3:1–6, all of which Bultmann regards as variants of one original story.

A similar analysis is given by Dibelius, 94f., and E. Lohse, TDNT VII, 25f., who hold that the content of v. 15 is a literary contrast between the loosing of the animal from the stall and of the woman from sickness, and that the whole story has been given a novellistic expansion; Luke has fitted the story into its context with the motifs of hypocrisy (v. 15) and impenitence (v. 17).

Bultmann's sceptical verdict is unjustified, and rests on little more than an arbitrary claim that primitive gospel material *must* fall into certain forms. Roloff, *Kerygma*, 67, observes that v. 15 could never have stood by itself, but requires v. 16 as the answer to the literary riddle which it contains. He argues that v. 15 is not authentic, since rabbinic practice was even more rigorous than is indicated here. Hence he conjectures that the story grew out of the historical reminiscences in vs. 16, 12–14a, and that it cannot have arisen simply from the desire to provide a setting for v. 15. But Roloff's verdict on v. 15 is faulty (see below), and the kernel of the story can stand as a whole. M. Hengel, TDNT IX, 53, correctly observes that v. 15 could well come from a polemical speech by Jesus. The detail in the story shows that it is more than a secondary variant to Mk. 3:1–6, and at most the story has been written up by Luke to fit its present place in the Gospel (Grundmann, 278f.).

See J. Wilkinson, 'The Case of the Bent Woman in Luke 13:10–17', EQ 49, 1977, 195–205.

(10) The situation described as the setting of the incident could have been deduced from the rest of the story and a knowledge of Jesus' normal habits. Note the use of the periphrastic imperfect to give the setting. ἐν τοῖς σάββασιν is generally regarded as referring to one particular Sabbath (Plummer; cf. 4:16, 31), especially in view of the reference to one synagogue, but Schürmann I, 227 n. 45, thinks that the plural may be meant literally. This is the last instance of Jesus teaching in a synagogue in Lk.

(11) After γυνή the verb ἦν is added by TR; *Diglot*; perhaps as a clumsy attempt to avoid anacolouthon with the following καὶ ἦν. πνεῦμα ... ἀσθενείας is a spirit causing an infirmity; for the thought cf. 11:14; 1QapGen 20:17, 21–29; Easton, 215f., argues that Luke took v. 16 too literally and so was led to transform an ordinary healing into an exorcism. Certainly the illness is attributed ultimately to the evil power of Satan, but the cure is not described as an exorcism, but as a release from a fairly literal 'bond'. Perhaps we should not try to give too definite a meaning to πνεῦμα and think of it simply as an evil influence. Medically the illness has been diagnosed as *spondylitis ankylopoietica* (a fusion of the spinal bones) or as *skoliasis hysterica* (Grundmann, 279), i.e. a hysterical rather than an organic paralysis. Since a disease lasting eighteen years would have produced organic changes, the former diagnosis is preferable; see the careful analysis by J. Wilkinson*, 197–200. The duration of the disease gives a numerical coincidence with v. 4 (see note there on the text), similar to that between Mk. 5:25 and 42. The woman was bent over (συγκύπτω**) and unable to raise herself (ἀνακύπτω, 21:28; Jn. 8:7, 10**), or possibly to raise her head (cf. 21:28; JB mg, Lagrange, 382). παντελής means 'complete, perfect' (Heb. 7:25**), but the precise force of the phrase here is uncertain. It may go with ἀνακῦψαι, 'unable to raise herself completely' (RSV; Lagrange, 382; A. Oepke, TDNT II, 427 n. 30; Grundmann, 279 n.; cf. Creed, 183,

'unable to lift up herself straight'), or with μὴ δυναμένη, 'completely unable to raise herself' (most translations; vg (*omnino*); G. Delling, TDNT VIII, 66f.). The latter translation, which stresses the severity of the complaint, is perhaps preferable.

(12) The action of Jesus is spontaneous (cf. 6:8; 14:3f.) and arises out of natural pity for the woman. He summons her from her position in the congregation and pronounces her cured: the perfect indicative no doubt stresses the permanent nature of the cure (cf. 5:20; 7:48).

(13) The action of laying on of hands on the woman (the addition of ἐπ' before αὐτῇ in *Diglot* gives an unparalleled construction) is to be regarded as accompanying the word spoken by Jesus; for the action cf. 4:40. The healing follows immediately (παραχρῆμα is Lucan, 1:64; *et al.*). ἀνορθόω, 'to rebuild, restore' (Acts 15:16; Heb. 12:12**), refers to the recovery of a normal upright posture (cf. Acts 14:10). The praising of God by the healed person is a motif not found in the similar stories in 6:10; 14:4, but is found in Acts 3:8f.; it may be due to Luke, but is entirely appropriate in the synagogue setting.

(14) The healing story has reached its climax, and by the rules of form criticism could end at this point. But as in other cases the sign wrought by Jesus becomes the occasion of controversy and teaching. The initiative is taken by the ruler of the synagogue (8:49) who responds to the healing: for ἀποκρίνομαι in this sense cf. 14:3; 17:17; 22:51; Mk. 9:5; *et al.* (This usage finds no mention in AG s.v. but F. Büchsel, TDNT III, 944f., notes it, and states that it means 'he began', a non-Greek use based on that of Hebrew '*ānāh*.) The ruler is indignant (ἀγανακτέω*) at the breaking of the Sabbath by Jesus, but he hesitates to attack him to his face and instead makes a comment to the crowd; ὅτι is *recitativum* (1:25). The comment echoes Ex. 20:9 par. Dt. 5:13. Let the people come on weekdays for healing, not on the Sabbath day (ἡ ἡμέρα τοῦ σαββάτου, 13:16; 14:5, is possibly a phrase typical of Luke's source).

(15) Behind the reply of Jesus lies his authority as ὁ κύριος (7:13); for the Hebraistic ἀπεκρίθη ... καὶ εἶπεν cf. 17:20. The plural form ὑποκριταί indicates that Jesus is addressing the ruler and any present who agreed with him; the singular form in p⁴⁵ D W f1 *pm* f 1 sy; Iren, is secondary. The question asks whether it is not true that any of them would loose his ox (βοῦς, 14:5, 19*) or ass (ὄνος, 14:5 v.1.*) from its stall (φατνή, 2:7) in order to take it to a source of water and give it a drink (ποτίζω*). The Mishnah presupposes that cattle may go out on a Sabbath – provided that they do not carry burdens (Shab. 5:1–4). There was dispute as to what kinds of knots might be tied or untied on the Sabbath; despite the general prohibition (Shab. 7:2; 15:1), it was permissible to tie up cattle lest they stray (Shab. 15:2). Moreover, special provisions were made so that cattle might be watered at wells without transgressing the limits for Sabbath travel (Erub. 2:1–4); the Qumran sect limited to 2000 cubits the distance that cattle might be taken in order to pasture

them (CD 11:5f.). Cf. SB I, 629f.; II, 199f. Roloff's claim that Pharisaic practice was more rigorous than Jesus depicts here seems to be unfounded; in any case there were variations of opinion among the Pharisees. For ἀπαγαγών the present form ἀπάγων is attested by ℵ* B* Θ 1 pc and adopted by *Diglot*, probably rightly.

(16) Having established his ruling, Jesus draws a conclusion *a minore*: what is right for cattle is all the more right for man; cf. 14:5; Mt. 12:11. The force of the argument, however, has been contested. Montefiore asked why the crippled woman could not wait another day to be healed; her need was not as great as that of thirsty cattle. The objection is trivial. For Jesus, although she is a woman (and therefore regarded as less important than men in Jewish thought), she is nevertheless a descendant of Abraham (cf. 1:55), and like Zacchaeus (19:9) a member of God's people (Acts 13:26). It may be that the Jews denied her this position, since her illness might have been regarded as a sign of sinfulness (cf. 13:2), but Jesus affirms it. She ought, therefore, to be freed from an alien master who had kept her bound for 18 years: the aorist ἔδησεν is the past equivalent of the present form ('He has kept her bound'; cf. 13:7), and is appropriate since the woman is now free (cf. BD 332¹). She should not remain bound a moment longer, for, look, she has already suffered 18 years (for the use of ἰδού cf. 13:7, and especially the fourth cent. papyrus (BU 948) cited by MH I, 11 n. 1). Hence it was necessary (ἔδει) for her to be released immediately, even though it was the Sabbath, perhaps indeed all the more fitting on the Sabbath, since Satan evidently does not stop his work on the Sabbath; in this way the Sabbath is positively hallowed (cf. Grundmann, 280).

(17) The story reaches its second climax with those opposed to Jesus (ἀντίκειμαι, 21:15*) being put to shame (καταισχύνω, cf. 1 Cor. 1:27; 1 Pet. 3:16). The phrase is strongly reminiscent of Is. 45:16 αἰσχυνθήσονται ... πάντες οἱ ἀντικείμενοι αὐτῷ, and may perhaps imply that for the narrator the messianic promises are being fulfilled in Jesus. Not only so, but the crowds rejoice (cf. 19:37) at the glorious (7:25) deeds done by Jesus; the expression is reminiscent of Ex. 34:10, and stresses that the deeds of Jesus are the work of God (cf. 7:16 for the thought). These are Lucan motifs.

viii. The Parables of the Mustard Seed and the Leaven 13:18–21

These two parables formed a pair in Luke's source (Q), as is attested by Mt. 13:31–33. It is disputed whether they were originally a pair, since the former appears on its own in Mk. 4:30–32, while the latter has a different companion in G. Thomas 96–97 (Bultmann, 186; Dodd, *Parables*, 143; Schulz, 300, 307); but the objections cited are quite unconvincing (so rightly Kümmel, 132 n. 98).

For Q and Luke both parables obviously have the same essential point. If the former speaks of the growth of a proverbially tiny seed, the latter describes the great influence of a small amount of leaven. In both cases the kingdom of God is compared to the process involved. From tiny beginnings it will grow and extend its influence to a tremendous extent. Thus the ideas of growth and of the contrast between the small beginning and the great end result are both present (cf. Schulz, 302). In the present Lucan context the parables are a commentary on what has preceded. The defeat of Satan is a sign of the advance of God's rule (11:20). The evidence may be slight – such an apparently trivial incident as the cure of a crippled woman – but the potential is beyond description. The small beginning is an earnest of certain victory, despite the opposition which Jesus experiences throughout his ministry.

Luke's source is Q. In the parallel passage in Mt. 13:31f. Matthew has conflated material from Q and Mk. 4:30–32. Streeter, 246–248, holds that Luke used Q alone, but Schramm, 50, argues that the double introduction, found here only in a Lucan parable, reflects Mk. Certainly there is no other trace of influence from Mk., and his form of the parable describes a fact by means of a comparison while Luke describes a process by means of a story (C.-H. Hunzinger, TDNT VII, 290). It is possible that Mark's introduction reflects an original double question found also in Q. The relation between the Q and Marcan forms of the parable is not clear. While the Marcan form is more Semitic in its wording (Black, 165f., 189 n. 3), the Q version of the mustard seed is structured more simply. Mark has nothing corresponding to the parable of the leaven.

Schulz, 301, 309, assigns both parables to the later strand of Q material and implicitly denies that they contain authentic teaching of Jesus. He argues that the concept of the kingdom as an eschatological phenomenon which spreads and grows in Israel – in the limited time before the imminent parousia – stands in contrast to the earlier apocalyptic idea of the kingdom. The thought of the final entry of the nations into the kingdom, as an eschatological event at the parousia and not as the result of a gradual mission – is likewise a late concept. These arguments are insufficient to overturn the generally accepted conclusion that the parables reflect the self-consciousness of Jesus. They rest on a schematic view of the development of eschatology in the Q community which lacks a firm basis. The presupposition that Jesus expected the kingdom to come suddenly and soon without any preparation leads to grave misinterpretation of the synoptic material.

See Dodd, *Parables*, 141–144; O. T. Allis, 'The Parable of the Leaven', EQ 19, 1947, 254–273; Jeremias, *Parables*, 146–149; N. A. Dahl, 'The Parables of Growth', ST 5, 1951, 132–166; Percy, 207–211; Grässer, 141–149; I. H. Marshall, *Eschatology and the Parables*, 24–28; Schulz, 298–307, 307–309.

(18) Luke's introduction differs from that in Mt. (cf. v. 20 diff. Mt. 13:33) and is close to Mk. 4:30. The οὖν links with the preceding narrative, and suggests that Jesus – apparently still in the synagogue – is commenting on what has just happened. For the τίνι ὁμοία . . . phrase cf.

6:47, and for τίνι ὁμοιώσω ... cf. 7:31 par. Mt. 11:16. The double introduction is found in Mk. 4:30, but the wording differs; cf. Is. 40:18. Possibly Matthew (who is stylising, cf. Mt. 13:24) has dropped half of the introduction rather than that Luke has copied Mk. Did the double introduction originally indicate that *two* objects of comparison were to follow?

(19) The kingdom is said to be like a grain of mustard seed; i.e. the situation in both cases is similar (Jeremias, *Parables*, 101f.). For κόκκος cf. 17:6; O. Michel, TDNT III, 810–812. σίναπι (neuter), 17:6*, is 'mustard', usually identified as *sinapis nigra*, 'black mustard'.This grows to form a bush about 4 ft. high, but greater growth, even to 9 ft., is known, and the description of it as a δένδρον is not inappropriate (C.-H. Hunzinger, TDNT VII, 288f.). Since the seed was proverbially extremely small (Nid. 5:2; cf. SB I, 669; O. Michel, TDNT III, 810 n. 1; Hunzinger, ibid.), there was no need for Luke to make explicit reference to this, although Mark does so. When a man takes it (λαβών is in Semitic, redundant style; cf. 13:21; B!ack, 125) and sows it (βάλλω, Mk. 4:26) in his garden (κῆπος, Jn. 18:1, 26; 19:41**), it proceeds to grow. According to rabbinic sources (Kil. 3:2; SB I, 669), mustard was not cultivated in gardens, but in fields (cf. Mt.); Luke presumably has rewritten the parable in non-Palestinian terms (*pace* Schulz, 299). The plant grows and becomes a tree: many MSS add μέγα (p⁴⁵ A W Θ f1 f13 *pl* lat syᵖ; TR; *Diglot*) to heighten the point (Metzger, 162). The birds are able to settle (κατασκηνόω, also Acts 2:26*, 'to dwell') in its branches (κλάδος*). Cf. Dn. 4:12, 21 (9, 18 Θ), where similar imagery is used of the relation of the nations of the world to Nebuchadrezzar, the ruler of Babylon; see also Ps. 104:13 (103:12); Ezk. 17:23; 31:6; 1 En. 90:30. For a related picture cf. 1QH 6:14–16.

The imagery suggests the growth of the kingdom of God from tiny beginnings to worldwide size, and the birds may represent the nations (an allusion which is regarded as secondary allegory by Grässer, 142); cf. Jeremias, *Parables*, 146–149. The stress is not so much on the idea of growth in itself as on the certainty that what appears tiny and insignificant will prove to have been the beginning of a mighty kingdom.

(20) The second parable reinforces the point. πάλιν is comparatively rare in Lk. (6:43; 23:20*; Mt., 17x; Mk., 28x) and hence is from Luke's source here (diff. Mt.).

(21) ζύμη, 'leaven' (12:1*), is old, fermented dough which is added to the new baking in order to start off the process of fermentation. Its working cannot be seen, cf. the use of κρύπτω (diff. Mt. ἐγκρύπτω**). But a small quantity will pervade three measures of wheat flour (ἄλευρον, Mt. 13:33**); σάτον is a transliteration of Aramaic s'âtâ (Hebrew sᵉ'āh), a quantity equivalent to 4¾ gallons or 13.13 litres (1½ times a Roman *modius*). The quantity is surprisingly large (sufficient to feed about 160 people), but the figure is traditional (Gn. 18:6; cf. Jdg. 6:19; 1 Sa. 1:24). The process of leavening (ζυμόω, Mt. 13:33; 1 Cor.

5:6; Gal. 5:9**) takes place overnight. By morning the whole mass of dough has been affected, cf. 1 Cor. 5:6; Gal. 5:9. Leaven often typifies evil influences (12:1), but here the point is the powerful influence of the kingdom of God; cf. H. Windisch, TDNT II, 905f.

e. The Way of the Kingdom (13:22 – 14:35)

Any division of the Gospel into sections must show some arbitrariness, and this is especially evident at this part of the narrative. The mention of Jesus' journey to Jerusalem in 13:22 suggests that we are perhaps to see the beginning of a new section at this point, but its limits are uncertain. On the one hand, the new section has close links with the preceding one, the theme of the need for repentance and decision forming an obvious link between 13:23–30 and 13:1–9. On the other hand, it is difficult to see where the section ends. There is an obvious change of theme at 15:1, and the section can be regarded accordingly as stretching to 14:35; but there is such a variety of contents in it that it is debatable whether we should regard all of what is to be found here as being linked in any kind of way. The opening part of ch. 14 has a unity around the table scene, and 14:24–35 might be regarded as an epilogue to this, although there is no clear connection of thought. Similarly, the two paragraphs in 13:22–30 and 31–35 have no very obvious connection with each other or with the rest of the proposed section. It would appear that Luke has had to do his best with a variety of material from more than one source, and that we should not look for too connected a theme running throughout the section.

Tentatively we may suggest that in 13:22–35 the theme is that of the demands made by the kingdom upon intending disciples and upon Jesus himself. Then in 14:1–24 there is a series of criticisms of Pharisaic attitudes and finally in 14:25–35 a further stress on the stringency of the situation and the radical nature of discipleship.

i. Entry to the Kingdom 13:22–30

The section opens with a reminder that Jesus is evangelising the people and is on his way to Jerusalem, the city of his passion. This provides the context for both of the following sections, the first dealing with the danger of not responding to the message of Jesus, and the second with the inevitability of the rejection of Jesus and his death in Jerusalem. A question by an enquirer introduces a saying of Jesus stressing the importance of entry to the kingdom by the narrow door before it is too late and the door is shut. Two thoughts are juxtaposed. The one is that the period of opportunity is limited by the imminence of judgment. The other is that entry to the kingdom depends not merely upon hearing the message of Jesus and having fellowship with him but above all on turning from evil in repentance. The unrepentant Jews of Jesus' own time are contrasted with the faithful men of OT times and believing gentiles who will find their way into the kingdom. The day of judgment will produce surprises with its overturning of human expectations.

The origins of this section are particularly obscure. There are parallels with Mt. 7:13f., 22f. and 8:11f., but in the first two of these the wording varies considerably. The setting in v. 22 is probably Lucan. The question in v. 23 may have been composed by Luke as an introduction to the following saying (if so, it is dependent on Mt. 7:14 diff. Lk. 13:24), but it is also possible that it constituted the original introduction to the saying (Lucan: Bultmann, 359f.; Dibelius, 162; P. Hoffmann*, 193 n. 16; Flender, 81f.; Schulz, 310; pre-Lucan: Manson, *Sayings*, 124; Rehkopf, 87 n. 2; Jeremias, *Parables*, 195 n. 9; Wrege, 134 (undecided)).

The metaphorical picture of the narrow door in v. 24 differs considerably from that of the narrow gate and difficult way in Mt. 7:13f. Manson, *Sayings*, 124–126, and Grundmann, 284, assign the two versions to different sources. Similarly, Wrege, 132–135, holds that different traditions have been used. J. Jeremias, TDNT VI, 922f., thinks that Luke has preserved the original form of the saying which has been developed by Matthew (cf. P. Hoffmann*, 195f.), but the view that Matthew has the original form is defended by Schulz, 309–311. In favour of this last view, it is argued that Matthew's saying preserves poetic parallelism and contains no specifically Matthaean vocabulary; Luke has altered the picture from a gate to a door in order to get a link with v. 25 (which is itself a redactional link with vs. 26f.). But since the 'two way' motif was current in Matthew's environment (Did. 1–6) it is possible that its introduction here is due to Matthew or his source. No certain answer to the problem of priority can be given, and the possibility of separate developments in the tradition is perhaps most likely.

V. 25 is peculiar to Lk. As it stands, it has affinities to Mt. 25:10–12, but this passage can hardly be its source. Jeremias, *Parables*, 95f., suggests that Luke has created this 'parable of the closed door' out of motifs preserved in various places in Mt. It is more probable that Luke has preserved a parabolic saying which was dropped by Matthew or his source in the reformulation of the material in Mt. 7:13ff., and that the same motif has been independently used in the parable of the ten girls. The parallelism between vs. 26f. and Mt. 7:22f. suggests an ultimate common origin, but the Matthaean material has been adapted to deal with the problem of nominal church members; the Lucan form has better claims to being original (cf. P. Hoffmann*, 200–202; Schulz, 424–426). It remains unclear whether the differences in Mt. are due to Matthew himself.

Vs. 28f. have a much closer parallel in Mt. 8:11 ff., where they conclude the story of the centurion's servant. The order of the clauses is inverted in Mt. Matthew's linking of the saying with the story of the centurion's servant may well be original; but it is significant that the present group of sayings occurs in the same order in Mt. and Lk., and this raises the possibility that in Matthew's source the present saying preceded the story which thus followed it as an example or confirmation of the point which is made in it.

V. 30 is an isolated saying paralleled in Mt. 20:16 (in the context of Matthaean special material) and (in a different form) in Mk. 10:31 par. Mt. 19:30. Whether it stood in Luke's Q material at this point is impossible to say with certainty, but it is probable that it did.

Luke has thus probably taken over a set of sayings from Q which were available to Matthew in a variant form. Their theme was the judgment on Israel for refusal of Jesus' message; Luke has underlined the ethical emphasis of the passage.

See Manson, *Sayings*, 124–126; Wrege, 132–135; 146–152; P. Hoffmann, '*Πάντες ἐργάται ἀδικίας*: Redaktion und Tradition in Lc 13, 22–30', ZNW 58, 1967, 188–214; Schulz, 309–312, 424–427, 323–330.

(22) The setting of the scene is fairly obviously the work of Luke (cf. 8:1). For διαπορεύομαι cf. 6:1 and especially Acts 16:4, and for the use of κατά with a δια-compound cf. 8:1; 9:6. πορεία, is 'going, journey' (Jas. 1:11**). No geographical information can be extracted from the verse (*pace* Lagrange, 387). It is simply a reminder of the background to the following teaching, and emphasises that the work which Jesus is doing will not be terminated – despite the threats of Herod (13:31–35) – until he reaches Jerusalem. At the same time it indicates that the following question in all probability comes from the crowds rather than the disciples.

(23) The introductory formula may be pre-Lucan (Rehkopf, 87 n. 2), but this is not certain (P. Hoffmann*, 193 n. 16). For εἰ introducing a direct question cf. 22:42 v.1.; 22:49; Acts 1:6; *et al.*; Mk. 10:2; Rehkopf, 59. The usage is Lucan and appears to be Semitic. οἱ σῳζόμενοι has a future sense (1:35 note); it is a stereotyped phrase in the early church (Acts 2:47; 1 Cor. 1:18; 2 Cor. 2:15). Van Unnik, 30f. notes that the term occurs in Is. 37:32 LXX, and suggests that it may have become a technical term in certain circles. It refers to the obtaining of eschatological salvation, and is tantamount to entry to the kingdom and the gaining of eternal life (Mk. 10:26; cf. 1 En. 102:7; 4 Ez. 7:66). The question whether those who gained final bliss would be (only a) few (cf. Jeremias, *Parables*, 39 n. 59) was debated in Judaism; cf. Sanh. 10:1. A pessimistic answer is given in 4 Ez. 8:1; cf. 7:47; 9:15; see also SB I, 883. Jesus himself spoke in similar terms (Mt. 22:14). The word 'few' appears in Mt. 7:14; this suggests that either Luke (or his source) constructed the question out of Jesus' answer, or the answer in its Matthaean form is based on the question posed in Lk.

(24) The question is not answered directly (cf. Acts 1:6–8),

although an answer is implicit in the second clause. Instead the point is applied existentially to Jesus' hearers: rather than speculate about the fate of others, let them make sure now that they enter by the door, however narrow and difficult it is, rather than put off decision, because at the last day many people who want to enter will find that they have left it until too late. ἀγωνίζομαι is 'to strive' (Jn. 18:36; 1 Cor. 9:25; Col. 1:29; 4:12; 1 Tim. 4:10; 6:12; 2 Tim. 4:7**; E. Stauffer, TDNT I, 134–140, especially 137). By using the term (diff. Mt.) Luke stresses that moral effort is necessary in order to enter the kingdom (cf. 16:16; P. Hoffmann*, 196f.). The metaphor of entry (Mt., 'to life') is developed in terms of a house with a narrow door (θύρα), within which there is a banqueting hall (v. 29; cf. J. Jeremias, TDNT III, 178). For στενός (Mt. 7:13f.**) see G. Bertram, TDNT VII, 604–608. The imagery is akin to that of the camel passing through the needle's eye, and suggests the difficulty of facing up to the demands of Jesus in self-denial. V. 27 indicates that (at least for Luke) the difficulty of repenting and turning from evil is in mind; although P. Hoffmann*, ibid., thinks that the saying has been ethicised, this is surely in line with its original meaning as a saying of Jesus.

Many people who fail to enter now will one day try to do so and will not be able to do so. The reason may be that a narrow door will only admit a few people. Luke, however, will undoubtedly have seen the explanation in the following verse which speaks of the door being shut. It is possible that v. 25 forms part of the sentence in v. 24 (WH; RV mg; Lagrange, 388; Luce, 241), but even without this unlikely punctuation this is surely the connection of thought.

It is not clear whether vs. 24 and 25 were originally connected to each other. It can be argued that the metaphors of the narrow door (v. 24) and the closed door (v. 25) are incompatible, and that Luke has joined them together secondarily. But the thought of the door being closed in the future is probably already present in v. 24 in its Lucan form. Also, the fact that vs. 22f. and 26f. probably belonged together in Luke's source is suggested by their occurrence in the same order in Mt. 7:13f., 22f. Whether we can work back from Luke's source to an earlier stage is less clear.

Closely connected with this problem is that of the original form of v. 24. In Mt. there is the developed metaphor of the two city gates and the two ways as pictures of the two possibilities open to men. It seems highly improbable that if Luke had known of the metaphor of 'the way' in Mt. he would have omitted it; on the other hand, there is nothing to suggest Matthaean formulation of the metaphor in Mt. The same basic thought of the narrow entrance has been developed in two different ways, probably in Christian catechetical usage.

(25) The sentence structure is not clear, since it is not clear how far the force of ἀφ' οὗ, 'from the time that' (13:7), extends. The difficulty is caused by the phrase καὶ ἀποκριθεὶς ἐρεῖ which should probably be

regarded as forming the apodosis despite the initial καί; the paratactic formulation is Semitic (cf. Beyer, I:1, 267f.). The clumsiness speaks against, rather than for, Lucan formulation (Wrege, 149f.; *pace* Bultmann, 137f.; P. Hoffmann*, 199f.). The picture is of an οἰκοδεσπότης (12:39; 14:21) who closes the door (ἀποκλείω**) of his house once he knows that all his guests are present (Easton, 218). The late-comers stand outside. The use of ἄρχομαι (cf. v. 26) may be Semitic redundancy (cf. 11:29; 12:1); in view of the repetition in v. 26 it is unlikely that both occurrences here are Lucan, and one at least may be from Q (cf. 3:8). Nor is it the case that κρούω must be Lucan (*pace* Hawkins, 19; P. Hoffmann*, 199 n. 35). The people outside address the master as κύριε (so p^{75} ℵ B *pc* lat sy^s sa bo^{pt}; in the other MSS the vocative is repeated (so *Diglot*), and despite the possibility of assimilation to Mt. 7:22 this reading may be original, since Luke likes double vocatives (cf. 10:41)). The request is shouted through an opening in the door (Grundmann, 286). The master's reply (repeated in v. 27) is tantamount to 'I do not acknowledge you' (cf. Is. 63:16; 2 Tim. 2:19; Mt. 7:23). It is similar to rabbinic formulations, but these stand closer to Matthew's wording (SB I, 469; IV:1, 293). For Luke's wording cf. Jn. 7:27f.; 9:29f.; it lays stress on the lack of knowledge about the people concerned and their antecedents, whereas Matthew's phrase is a simple denial that the speaker wishes to have anything to do with them.

(26) Luke continues with an address in the second person plural form, while Matthew has the third person. The repetition of ἄρχομαι is clumsy, and speaks against Lucan formulation. The rejected guests plead that formerly they had enjoyed table fellowship with Jesus (cf. 24:43 for the use of ἐνώπιον). They had also heard him teaching in their streets. What more could be needed in the way of qualifications for entrance? The description is of Jews who had companied with Jesus during his earthly ministry. But there is something hollow about their claim. They had only eaten in the presence of Jesus; the language does not necessarily describe a real fellowship. Likewise, although Jesus had taught in their presence, it is not said that they had responded to his teaching. In Mt. 7:22f. the claim is that they have prophesied, cast out demons and done mighty works in the name of Jesus, language which suggests a Christian setting. Bultmann's rejection of both forms of the saying as community creations (123) is unjustified as far as the form in Lk. is concerned. His objection is based on the identification of Jesus with the world judge; but if Jesus identified himself with the coming Son of man, this role would be an appropriate one for him to adopt.

(27) Luke has the third person form, as in v. 25, whereas Matthew makes the identification of Jesus with the Son of man explicit by letting Jesus speak in the first person (ὁμολογήσω). The text is uncertain. UBS has λέγων ὑμῖν with p^{75c}B *pc*; λέγω ὑμῖν is read by p^{75*} A D W Θ *pl*; TR; *Diglot*; ἀμὴν λέγω ὑμῖν by sy^s; and ὑμῖν by ℵ lat sy^p cop. λέγων could well have been regarded as pleonastic and altered by scribes; it could be

equivalent to a Hebrew infinitive absolute (Metzger, 163). But it may simply be due to a scribal error for λέγω. The wording of the reply οὐκ οἶδα πόθεν ἐστέ (p⁷⁵ B *al* it) is also disputed. UBS includes in brackets ὑμᾶς (ℵ A W Θ *pm* sy sa bo Orig). Did it arise from conflation with the reading οὐδέποτε εἶδον ὑμᾶς (D e) (itself an assimilation to Mt. 7:23)? Cf. Metzger, 163. The repetition of the formula implies the ineffectiveness of the plea made against it. And now the real reason for the rejection comes out in a quotation from Ps. 6:8 (6:9). In the LXX this reads: ἀπόστητε ἀπ' ἐμοῦ πάντες οἱ ἐργαζόμενοι τὴν ἀνομίαν. The words are those of a sufferer, vindicated by Yahweh, who tells his opponents to leave him. Luke's wording differs from that of the LXX. The first part of the quotation is the same, diff. Mt. which has ἀποχωρέω in place of ἀφίστημι (which is a favourite word of Luke). In the second part Luke has 'all you workers of iniquity'. For ἐργάτης cf. 10:2, 7 (all from Q); ἀδικία, 'wrong-doing, unrighteousness', is a Lucan word (16:8, 9; 18:6*; Acts 1:18; 8:23*; Mt., 0x; Mk., 0x). The indications are that Luke has altered the quotation to stress the element of iniquity, but this is not certain, since the two words appear as variants in the LXX (Pss. 7:14; 13 (14):4; 27 (28):3; 100 (101):8). Be this as it may, the text appears in Lk. as a clear assertion that lack of righteousness excludes men from the heavenly banquet.

(28) The rejection by the master leads to expressions of rage on the part of those who are ἐκεῖ, i.e. outside the door. The phrase is found in Mt. 8:12b; cf. Mt. 22:13b and (less close) 13:42, 50; 24:51; 25:30.

κλαυθμός is 'weeping' (Acts 20:37), and is expressive of sorrow at the thought of the loss which must be endured (cf. 6:25; Jas. 4:9; 5:1); how K. H. Rengstorf (TDNT III, 725f.) reads an attitude of 'mortal terror' into the word is far from obvious. βρυγμός is the chattering or gnashing of teeth. It can be an expression of rage (Acts 7:54), like the snarling of a lion (Pr. 19:9), and the verb expresses the hatred shown by enemies (Job 16:10; Pss. 35 (34):16; 37 (36):12; 112 (111):10; La. 2:16). The thought here is of anger directed against the master, rather than of 'despairing remorse' (K. H. Rengstorf, TDNT I, 641f.).

These feelings arise at the sight (through the opening in the door) of the company present at the banquet. The sentence construction here differs markedly from that in Mt., and it is generally thought that the Lucan form is secondary (but see below). The persons at the banquet include the three patriarchs (cf. Mk. 12:26 par. Lk. 20:37; Acts 3:13; 7:32; Heb. 11:9 for this triad which is based on Ex. 3:6), and all the prophets (Lk. only). The kingdom of God is here the transcendent future realm in which the righteous dead are present. The force of the utterance, however, lies in the second part: while the OT saints are present, the contemporaries of Jesus are cast out: the participle construction represents an Aramaic circumstantial clause and contains the main thought (Black, 82; Jeremias, *Promise*, 55 n. 185). This Aramaism shows that Luke has preserved the primitive form here over against Mt.

The present participle is clumsy and is perhaps meant to express the continuing state of those who are excluded. The word ἐκβάλλω does not quite fit the preceding picture, for the outsiders were never actually in the banquet; the thought is rather of the last judgment.

(29) The saying concludes with mention of another group who are present at the banquet. People (Mt. πολλοί) will come from all four points of the compass. For ἀνατολή, cf. 1:78; the plural form means 'the east'. The points of the compass are always anarthrous (BD 253⁵). 'East and west' together mean 'the whole world' (Mal. 1:11; Zc. 8:7; Is. 59:19), and the addition of the other two points is not absolutely necessary (but see Ps. 107 (106):3; Gn. 13:14; 1 Clem. 10:4). βορρᾶς, 'north' (Rev. 21:13**) is Hellenistic for Classical βορέας (BD 34³; 45). ἀνακλίνω (2:7; 12:37) refers to reclining at a meal and indicates that the heavenly banquet is pictured. For this idea cf. Is. 25:6f.; 64:3; 65:13f.; Ezk. 32:4; 39:17–20; 1 En. 62:14; 2 Bar. 29:4; 4 Ez. 6:49ff.; 2 En. 42:5; SB IV:2, 1148, 1154–59; Lk. 14:15; Mt. 22:2–14; Mk. 14:25; Rev. 19:9. In view of this clear tradition it is certain that the picture here is of the future heavenly banquet (cf. Jeremias, *Words*, 233f.; *Promise*, 60; Kümmel, 85; Wilson, 3f.); Hahn's suggestion (*Mission*, 34 n. 2) that it refers also to the present time is improbable. The present reference lies in the fact that the gentiles can qualify now for admission to the banquet in the future. The subject of the verse is of course the gentiles (Wilson, 33f.), and not Diaspora Jews (N. Q. King, 'Universalism in the Third Gospel', TU 73, 1959, 199–205).

(30) The closing saying is proverbial in form. The agreement between this verse and Mt. 20:16 in order against Mk. 10:31 par. Mt. 19:30 indicates that we are dealing with a Q doublet to a Marcan saying. καὶ ἰδού is a Lucan transition. For people who are in the 'last' place cf. 14:9f.; Mk. 9:35; 1 Cor. 4:9; contrast Mt. 20:8. The future ἔσονται indicates the reversal of places that occurs in the age to come. The saying is an isolated logion of general application. It may mean here that those who regard themselves as oppressed and hopeless will gain entry to the kingdom, while those who think that they alone are worthy will be excluded (cf. 1:51–53). It is possible that the saying contrasts the Jews, who were first to hear the gospel, with the gentiles (J. Weiss, 476; Grundmann, 286f.). Yet another possibility is that the saying places both groups on an equal footing (cf. W. Michaelis, TDNT VI, 868 n. 14). It is probable that the saying is applied here especially to the relation between Jews and gentiles.

ii. A Warning against Herod 13:31–33

The theme of Jesus' journey to Jerusalem, announced in v. 22, comes into sharper focus as the significance of Jesus' activity is brought out in this brief story, variously characterised as a biographical apophthegm (Bultmann, 35, 58f.) or chria (Dibelius, 162f.). Some Pharisees warn

Jesus to flee from the murderous intentions of Herod Antipas, but he replies with an expression of contempt for that 'fox'; he has a task to perform, which will conclude with his 'perfecting' in Jerusalem, and no Herod will be able to divert him from it. He has, therefore, no need to flee at this juncture. If Herod wants to kill him he had better go to Jerusalem!

Older scholars found no difficulty in regarding the pericope as substantially historical, claiming that its very obscurity spoke against its being a literary invention (cf. Taylor, *Sacrifice*, 167–171; J. Jeremias*; Hoehner, 214–224, for recent supporters of this view). The story certainly raises no historical difficulties.

The story is, however, open to literary criticism, especially because of the apparent repetition and possibly contradiction between vs. 32 and 33. Thus Dibelius regarded the introduction (v. 31) as a creation by Luke who likes to produce settings for the sayings of Jesus and in this case displays his interest in the 'mighty ones' of the world. Bultmann reckons with two possibilities: either vs. 31f. and 33 are two separate logia (joined together by a catchword connection) or v. 32b is a redactional addition. The former solution is taken up by J. Jeremias*, who finds that two parallel statements about the way of Jesus have been juxtaposed. Similarly, Steck, 44, argues that v. 33 must be separated from vs. 31f., but regards it as a Lucan creation in order to give a link with vs. 34f. A different kind of solution was initiated by Wellhausen, 75f., who attempted to produce one statement out of vs. 32 and 33 by excision of apparently repetitious phrases, and similar solutions have been offered by Black, 205–207; J. Blinzler* and W. Grimm*, the last mentioned of whom offers the view that a complicated OT typology based on Ex. 19:10f. is concealed in the wording (concealed even from Luke).

The most recent tendency is to solve the problems of the pericope by means of redaction criticism. A. Denaux* claims that the vocabulary of the section can all be attributed to Luke, and that there is no evidence that any source has been used at all. The motifs present agree perfectly with Luke's outlook, and the passage was composed to show how the divinely ordained pattern for Jesus' ministry will be fulfilled regardless of human opposition. A similar result is reached by M. Rese*, but he holds a different understanding of Luke's view of the role of the Pharisees and Herod in the story. For Rese the story brings out openly what was revealed secretly to Jesus at the transfiguration: Jesus' way is characterised by healings and exorcisms, no mention being made of his teaching for 'tactical' reasons in relation to Herod and his treatment of John; the divinely ordained end of the journey is Jesus' 'perfecting' in Jerusalem.

These redactional explanations of the story at once arouse some suspicion since Denaux and Rese are able to argue that entirely opposed evaluations of the Pharisees (as hostile or friendly to Jesus respectively) can equally well be regarded as due to Luke's redaction. The fact that the picture of Herod fits in with Luke's other information about him is more likely to be due to reliance on a source than on Luke's imagination. Attempts to explain the sayings in vs. 32 and 33 as Lucan compositions are quite unconvincing. The fact that the vocabulary throughout can be Lucan is no proof that a source has not been used.

Theories which involve rewriting the text to make sense of it are improbable if the text can yield sense as it stands. Recognition of the idioms involved makes the sayings comprehensible. Further, the incident makes good historical sense, and satisfactory motives for inventing it have not been established. The question is, therefore, one of redaction of existing tradition. Since v. 32 can hardly have existed without some kind of situation, v. 31 is not a separate creation. V. 33 may then be a separate saying, or a redactional link, or part of the same saying. But v. 32 is by itself an inadequate reply to the warning in v. 31, and hence v. 33 is an integral part of the reply of Jesus. The pericope as a whole rests on tradition or is a Lucan creation to provide an introduction to vs. 34f. It is more probable that the former is the case.

See Taylor, *Sacrifice*, 167–171; J. Blinzler in Schmid, *Studien* 42–46 (cf. bibliography for 9:51–19:10); Steck, 40–47; J. Jeremias, 'Die Drei-Tage-Worte der Evangelien', in Jeremias, *Tradition*, 221–229; Hoehner, 214–224; A. Denaux, 'L'hypocrisie des Pharisiens et le dessein de Dieu. Analyse de Lc., xiii, 31–33', in Neirynck, 245–285; W. Grimm, 'Eschatologischer Saul wider eschatologischen David. Eine Deutung von Lc. xiii 31ff.', Nov.T 15, 1973, 114–133; M. Rese, 'Einige Überlegungen zu Lukas xiii, 31–33', in Dupont, *Jésus*, 201–225.

(31) The opening time phrase is Lucan (2:38 note). προσῆλθαν is the only example of a first aorist ending with this verb in Lk. For the word order τινες Φαρισαῖοι cf. Acts 5:34. Jesus is advised by the Pharisees to get out of Herod's territory (Galilee and Peraea, probably the former; cf. Hoehner, 217) because of the latter's murderous designs on him. The motives of Herod and the Pharisees are uncertain. Herod liked tranquillity (Jos. Ant. 18:245) and may simply have wished to get rid quietly of a possible trouble-maker; he may have hoped that a threat would be sufficient. It is possible that the report was a fabrication by the Pharisees; A. Denaux*, 263–268, thinks that Luke has invented a hypocritical assertion by the Pharisees which stands in contrast to Luke's generally mild picture of Herod's attitude to Jesus, and that Luke has made use of language from Mk. 6:19. But this is a misrepresentation of Luke's picture of Herod (Lk. 3:19f.; Acts 4:27), and it is more probable that Luke wished to report Herod's hostility to Jesus. As for the Pharisees, they have been variously regarded as acting in a friendly fashion to Jesus by warning him of possible danger (M. Rese*, 209–212), or as being opposed to Jesus and therefore misrepresenting Herod (A. Denaux*, 261–263), or acting in concert with him, or making use of their knowledge of his intentions to get Jesus out of Galilee. Appeal to Luke's picture of the Pharisees elsewhere is not especially helpful; while he certainly emphasises the friendliness of some of them to Jesus and later regards them as better disposed to the church than the

Sadducees were, he also brings out their hostility to Jesus and the bitterness of his attacks on them. It is most likely that their action here is motivated by malice, and that they were trying (like Herod) to get Jesus to make himself scarce. For Jesus the warning presented itself as a temptation to follow human advice and ignore God's plan for his ministry.

(32) Jesus takes the Pharisees at their face value as agents of Herod and gives them a message for that 'fox' (9:58). In rabbinic literature the fox was typical of low cunning (Ber. 61b, citing R. Akiba; SB II, 200f.), but it was also portrayed as an insignificant creature in comparison with the lion: 'Be first in greeting every man; and be a tail to lions and be not a head to foxes' (P. Ab. 4:15). Both ideas have been detected here, the former by Easton, 221; Stuhlmueller, 147; and the latter by Creed, 186; Grundmann, 288; probably both are present (Manson, *Sayings*, 276). W. Grimm*, 114–117, takes the point further and sees an allusion to king Saul (*šā'ûl*; cf. Hebrew *šû'āl*, 'fox') in contrast to the messianic 'lion' of the house of David (Gn. 49:9; Rev. 5:5). The saying would then contain an implicit messianic identification by Jesus; but in the absence of an explicit reference to the lion, this proposal is too speculative to be convincing.

Jesus' message is that he will go on with his work (present tenses referring to the future). It consists in the exorcism of demons (11:14, 20) and the accomplishment of healings; ἴασις is a Lucan word (Acts 4:22, 30**). ἀποτελέω, 'to complete' (Jas. 1:15) may represent Aramaic *shakhlᵉleth*, giving a wordplay with *ithkallᵉleth* (τελειοῦμαι, Black, 233). M. Rese*, 218f., thinks that it is significant that Jesus makes no mention of his preaching; he argues that Luke is deliberately omitting the element which would make Jesus appear like John, who was imprisoned by Herod because of his preaching, and that Herod is meant to realise that Jesus is rather one of the old prophets (9:8). This is more ingenious than convincing.

The phrase σήμερον καὶ αὔριον is to be explained from a Semitic background. 1. It can mean 'for two days' quite literally (Ex. 19:10f.). W. Grimm*, 121–127, claims that Ex. 19:10f. is the direct background to the present passage: a period of preparation and cleansing is followed on the third day by the revelation of God in fire; but the analogy between these events and the healings and exorcisms of Jesus followed by the cross is highly remote. 2. The phrase can mean 'two days' (cf. Ho. 6:2, if this is not meant literally), and indicate an indefinite period of time, culminating at a definite but uncertain point. Rabbinic usage indicates that this was a continuing idiom (SB II, 203f.). 3. Black, 205–207, suggests that in the present case the Aramaic phrase *yoma den wᵉyomaḥra*, 'day by day', underlies the phraseology (cf. 11:3 note). Since there is no LXX parallel (Ho. 6:2 is differently formulated), it is improbable that Luke himself is responsible for the expression. The significance then is that Jesus is going to carry on his beneficent work for an uncertain, but limited period. The decisive point comes on the 'third day'. τελειόω, 'to complete' (2:43*; Acts 20:24*), is here used in the passive, perhaps implying that God is the agent (J. Blinzler*, 45 n. 67). The verb is unlikely to refer here to a 'consecration' of Jesus as priest (O. Michel, *Der Brief an die Hebräer*, Göttingen, 1960[11], 76f.). It may refer to the completion of Jesus' work of exorcism and healing (Manson, *Sayings*, 276; G. Delling, TDNT VIII, 84), or to the completion of his ministry in death (cf. Wis. 4:13). This latter sense can include the former, and should probably be adopted, especially since the context refers to Jesus' death (Grundmann, 289; W. Grimm*, 119f.). J. Jeremias* suggests the meaning 'I reach the goal' (cf. Heb. 7:28; 10:14; Jn. 19:30; A. Denaux*, 271–274, also stresses the ideas of termination and fulfilment, and also (less probably) finds an intended Lucan allusion to resurrection on the third day). In order to avoid repetition of the idea in v. 33 Wellhausen, 75f., proposed to delete καὶ τῇ τρίτῃ τελειοῦμαι (v. 32) and σήμερον καὶ αὔριον καί (v. 33) as interpolations (so J. Weiss, 477; Creed, 187). But attempts to find a motive for the former of these interpolations (e.g. in the desire to create an Easter prediction) are unconvincing (J. Blinzler*, 44f.; Steck, 41f.), and the text should be accepted as it stands.

(33) The introductory πλήν is usually regarded as drawing a sharp contrast with the thought of 'completion' in v. 32: before the end can come Jesus must continue his way. But πλήν can have the sense 'moreover, and indeed' (M. E. Thrall, *Greek Particles in the New Testament*, Leiden, 1962, 20f.), and this gives a good connection here (M. Rese*, 217). The thought in v. 32 is developed in terms of the necessity of Jesus continuing his divinely appointed way to its end, because the end cannot come except in Jerusalem. ἐχόμενος is used with the sense 'next, neighbouring' (Mk. 1:38; Acts 13:44; 20:15; 21:26). The whole phrase σήμερον καὶ αὔριον καὶ τῇ ἐχομένῃ may reflect a Hebrew idiom referring to a short, limited period of time (2 Esd. 8:32; Jdt. 12:7), but the parallels actually refer to 'three days' followed by a fourth, decisive day. The expression can be taken in two ways: 1. It may be understood as an alternative expression for a short time, corresponding to 'today and tomorrow' in v. 32. Then πορεύομαι is used of the wanderings of Jesus (F. Hauck and S. Schulz, TDNT VI, 574), which Herod cannot hinder. (W. Grimm's view that Jesus wanders, like David, in order to avoid being caught by his enemy completely misunderstands the saying.) 2. Alternatively, the phrase in v. 33 corresponds to the whole of the 'three days' in v. 32, so that Jesus is saying that his 'way', which includes exorcisms, healings and reaching his goal, must carry on till it reaches its divinely intended conclusion (M. Rese*, 218). On this view, the two temporal expressions have the same reference, and the problem of their apparent inconcinnity is solved. πορεύομαι then has a metaphorical reference to the 'way' of Jesus. Jesus is thus represented as making his way to Jerusalem because it is only there that he can share the fate of

the prophets (cf. G. Friedrich, TDNT VI, 843). ἐνδέχομαι** is 'to be possible, permitted', and suggests the appropriateness of death in Jerusalem; the force of the verb should not be pressed to produce the false general rule that all prophets perished in Jerusalem. Rather, since Jerusalem does kill prophets (v. 34), it is appropriate that Jesus as a prophet should die there too. The saying is not a quotation of an existing proverb.

If this interpretation is accepted, there is no need to emend v. 33, but for the sake of completeness the various possibilities may be listed: 1. The Peshitta adds a verb: 'But today and tomorrow I must *work* and on the next day go my way (i.e. die).' On this basis Torrey, 310f., and Black, 206, argue that a verb has fallen out of the text. 2. Wellhausen, 75f., proposed to omit σήμερον καὶ αὔριον καί (see also on v. 32 above). This part of his proposal is adopted by J. Blinzler* who takes τελειοῦμαι to refer to the end of Jesus' healing ministry and πορεύομαι to refer to his death, with τῇ ἐχομένῃ referring to a fourth day. 3. W. Grimm*, 127f., omits καὶ τῇ ἐχομένῃ, claiming that Luke has created a false parallel with v. 32: πορεύομαι refers to the wandering that accompanies Jesus' ministry 'today and tomorrow'. None of these proposals carries conviction.

iii. Lament over Jerusalem 13:34–35

The thought of Jesus' death as a prophet at Jerusalem merges into a lament over the city which had rejected God's messengers. Speaking in a manner reminiscent of wisdom literature, Jesus states how he had longed to gather the people of Jerusalem into his arms, like a mother bird, but found himself rejected. He could only pronounce the judgment of God on the city which would be abandoned by God's presence. He would not be seen again there until the fulfilment of the hope of the coming of the Messiah.

The saying appears to have been joined to the previous section by a catchword link. It appears with insignificant differences in wording in Mt. 23:37–39, and is therefore from Q. In Mt. it follows the 'wisdom' saying Mt. 23:34–36 par. Lk. 11:49–51, and this order was probably that in Q (11:49 note). Whether, however, the two sayings were originally linked or were independent is less certain. The arguments against linking them depend largely on the assumption that they contain sayings of divine wisdom who looks forward in the former saying and backward in the present saying; if, however, the sayings are understood as sayings of Jesus, this difficulty loses its force, since vs. 34f. can then be understood as a comment of Jesus on the present situation. For the exegesis of Lk. the question is of lesser importance.

The origin and background of the saying pose considerable difficulty. It is generally agreed that the broad background is to be found in the Deuteronomistic tradition of the violent fate of the prophets coupled with the concept of wisdom as the sender of divine messengers to Israel. The rejection of God's messengers leads to judgment upon Israel, here pronounced in an emphatically final manner. The question of the immediate origin is less clear. 1. Many scholars hold that the saying is to be understood as an utterance of a supra-historical being, i.e. wisdom, who has sent messengers to men and has herself tried to find a dwelling among them, but in vain (cf. Sir. 24:7–12; 1 En. 42; Wis. 7:27f.; Bultmann, 120f.; U. Wilckens, TDNT VII, 515; Steck, 230f.; Christ, 136–152; Suggs, 63–71). On this view, the saying has been taken from a Jewish source. Opinions differ, however, as to whether v. 35b is a Christian addition to an originally Jewish formulation (E. Haenchen, ZTK 48, 1951, 57 (see 11:37–54 bibliography); U. Wilckens, ibid.; Christ, 141f.; Hoffmann, 175–177) or is an original part of the wisdom saying, in which wisdom threatens to depart from men until she returns in the person of the Messiah or Son of man (Bultmann, 120f.; Steck, 56f.). For Steck, 237–239, the saying comes from Jewish sources shortly before AD 70. 2. A second type of view is that the saying is a Christian formulation based on Jewish wisdom material; in it the speaker is wisdom (not Jesus), and the saying expresses the conviction of the Q community that judgment has come finally upon Israel for its rejection of Jesus (Schulz, 346–360). 3. Third, the saying can be regarded as a saying of Jesus who makes use of wisdom terminology to express his feelings regarding his rejection by Jerusalem. On this view Jesus does not necessarily identify himself with wisdom but sees himself as one of wisdom's messengers (Kümmel, 79–82; cf. Hoffmann, 173f.).

Although Schulz, 349 n. 193, claims that the saying cannot be interpreted except against the background of the situation of the Q community, there is no compelling reason for this claim; even if the saying is interpreted as an utterance of wisdom, it can still be understood as a form of words used by Jesus (so rightly Christ, 148). The difficulty of the saying lies in the identification of Jesus in v. 35b with the coming Messiah or Son of man (cf. 13:25–27), but the identification is cryptic and by no means impossible on the lips of Jesus.

The exegesis of the saying suggests that view 3. above fits its interpretation best. The saying is probably not a citation of an existing wisdom saying, but represents a free use of wisdom terminology by Jesus as the messenger of divine wisdom.

See Kümmel, 79–82; U. Wilckens, TDNT VII, 515; Steck, 48–50, 53–58, 227–239; Christ, 136–152; Suggs, 63–71; Hoffmann, 171–180; Schulz, 346–360.

(34) The speaker has been variously identified with 1. God (B. W. Bacon, in Hasting's *Dictionary of Christ and the Gospels*, Edinburgh, 1908, II, 825–829); 2. Jesus (Kümmel, 80f.; Hoffmann, 173f.); or 3. Wisdom (U. Wilckens*; Steck, 53f., 230–232; Schulz, 349 n. 194). In favour of 3. it is argued that the reference to Jerusalem's past history as an opponent of God's messengers demands that ποσάκις ἠθέλησα ... must refer to the same period and to wisdom's sending of these messengers. But the saying was understood by Matthew and Luke as a

saying of Jesus, in which case Jesus aligns himself with the earlier messengers of wisdom and expresses his own repeated attempts to win over the people of Jerusalem; there is no good reason for thinking that the saying had a different meaning at an earlier stage. E. Lohse, TDNT VII, 328f., suggests that Jesus may be quoting a wisdom saying which did not fully apply to himself.

The Aramaic form ʼΙερουσαλήμ (2:22 note) is found here only in Q; for the double vocative see 6:46 note. The present participles indicate the way in which Jerusalem was 'ever ready to kill and stone' God's messengers. For the murder of prophets cf. 1 Ki. 18:4, 13; 19:10; Je. 26:20ff.; Ne. 9:26; J. Jeremias, TDNT V, 714; G. Friedrich, TDNT VI, 834f.; Steck, 60ff. λιθοβολέω is 'to stone' (Mt. 21:35; 23:37; Acts 7:58f.; 14:5; Heb. 12:20**; cf. Jn. 8:59; 10:31; J. Blinzler, 'The Jewish Punishment of Stoning in the New Testament Period', in Bammel, 147–161). For stoning in Jerusalem see 11:51 (2 Ch. 24:21), and in Israel generally see 1 Sa. 30:6; 1 Ki. 12:18; 21:10–15. There is no need, therefore, to find a *vaticinium ex eventu* of Christian martyrdoms here (*pace* E. Haenchen, op. cit. 55). ἀποστέλλω can be used of the prophets (e.g. Is. 6:8; Je. 1:7; K. H. Rengstorf, TDNT I, 402 n. 25); the perfect participle is not otherwise used of apostles (cf. 19:32; Acts 10:17; 11:11; Rev. 5:6), and a reference to God's messengers in OT and pre-Christian times is more appropriate (see also 11:49 note). The use of the third person pronoun αὐτήν in a direct address is Semitic (Grundmann, 289).

ποσάκις is 'how often' (Mt. 18:21; 23:37**). If taken literally, it implies several visits by Jesus to Jerusalem (as attested in Jn.); possibly Jerusalem's 'children' signify the Jews generally. Matthew's setting of the saying in Jesus' last (and, for the Synoptics, only) visit to Jerusalem is appropriate historically. ἐπισυνάξαι is the colloquial first aorist infinitive of ἐπισυνάγω (BD 75); Matthew has the more usual second aorist form ἐπισυναγαγεῖν, and since he makes other alterations in the wording it is probable that he is responsible for this one too. The 'children' of a city are its inhabitants (19:44). τρόπον* is an accusative of respect attracted into the relative clause (cf. Acts 1:11; 7:28; 2 Tim. 3:8). For ὄρνις, 'bird', the Koine form ὄρνιξ (a Doricism; BD 47[4]) is read by א D W; *Diglot* and may be original. νοσσία** can mean 'brood' or 'nest'; in Dt. 32:11 it translates qēn, 'nest', but the poetic parallelism indicates that the word is used by metonymy for the young birds in the nest. Matthew has νοσσίον**, 'young bird' (Ps. 84:3 (83:4)). Both Evangelists picture the mother bird brooding over her young ones in the nest to protect them, and attempts to find a subtle difference in the imagery (Steck, 49f.) are artificial (Hoffmann, 171f.). πτέρυξ, 'wing' (Mt. 23:37; Rev. 4:8; 9:9; 12:14**), conjures up the picture found in Dt. 32:11; Pss. 17:8 (16:8); 36:7 (35:8); 57:1 (56:2); 61:4 (60:5); 63:7 (62:8); 91:4 (90:4); Ru. 2:12; Is. 3:5; 2 Bar. 41:3f.; 4 Ez. 1:30; rabbinic sayings refer to proselytes coming under the wings of the Shekinah (SB I, 927, 943). It should be noted that the saying does not speak of 'wisdom' finding a home among men, but of the care exercised by Jesus like a mother bird. The basic sense is 'the quite simple one of bringing men into the kingdom of God' (Manson, *Sayings*, 127). Over against the ἠθέλησα of Jesus is deliberately placed the οὐκ ἠθελήσατε of the people of Jerusalem.

(35) Following the lament comes the prophecy of judgment. The phraseology alludes to Je. 12:7 ἐγκαταλέλοιπα τὸν οἶκόν μου, ἀφῆκα τὴν κληρονομίαν μου, and 22:5 εἰς ἐρήμωσιν ἔσται ὁ οἶκος οὗτος. Here God speaks of deserting the sinful people of Judah and the royal palace in view of their continued rejection of him. οἶκος here can thus be understood in several ways: A reference to the 'world' as in the Mandaean writings (Bultmann, 121) has nothing to commend it. A better possibility is that the word refers to the temple (1 Ki. 6:2ff.; 2 Ch. 3:6ff.; Je. 26 (33):6; 2 Bar. 8:2; Jeremias, *Parables*, 168; Kümmel, 81; Ellis, 191; Schulz, 356 n. 230). But SB I, 943f., notes than when a pronominal suffix is attached to 'house' in this sense, it always refers to God. Hence it is more probable that 'house' here means the city or people of Jerusalem (cf. 1 En. 89:50ff.; T. Levi 10:5; O. Michel, TDNT V, 125; Easton, 223; Steck, 228 n. 3; Hoffmann, 174; Christ, 150 (but he prefers 'temple' in the original form of the saying)). ἀφίημι, 'to abandon', can refer to the abandonment of Jerusalem by God absolutely (Je. 12:7) or its abandonment to its enemies (the present tense is equivalent to a future, BD 323). The latter interpretation is supported by the addition of ἔρημος as a variant reading in Mt. (where it is well supported by all evidence except B L ff² sy² sa bo) and in Lk.: it is included by D Θ *al* lat syᶜ ᵖ boᵖᵗ Ir Or Eus; TR; and omitted by 𝔭⁴⁵ 𝔭⁷⁵ ℵ A B W f1 565 *pm* it vgᶜᵒᵈᵈ syˢ sa boᵖᵗ. The status of the word is thus problematic, and in any case it is not a part of Luke's text. The context of the saying in Q would also support the second understanding: judgment is to come upon this generation for its share in the murder of the prophets. Taken on its own, however, the saying surely refers primarily to the abandonment of Jerusalem by God, which results (incidentally) in its becoming a prey to its enemies. Ellis, 191, sees a reference to the departure of God's presence from the 'old temple' to the 'new temple' constituted by the church after the resurrection (cf. Acts 7:48; 1 Cor. 3:16f.; 4QFlor 1:5f., 12; Gärtner, 110f.). This is doubtful, since the positive side of the transfer is absent, but the saying could fit into such a theological framework. A closer parallel lies in Jesus' prophecy of the destruction of the temple.

In the second part of the verse Jesus announces that the people of Jerusalem are no longer to see him; the dramatic situation in his last visit to the city (so Mt.). The connective δέ, omitted by 𝔭⁴⁵ ℵ* *pc* it syᶜ sa bo.ᵖᵗ; *Diglot*; is bracketed by UBS. It may have been added to avoid asyndeton, or dropped because the clause does not really contrast with what precedes; Matthew's use of γάρ, which is probably editorial, suggests that some connective stood in Q. Much more uncertain textually is the phrase ἕως ἥξει ὅτε (D *al* lat syˢ ᶜ; *Diglot*). Many MSS have ἕως ἂν ἥξει (or ἥξῃ) ὅτε (A W pm; TR). UBS brackets ἥξει ὅτε in view of the simple ἕως read by p⁷⁵ B L syᵖ sa; ἕως ἄν is read by p⁴⁵ ℵ Θ f1 f13 pc. The text in *Diglot* and (UBS) could well be original despite its poor attestation. Scribes could have taken offence at the use of εἴπητε in the subjunctive after ὅτε (but this is not an impossible construction; see BD 382² and the somewhat similar cases in BD 379), and also in the use of ἥξει in the future indicative after ἕως. Since Luke always has the subjunctive after ἕως, however, the future indicative may be due to his source. Assimilation to the simpler form in Mt. (ἕως ἄν εἴπητε) may also have affected the text (Metzger, 163). Wellhausen, 76, suggested that the cause of the difficulty was a mistranslation of the Aramaic relative pronoun (equivalent to *is cui*) as a temporal conjunction ('Until he comes to whom you will say ...'), but this suggestion is not supported by the simpler wording in Mt. The phrase simply means 'until the time when you will say'. Matthew has the phrase ἀπ' ἄρτι which fits in with his setting of the saying in the final visit of Jesus to Jerusalem. The saying of the people is identical with Ps. 118 (117):26 LXX, also cited in 19:38 (cf. Gundry, 40–43; Holtz, 160). The reference here may be to the triumphal entry of Jesus into Jerusalem (Danker, 162), but if so it is heavily ironical; the saying is not quoted exactly at 19:38, nor is it there placed on the lips of the people of Jerusalem. In Mt. the saying follows the triumphal entry, and the point is that the Jewish leaders failed to join in the acclamation then. Hence the ultimate reference must be to the final consummation when the promise of the coming of the Messiah is fulfilled. (An allusion to the Son of man is unjustified.) The Psalm appears to have had a messianic interpretation (SB I, 849f., 876). The question is whether the coming of the Messiah affords a last hope of salvation to the Jews (as in Rom. 11:26; cf. Acts 3:19f.; Grundmann, 290; H. van der Kwaak, 'Die Klage über Jerusalem (Matth. xxiii. 37–39)', Nov.T 8, 1966, 156–170, argues that the construction in Mt. (not Lk.!) should be taken conditionally with regard to the possibility of the Jews welcoming the Messiah with faith). Or is it simply a threat of final judgment (Manson, *Sayings*, 128; Schulz, 358)? Ellis, 191, states that the question must be left open, but the former possibility is a live one (Marshall, 186f.).

Did Jesus speak in this way of his own future coming as Messiah? He did so in terms of the future coming of the Son of man. Here, however, the symbolism is messianic (perhaps as a result of assimilation of the two figures) and contains an implicit identification as the coming One, the Messiah. There is no difficulty about this identification (cf. 7:18–23). Nor is it made absolutely explicit in the present saying, which is sufficiently indirect in phrasing to be genuine (cf. Kümmel, 81f.).

iv. The Healing of a Man with Dropsy 14:1–6

14:1–24 forms a unity round the theme of Jesus at table in the house of a Pharisee, but the unity is probably secondary; it is not certain whether the unity was created by Luke (Ellis, 191) or was already in his source (Schürmann, *Abschiedsrede*, 96 n. 325). The general theme of the section, which continues into the following sections, is criticism of the Pharisees.

The opening incident in the *Tischrede* is the healing of a man with dropsy; the story is very similar in construction and content to 13:10–17, and Easton, 225, suspects that it may have formed a pair with it, especially since both stories come from Luke's special source and the intervening material is all, or nearly all, from Q. This story, however, may be from Q (see 14:5 note; Schürmann, *Untersuchungen*, 213). Bultmann, 10, 48, regards the story as a variant of Mk. 3:1–6, more precisely as a framework created on the basis of the Marcan story to incorporate the saying in v. 5 which Matthew has actually included in the Marcan story; v. 1 is a Lucan introduction. A similar view is taken by E. Lohse, TDNT VII, 26, and Roloff, *Kerygma*, 66–69. Precisely the opposite view is taken by E. Stauffer (as reported by Grundmann, 291) who holds that v. 5 is a later addition to the story. Grundmann himself points out that the story differs markedly in detail from Mk. 3:1–6, and that Jesus' sabbath conflicts were not confined to one incident in a Galilean synagogue. Since Bultmann offers no evidence for his view of the story, we are justified in rejecting it as arbitrary assumption and assessing the story as historical.

(1) It is simplest to regard v. 1 as a complete sentence with the ἐγένετο ... καί ... with finite verb construction (5:1; *et al.*). The significance of ἄρχοντες is not clear. It may refer to rulers who belonged to the Pharisaic party (cf. Jn. 3:1; RSV; Creed), or to rulers of the synagogues (cf. 8:41) or to leading men among the Pharisees (RV; NEB; JB; TEV; TNT; NIV). The objection that the Pharisees did not have leaders (Stuhlmueller, 147) is met by reference to Jos. Vita 21 (cf. J. W. Bowker, *Jesus and the Pharisees*, Cambridge, 1973, 35). The omission of τῶν after ἀρχόντων by p[45] p[75] ℵ B *pc*; (UBS) is surely due to haplography, even though it could be argued that the article was so obviously required here that scribes almost uniformly supplied it. For the anarthrous use of σαββάτῳ cf. 6:1; 23:54; Acts 1:12. The situation indicated is doubtless a meal after the service in the synagogue (cf. 7:36; 11:37; SB II, 202f.). If the Pharisee was a ruler, i.e. member of the sanhedrin, the scene may have been in Jerusalem (Grundmann, 291). The motives for the invitation may have been mixed. αὐτοί must refer to other Pharisees who were present (14:3). For παρατηρέω see the similar story in 6:6–11 (v. 7). Klostermann's claim that the detail comes too soon in the story is unjustified; by now the Pharisees were suspicious of Jesus and looking for evidence against him, and it is possible that the man was planted there as a trap for him.

(2) The man was suffering from dropsy (ὑδρωπικός**), a disease in which the body swells up due to fluid forming in the cavities and tissues;

according to the rabbis the disease was the result of immorality (SB II, 203f.), but the evidence does not reach back beyond the third century. The ἔμπροσθεν phrase indicates that Jesus could not help noticing the man.

(3) Jesus responds (ἀποκρίνομαι, 13:14) to the unspoken challenge, by addressing the lawyers (who have not previously been mentioned in the story) and Pharisees. The question is similar to that in 6:9, but the vocabulary differs. For θεραπεῦσαι the present infinitive is read by TR; Diglot. As in the earlier story, the question precedes the healing; contrast 13:10–17.

(4) Just as in 6:9 (and especially Mk. 3:4) the audience can offer no answer and remain silent (ἡσυχάζω, Acts 11:28; 21:14; also 'to rest', 23:46; 1 Thes. 4:11**). Did the nature of the disease make it uncertain to casuistically minded people whether or not life was in danger? In the absence of objections Jesus takes the man (ἐπιλαμβάνομαι 9:47; et al, is Semitic redundant style), heals him and dismisses him.

(5) Thereafter Jesus takes the initiative with a question regarding the legitimacy of his act. (The question of his ability to perform the healing is not raised.) The participle ἀποκριθείς is inserted by ℵ* A W Δ Θ pm aur f vg; TR; Diglot, thus giving a Semitic word order (Kilpatrick, 198). The saying bears some resemblance to 13:15, but this is not very close. More important is the parallelism with Mt. 12:11, which expresses the same thought in different wording and appears to be a translation-variant from Aramaic. The question is worth raising whether Matthew knew a similar story to that in Lk.; there is a very slight amount of verbal parallelism between Mt. 12:10 and Lk. 14:2f. which might suggest that Matthew was influenced by such a story in editing his version of Mk. 3:1–6. This would explain how Matthew knew the saying found here.

The question form conceals a condition (11:5 note; Black, 118f.). φρέαρ (Jn. 4:11f.; Rev. 9:1f.**) is an artificially constructed well, by contrast with a natural spring, πηγή (Jn. 4:6). Mt. has βόθυνος, 'pit' (Lk. 6:29); both words are used in the LXX to translate gēḇ (Je. 14:3; 2 Ki. 3:16), and hence could be translation-variants. φρέαρ, however, is usually the equivalent of Hebrew beʾēr. What falls in is textually doubtful. The MSS offer: 1. υἱὸς ἢ βοῦς (p⁴⁵ p⁷⁵ A B W Δ al e f q syᶜᵖsa; TR; WH App., 62; Synopsis; UBS; Diglot); 2. ὄνος ἢ βοῦς (ℵ L f1 f13 33 pm lat bo; NEB; TNT); 3. βοῦς ἢ ὄνος (syˢ); 4. υἱὸς ἢ βοῦς ἢ ὄνος (syᶜ), 5. ὄνος υἱὸς ἢ βοῦς (Θ); 6. πρόβατον ἢ βοῦς (D d). So far as the Greek text is concerned, reading 6. may be due to assimilation to Mt. 12:11. Readings 4. and 5. are poorly supported and are conflations of readings 1. and 2.; it is noteworthy that the order υἱὸς ἢ βοῦς is retained in both of them, and this is a point in favour of reading 1. as the original, determinative text. Reading 3. is evidence for the existence of the better attested reading 2. and is due to assimilation to 13:15. Reading 1. has the best external support, and it is easy to understand its being altered in transmission, since the conjunction of a son and ox would seem in-congruous, especially in the light of such OT texts as Ex. 21:33f.; 22:4; 23:5 and Dt. 22:4 (cf. Is. 32:20). Furthermore, this reading gives a good sense: the meaning is 'a child or even just an ox' (E. Schweizer, TDNT VIII, 364 n. 209). It fits in with the rabbinic ruling in B. Kamma 5:6 which compares culpability in the cases of men or oxen falling into someone's well. As regards the Sabbath, Shab. 128b gives both a mild ruling, allowing helping an animal out of a pit, and a harsh ruling, allow-ing only the provision of fodder to it in the pit; SB I, 629, claims that the milder ruling must have been in force in the time of Jesus. The Qumran sect, which appears to have been stricter than the Pharisees, allowed that a man could be pulled out, so long as no implements were used, but an animal might not be pulled out (CD 11:13–17; cf. K. G. Kuhn, TDNT V, 287 n. 26). Finally, the text gives paronomasia when rendered into Aramaic, with $b^e ra$ (son), $b^{e\prime}ira$ (ox), and $bera$ (well) (O. Michel, TDNT V, 287). This, then, gives a satisfying explanation of the text. Other possibilities, however, have been suggested. Wellhausen, 78, favoured the earlier conjecture of Mill that υἱός was a corruption for an original ὄϊς (sheep) (cf. the reading of D), but this word is poetic and rare in Greek prose. Roloff, *Kerygma*, 66, takes up a suggestion mentioned by Black that the original Aramaic contained *bar ḥamra* (ass) and $b^{e\prime}ira$, and that the former was misunderstood as 'son'. Black himself, holds that the original Aramaic saying had the one word $b^{e\prime}ira$, a generic word for beasts of burden; this was variously interpreted in the Greek ver-sions, and also misread as $b^e ra$ (son). But this suggestion does not ex-plain how two or even three Greek words replaced one Aramaic word; nor can recourse to the Aramaic explain Greek textual variants in this way. There is more to be said for the variant suggestion of J. Jeremias (reported in E. Lohse, TDNT VII, 26 n. 203) that an original pun on beast/well underwent development to include $b^e ra$ at the Aramaic stage of transmission. The use of ἀνασπάω, 'to draw, pull up' (Acts 11:10**), suggests Lucan editing. For ἡμέρα τοῦ σαββάτου cf. 13:16.

(6) In Mt. 12:12 the argument is concluded by an *a fortiori* statement, 'How much more valuable is a man than a sheep'. This would be incongruous in the Lucan form of the saying, which has already referred to a son. It could therefore be argued that Luke's version of the saying with 'son' is secondary to the form posited by Black and attested by Matthew. On the other hand, the application in Mt. could be an in-dependent development on the lines of Lk. 12:24, 28. Luke's form con-tains an unexpressed *a fortiori* argument from what *men* do on the Sab-bath to what *God* does (Alford, 577). The point was unanswerable (ἀνταποκρίνομαι, 'to answer in turn', Rom. 9:20**; αὐτῷ is added by A W Δ Θ f13 *pm* lat; TR; *Diglot*).

v. Places of Honour 14:7–11

14:8–10 contains a saying which recommends guests at a meal not to take the highest places and run the risk of being humiliated by being asked to move down the table, but to take a low place and then enjoy the 'glory' of being asked to take a higher place. This could be simple, worldly advice to guests, and it is amply paralleled in Jewish writings (cf. Pr. 25:6f.; SB II, 204). But it is presented here as a parable, according to Luke's introduction. This is confirmed by the conclusion in v. 11 which speaks of the humiliation and exaltation of men by God. Hence the advice given (while good and valid on a worldly level) is a parable of how men should behave over against God (Flender, 81f.). There is no reason to doubt its authenticity, as is done by Bultmann, 108, on the grounds that the saying is purely Jewish worldly wisdom. Elsewhere Jesus warned his disciples about seeking positions within the kingdom of God (22:24–27; Mk. 10:35–45), and he also criticised the Pharisees for their religious pride (11:43; 20:45–47). There is thus nothing improbable about the setting here. Against the suggestion that a secular saying has been reinterpreted as a parable by the addition of v. 11, it has been noted that a similar sequence of teaching is found in a rabbinic source (see below).

A similar saying is found in Mt. 20:28 D. This appears to be a piece of floating tradition and is not part of Matthew's text (cf. Metzger, 53); it is, however, not derived from Lk. but represents a translation-variant of the same Aramaic original (Black, 171–175; Jeremias, *Parables*, 25f.), with Luke giving the more literary version.

See Jeremias, *Parables*, 25f., 191–193.

(7) For the device of giving an introduction to a parable which sets the scene or gives the purpose cf. 19:11; also 18:1, 9. On the phraseology see 5:36 note; 6:39 note. καλέω is the key word which binds the whole of this section together: 14:8, 9, 10, 12, 13, 16, 17, 24; cf. 5:32; 7:39. παραβολή here may simply mean a 'rule' of etiquette (Jeremias, *Parables*, 20, 192), but in fact the 'rule' which Jesus gives has a deeper significance, so that the nuance of 'parable' is not absent. ἐπέχω has a variety of meanings: 'to hold out' (Phil. 2:16); 'to pay attention to (sc. τὸν νοῦν) ', Acts 3:5; 1 Ti. 4:16 (cf. Creed, 189); also, 'to stay' (Acts 19:22**). Here it has the second meaning and is followed by an indirect question. πρωτοκλισία is a 'place of honour' (14:8; 20:46 par. Mk. 12:39 par. Mt. 23:6**; W. Michaelis, TDNT VI, 870f.). Precedence depended on the rank and distinction of the guests at this time; after AD 300 it depended upon age. The most important guests arrived late for banquets. For Jewish love for position and warnings against it cf. Sir. 3:17f.; Arist. 263; SB I, 774, 914f.; II, 204, 402; for the same motif in Hellenistic thought see Theophrastus, *Characters* 21:2; Lucian, *Conviv.* 9. The top place at a Jewish meal was at the head end of the table or the middle of the middle couch (cf. SB IV:2, 618).

(8) The parable begins with a general injunction in Mt. 20:28 D, which is missing from Lk. (ὑμεῖς δὲ ζητεῖτε ἐκ μικροῦ αὐξῆσαι καὶ (μὴ, syᶜ) ἐκ μείζονος ἔλαττον εἶναι). Luke speaks of the host from the outset of the parable (ὑπό τινος, diff. 'Mt.'), and has καλέω, diff. 'Mt.' παρακαλέω; the uncompounded form is closer to the Aramaic wording, since Aramaic has no compound verbs. For γάμος cf. 12:36. The underlying Aramaic word mištutha can mean 'marriage' or 'banquet': cf. 'Mt.', δειπνῆσαι. For πρωτοκλισίας 'Mt.' has ἐξέχοντας τόπους. μήποτε expresses apprehension or fear (BD 370²). For ἐντιμότερος (diff. 'Mt.' ἐνδοξότερος) cf. 7:2. The perfect ᾖ κεκλημένος has the sense 'has (already) been invited'.

(9) For the cumbersome ὁ σὲ καὶ αὐτὸν καλέσας 'Mt.' has ὁ δειπνοκλήτωρ (a rare word). The future indicative ἐρεῖ is used loosely for the more correct aorist subjunctive (12:58 note). τόπος can mean 'a place at table' (AG s.v.), 14:9b, 10. 'Mt.' has ἔτι κάτω χωρεῖ. κατέχω is 'to occupy' (cf. AG s.v.). 'Mt.' again has simpler wording: καὶ καταισχυνθήσῃ.

(10) The parabolic instruction continues with a positive command, similar in structure to the preceding negative command. 'Matthew' has a conditional clause and differs considerably in wording. He shares the use of ἀναπίπτω, but speaks of the 'worse' place (ἥττων) and the arrival of an inferior (ἥττων) guest, where Luke has ἔσχατος; both forms may reflect the one positive adjective in Aramaic. ἵνα may express result rather than purpose (16:9; Lagrange, 400). The perfect κεκληκώς is literary variation for the earlier καλέσας. ἐρεῖ is again used in the future indicative when a subjunctive form would be more normal after ἵνα; cf. 20:10; Gal. 2:4; BD 369². For the vocative φίλε cf. 7:6; et al. προσαναβαίνω**, 'to go up, move up', contains an invitation to sit near the host; cf. 'Mt.' συνάγω. For the comparative ἀνώτερον cf. Heb. 10:8**, diff. 'Mt.' ἔτι ἄνω. δόξα corresponds to 'Mt.' χρήσιμος, 'useful, beneficial, advantageous'. Black suggests that the two versions reflect the root ytr; the rendering of 'Mt.' in syᶜ is 'excelling honour' (teshbohta mᵉyattarta), which suggests an Aramaic yithron shᵉbhaha ('great honour'). The 'great' has been omitted in Lk. and the 'glory' in Mt., leaving the word yithron (or perhaps mᵉyattᵉra), which could mean 'advantage, usefulness, profit', and the translator did the best he could with it. A simpler solution is suggested by Jeremias; Aramaic šibhḥa is ambiguous and could mean 'praise, honour, fame' or 'gain, share'; here the correct meaning is 'honoured'. The open shame of the first alternative is contrasted with the public honour in the second. This is the worldly understanding of the situation, and it could be argued that here an (unworthy) appeal is being made to human pride, which does not really get to the root of the matter. In effect, blatant seeking for prestige, which can lead to dishonour, should be replaced by a more cunning approach which will result in greater honour.

(11) That this is not Jesus' meaning is proved by this verse which states that anybody who tries to exalt himself (ὑψόω, 1:52; G. Bertram,

TDNT VIII, 608) – blatantly or cunningly – will be humbled (sc. by God; ταπεινόω, 3:5; cf. 1:48; W. Grundmann, TDNT VIII, 16), and vice versa. A man's position depends on God and not on his own self-seeking. The saying is identical with 18:14; cf. Mt. 23:12 and the somewhat similar Mt. 18:4. For the thought cf. Mt. 11:23; 2 Cor. 11:7; Jas. 4:10; 1 Pet. 5:6; and also Lk. 16:15; Rom. 12:16; 1 Tim. 6:17. The verse may appear to be a wandering saying which has been attracted here by community of theme. However, Jeremias, *Parables*, 107, 191–193, has shown that a similar train of thought is to be found in Lv. R. 1:5, where we have a Jewish proverb, ascribed to R. Hillel, which was traditionally associated with table-manners: 'My humiliation is my exaltation, and my exaltation is my humiliation'; Jeremias claims that Jesus has taken this over. But whereas for the rabbis the saying was merely a piece of worldly wisdom, for Jesus it is an expression of God's verdict upon men.

vi. The Choice of Guests 14:12–14

This passage, peculiar to Lk., contains advice to a host on his choice of guests for a meal. He should not invite his friends lest they invite him back, and that is the sum total of his reward. Rather, he should invite the poor and needy, who cannot repay him, and he will receive a heavenly reward. Put thus bluntly, the saying is alarmingly open to misunderstanding. It can surely not be Jesus' meaning that one is never to have a party for one's friends, especially since this goes counter to the spirit of his own way of life. What, however, is stated as a plain 'not X ... but Y ...' really means in Semitic idiom 'Not so much X ... as rather Y ...' (10:20 note). Again, it can surely not be Jesus' meaning that one is to do good deeds simply because they bring a better and more durable reward. The point is rather that one should seek to do good to those who are so needy that they cannot do anything in return, and leave the whole question of recompense to God; (cf. 6:32–35).

The teaching is doubtless to be taken literally, but it forms the prelude to a parable in which it is seen that the attitude recommended to men is in fact that which is taken by God.

Easton, 227, suggests that it would have been out of place for Jesus to address his host in this way. This may well indicate that the present discourse is composite. Bultmann, 108, thinks that the saying has the atmosphere of 1 En. 108 rather than of the proclamation of Jesus, and is Jewish in character. But the sentiments are those of 6:32–35, and while the thoughts would be congenial to Luke, there is no evidence that they are created by him or by the early church.

(12) For ἄριστον cf. 11:38. δεῖπνον, 'meal' (14:16, 17, 24; 20:46*), is used here for the main meal of the day, held in the late afternoon (11:37 note). Guests might be invited to the earlier or the later meal;

φωνέω is a variant for καλέω. Four categories of people are mentioned, just as four categories appear in the second part of the parable. ἀδελφοί, 'brothers', may mean 'near relations' here; for συγγενής cf. 1:58; 21:16. γείτων is 'neighbour', 15:6, 9; Jn. 9:8**. For μήποτε cf. 14:8. ἀντικαλέω** is 'to invite in return', and ἀνταπόδομα (Rom. 11:9**) is 'repayment'. The word order ἀνταπόδομά σοι is reversed in TR; Diglot. The main point, however, is unexpressed: supply 'and you will get no heavenly reward' (J. Weiss, 478).

(13) For the literary variant δοχή, cf. 5:29**; the word order δοχὴν ποιῇς B (ποιήσῃς, p⁷⁵ ℵ M 579) is reversed in the other MSS; TR; Diglot. ἀνάπηρος (14:21**) is 'crippled'. For the motif cf. Dt. 14:29; 16:11, 14; 26:11f.; P. Ab. 1:5; SB II, 206f., and contrast 2 Sa. 5:8; 1QS 2:4ff.; 1QSa 2:5-7; CD 13:4-7; from which it is clear that on this point Jesus was opposed to the Qumran viewpoint (Braun, Qumran, I, 90), and indeed to the principle of reciprocity widely current in the ancient world (G. Stählin, TDNT IX, 160f. and n. 117).

(14) The person who cares for the needy in this way will be truly happy (μακάριος), even if his guests are unable (ἔχω, 7:40, 42; 12:4, 50) to repay him (cf. 7:42; ἀνταποδίδωμι, 14:14b*). For God will give him his reward at the resurrection of the just. For this concept cf. 2 Mac. 7:9; Lk. 20:35; Jn. 5:29. A resurrection of all men is taught in Acts 24:15; cf. Lk. 10:12; Jn. 5:28f.; Rom. 2:5; 2 Cor. 5:10; 2 Tim. 4:1; and for a full discussion see SB IV:2, 1166-1198.

vii. The Great Supper 14:15-24

When a guest piously remarks that a man who can look forward to sharing in God's heavenly banquet is truly happy, Jesus replies with a parable which deals with the question of invitations to a banquet. When a certain man prepared a banquet and invited his guests to it, they one and all rejected his invitation, pleading other pressing engagements. So the man, angry at their refusal and determined that none of the original guests should share in the meal, sent out repeatedly and summoned in poor and needy people from both inside and outside the town until his table was filled.

A very similar parable appears in Mt. 22:1-14, but with considerable alteration and addition. It is generally accepted that the two parables are variants of one original theme, and considerable progress can be made towards reconstructing a basic form of the parable (which turns out to be very close to the Lucan form). There is also a third form of the parable in G. Thomas 64 which represents yet another adaptation of the basic theme. It is not, however, certain that the various forms go back to one original Q form, and the possibility of redactional activity prior to the work of the Evangelists is to be taken seriously.

Jeremias, Parables, 176-180, interprets the parable in its original form as a warning to 'pious' Jews that if they pay no heed to the gospel call, they will be replaced by the despised and ungodly, and find that they have left it until too late to come. Additional force is given to this interpretation by the suggestion that the parable is deliberately modelled on the story of the rich tax-collector Bar Ma'jan who performed one good deed in an otherwise ungodly life: 'He had arranged a banquet for the city councillors, but they did not come. So he gave orders that the poor should come and eat it, so that the food should not be wasted' (j. Sanh. 6.23c; cited by Jeremias, op. cit. 179). The implication is that the Jews are treating God with the same contempt as the aristocracy showed to the *nouveau riche* tax-collector.

The difficulty with this interpretation is that it suggests that it is only when the 'pious' have rejected the gospel that Jesus turns to the poor and needy. F. Hahn* also suggests that the difference in conduct between the tax-collector and God is so great that it is unlikely that Jesus was drawing any comparison between them. Both of these objections, it may be suggested, arise from an over-allegorisation of the parable and do not affect the basic point.

Hahn himself suggests that on the lips of Jesus the parable is clearly a picture of salvation; the stress lies not on the refusal of the guests to come, but on the readiness of the host to fill the table. So the parable becomes an interpretation of Jesus' own behaviour in eating with tax-collectors and sinners, and the point is basically the universal offer of the gospel with a subsidiary warning not to refuse the offer. In the Lucan version a certain amount of allegorisation has taken place. This is to be seen in the two-fold effort to reach the new guests (vs. 21–23). But who are meant by these two groups? If they represent Jews and gentiles, who were the original guests? The 'pious' Jews? Or were the original guests those called by Jesus himself and the new guests the Jews and gentiles addressed by the post-Easter mission of the church? Alternatively, the distinction may be between the rich and the poor (Jülicher). Or again two contrasts may be intended at the same time, between the 'pious' and sinners in Israel (vs. 17–20/21), and between Israel and the gentiles (vs. 21/22f.; cf. Jeremias, op. cit. 64, 69). Hahn himself appears to favour this third view, but insists that the servant in the parable represents not Jesus but the disciples collectively. On this view, it would seem that an original 'pious'/sinners contrast has been complicated by a later reference to the gentiles.

Yet another view is taken by Schlatter, 336–340, who holds that the basic contrast is between Jews and gentiles. It is taken up and developed by Vögtle, 194–196. He rightly criticises Hahn for ignoring the temporal elements in the parable and seeing in it one universal offer of salvation. Having dropped the detail about the poor in v. 21 from the original version of the parable, Vögtle is able to claim that Jesus threatens the Jews who refuse the message with the possibility that they will be replaced by the gentiles. Thereafter, what Jesus had merely threatened became a reality in the experience of the early church when it

undertook the successful mission to the gentiles (something not envisaged by Jesus) and was rejected by the Jews. Hence there was a shift
in the interpretation of the parable; it now provided a prophetic explanation of what was happening. The gentiles are seen as poor and needy
people over against the well-to-do Jews described in the first part of the
parable, and the purpose of the second invitation to the people outside
the city is to indicate to the church that it still has an unfinished task until the house is filled with guests.

The weakness in this view is the interpretation of the poor as the
gentiles, for which Vögtle offers no real proof.

A totally different approach is taken by Derrett, 126–155, who interprets the parable as consisting of midrashic elements based upon
various OT texts. Essentially the parable is concerned with the feast of
victory which follows a holy war, and with the muster of troops
beforehand to see who is fit and faithful to take part in the battle and enjoy the following feast (Zp. 1:7–9). The excuses offered by the guests
reflect Dt. 20, in which various reasons for refraining from going to war
are listed. The instruction following the parable, Lk. 14:25–35, deals
with the whole-hearted commitment required on the part of those who
side with Jesus in his holy war. The king regards the refusal to come to
the feast (and hence to take part in the preceding obligation of going to
war) as a sign of unworthiness and proceeds to punish it by a social
penalty; they are replaced by others at the meal, and they do not even
have portions of the meal (like pieces of wedding cake today) sent to
them.

The details of this exceedingly intricate interpretation, which attempts to account for all the features of both Synoptic narratives, cannot
be set out here. A basic difficulty is that the features of the king and the
element of war are absent from Luke's version, and it is difficult to
regard them as determining the interpretation of Luke's parable. P. H.
Ballard*, 344 n., 350 n., is therefore sceptical of Derrett's reconstruction, although he thinks it possible that some elaboration of themes
along midrashic lines may have taken place in the Matthaean version. At
most the series of excuses in Lk. may bear some relationship to Dt.
20:5–7; cf. 28:30–33.

From our discussion it emerges that difficulty is caused by attempting to take all the details of the story in too literal a sense in order
to construct a coherent allegory, whether at the level of Jesus' original
intention or at the level of subsequent interpretation. It is best to see in
the story Jesus' comment on the 'pious' in Israel who neither entered the
kingdom themselves nor allowed others to enter (11:52); they are warned that they will be excluded from the kingdom, and the way will be
opened up (as it was by Jesus) to the needy and the outsiders. The element of substitution and succession (the poor replace the 'pious' and
come in only after their refusal) should not be pressed in the interpretation; F. Hahn*, 72 n. 91, rightly comments how difficult it was for the

teacher in parables to remain within the limits of the imagery. It is possible that Jesus intended a conscious allusion to the gentile mission: it may well be that this feature was developed more fully in the course of the tradition, so that the parable was seen as giving a summons to the gentile mission.

See Jeremias, 63–69, 176–180; Linnemann, 88–97; E. Haenchen, 'Das Gleichnis vom grossen Mahl', in *Die Bibel und Wir*, Tübingen, 1968, 135–155; Derrett, 126–155; F. Hahn, 'Das Gleichnis von der Einladung zum Festmahl', in Böcher, 51–82; Vögtle, 171–218; P. H. Ballard, 'Reasons for refusing the Great Supper', JTS ns 23, 1972, 341–350.

(15) The occasion for the parable is given by a remark from one of the guests which expresses in typical Jewish form the hope of participation in the heavenly banquet. There is no evidence to show that the verse has been created by Lucan redaction (*pace* E. Haenchen*, 144), and it probably belonged to the tradition (Schürmann, *Abschiedsrede*, 98; F. Hahn*, 74). Indeed, there is no reason why the parable should not originally have been told by Jesus as a comment on this remark: future blessedness depends on acceptance of the invitation. For ἀκούσας as a link cf. 7:3, 9, 29; 8:50; 18:22; 23:6. μακάριος may link with 14:14: the guest may perhaps be regarded as offering a corrective to the restriction of blessedness implicit in Jesus' saying: *all* who attain to the heavenly banquet will be blessed. The phrase 'to eat bread' refers to eating a full meal (14:1; cf. 7:33). The future tense and the reference to the kingdom indicate that the thought is of final bliss. (The suggestion that the saying implies a delay in the coming of the kingdom (Grässer, 196) is baseless.) For this concept cf. 13:28f. Bultmann, 113, cf. 136, 360, claims that it is pure chance that the saying has not been attributed to Jesus as part of his preaching of salvation, and SB I, 180, comments that the use of the term 'kingdom of God' bears the impress of Jesus' teaching, since a Jew would have used some other expression. It is more likely that the saying has undergone some conformation to Christian style in the course of transmission.

(16) 'A certain man' often figures in parables (10:30; 12:16; 15:11; 16:1, 19; 19:12). The great supper (δεῖπνον, 14:12) is so much a standing figure for salvation that it need not be regarded as having any other meaning (cf. F. Hahn*, 68). Many guests are invited, apparently from the man's friends. The invitation may be taken to represent God's call to Israel, given in various ways, and not necessarily restricted to one particular group of people (i.e. the parabolic detail should not be pressed to produce minute allegorical results).

In Mt. the host is a king who holds a marriage feast (cf. 14:8 diff. Mt. 20:28 D) for his son; this looks like allegorical expansion, although the figure of Jesus as the bridegroom is firmly based in the Synoptic tradition. It is much less likely that these features have been trimmed away to produce the Lucan picture (cf. Vögtle, 174f.).

(17) The invitation is followed by an actual summons to the meal when it is ready. This detail corresponds with actual upper-class

courtesy attested for both the Jewish and the Roman worlds (Est. 6:14; La. R 4:2 (SB I, 880f.); Philo, Opif. 78 ('Just as givers of a banquet, then, do not send out the summonses to supper till they have put everything in readiness for the feast . . .'); Terence, Heaut. 169f.; Apuleius, Met. 3:12). ὁ δοῦλος αὐτοῦ may mean 'the servant appointed as "vocator"' (Zerwick, 168), or the picture may simply be of a rich man with one slave. In Mt. the king employs a number of servants, which corresponds to the dramatic situation. While, therefore, it has been argued that Luke's form has reduced the number to 'one' to give an allegorical reference to Jesus (Easton, 228; Klostermann, 151), it is more probable that the one is original. In both forms of the parable, however, there were allegorical possibilities (cf. Weiser, 64–66, who thinks that Luke does not take these up). The message delivered by the servant is that the feast is now ready. (The text is variously transmitted: ἕτοιμά ἐστιν (p⁴⁵ ᵛⁱᵈ B); ἕτοιμά εἰσιν (p⁷⁵ ℵ L Θ); ἕτοιμά ἐστιν πάντα (A W Δ f1 f13 pl vg sa bo: TR; Diglot); πάντα ἕτοιμά ἐστιν (D a e sy). πάντα is assimilation to Mt., and ἐστίν is better attested than εἰσίν (Metzger, 164).) This message emphasises that refusal to respond to the invitation at this point is an act of great discourtesy. The ἤδη is natural enough in the dramatic situation. But is the parabolic implication that the salvation, portrayed by the meal, is already available and not a matter of the distant future? What was regarded as future in v. 15 is already present. Admittedly, there may be a gap between the invitation (by Jesus or the disciples) and the actual consummation, in which case the interpretation again breaks the limits of the picture. It may be best to assume that the meal stands for salvation in its totality, including both the present experience of those who respond to the gospel and the future consummation.

(18) But the invited guests rejected the invitation. Three particular examples are given, typical of all of them (πάντες): ἀπὸ μίας is probably a Greek phrase (sc. γνώμης) meaning 'unanimously' (AG s.v. ἀπό VI; BD 241⁶; Plummer, 361), rather than a literal translation of min hᵃda, 'all at once, immediately' (Black, 113; Jeremias, Parables, 176). παραιτέω here has the sense 'to excuse'; the passive is used reflexively; cf. Acts 25:11.

Although the description of the excuses is fuller in Lk. than in Mt., they form an integral part of the original parable (F. Hahn*, 54–56; Vögtle, 177–183; pace Grundmann, 297; Schulz, 394f.). The excuses bear a certain resemblance to those that are advanced in Dt. 20:5–7; 24:5; cf. Sotah 8:1–6, as reasons for withdrawing from a holy war. Nevertheless, the correspondence is far from exact, and it is therefore improbable that this should be regarded as a main motif in the parable. All three excuses are concerned with the details of commercial and family life, and fit in with the teaching of Jesus regarding the danger of letting love of possessions or domestic ties interfere with total commitment to the call to discipleship; they do not need to be allegorised in order to be interpreted outside the parable. At the same time, however,

there are undoubted reminiscences of Dt. throughout Lk., and hence the
lesson may well be that the kind of reasons which were valid for non-
participation in the holy war are improper excuses for refusal to accept
the gospel invitation.

The first man has just bought a field; for the aorist translating a
Semitic perfect referring to an act just completed see Black, 129. It may
seem strange that a visit to the field should follow rather than precede
the purchase, but the purchase may well have been arranged on condition of a later inspection and approval (AZ 15a, in SB II, 208; Alfenus,
Digest 9:252:3). Although some commentators find a growing discourtesy in the guests' replies (cf. the omission of the excuse formula in
v. 20), the impossibility of attendance is emphasised from the beginning
by the use of ἀνάγκη, which implies the legal obligation of the purchaser
to complete the sale. The formula ἐρωτῶ σε, ἔχε με παρῃτημένον may be
a Latinism (Martial 2:79, 'Excusatum habeas me rogo'), but is found in
the papyri (AG s.v. ἔχω I, 5; cf. BD 471³).

(19) The second excuse is likewise concerned with rural life (contrast the more urban, upper-class excuses in G. Thomas 64). The
purchase of five pairs (ζεῦγος, 2:24) of oxen suggests a farmer of some
means, since in general one or two pairs of oxen were adequate for a
small farm (Jeremias, Parables, 177). As in the former case, inspection
followed the purchase.

(20) The third excuse is strange. It may be assumed that women
were not invited to the banquet (a detail that obviously is not to be
pressed allegorically). The man had no doubt been recently married (on
the aorist cf. 14:18 note; for ἔγημα see BD 101). In such circumstances
a man was excused going to war (Dt. 20:7; 24:5; cf. Herodotus 1:36),
but this is hardly an adequate parallel to missing a banquet. No doubt
the banquet would last into the night, and the newly-wed bridegroom felt
under obligation to sleep with his wife. The importance of begetting a
child may be the dominant factor. Here, if anywhere, there is perhaps
support for Derrett's view that not only a banquet but also participation
in war is envisaged. The difficulty is reflected in G. Thomas where the
excuse has become that of making arrangements for a friend's wedding.
Or is the reason meant to be seen as a possible, but weak excuse? Was
the man under his wife's thumb? Note how the man simply states that he
cannot come without asking to be excused: did he think that such a request would be refused by the host?

(21) Although the guests acted independently, their combined
refusal to come is surprising and goes beyond normal events. But the
host's response is in part at least normal. When the servant (ἐκεῖνος is
added by TR; Diglot) returns with the news, he breaks out in anger
against the guests. τότε and ὀργίζομαι recur in Mt., but the motif is expanded into an account of a punitive campaign against the guests, which
fits in with the royal setting. But the emphasis lies on the positive action
of the host. The same servant is sent out as a matter of urgency (ταχέως)

– since the feast waits for guests – to bring other people in. πλατεῖαι (sc. ὁδοί) indicates broad, main streets or public squares, probably the latter in view of the contrast with ῥύμη, 'narrow street, lane, alley' (Acts 9:11; 12:10; Mt. 6:3**); cf. Is. 15:3; Tob. 13:17f. Matthew has εἰς τὰς ὁδούς (but also ἐπὶ τὰς διεξόδους τῶν ὁδῶν) which may be original. In such places one would find the beggars of the town, since all four categories of people specifically listed would fall into this category. The same list is found in 14:13, and is generally thought to be a secondary insertion from there, Matthew simply has 'all whom you find', which may be original, and could have been understood to refer to beggars. But the story of Bar Ma'jan refers specifically to the poor, and it is therefore possible that the list in Lk. is original, and has been inserted in 14:13, while Matthew's form of the parable has generalised, especially since Matthew's parable is concerned with the final presence of both good and bad at the feast.

(22) The servant returns after carrying out his task to explain that the table is not yet filled.

(23) He is therefore sent out again, this time into the country, along the roads and by the fences (φραγμός, 'wall, hedge') along which beggars might rest for protection. He is to urge (ἀναγκάζω) more people to come in; the use of the word implies the situation of oriental courtesy in which an invited guest will at first politely refuse to come until he is pressed to do so (cf. Gn. 19:3). This second invitation is absent from Mt., and is generally conceded to be a secondary development (Weiser, 62); F. Hahn*, 59, rightly comments that we should not in this case regard either the first or the second invitation as original, but both as being derived from one basic invitation. But why did this development take place? Two motifs appear to be present. The one is to indicate a call to a wider circle of people, who can most plausibly be identified with the gentiles; the other is to indicate that the task of inviting the guests is still incomplete and hence to stress the continuing task that must be carried on by the disciples. Can such an outlook be assigned to Jesus? It is by no means impossible. Nor is it impossible that Matthew's form has reduced the two invitations to one (W. Michaelis, TDNT V, 108), and the presence of two invitations in the earlier part of Matthew's parable may indicate a memory of the two invitations at this point. Hence it is far from certain that Luke has expanded the original parable here.

(24) The final comment is often regarded as an expansion, since with its address to 'you' it is thought to be a comment addressed by Jesus to his hearers about the messianic banquet (Creed, 192); cf. 11:8; 15:7, 10; 16:9; 18:14; Mt. 21:43. Even Jeremias (*Parables*, 171f.) who admits that the remark is possible within the limits of the parable argues that the threat has significance only if addressed to Jews who might be excluded from the messianic banquet. Plummer, 361, and Linnemann, 88–97, hold that the guests' excuses were really requests to be allowed to postpone their arrival, so that this saying is a warning that late-comers

will not be accepted; but this view of the parable is to be rejected. The right interpretation is suggested by Derrett, 141, who argues that the reference is to sending portions of food from the banquet to guests who were unable to come (Ne. 8:10–12). The saying therefore fits into the situation in which the host addresses the company of people already gathered in response to the first invitation to the poor; the saying follows on directly from the instruction to the slave to go out for the second time. It may be significant, however, that by this point in the story the host has become ὁ κύριος, with an obvious allegorical indication. There is no way to the messianic feast except by responding to the invitation once given.

viii. The Conditions of Discipleship 14:25–35

The theme of the cost of accompanying Jesus runs like a refrain throughout Lk. (9:57–62; 18:24–30). If the guests in the preceding parable refused to face the cost of accepting the invitation, other men may be tempted to underestimate the cost of discipleship and to embark on a course which is beyond their abilities. Hence this section takes up the theme of 14:18f. and develops it further, and is thus integrally joined to the table scene, although there is a change of scenery and audience.

The section consists of an introduction (v. 25), two parallel sayings on discipleship (vs. 26f.), two parabolic sayings with an application (vs. 28–30, 31f., 33) and a conclusion (vs. 34f.). The opening sayings and the application express the total commitment required from disciples; they repeat teaching found in 18:29f. and 9:23, and the parallel in Mt. 10:37f. indicates that they form a Q doublet to the Marcan teaching. The summary in v. 33 is probably an editorial composition, based on Q.

The two parables are peculiar to Lk., but have a formal parallel in G. Thomas 98. They are concerned with the need for correct evaluation of the situation before making a venture: the person who has inadequate resources should refrain from an unequal task. The disciple should be sure that he is able to pay the cost, lest his life should resemble a task half-completed and worthy of scorn.

The closing saying appears to express the ultimate uselessness of the half-hearted disciple, who can expect only judgment. The saying is found in Q material at Mt. 5:13, but there is also a parallel in Mk. 9:49f. Luke's form is basically from Q, and may possibly reflect Mark's wording; in any case we are dealing with variant forms of one basic saying.

The passage as a whole is probably a Lucan composition, based on Q material, but also including material from other sources.

See H. Gressmann, 'Mitteilungen. 14. Salzdüngung in den Evangelien', TLZ 32, 1911, 156f.; W. Nauck, 'Salt as a Metaphor in Instructions for Discipleship', ST 6, 1953, 165–178; C.-H. Hunzinger, 'Unbekannte Gleichnisse Jesu aus dem Thomas-Evangelium', in Eltester, 209–220; E. P. Deatrick, 'Salt, Soil, Savior', BA 25, 1962, 41–48; J. Dupont, 'Renoncer à tous ses biens (Luc 14, 33)', NRT 6, 1971, 561–582; Schulz, 446–449, 430–433, 470–472.

(25) The theme of Jesus' journey to Jerusalem is kept before the reader by the use of συνπορεύομαι (7:11; cf. J. Weiss, 479). The accompanying crowds are great (cf. 5:15), and their enthusiasm must be dampened by a sense of the realities of the situation. For ὄχλ~ι πολλοί cf. 7:9; *et al.* The language is Lucan and the verse is probably redactional (cf. Klostermann, 153).

(26) The εἴ τις formulation, diff. Mt. ὁ with participle, may reflect 9:23 par. Mk. 8:34, or represent a variant oral tradition. To come *to* Jesus is the initial step in response to his call (cf. 6:47; Jn. 5:40; 6:35; *et al.*; Mt. 11:28). It has to be complemented by coming *after* (ὀπίσω) Jesus (14:27; cf. 9:23). μισέω, 'to hate', is usually said to have its Semitic sense, 'to love less' (16:13 par. Mt. 6:24; Gn. 29:31–33; Dt. 21:15–17; 2 Sa. 19:7; Pr. 13:24; Is. 60:15; Mal. 1:2f.; Rom. 9:13; 1 Jn. 2:9; SB I, 434). This is no doubt how the phrase was understood by Matthew's tradition which has φιλῶν ... ὑπέρ.... At the same time, however, it should be noted that the Hebrew *śānē'* has the sense 'to leave aside, abandon', and this sense may be present: cf. the use of ἀρνέομαι in 9:23 diff. 14:26, and the use of ἀφίημι in 18:29 par. Mk. 10:29. The thought is, therefore, not of psychological hate, but of renunciation (O. Michel, TDNT IV, 690f.). Matthew's form has toned down the force of the original (Lucan) saying in the interests of a comparison between the claims of family and of Jesus; Luke retains the hyperbolical form, which is an authentic part of Jesus' teaching. The use of οὐ in a condition with the indicative is normal in the NT, in contrast to Classical usage (cf. 11:8; BD 428[1]). Matthew has a two part saying referring to a. father and mother, and b. son and daughter. Luke has one clause with seven objects, on the analogy of 18:29, and his wording may be a secondary expansion (Grundmann, 302). Behind the saying lies the expression of Levi's devotion to the Torah expressed in Dt. 33:9 (cited in 4QTest. 15f.; cf. Lv. R. 19:1 in Grundmann, 302f.; cf. Schulz, 448f.). Luke alone has a reference to renunciation of one's wife (cf. 14:20 and 18:29 diff. Mk. 10:29); it is unlikely that we should see a deliberate Lucan theme here, and more probable that he is stressing the link with 14:20. For 'son or daughter', Luke has τέκνα, possibly by assimilation to 18:29. He includes 'brothers and sisters', possibly from Mk. 10:29 (Lk. 18:29 omits 'sisters').

τε (B *pc* it) is omitted by p[75] a e r[1]; *Diglot*; and replaced by δέ in TR; ἔτι τε καί (Acts 21:28) means 'and in addition'. For ψυχή cf. 9:24; 17:33; Mt. 10:39; *Diglot* has αὐτοῦ for ἑαυτοῦ. There is no reference to ψυχή in the Matthaean saying, but the immediately following saying, Mt. 10:39 (cf. Lk. 17:33), is the Q equivalent to Lk. 9:24 par. Mk. 8:35, and the indications are that Luke has run the Matthaean sayings together (cf. Schulz, 447 n. 327). But the occurrence of Luke's phrase μισεῖν ... τὴν ψυχήν in Jn. 12:25 warns against any facile conclusions, and suggests that the Lucan form was one of several similar sayings in circulation (Dodd, 338–343). For μαθητής cf. 14:27, 33. Matthew has the form οὐκ ἔστιν μου ἄξιος (10:37 and 38); cf. G. Thomas 55 with the same emphatic position of μου. Manson, Teaching, 237–240, argues that Matthew's form arose from a misreading of an Aramaic phrase š⸗ʷwilyî ('my disciple') as š⸗ʷwê lî ('worthy of me'). See, however, J. Dupont*, 566 n. 11. The different forms may arise from application to different audiences (P. S. Minear, 'Jesus' Audiences, according to Luke', Nov.T 16, 1974, 81–109, especially 98f.).

(27) The whole verse is omitted by homoioteleuton in 69 544 *al* sy^s bo^pt (Metzger, 164). Before ὅστις the conjunction καί is added by ℵ^c A (D) W Θ f1 f13 *pm*; TR; *Diglot*. βαστάζω (7:14) is used of Jesus carrying his cross at Jn. 19:17; diff. Mt. λαμβάνω and Lk. 9:23 par. Mk. 8:34 αἴρω, all of which may represent Aram. š⸗qal (Black, 195f.). For ἑαυτοῦ, αὐτοῦ is read by p^45 p^75 ℵ D Θ *pm* TR; *Diglot*. On the meaning of the phrase see 9:23 note. To come after Jesus is the same as to follow him (9:23; Mt. has ἀκολουθέω ὀπίσω; cf. Black, 195). The phrase is used in the OT of going after false gods and walking in the ways of Yahweh (Dt. 13:4; 1 Ki. 14:8; 18:21; 2 Ki. 23:3; H. Seesemann, TDNT V, 289–292; cf. J. Schneider, TDNT II, 669). Jesus, however, calls men not to follow God but to follow himself in the path of self-denial: cf. Dt. 13:4, where following after other gods and total love for Yahweh are contrasted. Davies, 422f., however, sees the background in the rabbinic technical terms for following a rabbi as his servant (cf. Mk. 15:41). This seems less suitable in the present context, where serving a rabbi would be an anticlimax after the thought of utter self-sacrifice.

(28) The two parabolic sayings are very similar, though not identical, in form, and obviously make essentially the same point. A third parable of a similar kind is found in G. Thomas 98, where the kingdom is likened to an assassin who before killing a man tests his strength by driving a sword into a wall. For the thought cf. Philo, Abr. 105; Epictetus 3:15:10–12. C.-H. Hunzinger* argues that the three parables draw a lesson about God from human behaviour: if men so carefully test their ability to complete an action, how much more does God, so that whatever he begins he carries through to completion. This interpretation is forced; nor does it fit the context (cf. Jeremias, *Parables*, 197 n. 23).

τίς ἐξ ὑμῶν ... is a parabolic introduction in the form of a rhetorical question with a conditional participle (cf. 11:5 note). The force of the connective γάρ appears to be: would-be disciples must be ready for the ultimate in self-denial (vs. 26f.), for anybody who undertakes a task without being ready for the total cost involved will only make a fool of himself. πύργος (13:4) may here mean a farm building (AG), apparently of some size, since even the foundation for it may take the builder's total resources. Possibly one should think of an even more ornate building of palatial dimensions (as in Jos. Bel. 5:168), but the more natural view is that Jesus is addressing an audience including small farmers. καθίζω conveys the idea of settling down to make a deliberate calculation (cf. Virgil, Aen. 10:150; Klostermann, 154).

ψηφίζω is 'to count up, calculate' (Rev. 13:18**), and δαπάνη** is 'expense'. εἰ introduces a loosely attached indirect question (cf. 6:7). For ἔχω used absolutely cf. 8:18; 19:26; AG s.v. I 2a. ἀπαρτισμός** is 'completion'.

(29) ἵνα μήποτε appears to be a strengthened form of ἵνα μή, expressing apprehension; ἐκτελέω (14:30**) is 'to complete'. For ἐμπαίζω, 'to ridicule, mock', cf. 18:32 par. Mk. 10:34; Lk. 22:63; 23:11, 36*; the word-order αὐτῷ ἐμπαίζειν is inverted in TR; Diglot.

(30) ὅτι is recitativum. The lesson of the parable is left implicit.

(31) The same point is now made on a larger scale; for ἤ in this sort of context cf. 15:8. ἐξ ὑμῶν is omitted from the introductory formula, since there were no kings in Jesus' audience. συμβάλλω (2:19) here means 'to meet, engage' (11:53 v.1.; Acts 20:14), here for purposes of war; the word order συμβάλλειν ἑτέρῳ βασιλεῖ is given in W Δ Θ f1 f13 pm lat; TR: Diglot. βουλεύομαι is 'to deliberate' (also, 'to decide', Acts 27:39), here followed by an indirect question. ἐν is 'with', as in 1 Mac. 4:29, and ὑπαντάω (8:27) has the sense 'to oppose'.

(32) For εἰ δὲ μή γε, cf. 5:36; et al. From this point the parallelism with the previous parable breaks down. The lesson is that one should come to terms with the enemy before it is too late. πόρρω is 'far' (24:28; comparative in Mk. 7:6 par. Mt. 15:8**). πρεσβεία, 'embassy', is an example of use of abstract for the concrete, 'ambassadors' (19:14*). The force of ἐρωτᾷ τὰ πρὸς εἰρήνην is uncertain, and the text is confused. In addition to the UBS text (A D W Θ f1 f13 al lat; TR), there are the variants πρὸς εἰρήνην (ℵ* al); εἰς εἰρήνην (B); τὰ εἰς εἰρήνην (K al; Diglot); εἰρήνην (p⁷⁵ it). The short reading of p⁷⁵ may be due to the influence of Acts 12:20, and the longer reading with τά is more likely to be original and to have caused difficulty to scribes. τὰ πρός could be due to assimilation to 19:42, and hence the Diglot reading may be original, supported indirectly as it is by B. The whole phrase appears to represent Hebrew ša'al bᵉšālôm 'to greet (an opponent)', hence 'to do homage, surrender unconditionally' (1 Sa. 30:21; 2 Sa. 8:10; 11:7; 1 Ch. 18:10; Ps. 121:6; cf. T. Jud. 9:7; W. Foerster, TDNT II, 412), rather than 'to ask for terms of peace' (as AG); on this view the τά (if original) is an accommodation to Greek syntax. Although this point is developed in the parable, it does not appear to have any parabolic significance, unless it emphasises the ridiculous situation of the man who so far from surrendering plunges his army into complete destruction.

(33) The lesson is now drawn. The verse essentially repeats the thought of vs. 26f. in Lucan language; and takes up the theme: 'he cannot be my disciple'; discipleship means saying a final 'good-bye' (ἀποτάσσομαι; 9:61; cf. Philo, LA 3:142) to one's possessions. Just as one should not attempt a venture without having sufficient resources to complete it, but will need to put everything into it in order to be successful, so the disciple must be continually ready (present tense) to give up all that he has got in order to follow Jesus (cf. 9:23; J. Dupont*). The

connection of thought could be smoother, and this confirms that originally independent sayings have here been joined together.

(34) The final saying in the section speaks about the uselessness of salt which has lost its saltiness, and in the present context makes the same point as the two parabolic sayings: there is no point in beginning something which cannot be completed, for the person who cannot sustain the course to the end comes under judgment. The saying is found in Mt. 5:13 and Mk. 9:50, and the evidence suggests that we have separate Marcan and Q versions of the same basic saying; the agreements between Mt. and Lk. against Mk. cannot be explained otherwise. The Lucan saying may have been slightly influenced in wording by Mk., but is essentially from Q. Bultmann, 102, suggests that the saying is originally a piece of secular wisdom, but his conclusion (107) that it was probably not spoken by Jesus is unjustified. He further claims (91, 95) that the introduction and the whole of v. 35 are secondary additions to the basic saying found in Mk. 9:50.

The opening clause is the same as in Mk. καλός here has the sense of 'useful' (AG). The connective οὖν is omitted by p⁷⁵ A D W *pm* lat; TR; *Diglot*. ἅλας, 'salt', replaced the Classical masculine form ἅλς (which survives in Mk. 9:50c); Mt. 5:13; Mk. 9:50; Col. 4:6** (F. Hauck, TDNT I, 228f.). Salt was regarded as an indispensable necessity for life (Sir. 39:26; cf. Sopherim 15:8; SB I, 232–236), and was used as a preservative and flavouring for food, and also as an ingredient in sacrifices. In the present context the thought of its seasoning effect is uppermost. There is no particular application of the specific usefulness of salt to some characteristic of men, as there is in Mt. 5:13 (but cf. W. Nauck*, who argues that salt is a metaphor for wisdom). The thought is simply of loss of usefulness. This may happen even (καί Lk. only) to salt. The verb used, however, is strange. μωραίνω means 'to be, make foolish' (Mt. 5:13; Rom. 1:22; 1 Cor. 1:20**), and no other meaning is attested. Hence the meaning here cannot be 'to make tasteless, insipid' (passive, 'to lose its savour', AV; RV; cf. RSV; NEB; JB; TEV; NIV; TNT). Yet all of the common modern translations adopt this meaning, and the parallel in Mk. is ἄναλον γένηται, which gives the required meaning. The solution to the problem is that the Hebrew root *tpl* has the double meaning of 'saltlessness' (*tāpēl*, Job 1:6) and 'folly' (*tiplah*, Je. 23:13; Job 1:22; 24:12); it is to be presumed that the same root was used in Aramaic in the same way, especially since this would give a word-play with *tabbēl*, 'salted, seasoned' (Black, 166f., adopting a suggestion of J. Lightfoot; Jeremias, *Parables*, 168f.). If so, Mark's version has reproduced the literal meaning of the verb, which fits 'salt' as a subject, whereas the Q version (followed by both Mt. and Lk.) has used the other meaning of the verb, so that what fits the disciples has been inappropriately used within the metaphor in order to bring out the application. Probably one should continue to translate by 'lose its taste', but a footnote explanation should be added. Once this has happened to salt, the question arises: with what can it be made to regain its flavour (ἀρτύω (Mk. 9:50; Col. 4:6**), 'to season', diff. Mt. ἁλίζω, 'to salt')? It is unlikely that the subject of ἀρτυθήσεται is 'food', since this word is not present in the context, and the change of subject in the next clause back to 'salt' would be awkward; moreover, in Mk. the reference is plainly to the salt. But what does the question mean? Strictly speaking, salt cannot lose its flavour; a rabbinic story attributed to R. Joshua b. Hananiah (c. AD 90) states that salt can no more easily lose its flavour than a mule can bear a foal (Bekh. 8b; SB I, 236; TDNT I, 229). This saying may be a deliberate contradiction of the saying of Jesus. (G. Bertram, TDNT IV, 837–839, thinks that the rabbinic saying has preserved the original point: just as salt cannot become inactive, so the gospel which Jesus gave to his disciples cannot become insipid and perish. This point was then lost in transmission, and the saying was taken to refer to the possibility of a change in the disciples. This hypothesis is speculative, and is unnecessary if in fact salt can lose its flavour.)

The explanation probably lies in the nature of Palestinian salt. It was obtained by evaporation from the Dead Sea. Since the water of the Dead Sea contains various substances, evaporation produced a mixture of crystals of common salt and carnallite ($KCl\ MgCl_2\ 6H_2O$); since the former crystallises out first, it is possible to collect relatively pure salt by fractional collection of the first crystals, but it would be easy to mistake crystals of bitter-tasting carnallite for salt, especially if contaminated with fine clay, etc, which would also produce a stale taste. Carnallite, or gypsum out of which the salt content had been dissolved away, would be 'salt that had become tasteless' (cf. F. Hauck, TDNT I, 229; Jeremias, *Parables*, 168f.; further information supplied by J. Tinsley, Professor of Soil Science in the University of Aberdeen). An alternative, but much less likely explanation is that blocks of salt were used in ovens to catalyse the burning of the dung which was used as fuel; after a time the salt loses its catalytic power and hinders the burning (F. Scholten, cited by Jeremias, ibid; L. Köhler, cited by G. Bertram, TDNT IV, 838; E. H. Riesenfeld, 'Salz als Katalysator und Antikatalysator', *Die Naturwissenschaft* 23, 1935, 311–320 (not accessible to me)). But the saying refers to 'taste' rather than usefulness.

(35) Disciples who cannot stay the course are as useless as 'salt' which has lost its flavour. It has no further use. Luke here differs from Mt. by including the detail that the salt is not useful (εὔθετος, 9:62) for the land or the manure heap (κοπρία**, cf. 13:8). This saying was sufficiently difficult to lead F. Perles to propose that the original Aramaic should have been translated, 'It is fit neither for seasoning nor for dunging', but Black, 166f., shows that this is not possible linguistically. The difficulty arises because it is not clear that salt could be used as a fertiliser or kept on a manure heap. Jeremias, *Parables*, 27 n. 12, states that there is no Palestinian evidence for the use of salt as fertiliser; the practice of 'sowing with salt' and references to salty wastes suggest that

salt made land infertile (Dt. 29:22; Jdg. 9:25; Je. 17:6; Zp. 2:9; Job 39:6; Ps. 107:34). However, H. Gressmann* was able to adduce evidence for the use of salty earth as a fertiliser in modern Egypt. E. Deatrick* claims that while salt kills weeds it also improves the soil at a deeper level, possibly by the liberation of potassium (from the potassium chloride in Dead Sea salt), and also that when added to fermenting dung it would slow down the process of fermentation until the dung is ready to be used. Possibly these two uses of salt are in mind here. On the other hand, J. Tinsley thinks that if the 'salt' were applied directly to the soil, the magnesium chloride in carnallite would be more harmful to it than the potassium chloride would be beneficial. No explanation of the saying is thus free from difficulty. While it seems clear that the substance referred to by Jesus would have been useless as a fertiliser, it is possible that it might have been used as a weedkiller or to slow down the fermentation of dung. But in any case, the intention of the saying is plain. The difficult phrase is not present in Mt., and it may be a Lucan expansion of an original 'it is good for nothing'. Such salt is good for nothing; people simply throw it out: Matthew has 'to be trampled down by men' – they regard it with contempt (cf. Lk. 14:30).

Luke follows the saying with an injunction to hear it with care, repeated from 8:8; here it may be drawn from Q (cf. Mt. 11:15).

The whole saying is addressed to the disciples in Mt. 5:13. Here it is addressed to a group including would-be disciples (Jeremias, ibid.) and committed disciples who are warned against failure to persevere (J. Dupont*, 576–579). It is unlikely that it was originally meant as a warning to the Jewish leaders who thought that God would never cast them off (Schniewind, *Matthäus*, 51; Schulz, 472).

f. The Gospel for the Outcast (15:1–32)

There can be no doubt that ch. 15 forms one self-contained and artistically constructed unit with a single theme. The theme is announced at the outset: Jesus is criticised for welcoming sinners and having fellowship with them, and he gives parabolic teaching to justify his attitude. The introduction (15:1–3) is followed by two short, similarly constructed parables (15:4–7, 8–10) and one longer parable (15:11–32) which all make the same point: the joy which is experienced by a person who recovers what he has lost. The applications of the first two parables make it quite explicit that such joy is a reflection of the joy felt by God when he recovers what he has lost (cf. E. Rasco*). The third parable, however, broadens out the theme by investigating the situation of the lost person and by looking at the attitude of the person who was apparently not lost and yet resented the joy felt over the returning prodigal.

The section has obvious thematic links with the surrounding material. The thought of God's love, demonstrated in the ministry of

Jesus, for the outcasts of society and the poor has been a frequent topic in the Gospel already, and came to expression in 14:15–24. The wasteful ways of the prodigal son give a forward link with the character of the unjust steward, although the link here is not a strong one:

The literary pattern of the section has been studied by W. R. Farmer* who finds here a pattern of an introduction followed by two short, similarly constructed parables and a longer parable, exactly as in 13:1–9; the structure is that of the *chreia* with a parable added to illustrate the point. The language is not Lucan, and indicates that the section as a whole was drawn from Luke's special source. This conclusion has been largely confirmed by the linguistic investigation of J. Jeremias* with the important qualification that Jeremias regards vs. 1–3 as being a Lucan formulation that may have replaced an original introduction which is now lost. A similar conclusion is reached by Dupont, II, 233–249.

A different approach to the section is offered by H. B. Kossen*: the unifying principle is held to be the use of Je. 31:10–20 in which are depicted God as a shepherd, Rachel weeping for her children, and Ephraim as the dear son who returns to God. But while the picture of God's love for Ephraim may lie behind the imagery of the third parable, the earlier allusions are too vague to compel the view that this chapter has dictated the composition of Lk. 15.

See H. B. Kossen, 'Quelques remarques sur l'ordre des paraboles dans Luc xv et sur la structure de Matthieu xviii 8–14', Nov.T 1, 1956, 75–80; W. R. Farmer, 'Notes on a Literary and Form-Critical Analysis of Some of the Synoptic Material peculiar to Luke', NTS 8, 1961–62, 301–316; Perrin, 90–102; E. Rasco, 'Les paraboles de Luc XV', in de la Potterie, 165–183; Linnemann, 65–73; Dupont II, 233–249; J. Jeremias, 'Tradition und Redaktion in Lukas 15', ZNW 62, 1971, 172–189; K. E. Bailey, 142–206.

i.. Introduction 15:1–3

The problem of the introductory verses is simply whether they are pre-Lucan (with some Lucan editing) or a Lucan composition, views supported by W. R. Farmer and J. Jeremias respectively (see previous section). Both agree that the language of v. 3 is Lucan. Farmer claims that the rest of the section is relatively free of Lucan mannerisms, but Jeremias is able to assemble a number of these. There is little that might be regarded as pre-Lucan. For Jeremias the decisive point is that the section is closely parallel in wording to Luke's own redaction (5:29–32) of Mk. 2:15–17, and hence is probably based on it. Moreover, the introduction indicates that Jesus was speaking to the Pharisees and scribes, but the immediately following parable assumes that the audience included herdsmen; herdsmen, however, belonged to a despised occupation, and would not be included in Pharisaic circles. Hence the parable and the introduction were originally separate, and the linking of them was done by a non-Palestinian who did not understand the social set-up. Finally, while the introduction refers only to one parable (v. 3; but see note there), it is in fact followed by three parables. The weight of the argument linguistically is on the side of Jeremias, and it should probably be concluded that the introduction is Lucan (cf. Dupont II, 233–237); nevertheless, this does not exclude the possibility that Luke has to some extent made use of existing material which he has rewritten in the manner of 5:29–32. It is possible that the introduction originally was linked to the parable of the prodigal son (Grundmann, 304), in which case it was pre-Lucan, and then separated from the parable by the two short parables still at a second, pre-Lucan stage. K. E. Bailey, 147, goes so far as to claim that Jesus deliberately addressed an audience of Pharisees as shepherds in order to shock their sensitivity and expose their prejudice against a despised occupation.

(1) The introduction depicts the situation in the imperfect tense; the periphrastic form ἦσαν ... ἐγγίζοντες is perhaps meant to indicate that the general circumstances of Jesus' ministry rather than one particular incident are in mind. The order αὐτῷ ἐγγίζοντες is reversed in TR; Diglot. ἐγγίζω (7:12; et al.) is used here only of the crowds. πάντες is Lucan and hyperbolic; cf. 5:17. Grundmann, 305, suggests that the meaning is almost adverbial – 'überall'. For the combination of τελῶναι and ἁμαρτωλοί cf. Mk. 2:15 diff. Lk.; Mk. 2:16 par. Lk. 5:30. The use of ἀκούειν gives a verbal link with 14:35: such were the kind of people who did have ears to listen to Jesus.

(2) διαγογγύζω, 'to murmur' (19:7**), diff. 5:30, γογγύζω, could be pre-Lucan, but Luke himself frequently uses δια- compounds (J. Jeremias*, 186 n. 48). The unusual word order 'Pharisees and scribes' (5:30, diff. Mk.; Mk. 7:1, 5; Mt. 15:1; contrast Lk. 5:21; 6:7; 11:53; Mk. 2:16; Mt. 5:20; et al.) is a further link to 5:30. The use of τε (omitted by A W Δ fl f13 pm; TR; Diglot) is probably Lucan (J. Jeremias* 186; correcting his earlier view in Parables, 100 n. 42). It joins two closely associated words more tightly together (MH III, 339). It is not clear whether ὅτι should be taken as recitativum or as an interrogative (a possibility raised for this passage; 19:7; and Acts 11:3 by H. J. Cadbury, 'Lexical Notes on Luke-Acts. IV. On Direct Quotation, with some Uses of ὅτι and εἰ', JBL 48, 1929, 423–425; Jeremias, Parables, 39), but there are no strong reasons for abandoning the accepted interpretation. οὗτος is strongly derisory; cf. 14:30. J. Jeremias*, 187f., argues that προσδέχομαι (2:25) is used here alone of receiving guests, and may be pre-Lucan, since in 5:29f. Jesus himself is a guest and not the host. However, the word has probably a wider meaning than that of welcoming guests (cf. Rom. 16:2; Phil. 2:29; Dupont, II, 234 n. 2). συνεσθίω, 'to eat with', is Lucan (Acts 10:41; 11:3; 1 Cor. 5:11; Gal. 2:12**). The Pharisees were unable to share table-fellowship with those whom they considered sinful; cf. M. Ex. 18:1 (65a): 'Let not a man associate with the wicked, not even to bring him to the law' (SB II, 208; cf. I, 498f.).

(3) The statement is thoroughly Lucan in style; cf. 4:23; 5:36; *et al.* The singular form παραβολή is also followed by more than one parable in 5:36 (cf. 12:41 for a similar backward reference), and it is possible that Luke understood the word collectively ('a parabolic discourse' – Lagrange, 416; Grundmann, 305).

ii. The Lost Sheep 15:4–7

The parable of the lost sheep in its Lucan form describes the joy of the shepherd who finds one of a large flock of sheep which has become separated from its companions and lost. The picture is applied to the joy of God over the sinner who repents. The conclusion brings out the greater joy felt over the one sinner who repents in comparison with the 'just' people who do not need to repent, and thus takes up a feature which is brought out more explicitly in Matthew's version of the parable than in Luke's. The application in the Matthaean form of the parable stresses the desire of God that none should be lost, and in its context backs up an exhortation to the disciples (or their leaders) to exercise pastoral care over the weaker members of the community. A third form of the parable in G. Thomas 107 draws a gnostic lesson from it, by making the shepherd love the lost sheep, which was the biggest in the flock, more than the others.

The differences between the Lucan and Matthaean forms are sufficiently great to make it unlikely that both Evangelists are directly dependent upon the same source. Even when allowance is made for their editorial work, we are still left with two independent versions of the parable. There is no reason why Jesus himself should not have used the same basic parable more than once and for different purposes. Nevertheless, it is also possible that one original parable has been developed differently in two separate traditions. A decision depends on the nature of the varied applications of the parable in Lk. and Mt.: does either of these form an original part of the parable? The Lucan application is generally thought to be secondary (Dupont, II, 244; cf. Bultmann, 184), and to be based on Mt. 18:13b, but J. Jeremias*, 181–185, has argued on linguistic grounds that only v. 7c is due to Lucan redaction, the rest of the application being pre-Lucan. The λέγω ὑμῖν application is so frequent in the parables that it appears to be original. The difficulty with this view is that v. 7 then gives a close parallel to Mt. 18:13b, and it can be argued that it is strange to have an ἀμὴν λέγω ὑμῖν statement within the parabolic framework followed by a λέγω ὑμῖν application. Further, it can be argued that Lk. 15:5f. is a Lucan expansion to bring out the motif of joining in rejoicing and thus act as a foil to the motif of the elder brother who would not join in the rejoicing. Mt. 18:13 would then be the original ending of the parable and Mt. 18:14 a secondary application by Matthew. Despite the plausibility of this view, it is on the whole more likely that Luke has preserved the original ending of the parable and that Matthew has abbreviated it in order to introduce his v. 14: So far as the actual content of the parables is concerned, there are no decisive grounds for regarding one form as more original than the other: contrast the defences of Matthaean originality (Bultmann, 184f.; Linnemann, 67–70; J. Dupont*, 336; Schulz, 387–389) and of Lucan originality (W. Pesch, *Matthäus der Seelsorger*, Stuttgart, 1966, 28–30; K. E. Bailey, 152–153).

See 15:1–32 note; Schulz, 387–391; J. Dupont, 'Les implications christologiques de la parabole de la brebis perdue', in Dupont, *Jésus*, 331–350; K. E. Bailey, 142–156.

(4) The parable begins with a rhetorical question (τίς ... ἐξ ὑμῶν ...) which is characteristic of the teaching of Jesus (11:5 note). The addition of ἄνθρωπος seems unnecessary, but is also found in Mt. 18:12, and similar additions are found in 11:5; 14:31; 15:8; Mt. 7:9; 12:11; it may be meant to give a deliberate contrast with γυνή in 15:8, in which case the two parables will originally have formed a pair. Although Bultmann, 184, regards Matthew's introduction (τί ὑμῖν δοκεῖ;) as original, it is in fact editorial (Schulz, 387). ἔχων is conditional (cf. Mt. ἐάν γένηται ...), as in 11:5, 11; the variant ὃς ἔξει (D; ὃς ἔχει, *Diglot*; cf. ἀπολέσῃ (B* D) for ἀπολέσας) is secondary. A hundred sheep would be a herd of fairly normal size for a small farmer (Jeremias, *Parables*, 133). For πρόβατον (15:6*; cf. 10:4) see H. Preisker and S. Schulz, TDNT VI, 689–692. ἀπόλλυμι (9:24; 15:8f.; 17:33) is the appropriate word for losing an animal – or a son (15:24) – and forms the connecting link between the three parables. The reference is no doubt to the shepherd counting his sheep in the evening and discovering that the number is one short. Matthew has πλανάομαι (Lk. 21:8) throughout, which emphasises more the foolish action of the sheep. It is probable that πλανάομαι is original, and that the Lucan form is an alteration to conform the parable to 15:8f., 24 (cf. Lagrange, 417; Schulz, 387). καταλείπω (5:28) and ἀφίημι (Mt.) could be translation variants; Luke uses the latter to mean 'to leave' only when following Mk. (Lagrange, 417). The same is true of ἐν τῇ ἐρήμῳ and ἐπὶ τὰ ὄρη, which represent Aramaic bᵉṭura (Black, 133; Jeremias, *Parables*, 133). Perrin, 99–101, argues that the shepherd, forgetful of normal caution, simply leaves the flock untended in the wilderness, while he hastens off after the lost sheep. The point of the parable is not the love shown by God, but the joy that arises from the new situation in the kingdom of God. This is most unlikely; it is obviously presupposed that the sheep are left in the care of a helper (cf. Jn. 10:3). On the contrary, the parable takes up the theme of God's care for his flock (Ezk. 34:12, 23f.) which is now fulfilled in the Messiah (Grundmann, 307). The search is carried on until it is successful (ἕως), diff. Mt. who leaves the result uncertain (ἐάν ...).

(5) When the sheep has been found the shepherd carries it home on his shoulders (ὦμος, Mt. 23:4**); cf. Is. 40:11; SB II, 209. The action illustrates the care of the shepherd, perhaps also his triumphant air, and represents normal rural practice. He is full of joy at his success. The

verb belongs to the story (Mt. 18:13), but the use of the participle in this way is probably Lucan (cf. 19:6, 37; Acts 5:41; 8:39).

(6) This motif is expanded in the shepherd's summons (συγκαλέω, 9:1, but the use of the active for the middle here (corrected in some MSS, BD 316¹) is pre-Lucan) to his friends and neighbours (14:12) to share in his rejoicing, no doubt at a feast. This motif is lacking from Mt., but corresponds to 15:9. This may suggest that the simpler form attested by Mt. was expanded when this parable was linked to the next parable; but we have already seen that the parables probably formed a pair from the start. It is therefore more probable that if both Gospels are following the same ultimate source Matthew's form is an abbreviation. If so, Mt. 18:13 may well be an adaptation of Lk. 15:7 rather than vice versa.

(7) In Mt. the λέγω ὑμῖν formula (with an original ἀμήν prefixed) introduces Jesus' comment on the shepherd, but here it introduces the application of the parable. The οὕτως is also found in Matthew's separate application (Mt. 18:14). χαρά is a Lucan motif (1:14; 15:10), but is here pre-Lucan, since retranslation into Aramaic (ḥedhwa) gives paronomasia at this point (Black, 184). (This shows that Jeremias's earlier attempt, Parables, 40, to explain Mt. θέλημα as a translation-variant for ra'ᵃwa, is wrong). ἐν τῷ οὐρανῷ veils a reference to God (so rightly Mt. 18:14) and probably (cf. 15:10) to the angels. The joy is over a sinner who repents, and thus obeys the call in 5:32; cf. 15:10. By contrast, a rabbinic quotation speaks of God's joy over the downfall of the godless (t. Sanh. 14:10; SB II, 209). The comparative indicates that μᾶλλον is to be supplied, and the comparison may mean 'more than' (AG; Grundmann, 307f.) or 'instead of' (cf. 18:14 for the thought). The former interpretation is more likely: God is, after all, also pleased with the righteous (1:6). The latter interpretation fits only if the phrase is ironic, and 'who do not need to repent' refers to 'people who think that they are righteous and have no need to repent' (so L. Schottroff* (15:11–32 note), 34f.). This last phrase is Lucan (cf. 5:31f.), and may have been inspired by the presence of the participle μετανοοῦντι. L. Schottroff*, 32–35, thinks that the whole verse is a summary of Lucan theology (salvation only for those who repent and not for the seemingly righteous; joy now in heaven over the repentant, rather than at the last judgment), and that it stands in tension with the parable itself which is concerned with God's joy and not with the attitude of the sinner. In fact, however, only the motif of repentance is Lucan and does not spring directly from the parabolic situation.

iii. The Lost Coin 15:8–10

The construction of the parable of the lost coin is almost identical with that of the lost sheep, and it is likely that the two parables originally formed a pair in the teaching of Jesus. The hypothesis that one parable has been formed by the tradition (Bultmann, 185; Klostermann, 155) or even by Luke himself (Conzelmann, 103; Drury, 155f.) on the pattern of the other rests on the unlikely assumption that Jesus could never have repeated himself, and on the postulate that two similar parables could not have been separated by an application attached to the first of them (Bultmann): Dupont, II, 248, rightly observes *ad hominem* that, if Bultmann regards the application as itself secondary, it need not originally have separated the two parables, and that in any case each of the two parables requires an application.

Perrin, 101f., who regards v. 10 as secondary (without any evidence, beyond an appeal to the 'parallel' in v. 7), argues that the parable has a message akin to that of the treasure hidden in the field. But in the latter case the joy is over finding something *new*, and the situations are not parallel. Nothing justifies us in finding any other lesson than that recorded by Luke.

The thought and situation in the parable are Palestinian. The language, however, shows greater signs of Lucan editing than in the previous parable (J. Jeremias* (15:1–32 note), 184).

(8) For ἤ, cf. 14:31. The parable has the form of a rhetorical question, which Jeremias, *Parables*, 134, regards as extending to the end of v. 9, although translators find it easier to put the question mark at the end of v. 8. The preceding parable was about a man; now the picture is complemented by that of a woman who possesses ten drachmae. The δραχμή** (cf. δίδραχμον, Mt. 17:24**) was a Greek silver coin, roughly equivalent in value to the Roman *denarius*. About 300 BC it represented the value of a sheep, but it was considerably devalued during the first century AD. It is not certain whether such coins were generally available in Syria during AD 20–60, and it may be that Luke is using the name of a coin familiar to his readers (cf. O. Roller, *Münzen, Geld und Vermögensverhältnisse in den Evangelien*, 1929). The money would appear to represent the woman's savings or dowry, and it is often suggested that the ten coins may have been worn on a string as a headdress (cf. Kel. 12:7; Jeremias, *Jerusalem*, 100; *Parables*, 134f.); but there is no proof that this was so (Klostermann, 157).

If one is lost, great efforts are made to find it. The picture is similar to that in a rabbinic parable from about AD 200 of a man who loses something valuable in the house, lights many lamps and hunts until he finds it: so ought men to study the Torah which is of eternal value (M. Cant. 1:1 (79b); SB II, 212). The woman lives in a peasant's house with a low door and no windows. She must light a lamp (11:33) and sweep the house (11:25), and search carefully (ἐπιμελῶς**; possibly Lucan, cf. 10:34f.; Acts 27:3; Dupont, II, 248 n. 6), until she finds it.

(9) The discovery leads to rejoicing, which the neighbours are invited to share – no doubt on a modest scale (Jeremias, *Parables*, 135), but none the less with great feeling.

(10) In the same way, says Jesus (did the original saying com-

mence with ἀμήν?) there is joy over a repentant sinner in the presence of the angels (cf. 12:8). As the text stands, the reference to the angels is hardly a periphrasis for the name of God, since God is mentioned in the verse – unless we are to assume that τοῦ θεοῦ is secondary (cf. 22:69 diff. Mk. 14:62). The thought is of the angels rejoicing along with God (for angels rejoicing cf. SB II, 212); Lagrange, 417; A. F. Walls, ' "In the Presence of the Angels" (Luke xv. 10)', Nov.T 3, 1959, 314–316).

iv. The Lost Son 15:11–32

Of all the parables this one is perhaps the easiest to interpret in broad outline and yet the most open to a variety of interpretation, dependent on where the main emphasis is thought to lie. In its present context it is meant to illustrate the pardoning love of God that cares for the outcasts; the sinful son is welcomed home by the father and his former status is restored. The central figure is the father, just as in the previous parables the shepherd and the housewife stand at the centre, and H. Thielicke's famous description of the parable as being concerned with 'the waiting Father' is correct. But at the same time the figure of the son is developed; we see his sin and his need, his repentance and his return, and so the parable is also concerned with 'the joy of repentance' (J. Schniewind's phrase). Nevertheless, in the end it is not so much the repentance of the son as the communal joy of the restored and reunited family which is the culminating note in the parable. What, then, is the place of the other son? It would not be inapt to regard the story as 'the parable of the lost sons' (cf. Jüngel, 160–164), since it emerges that the elder son's relationship to his father is not what it should be. But this is a subordinate detail, and the question of the elder brother's relationship to his younger brother is more important: will the elder brother share the father's joy at the return of the prodigal? – this is the unanswered question which is addressed to the hearers of the parable. So the parable is ultimately concerned to justify the attitude of God to sinners. In this way it justifies the attitude of Jesus himself, since he is able to defend himself and his attitude to sinners by appeal to the attitude of God. Implicit, therefore, in the parable is the claim that Jesus acts as the representative of God in pardoning sinners.

What is portrayed in the parable, therefore, is the love of God for his wayward children, a theme already developed in the OT: with reference to Je. 3:22 G. Quell notes how the backsliding Israelites are summoned to return to God as to a Father, and 'in Jer. 31:18–20, where the sons of Ephraim are now the son, one may clearly perceive the original of the parable of the prodigal'; cf. Ho. 11:1–9; Is. 63:15f. (TDNT V, 973).

At the same time the theme of the parable is drawn from contemporary experience (cf. SB II, 216), Danker, 170, cites appositely a papyrus letter from a son to his mother: 'Greetings: I hope you are in good health; it is my constant prayer to Lord Serapis. I did not expect you to come to Metropolis, therefore I did not go there myself. At the same time, I was ashamed to go to Kanaris because I am so shabby. I am writing to tell you that I am naked. I plead with you, forgive me. I know well enough what I have done to myself. I have learned my lesson. I know I made a mistake. I have heard from Postumus who met you in the area of Arisnoe. Unfortunately he told you everything. Don't you know that I would rather be a cripple than owe so much as a cent to any man? I plead, I plead with you . . . (Signed) Antonios Longus, your son.'

It has been left to G. V. Jones* to show that the parable expresses universal truths of human experience and to offer an existential interpretation in terms of freedom and estrangement, the personalness of life, longing and return, anguish and reconciliation. Jones, however, is careful to point out that this discovery of existential truth in the parable does not exclude the presence of religious truth.

Despite the proposals of earlier scholars such as Wellhausen, 81–85, and (cautiously) J. Weiss, 483f., to separate the parable into two parts, vs. 15–24a and 24b–32, Bultmann, 212, is justified in maintaining the unity of the parable; cf. Manson, *Sayings*, 284. More recently dissection has been attempted by J. T. Sanders*, on the grounds that no other parable is *zweigipfelig* and that there is a concentration of Lucanisms in the second part of the parable. He proposes that an original parable which deferded Jesus' association with the lost was altered by Luke into an attack on the Pharisees so as to make a bridge with the development of this theme in ch. 16. But while the parable has two parts, it has one point. Above all, Sanders' linguistic arguments have been completely refuted by J. J. O'Rourke* and J. Jeremias* 172–181.

The unity of the parable is also defended by L. Schottroff*, but this is achieved by ascribing the whole parable to Luke himself (cf. Drury, 156). The themes of the parable, repentance and forgiveness leading to joy, are those of Lucan theology, especially as seen in Acts, and hence the parable reflects the mind of Luke. The elder son represents a religion which relies on its own ability and imposes a claim upon the Father, instead of recognising its dependence on the kind of fatherly love shown in ordinary human relations (this theme is illustrated from a speech of Pseudo-Quintilian). The Pharisees could not have recognised themselves in the figure of the elder son, since that would mean that they recognised Jesus as bringing God's salvation to sinners (which they did not recognise), and also that their religion was one of self-righteousness (which it was not). Rather, the parable exemplifies later Christian polemic against the Pharisees.

This thesis is vulnerable at several points. First, it fails to reckon with the linguistic evidence for a pre-Lucan origin assembled by Jeremias. Admittedly, this in itself does not guarantee authorship by Jesus, but it rules out composition by Luke himself. Second, it does not examine the soteriology of Jesus himself, whose teaching was certainly concerned with sin and repentance, nor does it ask what continuity there may have been between the teaching of Jesus, as mediated by early tradition, and the thought of Luke himself. It is true that Luke himself is particularly interested in stressing repentance (5:32 diff. Mk. 2:17; cf. 15:7; 17:3f.), but it should also be noted that the term 'repentance' does not occur in the parable. Third, it is doubtful whether the elder son plays the part in the parable ascribed to him by Schottroff; she is guilty of un-justifiable allegorisation in finding a picture of Pharisaic religion in his attitude.

Attempts have been made to illuminate the parable from other points of view. K. H. Rengstorf* argues that the symbolism associated with the son's return suggests that it had been preceded by k*etsatsah*. This was a Jewish ceremony of cutting off a member of a society who had broken its rules, especially by selling property or marrying without permission. The rite could be reversed by an appropriate ceremony and in this case it involved reinstatement as a son. The bestowal of the robe, ring and shoes fit into this pattern and indicate the presence of kingly motifs. While this suggestion throws considerable light on the background of the parable, it is probable that it goes too far in regarding the parable as being built round this motif. The actual act of k*etsatsah* is not mentioned or even hinted at, and is a deduction from the language in vs. 24 and 32 where the son is said to have been 'dead'. The attitude of the father hardly suggests that he had rejected the son. Moreover, to make the theory fit, Rengstorf has to admit that the original 'kingly' ele-ment in the parable has been edited away in order that it might be more intelligible to a non-Palestinian audience. It is always dangerous to postulate an earlier form for a narrative, and then to admit that it has been almost entirely removed; one may well ask whether the hints are sufficient to demonstrate the earlier form. What Rengstorf has done is to show the kind of thought-world which surrounds the parable, to indicate the kind of emotions which would arise in such a Jewish situation.

Another important aspect of the parable is the legal situation represented in it (D. Daube, art. cit. in 12:13 note; Derrett, 100–125; cf. Schottroff, 39–41). While there is some uncertainty about the precise details, the general picture is clear. It should be remembered that neither Jesus nor the Evangelists were lawyers, and we should not expect from them the legal finesse which contemporary lawyers may be tempted to expect.

See Jeremias, *Parables*, 128–132; Jüngel, 160–164; G. V. Jones, *The Art and Truth of the Parables*, London, 1964, 167–205; Linnemann, 73–81; K. H. Rengstorf, *Die Re-Investitur des verlorenen Sohnes in der Gleichniserzählung Jesu Luk. 15, 11–32*, Köln, 1967; J. T. Sanders, 'Tradition and Redaction in Luke xv. 11–32', NTS 15, 1968–69, 433–438; Derrett, 100–125 (originally as 'Law in the New Testament: The Parable of the Prodigal Son', NTS 14, 1967–68, 56–74); J. J. O'Rourke, 'Some Notes on Luke xv. 11–32', NTS 18, 1971–72, 431–433; L. Schottroff, 'Das Gleichnis vom verlorenen Sohn', ZTK 68, 1971, 27–52; I. Broer, 'Das Gleichnis vom verlorenen Sohn und die Theologie des Lukas', NTS 20, 1973–74, 453–462; C. E. Carlston, 'Reminiscence and Redaction in Luke 15:11–32', JBL 94, 1975, 368–390; K. E. Bailey, 158–206. See also D. Daube (as in 12:13 note); J. Jeremias (as in 15:1–32 note).

(11) The parable is very simply added to the preceding ones: εἶπεν δέ (cf. 4:24; et al.). For the parabolic beginning cf. 10:30; 12:16; et al.; and especially Mt. 21:28 for the 'two sons' motif. At the outset the audience is made aware of the elder son, although he does not play any part in the story until v. 25. On the motif of the younger son cf. Derrett, 116–121.

(12) The younger son (νεώτερος, 15:13; 22:26; Jn. 21:18; Acts 5:6; 1 Tim. 5:1; et al.) may well have been about 17 years or more, since the story implies that he was unmarried (marriage took place normally at about 18–20 years, but by no means universally). The story begins with his request for the portion (μέρος, 11:36; et al.) of the family property (οὐσία, 15:13**) that fell to him (ἐπιβάλλω, 5:36; et al.; cf. τὸ μέρος τὸ ἐπιβάλλον, Ditt. Syll.³ 346, 36). The OT law prescribed that the first son was entitled to a double share of the property, so that here the younger son might expect one-third on the death of his father; if, however, a disposition was made to take effect earlier, the share would be less, possibly two-ninths (Derrett, 107). In the latter case, the son usually gained the right to the capital, but since the father retained the usufruct, he could not dispose of the property (cf. BB 8:7). This practice, however, does not quite fit the situation here. The younger son asks for, and obtains, the right of disposal of his share. The law allowed for this possibility, but the son may have remained under a moral obligation to his father with regard to what he did with his inheritance. In any case, the younger son thereby deprived himself of any further claims on the father's estate, as he himself later recognised (v. 19). When the younger son received his portion absolutely, the father apparently also made over the rest of the inheritance to the elder son, while himself retaining the usufruct; hence his remark in v. 31. If so, however, this means that the father could hardly reinstate the prodigal as a son without making in-roads upon the property already granted to the elder son (L. Schottroff*, 39–41). D. Daube* therefore suggests that the father may not have followed the strict letter of the law; he may have given the younger brother his share without making a special gift to the elder son. But this solution does not do justice to vs. 12 and 31. It is more probable that the father followed the letter of the law (which Daube allows to be possible), and that the question of any further inheritance by the younger son is simply not raised in the dramatic setting of the parable.

Whatever, then, be the precise position, the father acted in accordance with the son's wish. For ὁ δέ, א° A B L pc the variant καί is read by א* D W Θ f1 f13 pl latt; TR; Diglot; p⁷⁵ omits the connective. διαιρέω is 'to distribute, divide' (1 Cor. 12:11**), and βίος (8:14) here means 'means of subsistence' (15:30; 21:4 par. Mk. 12:44; 1 Jn. 2:16; 3:17).

(13) The litotes οὐ πολύς, 'few', is Lucan (Acts 1:5). συνάγω has the sense 'to turn into cash' (AG; Creed, 199), rather than 'to gather together'. The younger son accordingly realised his assets, and

proceeded to ignore any moral claim that his father might have on the property. On the forms πάντα (א A W Θ f1 f13 pl; TR; Diglot) and ἅπαντα (p⁷⁵ B D pc) cf. 2:39 note. ἀποδημέω is 'to go on a journey', 20:9; μακρός is 'far away, distant' (19:12), usually 'long' (20:47; Mk. 12:40**; cf. Lk. 15:20 for the adverbial use). Jeremias, Parables, 129, comments on the vast number of Jews who left their homeland for the money-making possibilities of the big cities. The son's motive, however, was different. He proceeded to waste his money (διασκορπίζω, 16:1 in this sense; cf. 1:51) by living ἀσώτως**, i.e. 'recklessly' or 'on dissolute pleasures'; cf. Eph. 5:18; Tit. 1:6; 1 Pet. 4:4. In view of Athenaeus 11, p. 485A ἀπὸ τῶν εἰς τὰς μέθας καὶ τὰς ἀσωτίας πολλὰ ἀναλισκότων (cited by AG) the two senses should probably be combined. The younger son's way of life was by no means unique, as is indicated by the interesting parallel in P. Flor. 99, 6ff. (cited by AG s.v. ἀσώτως; W. Foerster, TDNT I, 507 n. 4).

(14) δαπανάω, 'to spend' (Acts 21:24; cf. δαπάνη, 14:28), may have the connotation of wasteful spending (AG, quoting Suidas). It is when the young man's resources are at an end that the realities of life hit him. ἰσχυρά is the standing Greek epithet with λιμός (Thucydides 3:85). ὑστερέομαι (22:35) is 'to be in want, lack'. The use of ἄρχομαι (3:8; et al.) is Semitic and probably from Luke's source.

(15) κολλάομαι (10:11) can be used of attachment to a person (Acts 5:13; 8:29; 9:26; 10:28; 17:34). For εἷς used as an indefinite pronoun cf. 5:3; et al. πολίτης, 'citizen', may be Lucan (19:14; Acts 21:39; Heb. 8:11**), but could equally well be from his source. The change of subject (unannounced) with ἔπεμψεν is Semitic (Jeremias, Parables, 129). ἀγρός may be used in the plural to mean 'farm(s), hamlet(s)', and this meaning is suggested for the present passage by AG. But the evidence (Jos. 19:6 – a mistranslation – and Jos. Ant. 17:193) is weak; it would appear that the word can mean 'countryside', i.e. areas where farmhouses can be found (cf. 8:34; 9:12), and possibly 'farm' (singular); but here the reference is to the fields that formed part of the man's farm. The man was a gentile, and therefore able to keep pigs (8:32f.), an occupation forbidden to Jews ('None may rear swine anywhere', BK 7:7). Feeding (βόσκω, 8:32) them was an unclean occupation (Lv. 11:7), and thoroughly degrading for a Jew: 'Cursed is the man who rears swine or who teaches his son Greek philosophy' (BK 82b; cf. SB I, 492f.; cf. 448–450). See also Ahikar 8:34 syr.

(16) Feeding swine was thus about as low as Jews could go. To wish to share their food was the nadir of degradation. The imperfect ἐπεθύμει may represent an unfulfilled desire (Jeremias, Parables, 129 n., 184; Words, 208, citing 16:21; 17:22; 22:15; but such food was eaten, and the linguistic point is not compelling (Schürmann, Paschamahlbericht, 11). χορτασθῆναι (6:21) is the reading of p⁷⁵ א B D L f1 f13 al e f sy⁽ᶜ⁾ sa, and was accepted by UBS on the basis of the external evidence (Metzger, 164; cf. WH App., 62). Other MSS have γεμίσαι τὴν

κοιλίαν ('to fill his stomach'); so A *Θ pm* lat sy^{s p} bo; TR; *Synopsis; Diglot* (and RSV mg; NEB t; JB; TEV; NIV). It is more likely that this strong, almost crude expression was corrected by scribes (Grundmann, 312 n. 23), than that it was later added to the text; here, therefore, the inferior MSS may preserve the correct reading. The UBS text has the preposition ἐκ; the alternative reading should have ἀπό (A W *Θ pm*; TR; *Diglot*), but *Synopsis* prints ἐκ, since it does not regard the two variants as being connected. κεράτιον**, literally 'little horn', is used in the plural for carob pods (*ceratonia siliqua*), the fruit of a Palestinian tree, used for fodder and eaten only by very poor people: 'When the Israelites are reduced to carob pods, then they repent' (R. Acha, *c.* AD 320, in Lv. R. 35 (132c); SB II, 213–215). K. E. Bailey, 171–173, thinks that a wild, almost inedible variety is meant. ὧν is by relative attraction for ἅ (cf. 1:4 note). Whatever friends the young man had had in the days of his wealth had melted away, and he experienced the fulfilment of Sir. 12:4–6. The omission of the object with δίδωμι is Semitic (Jeremias, *Words*, 177). It is not necessary to assume (with Jeremias, *Parables*, 130) that the youth was reduced to stealing: would he not have received some tiny wage for looking after the swine?

(17) In his misery he realised that his own wrongdoing had brought about his fate: 'When a son (in need in a strange land) goes barefoot, then he remembers the comfort of his father's house' (M. Lam. 1:7 (53b); SB I, 568, II, 215f.). εἰς ἑαυτὸν ἔρχεσθαι, literally 'to come to one's senses', represents a Semitic phrase 'to repent' (SB II, 215); but see K. E. Bailey, 173–175, who thinks that the phrase has a weaker sense. For ἔφη (p⁷⁵ ℵ B L), *Diglot* adopts the less Atticist εἶπεν (A D W *Δ Θ* f1 *pl*; TR). μίσθιος is 'day labourer, hired man' (15:19**). περισσεύω can mean 'to have an abundance of' (with genitive, BD 172); the passive form (p⁷⁵ A B f1 *pc*) is adopted by editors, but AG prefer the active form.

(18) ἀναστὰς πορεύσομαι represents an Aramaic phrase ('ᵃqum wᵉ'ezel) meaning 'I will go at once' (Jeremias, *Parables*, 130). The youth is determined to act swiftly and decisively. He is prepared to accept the lot of a servant – at home – in preference to his present misery. He knows that he does not deserve anything higher. He has sinned by squandering his money and ignoring whatever obligation, legal or moral, that he had to his father; he has acted as a bad steward (16:1, 10–12). εἰς τὸν οὐρανόν means 'against God' in view of the parallelism with ἐνώπιόν σου, and not 'to highest heaven' (Ezr. 9:6); cf. Ex. 10:16; SB II, 217. For ἐνώπιόν σου cf. 1 Sa. 7:6; 20:1, and for the son's confession as a whole cf. Ahikar 8:24b arm. The wording indicates that there is not a direct allegorical equation of the father with God, although the attitude of the father is meant to depict that of God.

(19) The connective καί is inserted here and in v. 21 by TR; *Diglot*. The idea of worthiness is used religiously in Mt. 10:37f. The youth is morally unfit to be regarded as a son, whether or not he has been legally disowned. He has no claims on his father after the earlier settlement of

his portion, and can only ask to be given the position of a servant in a household where servants are known to be well-treated (v. 17).

(20) The use of ἑαυτοῦ is unemphatic (Zerwick, 197) and probably pre-Lucan (J. Jeremias*, 177). For μακρὰν ἀπέχοντος cf. 7:6; the genitive absolute is illogical. The verb σπλαγχνίζομαι (7:13; 10:33) expresses the heart of the story: the father's feeling precedes any confession of repentance by the son and corresponds to the seeking and searching in the two preceding parables. He ran (Tobit 11:9) to meet him, embraced him (ἐπέπεσεν ἐπὶ τὸν τράχηλον αὐτοῦ) and kissed him (for the combination cf. Acts 20:37 – the phrase is thus Lucan; Gn. 45:14f.; 33:4). The action is a sign of forgiveness (2 Sa. 14:33) and of the restoration of the broken relationship, with the initiative being taken by the father (K. H. Rengstorf*, 19).

(21) The boy begins to repeat the words of his pre-determined confession. But before he can complete what he intends to say, his father interrupts him. Pedantic scribes, however, completed the verse by adding the missing words from v. 19 (א B D 33 pc); despite the authority of these MSS the shorter reading is to be preferred (Metzger, 164).

(22) The father now issues the instructions which show the nature of the welcome he gives to his lost son. δοῦλος is the appropriate term to use for the servants in the present relationship; the reference is to household servants who are probably to be distinguished from the hired men who worked on the farm; παῖς (26) will then be a variant for δοῦλος. K. H. Rengstorf*, 18, distinguishes two sets of instructions to be carried out by the house servants (v. 22) and the farmyard workers (v. 23) respectively. The first set of instructions is concerned with the decking out of the youth in the garments appropriate to a son. No time is to be wasted (ταχύ*, 'quickly'). They are to bring the best robe for him to wear. For στολή, cf. note on 20:46 (par. Mk. 12:38). The word order noun-article-adjective is Hellenistic (7:32 note; but the article is added before the noun in TR; Diglot). πρῶτος with the meaning 'best' is Classical (but cf. Ezk. 27:22; Am. 6:6; Ct. 4:14). This is not so much a sign of 'the New Age' (Jeremias, Parables, 130) as an indication of status, reminiscent of Gn. 41:42 (cf. U. Wilckens, TDNT VII, 687–691). A different interpretation is taken up by K. H. Rengstorf*, 40–45, who takes πρῶτος in the sense of 'former' (Acts 1:1; cf. Lk. 11:26) and regards the garment as that which the son wore before he left home and was disinherited; it is now the insignia of his reinstatement. But would not this interpretation require the insertion of an αὐτοῦ?

The second item is a ring (δακτύλιον**); the use of δίδωμι, 'to place', and εἰς (for Classical περί; BD 207¹) is Semitic. Here again it is not simply an ornament, but a symbol of authority, especially of royal authority (1 Mac. 6:15; Jos. Ant. 12:360; Est. 3:10; 8:8; fuller evidence in K. H. Rengstorf*, 30–39). Third, the shoes were a sign that a person was a freeman, not a slave; at the same time, they were worn in the house by the master, and not by the guests, who took them off on arrival. Hence they indicated authority and possession as well as freedom (K. H. Rengstorf*, 28f., 45–51).

(23) The second set of instructions leads to the celebration of the son's return at a feast – the inevitable accompaniment of rejoicing. μόσχος is a 'calf' (15:27, 30; Heb. 9:12, 19; Rev. 4:7**), and σιτευτός is 'fattened' (15:27, 30**). The reference is to an animal specially fed and kept to be slaughtered on a special occasion. θύω is simply 'to lay' (15:27, 30; Mt. 22:4; Jn. 10:10; Acts 10:13; 11:7); elsewhere 'to sacrifice' (22:7; Acts 14:13; 15:18; et al.). φάγοντες is tantamount to φάγωμεν καί (BD 420³). εὐφραίνω is especially used of the enjoyment of meals (12:19; 16:19).

(24) The father expresses the reason for his joy in what seems to be extravagant language. His son was dead but has come to life (ἀναζάω, Rom. 7:9**); he was lost, but has been found (ἦν ἀπολωλώς, p⁷⁵ 𝔑* A B L pc; ἀπολωλώς ἦν, 𝔑ᶜ Θ f1 f13 pm; καὶ ἀπολωλώς ἦν, Δ al; TR; ἀπολωλώς, D al; καὶ ἦν ἀπολωλώς, Diglot; the variants show signs of assimilation to the preceding phrase, and the desire to avoid asyndeton). The second statement links the parable to the preceding two. (15:4, 8). The first statement is so strong that it led Rengstorf to his new inter- pretation of the parable: only the act of kᵉtsatsah gives full meaning to a phrase which cannot be taken merely ethically, still less to mean that the son was thought to be physically dead. Whether or not one goes so far as to see a legal act of disinheritance behind the parable, the language certainly suggests that the son had announced his intention never to return, and that therefore he was as good as dead. His unexpected return leads to great rejoicing.

(25) But now the 'elder brother' theme, familiar from other literature (Derrett, 116–119) makes its appearance in order to drive the lesson home: the Pharisaic audience may perhaps approve of the story as a story, but their own attitude to returning prodigals must be clarified. The elder son was out at work while all this was going on. It is strange that nobody went to tell him what had happened, and that he must find out for himself: is there some suggestion that he was not on the best of terms with his father (cf. K. H. Rengstorf*, 53f.)? Or is the point simply that he slaves away all day in the fields until his duty is complete? The language is redundant and pre-Lucan (ἐρχόμενος, cf. 13:14; 16:21; 18:5). συμφωνία** can mean '(the sound of) music', 'band, orchestra', 'a wind instrument' (cf. Dn. 3:5; O. Betz, TDNT II, 304–309, thinks a double flute is meant), and χορός** is 'dancing'; cf. 6:23; 7:32. Jeremias, Parables, 130, suggests that clapping and singing and dancing by the men are indicated.

(26) The son has to summon one of the slaves in order to learn what is going on (πυνθάνομαι, 'to inquire, ask, seek to learn' is Lucan (18:36; Acts, 7x), as is the use of τί ἂν εἴη; cf. 18:36; Acts 21:33. For the use of ἄν cf. 1:29 note). For ταῦτα after τί see BD 299¹.

(27) The servant simply narrates the facts as they would have ap-

peared to an 'outsider' (Grundmann, 314). The first ὅτι is *recitativum*. ὑγιαίνω means that the boy is safe and well.

(28) Maybe the elder brother hated the younger. At any rate he objected to the welcome given to one who had done nothing to deserve it, but rather had done harm to his father. Perhaps too he feared some loss to himself as heir to what remained. So he was angry (14:21) and refused (οὐκ ἤθελεν) to go in. Once again, the father took the initiative, going out to him as he had done to the younger son (Geldenhuys, 409). Jeremias, *Parables*, 130, stresses the significance of the imperfect παρεκάλει: 'he spoke kindly to him'.

(29) The elder son's attitude is reminiscent of that in Mt. 20:12 (Dupont, II, 239). He omits any respectful address to his father, criticises him, and casts aspersions on his brother's character. For ἰδού with an expression of time cf. 13:7, 16. The son feels that he has the position of a slave (cf. Gal. 4:1f.); moreover, he has scrupulously obeyed his father's commands (for παρέρχομαι, cf. 11:42). He reflects the outlook of the Pharisees (18:9ff.; 18:21; Gal. 1:13f.; Phil. 3:6) as seen by Jesus and the early church. L. Schottroff*, 50f., argues that the Pharisees could not have identified themselves with this characterisation, since it represents what the early church thought of them rather than what they were really like or thought themselves to be like; hence Jesus cannot have spoken in this way in order to bring them into the parable. Whether or not the characterisation is correct (cf. H. Merkel, 'Jesus und die Pharisäer', NTS 14, 1967–68, 194–208; H.-F. Weiss, TDNT IX, 11–48) is beside the point: the picture here agrees with what Jesus said elsewhere about the Pharisees, and it should be regarded as a 'persuasive definition' rather than as a statement with which they could at once identify themselves. Jesus' description is meant to make them re-examine themselves, and the charge of inauthenticity is without foundation. If the son is conscious of faithful service to his father, he is at the same time critical that it seems to have brought him no reward, not even a kid (ἔριφος, Mt. 25:32**), a much cheaper meal than a fatted calf (Grundmann, 314).

(30) He cannot bring himself to speak of his 'brother', but talks contemptuously of 'this son of yours' (14:30; Acts 17:18; BD 290⁹). κατεσθίω is here 'to consume, devour' (8:5). The father's livelihood had been destroyed in the sense that the younger son's portion which might have continued to contribute to the family fortunes had now disappeared, so that the father was the poorer. The mention of harlots (πόρνη, Mt. 21:31f.; τῶν is inserted by A (D) L Ψ 579 sa bo; *Diglot*) is made without evidence but on grounds of probability. For τὸν σιτευτὸν μόσχον, the variant τὸν μόσχον τὸν σιτευτὸν is read by A W Δ Θ f1 f13 *pm* lat; TR; *Diglot*.

(31) The father addresses the son affectionately (τέκνον) and assures him that he is constantly (πάντοτε, contrast οὐδέποτε, v. 29) with him, and that all his father now possesses is his. The saying must be in-

terpreted to mean that legally the son will inherit the farm, since it has already been promised to him. If the son has not already enjoyed the fruits of it, it is because he has not asked rather than because the father was unwilling to give it. 'If the sinner is received into pardoning fellowship with Jesus, he is at home in the Father's house, and this fact puts to the man who is legally righteous the challenge whether he is building on his obedience to the commandment as hard-earned merit – this seems to be suggested by his grumbling at the reception of the prodigal – or whether he regards his perseverance in obedience as a joyous being at home in the Father's house' (W. Gutbrod, TDNT IV, 1060).

(32) Jeremias suggests that with ἔδει the pronoun σε should be supplied (*Parables*, 131): it is the elder brother who ought to have joined in the rejoicing. Recent translations, however, fairly uniformly supply ἡμᾶς. The demonstrative οὗτος is not superfluous (against Jeremias, ibid.) but brings out the stress, 'it is your brother who was . . .'. ἔζησεν has the sense of ἀνέζησεν (v. 24; cf. Rom. 14:9); καὶ ἀπολωλώς has undergone assimilation to v. 24 in various groups of MSS. With the father's statement the parable comes to an end, leaving his words as the climax, but also leaving the question for the hearers to answer: will the elder brother go in?

g. Warnings about Wealth (16:1–31)

If the purpose of the previous section was to vindicate the attitude of Jesus to the poor and needy, a contrast is now supplied by a series of warnings concerned with the dangers of wealth. The teaching is addressed in the first instance to the disciples (16:1–13), and warns them against the false use of wealth; they can learn a lesson from the behaviour of the prudent steward who put his wealth to good account, and, more generally, they are called to be good stewards of wealth and to avoid being enslaved by the desire for it. But the Pharisees, who were the audience in ch. 15, are still in view, and the rest of the section is devoted especially to them. They are accused of a hypocritical attitude in that their outward piety masked their greedy hearts. But while it was true that the coming of Jesus signalled the arrival of a new age, the old law, which contained clear enough teaching to condemn them, still remains in force; indeed, it is sharpened by the teaching of Jesus, for example, on divorce (16:14–18). To men who are slaves to wealthy living and ignore the poor Jesus has nothing further to say. Not even the message of the resurrection, with its threat of judgment to come, can move those who have not responded positively to the revelation of God's will in the Old Testament (16:19–31). The wealthy will be brought low, and the poor exalted.

Such appears to be the general trend of the section. But the unity gives the impression of artificiality. The sayings on stewardship (16:10–13) are appendages to the preceding parable, with catchword links. The restatement of the law on divorce appears oddly in a section devoted primarily to teaching about wealth. While most of the material is from Luke's special source, there is also material from Q (16:13, 16, 17, 18). Moreover, the various items in the chapter have multiple meanings: the opening section has something to say both to the disciples and to the Pharisees, and the various applications appended to the parable indicate that it could be the basis of several lessons. It is not surprising, therefore, that the section shows links with many Lucan themes, and that it is hard to find one simple thread of thought uniting its various parts. All this means that it is even more difficult to trace back the various sections to their original situation and purpose in the teaching of Jesus. This problem is accentuated by the fact that we may be dealing in part with a pre-Lucan combination of material from L and Q.

See A. Descamps, 'La composition littéraire de Luc xvi 9–13', Nov.T 1, 1956, 47–53; C. J. A. Hickling, 'A Tract on Jesus and the Pharisees? A Conjecture on the Redaction of Luke 15 and 16', *Heythrop Journal* 16, 1975, 253–265.

i. The Prudent Steward 16:1–9

Few passages in the Gospel can have given rise to so many different interpretations as the parable of the prudent steward. We have in effect to deal with three closely linked problems. What was the steward doing? What was the point of the parable, as told by Jesus? What did Luke regard as the point of the parable?

Essentially there are two main interpretations of the steward's action. The traditional interpretation is that he acted corruptly throughout the story: having wasted his master's goods during his stewardship, he finally proceeded to falsify the accounts of the master's debtors by reducing the amounts owed in order to obtain their goodwill. This is the 'obvious' interpretation of the story. It raises the difficulties that the steward is praised for his conduct and that he is made an example for the disciples to follow. To be sure, neither objection is insurmountable: it is not the steward's dishonesty but his foresight in preparing for the future which is commended, and Jesus was prepared to draw lessons (usually by contrast) from the behaviour of sinful men (11:13; cf. 18:6f.).

These objections can, however, be met by a different interpretation according to which the steward's final set of actions was legal and praiseworthy. Derrett, 48–77, made the suggestion that the steward had included in the original accounts the interest due on the deferred payments. By God's law the charging of interest was strictly illegal, although man's law had found ways of evading God's law. What the steward did was to reduce the debtor's accounts by the amount of interest due, thus pleasing the debtors, acting legally himself and putting his master in a good light. There is then no difficulty about the steward's changed way of life being praised and used as an example to be imitated.

Derrett's discussion (72f.) appears to assume that the interest charges would have gone to the master, to whom the debts were due, so that the steward's action deprived him of what he would otherwise have been paid. A variant view is that adopted by Findlay, 1049, and Fitzmyer, 161–184, who claim that the 'interest' was actually the steward's 'commission' on the transactions. What happened was simply that the steward forwent his own profit on the debts, and the master suffered no loss. The steward, as it were, paid out of his own pocket by renouncing the profit that he had hoped to gain, in order to obtain a lasting welcome from the debtors instead. (This is preferable to the view sometimes put forward that there was no question of interest or commission, and that the steward simply paid out of his own pocket the difference between the original and the reduced sums due to the master.) This interpretation gives a closer link to the interpretation (16:9) in that the steward was making use of his own money (in this case, what was owing to him personally), and the disciples are called to act wisely with their own money. But no evidence is cited to support this view over against that of Derrett, which is accordingly to be preferred.

It is more difficult to decide between Derrett's view and the older one. Danker, 173, states that there is not sufficient evidence to justify decision. The evidence adduced by Derrett shows that his interpretation is feasible for a first-century situation. What is not clear is whether an audience, especially an audience outside Palestine, would have got the point. Perhaps Jesus intended the full meaning, but the subsequent tradition failed to do so and hence the less adequate interpretation came to dominate exegesis from a very early date. K. E. Bailey*, holds that what the steward did was simply to show generosity by reducing the debtors' bills in faith that the master would be unwilling to countermand the changes and thereby lose *his* reputation for generosity.

We can now proceed to look at the application of the parable, taking into account the original meaning and the meaning seen by the Evangelist simultaneously. In his useful, brief history of interpretation H. Preisker* discerns two main types of interpretation, both based, of course, on the older view of the point of the parable. On the one hand, many commentators found the application in v. 9 where the disciples are commanded to use the wealth at their disposal as wisely as possible in order to secure places for themselves in heaven (Plummer, 380f.; Lagrange, 435; Zahn, 575f.; Klostermann; and many others). The wise use of money is then to be seen in almsgiving (so recently F. E. Williams*). On the other hand, commentators who eschewed allegory (such as Jülicher; Jeremias, *Parables*, 45–48, 181f.) limited the lesson to imitation of the steward's prudence in recognising the imminence of catastrophe and acting appropriately.

Preisker notes that a decision between these two possibilities depends on where the parable, as originally spoken by Jesus, comes to an end. Here the commentators are of very varied minds (cf. Fitzmyer, 165–168). All are agreed that vs. 10–13 represent secondary applications of the parable or further developments of its theme. V. 9 is obviously meant to be an application of the parable by Jesus; similarly, v. 8b must be seen as a comment on the parable. But v. 8a could be regarded as a comment by Jesus ('the Lord') or as a statement about the steward's master's reaction. If the former view is correct, the parable proper concludes with v. 7. V. 9 shows how Luke understood the parable: it has to do with the proper use of wealth. If it is detached as a secondary addition, then the original application of the parable must be determined from the parable itself, the presence or absence of the whole or part of v. 8 making little difference to the verdict. In this case, both the 'use of money' application and the 'act prudently' application are possible.

Preisker himself limits the parable to vs. 1–7. He finds the clue to the meaning in the somewhat parallel stories in 12:13–21 and 16:19–31, both of which are concerned with men in the grip of mammon, from which they cannot get free. So too this parable describes a steward who is so much in the grip of mammon that he crowns a career of dishonesty by one great final act of dishonesty which involves his master's debtors in his own wrongdoing; so far from repenting in view of his summary dismissal, he continues in his dishonesty, and thus constitutes an 'awful warning' of the demonic, enslaving power of mammon. The parable thus gives the contrast to the prodigal son who, after wasting his wealth, repented. A somewhat similar interpretation is given by D. R. Fletcher* who finds the lesson: You cannot expect to emulate worldly people. How far will their sort of behaviour get you when the end comes? Rather be honest and faithful in your use of money.

Preisker's interpretation is questionable. It makes too much of the redactional link with 15:11–32 (a link due to Luke, who did not interpret the parable in this way), and it rejects 16:8a without adequate reason.

An entirely different approach is taken by E. Kamlah*, who finds the clue to the parable in Jesus' use of the term 'steward' in relation to his underlings; it is a criticism of the Pharisees who are commanded to forgive those who cannot keep their stringent laws and so to act as God's stewards. But this is most unconvincing.

Finally, we come to the interpretations based on Derrett and Fitzmyer's view of the parable. It is now to be seen positively as an injunction to repentance and to the right use of wealth in order to gain the approval of God. For Fitzmyer, 177f., the point lies in the steward's use of his own wealth to ensure his future. For Derrett, 74, the point lies in the proper stewardship of God's wealth entrusted to the disciples (cf. his view of the prodigal son). So understood, there is no real incompatibility between the parable and the interpretation found in Luke, and this is a point in favour of this view.

The detailed exegesis below will take account of these various possibilities but will show that Derrett's interpretation has most to be said for it.

See H. Preisker, 'Lukas 16, 1–7', TLZ 74, 1949, 85–92; Jeremias, *Parables*, 45–48, 181f.; D. R. Fletcher, 'The Riddle of the Unjust Steward: Is Irony the Key?' JBL 82, 1963, 15–30; E. Kamlah, 'Die Parabel vom ungerechten Verwalter (Luk. 16.1ff) im Rahmen der Knechtsgleichnisse', in O. Betz, 276–294; H. Kosmala, 'The Parable of the Unjust Steward in the Light of Qumran', ASTI 3, 1964, 114–121; F. E. Williams, 'Is Almsgiving the Point of the Unjust Steward?' JBL 83, 1964, 293–297; H. Drexler, 'Miszellen: zu Lukas 16, 1–7', ZNW 58, 1967, 286–288; I. H. Marshall, 'Luke xvi. 8 – Who commended the unjust steward?' JTS ns 19, 1968, 617–619; Derrett, 48–77 (originally as 'The Parable of the Unjust Steward', in NTS 7, 1961, 198–219); J. D. M. Derrett, ' "Take thy Bond ... and write Fifty" (Luke xvi. 6) The nature of the Bond', JTS ns 23, 1972, 438–440; Fitzmyer, 161–184 (originally as 'The Story of the Dishonest Manager (Lk. 16:1–13) ', in *Theological Studies* 25, 1964, 23–42); L. J. Topel, 'On the Injustice of the Unjust Steward: Lk. 16:1–13', CBQ 37, 1975, 216–227; K. E. Bailey, 86–110.

(1) No change of scene from the previous section is implied (cf. Klostermann, 161), but Jesus directs his teaching particularly to his disciples (αὐτοῦ is read by A W Θ f1 *pm* lat sy sa bo[pt]; TR; *Diglot*) in the hearing of the Pharisees (16:14). Luke thus implies that the parable has significance for both groups of hearers, but is meant primarily for those who are disciples. In the opening sentence of the parable πλούσιος is attributive: 'There was a certain rich man who ...' (Klostermann, 161). He is to be regarded as the absentee landlord of a *latifundium*, such as were common in Galilee at the time (Grundmann, 317). His affairs were therefore in the hands of an οἰκονόμος (12:42), here an estate-manager (Scottish 'factor'), who acted as his agent with considerable legal powers (Derrett, 52–55). διαβάλλω** means 'to bring charges against with hostile intent', and in itself does not imply whether the charges were true or false; nor does ὡς necessarily imply falsity (BD 425[3]). But the fact that the charges are taken seriously by both master and steward indicates that they were correct. διασκορπίζω (15:13) could imply neglect of duty or misappropriation of funds, but since there is no suggestion of having to pay compensation, the former is more likely.

(2) The master forthwith took action. For τί τοῦτο, sc. ἐστίν, cf. Gn. 42:28; BD 299[1]. The servant was called to render an account (ἀποδίδωμι, Mt. 12:36; Acts 19:40; Heb. 13:17; 1 Pet. 4:5) of the state of the property entrusted to him, for he was no longer to continue as steward. For δύνῃ cf. BD 93; it is attested by p[75] ℵ B D W Θ f1 f13 *al*; the variant δυνήσῃ is attested by A *pm* Orig; TR; *Diglot*. οἰκονομέω** is 'to act as steward'. The master's action is clear. It is a summary dismissal of the steward, coupled with a demand for a statement of the accounts for the benefit of his successor (cf. P. Eleph. 9:4–7, cited by Lagrange, 431, for such a reckoning). The steward's actions are consistent with this. He knows that he is being dismissed (16:3a), and he therefore uses his last hours in office to alter the accounts for his own

advantage. The self-contradictions discovered in the story by H. Drex-ler* are simply not there.

(3) Soliloquy is not uncommon in the parables (12:17; 15:17–19; *et al.*). For εἶπεν . . . ἐν ἑαυτῷ, cf. 3:8; 7:39; 18:4, and for τί ποιήσω, cf. 12:17. ἀφαιρεῖται signifies the process of dismissal, which will not be completed until the steward has had time to set down his accounts. The steward is unable to see any future chance of employment. He will not easily find another job as steward. He does not have the strength to dig: this was regarded as especially strenuous, and the thought had become proverbial (Aristophanes, Birds, 1432; cf. AG s.v. σκάπτω). He is ashamed (αἰσχύνομαι*) to beg (ἐπαιτέω, 18:35**; καί is prefixed by B; *Diglot*). He has no future, unless he does something quickly about it.

(4) The aorist ἔγνων has been taken to express the sense 'suddenly the idea has come to me' (Bengel; MH III, 74). Stuhlmueller, 149, suggests, 'I have known all along what to do in a situation like this', but this does not fit in with the uncertainty expressed in v. 3. A gnomic aorist (mentioned by MH III, 74) seems impossible. Moule, 7, 11, produces the correct answer by noting that an instantaneous action is over before it can be commented on, and that a Greek punctiliar has to be translated on occasion by an English simple form; so the meaning is 'I know what I will do', more exactly, 'I found out (a moment ago) what I will do'. Cf. Mk. 1:11; Lk. 12:32. μεθίστημι is 'to remove' (Acts 13:22; cf. 19:26**; 1 Cor. 13:2; Col. 1:13**). The subject of δέξωνται is not stated: the steward's thoughts have leapt ahead to the debtors who ap-pear in the next verse. See also on 16:9. For ἑαυτῶν, αὐτῶν is read by p⁷⁵ A D L W Θ f1 f13 *pl*; TR; *Diglot*.

(5) The nature of the steward's plan is explained by telling what he did. He summoned each of his master's debtors (7:41; for ἑαυτοῦ *Diglot* again has αὐτοῦ with ℵ* D *al*). These may have included tenants of the estate who paid their rents in kind or (more probably) merchants who had received goods on credit from the estate and had given promissory notes in their own handwriting (Phm. 18) to the steward. The bills may have been for the receipt of the goods specified, or they may have been for amounts of money that had been restated in terms of amounts of oil and wheat, so as to get round the Jewish laws on usury. The story proceeds to give two examples of how the steward treated the debtors.

(6) The first man was asked how much he owed and gave his reply (ὁ δὲ εἶπεν; Kilpatrick, 201, prefers καὶ εἶπεν (Δ Π *al*; *Diglot*) on the grounds that scribes normally altered καί to δέ rather than vice versa; but the external evidence is too weak in this case). He owed in respect of 100 measures of oil. The size of the measure (βάτος**) is uncertain. Ac-cording to Jos. Ant. 8:57 the *bath* was equivalent to 72 *sextarii*, from which its value can be determined as 72 x .96 pints, i.e. roughly 8.6 gallons or 39 litres. A jar discovered at Qumran suggests a figure of 10 gallons (R. B. Y. Scott, PC, 38). On the other hand, a variety of archaeological finds from OT and Graeco-Roman times give a figure of

about 5 gallons or 21–22 litres, a figure which is beyond doubt for OT times. Different standards may thus have been in use in different times and places. Working on the former estimate, Jeremias, *Parables*, 181, suggests that the debt was about 1,000 denarii. The debtor is asked to take his bill (τὰ γράμματα, plural used for one document: here, a promissory note; cf. AG; Jos. Ant. 18:156) and either alter it in his own handwriting or more probably write out a new one to half the amount. On Derrett's view this represents interest at 100%, which seems excessively high, but which is not impossible under oriental conditions. In the case of the wheat the amount of interest is much more realistic. In a later article J. D. M. Derrett* has produced evidence a. that in the conditions of the time both Jewish and Greek readers would understand the original bill to contain an interest charge, and b. that in Egypt the rate of interest on comestibles was rationalised at 50%. There is, therefore, no real difficulty about the figures, the Egyptian amount representing a lowering of the rate for oil and an increasing of the rate for wheat to a common level.

(7) Then (ἔπειτα*) the process is repeated with a second, typical debtor, whose payment is in terms of wheat. The amount is again uncertain. κόρος** represents the *kor*, a dry measure, equivalent to the *homer*. In OT times it was approximately 220 litres or 48 gallons. Jos. Ant. 15:314 gives a larger value, 525 litres (131 gallons), which appears to be erroneous. The price of wheat was said to be 25–30 denarii per cor (BM 5:1), giving a total price here of 2500 denarii or so; if so, the reduction in price was about 500 denarii (the same amount as in the case of the oil (Jeremias, *Parables*, 181), but this is probably coincidence). In any case, the reduction represents an interest charge of 25%, which fits in with ancient practice. The asyndetic λέγει (p⁷⁵ B L *al*) is altered in the MSS: καὶ λέγει (A W Δ Θ f1 *pm*; TR; *Diglot*); ὁ δὲ λέγει (D); λέγει δέ (א); the variety of readings suggests that the UBS reading gave rise to the others (cf. Black, 57).

(8) Did the parable end with v. 7, so that what follows is secondary? There are three possibilities: 1. The actual story continues to v. 8a, with v.8b as a comment by the narrator; v. 8a is then a description of the master's attitude. 2. The actual story finishes with v. 7, with v. 8a giving the narrator's comment about what the Lord (Jesus) went on to say. 3. The story finishes with v. 7, with v. 8a as a comment on the master's attitude added by the tradition. The following factors are relevant: a. Grammatically, there is no difficulty about ὁ κύριος referring to Jesus, since the clash with καὶ ἐγὼ ὑμῖν λέγω . . . in v. 9 can be explained in terms of a statement in indirect speech being carried on in direct speech (cf. 5:14 note; I. H. Marshall*; Ott, 39f.). Less probably, the clash may be alleviated by suggesting that v. 9 is clumsily added from a different source (Jeremias, *Parables*, 45f.). b. In the somewhat similar case of 18:6, ὁ κύριος certainly means Jesus. By analogy of style the same could be true here. On the other hand, the equally valid parallel in

14:23f. refers to the householder in the parable, and the use of κύριος in 16:3, 5 suggests that here too the steward's master is meant. c. It has often been objected that the master would not have commended a servant who had cheated him. But it may forcefully be urged, *either* (on the older view) that the master simply admired the foresight of the servant in looking after his own interests (Manson, *Sayings*, 292) *or* (on Derrett's view) that the master applauded the servant's return to legal dealings and was happy to bask in the undeserved reputation for fair dealing which he himself could now enjoy. d. If the parable ends with v. 7, it does so with decided abruptness (Fitzmyer, 166f.). After the mention of the master at the beginning, we expect to hear of his reaction at the end, and, although the tradition could have added the missing reaction, it is more probable that it was included in the original form of the story. These considerations show that there is no evidence that *demands* that ὁ κύριος be taken to mean Jesus (i.e. view 2. has no positive support), and that it is probable that v. 8a is an original part of the parable (view 1; Lagrange, 433). We thus go against the view of the majority of interpreters that ὁ κύριος represents Jesus (Klostermann, 163; Rengstorf, 185; Schmid, 258f.; Ellis, 201; Jeremias, I. de la Potterie, in Descamps, 143; Grundmann, 320, suggests that originally ὁ κύριος referred to the master and was taken by Luke to refer to Jesus; while A. Descamps*, 47, adopts the opposite view).

ἐπαινέω, 'to praise', occurs here only in Lk. and is not a sign of Lucan composition (*contra* Ott, 39f.). τῆς ἀδικίας is a Hebraic genitive, equivalent to an adjectival phrase; cf. 13:27. ἀδικία usually means 'wrongdoing, unrighteousness, wickedness, injustice' (13:27; Acts 1:18; 8:23). If so, the adjective may refer to the whole of the steward's career (the traditional interpretation) or only to that part preceding his final dealings (Fitzmyer, 172–174). A different view is suggested by H. Kosmala* who argues that ἀδικία denotes the standing characteristic of this world, corrupted as it is by sin. The steward is simply a worldly man who acts in worldly fashion (i.e. sinfully), and the point of the description is to contrast him with the disciples; understood in this way, the phrase then links closely to v. 8b and v. 9. Cf. 1 Jn. 5:19; Jas. 3:16; 1QH 5:25 (Delling, 214f.). The steward is praised for acting φρονίμως (12:42 note), a word which is often used of the attitude which disciples should adopt in regard to the coming of the Son of man. The steward had seen the urgency of the situation and reacted sensibly towards it; so too, it is implied, should men react to the impending judgment of God.

Whatever verdict is passed on v. 8a, the second part of the verse is clearly a comment on the parable ascribed to Jesus. The ὅτι forms a rather loose connection, justifying the statement that the steward is said to have acted φρονίμως by the fact that this is what is expected of worldly people. οἱ υἱοί with a genitive is a common Semitic phrase to denote people belonging to a particular class (cf. 10:6 note; E. Schweizer, TDNT VIII, 365). Jewish phraseology refers to 'sons of the age to come' and to 'sons of the age (world)', i.e. men (SB II, 219), but does not include 'sons of this age' (Lk. 20:34). But the use of 'this age' in contrast to 'the age to come' is found (H. Sasse, TDNT I, 206f.), and hence the creation of the present phrase is a perfectly natural development. The men of this world are contrasted with 'the sons of light', (cf. Jn. 12:36; 1 Thes. 5:5; cf. Eph. 5:8; 1 En. 108:11), a phrase now shown to be Palestinian (1QS 1:9; 2:16; 3:13, 24f.; 1QM 1:3, 9, 11, 13; Braun, *Qumran*, I, 90f.; *Radikalismus*, II, 39 n. 1), although not used by the rabbis. The verse thus makes use of a dualism similar to that found at Qumran; it distinguishes those who belong to, are destined for, God's kingdom of light. Jesus in effect upbraids them for being less alert to the eschatological situation (ὑπέρ, expressing comparison; Heb. 4:12; BD 185³) than worldly people are in their own generation, i.e. in their dealings with each other. Derrett, 79 n. gives 'by the standard of their generation'. For this last phrase cf. 1QS 3:14, where *dôrôṯ* expresses types of character rather than a chronological succession of generations.

The thought of this part of the verse is thus Palestinian, and not Hellenistic (as Bultmann, 190 n., thought before the Qumran discoveries). Fitzmyer, 167f., regards the comment as a secondary addition, since in his view it follows strangely on the parable itself and generalises its meaning; if the steward is an example to be followed in the parable, here he is contrasted with the disciples. This is unconvincing.

(9) The application to the hearers and readers now follows (ὑμῖν λέγω); cf. 11:9; *et al.* ἑαυτοῖς stands emphatically at the beginning of the exhortation in p⁷⁵ ℵ* B L *pc*; the order is reversed in TR; *Diglot*. The disciples are commanded to make friends for themselves by means of 'worldly wealth'. μαμωνᾶς (16:11, 13; Mt. 6:24**; cf. Sir. 31:8) is formed from Aramaic *māmôn*, possibly originally meaning 'that in which one puts one's trust', hence 'wealth' (SB I, 434f.; F. Hauck, TDNT IV, 388–390). It can express wealth of all kinds, and may have a good or a bad sense. H. Kosmala* shows that it is equivalent to *hôn* in the Qumran texts (1QS 6:2, 19; CD 14:20). Hence the addition of τῆς ἀδικίας points not to the rabbinic *māmôn šel šeqer* ('possessions acquired dishonestly') but to the Qumran phrase *hôn hārīšāh* (CD 6:15; cf. 1QS 10:19; Braun, *Qumran* I, 91). Hence the meaning is 'worldly wealth', as opposed to heavenly treasure. It is to be used to win friends, no doubt by almsgiving. For one day wealth will come to an end; there will be none left (see 1 Mac. 3:29 for this meaning of ἐκλείπω; cf. 22:32; 23:45; Heb. 1:12**; the word is probably but not necessarily Lucan). The poorly attested variant ἐκλίπητε (W 33 69 131 *pm* lat; TR) gives the euphemism, 'when you die' (cf. Gn. 49:33). Then the givers of alms will be received into the eternal dwellings; this is an unusual phrase, not found in the Rabbis; see, however, 4 Ez. 2:11; 1 En. 39:4. Although a σκηνή is usually a temporary dwelling, here it refers to something permanent. Perhaps it refers to the place where the presence of God dwells (cf. W. Michaelis, TDNT VII, 378f.). δέξωνται may have as its implied subject: 1. the angels, as a

circumlocution for the name of God; cf. 6:38 note; 12:20; Yoma 8:9, as cited by Creed, 205; so G. Stählin, TDNT IX, 164. 2. the recipients of the alms, who act as intercessors with God (cf. 1 En. 39:4f.). 3. the personified alms (cf. P. Ab. 4:11; t. Peah 4:21, cited by Jeremias, *Parables*, 46 n. 85). Lucan usage supports view 1. This may sound suspiciously like salvation by works but the point is surely that the giving of alms is a testimony to the reality of discipleship and self-denial; in any case, Jesus makes it quite clear that it is the attitude of the heart to God that ultimately matters and not any outward show of giving charity.

Few scholars are willing to see the original application of the parable in this verse. Derrett, 80, is apparently prepared to do so, but is almost alone. But the arguments against it being originally attached to the parable are weak. The style is not especially Lucan, but is close to that of Luke's special source. The vocabulary has parallels in the context, but this does not prove that it has been constructed on the basis of material from the context (*contra* A. Descamps*, 49–51). The main reason for separation is the claim that the application does not correspond to the original meaning of the parable, but our exegesis has led us in the direction of this application. Accordingly, the verse should be accepted as the original application of the parable.

ii. Faithful Stewardship 16:10–13

The sayings in this section take up two motifs found in the preceding parable, and can be regarded as secondary lessons that may be drawn from it. The first motif is that of faithfulness in stewardship, and in their present context the sayings implicitly draw a contrast between the unfaithfulness of the steward in the parable and the faithfulness required in disciples. The basic principle, which contrasts small and great responsibilities, is in no sense an application of the parable itself, however, and is an anticipation of 19:17. The principle is then applied to worldly and heavenly wealth, which are equated with small and great responsibilities, and (in a further comment) with alien and native wealth respectively. Disciples will not be entrusted with heavenly wealth and responsibilities if they have not already shown themselves faithful over against worldly wealth; cf. the application of this principle to church government in 1 Tim. 3:5.

The second motif is that of mammon (which has already cropped up in v. 11), but this is also linked with the idea of service to a master. A servant cannot properly attend to the claims of God and wealth as his masters: undivided loyalty is demanded.

V. 13 is from Q material, while the rest of the section is peculiar to Lk. This in itself suggests that we have a compilation of related sayings here; they have been added by a compiler to the parable on the basis of a broad community of theme. (But see K. E. Bailey* for a defence of the original unity of vs. 9–13 as a poem on mammon and God.) The authenticity of v. 13 is not in doubt. Bultmann, 90, and A. Descamps* regard vs. 11f. as an explanatory addition to v. 10. This is improbable. V. 12 is too obscure to be regarded as an explanation of anything, and v. 11 contains an Aramaic play on the words for 'faithful' and 'mammon'. There is a stronger case that v. 10 is an imitation of 19:17 par. Mt. 25:21, but the careful antithetical form, and the use of ἄδικος in a slightly different sense from ἀδικία in the context strongly suggest that an existing saying is being used. Accordingly, Luke is using traditional material which it was appropriate to insert at this point.

See A. Descamps (16:1–31 note); Schulz, 459–461; K. E. Bailey, 110–118.

(10) The saying is a good example of a secular truth being used as a basis for a religious lesson. It is true in the world at large that a person who is faithful in a small responsibility can be trusted in a larger one. The contrasting statement is not that a person faithful in a large responsibility will (or will not) be faithful in a small one – this thought is not in mind – but that a person who is unfaithful in small things cannot be trusted in big ones. For πιστός as a quality expected in a steward see 12:42; 19:17; 1 Cor. 4:2. ἐλάχιστος (19:17) is elative: 'in a very little'. ἄδικος, 'unjust' (16:11; 18:11; Acts 24:15; Mt. 5:45), here has the meaning 'dishonest, untrustworthy'; this is a stronger sense of the root than in v. 8, if we accept Kosmala's view of it there. In any case, ἄδικος certainly typifies the dishonesty which is characteristic of worldly people.

(11) The application follows in two stages. It is possible that disciples may not act faithfully in respect of ἄδικος μαμωνᾶς; the phrase here must mean 'worldly wealth', rather than 'wealth dishonestly acquired or used', but the use of πιστός indicates that even such material wealth is regarded as something of which men are the stewards, not the owners. It is contrasted with 'true' (wealth); ἀληθινός refers to what is characteristic of the new age (Jn. 1:9; 6:32; et al.; Heb. 8:2; 9:24; Ellis, 202) and hence has an abiding, permanent quality. It is thus 'real'. πιστεύω here has the meaning 'to entrust' (1 Cor. 9:17; cf. Jn. 2:24; Rom. 3:2; Gal. 2:7; 1 Thes. 2:4; 1 Tim. 1:11; Tit. 1:3). Behind the τίς of the rhetorical question lies the figure of God. The contrast of tenses between the two clauses suggests that the thought is of the bestowal of heavenly treasure in the age to come, rather than of the entrusting of the gospel to disciples called to be evangelists.

(12) In the second stage of the application a new thought is injected. The parallelism suggests that now worldly mammon is to be equated with what is ἀλλότριος*, 'belonging to another person'. Worldly wealth does not really belong to the disciples; they hold it on trust from God. (This is one of the few places in the NT where the idea of stewardship is applied to material possessions; mostly it is applied to the gospel.) Correspondingly, the true wealth is yours, ὑμέτερον (UBS; so the translations). The variant ἡμέτερον is attested by B L 1574 Origen pc, and adopted by Synopsis; Diglot (cf. AG s.v.); cf. ἐμόν, 157 e i l Mcion. The

variant arises from a simple copying error; it could only be interpreted to mean 'belonging to the Father and the Son', a theological nicety which is unlikely at this stage (Easton, 245; Metzger, 165). The passage demands a contrast between what does not belong to the disciples and what will really belong to them. The treasure of heaven will be their own in-alienable possession. For the thought cf. Epictetus 4:5:15: οὐδὲν ἴδιον τῷ ἀνθρώπῳ ἐστίν, ἀλλὰ πάντα ἀλλότρια. The inverse statement is found in Ahikar 8:35 syr. 'Thou hast not been industrious in what is thine own, and how wilt thou be industrious in what is not thine own?' This senti-ment is equally true, but is irrelevant here. The form of Jesus' saying, which is negative, shows that it is really a command to be faithful now, so that one may possess then.

(13) The closing saying of the series can be regarded both as a warning against being unfaithful in God's service and as a warning against being enslaved by mammon. οἰκέτης, 'servant', especially in a household (Acts 10:7; Rom. 14:4; 1 Pet. 2:18**) is absent from Mt. here. The saying is often taken to mean that in the conditions of ancient slavery it was not possible for a person to have two masters, as, for ex-ample, someone might work part-time for two different employers today. This is false. A slave might work for two or more persons in partnership (Acts 16:10, 19) or for two different masters (Pes. 8:1) or he might even have been freed by one master while still a slave to another (SB I, 433f.). Hence the point of the saying is that a man cannot render the exclusive loyalty and service which is inherent in the concept of δουλεία to more than one master (K. H. Rengstorf, TDNT II, 270f.). His temptation will be to love one more than the other (μισέω, 14:26 note), or at least (ἤ, Plummer, 387) to be devoted to one (ἀντέχομαι, literally, 'to cling to', 1 Thes. 5:14; Tit. 1:9**) and to despise the other (καταφρονέω*, Mt. 18:10). If a man tries to serve mammon as well as God, he will fail to give God the exclusive loyalty that God demands. Cf. G. Thomas 47 for an expansion of the saying.

iii. Reproof of the Pharisees 16:14–15

Such teaching on the need for faithful stewardship of wealth drew forth criticism from the Pharisees, because they attempted to combine the worship of God and of mammon. Jesus reproves them, first of all, by arguing that although they may win the esteem of men, God judges their hearts and condemns their proud desires.

The connection of thought at this point in the section is far from obvious. Although the theme of wealth returns in vs. 19–31, the theme in vs. 16–18 is the law. It may be best to assume that Luke was governed by the order of the material in his sources, and that he has put it together as best he could, but not with complete success. The linguistic evidence together with Luke's known propensity to create links between his pericopes suggests that he has composed v. 14 as a transition

(Bultmann, 360; W. G. Kümmel* 16:16–17 note), 91f.). V. 15, however, or at least the second part of it, is an authentic saying of Jesus (Bultmann, 110; cf. 77, 84).

The Lucan connection with the preceding section would then appear to be that the Pharisaic love of money was rooted in a hidden covetousness, possibly masked by almsgiving. The connection, however, is artificial. Luke's train of thought in relation to the following verses is even more difficult. It is not surprising that Ellis, 200f., has a break between sections at this point (13:22 – 16:13; 16:14 – 18:14), although this particular division of the material is itself unlikely. He argues further that vs. 14f. point forward to vs. 19–26, and vs. 16–18 to vs. 27–31, so that the two parts of the parable illustrate the earlier sayings: exaltation by men forecasts rejection by God (and vice versa), and the abiding witness of the OT is an adequate basis for believing the message of the kingdom. *Pace* W. G. Kümmel, 92, this is the only way to see a thread in the passage; the alternative is to see no thread at all. Again, however, the connection is artificial and suggests that vs. 16–18 (probably Q sayings) have been inserted into an alien context.

(14) The use of ἀκούω as a connective is Lucan (cf. 14:15). The reading οἱ Φαρισαῖοι is supported by p⁷⁵ ℵ B D L *al*; καὶ οἱ Φαρισαῖοι is attested by A W Δ Θ f1 f13 *pm*; TR; *Diglot*; and other variants are found. Metzger, 165, explains the addition of καί as due to a scribal desire to soften the abrupt mention of the Pharisees, who have not figured in the story since 15:2. φιλάργυρος is 'money loving' (2 Tim. 3:2**; cf. the noun, 1 Tim. 6:10**). ὑπάρχω is Lucan (7:25; *et al.*) and ἐκμυκτηρίζω, 'to turn up the nose', hence 'to ridicule, sneer at', is also Lucan (Lk. 23:35**, diff. Mk.). Manson, *Sayings*, 295f., 350, has suggested that mention of the Sadducees would be more appropriate here: 1. The Sadducees were more obviously lovers and possessors of money than the Pharisees. 2. The Sadducees would be more likely to scoff at teaching about heavenly treasure. 3. 'Sadducee' and 'justify' (v. 15) would give a word-play in Aramaic (*sdk*). 4. The Sadducees were wealthy and proud (Jos. Ant. 13:298; Pss. Sol. *passim*) and considered themselves just (1 En. 102:10; Ass. Moses 7:3). 5. The parable of Dives and Lazarus would fit a Sadducean audience. There is sufficient weight in these points to show that the Sadducees would be a suitable audience at this point, but there is also sufficient evidence of the avarice of the Pharisees to make it unnecessary to suppose that there is an error here; cf. t. Men. 13, 22 (533), dated *c.* AD 110, describing the greed of the scribes (SB I, 937; cf. SB II, 222; IV:1, 336–339; Jeremias, *Jerusalem*, 114; Grundmann, 322f.).

(15) Jesus' reply accuses the Pharisees of belonging to the class of those (οἱ with predicative adjective, Zerwick, 166) who justify (7:29) themselves in the eyes of men, i.e. who endeavour to demonstrate to other men that they are righteous. Creed, 206, suggests that the force is:

'You do indeed give alms, but you only do so to justify yourselves before men' (cf. 18:9, 11f.). This is more likely than Klostermann, 166: the Pharisees claimed that their wealth was God's reward for their piety. It fits in with the criticism made in Mt. 6:1–4. God, however, sees into the motives that lie behind the outward act of piety (cf. 2:35; 1 Sa. 16:7; 1 Ch. 28:9; Ps. 7:10).

The force of ὅτι is doubtful, unless we assume that 'knows your hearts' carries the implicit consequence 'and judges them', *because* he hates pride. ὑψηλός*, 'high', signifies 'exalted, proud, haughty' (Rom. 11:20; 12:16; cf. 1. Tim. 6:17); cf. 1:52 and especially 14:11. βδέλυγμα, 'abomination, detested thing', is used of things hated by God (Is. 1:13; Pr. 11:1; cf. Mk. 13:14 par. Mt. 24:15; Rev. 17:4f.; 21:27; W. Foerster, TDNT I, 598–560). France, 245, finds here a possible echo of Pr. 16:5 MT; cf. 6:16f. MT (tô'ēbâ). The saying is a threat of judgment; cf. Is. 2:11–19; 5:14–16; Lk. 1:51–53; 14:7–11; Grundmann, 323, notes that this judgment is now at hand with the coming of the kingdom of God (16:16).

iv. The Law and the Kingdom 16:16–17

This section contains the second and third in the brief sequence of four sayings which Luke records at this point. V. 16 draws a distinction between the times before and after John the Baptist. The period of the law and the prophets has given place to the period during which the kingdom of God is the content of God's message to men, and everybody acts forcefully with regard to it. Nevertheless, according to v. 17 the law continues to remain valid down to the smallest detail. This collocation of sayings lays stress on the second part – the abiding validity of the law; the fourth saying (v. 18) then serves as an example of the permanent force of the law.

The stress, then, is on the continuing significance of the law in the time of the gospel (cf. 16:29). Luke's purpose is to underline the fact that the Pharisees – and the disciples – still stand under the law; and this may be regarded as a qualification of the apparently absolute distinction made in v. 16. It follows that v. 16 does not have the programmatic significance for Luke which is assigned to it by Conzelmann, 17 (W. G. Kümmel*, 91).

V. 16 appears in a variant form in Mt. 11:12f., and v. 17 in Mt. 5:18. Both sayings were probably in the Q material, but it is disputed whether they were linked together in Luke's source. Schürmann, *Untersuchungen*, 126–136, claims that 16:14–18 was a unity in Q (together with Mt. 5:19), and its influence can be traced in Mt. 5. Hoffmann, 53–56, however, argues that Schürmann's view depends upon Luke preserving the original wording in 16:16b (contrary to the general opinion on the matter), and that the passage has been put together by Luke in terms of his interest in the law. A weakness in

Hoffmann's case is his argument that Luke introduced v. 18 at this point; it is almost impossible to ascribe the change in theme to Luke. This suggests that vs. 17 and 18 belonged together in Luke's source. It is less clear whether vs. 16 and 17f. formed a unity in Luke's source; one can be reasonably sure that the placing of Mt. 11:12f. in its present Matthaean context is secondary, but this does not prove that the Lucan setting is original.

V. 16 and Mt. 11:12f. are variant forms of the same saying (*pace* E. Bammel*, 104). They express essentially the same thoughts but with reversed order. Originally the saying will have expressed the consciousness of the new era brought about by the coming of the kingdom, although the precise significance of the statement is much debated. While E. Bammel* argues that it reflects a tradition from a Baptist community, many scholars hold that it is a creation by the early church (Bultmann, 178; G. Braumann*; Schulz, 263). A different view is argued by F. W. Danker* who claims that the saying reflects a charge made against the message of Jesus and the early church by Pharisaic opponents who claimed that it was bringing moral chaos and lawlessness in its train: 'not only the righteous, but *everyone*, including publicans and sinners, forces his way in' (F. W. Danker*, 237; cf. Jeremias, *Theology*, I, 111f.). This view depends on Danker's interpretation of βιάζομαι (see below). In this case, the saying could have been used ironically by Jesus himself, although Danker does not so regard it. But while it has been argued that the saying looks back on the ministry of Jesus as the period during which the kingdom became a present reality and that it must therefore be late, it is more probable that the enigmatic nature of the saying and its positive estimate of the Baptist point to a setting in the ministry of Jesus (Kümmel, 121–124; Percy, 199; Hahn, 165 n. 1; Jüngel, 191; Perrin, 74–77).

V. 17 is a variant form of Mt. 5:18. As it stands, it is a statement of the permanency of the OT law; this is made without any restriction in Lk. The saying has been thought to represent a legalistic Jewish-Christian point of view, but this is improbable. Manson, *Sayings*, 135, certainly found it so legalistic in tone that he was reduced to the suggestion that originally it was an ironical comment on the attitude of the Pharisees. But this desperate solution is unnecessary. Rather, the saying is to be understood as Jesus' rhetorical stress on the permanence of the law, but of the law as transformed and fulfilled in his own teaching (R. J. Banks*, 218). It has been correctly understood by both Evangelists, and there is no real objection to its authenticity; Schulz's claim, 115, that a Palestinian prophet here pronounces the permanent validity of the entire Mosaic law remains pure hypothesis.

On v. 16 see G. Schrenk, TDNT I, 609–614; Kümmel, 121–124; W. G. Kümmel, ' "Das Gesetz und die Propheten gehen bis Johannes" – Lukas 16, 16 im Zusammenhang der heilsgeschichtlichen Theologie der Lukasschriften', in Böcher, 89–102; Percy, 191–202; Conzelmann, *passim*; E. Bammel, 'Is Luke 16, 16–18 of Baptist's Provenience?' HTR 51, 1958, 101–106; F. W. Danker, 'Luke 16:16 – an Opposition Logion', JBL 77, 1958, 231–243;

Schürmann, *Untersuchungen*, 126–136 (' "Wer daher eines dieser geringsten Gebote auflöst . . ."
Wo fand Matthäus das Logion Mt. 5, 19?'. Originally in BZ 4, 1960, 238–250), cf. 117f.; G.
Braumann, 'Dem Himmelreich wird Gewalt angetan', ZNW 52, 1961, 104–109; Schnacken-
burg, 129–132; K. Chamblin, 'John the Baptist and the Kingdom of God', Tyn.B 15, 1964,
10–16; Jüngel, 190–193; Ladd, 154–160; Perrin, 74–77; Wink, 20–22; P.-H. Menoud, 'Le sens
du verbe *biazetai* dans Lc 16, 16', in Descamps, 207–212; Hoffmann, 50–79; Schulz, 261–267;
W. E. Moore, '*BIAZΩ, ΑΡΠΑΖΩ* and Cognates in Josephus', NTS 21, 1974–75, 519–543.
   On v. 17 see Schulz, 114–116; R. J. Banks, *Jesus and the Law in the Synoptic Tradition*,
Cambridge, 1975, 203–226.

(16) The first clause is probably preserved by Luke in its original,
sharp form. (The introductory Ἐστίν in X *al* it vg; *Diglot* is very weakly
attested; Tischendorf included it as a marginal reading, but with the last
clause of the previous verse.) The order ὁ νόμος καὶ οἱ προφῆται is standard (24:44; Mt. 5:17; *et al.*; Acts 13:15; 24:14; 28:23), and fits in with
Luke's stress here on the law. Although, therefore, the tendency could
well have been to reverse the unusual order found in Mt., it is likely that
Matthew's form is secondary, and is linked to his placing of the saying in
the context of teaching about John the Baptist as a prophet (so most
scholars; Schulz, 261 n. 585). μέχρι, usually μέχρις before a vowel, is
'until' (Acts 10:30; 20:7), diff. Mt. ἕως, and may be secondary (so
Schulz, 261; but it could have been altered by Matthew to produce his
ἕως ἄρτι phrase). It is disputed whether μέχρι Ἰωάννου means 'up to,
and including, John' or 'up to, but not including, John', i.e. whether John
is regarded as belonging to the era of the law and prophets or not. The
evidence is indecisive, and the question can be settled only when the
opening phrase of the next clause is taken into consideration. Luke has
no verb (but see textual note above). Matthew has προφητεύω, which
Hoffmann, 56–60, is inclined to regard as original, but which is more
probably redactional (W. G. Kummel*, 97 n. 29). But if there is no verb,
what is the meaning of the clause? The difficulty is to find a verb that
will take both nouns as its subject. Does 'the prophets' mean the men or
their books? Usually in the stereotyped phrase it means the latter.
Probably the sense is that the period of time marked by the law and the
prophets lasted until John. The next verse indicates that for Luke the
validity of the law and prophets has not ended; it is the activity which
produced them which has ended.
   A new era has begun ἀπὸ τότε, i.e. from the time of John (cf. Mt.
11:12 which is a secondary expansion). But does this expression exclude
John from the new era (Conzelmann, 16–21; Ellis, 202f.; Schulz, 264)
or include him as its beginning (Percy, 5 n., 198f.; E. Bammel*, 103 n.
14; Daube 285f.; Wink, 51–55; W. G. Kümmel*, 98–102)?
Linguistically either view is possible (cf. Mt. 16:21; 26:16 and 4:17). The
facts that Luke presents John as a preacher of good news in 3:18 (cf.
1:77), and that he regards the ministry of John as the beginning of the
gospel (Acts 1:22; Wink, ibid.) are decisive for his understanding. The
same meaning is required in Mt. (Percy, ibid.; cf. K. Chamblin*). It
remains possible that Luke has reinterpreted a saying which originally

meant to exclude John the Baptist from the era of the kingdom (Jüngel, 191–193; Schulz, 265), but this presupposes a division between John and Jesus which is improbable on the lips of Jesus.

During this period the kingdom of God is preached as good news. The verb εὐαγγελίζομαι is a favourite of Luke, and he frequently inserts it in his sources; he alone uses it with 'the kingdom of God' (4:43; 8:1; Acts 8:12; W. G. Kümmel, 95). These considerations indicate that Luke has substituted the verb for βιάζομαι (Mt.), which will have been original in the Q saying. The problem is then whether Luke has given a correct paraphrase of the saying. The verb βιάζεται can be understood as a middle or a passive. The active βιάζω is 'to constrain, force'; the middle is 'to overpower by force, press hard; to act with violence'; the passive is 'to be hard-pressed, overpowered' (cf. AG; G. Schrenk, TDNT I, 609–613). So here the meaning can be: 'the kingdom exercises its force' (Otto, 84–88; Manson, *Sayings*, 134; Percy, 196; Schnackenburg, 129–132; Ladd, 155–160; O. Betz, 'The Eschatological Interpretation of the Sinai Tradition in Qumran and in the New Testament', RQ 6, 1967, 89–107), or 'the kingdom suffers violence' (G. Schrenk, ibid.; Kümmel, 121–124; W. G. Kummel*, 97; F. W. Danker*, 233–236, 240; Schulz, 265). If the former meaning is accepted, Luke has paraphrased a positive statement about the powerful coming of the kingdom; if the latter meaning is original, then Luke has taken a negative statement (which *implies* the presence of the kingdom as a powerful force which creates opposition to itself) and reinterpreted it positively in order to get a contrast between law and gospel. The former interpretation is the more probable, and fits in with Jesus' other positive statements about the coming of the kingdom. It is linguistically possible, and it is not out of harmony with the following clause.

The remaining clause καὶ πᾶς εἰς αὐτὴν βιάζεται differs considerably from Mt. καὶ βιασταὶ ἁρπάζουσιν αὐτήν. Here too it is probable that Matthew has the original wording, since a double use of βιάζομαι in the saying is not very likely. The meaning is much debated. The passive sense 'everyone is forced into it' (Easton, 248; Käsemann, *Essays*, 42) is unlikely. It is not required by the parallel in 14:23, and the Matthaean form of the saying suggests a different view. A more acceptable version of this suggestion is proposed by P.-H. Menoud* who takes the verb to mean 'to invite' (cf. παραβιάζομαι, 24:29; Acts 16:16). Most commentators, however, prefer the middle form. This can be positive: 'everybody forces his way into it' (Klostermann, 167; G. Schrenk, ibid.; Manson, *Sayings*, 134; W. G. Kümmel*, 96); or it may be understood in a bad sense of 'everybody' forcing his way in by wrong means (F. W. Danker*, 235, insists that εἰς implies hostile intent, but this seems doubtful). Or again it may be used of opponents, whether the Pharisees (Ellis, 203f.) or demonic powers, oppressing the kingdom (Black, 116). This last possibility, however, is unlikely in view of the use of εἰς (G. Schrenk, ibid. 612). For Luke the saying would certainly seem to express the zeal and single-mindedness with which men must respond to the proclamation of the kingdom (13:24). The difficulty is the $\pi\tilde{\alpha}\varsigma$, which is hardly realistic in view of Jewish rejection of the gospel. Lagrange, 440, takes it to mean, 'Anyone who wishes to enter must strive to do so'. Again, we have to take the meaning of the Matthaean parallel into consideration. $\beta\iota\alpha\sigma\tau\eta\varsigma$ is a 'violent person', and $\dot{\alpha}\rho\pi\dot{\alpha}\zeta\omega$ means 'to snatch' or 'to snatch away' (Mt. 13:19). Hence the saying can also be taken positively, 'Men of violence seize at the opportunity of entering the kingdom', or negatively, 'men of violence snatch away the kingdom from those trying to enter'; the arguments in favour of the former meaning are the stronger (Schnackenburg, ibid.). Hence it appears probable that the saying in both of its forms refers to the effort men should make in order to get into the kingdom; but few sayings in the Gospels are so uncertain in interpretation as this one.

(17) The saying appears in different form in Mt. 5:18 where it forms part of a group of sayings about the permanency of the law. Luke's construction with $\varepsilon\dot{\upsilon}\kappa\sigma\pi\dot{\omega}\tau\varepsilon\rho\sigma\nu$ (5:23; 18:25) and two accusative and infinitive phrases differs from Matthew's rather redundant use of 'until' clauses, and may represent a stylistic revision (cf. Schulz, 114). $\dot{o}$ $o\dot{\upsilon}\rho\alpha\nu\dot{o}\varsigma$ $\kappa\alpha\dot{\iota}$ $\dot{\eta}$ $\gamma\tilde{\eta}$ (21:33 par. Mk. 13:31 par. Mt. 24:35) is the created universe (cf. Job 14:12; Is. 51:6). It is a symbol of permanency, but the law is more permanent. $\kappa\varepsilon\rho\alpha\dot{\iota}\alpha$, literally 'horn', can mean 'projection, hook' and may be used of some tiny part of a letter (Mt. 5:18**). It has been variously understood of the small additions which distinguish similar Hebrew characters (Origen, in Creed, 207) or of the scribal ornaments added to various letters (SB I, 248f.). The latter view is generally accepted (Schulz, 115 n. 155). $\kappa\varepsilon\rho\alpha\dot{\iota}\alpha$ may be a mistranslation of the ambiguous Aramaic $w\bar{a}w$, the name of the seventh letter of the Hebrew alphabet (G. Schwarz, '$\dot{\iota}\tilde{\omega}\tau\alpha$ $\dot{\varepsilon}\nu$ $\tilde{\eta}$ $\mu\dot{\iota}\alpha$ $\kappa\varepsilon\rho\alpha\dot{\iota}\alpha$ (Matthäus 5, 18)', ZNW 66, 1975, 268f.). In any case the most insignificant detail of the law is meant (cf. Philo, Flac. 133), so that the saying is a hyperbolic way of emphasising the abiding validity of the law: Matthew adds $\dot{\iota}\tilde{\omega}\tau\alpha$ $\dot{\varepsilon}\nu$; for $\pi\dot{\iota}\pi\tau\omega$ he has $\pi\alpha\rho\dot{\varepsilon}\rho\chi\sigma\mu\alpha\iota$ with the same sense. For the thought cf. Bar. 4:1; 4 Ez. 9:37; 2 Bar. 77:15; Luke understands the saying literally: the law has lost none of its validity despite the coming of the kingdom. It is, however, 'in the demands of the kingdom, not in its own continued existence, that the Law is validated' (R. J. Banks*, 218), as is seen by the way in which the saying is followed in both Mt. and Lk. by teaching in which the OT law is restated in a new way.

v. The Law concerning Divorce 16:18

Jesus pronounces that for a man to divorce his wife and remarry is tantamount to adultery on his part, and likewise for a man to marry a divorced woman is to commit adultery. The statement is essentially the same as that in Mt. 5:32 and is probably from Q. There is one important difference: Matthew states that the man who divorces his wife causes *her* to commit adultery (i.e. if she remarries), while Luke makes the man himself guilty of adultery if he remarries. Luke is here closer to Mk. 10:11 par. Mt. 19:9, and may have conformed the saying to the wording in Mk. (Schulz, 116f.). However, it is also possible that he has used an independent form of the saying in Mt., since there is no other influence from Mk. in the saying, and the whole has a neat parallel structure (Wrege, 66–70). In any case, Luke's saying goes against Jewish ideas, according to which a husband had freedom to divorce his wife and remarry, and condemns this as adultery. Similarly, the saying condemns the second husband for committing adultery; Jewish law allowed such marriages, except in the case of a woman marrying her co-respondent. Thus the saying sharpens the teaching of the OT law, and in no sense undermines it.

This suggests that the saying is included by Luke at this point in order to illustrate the continuing validity of the law but in the new form given to it by Jesus. To be sure, the change of subject to divorce is strange, but if Luke was following Q, this may well have been the next most suitable saying in that source; in Matthew's order, Lk. 16:17 par. Mt. 5:18, is followed by Q material in Mt. 5:25f. (cf. Lk. 12:57–59) and then by this saying, the intervening material being from other sources; see 16:16 note for the possibility that vs. 17 and 18 were linked in Q.

The authenticity of the basic saying as teaching of Jesus stands beyond all dispute (D. R. Catchpole*, 113).

See Wrege, 66–70; Derrett, 363–388; Schulz, 116–120; D. R. Catchpole, 'The Synoptic Divorce Material as a Traditio-Historical Problem', BJRL 57, 1974–75, 92–127.

(18) ἀπολύω has the meaning 'to divorce' in Mk. 10:2–12 par. Mt. 19:3–9; Mt. 1:19; 5:31f. For the participial form cf. Mt. 5:32. Jewish law permitted a man to divorce his wife provided that he went through the prescribed legal forms (Dt. 24:1–4). In such cases remarriage was possible, and this eventuality is envisaged as taking place here (cf. Mk. 10:11). The use of ἕτερος is probably editorial. Jesus declares that such a person is committing adultery (μοιχεύω, 16:18b; 18:20 par. Mk. 10:19; par. Mt. 19:18; Mt. 5:27, 28, 32; Jn. 8:4; Rom. 2:22; 13:9; Jas. 2:11; Rev. 2:22**; cf. Ex. 20:14 par. Dt. 5:17). The Marcan saying has μοιχάομαι (Mk. 10:11f.; Mt. 19:9; Mt. 5:32b**; cf. F. Hauck, TDNT IV, 729–735). The verbs are used of violating a person's marital relationships. Whereas in Jewish law a man who divorced his wife and married another was not guilty of any offence, Jesus here declares that this act is one of adultery; the implied object of the sin is the first wife (cf. ἐπ' αὐτήν, Mk. 10:11, unless this phrase refers to committing adultery (by intercourse) *with* the second wife). Thus Jesus places the husband and wife on the same level, and condemns the breaking of the marriage bond by the husband who is attracted by another woman. The parallel saying in Mt. states that a husband who divorces his wife causes *her* to commit adultery (when she contracts a second marriage),

presumably since she is then living with a second husband while her first husband is still alive.

In the second part of the saying Luke is closely parallel to Mt. 5:32b but has the better parallelism. The situation here is that of a man (a generalising πᾶς is added in ℵ A W Θ f1 *pm* sy^p; TR; *Diglot*) who marries a woman divorced ἀπὸ ἀνδρός (Lk. only; cf. Mk. 10:12); he is also committing adultery, i.e. against the first husband. (The situation in Mk. 10:12, however, is that of a wife who divorces her first husband and marries a second husband.) Here again Jesus goes beyond Jewish law, which regarded such a marriage as inadvisable (SB I, 320f.) but did not disallow it. The first marriage is regarded as permanent, so that the second husband of a divorced woman is regarded as offending against the first husband.

vi. The Rich Man and Lazarus 16:19–31

The editorial comment in 17:1 reminds us that the audience for this parable is still the Pharisees; there has in fact been no break in the teaching of Jesus since v. 15. Two themes are combined in the parable. The first is the reversal of fortunes in the next world for the rich and the poor; this sums up the theme found in 1:53 and 6:20–26 and the warning against covetousness in 12:13–21. The earlier part of the parable indicates that the rich man did not go out of his way to help Lazarus; the latter received only the left-overs from the table as they casually fell on the ground, and was not the object of any decent charity. The poor man is not specifically stated to be righteous or pious, but this is perhaps to be deduced from his name and from Luke's general equation of poverty and piety. Thus the rich man may possibly be intended as an example of the misuse of wealth over against the example of the proper use of wealth earlier in the chapter (cf. Schlatter, 376).

The second theme is that if the law and the prophets are insufficient to call the rich to repentance, even the return of someone resurrected from the dead will not achieve the desired effect. Miracles in themselves cannot melt stony hearts. Here again there is a link with the earlier part of the chapter in which the validity of the law and the prophets during the era of the gospel is upheld.

The parable is thus given as an example, or rather a warning, with regard to human conduct. The attempt by J. D. Crossan* (10:29–37 note), 297–299, to find a parable of the kingdom in an original form of the story is highly unconvincing.

It is, therefore, appropriate to see in the story some connection with similar OT teaching on attitudes to the poor, especially in Dt. 24:6ff., but the links are not very strong. Other attempts to find an OT basis for the story are more doubtful. The most plausible is a connection between Abraham and Lazarus in the story and Abraham and his servant Eliezer in Gn. 15:1f.; cf. Derrett, 85–92, who finds in Lazarus the servant of

Abraham sent to discover whether the Jews are acting hospitably (just as in Jewish tradition Eliezer visited Sodom). C. H. Cave* notes that Eliezer was a gentile and suggests that the parable teaches the severity of the judgment that will come upon the sons of Abraham if they fail to repent: they will see the gentiles finding mercy instead of themselves. But it is questionable whether either of these views reaches the heart of the parable.

We have in fact one of the cases where the background to the teaching is more probably found in non-biblical sources. An Egyptian folk tale, to which attention was drawn by H. Gressmann*, tells the story of an Egyptian who was reincarnated after his death as Si-Osiris, the miraculous son of a childless couple. When his 'father' one day remarked on how a rich man had had a sumptous funeral while a poor man had been simply buried, Si-Osiris took him to Amnte, the land of the dead, where he was able to see the rich man in torment and the poor man in luxury. The explanation is added that the good deeds of the poor man had outweighed his evil deeds, but the opposite was true of the rich man. The general motif of this story found its way into Jewish lore, and it is attested in some seven versions, the earliest of which concerns a poor scholar and the rich publican, Bar Ma'jan. Part of this story has been quoted above as a possible background to the parable of the great supper (14:15–24 note). Because of his one good deed Bar Ma'jan had a great funeral, but the poor scholar had a simple burial. One of the scholar's friends, however, had a dream in which he saw the poor man after his death in paradisial gardens beside flowing streams, while the publican was standing on the bank of the river but unable to reach the water. Thus the scholar received no reward in this life, in order that he might have a full reward in the next, while the publican received his reward for his one good deed in this world, so that he might have no reward in the next. It is clear that Jesus' parable bears some relation to this folk tale. Jeremias (*Parables*, 182–187) draws the parallel, and concludes that the point of Jesus' parable is to be found where it goes beyond the Jewish story, namely in the lesson that no sign will be given to this generation to lead it to repentance if it refuses to hear the word of God. This interpretation does not do justice to the first part of the parable with its lengthy description of the two men.

The relation between the Egyptian tale and the parable has been raised afresh by the fact that in some textual authorities a name is given to the rich man, Nineveh. The authorities in question are Egyptian, and it may be that the name is derived from some Egyptian form of the story. K. Grobel* has accordingly taken a fresh look at the story and is able to explain several of its difficulties in the light of the Egyptian parallel.

The unity and authenticity of the parable are problematic. The fact that the parable has two parts and two points inevitably suggests that the second part is secondary. Bultmann 212f., argued that the story resembles a Jewish legend in which a husband repents after his wife (who had died earlier) sent him a warning message from the underworld; the present story originally had the same point, but has had a secondary ending added in order to show that messages from the dead will not convert anybody. For further difficulties in the story see C. F. Evans*. The basic question is whether two themes may be linked in the one parable, especially since the second may be seen as a post-Easter addition by the early church in the light of Jewish failure to respond to the message of the resurrection, whether of Jesus or of Lazarus (Jn. 11). The parable thus falls under some suspicion of being a Lucan composition along with the other parables peculiar to this Gospel (cf. Drury, 161f.).

In the present case, however, the two-tier structure arises as a result of the adaptation of an existing story. Moreover, this story already contains the basic elements, including the thought of a messenger from the world of the dead, which are found in the parable. Although a much more concrete interpretation would be given to it by Christians, v. 31 could have been spoken in a pre-Christian setting. Grobel's treatment shows that the parable can be successfully explained as a unity. There is no 'law' that parables of Jesus must conform to a particular one-point pattern. The present parable probably rests on tradition traceable back to Jesus himself.

See H. Gressmann, *Vom reichen Mann und armen Lazarus*, Berlin, 1918 (not accessible to me); Jeremias, *Parables*, 182–187; Derrett, 78–99 ('Fresh Light on St Luke xvi. II. Dives and Lazarus and the preceding Sayings', NTS 7, 1960–61, 364–380); H. J. Cadbury, 'A Proper Name for Dives', JBL 81, 1962, 399–402; K. Grobel, '... Whose Name was Neves', NTS 10, 1963–64, 373–382; C. H. Cave, 'Lazarus and the Lucan Deuteronomy', NTS 15, 1968–69, 319–325; C. F. Evans, 'Uncomfortable Words – V. (Lk. 16:31)', Exp.T 81, 1969–70, 228–231; O. Glombitza, 'Der reiche Mann und der arme Lazarus', Nov.T 12, 1970, 166–180.

(19) The opening phrase is reminiscent of 16:1, but here the rich man is of importance in his own right. After πλουσιος p[75] has the doubtless secondary insertion ὀνόματι Νευης; cf. the addition of the name *Nineue* in sa; the rich man is given the name 'Finaeus' in Pseudo-Cyprian, 'Finees' in Priscillian, and 'Amonofis' in Peter of Riga (Metzger, 165f.). The origin of these names is uncertain. 'Amonofis' is a form of 'Amenophis', a name of several ancient Pharaohs. Finaeus/Finees may be based on the Phinehas who appears along with Eleazar in Ex. 6:25; Nu. 25:7, 11; Jos. 22:13, 31f.; 24:33. Alternatively, it may be explained as a combination of the Coptic article with Neues (K. Grobel*, 381f.). Neues is most plausibly explained as due to haplography of the longer form Νινευης, as attested by sa, and no doubt crept into the Greek text from the Sahidic tradition. As for *Nineue*, this has been explained as a corruption of Μιναῖος, which in its turn is equivalent to Bar Ma'jan (H. Gressmann, cited by Creed, 211, who comments rightly that this is a precarious identification). More obvious is an allusion to the rich city of Nineveh and God's judgment upon it. Most ingenious is the suggestion of Grobel that it represents a Coptic word meaning 'Nobody', a derisory word to describe the status of the

rich man in the underworld, which was used in an Egyptian version of the basic story and thence was added by a scribe to the Lucan version.

The rich man's sumptuous way of life is now described. It was his custom (ἐνεδιδύσκετο, imperfect) to wear garments of purple and fine underwear. πορφύρα, originally the purple fish (murex), was used of the dye obtained from it, and then of cloth so dyed (Mk. 15:17, 20; Rev. 18:12**). A costly mantle of wool, such as would be worn by royalty is meant (cf. SB II, 222). βύσσος (Rev. 18:12 v.l.**) is a loan word, Hebrew bûṣ, (Est. 1:6; cf. Pr. 31:22), 'fine linen' (cf. SB II, 222; J. Weiss, 488, however, claims that fine Egyptian cotton is meant). For linen and purple see Pr. 31:22; 1QapGen. 20:31. εὐφραίνομαι (12:19) here has the sense of feasting, and λαμπρῶς**, 'splendidly', can be applied to feasting (ἐξαρτίσαι τὸ δεῖπνον λαμπρῶς, PGM 1, 111, cited by AG).

(20) The poor man is deliberately contrasted with the rich man. Unlike the rich man he is named, as Λάζαρος, i.e. la'ªzar, an abbreviation of 'el'āzār, 'He (whom) God helps' (SB II, 223; cf. Vermes, 53, 190f., on the currency of the shortened, dialectical form). This is the only instance of a name being given to a character in the parables of Jesus. Its significance may be that it hints at the piety of the poor man, although the general use of πτωχός in Lk. (4:18; 6:20; 7:22; 21:3) already indicates that the poor are in general pious and the recipients of God's grace (cf. 14:13, 21). The name may be included also because it facilitates the dialogue in vs. 24ff. The coincidence of the name with that of Abraham's servant has also been noted, and hence a symbolical significance has been seen in it. Although the name was an extremely common one, it remains surprising that the man whom Jesus raised from the dead in Jn. 11 bore the same name, and that his resurrection failed to convert the Jewish leaders and divert them from plotting against Jesus. Hence it has been argued that either the parable has influenced the form of the miracle story, or vice versa (R. Schnackenburg, *Das Johannesevangelium*, Freiburg, 1971, II, 429f.). The structure of the sentence is altered by the addition of ἦν and ὅς in A W Θ f1 f13 *pm* lat; TR; Diglot. The pluperfect ἐβέβλητο could mean that he had been laid by friends in a suitable place for begging, but more probably it means 'he was lying' (BD 347²; AG, citing Jos. Ant. 9:209); the implication is that he was ill or crippled. πυλών*, 'gate', refers to a large, ornamental gateway to a city or a mansion (Mt. 26:71; Acts 10:17; 12:13f.; 14:13). ἑλκόω** (BD 68) is 'to cause sores, ulcers'; the perfect participle means 'covered with ulcers'. Manson, *Sayings*, 298, suggests that he may have been a leper (but would he then have begged in public?).

(21) As in 15:16 ἐπιθυμέω may represent an unfulfilled wish, since the beggar lay at the gate, and not beside the table from which the scraps fell; the words καὶ οὐδεὶς ἐδίδου αὐτῷ are added from 15:16 by f13 1 vg^cl. ἀπό is partitive, and the noun τῶν ψιχίων is added in most MSS from Mt. 15:27 (omitted by p⁷⁵ ℵ* B L it sy^s; Metzger, 166). πίπτω is used as the passive of βάλλω (10:18); the reference may be, therefore,

not to crumbs that fell unwittingly from the table, but to pieces of bread which the guests used to wipe their hands and then threw under the table (Jeremias, *Parables*, 184; but no evidence is provided, and the description is strange). Such crumbs were normally eaten by the dogs (Mt. 15:27; note the close correspondence in language), which also turned their unwelcome attention to the beggar. ἀλλὰ καί has the sense 'and worse than all' (Easton, 252). The dogs aggravated the sores by licking them (ἐπιλείχω**, apparently a *hapax legomenon*; cf. ἐκλείχω, 1 Ki. 22:38; ἕλκος, 'sore, ulcer', Rev. 16:2, 11**); they were also ceremonially unclean (Klostermann, 168). J. Weiss, 488, suggests that they treated the beggar as if he was already dead. The main point is clear: the rich man and his associates did nothing to help the beggar, beyond possibly throwing him some scraps. It is quite false to infer that the rich man's lack of charity does not figure in the story.

(22) The decisive point in the story is introduced with an ἐγένετο δέ construction (3:21). The poor man dies and is carried away (ἀποφέρω, Acts 19:12; Mk. 15:1; 1 Cor. 16:3; Rev. 17:3; 21:10**) by the angels to Abraham's bosom. The imagery is unusual. The thought of angels accompanying the souls of the righteous is not found in rabbinic sources before AD 150 (SB II, 223–225; the text of T. Ash. 6:6 is uncertain). K. Grobel*, 378, suggests that the angels are a Jewish substitute for some bearer of the dead in the Egyptian version of the story. In any case, the point is the divine care lavished upon Lazarus. The metaphor of the bosom (κόλπος; cf. 6:38 for a different meaning) may suggest: 1. a child lying on its parent's lap (Jn. 1:18; Jeb. 77a in SB I, 25; cf. Creed, 212; Manson, *Sayings*, 299); 2. the proximity of a guest to the host at a banquet (Jn. 13:23; cf. 2 Clem. 4:5; Jeremias, *Parables*, 184; R. Meyer, TDNT III, 824–826); 3. a late form of the idea of being gathered to one's fathers (Gn. 15:15). See further SB II, 225–227. We should probably combine suggestions 1. and 2., so that the poor man enjoys close fellowship with Abraham at the messianic banquet (cf. 13:29). For Abraham receiving the righteous martyrs cf. 4 Mac. 13:17. Nothing is said about where Abraham is thought to be. 'Abraham's bosom' is not a synonym for Paradise, although Abraham may be thought to be in Paradise (Test. Abr. 20A, cited by J. Jeremias, TDNT V, 769, n. 37). K. Grobel's* suggestion (379) that the four depressions (κοῖλοι) in the abode of the dead in 1 En. 22 could be called κόλποι is not very helpful.

The rich man simply died and was buried, without any heavenly honours. To the end of his life he enjoyed luxury, and did not suffer any earthly loss (such as lying unburied) which might have mitigated his fate in the next world (SB II, 227). A reversal of position was all that he could expect (1 En. 103:5–8).

(23) So the rich man found himself in ᾅδης (10:15 note). Since the reference is to the state of the man immediately after his death, it is most likely that the intermediate abode of the dead before the final judgment is meant (cf. 1 En. 22; SB II, 228; IV:2, 1019f.; J. Jeremias, TDNT I,

146–149; V, 769 n. 37). An allusion to the final abode of the dead (Gehenna; so J. Weiss, 489; Klostermann, 168f.) is less likely. The reason for the suggestion is that only the rich man appears to be in Hades. But this depends on where we regard Abraham's bosom as being situated. Lazarus is separated from the rich man by a great gulf, which suggests that they are adjacent to each other, as in 1 En. 22; cf. 4 Esd. 7:85, 93; 2 Bar. 51:5f., but the visibility of the blessed from the abode of the damned also seems to be possible after the last judgment (Lk. 13:28, but this may be to over-press the language). The Egyptian background supports the view that we have a picture similar to that in 1 En. 22. The difficulty is due to the fact that Jewish representations of the after-life were fluid and developing, so that consistent pictures are hardly to be expected (cf. SB IV: 2, 1016–1165). The fact that the rich man 'lifted his eyes' (cf. 6:20) to see Lazarus does not necessarily indicate that the latter was above him; the phraseology is stereotyped (see especially 2 Sa. 18:24; K. Grobel*, 379). Torment (βάσανος, 16:28; cf. Mt. 4:24**) is a feature of the intermediate state as well as of the final state of the wicked (1 En. 22; cf. Wis. 3:1; 4 Mac. 13:15; 2 Clem. 17:7; 10:4). The historic present ὁρᾷ is pre-Lucan (Rehkopf, 99). The use of μακρόθεν (18:13; 22:54; with ἀπό (strictly redundant) as here, 23:49*; for Classical πόρρωθεν, BD 104³) shows that the wicked and righteous are well separated from each other, so that neither can reach the other; nevertheless, the story requires that communication by shouting is possible. The dead are visualised in bodily terms, since there is no other way in which they can be visualised (cf. SB II, 228–231); the story has no bearing on the question of the resurrection of the body. It is manifest too that the details are not to be taken literally. For the plural ἐν τοῖς κόλποις cf. BD 141⁵.

(24) Abraham occupies a position of authority and importance because he is the spiritual father of Israel; the rich man's address to him echoes 3:8 (Danker, 176), and lays claim to his share in his merits (SB I, 116–121; J. Jeremias, TDNT I, 8). He calls out for mercy (ἐλεέω, 17:13; 18:38f. par. Mk. 10:47f.), i.e. gracious help in time of need and helplessness. He thinks that Abraham will send Lazarus to help him. Even in Hades he thinks of Lazarus as there to look after *his* wants, while in his lifetime he had never spared a thought for Lazarus's wants; he remains totally blind and unrepentant. The fact that he knows the beggar's name indicates that he knew who he was, even if he never did anything for him.

His great need is thirst (4 Ez. 8:59; 2 En. 10:1f.; SB II, 232) consequent upon the burning heat of the fire in Hades (1 En. 63:10; SB IV:2, 1075–1083). βάπτω is 'to dip' (Jn. 13:26; Rev. 19:13**) and takes the accusative of the thing dipped and the genitive of that into which it is dipped (BD 172). ἄκρον is 'high point, top', hence 'tip' (Mk. 13:27; Mt. 24:31; Heb. 11:21**). καταψύχω**, is 'to cool, refresh', and φλόξ is 'flame' (Acts 7:30; 2 Thes. 1:8; Heb. 1:7; Rev. 1:14; 2:18; 19:12). It is presupposed that Lazarus has access to water, as is the case in the stories of Satme and Bar Ma'jan (cf. 1 En. 22); the association of water with Osiris is frequent (K. Grobel*, 379f.).

(25) It is not clear whether Abraham's use of the address τέκνον to the rich man is merely formal (cf. Mk. 2:5; 10:24) or represents an acceptance of his claim to kinship (cf. Jn. 8:37). In any case, the physical relationship is no entitlement to favour. The person who has enjoyed good things in life now experiences a reverse of fortune. After ἀπέλαβες an emphatic σύ in W Δ Θ f1 pm; TR; Diglot; draws the contrast with Lazarus. τὰ ἀγαθά (12:18) is not simply 'possessions', but is contrasted with τὰ κακά. ζωή is used non-theologically of earthly life (cf. 12:15, but here the sense is more 'real life'; cf. Acts 8:23; 17:25). For ὧδε a few witnesses have ὅδε (f1 pc Mcion), which is preferred by MH III, 44; the usage would then be akin to 10:39. The sufferer on earth is comforted in the next life (παρακαλέω, Mt. 5:4). The rich man's fate is pain; ὀδυνάω (2:48; 16:24; Acts 20:38**) can refer to physical pain, but F. Hauck, TDNT V, 115, holds that in this verse it is 'the spiritual torture of remorse'.

(26) Not only is help unavailable because of the action of retributive justice; it is also impossible because of the eternal separation between the two parts of the abode of the dead. ἐν πᾶσι τούτοις is said to mean 'in spite of all this' (C. F. Evans*, 229, but no evidence is cited). The literal meaning 'in all these regions' (Plummer, 395f. with caution; Lagrange, 447) is unlikely. The variant reading ἐπί suggests the sense 'in addition to all this' (most translations; Creed, 213). Could it mean 'because of all these things' (cf. AG s.v. III, 3)? χάσμα, 'chasm', is found here only; ἐστήρικται is the perfect passive of στηρίζω (9:51); the ὅπως clause is tantamount to result; διαβαίνω is 'to go across' (Acts 16:9; Heb. 11:29**) ἔνθεν is 'from here' (Mt. 17:20**); the v.l. ἐντεῦθεν is found in K Π al; TR; Diglot. After μηδέ supply οἱ θέλοντες διαβῆναι (οἱ is added in most MSS except p⁷⁵ ℵ* B D). διαπεράω is 'to cross over' (Acts 21:2). For the separation of the two groups of people cf. 1 En. 22:8ff. The judgment is thus irrevocable; there is no suggestion of purgatory (Jeremias, Parables, 186).

(27) The change of subject is not announced. The rich man now bends his efforts to doing what may still be possible, namely to prevent his brothers from joining him. For ἐρωτῶ σε cf. 14:18f. The rich man still thinks of Lazarus as a possible messenger; he has evidently not yet realised that he has no jurisdiction over him. The possibility of a messenger from the dead was a recognised one (Plato, Rep. 10, 614d).

(28) The five brothers are envisaged as living at home with their father, probably because the family estate has not been broken up (cf. 15:12; 12:13f.); it is not clear whether the rich man had also lived with them, but the story suggests that he had his own independent establishment. Five is no doubt a round number; attempts to find allusions to the Herod family are ill-directed. After the parenthetic γάρ clause, a purpose

clause continues the construction of v. 27. διαμαρτύρομαι is 'to warn' (AG) or 'to bear witness' (Acts 2:40; *et al.*). The thought is that if the brothers know that their present way of life will bring them into torment, as testified by a witness from the dead, then they will amend their ways. It is unnecessary to suppose that they are Sadducees who did not believe that there was any life after death (so Manson, *Sayings*, 300f.); they simply thought that they were secure from any post-mortem penalties by reason of their descent from Abraham. Nor is the rich man necessarily showing the saving grace of compassion; he failed to show it to Lazarus, and in any case it is now too late to show it, even to wealthy brothers (cf. O. Glombitza*, who stresses the element 'too late' in the story).

(29) For λέγει δέ, *Diglot* has λέγει αὐτῷ with weak external evidence. The brothers have Moses, i.e. the Torah (24:27; cf. Jn. 5:46 and the prophets (cf. 16:16, 31; 24:27, 44; for the combination cf. 1QS 1:3; 8:15f.; cf. CD 5:21; 6:1; it is not found in rabbinic Judaism; SB IV:1, 415–417; Braun, *Qumran*, I, 91). let the brothers listen to them, i.e. in the readings in the synagogue (O. Glombitza*, 175–177), and take in the force of what they say.

(30) But the rich man knows from personal experience that his family do not take seriously what the law and the prophets say. Something more is needed, and he persists with his request to Abraham. If someone visits them from the dead, perhaps in a dream or vision, this will lead them to repent. For Luke's readers there would be an inescapable allusion to the resurrection of Jesus (9:22; 11:29f.; 13:32), and for readers of the New Testament a reference to the story of Lazarus in Jn. 11. The reference in the story would also have point for the original hearers, since the idea of messages from the next world was by no means unheard of; angels were known to visit men, and in Jewish and pagan thought men might appear from the dead. Hence there is nothing specifically Christian in this verse.

(31) But the request is refused, because it will not work. Note the double condition, expressive of present fact (they do not listen to the law and the prophets) and future possibility (if someone rises from the dead). The possibility is couched in terms of resurrection, rather than simply a messenger from the dead, and fits in with the language of Jesus and the early church. Miracles will not convince those whose hearts are morally blind and unrepentant; they will not be persuaded. The parable ends on a note of solemn warning.

h. Teaching for Disciples (17:1–10)

Luke oscillates between teaching addressed to the crowds and Pharisees and instruction for the disciples. The present section reverts to the disciples and contains miscellaneous advice to them about the danger of putting stumbling blocks in the way of one another (17:1–3a), the need to forgive one another (17:3b–4), growth in faith (17:5f.), and the need for humble performance of duties (17:7–10). The material is drawn from more than one source, and this is reflected in the lack of logical connection.

i. Stumbling-Blocks 17:1–2

Jesus' saying admits that there are bound to be causes of sin in the world, but men are morally responsible if they act as such; it would therefore be better for them to die before they commit such an offence than to do so and then suffer divine judgment.

The saying has a parallel in Mk. 9:42 and Mt. 18:6f. Although the passage is not discussed by Schulz, it is clear that Luke and Matthew are both dependent on Q at this point, which had a doublet of the Marcan saying. There is nothing corresponding to v. 1 in Mk. One or two agreements in wording between Mk. and Lk. against Mt. suggest that Luke may have made some use of Mk. at this point. Bultmann, 155, and W. Pesch, *Matthäus der Seelsorger*, Stuttgart, 1966, 21–24, suggest that Matthew has first copied down what was common to his two sources and then added what was peculiar to one of them.

Bultmann, ibid., regards the saying as originally taken over by the Christian tradition from an unknown source, and given some Christian touches by Mark. No evidence is offered for this surmise. An origin in the teaching of Jesus is at least as likely.

(1) The introduction to the saying is Lucan (9:14; 12:22; 17:22). The reference to the disciples as the audience may be Luke's deduction from the content of the saying, or may be drawn from his source (Klostermann, 171). Grundmann, 331f., thinks that the saying is meant as a commentary on the preceding parable: the rich man was a stumbling-block in failing to show mercy to Lazarus, and his fate illustrates the judgment on such people. This seems rather artificial.

The first part of the saying is parallel to Mt. 18:7b, but the wording differs in detail. Matthew prefixes 'Alas for the world because of stumbling-blocks', which Luke may have omitted if he regarded the saying as addressed to disciples. ἀνένδεκτος**, 'impossible', may be Lucan (cf. οὐκ ἐνδέχεται, 13:33). The construction with τοῦ and infinitive (BD 400⁴) is Lucan (cf. 4:42; 24:16), but is rather awkward; Matthew has a simpler construction (ἀνάγκη with accusative and infinitive), regarded as primitive by Lagrange, 450. The word order τὰ σκάνδαλα μὴ ἐλθεῖν (p⁷⁵ ℵ B L *pc* e) is reversed in TR; *Diglot*, giving what Kilpatrick, 198, regards as a more Semitic word order. σκάνδαλον is 'stumbling-block, cause of offence' (Mt. 13:41; 16:23; 18:7; for the verb see Lk. 7:23; 17:2; cf. G. Stählin, TDNT VII, 339–358, especially 351). The thought here is of causing people to stumble (Ps. 140:5), in the sense that they are led into sin (Ps. Sol. 16:7) or apostasy (Wis. 14:11). Such temptations are inevitable, presumably because of the evil influence of Satan in the world. Nevertheless, it is a sad thing for the person responsible for causing temptation in view of the judgment which he will have to face. πλήν is read by p⁷⁵ ℵ B D f1 f13 *pc* it syˢ sa bo and should be preferred to δέ (*rell*; *Synopsis*) despite the possibility of assimilation to Mt. For οὐαί see 6:24. The saying is formally parallel to 22:22 (par. Mk. 14:21) which contrasts the plan of God regarding the suffering of the Son of man with the responsibility of the man who betrays him.

(2) So fearful is the judgment that it would be better for a man to die before he can act as a stumbling-block. Luke's order of the sayings is original, as compared with Mt. Matthew follows the construction in Mk. with an introductory relative clause; this appears to be secondary to the Q form, and to have developed once the introduction in the Q form had been dropped to give a more general form of statement which could stand on its own. λυσιτελεῖ**, 'to be profitable', is peculiar to Lk.; the verb must be taken in a comparative sense (BD 245³; cf. Mk. μᾶλλον). Luke's use of εἰ aligns him with Mk. against Mt. (ἵνα), and his phrase λίθος μυλικός, may be from Q or be a simplification of Mk. μύλος ὀνικός. μυλικός**, 'belonging to a mill', here describes the round upper stone of a grinding mill, pierced with a hole in the centre so that it could be rotated (cf. SB I, 775–778). περίκειμαι is 'to lie, be placed round' (Acts 28:20; Mk. 9:42; diff. Mt. κρεμάννυμι). The thought of a millstone round the neck was used proverbially by the Jews, as in modern English, to signify an encumbrance. The use of the millstone to weigh down a person so that he drowned is not found, but the use of a heavy weight to sink a light object or to drown a person is attested (Je. 51:63; Jos. Ap. I, 307). The use of the perfect ἔρριπται (4:35; diff. Mk. βέβληται; Mt. καταποντισθῇ) expresses the state of the man before he can pursue his sinful intent; the tenses are unusual in an unreal condition (BD 360⁴; 372³). The comparison is expressed by means of a ἵνα clause. The problem here is the identity of the 'little ones' (μικροί, cf. Mt. 10:42; 18:10, 14; the order τῶν μικρῶν τούτων ἕνα (ℵ* B L) is inverted in TR; *Diglot*). The word may refer literally to children (cf. Manson, *Sayings*, 138f., who thinks that this was the original meaning), or to the disciples (cf. 12:32; Klostermann, 171; O. Michel, TDNT IV, 651f.), or to the 'poor' to whom the gospel is preached (Kümmel, 93f.; cf. Grundmann, 332, who sees Lazarus as an example of this group). Mt. 18:6 clearly identifies them as those who believe in Jesus, but this is generally regarded as a clarification. The curious feature is the uniform use of οὗτοι in the phrase, presumably referring to people present.

ii. Unlimited Forgiveness 17:3–4

Closely allied to the subject of not leading other people, especially other disciples into sin, is the theme of helping them when they fall into sin. Here one particular kind of sin, namely personal offence, is discussed.

The disciple has the duty to admonish an offender so that he does not remain guilty of sin but has the opportunity to repent; the willingness to forgive that is inherent in the admonition is to be limitless.

The first part of the saying (17:3) appears as the first part of a more developed three-stage system of discipline within the community in Mt. 18:15. It is generally agreed that the Matthaean form is a development, so that a church rule has evolved out of what was originally more like a wisdom saying (Bultmann, 81, 151). But Matthew's material here is probably not the result of his own redaction, and therefore the question arises whether he has used a different recension of Q from Luke, or has employed a different source which had incorporated and developed Q material (cf. Lührmann, 111–114, who claims that Matthew's Q material was transmitted to him via a Jewish-Christian community), or has utilised a different saying of Jesus (K. H. Rengstorf, TDNT II, 631 n. 29). The parallelism is sufficiently close to suggest that Matthew is ultimately dependent on the Q saying.

This is confirmed by the fact that Matthew 18:21f. continues with a parallel to the second part of the saying (17:4). Here, however, it has the form of a dialogue between Peter and Jesus, and this may be due to Matthaean editing (Bultmann, 151; Schulz, 321). Luke then has the original form with two parallel sayings, the second of which goes beyond the first and makes the whole saying more forceful; Bultmann's view (90; cf. Lührmann, 112 n. 1) that the second part is a secondary development is thus improbable (Schulz, 322 n. 486). Similarly, his claim that the first part is a Christian construction (Bultmann, 158) is unfounded.

See Lührmann, 111–114; Schulz, 320–322.

(3) The opening words προσέχετε ἑαυτοῖς (cf. 12:1) may be linked with the preceding section (*Synopsis*; NEB; TEV; NIV; Plummer, 399; Lagrange, 452; Klostermann, 171) in the sense: 'Let each person take heed to himself'. They then form a reinforcement of the warning that has just been given. But this sounds rather like an anticlimax, and more probably the phrase introduces the present section (RV; RSV; TNT; Stuhlmueller, 150). In this case ἑαυτούς may be equivalent to ἀλλήλους, giving the sense: 'Take heed to one another' (Zahn, 593), but the usual meaning is better. The phrase really serves as a link between the two sections (Creed, 215) and may have been inserted by Luke (Schulz, 320).

The verb ἁμαρτάνω can be used of offences against God and also against man (cf. the clarifying εἰς σέ in D Γ Δ Π pm c e q; TR; *Diglot*; similarly in Mt. 18:15 TR; *Diglot*); cf. 15:18, 21; Acts 25:8; 1 Cor. 8:12. ὁ ἀδελφός σου (6:41) indicates that fellow-disciples are in mind. ἐπιτιμάω (4:35; *et al.*) can mean 'to censure' or 'to speak seriously, warn in order to prevent an action or bring one to an end' (AG). Matthew uses ἐλέγχω (Lk. 3:19*), which may be original (Schulz, 321). The saying implicitly forbids the nursing of grudges and criticism of the offender behind his back.

The hoped for result is positive. The offender may respond by an expression of repentance (diff. Mt. σου ἀκούσῃ, which is probably secondary). When this condition is fulfilled, forgiveness is to be granted; Mt. ἐκέρδησας is again probably secondary.

(4) So far the instruction fits in with Jewish thought which also recognised the need for repeated forgiveness (SB I, 795–797); but here the thought is expressed more sharply than in Judaism (Braun, *Radikalismus* II, 87). ἑπτάκις signifies an indefinite number of times (Ps. 119 (118): 164). τῆς ἡμέρας (genitive of time within which) heightens the force of the saying (diff. Mt.). εἰς σέ emphasises the personal nature of the insult, already implicit in v. 3. After the second ἑπτάκις many MSS insert τῆς ἡμέρας (so TR; *Diglot*). The use of ἐπιστρέφω may be Lucan (cf. 1:16f.). The use of λέγων does not imply that the repentance is merely outward. ἀφήσεις is a command.

iii. The Power of Faith 17:5–6

The saying of Jesus is given in reply to a request for greater faith by the apostles: even the tiniest 'amount' of faith is capable of mighty tasks.

The connection of the paragraph with what precedes and follows is imperceptible, and it is best to assume that Luke is following a source which simply listed sayings of Jesus. In G. Thomas 48 (cf. 106) the establishment of peace between two people is the condition for their successfully praying that a mountain may be moved; this reflects a connection of thought between Lk. 17:3f. and 5f., but hardly represents the original one. Ellis, 207, understands the connection in the opposite way: the greatness of the task in 17:3f. leads to the request for resources with which to tackle it.

The introductory request of the disciples in v. 5 could be seen as a response to the sort of remark made by Jesus in Mk. 9:28f. or 11:22; but the language is Lucan, and, if it is not a Lucan composition, it is an edited form of an original introduction which cannot now be reconstructed (cf. Schulz, 465f.). The saying of Jesus is paralleled in Mk. 11:23 par. Mt. 21:21 and more closely in Mt. 17:20; the latter saying is a Matthaean insertion in a Marcan setting, but while it agrees with Lk. in a reference to a grain of mustard seed (Q), it has been assimilated to Mk. by the substitution of mountain for 'tree'. Luke's form of the saying appears, therefore, to reflect Q. See Schulz, 465–468.

The relation between the Q saying and the Marcan saying is less certain. Some argue that the Q form is the oldest form, that it has been assimilated to current Jewish expressions which spoke of a mountain in Mt. 17:20 (cf. Is. 54:10; SB I, 759; 1 Cor. 13:2), and that Mark has combined the two forms (C.-H. Hunzinger, TDNT VII, 289f.; Schulz, 467 n. 493). But how could Mark have known these two forms? Others postulate the existence of two independent sayings (Mt. 17:20 and Lk. 17:6) which have been conflated in Mk. (Manson, *Sayings*, 140f.;

Lohmeyer, 238f.). Schweizer, *Markus*, 133; *Matthäus*, 230, regards Mt. 17:20 as the oldest form; this was then linked to the story of the cursing of the fig-tree in pre-Marcan tradition, and in the version of the oral tradition that reached Luke, 'tree' was substituted for 'mountain'. The weakness in this view is that the fig-tree is *not* a mulberry or fig-mulberry, and that the 'mountain' has survived in Mark's account. It remains most probable that Lk. 17:6 and Mk. 11:23 are separate sayings which have been conflated in Mt. 17:20. Since there is no reason why 'mountain' should be altered to 'tree', the Lucan (Q) form must be original; whether the Marcan saying is an independent saying of Jesus or a secondary version of the Q form can scarcely be decided.

See Manson, *Sayings*, 140f.; C.-H. Hunzinger, TDNT VII, 287–291; Schulz, 465–468.

(5) The use of οἱ ἀπόστολοι is generally regarded as Lucan (6:13; *et al.*). It may be meant here to associate the apostles with the gift of wonder-working faith, although there is nothing in the context to suggest this motif. προστίθημι is probably also Lucan (3:20; *et al.*). The phrase may mean simply 'give us faith' (AG), or 'give us also faith (in addition to other gifts)' (Klostermann, 171; Creed, 215), or 'give us more faith' (cf. Is. 2:19; 26:15; Turner, 51 n.; most translations). The third possibility fits in best with the thought in the next verse, which in effect denies that faith can be quantified.

(6) Jesus' reply has the form of a mixed condition with the present indicative in the protasis (but altered to εἴχετε in D E G *al* lat) and the imperfect with ἄν in the apodosis. The curious form (diff. Mt.) may be due to politeness: the disciples' request presupposes that they have some faith, and 'if you had faith' might seem to deny this assumption too bluntly (BD 372[la]; MH III, 92). For πίστιν ἔχω cf. Mk. 11:2. For the proverbially small κόκκος σινάπεως see 13:19; SB I, 669. συκάμινος** is usually the 'mulberry' (*morus nigra*), a different tree from the συκομορέα (19:4), 'fig-mulberry' (*ficus sycomorus*), συκῆ (13:6), 'fig', and the English sycamore. But the names tended to get confused: Hebrew *šiqmāh* (*ficus sycomorus*) is rendered by συκάμινος in the LXX but by συκόμορος in Aquila and Symmachus (Ps. 78 (77):47; Is. 9:10). The fact that Luke uses the two different words here and in 19:4 may suggest that he did intend the mulberry here. In fact, however, it was the fig-mulberry which was traditionally deep-rooted (SB II, 234), and hence it is probably that tree which is meant here (Plummer, 400 n.; C.-H. Hunzinger*). The demonstrative ταύτῃ, suggesting a reference to an actual tree, is omitted by p⁷⁵ ℵ D pc sy[c] and bracketed by UBS. The disciples are to command such a tree to be uprooted (ἐκριζόω**) and to be planted in the sea; if they do so, it would obey them. The verb ὑπήκουσεν ἄν strictly refers to a time prior to the command; the peculiar tense is perhaps meant to emphasise the certainty of the fulfilment. It is not clear why anybody should want to transplant a deep-rooted tree into the sea. Lagrange, 454, notes that there were trees on the shore at Jaffa which

one could imagine throwing themselves into the sea. Matthew refers simply to transfer to another site; this could be original, and Luke's reference to the sea due to assimilation to Mk. 11:23, but more probably Matthew's less vivid wording is secondary. On the relation between Luke's 'tree' and Mark's 'mountain' see introduction to section. Mark's saying is more fully developed in terms of the need to avoid doubt and believe. The saying is not to be taken literally in any of its forms. It may originally have referred to the ability to work miracles (cf. 10:9; Schulz, 467f.), but there is no hint of this in the present context. Manson, *Sayings*, 141, holds that the absurdity of transplanting a tree is a warning against misunderstanding: 'This word of Jesus does not invite Christians to become conjurers and magicians, but heroes like those whose exploits are celebrated in the eleventh chapter of Hebrews.' There is no reason to doubt the authenticity of the saying.

iv. The Parable of the Unprofitable Servant 17:7–10

Without any break Jesus describes how when a slave has finished his daily work in the field he does not receive any special reward from his master, such as being provided with a meal; he still has to perform his household duties before he can rest. The performance of duty does not entitle one to a reward. So too when disciples have accomplished all that God has commanded them, they have no claims upon him.

The saying can be understood as an attack upon the Jewish attitude, especially that of the Pharisees, which argued that the performance of good works constituted a claim upon God for due reward. Jesus repudiates such an attitude; men cannot put God in their debt. To be sure, this does not mean that God does not reward his faithful people; the corresponding parable in 12:35–37 stands in sharp contrast to this one and indicates that God will treat his servants with gratitude and reward. What is wrong is the attitude that seeks reward and thinks that it can lay claim upon God. By contrast, the teaching of Jesus and his followers stresses the element of divine grace, to which the appropriate human response is gratitude (cf. 17:11–18: the disciples are not to seek thanks, but to give thanks, Klostermann, 171).

In its present context, however, the parable is addressed to the disciples, more specifically the apostles, and it may well be understood as a warning against the attitude of church leaders who think that their service in the church entitles them to some reward and that they can be proud of what they have done (Weiser, 117–120; P. Minear, 82–87).

The teaching of the parable is not unparalleled in Judaism, where one or two voices spoke against the prevailing trend of righteousness by works (P. Ab. 1:3: 'Be not like slaves that minister to the master for the sake of receiving a bounty'. P. Ab. 2:8: 'If thou hast wrought much in the law, claim not merit for thyself, for to this end wast thou created').

Despite this, there is no reason to doubt the authenticity of the parable
as coming from Jesus (it is apparently accepted by Bultmann, 218–222);
the 'which of you . . .?' formula is a sign of authenticity (11:5 note).
Some of the wording, however, may show signs of redaction. P. S.
Minear* claims that the application in v. 10 is a secondary addition by
Luke, since it has a slightly different point from the parable and makes
the application to the apostles. There is no linguistic evidence to support
this suggestion, and it is unnecessary (Bultmann, 184; Weiser,
112–114); the tension between the fact that in the parable the master is
the actor while in the application the attitude of the slaves is taken up is
no argument against this, since the attitude of the slaves is the one that is
fitting in view of what they experience of the master's character. There is
more to be said for the view that v. 8 is a Lucan addition (Weiser,
108–110). The syntactical structure of the parable as it stands is complicated, the verse shows signs of Lucan editing, and it can be argued
that it is really unnecessary since anybody who understood ancient
master-slave relationships would automatically answer the question in
v. 7 correctly. But it remains possible that the original parable went to
the trouble of making the meaning absolutely clear.

While most commentators assign the parable to Luke's special
source, Weiser, 106–112, claims that it stood in Q on the basis of weak
linguistic evidence and also because the rest of the section is from Q and
Luke is unlikely to have made an addition at this point. This reasoning is
weak; it is more probable that the parable was added in a pre-Lucan
stage or by Luke himself. The structure of two or three sayings followed
by a parable is not uncommon in the Gospel, and it is possible that the
whole section was put together as teaching for disciples at some stage.

See Jeremias, *Parables*, 193; Weiser, 105–120; P. S. Minear, 'A Note on Luke 17, 7–10',
JBL 93, 1974, 82–87.

(7) The parable begins with the τίς ἐξ ὑμῶν . . . construction (11:5
note), introducing a rhetorical question. There is no verb with the opening phrase; we must either supply ἐστίν with the participle ἔχων, or else
regard μὴ ἔχει in v. 9 as the main verb of an extended conditional sentence (Beyer I:1, 292f.). The latter view is difficult in view of the considerable amount of material inserted in between – unless v. 8 is regarded as an interpolation. On the former view vs. 7–8 build one sentence
with a contrast expressed in the relative clause which bears the main
weight of the sentence (cf. RV). In translation it is best to take vs. 7, 8
and 9 as three separate rhetorical questions. The situation is that of a
small farmer who has one slave to look after his outside work
(ploughing; ἀροτριάω, 1 Cor. 9:10**) and tending the flock (ποιμαίνω, 1
Cor. 9:7; Jn. 21:16; Acts 20:28; *et al.*) and to do any housework. The
language may suggest an allusion (for Luke's readers) to the 'pastoral'
tasks of the apostles (Zahn, 596 n. 34; P. S. Minear*), but this was scarcely the original intent of the parable. At the end of the day when the
slave returns to the house is it likely that the master will order him to

come (παρέρχομαι, 12:37, but there of a servant at table) and take his place at the meal (ἀναπίπτω, 11:37)? Weiser, 108f., claims that the answer to the question ('No') would be obvious at this point.

(8) The account of what the master is more likely to do follows in what is essentially a continuation of the ὅς ... clause; ἀλλ᾽ οὐχί is 'and not rather' (BD 448⁴; cf. 21:9; Acts 7:48). The difference in *Aktionsart* between ἑτοίμασον, 'prepare my meal', and διακόνει, 'go on serving me until I have finished it', is noted by Moule, 20, 135. ἑτοιμάζω is frequent in Lk. τί is used as a relative, 'that which' (BD 298⁴; contrast 11:6 ὅ). δειπνέω, 'to eat, dine' (22:20; 1 Cor. 11:25; Rev. 3:20**), is used of formal meals, and perhaps indicates the formal character of the master's meal compared with the slave's simple supper (Weiser, 109). For περιζώννυμι and διακονέω cf. 12:37; the language may be Lucan. ἕως with the aorist subjunctive conveys the sense 'until I have finished eating and drinking'. For the forms φάγεσαι and πίεσαι see BD 87. The answer to the rhetorical question is obvious, but a different answer, given in 12:37 and implied in Jn. 13:4, demonstrates that this parable contains only half the story.

(9) The point of the parable is now established on the basis of the hearers' assent to what has already been related. The master does not express thanks (ἔχω χάριν, 1 Tim. 1:12; 2 Tim. 1:3 in this sense) to the slave for doing what he has been commanded to do (διατάσσω, 3:13), i.e. in the fields rather than at table. The point is then simply that slaves have to carry out their duties without expecting that they thereby place their masters under obligation (for other possible meanings see Weiser, 111). The application is made within the context of the ancient idea of slavery, and modern ideas about the responsibility of employers to employees should not be read into it or allowed to confuse the interpretation. The text of the verse shows some variations. For δούλῳ the variant δούλῳ ἐκείνῳ is attested by Γ Δ; TR; *Diglot*, but the fact that the variant ἐκείνῳ τῷ δούλῳ is also found (K Π) suggests that ἐκείνῳ is an insertion. At the end of the verse we have the additions: αὐτῷ (X a syᶜˢ sa bo); οὐ δοκῶ (A W Δ Θ Π pl c s syʰ); αὐτῷ, οὐ δοκῶ (D f13 it vg sy ᵖ; TR; *Diglot*). Metzger, 166, rightly explains αὐτῷ as an obvious scribal addition and οὐ δοκῶ as a marginal comment which has found its way into the text; it is difficult to see why either reading should have been omitted if original.

(10) For the form of the application cf. 14:33; 15:7, 10. The thought is now of God's commands to his servants. (The variant ὅσα λέγω in D gives the parable a christological emphasis). λέγετε is equivalent to 'think' (Mt. 9:3; 14:26; Jeremias, *Parables*, 193), and ὅτι *recitativum* is probably pre-Lucan (Weiser, 113). ἀχρεῖος (Mt. 25:30**) means 'unworthy' rather than 'useless', and is simply an expression of modesty, underlining the meaning of δοῦλος (cf. 2 Sa. 6:22; Klostermann, 173; Jeremias, *Parables*, 193 n. 98; Weiser, 113f.). TNT paraphrases with 'There is no need to thank us'; syˢ omitted the word,

probably because it was difficult, and Marcion omitted the whole clause. Before ὁ the conjunction ὅτι is inserted by TR; *Diglot*. The use of ὀφείλω conveys the idea of man's obligation to serve God. πεποιήκαμεν is 'we have *only* done' our duty; the Pharisee in 18:12 thought that he had done more, and was therefore entitled to special favour from God, and the parable was probably originally directed against such an outlook.

i. The Coming of the Son of Man (17:11 – 18:8)

With considerable hesitation we regard a new section as commencing at 17:11. The geographical marker in 17:11 with its emphasis on Jesus' way to Jerusalem suggests that a new section is commencing, although the opening incident has little connection with the rest of the section and may be regarded as having some affinity of thought with what has preceded; it may be best, therefore, to regard it as a bridge passage (cf. the incident in 14:1–6 which has little connection with the theme of the remainder of the meal scene).

The remainder of the section falls into three clear parts, the question by the Pharisees regarding the coming of the kingdom (17:20f.), an extended discourse to the disciples on the coming of the Son of man (17:22–37), and a closing parable with reference to the time that must elapse before the coming of the Son of man (18:1–8). Since this parable is concerned with prayer, which is also the theme of 18:10–14, it is perhaps artificial to make a break at 18:8, but this is simply another example of the compiler's skill in avoiding sharp breaks in his narrative.

The section contains material from Q surrounded by material from L, and the connections are probably artificial.

i. The Grateful Samaritan 17:11–19

The story, set apparently on the borders of Samaria, describes how Jesus met a group of ten lepers who sought healing from him. Instead of healing them on the spot, he simply commanded them to go and show themselves to the priests, something that needed to be done by lepers who had been cleansed. As they went in obedience to his word, they found that they had been cured. Thus far the story is like a typical miracle story, with the significant feature that the cure is delayed and wrought at a distance (cf. 2 Ki. 5:10–14). But, like other miracle stories in Luke's special source (13:10–17; 14:1–6; cf. Pesch, *Taten*, 129), the story takes a fresh step forward with the account of how one of the lepers gave praise to God for his cure and returned to thank Jesus. Jesus' comment is twofold: a remark on the fact that only one man – and a Samaritan at that – returned to give thanks to God, and a declaration of salvation to the man on account of his faith. Thus the story is not simply a testimony to the ability of Jesus to cure lepers (5:12–14) but is also concerned with the attitude of the person cured. Jesus' mercy is offered to all men, but they must acknowledge what God has done through him; to faith must be added thanksgiving. Moreover, this may be missing from the attitude of Jews who might be expected to appreciate the obligation better than Samaritans. The person who makes such acknowledgement experiences a salvation which goes beyond the merely physical cure. H.-D. Betz* goes further and claims that the story reflects the church's attempt to show that a healing miracle is not the same thing as salvation itself; the miracle is in itself ambiguous, and it is not properly experienced unless it leads to a change of inner orientation. Naturally, the reality of the miracle is not disparaged, but a way is opened up for a faith in Jesus which is independent of the occurrence of miracles.

The story is peculiar to Lk. The introduction, v. 11, is probably Lucan, but the ending is probably part of the tradition. Luke has another story of the healing of a leper in 5:12–14. It is, therefore, unlikely that he has created this particular story, since he avoids doublets in his narrative (cf. Pesch, *Taten*, 114). Nevertheless, this story could be an expanded version of the earlier story by the church (Bultmann, 33; Klostermann, 173; Creed, 216f.). Thus Bultmann regards this story as a Hellenised version of the earlier one, designed to bring out the motif of gratitude. The sending of the lepers to the priests is here unmotivated and serves the literary purpose of making it necessary for the one leper to return to Jesus (Pesch, *Taten*, 126f.). The evidence for regarding the story as Hellenised is weak; Knox II, 112, speaks only of a light Hellenisation by Luke. The theory that this story is a variant of the Marcan one appears to have no stronger basis than the questionable assumption that there can originally have been only one story of the cure of a leper. The sending to the priest was a necessary epilogue to the cure of a leper.

A more refined analysis is offered by H.-D. Betz*. For him the oldest form of the story dealt with ten lepers, of whom only one showed gratitude. At a second stage v. 16b was added, giving more colour to the narrative and turning it into an anti-Jewish story. The story itself is based on such a miracle story as Mk. 1:40–45; the first part is a parody of this sort of story, with the nine lepers presented satirically and caricatured to provide a foil for the Samaritan leper who is the hero of the second scene. The theological interest shown in the story demands that its composition be placed fairly late, and the anti-Jewish polemic likewise suggests a date after the breach between the church and the synagogue.

Betz's description of the first part of the story is itself a caricature with no basis in the text. The Samaritan motif is found elsewhere in Luke's special source, and the point need not be a late development.

The historicity of the story is naturally denied by scholars who think that it is based on Mk. 1:40–45 (Pesch, *Taten*, 130f.). For Pesch it lacks concrete details and is designed to convey a lesson to the readers. These considerations, however, do not disprove historicity, and it is better to leave the question open.

See Pesch, *Taten*, 114-134; H.-D. Betz, 'The Cleansing of the Ten Lepers (Luke 17:11-19)', *JBL* 90, 1971, 314-328.

(11) The story begins with typical Lucan phraseology (5:1), and the theme of Jesus' journey to Jerusalem (9:51; 13:22) is reintroduced. There does not appear to be any organic relationship between this theme and the story; more probably the fact that the story involves Jesus' journeying in the neighbourhood of Samaria enabled Luke to give a reminder to his readers that the whole of this major section of the Gospel leads up to Jerusalem; if so, the geographical comment in the second part of the verse may represent traditional information of which he has made use. After πορεύεσθαι (p⁷⁵ ℵ B L *pc*) αὐτόν is added in many MSS; TR; *Diglot*. It may have been omitted because it seemed redundant before the following καὶ αὐτός, or it may have been added to provide the infinitive with a subject. The phrase διὰ μέσον (p⁷⁵ ℵ B *pc*) seemed difficult. Variants are διὰ μέσου (A W Θ *pl*; TR); ἀνὰ μέσον (f1 f13); and μέσον (D; Creed, 217); but these are no doubt simplifications. διὰ μέσον means 'through the midst of' (cf. 4:30; 11:24; Jn. 4:4; Acts 9:32; *et al.*), and could refer to a journey through both of the regions named, or more probably along the border between the two regions. διὰ μέσον could mean 'between', and may simply be a Hellenistic form of the more correct idiom. If so, a journey along the border between Samaria and Galilee is meant (cf. Lagrange, 457; Ellis, 209). The fact that Samaria is mentioned first is due to the important role of the Samaritan in the story, and no recondite explanation is necessary. Nevertheless, Conzelmann, 60-62, holds that Luke's geography is erroneous, J. Blinzler (in Schmid, *Studien*, 50-52; cf. 9:51-19:10 note) emends the text by omitting μέσον Σαμαρείας καί without it being clear how these words ever got into the text if they are not original; and Pesch, *Taten*, 116-119, regards the words as Luke's addition to the tradition. Grundmann, 336, follows the view that the geography is described from the perspective of Jerusalem, so that Samaria is named first. Yet another possibility is that the reference is to the border between Samaria and Peraea (the latter being reckoned as part of Galilee).

(12) The genitive absolute is illogical. The reference to the village entered by Jesus is vague (cf. 5:12; *et al.*); it serves to show that Jesus rested from his journey and therefore could easily be found by the cured leper. It also places the incident on the outskirts of habitation where a group of lepers might be found. ἀπαντάω, 'to meet', is rare (Mk. 14:13), and the text shows variations. For ἀπήντησαν (p⁷⁵ ℵᶜ A B W Δ 700 *pm*; TR), we find ὑπήντησαν in ℵ* L Θ f1 f13 157 a; *Diglot* (and the erratic variations ὅπου ἦσαν, D e; *et ecce*, it syˢ ᶜ); αὐτῷ, read by TR; *Diglot*; (UBS); is omitted by p⁷⁵ B L (D) *pc*. λεπρός appears as an adjective here only in the NT; on the disease see 5:12 note. For lepers grouping

together cf. 2 Ki. 7:3. πόρρωθεν is 'from a distance' (Heb. 11:13**). The lepers were conforming to the law by avoiding physical contacts with other people (Lv. 13:45f.; Nu. 5:2), but staying close to habitation so that they might receive charitable gifts. It is not surprising that they knew about the reputation of Jesus.

(13) αἴρω φωνήν (Acts 4:24) is here 'to shout'; cf. ἐπαίρω φωνήν, 11:27. The vocative Ἰησοῦ is common enough (4:34; et al.). More difficult to account for is the title ἐπιστάτης (5:5 note) which is normally placed on the lips of disciples in Lk. Grundmann, 336f., accordingly assumes that they stood in some close relationship to Jesus. It is more probable that the word is used loosely without any deeper implications. It may be a Lucan equivalent for an earlier διδάσκαλε (cf. P. Eger. 2:8; Pesch, Taten, 120). For ἐλεέω cf. 16:24; 18:38f. (par. Mk. 10:47f.); Mk. 5:19; Mt. 15:22; 17:15.

(14) Normally, a command to visit the priest would follow a cure (5:14; cf. Lv. 13:49; 14:2f.), so that the cured man might officially resume his place in society. Here the use of the plural ἱερεῖς arises from the fact that a mixed group of lepers, Jewish and Samaritan, is described, and each man would go to the appropriate priest. It is not clear whether it was necessary to go to the temple; the OT legislation assumes that this is the case, since sacrifice had to be offered, but the other aspects of the ritual could perhaps be carried out wherever a priest was to be found. The command to go to the priests is a test of faith and obedience. It also implies that the completion of the cure took place at a distance without Jesus having touched the men; cf. the cure of Naaman, 2 Ki. 5:10–14. In this way too the scene is set for the return of the Samaritan leper.

(15) The use of ἰάομαι demonstrates the meaning of καθαρίζω in v. 14. The language of the verse (ὑποστρέφω, 1:56; et al.; δοξάζω τὸν θεόν, 2:20; et al.) is Lucan; it may be an expansion but is required by v. 18 as an integral part of the story (Pesch, Taten, 121).

(16) In the story in 5:12 the leper kneels before Jesus *before* his cure; cf. 8:41; Acts 5:10. The action is one of respect (Matthew stresses the element of worship), here accompanied by thanksgiving (εὐχαριστέω, 18:11; 22:17. 19; cf. Jn. 11:41; Acts 28:15). It is also found in stories of pagan wonderworkers (H.-D. Betz*, 318f.). Then comes the surprise for Jewish readers. The construction is that of an Aramaic circumstantial clause (Black, 83). The man is a Samaritan (and by implication the other nine are Jews). Braun, Radikalismus II, 60 n. 1 and H.-D. Betz*, 319, hold that the phrase is a secondary expansion (but pre-Lucan); this judgment, however, ignores the dramatic art of the story which holds back the detail to this point for emphasis.

(17) Jesus responds to the situation (and the words of thanks which are implied in v. 16) with a series of three questions. Bultmann, 33, rightly points out that the saying of Jesus could not have been transmitted on its own apart from the story (i.e. we do not have an imaginary story constructed to give a framework for the saying), from

which H.-D. Betz*, 320, illogically concludes that the saying was composed for this story and cannot be original. This *assumes* the non-
historical nature of the story without any justification. The first question
begins with οὐχί (ℵ A Θ f1 f13 *pl* lat; TR; UBS; *Diglot*; οὐχ, B L V *pc*;
Synopsis; omitted by D it sy^sc). The second is constructed chiastically;
for the order of words cf. Plato, Tim. 17a. The connective δέ is omitted
by A D *pc* it sy; *Diglot*.

(18) The use of εὑρίσκω with the participle is unusual; it is
equivalent to the niphal of *māṣā'*, 'to be found, appear, prove, be shown
(to be)' (AG); cf. Mt. 1:18; Rom. 7:10; Acts 5:39; *et al.* With the verb
supply τινές as subject. δοῦναι is dependent on ὑποστρέψαντες. For the
phrase cf. 4:6; Jn. 9:24; 17:22; Acts 12:23; 1 Sa. 6:5; Ps. 29:1; *et al.* εἰ
μή is used exclusively. ἀλλογενής**, 'foreign', is used of non-Jews in the
LXX and on the well-known 'keep out' signs on the inner barrier in the
temple. The non-Jew with no religious privileges has shown a better understanding of the situation than the Jews.

(19) So it is he alone who hears the word of Jesus, bidding him rise
from worship and go his way (Acts 8:26; 9:11; *et al.*). His faith has been
the means of his cure – and of his salvation. Most commentators regard
the verse as a schematic, redactional addition; it may well be pre-Lucan,
but this does not solve the problem whether it is secondary to the
original story. It is, however, an integral part of the story, since the
whole point of the second part of the story lies in the relationship of the
man to Jesus, and not simply in the fact that he gives thanks. The story
does not necessarily imply that the other nine lacked faith; the point is
rather that their faith was incomplete because it did not issue in
gratitude.

ii. The Coming of the Kingdom 17:20–21

At this point Luke follows a pattern, familiar in Mk., in which teaching
given by Jesus to non-disciples, in this case the Pharisees (17:20f.), is
followed by fuller explanation to the disciples (17:22–37). The Pharisees,
aware that the kingdom of God is coming, ask when it is coming. Jesus
answers briefly with a negative statement which rules out the possibility
of calculating the date of its arrival, and then states positively that the
kingdom is in their midst.

In an attempt to link the passage to the preceding context, Danker,
181, suggests that the Pharisees show a misunderstanding similar to that
displayed by the nine lepers in failing to see the presence of the kingly
power of God in Jesus. This is not impossible in view of the somewhat
similar connection between 13:10–17 and 18–21. There is also a link in
thought with 11:29.

The link with what follows is also difficult. The following discourse
to the disciples manifestly deals with future events including the coming
of the Son of man. The tension between the reference here to the

presence of the kingdom and the accent on the future in the discourse has motivated attempts to understand the present text in a future sense ('the kingdom of God will (suddenly) be among you'). The solution may lie partly in the way in which Luke likes to bring present and future together (Ellis, 210). In their different ways the present saying and the discourse both discourage apocalyptic speculation. Having established that the kingdom is already present, Luke recounts how Jesus deals with the unspoken question, 'But what is still to happen?', by assuring them of the coming of the Son of man, but stressing that his coming, like that of the kingdom, will not be predictable in advance by means of signs.

The pericope has the form of a pronouncement story. More precisely, Bultmann, 24 (cf. Dibelius, 162), holds that it is like a Greek *chreia*, composed by Luke himself (cf. 2 Clem. 12:2; Lk. 6:5D; Kümmel, 32). As for the saying itself, it may be compounded of several elements. H. Riesenfeld, TDNT VIII, 150 n. 16, states that v. 20b can be translated into Hebrew only with difficulty and therefore stems from the Greek stage of the tradition; v. 21a may be based on the saying of Jesus in v. 23 (cf. Mk. 13:21), and v. 21b is authentic. The most radical opinion is that of A. Strobel* who holds that the whole saying is a creation by Luke to combat the Pharisaic view, current in his day, that the Messiah would come on the night of the Passover. Geiger, 45–50, also regards the pericope as a redactional construction to show that the future aspect of Jesus' teaching is concerned not with the kingdom but with the Son of man – a view that comes to grief on 21:21 diff. Mk. Zmijewski, 378–386, holds that the tradition contained vs. 20b and 21b which form an antithetical couplet; Luke has created the setting in order to reflect a Pharisaic tendency in the church which required to be corrected.

The attempt to separate tradition and redaction is complicated by uncertainty regarding the source of the material. While Schürmann, *Untersuchungen*, 237, holds that 17:20f., 22–24, formed a unity in Q, most scholars deny that vs. 20f. are from Q.

Strobel's view that Luke has created the entire pericope has rightly not found acceptance (Perrin, 69–72; Zmijewski, 379f.). The difficulty of the passage speaks against Lucan creation and points rather to the use of source material. The change in address at v. 22 suggests that some linking has taken place, and that some degree of Lucan editing is present. It is unlikely, therefore that 17:20–24 comes directly from Q. R. Schnackenburg*, 217–220, discusses the possibility that v. 21b and most of v. 22 are a Lucan addition to material from Q. The alternative is that v. 21a is a Lucan addition to vs. 20f. to link the pericope with the following material from Q, and this is perhaps the best solution; on this view, Luke has used v. 21a to draw out the parallelism between the two situations in v. 20 and vs. 22f. If so, the original source of vs. 20f. must remain obscure. A final question is whether Luke has created the framework for the saying in v. 20. This is possible, since Luke has created similar settings elsewhere and since similar questions are characteristic of his work (19:11; 21:7; Acts 1:6; Zmijewski, 381–384). But the mention of the Pharisees could well be traditional, since the question fits in with their interests, and therefore the introduction may have had a basis in tradition (cf. Perrin, 70, who holds that the pericope has the marks of oral tradition).

See Dalman, 143–147; A. Sledd, 'The Interpretation of Luke xvii. 21', Exp.T 50, 1938–39, 235–237; B. Noack, *Das Gottesreich bei Lukas: eine Studie zu Luk. 17, 20–24*, Uppsala, 1948; C. H. Roberts, 'The Kingdom of Heaven (Lk. xvii. 21)', HTR 41, 1948, 1–8; H. Riesenfeld, ''Εμβολεύειν – 'Εντός', and A. Wikgren, 'ΕΝΤΟΣ', *Nuntius* 4, 1950, 27f. (not accessible; see Moule, 83f.); J. G. Griffiths, ''Εντὸς ὑμῶν (Luke xvii. 21)', Exp.T 63, 1951–52, 30f.; Percy, 216–223; Kümmel, 32–36; A. Strobel, 'Die Passa-Erwartung als urchristliches Problem in Lk. 17:20f.', ZNW 49, 1958, 164–174; id. 'In dieser Nacht (Lk. 17:34)', ZTK 58, 1961, 16–29; id. 'Zu Lk. 17:20f.', BZ nf 7, 1963, 111–113; A. Rüstow, 'ΕΝΤΟΣ ΥΜΩΝ ΕΣΤΙΝ. Zur Deutung von Lukas 17:20–21', ZNW 51, 1960, 197–224; F. Mussner, 'Wann kommt das Reich Gottes?' BZ 6, 1962, 107–111; R. J. Sneed, ' "The Kingdom of God is within you" (Lk. 17, 21)', CBQ 24, 1962, 363–382; Perrin, 68–74; R. Schnackenburg, 'Der eschatologische Abschnitt Lk. 17, 20–37', in Descamps, 213–234 (reprinted in R. Schnackenburg, *Schriften zum Neuen Testament*, München, 1971, 220–243; Zmijewski, 361–397; Geiger, 29–52.

(20) The ascription of the question to the Pharisees reflects the apocalyptic expectations which they held (W. D. Davies, *Christian Origins and Judaism,* 1962, 19–30). The present ἔρχεται may be equivalent to a future: 'When will the kingdom of God come?' H. Riesenfeld, TDNT VIII, 150 n. 15, suggests that the meaning is rather 'When does one know that the kingdom of God is there?', but this is over-subtle. The Pharisees appear to be concerned with premonitory signs, and expect an answer of the form, 'The kingdom will come when you see so-and-so taking place' (cf. J. Weiss, 493).

Jesus' reply denies that the kingdom will come with παρατήρησις**. This rare word means 'watching', 'spying' (cf. the use of the verb, 6:7; 14:1; 20:20; Acts 9:24), 'observation', 'observance (of rules)' (cf. Gal. 4:10). The following meanings are possible here: 1. Concrete observations of signs and symptoms (H. Riesenfeld, TDNT VIII, 150; cf. Klostermann, 175; SB II, 236); 2. A. Strobel* argues that the verse refers to the Pharisaic expectation that the Messiah would come on the night of observation, i.e. the night of the Passover (Ex. 12:42; cf. Aquila's translation of this verse). See the criticisms by Perrin, 69f. 3. R. J. Sneed* holds that the reference is to religious observances (such as Pharisaic ritual rules) by which the coming of the kingdom might be expedited. Sneed bases his case partly on Rom. 14:17, which he regards as a parallel to this text, but the parallel is not strong, and Luke's context hardly supports the presence of ritual ideas. 4. Beasley-Murray, 173 n. 2, draws attention to a suggestion of A. Meyer that the word is equivalent to Aramaic *nᵉṭîr*, 'observation'; the whole phrase μετὰ παρατηρήσεως, however, is equivalent to *binṭîr*, which means 'secretly'; the kingdom comes openly, so that nobody can mistake its coming. As Beasley-Murray admits, this suggestion is very hypothetical. It seems most likely that the first meaning should be accepted (cf. Geiger, 42).

The coming of the kingdom is not accompanied by ratifying or premonitory signs that men can observe. To look for such is to misunderstand the character of the kingdom.

(21) There will in fact be people who say, 'it is here' (cf. 17:23), but they will be mistaken in finding signs of the coming of the kingdom because there will be none to see. The wording is compressed: ἰδού should be supplied before ἐκεῖ, and is in fact added by A D W Δ Ψ f1 f13 700 *pl* lat sy^{cph} Mcion; TR; *Diglot*. The phrase is close to Mk. 13:21, which warns the disciples against those who state that the Messiah is here or there; cf. Lk. 17:23 (with reversed order). Here the reference is to the kingdom, but a kingdom can hardly be 'here' or 'there', and so the reference must be to the ruler himself.

The meaning of the final clause depends upon the translation of ἐντός. The word occurs in Mt. 23:26** with the meaning 'inside'. A long tradition accordingly translates ἐντὸς ὑμῶν as 'within you' (*intra vos*, it vg; Origen; AV; Barclay; NIV; Turner, 61–63; Dalman, 145–147; Easton, 262; Creed, 218f. (as Luke's view); Percy, 216–223; R. J. Sneed*). It is not an objection to this view that Jesus is addressing the Pharisees, for the 'you' is quite indefinite. More important is the fact that nowhere else is the kingdom regarded as something internal (cf. Kümmel, 33f.; Manson, *Sayings*, 304). R. J. Sneed* uses the analogy with Rom. 14:17 to show the equivalence of the Spirit and the kingdom, but this does not prove the point. Jesus speaks of men entering the kingdom, not of the kingdom entering men. A different translation is demanded, and is not difficult to find. With a plural noun ἐντός means 'among, in the midst of' (NEB t; cf. A. Sledd*; Kümmel, 33 n.; Grässer, 194). Considerable discussion has surrounded the use of the word in the papyri. C. H. Roberts* drew attention to various papyri in which he claimed the word had the meaning 'in the hands of, in the control of, within the power of'; hence the force here is 'within your reach' or 'within your grasp' (cf. Dodd, 401 n., withdrawing his earlier support for 'within'; A. Rüstow*). The papyri were reinterpreted by H. Riesenfeld* and A. Wikgren* who suggested the meaning 'in the house of', i.e. 'in your domain, among you'. Such a meaning gives good sense. Jesus is speaking of the presence of the kingdom of God among men, possibly as something within their grasp if they will only take hold of it.

The force of the saying may then be present or future. Looking for the kingdom is rejected because it is always present in the ministry of Jesus (J. Weiss, 493f.; Lagrange, 666f.; B. Noack*; Kümmel, 32–35; Schnackenburg, 134–137; Ellis, 211; Zmijewsky, 375–377). Alternatively, the meaning is that the kingdom will (suddenly) be among men, so that there will be no question of looking for its coming (Klostermann, 175; Bultmann, 128; Hauck, 215; Manson, *Sayings*, 304). This second view fits in with the future tenses in the following verses, but it undoubtedly requires that something be read into a saying which is more naturally interpreted as referring to the present time. The saying then fits in with other sayings which speak of the kingdom having reached men in the sense that its saving benefits are now available for them (10:9; 11:20). B. Noack*, 39–50, claims that the kingdom is present in this way only during the earthly ministry of Jesus, so that the following verses deal with the hard times between the departure of Jesus and the coming of the Son of man as king.

iii. The Day of the Son of Man 17:22–37

Jesus' answer to the Pharisees' question is followed immediately by a long discourse addressed to the disciples. They too are concerned about what is to happen in the future. A time will come when they will long to see some visible evidence of the coming of the Son of man, but there will be nothing to see. It is true that people will spread rumours of the coming of the eschatological event, but the disciples must not be misled by them. For when the Son of man appears, there will be no mistaking his appearance in glory – a glory that contrasts with his earlier suffering and rejection by the present generation. This same generation will give itself up to worldly, godless living, as in the days of Noah and Lot. It will pay no heed to the gospel and consequently the day of the Son of man will take it by surprise with its sudden judgment and destruction. If that day brings redemption for God's people, it also brings judgment on the ungodly. Therefore, let the disciples not be attracted by worldly desires which may divert them from being instantly ready for the Son of man. Even Lot's wife, though rescued from Sodom and Gomorrah, fell under the same judgment. Only those who are prepared to lose their lives will survive the judgment which will come and separate between men. It is as senseless to ask for a map of what will happen as it is to ask for a timetable: just as the location of a corpse in the wilderness is obvious from the crowd of circling vultures, so the Son of man will appear for judgment in an unmistakable manner, and there will be no need to ask where he is.

Luke's teaching is closely parallel to Mt. 24:23 (or 26), 27, 28, 37–39, 17f., 40f.; and it can be assumed that both writers are dependent on Q which contained a brief 'apocalypse'. The precise limits of the Q material are uncertain. There are no clear parallels in Mt. to Lk. 17:22, 25, 28f., 32, (34), 37a. Lk. 17:33 is paralleled in Mt. 10:39. Manson, *Sayings*, 141–147, ascribes all of this Lucan material to Q, but more recent scholars tend to regard most or all of it as coming from other sources or being created by Luke. The problem of origins is complicated by the fact that some of the material is paralleled in Mk., especially in Mk. 13, and influence from Mk. cannot be ruled out. Thus 17:23 may be based on Mk. 13:21. V. 25 is widely regarded as being based on the passion predictions in Mk. V. 31 may be based on Mk. 13:15f. and v. 33 on Mk. 8:35 (par. Lk. 9:24). The remaining verses (vs. 22, possibly 28f., 32,

34, and 37a) will then be Lucan additions to give unity to the enlarged discourse.

The sources of the material will be discussed below in the exegesis, but firm conclusions are hard to reach. In general, however, it can be seen that the effect of Luke's editing has been to apply the teaching more directly to the disciples. It may be intended to counter any ideas that the Son of man remains hidden on the earth or that his appearance would be immediate (Ellis, 210). If the original teaching in Q had more the form of warnings to non-disciples, Luke warns the disciples against being deceived by the world and falling away. They must endure patiently, whatever the cost in self-sacrifice. The Q material that remains when possible additions have been separated off has essentially the same message, so that Luke has not substantially altered its force, but has rather underlined the message for his particular audience.

The relation of this teaching to the actual words of Jesus is variously estimated. Schulz, 282f., assigns the whole section to the later strata of Q (cf. Grässer, 170–172). He claims that the existence of an 'apocalypse' in Q, similar to that in Mk., is a sign of late origin, and that this is confirmed by the assumption of the delay of the parousia, the developed picture of the Son of man, and the use of the OT (in the LXX translation) in exact comparisons. These arguments are unconvincing. They certainly do not rule out the possibility that isolated sayings go back to Jesus; but even on the broader front they lack force. It is highly probable that Jesus himself reckoned with some kind of the interval before the parousia, and that he identified himself with the coming Son of man (cf. 9:26; 12:8f.). Nor is there any real evidence that Jesus could not have used the OT in the way it is used in this passage. R. Schnackenburg*, 233, rightly concludes that there is no good reason to deny to Jesus himself the substance of the Q material in this discourse.

See Manson, *Sayings*, 141–147; Kümmel, 29, 37–39, 43–45, 70f.; Vielhauer, 74–76, 108–110; A. Strobel, 'In dieser Nacht (Lk. 17:34)', ZTK 58, 1961, 16–29; Tödt, 48–52, 104–108; Higgins, 82–91; Flender, 13–15, 94–96; Borsch, 356f.; C. Colpe, TDNT VIII, 433f., 450f; Lührmann, 71–83; R. Schnackenburg, in Descamps, 213–234 (see 17:20–21 note); B. Rigaux, 'La petite apocalipse de Luc (xvii, 22–37)', in *Ecclesia a Spiritu Sancto edocta* (Festschrift Mgr. G. Philips), Gembloux, 1970, 407–438; Schulz, 277–287, 444–446; Zmijewski, 326–540; Geiger, 53–169; J. Schlosser, 'Les Jours de Noë et de Lot. A propos de Luc xvii, 26–30', RB 80, 1973, 13–36.

(22) The opening verse is peculiar to Lk. and usually regarded as redactional (Bultmann, 138; Klostermann, 175; Creed, 220; Conzelmann, 96 n. 3; R. Schnackenburg*, 221; Zmijewski, 417–419; Geiger, 53–58; *contra* Kümmel, 29 (with hesitation); Borsch, 356 n. 2; C. Colpe, TDNT VIII, 450f.; Higgins, 88; B. Rigaux*, 413). Certainly the introductory framework is Lucan (cf. 17:1; αὐτοῦ is added by A X *al* cop; *Diglot*). The phrase ἐλεύσονται ἡμέραι may be Lucan (Zmijewski, 417; cf. 21:6 diff. Mk.; 23:29; but also Mk. 2:20); it is used in the OT of future periods of judgment (Is. 39:6). ἐπιθυμέω is found in Q and L material, and is not necessarily Lucan; it may denote an unfulfilled wish,

as is indicated here by the addition of καὶ οὐκ ὄψεσθε.

The next phrase is highly problematic. εἷς usually means 'one', and can mean 'even, just one' (so B. Rigaux*, 410). It can also be used as a synonym for πρῶτος, 'first', a Hebraism found in Koine Greek (Plummer, 407; AG s.v. 4); the omission of the article is possible in this idiom. In the latter case the longing will be to see the first day of a period. 'The days of the Son of man' is a phrase peculiar to this verse and v. 26, where it stands in parallel with 'the days of Noah' and may have been formed by analogy with it. The usual phrase is 'the day of the Son of man' (17:24, 30). 1. The phrase may have been formed on the analogy of 'the days of the Messiah', i.e. the period of the Messiah's reign (Ber. 1:5; SB II, 237; IV:2, 826ff.). It would then refer to the period inaugurated by the parousia, and the whole phrase would refer to a day of the Son of man's rule or to the first day, i.e. the day of the parousia itself (Klostermann, 175; Creed, 220; Tödt, 105). The difficulty with this view is that it is hard to see why the simple singular phrase could not have been employed. But Luke may have been unwilling to deny his readers the possibility of experiencing the day of the parousia in their lifetime, and may therefore have preferred this less definite phrase. 2. The analogy with 17:26 suggests that the phrase refers to the days which will be brought to an end by the parousia (Manson, *Sayings*, 143, with reference to v. 26. For the present verse, however, Manson prefers the view of Torrey, 160, 312, that there has been a misunderstanding of Aramaic *lakhda*, 'very much', as the numeral 'one'). On this view, the reference is to the days immediately preceding the parousia in which the signs of its imminence are clear. 3. Alternatively, the reference is to the whole period between Easter and the parousia, the period of Jesus' exaltation. This exaltation remains hidden from the disciples who long for the parousia when it will be revealed (Flender, 94–96; Zmijewski, 400–403). This is highly artificial and unconvincing, and places far too much stress on ἰδεῖν. 4. The phrase may refer to the earthly days of the Son of man; during the future time of tribulation the disciples will long to experience again even one day of that glorious period of Jesus' earthly presence with them (Dodd, *Parables*, 81 n. 31; T. F. Glasson, *The Second Advent*, London, 1945, 83–88; J. A. T. Robinson, *Jesus and His Coming*, London, 1957, 74f.; Conzelmann, 96 n. 3; E. Schweizer, 'Der Menschensohn', ZNW 50, 1959, 185–209, especially 190; R. Maddox, 'The Function of the Son of Man according to the Synoptic Gospels', NTS 15, 1968–69, 45–74, especially 51; C. Colpe, TDNT VIII, 458 n. 396; cf. Grundmann, 343). 5. Somewhat similar is the view that the phrase refers to the various glorious manifestations of the Son of man at the transfiguration, resurrection and ascension, the visions of Stephen and Paul, the restoration of Jerusalem and Israel and the final consummation (Leaney, 68–72; Stuhlmueller, 151). 6. Luke may have formed the phrase to show that the coming of the Son of man does not take place in an instant but over a period of time (Conzelmann, 115; Schulz,

278 n. 90). Since, however, Luke retains the traditional idea of *the* day of the Son of man in vs. 24, 30, this view is implausible.

A decision between these possibilities is not easy, although some of them are manifestly unlikely. It is clear from the following verses that a future appearance of the Son of man is in mind. The concept of longing for a return of past days is unparalleled, and unlikely for Luke whose understanding of the ministry of Jesus appears in v. 25. On the whole, therefore, view 1. has most to be said for it, or rather is the least unsatisfactory.

Although the verse could be Lucan, it is difficult to credit Luke with creating a saying with the repetition of ἡμέραι in it or a saying in which a crucial phrase has a different meaning from that in v. 26. If the saying originally spoke of the day (singular) of the Son of man, the change to the plural is probably pre-Lucan. The absence of the saying from Mt. does not rule out the possibility of the saying coming from Q, since he could have omitted it when conflating his Q and Mk. material, and since v. 23 demands an introduction. Since Luke does not in general create Son of man sayings, it is probable that he found the saying in a source, whether Q (Schürmann, *Untersuchungen*, 222) or L (C. Colpe, TDNT VIII, 450f.). Since the saying does not overtly identify Jesus with the Son of man, and since Jesus allowed for an interval between his ministry and the parousia, the saying can well be authentic (Kümmel, 29; Borsch, 356 n. 2), although this is denied by most scholars.

(23) The next saying warns the disciples against being misled by people who fancy that the Messiah has already come. The sentence structure, a statement followed by an imperative, is tantamount to a condition (cf. Mk. 13:21; Mt. 24:23, 26). The use of the impersonal plural in the first clause, par. Mt., diff. Mk., and the fact that both the present saying and the parallel in Mt. 24:26 are followed by the same 'lightning' saying points to the use of Q material. There is, however, a very similar saying in Mk. 13:21 par. Mt. 24:23, and the present saying is closer in wording to Mk. 13:21 than to Mt. 24:26. The comparison of the sayings is complicated by the presence of a textual variant. UBS reads ἰδοὺ ἐκεῖ (ἤ) ἰδοὺ ὧδε (p⁷⁵ B). ἤ is replaced by καί in ℵ syᶜˢ, and omitted in L (followed by *Synopsis; Diglot*; Zmijewski, 398). The reverse order of adverbs ἰδοὺ ὧδε ἤ ἰδοὺ ἐκεῖ is found in A Δ Θ Ψ *pl* it; TR (and with the omission of ἤ in D W 33 69 *pc* e q vg^codd). According to Metzger, 166f., the succession of vowels led to confusion, and there could have been assimilation to the order in 17:21; Mk. 13:21. The status of ἤ is uncertain; it could have been added or omitted by assimilation to the parallels, probably the former. UBS thus has the same wording as in Mk. 13:21 (and Lk. 17:21), but with reversed order, whereas Mt. 24:26 has ἐν τῇ ἐρήμῳ . . . ἐν τοῖς ταμιείοις. Luke's order 'there . . . here' corresponds to Mt. ' (out there) in the desert . . . (here) in the inner rooms'. It is not clear whether Matthew has the original wording (Schulz, 278; Lambrecht, 101–103; Zmijewski, 410f.) or Luke (Manson, *Sayings*, 142; Geiger,

63), but probably the former. If so, Luke has altered the wording under the influence of Mk. 13:21 or Lk. 17:21 (but see note above, where the possibility that Lk. 17:21 is based on the present verse is discussed). But who is in mind? In Mk. there is explicit mention of the Messiah appearing, and in Mt. there is the possibility of the Messiah appearing in the desert, as several Jewish messianic pretenders and false prophets actually did (R. Meyer, TDNT VI, 826f.). Such people admittedly did not use the title 'Messiah' so far as we know; certainly Josephus is silent on the matter (M. de Jonge, TDNT IX, 520f.). Although in both Mk. and Q the appearance of these pretenders is contrasted with the coming of the Son of man, it is false to assume with Vielhauer, 75f., that the reference is to pretenders to be the Son of man, and that therefore the saying must be a creation by the early church which identified the figures of Messiah and Son of man; the contrast is between messianic pretenders and the coming of the Son of man (Tödt, 337f.; C. Colpe, TDNT VIII, 433). In this form the saying could go back to Jesus, as Vielhauer admits is possible (cf. Bultmann, 128). The disciples are warned not to be attracted by such false prophets (or the people to whom they testify). ἀπέλθητε μηδέ is omitted by p⁷⁵ B f13 pc sa, possibly because it seemed superfluous (Metzger, 167). Matthew's ἐξέρχομαι is more appropriate for going into the desert. διώκω has the sense 'to run after, pursue' (Phil. 3:12; AG), rather than its more common bad sense, 'to persecute'. This makes it less likely that it is due to Lucan redaction (Schulz, 279 n. 99); more probably Matthew's μὴ πιστεύετε is due to assimilation to Mk. 13:21.

(24) The reason why the disciples need not be taken in by pretenders is that when the Son of man appears on his day, there will be no mistaking the fact any more than one can mistake the occurrence of lightning which is universally visible. Most commentators think that Matthew's wording is more original in the first half of the saying, while Luke is more original in the second half (cf. Klostermann, 175; Tödt, 49; Schulz, 279; Zmijewski, 412–414; Geiger, 65). ὥσπερ, 'just as' (18:11*; here par. Mt.), introduces a comparison. For ἀστραπή see 10:18. ἀστράπτω, 'to flash, gleam' (24:4**) is probably Lucan; cf. ἐξαστράπτω, 9:29. Luke's description resembles that of Jesus at the transfiguration and suggests that he saw in the lightning not merely a symbol of something universally visible but also a picture of the glory of the Son of man (Zmijewsky, 404–406). λάμπω is 'to shine' (Acts 12:7; Mt. 5:15f.; 17:2; 2 Cor. 4:6**), diff. Mt. φαίνω (which is a favourite word of Matthew). ἐκ τῆς ὑπὸ τὸν οὐρανὸν εἰς τὴν ὑπὸ τὸν οὐρανόν is a difficult phrase. With τῆς supply χώρας or γῆς or even μερίδος, and correspondingly with τήν (BD 241¹; H. Traub, TDNT V, 534 n. 312). ὑπὸ τὸν οὐρανόν, 'beneath heaven', means 'on the earth' (Ex. 17:14; Job 28:24; Ec. 1:13; 3:1; Acts 2:5; 4:12; Col. 1:23; cf. Plato, Ep. 7, 326c). For the first half of the whole phrase (ἐκ τῆς ὑπὸ τὸν οὐρανόν) cf. T. Levi 18:4. The meaning must be 'from one place on earth to another (place on earth)'. Possibly the idea is of lightning flashing from one place below

heaven (conceived as the upper limit of space) to another. Grundmann, 343, thinks that the phrase refers to the two points on the horizon where the heaven appears to rest on the earth (cf. TNT, 'from one horizon to another'), but this does not square with how lightning actually flashes. Matthew's phrase 'from the east to the west' (cf. Mt. 8:11 par. Lk. 13:29) may be a simplification (B. Rigaux*, 416), or Luke may have substituted a more general expression (so most scholars). For lightning in apocalyptic contexts cf. 2 Bar. 53:9; it is also associated with theophanies in the OT (W. Foerster, TDNT I, 505). Here the point is its brightness and visibility rather than its sudden appearance (C. Colpe, TDNT VIII, 433 n. 251; *pace* Grässer, 170). The comparison is now made with the Son of man ἐν τῇ ἡμέρᾳ αὐτοῦ, a phrase omitted by p⁷⁵ B D it sa; (UBS), possibly as a result of homoioteleuton (Metzger, 167); but the external evidence for omission is strong. The comparison is strengthened by the addition of καί after ἔσται in D *al*; *Diglot*. Matthew's reference to the parousia is generally considered secondary (cf. Mt. 24:37, 39b diff. Lk. 17:26, 30). The original references may have been to the *day* of the Son of man (Geiger, 66). In its Lucan form the verse prophesies the unmistakable presence of the Son of man on his day when he is revealed (17:30). The day of Yahweh in Jewish expectation has been replaced by the day of the Son of man (cf. 1 En. 45:3; 61:5; 4 Ez. 13:52; G. Delling, TDNT II, 951; Higgins, 90f.): he manifests the glory of Yahweh (Geiger, 66–70). The lack of apocalyptic premonitory signs and the absence of political-messianic ideas favour the genuineness of the saying (Bultmann, 133; Tödt, 337f.; Higgins, 89f.; Borsch, 356 n. 3; C. Colpe, TDNT VIII, 433f.); the arguments to the contrary by Vielhauer, 75f., 108–110, are concerned with v. 23 and do not affect the content of v. 24. Admittedly, the defenders of the authenticity of the saying cited above assume that Jesus meant someone other than himself by the Son of man; since the present saying does not explicitly identify Jesus with the Son of man, there is no real difficulty concerning its authenticity even on the assumption that Jesus did identify himself with the Son of man (cf. Jeremias, *Theology*, I, 276; Goppelt, 231–233).

(25) This saying appears to be a warning to the disciples of Jesus against expecting the manifestation of the Son of man before he has suffered and been rejected; it assumes the identity of Jesus with the Son of man. For the same thought see 19:11. Such a saying appears pointless when addressed to Luke's readers who know that Jesus has already suffered and died, but this difficulty disappears if the saying is meant to establish the theological necessity of suffering preceding glory (24:26) and hence to show that, although Jesus suffered and was rejected, he will nevertheless come as the Son of man. There may also be the suggestion that the rejection of Jesus foreshadows the experience of the disciples in the interim period.

The saying is almost universally regarded as an insertion into the Q material, since it is not paralleled in Mt. and it breaks the connection between vs. 24 and 26. Manson, *Sayings*, 142f., is a notable exception to this *communis opinio* (cf. the earlier views of B. Weiss and W. Bussmann, cited by Taylor, *Sacrifice*, 173 n. 3). He points to the vague character of the saying and claims that it refers to the sufferings of the collective Son of man (Jesus and his disciples) before the end; this is a view worthy of more consideration than it usually receives.

If the saying is an insertion, it may be from the hand of Luke (so most scholars; e.g. Higgins, 78f.; R. Schnackenburg, 222f.; Zmijewski, 406–410, 419; Geiger, 76–85). If so, it is probably based on the earlier passion predictions. It is close in wording to the longer saying in 9:22, but with ἀπό (for ὑπό) τῆς γενεᾶς ταύτης (cf. 7:31). The use of γενεά may indicate that it is the same generation which rejected Jesus which will also be unprepared for the parousia (Ellis, 212). What remains difficult on this view is the absence of mention of the resurrection (contrast 24:26); but this feature is paralleled in 9:44 (cf. Mk. 9:12). The use of πρῶτον links the saying to its present context (cf. 21:9 diff. Mk. 13:7; Mk. 9:11f. par. Mt. 17:10; Mk. 13:10).

On the other hand, the literary evidence fails to *prove* Lucan composition (Schramm, 131 n. 2; Schürmann, *Abschiedsrede*, 85 n. 287), and this opens up the possibility that Luke instead of being dependent on the Marcan predictions drew the saying from some other source (Kümmel, 70f.; Patsch, 188f.). Earlier we saw that in 9:44 Luke may have been influenced by an independent form of the passion prediction, and it is significant that the same brief form is found here. This suggests, although it does not prove, that the present saying may reflect a tradition of the passion predictions independent of Mk., adapted by Luke to its present context. The absence of reference to the death and resurrection of Jesus may be due to Luke's concept of Jesus suffering and being rejected in his representatives, the disciples.

(26) Vs. 26–30 offer a double comparison between the day of the Son of man and the time of Noah and Lot. Lührmann, 75–83, has shown that these two OT events were often connected with each other as examples of the punishment of the wicked and often also of the redemption of the pious (T. Naph. 3:4f.; 3 Mac. 2:4f.; Wis. 10:4, 6; Philo, Vit. Mos. II, 52–65; Gn R 27; Sanh. 10:3; *et al.*). On this basis he confirms the suggestion of earlier writers that the Lot-comparison is a secondary addition, constructed on the analogy of the Noah-comparison (perhaps by Q, Bultmann, 123; Geiger, 91–94; or by Luke, Vielhauer, 67; Creed, 220; undecided: Schulz, 278 n. 93; Zmijewski, 452–457). The Lot-comparison is omitted by Matthew, and this has suggested that it may not have stood in Q; C. Colpe, TDNT VIII, 434 n. 257, regards it as a detached, but authentic saying, not known to Matthew. But the view of Manson, *Sayings*, 143; R. Schnackenburg*, 223; and B. Rigaux*, 422, that the whole saying was in Q and was abbreviated by Matthew is more probable. The repetition in Mt. 24:37 and 39b may suggest that something has been omitted. It is a moot point whether the Evangelists

had the same form of Q here; editorial activity by the Evangelists could account for the differences. So far as authenticity is concerned, Vielhauer, 79f., admits that there is nothing in vs. 26f. themselves that suggests inauthenticity, but they fall (by analogy) under his general rejection of *all* Son of man sayings. Perrin, 197, holds that the development of the apocalyptic concept of the coming of the Son of man took place in the early church. Schulz, 282f., draws attention to the use of the LXX and the use of the 'exact comparison' construction which he regards as characteristic of Hellenistic Jewish Christianity. But the use of the LXX was natural once the Q material was turned into Greek, and attribution of exact comparisons to a late stage in the tradition is quite arbitrary. The saying is without doubt authentic (C. Colpe, TDNT VIII, 434; Jeremias, *Theology*, I, 263). It warns of the unexpectedness and of the certainty (J. Schlosser*) of judgment upon sinners.

Luke's καί is probably original, diff. Mt. γάρ (v.1. δέ; pace Zmijewski, 445), since Matthew has adapted the saying to show how the day of the Son of man is unknown (Mt. 24:36). The use of καθώς (11:30; 17:28) may be Lucan (diff. Mt. ὥσπερ, but the latter is a favourite word in Mt.). The days of Noah (1 Pet. 3:20) is a general reference to Noah's lifetime. In Mt. the comparison is between the days of Noah and the parousia. A more exact comparison is found in Lk. with the use of ἐν ταῖς ἡμέραις τοῦ υἱοῦ τοῦ ἀνθρώπου. The plural refers to the days preceding the parousia (R. Schnackenburg*, 226), and is not the plural of 'the day of the Son of man' (so rightly Manson, *Sayings*, 143). The vagueness of the phrase is due to its having been formed on the analogy of 'the days of Noah' (not on the analogy of 17:22, where the phrase probably has a different meaning). It may be due to Lucan editing of an original singular (Schulz, 279), but could well be original in Q (Lührmann, 73 n. 1). E. Schweizer, art. cit., 190, and R. Maddox, art. cit., 51 (17:22 note), think that the reference is to the days of Jesus' earthly ministry, when he acted like Noah as a preacher of righteousness; the future tense is against this attractive interpretation (but cf. 11:30), unless 'Son of man' is interpreted corporately, or the saying is regarded as originally referring to the crisis of judgment following upon the ministry of Jesus.

(27) The comparison is now detailed. During the days of Noah men and women were going about their normal life, eating and drinking, marrying and getting married. Luke does not have the repeated comparison form (ὡς) found in Mt., and has imperfects instead of participles; for τρώγω he has the more elegant ἐσθίω; and for γαμίζω, 'to give in marriage', he has the better contrast, γαμίζομαι, 'to be given in marriage' (of a woman). For the thought of marriage cf. Gn. 6:4. The people were unprepared for what happened; Matthew (καὶ οὐκ ἔγνωσαν) stresses their ignorance of the day of reckoning. Tödt, 50f., emphasises that they had not heeded the preaching of Noah. There came the day of 'salvation' for Noah and his family when he entered the ark (κιβωτός,

Mt. 24:38; Heb. 11:7; 1 Pet. 3:20; also 'ark of the covenant', Heb. 9:4; Rev. 11:19**), and the deluge (κατακλυσμός, Mt. 24:38f.; 2 Pet. 2:5**) destroyed them (following Gn. 7:7 LXX, but there is hardly any other way of rendering the MT); Luke has ἀπόλλυμι, diff. Mt. αἴρω, UBS has πάντας (p⁷⁵ B D Θ pc; v.l. ἅπαντας) in Lk., while Mt. has ἅπαντας; it is strange that Matthew has this form and not Luke, so perhaps ἅπαντας should be read in Lk. with *Diglot* (cf. the same problem in v. 29).

(28) The comparison is not worked out. Instead Luke proceeds to record the further example of what took place in the days of Lot. ὁμοίως (3:11) may be Lucan. Λώτ is not especially named as an example of virtue; the emphasis is rather on the behaviour of the men of Sodom and the consequent, unexpected judgment. A fuller list of activities is given (buying, selling, planting and building), and there is surprisingly no mention of the sins of Sodom. It is the thought of unpreparedness and attachment to earthly pursuits rather than of sin which is uppermost.

(29) The relative phrase should be expanded to τῇ ἡμέρα ᾗ. For βρέχω cf. 7:38, 44; the subject is God (cf. Gn. 19:24; Mt. 5:45), unless the verb is used intransitively (cf. 5:17; BD 129). θεῖον is 'sulphur' (Gn. 19:24; Rev. 9:17f.); the text is confused with πῦρ καὶ θεῖον as the best attested reading (ℵ B ΓΔ al vg cop). The inverted wording in A D K syᵖ is assimilated to the LXX; πῦρ alone is read by it syᶜ; (*Diglot*).

(30) κατὰ τὰ αὐτά (κατὰ ταῦτα p⁷⁵ ᵛⁱᵈ ℵ* A W Θ f1 f13 pm lat; TR; *Diglot*) is perhaps Lucan (6:23, 26; cf. Acts 14:1), diff. Mt. οὕτως. The dative phrase ᾗ ἡμέρα may be due to assimilation to v. 29; Mt. has the nominative ἡ παρουσία, which is in any case probably secondary. The use of ἀποκαλύπτεται corresponds exactly to Mt. παρουσία (cf. 1 Cor. 1:7; 2 Thes. 1:7; 1 Pet. 1:7, 13; 4:13), and is probably original (*pace* Schulz, 280).

(31) The thought now moves to practical warning in face of the coming catastrophe. The picture employed is that of people fleeing without stopping to collect their possessions; the contrast is provided by Lot's wife who lingered and was lost. V. 31 has a close parallel in Mk. 13:15f., where the thought is of flight from Judaea in time of war, and the reference appears to be to the events of AD 66–70. But precipitate flight will be out of the question when the Son of man appears, and so the saying must here be taken metaphorically: attachment to earthly things will lead to disaster (Creed, 221). Luke may have taken the material from Mk. 13:15f. (contrary to his general practice of not inserting Marcan material in a Q context); if so, it is probable that v. 32 is his own creation (Bultmann, 123; R. Schnackenburg*, 223f.; Zmijewski, 473–478; Geiger, 111–118). This hypothesis is strengthened if v. 33 is an isolated Q saying (cf. Mt. 10:39) which he has also inserted at this point. But Manson, *Sayings*, 144f., argues that Luke is unlikely to have added inappropriate material at this point from Mk.; more probably vs. 31 and 32 were already joined by association of ideas, and the whole unit was added on the basis of the catchword 'Lot' in the oral stage.

Luke then omitted the Marcan saying at the corresponding point in 21:21f. to avoid a doublet or because he was following another source there. The language, it is true, is close to that of Mk., but there is sufficient difference and common omissions with Mt. to make it possible that the saying originally stood also in Q (cf. Lambrecht, 157f.).

For ἐν ἐκείνῃ τῇ ἡμέρᾳ cf. 21:34; 6:23; 10:12; this may be a Lucan connection, but it could belong to the Q form of the saying. Luke has ὅς ἔσται followed by a hanging nominative phrase, diff. Mk. and Mt. ὁ ἐπί...; contrast v. 31b. There is no obvious reason for Lucan redaction here, and the phrase may betray his use of a different tradition from Mk. The roof (δῶμα, 5:19) is a place where one might rest. σκεῦος could be Lucan (8:16 diff. Mk.; Acts, 5x), but the plural, 'possessions', is found here only in Lk. and Acts. It is not coming down from the roof (to flee) that the saying forbids, but coming down in order to collect one's possessions; this is clearer in Mk. with the addition μηδὲ εἰσελθάτω; the omission by both Matthew and Luke may reflect use of a non-Marcan source. Similarly, the plural form αὐτά par. Mt. τὰ ἐκ τῆς οἰκίας αὐτοῦ, diff. Mk. τι may also indicate a non-Marcan tradition. For ἐν, par. Mt., Mark has εἰς (loose Hellenistic use of prepositions); the correction may be coincidental or due to non-Marcan influence. After ἐν the article is added by A D W Δ Θ Π f1 pm; TR; Diglot, probably by assimilation to the parallels. ὁμοίως (17:28) is probably a Lucan addition. μὴ ἐπιστρεψάτω εἰς τὰ ὀπίσω is reminiscent of Gn. 19:26 (καὶ ἐπέβλεψεν ... εἰς τὰ ὀπίσω) and also of Lk. 9:62. Luke does not have the epexegetic phrase ἆραι τὸ ἱμάτιον αὐτοῦ, diff. Mk. and Mt. The effect is to give a closer link with the following verse. The thought of turning back to get something has to be supplied from the first part of the verse. The omission may reflect use of a non-Marcan source, or it may have been made in order to get a closer link with v. 32.

(32) The warning not to turn back is reinforced by a reference to the fate of Lot's wife. To remember (μνημονεύω*; Acts 20:31, 35*) is more than an intellectual act; it is to pay heed to something and so to be encouraged or, as here, warned by it (cf. O. Michel, TDNT IV, 682f.). The allusion is to Gn. 19:26, and serves to warn those who have been saved against the danger of falling back into worldliness and sin and hence into judgment.

If v. 31 has been drawn from Mk., it will originally have applied to the need for flight in face of war and disaster; Luke has then applied it to the day of the Son of man. It could then be a warning to unbelievers, but with the metaphorical force that flight will in fact be impossible. However, more probably (especially in view of v. 32) it is meant as a metaphorical warning to disciples not to be concerned about worldly pursuits and possessions. This use appears to be secondary to that in Mk.; if so v. 32 is a comment by the Evangelist (or possibly his source, if he is drawing on Q) which binds the warning more closely to the preceding illustration and brings out its force.

(33) There now follows a general principle which undergirds the warning. It is paralleled in 9:24 par. Mk. 8:35 and Mt. 16:25, and also in Mt. 10:39 and Jn. 12:25. Whereas most scholars regard the saying here as a parallel to Mt. 10:39 based on Q (Schulz, 444–446; Geiger, 120), Zmijewski, 479–482, argues that both Evangelists were in fact drawing on Mk. It must be admitted that in any case the Marcan and Q forms are close in wording; Black, 188, regards them as translation variants. On the other hand, it is remarkable that both Matthew and Luke should have made the same addition from Mk., each in the context of Q material (Mt. 10:37f. par. Lk. 14:26f.; Mt. 10:40 par. Lk. 10:16), and it is also remarkable that Luke should have used the same saying from Mk. twice, since he never does so anywhere else and has an aversion to 'doublets' (Schürmann, *Untersuchungen*, 272–278). Both Evangelists have assimilated the wording in the present saying to Mk., which is not surprising in the case of so important a saying. A difficulty for the Q hypothesis is the question of the original context of the saying. It may originally have belonged in its present Lucan context (Manson, *Sayings*, 145; R. Schnackenburg*, 224f.), and have been transferred by Matthew to his mission discourse, a supposition supported by the facts that Matthew uses other eschatological material in Mt. 10 and that he appears to be drawing material from different parts of Q. The alternative is that the Matthaean context is original (Schulz, 445), especially since this gives a parallel with Mk. 8:34f. The omission of the saying in Mt. 24:37–39, 40f., gives some support to the latter alternative. It is just possible that the saying is an isolated one and that it appeared in different contexts in different recensions of Q.

Luke's ὅς ... construction, diff. Mt. ὁ with participle, may be due to assimilation to 9:24 (par. Mk.). ζητέω could be a translation variant of Mk. θέλω (Black, 244), but the word is a favourite of Luke (5:18 note), and περιποιέομαι may also be Lucan (Acts 20:28; 1 Tim. 3:13*). Matthew uses εὑρίσκω, which may be from Q or be due to his own editing (cf. Mt. 16:25 diff. Mk. 8:35; E. Schweizer, TDNT IX, 643). περιποιέομαι is 'to leave alive' (Gn. 12:12; Ex. 1:16) or 'to win, acquire' (Gn. 36:6; Acts 20:28; 1 Tim. 3:13); the variants σῶσαι and ζωογονῆσαι are due to assimilation to 9:24 and 17:33b respectively, and the reading of p75 B pc it is to be preferred (Metzger, 167). For ψυχή see 9:24 and especially Gn. 19:17 (Geiger, 125). The use of αὐτοῦ suggests that the former meaning of περιποιέομαι is preferable: the thought is of holding on to what one considers to be one's real life (not of escaping physical death; cf. E. Schweizer, TDNT IX, 643f.). There may be influence from Ezk. 13:18f. (Geiger, 121f.).

In the second part of the saying the indicative ἀπολέσει should possibly be read in the indefinite relative clause (so ℵ A al; *Synopsis*; ἀπολέσῃ, rell; TR *Diglot*; cf. 12:8 v.1.; Mk. 8:35; BD 380³; MH III, 110).

αὐτήν is added as object in A L Δ Π; *Diglot*, probably as clarification. Luke does not have ἕνεκεν ἐμοῦ diff. Mt. 10:39 and Lk. 9:24 and parr. It is also missing in Jn. 12:25. While it could be an addition from Mk. 8:35 in Mt. 10:39, Schulz, 445, holds that it is original in Mt. in a context of teaching about discipleship, and that Luke dropped it because it was unnecessary in the present context; this explanation is less likely. ζωογονέω can mean 'to keep alive' (Acts 7:19) or 'to bestow life' (1 Tim. 6:13**; R. Bultmann, TDNT II, 873f.); here the former meaning is required. The word is probably a Lucan literary expression here (cf. Mk. σώζω; Jn. φυλάσσω). For the thought as a whole cf. 21:19 par. Mk. 13:13b.

(34) These sayings follow on directly from the Noah saying in Mt. If the day of the Son of man comes unexpectedly, there will be a division among men between those who are ready and those are unready. Three illustrations are offered, of which each Evangelist has two (unless v. 36 is authentic). It is a moot point whether one Evangelist has altered the original text of Q (change by Matthew: Bultmann, 123; Schulz, 280; change by Luke: Schlatter, 555; Zmijewski, 497–501), or each Evangelist has chosen two out of an original triad of examples, or we have two independent developments of the same tradition at the oral stage (cf. 11:11f.; 12:27 for similar problems). The argument that Matthew missed the point of the close companionship found in Lk. (i.e. Q) and substituted a more accidental association of people at the same task (Wellhausen, *Matthäus*, 127) is weak: two women at the mill are not more closely linked than two men in the same field. Zmijewski argues that Luke introduced the thought of 'night' and altered the illustrations accordingly. (cf. 9:32, 37a; 12:20). It is more probable that Matthew or his source assimilated the picture to that in Mt. 24:18 par. Lk. 17:31. The original picture is that of a farmer and his wife still in bed while the members of the household are beginning their daily tasks.

The introductory λέγω ὑμῖν is used in Q to introduce conclusions and applications (cf. 14:24; 19:26; Mt. 18:13) and is probably original, diff. Mt. τότε (Schulz, 280; *pace* Zmijewski, 490f.; Geiger, 135). The use of ταύτῃ τῇ νυκτί is associated with the following picture. A. Strobel* holds that the phrase reflects the Jewish expectation that redemption would come on the night of the Passover (cf. Jeremias, *Words*, 206f.); cf. the Christian use of the imagery in 1 Thes. 5:2. This thought may be present here, or Christians may have read it back into the saying, but the mention of work is inconsistent with the thought of Passover night. In fact the passage refers to the period just before dawn when some people are still asleep and others are up early to perform their tasks, and the point is that the night is followed by the day of the Son of man. Moreover, the saying is not concerned with being asleep or awake (contrast the admonitions to watchfulness in 12:35–40); the point is the separation between closely related people. This freedom from parenetic development in terms of spiritual wakefulness points to the primitive nature of the saying and suggests that the thought of the parousia occurring at night is not necessarily present; the mention of night is simply part of the metaphor.

The opening clauses in vs. 34 and 35 represent Semitic noun phrases giving the situation (cf. 12:52f.). The first picture is of two people on the same bed. Zmijewski's claim, 493f., that κλινή means a couch on which people lie to eat a meal is improbable, especially after the mention of night-time. Luke has ὁ εἷς ... ὁ ἕτερος ... diff. Mt. εἷς ... εἷς ...; the former may be a Semitism and hence original (7:42 note; cf. 16:13; A. Strobel*, 21) rather than a Lucan correction (*pace* Schulz, 280). Both pronouns are masculine, since either the man or his wife may be taken/left. παραλαμβάνω (9:10) can mean 'to be taken (into the kingdom, away from judgment)' (Jn. 14:3; cf. the thought in Mk. 13:27; 1 Thes. 4:17; G. Delling, TDNT IV, 13) or 'to be taken (for judgment)' (an older interpretation, mentioned and rejected by A. Strobel*, 20 n. 1). ἀφίεμαι must then mean 'to be left behind', sc. for judgment or salvation respectively. Zmijewski, 501, holds that the latter set of meanings is required in Q (where the saying, on his view, was closely linked with the Noah saying), while the former set of meanings is intended by Luke. But in fact Noah was saved by being taken away from the flooded earth. The picture is of an act of God (a divine passive?), taking away his people from the scene of judgment. Geiger, 140, thinks that originally the saying was meant unapocalyptically of accepting or rejecting the call to discipleship; this is speculative.

(35) The second picture is that of two women grinding (ἀλήθω, Mt. 24:41**) at the mill, one turning the stone and the other pouring out the meal. ἐπὶ τὸ αὐτό, 'together' is probably Lucan (Acts 1:15; 2:1, 44, 47; 4:26) diff. Mt. ἐν τῷ μύλῳ. Again one is taken, but the other is left (ἡ δέ, p75 ℵ B L R f13 *pc*; καὶ ἡ *rell*; TR; *Diglot*). According to Rengstorf, 197, the grinding of meal for each day's fresh baking of bread was done just before dawn, but Schlatter, 555, denies that grinding was done at night.

(36) This verse is omitted by the best MSS (p75 ℵ A B L W Δ Θ Ψ fl 28 33 565 sa bo). It appears, with variations in wording, in D *pm* lat sy; TR. Most editors reject it as due to assimilation to Mt. 24:40 (Metzger, 168). It is just possible that it was omitted by homoioteleuton (cf. the omission of v. 35 by ℵ* *pc*). Manson, *Sayings*, 145f., argues that the style is Lucan, and that the inclusion gives a triad of examples with a 'complete' family of the farmer and his wife, two maidservants and two menservants. The verse could have been omitted by a scribe who thought that agricultural activity was unlikely at night. These are valid points, but it is doubtful whether they can overturn the strong weight of external evidence.

(37) The closing verse is enigmatic. It comes earlier in Matthew's discourse, immediately following Mt. 24:27 par. Lk. 17:24. Most scholars argue that Luke has moved it to its present position, possibly as a result of his insertion of v. 25, and also in order to get a climax for the

discourse as a whole. If so, v. 37a is presumably editorial, despite the use of the historic present λέγουσιν (cf. 11:37, 45; Schürmann, *Paschamahlbericht*, 83).

The disciples' question is concerned with locality, and does not follow very logically from the preceding sayings. It takes up the point in v. 23. In Mt. the point is that there is no need to ask 'Where?' or to seek for the coming of the Son of man. His coming will be as obvious as lightning. His presence will be clearly indicated, just as the presence of carrion is clearly indicated by the gathering of vultures overhead. Alternatively, the thought is that men will no more be able to miss seeing the Son of man than vultures can miss seeing carrion (Klostermann, *Matthäus*, 195, cited by Schulz, 284 n. 153). Others take the force to be that the Son of man will appear when the world is ripe for judgment (Zahn, 607; Geldenhuys, 445), or that judgment will operate wherever it is needed (Creed, 221), or that men should avoid being like carrion, waiting to be devoured (Danker, 183). J. Weiss, 495, thinks that the disciples' question means, 'Where do those who are left behind stay?' with the answer being 'at the scene of judgment'; but this is rather forced. Zmijewski, 513–517, holds that the point is the universality of the separation in vs. 34f. This last view seems best for Lk.

Luke has the simple relative ὅπου, diff. Mt. ὅπου ἐάν. σῶμα, diff. Mt. πτῶμα, means 'corpse', and is perhaps a literary refinement (Tödt, 50 n.). ἀετός can mean 'eagle' (Ezk. 17:37; Rev. 4:7; 8:13; 12:14) or 'vulture' (Mt. 24:28**; Lv. 11:13; Dt. 14:12). Here the latter meaning is required, since eagles do not search out dead prey. The use of ἐπισυνάγω, diff. Mt. συνάγω, is Lucan (12:1).

There is no reason to doubt the authenticity of the saying as a warning by Jesus against the fact of impending judgment. Jeremias, *Parables*, 162, assumes that it was originally addressed to Jesus' opponents and reproached them for not being able to see the signs of coming judgment in contemporary events (cf. 12:54–56). Manson, *Sayings*, 147, thinks that it refers to the swiftness with which the Son of man will come in judgment.

iv. The Parable of the Unjust Judge 18:1–8

The teaching about the coming of the Son of man (cf. 18:8) is concluded with a parable about prayer. As it stands, the purpose of the parable is said to be that of encouraging the disciples to pray until the parousia and not give up hope (18:1): an interval before the parousia is presupposed, as is clear from 17:22–37. The parable proper concerns a widow who at first fails to get a judge to take up her case, no doubt out of deference to a wealthy opponent and his bribes. Weak though she is, she gains her end by persistence. The application is similar to that in 11:5–8. But the parable has a further point. In the application made in vs. 6–8 the point made *a peiore ad melius* (C. Colpe's apt phrase, TDNT VIII, 435 n. 265) is that God too will certainly vindicate his elect people in the end. He will act speedily (or suddenly): but the decisive question is whether they will continue faithful (and therefore prayerful) right through until the parousia of the Son of man.

The exegesis below supports the interpretation of v. 1 given in the above summary, and shows that Luke has not wrongly generalised the message of an eschatological parable into a comment on the need for persistent, importunate prayer (*pace* Bultmann, 209, 360). Indeed, there is more to be said for the suggestion that a parable about prayer in general has been turned into a parable about the need to be ready for the coming of the Son of man. Acceptance of this view depends upon the view taken of vs. 6–8. These verses offer an interpretation of the parable. Taken on its own the parable could be regarded as a companion to the parable of the friend at midnight (11:5–8), and giving teaching on the need for importunity in prayer (cf. Ott, 19–72). Then vs. 6–8 are an addition or series of additions in which the parable is turned into a lesson about the character of God (vs. 6–8a, or 6b–7), and finally applied to the disciples (v. 8b). Most commentators regard 8b as an addition to the parable, probably by Luke (Bultmann, 189; Grässer, 36f.; Kümmel, 59; Kümmel, *Heilsgeschehen,* 461f.; Grundmann, 346; Ellis, 213; Ott, 32–34), and many regard vs. 6–8a as an addition also (Bultmann, 209; Grässer, 36; Grundmann). Ott, 32–72, holds that v. 8a was added with v. 8b by Luke, and that v. 6a is a Lucan introduction; vs. 6b–7 are a pre-Lucan addition.

These attempts at dissection are not universally accepted. C. Spicq*, G. Delling*, and Jeremias, *Parables*, 153–157 (reversing his earlier opinion) accept the whole of vs. 6–8; and Kümmel and Ellis accept all except v. 8b. The language of vs. 6b–7 is not Lucan, and the Aramaising construction is proof of its age. Delling has listed the differences in construction between this parable and 11:5–8 which show that neither should be interpreted narrowly in the light of the other, e.g. by removing the eschatological features here. As it stands, the parable requires an application, and since the judge is the principal character, the application is appropriate; the point of the parable is the contrast between the judge and God (Lagrange, 472). As for the Lucan style of v. 6a, this proves nothing more than that Luke has edited at this point. There is greater difficulty with v. 8b, which reverts to the attitude of the disciples. But the saying in itself is unexceptionable as teaching of Jesus (C. Colpe, TDNT VIII, 435), and it is not necessarily Lucan. In fact, we have a structure similar to that in the parable of the prodigal son, where a story, whose central character appears to be the father and whose central concern is to depict the character of God, turns out to have a 'sting in the tail' as it presents the picture of the elder brother and asks the audience whether they behave like him. So here, after depicting the character of God, the parable turns in application to the disciples and asks whether they will show a faith as persistent as the nagging of the widow. Since these two factors, the attitude of the judge and the attitude of the woman, are tightly woven into the parable, it is probable that the double application is also original; certainly it flows perfectly naturally from the parable itself. It seems unnecessary, therefore, to suppose that vs. 6–8 are a later addition. As for v. 1, this is a Lucan introduction which links up closely with v. 8b. It stresses the fact that there may be an interval before the parousia (cf. 19:11), but does not distort the teaching of the parable.

Delling suggests that the parable was originally addressed by Jesus to a group of pious Jews who were waiting impatiently for the Son of man to vindicate them against their opponents. This reconstruction is quite conjectural, since we have no evidence for the existence of such a group (Jeremias, *Parables*, 156 n. 18). Rather, the parable presupposes the same persecution for disciples as is found elsewhere in the teaching of Jesus.

The parable is from Luke's special source material, and Luke has used v. 1 to link it to Q material.

See H. Sahlin, *Zwei Lukasstellen* (*Symbolae Biblicae Upsalienses*, 4) Uppsala/Copenhagen, 1945, 9–20; Jeremias, *Parables*, 153–157; C. Spicq, 'La parabole de la veuve obstinée et du juge inerte, aux décisions impromptues (Lc xviii. 1–8)', RB 68, 1961, 68–90; Delling, 203–225 (originally as G. Delling, 'Das Gleichnis vom gottlosen Richter', ZNW 53, 1962, 1–25); Linnemann, 119–124; C. E. B. Cranfield, 'The Parable of the Unjust Judge and the Eschatology of Luke-Acts', SJT 16, 1963, 297–301; H. Riesenfeld, 'Zu μακροθυμεῖν (Lk. 18, 7) ', in Blinzler, *Studien*, 214–217; H. Ljungvik, 'Zur Erklärung einer Lukas-Stelle (Luk. xviii. 7) ', NTS 10, 1963–64, 289–294; A. Wifstrand, 'Lukas xviii. 7', NTS 11, 1964–65, 72–74; Ott, 19–72; J. D. M. Derrett, 'Law in the New Testament: The Parable of the Unjust Judge', NTS 18, 1971–72, 178–191; D. R. Catchpole, 'The Son of Man's Search for Faith (Luke XVIII 8b)' Nov.T 19, 1977, 81–104.

(1) The introductory statement shows features of Lucan style, and has at least been edited by him (Delling, 206–208; Ott, 19). For the opening phrase cf. 5:36; after δέ, καί is added by A D W Δ Θ Π Ψ f1 *pm* lat sy; TR; *Diglot*. In context αὐτοῖς must refer to the disciples. πρὸς τό with the infinitive to express purpose is found only here in Lk. (cf. Acts 3:19; cf. BD 402⁴; MH III, 142; and the use of εἰς τό 5:17; Acts 7:19). But the use here is not so much to express purpose (in which case the δεῖν would be unnecessary), as rather reference (compare the use of πρὸς αὐτούς, 20:19.). πάντοτε (15:31) is generally understood to refer to continuous prayer (cf. 1 Thes. 5:17). Jewish teaching in general rejected the idea of perpetual prayer, although there were exceptions (SB II, 237f.; I. 1036). But the thought here is of continual prayer, rather than continuous prayer. The fear is that men will give up before they are answered. Hence Ott, 68–71, rightly concludes that the verse is concerned with praying throughout the period until the parousia rather than with continuous prayer. This is supported by the use of ἐγκακέω, 'to become weary, tired' (2 Thes. 3:13; Gal. 6:9), 'to lose heart, despair' (2 Cor. 4:1, 16; Eph. 3:13; in addition to W. Grundmann, TDNT III, 486, see especially Delling, 207 n. 23, who adduces evidence from Gk. tran-

slations of the OT for the meaning 'überdrüssig sein', 'to grow tired of';
Gn. 27:46; Nu. 21:5; Pr. 3:11; Is. 7:16).

(2) The parable is about a judge (11:19; 12:14, 58) apparently in a
small town where local people of prominence were appointed to act as
required; there does not appear to have been a uniform, organised
system (cf. Schürer II:1, 149f.; SB I, 289). Jeremias, *Parables*, 153,
states that monetary cases could be settled by a single judge rather than
by a tribunal. Derrett*, 180–186, thinks that the woman had bypassed
the Jewish courts and gone to a secular judge who would have more
power to gain her end for her.

The corruption of the judge is indicated by his double characterisation as one who neither feared God nor had regard for men (ἐντρέπομαι,
20:13; Heb. 12:9; also (active) 'to make ashamed', 1 Cor. 4:14; *et al.*).
The description is proverbial (Jos. Ant. 10:83; Dion. Hal. 10:10:7; Livy
22:3); Delling, 208 n. 26, notes that in the OT fear of God is especially
fear of his *as judge*, so that the point here is that the judge does not take
the judgment of God seriously.

(3) The other character in the story is a widow (χήρα, 2:37; *et al.*
τίς is added by *Diglot*), who is the typically needy and helpless person
(La. 1:1; Ex. 22:22–24; Ps. 68:5 (67:6); Jas. 1:27). She came repeatedly
(ἤρχετο) to the judge with a request that he would take up her case.
ἐκδικέω, 'to avenge', can mean 'to procure justice for someone' (Rom.
12:19), in the sense of securing the rights of the wronged person (e.g. the
payment of compensation) or of punishing the offender (Acts 7:24; 2
Cor. 10:6; Rev. 6:10; 19:2; cf. G. Schrenk, TDNT II, 442–444; Delling,
209–212). Here the former interpretation is required; what the widow
wants is not the punishment of her opponent but the payment of
whatever is due to her (Plummer, 412).

(4) For a long time (ἐπὶ χρόνον; cf. 4:25) her pleas were in vain.
Although the judge was legally required to give precedence to a widow's
case (G. Stählin, TDNT IX, 450 n. 86), he was either unwilling to do so
(perhaps through laziness) or he would not dare (θέλω, 18:13; Mk. 6:26;
Jn. 7:1) to withstand her powerful opponent (Jeremias, *Parables*, 141 n.
45, 153). Finally, he gave in. μετὰ δὲ ταῦτα is read by א A D W Θ fl f13
pl; TR; UBS; *Diglot*; μετὰ ταῦτα δέ is read by B L Q *pc* lat; *Synopsis*,
and looks like a correction. μετὰ ταῦτα is Lucan (5:27; *et al.*), and solilo-
quies are not infrequent in Lucan parables (12:17; for the Semitic λέγειν
ἐν ἑαυτῷ, cf. 3:8; *et al.*) The concessive clause in the judge's comment
gives the same structure as in 11:8. For οὐδὲ ἄνθρωπον the variant καὶ
ἄνθρωπον οὐ is read by A D W Δ fl f13 *pl*; TR; *Diglot*.

(5) The use of διά γε is also found in 11:8, and the thought of causing trouble for someone also appears in the earlier parable (κόπος, 11:7).
ταύτην could be derogatory (15:30), but not necessarily so. The judge is
now willing to see that the widow receives justice because of the consequences to himself if he fails to take her side. He fears that she may keep
on coming (ἐρχόμενος, present participle, as in 13:14; 16:21; but a single

coming could be meant, as in 15:25). ὑπωπιάζω means literally 'to strike under the eye', i.e. 'to give a black eye to' (cf. 1 Cor. 9:27** in a metaphor drawn from boxing); so C. Spicq*, 75 n. 6; Delling, 213; G. Stählin, TDNT IX, 450 n. 88; AG (with doubt). Most translations adopt the weak metaphorical meaning 'to wear out' (BD 207³; Jeremias, *Parables*, 154; Grundmann, 345; K. Weiss, TDNT VIII, 590f.). This view is supported by the Syriac and Georgian versions (Jeremias, ibid.), and there is some Greek evidence for it (Plutarch, Fac. Lun. 5 (II, 921f.), cited by K. Weiss, ibid.). Derrett, 189–191, argues that the Greek word is meant as a translation of taš^ehîr pānay, with the sense 'to blacken one's face', i.e. 'to defame, disgrace' (p. Hag. II, 771; Jastrow, *Dictionary*, 1551). Although the OT parallels which he cites do not support his case, and a black eye is not the same thing as a blackened face, the later history of the word supports this view. The problem is complicated by the phrase εἰς τέλος; this can mean 'finally' (AG 819; A. Oepke, TDNT II, 426 n. 25; G. Delling, TDNT VIII, 56; and most translations); 'completely' (BD 207³; Jeremias, *Parables*, 154); or 'for ever', 'unceasingly' (Ott, 21f.). The phrase may go with ἐρχομένη or with ὑπωπιάζῃ. We thus get a variety of possibilities: 1. 'lest she finally comes and assaults me'; 2. 'lest by her unceasing coming she wears me out'; 3. 'lest by her continually coming she finally wears me out; 4. 'lest by keeping on coming she blackens my face'. Although Delling argues that ἐρχόμενος can be used of a single coming, Jeremias and Zerwick, 249, argue that the use of the present tenses (including ὑπωπιάζῃ) rules out view 1. Moreover, it is unlikely that the judge would fear a physical attack by the woman. The parable is concerned with continual nagging rather than a single attack. The judge's fear is that the woman's continual nagging will wear him out or get him a bad name for refusing to hear her entreaties. The evidence favours view 4.

(6) The parable in itself contains no application, but now an application follows. It is odd, however, that the flow of words is interrupted. εἶπεν δέ is common in Lk. and ὁ κύριος may be Lucan (Ott, 34–40) or pre-Lucan (Delling, 214 n. 52; cf. 7:13 note; 16:8). The insertion signals the change from parable to application and underlines the solemn utterance about the character of God drawn by Jesus. For τῆς ἀδικίας cf. 16:8 note; the phrase characterises the judge as one who belongs to this present evil age, and thus stands in strong contrast to God (Delling, 214f.); whether it is intended to indicate that we are dealing with a secular judge rather than a Jewish judge (Derrett's view) is not certain, since Jewish judges too could be corrupt. The whole ἀκούσατε . . . clause is virtually a protasis to the following statement about God.

(7) With the mention of God's name the application moves to a description of his character comparable to that in Sir. 35:12–20, the language of which is reflected here. The οὐ μή construction is used to give a strong question expecting an emphatic answer, 'Yes' (Jn. 18:11; Acts 15:4; BD 365⁴). ποιέω τὴν ἐκδίκησιν means 'to vindicate', in the

sense of punishing offenders (T. Levi 3:3) and or of rescuing those who
are in trouble (cf. Acts 7:24; Test. Sol. 22:4; Jeremias, *Parables*, 154 n.
8). Here the latter thought is uppermost, since there is no mention of the
opponents of the elect (Delling, 216f., especially n. 68; G. Schrenk,
TDNT II, 445f., thinks retribution is in mind). The thought, therefore, is
not in any sense vindictive. The ἐκλεκτοί are God's own, chosen people:
Delling, 215, rightly notes that if the judge vindicated the widow who
was a stranger to him, God is all the more bound to help his own people.
The widow symbolises God's elect (G. Stählin, TDNT IX, 458).

ἐκλεκτός is used in 23:35* of Jesus, and of God's people (especially
in an eschatological context) in Mk. 13:20, 22, 27; Mt. 22:14; for the
background see G. Schrenk, TDNT IV, 181–192; Delling, 215 n. 63.
The use of the term implies that eschatological vindication is in view,
and not a purely this-worldly answer to prayer (cf. the discussion in Ott,
61f.). βοάω can be used of the cry of the needy to God (cf. Jdg. 10:10;
Nu. 20:16; *et al.*; Jas. 5:4f.; Mk. 15:34; E. Stauffer, TDNT I, 625–628),
and it here describes the standing characteristic of God's people. For
αὐτῷ (p⁷⁵ ℵ B L Q *pc*), πρὸς αὐτόν (A W *Δ Θ* f1 f13 *pl*; TR; *Diglot*) and
αὐτῶν (D) are also found. For ἡμέρας καὶ νυκτός as a description of in-
cessant prayer cf. 2:37 note. Those who depend entirely on God may be
sure that he will vindicate them.

The final clause is a *crux interpretum*. μακροθυμέω can mean: 1. 'to
wait patiently' (Jas. 5:7). Hence, either 2. 'to be dilatory, slow' (secular
examples in F. Horst, TDNT IV, 374–387, especially, 375), or 3. 'to be
forbearing', especially in the sense of being patient with recalcitrant people (cf. Mt. 18:26, 29; 1 Cor. 13:4; 1 Thes. 5:14; 2 Pet. 3:9). It is used
especially of God delaying his wrath in the hope that sinners will repent
before it is too late. In Sir. 35:19 (καὶ ὁ κύριος οὐ μὴ βραδύνῃ οὐδὲ μὴ
μακροθυμήσῃ ἐπ' αὐτοῖς), the meaning is uncertain: when the righteous
cry to God in the face of human oppression, 'the Lord will not be slow,
neither will he be patient with the wicked, until he . . . sends retribution
on the heathen' (NEB; but JB translates: 'And the Lord will not be slow,
neither will he be dilatory on their behalf, until he has . . . exacted
vengeance on the nations'; in favour of NEB cf. 2 Mac. 6:14). In the present verse ἐπ' αὐτοῖς must refer to the elect rather than their opponents
who have not been mentioned (*pace The Moffatt Bible*). ἐπί, however, is
ambiguous, and may mean 'towards' or 'on account of'. The third aspect
of the problem is the syntactical relation of this clause to the previous
clause: is it a continuation of the same question, or is it a different kind
of clause? The following possibilities have been suggested: 1. Despite the
change in mood, from subjunctive to indicative, the clause might be understood as a continuation of the previous question: 'and does he not
show patience towards them (i.e. listen patiently to their prayers)?' But
this comes rather lamely after the promise of vindication, and it gives an
odd meaning to μακροθυμέω. 2. In view of the difficulty in regarding the
clause as a continuation of the question, F. Horst, TDNT IV, 381 n. 56,

thinks that it is a parenthetic statement: 'and he shows patience (even) with them'. This view is open to the same objection as the preceding one. 3. Manson, *Sayings*, 307f., argued that the clause was based on misunderstanding of an Aramaic original which should have been rendered 'and he postpones the wrath which he has on their account (sc. against their opponents)'. The corresponding Hebrew is *he'erîk 'ap* (F. Horst, TDNT IV, 376). On this view, the clause should be presumably regarded as concessive in effect, or else it should be regarded as a positive question: 'Surely God will vindicate his elect, although he postpones his wrath against their opponents?' This is a possible sense, but it is not the obvious way of taking ἐπ' αὐτοῖς. 4. H. Sahlin* also had recourse to a Hebrew background and postulated a conditional expression (participle, followed by finite verb): 'Shall not God vindicate his elect, those whom, if they cry to him day and night, he patiently hears?' 5. H. Ljungvik* argues that the introductory καί should be taken adversatively, to give the rejected possibility, and that μακροθυμέω be taken in sense 2. 'will God not vindicate his elect but rather remain unmoved toward them?' The answer is then that God will vindicate them – and quickly. 6. Rengstorf, 197f., H. Riesenfeld*, A. Wifstrand* and Jeremias, *Parables*, 154f., regard the clause as concessive; Jeremias explains it as being based on an Aramaic stative clause, with the force: 'will not God vindicate his elect, even if he keeps them waiting for him?' (cf. Je. 14:15; Jn. 5:44; 2 Jn. 2; Rev. 3:7; BD 468³). For this type of interpretation see also Plummer, 414; Lagrange, 471f., who saw that καὶ μακροθυμεῖ . . . could be linked to τῶν βοώντων . . ., but did not recognise the Aramaic basis. 7. Beyer, I:1, 268 n. 1, adopts the same Aramaic basis, but understands the clause as causal, equivalent to ἅτε μακροθυμῶν ἐπ' αὐτοῖς: this gives the sense: 'who cry to him, inasmuch as he is patient with them'. 8. C. E. B. Cranfield*, 300, follows view 6. but takes μακροθυμέω in sense 3. and ἐπί in the sense 'with regard to': 'It is true that He is patient with regard to them – i.e. He is patient and longsuffering toward their persecutors in mercy'. 9. Ott, 44–59, holds that the clause is tantamount to a relative (cf. 2 Jn. 2), and takes μακροθυμέω as 'to hear graciously': 'who cry to him day and night and (whom) he hears graciously': God is thus contrasted with the judge who refused to hear the widow. Several of these solutions are linguistically unlikely in that they misunderstand the construction or give a wrong sense to μακροθυμέω. It seems most likely that an Aramaic stative clause lies behind the construction, that Sir. 35:19 has had some influence on the passage, and that μακροθυμέω has the sense 'to delay'. (The meaning 'to hear graciously' is unlikely.) Hence views 5., 6. and 7. come closest to the probable meaning. The elect cry to God night and day, but he puts their patience to the test by not answering them immediately (Jeremias, *Parables*, 155), or they call to him night and day even though (it seems as if) he is dilatory towards them (H. Riesenfeld*).

(8) Jesus answers his own question authoritatively with a λέγω ὑμῖν

construction which is probably pre-Lucan (Delling, 219 n. 82; *pace* Ott, 41f.). God will act on behalf of the elect ἐν τάχει. This phrase can mean 'soon' (Klostermann, 179; Kümmel, *Heilsgeschehen*, 462; Delling, 219f. and n. 83; C. E. B. Cranfield*, 299 n. 1) or perhaps 'suddenly, unexpectedly' (cf. Dt. 11:17; Jos. 8:18f.; Ps. 2:12; Ezk. 29:5; Sir. 27:3; Zahn, 610; Jeremias, *Parables*, 155; C. Spicq*, 81–85). In the OT passages cited the phrase can refer to something which happens after a very short interval, i.e. 'soon', or which happens in a very short space of time, i.e. 'quickly', or which happens before men are ready for it and when they do not expect it. The context and the normal use of the phrase (cf. Acts 12:7; 22:18; 25:4; Rom. 16:20; Rev. 1:1; 22:6**) suggest that 'soon' is the meaning. For the parable is concerned with two points: 1. Will God vindicate his people? Answer: Yes, even more certainly than the unjust judge who eventually acted contrary to his character. 2. Will they have to wait a long time? Answer: God is not like the judge who had to be pestered before he gave in to the widow. He will answer soon. V. 7b is concerned with the apparent delay in God's action. To the elect it may seem to be a long time until he answers, but afterwards they will realise that it was in fact short (Delling, 219f.). Ott, 41f., thinks that the phraseology here betrays the hand of Luke, but while he uses ἐν τάχει 3x in Acts this is not a sufficient basis for such an argument.

There is a somewhat abrupt shift in v. 8b which directs attention away from God to men and draws a further lesson from the parable. πλήν (6:24 note) is a strong adversative, regarded as pre-Lucan by Jeremias, *Parables*, 155 n. 13; Delling, 220 n. 87, but as Lucan by Ott, 33f. The evidence shows that it can be either, and that the word cannot be used as proof of Lucan composition. The reference to the Son of man links the parable to 17:22–37, and is clearly meant to be eschatological. Since Luke does not create 'Son of man' sayings, there is a *prima facie* case that he has not done so here (C. Colpe, TDNT VIII, 435). The only real ground for the opposite view (held by Bultmann, 189; Kümmel, 59 n. 126; Vielhauer, 62; Higgins, 91f.; Tödt, 99f.; Ott, 32–34) is that the figure of the Son of man may be a redactional link between 17:22–37 and 18:1–8a. Since, however, the Son of man is the eschatological vindicator of the elect, the concept fits naturally into the parable. ἐλθών implies a coming of the Son of man to earth, a motif that arises out of Dn. 7:13. For ἄρα as an interrogative particle see Acts 8:30; Gal. 2:17**; and for εὑρίσκω used in an eschatological context cf. 11:25 par. Mt. 12:44; Lk. 12:37, 43 par. Mt. 24:46. The use of πίστις with the article is unusual. It could refer to acceptance of Jesus and his message, which would be a developed Christian usage (Klostermann, 179; Grässer, 38), but more probably it signifies faithfulness, expressed in unfailing prayer. The presence of the article is an Aramaism (Jeremias, *Parables*, 155 n. 13; Borsch, 364 n. 1). The question as a whole presupposes a time of tribulation for the disciples in which they may be tempted to give up faith because their prayers are not answered; it is meant as an exhortation to take seriously the lesson of the parable that God will certainly act to vindicate them. Thus an interval before the parousia is presupposed, but the sense of imminent expectation is not abandoned.

j. The Scope of Salvation (18:9 – 19:10)

The catchword 'prayer' spans the break between the two sections at this point, but the real connection of thought appears to be that the present section deals with the question of who will be found faithful when the Son of man comes; in other words, it deals with the qualifications required for entry to the kingdom and demonstrates in a radical manner that entry is on the basis of divine grace and human faith, all claims based on legal righteousness being rejected. Although the material is drawn from more than one source, it has thus a certain unity of theme. In effect, Luke has here returned to the question of qualifications for discipleship and characteristics of disciples with which the long non-Marcan section began and which is prominent in the Marcan material which he now begins to use again.

Thus it is demonstrated that tax-collectors who cast themselves on the mercy of God are accepted by him rather than legalistic Pharisees (18:9–14); to be sure, this does not mean that tax-collectors are excused from making restitution for their extortion, as 19:1–10 makes clear. What is demanded is the attitude of childlike faith and trust (18:15–17) which the rich ruler was unwilling to show (18:18–34), but which was demonstrated by Bartimaeus (18:35–43). In this way the ministry of Jesus on the way to Jerusalem reaches something of a triumphant climax in the account of what Jesus did at Jericho.

i. The Pharisee and the Tax-Collector 18:9–14

Like some other parables (15:11–32; 16:19–31; Mt. 21:28–32), this one contrasts the behaviour of two characters, a Pharisee who is conscious of his own righteousness which went beyond the requirements of the OT law, and knew that he was better than other men; and a tax-collector who was conscious of his sin and could only plead for divine mercy. Jesus pronounces authoritatively that it is the latter who is accepted by God, and not the former. God accepts the humble and needy, and not the proud and disdainful. In other words, the point is that even tax-collectors are accepted by God; even they can be acceptable to him.

The story is unusual in being a real story and not a 'comparison' such as is usually found in the parables. It goes beyond being a story when Jesus claims to know God's verdict on the two men.

The picture of the Pharisee is drawn from life, although the picture may be slightly over-drawn: it is a deliberate attack on the type of character which could result in Pharisaism. H. F. Weiss, TDNT IX, 42, comments: 'Here the whole, subjectively honest concern of Pharisaic Judaism to fulfil the Law correctly and thereby to contribute to the coming of God's kingdom is radically set aside in favour of the attitude of those who expect nothing of themselves and their works but everything from God'; this verdict perhaps underplays the element of pride that could corrupt the Pharisaic concern to please God. L. Schottroff* argues that the picture is a caricature, but this is to press the presence of exaggeration much too far. As for the tax-collector, there may not have been many who prayed like this one, but Jesus' point is part of his more general purpose, expressed in his table fellowship with them, to bring about a new social and religious valuation of them. L. Schottroff*, 456, doubts whether Jesus' affirmation in v. 14a would have been comprehensible except to a group that already recognised his authority; but this ignores the fact that prophets do not always speak solely to their followers.

The general content of the story is typical of Palestinian religious life, and the language is particularly Semitic in character (Jeremias, *Parables*, 140). There is no reason to doubt its authenticity as teaching of Jesus, although L. Schottroff* raises some doubts on this score (without, however, delivering a verdict). She draws attention particularly to the literary level of the story, which cannot be proved to have an oral pre-history. Further, the closing comment, v. 14b, also found in 14:11, fits in well with the lesson of the parable, and the introduction (which could be drawn from tradition, Bultmann, 193 note) also ties in closely with it. The parable, which contains a lesson particularly congenial to Luke, could thus be regarded as a Lucan creation, or as stemming from a group in the church which shared his outlook. But one has yet to provide evidence that Jesus, the friend of tax-collectors, did not also share Luke's outlook, and the case that Jesus is unlikely to have used this story, or that the story would have been persuasive only in the situation of the church, remains unconvincing.

See Manson, *Sayings*, 308–312; Jeremias, *Parables*, 139–144; Linnemann, 58–64; L. Schottroff, 'Die Erzählung vom Pharisäer und Zöllner als Beispiel für die theologische Kunst des Überredens', in H.-D. Betz, 439–461.

(9) The feature of prefixing an explanation of the purpose of a parable is characteristic of Luke (18:1; 19:11), but may be due to his source. πρός may indicate the persons to whom the parable is addressed (Klostermann, 179) or possibly the people 'against' whom it is directed (20:19). That the Pharisees are meant is clear from v. 10, and did not need to be spelled out here. For πρός followed by the article and participle cf. BD 412⁴. πεποιθότας (cf. 11:22) ἐφ' ἑαυτοῖς is taken by Jeremias, *Parables*, 139 n. 38, to mean that they trusted in themselves rather than in God (cf. 2 Cor. 1:9); if so, ὅτι must be translated 'because', giving the reason for their self-confidence, rather than 'that', stating the content of

their self-confidence. δίκαιος (1:6) has the sense of practising conduct that makes one acceptable to God.

ἐξουθενέω is 'to treat with contempt' (23:11; Acts 4:11). οἱ λοιποί is the rest of mankind, especially other Jews (since gentiles did not even come into the reckoning) – the *Am ha-aretz*. The Pharisaic claim to superior righteousness is well attested (Jos. Bel. 1:10; Phil. 3:4ff.; Sanh. 101a; Sukka 45b; Grundmann, 350).

(10) Since Jerusalem stood on a hill, ἀναβαίνω became the appropriate verb to use of visits to the temple (cf. καταβαίνω, 18:14; Jos. Ant. 12:164f.; see 2:42 note). Daily prayer took place in the morning and afternoon (1:10 note), but at any time individuals might engage in their own private prayers. For ὁ εἷς ... ὁ ἕτερος cf. 7:41.

(11) Standing was a normal posture for prayer (SB I, 401f.; II, 240); it need not necessarily imply a pompous attitude but is probably meant to do so here (cf. Mt. 6:5 and the contrast in Lk. 18:13); σταθείς is found only in Lk. and Acts (18:40; 19:8; Acts 6x**). πρὸς ἑαυτὸν ταῦτα (A W f13 *pm*; TR; UBS) is difficult. πρὸς ἑαυτόν should be understood as representing an Aramaic ethic dative, which emphasises the verb: 'The Pharisee, taking his stand, prayed' (Black, 103f., 299; Jeremias, *Parables*, 140; cf. Manson, *Sayings*, 310). The phrase is softened to καθ' ἑαυτὸν ταῦτα in D. The reverse order of words ταῦτα πρὸς ἑαυτόν has good external attestation (p⁷⁵ ℵ L Θ f1 *pc* e vg; so *Synopsis*; *Diglot*)*. This could mean that he prayed silently rather than aloud. But this is unlikely in the context; Jewish practice was to pray aloud, but quietly in the manner of Hannah (1 Sa. 1:13). There was criticism of rabbis who prayed loudly (SB IV:1, 231f.). Grundmann's suggestion (350) that he prayed to himself rather than to God is too sophisticated. The reading ταῦτα in ℵ* it sa; NEB, may be an attempt to avoid the problem (so Metzger, 168) or may be regarded as evidence (along with the fluctuating position of the words) that πρὸς ἑαυτόν is a gloss (Tasker, 422).

ὁ θεός is a nominative of address; for εὐχαριστέω cf. 17:16. ὥσπερ is altered to ὡς in D L *al* Or; *Diglot*; perhaps by assimilation to the following ὡς. ἅρπαξ is 'robber, swindler' (Mt. 7:15; 1 Cor. 5:10f.; 6:10**). ἄδικος (16:10) here means 'swindler, cheat' (1 Cor. 6:9; cf. Lv. 19:13; T. Ash. 2:5). μοιχός is 'adulterer' (1 Cor. 6:9; Heb. 13:4). ἢ καί is 'for that matter' (Manson, *Sayings*, 311): the tax-collector is not a worse person than those just listed, but is simply contemptible, especially perhaps as one who even dares to say prayers in his unclean state. οὗτος could carry a derogatory tone.

(12) The verse logically continues the list of things for which the Pharisee thanks God. His fasting (5:33) takes places twice a week, thus going well beyond legal requirements (5:33–39 note). ἀποδεκατεύω** is 'to give a tithe of', and takes an accusative of respect; cf. ἀποδεκατόω 11:42. The use of κτάομαι, 'to acquire', suggests that the Pharisee went beyond the letter of the law in paying tithes on what he bought, although

the producer would already have paid the requisite tithes (Jeremias,
Parables, 140; for other possibilities cf. SB II, 244–246).

The prayer as a whole is not a caricature but is fairly true to life; cf.
1QH 7:34; p. Ber. 4, 7d, 31; Ber. 28b (SB II, 240f.; translation in
Jeremias, *Parables*, 142). Jesus is attacking the Pharisaic religion as it
was, not an exaggeration of it; the Pharisee's prayer is disqualified
because of its pride and contempt the other men.

(13) By contrast (ὁ δέ, p⁷⁵ ℵ B G L f13 *pc*; καὶ ὁ, rell; TR; *Diglot*)
the tax-collector stands at a distance, possibly in the outer court of the
temple (SB II, 246). θέλω is again 'to dare' (18:4). To lift one's eyes
(6:20) was not very usual in prayer according to SB II, 246f., but in fact
it is well attested (Mk. 6:41; 7:34; Jn. 11:41; 17:1; Ps. 123:1; 1 Esd.
4:58; Jos. Ant. 11:162; *et al.*; J. Jeremias, TDNT I, 185f.; W. Foerster,
TDNT V, 377 n. 11). The significance of οὐδέ, 'not even', is that he did
not even raise his eyes, still less his hands in prayer. Instead he beat
(τύπτω, 6:29) upon (εἰς is added by A W Δ Θ f13 *pl sy* sa bo; TR;
Diglot) his breast (cf. 23:48). The breast or heart is regarded as the seat
of sin, and hence the act is one of grief or contrition. Although the act
was not unusual in prayer, it was not uncommon in itself (G. Stählin,
TDNT VIII, 260–269, especially 262 n. 18 and 264). The words of the
man's prayer express his longing for forgiveness. ἱλάσκομαι is 'to be
propitiated' (Heb. 2:17**; cf. F. Büchsel, TDNT III, 314–317; L.
Morris, *The Apostolic Preaching of the Cross*, 1965³, 144–213 (this
passage is ignored); D. Hill, *Greek Words and Hebrew Meanings*, Cambridge, 1967, 23–48, especially 36). The petition appears to be that God
will show mercy to the sinner (cf. Ps. 51:1) by forgiving his sin, and Hill
suggests that a trace of the idea of propitiation lies in the background.
The ground for the appeal lies solely in the mercy of God.

(14) Jesus' authoritative comment is that the latter person (οὗτος,
in contrast to ἐκεῖνος, 'the former', AG 238) went back down from the
temple 'justified', i.e. declared to be acquitted by God. For δικαιόω cf.
7:29. This is the only occurrence in the Gospels of this characteristically
Pauline use (for ἱλάσκομαι and δικαιόω cf. especially Rom. 3:24f.), but
the language is not based on Paul (cf. Ps. 51:19; 1QSb 4:22; 4 Ez. 12:7;
Braun, *Qumran* I, 92; F. F. Bruce, 'Justification by Faith in the non-
Pauline Writings of the New Testament', EQ 24, 1952, 66–77). In παρ'
ἐκεῖνον the preposition represents Aramaic *min* used comparatively, and
probably in an exclusive sense, i.e. not 'rather than the former', but 'and
not the former' (Klostermann, 181; G. Schrenk, TDNT II, 215 n. 16;
Jeremias, *Parables*, 141f. with examples, e.g. 2 Sa. 19:44; Ps. 45 (44):8).
The same sense is conveyed by the variant ἤ ἐκεῖνος (W Θ 61* 69; cf.
Gn. 38:26). Thus, the Pharisee was not accepted by God on the basis of
his prayer.

The reason for his rejection is stated in the final comment, which is
identical with 14:11 (q.v.; ὁ δέ is altered to καὶ ὁ in A *al lat*; *Diglot*, but
this may be due to assimilation to 14:11). Bultmann, 193 (cf. Dibelius,

254; Ellis, 216) regards the comment as secondary because the tax-collector does not really humble himself; but this is to ignore the content of his prayer (cf. especially W. Grundmann, TDNT VIII, 16; Grundmann, 353, also notes that the comment paves the way for 18:15–17; cf. Mt. 18:4 for the thought). The comment, therefore, *may* belong organically here (cf. Jeremias, *Parables*, 144). It is true that the tax-collector does not show 'works of repentance', e.g. in restoring ill-gotten wealth, and therefore the Pharisees would have disagreed with Jesus that he was justified by God (SB II, 247–249), but Jesus' lesson is precisely that the attitude of the heart is ultimately what matters, and justification depends on the mercy of God to the penitent rather than upon works which might be thought to earn God's favour; when Zacchaeus restores his ill-gotten gains – a responsibility from which he is not excused! – this follows his acceptance by Jesus and does not precede it.

ii. Jesus and Children 18:15–17

Luke ceased to use Mk. as a source at 9:50 par. Mk. 9:40. He now resumes use of Mk. as a framework for his narrative and its main source, and takes up the story in Mk. 10:13–16. On the reasons for his omission of Mk. 9:43 – 10:12 see 9:51 – 19:10 note; some of the material has already been paralleled in other contexts, and it is not included now because Luke's theme is that of the kind of people whom Jesus receives into the kingdom of God. Luke is thus able to get a neat link between the preceding story from his special source and this Marcan story by means of the common idea of humility.

The story is a brief pronouncement story in which the disciples attempt to prevent parents from bringing their children to Jesus for his blessing. Jesus replies by stating that the kingdom belongs to children and people like them; in a further solemn statement he denies entry to anybody who is not prepared to enter like a child. The narrative is based exclusively on Mk. as a source. Luke stresses that the children were infants, and he omits the details about Jesus' annoyance at the disciples and his embracing of the children; in this way he generalises the story, and stresses its significance for the character of adults.

In Lk., therefore, the point is somewhat different from what it is in Mk. In Mk. it forms part of a series of incidents giving teaching of Jesus in respect of marriage, children and possessions (Mk. 10:1–12, 13–16, 17–31); here, however, it is part of a series describing what is involved in becoming a disciple.

Bultmann, 32, rightly rejects the view that the scene was created in order to provide a framework for Mk. 10:15. On the contrary, he regards this verse as an isolated logion which has been added to the story; it has a different point from Mk. 10:14. The story that remains is, however, an ideal construction based on the Jewish custom of blessing, the analogy of 2 Ki. 4:27 and the rabbinic story of R. Akiba being dissuaded by his disciples from being greeted by his mother (Keth. 63a; SB I, 808). This dissection of the narrative is unwarranted (cf. Percy, 31–37). It is natural that Mk. 10:15 should have a different point from v. 14 or else it would be tautologous. What it does is to apply what has been said about children to adults, and there is no reason why Jesus should not have made the application himself. In any case, the genuineness of v. 15 is beyond suspicion. It reappears in a different form in Mt. 18:3 and Jn. 3:3, 5. On the historical basis of the narrative see J. Jeremias*, 49–55.

See Percy, 31–37; J. Jeremias, *Infant Baptism in the First Four Centuries*, London, 1960, 49–55; G. R. Beasley-Murray, *Baptism in the New Testament*, Exeter, 1972, 320–329; Légasse, 36–43, 187–209.

(15) The background to the story appears to be the practice of bringing children to the elders or scribes for a prayer of blessing upon them on the evening of the Day of Atonement (Soph. 18:5; SB II, 138; J. Jeremias*, 49). προσέφερον is an impersonal plural, par. Mk. καί is 'even', and the point is emphasised by the use of βρέφος (2:12), diff. Mk. παιδίον. The use of the article may emphasise the idea of the class; the children are representatives of the class, and the point that Jesus is concerned even about infants as such is stressed, although, as has been noted, Luke's interest in the pericope is more with children as an example to adults. ἅπτομαι is used of the physical accompaniment of an act of blessing (5:13; cf. Gn. 48:14; SB I, 807f.). ἰδόντες is used as a connective, diff. Mk. (but probably brought forward from Mk. 10:14). ἐπετίμων is probably conative, diff. Mk., aorist.

(16) The use of προσκαλέω (7:19), diff. Mk. (but cf. Mt. 18:2), enables Luke to avoid Mark's use of ἀγανακτέω, and at the same time stresses the positive call of Jesus. J. Jeremias*, 54 n. 5, thinks that Jesus here addresses the parents rather than (as in Mk.) the disciples, but this is reading too much into the wording.

ἔρχεσθαι is meant quite literally, but is open to a deeper understanding. μὴ κωλύετε αὐτά is perfectly intelligible in the situation, but O. Cullmann, *Baptism in the New Testament*, 1950, 73f., and J. Jeremias* argue that the presence of the word, which echoes the use in baptismal texts (Mt. 3:14; Acts 8:36; 10:47; 11:17; G. Ebionites 4 (NTA I, 157f.)), enabled the church to use the pericope as an answer to doubts about the legitimacy of infant baptism; the speculative nature of this suggestion is brought out by G. R. Beasley-Murray*. Children may come to Jesus for the kingdom of God belongs to them: τοιοῦτος (9:9) refers to children and such people. In view of the following verse the adverb 'only' should be understood before τῶν τοιούτων (J. Jeremias*, 49). But if the kingdom is for those who are like children, what is the point of comparison? The thought of humility is perhaps still present (cf. 9:46–48; Mt. 18:4; Cranfield, 324), but more probably the basic thought is that of the sheer receptivity of children, especially infants, who cannot do anything to merit entry into the kingdom (Percy, 35–37.; Schweizer, *Markus*, 117).

(17) The story reaches its climax in an authoritative saying of Jesus with a solemn ἀμήν introduction (4:24 note). For ἄν the variant ἐάν is attested by A Γ Δ Θ f1 *pm*; TR; *Diglot* (cf. 17:33). The saying is concerned with the condition for entry to the kingdom. There is some debate whether the entry is to be regarded as future entry into the consummated kingdom (Kümmel, 52f., 126; Percy, 35f.) or as present entry into enjoyment of the blessings of the kingdom (Taylor, 423f.). The former view, however, fits in best with the other teaching of Jesus. The problem arises because the first part of the verse refers to receiving the kingdom, and Taylor, ibid., thinks it unlikely that the present and future aspects of the kingdom are contrasted in this way. But this difficulty is unreal (cf. Percy), and is resolved by taking the phrase to mean 'receiving the message of the kingdom'. Lohmeyer, 204f., and Kümmel, 126 n. 77, question the authenticity of this phrase and regard it as influenced by the language of the church, but the difficulties seem unreal.

iii. The Rich Ruler 18:18–23

Still following Mk., Luke continues with the story of the rich man who came to Jesus to ask how he might gain eternal life. The conversation falls into three parts: 1. Jesus takes up the address used by the rich man, 'Good master', and protests that only God is good. 2. Jesus directs the man to the second part of the decalogue, to which he replies that he has kept all these commandments. 3. Jesus summons the man to sell his possessions and give the proceeds in alms; so he will have treasure in heaven. But the man goes away sadly, unable to bear the thought of surrendering his wealth.

The significance of the story is brought out in the appended comment, that riches make it impossible for a man to enter the kingdom. Although his principle of organisation of the material at this point is not the same as in Mk., Luke has retained the interpretation of the story given there. He has, therefore, been able to take over the story with little more than stylistic revision. It is to be seen in the wider context of the teaching about the way to gain eternal life given earlier in the Gospel (10:25; cf. 12:15) and about the attitude of disciples to riches (cf. 6:24; 8:14; 11:41; 12:13–34; 16). Its purpose is to reinforce this earlier teaching that the way to the kingdom is by loving God and one's neighbour, by showing concretely that this is realised by obedience to the commandments and limitless charity.

The incident may owe its present position in the tradition to its thematic contrast with the preceding story. It is regarded by Bultmann, 20f., as an apophthegm, and its unity is not seriously questioned, although P. S. Minear*, 160f., suggested that Mk. 10:19f. was an addition in the interest of the Law (*contra* Percy, 116 n.).

See P. S. Minear, 'The Needle's Eye. A Study in Form-Criticism', JBL 61, 1942, 157–169; N. Walter, 'Zur Analyse von Mk. 10:17–31', ZNW 53, 1962, 206–218.

(18) Luke omits Mark's journey setting. Although it would have been appropriate enough in his own travel section, it is unnecessary at this point and the omission brings out the contrast with the preceding incident more strongly. Similar omissions by Matthew are probably coincidental, since there is no other evidence of significant agreement between Lk. and Mt. here. ἐπηρώτησεν (aorist) is stylistically better than Mark's imperfect, as is the use of τις, diff. Mk. εἷς. Luke omits the detail of the man running to Jesus and kneeling before him (par. Mt., diff. Mk.), but he has added a description of the 'certain man' as an ἄρχων. This may mean a leader of the synagogue (cf. 8:41) or a member of the sanhedrin (23:13, 35; 24:20; cf. 14:1). Bultmann, 72, regards the detail as 'novellistisch', but it could be derived from oral tradition. It is possibly a deduction from the fact of the man's riches (Creed, 225; cf. 14:1 for a possible use in the same kind of way). F. Hauck and W. Kasch, TDNT VI, 328, think that Luke is here (and elsewhere) equating the rich with the opponents of Jesus; but in fact the rich man is here presented sympathetically. Luke does not know that he was a νεανίσκος (Mt. 19:20, 22). For διδάσκαλε as an address to Jesus cf. 7:40. The addition ἀγαθέ is strange in an address to a rabbi (the one example, Taan. 24b (in SB II, 24f.), is fourth century AD). While the Jews tended to reserve the attribute for God, it certainly was used with regard to men (Pr. 12:2; 14:14; Ec. 9:2; Lk. 6:45 par. Mt. 12:35; T. Sim. 4:4; T. Dan 1:4; T. Ash. 4:1; *et al.*). Although, therefore, there was nothing strange in speaking of a man as 'good', it may have seemed unusual to address a man as 'good'; it could be regarded as flattery, in which case it was a cheapening of a word that strictly applied only to God. The following question is identical with 10:25b; Luke has slightly altered Mark's formulation.

(19) Jesus first takes up the title by which he has been addressed. λέγω is here 'to call'. He questions the propriety of being called 'good' because the description properly belongs to God alone: 'nobody is good except one, (namely) God'. Jesus' answer is meant to do away with any cheapening of the idea of goodness. True goodness belongs to God, as the OT testifies (Pss. 106:1; 118:1, 29; 136:1; 1 Ch. 16:34; 2 Ch. 5:13). There is no reason to regard Jesus' statement as a confession of sinfulness, since this would be at variance with the rest of the Synoptic tradition (Taylor, 426). The Christian reader may go to the other extreme and see here a tacit identification of Jesus with God, but this lies beyond what the passage actually says. It is a criticism of the view which sees Jesus as a teacher, even a 'good' teacher, and nothing more. The man's ultimate refusal to obey the 'good teacher' shows that he did not really take his goodness seriously, and therefore he could be criticised for using the word in an empty fashion.

(20) 'You know the commandments' (ἐντολή, 1:6) is tantamount to

an injunction to obey them. Jesus quotes the so-called second table of the decalogue in a form that raises some problems. In the first place, he does not quote the first part of the decalogue. The implication is that he was concerned with the man's attitude to his neighbour; the question of love for God is not raised, possibly because nobody could claim to fulfil that commandment fully. Possibly the reply focuses on those commandments obedience to which could be determined in terms of overt behaviour; here was a criterion by which the man could measure his performance. Second, the form of the commands (μή with aorist subjunctive) differs from that in the LXX (οὐ with future indicative; so Mt.). Luke is here dependent on the tradition followed by Mk. Third, the order of the commandments is odd. In terms of the usual order, Luke has: vii, vi; viii; ix; v. Mark has the order: vi; vii; viii; ix; (x); v, but the text is uncertain. Both Luke and Matthew omit the unusual 'Thou shalt not defraud', which Mark has in place of the tenth commandment. The inversion of commandments vi and vii is also found in Dt. 5:17f. LXX ᴮ; the Nash papyrus; Rom. 13:9; Jas. 2:11, and the evidence suggests that Luke is here following an early church catechetical pattern. The postplacing of the fifth commandment suggests that it is an addition to an originally briefer text. (After μητέρα, σου is added by א Γ Δ f13 pm a b c sy sa bo; TR; Diglot). No solution to the problems has yet been found, beyond the suggestion that the commandments were used in early catechetical teaching with considerable freedom (cf. Gundry, 17–19; Holtz, 81f.).

(21) Whatever be the right order of the commandments is a matter of indifference; the man claimed to have kept all of them throughout his life. The address διδάσκαλε is omitted, par. Mt., diff. Mk. Luke uses the active of φυλάσσω, par. Mt., diff. Mk. middle, and thus follows the more normal use of the verb (11:28). For νεότης cf. Mk. 10:20; Acts 26:4; 1 Tim. 4:12**. The statement is not untypical of Pharisaic claims: cf. 18:11; Phil. 3:6; SB I, 814f.; and even Lk. 1:6.

(22) Luke, like Matthew, omits mention that Jesus looked at the man and loved him (cf. 18:27 diff. Mk.). The emotion shown by Jesus is ignored, and in this way the story is generalised. ἀκούσας is used by Luke as a link (14:15; 19:11). The man's obedience to the commandments is not condemned – or praised. Jesus rather gives him a further command: ἔτι is also added by Matthew but in the previous verse (19:20). For ὑστερέω he uses λείπω*, 'to lack, fall short'. He drops the command ὕπαγε and adds the antecedent πάντα, of which he is fond. Although only one thing is lacking, it is all-embracing: it involves the selling of all the man's possessions and the distribution of the proceeds to the poor (διαδίδωμι, diff. Mk.; cf. 11:22). If he does this (imperative equivalent to apodosis), he will have 'treasure' in heaven, i.e. eternal life; cf. 12:33f. (For τοῖς οὐράνοις, B D; Synopsis; (UBS), there are also attested οὐράνοις, א A L R pc; and οὐράνῳ, W Γ Δ Θ f1 f13 pl lat; TR; Diglot.) But there is in fact one further command: a call to discipleship.

δεῦρο is equivalent to an imperative, 'come here' (Acts 7:3, 34; Jn. 11:43; Rev. 17:1; 21:9; cf. the plural δεῦτε, Mk. 1:17; *et al.*).

(23) For ἀκούσας, par. Mt., diff. Mk., cf. v. 22. Luke omits mention of the young man's emotion (στυγνάσας ἐπὶ τῷ λόγῳ), but retains the fact of his grief (περίλυπος (Mk. 6:26; 14:34 par. Mt. 26:38**), diff. Mk. λυπούμενος). He also paraphrases the closing words, so that the theme-word πλούσιος comes to expression (6:24). σφόδρα* is 'exceedingly'.

iv. Riches and Rewards 18:24–30

The episode contains a comment by Jesus on the preceding incident: it is hard, indeed impossible, for rich people to enter the kingdom of God. Pressed by the disciples to explain such a drastic statement, which appears to rule out all hope of salvation for anybody, Jesus replies that, while it is certainly impossible from a human point of view, it is possible in terms of the power of God. The statement is not explained, but the point is that God can work the miracle of conversion in the hearts even of the rich.

There follows a statement by Peter to the effect that the disciples have fulfilled the condition which the rich man was unwilling and unable to fulfil. Jesus replies with the promise that those who have given up family and possessions will receive a much greater return in this present time and will gain eternal life in the new world.

The narrative shows considerable abbreviation as compared with Mk. Luke omits reference to the disciples as the participants in the discussion, and thereby makes it clear that the comments of Jesus are to be understood as directed to non-disciples, attempting to stir them up to realise the danger of riches. So Mk. 10:24 disappears with the disciples' surprise and the consequent repetition of Jesus' statement. This means that the conversation is concerned solely with the rich, and the general comment on the impossibility of anybody entering the kingdom disappears (which leads to a slight anacolouthon in v. 26 which assumes the general statement). In the second part of the conversation, which is concerned with disciples, Luke notes the possibility of leaving one's wife for the sake of the kingdom, and he omits mention of persecution. The generalising saying in Mk. 10:31 also disappears. These differences, and the fact that Matthew offers a similar picture, are sufficient to suggest to Grundmann, 355 n. 3, that Luke and Matthew preserve a more primitive text here, but the more probable explanation is in terms of independent editing and abbreviating of Mk.

The basis of the Marcan pericope is uncertain. While Taylor, 430–432, thinks that the original text of Mk. inverted the order of vs. 25 and 24, and that in this form the conversation is substantially traditional (with v. 31 as a Marcan addition), Bultmann, 20f., holds that the basis is Mk. 10:23, 25, with vs. 24 and 26f. as Marcan additions; 28 is a redactional link to the separate saying in vs. 29f., or possibly it is the introduction to an apophthegm whose original content has been displaced by vs. 29f. Schweizer, 119, gives essentially the same analysis, but regards v. 27 as traditional. Cranfield, 325f., argues that the conversation was originally connected with the story of the rich man, but the second part of it (Mk. 10:28ff.) is probably an addition.

See 18:18–23 note for literature.

(24) The connective ἰδών replaces Mk. περιβλεψάμενος (a favourite verb in Mk.; Lk. 6:10*); it serves the same function of making the verse a comment on what has just happened. If we are looking for an original context for the present saying, no better one can be provided than the present one. After 'Ιησοῦς an object to the participle is supplied in many MSS: περίλυπον γενομένον (A W Γ Δ Θ f13 28 pm lat sy; TR; (UBS); Diglot; before ὁ 'Ιησοῦς, D it; omitted by ℵ B f1 1241 pc; Synopsis). Stylistically, the phrase could be a Lucan repetition from v. 23 (cf. H. J. Cadbury, 'Four Features of Lucan Style', SLA, 87–102), but the external evidence strongly suggests interpolation (cf. Metzger, 168f.).

δυσκόλως (Mk. 10:23; Mt. 19:23**) is 'hardly', and πῶς δυσκόλως should be translated 'with what difficulty'. χρῆμα, plural, 'wealth', is found here only in the Gospels (Mk. 10:23; cf. Acts 8:18; 20; 24:26; sing., 4:37**). εἰσπορεύονται, diff. Mk. εἰσελεύσονται, is probably literary variation (8:16). Luke has the present tense, diff. Mk. and Mt. future. Klostermann, 181, suggests that he thinks of the kingdom as present; Conzelmann, 105 n. 3, as timeless. But the future of this verb is not used in the NT, and in 22:10 (redactional) Luke uses it in a futuristic sense, so that a theological nuance is unlikely here.

(25) Luke omits the account of the disciples' reaction (par. Mt.) and proceeds straight to the further, confirmatory remark of Jesus about the rich. The statement is a hyperbolical expression of what is impossible (O. Michel, TDNT III, 592–594); it has a rabbinic parallel in a saying about the impossibility of an elephant passing through the eye of a needle (Ber. 55b; BM 38b;SB I, 828), but this is not attested until the third century AD and could be based on the saying of Jesus. κάμηλος* is 'camel'; the v.1. κάμιλον (ℵ pc), 'rope', is a late attempt to tone down the saying (Metzger, 169). τρῆμα (Mt. 19:24 v.1.**; τρύπημα, UBS) is 'opening, hole', diff. Mk. τρυμαλιά**, which is rare. βελόνη**, 'needle', is a more literary word than Mk. ῥαφίς (cf. H. J. Cadbury, 'Lexical Notes on Luke-Acts v. Luke and the Horse Doctors', JBL 52, 1933, 55–65, especially 59f.). The MSS show assimilation to the parallels. Luke's εἰσελθεῖν, diff. Mk. διελθεῖν, is due to assimilation to the second part of the saying.

(26) Luke omits the note of surprise on the part of the hearers recorded by Mark, and inserts the generalising οἱ ἀκούσαντες to bring out the universal significance of the saying of Jesus. 'To be saved' is the

same as 'to enter the kingdom' (cf. 13:23f.). The implied thought is: 'If even the rich (whose prosperity is generally regarded as a sign of blessing) cannot enter the kingdom, how can anybody else enter it?', or else Luke has forgotten to allow for his omission of the general statement in Mk. 10:24.

(27) Luke again omits Mark's ἐμβλέψας (cf. 18:22; but contrast 20:17 diff. Mk. 12:9). He shortens Mark's saying into a brief, pointed one. The things that are impossible for men to do are possible for God (note the inversion ἐστὶν παρὰ τῷ θεῷ in A Γ Δ Θ f13 pm; Diglot). For the use of παρά see H. Riesenfeld, TDNT V, 733; the background is to be found in Gn. 18:14; cf. Lk. 1:37. It is impossible for a man to break free from the lure of riches – even at the command of Jesus. But God can work what is impossible, although how this is related to human response is not indicated.

(28) The conversation now takes a turn with Peter's comment. Luke avoids Mark's asyndeton and redundant use of ἄρχομαι. The disciples have left their possessions (τὰ ἴδια, diff. Mk. πάντα) and followed Jesus (cf. 5:11; 18:22); the use of the aorist ἠκολουθήσαμεν, par. Mt., is less apt than the perfect in Mk. (Taylor, 433). The unspoken thought is, 'Have we qualified for entry to the kingdom?' or 'What shall we get in return for our self-sacrifice?' It is surprising that, although generally Jesus does not think in terms of seeking reward, here he is prepared to respond to Peter's saying. This suggests that Peter's question was not regarded by the Evangelists as an implicit claim for a selfish reward. Rather it is seen as an opportunity to give a promise that self-denial for the sake of the kingdom will be vindicated.

(29) For λέγω diff. Mk. φημί, cf. 18:21. Jesus' reply is directed to all the hearers (αὐτοῖς, par. Mt.). Here Luke retains ἀμήν (4:24 note) to confirm the solemn promise made by Jesus, and adds ὅτι par. Mt. His list of things and persons given up differs from that in Mk. He includes ἢ γυναῖκα (cf. 14:26), an addition regarded as inappropriate by Klostermann, 183; but the thought may be of renouncing the possibility of marriage rather than the breaking up of an existing marriage. ἀδελφοί will include both brothers and sisters (AG xxiv, 15), just as Luke uses γονεῖς for 'father and mother'. He omits Mk. ἀγρούς, which suggests that he is thinking here entirely of personal relationships and that accordingly οἰκία should be understood as 'household' or 'family' rather than as a building (cf. O. Michel, TDNT V, 131). The thought is then of the possible disruption in family relationships (12:52f.; 14:26) which may result from discipleship. If so, the idea of material loss and reward is not present in Lk., possibly because he wished to avoid the idea of material reward for disciples. εἵνεκεν (4:18 (LXX); Acts 28:20; 2 Cor. 3:10**) is a Hellenistic variant for ἕνεκεν (BD 30³). Mark's phrase 'for the sake of me and for the sake of the gospel' is independently altered by both Luke and Matthew; Luke assimilates to v. 25 and thereby gains greater unity in the pericope.

(30) The promise of Jesus is strengthened (and the Greek improved) by the substitution of ὃς οὐ μή for Mk. ἐὰν μή. For ἀπολάβῃ (ℵ A W Θ f1 f13 *pm*; TR; UBS; *Diglot*) the variant λάβῃ is attested by B D *pc*; *Synopsis*. The former reading fits in with Luke's style (6:34; 15:27; 16:25; 23:41) while the latter may be due to assimilation to Mk. Luke has πολλαπλασίων (Mt. 19:29**), 'many times as much', diff. Mk. ἑκατονταπλασίων; but the variant ἑπταπλασίων, 'seven times as much' (D it sy[h mg]) is preferred by Creed, 227; G. D. Kilpatrick, in Ellis, *Neotestamentica*, 203, on the grounds that Luke often echoes the LXX (here Sir. 35:11), and it is unlikely that the reading is due to a scribe. Luke omits the list of blessings received, par. Mt. (probably because it seemed redundant), and the qualification μετὰ διωγμῶν (but cf. Acts 8:1; 13:50). The self-denial is the condition of blessing; it would perhaps be misleading to associate persecution with the reward for self-denial. Luke also omits Mk. 10:31, to which he has a parallel at 13:30. Thus the promise of eternal life (cf. 18:18) concludes the pericope. The disciples are to be seen as those for whom God has made salvation possible.

v. The Passion draws near 18:31–34

In Mk. this is the third of the formal series of predictions of the passion, and it forms the prelude to the request of James and John for places in the kingdom. Luke will omit this section, and he does not preserve the three-fold announcement of the passion as a basic item in the pattern of the Gospel. In Mk. too, the prediction could well be regarded as strengthening the reference to persecution in Mk. 10:30, which Luke has omitted. For Luke the prediction is much more part of the 'travel'-motif which brings Jesus nearer to Jerusalem. There is fresh information in the announcement: the relation of the fate of the Son of man to OT prophecy is indicated, and (following Mk.) the place of the gentiles in putting him to death is depicted. (This motif is significant, since Luke is usually thought play down the role of the gentiles in the passion story.) Above all Luke has omitted the difficult reference to the astonishment and fear of the disciples in Mk. 10:32 and has in effect substituted a note on the way in which understanding of the prophecy was kept from them (cf. 9:45 par. Mk. 9:32). In this way, the theme of the failure of the disciples to appreciate what was going to happen in Jerusalem is emphasised (cf. 19:11). Thus alongside the theme of the response of men to the gospel we have also the theme of the disciples faced by the approach to Jerusalem. In a subtle way the pericope affords a commentary on the preceding saying of Jesus: although eternal life is promised, the path to it is by way of the suffering of Jesus.

The material is based on Mk. The use of a non-Marcan source is defended by Easton, 275, and Schramm, 133, but the arguments offered for this point of view are lacking in substance and conviction. It is more probable that Luke has simply edited Mk. Possibly the motif of fulfil-

ment of Scripture comes from a separate tradition of the predictions
(Patsch, 192).

See 9:21–22 note for literature.

(31) Luke omits almost the whole of Mk. 10:32. V. 32a is in effect
repeated in the first part of the saying of Jesus; v. 32b is difficult to understand; v. 32c is retained in abbreviated form. For παραλαμβάνω cf.
9:10. Mark's πάλιν is dropped because it is unsuitable in view of the
longer gap in Lk. since the last passion prediction. Luke also omits
Mark's summary of the following saying: τὰ μέλλοντα αὐτῷ συμβαίνειν,
possibly because he regards πάντα τὰ γεγραμμένα as an equivalent to it.
Similar omissions in Mt. hardly prove that Luke and Matthew had an
abbreviated text of Mk. before them. ἰδοὺ ἀναβαίνομεν εἰς Ἰερουσαλήμ is
drawn from Mk. For the mention of Jerusalem as the place of the passion see 9:31; 13:33f., but it is already implicit in the reference to the
Jewish rulers in 9:22. Luke has Ἰερουσαλήμ, diff. Mk. Ἱεροσόλυμα (but
many MSS assimilate to Mk.), but there is no obvious significance in the
change. The notion of scriptural fulfilment is peculiar to Lk. here. For
τελέω (2:39; et al.) cf. 12:50; 22:37; Acts 13:29 and cf. Lk. 13:22; this
appears to be a Lucan motif (Schürmann, Abschiedsrede, 125; G. Delling, TDNT VIII, 60 n. 16, raises the possibility that Luke is following
his special source). But it fits in with the Marcan idea of the 'necessity' of
suffering for the Son of man (Mk. 8:31). For τὰ γεγραμμένα in this connection cf. 22:37; 24:46; Acts 13:29; 24:14; Mk. 9:12; 14:21; and also
Lk. 21:22; 24:44. Here again Lucan phraseology is evident. The dative
τῷ υἱῷ is equivalent to περί with the genitive (cf. the variant in D f13 pc)
and hence the phrase is to be linked to γεγραμμένα rather than
τελεσθήσεται (Klostermann, 183; Grundmann, 355).

(32) Luke retains Mark's παραδοθήσεται (cf. 9:43); the passive
may conceal a reference to God as the real subject, but clearly this does
not apply to the remaining verbs in the clause; perhaps the reference is
to the action of the Jews which is otherwise passed over in silence, so
that Luke's verb corresponds in content to παραδώσουσιν in Mk. The
action of the gentiles is described in detail, using Mark's vocabulary but
altering the construction to the passive. For ἐμπαίζω cf. 14:29; 22:63;
23:11, 36*; G. Bertram, TDNT V, 630–635. ὑβρίζω (11:45*) is added
by Luke; the verb strengthens the preceding one, and is perhaps meant
to show that Jesus suffers in the same way as the righteous do in the OT
(G. Bertram, TDNT VIII, 295–307, especially 306), but in the OT the
thought is more of the sin of the person who shows this attitude than of
the suffering of the victim. Grundmann, 356, thinks that the ὕβρις motif
of Greek tragedy is present, but this is improbable. For πτύω*, 'to spit',
cf. Mk. 14:65; 15:19.

(33) The construction changes to the active form. μαστιγόω* is 'to
scourge'; cf. Mk. 15:15 for the fulfilment. The form τῇ ἡμέρᾳ τῇ τρίτῃ,
diff. Mk. μετὰ τρεῖς ἡμέρας, resembles that in Mt. and in 9:22 (diff. Mk.);
24:6, 46 (τῇ τρίτῃ ἡμέρᾳ), but the difference is probably simply due to

literary variation. Although Luke altered Mark's ἀνίστημι to ἐγείρω at 9:22, he keeps the verb here (cf. 24:7, 46; also 8:55; 9:8, 19; 16:31).

(34) The closing comment is peculiar to Lk., and may be meant to replace Mk. 10:32; cf. the expansion of Mk. 9:32 in Lk. 9:45. It may also be meant to replace the James and John scene which Luke omits, and it anticipates the Emmaus story (24:16, 25f.). The language is strong. The disciples were not able to understand any of these things (contrast 24:45); the matter was hidden from them (cf. 9:45, but with κρύπτω here instead of παρακαλύπτω; cf. 19:42), and they did not know what was being said. In the light of 9:45 it would seem that the disciples could not understand that Jesus was going to suffer and be raised from the dead. But his statement is so clear that it is difficult to see how they could have been so blind. Possibly Luke's point is that they could not understand how these events would fulfil Scripture (what OT texts were in mind?), but the strong stress on the matter being hidden from the disciples suggests that a divine 'veiling' of what was said is in view; or it may simply be that they could not believe that such things would happen to Jesus (Grundmann, 356).

vi. The Healing of a Blind Man 18:35–43

Luke passes over Mk. 10:35–45; the theme of the implications of discipleship is irrelevant to his present concern with the way of Jesus to Jerusalem and with the significance of faith as the means of salvation; in any case he has parallels to the incident in 12:50 and 22:24–27. The cost of the omission is the loss of the ransom saying in Mk. 10:45, but among the passages in Acts which take up phrases from Mk. omitted in the Gospel we may perhaps regard Acts 20:28 as the equivalent to Mk. 10:45.

The present story is a simple account of a healing miracle performed upon a blind man in response to his persistent cries for help; the story makes it clear that the man displayed faith in Jesus and culminates in the glorification of God by the healed man and the audience. In Lk. the story is closely associated by means of the geographical location with the separate tradition of the conversion of Zacchaeus, so that we have a climax to the ministry of Jesus in his call to the poor and the outcasts. The narrative brings out the significance of the person of Jesus as the 'Son of David', a messianic title, and the importance of faith (and perhaps also of following Jesus), but its major significance for Luke would appear to be in its testimony to the concern of Jesus for the poor and needy over against those who were unconcerned about them (cf. 18:15f.).

The narrative substantially follows Mk. without use of any other source (Schramm, 143–145). The alterations are typical of Luke's editing. The introduction has been altered, the story generally abbreviated and smoothed out (Burger, 107–112), and the characteristic note of glorifying God added by way of conclusion.

The original Marcan story is regarded by Bultmann, 228, as a miracle story created by the community. Signs of lateness are evident in the naming of the beggar and the use of the address 'Son of David'. It is no longer possible to reconstruct an original miracle story, and one gains the impression that for Bultmann the story has been composed to fit into its present position. Dibelius, 49f., suggested that the story has the form of a 'paradigm' rather than a miracle story, since the miracle itself receives little emphasis and the stress is more on the mercy shown by Jesus. Originally the story made this point briefly; it was later filled out with details and the originally anonymous beggar was identified with a well-known figure at Jericho. By contrast Taylor, 446f., sees in the story evidence of an eye-witness tradition; the story has not yet been reduced to the rounded form of a miracle story. Mark has recorded it at this point because of its messianic testimony which affords a good prelude to the story of the entry to Jerusalem. Similarly, Schweizer, *Markus*, 127f., appears to accept the story as it stands, with a certain amount of editorial change to fit it into its present position in Mk. Such a verdict seems most probable; there may well have been some development in the story (cf. Lohmeyer, 223–227; Hahn, 262–264), but this should not be exaggerated.

See Kertelge, 179–182; Roloff, *Kerygma*, 121–126; Schramm, 143–145; Burger, 42–46, 59–63, 107–112.

(35) The opening is Lucan in style (cf. 1:8). ἐγγίζω is Lucan (7:12). The incident is thus placed outside Jericho as Jesus approaches the town, and presumably the beggar is regarded as being near the gate of the town. Schramm, 143f., follows the suggestion of Easton, 277, that the opening clause originally belonged to the Zacchaeus story, and that the inclusion of the story of the blind man led Luke to substitute a fresh introduction in 19:1. This argument depends on the supposition that the ἐγένετο δέ construction is pre-Lucan (Schramm, 94–96), which is however, doubtful. In any case, the effect is that the Bartimaeus incident is now located outside Jericho as Jesus enters, whereas in Mk. it takes place outside Jericho as Jesus leaves the town. 1. The alteration may have been made simply to accommodate the Zacchaeus incident which takes place in Jericho, and which Luke wishes to place after the healing of Bartimaeus as a climax to the series of incidents. At the same time, Luke avoids separating the Zacchaeus story from the following parable, which also comes from his non-Marcan material (although this is very much of secondary importance). 2. On Schramm's view, the discrepancy arises from the use of the introduction to the Zacchaeus story with the Bartimaeus story. 3. An attempt to avoid geographical contradiction rests on the assumption that the name of Jericho is used in two different senses by the Evangelists. For Mark it means the old town on the hill, whereas for Luke it means the larger Herodian town (cf. Jos. Bel. 4:459)

built to the south of the old site (Geldenhuys, 467). There is, however, no evidence that old Jericho was now inhabited or that the name continued to be used for the old town as distinct from the new (Plummer, 429).

Luke omits the details about Jesus' retinue and concentrates attention on the blind man (4:18; 7:21f.) who was sitting by the side of the road as a beggar (ἐπαιτέω, 16:3, diff. Mk. προσαίτης which is less literary). He omits his name as unimportant.

(36) Luke clarifies what the blind man heard by referring at this point to the crowd which was accompanying Jesus (Mk. 10:46); the language is Lucan (διαπορεύομαι, 6:1; πυνθάνομαι, 15:26; τί εἴη τοῦτο, cf. 1:62). Luke has added vigour to the story by supplying the conversation between the blind man and passers-by, but has produced a mixture of indirect and direct discourse.

(37) The impersonal plural ἀπήγγειλαν (7:18; et al.) refers to the passers-by. Ναζωραῖος, 'Nazarene' (Acts, 7x; Mt. 2:23; 26:71; Jn. 18:5, 7; 19:19**), diff. Mk. Ναζαρηνός (4:34 par. Mk. 1:24; Lk. 24:19; cf. Mk. 16:6) probably simply means 'of Nazareth' (contra Burger, 108: a title). παρέρχομαι (cf. Mt. παράγω), diff. Mk. εἰμί, here means 'to go by, pass by' (11:42, transitive); it may perhaps be used to signal a miracle or epiphany (cf. Mk. 1:16; J. Schneider, TDNT II, 681f., following a suggestion by E. Lohmeyer). The link with Mt. παράγω is interesting, but is so isolated that no conclusions about a common tradition can be drawn.

(38) Luke uses βοάω (cf. 9:38; 18:7), diff. Mk. κράζω, for the man's cry for help. His words show that he is aware of the power of Jesus to help. Jesus is addressed as 'Son of David' (cf. 1:27, 32), a phrase which is messianic; it is usually said that it was not related in Judaism to the performing of saving miracles (cf. E. Lohse, TDNT VIII, 478–488; Burger, 44; Hahn, 242–279); hence the title is usually regarded as one applied by the church to Jesus and secondarily linked to his activity as a miracle worker (cf. Mt. 9:27; 15:22). See, however, K. Berger, 'Die Königlichen Messiastraditionen des Neuen Testaments', NTS 20, 1973–74, 1–42. But in any case was it beyond the ability of the blind man (or anybody else) to link together a. the fact that Jesus was believed to work miracles, and b. the fact that his mission could be understood in messianic terms, and hence to draw the conclusion that Jesus performed his mighty works in virtue of his divinely-given office? Such a conclusion is more probable than complex processes of Traditionsgeschichte. For ἐλεέω, cf. 16:24; 17:13 and Mk. 5:19.

(39) Luke has οἱ προάγοντες, diff. Mk. πολλοί, to indicate the people who replied to the blind man; the verb has probably been drawn from Mk. 11:9 (or 10:32), and is used to give a realistic picture of the people who preceded Jesus in the crowd, so that the conversation is able to take place before, or just as, Jesus approaches. σιγάω (diff. Mk. σιωπάω) is Lucan (but cf. 1:20; 19:40).

(40) Jesus responds to the cry for help by coming to a halt (σταθείς

(18:11; et al.), diff. Mk. στάς) and issuing a command; κελεύω*, diff. Mk. λέγω, is Lucan (Acts, 17x; Mk., 0x; Mt., 7x). The blind man is to be led to him (for the phrase cf. 25:6, 17). Luke omits the Marcan dialogue in which Jesus tells the people to summon the beggar and the message is passed on. Likewise, he omits the vivid details of the man casting aside his garment and jumping up; by comparison the genitive absolute ἐγγίσαντος ... αὐτοῦ (cf. 18:35) is distinctly colourless.

(41) But the details of the vital conversation are preserved. Jesus asks the blind man what he wants done to him: θέλεις is syntactically parenthetical (BD 465²), but it may be better to regard the construction as due to the omission of ἵνα before ποιήσω (9:54). The question is designed to elicit faith rather than to gain information, since it is clear enough what the blind man wants. The blind man addresses Jesus as κύριε, par. Mt., diff. Mk. ῥαββουνί; Luke avoids such Aramaisms (cf. 9:33, diff. Mk.) and is here perhaps influenced by 19:8 (Schramm, 143). Before ἵνα supply θέλω.

(42) Jesus replies with a command, 'see' (diff. Mk. ὕπαγε, which Luke on the whole avoids; cf. 8:42), and the formula 'your faith has cured you' (7:50; 8:48; 17:19). The healing is performed by divine power in response to human faith.

(43) The healing is immediate (παραχρῆμα (1:64; et al.), diff. Mk. εὐθύς), and the man follows Jesus. The word simply means that the man attached himself to the crowd who were accompanying Jesus, but it may well be meant to convey the deeper sense that he became a disciple. Luke adds the characteristic notes that he glorified God (2:20; et al.; cf. 5:25), and that the people present (2:10) also offered praise (αἶνος, Mt. 21:16**; cf. αἰνέω, 2:13; et al.) to God. The attitude of the people stands in contrast to that of the rulers (19:47f.; 21:19; 22:2; 23:13ff.; Ellis, 220).

vii. Zacchaeus the Tax-Collector 19:1–10

The final story in the long account of Jesus on his journey to Jerusalem is meant to be a climax in the ministry of Jesus, and it brings out several notable features which Luke considered important. It is a supreme example of the universality of the gospel offer to tax-collectors and sinners, with Jesus taking the initiative and inviting himself to the house of Zacchaeus. In doing so Jesus was certainly responding to the interest shown in him by Zacchaeus, but the decisive action, contrary to all that would be expected at the time, stemmed from Jesus. Zacchaeus for his part responds with joy, and also by promising to use his wealth, honestly and ill-gotten, to help the poor and to make restitution for his former evil habits; in this way the meaning of discipleship, especially in regard to wealth, is clearly expressed. Jesus affirms that, tax-collector though he is, Zacchaeus is entitled to salvation, for he too is a Jew, a member of the people to whom salvation was promised by God in the coming of the

Messiah. But salvation comes even to Jews only when Jesus goes after them and brings them home. So the narrative concludes with the great declaration of the task of the Son of man as a shepherd, which may fittingly be regarded as the epitome of the message of this Gospel.

In form the story is what Dibelius, 115, calls a 'personal legend', full of anecdotal detail which is essential to the narrative; he contrasts it with the preceding story of the blind man which is much more a 'typical' healing story, and he rightly regards it as having a historical core (293). He thus implicitly refutes the claim of Bultmann, 33f., that it is an ideal scene.

Essentially the story is a unified composition. Bultmann, 33f., 58f., 65, is disposed to regard vs. 8 and 10 as Lucan additions. (cf. Grundmann, 358). The difficulty with v. 8 is that it breaks the connection between v. 7 (where the bystanders grumble) and v. 9 (which, despite the πρὸς αὐτόν, appears to be addressed to them, since it refers to Zacchaeus in the third person); moreover, v. 9 makes no allusion to the proposal of Zacchaeus in v. 8. There is certainly an inconcinnity in the narrative here, but the material has been so thoroughly edited by Luke and his source that it is hard to offer a certain analysis. If the thought of v. 8 was congenial to Luke, the same is also true of vs. 9 and 10, so that a decision on grounds of content is scarcely possible; cf. the detailed analysis by Dupont, II, 249–254. There are some grounds for regarding the legal details in v. 8 as forming an integral part of the story (Derrett, 278–285), and there are also sound reasons for regarding v. 10 as a saying of Jesus, although possibly a misplaced one. It seems probable that v. 10 is an isolated saying, and that we should regard v. 9 as addressed to Zacchaeus and the bystanders simultaneously; it has possibly been reformulated by Luke in order to give a comment on the story for the benefit of the readers, and to give a link to v. 10.

The story is from Luke's special source, and probably stood in juxtaposition with the parable of the Pharisee and the tax-collector with a catchword connection. Bultmann's view that it is a developed variant of the simpler story in Mk. 2:14–17 is pure speculation; the preservation of the name Zacchaeus speaks in favour of its historicity.

See Dupont, II, 249–254; Derrett, 278–285; W. P. Loewe, 'Towards an Interpretation of Lk. 19:1–10', CBQ 36, 1974, 321–331.

(1) The opening verse links with the preceding story of the blind man which was located outside Jericho. διέρχομαι may be Lucan (19:4; 2:15; et al.). It is difficult to know whether the detail originally belonged to the story of Zacchaeus or is a redactional addition. Schramm, 143f., argues that 18:35a contains the original introduction to the story, and that Luke created 19:1 to replace it when he repositioned the original introduction before the story of the blind man. It is true that the story of the blind man is associated with Jericho in Luke's source (Mk. 10:46), and the story of Zacchaeus could have been secondarily placed in the same location. But the fact that Jericho was a likely post for a tax-

collector means that the Zacchaeus story could well belong to this locality also. It has further been claimed that Zacchaeus would not have climbed a tree within Jericho but rather a roof (Wellhausen, 103), but Lagrange, 488 (cf. Bultmann, 69), has indicated that trees still grow in Herodian Jericho, which was spaciously laid out.

(2) The action is introduced, as often, with καὶ ἰδού (cf. 5:12; *et al.*). The combination of ὀνόματι (1:5; *et al.*) and καλούμενος (1:36; *et al.*) is odd and unique. Perhaps it is meant to draw especial attention to the man's name, Ζακχαῖος, Hebrew *zakkay*, an abbreviation of 'Zachariah', meaning 'the righteous one' (2 Mac. 10:19; Jos., Vit. 239); Zacchaeus thus has a thoroughly Jewish name. ἀρχιτελώνης**, 'chief tax-collector', is found only in this passage, and implies that Zacchaeus was probably head of a group of tax-collectors who were responsible for customs dues in the area on goods passing from Peraea into Judaea (cf. O. Michel, TDNT VIII, 97–99). From the fact that Zacchaeus was rich (6:24; *et al.*) we are already entitled to assume that, like others of his trade, he was none too scrupulous in making sure that he got a good profit on his transactions. More important is the allusion to the earlier question whether a rich man can be saved (Danker, 191).

(3) We are not told why Zacchaeus made an effort (ζητέω, cf. 9:9; 23:8) to see who Jesus was (cf. 4:34 par. Mk. 1:24 for this construction); curiosity is presumably the motif. The reader at least knows that Jesus has a reputation as the friend of tax-collectors, and Zacchaeus may be presumed to be in the same position. But he was unable to see Jesus because of the crowd: ἀπό is commonly used in this sense (Acts 11:19; 22:11; Mt. 18:7; *et al.*; AG s.v. V). ἡλικία (2:52) here obviously means 'height'; Danker's allusion (191) to 12:25 is fanciful. Clearly it is Zacchaeus and not Jesus who is small in height, despite the doubts expressed by Findlay, 1052.

(4) In order to gain a glimpse of Jesus, Zacchaeus runs on ahead (προτρέχω, Jn. 20:4**) in front of the crowd which is surrounding Jesus. εἰς τὸ ἔμπροσθεν is pleonastic (cf. Tob. 11:3 B; BD 484), and Black, 116, suggests that it equals Aramaic *lᵉqadhmutheh*, 'to meet him', but Zacchaeus' action in climbing a tree hardly supports this. συκομορέα** (17:6 note) is the 'fig-mulberry' or 'sycamore fig' (*Ficus sycomorus* L; C.-H. Hunzinger, TDNT VII, 758f.), a tree rather like an oak and easy to climb; it had evergreen leaves and bore an edible fruit, and should not be confused with the European sycamore or the North American plane (F. N. Hepper, NBD, 1294). With ἐκείνης sc. ὁδοῦ (cf. 5:19). The preposition δι' is prefixed in Θ Ψ f1 69 *pm* a l s; *Diglot*.

(5) Whether Zacchaeus intended to remain hidden from view or not is not stated, but it may be assumed that this was his intention, since it would hardly be consistent with his dignity to be found up a tree. But in any case, Jesus knew that he was there and knew his name (cf. Nathanael, Jn. 1:47f.); this may be a case of supernatural knowledge, but it is perfectly possible that Jesus could have known his name. After

'Iησοῦς the words εἶδεν αὐτὸν καί are added by A (D) W ΓΔ f13 pl; TR; Diglot, but they seem redundant after ἀναβλέψας. Zacchaeus is told to waste no time (σπεύδω, 2:16; et al.) in coming down, for today Jesus must stay in his house. σήμερον is to be taken quite literally, but it may convey the idea that the time has come for the fulfilment of God's plan of salvation (19:9; cf. 2:11; et al.; Ellis, 221). Behind Jesus' summons lies a necessity imposed on him by God (δεῖ); the implication is that a divine plan is being worked out. μένω is the usual word for staying at a person's house (Jn. 1:38f.), equivalent here to καταλύω, 'to stay a night' (19:7).

(6) Zacchaeus does exactly what he is told; the repetition in σπεύσας κατέβη is no doubt deliberate. He welcomes Jesus into his home (ὑποδέχομαι, 10:38), and he does so with joy (1:14), since the coming of Jesus to share his home is a sign of fellowship and ultimately of forgiveness.

(7) But now the objections begin. All the people who see what has happened (πάντες, but Diglot has ἅπαντες with poor support) begin to grumble (διαγογγύζω, 15:2*); it is the same reaction as on previous occasions (5:30; 15:2). Not only to Pharisees but also to Jews in general the tax-collector was a ἁμαρτωλὸς ἀνήρ (cf. 5:8 of Peter); to stay in such a person's home was tantamount to sharing in his sin.

(8) The statement of Zacchaeus is to be understood as a reaction to the initiative of Jesus and to the objections of the crowd. In order that Jesus may be freed from the suspicion of consorting with a sinner he makes a public declaration of his intention to live a new life. In such a situation a declaration of intent was an adequate sign of repentance (Derrett, 283–5). At the same time, his action is to be seen as an expression of gratitude to Jesus for his gracious attitude to him, and as an example of the sort of change in life that should follow upon the reception of salvation. σταθείς (18:11; et al.) prefaces a significant statement, envisaged as taking place at the meal in Zacchaeus's house or, perhaps more probably, outside in the presence of the people (as often in the Gospels, changes of scene are passed over in silence). The use of κύριος is indicative of pre-Lucan or Lucan style. ἰδού may express a sudden resolve. ἥμισυς, 'half', can be used as an adjective followed by a noun in the genitive case and takes the gender of the noun, as here; or it can be used as a singular neuter noun (Mk. 6:23; Rev. 11:9, 11; 12:14**; BD 164⁵); the neuter plural is variously spelled ἡμίσεια (L; UBS; Diglot); ἡμίσια (ℵ B* Θ al); and ἡμίση (Synopsis); cf. BD 48; MH II, 176–178. μου τῶν ὑπαρχόντων is inverted in A (D) W ΓΔ f13 131 pm; TR; Diglot. The very late position of κύριε in the sentence is due to the heavy emphasis placed on the object. The amount to be given in charity was well beyond the normal requirement; 20% of one's possessions or (in subsequent years) of one's income was a recognised figure among the rabbis (SB IV:1, 546–551). The present tense τοῖς πτωχοῖς δίδωμι (the order is inverted in A W ΓΔ f13 131 pl lat; TR; Diglot) is futuristic, and

expresses a resolve (NEB; TEV; TNT; Barclay; cf. NIV: 'Here and now I give'); self-justification (Godet, II, 217f.) would be quite inappropriate at this point. For συκοφαντέω cf. 3:14** where it is used of a characteristic sin of soldiers who may have aided tax-collectors. The conditional clause is to be translated 'From whomsoever I have wrongfully exacted anything', and thus does not put the fact of extortion in doubt, but rather its extent. The normal recompense for money illegally acquired was the amount plus one fifth (cf. Lv. 6:1–5; SB II, 250), but fourfold recompense (τετραπλοῦς**), i.e. the amount plus a threefold penalty was demanded of rustlers (cf. 2 Sa. 12:6; Ex. 22:1; Jos. Ant. 16:3); similar practices appear to have been known in Roman law and in Egypt (Derrett, 284; O. Michel, TDNT VIII, 105 n. 154).

(9) The story ends with a comment by Jesus (curiously not designated ὁ κύριος here). πρὸς αὐτόν would normally mean 'to him', but since the saying is couched in the third person, it may mean 'about him' (cf. 18:9 and 20:19, although here πρός has a rather hostile sense; cf. Klostermann, 185). σωτηρία was a motif in the birth stories (1:69, 71, 77*) and does not occur elsewhere in the Gospels. The reference to Zacchaeus's house (19:5) is surprising, and may perhaps be linked with the salvation of households in Acts (10:2; 11:14; 16:15, 31; 18:8). For καθότι cf. 1:7; et al. καὶ αὐτός means 'even this tax-collector'. The saying probably means 'salvation must be extended to this man because even a tax-collector is a Jew' (O. Michel, TDNT VIII, 104; E. Schweizer, TDNT VIII, 365). Ellis, 220f., however, takes the view that the reference is rather to 'spiritual' sonship of Abraham, which is seen in those who share his faith and works. But καθότι is used to introduce an antecedent reason rather than a subsequent proof, so that the point of the saying is that a Jew, even though he has become one of the 'lost sheep of the house of Israel', is still a part of Israel; the good Shepherd must seek for such (v. 10; J. Jeremias, TDNT VI, 500). Cf. Lk. 13:16 for the same theme. The language and themes of the verse are Lucan, and hence it is probable that this is either a Lucan comment or an edited statement.

(10) The second part of the saying of Jesus is a Son of man saying, and is probably traditional, since Luke does not create Son of man sayings. For the ἦλθεν form cf. 5:32 par. Mk. 2:17; 7:34 par. Mt. 11:19; Mk. 10:45 and notes on these verses. ζητέω uses the image of seeking for lost sheep (Mt. 18:12; Ezk. 34:16) and σῴζω can also be used in the same metaphorical area (Ezk. 34:22; Jn. 10:9); similarly ἀπόλλυμι is used of sheep (15:4, 6; cf. Ps. 119 (118):176; Ezk. 34:4, 16; A. Oepke, TDNT I, 395). The saying as a whole is thus couched in Shepherd imagery (J. Jeremias, TDNT VI, 492), and this strongly anchors it in the teaching of Jesus. The argument that the saying is Hellenistic (Bultmann, 155) is unconvincing: 1 Tim. 1:15 shows what the saying would have been like in a Hellenistic form. The idea of present salvation as the purpose of the earthly work of Jesus has been found difficult by some

scholars (Hahn, 45; cf. W. Foerster, TDNT VII; 991f.), but the thought is already present in Jesus' 'realised eschatology'. In short, there is nothing in the saying itself that would make it inauthentic (*pace* Tödt, 133–135; Higgins, 76f.). The one point that causes real difficulty is the presence of the term 'Son of man' with reference to Jesus' earthly ministry in a public saying. C. Colpe, TDNT VIII, 453, accordingly regards the title as an addition to the saying, but admits that the saying might be based on Mk. 2:17 or Mt. 15:24 (cf. Mk. 8:35). But the case that Jesus did use the phrase 'Son of man' with respect to his earthly activity is a strong one (Borsch, 326; I. H. Marshall, NTS 12, 1965–66, 339–343), and the saying should be accepted as authentic. The variants of the saying in Mt. 18:11 v.l. and Lk. 9:56 v.l. appear to be late developments.

VI

THE MINISTRY IN JERUSALEM

19:11 – 21:38

FROM Jericho Jesus moves to Jerusalem. Luke has no special information about his ministry there, and therefore the contents of this section are in all essentials drawn from Mk. and follow the pattern presented there. The opening 'bridge' passage (19:11–27) is non-Marcan and is dramatically situated at Jericho. Thereafter Jesus approaches Jerusalem on a colt and prophesies the destruction of the city (19:28–40, 41–44). Luke is especially concerned with the temple as the scene of Jesus' action and ministry (19:45–48). He proceeds to describe the conflict between Jesus and the Jewish authorities, as recorded in Mk., omitting only the question about the great commandment (cf. Lk. 10:25–28). The section concludes with the apocalyptic discourse addressed to the disciples (21:5–38). Throughout the section it is significant that the people are prepared to listen to Jesus, but the rulers are opposed to him. From the very outset, Jerusalem stands under condemnation.

a. The Parable of the Pounds (19:11–27)

Luke regards the parable as being delivered to the same audience as was present in the last scene; it is necessitated by their belief that when Jesus came to Jerusalem the kingdom of God would appear. Such a hope makes sense in the context of what has preceded in this Gospel. The disciples had been taught that the kingdom had in some sense arrived, and it was natural for them to assume that its consummation would follow once the activity of Jesus extended to the capital city. Luke regards the parable as being told in order to dispel such hopes. Two strands of thought are interwoven in it. One is the idea that Jesus is departing, and will not be appointed as king until his return; meanwhile, the Jewish people, over whom he ought to rule, will reject him, and can expect only judgment on his return. This attitude of rejection belongs to the post-resurrection period, but it corresponds to the rejection that Jesus would suffer on his arrival in Jerusalem. The other strand of thought is that the servants of Jesus must occupy themselves in profitable service during the time of his absence, and that judgment and deprivation await the unprofitable servant. Thus the parable looks backwards with its theme of the meaning of discipleship and forwards with its stress on the rejection of the claimant to the throne (Ellis, 222).

The parable is similar in form and content to the parable of the talents in Mt. 25:14–30; the latter lacks the element of the rejection of the king (cf. Mt. 22:7 for this motif), which in any case fits rather awkwardly into Luke's parable. It is, therefore, almost universally agreed that this theme is a secondary addition to the parable (19:12, 14, 15a, 27; *contra* Lagrange, 497). It reflects contemporary history, especially the story of Archelaus (Jos. Bel. 2:80–100; Ant. 17:299–320). What is uncertain is whether it ever existed as a separate parable (Jeremias, *Parables*, 59) or is simply an expansion of the main parable (Bultmann, 190; Schulz, 288 n. 178; and many others); equally uncertain is whether it was added in pre-Lucan tradition (Jeremias) or by Luke himself (Bultmann; Schulz).

Once this addition has been removed, there are still considerable differences between the two parables. Essentially, Matthew has three servants who each receive different, large sums of money; the first two of them double their capital: Luke has ten servants who each receive the same small sum of money, and two of them make different profits. There are indications that a common basis for the parables can be found in one story of a man who gave the same, small sums to each of three servants, two of whom traded successfully. We may take it, therefore, that one original parable lies behind the two versions, although it is not absolutely excluded that Jesus himself told two similar parables on different occasions (so Zahn, 628 n. 23; Plummer, 437; Geldenhuys, 476f.). It has been developed in different ways. Granted that signs of Lucan editing can be seen in the present form of the parable, the question arises whether the development of the parable from the hypothetical original form is due entirely to the editorial work of Luke or is partly due to development in the tradition. Two detailed linguistic analyses come to different conclusions on the matter. Schulz, 288–293, explains all the differences between Lk. and Mt. at this point in terms of their separate editorial activity on one common parable recorded in Q. Weiser, 229–258, argues that Matthew and Luke have taken their accounts from separate traditions in which the basic parable had been modified. The more probable solution is offered by Weiser, who pays greater attention to Luke's redactional motives and shows that the development of the parable cannot be entirely explained in terms of his purposes. It would be a remarkable coincidence if both Evangelists had indulged in very considerable redactional activity at the same point in this way.

Moreover, a good deal of the elaboration is typical of popular story-telling rather than of the theological and stylistic re-working of existing traditions which is the usual characteristic of the final redaction of the Gospels (cf. the further elaboration of the parable in the Gospel of the Nazarenes, NTA I, 149). If this view is correct, it leaves unsolved the question of the source or sources employed by the Evangelists. Probably, however, we have further evidence for the two recensions of the Q material which have been detected elsewhere in the course of this commentary. It is less likely that the parable is from Luke's special source, since there is no real link with the preceding story of Zacchaeus, and the content of the parable is closer to the themes found in Q (cf. Schulz, 293–298).

Jülicher claimed that the original form of the parable was meant simply to teach a moral lesson about using the gifts which God has given to man. Dibelius, 255, vigorously criticised such views, and noted the possibility of the use of metaphors which are 'half-allegorical' and lead to fuller allegorisation. This appears to be the case in the present parable where the original form could not but have an allegorical significance for the hearers. Such incipient allegorisation was possible on the lips of Jesus who reckoned with the facts of his departure and of his return as the Son of man. The parable, therefore, presupposes an interval between the time of Jesus' ministry and the parousia, but belief in this interval was part of the teaching of Jesus and not a later development in the early church. It is consequently unlikely that the parable is a later composition by the early church designed to enable it to come to terms with the delay of the parousia (so apparently Schulz; cf. Grässer, 114 who raises this possibility). Nor is it probable that the parable was originally addressed to the Jewish leaders to warn them about the coming of national catastrophe (so Jeremias, *Parables*, 58–63). Rather the parable is concerned with the entrusting of the kingdom to men and their responsibilities to use its spiritual benefits until the consummation (M. Didier*, 266–269; cf. Weiser, 259–266). In this form the parable contained the seeds of the christological and eschatological development which it underwent in the early church; the identity of the absent man with Jesus, portrayed in a kingly role, and the significance of the man's return as a metaphor of the parousia and last judgment were brought out. In its earliest form the parable stressed the importance of human attitudes before the consummation of the kingdom, and this ecclesiological feature too was easily open to development. Luke particularly has used the parable to warn his readers that the kingdom would not come immediately; possibly he had to face the misunderstanding that the resurrection *was* the parousia, for otherwise it is hard to see why he should stress a point which ought to have been obvious to his readers after Easter.

See Manson, *Sayings*, 312–317; Jeremias, *Parables*, 58–63; Grässer, 114–119; Derrett, 17–31 (originally as 'The Parable of the Talents and two Logia', ZNW 56, 1965, 184–195); M.

Didier, 'La parabole des talents et des mines', in de la Potterie, 248–271; Weiser, 226–272; Schulz, 288–298.

(11) There is general agreement that the framework for the parable has been composed by Luke, but it is possible that to some extent it is based on a source (Jeremias, *Parables*, 99 n. 40, gives a list of Lucan and pre-Lucan characteristics; cf. Knox, II, 112). For the use of ἀκούω cf. 16:14; 20:45; *et al.* The effect is to tie the parable closely to the preceding scene with its audience of followers of Jesus (cf. 5:27–32/33–39; Klostermann, 185). The point will then be that, although salvation has come *today* (19:9f.), the End, and the coming of the Son of man to judgment, still lie in the future. The present participle suggests that the preceding sayings are still ringing in their ears or being turned over in their minds. On προστίθημι see 3:20 note; the meaning is that Jesus went on to say something else, namely a parable. εἶπεν παραβολήν is Lucan (6:39; *et al.*, possibly pre-Lucan). Luke also gives a reason for parabolic teaching in 18:1, 9. If the scene envisaged is Jericho, then Jerusalem was ἐγγύς, about 17 miles away (10:30 note); the implication is, of course, that Jesus is nearly at his intended destination (18:31). ἀναφαίνω is 'to sight' (Acts 21:3**), here, passive, 'to appear' (cf. Ass. Moses 10:1). The verb refers to the final revelation (cf. 2 Tim. 4:1) of God's rule associated with the coming of the Son of man. From the point of view of Luke's readers it is possible that the verse is meant to contradict the view that the resurrection appearances of Jesus constituted the revelation of the kingdom of God (H.-W. Bartsch, 'Early Christian Eschatology in the Synoptic Gospels', NTS 11, 1964–65, 387–397, especially 393; C. H. Talbert, in JMH I, 172–174). The parable itself, however, assumes the fact of an interval before the end, rather than proves it, and to this extent Luke's introduction does not reflect the main thrust of the parable (cf. Wilson, 68f.).

(12) The parable concerns ἄνθρωπός τις who is described as εὐγενής, 'noble' (Acts 17:11; 1 Cor. 1:26**), a word that may have been introduced in connection with the motif of his claim to a kingdom; it is used in a different sense in Acts 17:11, and so is not necessarily Lucan. πορεύομαι, diff. Mt. ἀποδημέω, is probably secondary; εἰς χώραν μακράν is a traditional phrase (15:13). The departure of the man is essential for the theme of stewardship (cf. Mk. 13:34), and allegorically depicts the absence of Jesus after the resurrection (cf. perhaps 22:22). Luke, however, gives a motive for the departure which is lacking in Mt. The man departs in order to acquire kingly rule or a kingdom (22:29f. has both senses together) for himself and thereafter to return (ὑποστρέφω, 1:56; *et al.*; the infinitive is rather loosely added). The story resembles that of Archelaus who on the death of his father Herod made his way to Rome in order to get confirmation of the kingship bestowed on him in his father's will. The rest of the story fits in with this allusion, for Archelaus was followed by a deputation of Jews who resisted his appointment and who succeeded in persuading Augustus to give him only

half his father's kingdom and the status of an ethnarch (Jos. Bel. 2:80–100; Ant. 17:299–320). In the same way Herod the Great (Jos. Ant. 14:370–385), Antipas (Jos. Bel. 2:20–22; Ant. 17:224–227), Philip (Jos. Ant. 17:303) and Agrippa I (Jos. Ant. 18:238) all had to seek the decision of Rome, but the story of Archelaus provides the closest parallel to the parable. The motif of kingship features in Lk. from this point (cf. 1:33; 19:38; 22:29f.; 23:3, 11, 37f.; Ellis, 222), and Luke appears to be thinking of the acquisition of kingly power by Jesus (19:11). This might suggest that the motif of acquiring rule here is due to Luke himself rather than to his tradition, but the development of the motif later in the parable bears signs of pre-Lucan origin. For Luke Jesus' rule and his glory can come only by the path of suffering and death.

(13) The action begins as the man summons his servants (par. Mt.). Derrett, 18f., argues that they are not his slaves in view of the powers which he entrusts to them. Luke has ten servants, Matthew three; the use of ὁ ἕτερος in v. 20 suggests that the smaller number is original, and the larger number may be due to the elevation of the man into a nobleman; in any case, the number 'ten' plays no further part in the story. Luke has ἑαυτοῦ, diff. Mt. ἴδιος; his phraseology suggests that the man had a larger number of servants, whereas in Mt. there appear to be no more than three. Hence the formulation here may be secondary (Schulz, 289), but it is equally possible that Matthew has substituted ἴδιος (Weiser, 231). In Mt. the man apparently gives the whole of his possessions to the servants, but the amount is exceptionally large: he has a capital of 8 talents. In Lk. the comparatively small sum of 10 minas is divided among the servants. The μνᾶ (19:16, 18, 20, 24f.**) was a Greek coin worth 100 drachmas. It is hardly possible to give a modern equivalent; Barclay suggests £5, but NIV mg, 'about three months' wages', is better. The small sum involved shows that a test of faithfulness is being given. The noble himself would have to expend far greater sums in order to secure his kingdom. πραγματεύομαι** is 'to do business, to trade', and expresses what was implicit in the handing over of the money; since the phrase is absent from Mt., it may be an addition. It is not clear whether the giving of equal sums (Lk.) or varying sums (Mt.) to the servants is original; if Matthew describes how different opportunities were equally used, Luke describes how equal opportunities were differently used by the successful servants. It seems probable that, if we are dealing with one basic story, the varying sums disappeared when the number of servants was increased. The sums are to be regarded as loans of capital by the master, and he would expect to receive the profit on his return; there may have been an agreement regarding the amount of profit to be given to the servants, and also regarding their making up any loss of capital to the master (Derrett, 22–24).

(14) Luke has nothing to correspond to the description of the servants' activity in Mt. 25:16–18, which is strictly unnecessary and may be an addition by Matthew or his source; on the other hand, it is possible

that Lk. 19:13b is an equivalent for this description. In any case the theme of the kingdom is taken up again at this point. The absent nobleman is thought of as having 'citizens' (πολίτης, 15:15*), i.e. the persons in the country over which he wishes to rule. They hated him (imperfect) and so sent (aorist) an embassy (14:32**) after him to state that they did not wish him to rule (1:33; 19:27*) over them (cf. Jos. Ant. 17:300 of Archelaus). A reference to Jewish rejection of Jesus as king (cf. Acts 17:7) would be seen by Luke's readers. For the thought cf. Mt. 22:6f. which suggests that this is a traditional feature, not due to Lucan redaction.

(15) The first half of the verse continues the same motif. For ἐπανέρχομαι cf. 10:35**. λέγω again means 'to command'; for the use of the passive infinitive cf. 18:40. The description of the servants is introduced to regain the connection with the earlier part of the story after the addition. For δεδώκει (pluperfect without augment, as is usual) ἔδωκεν is read by A W Γ Δ Θ f13 118, 209, pl; TR; Diglot; the pluperfect could be a grammatical correction, but is well supported. γνοῖ is aorist subjunctive (Mk. 5:43; 9:30; BD 95²). After γνοῖ the interrogative τί is read by ℵ B D L Ψ pc e Origen. The main variant is τίς τί (with διεπραγμεύσατο): A K Γ Δ Θ f1 f13 pm lat; TR; Synopsis; Diglot. In this case τι may be indefinite ('who had gained something') or interrogative ('who had gained what'; cf. Mk. 15:24; BD 298⁵). Metzger, 169, thinks that the latter reading is due to scribes trying to make the narrative more precise; but the former reading could well be a simplification. διαπραγματεύομαι** is 'to gain by trading' (in Classical Greek, 'to examine thoroughly'). Matthew's text is different. He refers to the long period of the master's absence, a thought which is probably a secondary stress on an original and necessary feature of the story (cf. Weiser, 238f.), and he describes the reckoning with the phrase συναίρω λόγον (cf. Mt. 18:23f.).

(16) The examination of the servants follows the same pattern as in Mt. but the wording differs and the form is simpler. παραγίνομαι, diff. Mt. προσέρχομαι, is Lucan (7:4; et al.). The designation of the servants as ὁ πρῶτος, and so on, must be from Luke's tradition in view of the difficulty of ὁ ἕτερος (v. 20) when there are in fact ten servants involved. The Matthaean form looks like popular elaboration at this point. The first servant's capital has gained (προσεργάζομαι**, 'to make more, earn in addition') a 1,000% profit, which may seem large to the modern reader but was quite possible under ancient conditions with enormous interest and commission rates (Derrett, 24).

(17) The omission of the subject ὁ κύριος, diff. Mt., is surprising, and suggests that its inclusion by Matthew is editorial. But the use of λέγω, diff. Mt. φημί, is original. Luke has εὖγε (punctuated as two words in Synopsis; Diglot; AG), 'well done! excellent!', diff. Mt. εὖ. The servant is commended as good because he has fulfilled his duty. Matthew adds πιστός, the appropriate phrase to use of a good servant who has

fulfilled his commission. The same use appears in Lk. 12:42, and it is possible that Luke has omitted the word here to avoid pleonasm with the next phrase (Schulz, 291). Luke's use of ὅτι avoids the asyndeton in Mt. which may be original. The servant has been faithful ἐν ἐλαχίστῳ, diff. Mt. ἐπὶ ὀλίγα. Luke's phrase is reminiscent of 16:10**, and may be due to the influence of that verse (H. Seesemann, TDNT V, 172). The use of the periphrastic form ἴσθι ἔχων seems unmotivated, but may be meant as a sign of eternal reward. For ἐπάνω in the sense of authority over something cf. Dn. 6:3; Jn. 3:31. Matthew has the quite different phrase ἐπὶ πολλῶν σε καταστήσω (cf. Mt. 24:45, 47 Q). Luke gives the new sphere of authority as ten cities, corresponding to the ten minas. This is a disproportionate reward, which brings out the principle, 'faithful in little, great reward', and does not fit the picture of the wealthy master, although it does fit the picture of the nobleman, now become a king. E. Nestle suggested that the Aramaic word for 'talents' (kakʻrin) had been misread as 'cities' (kʻrakin), a hypothesis defended by Black, 2f., and this may be the right solution. But there is no entirely satisfactory explanation. Luke does not have the Matthaean phrase 'enter into the joy of your master'.

(18) The description of the second servant's interview follows the same pattern, but there is literary variation, whereas Matthew's wording is much more stereotyped. In place of ὁ δεύτερος D has ὁ ἕτερος, probably by assimilation to v. 20. For ποιέω in the sense of 'earning, gaining', cf. Black, 302.

(19) The word order ἐπάνω γίνου (ℵ B L f1 157 pc) is inverted in rell; TR; Diglot (assimilation to v. 17).

(20) A third servant is described as ὁ ἕτερος, which implies that the story originally contained only three servants. The reading of D in v. 18 hardly supports the view that ὁ ἕτερος can mean 'another'. Plummer, 441, and Ellis, 224, suggest that the phrase refers to a third type of servant, one individual representative of several of the same kind; but this does not avoid the difficulty caused by the presence of the article. The third servant simply returns the mina to his master. He had kept it, laid aside (ἀπόκειμαι, Col. 1:5; 2 Tim. 4:8; Heb. 9:27**) in a cloth; σουδάριον, a loanword from Latin sudarium, is a scarf or neckcloth used to protect the back of the head from the sun (Jn. 11:44; 20:7; Acts 19:12**). The practice of keeping money in this way is attested in rabbinic writings (Keth. 67b; SB II, 252), but was regarded as unsafe (BM 3:10f.; SB I, 970f.); by contrast, burying money in the ground, as practised in Mt. 25:25, was much safer (cf. Jeremias, Parables, 61). In Lk. the description of what the servant has done precedes his comments on the master's character, diff. Mt.; Schulz, 291, prefers Matthew's order as original.

(21) The servant justifies his action by stating that he was afraid of his master (cf. φοβηθείς, Mt. 25:25, but at the corresponding point Mt. has ἔγνων, which seems to be original in view of ἤδεις, v. 22; Schulz,

292). The master is 'exacting, strict' (αὐστηρός**, diff. Mt. σκληρός, which is harsher and hence original). He is a grasping person who wants money without the labour of earning it. He takes what he has not put aside (for this use of τίθημι, cf. 1 Cor. 16:2): the metaphor is drawn from banking, and is used here to describe a person who seeks a disproportionately high return from his investments. For the proverbial nature of the phrase cf. Jos. Ap. 2:216; Aelian, VH 3:46; Philo, Hypothetica 7:6 (Derrett, 25 n. 1). Matthew has 'gathering where you have not scattered', an agricultural metaphor, which fits in with the other half of the saying, 'harvesting what (Mt.: where) you have not sown'. The servant appears to have feared that he would get no return for his work: all the profit would have been taken by the master. At the same time, he may have feared that if he incurred a loss on the capital he would have to make it up to the master (Derrett, 25f.). These details belong to the setting, and are not meant to be allegorised.

(22) The historic present λέγει indicates that Luke is following a source here; Matthew has a more solemn introduction. The master proposes to judge the servant by what he himself has just said: ἐκ τοῦ στόματός σου (cf. Job 15:6; cf. SB II, 252) is not in Mt. The ᾔδεις ... clause should probably be taken as a question, but it is equivalent to a conditional protasis. The master is willing to adopt the character given him by the slave. Even on that basis the slave stands self-condemned; he is even more to be condemned if his estimate of the master is false.

(23) If, then, the master seeks profit for which he has not worked, why had the slave not taken the elementary step of banking the money – not for safe-keeping, but in order that it might earn interest? In this way he would have earned money for the master without doing any work himself. Luke has the question form διὰ τί..., diff. Mt. ἔδει σε οὖν (cf. Mt. 23:23), but in view of his own preference for δεῖ, it is hard to see why he has avoided it here, and hence he is following his source. The word order μου τὸ ἀργύριον (א A B L W* Θ 33 157 pc) is inverted in TR; Diglot to the more usual order; Mt. τὰ ἀργύρια (plural) is appropriate with a larger amount of money. τράπεζα (with the article prefixed in K al; TR; Diglot) is the table used by money-changers, hence 'bank' (cf. Mk. 11:15; Mt. 21:12; Jn. 2:15); Mt. τραπεζίτης** is a variant tradition. τόκος (Mt. 25:27**) is 'interest'; the rate would have been high by modern standards, but low in comparison with what the other servants had been able to earn by trading (Derrett, 26). πράσσω (3:13) is used of collecting money (diff. Mt. κομίζομαι, the less technical term): the order αὐτὸ ἔπραξα (א B L pc) is again inverted by TR; Diglot.

(24) In Mt. the command of the master follows without a break, but here it is addressed to the bystanders (παρίστημι, 1:19; 2:22*) who begin to speak in the next verse. Hence the introduction here is probably Lucan. The identity of the bystanders it is not clear, since there is no indication that the other nine servants are present at the interview; presumably other, lesser servants are in mind. They are to give the

servant's mina to the servant who had the ten. This implies, what had not been stated earlier, that the servants were rewarded with the profit that they had made and encouraged to use it for further profit; it may be presumed that this was the reward in the Matthaean form of the parable. In the Lucan form, however, it is very strange that a person who has just been given ten cities should receive a further reward of a small sum of money, unless the thought is that the responsibility given to the third servant has still to be carried on and is therefore transferred to a more capable servant. The detail confirms that the mention of the cities is secondary.

(25) The objection of the bystanders is, therefore, because the first servant has already profited to the tune of ten minas (not ten cities). The attitude is one of legalism, working in terms of strict reward and disliking the idea of a bonus. The verse is not in Mt., and is textually suspect in Lk., being omitted by D W 69 *pc* b e ff² sy^{s c} bo^{pt}; Wellhausen, 107; Klostermann, 188f.; Creed, 235. But the majority of editors and commentators accept the verse, since it is difficult to explain its entry to the text (e.g. as a marginal comment), and easier to explain its omission in view of its absence from Mt. and the difficult transition to v. 26 (Metzger, 169). But this still leaves the possibility that it is a secondary addition to the parable. Since it belongs to the stage of transmission at which the kingdom motif was not yet present, it is probably pre-Lucan (cf. Weiser, 251f.), but its absence from Mt. suggests that it belongs to the pre-Lucan stream of tradition rather than to the original form of the parable.

(26) The reply of the master follows directly on from v. 24, as if v. 25 had not intervened; but such changes of speaker without announcement are not unknown in Lk. (7:29f./31). The saying is found in very similar form in 8:18, par. Mk. 4:25, and is thus a Q doublet to the Marcan saying. It could be used proverbially in the parabolic situation (Derrett, 29–31) in the sense that the person who has capital and uses it to make a profit will be rewarded with further opportunity, whereas the person who has no profit to show will have even 'what he has' (i.e. his capital) taken from him (ἀπ' αὐτοῦ is added, par. Mt., in many MSS; TR; *Diglot*). Indeed, it is this situation which makes sense of the paradoxical second half of the saying. Nevertheless, the authoritative form of the saying, introduced by λέγω ὑμῖν (omitted by Mt.), suggests that it is to be seen as a comment by Jesus, drawing out the lesson of the parable, which is the promise of reward for faithful service and loss for unfaithfulness. The saying has been regarded as a 'sentence of holy law' in which the proverbial sense has been replaced by an eschatological meaning (Käsemann, *Questions*, 98f.); cf. how the following verse in Mt. 25:30 refers to eschatological punishment and falls outside the parabolic picture.

(27) Luke says nothing about the fate of the third servant, which appears to be a Matthaean addition, but he does return finally to the fate

of the citizens who refused to accept the nobleman's rule. The language is not decisive as to the origin of the verse; it may be pre-Lucan. ἐχθρός is used to characterise the disobedient citizens, whose unwillingness to serve their new monarch is described in terms drawn from v. 14. They suffer the typical fate of ancient rebels.

κατασφάζω** is 'to slaughter, strike down', and it was not uncommon for such massacres to take place before the ruler's presence (1 Sa. 15:33; Rev. 14:10; frequent examples in ancient history, e.g. Jos. Ant. 13:380). This revenge is not attested of Archelaus, although he ruled in cruel fashion and it would not be out of character (cf. Jos. Ant. 17:342). What is difficult is the use of this imagery with regard to the judgment of the Son of man on unfaithful people who reject his rule over them; but the language, although strange to us, is such as would make sense to Jesus' hearers and convey to them the seriousness of their position.

b. Jesus approaches Jerusalem (19:28–40)

Now at last Jesus approaches Jerusalem from the east. He gives instructions to his disciples to bring him a previously unridden young ass. Then, seated on it, he makes his way down from the Mount of Olives to the accompaniment of praise to God by his disciples as they celebrate the coming of the king. Only Luke describes how the Pharisees told Jesus to curb his disciples, but he replied that it was impossible for them to do anything else.

Luke's story follows Mk. quite closely, but shows differences from it in v. 37, and vs. 39f. have no Marcan parallel. It is debated whether he is simply editing Mk. freely (Creed, 240f.) or is using alternative source material (Schramm, 145–149; H. Patsch*, 7–10; cf. earlier B. Weiss, 592; Taylor, *Behind*, 94f.; Manson, *Sayings*, 317; Schlatter, 408–412). Since it is probable that Luke uses non-Marcan material in the next section, the likelihood that he has done so here also is increased. If so, Luke knew a version of the story (including parts of vs. 29, 37f.) which apparently did not mention Jesus' ride on the ass.

The result is that Luke's story is simpler than that in Mk. – there is no mention, for example, of the palm branches. The acclamation by the disciples is reworded, and Jesus accepts in substance the disciples' understanding of what is happening. The possibility of a political misunderstanding of the incident is greatly reduced (Burger, 112–114).

The historical analysis of the incident is difficult. H. Patsch* in effect distinguishes three elements. The first is the story of the finding of the animal, apparently as the result of supernatural foreknowledge by Jesus; this is generally regarded as a legendary accretion to the story, made in Hellenistic-Jewish circles under the influence of the LXX (Zc. 9:9; cf. Bultmann, 281; H. Patsch*, 16). Second, there is the riding of the ass which is seen as a fulfilment of Zc. 9:9. Third, there is the acclamation by the disciples. These two last features raise problems individually and in combination. Any kind of public demonstration of a messianic nature would, it is argued, have led to police action; and this is often regarded as a decisive argument against historicity. Patsch himself is more concerned with the problem of how Jesus' ride could have led to the disciples' response. It was normal for a rabbi to ride, followed by his disciples on foot. At the same time it seems to have been normal for pilgrims to enter Jerusalem on foot. If, however, Jesus deliberately intended to act out Zc. 9:9, then his action would have been regarded as that of a political Messiah, and it is highly unlikely that Jesus would have intended this. At the same time there is the problem of interpreting the response of the disciples: is it historical, and if so what did it mean, or is it a church creation? While some critics dispute the historicity of both of these items, there seems to be agreement that at least the fact of Jesus' entry to Jerusalem with his disciples can be historical, but that the account of this has been overlaid with legend and messianic colouring. Patsch himself argues that the difficulties are substantially reduced if the two incidents are regarded as originally separate and unconnected. A story of how Jesus entered Jerusalem on an ass has been conflated with the story (found in Luke's special material) of how Jesus was acclaimed by his disciples as Messiah on a different occasion. Neither of these stories is historically incredible; it is their conjunction which raises difficulties.

Although the story has the form of a 'legend', this obviously does not rule out the possibility of a historical basis for it (Dibelius, 118f.). The most obviously legendary part of the story is the first part which appears to include various supernatural features (the foreknowledge of Jesus; the possibility of riding an unbroken colt), to be based on OT motifs (Gn. 49:11; Zc. 9:9), and to be constructed on the same plan as the similar story of the preparations for the passover meal. Nevertheless, Derrett*, 241–253, has shown quite plausibly how the details of the story fit in with Jewish concepts of commandeering and borrowing animals. In Mark's form of the story the OT motifs are present as implicit allusions, and it is only in Mt. and Jn. that Zc. 9:9 is explicitly quoted. There is thus a messianic significance in the story, and it is an open question whether this was intended by Jesus – a possibility that cannot be dismissed, with Bultmann, as 'absurd'. It is doubtful whether supernatural elements are present. The finding of the animal may rest on a previous arrangement or on the knowledge that animals were kept in the village for travellers, and the point in Jesus' riding an untried animal lies in the ritual purity of the animal and not in the peaceableness of the animal. In short, there can well be a historical basis for this part of the narrative.

If so, there is even less difficulty about Jesus riding into Jerusalem. The incident itself will have been so minor as not to attract the attention of the police; it will not have been any more noisy or demonstrative than

the arrival of any large group of pilgrims, filled with elation at their journey's end, and it took place outside the city walls where it was less likely
to cause a disturbance or attract the attention of the city police. The
question is, then, whether Jesus intended some special significance to be
seen in his action. If he had any such intention, then Zc. 9:9 must have
been in his mind: his action was that of the king laying claim to his city.
Of course this could be misunderstood, but a reader of Zc. 9:9 would get
the point. It may well be that the disciples did not realise the point fully
at the time. It is probable that the sort of expectation reflected in Lk.
19:11 was alive among the disciples. Luke's stress on the kingship of
Jesus is an accurate insight into the situation (cf. Jn. 12:13). What was
significant for the disciples was that it was *Jesus* who was coming to
Jerusalem; they hoped that their messianic expectations concerning him
would be fulfilled. Jesus' action was intended as a tacit acceptance of this
role, but the disciples probably failed to understand the fact that he was
deliberately claiming to be a figure of peace. If this view is correct, there
is no need to postulate the existence of two separate incidents which
have been conflated in the tradition. (The fact that there is no mention of
Jesus riding in Luke's special tradition may be due simply to the
fragmentary nature of this source, as it has been preserved for us in the
Gospel, and does not necessarily mean that this motif was absent from
it.)

See Manson, *Sayings*, 317–319; W. Bauer, 'The "Colt" of Palm Sunday', JBL 72, 1953,
220–229; H.-W. Kuhn, 'Das Reittier Jesu in der Einzugsgeschichte des Markus-evangeliums',
ZNW 50, 1959, 82–91; H. Patsch, 'Der Einzug Jesu in Jerusalem', ZTK 68, 1971, 1–26;
Schramm, 145–149; J. D. M. Derrett, 'Law in the New Testament: The Palm Sunday Colt',
Nov.T 13, 1971, 241–258; A. Frenz, 'Mt xxi 5.7', Nov.T 13, 1971, 259f.

(28) The opening verse is a Lucan link with the preceding section;
the phrase εἰπὼν ταῦτα is meant to emphasise that Jesus has removed
any basis for misunderstanding of the present incident, and the reformulation of the story itself is perhaps meant to smooth out any grounds
for misunderstanding in Mk. ἔμπροσθεν means that Jesus went in front
of his followers (cf. Mk. 10:32 for the motif). For ἀναβαίνω cf. 2:42;
18:31. εἰς Ἱεροσόλυμα is drawn from Mk. 11:1. Although Jesus is not
actually said to enter Jerusalem until the last supper, Conzelmann's view
(68) that for Luke Jesus does not enter Jerusalem but only the temple is
implausible (Marshall, 155 n. 1); the present verse surely implies that
Jerusalem is his intended goal.

(29) The καὶ ἐγένετο ... construction is again regarded by
Schramm, 145f., as pre-Lucan; he suggests that the opening of this verse
belonged, with vs. 37f., to Luke's special source. This is possible, but the
linguistic basis is not strong. ἤγγισεν is singular, diff. Mk. plural, thereby
emphasising the leading position of Jesus (cf. v. 28). βηθφαγή, i.e. bēṭ
paggē', 'house of unripe figs' (Mk. 11:1; Mt. 21:1), was a hamlet between Jerusalem and Bethany. βηθανίαν (so (UBS), but ℵ* B D* have
βηθανία, an indeclinable form, BD 56²; cf. 24:50; Mk. 11:11f.; 14:3), i.e.

bēt ʿᵃnniyāh, 'house of dates', is to be identified with El Azariyeh, two miles SE of Jerusalem and on the E of the Mount of Olives; for the topography see Finegan, 88–92. The places are named in a surprising order, since Bethany was further away from Jerusalem than Bethphage; it is possible that Bethany, the better-known place, was added to elucidate the situation of Bethphage. It is also notable that Bethphage appears to have marked the outer limit of the area which ritually belonged to Jerusalem itself. πρός means that Jesus came towards the Mount of Olives: ἐλαιῶν is genitive plural (cf. 19:37), but E. Nestle, followed by AG, preferred the nominative form ἐλαιών ('olive yard', Acts 1:12) here and in 21:37; see the discussion in BD 143; MH I, 235; W. Foerster, TDNT V, 484 n. 100); surely, however, an accusative form would have been needed here. In view of Zc. 14:4 (cf. Ezk. 11:23) the hill came to have eschatological associations (SB I, 840–842), but these are not developed in the NT, and it figures solely as the place of the ascension in Acts; whether Luke expected the parousia to take place at the same location is not clear.

(30) The village opposite (κατέναντι*) to which Jesus sent the two disciples is no doubt Bethphage. Mark's paratactic style (καὶ εὐθύς . . .) is improved by the use of ἐν ᾗ. According to W. Bauer* (summarised in AG s.v.), πῶλος means a 'young animal' when another animal is named in the context, but a 'horse' (not a 'colt') when it stands alone; he therefore adopts the meaning 'horse' here and in Mk. 11:2. The linguistic basis for this conclusion is inadequate (H.-W. Kuhn*, O. Michel, TDNT VI, 959–961); Mark follows the meaning of the word in the LXX (cf. Gn. 49:11; Zc. 9:9), and this is confirmed by Matthew's interpretation; the young of the ass is meant. This interpretation is also demanded by the circumstances of the story; it is more likely that an ass would be found in a village than the much rarer horse which was used more by the upper class. J. D. M. Derrett*, 244, states that animals would be kept for the benefit of travellers who might borrow or hire them to aid them on their journeys (cf. similar arrangements for stage coaches in later history). The animal is described as tied up (an echo of Gn. 49:11, which has messianic associations) and not previously ridden (cf. Nu. 19:2; Dt. 21:3; 1 Sa. 6:7; 2 Sa. 6:3 ; cf. νέος, Zc. 9:9). Animals for sacred use could not be put to ordinary use, but the same was also true for animals to be used by a royal personage (J. D. M. Derrett*, 248f.). We are probably to think of a young, unridden animal tethered alongside its mother, who would naturally accompany the young animal (cf. A. Frenz*, who thinks, however, that Jesus rode the mother). πώποτε, 'ever' (Jn., 4x; 1 Jn. 4:12**), replaces Mk. οὔπω (Lk. 23:53): does Luke try to avoid the possible deduction from Mk. that a mere *man* was now about to ride it? ἄγω, par. Mt., is preferable to Mk. φέρω in the case of leading an animal (cf. v. 35; 9:41).

(31) Jesus' instructions take care of the possibility that somebody will ask (ἐρωτάω, diff. Mk. λέγω) the disciples why (διὰ τί, diff. Mk. τί)

they are untying the animal (diff. Mk. 'doing this'). If they are asked, they will answer: because the master needs it. ἐρεῖτε is a polite imperative, par. Mt., diff. Mk. (cf. 22:11). αὐτῷ is added by A W Γ Δ Θ f1 f13 *pm*; TR; *Diglot*; the omission in ℵ B D L R *pc* could be due to assimilation to Mt. and Mk. ὅτι is here causal (in Mt. it may introduce indirect speech). The word κύριος is ambiguous. It is unlikely to refer to God; it is more likely that it refers to the animal's owner (αὐτοῦ should perhaps be taken with κύριος rather than χρείαν, at least in Mk.; cf. J. D. M. Derrett*, 246 n. 2), but in Lk. there is a reference to οἱ κύριοι αὐτοῦ in v. 33 which indicates that this is not the meaning here. Accordingly ὁ κύριος must mean 'its (real) owner' (J. D. M. Derrett*, 246f.) or 'the Master' (123), as a term used to refer to Jesus. On the first view, Jesus is the 'real owner', in contrast to 'its owners' below. Readers of the Gospels probably accepted the second of these two possibilities. It is not clear how much significance was originally present in the phrase. Luke omits the remainder of Mk. 11:3 which probably seemed unnecessary to him.

(32) Luke introduces the subject οἱ ἀπεσταλμένοι (cf. 13:34) which stresses the solemn nature of the mission; he states simply that the disciples found everything just as Jesus had said (cf. 22:13, 21, 34; Jn. 14:29); the phrase is brought forward from Mk. 11:6, where it indicates the disciples' obedience to Jesus' command, in order to indicate that his prophecy was fulfilled. The story does not make it clear whether what happened took place in view of a prior arrangement made by Jesus or was a matter of supernatural prescience. A prior arrangement is certainly possible. If animals were kept for the purpose of hiring or lending out to travellers, no such arrangement need have been made, nor is prescience necessary, except if Jesus knows that the animal will be an unridden foal. The story thus gives the impression of prescience, but may originally have referred to a normal human arrangement.

(33) The rest of the story unfolds as Jesus foretold. While the disciples were untying the animal to take possession of it (genitive absolute, diff. Mk.), the persons responsible for it (cf. Acts 16:16, diff. Mk., 'some of the bystanders') asked them what they were up to. The question may simply be about the authority of the disciples to impress or borrow the animal, but more probably it arises because of the odd action of the disciples in taking a foal that was not used for riding.

(34) The disciples answer with the words provided by Jesus, and these suffice to satisfy the questioners. It is unlikely that ὁ κύριος here means the actual owner of the animal, and the implication is that a higher authority is recognised who has the right to impress the animal. On the whole, it is most reasonable that Jesus was already known in the area – cf. the tradition of his contacts at Bethany – and that he was understood to be a kind of rabbi with authority to make a request of this kind. The fact that the trivial detail of obtaining the animal is told at such length (cf. 22:7–13) suggests that the Evangelists saw some

importance in it, and this lay in its testimony to the authority and perhaps the prescience of Jesus.

(35) When the animal had been brought to Jesus (ἄγω, as in v. 30), the disciples threw garments upon it, and seated Jesus on it. ἐπιρίπτω (1 Pet. 5:12**) is 'to throw upon', diff. Mk. ἐπιβάλλω (Mt. ἐπιτίθημι); the clothes are apparently meant to do duty for a saddle, and would be needed if the foal was not normally intended to be ridden. Luke alone draws attention to the action of the disciples in mounting Jesus on the animal (diff. Mk. ἐκάθισεν), and the use of ἐπιβιβάζω (10:34; et al.), may reflect the influence of Zc. 9:9 LXX, although it is admittedly the normal word for the process. The act is to be regarded as one of honour; such homage was a sign of kingship (1 Ki. 1:33).

(36) Luke has dropped the vague subject in Mk. (πολλοί), so that it is apparently the disciples who continue to act here (diff. Mt., 'the crowd'), and he inserts a genitive absolute phrase to bring out the fact that Jesus actually proceeded on the foal. While he did so, the disciples strewed their garments on the way. ὑποστρώννυμι** is 'to spread something out beneath' (cf. Jos. Ant. 9:111; 18:204), diff. Mk. στρώννυμι; αὐτῶν (ℵ D f1 f13 pm; TR; UBS; Diglot) is perhaps more likely than ἑαυτῶν (A B W Θ al; Synopsis) in view of the usage in v. 35. The placing of garments for the animal to walk over is another expression of respect, perhaps indicating willingness to let a ruler trample on one's own property; cf. 2 Ki. 9:13; Jos. Ant. 9:111; SB I, 844f.; Plutarch, Cato Mi. 7; Acts of Pilate 2 (NTA I, 451). Luke makes no mention of the use of palm branches; was their use not regarded as part of the kingly symbolism?

(37) Luke's account here differs considerably from Mark's, and raises the question whether another source is being used. The use of ἐγγίζω (repeated from v. 29) and the genitive absolute indicates a Lucan connection with what precedes, but the combination with πρός (instead of the simple dative) is surprising (Schramm, 147); πρός with dative is rare (Mk. 5:11; Jn. 18:16; 20:11f.; Rev. 1:13**). κατάβασις** is 'descent, road leading down', and the description indicates that the procession has reached the summit of the Mount of Olives and is now beginning the descent, with Jerusalem spread out before it. The use of the phrase τὸ ὄρος τῶν ἐλαιῶν is not Lucan (cf. 19:29, diff. Mk.; Schramm, 147). ἤρξαντο is plural with a collective noun as subject (Mt. 21:8; Acts 6:7; 25:24; Jn. 7:49; Rev. 8:9; 9:18; BD 134[c]); the construction is Lucan (Acts 25:24 is a close parallel). Luke's phrase, 'the whole crowd of disciples' (cf. 8:37; et al.), is clearer than Mark's 'those who preceded and those who followed', and could be regarded as an improvement of it. The motif of praising God is also Lucan, but may be from a source (cf. 2:13, 20; 19:37; Acts 2:47; 3:8f.), and the language of the rest of the verse is Lucan. The δύναμεις which the disciples have seen are simply those reported earlier in the Gospel (but cf. Mt. 21:14; Jn. 12:17 for a similar motif). Hence there is no need to adopt the variant γινομένων (D

r¹; Creed, 241). The verse is reminiscent of the praise which greeted
Jesus on his entry into the world at Bethlehem in Galilee from the angels
and the shepherds (2:13, 20); his entry to Jerusalem is hailed in the same
way by those who have seen what has already happened.

(38) What now follows is to be understood in its Lucan context as
the wording of the praise expressed to God for the mighty acts done by
Jesus, although the saying itself does not at first sight have this character. Luke has omitted the Hebrew word ὡσαννά at both the beginning
and the end of the saying; it would not have been intelligible to gentile
readers. He has the formula 'Blessed is he who comes in the name of the
Lord', which is based on Ps. 118:26 (117:26), and which was used as a
greeting for pilgrims. In the Ps., however, it appears to have been
originally a greeting addressed to the king as he approached the temple
to worship God (G. W. Anderson, PC, 439). This original force reappears in Lk. with the addition of ὁ βασιλεύς (the text is confused: ὁ
ἐρχόμενος ὁ βασιλεύς is read by B; UBS; Synopsis; Diglot; ὁ ἐρχόμενος,
D W pc it; ὁ βασιλεύς, ℵ* pc Origen; ὁ ἐρχόμενος βασιλεύς, ℵᶜ A L Γ
Δ Θ f1 f13 pm; TR. Metzger, 169f., regards the reading of B as the most
difficult; the others can be explained as assimilation to the LXX and the
parallels. The presence of βασιλεύς in the text is unquestionable; D adds
it in a separate phrase). Several motifs may be involved here. Luke may
be following a tradition also attested in Jn. 12:13, which alludes to Zc.
9:9 (cf. Lindars, 114f.). He has replaced a reference to the coming
kingdom of David with a reference to the coming of the king (Burger,
112–114). For Luke the kingdom is not yet to appear (19:11) but the
one who is to be king is at hand. The wording (without ὁ βασιλεύς) also
appears earlier in 13:35, but we argued that this verse was probably not
prophetic of the present occasion, since here it is the disciples from
Galilee who utter the greeting and not the people of Jerusalem; the
significance of the present scene is that the prophecy in 13:35 is *not*
fulfilled at this point, as the next verse makes clear. The greeting closes
with an enigmatic couplet, peculiar to Lk. and reminiscent of, but
significantly different from 2:14. It replaces the Marcan 'hosanna in the
highest (places) i.e. in heaven', which is to be regarded as a 'summons to
strike up songs of praise in the heavenly heights' (E. Lohse, TDNT IX,
683). Hence δόξα ἐν ὑψίστοις is to be understood as an ascription of
praise in view of the coming of the king. The praise is regarded as addressed to Jesus by J. H. Davies, 'The Acclamation in Luke 19:38' (unpublished paper), who notes that to ascribe glory to Jesus is especially
Lucan (9:26; 24:26), but this seems less probable than the view that
glory is ascribed to God, since this is what is meant in Mk., and it is
demanded by v. 37. The preceding phrase is difficult (ἐν οὐράνῳ εἰρήνη,
ℵ B L; inverted by rell; TR; Diglot, but the chiastic form is surely
original). To speak of peace in heaven is unusual; contrast 2:14 where
the effect of the Messiah's birth is peace on earth among men, i.e. salvation. W. Foerster, TDNT II, 413, takes the view that salvation is present

and fashioned in heaven (cf. Rev. 12:10; 19:1); it is not yet present in Jerusalem (cf. 19:39–44; Klostermann, 189; Ellis, 225). H. Traub's explanation of the relation to 2:14 (TDNT V, 519 n. 169) is not perspicacious. J. H. Davies suggests that peace is given to Jesus in order that he may give it to men (cf. the Spirit, Acts 2:33), but this does not explain why this happens in heaven. Perhaps the phrase means that there is peace in heaven, i.e. between God and man as a result of the exaltation of Jesus as king (cf. Acts 10:36), or more probably the force of the saying is the same as in Rev. 7:10 where God is praised by the ascription of salvation to him, i.e. he is praised as the author of salvation. The same liturgical use is present here, so that ἐν οὐράνῳ is virtually a periphrasis for the name of God. The coming of the king who brings peace (Zc. 9:9f.) is the appropriate occasion for ascribing praise to God as the author of peace.

(39) Although the actors so far have been the disciples of Jesus, there is an audience, among which are to be found some Pharisees (for ἀπὸ τοῦ ὄχλου cf. 9:38). It is possible that they are to be regarded as friendly to Jesus, as elsewhere in Lk. (7:36; 11:37; 14:1; possibly 13:31–33), but their advice is unacceptable. They think that Jesus should restrain the fervour of his disciples. They may possibly have feared for Jesus' safety (and their own skins) if such outbursts led to a messianic demonstration. Or they may have felt simply that Jesus should not tolerate such extravagant and (in their eyes) unwarranted sentiments. The same motif appears in Mt. 21:14–16 where the chief priests and scribes are annoyed by the messianic acclamation of the children in the temple. A common tradition may lie behind the two Gospels here, especially as a similar motif occurs yet again in Jn. 12:18f. Cf. Bultmann, 34, who holds that an 'ideal scene' is being described.

(40) Jesus' reply is peculiar to Lk. After λέγω ὑμῖν the conjunction ὅτι is added in א A D Γ Δ f1 pm; TR; Diglot. The use of ἐάν with the future indicative is rare (1 Thes. 3:8; 1 Jn. 5:15; MH I, 168, 187; BD 372^la 373²). For σιωπάω cf. 1:20; Acts 18:9; Mk. 10:48; et al.; see also 18:39 note. The force of the saying as a whole is uncertain: 1. It is no more possible for the disciples to keep silent than it is for stones to speak. 2. If the disciples keep silent, the stones will be forced to proclaim the mighty acts of God instead of them (cf. Grundmann, 367f.). 3. Hab. 2:11 was taken up in the Targum and rabbinic writings to indicate that the stones could cry out against those who do evil (SB II, 253). This may be taken to refer to the stones crying out against the disciples who would sin by keeping silent (J. Jeremias, TDNT IV, 270; cf. Gn. 4:10; Job. 31:38, or, 4. to the stones crying out against the people who rejected Jesus and silenced the disciples (cf. Schlatter, 409f. who thinks that the reference is not to the stones speaking, but to the testimony of their being overthrown in AD 70). The portents in Jos. Bel. 6:288–300 are of a different kind. In any case, the saying serves to underline the truth of the messianic acclamation in v. 38. Its authenticity was strongly defended

by J. Weiss, 501. The Jewish terminology is a sign that it is not a Lucan creation, and a traditional origin is likely; it may well be authentic.

c. The Fate of Jerusalem (19:41–48)

This brief section bridges the gap between Jesus' approach to Jerusalem and his teaching ministry in the temple, and falls into two parts. In the first, Jesus is still outside Jerusalem and weeps over the prospect that lies before the city which, he knows, will reject his message. Nevertheless, Jerusalem is given its chance to hear the message, and in the second scene Jesus enters the temple and cleanses it of avaricious practices so that it may be a place of prayer to God and teaching for the people.

In order to accommodate the first scene, Luke has removed Mark's story of the cursing of the fig tree, whose two parts bracketed the story of the cleansing of the temple (Mk. 11:12–14, 20–25). He has already related a parable which might be considered an equivalent to this dramatic parable (13:6–9), and the new material expresses the same theme. At the same time, the cleansing of the temple appears more clearly as a prelude to Jesus' teaching there.

i. Jesus Weeps over Jerusalem 19:41–44

As Jesus sees Jerusalem spread out before him, he weeps over the destruction which will come over it unawares. The city could have learned the way of peace from his teaching, but it would fail to recognise in his coming the gracious presence of God offering a last opportunity of repentance; the attitude of the Pharisees (vs. 39f.) would prevail. There would be a different kind of visitation in due course, a judgment in which enemies would destroy the city stone by stone.

The section is peculiar to Lk., but is unlikely to be a Lucan composition. The language shows at least one Aramaic feature (v. 44), and the theme is found elsewhere in Luke's special material (cf. 13:34f.; 23:28–31, and possibly 21:5f., 20–22). The material may have formed part of an apocalyptic discourse, traces of which can be seen in 21. The thought is dependent on Je. 6:6–21 (Hastings, 116–120) and Is. 29:1–4, and it is therefore unnecessary to hold (with Bultmann, 130; Wilson, 71) that it was composed after AD 70: 'To describe these verses as a Christian composition after the event is the kind of extravagance that brings sober criticism into disrepute' (Manson, *Sayings*, 320). This comment may itself be exaggerated; but, although the passage may have been edited in the light of AD 70 (J. Weiss, 501), there is no reason to doubt that the Christian interpretation of the fall of Jerusalem as the outcome of failure to accept the message of Jesus goes back to Jesus himself (Ellis, 226).

See Manson, *Sayings*, 319–322.

(41) The connecting verse is probably Lucan (ὡς, ἐγγίζω, κλαίω (6:21; *et al.*) with ἐπί, 23:28). Only here and in Jn. 11:35 is Jesus said to weep.

(42) The sorrow of Jesus over the impending fate of Jerusalem (cf. 23:28f.) is matched by that of Jeremiah (Je. 8:18ff.; 15:5; cf. 2 Ki. 8:11f.). ὅτι is *recitativum*. It is followed by the protasis of a present, unfulfilled condition, with the apodosis suppressed (BD 482; cf. Nu. 22:29; Jos. 9:7; Is. 48:18; Jn. 6:62; Acts 23:9). The force is: 'If only you knew now . . ., the future would hold something better for you, *or* it would be pleasing to me'. For ἐν τῇ ἡμέρᾳ ταύτῃ καὶ σύ (‭א‬ B L 579 *pc*) there are the variants καὶ σὺ ἐν ταύτῃ τῇ ἡμέρᾳ (Θ *pc*); καὶ σὺ καί γε ἐν ταύτῃ τῇ ἡμέρᾳ ((A D f1 *al*) W f13 *pm* lat; TR): Metzger, 170, argues that καί γε (Acts 2:18; Acts 17:27) is a secondary addition. With the meaning 'at least' (BD 439²), it would stress that this was Jerusalem's last opportunity after she had rejected many previously. The force of καὶ σύ, 'even you', may possibly be to draw attention to the significance of 'Jerusalem' as the city of peace (Heb. 7:1f.; cf. Je. 15:5; Pss. 122:6; 147:12–14), but since the city is not named in the context this allusion must remain doubtful.

τὰ πρὸς εἰρήνην (14:33) here signifies 'the things that make for your peace' (σου is added by A W Γ Δ f1 *pm*; TR; *Diglot*; and σοι by D f13 157 *pc* lat; cf. Metzger, 170), i.e. for salvation (W. Foerster, TDNT II, 413). Possibly there is an allusion to the Jerusalem which thought it had peace when in reality it had none (Je. 6:14). νῦν δέ is 'but as it is'. κρύπτω (18:34; Mt. 11:25) may refer to the action of God who has given up the city that has for long rejected those who were sent to it (13:34; 11:50f.).

(43) The ὅτι . . . clause is to be taken with εἰ ἔγνως . . .: 'if only you knew . . ., for the consequences of your ignorance are fearful'. For ἡμέραι cf. 5:35; 17:22; 21:6; 23:29; and for ἥκω cf. 13:35. The addition of ἐπὶ σέ is unusual and indicates the menacing character of the future period. καί is equivalent to 'when' (BD 442⁴; cf. Mk. 15:25; Lk. 23:44; Mt. 26:45; Heb. 8:8). παρεμβάλλω**, 'to throw up against', is a military term, and χάραξ**, is 'stake, palisade' (cf. Is. 29:3 LXX; Je. 6:6 MT); for the adoption of this manoeuvre by the Romans cf. Jos. Bel. 5:262ff., 491ff.: when the palisade erected by the Romans was burned down by the Jews, it was replaced by a stone siege-dyke. This latter may be referred to by περικυκλόω**, 'to surround, encircle' (Jos. 6:13; 2 Ki. 6:14; cf. Lk. 21:20; Is. 29:3), but this verb may simply stress that the siege-works extend all round the city. συνέχω (4:38; *et al.*) here means 'to press hard upon' (2 Mac. 9:2); πάντοθεν is 'from all sides' (Mk. 1:45; Heb. 9:4**).

(44) ἐδαφίζω** (here with an Attic future) can mean 'to dash something to the ground' (Ps. 137 (136):9; Ho. 10:14) or 'to raze something to the ground' (Is. 3:26). Here the two meanings may be combined (AG), in which case τὰ τέκνα is a second object, or the second

meaning is intended, and καὶ τὰ τέκνα . . . is to be taken as a circumstantial clause: 'while your children are in you' (Manson, *Sayings*, 320). The τέκνα are the inhabitants of the city (1 Mac. 1:38; *et al.*; A. Oepke, TDNT V, 639), but the destruction of children is a traditional feature of descriptions of siege (Ho. 13:16; Na. 3:10) and this idea is possibly present here. Not a stone will be left in position; cf. 2 Sa. 17:13, and Lk. 21:6 par. Mk. 13:2. The active form ἀφήσουσιν, diff. 21:6 passive, may be due to assimilation to the preceding verb forms, but in any case it is probably a sign of use of a source: Luke had no need to conflate with Mk. 13:2 here. For λίθον ἐπὶ λίθον ἐν σοί (א B L 33 *pc*), *Diglot* has ἐν σοὶ λίθον ἐπὶ λίθον, possibly a misprint for ἐν σοὶ λίθον ἐπὶ λίθῳ (A C W (Γ) Δ f13 *pl*; TR). For ἀνθ᾽ ὧν cf. 1:20; *et al.* γινώσκω is here 'to recognise', and for καιρός cf. 12:56. ἐπισκοπή is 'visitation', the coming of God whether for good (Gn. 50:24f.; Ex. 3:16; Wis. 2:20; 3:7; Job 10:12; 29:4; *et al.*) or for judgment (Je. 6:15; 10:15; Is. 29:6; cf. 1QS 3:14, 18; 4:6, 11, 19, 26; Braun, *Qumran* I, 92; H. W. Beyer, TDNT II, 606–608); cf. 1:78; 7:16; 1 Pet. 2:12. Here the visitation is intended to be the occasion of salvation as proclaimed by Jesus; unrecognised as such, the same visitation becomes the basis for a judgment yet to follow.

ii. The Cleansing of the Temple 19:45–46

The Lord's visitation (v. 44) is concerned with the temple, perhaps as an intended fulfilment of Mal. 3:1 (a text which curiously is not linked with the incident). Jesus enters the sacred precincts and drives out the people carrying on trade in the Court of the Gentiles, alleging that they have made the temple into a haunt of robbers rather than a place of prayer.

The story is related with the utmost brevity and is an abbreviation of Mk. 11:15–17. The details about the variety of pursuits carried on in the temple disappear, as does Mark's stress on the place of the gentiles in the temple (cf. Mt.). There is no suggestion of any future use of the temple. The incident has become the prelude and necessary preparation which preceded the teaching ministry of Jesus in the temple, and it thus has less significance in its own right (E. Trocmé*, 4, 6f.). At the same time it also serves to provide part of the motive for the action taken against Jesus by the Jewish leaders (v. 47; Roloff, *Kerygma*, 101f.).

Bultmann's view (36) that Mk. 11:17 is an addition to vs. 15f. by the early church to bring out the significance of the scene has found many adherents. He argued that the climax of the scene lay in the action of Jesus, but it is hard to see how the narrative could have been transmitted without some explanation of its significance. Hence it has been suspected that some other saying may originally have concluded the narrative (cf. Schweizer, *Markus*, 131; C. K. Barrett*, 19f.). The reasons for such surgery are to be found in tensions in the narrative. For Mark himself, the context suggests that he saw the incident as prophetic of the destruction of the temple (C. K. Barrett*, 13f.). But the incident itself appears to represent a purification of the temple to accomplish its proper task. Was Jesus perhaps giving a warning to Israel that if it did not reform itself judgment would follow? In any case, there is no real conflict here between the action and its interpretation. C. K. Barrett*, 14–18, however, thinks that ληστής must refer to nationalist rebels, and that the saying refers to the presence of violent men in the temple who were in effect making it into a nationalist stronghold (as it became during the siege of Jerusalem). But, Barrett continues, this comment hardly fits an attack on the petty dishonesties of the shopkeepers in the temple. Hence the saying should be separated from the incident. It may be based on a genuine word of Jesus, consistent with his lamentations over Jerusalem, spoken on a different occasion. E. Trocmé*, 15, draws attention to the unlikelihood that Jesus could have made a serious pronouncement in the chaos following his action, which he interprets as a 'zealous' action on behalf of the law.

Barrett's case rests on his interpretation of ληστής in the light of its usage by Josephus. But the word can be used of an ordinary robber or brigand, and there is no evidence that the corresponding Hebrew word meant a nationalist rebel. The word is drawn here from Je. 7:11 and has no nationalist connections. If it is inappropriate to use it for thieving traders, this arises from the reapplication of Je. 7:11 to a new situation. Thus the alleged tension between the incident and the comment does not exist. It then remains an open question whether the incident and the comment belong to the same occasion or not.

The historicity of the incident has been doubted. While there is no absolute proof that crooked dealing was being carried on in the temple, this is by no means improbable. But it is possible that it was simply the use of the temple court for trading that attracted Jesus' ire, if we accept the suggestion of V. Eppstein* that the introduction of traders to the temple was a comparative novelty. It is more difficult to see how the action could have taken place without some intervention by the temple police. (It is not clear whether the Roman garrison in the overlooking Fortress of Antonia would have intervened in a minor riot in the temple.) If, however, there was some difference of opinion among the Jewish authorities over the matter (as Eppstein suggests), and if Jesus had some measure of popular support, the authorities may have considered it wisest not to act summarily against him; they certainly did not let the action pass without comment, and it may be that Jesus' statement (Mk. 11:17) was addressed to the officials who came to ask, 'What's all this going on here?'

See V. Eppstein, 'The Historicity of the Gospel Account of the Cleansing of the Temple', ZNW 55, 1964, 42–58; E. Trocme, 'L'expulsion des marchands du temple', NTS 15, 1968–69, 1–22; C. K. Barrett, 'The House of Prayer and the Den of Thieves', in Ellis, Jesus, 13–20.

(45) Luke omits Mark's opening remark about Jesus' entry into Jerusalem, which is unnecessary in his narrative, since Jesus goes straight from the entry to the temple, whereas in Mk. the incident of the cursing of the fig-tree outside Jerusalem intervenes. The rest of the verse follows Mk. word for word. Luke refers merely to those who were selling in the temple. The Court of the Gentiles was occupied by merchants selling the requisites for sacrifice – animals, wine, oil, salt and so on (cf. SB I, 850–852). The text is expanded in many MSS (ἐν αὐτῷ καὶ ἀγοράζοντας, A C W Θ pl; TR; Diglot; an even longer addition is found in D pc it).

(46) Instead, Luke passes straight to the comment of Jesus on the state of the temple. It is formed from two quotations, the first from Is. 56:7. Mark quotes it verbatim from the LXX, but Luke has altered the wording slightly with καὶ ἔσται instead of κληθήσεται. There is no very obvious motive for the change (cf. Gundry, 19; Holtz, 163–165). God's house is intended to be a house of prayer. Luke omits reference to the gentiles, probably because he is aware that in fact the temple did not become such, and he did not want to make Jesus the author of a false prophecy. Gundry, 19, suggests that Matthew and Luke follow a pre-Marcan tradition of the wording. The temple is to be for people like the tax-collector who came to pray and seek forgiveness (18:11–14). But Jewish avarice has destroyed this purpose and made the temple, in Jeremiah's words (7:11), into a cave or den (σπήλαιον) for robbers (λῃστής, 10:30). The implication is that the legitimate sale of sacrificial victims was accompanied by money-grabbing and commercial rivalry.

It is not clear whether Luke regards the action as having any deeper significance. The cleansing of the temple was expected in the end time (Mal. 3:1ff.; Zc. 14:21; cf. Ezk. 40–48) and hence could be regarded as a messianic sign, but Luke makes so little of the incident that it is hard to believe that he saw this significance in it. He may well have played down the details of the action in order to avoid any suspicion that Jesus was a man of violence. Nor is it clear whether he regards Jesus' action as prophetic of the destruction of the temple, although it is likely enough that he saw this nuance; the coming of Jesus to Jerusalem signifies judgment upon a people which rejects the Messiah and his message. The implication of the following scene is that the temple became briefly the place of teaching by the Messiah to the expectant people, but the Jewish leaders could not tolerate what was going on.

iii. Jesus teaches in the Temple 19:47–48

The introduction to Jesus' ministry in Jerusalem concludes with an account of his teaching in the temple, the opposition that this raised, and the popular support which it enjoyed. These points are then developed in the ensuing section which shows what Jesus taught and how it was received. The present paragraph has a role similar to that of 4:14f. at the beginning of the Galilean ministry.

The narrative is modelled on Mk. 11:18, but the wording has been considerably altered to bring out the points that Luke considered important. There is no reason to suspect use of another source.

(47) The opening clause which describes the daily teaching of Jesus in the temple is based on Mk. 14:49 par. Lk. 22:53 (omitting διδάσκων) and is repeated at 21:37. Thus a historical basis is provided for the later descriptions of what Jesus did in Jerusalem; the periphrastic verb and καθ' ἡμέραν, both from Mk., indicate that Luke is describing what Jesus proceeded to do for several days. He emphasises that Jesus' task in Jerusalem was teaching – there is no mention of healing, since the teaching is largely condemnatory and not a presentation of the gospel. Conzelmann, 71, sees here Jesus taking 'possession' of the temple. Such an act leads to opposition. The chief priests (9:22) and scribes join forces together with the rather belatedly added leaders of the people; for πρῶτος in this sense cf. Acts 13:50; 25:2; 28:17; Mk. 6:21. Presumably the lay elders of the people, the third group in the sanhedrin, are meant (for the use of the word cf. Jos. Ant. 4:140; et al.; W. Michaelis, TDNT V, 866). Alternatively the phrase stands in apposition to the preceding ones, but the parallel in 20:1 makes this unlikely. ζητέω probably refers to looking for a way of getting rid of Jesus rather than simply making up their minds to get rid of him; the decision is regarded as having already been taken, although it is not clear when it was taken.

(48) For the moment, however, it cannot be put into effect. The people must first hear Jesus, and their support prevents police measures being taken. For εὑρίσκω cf. 5:19 note, and for the τὸ τί . . . construction see 1:62. The deliberative subjunctive of the original question (τί ποιήσωμεν) is retained in the indirect form. λαός, diff. Mk. ὄχλος, is the Jewish people as God's people, the nation apart from its leaders; it is favourable to Jesus at this stage (cf. G. Rau, 'Das Volk in der lukanischen Passionsgeschichte. Eine Conjectur zu Lk. 23, 13', ZNW 56, 1965, 41–51).

ἐκκρεμάννυμι** is used in the middle 'to hang on' (cf. Gn. 44:30; BD 93). For the metaphorical use cf. Eunapius, Vi. Soph. 29 (cited by AG) and Virgil, Aen. 4:79, '*pendetque iterum narrantis ab ore*.' The expression is more positive than Mark's use of ἐκπλήσσομαι.

Mark concludes the section by noting that Jesus went outside the city (11:19); Luke retains this detail for 21:37, and proceeds straightaway to give characteristic examples of Jesus' teaching. He is not interested in Mark's chronological scheme.

d. Teaching in the Temple (20:1 – 21:4)

From now on Jesus carries on his ministry of teaching the people in the temple (Lagrange, 505). It takes place amid continued questioning by the Jewish leaders, and it is the details of these encounters which give content to the narrative. Three times deputations approach Jesus and question him about his teaching, seeking to find out what authority was claimed by him and where he stood in relation to the teaching of the Torah (20:1–8, 20–26, 27–40). Then Jesus warns the people against their leaders. He compares the latter to unfaithful tenant farmers (20:9–18); he attacks their teaching about the Messiah (20:41–44), and he denounces the false piety of the scribes which stands in strong contrast to the true piety of a poor widow (20:45–47; 21:1–4).

Throughout this section Luke closely follows Mk., omitting only the question about the chief commandment, to which he has an earlier parallel (Mk. 12:28–34; cf. Lk. 10:25–28). The whole complex may rest on a pre-Marcan collection of conflict stories (Taylor, 101), and this in turn may reflect a rabbinic pattern incorporating four types of question (a question of wisdom, concerning a point of law, Mk. 12:13–17; a mocking question, Mk. 12:18–27; a question on conduct, 12:28–34; and an exegetical question, 12:35–37; these four types of question are found in this particular order in the Passover liturgy; see Daube, 158–169).

i. The Question about Authority 20:1–8

The first episode follows Mk. fairly closely, and there is no real indication that any other source has influenced Luke (*pace* Schramm, 149f.; Schneider, 103, who allow for this possibility). Luke stresses that it was while Jesus was teaching that he was interrupted by a deputation which wished to know the source of his authority for what he was doing. Jesus replied with a counter-question: did they think the authority of John the Baptist was human or divine? This placed them in a quandary, since either answer could lead to difficulties, and they pathetically replied, 'We do not know'. Jesus then refused to enlighten them about his own authority, but the implications of his question were clear enough.

Bultmann, 18f., finds that the basis of the story is a Palestinian apophthegm in Mk. 11:28–30 which closes with Jesus' counter-question, to which the answer and Jesus' rejoinder would have been self-evident: if the opponents admitted that John got his authority from heaven, Jesus could reply, 'So do I'. Then a redactor adopted the Christian viewpoint that the opponents of Jesus did not accept the authority of John and developed the story accordingly. This reconstruction is based upon the two faulty premises that the structure of a Gospel apophthegm *must* be the same as that of a rabbinic debate, and that the Jewish hierarchy *did* accept the authority of John. In fact the elements in the story which Bultmann regards as secondary do fall into a rabbinic pattern (Daube, 151f.). It has been claimed that the reply of the authorities to Jesus is lame (Schweizer, *Markus*, 134f.), but what else could they have said?

Many a government official's answer to an awkward question is equally lame. G. S. Shae* suggests that the original nucleus of the story dealt with Jesus' reply to questions about his credentials for proclaiming the kingdom in a manner different from that of John. But in fact it would appear to be Jesus who brings John into the discussion rather than his opponents; consequently this suggestion remains speculative. Creed, 244f., strongly supports the basic historicity of the story as 'a powerful and coherent whole' (cf. Taylor, 468f.), and this remains the most sensible verdict.

See G. S. Shae, 'The Question on the Authority of Jesus', Nov.T 16, 1974, 1–29.

(1) The opening construction (1:8; *et al.*) suggests to Schramm, 149f., that v. 1a is a fragment from Luke's special source, but this is insufficient evidence. Luke has made the time quite indefinite (5:12; *et al.*) in contrast to Mark who locates the dialogue on the day after the cleansing of the temple. While Mark simply states that Jesus was walking in the temple, both Matthew and Luke say that he was teaching (cf. Mk. 12:35); the deduction was perhaps an obvious one, although περιπατέω does not in itself carry the implication of teaching. Luke characterises the teaching as preaching the gospel: the people (λαός) in Jerusalem are a receptive audience and the gospel is available for them as well as for Galileans. For ἐφίστημι cf. 2:9 note; Acts 4:1; 6:12. In place of ἀρχιερεῖς· the variant ἱερεῖς (A W Γ Δ *al*; TR) is defended by H. Greeven, 'Erwägungen zur synoptischen Textkritik', NTS 6, 1959–60, 281–296, especially 295f., and B. M. Metzger, *The Text of the New Testament*, Oxford, 1964, 238f., but ἀρχιερεῖς is defended by G. D. Kilpatrick, in Ellis, *Neotestamentica*, 203–208, since there are no good reasons for supposing that Luke abandoned his usual terminology, whereas scribes often avoided the plural of ἀρχιερεύς. The listing of the three groups of people indicates that an official deputation of representatives of the sanhedrin is meant, and the grouping suggests that the religious groups took the initiative against Jesus; in Mk., however, all three groups are on the same footing.

(2) The redundant form εἶπαν λέγοντες (ℵ B L (f1) *pc*) is reduced to εἶπαν in C D *pc* f q; *Diglot*; and the word order is altered in *rell*; TR; the UBS text represents the *lectio difficilior*. Luke adds εἰπὸν ἡμῖν to the question (cf. 22:67). For ἐξουσία cf. 4:6; ποῖος indicates that the question concerns the kind of authority possessed by Jesus: was it rabbinic, or prophetic, or what? Hence the question is not tautologous alongside the second one which asks who gave him whatever authority he had. The double question form is Jewish (Mk. 12:14; 13:4; 15:29; Acts 4:7). The antecedent of ταῦτα is as obscure in Lk. as in Mk. Here it may well refer to the teaching of Jesus (19:47; 20:1; Klostermann, 193; J. Weiss, 503). But ποιεῖς refers more to doing something, and it is often suggested that the question originally referred to the cleansing of the temple; indeed it would be surprising if that event had not provoked a reaction (cf.

Jn. 2:13–22). Perhaps the whole activity of Jesus in the temple is in mind.

(3) Jesus replies (ἀποκριθείς, par. Mt., diff. Mk.) with his counter-question. Luke and Matthew both add the emphatic κἀγώ (but this may have been in Mk.; cf. *Diglot*), and substitute λέγω for ἀποκρίνομαι. Luke omits the last part of Jesus' reply, 'and I will tell you by what authority I do these things', with the result that the dialogue is speeded up. The device of a counter-question was frequent in rabbinic discussions, and there is nothing surprising in Jesus' use of it.

(4) Jesus' question is repeated from Mk. with the omission of the final ἀποκρίθητέ μοι (par. Mt.). Did the baptism of John derive its authority from heaven, i.e. God, or from men? Cf. Dn. 4:26; 1 Mac. 3:18; Lk. 15:18, 21; Jn. 3:27. John's authority was that of a prophet, in-deed (according to Jesus) of more than a prophet. Jesus ranges himself beside John, acknowledging the latter's divine commission and implicitly claiming the same for himself.

(5) The narrator pictures the reaction to Jesus' question; the leaders are probably thought of as whispering among themselves. Luke uses συλλογίζομαι**, 'to reason, discuss, debate', diff. Mk. διαλογίζομαι, which he adds in 20:14; Luke likes συν- compounds. The imperfect συνελογίζοντο is read by א C D W Θ *al*; *Diglot*, but this could be due to assimilation to Mk. Luke adds ὅτι *recitativum*. Creed, 244, suggests that the leaders' problem was that if they assented to John's claims, they were obliged to allow that he had fewer credentials than Jesus could show. In fact, however, they realise that if John was a prophet they had failed to accept his message and submit to his baptism. Bultmann, 19, thinks that the use of πιστεύω is Hellenistic, possibly due to Mark himself, but this is purely speculative.

(6) The other horn of the dilemma (ἐὰν δέ, par. Mt., diff. Mk. ἀλλά) arises if they allow John a purely human authority. Mark has a dramatic aposiopesis – 'they feared the people'. This has been worked into the reply by Matthew, and correspondingly Luke makes them express the content of their fear: the people (λαός, diff. Mk. ὄχλος, has a theological nuance) will stone them (καταλιθάζω**, is not found earlier, but καταλιθόω is attested). The penalty for a false prophet was stoning (Dt. 13:1–11); here the same penalty is inflicted on those who deny the legitimacy of a true prophet, and the people appear as the represen-tatives of the true Israel in threatening to stone unworthy leaders. For the people were convinced (πείθω, 11:22; *et al.*; Mk. uses ἔχω) that John was a prophet; Mark's ὄντως is dropped.

(7) The dilemma is insoluble and so the leaders take refuge in ignorance. Luke has put their reply in the indirect form and adds πόθεν (cf. Mt. 21:25 for the same addition).

(8) The final verse follows Mk. almost exactly. Since the leaders will not reply to Jesus' question, he refuses to answer theirs. He had, however, sufficiently implied what the source of his own authority was,

and thus had answered in keeping with his usual policy of not giving clear 'signs' but summoning men to take note of what was happening in his ministry and to draw their own conclusions.

ii. The Parable of the Wicked Husbandmen 20:9–19

Luke has made it clear, following Mk., how he has understood this parable: it is directed against the religious leaders of the people (20:19). It is addressed to the people, and Jesus takes the initiative in issuing this warning to them against their leaders. The parable follows essentially the same lines as in Mk. It is a description of tenants – note how the motif of stewardship once again is prominent – who refuse to pay proper respect to their employer, but attempt to gain possession of his property for themselves, and are ready to go to any lengths, even murder, in order to do so. There is no indication that they have been dilatory in their duty of looking after the vineyard: on the contrary, they have presumably been so successful in tending it that they are unwilling to share the profits with anybody else. But such rank insubordination will bring its own reward: the owner will turn them out and let out the vineyard to other tenants. The lesson is then drawn with the aid of a quotation from Ps. 118 (117):22 which is followed by an OT allusion peculiar to Lk. from Dn. 2:34f., 45f. The point is made that the messenger rejected by the tenants is indeed the person favoured by God, so that a person's destiny is determined by his attitude to him.

The context and content of the parable indicate that Luke and the tradition which he followed recognised Jesus to be the son who would be put to death and also identified the stone with him. The parable itself contains some allegorical reference to the history of Israel and the rejection of God's messengers by its leaders, although this element is much less prominent in Lk. than in Mk. and Mt. In this respect Luke is closer to G. Thomas 65.

It is a moot point how far these allegorical features belong to the original form of the parable. There can be no doubt that there has been allegorical expansion in the Gospels, as a comparison between them demonstrates (Jeremias, *Parables*, 70–77). But was the original parable basically allegorical? The case for allegory has been strongly defended by Kümmel, *Heilsgeschehen*, 207–217 (cf. Grässer, 34). There are two aspects to the question.

On the one hand, there is the question whether the parable can be explained as a reasonably coherent picture, or must be regarded as an unnatural and fantastic story of something that could not happen in real life; i.e. is the story a real story, or has it been constructed in order to serve as an allegory, without due regard to what was possible in real life? This question can be regarded as convincingly answered in the first sense as the result of research by various scholars (especially Dodd, *Parables*, 93–98; Jeremias, *Parables*, 175f.; E. Bammel*; Derrett, 286–312; M.

Hengel*, 9–31). They have shown that the general background of the story fits in with known conditions in Palestine. Many estates were let out by absentee landlords, and in certain circumstances the tenants might attempt to take possession of the property for themselves by fair means or foul. Even the sending of the son, which is the most obviously allegorical feature in the story, will fit into this framework. Accordingly, what we have is a real story, but one that could easily lend itself to allegorisation.

On the other hand, there is the question whether Jesus would have told a story with allegorical features. It is impossible to work back to a version of the story which had no allegorical possibilities, and consequently it is often denied that Jesus could have told the parable, especially since it allegorically gives him a position of divine sonship, which in any case would have been unintelligible to a Jewish audience. But the fact that divine sonship would not have been an obvious allegorical key to the parable for the Jews speaks rather in favour of its authenticity, and the suggestion that Jesus did speak in this way to warn the Jews of the consequences of refusing to hear his message is by no means unlikely; moreover, M. Hengel*, 35f., has shown good reason why the parable is not to be assigned to a *Sitz im Leben* in the early church.

It seems possible, therefore, indeed probable, that we have here an authentic parable of Jesus which had obvious allegorical possibilities; these were developed in the tradition, but in such a way that the genuine latent thrust of the parable was expressed more clearly for a Christian audience.

In the above discussion it has been assumed that Luke is here following Mk. Schramm, 150–167, gives a detailed argument that an independent version of the parable, also attested in G. Thomas 65, has also been used by Lk.; the point of this parable was the determination with which the tenants strove to get hold of the inheritance, and the lesson was that men should display the same determination to inherit the kingdom of God. A very similar understanding of the parable, based on the view that G. Thomas offers the earliest form of the tradition, is defended by J. D. Crossan*. This interpretation depends upon the assumption that G. Thomas is based on primitive tradition, independent of the Synoptic tradition (Schramm, 10–21), an assumption which remains uncertain (B. Dehandschutter*; K. R. Snodgrass*). Further, the version in Thomas seems to me to have the same basic allegorical possibilities as the Synoptic version. The theory that Luke had an independent form of the parable remains doubtful.

See Dodd, *Parables*, 93–98; E. Bammel, 'Das Gleichnis von den bösen Winzern (Mk. 12, 1–9) und das jüdische Erbrecht', RIDA 6, 1959, 11–17; Kümmel, *Heilsgeschehen*, 207–217 (originally as 'Das Gleichnis von den bösen Weingärtnern (Mk. 12, 1–9) ', in *Aux Sources de la Tradition Chrétienne* (Mélanges offerts à M. Goguel), Neuchâtel/Paris, 1950, 120–131); Jeremias, *Parables*, 70–77; Derrett, 286–312 (originally as 'Fresh Light on the Wicked Vinedressers', RIDA 10, 1963, 11–41); Schramm, 150–167; J. D. Crossan, 'The Parable of the

Wicked Husbandmen', JBL 90, 1971, 451–465; J. Blank, 'Die Sendung des Sohnes. Zur
christologischen Bedeutung des Gleichnisses von den bösen Winzern Mk. 12, 1–12', in Gnilka,
Neues Testament, 11–41; B. Dehandschutter, 'La parabole des vignerons homicides (Mc., XII,
1–12) et l'évangile selon Thomas', in Sabbe, 203–219; K. R. Snodgrass, 'The Parable of the
wicked husbandmen: is the Gospel of Thomas version the original?' NTS 21, 1974–75,
142–144.

(9) The introduction has been reworded by Luke. Kilpatrick, 198,
prefers the Semitic word order λέγειν πρὸς τὸν λαόν, attested by Q *pc* lat
cop sy[p]; *Diglot*, but the external evidence is weak. In Mk. Jesus' audience
appears to be the Jewish leaders, although Mk. 12:12 implies the
presence of the people; in Lk. Jesus is represented as speaking to the
people about the leaders. Luke has παραβολή sing., diff. Mk. ἐν παραβ-
ολαῖς which indicates the manner of his teaching; for the use of οὗτος cf.
4:23; 20:19.

The parable begins with ἄνθρωπός τις (A W Θ f13 *pc* sy; (UBS); τις
is omitted by *rell*; cf. Metzger, 170f.); the word order (par. Mt.) differs
from Mk. and resembles that in the parables in Luke's special material
(10:30; 12:16; 15:11; 16:1, 19). Schramm, 154–156, finds here evidence
of a parallel source; but his case rests on cumulative evidence, and this
detail by itself could be due to Luke following the style found in other
parables. For ἀμπελών and φυτεύω see 13:6. Luke does not have the
detailed description of the fence, winepress and tower found in Mk. and
Mt. (cf. Is. 5:1f.). This weakens the identification of the vineyard with
Israel. The omission may be deliberate, since the allegory is hard to
carry through in detail. This does not, however, mean that it is not an
original part of the story, since such difficulties are common in the construction of allegories. The simpler form may claim originality
(Schramm, 156–158), and this would support the view that Luke knew a
variant form of the parable to that in Mk. But abbreviation of apparently
irrelevant information is equally possible, and the significance of the
details in Mk. is to show that the story is about a newly-planted vineyard
– a factor which may be important for the subsequent development of
the story (Derrett, 289ff.). The owner in any case let out the vineyard to
tenant farmers. ἐκδίδομαι is 'to farm out, let out for advantage' (Mk.
12:1; Mt. 21:33, 41[**]; ἐξέδετο is a vernacular form of ἐξέδοτο
(*Synopsis*); cf. BD 94[1]). γεωργός is 'farmer, husbandman' (20:10, 14,
16[*]). Thereupon the owner departed (cf. 15:13; Mt. 25:14f.) for a long
time (χρόνους ἱκανούς is not found elsewhere in Lk., but cf. 8:27, 29).
The picture is that of an absentee landlord, and the probability is that he
resided outside Galilee (Jeremias, *Parables*, 75); M. Hengel[*], 21f., notes
that anywhere outside Galilee (even Judaea) would count as 'foreign
parts'. There is good evidence that substantial estates in Galilee were
owned by such people. In such cases agreements were made covering
the amount of rent in kind to be paid by the tenants; the remainder of the
produce was at their disposal, but in the early years of a vineyard this
would not amount to very much since it took four years before the vines
reached maturity (cf. Derrett, 289–295). Allegorically, the 'long time'

has been thought to reflect the delay of the parousia (Grässer, 113), but the reference, if any, is rather to the long period during and since the sending of the prophets, since there is no reference to the parousia or the final judgment in the parable (Grundmann, 372 n.).

(10) The use of the absolute καιρῷ (preceded by ἐν in A W Γ Δ f13 pm; TR; Diglot; ἐν τῷ is added by C Θ pc), diff. Mk., seems to be idiomatic for 'at (harvest) time' (cf. 12:42). It would be normal to send one slave to get the owner's share (ἀπὸ τοῦ καρποῦ is partitive) of the produce, since trouble would not be expected; it was necessary for the owner to do so, since failure to collect the rent would give the tenants a chance to claim possession for themselves in due course. For ἵνα with future indicative cf. 14:10. Luke has δίδωμι, diff. Mk. λαμβάνω, perhaps stressing the free response expected by the owner (cf. Mt. 21:41; Schramm, 161, argues that the motif, found in G. Thomas, is from Luke's tradition). The repetition of οἱ γεωργοί in the second part of the verse, par. Mt., seems unnecessary. The tenants not only sent him away (ἐξαποστέλλω, 1:53; et al., diff. Mk.) empty-handed but gave him a beating as well (δέρω, 12:47). Derrett, 296f., suggests that the beating was because the messenger refused to go away without receiving the rent; he also claims that κενός implies that the messenger was robbed of his possessions – the tenants felt entitled to some pay from the master, since the vineyard was as yet producing very little. This is speculative, but makes good sense of the story.

(11) The rest of the story is told in similar terms, the accounts of the three messengers having been stylised by Luke or his source. For προστίθημι cf. 3:20 note; it means 'to do another act of the same kind'. πέμπω is a literary variant for ἀποστέλλω, diff. Mk.; the word order ἕτερον πέμψαι is reversed in C W Γ Δ Θ f1 f13 pm; TR; Diglot (cf. 20:9 note for this more Semitic order). The second servant may have been sent at next year's harvest, in the hope that the tenants' attitude might have changed as the result of a better harvest. It had not done so, for the messenger was again beaten and treated to insults (ἀτιμάζω; Acts 5:41); Luke has avoided Mark's difficult κεφαλαιόω, and paraphrased in the light of the previous verse.

(12) The process was repeated a third time, possibly again after a year's interval. This servant too (καὶ τοῦτον) was attacked. Whereas in Mk. he is killed, here he is simply wounded (τραυματίζω Acts 19:16**; cf. τραῦμα, 10:34**) and thrown out. The language suggests Lucan modification of Mk., so that the supreme act of defiance is reserved for the son. The tenants had now refused to pay rent three times over, and the idea was developing that they could claim possession of the vineyard.

Mark relates how the owner sent many other slaves who were maltreated by the tenants. This detail is omitted by Luke, whereas Matthew has simply two groups of slaves. The differing forms represent various attempts at allegorisation, and many commentators think that

Mark has added an allegorical reference to the prophets. Luke has either omitted it, as superfluous, or followed a different version of the story which retained a primitive simplicity. Mark's grammar is so rough here as to be reason enough for Luke's omission.

(13) Only one move was left to the owner, short of coming himself to deal with the situation. He must send somebody with greater legal powers than a slave possessed in order to deal with the matter conclusively. His son would be appropriately qualified. So the owner is represented as soliloquising what to do. The soliloquy is a common feature in Lucan parables, but here it is taken over from Mk., brought forward and enlarged, so that what appears as narrative in Mk. becomes direct discourse here. It is unlikely that another source has been utilised here (*pace* Schramm, 162f.). ὁ κύριος τοῦ ἀμπελῶνος is borrowed from Mk. 12:9. The deliberative question τί ποιήσω is also found at 12:17; 16:3, but here it may be suggested by Mk. 12:9 or by Is. 5:4. The owner speaks of his son as ἀγαπητός (cf. 3:22); this means 'only' and would certainly raise echoes for a Christian audience. The insertion of the word (in Mk.) could therefore be due to allegorical motives, although it makes good sense on the parabolic level: he is the only heir with whom the tenants have to deal. The owner's hope that they will respect the son (ἐντρέπομαι, 18:22) is tempered in Lk. by ἴσως**, 'perhaps' (cf. G. Thomas), which may be meant to avoid the impression of the owner's (i.e. God's) mistaken expectation more strongly expressed in Mk. (Klostermann, 193). After τοῦτον the participle ἰδόντες is added in A W Θ f13 *pm* e f vg sy^p; TR; *Diglot*; this could be an anticipation of the use in the next verse.

(14) Luke has ἰδόντες, par. Mt., diff. Mk., and omits ἐκεῖνοι, par. Mt.; oral variation may be at work. διαλογίζομαι (1:29; *et al.*) replaces λέγω and ἀλλήλους is better than ἑαυτούς (cf. 20:5). The tenants are represented as making a spur-of-the-moment decision, although they presumably had their plans ready. They know that the newcomer is the only son, and so presume that he is the heir (κληρονόμος*) to the estate; and they resolve to murder him so that they may take possession of the vineyard. Their line of thinking is not absolutely clear. Their original hope may have been simply to avoid paying rent for a fourth time, and thereby to establish finally their claim to possession of the vineyard (Derrett, 300–302). But the fact that the messenger was the son led to a new idea. They may have assumed that the original owner had died, so that if they killed the new owner, the vineyard would pass into their hands as the first claimants; it would be regarded as ownerless property, and they would have a good chance of maintaining their claim (Jeremias, *Parables*, 75f.). Again, the original owner might be regarded as having made over the property to the son during his lifetime (E. Bammel*; Derrett, 300–306). In any case, the tenant's act was foolish because they forgot that the owner, although distant, was still alive and could take proceedings against them.

(15) So they acted. They expelled the son from the vineyard and put him to death. The order (cf. 1 Ki 21:12) is the reverse of that in Mk. where the son is killed inside the vineyard, and then his body is thrown out. In any case, there would be objections to leaving the body in the vineyard to contaminate the place and make it unfit (ritually) for crops. Luke and Matthew may have this thought in mind, but commentators generally assume that the change is for allegorical purposes: the vineyard is identified with Jerusalem and the tradition that Jesus died outside the city (Jn. 19:17; Heb. 13:12f.) has been worked into the story. This assumption rests on the view that the vineyard allegorically represents Jerusalem rather than Israel. It is unlikely, and it is more probable that the order in Lk. and Mt. is designed to make the murder the climax; the 'casting out' is seen as a rejection of the son's claim to the vineyard rather than as an insult to his corpse. There is no indication that the death of Jesus *outside* Jerusalem had significance for the early church (except Heb. 13:12f.), and Luke tends to assign the guilt for Jesus' death to Jerusalem so strongly that he is unlikely to have appreciated the theological significance of his death outside the city. The agreement between Lk. and Mt. at this point (not in G. Thomas) may again be due to oral variation.

The narrator breaks off the story to put a question to the hearers. What do they think that the owner of the vineyard will do in such circumstances? Various commentators hold that this final question, which is not to be found in G. Thomas and whose language is reminiscent of Is. 5:4, is an addition to the original parable which closed with the son's murder (Jeremias, *Parables*, 74; Schramm, 163f.). But Jesus could use a question in this way (17:9), the value of G. Thomas as evidence is doubtful, and the language of Is. 5:4 LXX is only superficially similar. The question, therefore, is probably original.

(16) In Mk. and Lk. the question is answered by Jesus himself, but in Mt. it is put on the lips of the hearers. In any case, it is self-evident what the answer will be, and the case that this is a secondary addition to the parable is stronger, but by no means conclusive. The master himself will come to assert his rights; he will destroy the tenants (possibly an armed attack is envisaged, but a legal process of trial for murder is possible) and he will let the vineyard to new tenants. The details are again quite plausible in the dramatic setting, although the early church may have seen a reference to the gentiles entering the church (so in Mt. 21:43, where the vineyard is equated with the kingdom of God). But the allegorical application is not obvious in Mk. or Lk. (*pace* Wilson, 7 n. 1), although it might be urged that Lk. 21:24 points in the direction of this explanation.

Luke adds the reaction of the crowd: μὴ γένοιτο is a negative form of wish, using the optative, otherwise found only in Paul in the NT (Rom. 3:4; *et al.*). The remark may be taken as expressing horror at the reaction of the owner or at the whole course of events; in either case the application of the story to the Jewish leaders is in mind. While it is generally assumed that the former interpretation is correct, it is more probable that the horror is at the fact that the Jewish leaders would act in such a way towards God and suffer the inevitable consequences.

(17) Having inserted a dialogue here, Luke has to reintroduce Jesus as speaker. ἐμβλέπω is 'to look at, fix one's gaze upon' (22:61* par. Mk. 14:67; Acts 22:11; Mk. 10:21, 27 diff. Lk.). It stresses the solemnity of the occasion. τί οὖν ... means 'what else then can be the meaning of this Scripture which speaks of judgment on the builders?'; the use of τὸ γεγραμμένον as a quasi-noun is Lucan (cf. 18:31; 21:22; 22:37; 24:44; Acts 13:29; 24:14). Mark's introduction is different. The quotation is from Ps. 118 (117):22 LXX, with the omission of v. 23 which is quoted by Mark and Matthew; the omission enables a closer link with v. 18 which keeps up the stone imagery. The quotation is about a stone which the builders rejected as useless but which was destined to be a keystone, and its significance in the early church was primarily christological (Acts 4:11; 1 Pet. 2:7), although in each case the thought of rejection by unbelievers is present. Hence the basic thought here is that, although the stone has been rejected, nevertheless it will have the place of honour. The link with the parable is thus not very direct, and may be secondary. This lack of direct connection may explain the introduction of the following verse in Lk. (Lindars, 174). λίθον is accusative by attraction to the relative pronoun, and is caught up by οὗτος. On the significance cf. J. Jeremias, TDNT IV, 268–280, especially 275f.

(18) The element of judgment upon those who reject the stone is now brought out in a saying peculiar to Lk. (The verse appears as Mt. 21:44 in most MSS, but is omitted by D 33 b ff¹ ff² r¹ syˢ Ir Or Eus; it is probably an 'accretion to the text', Metzger, 58). The imagery may be that of a pot falling on a stone and being dashed in pieces (συνθλάω**); alternatively the stone may fall on the pot and destroy it (λικμάω**, usually 'to winnow, scatter', but here 'to pulverise', Dn. 2:44; cf. G. Bornkamm, TDNT IV, 280f.). The language reflects Dn. 2:34., 44f. and Is. 8:14f. (Lindars, 183–186), and the thought has a parallel in M. Est 3:6 (SB I, 877); cf. Sir. 13:2. The point is the inevitability of judgment, expressed in proverbial form. The origin of the saying is obscure, preserved as it is only here. Manson, Sayings, 322, regards it as a detached saying originally unconnected with what precedes, since there is a difference between a keystone and a stone that can fall in judgment. See further France, 98f.

(19) The reaction of the authorities in described as in Mk. Their desire was to lay hands on him (21:12; Mk. 14:46; Acts 4:3; et al.; diff. Mk. κρατέω; cf. 8:54 note) at that very moment (2:38 note), but (they were unable to act because) they feared the people. The final γάρ clause qualifies ἐζήτησαν, not ἐφοβήθησαν. The incident thus closes with the appreciation of the people and the discomfort of the leaders who have nothing to say in reply.

iii. Tribute to Caesar 20:20–26

The second deputation to Jesus had the specific aim of persuading him to say something incriminating which would form the basis of an accusation against him to the governor; the questioners adopted the role of righteous men, seeking an answer from Jesus which would be in conformity with Jewish ideas of righteousness but which would thus be contrary to Roman demands. Their question was preceded by some flattery which praised Jesus as one who followed the way of God and showed subservience to no man; surely such a teacher would hold that it was wrong to pay tribute money to a foreign ruler? Jesus' answer was the opposite of what they expected, but was so framed that it could not be attacked as contrary to the law of God. Men who use Caesar's money must pay Caesar's taxes; but at the same time they must pay God what is owed to him. There may be the thoughts that obeying the ruler is part of one's obedience to God, and also that there is no question of absolute obedience to any human ruler, since this would be inconsistent with giving God his due. Such teaching was not out of harmony with that of Judaism where the thoughts of obedience to earthly rulers and to God are both expressed. The trap thus failed to close on its prey; yet in 23:2 Luke records how the Jews nevertheless accused Jesus before Pilate of forbidding the payment of taxes; he means us to see plainly that the teaching of Jesus was not hostile to the state as such, and that the accusations brought by the Jews against him had no substance in them.

The narrative is based on Mk. and there is no evidence for use of any other source (Schramm, 168–170). The version in P. Egerton 2 is secondary, as is the version in G. Thomas 100. Luke's wording differs in detail from Mk., especially at the beginning of the narrative where he has omitted reference to the Pharisees and Herodians and has introduced the motif of finding evidence to accuse Jesus before Pilate. At the end of the parable he stresses how the plot failed; Jesus was too clever for his adversaries.

The story itself falls into the category of a pronouncement story with some detail and dialogue (cf. Bultmann, 25, who expressly admits its authenticity).

See H. Loewe, 'Render unto Caesar', Cambridge, 1940; E. Stauffer, Christ and the Caesars, 1955, 112–137 (with excellent illustration of a denarius); Derrett, 313–338; G. Bornkamm, Jesus of Nazareth, 1966, 120–124; C. H. Giblin, 'The "Things of God" in the Question concerning Tribute to Caesar (Lk. 20:25; Mk. 12:17; Mt. 22:21)', CBQ 33, 1971, 510–527; F. F. Bruce, 'Render to Caesar', in C. F. D. Moule and E. Bammel (ed.), The Zealots and Jesus (forthcoming).

(20) The subject of the clause is not given, but from the context it must be understood to be 'the scribes and high priests' (20:19). παρατηρέω (6:7) means that they watched him (RSV) or 'watched their opportunity' (AG; NEB; TNT; TEV). The unusual use of the verb absolutely has led to alteration in the text (ἀποχωρήσαντες, D Θ pc it;

ὑποχωρήσαντες, W; cf. Metzger, 171). Luke has dropped the description of the deputation as being composed of Pharisees and Herodians, possibly because the latter group were no longer significant, or because an association of the two groups seemed unlikely to him. Instead he takes up the hint provided by Mk. 12:15 which speaks of the hypocrisy of the deputation and interprets them (no doubt correctly) as persons who pretended to be righteous by Jewish standards but at a deeper level were malicious and evil in seeking the downfall of Jesus. ἐγκάθετος** is a 'person hired to lie in wait, spy'. ὑποκρίνομαι**, 'to pretend, make believe', occurs surprisingly only here, although the theme of hypocrisy is common enough in the NT; on the construction (with accusative and infinitive) see BD 397², and on the non-Classical use of the reflexive pronoun see BD 406¹. δίκαιος may have the sense of 'honest', but more probably it has the sense of loyalty to the Jewish law. In this context it could conceivably refer to the outlook characteristic of the Zealots whose opposition to Roman rule was based on their religious devotion to God and his law. If Jesus were to side with the Zealots, he would certainly place himself in opposition to the Romans. ἐπιλαμβάνομαι is Lucan (9:47; et al.), diff. Mk. ἀγρεύω**, which is rare; it takes the genitive of the person and of the thing by which the person is grasped.

ὥστε here must be final rather than consecutive (4:29 note). ἡγεμών is 'governor' (21:12 par. Mk. 13:9; Acts, 6x; Mt., 9x; 1 Pet. 2:14), and the genitive goes with both preceding nouns, ἀρχή and ἐξουσία, which describe his jurisdiction and power (contrast 12:11).

(21) The actual question of the deputation (cf. ἐπερωτάω) is preceded by a lengthy captatio benevolentiae by means of which it was hoped to persuade Jesus that there was only one way in which the question could be answered. The question concerns the interpretation of the law (halakhah; cf. Daube, 158–163), and so Jesus is appropriately addressed as a teacher. The questioners claim in effect to accept his teaching; they are on his side for he teaches ὀρθῶς, 'correctly' (7:43; 10:28; Dt. 5:28; Klostermann, 194, suggests 'candidly', but this is unlikely). Luke has altered Mark's ἀληθὴς εἶ for no very obvious reason. λέγεις καὶ διδάσκεις is somewhat redundant, but is perhaps meant to compensate for the omission of καὶ οὐ μέλει σοι περὶ οὐδενός, a difficult phrase which Luke has dropped. The phrase λαμβάνω πρόσωπον means 'to show favour' (Gal. 2:6; Barn. 19:4; Did. 4:3) and is used in the LXX to translate nāśā' panîm (Lv. 19:15; 2 Ki. 3:14; Job 42:8; et al.; cf. E. Lohse, TDNT VI, 779f.); Luke has substituted the LXX phrase for Mark's βλέπω εἰς πρόσωπον, which may also reflect a Hebrew expression (Cranfield, 370). The force is that Jesus is not influenced in his teaching by obsequiousness to men – not even to his questioners, as they found out to their chagrin. On the contrary, he teaches the way of God truly (cf. 1QapGen. 2:5), i.e. the kind of life God requires from men (cf. Dt. 8:6; 10:12f.; Job 23:11; Pss. 27:11; 119:15; CD 20:18; Acts 18:26; 1QS 3:10; W. Michaelis, TDNT V, 51f.).

(22) After this lengthy preamble the questioners come to the point. Their question concerns what is lawful, i.e. permitted by the law. Derrett's query (315) whether the law might be expected to answer such a question is strange. He himself suggests that the law gave no direct guidance on this particular question, and that therefore what was sought was the wisdom of a prophet or teacher in finding an answer. After the verb Luke adds ἡμᾶς (cf. 6:4; BD 409³ for the use of the accusative), a device which enables him to dispense with Mark's second, rather redundant question, and which brings out the stress, 'Is it lawful for us *Jews*?' The legitimacy and necessity of taxes was not of course in doubt. The difficulty arose because it was a poll tax paid to a foreign ruler, Caesar. Luke has substituted φόρος, 'tax, tribute' (23:2; Rom. 13:6f.**), for Mk. κῆνσος, a Latin loanword. The reference is to the taxes imposed in connection with Roman rule of Judaea (cf. 2:1 note). These were particularly hated by the Jews, and their introduction had been accompanied by rioting. An affirmative answer to the question (such as in fact Jesus gave) would lead to his losing the sympathy of Jewish patriots, but, as we have noted, it is more probable that the hope was that he would answer in the negative and thereby incur the displeasure of the Romans. If, then, the tax was hated, Jews might well look for indications that payment of it was not according to the way of God. It seems unlikely at this stage in the dialogue that the thought is of the idolatrous representations on the Roman coinage which made them unacceptable to the Jews – at least for paying taxes: they do not seem to have objected to using them for commercial gain (cf. Bornkamm, 112). The question is rather whether *God's* people are not free from the requirement to make payment to Caesar.

(23) The effect of the next comment is to show that Jesus was not taken in by his questioners. He recognised (κατανοέω, 6:41; *et al.*, in the aorist is more apt than Mk. εἰδώς) their cunning (πανουργία, 1 Cor. 3:19; 2 Cor. 4:2; 11:3; Eph. 4:14**; O. Bauernfeind, TDNT V, 722–727); cf. Mt. πονηρία, diff. Mk. ὑπόκρισις (a motif already used in v. 20). According to Mk. Jesus begins his reply with the question τί με πειράζετε, which is omitted by Luke. Jesus does not so much unmask their evil design as lead them into a trap.

(24) Jesus therefore asks to be shown a denarius. Luke makes less of the request that the questioners should produce the coin in order that Jesus may see it. It is assumed that they will have a coin to hand and not need to go and look for one; hence Jesus can go straight on without pause to ask his question about the coin. Matthew brings out the point that the coin requested was that actually used in payment of the Roman tax. The δηνάριον (7:41; 10:35) was a Roman coin, and the implication of the story is that it had been issued by the current emperor; if so, it would be a silver coin, bearing on one side the head of the emperor wearing a laurel wreath and the legend '*Ti. Caesar Divi Aug. F. Augustus*' (Tiberius Caesar, son of the deified Augustus, Augustus), and on the

other side the figure of the emperor's mother Livia as an earthly incarnation of the goddess Pax (peace) and the legend '*Pontifex Maximus*' (high priest). The coin symbolised the power of the emperor and made religious claims for him that Jews would consider blasphemous (E. Stauffer*, 124–127). In the complex monetary situation of the ancient world many types of coins issued by different authorities were in circulation (compare the situation in a modern international airport); but this particular coinage was required for payment of Roman taxes, just as the Jewish temple tax had to be paid in an appropriate coinage. For it was Caesar's money, as Jesus elicited by his question; it bore his likeness (εἰκών*) and his inscription (ἐπιγραφή, 23:38*). Granted that money belongs to the person who possesses it (Derrett, 321 n. 3), there is still a sense in which it expresses the lordship of the person whose claims to rule are expressed on it, and this is the point at issue. Caesar is the *de facto* ruler. (For οἱ δὲ εἶπαν, א B L 33 *pc*, the variant ἀποκριθέντες δὲ εἶπαν is read by A C Δ f13 *pm*; TR; *Diglot*; and ἀποκριθέντες εἶπαν by D W Γ Θ f1 *pc* it lat; in terms of Lucan usage either of the first two readings is possible, but the second looks like a conflation of the first and the third.)

(25) If therefore (τοίνυν, 1 Cor. 9:26; Heb. 13:13**) the coin expresses Caesar's rule, the questioners should pay him what is due to him. ἀποδίδωμι (4:20; *et al.*) is the word used for giving back something to somebody; hence it has been suggested that the idea here is of giving back to Caesar what belongs to him (E. Stauffer*, 128–130). But the word can simply mean 'to pay', and is used generally of payments. τὰ τοῦ Καίσαρος goes beyond the payment of taxes and refers to rendering to the ruler whatever he may lawfully prescribe. The saying affirms the general principle of submission to political authority, a principle repeated in Rom. 13:1–7; 1 Pet. 2:13–17. But this answer by itself would not have been forceful to Zealots and others of like mind. Jesus' answer goes further. It culminates in the command to give God what belongs to him. It is improbable that this refers to the payment of the temple tax as a symbol of obligation to God (as E. Stauffer*, 132f. suggests). Both parts of the saying go beyond the strict question of paying taxes. There may be the thought that men, as bearers of God's image, should recognise his authority over them (G. Bornkamm*, 113). C. H. Giblin* finds a reference to God's inscription (Is. 44:5) on men. This, however, is more of a (correct) theological deduction from the saying than an inherent element in the argument, the comparison being more between Caesar and God than between coins and men. The relation of the two halves of the saying is disputed. It is safe to say that Jesus is not setting up two parallel and separate realms. In the light of Jewish and biblical teaching it is more likely that Jesus is grounding obedience to the earthly ruler in obedience to God – the law of God requires that men obey his delegated authority on earth. The context requires that Jesus should make this the positive point of the saying over against those who

denied that men should obey Caesar. At the same time the wider context of the saying in the early church (cf. Acts 5:29) indicates that the power of the earthly ruler is circumscribed by that of God, and that the climax of the saying lies in its assertion of the supreme authority of God's demands, especially when these run counter to those of an earthly ruler. Bornkamm's suggestion (113), that the saying implies the temporary, transient nature of Caesar's kingdom over against the kingdom of God, reads too much into the saying. Derrett, 324–337, draws attention to Ec. 8:2 and its rabbinic interpretation; he suggests that an allusion to the king's mouth, depicted on the census coin, is present in the response of Jesus, but, although the Jewish teaching about obedience to a ruler in this tradition is in line with the teaching of Jesus, it is doubtful whether the allusion to the king's mouth can be pressed, especially since there is no explicit reference to it in the story.

(26) Luke's closing comment stresses the inability of the questioners to trap Jesus (cf. 14:6 with the same use of ἰσχύω). The use of ἐπιλαμβάνομαι echoes 20:20 and so rounds off the narrative. The reading αὐτοῦ ῥήματος (A C (D) W f1 f13 pl; TR; UBS; Diglot) could be due to assimilation to v. 20, and τοῦ ῥήματος has good external support (ℵ B L 892 pc), but the former remains the more difficult construction (Metzger, 171). The favour enjoyed by Jesus with the people is again stressed by Luke. The motif of surprise is taken over from Mk. (for ἀπόκρισις cf. 2:47), but only Luke states that Jesus' answer reduced his opponents to silence (cf. 20:40 par. Mk. 12:34). There are no grounds for denouncing him (or his followers) to the governor on a charge of political insurrection. (It goes without saying that attempts to extract a pro-Zealot attitude on the part of Jesus from this story are thoroughly misdirected.)

iv. The Problem of the Resurrection 20:27–40

If Daube's analysis (158–169) of this area of the Gospel is correct (20:1–21:6 note), we now have an example of a mocking question, intended to ridicule the teaching of Jesus. For the first and only time in Lk. the Sadducees feature in the narrative. They appear as opponents of belief in the resurrection, a doctrine which was held by Jesus (14:14), and ridicule it by citing a possible but far-fetched case which makes nonsense of it: in the resurrection what is the situation of a woman who has had seven husbands? Which, if any, of them, is her real husband? The implication is that polyandry is the only solution, and that a belief which leads to such an immoral suggestion must itself be false. Jesus' reply has two parts. First, he attacks the basis of the case by claiming that in the resurrection conditions are so different that human relationships are raised to a new level; in a situation of immortality questions of marriage and procreation are irrelevant and misconceived, and the basic relationship is one of divine sonship, perhaps with the implication that men and women are related to one another as brothers and sisters. Second, Jesus mounts a positive defence of the doctrine of the resurrection by reference to God's promise to the patriarchs, which implies that he continues to stand in a covenant relationship to them (and their descendants), and that death cannot break this relationship. If God is still the God of Abraham after his death (i.e. at the time when he spoke to Moses), then Abraham cannot be finally dead: either he is in some sense alive, or he will be raised from the dead. The former of these possibilities is the traditional interpretation of the passage, but is exposed to the difficulties that it presupposes a body-soul dualism which is not characteristic of biblical thought and it implies immortality rather than resurrection. The latter view is advocated by E. E. Ellis*. This interpretation is necessary in order to do justice to the theme of resurrection: the covenant guarantees that God will raise its members (F. Dreyfus*; Lane, 429f.). A synthesis of the two views is achieved by Gundry, 20–22, especially 22 n., where he argues that the present 'spiritual' existence of the patriarchs demands the restoration of full 'bodily' existence at the resurrection; on this view we get a better understanding of v. 38b which constitutes a major difficulty for Ellis's view.

The narrative follows Mk. closely, except in vs. 34–36 and 38b–39. Schramm, 170f., posits the use of another source on the basis of the Semitic style in vs. 34–36, but it is more likely that we have an example of Lucan explanation (Neirynck, 176f.). The narrative is generally held to reflect Pharisaic types of discussion and to represent the use of similar techniques by the early church (Bultmann, 25; Schweizer, *Markus*, 140). The church has taken up the method of argument, perhaps the actual arguments, used in Jewish circles and utilised it for its own purposes. But the lack of specific Christian elements in the discussion, seen in the reference to angels and the appeal to Ex. 3:6 instead of the resurrection of Jesus, speaks against formation by the early church (Jeremias, *Theology*, I, 184 n. 3); and it remains unproven that Jesus did not respond to Jewish arguments by employing counter arguments in the same style (Taylor, 480, following Lohmeyer, 257). We may confidently accept the authenticity of the story. Bultmann's claim that Mk. 12: 26f. is a later addition fails to recognise that Jesus' reply has a chiastic structure (Mk. 12:24a and b are taken up in reverse order).

Luke uses the story to form the climax of the disputes with Jesus by his opponents; it stresses the inability of the opponents to overcome him in argument, and it leaves the field clear for Jesus to take the initiative in an attack on scribal teaching and practice.

See F. Dreyfus, 'L'argument scripturaire de Jésus en faveur de la résurrection des morts (Marc XII, 26–27)', RB 66, 1959, 213–224; E. E. Ellis, 'Jesus, the Sadducees and Qumran', NTS 10, 1963–64, 274–279; Gundry, 20–22.

(27) The narrative opens with the approach (προσέρχομαι, par. Mt. (cf. 4:38 note), diff. Mk. ἔρχομαι) of some representatives of the Sadducees to Jesus. The Sadducees figure rarely in the Gospels (Mk. 12:18;

Mt. 22:23, 34; Mt. 3:7; 16:1, 6, 11f.; Acts 4:1; 5:17; 23:6–8**). They were a party opposed to the Pharisees in theology and associated with the priests (SB IV:1, 334–352; R. Meyer, TDNT VII, 35–54). They opposed what they regarded as the new-fangled doctrines of the Pharisees and clung to the literal wording of the Torah. Their disbelief in the resurrection is fully attested in Jewish sources (Acts 23:8; Jos. Ant. 18:16; Bel. 2:165; cf. SB I, 885f.; A. Oepke, TDNT I, 370). The nominative case, οἱ ἀντιλέγοντες, is strange after the preceding genitive (Zerwick, 14). The reading ἀντιλέγοντες (A W Γ Δ f13 pm lat; TR; (UBS); Diglot) has poorer attestation than λέγοντες (ℵ B C D L Θ f1 pc e r¹ sy sa bo) but is the more difficult (because of the double negative); the latter could be due to assimilation to Mt. 22:23 (Metzger, 172f.). Since ἀντιλέγω is Lucan (2:34; Acts, 3x), it should perhaps be preferred. For ἀνάστασις cf. 2:34. For ἐπηρώτησαν (aorist) the imperfect ἐπηρώτων is read by B (f13) pc; Diglot; although it is arguable that copyists turned imperfects into aorists, there is no clear internal evidence for either reading here, but the external evidence for the aorist is stronger.

(28) Again Jesus is addressed as a teacher and asked for his opinion on a point that concerns interpretation of the law and its bearing on doctrine. The starting point is what Moses wrote in the law about levirate marriage; the language is based on Dt. 25:5 and Gn. 38:8, which are loosely cited. Luke follows Mk. with slight modifications (cf. Holtz, 68–70). Mark's construction is difficult; Luke eases it by omitting Mark's ὅτι which is unnecessary before the following ἵνα. The difficulty is in fact caused by the presence of ἵνα which should probably be taken in the rare imperatival sense (BD 470¹); alternatively Mark has confused two separate constructions (Taylor, 481). A further difficulty is caused by the double use of ἀδελφός to refer to the deceased husband and his brother respectively; to avoid the difficulty the second occurrence of the word should be translated simply by 'he': 'if a man's brother who was married dies childless, let him marry the widow and raise a family for his brother'; Luke's ἔχων γυναῖκα is less elegant than Mk. καὶ καταλίπῃ γυναῖκα, but he avoids Mark's monotonous parataxis. ἄτεκνος (20:29**) is 'childless'. For ἤ there is the variant ἀποθάνῃ (A W Γ Δ Θ f13 pm; TR; Diglot), which looks like a copyist's repetition of the preceding use of the verb. ἐξανίστημι (Acts 15:5) is 'to raise up'; σπέρμα (1:55*) is 'offspring'. For the law concerning levirate marriage see Dt. 25:7–10; Ruth 3:9 – 4:12; Yebamoth; M. Burrows, 'Levirate Marriage in Israel', JBL 59, 1940, 23–33; 'The Marriage of Boaz and Ruth', JBL 59, 1940, 445–454. The law concerned brothers who lived together and its purpose was to keep property in the family by raising up an heir to inherit it.

(29) Having stated the Mosaic principle the questioners proceed to outline a problem that it could lead to on the assumption of resurrection life. The round number 'seven' also appears in the context of repeated marriages in Tob. 3:8, and the idea of levirate marriage is likewise

present in that story (Tob. 6:9–12; 7:12f.); this suggests that we have a popular theme in folklore here put to a new use (cf. Lane, 427). The story of the seven brothers, each of whom married the same wife in turn and died childless, is told in popular style with a certain amount of repetition in Mk., and both Matthew and Luke modify the wording. Luke has remodelled this verse by using the participle λαβών (cf. Mt.) and the adjective ἄτεκνος.

(30) In the UBS text Mark's full-length repetition of the story with reference to the second brother is abbreviated to καὶ ὁ δεύτερος and this becomes the subject, along with καὶ ὁ τρίτος, of the singular verb ἔλαβεν in v. 31. This is difficult grammatically, for the verb following two subjects is normally plural; the exceptions (Mk. 4:41; Mt. 24:35; et al.; MH III, 314) are pairs that form single entities. This difficulty is avoided in the variant reading: καὶ ἔλαβεν ὁ δεύτερος τὴν γυναῖκα καὶ οὗτος ἀπέθανεν ἄτεκνος (A W Γ Δ (Θ) f1 f13 pm lat; TR; Diglot), but the weakness of the external evidence and the difficulty of explaining how the short reading arose out of the longer (assimilation to Mt. is a possibility) suggest that the lectio difficilior (which is not impossibilis) should be preferred.

(31) The second and third brothers are simply said to take the woman to wife; the laws of popular story telling enable us to supply the rest of the details from the account of the first brother. ὡσαύτως (adapted from Mk.) signifies that in this way the whole seven married her in turn, and died without leaving (καταλείπω, suggested by Mk. 12:19) children. Thus none of the brothers could claim to be the 'real' husband in terms of having begotten an heir.

(32) Finally, the woman died. ὕστερον, 'later, finally', is omitted by a c i syˢᶜ arm; (Diglot): Kilpatrick, 193, suspects that it is a harmonising addition from Mt. 22:27 (Mk. has ἔσχατον πάντων), but the external evidence is far too weak to support this suggestion.

(33) Now comes the question: which brother will be accounted as the woman's husband in the resurrection, granted that polyandry is not permitted? The introductory ἡ γυνὴ οὖν is somewhat unnecessary, and has perhaps been added as compensation for the dropping of Mark's redundant ὅταν ἀναστῶσιν. The text (so B L pc) is, however, uncertain. The whole phrase is omitted by ℵ* 157 pc it; ἐν τῇ οὖν . . . is read by ℵᶜ A D W Γ Δ Θ (f1) f13 pl lat; TR. Diglot reads ἡ γυνὴ (οὖν) ἐν τῇ . . ., but there seems to be no MSS evidence for omitting οὖν. There may have been some assimilation between Mt. and Lk. here.

(34) ἀποκριθείς is inserted before εἶπεν by A W Γ Δ Θ f1 f13 pm; TR; Diglot; possibly by assimilation to Mt. In Jesus' reply Luke omits the opening sentence found in Mk.: 'Is not this why you are wrong, that you know neither the scriptures nor the power of God?' (cf. Mk. 12:27b). Instead he poses a contrast between conditions in this life and the next, and elaborates the status of those who participate in the resurrection as sons of God. In this way Luke brings out more clearly

the difference between the two ages and stresses that not all men qualify for life in the new age. For 'the sons of this age', i.e. people who belong to this world, cf. 16:8. The MSS are very confused with regard to the following words. Modern texts have 1. γαμοῦσιν καὶ γαμίσκονται, i.e. (men) marry and (women) are given in marriage. (γαμίσκω, 'to give in marriage' (20:35 v.1.**), is attested by ℵ B L 33 157 pc; the variants are ἐκγαμίσκονται, ἐκγαμίζονται, γαμίζονται and γαμοῦνται; see Synopsis.) The other readings are: 2. γεννῶνται καὶ γεννῶσιν (ff² i q), i.e. 'are born and beget' (Grundmann, 375; Ellis, 236; cf. Klostermann, 195; Creed, 249). 3. γεννῶνται καὶ γεννῶσιν, γαμοῦσιν καὶ γαμοῦνται (D r¹ syˢᶜ). 4. γεννῶσιν καὶ γεννῶνται (c e l). 5. γεννῶσιν καὶ γεννῶνται, γαμοῦσιν καὶ γαμίσκονται (a Ir Or Cypr Aug). Black, 226f., argues that the Syriac evidence (yaldin wᵉmauldin) gives the sense 'bear and beget children'; he combines this wording with the order of the words attested in variants 4. and 5. to get a hypothetical original form, 'The children of this world beget and bear children, marry and are given in marriage'. But this is too conjectural to carry much weight. Moreover, as Black admits, the order (procreation, marriage) is odd. It is more plausible that the text refers first to the origin of human life in procreation, and this gives the required contrast with the stress on resurrection and immortality which make marriage unnecessary in the next world. Variants 3. and 5. are probably conflations. It is possible, then, that variant 2. preserves the original text and that most MSS have been assimilated to v. 35 (cf. Mk. and Mk.), but the lack of Greek attestation and the variety of wording in the Latin and Syriac MSS weigh strongly against it. The issue must be left open. In any case, variant 2. correctly indicates the line of thought in the passage.

(35) The contrast is now drawn with those who take part in the life of 'that age' (a unique phrase for 'the age to come', cf. 18:30). Luke stresses that not all men share in the life of the new age. They must be accounted worthy (καταξιόω, Acts 5:41; 2 Thes. 1:5**) to attain to it (τυγχάνω, Acts, 5x.; rest of NT, 6x**). Cf. Acts 13:46; the thought may be Pauline, but the language is Jewish (SB II, 254f.). The 'resurrection from the dead' (Acts 4:2; cf. Lk. 9:7; 16:30f.; 24:46) here means the resurrection of the just (14:14; cf. Plummer, 469, who thinks that the ἐκ gives a partitive sense to the phrase). The question of what makes a person worthy is not raised here. The point is that in the new age such people are not involved in marriage relationships. This can be understood to mean the abolition of earthly relationships. It is more likely, however, that the marriage relationship is transcended in a new level of personal relationships, and the basic point being made is that marriage as a means of procreation is no longer necessary.

(36) This is brought out in the next statement in which Luke elucidates Mark's comparison between men and angels (ἰσάγγελος**, a hitherto unattested word, diff. Mk. ὡς ἄγγελοι) by showing that the point of comparison is immortality: the heavenly life is eternal. For the comparison cf. Philo, Sacr. 5; and for the thought cf. 2 Bar. 51:10;

1QSb 4:24–28. But the thought of immortality rests on a higher basis. Inasmuch as they are 'sons of the resurrection', i.e. share in the resurrection (for this type of phrase cf. 10:6; 16:8; 20:34), men become sons of God (a status also ascribed to angels, G. Fohrer and E. Schweizer, TDNT VIII, 347–349, 355). Cf. 6:35; Mt. 5:9, 45 for this eschatological use of the term. While E. Schweizer (TDNT VIII, 390) derives the description from the thought of the angels as God's sons, the text suggests rather that men become God's sons as a result of the resurrection; we may have a parallel thought to the way in which Ps. 2:7 is applied to Jesus being begotten as his Son by God by means of the resurrection (Acts 13:33). Thus divine Fatherhood replaces human parentage (Danker, 205). Before θεοῦ the article is inserted by W Γ Δ Θ pl; TR; Diglot.

(37) The Sadducean objection to the possibility of resurrection life has now been shown to be invalid, since it wrongly assumes that earthly conditions persist in the heavenly world. It remains to offer a positive argument in favour of the resurrection. Luke simplifies Mark's introduction and loses his vivid question, 'Surely you have read...?' Even Moses – the accepted authority who wrote so long ago – revealed the fact of the resurrection (μηνύω, Acts 23:30; Jn. 11:57; 1 Cor. 10:28**) in the story of the burning bush. ἐπί means 'in the passage about' (Mk. 12:26; cf. Rom. 11:2 and ἐν, Heb. 4:7). βάτος (6:44) is feminine, diff. Mk. who adopts the Classical masculine gender (cf. AG). In Mk. Moses is said to describe how God said to him, 'I am the God of Abraham ...' Luke says that Moses called the Lord the God of..., so that Jesus is made to appeal more directly to the authority of Moses for this usage. The allusion is to Ex. 3:6; cf. Acts 7:32. For the use of λέγει, diff. Mk. εἶπεν, cf. 20:42; the present tense implies that Moses still speaks. The point of the quotation is that, after their deaths, God could still speak of himself as the God of the patriarchs (cf. the εἰμί in Mt. 22:32; Ex. 3:6 LXX). The phrase implies that God was the saviour of the patriarchs in accordance with his promises to them (Lane, 429f.), and in its original context it carries the thought of his continuing care for their descendants. But more is implied than this. On the one hand, there may be the thought that if God spared the patriarchs from danger during their life, he would not forsake them in the greater danger of death. On the other hand, the timing of the statement shows that God is still the God of the patriarchs after their death, and therefore they either must be still alive in some way and/or can confidently expect that he will raise them from the dead. This latter thought seems to be uppermost in view of the following verse. Ellis, 236, rightly sees the difficulty that if Abraham and the others are regarded as now living in heaven the passage witnesses to immortality rather than future resurrection; he also argues that a body/soul dualism is not characteristic of the NT view of man. Granted, however, that Jesus and his opponents accepted the concept of Sheol, then it can be argued that it would be inconsistent with God's promises

for him to leave the patriarchs there; but it is a moot point whether the Sadducees believed in Sheol. More probably the argument is not concerned with the niceties of Sheol, immortality and resurrection, but simply asserts that God will raise the dead because he cannot fail to keep his promises to them that he will be their God.

(38) For God cannot be the God of dead people (θεός is predicative); only living people can have a God, and therefore God's promise to the patriarchs that he is/will be their God requires that he maintain them in life. This statement is grounded in the further affirmation, peculiar to Lk., that all men live 'to' God. The line of thought is not clear. A close parallel is given by 4 Mac. 7:18; 16:25 which states that the martyrs, like the patriarchs, do not die to God, but live to God; here the meaning is that although they may die in the eyes of men, they are not dead, but alive, so far as God is concerned and because God gives them life. So the force here is that all men (i.e. all men thought worthy of the age to come, including the patriarchs) receive life from God, so that as living men they can continue to know him as their God. Ellis, 237, suggests that the phrase can be understood proleptically of the future resurrection, but prefers the less likely view that it refers to the present, hidden 'spiritual' life of believers in Christ (cf. Phil. 1:23): 'the Christian's present (corporate) existence in Christ continues in spite of his (individual) death. What the Christian now shares corporately, "in Christ", will be fulfilled individually at the *parousia*' (Ellis, 237). This view reads too much into the verse and demands that we understand Luke on a Pauline wavelength.

(39) The incident closes with a 'choral' response from some of the scribes – presumably Pharisaic scribes who accepted the viewpoint of Jesus. (The Pharisees were open to ideas of immortality and resurrection. Ellis, 234f., argues that the Qumran sect may have been nearer to Jesus in believing in immortality *via* resurrection; cf. 1QH 3:21f.; 6:29f., 34.) The statement is peculiar to Lk., and appears to be a generalisation of the sentiments expressed by one scribe in Mk. 12:28, 32, where καλῶς is used. The view of Klostermann, 196, that the saying expresses resignation or hypocrisy, is wrong.

(40) Luke has brought forward the statement in Mk. 12:34b that nobody dared to ask Jesus any more questions, since he has omitted the intervening story of the scribe's question about the great commandment. If the γάρ has its usual force, the clause will refer especially to the unwillingness of the Sadducees and unfriendly Pharisees to engage in further controversy.

v. The Person of the Messiah 20:41–44

Having silenced his opponents, Jesus proceeds to take the initiative by posing a theological question to them and then (in the next pericope) by criticising their practice. The present narrative is taken from Mk. with minor alterations. In Mt. it has undergone a more thorough revision and has been turned into a conflict dialogue between Jesus and the Pharisees. Matthew's form is probably a secondary elaboration (cf. Mk. 12:9–11 and parr.), but it has been suggested by R. P. Gagg* that the original form of the story was that of a dialogue, from which only Jesus' answer has been preserved; this view is unsubstantiated, especially since it is not clear what question from his opponents might have provoked Jesus' counter-question.

Jesus asks how it is possible that the Messiah can be called David's son in view of the fact that David himself speaks of the Messiah as his lord in Ps. 110 (109):1. This question is open to varied interpretations (see especially the survey of modern exegesis in G. Schneider*, 66–81). First, the question (introduced by πῶς) may be taken either as a rhetorical denial that the Messiah can be David's son, or as a request for an explanation of how he can be both David's son and David's lord. Second, there is the question whether 'David's son' means a person genealogically descended from David or a person of Davidic character. Third, there is the question of what status is to be attributed to David's 'lord': is he perhaps the Son of God or the Son of man? Fourth, there is the question whether the saying was understood in different ways during the history of the tradition.

An important point is made by F. Neugebauer*, 81f., who distinguishes between 'messianology', which is concerned with the character of the Messiah (it being not yet decided who the Messiah is), and 'christology', which is concerned with the identity of the Messiah. Strictly speaking, the present question is one of messianology. But this point has not always been observed, and of course the question leads into christology.

It can be taken as certain that Jesus' opponents believed that the Messiah would be a descendant of David. Various scholars have argued that the present saying rejects this view: since Jesus was thought *not* to be a descendant of David, the early church had to defend his messiahship by denying that the Messiah was to be a descendant of David (Burger, 52–59; cf. G. Schneider*, 83). But we have no evidence that this accusation was brought against Jesus, or that the early church did not know of Jesus' Davidic descent. Further, the Davidic descent of the Messiah is so clearly attested in the OT and Judaism that it is impossible that Jesus or the early church could ever have denied it. It follows that the saying is not a denial of the Davidic descent of the Messiah.

Alternatively, the saying can be regarded as a denial or a qualification of the expectation of a Davidic type of Messiah. Thus Cullmann, 130–133, thinks that Jesus is not denying the fact of Davidic sonship but its christological value understood in terms of political kingship. Hahn's objection to this view (260) rests on the assumption that the saying belongs to the Hellenistic church where it had acquired a Christian sense. A weightier objection is that Ps. 110:1 appears to speak in similar, political tones to the view which is said to be rejected by Jesus.

A different type of solution was proposed by Daube, 158–163, who argued that Jesus was raising a rabbinic question in which an apparent contradiction between two verses is brought to light, the resolution of the difficulty being achieved by showing that each verse is right in its own context. In the present instance there is no specific citation of one of the texts but a statement clearly based on the OT. On this view, the effect of Jesus' question is to qualify the characterisation of the Messiah as David's son. G. Schneider*, 83–85, objects that this view of the question as being haggadic arises only in Mark's context, and that the two texts which are being contrasted are not really in conflict if Ps. 110:1 is not given a messianic interpretation. Neither objection is justified. The question can still be haggadic in character when taken on its own, and it is probable that the Jews did understand Ps. 110:1 messianically (see below).

On the assumption that the question arose in the early church, Hahn, 259–262, holds that it finds its solution in a two-stage christology in which Jesus was regarded as 'Son of David' during his earthly life and 'David's lord' during his exaltation (cf. E. Lohse, TDNT VIII, 484f.; Schweizer, Markus, 147; Jeremias, Theology, I, 259). The answer to the question posed by Jesus: how can the Messiah be both David's son and lord? is implicitly answered by saying: 'By means of the resurrection through which David's son, Jesus, was exalted to God's right hand as his lord'. This answer is not given in the passage, but is later found in Acts 2:32–36 (Burger, 114–116). Later the early church understood Jesus in terms of a two-nature (rather than a two-stage) christology as being both Son of David and the exalted Lord.

F. Neugebauer*, 82–92, argues that the 'genealogical' title 'Son of David' had an eschatological sense and referred to a Messiah who stood under the Torah. Jesus rejects this type of Messiahship in favour of one based on Ps. 110:1, a text which reflects David's vision of one seated beside God; this must refer to the Son of man. Then before the sanhedrin Jesus expresses messiahship in terms of Dn. 7:13 and Ps. 110:1. As a background to the whole issue Neugebauer claims that John the Baptist's hope of the 'coming One' was expressed in terms of the Son of man rather than the Davidic Messiah.

From the foregoing survey it emerges that Jesus' unanswered question was regarded by Luke as a mystery which found its solution in the resurrection. The one who was David's son (as Luke clearly believed, 3:23–38) became David's lord by being exalted. But this means that for Luke the question was 'If the Messiah is David's son, how can he be his lord?', rather than 'If the Messiah is David's lord, how can he be his son?' (Burger, 115). If this understanding of Luke's use of the pericope is correct, it follows that the original force was somewhat different. It also makes it less likely that the pericope arose in the early church. The original force of the question is rather how a Messiah who is David's lord can also be his son. We have seen above that one possible way of answering this question is by denying that the Messiah can be David's son, but that the early church could not have accepted this answer. A more probable answer is that the question is designed to show that the Messiah cannot be merely the Son of David, i.e. a human descendant. The Messiah must be a person who embraces within himself the characteristics of being both an exalted figure and the Son of David. Such a figure can be seen in the Son of God: this would give an answer to the question in terms of 2 Sa. 7:12–16. Alternatively, the reference is to the Son of man; this would tie up with the answer of Jesus in the trial scene (22:69). Admittedly, the Jewish evidence for assimilation of the Son of man to the Messiah is not strong, but this creative step may have been taken by Jesus and the early church. It fits in with the way in which there is a transition from Messiah to Son of man in 9:20/22 par. Mk. The question is thus one of messianology, but it finds its answer in christology: it is in Jesus that this fusion of figures becomes a reality. In this form too the question is meant to show up the inadequacy of Jewish messianic expectation.

Hahn, 113–115, argues that the question arose in the Hellenistic church. For 1. Jesus takes the initiative in a discussion which is about Jewish messianic teaching (cf. Bultmann, 70). 2. The question cannot be answered on the basis of Jewish teaching. 3. The saying shows a pronounced christological interest, making use of Christian christological titles. 4. The type of argument and the use of the OT is rabbinic and fits the early church rather than Jesus. 5. The concept of exaltation is not only post-Easter (Acts 2:34; Lindars, 46f.) but in Hahn's view Hellenistic. 6. The argument rests on use of the LXX. Neither Jesus nor the Palestinian church would have applied Hebrew *'ᵃdōnî* to the Messiah or Jesus, since this was a divine title (cf. how *YHWH* in Ps. 110:1 would have been replaced by *'ᵃdōnāy*.

These arguments are, however, lacking in force. 1. It is a misuse of form criticism to argue that Jesus could never take the initiative in a discussion. 2. Jesus was deliberately asking a question that could not be answered in terms of Jewish messianology. 3. The saying lacks a clear Christian explanation (Lohmeyer, 263; Taylor, 492f.). It is a mistake to assume that Jesus totally ignored the titles used in Jewish messianology. 4. The case that Jesus did not use the OT in the present manner requires the jettisoning of far too much of his teaching to be convincing. 5. Hahn's view of the origin of the concept of exaltation in the Hellenistic church has failed to convince most scholars. The view that Jesus expected some kind of vindication is firmly planted in the sources, and in any case the allusion here is quite indirect. 6. The linguistic point is unconvincing. There is a clear distinction between the two uses of 'lord' in Ps. 110:1, especially in the Hebrew wording, and no danger of *'ᵃdōnî* being taken in a divine sense. J. A. Fitzmyer (NTS 20, 1973–74, 389f.; cf. 1:32 note) holds that in Aramaic the title *mārē'* could have stood behind both uses of κύριος here, and that this helps to make arguments for the authenticity of the saying more plausible. It thus remains possible, and indeed probable, that the saying goes back to Jesus, especially since it has no convincing *Sitz im Leben* in the early church.

See Bultmann, 144–146; R. P. Gagg, 'Jesus und die Davidssohnfrage. Zur Exegese von Markus 12:35–37', TZ 7, 1951, 18–30; Daube, 158–169; Cullmann, 130–133; Hahn, 113–115, 191, 259–262; Burger, *passim*; France, 101f., 163–169; G. Schneider, 'Die Davidssohnfrage (Mk. 12, 35–37)', Bib. 53, 1972, 65–90 (with earlier bibliography); D. M. Hay, *Glory at the Right Hand: Psalm 110 in Early Christianity*, Nashville, 1973; F. Neugebauer, 'Die Davidssohnfrage (Mark xii, 35–37 parr.) und der Menschensohn', NTS 21, 1974–75, 81–108.

(41) The introduction to the saying has been abbreviated. Luke omits the redundant ἀποκριθείς in Mk. (which might give some support to R. P. Gagg's view that the beginning of the pericope has been suppressed) and the detail that Jesus was teaching in the temple, since this has already been made clear (20:1 par. Mk. 11:27). The audience is identified by Matthew as the Pharisees (cf. 20:40 note). πῶς can mean 'in what sense?' or 'how is it possible that?' λέγουσιν (third person) is odd. In Mk. the inclusion of the subject, οἱ γραμματεῖς, suggests that Jesus was speaking about them to the crowds; in Lk. the audience is the Pharisees (or the scribes) so that a question in the second person (cf. Mt.) would be more appropriate. Perhaps 20:45 suggests that the crowds are in Luke's mind as the audience. Mark's ὅτι construction is replaced by the accusative and infinitive. The scribal belief that the Messiah would be a son of David is based on such passages as 2 Sa. 7; Ps. 89:20–37; Is. 9:2–7; 11:1–9; Je. 23:5f.; 33:14–18; Ezk. 34:23f.; 37:24; and is attested in Ps. Sol. 17:21; 4QFl 1:11–13; cf. 4QPB 4; 4 Ez. 12:32; Shemoneh Esreh 14. 'Son of David' is the regular title for the Messiah in rabbinic texts (e.g. Sanh. 98a); cf. SB I, 11–14, 525; E. Lohse, TDNT VIII, 480–482; Burger, 16–24.

(42) The question has implicitly contained the OT evidence that constitutes one part of the apparent contradiction that Jesus is putting before his hearers. The second part is given in a citation. αὐτὸς γάρ apparently gives a better connection than καὶ αὐτός (A D W Γ Δ f13 *pm* lat; TR; *Diglot*), but the latter phrase could mean 'and yet he himself calls . . .', and so be original. As in 20:37 Luke has λέγει, diff. Mk. εἶπεν, to introduce a citation. He drops Mark's note of Davidic inspiration, ἐν τῷ πνεύματι τῷ ἁγίῳ; contrast Acts 1:16; 4:25. Instead he substitutes ἐν βίβλῳ ψαλμῶν, possibly as a reminiscence of Mk. 12:26; for βίβλος cf. 3:4* and for ψαλμός, 'psalm', cf. 24:44; Acts 1:20; 13:33. (cf. G. Delling, TDNT VIII, 499f.). The quotation follows the wording in Mk. which differs from the LXX of Ps. 110 (109):1 only in omitting ὁ before κύριος and in substituting ὑποκάτω, 'underneath', for ὑποπόδιον, 'stool'; Luke has reversed the second change (cf. Acts 2:35; Heb. 1:13; 10:13; Holtz, 51–53).

France, 163–169, correctly observes that Jesus' use of the Psalm depends upon the assumptions that 'my lord' denotes superiority (strangely denied by Lindars, 47), that the person addressed as 'my lord' is the Messiah, and that the speaker is David. Both of these two latter assumptions are very much open to question. The form of the Psalm is usually thought to be that of a royal psalm in which the king is being addressed by a loyal subject; the speaker relates an oracle in which Yahweh addresses the king and makes promises to him. Although the Psalm used to be given a late date, recent criticism has pushed its date backwards, and there is a sound case that it belongs to the early days of the monarchy, possibly even to the reign of David. The case for composition by the king himself has never won much favour. Gundry, 228f., argues that David could have composed it to legitimize Solomon on the throne, referring to the new monarch as his 'lord'; when Solomon failed to live up to the high ideal set forth here, the psalm began to be interpreted messianically. France, however, argues that the claims made for the future king here go beyond the limits even of extravagant, courtly language, e.g. in the attribution to the ruler of priesthood and of a seat at God's right hand. He claims, therefore, that this is not a royal psalm but that it refers to the Messiah. A similar interpretation of the psalm is advanced by F. Hesse, TDNT IX, 505f., although in his view the psalm reflects disillusionment with the monarchy and is the work of a cultic prophet who hopes that the next ruler will have the world dominion which ought to belong to Israel. It seems fairly certain that the psalm does go back to the monarchy and is messianic in outlook; whether we can proceed from this point to affirm that it goes back to David is not so clear. It is certainly not impossible that a hope which is as old as Is. 9 may be dated even earlier.

In any case, what matters is how the psalm was understood by Jesus and his contemporaries. For them there was no question about the Davidic authorship, but it is uncertain whether the psalm was interpreted messianically. The available rabbinic evidence shows that c. AD 130–250 the psalm was applied to Abraham or Hezekiah (SB IV:1, 452–465). This interpretation may go back earlier (cf. Schweizer, Markus, 145f. who notes the lack of messianic use in the Qumran and other early Jewish writings), but it is also possible that Billerbeck is right in arguing that the second-century Jewish interpretation dates back only to R. Ishmael (c. 100–135) who sought to remove a debating weapon from the Christians by repudiating an earlier Jewish messianic interpretation of the psalm. France claims that Jesus' opponents would have had to accept this if his argument was to be forceful to them. But this is not completely certain. It is possible that Jesus was putting before them a text which they did not previously interpret messianically, and asserting that it was messianic and that it should modify their understanding of messiahship. The fact that the early church frequently used the psalm with a messianic reference (Mk. 14:62; Acts 2:34; 7:56; Rom. 8:34; 1 Cor. 15:25; Eph. 1:20; Col. 3:1; Heb. 1:3, 13; 5:6; 7:17, 21; 8:1; 10:12f.; 1 Pet. 3:22; Rev. 3:21) gives some credence to the view that the psalm's messianic interpretation was not disputed by the Jews.

(43) Luke's restoration of ὑποπόδιον (so LXX), diff. Mk. ὑποκάτω, gives a literal rendering of the MT. Cf. Mt. 5:35; Acts 7:49; Jas. 2:3.

(44) The conclusion is arranged chiastically, and is introduced by οὖν, par. Mt. Similarly, Luke and Matthew both use καλέω diff. Mk. λέγω. The first part of the sentence is equivalent to a conditional protasis. The order αὐτοῦ υἱός is inverted by ℵ D L W Γ Δ f13 pm; TR; Diglot. For the probable solution to the question see above.

vi. Woes to the Scribes 20:45–47

Luke has already included a lengthy series of criticisms of the scribes in 11:37–54. It is, therefore, mildly surprising that he has included the similar sayings of Jesus against the scribes recorded by Mark at this point, and has not troubled to avoid the doublet found in 11:43 with 20:46b (contrast his omission of Mk. 12:28–34). But Luke had good reasons for his procedure. By his inclusion of this passage he was able to add a second prong to Jesus' attack on the scribes and to complement the criticism of their theology (20:41–44) with a criticism of their way of life. The falsity of scribal religion is thus seen to come to a climax in pride and greed and hypocrisy. Is there the suggestion that false theology leads to immoral behaviour? Implicitly, the section constitutes a warning to the disciples not to fall into the same errors.

The scribes are attacked for using their position as teachers to further their own prestige in both religious and secular life. At the same time they made a good thing financially out of their function as lawyers by abusing positions of trust as guardians of property; to this end they put up a show of religiosity in the hope that it would encourage people to trust them in matters of business (J. D. M. Derrett*).

The material is again taken from Mk. with some possible influence from the source utilised in 11:43 (cf. Schramm, 29).

See K. H. Rengstorf, 'Die ΣΤΟΛΑΙ der Schriftgelehrten', in O. Betz, 383–404; J. D. M. Derrett, ' "Eating up the houses of widows": Jesus's comment on lawyers?', Nov.T 14, 1972, 1–9.

(45) Luke again substitutes λαός for Mk. ὄχλος, thereby distinguishing the people of Israel from their religious leaders. He transforms Mark's comment that the people heard Jesus gladly into a simple statement that they now continued to listen while Jesus taught his disciples; the reference to the disciples is brought forward from Mk. 12:43 (cf. Mt. 23:1). After τοῖς μαθηταῖς (B D pc) αὐτοῦ is added by ℵ A L W Δ Θ f1 f13 pm lat; TR; (UBS); Diglot (cf. Metzger, 172, who holds that there was a scribal tendency to drop αὐτοῦ in this situation, since 'the disciples' were self-evidently Jesus' disciples; in this particular case, however, the 'later' reading has good support from B and D).

(46) προσέχω ἀπό (12:1), diff. Mk. βλέπω ἀπό, is a Hebraism and may have been drawn from Luke's source in 12:1 (Schramm, 49 n.).

θέλω here has the sense 'to like' (cf. MM, 286). The στολή (15:22) has been traditionally identified with the long, flowing garment of the learned (*tallith*) (SB II, 31–33; U. Wilckens, TDNT VII, 687–691). K. H. Rengstorf* claims that festal garments worn on the Sabbath are meant. In both cases it is the ostentation of the scribes which is attacked. The addition of καὶ φιλούντων eases Mark's phraseology (θελόντων constructed in two different ways) and may reflect the source behind 11:43 par. Mt. 23:6 (on the verb, used in this sense here only in Lk., see G. Stählin, TDNT IX, 114–116, especially 128f.). The first two items beloved by the scribes have already appeared in 11:43 and the third in 14:7–11.

(47) The structure changes to a relative clause (avoiding Mark's difficult construction). The new charge is of devouring (8:5) the houses of widows. Jeremias, *Jerusalem*, 114, reviews various interpretations, including making payment for giving legal advice, and concludes that abusing the hospitality of people of limited means is most probable. T. W. Manson thought the reference was to mismanaging the property of widows who had dedicated themselves to the service of the temple (2:36f.). J. D. M. Derrett*, holds that the verse refers to lawyers acting as guardians appointed by a husband in his will to care for his widow's estate. They were entitled to some remuneration for their task and some of them helped themselves lavishly out of the estates committed to them (cf. Gittin 52a, b). On Derrett's view, the long prayers (cf. Mt. 6:7) were said publicly in order to give an impression of piety and trustworthiness and so to induce people to appoint them as trustees. πρόφασις can mean 'actual motive' (Jn. 15:22) or 'pretext' (Acts 27:30; Phil. 1:18; 1 Thes. 2:5). While most scholars prefer the latter meaning ('for appearance sake'), Derrett prefers the former ('with such an end in view'). Persons guilty of such conduct will receive all the greater judgment (κρίμα, 23:40; 24:20*; Acts 24:25*), i.e. those who abuse positions of trust (cf. 12:47). For similar accusations cf. Ass. Moses 7:6f; Ps. Sol. 4:11–13.

vii. The Widow's Offering 21:1–4

The final incident in this section is joined to what precedes both by the catchword 'widow' and by the contrast between the false piety of the scribes and the widow, although in the story itself the contrast is between the rich and the poor rather than between the scribes and the widow; in both contrasts, however, true and false piety is the issue. The incident fits in with Luke's emphasis on the way in which true religion affects a person's attitude to wealth, and brings out the lesson that what matters is not the amount that one gives but the amount that one keeps for oneself; in the present case the widow gave all that she had and thereby expressed her faith in God to provide for her needs.

The story is a good example of how Luke can considerably alter the wording of a Marcan narrative while preserving the element of discourse almost unaltered. There is no trace of use of another source. The original story in Mk. is regarded by Bultmann, 32f. (cf. Lohmeyer, 265f.; Schweizer, *Markus*, 148; Nineham, 334f.) as an ideal construction, since 1. Jesus could not have seen how much the woman gave nor known how much she had left over, and 2. the story has parallels in rabbinic and Indian tales (Lv. R 3 (107a), in SB II, 46) and the point is already made in Greek literature (cf. also Jos. Ant. 6:148f.). The story has, therefore, been thought to be originally a parable or fable, perhaps told by Jesus, which has been transformed into a story about Jesus.

There is nothing surprising in the fact that Jesus could take over a well-known and sound religious idea, and it is quite possible that he may have used the incident of a widow as an illustration of the principle. Nor can we rule out the possibility that he had knowledge, natural or perhaps clairvoyant, of the nature of the woman's gift (see below). In any case the point of the story is not concerned with the possible prophetic knowledge of Jesus but with his verdict on the question of giving. As for the parallels to the story, these are not of such a kind as to force us to conclude that the story has developed out of them (Taylor, 496). The question of the historicity of the narrative must thus at least be kept open.

(1) While Mark introduces the narrative as a separate scene, Luke pictures Jesus as already sitting as he teaches and looking up to see what is going on in the vicinity; the incident is thus connected more closely with what precedes in order to emphasise the contrast (Grundmann, 377). Luke uses εἶδεν diff. Mk. ἐθεώρει (contrast 21:6), a word which suggests here a sudden glance rather than a conscious gaze. Luke omits reference to the crowds putting their money into the receptacles and concentrates on the rich people. γαζοφυλάκιον (Mk. 12:41, 43; Jn. 8:20**) can mean 'treasury', i.e. a room for keeping treasure; AG prefer in the present case the meaning 'contribution box, receptacle'. There were a number of rooms for keeping valuables in the temple (Jos. Bel. 5:200; 6:282), one of which in particular was known as 'the treasury' (Jos. Ant. 19:294; cf. Jn. 8:20). There were also thirteen trumpet-shaped collection boxes for offerings of various kinds, and SB II, 37–45, argues that they were in this treasury which opened off the Court of the Women. Although many commentators think that the reference here is to one of these receptacles, SB points out that this meaning for the word is otherwise unattested, and that it is more probable that Jesus was seated near the room where the receptacles were kept. Evidence is also adduced (t. Shek. 3:1ff. (177)) that gifts were offered for various purposes, especially in relation to vows, and the offerer declared the amount and purpose of the gift to the officiating priest. In these circumstances it is not surprising that Jesus knew how much the various people were offering. Mark refers to the copper coins put in by the people; Luke

substitutes a vaguer reference to 'gifts' (δῶρον, cf.21:4*), which allows for more valuable coins being given by the rich.

(2) Where Mark describes what happened in narrative style, Luke describes what Jesus saw: a poor (πενιχρός**; cf. F. Hauck, TDNT VI, 40, who gives the meaning 'very poor') widow. For δέ τινα there are the variants δέ τινα καί (A Δ Θ f1 pm; TR); δὲ καί τινα (D al; Diglot); and τινα καί (W pc); the fluctuating position of καί suggests that it is a scribal addition. For λεπτόν see 12:59; Luke omits Mark's statement of the equivalent in Roman coinage. The statement that a gift of one lepton was forbidden (Plummer, 475) rests on a misreading of BB 10b (cf. SB II, 45). The widow, therefore, could have given even less than her tiny gift (Schmid, Mark, 230).

(3) Luke has no need to mention that Jesus called his disciples (Mk.) for they are already present to be instructed. Jesus solemnly draws attention to what he has witnessed with ἀληθῶς (diff. Mk. ἀμήν, cf. 9:27; 12:44*). This widow, who belongs to the class of the poor – who trust in God and for whom the good news is especially meant (cf. Danker, 209) – has given proportionately more than all the others. The word order αὕτη ἡ πτωχή is inverted in A W Γ Δ Θ f1 pm; TR; Diglot, and this looser order may be correct, the other reading being due to assimilation to Mk.

(4) Jesus explains his verdict. For πάντες (א B D Δ pc) ἅπαντες is read by rell; TR; Diglot (cf. 2:39 note). The rich gave out of their abundant wealth (cf. 12:15). εἰς τὰ δῶρα can mean 'into the gifts', i.e. 'as gifts' or 'into the offering (chest)' (AG). The addition τοῦ θεοῦ (A D W Γ Δ Θ f1 f13 pl lat sy^p; TR; Diglot – an explanation for gentiles, Metzger, 172) suggests the latter interpretation. ὑστέρημα, 'need, want, deficiency', replaces Mark's rare ὑστέρησις (Phil. 4:11**). For πάντα Diglot again has ἅπαντα (A W Γ Δ Θ f1 pm; TR). For βίος, 'livelihood', cf. 8:43; 15:12, 30. In a condition of need the widow gave away even the little which she had to support life. If the leaders of Jewish religion treated such pious people in the way criticised by Jesus in 20:47, it followed that the system was ripe for judgment. It is no accident that the prophecy of the destruction of the temple follows: the priests were no better than the scribes in their attitude to wealth (20:45f.).

e. The Coming of the End (21:5–38)

Jesus is portrayed (diff. Mk.) as still teaching in the temple in the presence of the people and his disciples, so that this section marks the climax of his public ministry (Zmijewski, 53). After a statement concerning the destruction of the temple (cf. 13:35; 19:42–44), his hearers ask him when it is going to happen and what indications there will be in advance of the event itself. The character of Jesus' answer implies that his

questioners assumed that there was some link between the destruction of
the temple and the end of the world.

Ellis's analysis (241) of the discourse suggests that it falls into four
main 'sign' sayings. The first of these (21:8–11) prophesies the coming
of false prophets and wars which might be mistaken for signs of the End;
in fact there will still be further wars and earthly and heavenly convul-
sions. Second, before all these things happen, there will be persecution
for the disciples, during which they must rely on the help given them by
Jesus and persevere faithfully to the end (21:12–19). Third, the encircl-
ing of Jerusalem by troops will be a sign that its prophesied fate is at
hand. There will be terrible suffering for the Jews and Jerusalem will
remain in the power of the gentiles for an indefinite period (21:20–24).
Then, fourth, there will be heavenly and earthly portents which will be
followed by the glorious coming of the exalted Son of man. These events
will signal the coming of final redemption for the people of God
(21:25–28). These sayings are followed by an assurance that the End
will follow the signs of its coming, and that Jesus' words will be fulfilled
(21:29–33). It follows, as a practical admonition, that the disciples must
not be deluded by sin into failing to recognise the signs and so being unready for the sudden, unexpected coming of the Son of man (21:34–36).

Luke has already given his readers apocalyptic teaching by Jesus;
in 12:35–48 there were warnings about being ready at all times for the
coming of the Son of man, and in 17:20–37 Jesus spoke about the
danger of being misled by false prophets; when the Son of man comes,
there will be no mistaking his arrival, which will bring judgment on all
who are not ready for it. Why has Luke included this further discourse,
which covers much the same ground? Elsewhere, he has omitted
material from Mk. to which he had already provided an equivalent.
Clearly he must have felt that the lesson needed repetition or that there
were fresh things to be said.

A solution to this problem may be found by reconsidering the contents of the discourse. First, it is concerned with a point not treated
earlier in the apocalyptic teaching of Jesus. Jesus had spoken of the
desolation of the temple (13:35) and the destruction of Jerusalem
(19:42–44), but he had not related these to the coming of the Son of
man. It is clear that the problem of the relation between these two sets of
events needed to be solved. Was the End linked chronologically with the
fall of Jerusalem? The present discourse takes up this point, and it shows
that the two sets of events are chronologically separate, although both
are the fulfilment of prophecy and take place in the last days.

Second, the discourse is concerned with the question of 'signs' of
the End. Contemporary apocalyptic teaching offered various signs by
which men might know that the End was near. Luke has already shown
that Jesus rejected any such use of signs to calculate when the kingdom
of God would come, and that he taught that the Son of man would come
suddenly and unexpectedly; men, therefore, could not live carelessly

until the End was drawing near and then reform themselves at the last minute. This lesson needed to be reinforced, especially in relation to the tradition that Jesus had given teaching on signs indicating the approach of the End. Luke, therefore, tries to show that various events, which might be regarded as signs of the End, were not in fact such signs. Even the fall of Jerusalem would not be followed immediately by the End. But the fact that Jesus had spoken of signs could not be edited away, and there is a certain tension in the discourse between the recognition that there will be signs of the End and the fact that the End will be sudden and unexpected.

Third, Luke has underlined the fact that the disciples will face persecution and temptation to give up their faith, and he stresses the encouragements given to them by Jesus to hold fast to the end.

Ellis has suggested that in all four 'sign' sayings we have the same span of time: each culminates in the End, but whereas the first two deal with the period from the resurrection onwards, the third begins with the judgment on the Jews, and the fourth begins with the cosmic signs which were the climax of the first saying. This interpretation is required in the light of v. 12a and the parallelism between vs. 11 and 25. The effect is to make it clear that there are no premonitory signs until the End itself: the 'times of the gentiles' are of uncertain duration. This may suggest that Luke was writing after the fall of Jerusalem at a time when it had become obvious that it did not herald the End.

The preceding discussion has already shown that the discourse must be analysed in relation to the parallel discourse in Mk. 13. After much discussion of the problem it seems to be established that the fundamental points of view in the two discourses are not dissimilar. Thus Luke agrees with Mark in stressing the certainty of the End, but showing that it would not happen immediately after the resurrection of Jesus and that, although various 'signs' might be seen, it would be impossible to forecast when it would take place. Further, the thrust of both discourses is paraenetic rather than apocalyptic. Jesus is not concerned to impart apocalyptic secrets to the disciples, but to prepare them spiritually for what lies ahead. Both Evangelists teach the need to be ready at all times for the coming of the Son of man, but Luke, writing later than Mark, indicates more clearly that it would not happen immediately after the resurrection of Jesus – although it might be very near indeed for his readers. Where Luke differs from Mk. is in bringing out more clearly that the destruction of the temple is not associated chronologically with the End, and in demonstrating that the destruction of the temple is part of the divine judgment upon Jerusalem. In so doing, Luke's discourse draws upon a different OT background from that in Mk.

Obviously Luke knew Mk. 13 and used it as a source. The wording is almost identical with that in Mk. in vs. 5–11a, 16f., 21a, 23a, 27, 29–33; elsewhere there is parallelism in structure and thought, but the wording differs considerably. On any account of the matter, due allowance must be made for the editorial activity of Luke. The question is whether this is a sufficient explanation of the relationship.

1. The 'orthodox' view is that Luke had Mk. 13 as his sole source, and that all differences are due to Lucan editing in the light of the events of AD 70 (now past) and the delay of the parousia (so, for example, Bultmann, 129; F. C. Burkitt in BC II, 106–120; Klostermann, 197–199; Creed, 252–254; Conzelmann, 116–124; Grässer, 152–168; Neirynck, 177–179; Zmijewski, 59–65, 311; Geiger, 150f.). Klostermann suggests three main motives that influenced Luke. First, he omitted material to which he had earlier provided parallel traditions (Lk. 17:23 par. Mk. 13:20–23; Lk. 12:39–48 par. Mk. 13:34–36), and rewrote these sections in his own words. Second, he dropped Mk. 13:32 with its confession of Jesus' ignorance, and regarded Acts 1:7 as a less controversial substitute. Third, he brought Mark's prophecies up-to-date in the light of the fulfilment of some of them and the delay of others. 21:12–19 dealt with prophecies that could be regarded as largely fulfilled in the history of the church, and this was brought out in the wording (e.g. 21:14f. par. Acts 6:10); 21:12 indicates that Luke regarded these events as happening at an early point. 21:20–24 was rewritten to clarify that the events of AD 70 were in mind, and to distinguish the fall of Jerusalem from the parousia. Only after the fulfilment of the earlier prophecies could the Son of man come. Conzelmann, 123f., adds that the thought of the delay of the parousia has led to a stress on ethical paraenesis, especially to a call for perseverance during the long wait for the parousia.

These observations are broadly convincing, and subsequent studies have not brought any substantially new understanding of Luke's motives (see Zmijewski, 311–325; Geiger, 249–268), although they have clarified these in detail. It has become clear that Luke's outlook is not fundamentally different from that of Mark, although his own distinctive concepts have coloured his presentation.

2. It is not certain, however, that the hypothesis of Lucan editing of Mk. 13 furnishes a satisfactory explanation of all the material in Lk. 21. There is a strong minority opinion that Luke was partly dependent on other source material (Taylor, *Behind*, 101–125; Easton, 311; Schlatter, 412–420; Manson, *Sayings*, 323–327; Beasley-Murray, 226f.; P. Winter, 'The treatment of his sources by the Third Evangelist in Luke xxi-xxiv', ST 8, 1954, 138–172; W. Nicol*; L. Gaston*; cf. Gaston, 355–365; Caird, 227–229; Hartman, 226–235; Schramm, 171–182). Taylor argues that Luke is dependent on Mk. in 21:5–11, but on other sources in 21:12–15, 18f., 20, 21b, 23b–26a, 28, 34–36; while Gaston assigns 19:41–44; 21:20, 21b, 22, 23b–24, 10f., 25f., 28, 37f. to one source and 21:12–15, 18f. to separate traditions.

The arguments in favour of this position are: 1. It is odd that Luke should have omitted references to the gentile mission and to the gift of the Spirit (Mk. 13:10, 11) if he was following Mk. 2. There are a number of sutures in the text which suggest that Luke was combining two sources. V. 21a appears to be an interruption, since αὐτῆς and εἰς αὐτήν in v. 21b refer to Jerusalem (v. 20) and not to Judaea. Vs. 26b–27 disturb the connection between vs. 25f. and 28. 3. The poetic parallelism in vs. 20–24 is hardly the result of Lucan editing. 4. The subtle use of the OT (MT not LXX) in vs. 20–28 does not seem to be typical of Luke himself (Hartmann, 229–234). 5. When the Marcan material is set aside, we are left with a reasonably continuous discourse instead of a set of *disiecta membra*.

These arguments vary in force. W. G. Kümmel, *Introduction to the New Testament*, London, 1966, 94, attempts to weaken them by arguing: a. The connection of thought in the postulated source is not always coherent. b. It is as easy to account for the sutures in the discourse on the view that other traditions have been added to a Marcan basis. c. Luke has so obviously reworded Mk. in other places where dependence cannot be denied that it is not difficult to believe that he has also done so in other places where dependence is not so obvious. The highly detailed treatment by Zmijewski elaborates these points.

The discussion below will show that point 1. above is certainly contestable. The other points retain considerable force, especially point 2. Arguments based on the coherence of the alleged source (point 5.) are not compelling one way or the other, since the material may have been re-ordered in the editorial process.

Could such an alternative source have existed? Taylor, 118–125, argues that in the period around AD 70 there may have been various attempts to explain the significance of the events in Palestine; the hypothetical source of Lk. 21:20–36 could have been such an oracle, based to some extent on earlier materials. Manson, *Sayings*, 336f., argues that Mk. 13 and Lk. 21 contain two versions of an apocalyptic discourse whose earlier form is preserved in Q (Lk. 17:22–30). Such a view would explain how there is close parallelism in thought between Mk. 13 and Lk. 21 despite considerable divergence in wording.

3. It will be clear that Manson's view does not differ greatly from the 'orthodox' view, in that it postulates an intermediate stage between Mk. 13 and Lk. 21 in the shape of an earlier version of the material in Mk. 13. Where, however, Manson thinks that Luke's source was an *earlier* form of the material in Mk. 13, there is reason to believe that it was in fact later. The advantage of this view is that it satisfactorily accounts for those features in Lk. 21 which are hard to explain on the hypothesis that Luke was merely using Mk. 13. It is very significant that Kümmel, who completely rejects the theory of an alternative source, has to admit that Luke's editing of Mk. 13 involved 'the use of additional pieces of tradition'. At the same time, it is clearly difficult to distinguish between Lucan use of Mk. 13 and of a source very similar to Mk. 13. Taylor, *Behind*, 125, poses the problem: 'Mk. xiii supplies the groundplan on which the Lukan Discourse is built; *but in the Discourse, as in*

the Passion narrative, non-Markan matter is given the preference, and into it Markan extracts have been inserted.' It is this ambivalent nature of the material – Marcan structure but non-Marcan wording – which makes it difficult to decide whether Luke has heavily edited Mk. or used a similar source alongside Mk. On balance it is probable that Luke was using a connected source, related to 19:41–44 and concerned with the fall of Jerusalem, which he has joined with Marcan material.

The origins of the material in Mk. 13 have still not been solved satisfactorily despite several major treatments in recent years (for earlier studies see Beasley-Murray; for surveys of recent works see D. Wenham*; K. Grayston*). Beasley-Murray was concerned to dispute the view that much of Mk. 13 was based on a 'little apocalypse' composed in the early church and could not be traced back to the teaching of Jesus; he argued that while it could not be demonstrated that the discourse as a whole was a single utterance of Jesus, nevertheless its individual contents had high claims to authenticity. Beasley-Murray's work came just before the development of redaction criticism, and it could justly be claimed that he did not pay sufficient attention to the problems of how the discourse came to assume its present form and what share Mark himself had in this. A first attempt to discuss the material from this point of view was provided by Marxsen, 101–140.

From a different point of view Hartman explained much of Mk. 13 as being based on midrashic use of OT material, especially from Dn.; he traced a midrashic nucleus in Mk. 13:5b–8, 12–16, 19–22, 24–27, which was then supplemented in various ways. Although this tradition has undergone considerable developments, as may be seen from the different imprints left in Mk. 13, Lk. 21 and 1 Thes., Hartman was prepared to trace its ultimate origins to Jesus himself.

Redactional study was developed by Lambrecht who made three main points. 1. He argued for a careful, conscious structure in Mk. 13 as a whole. 2. He traced very considerable redactional activity by Mark himself. 3. He argued that Mark was working on a collection of sayings from Q together with verses taken from the LXX.

But the most thorough and influential study is that of Pesch, which is a refurbishing of the 'little apocalypse' theory. He postulates a Jewish or Jewish-Christian tract which announced the coming of the Son of man soon after catastrophic events in Jerusalem; originally the event in mind was Caligula's threatened erection of a statue in AD 39–40, but later the text was reinterpreted with reference to the siege of Jerusalem. This was taken over by Mark and given a new, less apocalyptic meaning by means of considerable editorial activity and the inclusion of other sayings. While retaining the hope of an imminent parousia, Mark concentrated attention on the persecution of the church, the rise of false prophets (such as were responsible for producing the apocalyptic tract itself), and the need for faithful and watchful discipleship.

Somewhat similar is the approach of Gaston who finds the basis of

Mk. 13 in the unfulfilled oracle in vs. 14–19 which originated c. AD 39–41. This was combined with the prediction of the parousia in vs. 20, 24–27, and then a Christian prophet included this oracle in an exhortation which included vs. 5–13, 21f. and perhaps 33–36. Finally, other sayings of Jesus were added, and Mark gave the discourse a new setting. The original prophetic discourse had referred to the destruction of Jerusalem, but Mark shifted the emphasis to the destruction of the temple.

A somewhat original approach is taken by K. Grayston* who postulates an original 'instruction leaflet', giving Christians warnings apropos of the prospect of war, persecution, sacrilege in Jerusalem and a messianic military leader; these were couched in the second person plural (Mk. 13:7a, 9, 11, 14–16, 18, 21, 23) and followed by reassurances of relief to follow (Mk. 13:28f.) and exhortation (Mk. 13:33–35). Then this was expanded by additions in apocalyptic style and related to the coming of the End. Mark himself carefully tied the discourse into his Gospel and linked it to the passion story so that the significance of each might be seen in the light of the other.

This brief summary cannot do justice to the complexity of the issues, but at least it shows that there is no unanimity regarding the origins of the apocalyptic discourse. There would appear to be valuable points in each of these treatments, but no final synthesis has been reached. It is probable that contemporary enthusiasm for redaction criticism has led to over-estimation of the place of Mark himself in the formation of the discourse. That some kind of pre-Marcan nucleus forms the basis of the discourse is beyond doubt; there is, however, no agreement regarding its content, character or origin. If we are right in thinking that Luke had access to a parallel version of the discourse, this would give some support to the view that a basic nucleus of teaching regarding the judgment on Jerusalem, the coming of the Son of man, and the behaviour of the disciples in the last days, was in existence; this has been developed in different ways in the light of OT prophecies and has left its influence on Paul and Rev. as well as in the Gospels. Its contents cohere sufficiently with the teaching of Jesus elsewhere in the Gospels to make it probable that the ultimate origin lies in his teaching, although the task of working back to this origin through traditio-historical criticism is one of extreme intricacy.

See Bultmann, 125–130; Taylor, *Behind*, 101–125; Manson, *Sayings*, 323–327; Kümmel, 95–104; Beasley-Murray; cf. Beasley-Murray, *Commentary*; Conzelmann, 116–124; Grässer, 152–168; W. Marxsen, *Der Evangelist Markus*, Göttingen, 1959, 101–140; L. Gaston, 'Sondergut und Markusstoff in Luk. 21', TZ 16, 1960, 161–172; Gaston, 8–64, 355–365; Hartman; Lambrecht; Pesch; Schramm, 171–182; Zmijewski, 43–325, 541–572; Geiger, 149–268; K. Grayston, 'The Study of Mark XIII', BJRL 56, 1974, 371–387; D. Wenham, 'Recent Study of Mark 13', *Theological Students Fellowship Bulletin* 71, Spring 1975, 6–15; 72, Summer, 1975, 1–9; W. Nicol, 'Tradition and Redaction in Luke 21', *Neotestamentica* 7, 1973, 61–77 (as summarised in NTA 20, 1976, § 482); C. Brown, 'The Parousia and Eschatology in the NT', in NIDNTT, II, 901–931, especially 909–917.

i. The Destruction of the Temple 21:5–6

The discourse as a whole consists of an opening remark by Jesus followed by a detailed exposition which goes well beyond the original statement.

A comment on the splendour of the temple from a bystander leads to a statement by Jesus that it will be completely destroyed in the coming days. The introduction thus has the form of an apophthegm or pronouncement story (Bultmann, 36).

Luke's narrative is similar in form to that in Mk., but the wording differs and the scene is different. In Mk. the *disciples* are *outside* the temple and comment on its *exterior* appearance, but in Lk. *unnamed hearers inside* the temple comment on its *internal* decoration. On the assumption that Luke is using Mk., these differences can be explained by his desire to give the discourse a public setting in the temple as the climax to Jesus' teaching there. The doom of the temple is announced publicly to the Jews (Zmijewski, 89). This change has landed Luke in a certain tension between the opening and the rest of the discourse which is clearly meant for disciples. Hence Manson, *Sayings*, 324f., argues that Luke is here following a source in which 21:5–7 was followed directly by vs. 20–24; but this hypothesis raises fresh difficulties. Luke appears to be assuming the kind of situation found in 20:45 where people and disciples form the audience of Jesus.

See Manson, *Sayings*, 324.; Beasley-Murray, *Commentary*, 19–24; Hartman, 219–222; Lambrecht, 68–79, 88–91; Pesch, 83–96; Gaston, 10f.; Zmijewski, 73–98; Geiger, 161–165.

(5) Luke omits Mark's statement that Jesus was on his way out of the temple, so that the impression given is that Jesus is still teaching there. Some people are commenting on the temple and observe how it had been adorned (κοσμέω, 11:25; for this use with respect to buildings cf. AG s.v.) with beautiful stones and offerings by worshippers in fulfilment of vows (ἀνάθημα**; cf. 2 Mac. 9:16). The magnificence of the temple and its contents constantly aroused wonder among spectators and visitors (cf. the description in Jos. Ant. 15:391–402; Bel. 5:184–226; Middoth). The general thrust of the saying is the same as in Mk. – a comment on the magnificence of the temple – but Luke has substituted indirect speech.

(6) Jesus' reply begins with a hanging nominative (ταῦτα) which is not taken up into the remainder of the sentence (1:36 note; BD 466¹; cf. Acts 7:40). Luke uses θεωρέω, diff. Mk. βλέπω, possibly a reminiscence of Mk. 12:41. The prophecy is then introduced (as in 17:22; Geiger, 164) with the phrase ἐλεύσονται ἡμέραι (cf. 5:35 par. Mk. 2:20; 19:43; 23:29) which may be Lucan. The point of the addition may be to indicate that there would be a time during which the temple would remain destroyed, and thus to avoid the misapprehension that with its destruction the end would immediately come. The fall of the temple is one of the various eschatological events in the last days (Zmijewski, 90). The

prophecy itself is close in wording to Mk. Luke has οὐκ with the future, diff. Mk. οὐ μή with the aorist subjunctive in both clauses. For λίθῳ some MSS read λίθον (ℵᶜ L W f1 33 al), probably by assimilation to Mk. or Mt. Some MSS add ὧδε (ℵ B L f13 cop; with reversed order X f1 33 e syˢᶜ), by assimilation to Mt. (Metzger, 172). The language is close to 19:44 where a similar prophecy is made against Jerusalem itself. It should also be related to the sayings in which Jesus speaks of the destruction of the temple (Mk. 14:58; Acts 6:14; Jn. 2:19).

The question now arises whether this saying and its setting are authentic. For the case against authenticity see especially Pesch, 83–96; Lambrecht, 68–79, 88–91; they argue that the whole scene has been created by Mark, the saying itself being based on Mk. 14:58; the saying and its framework could not exist without each other, and they were composed to fit together; the disciples are unlikely to have spoken about the temple in the way they do here, and Jesus' saying does not fall into the prophetic tradition of threats against Jerusalem and the temple; the saying can date only from after AD 70. These arguments are unconvincing. They assume that only one form of the saying about the temple can have existed originally, and have little justification for excluding the possibility that Mk. 13:2 is independent of 14:58 (cf. Hartman, 220). The saying could certainly not have been transmitted without a framework such as is provided here. Is, then, the framework possible? The remark of the interlocutor seems to be unmotivated and to have the literary purpose of introducing the saying of Jesus; yet is there any reason why some such remark could not have been made by the disciples – and at any time during their stay in Jerusalem? A great building continues to evoke such emotions long after the first time it has been seen, and the writings of Josephus indicate the national pride that Jews had in their temple.

Moreover, the teaching that follows in Mk. bears little relation to the theme of the destruction of the temple, and it is unlikely that the opening dialogue was composed as an introduction to it. It has more the impression of an independent conversation in which an apparently pious remark by one of his audience is used by Jesus to give a spiritual corrective (cf. 11:27f.; 14:15–24). There is no point in trusting in the temple, for one day it will be destroyed.

ii. Deceptive Signs of the End 21:7–11

Jesus' prophecy of the destruction of the temple prompts a question from his hearers: when are these events going to happen? What sign will indicate that they are about to happen? Luke does not have the shift of scene from the temple to the Mount of Olives found in Mk., and he does not restrict Jesus' audience to an inner group of disciples; it is public teaching which Jesus gives, and the warnings given to the disciples can also be heard with profit by the crowds. The question asked pertains to the destruction of the temple; but, although the use of συντελέω is dropped, the retention of the plural ταῦτα suggests that the scope of the question still includes the last things, and this is confirmed by the nature of Jesus' answer; Jesus' hearers may be presumed to have regarded the destruction of the temple as an eschatological event.

Jesus' answer falls into two parts. First, he warns the hearers not to be deceived by false prophets who make messianic claims and announce that the denouement is at hand. Nor must they be shaken in their faith by wars and tumults. These things are certainly part of God's plan for the last days, but they are not indications that the End is to follow immediately. Here Luke follows Mk. closely, bringing out more forcefully the danger of the audience being led astray. He does not basically alter the point already clearly present in Mk., that these events do not signify the imminence of the End.

Second, Luke sharply separates off a further description of national wars, natural disasters and fearful heavenly portents. The description of these is fuller than in Mk., and Mark's note that these are the beginnings of birthpangs is omitted. This may suggest that for Luke even large-scale disasters are not a sign of the End. On this view, vs. 10f. are the beginnings of a more detailed account of the things contained in vs. 9f. (Zmijewski, 121f., following Conzelmann, 118f.). But it is more likely that in vs. 8f. Jesus is describing local conflicts in Palestine, while in vs. 10f. he describes more widespread conflicts and cosmic signs. Geiger, 169–172, argues that Luke is moving from past history to the future at this point. This is possible, but it should be borne in mind that the kind of events described here were associated with the Jewish war in AD 66–70 (Schlatter, 413). It is thus more probable that the events leading up to AD 70 are in mind throughout this section.

The teaching is mostly taken from Mk. But the new introduction in v. 10, for which no redactional explanation is entirely satisfactory, and the differences in wording from Mk. give some support to the view that another source is being utilised alongside Mk. (L. Gaston*, 168f.). It seems possible that Luke did have another version of the discourse, but the evidence is not too strong.

Most scholars regard the introduction to this section as stemming from Mk. and the warnings as being drawn from an 'apocalyptic tract' giving advice in a time of disaster (cf. Pesch*). Hartman* finds a 'midrashic nucleus' based on Dn., while Lambrecht* thinks that Mark has composed the section on the basis of Q material (cf. Lk. 17:21, 23). K. Grayston* holds that vs. 5f. are Mark's introduction to the discourse, v. 7a is from a 'warning leaflet', and the rest is expansion by means of apocalyptic material. It is clear that there is no unanimity regarding the history of the tradition in this section. On the whole it is probable that Mk. 13:3f. is a link between this section and the preceding apophthegm. As for the teaching in vs. 5–8, the objections raised by Beasley-Murray to the 'little apocalypse' theory still stand, and to them should be added

Hartman's point that facilities for multiplying copies of tracts are unlikely to have existed in the first century. Even if such a document existed, we cannot assume without further ado that its contents were Jewish or Jewish-Christian; the possibility that the teaching is based on sayings of Jesus must be taken into account. When we examine it from this point of view, it is clear that while the teaching would be of great relevance to the early church in the confused situation before and after AD 70, it nevertheless coheres with other teaching of Jesus. The note of warning against false prophets fits in with his other teaching, and the warning against misunderstanding catastrophes as signs of the end fits in with his general warnings against seeking for messianic signs and his teaching on the sudden coming of the kingdom. The use of the OT also coheres with his teaching. A dominical basis for the teaching is in fact more than likely. If so, the question is how this basis has been used in the present section; see the exegetical notes below for some tentative discussions of this point.

See Manson, *Sayings*, 324–326; Beasley-Murray, *Commentary*, 25–39; Hartman, 147–150, 159–162, 220–224; Lambrecht, 80–114; Pesch, 96–112, 118–125; Gaston, 11–16 (cf. L. Gaston, as cited in 21:5–38 note); Zmijewski, 73–98, 98–128; Geiger, 165–172.

(7) Those who question Jesus here are implicitly the 'certain people' who commented on the splendour of the temple. They address Jesus as διδάσκαλε, a title probably taken from Mk. 13:1; Luke could not use it in v. 5 where he has indirect speech, and brings it in now. The title is generally used by non-disciples in Lk., and the implication is that Jesus continues to give public teaching here, although later his reply appears to be directed especially to disciples (21:12ff.). Luke omits Mark's εἰπὸν ἡμῖν, for which οὖν is perhaps a substitute with weak force. In context ταῦτα must refer primarily to the destruction of the temple (Manson, *Sayings*, 324f.; Ellis, 243). Zmijewski, 93–95, however, observes that a reference to events generally in the coming days (v. 6) is likely. It is probable in any case that the destruction of the temple was associated with the last days. The second part of the question asks for a sign that these things are about to happen. Luke drops Mark's πάντα and substitutes γίνεσθαι for συντελεῖσθαι. This could be an indication that he is not concerned here with the end of the age and is concentrating attention solely on the destruction of the temple (Geiger, 168f.). But this is unlikely in a post-70 document (if Luke is as late as that), and ignores the teaching on the parousia that follows later in the chapter.

The language suggests that the material has been composed by Mark, and it is not clear how far he has based it on tradition. Pesch, 105f., claims that the origin is a situation in which people were asking whether the fall of the temple (which had already taken place) was a sign of the imminence of the end. But Jesus' prophecy of the destruction of the temple would be a perfectly adequate stimulus to make people ask when it would happen, and in its context this is what the saying refers to.

(8) Luke drops Mark's ἤρξατο λέγειν, which would be appropriate

enough before a discourse. The warning to beware lest anyone lead the hearers astray is changed to a direct imperative – beware lest you be led astray – perhaps to make it more stringent, or under the influence of catechetical usage (1 Cor. 6:9; 15:33; Gal. 6:7; Jas. 1:16). The verb πλανάω* is used elsewhere of being led astray in the last days (Rev. 2:20; 12:9; 13:14; et al.; H. Braun, TDNT VI, 228–253, especially 246f.). The stress of the last days will make men particularly open to any charlatan who promises them deliverance. Hartman, 176, thinks that the warning here has been derived from the prophecy in the following verse in Mk. Pesch, 107f., regards the saying as a creation by Mark which sets the parenetic tone of what follows; but his argument, that the second person style belongs to Christian parenesis and not to apocalyptic, in no way proves the point. Lambrecht, 93–95, ascribes the use of βλέπετε (Mk. 13:5, 9, 23, 33) to Mark.

The warning is directed against people who come in the name of Jesus bringing what are to be regarded as false messages. Luke adds γάρ (par. Mt.) to improve the connection. πολλοί is not too strong a word to use in view of the number of false prophets who flourished in the first century (cf. R. Meyer, TDNT VI, pp. 826f.). After λέγοντες many MSS add ὅτι (A D W Γ Δ Θ f1 f13 pl; TR; Diglot). ἐπὶ τῷ ὀνόματί μου is variously interpreted: 1. 'under my authority'; 2. 'claiming to be me'; 3. 'claiming the name of 'Messiah' which belongs rightfully to me. The phrase must be taken in conjunction with the claim ἐγώ εἰμι, which can mean: a. 'I am the Messiah' (so Mt.); b. 'I am Jesus, risen and returned'; but hardly c. 'I am God'. Probably we should combine views 2. and a. (H. Bietenhard, TDNT V, 277 n. 224; Cranfield, 395). The second part of the false prophets' claim is that 'the time has drawn near', a prophecy which echoes Rev. 1:3; 22:10; cf. Dn. 7:22. The view that Luke is implicitly contradicting Mk. 1:15 is quite improbable, since the wording differs and since Luke has already used expressions equivalent to Mk. 1:15. Here the point is the false claim that the prophet is an eschatological figure whose appearance signifies that the End has drawn near; the disciples might be tempted to follow such people, i.e. become their disciples, in order to gain salvation (cf. Zmijewski, 114–118), and might perhaps follow them literally into the wilderness (cf. Acts 5:37; 20:30; Lk. 17:23). Note that the saying – and the chapter generally – presupposes an interval between the ministry of Jesus and the End. If the saying is based on authentic teaching of Jesus, it indicates that such an interval (rather than a 'delay') before the End was part of his eschatological understanding.

But the saying stands under critical suspicion, since it implies that Jesus himself will return as a messianic figure (cf. Mt. 24:5) or as the Son of man, and since it prophesies the appearance of men like Simon Magus (Acts 8:9). Pesch, 207ff., assigns it to the opening of the 'apocalyptic tract' used by Mark; the phrase λέγοντες ὅτι ἐγώ εἰμι is an addition by Mark. In Luke's version the phrase 'the time has drawn near' is generally regarded as an addition by Luke to underline the fact that the End is not imminent. For similar teaching see 17:23; Mk. 13:21-23; Mt. 24:23, 26; earlier we saw that 17:23 is a Q saying, and Lambrecht, 100–105, argues that both Marcan forms of the saying are based on Q. But the view that Mk. 13:6 is a Marcan variant of Mk. 13:21, which in turn is based on Marcan redaction of Q, is dubious. It is more probable that the traditions are independent and confirm that Jesus did warn against false messianic claimants. The redundancy in Mk. 13:6 suggests that 'in my name' may be a clarification. Since Jesus in all probability identified himself with the coming Son of man, a warning to his disciples not to be misled by charlatans makes good sense. Since, however, the text could well have been influenced by the experiences of the church, it is difficult to be certain how far the wording goes back to Jesus.

(9) The thought now shifts from false prophets to political upheavals. The disciples will hear of wars (πόλεμος, 14:31*) and insurrections (ἀκαταστασία, Jas. 3:16; 1 Cor. 14:33**), i.e. probably civil wars; the latter word replaces Mark's 'rumours of wars'. These may be interpreted in terms of the Roman civil war or of internecine struggles in Palestine. War is a standard topic in apocalyptic (cf. Is. 19:2; 2 Ch. 15:6; Dn. 11:44; Rev. 6:8; 11:13; 4 Ez. 13:31), and such disturbances could lead to a belief that the end was at hand and perhaps fill men's hearts with fear that they would not live to see it or make them believe that evil had the upper hand and the end would never come. So the disciples are warned not to be terrified (πτοέω, 24:37**; diff. Mk. θροέω (cf. 2 Thes. 2:2) which is not quite so strong). Such events are in God's plan; they must happen as his plan unfolds (cf. Dn. 2:28; Rev. 1:1; 4:1; 22:6; France, 254), but they do not signify that the end will follow immediately. Luke has two changes from Mk. here. He inserts πρῶτον – these things must happen 'first', i.e. before the end (cf. 17:25; 2 Thes. 2:3). It is unnecessary to press the word to suggest that these are the very first events in the apocalyptic timetable (cf. W. Michaelis, TDNT VI, 869 n. 5). Luke has also replaced Mark's οὔπω by οὐκ εὐθέως; Grässer, 158, claims that the effect is to separate the events of AD 70 from the 'real' final events; but in fact the thought is already present in Mk., and the change is stylistically conditioned, since Luke generally avoids οὔπω (8:25 and 19:30 diff. Mk.; 23:53 may be from a source; cf. Jn. 19:41). τέλος is the end of the age (1 Cor. 15:24). There is nothing in the saying as a whole which cannot have been uttered by Jesus; the content is familiar from apocalyptic, and the hortatory, anti-apocalyptic tone is appropriate.

(10) The break in the discourse and introduction of the connective τότε ἔλεγεν αὐτοῖς is puzzling, since Luke is apparently still following Mk., there is no break in Mk. at this point, and the theme remains the same. The alternative punctuation which would make τότε part of what Jesus said ('At that time', he said, 'nation will rise up ...') is improbable and unhelpful. Klostermann, 201, argues that here Luke sees a transition

to definitely future events (cf. Geiger, 170). There is more to be said for L. Gaston's* view (169) that here Luke is influenced by a different source (cf. Easton, 310; Schramm, 174f.), but the evidence is not compelling (cf. 5:36 for a similar insertion in Marcan material). Gaston must assume that originally v. 10f. preceded vs. 25f. and have been moved forward because of their similarity to Mk. 13:9. Nevertheless, this suggestion may be the best answer to the problem, since a redactional motive for the interruption is not discernible.

What we now have is essentially a repetition of v. 9a. The first part of the saying is parallel to Mk. and is based on Is. 19:2 and 2 Ch. 15:6 (but not on the LXX; cf. Gundry, 46f.); cf. 4 Ez. 13:31.

(11) The second part of the saying deals with natural disasters. The wording is similar to that in Mk. but has significant differences. The particle τε (omitted by A L *pc*; (*Diglot*)) (2:16; *et al.*) links forwards rather than backwards. σεισμός, 'earthquake', is found in apocalyptic contexts (Rev. 6:12; 8:5; *et al.*; cf. Is. 13:13; Hg. 2:6; Zc. 14:4); Luke qualifies with μέγας (Rev. 6:12; 11:13; 16:18; cf. Mt. 8:24; 28:2), which suggests that climactic events are in view. The word order καὶ κατὰ τόπους is reversed in A W Γ Δ Θ f1 f13 *pm* lat; TR; *Diglot*, probably by assimilation to Mk. and Mt. Some English versions suggest a limited meaning ('in various places', RSV; TNT; NIV; 'here and there', Barclay), but the context suggests a broader meaning, 'in place after place' (AG 407; cf. NEB; TEV). λιμός, 'famine' (Is. 14:30; 8:21; Rev. 18:8), is traditionally linked with λοιμός**, 'pestilence' (cf. the adjective, Acts 24:5); cf. Thucydides 2:54; BD 488². The order of words (B 157 1241 lat sy^{sc} Mcion) is inverted in *Synopsis; Diglot*.

Along with these disasters on earth there will also be terrible sights (φόβητρον**) and signs in the sky. The latter are probably signs conveying messages to astrologists or simply unusual phenomena, as in Joel 2:30f.; Am. 8:9; Rev. 6:12–14. The text is confused: καὶ ἀπ' οὐρανοῦ σημεῖα μεγάλα ἔσται (B f1); καὶ σημεῖα ἀπ' οὐρανοῦ μεγάλα ἔσται (A W Γ Δ Θ *pm*; TR; *Diglot*), and other variations in order are found (Metzger, 172).

The signs described are typical of apocalyptic, and recur in Rev. 6, a passage which bears some relation to the present sayings and is probably based on them (G. R. Beasley-Murray, *The Book of Revelation*, 1975, 137). Luke's version has a combination of earthly and heavenly signs, as in Acts 2:19f. The unusual wording may suggest that Luke is following a non-Marcan source. Such signs were believed to have occurred before the fall of Jerusalem (Jos. Bel. 6:288–315), and Luke may have regarded these sayings as referring to them, in which case there is a parallel between the signs before the fall of Jerusalem and before the End (v. 25; Zmijewski, 122–125). Geiger, 169–172, thinks that signs after the fall of Jerusalem are meant: worldwide, cosmic events signify the arrival of the End. The former view is preferable. These 'signs' stand under the rubric of v. 9b, and the omission of Mark's 'these are the beginning of travail' (possibly missing from Luke's non-Marcan source) confirms that 'final' signs are not in mind. The point is that such phenomena are *not* apocalyptic signs of the End.

iii. The Persecution of Disciples 21:12–19

There is a clear change of theme in v. 12. In the preceding section the disciples were warned against the danger of being misled; now they are warned against the danger of succumbing to persecution. The section falls into two parts. In the first (vs. 12–15), the danger is that of being arrested and tried in the courts. This is to be regarded by the disciples as an opportunity to bear witness or as a testimony to their faith. They must, however, meet the occasion with the courage and wisdom which Jesus will give them; his help is promised to those who suffer for the sake of his name. In the second part of the section (vs. 16–19), the theme is betrayal by one's closest relatives and general hatred by all men, leading to the death of some of the disciples. Yet, says Jesus, such experiences cannot really harm them, and by showing steadfast endurance they will ultimately attain to resurrection life.

The thought of this section is closely similar to that in Mk. 13:9–13 which has the same structure, but the wording shows considerable difference. Only v. 17 and (to a lesser extent) v. 12 show close contacts with Mk. By prefixing 'before all these things' at the beginning Luke has changed the section from being a further 'sign of the times' to a description of the situation of the disciples from the outset. It is remarkable that he has omitted the reference to the gentile mission in Mk. 13:10, but this may be because he was thinking primarily of the period before AD 70. It is also remarkable that he has dropped the reference to the Spirit in Mk. 13:11, but this may be due to a christological heightening. In general, the wording points forward to the experiences of the church recorded in Acts. Hence it can be argued with a good deal of plausibility that Luke was simply editing Mk. in this section. Nevertheless, there are some changes in wording and some awkward Greek (v. 12) which may suggest that Luke was influenced by another source (Manson, *Sayings*, 326–328; L. Gaston*, 169f.; Schramm, 175–178). On the whole, the evidence supports the former possibility (cf. Zmijkewski, 140f.; A. Fuchs*), although some points remain unexplained.

Scholars who hold that Jesus did not reckon with an interval before the End and could not have foreseen persecution for his followers regard these sayings as the creation of the early church (Bultmann, 129; Grässer, 158; cf. Pesch, 125–138). Lambrecht, 114–144, regards Mark as being dependent on Q, but does not discuss the origin of the Q material. A more cautious opinion is offered by Kümmel, 99, who holds that Mk. 13:9, 11, 13 can go back to Jesus (cf. Taylor, 510, who accepts the substance of Mk. 13:9, 11). This opinion is confirmed by the parallels in Q (Lk. 12:11f. and 51–53) to Mk. 13:11 and 12 respectively.

Whether Mark was drawing on the traditions incorporated in Q or following similar, independent traditions, a basis for the sayings in the teaching of Jesus is highly probable.

See Manson, *Sayings*, 326–328; Beasley-Murray, *Commentary*, 40–53; Grässer, 158–161; L. Hartman, *Testimonium Linguae*, Lund/Copenhagen, 1963, 57–75; Hartman, 150f., 167–172; Lambrecht, 114–144; Pesch, 125–138; Gaston, 16–23; A. Fuchs, *Sprachliche Untersuchungen zu Matthäus und Lukas*, Rome, 1971, 37–44, 171–191; Zmijewski, 128–179; Geiger, 172–193.

(12) The opening phrase πρὸ τούτων πάντων is probably Lucan (cf. similar phraseology in Acts 5:36; 21:38); it connects the new material with the preceding section, but indicates that what is now to be described will take place before the previously described events. Luke may be now describing things that are already past history for his readers (J. Weiss, 505f.; Klostermann, 201; Grässer, 160; Zmijewski, 151); he is thinking of the church's experience of persecution in the period before AD 70. But Luke presumably has in mind experiences that his readers may still undergo, so that the passage is unlikely to refer exclusively to the early days of the church. The point is that while cosmic disasters are more closely associated with the end, persecution set in from the beginning – and involved Jesus himself. The phrase ἐπιβαλοῦσιν τὰς χεῖρας is based on the LXX (1 Sa. 21:6; *et al.*; Hartmann, 229f.), and may be Lucan (20:19); for διώκω cf. 11:49. παραδίδωμι is frequently used of Christians being handed over to the authorities (Mk. 13:9, 11f.; Lk. 21:16; Acts 8:3; 12:4; 21:11; 22:4; 27:1; 28:17). The συναγωγή here functions as the Jewish court for trying minor cases; offenders might be beaten by the synagogue officials (cf. Mk. δέρω, omitted by Luke; W. Schrage, TDNT VII, 831). φυλακή (2:8 note) is here 'prison', and the mention could be due to Luke (22:33; Acts 8:3; 22:4); imprisonment was used as a punishment in the ancient world (cf. G. Bertram, TDNT IX, 244). Luke has no mention of disciples being brought before συνέδρια, local Jewish courts (Mk.); the word might well be obscure to gentile readers (E. Lohse, TDNT VII, 867 n. 47).

The loosely attached accusative participle ἀπαγομένους is not very felicitous, and it is hard to see why Luke should have altered Mark's easier expression. The order βασιλεῖς καὶ ἡγεμόνας is inverted in Mk.; Luke places kings (and emperors) first, possibly under catechetical influence (cf. 1 Pet. 2:13f.). For Mk. ἕνεκεν ἐμοῦ he has ἕνεκεν τοῦ ὀνόματός μου (cf. 21:17; 18:29 diff. Mk. 10:29; Zmijewski, 157–161). The phrase could be Lucan (cf. Acts 4:17f.; 5:28; 40f.; 9:15f.; 15:26; 21:13), but is based on a firm early church usage (e.g. 1 Pet. 4:14, 16; 3 Jn. 7; Rev. 2:3; Jn. 15:21). The whole saying envisages persecution among both Jews and gentiles for the sake of loyalty to Jesus. It could well rest on teaching of Jesus.

(13) Mark's phrase εἰς μαρτύριον αὐτοῖς is replaced by a separate clause. ἀποβαίνω (5:2 note; Jn. 21:9) here has the sense 'to turn out, lead to' (Phil. 1:19**). The traditional translation is 'This will be a time for

you to bear testimony' (RSV), and this fits in with the usual interpretation of Mark's phrase. L. Hartman* defends the meaning, 'For you it will have as a result a testimony'; on this view μαρτύριον does not mean the *activity* of bearing witness but the *evidence* that will be available on the day of judgment for the disciples and against their enemies; cf. Zmijewski, 161–169 (this sense is also found by Mk. by H. Strathmann, TDNT IV, 502–504, who holds that the phrase there means 'for evidence against the persecutors at the judgment'). In support Hartman cites LXX usage (cf. Job. 13:16; 30:31; but more especially the use of μαρτύριον, Dt. 31:26; Ho. 2:12; Mi. 1:2; 7:18; Zp. 3:8; cf. Mk. 6:11; 13:9; Jas. 5:3). The strong point in favour of this view is that in the NT generally μαρτύριον means 'evidence, testimony', not the activity of bearing testimony.

Luke omits Mk. 13:10 at this point. It is possible that he regards 21:24b or (much more probably) 24:47 as a substitute for it. Moreover, while Mark is thinking of a condition to be fulfilled before the parousia, Luke's discourse is perhaps concerned here more with the period before AD 70, during which the condition was not yet completely fulfilled.

The question of authenticity is related to that of sources. If the verse is based on Mk., a verdict depends on our view of Mk. at this point (Pesch, 128f. regards the phrase as an addition by Mark, but without adequate proof); if Luke is following an independent source, this could be evidence for a pre-Marcan formulation.

(14) Having assured the disciples that they will face court situations, Jesus instructs them in their consequent (οὖν) behaviour. θέτε ἐν ταῖς καρδίαις (εἰς with accusative, W Θ pm; TR; Diglot) here means 'decide' (cf. Acts 19:21; a different sense is found in Lk. 1:66; Acts 5:4). The phraseology resembles that of the LXX, and could stem from Luke. προμελετάω**, 'to practise beforehand, prepare', can be used of rehearsing a speech (Aristophanes, Eccl. 116); for ἀπολογέομαι cf. 12:11; et al. The sentiment expressed is the same as in Mk. 13:11 (cf. Lk. 12:11) and has a more literary form; again Lucan origin is possible.

(15) No anxiety is necessary, for Jesus promises that he himself (ἐγώ) will give his disciples both mouth and wisdom. The use of στόμα is reminiscent of Ex. 4:11, 15; Ezk. 29:21; here the sense is metaphorical, 'utterance, eloquence'; for σοφία in a court scene see Acts 6:10, where it is coupled with the Spirit. Adversaries (for ἀντίκειμαι cf. 13:17; 1 Cor. 16:9; Phil. 1:28; et al.) will not be able to resist (ἀνθίστημι, Acts 6:10; 13:8; 2 Tim. 3:8; 4:15) the eloquence or refute (ἀντιλέγω, Acts 4:14; cf. Lk. 2:34; 20:27*) the wisdom of the disciples. The language suggests Lucan formulation, and points forward to the experience of the disciples in Acts (Zmijewski, 136f.). The use of ἤ may also be Lucan (cf. 12:11 par. Mt. 24:19; 9:25; 12:14, 47; 14:12; 17:7). In the saying a reference to Jesus has replaced Mark's reference to the Holy Spirit as the source of inspiration. It is debated whether an original saying without mention of the Spirit has been developed in the tradition, or whether Luke has

rewritten Mk. 13:11/(A. Fuchs*, 171–191) and imposed a christological heightening on a Spirit-saying (Grässer, 160; E. Schweizer, TDNT VI, 398 n. 414). A Lucan tendency to stress the place of Jesus as the giver of gifts associated with the Spirit could have led to the rewording of the text. Ellis, 244, suggests that Luke is utilizing a saying of a Christian prophet, which is unlikely, or a variant form of tradition, but a firm linguistic basis for this view is lacking. The claim that the saying in its Marcan form is 'naturally of Christian origin' (Pesch, 132) is arbitrary; there is no reason why Jesus should not have spoken of persecution or of the Spirit.

(16) From action in the courts the thought turns to betrayal by relatives and general hatred by mankind. Luke has a smoother connection with the passive form παραδοθήσεσθε, diff. Mk. Where Mark lists pairs – brother (betraying) brother; father (betraying) child; children (betraying) parents (cf. Mi. 7:6) – Luke has simply a list of unfaithful people: parents, brothers, relatives and friends. Luke's list is more general and less complicated in expression. Luke also softens Mark's αὐτούς to the partitive ἐξ ὑμῶν, 'some of you' (Semitic – BD 164²; Black, 108; cf. Mt. 23:34; 25:8). The verse has thus a more personal thrust than in Mk. For the thought cf. 12:53 par. Mt. 10:35. There is general agreement that Luke is here following Mk.

(17) Mark is followed word for word. The saying forecasts that the disciples will be the object of hatred by all men because of the name of Jesus, i.e. because they profess loyalty to him. For the thought cf. 6:22, 27. The saying could reflect bitter persecution, but we do not know of anything so severe in the first century, and hence it is unlikely to be a *vaticinium ex eventu*.

(18) Jesus promises that not a hair from their head will perish; cf. 12:7; Acts 27:34; 1 Sa. 14:45; 2 Sa. 14:11; 1 Ki. 1:52. The closest parallel is Acts 27:34, but the saying sounds proverbial. It is peculiar to Lk., and seems odd in its present position in a context of persecution and martyrdom. 1. It has been suggested that the saying simply means that no harm will occur to the disciples without the Father's permission – '*sine praemio, ante tempus*' (Bengel; Geldenhuys, 527; cf. Zmijewski, 175); Klostermann, 202, calls this 'desperate'. 2. Others suggest that v. 16 refers to only a few martyrs, while this verse refers to the safety of the church as a whole (J. Weiss, 506). 3. Most commonly it is argued that the verse is referring to spiritual safety. The disciples may suffer injury and death, but nothing can really harm their essential being (Plummer, 480; Creed, 256). 4. It is possible that the difficulty is due to verses from different sources being placed together infelicitously, but this does not explain what meaning the juxtaposition had for Luke. Probably the third explanation remains the best. Schramm, 177f. suggests that Luke has taken the verse from his source (vs. 14f., 18) and has qualified its optimistic spirit by introducing the hard realities found in Mk. Conzelmann, 119, 121, and Grässer, 161, suggest the opposite: Luke wanted

to be more optimistic than Mk. That Luke invented the saying on the basis of 12:7 (Geiger, 189–191) is unlikely in view of the difficulties it raises.

(19) The final verse is an injunction to steadfastness. The indicative κτήσεσθε (A B Θ *al* lat sy sa bo; *Synopsis*) contains an element of promise that is not so prominent in the imperative κτήσασθε (א D L W *Δ pm*; TR; UBS; Metzger, 173, argues that scribes were more likely to conform to the surrounding future indicatives). Luke uses the noun ὑπομονή (8:15*) diff. Mk. ὑπομένω. κτήσασθε gives the force 'you will win your lives', i.e. participate in eternal life, rather than 'you will preserve your earthly life' (E. Schweizer, TDNT IX, 647). At least some of the disciples will not survive to the end (v. 16). Mark's use of σῴζω is ambiguous, and this may have motivated the alteration in wording. It appears to be due to Luke.

iv. Judgment upon Jerusalem 21:20–24

The third main section of the prophecy intimates the devastation of Jerusalem. Its encirclement by troops will be the sign that its end is near. That will be the signal for people to flee from the vicinity and to avoid entering the city. The plight of the Jews will be severe, especially for those who cannot stand the hardships of wartime, such as pregnant and nursing mothers. All this is to be seen as a fulfilment of Scripture and as an expression of divine judgment and wrath against the Jewish people. They will die or be carried into captivity; Jerusalem itself will be under the heel of the gentiles for a period of time.

The passage is parallel to Mk. 13:14–20, but the amount of verbal parallelism is slight (four words in v. 20, v. 21a and v. 23a). Mark refers cryptically to the 'desolating sacrilege' and to the need for the people of Judaea to flee; he emphasises the awful plight of the people under tribulation. By contrast Luke specifically names Jerusalem and refers clearly to a siege. Mark's warning about delay (cf. Lk. 17:31) is replaced by a warning to keep away from Jerusalem. The thought of divine vengeance and wrath is included – although there is no suggestion here that Jerusalem is being judged because it slew Jesus (for this motif see G. Braumann*). Mark's enigmatic reference to the shortening of the period of tribulation for the sake of 'the elect' is dropped. Luke speaks rather of the death and captivity of the Jews, and the subjugation of Jerusalem by the gentiles; it is possible that he has in mind the period of the conversion of the gentiles.

These changes can be explained in terms of the rewriting of Mk. by Luke. He will have clarified the allusion to the events of AD 66–70 in the light of history. He has removed the apocalyptic language which might make the fall of Jerusalem seem to be closely associated with the End, and he has replaced it by prophetic language, thereby bringing out more strongly the element of divine judgment upon the Jews. Thus he has pronounced the final verdict upon Jerusalem (cf. Creed, 256; Grässer, 162, Danker, 212f.; Zmijewski, 190–192; Geiger, 210–212). Other scholars argue that the rewriting of Mk. could have been carried out by Luke before AD 70 in order to make Mark's cryptic language intelligible to gentiles (Geldenhuys, 532; Beasley-Murray, 260; Ellis, 244). Yet another view is that Luke was independent of Mk. here. C. H. Dodd* argued that Luke was dependent on LXX descriptions of the siege of Jerusalem and not on Mk., nor on the actual event. Manson, *Sayings*, 328–331, claimed that Luke was drawing on a tradition older than that in Mk.; this tradition was reinterpreted by Mark in the light of Caligula's attempt to profane the temple in AD 40. Manson also argued that the poetic character of the passage spoke against its being a Lucan rewriting of Mk. Lucan independence of Mk. is also affirmed by L. Gaston*, 164–167; Schramm, 178–180.

Evidence for use of another source alongside Mk. is to be seen in the grammatical irregularity regarding the antecedent of αὐτῆς in v. 21b; no satisfactory explanation of this has been offered on the basis of Luke's dependence purely on Mk. The passage has links of thought with 19:41–44 and 23:28–31, and it is unlikely that all these passages come from Luke's own pen. Rather they reflect a stream of tradition of pre-Lucan origin which can also be seen in the Q saying 11:49–51 par. Mt. 23:34–36. The wording of the passage is based solidly on the OT, and suggests that the fate of Jerusalem is being compared with the earlier judgment upon the city at the hands of the Babylonians.

It thus seems probable that Luke has made use of traditional material in rewriting this paragraph from Mk. The close parallelism in structure with Mk. suggests either that Luke has simply rewritten Mk. or that he has used an alternative form of the tradition found in Mk. The latter view implies that the tradition had already undergone development before it reached Luke.

The origins of the material are particularly hard to determine. In both forms of the tradition we have midrashic use of OT material, more apocalyptic in Mk. and more prophetic in Lk. Both traditions have links with the teaching of Jesus. Since Jesus certainly spoke in prophetic terms, and could certainly have prophesied the doom of Jerusalem in a manner analogous to the OT prophets, the roots of the section could reach back to him; but since the early church would recognise the fulfilment of the prophecy as AD 66–70 approached or actually happened, it is well nigh impossible to distinguish the original sayings of Jesus from midrashic development by the church.

See Manson, *Sayings*, 328–331; C. H. Dodd, 'The Fall of Jerusalem and the "Abomination of Desolation"', JRS 37, 1947, 47–54; Beasley-Murray, *Commentary*, 54–82; Grässer, 161–163; G. Braumann, 'Die lukanische Interpretation der Zerstörung Jerusalems', Nov.T 6, 1963, 120–127; Hartman, 151–154, 162–164, 230–232; Lambrecht, 144–168; Pesch, 138–154; Gaston, 23–29; Schramm, 178–180; Zmijewski, 179–224; Geiger, 193–212.

(20) Luke begins the section, like Mk., with ὅταν δὲ ἴδητε (cf. 21:31 par. Mk. 13:29). The theme is a new one, not closely connected with

what has preceded. Those addressed are not necessarily disciples, but all who live in Judaea. They are going to see Jerusalem – named here only by Luke – surrounded by armies. κυκλόω is 'to encircle' (Heb. 11:30; cf. Jn. 10:24; Acts 14:20**); cf. Is. 29:3; 37:33; Je. 52:7 and the use of περικυκλόω in 19:43. στρατόπεδον** was originally 'camp', then 'body of troops, army, legion' (cf. Je. 34(41):1). The encirclement means that the destruction of the city has drawn near. For γνῶτε cf. 10:11; 12:39; 21:30f. par. Mk. 13:28f. It may be Luke's equivalent for Mk. ὁ ἀναγινώσκων νοείτω. (This phrase is generally regarded as a parenthesis in Mk., and most scholars attribute it to Mark himself; we would suggest that it is the apodosis to the ὅταν ... clause, and that the command to flee is a separate clause added asyndetically; the person who reads, sc. the book of Daniel, is to recognise that it is being fulfilled.) In Lk. the siege points to the nearness (ἐγγίζω, 7:12; et al.) of the threatened devastation of Jerusalem (ἐρήμωσις, Mk. 13:14; Mt. 24:15**; for Luke's use see 2 Ch. 36:21; Je. 4:7; 7:34; 22:5; 25 (32):18; 44 (51):6, 22; Ps. 73 (72):19). The OT background in Lk. is thus different from that in Mk. (Dn. 9:27; 11:31; 12:11; cf. 1 Mac. 1:54), despite the fact that the same word is being used. Note the link with 13:35: the force is perhaps that Jesus' prophecy then will be seen to be fulfilled.

(21) At the outbreak of the siege those who are in Judaea should flee to the mountains (i.e. rather than into Jerusalem itself). For this motif cf. Gn. 19:26; Is. 15:5; Je. 49:8; Am. 5:19f.; Zc. 14:5; 1 Mac. 2:28; 2 Mac. 5:27; Ass. Moses 9; and for escape to the mountains cf. 1 Ki. 22:17; Ezk. 7:16; Nah. 3:18; Je. 16:16. Since Judaea itself is mountainous, the reference is to flight into Transjordan, or into the remoter areas of Judaea itself, such as the inaccessible mountains and caves around the Dead Sea. The saying has been identified with the oracle mentioned in Eus. HE 3:5, as a result of which the Christian church fled from the Jewish war to Pella; but this is improbable, as Eusebius himself would surely have pointed out the Gospel passage. Luke here follows Mk. exactly. The result is that in the next phrase οἱ ἐν μέσῳ αὐτῆς, the pronoun must refer back grammatically to 'Ιουδαίᾳ (so in a figurative sense, of leaving Judaism, Zmijewski, 211), but the sense demands a reference back to Jerusalem; this suggests that Luke has incorporated the saying from Mk. in the middle of another source. ἐκχωρέω** is 'to depart'; χώρα is used of open country in contrast to the city (cf. 12:16; Acts 8:1). The command repeats that in Mk. by urging the inhabitants of Jerusalem to flee for safety, and then goes on to warn the people in the environs not to enter the city for refuge. This saying replaces Mark's command to people on housetops and in the fields to flee with all speed, to which Luke has a parallel in 17:31. It is, therefore, arguable that, having used Mk. earlier, Luke has avoided a doublet and at the same time created a saying more appropriate to siege conditions. But it is doubtful whether 17:31 is derived from Mk., and it is probable that Luke is not himself responsible for the change from Mk. here.

(22) The reason for flight is that the people may avoid being involved in the divine judgment upon Jerusalem, for these are to be days of vengeance. For ἐκδίκησις cf. 18:7f.; Acts 7:24; the whole phrase is found in Dt. 32:35; cf. Ho. 9:7; Je. 46 (26):10; cf. Sir. 5:7; 18:24; Je. 46 (26):21; 50 (27):27, 31; 51 (28):6. The events of these days will fulfil (πίμπλημι, 1:15; et al.; here only of the fulfilment of prophecy) all that has been written (a Lucan phrase: 18:31; 24:44; Acts 13:29; 24:14). The prophecies in mind may include 1 Ki. 9:6–9; Dn. 9:26; Mi. 3:12. The language suggests Lucan formulation, but there may be a traditional basis in the first part of the verse.

(23) Luke returns to Mk. for the first part of the verse. οὐαί is an expression of sorrow at the thought of the fate of women with child (cf. 1:31; Mt. 1:18, 23; 1 Thes. 5:3; Rev. 12:2) and nursing infants (θηλάζω, 11:27*). The motif is repeated in 23:29; and the thought may possibly lie behind 1 Cor. 7:26–31. Luke does not include Mark's prayer that the siege may not take place in winter; Stuhlmueller, 155, notes that in fact the final stage was in the summer; Luke, therefore, has not omitted an unfulfilled prophecy. Rather he has omitted any suggestion of relaxation in the rigours of the siege. He concentrates (as in Mk. 13:19) on the horrors of the time. There will be great distress (ἀνάγκη; 1 Cor. 7:26; 2 Cor. 6:4; 12:10; 1 Thes. 3:7; cf. Zp. 1:15) in the land: γῆ must here refer to Judaea (cf. 4:25) rather than the world (contrast 21:35). The wrath of God will be upon (ἐν is added by W Γ Δ Θ al; TR; Diglot) this people, i.e. the Jews. For ὀργή cf. 3:7; Zp. 1:15; 1 Thes. 2:16; it is not a Lucan word. Luke appears to be following a source.

(24) There is no thought of the shortening of the period of terror, as in Mk. Instead Luke depicts clearly what will be involved for the Jews. Some will fall by the mouth of the sword (cf. Je. 20:4–6; 21:7). μάχαιρα (an a-impure noun) is found in 22:36, 38, 49, 52, and the use of στόμα (Heb. 11:34) reflects the LXX. Others will be taken captive (αἰχμαλωτίζω, Rom. 7:23; 2 Cor. 10:5; 2 Tim. 3:6**) and carried off among the nations (cf. Tob. 1:10; Dt. 28:64; τὰ ἔθνη πάντα (ℵ B L R pc) is inverted in TR; Diglot). Jerusalem itself will be 'trodden down' (πατέω, 10:19); for this motif cf. Zc. 12:3; Dn. 8: 10, 13; Is. 63:18; Ps. 79:1; 1 Mac. 3:45; 51; 4:60; 2 Mac. 8:2; Ps. Sol. 17:25; Rev. 11:2; et al. These references show that this was a set theme in prophecy; the language is not dependent on the LXX which uses καταπατέω (cf. France, 257f.). The period is one of gentile domination of the city, but a limit is set to it, namely the fulfilment of an allotted time, here called the times of the nations. For the idea of a limit to the sufferings of this period cf. Mk. 13:20; Dn. 8:13f.; 12:5–13; 1QS 4:18. The language is reminiscent of Tob. 14:5 (Codex B), and the thought of a fixed period of rule is also found in Je. 27:7. The theory has been put forward that the period in question is one during which the gentiles will be converted (cf. Mk. 13:10, omitted by Luke earlier; Rom. 11:25); after the Jewish mission comes the period of the gentile mission (Acts 28:25–28). This thought is

found in Tob. 14:6, but the MS tradition is confused at this point, and Christian influence is to be suspected. (But the thought may be based on Zc. 8, 12–14, where the siege of Jerusalem by the nations is followed by the return of the Jews and the conversion of the gentiles.) This theme was known in the early church (Rom. 11:25–27) and it may be that it is also present here (Zmijewski, 217–219), although it is not expressed clearly. Elsewhere Luke is well aware that the gentile mission did not have to wait until after the fall of Jerusalem.

v. The Coming of the Son of Man 21:25–28

Luke omits the warnings about false prophets in Mk. 13:21–23, which largely repeat the material in Mk. 13:5f. (par. Lk. 21:8), and to which he has a partial parallel in 17:21, 23. He proceeds straight to the cosmic signs in heaven and on earth and their effect, which is to cause men to panic at the thought of what may lie ahead. These cosmic signs in fact herald the coming of the Son of man in glory. But if the signs spell panic for the rest of mankind, they are the signal for the disciples to take fresh heart, for the coming of the Son of man will bring them redemption.

The structure, language and thought are close to Mk. 13:24–27. There is close verbal similarity in vs. 26b, 27 and, to a lesser extent, in v. 25a. Hence the majority opinion is that Luke is here wholly dependent on Mk. (Zmijewski, 233f.). But the rest of the language differs from Mk., and in v. 28 the redemption of the disciples replaces the gathering of the elect by the angels. The thoughts of the fear of the people and the encouragement given to the disciples have no parallel in Mk. V. 26b is distinctly redundant in its present context, and it can be argued that v. 27 breaks the connection between vs. 26 and 28 (where the antecedent of τούτων is obscure). It is, therefore, possible that we have traces of a non-Marcan source in vs. 25, 26a and 28 (Taylor, *Behind*, 109–114; Schlatter, 416; Manson, *Sayings*, 331f.; L. Gaston*, pp. 165–167; Schramm, 180f.). This source apparently did not include a reference to the coming of the Son of man, unless a reference originally following v. 28 has been replaced by v. 27, drawn from Mk.; perhaps there is a trace of such a reference in v. 36.

Even when we allow for Lucan redaction, Luke's version here is more literary than that of Mk. Since the thought runs parallel to Mk., we again appear to have evidence of an alternative version of the tradition in Mk. In both forms the tradition is closely based on the OT and is related to the apocalyptic tradition found especially in Rev. Many scholars are sceptical of the possibility of linking it with the teaching of Jesus because of these features, but this is a doubtful verdict. There is good reason to believe that Jesus spoke of the coming of the Son of man in terms of Dn. 7:13, and round this nucleus there has developed, whether in the teaching of Jesus or in that of the early church, a midrash which portrays the End in greater detail (cf. Hartmann, 245–248).

See Manson, *Sayings*, 331f.; Beasley-Murray, *Commentary*, 87–93; Grässer, 163f.; Hartman, 156–159, 165–167; Lambrecht, 173–193; Pesch, 157–175; Gaston, 30–35; Schramm, 180f.; France, 227–239; Zmijewski, 225–257; Geiger, 212–223.

(25) Mark's connective material, which might lead to the assumption that the signs about to be described would occur in close connection with the fall of Jerusalem, is dropped, and Luke simply adds the next events in the series which, on his view, follow 'the times of the gentiles'. In Mk. 13:22 we hear of signs wrought by false prophets to delude the elect. Luke refers to astronomical signs in the heavens which indicate that the end is at hand (cf. 21:7, 11). The fabric of the universe shows signs of breaking up (K. H. Rengstorf, TDNT VII, 232). The brief reference to sun, moon and stars summarizes the lengthier description in Mk. based on Is. 13:10; cf. Ezk. 32:7f.; Joel 2:10; 3:15; Rev. 6:12f. and also 1 En. 80; Ass. Moses 10:5; Sib. 3:796–803. These heavenly signs are accompanied by panic on the earth. συνοχή (2 Cor. 2:4**) is 'distress, dismay, anguish', and is a word used in Greek astrological texts to signify the dismay caused by unfavourable omens (H. Köster, TDNT VII, 886f.). ἀπορία** is 'perplexity, anxiety'. With the text as it stands, the following genitive must give the sense 'anxiety at the roaring of the sea and the waves'. ἦχος is 'sound, tone, noise'; The word is found only here, unless we find it present in 4:37 (see note there). Luke is following Ps. 65 (64):8; cf. Is. 17:12. σάλος** is used of the 'rolling, tossing motion' of the waves of the sea; cf. Jon. 1:15; Ps. 89 (88):10. The construction is difficult; L. Gaston*, 166f., thinks that the text is corrupt. He conjectures καὶ ἀπορία (D) and ἠχούσης (D W Γ Δ pm; TR; *Diglot*). Black, 261f., offers a possible reconstruction of the original Aramaic (based on vg and syᵖ, *prae confusione sonitus maris et fluctuum*), but without suggesting what was the Greek wording. The transmitted text, though difficult, reflects the wording and thought of Ps. 65 (64):8. It is God who holds back the sea from engulfing men: now they fear that it is being let loose (Harvey, 283).

(26) The thought shifts from uncertainty to fear. ἀποψύχω** is literally 'to stop breathing', hence 'to faint' or 'to die', here the former. προσδοκία is 'expectation' (Acts 12:11**); ἐπέρχομαι may be Lucan (1:35; *et al.*), and is used of unpleasant future events (Acts 8:24; 13:40; Jas. 5:1); for οἰκουμένη cf. 2:1. The vocabulary suggests Lucan editing. The thought is based on Is. 13:6ff. and the phraseology is Jewish (SB II, 255).

The second part of the verse is taken from Mk. with little change, and is ultimately based on Is. 34:4 MT. For δύναμις meaning 'a heavenly body' cf. 2 Ki. 17:16; Dn. 8:10. For σαλεύω cf. 6:38. The shaking of the heavens (Hg. 2:21) is the appropriate prelude to the heavenly coming of the Son of man.

(27) The coming of the Son of man is described in language taken from Mk. 13:26. It follows the signs already described (καὶ τότε). The subject of ὄψονται is vague, but appears to be 'men in general'; cf. Mk.

14:62. The motif of seeing may be derived from Zc. 12:10 (not LXX), in view of the usage in Rev. 1:7 and Jn. 19:37; cf. Mt. 24:30 (Perrin, 180–185), but it is already present in Dn. 7:13 (ἐθεώρουν), and it may be that it was the use of ὄψονται in the Synoptic texts which led to the amalgamation with Zc. 12:10 in Rev. 1:7. The phrase 'Son of man' of course reflects Dn. 7:13, but here we have the Christian title instead of the descriptive ὡς υἱὸς ἀνθρώπου found in Dn. The 'coming' is described without any indication of its origin or destination; it simply takes place in the sky, as is seen by the accompaniment of the cloud. Luke's ἐν νεφέλῃ replaces Mk. ἐν νεφέλαις (plural) which rests on Dn. 7:13 LXX, ἐπὶ τῶν νεφελῶν τοῦ οὐρανοῦ (so Mt. 24:30); cf. Rev. 1:7 μετὰ τῶν νεφελῶν which follows Dn. 7:13 Θ. Clouds may be a means of heavenly transport, but 'cloud' (sing.) is an indication of the divine presence or rather of the glory which is associated with God and hides him from men (9:34 note); Luke's change here suggests that he is thinking of the Son of man accompanied by the glory of God (as the next part of the verse makes clear); there are links with 9:34f. and also with Acts 1:9 where Jesus ascends into a cloud, and it is prophesied that he will return in the same way (Acts 1:11). Perrin, 173f., notes that the change of word-order, as compared with Dn. 7:13, makes it clear that the cloud is associated with the movement of the Son of man. The words δύναμις and δόξα do not appear in Dn. 7:13 (the latter appears in Dn. 7:14 LXX in a different sense) but are a correct interpretation of the appearance of one who is judge and ruler over all nations. Since the vision is one seen by men, it is highly unlikely that it refers to an ascent to God. The original vision in Dn. refers to a coming to the earth (cf. Dn. 7:9, 22), and this is evidently what is meant here. The purpose of the coming is not explained. Zmijewski, 244–250, sees in it primarily a revelation of the exaltation of Jesus.

It is normally assumed that the verse refers to the parousia of the Son of man which brings about the gathering of the elect (Mk. 13:27) and judgment on the ungodly (the subject of ὄψονται). France, 227–239, attempts to defend a new form of the view advocated by J. S. Russell (discussed by Beasley-Murray, 167–171) that the parousia took place in AD 70; he adopts the development of this view by J. M. Kik (*Matthew Twenty-Four*, Philadelphia, 1948) and R. V. G. Tasker (*The Gospel according to St Matthew*, 1961, 225–228) that in Mk. 13 (and Mk. 8:38; Mt. 10:23) parousia language is used symbolically to describe the fall of Jerusalem as the vindication of Jesus, while elsewhere in the NT the same language is used of the vindication of Jesus at his resurrection (Mt. 28:18; Mk. 14:62) and of his vindication at the still future judgment of all nations (Mt. 19:28; 25:31). On this view the cosmic phenomena described in the preceding verses must be interpreted symbolically to refer to political disasters, and the gathering of the elect (Mk. 13:27) refers to the mission of the church. This interpretation deserves careful attention, but it is exposed to various objections. In particular it does not

do justice to the language in Lk. where the cosmic signs cannot be interpreted as purely political events; there is no evidence that Dn. 7:13 was
applied to different stages of the vindication of the Son of man, and
nothing in the context leads us to believe that an unusual sense is to be
found here; in fact the clear temporal sequence (Mk. 13:24, 26) suggests
that an event *after* the fall of Jerusalem is in mind. The solution is an attempt to deal with the problem that the parousia appears to follow immediately after the fall of Jerusalem, an impression which is more
pronounced in Mk. and Mt. than in Lk. where the 'times of the nations'
intervene.

The authenticity of the verse as a saying of Jesus is denied by
nearly all modern scholars (Taylor, 519 – 'a distorted echo of his
words'; Higgins, 60–66; C. Colpe, TDNT VIII, 450; Perrin, 173–185;
and many others; exceptions are Borsch, 361–364; Hooker, *Son of
Man*, 148–159). The basic arguments are that the verse occurs in a
pastiche of OT quotations which is part of a detailed apocalyptic
programme; the saying is secondary in form to 8:38 and 14:62 and
represents a development of Christian exegetical traditions based on Dn.
7:13; the relation of Jesus to the Son of man is obscure and there is no
hint of any relation between them. These arguments are not convincing.
There is a good case for the authenticity of the very similar saying in
Mk. 14:62 (cf. I. H. Marshall, NTS 12, 1965–66, 346f.), and the view
that this saying is a development from Mk. 14:62 has not been proved. It
was unnecessary to press the connection between Jesus and the Son of
man in a saying originally addressed to the disciples.

(28) Luke omits Mk. 13:27 which refers to the gathering of the
elect and does not materially forward his present theme (cf. 17:34f.). Instead he presents other material to encourage the disciples. When the
disciples see 'these things' commencing, they can take heart. The antecedent of τούτων is not clear; the phrase reflects 21:31 (cf. Mk. 13:28f.),
and has been interpreted of the cosmic signs in 21:25f. (Klostermann,
203) or of the whole series of events in 21:8–27 (Zahn, 658). But a
reference to the parousia is out of place, and therefore a reference to the
cosmic signs is more appropriate; only when these appear is the End in
sight. ἀνακύπτω (13:11) is used metaphorically. For the lifting
(ἀνακύπτω, 6:20) of the head as a sign of hope cf. Jdg. 8:28; Pss. 24:7;
83:3; Job. 10:15. ἐγγίζω must mean 'to draw near' (cf. vs. 30f.).
ἀπολύτρωσις* is here used of release from affliction and the consummation of salvation (cf. Is. 63:4; Ps. 111:9; Dn. 4:34; 1 En. 51:2; SB II,
256; F. Büchsel, TDNT IV, 351–356); elsewhere it signifies
'redemption' (Rom. 8:23; Eph. 1:14; 4:30). The language of the verse is
Lucan, but the use of ἀπολύτρωσις suggests that a source is being used.

vi. The Certainty of the End Events 21:29–33

The announcement that the arrival of certain events will show that redemption is at hand is followed by a parable which reinforces the point. Just as the summer follows swiftly and surely upon the new growth of trees in the spring, so the coming of the kingdom will follow quickly after the signs of which Jesus has spoken. 'This generation' can be sure that it will see the completion of all that has been prophesied, for Jesus' words will undoubtedly be fulfilled: they will remain valid even when this world comes to an end.

The wording follows that of Mk. Schramm, 181, finds the influence of a parallel source, but this is quite unnecessary. Luke has clarified the parable for his readers by making clear that it refers to the coming of the kingdom. He omits Mark's statement that nobody can know the day or time of the End. It is unnecessary, and perhaps takes away from the authority of Jesus' statement. It is improbable that Luke had a christological objection to it. He has an equivalent statement in Acts 1:7.

The parable is generally regarded as a genuine saying of Jesus, which originally referred, however, to the present signs of salvation in the ministry of Jesus rather than to future apocalyptic signs of the End. The following sayings are often regarded as creations by the early church (cf. Pesch, 181–190). See the individual discussions below on each saying.

See Manson, *Sayings*, 332–334; Jeremias, *Parables*, 119f.; Kümmel, 20–22, 59–61, 91f.; Beasley-Murray, *Commentary*, 94–104; Grässer, 164–166; Hartman, 223–226, 240f.; Lambrecht, 193–227; Pesch, 175–195; Gaston, 35–39; Vögtle, 324–328; Schramm, 181; Zmijewski, 257–286; Geiger, 225–239; G. Schneider, *Parusiegleichnisse im Lukas-Evangelium* (see 12:35–48 note), 55–61.

(29) Luke replaces Mark's introductory formulation with his customary wording for introducing a parable (6:39; *et al.*). This leads to the introduction of ἴδετε, corresponding to Mk. μάθετε. For συκῆ cf. 13:6f. Luke adds καὶ πάντα τὰ δένδρα, an addition which has been said to dull the point of the parable, since the peculiarly bare appearance of the fig tree in winter, followed by its early blossom, makes it stand out in Palestine as the harbinger of spring. Luke may have generalised for a non-Palestinian audience (Jeremias, *Parables*, 29, 120). Or he has played down the significance of the fig as an eschatological symbol (Grässer, 141 n. 1). An allegorical allusion to Israel and the nations is unlikely, as is Zmijewski's suggestion (266–268) that Luke intends a wider group of signs than Mark who is referring only to the destruction of the temple.

(30) The construction (ὅταν ... ἤδη ...) follows Mk. The force of ἤδη is '*after* they have put forth leaves'. προβάλλω normally means 'to put forward' (Acts 19:33**), here 'to put forth foliage, fruit' (Jos. Ant. 4:226), but the absolute use is unusual. Luke is paraphrasing Mk. βλέποντες ἀφ' ἑαυτῶν (cf. 12:57) gives the sense 'you can see for

yourselves'. θέρος is 'summer' (Mk. 13:28; Mt. 24:32**); Luke repeats ἤδη to stress that the period of proximity has already arrived. The point of the parable is clear: certain events convey the unmistakable message to any observer that a climax is about to happen.

(31) Let the hearers display the same spiritual discernment and observe the signs which point unequivocally to the coming of the kingdom of God. The spiritual signs are to be understood in the light of v. 28, which in turn refers back to vs. 25f. Luke has inserted ἡ βασιλεία τοῦ θεοῦ, diff. Mk., to make the point clear, and has dropped ἐπὶ θύραις as being unnecessary; in Mk. the reference may well have been to the coming of the Son of man, who is to be equated with the master who appears *at the door* in the following parable. Luke has substituted the abstract concept here, although he can also use Mark's concept (12:40). The kingdom is thus a future reality here (contrast 17:21), and Luke's point is that its advent is introduced by the coming of the Son of man. Lagrange's view (532) that Luke regarded the comings of the kingdom and of the Son of man as two separate events is false.

Many scholars think that a parable of Jesus which originally referred to the imminence of the salvation of God, to be seen in the works of Jesus himself, has been transformed into a warning of the imminence of judgment and the end of the world, to be seen in apocalyptic signs (Jeremias, *Parables*, 119f.; Kümmel, 20–22; C.-H. Hunzinger, TDNT VII, 757). One may compare 12:54–56 where Jesus directs the attention of his hearers to the signs visible in his ministry. Pesch, 179–181, 205, holds that the whole of the application is secondary; he does not consider a possible meaning of the parable on the lips of Jesus, although he allows that Jesus may have alluded to the imminence of the kingdom of God.

It will be seen that there is universal agreement that the reference in the parable is to the future coming of the kingdom of God. The problem is whether an allusion to the 'signs' in the ministry of Jesus has been replaced by reference to future apocalyptic events. If Jesus warned against being misled by signs and trying to reckon the time of the End, would he have spoken in this way about apocalyptic signs? In our view it has too easily been assumed that he did not do so. In its present context, especially in Lk., the parable is designed to give encouragement and hope to disciples looking for the coming of final salvation, and is not primarily a warning of judgment to come. Jesus certainly looked forward to the future consummation of the kingdom and the End, and the reference to 'signs of the times' in 12:54–56 may well be wider than simply to the mighty works of Jesus. A general instruction by Jesus to see the nearness of the End in various signs has probably been adapted here to refer to a more limited series of events, namely those following the fall of the temple and of Jerusalem.

(32) Jesus declares solemnly – note the retention of ἀμήν (4:24 note) – that 'this generation' will not pass away until everything takes

place. γενεά (1:48; *et al.*) can mean: a. the descendants of a common ancestor; b. a set of people born at the same time; c. the period of time occupied by such a set of people, often in the sense of successive sets of people. The meaning of the term is thus flexible. It has been understood in various ways here: 1. The (Jewish) contemporaries of Jesus (Kümmel, 60f.; Beasley-Murray, 260f.). If so, the event will happen presumably before the last of them or perhaps the majority of them have died. 2. The Jews as a race (cf. a. above; Rengstorf, 230). Then the saying is a word of hope to the Jewish race that God will not reject them but give them a share in final salvation. 3. Wicked men (cf. 9:41; Acts 2:40; W. Michaelis, as reported by Kümmel, 61). 4. The contemporaries of the Evangelist (cf. Klostermann, 204). 5. The generation of the end-time (Ellis, 246f.; cf. Conzelmann, 96 n. 1 – 'die Menschheit überhaupt'; Zmijewski, 281–283). Ellis refers to the usage in 1QpHab 2:7; 7:2 where 'last generation' appears to cover several life-times. On this view, the saying is meant to convince the hearers that they belong to the 'last generation' in which eschatological events are drawing to a climax. The events in question, described as πάντα (diff. Mk. ταῦτα πάντα), must surely be the totality of events prophesied in the earlier part of the discourse and not simply the fall of Jerusalem (as Geldenhuys, 538f. – everything up to v. 24). Like Mt. Luke has ἕως ἄν diff. Mk. μέχρις οὗ; μέχρι means 'up to the point at which', and might be thought to imply that 'this generation' would pass away at that point. The thrust of the saying may be either that the End is sure to come before the passing away of this generation (i.e. the date is limited) or that the End is as sure to come as that this generation will continue to exist, or that this generation can be sure that the last events have begun and will be brought to a consummation. The last of these three possibilities gives the best sense: the emphasis is on the certainty of the End rather than on limiting the date of the end. This fits the parallelism of the next saying. Or rather, since men did expect that there would be *some* kind of end, Jesus is emphasising that the *particular* kind of end (and premonitory signs) prophesied by him will certainly come to pass.

Many commentators regard the verse as a saying originally referring to the fall of Jerusalem which has been reinterpreted in terms of the parousia (Taylor, 521). Vögtle, 324–328, argues that the saying was used by Mark as a model for Mk. 9:1, while Pesch, 181–188, holds that Mark created the present saying on the basis of Mk. 9:1 (cf. G. Schneider*, 59; Lambrecht, 202–211, adds Mt. 23:36 as a basis). But the similarity between the sayings does not prove that either is a copy of the other; we are dealing with two separate sayings, both of which are concerned with the certainty of the fulfilment of Jesus' words. The note of authority is characteristic of Jesus.

(33) A further confirmation of Jesus' statement follows, in words taken directly from Mk. Although heaven and earth may pass away, the words of Jesus will not do so; the language is reminiscent of that used of

the law in 16:17 par. Mt. 5:18; cf. Pss. 102:25–27; 119:160; Is. 40:6–8; 51:6; Bar. 4:1; Wis. 18:4; 4 Ez. 9:36f. j. Sanh. 2:20c (SB I, 244). παρέρχομαι is used in slightly different senses in the two parts of the verse; applied to Jesus' words it refers to their enduring validity in this age and the next. The saying is accepted as genuine by Kümmel, 91 (*contra* Bultmann, 139); it reflects Jesus' claim to authority and knowledge of the will of God, and is an isolated saying included here on the catch-word principle to reinforce the previous saying. On this high note Luke leaves the Marcan wording of the discourse, omitting Mk. 13:32 for which he has an equivalent in Acts 1:7.

vii. Be Watchful and Ready 21:34–36

The discourse concludes with a practical appeal to the hearers. Whatever may have been said about misleading signs and the fulfilment of certain events before the parousia, it remains true that the day of the Lord will come upon the whole world suddenly and unexpectedly and catch men unawares. The disciples must not be like drunk men or absorbed in worldly worries so that they are unprepared for it. On the contrary, they must be continually alert and praying that they may be able to overcome every temptation to apostasy and so finally to stand unashamed before the Son of man.

For this pattern of apocalyptic teaching followed by exhortation cf. 17:20–37/18:1–8 (Ott, 73). The passage replaces the exhortation in Mark's version of the discourse which has parallels here and earlier in Lk. (see especially 12:35–40). For Mk. 13:33 cf. Lk. 21:36; for Mk. 13:34 cf. Lk. 19:12f.; for Mk. 13:35 cf. Lk. 12:38, 40; for Mk. 13:37 cf. Lk. 12:41. Elsewhere it has been seen that when Luke has used material from Mk. (or closely similar material) at an earlier stage in the Gospel, he avoids repeating Mark's wording when he comes to the corresponding point (cf. 21:14f.). The present passage shows features of Lucan style (Kümmel, 36 n. 56) and the language is often said to be Hellenistic (Bultmann, 126). It presupposes an interval before the parousia (Conzelmann, 131f.; Grässer, 167; Tödt, 96–98) – although it allows that the parousia may happen without warning in the lifetime of the hearers. Ott, 73–75, argues that, as in 18:1–8, we have the Lucan motif of praying for strength to persevere to the End. Hence it is arguable that the passage as a whole is purely due to Lucan redaction of Mk. (Zmijewski, 291–294; Geiger, 245).

It is, however, unlikely that this is the whole story. Easton, 314f., notes that the passage is a development from Is. 24:17, 20 LXX. C. H. Dodd (*More New Testament Studies*, Manchester, 1968, 19–21) argues that there is a common catechetical basis behind this section and 1 Thes. 5:1–3, 7, 8–10. C. Colpe, TDNT VIII, 434f., also argues that the Son of man saying in v. 36 is authentic. Finally, Manson, *Sayings*, 335, notes that vs. 34–36 follow on more naturally from v. 28 than from the

Marcan material in vs. 29–33. These points combine to justify the view of Jeremias, *Parables*, 78 n. 28, that Luke has worked over earlier material here, i.e. that he was not simply editing Mk. Schramm, 181f., concludes that Luke was using parenetic material from the Hellenistic church. It may be surmised that we have in fact further traces of an alternative tradition of the apocalyptic teaching of Jesus which has also left traces in the teaching of Paul in 1 Thes. 5, and which has been omitted in Mark's version of the tradition. This teaching is in harmony with that ascribed in Jesus in Lk. 12, but it has undergone some development in the church as well as at the hands of Lk. Despite its Hellenistic colouring, the underlying thoughts cohere with the teaching of Jesus.

See Manson, *Sayings*, 334–336; Grässer, 167f.; Lövestam, 122–132; Tödt, 96–98; Higgins, 92–94; Borsch, 319; Ott, 73–75; Hartman, 192f.; Schramm, 181f.; Zmijewski, 286–310; Geiger, 239–248.

(34) The opening phraseology is Lucan (προσέχετε ἑαυτοῖς, 12:1; 17:3; diff. Mk. βλέπετε; μήποτε, 3:15; *et al.*). For the use of βαρέω (9:32) with καρδία cf. Ex. 7:14, and for the thought here cf. Sallust, Jug. 76:6, *vino et epulis onerati*. The motif of being weighed down spiritually was not uncommon (Wis. 9:15; Philo, Gig. 7; Act. Thom. 109; Epictetus, Diss. 1:1:15; Lövestam, 125–127). κραιπάλη** is 'carousing, intoxication', and hence the effects of drunkenness – a 'hangover' (cf. Is. 24:20; Ps. 78 (77):65; Is. 20:9). μέθη is 'drunkenness' (Rom. 13:13; Gal. 5:21**; H. Preisker, TDNT IV, 545–548, overlooks the present verse); see Is. 24:20; Lk. 12:45; Mt. 24:49; Eph. 5:18; 1 Thes. 5:7. Clearly we have here a theme of catechetical instruction, expressed in language reminiscent of Is. 24:20. A warning against literal drunkenness is no doubt included, but the main force is probably metaphorical, warning disciples against succumbing to the intoxicating attractions of the sinful world (cf. CH 1:27; 7:2; Rev. 17:2, 6). For μέριμνα cf. 8:14 (cf. the verb in 10:41; 12:22–26). βιωτικός, 'belonging to (daily) life' is found only in 1 Cor. 6:3f., but cf. τοῦ βίου in Lk. 8:14. If men's attention to spiritual things is dulled by such worldly concerns, they will not observe the signs, and 'that day' (10:12; 1 Thes. 5:4) will come upon them unexpectedly. For ἐφίστημι, cf. 2:9; *et al.*; 1 Thes. 5:3); for ἐφ' ὑμᾶς cf. Is. 24:17; and for αἰφνίδιος, 'sudden', cf. 1 Thes. 5:3**.

(35) If we read ὡς παγὶς ἐπεισελεύσεται γάρ (ℵ* B D it pt sa bo; UBS; *Synopsis*; *Diglot*), ὡς παγίς must go with the preceding clause; if we read ὡς παγὶς γὰρ ἐπελεύσεται (A C W Γ Δ Θ f1 f13 *pl* it pt vg sy; TR), it will go with what follows. Metzger, 173, supports the former reading in view of the good external evidence and the likelihood that copyists would transpose the γάρ under the influence of Is. 24:17, φόβος καὶ βόθυνος καὶ παγὶς ἐφ' ὑμᾶς τοὺς ἐνοικοῦντας ἐπὶ τῆς γῆς (so Zmijewski, 287; Geiger, 246 n. 93). Zahn, 660 n. 7 and Ott, 73f., defend the latter reading; they argue that the former reading is unlikely to be original since a reference to the worldwide effects of that day does not back up the statement about suddenness in v. 34, whereas, with the latter

reading, v. 34 is confirmed by the statement that the day will come like a snare on everybody; the ὡς παγίς phrase could easily have been linked to what precedes by scribes. Ott notes that ἐπέρχομαι is Lucan (1:35; *et al.*) while ἐπεισέρχομαι, 'to rush in suddenly and forcibly', is found only here, but Alford, 633, had already observed that Luke likes double compounds.

For παγίς, 'snare', see Rom. 11:9; 1 Tim. 3:7; 6:9; 2 Tim. 2:26**; J. Schneider, TDNT V, 593–595. πάντας is probably Lucan. κάθημαι here means 'to dwell' (cf. Je. 32:15; diff. Is. 24:17 ἐνοικέω). For ἐπί with accusative cf. Jn. 12:15; Rev. 4:4; *et al.*; and contrast Acts 17:26 where the LXX phrase πρόσωπον τῆς γῆς is also found (Gn. 2:6; 7:23; *et al.*). Since the day of the Lord will affect all men, not even disciples can expect to escape from it if they are not ready.

(36) The positive exhortation is to spiritual wakefulness (ἀγρυπνέω, 'to keep oneself awake, be on the alert', Mk. 13:33; Eph. 6:18; cf. Heb. 13:17**). ἐν παντὶ καιρῷ may be taken with ἀγρυπνεῖτε (RV; RSV; NIV; Zahn, 660) or with δεόμενοι (18:1; 1 Thes. 5:17; cf. NEB; JB; TEV; TNT; Barclay; C. Colpe, TDNT VIII, 434 n. 259; Ott, 74 n. 6), or perhaps with both (Easton, 315); But the sense is unaffected – at all times men must be ready for the parousia. The stress on prayer is typical of Luke. κατισχύω is 'to be strong, be able' (23:23; Mt. 16:18**). It is attested by ℵ B L 33 sa bo; the variant καταξιώθητε (accepted by Zahn, 661 n. 8; Klostermann, 205; Ott, 73f.) may have come from 20:35 and gives a poorer sense. ἐκφεύγω, 'to escape' (1 Thes. 5:3; *et al.*), has the force of coming unscathed through the terrible events of the last days and not giving up the faith in view of them. σταθῆναι can be used of going before a judge (Mt. 25:32; 27:11; 1 Thes. 2:19; 3:13; C. Colpe, TDNT VIII, 434 n. 260). Here the thought is of securing a favourable verdict (Black, 134, for this Hebraism; see 1 En. 62:8, 13; 1QH 4:21f.; Lövestam, 124 n. 2), or (less likely) of being acknowledged as a disciple (Grundmann, 387). The Son of man here acts as judge (Dn. 7:13). The saying is widely regarded as inauthentic (Tödt, 96–98; Higgins, 92–94). Tödt, 97, implies that Luke created the saying as a counterpart to 18:8. But Colpe, ibid., rightly insists that there is no positive evidence against the authenticity of the saying which stands with 17:24, 26, 30; 18:8 (cf. Jeremias, *Theology*, I, 275). Thus the argument that the saying reflects the delay of the parousia – readiness for the coming of the Son of man at any time being replaced by prayer for strength to live through the intervening period of tribulation – depends on the false assumption that Jesus did not expect an interval before the parousia. The one real argument against the saying is the questionable character of its context, but the nature of the context does not exclude the possibility of a basis of authentic teaching of Jesus, however much it may have been developed in the church. It may be noted that if Luke is using a non-Marcan source which did not contain a saying corresponding to Mk. 13:26, then this saying may have been the equivalent.

viii. The Ministry of Jesus in the Temple 21:37–38

This brief paragraph, which describes how Jesus continued to teach the people daily in the temple and spent the nights on the Mount of Olives, forms the conclusion of the entire section and not simply of the eschatological discourse. It is similar in thought to 19:47f. and prepares the way for 22:39 (J. Weiss, 507); cf. also Acts 28:30f. As such it is a Lucan summary of the activity of Jesus, but it reflects the historical position described in Mk. 11:19. It brings the public ministry of Jesus to a triumphant conclusion with the eager crowds anxious to hear him.

(37) The opening words ἦν . . . ἐν τῷ ἱερῷ διδάσκων reflect 19:47; the order ἐν τῷ ἱερῷ διδάσκων is inverted in B K 0139 pc lat; Diglot. τὰς ἡμέρας, accusative of duration, has the force 'throughout each day', and stands in contrast to τὰς νύκτας; τὸ καθ' ἡμέραν, 19:47, would not have been quite so suitable. ἐξερχόμενος refers to departure from the temple. αὐλίζομαι 'to spend the night, find lodging' (Mt. 21:17** of Jesus staying at Bethany), does not necessarily imply sleeping out of doors, but this was a common practice at Passover (Jos. Ant. 17:217 speaks of encampments). For the Mount of Olives cf. 19:29. In view of 19:29 it is possible to regard Luke's phrase here as referring to Bethany (Mk. 11:11f.; Mt. 21:17), but in 22:39 similar phraseology refers to the place where Jesus was arrested, which was nearer the city at Gethsemane. Jeremias, Jerusalem, 61f., accordingly holds that in the present verse Luke has mistaken the place of arrest (Gethsemane) for Jesus' usual lodging place (Bethany) out of ignorance of local geography. But both Jn. 18:2 and Lk. 22:39 imply that Jesus had spent several nights in the area of Gethsemane, and it is possible that we have two separate traditions, or that Jesus stayed in both places on different nights.

(38) πᾶς ὁ λαός is Lucan. ὀρθρίζω can mean 'to get up very early in the morning' (Ex. 24:4; 2 Ki. 6:16; Ct. 7:13) or simply 'to seek someone diligently' (Job 8:5; Ps. 78 (77):34; et al.). The use of similar words in Lk. 24:1, 22; Acts 5:21; cf. Jn. 8:2, perhaps supports the former meaning (so all translations).

At the end of the verse the Pericope de adulteria (Jn. 7:53 – 8:11) is added by f13; JB is disposed to accept it as a piece of Lucan writing which fits admirably into this context; but it is probable that the floating tradition was added here because of the link in wording with Jn. 8:1f. (Metzger, 173). The repetitiousness in wording if Jn. 8:1f. is added shows that the placing is not original, and the weak MS attestation stands against JB's suggestion.

VII

THE PASSION AND RESURRECTION OF JESUS

22:1 – 24:53

THE closing major section of the Gospel covers the same ground as in the other Gospels – the Last Supper, the arrest and trial of Jesus, his death, the discovery of his empty tomb, and his appearances to his disciples. But although the story is essentially the same as that in Mk., Luke has added material from other sources, and has so arranged it that various distinctive motifs stand out. The precise extent of non-Marcan source material is disputed, but there can be no doubt of its presence. As a result of it, we have a fuller elaboration of the farewell sayings of Jesus at the Last Supper, a shift of the Jewish trial from the night to the early morning, various new details in the crucifixion, and new appearance stories. Throughout the section the death and resurrection of Jesus are depicted in terms of the death of a righteous man suffering as a martyr. But above all Jesus is presented as going through suffering to glory, following the path marked out for him by the will of God, prophesied in the OT and foretold in his own teaching to his disciples. It is the end of the Gospel, but at the same time it points forward to the new beginning in the Acts of the Apostles.

See Bultmann, 282–316; Dibelius, 178–218; Finegan, *Überlieferung*; Bornhäuser, *Death*; E. Lohse, *Die Geschichte des Leidens und Sterbens Jesu Christi*, Gütersloh, 1964; Benoit, *Exégèse*, I, 163ff.; Benoit, *Passion*; Schenke; Taylor, *Passion*; Schenk; W. Horbury, 'The Passion Narratives and Historical Criticism', *Theology*, 75, 1972, 58–71; R. Pesch, 'Die Überlieferung der Passion Jesu', in K. Kertelge (ed.), *Rückfrage nach Jesus*, Freiburg, 1974, 148–173.

a. The Last Supper (22:1–38)

Luke's account of the passion opens with the plot of the Jewish leaders, aided by Judas, to put Jesus to death (22:1–6). Jesus for his part proceeds to make his own plans to celebrate the Passover meal (22:7–13), and comes together with his disciples for what will be the last occasion of the kind before the consummation of the kingdom; but the meal itself differs from all previous meals by the way in which Jesus attaches symbolic significance to the bread and wine that formed part of the meal (22:14–20). There follows a series of brief conversational pieces with the disciples in which the treachery of one of them is foretold (22:21–23), there is strife over which of them is greatest (22:24–27), Jesus promises them heavenly reward (22:28–30), he foretells the denial of Peter (22:31–34) and finally he warns them that conflict lies ahead (22:35–38). Much of this material is drawn from non-Marcan sources and gives the Lucan narrative a unique character. The institution of the Lord's Supper becomes part of a larger whole. The willingness of Jesus to face martyrdom is placed in stronger contrast with the treachery, rivalry and weakness of the disciples who persist in incomprehension of what is really happening.

See (in addition to bibliography in 22:1 – 24:53 note) Jeremias, *Words*; A. J. B. Higgins, *The Lord's Supper in the New Testament*, London, 1952; Schürmann, *Paschamahlbericht*; Schürmann, *Einsetzungsbericht*; Schürmann, *Abschiedsrede*; H. Schürmann, *Der Abendmahls- bericht Lukas 22, 7–38 als Gottesdienstordnung, Gemeindeordnung, Lebensordnung*, Leipzig, 1967[4] (reprinted in Schürmann, *Ursprung*, 108–150); E. Schweizer, *The Lord's Supper according to the New Testament*, Philadelphia, 1967; Patsch.

i. The Plot Against Jesus 22:1–2

The approach of the festival of the Passover was the signal to the Jewish leaders to plan to do away with Jesus, or rather to find a way of putting their previously formed intention into effect (cf. 20:47; Jn. 11:47–53). The account follows Mk. 14:1f. with a certain amount of Lucan editing, and nothing suggests the use or influence of another source (Taylor, *Passion*, 42). The narrative, which probably belonged originally with the account of Judas's treachery (Mk. 14:10f.), is regarded as legendary by Bultmann, 282, and as a Marcan invention by Schenke, 12–66, but Taylor, 529, argues that it is too obscure to be an invention. Nevertheless, the omission of the pericope from Jn. and the problem of dating which it raises afford some reason to doubt whether it belongs to the oldest form of the passion narrative (cf. Schweizer, *Markus*, 165). On the other hand, the association of the death of Jesus with the Passover is firmly established, and the detail may be regarded as historical even if it was not formally part of the earliest narrative.

See Schramm, 182–184; Taylor, *Passion*, 42.

(1) Luke replaces Mark's precise dating μετὰ δύο ἡμέρας with a vague ἤγγιζεν (7:12 et al.); in fact Mark's own dating is imprecise since it is not clear how he is reckoning the days. He gives the impending festival (ἑορτή, 2:41f.) its full title in solemn fashion; for the use of ἑορτή with a genitive cf. 2:41; Jn. 13:1 Ex. 23:15; 34:18; Dt. 16:16. Luke has conformed to LXX style. ἄζυμος, 'unleavened' (1 Cor. 5:7f.), is used in the neuter plural to designate the feast of Unleavened Bread (22:7; Acts 12:3; 20:6; Mk. 14:1, 12; Mt. 26:17**). The feast was held from Nisan

15 to 21 (or 22) during the barley harvest (Ex. 12:1–20; 23:15; 34:18; Dt. 16:1–8). By NT times it was closely linked with the Passover (πάσχα, 2:41) held on Nisan 14–15, and the two were virtually identified, as here (Jos. Ant. 3:249; 14:21; 17:213; J. Jeremias, TDNT V, 898–904, especially 898 n. 17).

(2) The plot against Jesus is attributed to the chief priests and scribes, two of the three groups who composed the sanhedrin; the third group, the elders, are not mentioned at this point, possibly because they had not felt the censures of Jesus so keenly as the two religious groups. They had already formed the desire to get rid of Jesus; now they were plotting (ζήτεω) how they might do so; the imperfect sets the scene for the action of Judas. The use of τὸ πῶς, diff. Mk. πῶς, is typically Lucan. (1:62); ἀναιρέω, 'to take away, do away with' (23:32; Acts 19x*), is Lucan, diff. Mk. ἐν δόλῳ κρατήσαντες ἀποκτείνωσιν. Luke also omits Mk.'s phrase μὴ ἐν τῇ ἑορτῇ, perhaps to avoid a seeming discrepancy with the date of Jesus' arrest. The γάρ clause explains the τὸ πῶς ... clause; they wanted to know how to arrest Jesus without causing a reaction from the people (cf. 22:6) whom they feared (cf. 20:19). Mark's expression is clearer.

ii. The Betrayal by Judas 22:3–6

Luke has omitted the story of the anointing of Jesus at Bethany (Mk. 14:3–9). He has already recorded a similar incident at 7:36–50. It may be that he was influenced by the thought expressed in 23:55f.: Jesus is to be anointed after his death (Conzelmann, 72; Stuhlmueller, 156). Grundmann, 388, suggests that the story was not in Luke's copy of Mk., but it is more probable that Luke was acquainted with a form of the tradition in which the anointing story was not included at this point (cf. Jeremias, *Words*, 93 n. 5).

Whatever the reason for the omission, Luke has brought together the stories of the priests' and scribes' plot and the betrayal by Judas into a unified account. The need of the authorities for an opportunity to arrest Jesus quietly is met by the willingness of Judas to give them inside information as to when this could be done. The narrative is based solely on Mk. with Lucan editing (Taylor, *Passion*, 42–44). The one new point is the attribution of Judas's action to the inspiration of Satan, a feature shared with Jn. 13:2, 27. Those who take the view that John contains traditions independent of the written Synoptic Gospels will see here the influence of pre-Johannine tradition on Lk. – for which there is considerable evidence throughout the passion and resurrection narrative (Dodd, 27f.); others, who hold that John's links with Lk. at this point are due to his use of the Gospel, will claim that the present detail is due to Luke himself. Since, however, neither Luke nor John uses the name 'Satan' of his own accord, it is more probable that a tradition is here incorporated by Luke; in our view Luke's contacts with Jn. are to be explained in terms of common traditions (J. Blinzler, *Johannes und die Synoptiker*, Stuttgart, 1965, 41–46, 57f., surveys the discussion and opts for John's dependence on Lk.).

The view of Conzelmann, 72, that Luke here brings to an end a 'Satan-free' period between the temptation and passion of Jesus, finds support in the re-entry of Satan, but it is a misrepresentation of Luke's understanding of the ministry: see the criticism in Brown, *Apostasy*, 6–12.

The subjectivism of historical and form criticism is apparent when Bultmann, 282, states that the pericope contains scarcely any historical information (cf. Schenke, 119–140, who assigns it to free Marcan composition), while Taylor, 534, claims that its historicity is 'beyond question'. Similarly, Schweizer, *Markus*, 168, argues that the church is unlikely to have invented the treachery of one of the disciples.

See Brown, *Apostasy*, 6–12; Schramm, 182–184; Taylor, *Passion*, 42–44.

(3) For Σατανᾶς (ὁ Σατανᾶς, U Θ *pm* Eus; *Diglot*) cf. 10:18; 13:16; 22:31; Luke prefers διάβολος (8:12 diff. Mk., Schürmann, *Abschiedsrede*, 102f.). For εἰσέρχομαι cf. Jn. 13:27, and for the motif of Satanic influence in men's hearts cf. Jn. 14:30; Acts 5:3; 1 Cor. 2:8; Asc. Is. 5:1. The reference to Satan (cf. 22:31) shows how more than human decisions were involved in the passion of Jesus; the early church could see no other explanation of what had happened.

Ἰούδας appeared in the list of disciples in 6:16. His by-name there was Ἰσκαριώθ (Mk. 3:19; 14:10**), here altered to Ἰσκαριώτης (Mt. 10:4; 26:14; Jn., 5x**) – a further link with Jn. 13:2, 26. καλούμενον is read by ℵ B D L W X 69 *pc* (1:36; *et al.*); ἐπικαλούμενον by *rell*; TR; *Diglot*; both words are Lucan, and superior external attestation must be decisive here. For the additional description introduced by means of the participle ὄντα cf. 23:7; Mk. uses ὁ εἷς in apposition. Luke inserts τοῦ ἀριθμοῦ, 'number' (Acts, 5x): is the implication that Judas merely belonged to the group outwardly without really being one of them in true loyalty to Jesus?

(4) Luke describes a conversation (συνλαλέω, 4:36; *et al.*, diff. Mk.) between Judas and the authorities. In addition to the chief priests he mentions the temple police (στρατηγοῖς; with τοῖς prefixed, ℵ U W *pm*; TR; *Diglot*; τοῖς στρατηγοῖς τοῦ ἱεροῦ (cf. 22:52), C (Θ) *pc* sy^pEus; the whole phrase is omitted by D it). The textual variations are due to the unusual nature of the word. στρατηγός occurs 5x in Acts to refer to Roman magistrates (praetors); it is also used in the singular (Acts 4:1; 5:24, 26) for the ruler of the temple (s^egan, SB II, 628–631), the priest next in authority after the high priest. Here in the plural (cf. 22:52**; Bikk. 3:3) it refers to the 'ammark^elîn who functioned as temple police (Jeremias. *Jerusalem*, 165f.; G. Schrenk, TDNT III, 271; cf. O. Bauernfeind, TDNT VII, 709 n. 35). These would be the appropriate functionaries if the question of an arrest, possibly in the temple, was

envisaged. Luke again uses the τὸ πῶς construction (22:2), diff. Mk. ἵνα; παραδῷ (diff. Mk. παραδοῖ) is a form of the aorist subjunctive (MH II, 210f.).

(5) Luke follows Mk. in describing the joy of the authorities and their agreement to pay Judas for his services. He has συντίθημι, 'to make an agreement' (also 'to decide', Acts 23:20; Jn. 9:22**), diff. Mk. ἐπαγγέλλομαι (Acts 7:5), which is perhaps more informal.

(6) The use of ἐξομολογέω in the active, 'to promise, consent', is unparalleled (cf. AG), but there is an excellent parallel in Lysias 12:8f. (cited by Klostermann, 205), where a person who has been offered money to do a service to someone else then agrees to do it (ὁ δ' ὡμολόγησε ταῦτα ποιήσειν; cf. Mt. 14:7; Acts 7:17). Thereupon Judas sought for a favourable opportunity (εὐκαιρία, Mt. 26:16**; cf. Mk. εὐκαίρως; Cadbury, 199) to betray Jesus (the use of τοῦ with the infinitive is Lucan): ἄτερ, 'without', is Lucan (22:35**), and ὄχλος, 'crowd', could mean 'tumult' (AG; evidence in R. Meyer, TDNT V, 584): cf. Acts 24:18. αὐτοῖς follows ἄτερ ὄχλου in p⁷⁵ ℵ A B pc; is omitted by D lat; and precedes it in rell; TR; Diglot.

iii. Preparations for the Passover Meal 22:7–13

Against the sombre background of the plot against Jesus Luke now recounts how Jesus prepared to celebrate his last meal with his disciples. Following Mk., he relates the story of the preparations at some length, describing in great detail how the disciples appointed for the task were to recognise the person who would take them to the intended room and then prepare the room for the meal in the customary Jewish manner. Here especially the Passover character of the meal is evident. The story itself suggests that Jesus made arrangements to hold the meal secretly, possibly in order to avoid arrest before he had completed what he intended to do: he is presented in the Gospels as being in control of the situation. At the same time, Jesus is perhaps regarded as showing supernatural knowledge of the circumstances; it is a moot point whether he is simply giving directions in terms of a previously-made secret arrangement with the owner of the room or is acting with supernatural knowledge and authority. The story is similar in pattern to that of the preparations for the entry to Jerusalem (19:29–35), and in both cases it is probable that the historical basis lies in a previous arrangement.

It is generally agreed that Luke is here dependent solely on Mk. and has not used any other source (Schürmann, Paschamahlbericht, 75–104; Taylor, Passion, 44–46). Luke's editing stresses the initiative taken by Jesus and identifies the two disciples involved as Peter and John.

The historical basis of Mark's story is disputed. Bultmann, 283f., finds legendary features in the account of Jesus' foreknowledge (cf. 1 Sa. 10:1–9); the story is a secondary addition to the account of Jesus'

Passover meal, and the dating in Mk. 14:12 is unjewish. Schweizer, *Markus*, 169f., draws attention to the use of 'the Twelve' in Mk. 14:17, whereas this story speaks of 'the disciples'. More important, he holds that this account is the sole basis in Mk. for regarding Jesus' meal as a Passover meal, and on the assumption that the Johannine dating of the crucifixion (and hence of the meal) *before* the Passover is correct, he argues that this story is historically inaccurate. The parallelism between this narrative and the story of the preparations for the entry is also seen as a sign of late composition.

The basic problem here is that of the nature and date of Jesus' meal. The other arguments are of lesser weight. We have already suggested that the story is about a pre-arranged meeting rather than a piece of legend; the similarities in construction to Mk. 11:1-7 show merely that the same author is responsible for the final form of both stories, and a simpler form of story may lie behind the present account (Schürmann, *Paschamahlbericht*, 120–122). The mixture of 'the disciples' and 'the Twelve' in Mk. is possibly a sign of the use of different sources, but the essential point here is that the stereotyped use of 'the Twelve' in v. 14 is not really in conflict with the fact that two of them had been sent on to make preparations; they may well have returned to Jesus to announce the completion of their task.

The dating of the meal is the serious point. We accept the view of Jeremias, *Words, passim* (cf. Lane, 497f.), that in *character* the meal was a Passover supper, and that paschal features are present both in Mk. and in Jn. Whether the Synoptic *date* of the meal at the official Passover hour or the Johannine dating before the official Passover is correct is more difficult to decide, and there is certainly no scholarly consensus on the matter. The attractive theory of A. Jaubert (*The Date of the Last Supper*, New York, 1965; cf. Ellis, 249f.) that Jesus followed a sectarian calendar and held his meal on this basis before the officially prescribed date creates considerable difficulty (cf. briefly Lane, 498 n. 33). The view that John's chronology is correct (Lagrange, 539f.; and many others; cf. Taylor, 664–667; Brown, *John*, II, 555f.; E. Schweizer* (22:1–38 note), 29–22) removes many of the historical difficulties associated with the trial and crucifixion of Jesus. It is possible that Jesus held a meal with a paschal character a day earlier than the official day. If so, the Synoptic Gospels have assumed that the meal was held a day later than it was actually held. But the Synoptic chronology is self-consistent, and the historical difficulties created by it are capable of resolution (Jeremias, ibid.). We are inclined to adopt it, while recognizing that no solution to the problem as a whole is free from difficulties.

The age of the tradition is uncertain. Schürmann, *Paschamahlbericht*, 118–122, argues that the Lucan supper narrative (22:15–18) presupposes an introduction, and that this lost introduction lies behind Mark's account; he finds similarities in outlook (Jesus' prophetic knowledge; his initiative; and the concentration on Jesus' eating the

Passover) between Mk. 14:12–18a and Lk. 22:15–18. These points indicate the possibility of Schürmann's thesis, but in the nature of things no absolute proof is possible.

See Schürmann, *Paschamahlbericht*, 75–104, 110–123; Schramm, 182–184; Taylor, *Passion*, 44–47; Schenke, 152–198.

(7) In 22:1 the festival had been drawing near; now it has come (ἦλθεν, diff. Mk.) and the date is solemnly noted in an independent sentence, diff. Mk. ἡ ἡμέρα τῶν ἀζύμων (Mark adds πρώτη) by itself would mean Nisan 15, but the addition to the phrase indicates that Nisan 14 is meant, and this meaning is found in Jewish usage (M. Ex. 12:15; Jos. Bel. 5:99; SB II, 813–815); the alternative explanation that by using a midnight-to-midnight time-reckoning Mark (and Luke) could regard Nisan 15 as stretching backwards into Nisan 14 is improbable. ἐν (TR; *Diglot*; (UBS)) is omitted by p⁷⁵ ᵛⁱᵈ B C D L 579 892 *pc*; *Synopsis*, but corresponds to Lucan style (cf. Schürmann, *Paschamahlbericht*, 79). The use of ἔδει, diff. Mk., brings out the statutory character of the practice (cf. 11:42; 13:14); the construction enables Luke to avoid Mark's impersonal plural ἔθυον. πάσχα (2:41) must here mean 'the paschal lamb' (22:11; Mk. 14:12, 14). θύω (15:23) carries a sacrificial sense in this context (cf. Ex. 12:21; Dt. 16:2).

(8) In Mk. the disciples take the initiative in the matter of preparations and Jesus responds by sending two of them with the necessary instructions. Here the order is inverted; Jesus takes the initiative in a command, based on the wording of Mk. 14:12b; this is followed by the question of the disciples (Mk. 14:12b) and Jesus' detailed instructions (Mk. 14:13–15). The structure of the narrative is thus brought closer to that of 19:29ff. The two disciples are named as Peter and John, diff. Mk. (cf. 8:45; 9:10; and the place of Peter and John in Acts 3:1f.; 8:14). πορευθέντες (diff. Mk. ἀπελθόντες) is appropriate for the journey into Jerusalem. The task of preparation for the Passover (πάσχα here means the meal as a whole) included making ready the room, providing the lamb, the unleavened bread and other food, and cooking the meal or arranging for helpers to do this. Since Jerusalem was crowded at the Passover season, and the meal had to be eaten within the confines of the city, the obtaining of a room was a matter of importance.

(9) The question of the disciples in Mk. 14:12b is now utilised to provide the introduction for Jesus' detailed instructions. The changed context enables Luke to abbreviate the wording.

(10) Jesus' answer is rephrased in Lucan style with ἰδού (5:12; *et al.*) and a genitive absolute (with εἰσέρχομαι, diff. Mk. ὑπάγω, which Luke tends to avoid). As the disciples enter the city, they will be met (συναντάω, 9:37; *et al.*, diff. Mk. ἀπαντάω, reflecting Luke's preference for συν- compounds) by a man carrying a jar (κεράμιον, Mk. 14:13**) of water. This would be an unusual sight, since men normally carried leather bottles (cf. 5:37f. for these) and women carried jars or pitchers. The instruction sounds like a reference to a pre-arranged sign, and it

must be assumed that the time for the disciples to enter the city was pre-arranged. The disciples were then to follow the man to his destination; Luke has improved the style by his εἰς τὴν οἰκίαν ... phrase, corresponding to Mk. ὅπου ἐὰν εἰσέλθῃ in the next sentence. But what was the purpose of the arrangement? Why could Jesus not have told the disciples the address of the house? He may have wished not to be seen making the arrangement himself and so being tracked down. More probably he wished to avoid naming the rendezvous in the presence of Judas. Lohmeyer, 299f., prefers to see in the incident the way in which every detail of the passion is foreordained by God and foreknown by Jesus, but this explanation does not fully account for the peculiar character of the present incident.

(11) On arrival at the house the disciples are to deliver Jesus' message to the owner. For ἐρεῖτε as a polite imperative cf. 19:31. Since οἰκοδεσπότης had lost its original force, Luke felt at liberty to add τῆς οἰκίας (BD 484). λέγει is brought forward to stress the authoritative command of Jesus who here describes himself as ὁ διδάσκαλος (6:40 par. Mt. 10:24f.; Mt. 23:8; Jn. 13:13f.). Hahn, 80, sees here a formal christological title of Palestinian Jewish origin, but it is more probable that it is a term used by Jesus for himself, and certainly used by his disciples to describe him. This is how he was known to his disciples, and the presumption is that the householder was a disciple. The question, 'Where is the guest-room?' is a polite way of asking to see the room in order that the preparations may be made. For κατάλυμα see 2:7; Luke drops Mark's μου, i.e. 'the guest-room that I am going to use'; the ὅπου clause with the subjunctive is tantamount to a purpose clause (cf. 7:4).

(12) The paratactic construction (κἀκεῖνος, diff. Mk. καὶ αὐτός, is a stylistic improvement) is Semitic. In response to the query 'Where?' the owner will show them an upper room (ἀνάγαιον Mk. 14:15**; cf. ὑπερῷον, Acts 1:13; et al.), i.e. an extra room built onto the flat roof of a typical Palestinian house. It will be 'furnished' (στρώννυμι, usually 'to strew') sc. with cushions (Jeremias, Words, 48 n. 1); Luke omits Mk. ἕτοιμον which clashes with the following ἑτοιμάσατε.

(13) So the disciples (the subject is omitted, diff. Mk.) depart; they find everything as Jesus has said (εἰρήκει, pluperfect, diff. Mk. εἶπεν, is more correct; Schürmann, Paschamahlbericht, 103f.), and they make the necessary preparations.

iv. The Passover Meal 22:14–18

Luke's account of the actual supper begins with a description of the arrival of Jesus and the apostles at the table (22:14; cf. Mk. 14:17). Then Jesus expresses his desire to eat this Passover with his disciples before his suffering, since this will be the last occasion before its fulfilment in the kingdom of God. In the same way he shares a cup of wine with them with the comment that he will not drink wine until the kingdom of God comes. This last statement is parallel to Mk. 14:25, where, however, it follows the words of interpretation over the bread and wine. The significance of Jesus' words in Lk. is that this is to be his last meal with his disciples before his suffering; the next meal of the same kind will be the 'fulfilment' of such meals after the coming of the kingdom of God. The idea of a vow of abstinence from food and drink in order to intercede for Israel, found by Jeremias, *Words*, 207–218, does not seem to be present for Luke, whether or not it represents a more primitive strand in interpretation. The question whether Jesus participated in the present meal or abstained from it cannot be answered with certainty.

In Lk. this account is followed by the account of Jesus taking the bread and wine and pronouncing the words of interpretation over them (here we anticipate the discussion of the authenticity of 22:19b–20 in the next section). *Prima facie* we have a continuous account of what took place at the meal. But the twofold structure in 22:15–18, including the sharing of a cup, and the way in which the vow of abstinence follows the words of institution in Mk., has aroused the suspicion that in fact two separate accounts of the meal have been combined. On the one hand, there is the account of a meal at which Jesus said farewell to his disciples and in which there is no developed sacramentalism. This account is most fully developed in Jn. 13–17; it is related more briefly in Lk. 22:(14)15–18, 24–30, 35–38; and a fragment of it survives in Mk. 14:25 (cf. Bultmann, 285–287; Schürmann, *Paschamahlbericht*, 1–74; Stuhlmueller, 157; E. Schweizer*, 18–22). On the other hand, there is an independent 'eucharistic' narrative, a 'cult legend' (Bultmann), which is found in Mk. 14:22–24; 1 Cor. 11:23–26; Lk. 22:19–20).

For Bultmann the account in Mk. 14:22–24 is a Hellenistic, Pauline cult legend, which has displaced the original account. With this view may be linked Schürmann's understanding of the present passage; for him it was originally a simple double-prophecy of Jesus' imminent death, but this was then redacted to describe the last Passover held by Jesus as the scene of the institution of the eucharist at which the cup is shared among the disciples; thus the present narrative which indicates how Jesus founded the eucharist is due to redaction of an account of Jesus' last Passover, and this account in turn is based on a simple forecast of Jesus' imminent death. For Schürmann (*Einsetzungsbericht*, 133–150) the eucharistic narrative was composed as an appendix to this 'Passover narrative', to clarify what was obscure in it, on the basis of early tradition, and thus was added to it to form a single unit.

It is, however, also possible that the eucharistic narrative is primitive over against the Passover narrative. Dibelius, 210–212, argued that 22:15–18 was the product of the historicising tendency of Luke to put the eucharistic narrative into the setting of a Passover meal and so produce a scene in four acts with careful parallelism (cf. Schenke, 303f.). But linguistic analysis forbids this hypothesis; the Passover narrative is based on tradition, even if it shows signs of Lucan editing. E.

Schweizer*, 25–28, admits that it is unlikely that the Passover narrative would have been created as a second, independent account of the supper with no reference to the words of institution; nevertheless, he prefers the view that the eucharistic narrative is the earlier, and that the Passover narrative 'originated in a Jewish-Christian group which still held to the celebration of the Passover feast'. It cannot be claimed that this is a very strong case. On the other hand, the weakness that Schweizer sees in his view, namely the mention of the Passover when (on his view) the last supper was not a Passover, is of little weight; for the mention could be historical (see 22:7–13 introduction above) or it may be a secondary addition (Schürmann).

Jeremias, *Words*, 122–125, recognizes that we have two independent traditions, but holds that they represent two stages in the one historical meal held by Jesus, in which he declared his intention to abstain from the meal and then proceeded to reinterpret it for his disciples.

A solution to the problem involves the recognition that the eucharistic narrative has been handed down in the form of an independent tradition (cf. 1 Cor. 11:23–26) and this tradition contains the 'eschatological outlook' found in the Passover narrative. But this independent tradition is in all probability the distillation of a longer account and presupposes a fuller knowledge of the circumstances of the last supper; already in 1 Cor. 5:7 the paschal character of Jesus' death is recognised, and in 1 Cor. 10:16f. the idea of a new Passover is present. It is probable that the eucharistic narrative originally stood in a paschal context. It is a feasible hypothesis that the original form of the eucharistic narrative has been replaced by the liturgically shaped unit attested by Paul (cf. Taylor, 542f.). This would explain the lack of connection between the two pieces of tradition in Luke, and at the same time enable us to avoid the difficulties caused by positing that either narrative is older than the other.

See F. C. Burkitt and A. E. Brooke, 'St Luke XXII. 15, 16: What is the General Meaning?' JTS 9, 1908, 569–572; Bultmann, 285–287; Dibelius, 210–212; Jeremias, *Words*, 122–125, 207–218; Schürmann, *Paschamahlbericht*, 1–74; E. Schweizer (22:1–38 note), 18–22, 25–28; C. K. Barrett, 'Luke XXII. 15: To Eat the Passover', JTS ns 9, 1958, 305–307; G. J. Bahr, 'The Seder of Passover and the Eucharistic Words', Nov.T 12, 1970, 181–202; Taylor, *Passion*, 48–50; Schenk, 303f.; Patsch, 95–102.

(14) This verse should be regarded as the introduction to the story of the meal (UBS) rather than as the conclusion of the preparations (*Synopsis*). Jesus and his companions assemble when the hour has come, i.e. the appropriate time for the meal (though Grundmann, 392, sees a further allusion to God's hour in the phrase). Schürmann, *Paschamahlbericht*, 104–106, sees here Luke's editing of Mk. ὀψίας γενομένης, a phrase which Luke habitually avoids. Luke omits reference to Jesus coming to the room, and concentrates attention on his taking his place at table. He uses ἀναπίπτω (11:37; 14:10; 17:7*), diff. Mk. ἀνάκειμαι, another word which he usually avoids (cf. 22:27, however). For Mk.

μετὰ τῶν δώδεκα he has καὶ οἱ ἀπόστολοι σὺν αὐτῷ; ἀπόστολοι is read
by p⁷⁵ ℵ*B D 157 it (syᶜ); the other authorities assimilate to Mk. or conflate. Luke may be following a source, or may have wished to avoid a
reference to the Twelve if only ten were involved (but see introduction to
22:7–13), or more probably he wished to stress the position of the
Twelve as apostles at the institution of the Lord's Supper. The wording
tends to stress the initiative and dominant position of Jesus.

The verse can be understood as Lucan redaction of Mk. 14:17–18a
(Schürmann, *Paschamahlbericht*, 104–110), since it avoids Marcan expressions that Luke dislikes and displays Lucan features. But the case
falls short of positive proof, and it can be argued that Luke is here
following a source which provided the introduction to 22:15–18;
Rehkopf, 90 n. 4, claims that there are elements of pre-Lucan
vocabulary (ὅτε, ἀναπίπτω, ὥρα as 'the eschatological hour', and
ἀπόστολος); cf. Jeremias, *Words*, 99 n. 1; Taylor, *Passion*, 48f. Certainty on the point is unattainable, but Schürmann appears to have the
better case.

(15) At the very outset of the meal, according to Luke, Jesus expresses his desire to partake of it. The dative ἐπιθυμίᾳ is used to
strengthen the verb in the manner of a Hebrew infinitive absolute; this is
said not to be an Aramaic construction (but cf. 1QapGen. 20:10f.; J. A.
Fitzmyer, NTS 20, 1973–74, 401), but is found in the LXX (cf. Gn.
31:30; Acts 2:17 LXX; 5:28; 23:14; 16:28; 28:10, 26 LXX; Jn. 3:39;
18:32; Jas. 5:17; BD 198⁶). It may be Lucan. For ἐπιθυμέω cf. 15:16. τὸ
πάσχα can mean 1. the paschal lamb (C. K. Barrett*; Jeremias, *Words*,
207f.); 2. the Passover meal (Schürmann, *Paschamahlbericht*, 8f.).
Schürmann argues that Jesus is thinking more of the fellowship of the
meal than of the ritual requirement, and that at this stage of the meal the
lamb would not yet be on the table; the interest in general is in the meal,
not in the lamb as such. But we do not know at what precise point in the
meal the words were uttered. Further, the use of a meal as the object of
φαγεῖν is odd (14:24 and 1 Cor. 11:20 are not entirely convincing
parallels). In any case, a reference to a Passover meal yet to come (F. C.
Burkitt; see below) is ruled out by the τοῦτο. The suggestion that the saying originally referred to bread (to give parallelism with the wine; cf.
Bultmann, 286) is improbable, since the tendency of Christian alteration
would have been to proceed in the opposite direction (Jeremias, *Words*,
18 n. 5; Schürmann, op. cit., 9f.). A reference to the lamb remains likely.
μεθ᾽ ὑμῶν underlines the fellowship between Jesus and the disciples. It is
to be the last possible occasion, and this explains why Jesus took such
elaborate care to have the meal undisturbed. He knew that it would be
followed by suffering (for πάσχω cf. 9:22; 24:46; Acts 1:3; 3:18; 17:3;
et al.). The πρὸ τοῦ phrase (2:21 note) appears to be Lucan (Schürmann,
op. cit., 12f., 69f.; Jeremias, *Words*, 162, notes that πάσχω is untran-
slatable into Hebrew or Aramaic, but see 9:22 note). The thought of
Jesus' death is implicit in vs. 16 and 18, and it is not impossible that

Luke has edited an earlier phrase in his characteristic style. We can now ask whether Jesus was expressing 1. a wish that was fulfilled in his sharing in the meal (Creed, 265; Geldenhuys, 557; Schürmann, op. cit., 11); 2. an unfulfilled wish (looking forward to a still future Passover in which he would not be able to participate; F. C. Burkitt and A. E. Brooke*; Taylor, *Behind*, 37; Rengstorf, 235); or 3. his intention not to take part in the meal presently before him (Jeremias, *Words*, 208). The argument for the second and third possibilities rests on the use of ἐπιθυμέω to express an unfulfilled wish (15:16; 16:21; 17:22 and Mt. 13:17; but see 15:16 note). The first view fits the context best, for the point is that Jesus *is* able to share this meal with the disciples.

(16) The reason for Jesus' great desire to share this particular Passover meal with his disciples is that he will not be able to do so again. The general structure of the sentence is parallel to v. 18, which in turn is parallel to Mk. 14:25. The connective γάρ corresponds to ἀμήν in Mk. 14:25; it could be due to Lucan redaction (4:24 note), but this is not necessarily the case, since Luke does not elsewhere replace ἀμήν by γάρ (cf. Jeremias, *Words*, 163 n. 6; Schürmann, op. cit., 14f.). ὅτι is omitted by C* D X *pc*; (UBS), but the omission may be due to assimilation to v. 18; cf. Mk. 14:25. οὐ μή is read by p⁷⁵ ᵛⁱᵈ ℵ A B L Θ f1 a sa bo *al*; UBS; *Diglot*; οὐκέτι οὐ μή by *rell*; *Synopsis* (D has οὐκέτι μή). While Tasker, 422, regards the omission of οὐκέτι as assimilation to Mt. 26:29, Metzger, 173, more convincingly sees its addition as an attempt to alleviate an abrupt saying. Jesus' saying can be regarded as a straightforward prediction of what he is going to do, but Jeremias, *Words*, 207–218, argues that it is a declaration of intent, giving the reason why Jesus' wish in v. 15 remains unfulfilled. He further argues that Jesus abstains in order to fast in intercession for the Jewish people. But there is no mention of intercession in the context, and the emphasis lies more on the coming of the kingdom. There will be no more Passover meals until the coming of the kingdom. For ἕως ὅτου cf. 12:50; 13:8; it is probably pre-Lucan. πληρόω is common in Lk. (1:20; *et al.*). The passive is probably a circumlocution for an active verb with God as subject, and the subject of the verb is presumably the Passover lamb or festival. The thought is of the fulfilment of the Passover in heaven, or rather in the new age which is brought about by the death of Jesus. 'Jesus calls the banquet of the age of salvation a fulfilment of the Passover' (J. Jeremias, TDNT V, 900f.; G. Delling, TDNT VI, 296f.; see further Black, 229–238, and criticism by Schürmann, op. cit., 21 n. 102). The question then arises whether the thought is of the final consummation and the messianic banquet or of the presence of Jesus with his disciples in the Lord's Supper. Jeremias (*Words*, 122–125; TDNT V, 900–904) and Ellis, 252f., argue that vs. 15–18 refer to the parousia, and 19–20 to the Lord's Supper; the former section has to do with fasting, carried out on behalf of the Jews and in anticipation of the possible coming of the Lord at Passover-time; thus the two-fold pattern of

fasting and supper corresponds to the eucharistic practice of the Jerusalem church. It is however, more probable that the custom of the early church was based upon its reading of Lk. rather than that Lk. reflects this custom. Nothing in the text suggests the presence of the belief that the Messiah would come in Passover-night. It is, therefore, possible that Luke saw in the saying a hint of the fellowship between Jesus and his disciples in the 'new Passover' of the Lord's Supper, especially since the stress is not, as in Mk., on Jesus drinking the new wine, but on the coming of the kingdom.

(17) The second part of the action shows parallels with the first part and also with the description of the institution of the Lord's Supper (vs. 19f., par. Mk. 14:22b–23). Schürmann, *Paschamahlbericht*, 23–34, has demonstrated the improbability that Luke is here dependent on Mk., and claims that it is more likely that the tradition in Mk. is indebted to that used by Lk. The use of $\delta\acute{\epsilon}\chi o\mu a\iota$ in the sense 'to take hold of' is found only here and 16:6f. in Lk; otherwise, it has its usual meaning, 'to receive something from somebody'. The use of $\lambda a\mu\beta\acute{a}\nu\omega$ appears to be fixed in liturgical terminology, and Luke's difference from the usual word is unlikely to be due to literary variation. $\pi o\tau\acute{\eta}\rho\iota o\nu$ is used without the article (but it is added in p[75 vid] A D W Θ *al*; *Diglot*), as in Mk. 14:23; contrast 22:20; 1 Cor. 11:25.

On the assumption that the Passover meal is being described, there is some controversy as to which cup in the sequence of four is meant. Schürmann, op. cit., 48–50, argues that in the original, independent tradition 22:15–18, the third cup was meant, i.e. the cup of blessing drunk after the main meal; he argues that the same cup is meant in 22:20 (cf. $\mu\epsilon\tau\grave{a}\ \tau\grave{o}\ \delta\epsilon\iota\pi\nu\tilde{\eta}\sigma a\iota$), the two accounts originally being independent versions of the same incident (cf. Schürmann, *Einsetzungsbericht*, 86). For Luke, it would appear, the cup is then to be understood as an earlier one, but Schürmann is not clear on this point. Grundmann, 393, argues that for both the source and Luke the third cup is meant. Jeremias, *Words*, 211f., claims, however, that a vow of abstinence must have come at the outset of the meal, i.e. in connection with the first cup, which preceded the meal. The same position is adopted by L. Goppelt, TDNT VI, 153f., who notes a reference to the 'fruit of the vine' in the prayer over the first cup at the Passover meal. But this prayer was said with other cups also. Jeremias' argument depends also on his special interpretation of the saying as a vow of abstinence from the present meal. Daube, 330f., argues that the third cup is meant; Jesus drank from it, but not from the fourth one, and the meal finished abruptly before the fourth cup and the second part of the Hallel; this assumes, as in Mk., that we are dealing with one cup in the two accounts and not two. The detailed study of the passover meal by G. J. Bahr* discusses the uncertainty that must attach to any identification, and argues that the third cup after the meal is meant; the eucharistic cup is a separate, later one, that may perhaps rest on unusual practice. On the whole, if the same cup is meant as in v. 20, the third cup is likely; if, however, two separate cups are meant, the first cup may be intended here.

εὐχαριστέω (17:16) also appears in connection with the cup in Mk. 14:23, and in connection with the bread in Lk. 22:19; 1 Cor. 11:24. The word is often thought to be Hellenistic, in contrast with the more Jewish εὐλογέω (Mk. 14:23; cf. Jeremias, *Words*, 175), but Schürmann, *Paschamahlbericht*, 53–60, argues that the use without an object is not Greek, that the presence of the word here is not a late development, and that the choice of the less usual word, associated for Christians with the Lord's Supper, points up the unusual character of what was happening. The word refers to the normal thanksgiving or benediction spoken in connection with the drinking of wine. For Christian readers it would be an indication of the eucharistic character of the meal. λάβετε is found in the 'bread saying' in Mk. 14:22, but not in Lk. 22:19. Schürmann, op. cit., 30f., 60–63, argues that Luke is unlikely to have transferred the word from Mk. 14:22, that it is more probably secondary in Mk. 14:22 (where it is unnecessary after ἔδωκεν and since it has no parallel in 1 Cor. 11:24), and that it was necessary in Lk. because the sharing of a common cup was unusual. But this last point is doubtful, Jeremias, *Words*, 69f., having assembled the evidence that a common cup was not unknown. διαμερίζω is Lucan (11:17; *et al.*), but could have replaced an original μερίζω (cf. 11:17f., diff. Mk. 3:24f.). For εἰς ἑαυτούς cf. 7:30; 15:17. The command corresponds to the narrative καὶ ἔπιον ἐξ αὐτοῦ πάντες, Mk. 14:23, but is unlikely to have been constructed from the latter by Luke. The whole action is unusual, since the cup was usually passed round in silence (Jeremias, *Words*, 208f.), and we have to inquire regarding its meaning for Jesus and for the disciples. In the case of Jesus the question is whether he himself partook of this cup. V. 18 is compatible with either partaking or not partaking. V. 17 would most naturally imply that Jesus told his disciples to share a cup of which he was not partaking (Jeremias, *Words*, 208f., listing other supporters of this view; L. Goppelt, TDNT VI, 141, 154). But Schürmann, op. cit., 63–65, argues that it was customary for the host to partake first, and that there is nothing to suggest that Jesus departed from custom at this point. Luke's usage of ἀπὸ τοῦ νῦν (v. 18) normally refers to what is going to happen subsequent to the moment of speaking and does not include what is happening at the precise moment (1:48; 5:10; 12:52; 22:69; Acts 18:6); this supports the second view. The interpretation of 22:16 and Mk. 14:25 also supports this view. If the cup here is different from that in v. 20, the implication is that Jesus did not partake of the later, eucharistic cup (J. Weiss, 509); if it is the same cup, he did partake of it.

As for the disciples, their sharing in the cup is usually said to represent a sharing in the blessing bestowed by Jesus (Jeremias, *Words*, 232f.; Schürmann, op. cit., 60–63). This understanding is questionable. For the 'blessing' spoken over the cup is not a blessing of the contents, but a prayer of thanks to God: 'Blessed be thou, Lord our God, King of the world, who hast created the fruit of the vine'. Rather, the act of drinking together unites the participants into a table fellowship with one another. And the significance of the action is that this is the last occasion on which they can do so with Jesus.

(18) The saying corresponds closely in form and wording to Mk. 14:25 and Lk. 22:16. This has led to the suspicion that it is modelled on Mk. 14:25 (Schlatter, 137; Schenke, 303), but the case for independence is stronger (Schürmann, op. cit., 34–45). Nevertheless, the tradition in Mk. may be more primitive than that in Lk. The saying is regarded by Jeremias as the explanation for Jesus' abstention from the cup (implied in v. 17), and by Schürmann as the explanation for the command to the disciples to participate in the cup. In the introductory λέγω γὰρ ὑμῖν, Mark's ἀμήν is replaced by γάρ (cf. 22:16 note). It is not clear whether ὅτι should be read; p⁷⁵ ᵛⁱᵈ B C D L f1 pc e; Synopsis; (UBS) omit it, and since the temptation to assimilation to Mk. 14:25 and Lk. 22:16 and to Lucan style was strong, the omission should probably be accepted. ἀπὸ τοῦ νῦν corresponds to Mk. οὐκέτι (contrast Lk. 22:16) and is probably Lucan; see 22:17 note on its significance. ἀπό may be a Lucan alteration of Mk. ἐκ. For γένημα cf. 12:18 v.1.; ἄμπελος is 'vine' (Jn. 15:1–5; Jas. 3:12; Rev. 14:18f.). The phrase 'the fruit of the vine' occurs in the Jewish prayer of thanksgiving for wine; cf. Is. 32:12. οὗ (p⁷⁵ ᵛⁱᵈ ℵ B C²L f1 157 579 892 pc; om. C*ᵛⁱᵈ; ὅτου rell; TR; Diglot) is Lucan (12:50; et al.), diff. Mk. τῆς ἡμέρας ἐκείνης ὅταν, which is closer to an Aramaic formulation with its pleonastic demonstrative. The clause speaks of the coming of the kingdom, perhaps as a circumlocution for saying that God will establish the kingdom (Jeremias, Words, 210). There is an implicit reference to the thought of the banquet in the kingdom, perhaps to the anticipation of this banquet in the Lord's Supper. Schürmann, op. cit., 38–42, argues for the more primitive formulation in Mk. being original at this point, and this seems probable. Nevertheless, the occurrence of ἄχρι οὗ ἔλθῃ in 1 Cor. 11:26 may be a pointer to the primitive character of Luke's formulation.

v. The Institution of the Lord's Supper 22:19–20

The interpretation of this section is closely linked with the problem of the establishment of the original text. Until about 1950 there was a strong tendency among scholars to adopt the shorter form of text, i.e. omitting vs. 19b–20, with D a d ff² i l syʰ (and possibly the archetypes of c r²δ; cf. G. D. Kilpatrick*; Jeremias, Words, 142 n. 6; M. Rese*, 15 n. 4). The existence of this text is further attested by various authorities which rearrange the verse order (15, 16, 19a, 17, 18: b e; 15, 16, 19a: syᵖboᵖᵗ; for details see Metzger, 174f.). It is accepted by WH App., 63f.; Diglot; RSV (earlier editions); NEB; Plummer, 496f.; Klostermann, 207f.; Creed, 263f.; Easton, 321; K. Th. Schäfer*; H. Chadwick*; Leaney, 72–75), and there has recently been some reaction in its favour (A.

Vööbus*; M. Rese*). In favour of this shorter text it can be argued: 1. It is briefer and more difficult than the longer text. 2. The longer text can be explained as due to assimilation to 1 Cor. 11:24 and Mk. 14:24b, whereas it is hard to see why an original long text should have been abbreviated. 3. The style of vs. 19b–20 is not Lucan. 4. Luke's aversion to 'ransom'-theology (cf. 22:27, diff. Mk. 10:45) precluded him from incorporating sacrificial ideas into his understanding of the death of Jesus. 5. Redactional study suggests that the shorter text can be explained in terms of Lucan editing of Mk. to change an account of the institution of the Lord's Supper into an account of Jesus' last Passover meal.

The case for the retention of the longer text has been put especially by Jeremias, *Words*, 139–159; Schürmann, *Untersuchungen*, 159–192; K. Aland*, 202f.; K. Snodgrass*; and it appears in *Synopsis*; UBS[3]; JB; and versions dependent on UBS. For a balanced discussion see Metzger, 173–177. In its favour may be argued: 1. The shorter text, supported as it is by only *one* Greek MS is extremely unlikely to be original. Only part of the western textual tradition supports the shorter text, and an interpolation throughout the rest of the entire textual tradition is highly improbable. 2. The longer text is not based on 1 Cor. 11. Linguistic analysis shows that it contains several differences from Paul's text. These are pre-Lucan in style, and they reflect a more primitive version of the text. (Hence the un-Lucan features of the text do not point to a late interpolation.) 3. The omission produces a difficult narrative: Lk. 22:19a can hardly have stood on its own. 4. The omission in the shorter text may have been due to an attempt to preserve the secrecy of the words of institution (Jeremias, *Words*, 156–169) – although it is hard to see why this motif did not affect the text of Mt. and Mk. Or it may reflect liturgical practice in the second century (Schürmann, *Untersuchungen*, 185–190). Or again confusion may have arisen as a result of Luke's earlier mention of a cup shared by the disciples. 5. Elsewhere Luke retains sacrificial ideas (Acts 20:28), and it is unlikely that 22:27 is due to theological editing of Mk. 10:45 to remove the 'ransom' element. The argument that the present text is due to redaction of Mk. fails to convince.

The external evidence for the longer text is overwhelming. The weakness in the argument lies in accounting for the origin of the shorter text (Ellis, 255), but this may be due simply to some scribal idiosyncrasy. On balance the longer text is to be preferred.

The longer text is thus similar to Mk. 14:22 and 1 Cor. 11:23–25, but is sufficiently different from them to make it improbable that it is a literary derivation from them; on the contrary, it represents a more primitive form of text than 1 Cor. 11:23–26 and stands closer to Mk. 14:22–25. As for the differences between Lk. and Mk. at this point, it is not possible to affirm with certainty that one is more primitive than the other. The Marcan form is more Semitic, and Jeremias, *Words*, 189–191, claims that it stands closest to the original form. On the other hand, the claims of the Lucan text to come closest to the original form have been defended by Schürmann, *Einsetzungsbericht*. Patsch, 87–89, confirms the view of Jeremias, but stresses that there can be no possibility of reconstructing 'the oldest form', and hence of regarding the sayings as *ipsissima verba* of Jesus. Nevertheless, the basic motifs expressed in the sayings can be shown to be in agreement with what we otherwise know of the teaching of Jesus (Patsch, 106ff.), and hence in our opinion a line can be drawn from the historical Last Supper to the sayings recorded here, even if it is impossible to be sure as to precisely what Jesus said. It is in our view less likely that the sayings represent the early church's interpretation of the meaning of the Supper (*pace* E. Schweizer*, 26). There is certainly nothing in the sayings that cannot go back to Jesus who viewed his ministry in terms of the suffering Servant and who expected to die as a martyr (cf. J. Jeremias, TDNT V, 712–717; France, 110–135).

The fact that the institution narrative can be separated off from the tradition of the Passover meal does not lead to the conclusion that originally there was a report of the meal without the words of institution. It is more likely that the essential part of the story which related to the institution of the Lord's Supper was separated off from its framework for cultic use, as 1 Cor. 11:23–26 would appear to indicate, and was then replaced in a Passover setting when the passion narrative was being put together.

In its Lucan form the narrative describes how Jesus linked his self-giving with the bread, thus giving a parallel with the pouring out of his blood. This takes place for the benefit of the persons present ('you') rather than the 'many' in general. If the allusion to Is. 53 is played down by this wording, the link with the new covenant in Je. 31 is strengthened over against Mk. The inclusion of the command to repeat the rite makes it clear that the account represents the foundation of the Lord's Supper in the church.

See WH App., 63f.; G. Dalman, *Jesus-Jeshua*, London, 1929, 86–184; J. Behm, TDNT III, 726–743; L. Goppelt, TDNT VI, 135–158; G. D. Kilpatrick, 'Luke XXII.19b–20', JTS 47, 1946, 49–56; Jeremias, *Words*; Schürmann, *Untersuchungen*, 159–192 (originally as 'Lk. 22, 19b–20 als ursprüngliche Textüberlieferung', Bib. 32, 1951, 366–392, 522–541); id., *Einsetzungsbericht*; K. Th. Schäfer, 'Zur Textgeschichte von Lk. 22, 19b.20', Bib. 33, 1952, 237–239; D. Jones, 'ἀνάμνησις in the LXX and the Interpretation of 1 Cor. XI.25', JTS ns 6, 1955, 183–191; H. Chadwick, 'The Shorter Text of Luke XXII.15–20', HTR 50, 1957, 249–258; Leaney, 72–75; H. Kosmala, 'Das Tut zu meinen Gedächtnis', Nov.T 4, 1960, 81–94; Ellis, 249–256; A. Vööbus, 'A New Approach to the Problem of the Shorter and Longer Text in Luke', NTS 15, 1968–69, 457–463; id., 'Kritische Beobachtungen über die lukanische Darstellung des Herrenmahls', ZNW 61, 1970, 102–110; A. R. Millard, 'Covenant and Communion in First Corinthians', in W. W. Gasque and R. P. Martin, *Apostolic History and the Gospel*, Exeter, 1970, 242–248; Patsch; K. Snodgrass, 'Western Non-Interpolations', JBL 91 1972, 369–379; Metzger, 173–177; M. Rese, 'Zur Problematik von Kurz- und Langtext in Luk. XXII. 17ff.', NTS 22, 1975–76, 15–31; B. Klappert, in NIDNTT II, 520–538.

(19) The report commences in the same way as Mk., diff. Paul, but omitting Mark's reference to the meal (ἐσθιόντων αὐτῶν). For λαβών cf.

Mk. 6:41; 8:6; Lk. 24:30, 43; Acts 27:35; ἄρτος is a 'loaf', whether of leavened or unleavened bread. The reference is to the bread served at the beginning of the main course of the Passover meal, over which grace was said (Jeremias, *Words*, 86f.). For εὐχαριστέω cf. 22:17; Mk. 14:23; 1 Cor. 11:24; diff. Mk. 14:22 εὐλογέω; Schürmann, *Einsetzungsbericht*, 45–47, demonstrates that Luke can be using tradition here rather than editing Mk. κλάω, 'to break', is used in the NT solely of dividing up bread at a meal (24:30; Acts 2:46; 20:7, 11; 27:35; 1 Cor. 10:16; 11:24; Mk. 8:6, 19; 14:22; Mt. 14:19; 15:36; 26:26**; J. Behm, TDNT III, 726–743). The action was a customary part of the preparation for eating; but this does not explain why it is specially mentioned here, and why it became the basis of a technical term for the Lord's Supper (cf. Schürmann, op. cit., 30). The element of distribution of one loaf among many was probably decisive (1 Cor. 10:16f.). ἔδωκεν is found in Mk. but not in Paul, possibly because the use of ἔκλασεν was felt to include the idea of distribution. In the word of interpretation which accompanies the action Luke does not have the initial λάβετε found in Mk. (contrast 22:17); it is an open question whether it belongs to the original form of the saying, and has not been introduced as a liturgical direction (Schürmann, op. cit., 113f.). τοῦτο, referring to the bread (masc.) is neuter by assimilation to the predicate (BD 132). There would be no Aramaic verb corresponding to ἐστιν (Jeremias, *Words*, 201); the verb can mean 'it signifies' rather than 'it is identical with'. The meaning assigned to σῶμα depends on the meaning of the underlying Aramaic word (cf. Schürmann, op. cit. 119 n. 416). Here opinion is divided. 1. G. Dalman*, 141–143, suggested *gupâ* as equivalent, a word that means the person as a whole ('body' in contrast to 'soul'). He is followed by J. Behm; TDNT III, 736; Cranfield, 426; Kümmel, 119f.; E. Schweizer, TDNT VII, 1059. The phrase would then be reminiscent of 'the body of the Passover (lamb)' in Pes. 10:4 (cf. C. K. Barrett, *1 Corinthians*, London, 1968, 266). Jeremias's objections to this parallel (*Words*, 198f.) do not seem cogent. 2. The other possibility is *biśrâ*, 'flesh', championed by Jeremias, op. cit., 198–201, who argues that 'flesh and blood' form a pair, that Jn. 6:51 offers an independent parallel to the bread-word with σάρξ instead of σῶμα, and that σωμα can be used as a translation of *bāśar* in the LXX. In this way, we get a parallelism between the bread-word and the cup-word, and both sayings have a sacrificial sense, since they presuppose the separation of flesh and blood in death. The use of σῶμα rather than σάρξ may have been for the benefit of gentiles, and possibly to gain assonance with αἷμα. This view is criticised by Schürmann, op. cit., 18f., 107–110. He argues that in Lk. we do not have synthetic parallelism between the two sayings (as in Mk.), and that the use of σῶμα as a translation for *biśrâ* is unlikely; he also argues that originally the two sayings were separated by the meal, and therefore were not meant to be understood in the light of one another. These objections are not convincing. In particular the bringing together of the two sayings in the narrative suggests that the early church regarded 'body and blood' as a pair and understood the two sayings in the light of each other. The evidence that at an earlier stage they were understood differently is not compelling. In either case, however, the thought is of the offering made by Jesus, whether of himself in the sense of Mk. 10:45 or of his flesh along with his blood in sacrificial death.

It is in the part of the verse which belongs to the 'longer text' that Luke's wording goes beyond that of Mk. The body of Jesus is τὸ ὑπὲρ ὑμῶν διδόμενον; Paul lacks διδόμενον, but since his formulation is difficult in Aramaic, and since reasons can be adduced for regarding it as secondary, the Lucan tradition appears to be older at this point (Schürmann, op. cit., 17–30; cf. Jeremias, Words, 104, 167). The present participle has a future sense (1:35 note); the passive may refer to a being given by Jesus (Is. 53:10) or by God (Is. 53:6, 12), and Schürmann, op. cit., 20f., thinks that the former thought is uppermost (cf. Mk. 10:45). The phrase can be used with reference to sacrifice (Ex. 30:14; Lv. 22:14; cf. Lk. 2:24; Jn. 6:51) or to martyrdom (Is. 53:10). Similarly ὑπέρ can be used with reference to the action of a martyr (2 Mac. 7:9; 8:21; 4 Mac. 1:8, 10) or to a sacrificial offering for guilt or sin (Lv. 5:7; 6:23; Ezk. 43:21); in the NT it is used with reference to redemption (Gal. 1:4; 3:13) and can express representative or substitutionary action. We should perhaps combine the sacrificial and martyrological motifs. In Mk. the same phrase, suitably adapted, appears in connection with the cup (τὸ ἐκχυννόμενον ὑπὲρ πολλῶν), and this raises the questions whether the motif originally belonged to the bread or the cup sayings, and whether ὑμῶν or πολλῶν is original. Jeremias, Words, 166–168, holds that the phrase was formed on the analogy of the cup saying (cf. Patsch, 73–87), while Schürmann, op. cit., 115–123 (cf. 65–69, 112f.) holds that it is original and the wording of the cup saying is secondary. Jeremias argues that the phrase in Paul is due to Paul himself, that the Lucan form is unsemitic in its word order, that the πολλῶν form is earlier than the ὑμῶν form, and that the brevity of the bread saying called for completion and the tendency to parallelism with the cup saying led to assimilation. Schürmann argues that the phrase is possible in Aramaic, and this seems to be right. He further claims that the saying understands Jesus' death martyrologically in the light of Is. 53, and not sacrificially in the sense of v. 20b, so that a climactic parallelism is given to v. 20a (the martyrological death of Jesus leads to the establishment of the new covenant); but this train of thought is lost if the participial phrase is lacking. Finally, it would be unlikely for the bread saying to contain no soteriological explanation, and no explanation could be read back from the cup saying which (originally) was separated from it by the whole meal: it was Mark, therefore, who transferred the phrase from the bread saying to the cup saying, although Schürmann finds it difficult to explain why he did so.

Jeremias's reasons are on the whole the less compelling. Paul's phrase can be based on Luke's, which is not obviously non-semitic. The relative antiquity of πολλῶν and ὑμῶν is a separate issue. Jeremias's strongest point is that a brief saying was more likely to be given a soteriological explanation than a longer saying to be curtailed. The problem is whether this is less probable than that the saying originally contained no explanation. But the saying is so enigmatic without an explanation that it probably had one from the start. This does not necessarily commit us to Schürmann's view of the meaning of the saying, which we have already had reason to doubt, so far as the interpretation of σῶμα is concerned. But the idea of the self-giving of Jesus in death does make good sense in the context. If this reference to Is. 53 is present, then it becomes probable that Mark's ὑπὲρ πολλῶν preserves the original wording, and Schürmann's arguments to the contrary (op. cit., 75–77) are unconvincing. But the whole problem is still *sub judice*.

Finally, there is the command to perform the action, found with both bread and cup sayings in Paul, only with the bread saying in Lk., and entirely omitted in Mk. The repetition of the command in Paul is generally thought to be secondary. Jeremias, *Words*, 168, holds that the command is not part of the oldest liturgical text; nevertheless, he claims that it is probably historical, having survived in a separate tradition, since its thought fits in with that of Jesus. This argument depends on Jeremias' unusual (and, in our opinion, untenable) interpretation of the phrase, and is therefore dubious. Schürmann, op. cit., 30–34, 123–128, presents a case for the wording forming part of the original text. He argues that Luke did not derive the phrase from Paul, since in Lk. it is primarily a command to repeat the rite in the future, whereas in Paul it has become primarily a command to remember Jesus. But this argument is weak, because the difference in meaning arises out of the different literary character of the two reports. More weight attaches to the fact that the account presupposes a continuance of the rite (22:16, 18), and that continuance demands a command of Jesus to this effect; the main argument against the authenticity of the command is that Jesus expected the parousia so soon that there would be no time for a repetition of the rite, but this is an improbable assumption (cf. Kümmel, 64–83; Patsch, 142–150). Finally, Schürmann offers reasons why Mark may have omitted the command, especially that once the Lord's Supper had become established custom a command to repeat it was less necessary; we should remember that Paul's account is concerned with the institution of the Lord's Supper, and Mark's with a description of the Last Supper. Accordingly the command may have belonged to the original form of the narrative, and may even be historical. Its original position is probably as in Lk., and it was repeated in Paul's formula for the sake of the parallelism. τοῦτο will refer to the action of sharing the bread, since the meal came to be known as 'the breaking of bread', perhaps together with the associated words. ποιέω is used of repeating rites (Ex. 29:35; Nu. 15:11–13; Dt. 25:9; 1QS 2:19; 1QSa 2:21; Jeremias, *Words*, 250f.).

ἀνάμνησις (1 Cor. 11:24, 25; Heb. 10:3**) is 'remembrance', and the whole phrase is usually understood to mean, 'Do this so that you will remember me'; ἐμός is equivalent to μου. There is no connection with Hellenistic commemorative meals for the dead (see the study of the evidence by Jeremias, *Words*, 238–243). Jeremias himself, *Words*, 244–255, understands the saying as a request that God will remember Jesus by causing the kingdom to come at the parousia (cf. 1 Cor. 11:26 with ἄχρι οὗ understood as an expression of purpose; Did. 10:5f.). Cf. Lv. 24:7; Pss. 69:1 LXX.; 37:1 LXX; Sir. 45:9, 11, 16; 50:16; 1 En. 99:3; 97:7; 103:4; cf. H. Kosmala*; Grundmann, 398. But this interpretation is unlikely. Paul understood the action in terms of proclaiming the death of Jesus, i.e. to men and not to God. Moreover, the Jewish background adduced by Jeremias should be differently interpreted (D. Jones*; A. R. Millard*). We therefore prefer the view that the action is to remind the disciples of Jesus and of the significance of his death.

(20) Luke's introduction to the cup saying is almost identical with that in Paul. Paul's word-order ὡσαύτως καί is probably original, and Luke's is secondary (but pre-Lucan), giving parallelism with v. 19a and reflecting the later practice of placing both bread and cup after the church meal; Luke himself dislikes the present word-order (cf. 20:31, diff. Mk. 12:21; Schürmann, op. cit., 34–36; Jeremias, *Words*, 122, 154). Schürmann, op. cit., 83–85, further argues that this brief description, with ὡσαύτως replacing Mark's more detailed account, is more primitive, since Mark appears to be filled out liturgically, while Luke's wording is asymmetrical and has echoes in Jn. 6:11 and Mk. 8:7. *The* cup (diff. Mk. which is anarthrous) is the third cup in the Passover ritual which followed the meal, the so-called cup of blessing (1 Cor. 10:16; SB IV:2, 628, 630f.; IV:1, 58, 72; L. Goppelt, TDNT VI, 154–156; but see above on v. 17). The phrase μετὰ τὸ δειπνῆσαι separates the two parts of the new ritual from each other by the Passover meal; this may have been reflected in church practice by inserting a common meal between the two parts of the action, but the tendency was certainly to draw the two sayings together, as is seen in the omission of the phrase in Mk. For δειπνέω cf. 17:8; 1 Cor. 11:25 and Rev. 3:20**; the use of the word suggests that Rev. 3:20 has eucharistic associations. Both Luke and Paul omit Mark's note that all the disciples drank from the cup, which would seem an unnecessary statement of the obvious (see Schürmann, op. cit., 87f.). It may have been meant to justify the unusual action involved in sharing a common cup. The omission means that Mark's καὶ εἶπεν αὐτοῖς (which implies that the cup saying followed the act of drinking) is unnecessary, and a simple participle suffices.

The wording of the cup saying differs considerably from Mk. In Mk. τοῦτο refers to the wine in the cup which represents the blood of Jesus, understood as the blood of a covenant-inaugurating sacrifice (Ex. 24:8), poured out for the benefit of many. In Lk. and Paul τοῦτο is explained as referring to the cup, and it is the cup (with its contents) which is the symbol of the new covenant brought about by the blood of Jesus shed for the disciples. Once again Jeremias, *Words* 169–171, and Schürmann, op. cit., 94–112, stand on opposite sides in defending the relative priorities of Mk. and Lk. respectively. 1. In general, the lack of symmetry between the bread and cup sayings in Lk. favours the priority of Luke's form of the cup saying. 2. The equation of the cup with the covenant is odd, compared with the equation of the wine with the blood. For Schürmann the odd form is the older form, simplified to gain parallelism with the bread saying. For Jeremias, the odd form is the later form, arising out of a desire to avoid the implication that Christians drank blood. 3. The argument that Mark's phraseology is impossible in Aramaic has been shown to be without foundation. 4. Schürmann argues that the use of 'covenant' is more primitive in Lk. He argues that the clear reference to Ex. 24:8 in Mk. is later than the vaguer reference to the new covenant and the death of the Servant in Lk. It is unlikely that a clear allusion to Ex. 24:8 was given up in favour of a vaguer one to Jer. 31. 5. The addition of τὸ . . . ἐκχυννόμενον in the nominative case is stylistically very awkward in Lk., but the significance of this fact is uncertain. If the Marcan form was original, would the person who altered the first part of the saying have left the second part in this form: what is the antecedent of the participle? But if the Lucan form is original, the same question again arises: was this phrase added from the Marcan tradition, and if so, why was it not altered? The fact that the phrase is missing from Paul, however, suggests that it is an addition in Lk. from the Marcan tradition. On the other hand, 'cup' is used in Lk. by metonymy for its contents, and so the connection is a possible one; this suggests that the Lucan form may be original, and that the Marcan tradition has simplified it in one way, and the Pauline in another way. The arguments are so evenly balanced that decision is difficult (cf. Patsch, 80–87, who prefers Mk. as original), but on the whole it seems easier to explain both Mark and Paul as representing later forms of the tradition found in an earlier form in Lk.

For Lk. the cup, i.e. its contents (L. Goppelt, TDNT VI, 155 n. 70), symbolizes the new covenant, in the sense that the new covenant is brought into being by what it signifies, namely the sacrificial death of Jesus. For καινός with reference to the covenant see Je. 31 (38):31; 1 Cor. 11:25; 2 Cor. 3:6; Heb. 8:8, 13; 9:15. It signifies not a temporal repetition but a new, eschatological beginning. Jeremias, *Words*, 171f., 185, holds that the adjective is a pre-Pauline addition to the original formula, since the word order (article-adjective-noun) is not Semitic; but this argument is not conclusive since the order of words could easily be altered in a Greek translation. A more serious argument is the omission of the word from Mk., but this can be accounted for if Mark's wording was altered to include an allusion to Ex. 24:8. On διαθήκη see J. Behm, TDNT II, 133f., who stresses that it is not Jesus' testament which is in view, but God's 'disposition' of grace to men whereby he summons them to be his people. ἐν is causative, and τῷ αἵματί μου is an allusion to the death of Jesus; since there is no allusion to blood in Je. 31:31ff., and the death of the Servant is not connected with the establishment of the covenant, it is more probable that here we have an implicit reference to Ex. 24:8 which has been made more explicit in Mk. If so, one of Schürmann's main reasons for rejecting the following phrase from the original tradition of the saying (op. cit., 65–69, 73–79, 112f.) disappears: there is not a mixture of motifs. For ἐκχύννομαι cf. 5:37; there is possibly an allusion to Is. 53:12 MT. The placing of the preposition phrase ὑπὲρ ὑμῶν before the participle is less Semitic than the inverse order in Mk. (Jeremias, *Words*, 172), but Mark's order could be due to stylistic considerations (Schürmann, op. cit., 76f.); Luke's ὑμῶν is secondary to Mark's πολλῶν, which is an allusion to Is. 53:10, 12.

vi. Jesus foretells his Betrayal 22:21–23

In Mk. the account of the institution of the Lord's Supper is immediately followed by the departure of Jesus and the disciples from the upper room, but before they reach Gethsemane Jesus warns them on the way about the danger of their falling away. In Lk. a parallel account of this conversation precedes the departure from the upper room, and it forms part of a longer composition in which Jesus speaks with the disciples. In Jn. this didactic motif is carried further, and there is a substantial 'farewell discourse' by Jesus. The fact that much of the material in Lk. 22:21–38 is not based on Mk. suggests that it had already been gathered together in an account of the Last Supper before it reached Luke (cf. Schürmann, *Abschiedsrede*, 139–142).

The first section stands in the closest possible connection with the words of institution and announces the presence of one who will betray Jesus at the table; alas for the man who will betray the Son of man. Thus it is made clear that even presence at the Lord's table is no guarantee against apostasy, and a warning is laid before the readers of the Gospel. Since Jesus has already been speaking of his death, it is appropriate that a comment on the Son of man treading his appointed path should follow at this point.

The equivalent section appears in Mk. 14:18–21 before the account of the Supper, and the wording is different. There are three views of the relationship between the two passages. 1. Schürmann, op. cit., 3–21, follows most earlier scholars (e.g. Creed, 266f., Finegan, *Überlieferung*, 9f., 13) in the view that Luke has transposed Mark's narrative and reworded it. 2. Rehkopf, 7–30, argues that Luke here follows his special source. 3. An intermediate position is adopted by Taylor, *Passion*, 59–61, who thinks that Luke is following a special source, but has drawn v. 22 from Mk.

The position of the narrative leads to no firm conclusion. If it is drawn from Mk., Luke has departed from his procedure of generally (but by no means always) avoiding transpositions in order to place the narrative in the first convenient place after his account of the meal from his special source. But it is equally possible that this was the order in his special source, and it is given some support by the order in Jn. 13:1–20, 21–30. (But the reference to dipping a morsel in Jn. 13:26 may refer to the earlier part of the meal and thus support Mark's positioning.) The language of the section shows pronounced Lucan features, and Schürmann explains them in terms of Lucan redaction of Mk. But it is possible that Luke was redacting a source similar to Mk. In view of the possibility that Mark's tradition was based on, or closely related to, Luke's tradition, it is not impossible that Luke is here essentially following his own source. A further question is why Luke should have redacted Mk. so extensively here, and the explanation in terms of stylistic improvement seems inadequate. On the whole, it seems probable that Luke was editing a source closely related to Mk., and allowing himself to be influenced by Mark's wording, with which of course he was familiar.

Bultmann, 284, claims that the more original form of the narrative is to be found in Lk. 22:21, but allows that vs. 22f. have been modelled on Mk.

This conclusion has some bearing on the origin of the narrative. According to Schenke, 199–285, the whole of Mk. 14:17–21, with the exception of v. 21b, is a Marcan creation. If, however, the narrative in Lk. is at least partly independent of Mk., and if there is a further independent tradition in Jn. (so cautiously Dodd, 52–54; Brown, *John*, II, 576), Schenke's hypothesis becomes problematical, and the question of the origin of the narrative in pre-Marcan tradition must be reconsidered. Taylor's claim (539) that the historical value of the narrative 'is vindicated by the sayings it contains' has not yet been overthrown.

See Bultmann, 284; Finegan, *Überlieferung*, 9f., 13; Schürmann, *Abschiedsrede*, 3–21; Rehkopf, 7–30; Taylor, *Passion*, 59–61; Schenke, 199–285.

(21) Luke allows Jesus to continue speaking with no gap, so that the saying follows the cup saying as closely as possible. For Mark's introduction to the saying cf. v. 14. Luke's saying runs together the contents of Mk. 14:18b and 20. πλήν has strong adversative sense (cf. 6:24 note). It excludes the traitor from the blessing just promised (Jeremias, *Words*, 237). The word may be pre-Lucan (Rehkopf, 8–10; see, however, Schürmann, *op. cit.*, 14f.). The use of ἰδού may be Lucan, but this is not certain. The use of χείρ to indicate a person is Semitic, especially when a friendly or hostile relation is in mind (e.g. 1 Sa. 22:17; 18:21; 24:13f.; 2 Sa. 14:19). But the expression is a Septuagintalism, and could be due to Lk. (cf. 1:66; Acts 11:21, 'the hand of the Lord'). It may refer to the hand as that with which one partakes of food 'at the table' (E. Lohse, TDNT IX, 430), but Rehkopf, 12, holds that the OT idea of close fellowship is uppermost – as it also is in Mk. 14:20. μετ' ἐμοῦ may be metonymy for 'with my hand', but Rehkopf, 13 n. 3, thinks that the reference is to the presence of the traitor with Jesus, and

therefore ἐπὶ τῆς τραπέζης does not mean 'on the table', but at the table (as in 22:30; 20:37; Acts 5:23). ὁ παραδίδους is the betrayer; cf. the stereotyped use of the phrase in Mt. 10:4; Mk. 14:42, 44. This could be Lucan, but could also represent an Aramaic timeless participle referring to the future (Jeremias, *Words*, 178f.). The sudden reference to the betrayer is rather harsh (contrast Mk.), and it is possible that Mark's wording is more primitive with its ἀμὴν λέγω ὑμῖν introduction.

(22) The saying is attached to what precedes by ὅτι (but καί is read by A W Γ Δ Θ Ψ f1 f13 *pm* lat; TR; ὅτι καί by *Diglot*). The fact that there is a betrayer present (v. 21) is explained by the divine necessity for Jesus to face his appointed destiny – although this does not relieve the betrayer of his responsibility. The connection is less close in Mk., where it is disturbed by Mk. 14:19f., and this could be a sign of the greater originality of Luke's order. The position of μέν after the article and noun (diff. Mk., and corrected in many MSS) is odd; but while Luke is capable of odd positioning (Acts 3:21; 21:39), it is hard to see why he should have altered the order in Mk. here. The subject of the clause is ὁ υἱὸς τοῦ ἀνθρώπου; this is regarded as a secondary addition to an original 'I'-saying by Higgins, 50–52; C. Colpe, TDNT VIII, 446, and the title has been thought to express the dignity of the one who has foreknowledge of what is to happen to him (Tödt, 198f.). But this conclusion is not demanded by the evidence (Hooker, *Son of Man*, 159–161), especially since the rest of the saying shows signs of early origin. The play on words with ἀνθρώπου/ἀνθρώπῳ and the fact that the saying refers to the impending tragedy facing Jesus both suggest that the title is original; it may be regarded as falling within the idiomatic usage documented by Vermes, 162–168. κατὰ τὸ ὡρισμένον is Luke's equivalent for Mk. καθὼς γέγραπται. ὁρίζω, 'to determine, appoint', is a Lucan word (Acts 2:23; 10:42; 11:29; 17:26, 31; Rom. 1:4; Heb. 4:7**; K. L. Schmidt, TDNT V, 452f.). The passive is a circumlocution for divine activity. It is again hard to see why Luke should have altered Mark's wording (for cf. 2:23; Acts 7:42; 15:15), unless he wanted to bring out more the element of destiny in the fate of Jesus. For Mk. ὑπάγω Luke has πορεύομαι; this reflects his dislike of the former word (cf. 8:42; *et al.*) and preference for the latter (1:6; *et al.*; cf. especially 5:24; 8:48; 22:8). Both verbs could represent Aram. *ʰzal* (cf. Jn. 7:33, 35). Again Luke could be editing Mk., but the traditional use of πορεύομαι for the 'way' of Jesus (9:51; 13:33; 22:33; cf. Jn. 7:35; 14:12, 28; 16:7, 28) could have been present in a source.

In the second part of the saying Luke has πλὴν οὐαί, diff. Mk. οὐαί δέ. The change could be due to Luke. But the wording is similar to that in 17:1 par. Mt. 18:7, and this passage could have influenced the present one (cf. also Lk. 6:24). The change, however, if it is one, can be pre-Lucan; nor should the possibility of alteration by Mark be overlooked. The full form τῷ ἀνθρώπῳ ἐκείνῳ δι' οὗ follows Mk. (diff. 17:1; Mt. 18:7) and is probably based on Mk.; it brings out the specific character of the person being described. The subject ὁ υἱὸς τοῦ ἀνθρώπου is not included, diff. Mk., and this again could be due to Luke's editing of Mk. Luke also omits Mark's final clause, 'it were better for that man if he had not been born'; and again it is not easy to see any good reason for the omission if Luke was following Mk. The possibility that he was following a different source remains strong.

(23) In the final part of the section the wording is much less close to Mk. and characteristically Lucan; the change of order in the section did not require any rewording at this point. Rehkopf, 28f., holds that the vague character of the reaction in Lk. is the most primitive form. On the other hand, the indirect form could be secondary to Mark's direct form. καὶ αὐτοί is a necessary introduction after Jesus has been speaking; it is omitted in Mk. (giving asyndeton). The addition is not necessarily due to editing of Mk. ἤρξαντο is used par. Mk., and suggests dependence, but it is appropriate in the context of a continuing discussion of the question, and Rehkopf, 23, holds that it could have been present in two independent traditions of the incident (cf. the similar situation in 4:21 par. Mk. 6:2). συζητέω is 'to discuss, dispute, debate' (24:15; Acts 6:9; 9:29; Mk., 6x**, including 1:27, diff. Lk. 4:36; cf. συζήτησις, Acts 28:29**). The phrase could well be Lucan, especially since it prepares for the further strife among the disciples in 22:24 (Schürmann, op. cit., 11; but discussion and strife are not the same thing). The phrase replaces Mk. λυπεῖσθαι καὶ λέγειν, to which Luke could have taken exception (but this is by no means certain). The use of an indirect question, diff. Mk., is Lucan, and the whole construction is clearly Lucan (τό with indirect question, 1:62; et al.; ἄρα; 1:66; et al; the optative, 1:29; et al.; ὁ with participle; μέλλω, 12x in Lk.; πράσσω, 3:13 et al.; cf. especially Acts 5:35; 22:26). The question could be based on the wording in Mk. 14:18, and differs from the wording in Mk. 14:19, where each disciple asks, 'Is it I?' Here the disciples ask one another who can be meant (cf. Jn. 13:22). The question could thus be dependent on Mk., but it is not necessarily from Mk., and on the whole the cumulative impression of the pericope, set among non-Marcan material, is that it reflects a tradition that possibly lay behind Mark's account.

vii. Precedence among the Disciples 22:24–27

If there is the possibility of betrayal of Jesus by one of the group of disciples, there is also the possibility of strife among them as a result of a worldly desire for places of position and authority. Jesus is aware that worldly rulers are rewarded with power over their subjects and even receive titles expressive of the services that they have rendered, but he contrasts this practice with the entirely different state of affairs that must exist among his followers. The person who is, or who claims to be, the greatest must become like the youngest and most insignificant, and even like a servant. For while it is true that in human society the guest is greater than the servant, Jesus himself has come among men as a servant. The real leader is the person who is prepared to follow his example.

The account in Lk. is purely a dialogue; in Jn. similar sayings occur in the context of an acted parable which could have given rise to them. The same lesson is found in Mt. 23:1–11, and there is similar teaching in Mk. 9:35 par. Lk. 9:48, and especially in Mk. 10:41–45. This last passage is omitted by Luke, and the present passage is so similar to it, despite the differences in wording, that the question of the relationship of the two is a pressing one. While a number of scholars (e.g. Finegan, *Überlieferung*, 13f.) think that Luke has given an edited version of Mk. here, it would be unlike Luke to hold over a Marcan passage in this way, and the differences in wording indicate that he is not dependent on Mk. (Creed, 267; Schürmann, *Abschiedsrede*, 63–99; Taylor, *Passion*, 61–64). Nevertheless, the parallelism in structure suggests that there is some link between the passages. Schürmann distinguishes between vs. 24–26 and 27. He claims that vs. 24–26 are a reflection of a tradition secondary to that in Mk. 10:41–44, which is also to be seen in Mt. 23:11, but that v. 27 is a reflection of an earlier form of the tradition behind Mk. 10:45a (cf. Bultmann, 154). Further, the whole section was found by Luke in his source at this point, and is not an insertion by him. This case is broadly convincing: the Marcan passage is more Semitic in style than Luke's form, but Luke's setting at table is more likely to be original (*contra* Lagrange, 548f.), and Mk. 10:45 is better explained as a separate saying from Lk. 22:27 (see below).

The basic teaching in the passage is no doubt authentic; Bultmann's attempt to regard it as a development from the original saying in Mk. 10:43f., furnished with an introduction and conclusion, is unconvincing. The frequent repetition of the lesson in the tradition indicates how urgent it was for the early church.

See Bultmann, 154; Finegan, *Überlieferung*, 13f.; Schürmann, *Abschiedsrede*, 63–99; Taylor, *Passion*, 61–64; Patsch, 170–180.

(24) Luke's introduction the conversation is quite general compared with Mk. 10:41 which links up with the request of James and John for places of honour in the kingdom of God. It is closer to Mk. 9:33–35 par. Lk. 9:46f. It is hard to regard these three scenes as all variants of one original tradition, and the possibility that the same conflict arose more than once should be taken seriously. The καί links the strife to the argument in the previous verse. φιλονεικία** (otherwise spelled φιλονικία, so B; *Diglot*) is 'contention'; cf. 1 Cor. 11:16. For ἐν, 'among', cf. 9:46. The indirect question form is paralleled in 9:46; here it has the indicative, but in 9:46 the optative with ἄν is used. For δοκέω cf. Mk. 10:42 in the reply of Jesus; it is used intransitively to signify how the disciples would appear to people in general – for it is the question of how they will appear in the eyes of others that is worrying them. Lagrange, 549, observes that it is not who appears to be greatest but who ought to be greatest that is at issue. The comparative form μείζων is rare in Lk.;

in 9:48 he uses μέγας as a superlative; hence he is probably following a source here. Schürmann, op. cit., 67–69, argues that the verse is based on Luke's source, since the following sayings demand an introduction; he also argues that, while the question is concerned with 'who is the greatest?' the answer of Jesus is concerned with how the greatest ought to behave, and this slight discrepancy between question and answer is unlikely to be due to Luke. But this is pedantic: Jesus' answer to the question is in effect: 'Don't seek to be great; if you are content to serve, you will be (truly) great'. Schürmann's further point, that Luke is unlikely to have created a scene of strife among the disciples, has more weight, although it should not be overlooked that Luke stresses as much as Mk. the blindness of the disciples to the cross and its meaning.

(25) The introduction to Jesus' reply is in Lucan style; but it is unlikely to be redaction of Mk., since Luke would probably have retained Mark's οἴδατε ὅτι (cf. 20:21; Schürmann, op. cit., 70). The first part of the saying contains the same thought as in Mk. Rulers normally lord it over their subjects. For Mk. οἱ δοκοῦντες ἄρχειν Luke has οἱ βασιλεῖς; similarly Matthew has dropped δοκοῦντες which is slightly awkward, so that Luke could here be editing wording similar to that in Mk. Since the Jews had no ruler of their own, Jesus' saying was inevitably formulated in terms of gentile rulers. κυριεύω is 'to rule over' (Rom. 6:9, 14; 7:1; 14:9; 2 Cor. 1:24; 1 Tim. 6:15**), diff. Mk. κατακυριεύω (Mt. 20:25; Acts 19:16; 1 Pet. 5:3**). Luke normally prefers compound verbs, inserting them where they are lacking in his sources; if he has followed the opposite procedure here, it may have been to tone down the condemnation of rulers in Mk.; this, however, is uncertain, since he does not do so elsewhere, and is quite conscious of the failures of secular rulers. It is interesting that both verbs are used with reference to attitudes to be avoided by Christian leaders (2 Cor. 1:24; 1 Pet. 5:3). In the second part of the saying Mark repeats the same thought: the great men of the gentiles exercise authority over (perhaps, 'tyrannise') their subjects. In Lk. the expression differs slightly, moving to the thought of the reputation held by those who have authority (ἐξουσιάζω, 1 Cor. 6:12; 7:4**; cf. Ec. 8:9; 9:17; W. Foerster, TDNT II, 574f.): they are rewarded by being called 'benefactors' (εὐεργέτης; cf. εὐεργετέω, of Jesus, Acts 10:38;** εὐεργεσία, Acts 4:9; 1 Tim. 6:2**; G. Bertram, TDNT II, 654f.). This corresponds with known secular practice in both Egypt (Ptolemy III and Ptolemy VII) and Syria (Antiochus VII), and later in Rome (Trajan); the title was also bestowed on the Jewish high priest Onias III (2 Mac. 4:2). καλοῦνται may be passive, or perhaps middle ('hunc titulum sibi vindicant', Bengel); one suspects that there is an element of irony in the saying. This new motif is possibly due to Luke himself.

(26) After the contrast comes the statement of how the disciples are to act. The opening command is briefer in Lk. than in Mk. and carries the force: 'but you ought not to act in this way' (cf. BD 480⁵; is ποιήσετε to be supplied?). Mark's form (οὐχ οὕτως δέ ἐστιν ἐν ὑμῖν) is

easier, *pace* Schürmann, op. cit., 73. In the command which follows, Mark speaks of those who wish to be great (cf. Mk. 9:35 diff. Lk. 9:48), while Luke (par. Mt. 23:11) of those who are great, i.e. of those who actually are leaders. This appears to be a reformulation of the saying to deal with the situation of those who held office in the church. Where Mark has the contrasts μέγας/διάκονος and πρῶτος/δοῦλος, Luke has μείζων/νεώτερος and ἡγούμενος/διακονῶν. The same basic thought evidently existed in a variety of forms; cf. further Mk. 9:35; Mt. 23:11. μείζων is an example of the comparative form being used for the superlative, especially since μέγιστος was practically obsolete (2 Pet. 1:4; MH I, 78; III, 29f.). Here it could mean 'greatest' (AG s.v.) or 'eldest' (Zahn, 680f.; he interprets it, however, of the relation between Peter and John). But despite the contrast with νεώτερος, the former meaning is preferable. γινέσθω is better Greek than Mark's Semitic ἔσται as a polite imperative. νεώτερος is here 'younger' (cf. 15:12f.) or 'youngest' (Gn. 42:20). The word is also found in Acts 5:6; 1 Tim. 5:1; Tit. 2:6; 1 Pet. 5:5, and indicates a particular group in the church. But to regard this group as having particular official functions (Schürmann, op. cit., 76f.) is to run beyond the evidence; the point is rather that it is the youngest who perform the lowliest service, as in Acts 5:6 (AG s.v.). So the leader must behave as though he were called to menial service. ἡγέομαι, 'to lead, guide' (also, 'to think, consider, regard'), is used with this sense only in the participle in the NT (Mt. 2:6; Acts 7:10; cf. 14:12), and was applied to church leaders (Heb. 13:7, 17, 24; cf. Acts 15:22; F. Büchsel, TDNT II, 907f.), and this nuance is present here. Church leaders must behave as servants. διακονέω (22:27) in the participle replaces Mk. δοῦλος; Schürmann, op. cit., 78f., suggests that Luke has transferred it from the first part of the saying to the second to give a link with the next verse. But it is possible that the formulation is influenced by church language: the contrast between ἐπίσκοπος and διάκονος is perhaps to be found here in a more primitive form, and the point is that all church leaders must show the characteristics of those who were especially entitled 'deacons'. At the same time, the thought of the lowly position of the house servant is dominant, as v. 27 demonstrates. The force of Jesus' saying for church leaders is thus brought out by these small changes, probably made by Luke.

(27) The point is clinched by a brief parable (Manson, *Sayings*, 338f.; Jeremias, *Parables*, 95, 121) whose force is derived from contrast (cf. 11:5–8; 18:1–8). The saying is not found in Mk. in this form, but Bultmann, 154, and Schürmann, op. cit., 79–92, regard it as an earlier form of Mk. 10:45a. This view is doubtful. In fact v. 27a has no parallel in Mk. 10:45a, so that it would be more accurate to say that Mk. 10:45a is based on v. 27b, with Lk. 22:27a being omitted in Mark's tradition. But Mk. 10:45 could also be regarded as a comment on Lk. 22:27, grounding the behaviour of Jesus in the role assigned to the Son of man, in which case Mark and Luke have each omitted half of the double

saying (Lk. 22:27 + Mk. 10:45); this is the more probable view, since otherwise it is difficult to explain how Mk. 10:45b forms part of the saying (since its wording is incontestably genuine, and yet it can hardly have existed on its own).

The parable consists of a double question, a mark of Semitic style (cf. SB II, 257). τίς is equivalent to πότερος (cf. 5:23; 7:42). μείζων gives a catch-word link with the previous saying, but this connection is probably original. ἀνάκειμαι is 'to lie, recline' (Mk. 6:26; 14:18; *et al.*) and is used of guests at a meal; διακονέω is here used of table-service (12:37); the same metaphor is ultimately behind Mk. 10:45a, although the omission of the present saying hides the fact. The question is answered by a second, rhetorical question: in secular life it is recognized that the person served at table is greater than the servant (SB II, 257f.). Then comes the contrast which makes the point: Jesus himself is present with the disciples as a servant. If the saying is related to Mk. 10:45a, we have an example of an original 'I'-saying being turned into a 'Son of man' saying (C. Colpe, TDNT VIII, 448; see above, however, and Higgins, 36–40, who regards the Lucan saying as secondary to that in Mk.). For ἐν μέσῳ ὑμῶν εἰμι (p⁷⁵ ℵ B L T *pc* lat) the other MSS have εἰμι ἐν μέσῳ ὑμῶν (so *Diglot*). In its present context the saying suggests that Jesus has the role of a table servant; this does not fit in well with the actual scene, in which Jesus was host, but the difficulty is obviated if the foot-washing incident can be presupposed (cf. Creed, 267); the reading in D makes Jesus' statement arise simply out of the metaphorical language that is being used (J. Weiss, 512). Luke has no parallel to Mk. 10:45b; if he has not omitted it for theological reasons (an unlikely view: see the detailed refutation in H. Schürmann, *Biblica* 32, 523), it would seem that it was not in his source, or that he regarded it as unnecessary in the present context. On the v.1. in D see Black, 228f.

viii. The Future Role of the Twelve 22:28–30

In sharp contrast to the previous conversation, which emphasised the need for lowly service without thought of reward, but tightly connected with it, stands the promise of Jesus to the disciples who have been faithful to him during his trials. Just as his Father has appointed kingly rule for him, so Jesus promises a share in this rule to his disciples; they will enjoy the privilege of being seated at his table, and also of sitting upon thrones to rule the twelve tribes of Israel. The language is that of traditional apocalyptic, and appears to refer to the final coming of the kingdom of God, as is the case in Mt. where there is reference to the 'new birth' and the glorious coming of the Son of man. Nevertheless, it is possible that Luke has seen in the saying reference to the Lord's Supper and to the position of Jesus' faithful disciples as leaders in the church; the thought may also have been broadened to refer to disciples in general rather than to the Twelve in particular. The language is that of a covenant or testamentary disposition, so that the saying has a decisive significance in the establishment of the new covenant. This makes it attractive to adopt the hypothesis of Schürmann, *Abschiedsrede*, 54–63, that the saying was originally connected with the institution narrative, from which it has been separated by the insertion of other material.

But the saying raises considerable difficulties. It reappears in a different form in Mt. 19:28, where it is an insertion into Marcan material. There has been indecisive debate regarding which form of wording stands nearest to the primitive saying which, it can be safely assumed, underlies both texts. The majority of scholars regard the Matthaean wording as standing closer to the original (Bultmann, 170f.; Klostermann, 209; Kümmel, 47; Vielhauer, 67f.; Higgins, 107f.; Roloff, *Apostolat*, 148–150; Schulz, 330–332), but the basic originality of the Lucan form is upheld by Schweizer, *Matthäus*, 251f.; Schürmann, *Abschiedsrede*, 37–54; cf. Jüngel, 239f. With some hesitation we are inclined to accept the latter position, while acknowledging that to some extent Luke has edited the saying. Matthew has nothing corresponding to vs. 29–30a, and since these verses are unlikely to be due to Lucan redaction the possibility arises that the two Evangelists were dependent on different sources (Manson, *Sayings*, 216) or, more probably, on two different recensions of Q. E. Bammel* claims that the present passage may have formed the conclusion of Q, giving to the document the character of a testamentary disposition.

Bultmann, Vielhauer and Schulz ascribe the saying to the self-consciousness of the early church, and Schulz, 333, assigns it to the later stages of the Q tradition when the use of 'the Twelve' had developed. But Manson, *Sayings*, 217, rightly objects that it is hard to imagine the early church ascribing a throne to Judas – a difficulty which Luke may have attempted to meet by dropping 'twelve' before 'thrones'. Further, there is no evidence for the development of such a self-consciousness by, or on behalf of, the Twelve in the church, especially at the comparatively late stage suggested by Schulz. Although the saying stands somewhat isolated in the teaching of Jesus, its very uniqueness and dissimilarity from the teaching of the early church favour its authenticity. Certainly it fits in with the promise of rule made by Jesus to the disciples (cf. 12:32) and forms the background to the request in Mk. 10:37. It expresses the hope of Jesus in the ultimate coming of the kingdom of God. On the setting of the saying in the ministry of Jesus see especially J. Dupont*, 386–389.

See Bultmann, 170f.; Manson, *Sayings*, 216f., 339; Kümmel, 47f.; Schürmann, *Abschiedsrede*, 37–63; Tödt, 62–64; Higgins, 107f.; J. Dupont, 'Le logion des douze trônes (Mt. 19, 28; Lc 22, 28–30) ', Bib. 45, 1964, 355–392; Vielhauer, 67f.; Roloff, *Apostolat*, 148–150; E. Bammel, 'Das Ende von Q', in Böcher, 39–50; Schulz, 330–336.

(28) For Luke's connective δέ, Matthew has ἀμὴν λέγω ὑμῖν which is probably original, in view of Luke's known tendency to suppress ἀμήν; Luke's δέ brings out the contrast between Jesus (v. 27) and the disciples.

In Mt. the saying begins with a hanging nominative (ὑμεῖς οἱ ἀκολουθήσαντές μοι); this appears as a clause in Lk. with the addition of ἐστε. διαμένω (1:22*) is 'to continue'; the perfect tense expresses the situation which has existed during the ministry and still continues – loyalty to Jesus during his trials. The claim of Conzelmann, 74–76 (cf. Ott, 85–89), that the reference is not to the past, but to the present, comes to grief on the meaning of the perfect tense (Brown, 8f.); consequently the verse cannot be used to defend Conzelmann's view of a Satan-free or temptation-free period before the passion. For πειρασμός cf. 4:13. The word has more the force of 'dangers, tribulations' than 'temptations', as in Acts 20:19 (H. Seesemann, TDNT VI, 35; cf. Lk. 8:13 diff. Mk.). Behind the word lies the thought of Satanic opposition to Jesus; the saying, therefore, is not a promise that the disciples will rule over the Jews who formerly persecuted them. For the whole phrase Matthew has οἱ ἀκολουθήσαντές μοι. Schulz, 330f., argues that Luke's formulation is secondary: ἀκολουθέω is the traditional word for following Jesus, and the reference to πειρασμός is a sign of Lucan redaction and refers to the coming passion, as characterised by Luke (cf. C. Colpe, TDNT VIII, 447f.). It is a moot point whether ἀκολουθέω was the catchword which led Matthew to include the saying after Mt. 19:27, or was substituted by him to provide a link with Mt. 19:27, but the latter is perhaps more probable (Schürmann, op. cit., 37). The use of διαμένω is unusual, and Schürmann, op. cit., 38, conjectures (not implausibly) that it replaces an original ὑπομένω, reflected in 2 Tim. 2:12; Jas. 1:12 (for Luke ὑπομένω means 'to wait behind', 2:43). As for ἐν τοῖς πειρασμοῖς μου, this could be a Lucan insertion to give a link with the present context, but the linguistic evidence is not compelling.

(29) The saying continues in its Lucan form with a promise by Jesus; κἀγώ expresses the contrast between the faithfulness of the disciples and the action of Jesus in vindicating them. What he will do for them is on the pattern (καθώς; 1:2; et al.) of what his Father has done for him. For ὁ πατήρ μου cf. 2:49; 10:22 (par. Mt.) 24:49; the phrase is not especially characteristic of Luke (cf. 9:26, diff. Mk. 8:38; 22:42, diff. Mk. 14:36). διατίθεμαι can mean: 'to issue a decree'; 'to make a covenant' (Acts 3:25; Heb. 8:10; 10:16); 'to assign, confer'; 'to bequeath' (Heb. 9:16f.**). Since God is the subject, the idea of a will or testament is excluded (pace Zahn, 681 n. 58; Wellhausen, 124), and the meaning must be 'to assign' (J. Behm, TDNT II, 104–106; Schürmann, op. cit. 41 n. 145; similarly, Lagrange, 551; Klostermann, 212; Schlatter, 424). The object is βασιλεία, here in the dynamic sense of 'rule, authority' (cf. 19:12, 15; Mt. 16:28; 20:21; Lk. 12:32). It is not clear whether the idea of a covenant is contained in διατίθεμαι; elsewhere this is made clear by the use of διαθήκην with the verb. Here, however, διαθήκη is present in the context (22:20), and the thought may be present for Greek readers (cf. Morris, 308; Danker, 223, finds influence from 2 Sa. 5:3). In the same way, Jesus makes an assignment to the

disciples; the object is either βασιλείαν (supplied from the use in the sub-ordinate clause; NEB; JB; (TEV); NIV; Klostermann, 212; Schürmann, op. cit., 44f.) or in effect the ἵνα clause (RSV; TNT; Barclay; Lagrange, 551; Creed, 269; Morris, 308; J. Behm, ibid.). Both constructions give the same basic meaning, since the content of 'rule' is detailed in v. 30, but the former is perhaps to be preferred. The disciples are then promised a share in the rule of Jesus (cf. 2 Tim. 2:12; Rev. 2:26f.; 3:21). There is nothing that completely corresponds to this statement in Mt.; it is in effect replaced by a reference to the new birth, when the Son of man will sit on the throne of his glory, and the reward promised to the disci-ples is that of sitting on thrones, as in Lk. 22:30b. It seems likely that the reference to the Son of man is a Matthaean addition (cf. Mt. 25:31) to explain the meaning of the unusual phrase παλιγγενεσία, which will then have stood in Matthew's source (Schürmann, op. cit., 43f.). Arguments to the effect that Matthew would not have substituted this concept for that found in Lk. (Schulz, 331 n. 62) are thus beside the point. Now ἐν τῇ παλιγγενεσίᾳ in Mt. corresponds to ἐν τῇ βασιλείᾳ μου in Lk. 22:30a (Schürmann, op. cit., 50f.); it could be original here, and altered to an easier expression by Lk. So there is in fact nothing corresponding to v. 29 in Mt., and it is possible that Matthew or his source dropped the verse (although Schürmann's reasons for this (op. cit., 40f.) are not con-vincing). It is more likely that the verse is an addition to the present say-ing, which was not known to Matthew, but which was handed down in Luke's tradition as an authentic saying of Jesus. This is the more probable, since Luke may be dependent upon a different source from Matthew (who was presumably using Q) at this point (cf. Manson, *Sayings*, 216, who ascribes the two forms to M and L respectively).

(30) There is also nothing corresponding to v. 30a in Mt., and it gives the impression of being an insertion into the saying; but if v. 29 is an insertion, it is probable that vs. 29 and 30a originally belonged together (Creed, 268); despite the objections made by Schürmann, op. cit., 45–47, especially n. 176, there is no real discrepancy between v. 29 and v. 30a, since the thought of a meal in the heavenly kingdom is com-mon enough (14:15; 13:29; 22:16). The language (ἔσθω for ἐσθίω; cf. 10:7*; ἔσθητε rather than φάγητε) is not particularly Lucan, and the concept of the messianic banquet is traditional. It has been objected that in the phrase ἐν τῇ βασιλείᾳ μου we have a local sense of 'kingdom' in-stead of the dynamic sense in v. 29, but the phrase here is probably a Lucan insertion when the sayings were joined together. Again, Schürmann argues that in v. 29 the thought is of the handing over of office, whereas here it is of reward for faithful disciples; but this is being over-pedantic, since the two thoughts can well go together (cf. Rev. 3:20/21). The thought is primarily eschatological, but there could also be an allusion to fellowship with the risen Lord in the Lord's Supper.

In the second part of the saying the mood is indicative; this is pos-sible in a ἵνα clause (12:58; Jn. 15:8; Acts 21:24; *et al.*), but here it indicates that two sources have been joined. The disciples will sit on thrones (not seats) – a reminiscence of Dn. 7:9 – and share the judicial functions of the Son of man (cf. Mt.). Luke has probably deleted δώδεκα, since the promise is addressed in this context to the eleven disciples; perhaps too the aim is to generalise the saying to apply to all faithful disciples. The function is exercised over the twelve tribes of Israel (cf. 2:36; Jas. 1:1; Rev. 7:4–8; 21:12). Many commentators see a reference to the literal Israel (J. Dupont*, 388) which persecuted the disciples (Schürmann, op. cit., 53), but a reference to the new Israel is more likely, at least for Luke (Ellis, 255; Stuhlmueller, 158; Danker, 223); cf. Ps. 122:4f. for the thought. κρίνοντες (placed after φυλὰς in p 75 B T 892; before τὰς ... in rell; TR; Diglot) conveys the ideas of rule and judgment (cf. Dn. 7:10; 2 Cor. 6:2).

ix. The Prediction of Peter's Denial 22:31–34

The thoughts of apostasy, self-seeking and betrayal which have been thematic throughout the Supper scene reach a new peak in this brief episode in which the denial of Peter is prophesied; it is true that Peter protests his loyalty to the point of readiness for imprisonment and death, but this protestation only makes his eventual failure the more heinous. Nevertheless, although the denial is inevitable, there is a new motif in the Lucan account which sheds light on what is happening. Peter's fall is part of Satan's scheme which was aimed at procuring the apostasy of all the disciples; but it is withstood by Jesus who prays that Peter's faith may not completely lapse under temptation, so that he may ultimately be the means of strengthening his fellow-disciples. The temptation is thus placed in a cosmic setting.

Vs. 33f. have a parallel in Mk. 14:29–31 where they form part of an extended conversation held after the disciples have left the upper room (Mk. 14:26–31). Opinion is divided as to whether both verses are derived from Mk. (Schürmann, Abschiedsrede, 21–35; cf. Finegan, Überlieferung, 14f.), or only v. 34 is from Mk. (Manson, Sayings, 339f.; Taylor, Passion, 65f.), or neither verse is from Mk. (Zahn, 667; Plummer, 503; Schlatter, 137; Rengstorf, 240; Rehkopf, 84 n. 1). Apart from linguistic arguments, Schürmann, op. cit., 34, argues that, since Lk. 22:54–62 is based on Mk., and is a late addition to the passion narrative (see, however, 22:54–62 note), and since a source containing a prophecy of the denial must also have contained an account of the denial, Luke was not using an alternative source here. But this is not self-evident, especially if 22:31f. (which for Schürmann is not based on Mk.) was understood as a prophecy of the denial; the argument would apply only to v. 34, and it is not inconceivable that a non-Marcan source could have consisted mainly of sayings of Jesus. Other considerations must, therefore, be given weight. The change in address from 'Simon' to 'Peter' in v. 34 strongly suggests that at least this verse is from Mk. and the contents reinforce this conclusion; but it is noteworthy that similar wording is to be found in Jn. 13:38, and (if John is not dependent on the Synoptics at this point) this might suggest that Luke has remodelled a non-Marcan source on Marcan lines. The dependence of v. 33 on Mk. 14:29 and 31 is much less certain. It could well have stood as the last part of the source used in vs. 31f., especially in view of the continued dependence on 2 Sa. 15:20f. LXX which appears throughout the section.

Although Finegan, *Überlieferung*, 14f., regards vs. 31f. as a Lucan creation to replace the Marcan picture of the fleeing disciples (cf. Mk. 14:26–29, 50, diff. Lk.), there is general agreement that the verses contain a pre-Lucan tradition (Bultmann, 288; E. Fuchs, TDNT VII, 291f.; Klein, 61–65; Linnemann, *Studien*, 72). Luke's hand, however, may be visible in v. 32b. The verses combine the motifs of testing by Satan (Job 1–2), the sifting of faith, and the typology of David and Ittai (2 Sa. 15:20f.). While most scholars regard it as originally an allusion to the denial by Peter, this is doubted by Linnemann, *Studien*, 72–77 (cf. Dibelius, 201), who regards the saying as the utterance of a Christian prophet to prepare the church for a situation of persecution and temptation (cf. 1 Pet. 5:6, 8; Rev. 2:10). But we cannot solve our critical problems by inventing Christian prophets whenever we need them. Nor is it easy to imagine the kind of situation postulated by Linnemann. Klein argues that the saying is pre-Lucan; it cannot, however, go back to Jesus since he would not have prayed only for Peter; moreover, it stands in contradiction to the tradition of Peter's denial, since (on Klein's interpretation) Peter's faith does not fail. But Klein's interpretation of the saying is wrong (Dietrich, 118–139), since it does allow that Peter's faith will nearly vanish, and therefore it is not incompatible with the tradition of his denial of Jesus. Nor is it obvious why Jesus should not have prayed especially for Peter as the one who was to be exposed to the gravest temptation. The saying makes good sense in its present context.

While Schenke, 348–423, regards the pericope in Mk. as being entirely due to Marcan redaction, R. Pesch*, 52–58, claims that it belonged to the pre-Marcan passion story. This view is confirmed by the existence of what is probably a separate form of the tradition in Jn. 13:36–38 (Dodd, 55f.; Brown, *John*, II, 614–616). The problem of relating the various forms of the tradition to one another may well be insoluble. Lk. 22:31f. stand apart from the rest of the tradition, and therefore the saying is open to the suspicion of reflecting a theological development of the episode. On the other hand, it is possible that it derives from a separate tradition which has been associated with the prophecy of the denial at a secondary stage (cf. Manson, *Sayings*, 339f.).

See Finegan, *Überlieferung*, 14f.; Manson, *Sayings*, 339f.; Schürmann, *Abschiedsrede*, 21–35, 99–116; W. Foerster, 'Lukas 22, 31f.', ZNW 46, 1955, 129–133; Klein, 49–98 (originally as 'Die Verleugnung des Petrus', ZTK 58, 1961, 285–328); Ott, 75–81; Linnemann,

Studien, 70–108 (originally as 'Die Verleugnung des Petrus', ZTK 63, 1966, 1–32); Schenke, 348–423; Dietrich, 116–139; Taylor, *Passion*, 65f.; R. Pesch, 'Die Verleugnung des Petrus', in Gnilka, *Neues Testament*, 42–62.

(31) Just as the announcement of the treachery of Judas follows directly on from the cup saying, so the announcement of Peter's betrayal follows without a pause after the promise to the disciples (so p ^{75} B L T 1241 *pc* sy^s sa bo^{pt}; other MSS add εἶπεν δὲ ὁ κύριος, as in 22:35a; cf. Schürmann, op. cit., 100, n. 340). Whereas in Mk. Jesus is concerned first of all with the apostles as a group, and then Peter brings himself to the forefront, here Jesus takes the initiative – and does so with regard to Peter who stands at the centre of attention; the failure of the other disciples is incidental. Klein, 66f., sees evidence here of a Lucan tendency to paint the apostles as those who remained faithful to Jesus throughout the ministry, and did not flee or fall away. The use of the name Σίμων by itself appears to be characteristic of Luke's special source (5:3; *et al.*), and the doubling of the vocative (8:24, diff. Mk.; 6:46, par. Mt.; 10:41; 13:34, par. Mt.; Acts 9:4, par. 22:7; par. 26:14) is probably pre-Lucan. Dietrich, 134 n. 240 notes the suggestion of D. Gewalt in an unpublished dissertation, *Petrus* (Heidelberg, 1966), that the form of the present saying is close to that of 13:34f. This suggests that, unless Luke is imitating the latter passage (which is surely unlikely), the use of ἰδού to introduce a threat is pre-Lucan. For Σατανᾶς cf. 10:18; *et al.* and especially 22:3 where Satan instigates Judas to treachery; here the same idea is present, but the attack is not directed so much against Jesus as against the disciples themselves in order to lead them to apostasy and loss of salvation (cf. 8:12; Dietrich, 128f.). The background of thought is to be seen in Job 1:6f. ἐξαιτέομαι** is 'to ask for, demand', more precisely, 'to demand the surrender of' (G. Stählin, TDNT I, 1964); the verb is used of demonic activity in T. Benj. 3:3; Plutarch, Def. Orac. 14 (II, 417d) (ibid.). The implication is that the petition is directed to God; and the use of the aorist has been thought to imply the success of the petition (RV mg, Plummer, 503; cf. Lagrange, 553). All the disciples constitute the object of the request, and ὑμᾶς should be translated 'all of you' to make this clear in English. The expression of purpose by τοῦ ... is Lucan. σινιάζω** is a late form for Classical σήθω (BD 108^3), 'to shake in a sieve, sift'. The usage is metaphorical, but the precise manner of application is not clear. Three possibilities for the use of the sieve have been suggested: 1. to separate the wheat from the chaff (Grundmann, 406f.); 2. to hold back large pieces of foreign matter, while letting the wheat through (Sir. 27:4); 3. to hold back the corn while letting tiny waste (sand, etc.) through. If there is uncertainty about the precise metaphorical picture, there is even more about the application to the disciples: a. Jeremias, *Parables*, 216, thinks of the sifting of the disciples in 'the tempest of tribulation', apparently so that the true may be separated from the false believers. b. W. Foerster* envisages Satan collecting evil evidence in the sieve with which to accuse the disciples (cf. Rev. 12:10;

similarly, G. Stählin, ibid.; Dietrich, 123). c. Lagrange, 551; E. Fuchs, TDNT VIII, 291f.; Ott, 78f., and Schürmann, op. cit., 104f., think that the phrase refers simply to a shaking of the disciples (cf. Amos 9:9) in order to prove their faith; there is no stress on the result of the sieving. Since it is the disciples who are being sifted, view b. would seem less likely, and the picture is rather of the proving of the disciples themselves. But the point of sifting wheat is to separate off the rubbish, and it is unlikely that this point is missing here. The question is whether the disciples will survive the testing by Satan which leads to their standing or falling as believers.

(32) But the power of Satan (who has in any case to seek permission from God to sieve the disciples) is limited; over against him stands Jesus with the power of his intercession. The δέ contrasts Jesus and Satan (Dietrich, 124) rather than the rest of the disciples and Peter (Klein, 63). Nevertheless, there is a contrast between the disciples and Peter; the latter is singled out for special intercession by Jesus, but with the ultimate purpose that he may strengthen them. For δέομαι, cf. 5:12; although the word is a favourite of Luke, it expresses an essential thought in the saying (Schürmann, op. cit., 105). W. Foerster, TDNT VII, 156f., regards Jesus as acting as intercessor for the disciples over against the accusations of Satan (cf. Michael in Rev. 12:7–12); although this allusion is denied by Ott, 75–81, it is a probable one. But although these roles are associated with the last judgment, here the reference is to the present time, and to the continual opposition of Satan to the people of God. περί can mean 'in the interests of' (cf. 6:28 diff. Mt.; Acts 8:15; 12:5). σοῦ limits the interest of Jesus to Peter who is to be the means by which the other disciples will be strengthened. (This at least is true for the present form of the saying; if v. 32b is secondary, the original saying may have lacked this thought.) ἵνα expresses both the purpose and content of prayer, and is not Lucan (Schürmann, op. cit., 106). The verb ἐκλείπω (16:9; 23:45; Heb. 1:12**) has the force 'to disappear'. Although Klein, 63f., claims that the effect of the prayer is that Satan will have no success with Peter, it is more probable that Luke understood it rightly as being that Satan would not be able totally to destroy Peter's faith; the process of sifting would not lead to its intended end (cf. Danker, 224; Finegan, Überlieferung 15 n. 2). The nuance is important, since Bultmann, 288, and Klein, ibid., have argued that the saying precludes the denial by Peter and represents a different tradition which did not know of the denial. But the story of the denial – with Peter's tears of remorse – is perfectly compatible with the tradition here, especially since it is admitted that Satan's request has been granted. The aorist ἐκλίπῃ is replaced by the present ἐκλείπῃ in A Γ Δ pl; TR; Diglot; it is arguable that scribes substituted aorists for Hellenistic presents, but the MS evidence is weak. πίστις appears to have the sense of 'faithfulness' ('confessional fidelity', E. Fuchs, TDNT VII, 292); cf. 18:8. Bultmann, 288 (cf. Ott, 81), argues that in view of ἐπιστρέψας we

should expect the meaning 'faith', in the sense of Christian faith which may be lost by apostasy and regained by conversion; if so, ἐπιστρέψας is a Lucan addition which has misunderstood the original meaning of the saying. Schürmann, op. cit., 112, likewise finds the idea of 'faith' present (especially in view of the use of ἐκλείπω), and thinks that the word may be due to Lucan redaction. But the case for understanding πίστις as meaning anything other than fidelity (even for Luke) is weak, and the concept is best understood as in 18:8; Acts 14:22; 16:5.

If Jesus prays for Peter, an obligation also rests upon him (καὶ σύ). ποτε, used indefinitely, is found here only in the Gospels, and, since it has no Aramaic equivalent (Jeremias, *Parables*, 216 n. 39), it may be a Lucan addition. ἐπιστρέφω (1:16; *et al.*) can be used transitively ('to convert', 1:16f.; so here Zahn, 683), or intransitively ('to be converted', Acts 3:19; *et al.*; so here Plummer, 504; Schürmann, op. cit., 109; Ott, 79 n. 26). Jeremias, ibid., suggests that it is a Semitism for 'again' with the following verb (cf. his interpretation of στρέφω in Mt. 18:3), but this is not very likely. Behind the text we may trace the influence of 2 Sa. 15:20 LXX, which suggests that the intransitive use is present, not in the technical sense of Christian conversion, but in the sense of return to a former state (cf. G. Bertram, TDNT VII, 727). στηρίζω, 'to strengthen' (9:51; 16:26; Acts 18:23), is used elsewhere in the NT of strengthening Christians in their faith amid persecution and temptation (1 Thes. 3:2, 13; 1 Pet. 5:10; *et al.*; G. Harder, TDNT VII, 653–657); cf. Luke's use of ἐπιστηρίζω, Acts 14:22; 15:32, 41; the variant στήριξον (D Γ Δ *al*; TR: *Diglot*) for στήρισον is weakly attested. ἀδελφοί as a term for the other disciples may be used under the influence of 2 Sa. 15:20, but is also to be associated with the Christian use of the term, Acts 1:15f.; *et al.* Dietrich, 173f., goes so far as to link the two passages by suggesting that Peter's activity of 'strengthening' the brothers lay in his filling up the empty place in the Twelve caused by the defection of Judas; this is very speculative. The saying in any case presupposes defection on the part of the other disciples, and this makes it unlikely that the whole of v. 32b is a Lucan addition to harmonise vs. 31–32a with the denial tradition, since the latter (as recorded by Luke) does not refer to the defection of the other disciples. There is more reason to suspect the originality of ἐπιστρέψας, but in any case the denial of Peter is forecast in the earlier part of the saving.

(33) Peter's reply in Lk. is concerned simply with his own standing and ignores the scattering of the other disciples, diff. Mk. ὁ δὲ εἶπεν αὐτῷ could be redaction of Mk. 14:29, 31, but there is no proof that this is the case, especially since Luke prefers πρὸς αὐτόν to αὐτῷ. The use of the vocative κύριε could be Lucan (cf. 2 Sa. 15:21), but the link with Jn. 13:37 makes this verdict insecure (Rehkopf, 84 n. 1). For the sentiment expressed cf. Acts 21:13; 23:29. Peter expresses his readiness for imprisonment (φυλακή; cf. 23:19, 25) or death with Jesus (cf. 2 Sa. 15:21); cf. Jn. 13:37f. for the same thought. Ott, 80, suggests that Peter's words

here refer to what he actually did suffer for Jesus (Acts 12 and his martyrdom), so that he is here 'rehabilitated' in contrast to Mk. 14:31 where he promises to be faithful to Jesus, and then fails to keep his promise. But the presence of v. 34 makes this interpretation unlikely. The vocabulary of the saying is largely Lucan, but there is no clear evidence that it rests on redaction of Mk.

(34) This verse is more plausibly seen as being based on Mk. The addition of the vocative Πέτρε is odd, especially after v. 31, but may be due to the influence of Mk. 14:29; it is just possible that there is an ironic reference to the meaning of the name. The omission of ἀμήν, diff. Mk., is typically Lucan. For οὐ (p⁷⁵ ℵ B Q Θ pc) οὐ μή is read by rell; TR; Diglot; cf. Jn. 13:38. Mark's time note is abbreviated, and ἀλέκτωρ ('cock', 22:60f.*) becomes the subject, par. Jn. 13:38. The use of ἕως diff. Mk. πρίν, is another link with Jn. (ἕως οὗ). Only Mark refers to the cock crowing twice. After ἀπαρνήσῃ Luke adds εἰδέναι (cf. 22:57). But the text is uncertain. UBS has με ἀπαρνήσῃ εἰδέναι (p⁷⁵ ᵛⁱᵈ ℵ B L Θ f13 al); other readings are με ἀπαρνήσῃ μὴ εἰδέναι με (D; cf. Synopsis, omitting the final με); ἀπαρνήσῃ μὴ εἰδέναι με (A W Γ Δ pm; TR; Diglot); ἀπαρνήσῃ με εἰδέναι (Q Ψ f1 pc). Schürmann, op. cit., 26 n. 105, apparently follows Synopsis on the grounds that μὴ εἰδέναι is Lucan; but this text has no MS authority. The UBS text is the most difficult and should be preferred; the inclusion of μή is probably due to scribes who knew that ἀπαρνέομαι often takes this construction (cf. Sophocles, Ant. 442, cited by AG; cf. BD 429).

x. The Two Swords 22:35–38

This is the final conversation-piece in the extended dialogue in the upper room. It brings to a climax the misunderstanding and earthly-mindedness of the disciples which has already figured three times in the dialogue, and which stands over against the promises and warnings of Jesus (P. S. Minear*). The section begins with an appeal by Jesus to the experiences of their earlier mission when they went out in faith and yet experienced no lack. But now conditions are different: the growth of opposition to Jesus and to his followers means that they must go out well prepared, even going to the length of regarding a sword as an indispensable accompaniment. The saying can be regarded only as grimly ironical, expressing the intensity of the opposition which Jesus and the disciples will experience, endangering their very lives. They are summoned to a faith and courage which is prepared to go to the limit (Schlatter, 429). This situation arises for there is an OT prophecy which must be fulfilled in Jesus, the saying that associates the Servant of Yahweh with evil-doers; Jesus sees it as a prophecy of his death, for his life is now drawing to an end. But the disciples fail to understand; taking Jesus literally, they produce two swords, and Jesus has to rebuke them for their lack of comprehension – a lack that will become even more evident when Jesus is arrested.

This is the most probable interpretation of a difficult conversation (cf. Taylor, *Sacrifice*, 190–194; Manson, *Sayings*, 340–342). For a different view see H.-W. Bartsch*, who thinks that Jesus is reckoning with the outbreak of the final messianic conflict, which did not in fact take place; Luke has reinterpreted the saying with the aid of the citation from Is. 53 to show that Jesus placed no trust in the sword.

The view of Finegan, *Überlieferung*, 16, that the passage is a Lucan composition, preparing for the appearance of a sword in the arrest scene, comes to grief on the linguistic evidence for pre-Lucan origin (Black, 179; Schürmann, *Abschiedsrede*, 116–139; Taylor, *Passion*, 66–68) and on the utter improbability of v. 36 being anything other than a genuine saying of Jesus. The quotation from Is. 53:12, which is closer to the MT than the LXX, is also pre-Lucan. Opinions vary whether Luke took over the unit, substantially as it stands, from a source, or has himself joined together some traditional elements (H.-W. Bartsch*; Hahn, 167–170). It is the common difficulty of deciding whether Lucan language means Lucan creation or Lucan editing. But there is sufficient evidence of traditional origin at each point in the pericope to make it probable that Luke took it over more or less as it stands. There is no good reason for questioning its authenticity.

See Finegan, *Überlieferung*, 16; Manson, *Sayings*, 340–342; Taylor, *Sacrifice*, 190–194; id., *Passion*, 66–68; Schürmann, *Abschiedsrede*, 116–139; Hahn, 167–170; P. S. Minear, 'A Note on Luke xxii. 36', Nov.T 7, 1964, 128–134; France, 114–116; H.-W. Bartsch, 'Jesu Schwertwort, Lukas xxii. 35–38', NTS 20, 1973–74, 190–203.

(35) The conversation commences with Jesus taking the initiative in reminding the disciples of the situation when he sent them out on mission. The reference is to 10:3f., where the same basic items of vocabulary are found, rather than to 9:2f.; the implication is that the Twelve took part in the mission of the Seventy(-two) (but see 10:1), or that the mission charge in 10 was originally addressed to the Twelve. In either case, the fact that Luke refers here to the charge to the Seventy (-two) means that he is drawing here on the source which included the charge in ch. 10. When the disciples went out without purse, wallet, or sandals, they had not lacked anything; for οὐθενός (v.1. οὐδενός, אַ D L U f1 565 *al* Orig; *Diglot*) cf. 23:14; Acts, 3x; 1 Cor. 13:2; 2 Cor. 11:8**).

(36) Now the situation is different. The strong ἀλλὰ νῦν (here only in Lk.) has been regarded as drawing a contrast between the time of Jesus and the time of the church (Conzelmann, 9, 74, 97, 186), but it is more probable that the contrast is between the peaceable conditions of the mission and the impending crisis in the career of Jesus (P. S. Minear*). What is not clear is whether the new instruction is regarded as countermanding the earlier one so that a new ruling governs the mission of the church. Probably both instructions are meant to be taken

seriously, especially if the present saying is metaphorical and refers to an attitude of mind rather than to outward equipment. The precise meaning, however, is not clear. 1. The force may be, 'Let the person who has a purse and wallet take them, and let the person who does not have them sell his cloak and buy a sword' (RV t; Plummer, 505). On this view, the person who has a purse with money in it is to buy a sword, while the person who has no money is to exchange his cloak for a sword (Finegan, *Überlieferung*, 16). 2. ὁ ἔχων and ὁ μὴ ἔχων may be used to mean 'he who is well provided for/he who is destitute' (Klostermann, 214); this gives essentially the same meaning as the previous interpretation. In both cases, it is assumed that the disciple does not already possess a sword. 3. The implied object of ἔχων is μάχαιραν: 'Let the person who has a sword take his purse or wallet; and let the person who does not have a sword sell his cloak and buy one'. RV mg adopts this rendering for the second clause, but logically the same object is required in the first clause, and in both cases it is impossible to supply the unexpected object from the last word in the sentence. αἴρω is here 'to take with, carry' (Mk. 2:3; 15:21; Lk. 9:3, par. Mk. 6:8). The purse and wallet may be seen as providing means of subsistence in a situation where people are hostile and unlikely to provide hospitality. Here, however, they are a sign of the affluence which can purchase a sword, and so the translation above is to be accepted. It is curious that the sandals find no further mention: would their value be insufficient to purchase a sword? The fact that they are mentioned suggests that Luke is following a tradition, and not inventing. On μάχαιρα see W. Michaelis, TDNT IV, 524–527. The saying brings out the extreme plight of the disciples. A garment for wear at night was an utter necessity; to give it up for a sword implies that dire circumstances are at hand. A reference to preparation for an anticipated eschatological or messianic conflict is highly improbable, since this idea plays no part in the thinking of Jesus or the early church (except in a non-literal sense). Nor is it likely that Jesus is contemplating armed resistance in the manner of the Zealots (see the decisive criticism of this view by Hahn, 167–170). Nor again is it likely that the saying is primarily designed to explain why the disciples had the use of a sword in Gethsemane, and to show that in so doing they were disobedient to the will of Jesus (for this view see P. S. Minear*; Wilson, 65f.). Rather the saying is a call to be ready for hardship and self-sacrifice.

(37) The reason why the disciples must be ready for the worst is that their Master also faces the worst (cf. 10:24f.; Jn. 15:20). The solemn introduction λέγω γὰρ ὑμῖν (3:8; 10:34; 14:24; 22:16) is unlikely to be Lucan (Schürmann, op. cit., 124). After ὅτι the adverb ἔτι is added by Γ Δ Θ f13 *pl* lat; TR; *Diglot*; stylistically it could be original. The introduction to the quotation shows signs of Lucan formulation: cf. especially 18:31, and for τελέω 21:22; 24:44. The unusual phrasing brings out the point that it is in Jesus that what stands written in the OT must find fulfilment (Taylor, *Sacrifice*, 193). Here we have Luke's stress

(which is to a lesser extent that of his sources) that the progress of Jesus' career is governed by divine necessity expressed in Scripture. The use of τό to introduce a citation is found only here in Lk. (cf. 9:23; Mt. 19:18; Rom. 13:9; Gal. 5:14; Eph. 4:9; Heb. 12:27). The citation is from Is. 53:12 (LXX: καὶ ἐν τοῖς ἀνόμοις ἐλογίσθη (cf. 1 Clem. 21:13); Luke's version shows two differences from the LXX (use of μετά instead of ἐν; omission of the article). These differences bring the quotation nearer to the MT (J. Jeremias, TDNT V, 707 n. 404), and suggest that it is drawn from pre-Lucan tradition; indeed, it is 'surely indispensable to the context' (ibid., 716). H. W. Heidland (TDNT IV, 287 n. 12) holds that Luke has used another Greek version than the LXX (which is unlikely if he is drawing on tradition), while Holtz, 41–43, argues that he is quoting inaccurately from the LXX from memory. H.-W. Bartsch*, 196, however, suggests that the use of μετά, as in 23:39–43, suggests that Luke deliberately avoided any implication that Jesus was identified with the evil-doers; this is speculative, especially when there is concrete evidence in the MT for a different basis for the wording; see further Schürmann, op. cit., 126–128, who argues that Luke himself does not introduce quotations in the Gospel, and has ignored Mark's allusions to the suffering Servant in the passion story. For λογίζομαι, 'to reckon', cf. Acts 19:27; the comments of H. W. Heidland, ibid., are wide of the mark. ἄνομος*, 'unjust, lawless, ungodly' (Acts 2:23*), is used of the crucified brigands in Mk. 15:28 v.l., and this is the most probable allusion here; a reference to the disciples with their swords (P. S. Minear*, 132; Danker, 225) misses the point completely. The quotation has been seen as the early church's attempt to produce scriptural justification for the 'offence' of the cross (J. Weiss, 513; Klostermann, 214; Higgins, 31), but it is more probable that it reflects the mind of Jesus himself; cf. Taylor, Sacrifice, 193f., and France, 114–116, who see Jesus' preoccupation with the thought that hostile men will treat him as an evil-doer, and possibly also the deeper thought that he is prepared to be reckoned with evil-doers since he has taken their side and made himself like one of them. The final clause in the saying can be understood in two ways. Thus AG offer the translations 'the references (in the Scriptures) to me are being fulfilled' or 'my life's work is at an end'. The former translation is adopted by modern versions (cf. G. Delling, TDNT VIII, 54); Delling points to phrases where τέλος ἔχειν means 'to be carried out'. But on this view this clause simply repeats what has preceded and does not really strengthen it. But τέλος ἔχειν can also mean 'to come to an end' (Jos. Vita 154; cf. Plutarch, Mor. 615E), and the use of τὸ περὶ ἐμοῦ rather than the plural form (24:19, 27; Acts 1:3; et al.) is hardly due (as Schürmann, op. cit., 129, suggests) to attraction to the singular predicate. Hence the second translation is to be preferred (Klostermann, 214; Luce, 336; Taylor, Sacrifice, 193; Manson, Sayings, 342), it is the thought that his life is drawing to an end which demonstrates that the Scripture is being fulfilled. H.-W. Bartsch*, 197f., suggests that the wording is perhaps deliberately ambiguous.

(38) But the point is lost on the disciples who continue to fail to understand the necessity of the death of Jesus. They point out to their Master (κύριε; cf. 22:33) that they already have swords, two in fact. Since the wearing of swords was not uncommon (Shab. 6:4), there is nothing surprising about this detail. Later on, the swords will reappear – or rather one of them: cf. 22:49, which is no doubt intended as a reference back to this incident. But Jesus replies, 'It is enough'. Although the use of ἱκανός could be Lucan, the phrase has a Semitic equivalent (cf. Dt. 3:26; also Gn. 45:28; Ex. 9:28; 1 Ki. 19:4; 1 Ch. 21:15; Hahn, 168 n. 9; Manson, *Sayings*, 342; the arguments of K. H. Rengstorf, TDNT III, 295f., to the contrary are not convincing). It is most probable that this simply means 'That's enough (sc. of this conversation)' and is meant as a rebuke (J. Weiss, 513f.; Klostermann, 214f.; Manson, *Sayings*, 342; Hahn, 168). But the words have been taken in other ways: ironically: 'Two swords will be enough (Lagrange, 558), sc. to fulfil the prophecy and to make us look like brigands' (P. S. Minear*, 131; Danker, 225); or 'two swords will be sufficient to demonstrate the sheer inadequacy of human resources' (K. H. Rengstorf, ibid.). Neither of these alternatives is at all probable.

b. The Arrest and Trial of Jesus (22:39 – 23:25)

There is a fairly clear break at the end of the session in the upper room, but thereafter scene succeeds scene without any break in the action, so that any attempt to impose a scheme upon the story is arbitrary. For the purpose of the exposition it is convenient to regard the period between the last supper and the crucifixion as forming one whole. The narrative closely follows Mk., but there are significant differences at various points, and evidence that other source material was available. The narrative commences with the dedication of Jesus to whatever lies ahead on the Mount of Olives, and carries straight on with the story of his arrest and mockery in the house of the high priest (22:39–46, 47–53, 63f.); throughout the disciples persist in failure and misunderstanding, and this reaches its peak in Peter's denial of Jesus (22:54–62), after which the disciples simply disappear from the scene without comment. The spotlight falls on Jesus himself as he is subjected to examination by the sanhedrin (22:66–71), and then brought before Pilate (23:1–5, 13–25) and Herod (23:6–12). The proceedings move inexorably to his condemnation, despite the lack of evidence against him and the recognition by his judges that he had no case to answer.

In addition to bibliography for 22:1 – 24:53 see Blinzler; Catchpole; Winter.

i. The Prayer of Jesus 22:39–46

Since Luke has already incorporated all that Jesus said at this time in the last supper narrative (diff. Mk. 14:27–31), he is able to bring Jesus straight from the upper room to the Mount of Olives with his disciples. Having instructed them to pray that they may not enter into testing, Jesus withdraws and prays that what lies ahead of him in pain and suffering might be averted, while requesting that God's will, rather than his own, might be done; the moment may be seen as a reflection of temptation to turn aside from what he knew must happen, or, more accurately, to ask that it might be otherwise, but willingness to obey God triumphs. According to one part of the textual tradition the intensity of the struggle is reflected in the presence of a sustaining angel and in the appearance of symptoms of deep psychosomatic distress. Meanwhile the disciples have fallen asleep; they have to be awakened and reminded that they too must pray that they may not be tested and fall.

Such is the brief scene in Lk. It is simpler in construction and content than the similar scene in Mk. It is bracketed by the command to the disciples, which they fail (at this stage) to keep, but which Jesus himself carries out; thus we are justified in regarding the occasion as one of 'testing' for Jesus himself. The disciples certainly do not come out of it well, and, although it can be argued that Luke has attempted to whitewash them (Conzelmann, 74), the general intent of the whole section is to demonstrate their weakness and lack of comprehension (cf. T. Lescow*, especially 218). As for Jesus himself, it may be fair to say that the real struggle takes place here, rather than later: as martyr, Jesus here faces up to his fate, and, having done so, he is able to go through what lies ahead with comparative equanimity (R. S. Barbour*, 238–241); it is less certain, however, that in Lk. (and Mt.) Jesus' prayer has become an act of alignment with the will of the Father rather than (as in Mk.) a plain submission to it (ibid., 250).

But the question of the interpretation of the narrative cannot be isolated from that of its sources. This is heightened by the textual uncertainty of vs. 43–44, which, if genuine, stress the real conflict in the heart of Jesus that is overcome by heavenly help and his own persevering prayer; in general commentators find that the words fit in with Luke's thought, while textual critics point to the very strong textual evidence against them. If they are original, they may be in whole or part the work of Luke (in whole: K. G. Kuhn*; Linnemann, *Studien*, 38f.; v. 43 is Lucan: T. Lescow*, 217f.). But this point is related to whether Luke is here dependent upon Mk. (Creed, 272; Finegan, 18f.; Linnemann, 34–40) or upon another source (Lagrange, 558f.; K. G. Kuhn, 271; Rehkopf, 84; Grundmann, 410f.; T. Lescow*, 215–223; Taylor, *Passion*, 69–72). Since Luke had Mk. before him in any case, the question is not easy to answer. It is further complicated by the great uncertainty regarding the origin of Mark's narrative : 1. successive redactions of a primitive narrative (vs. 32, 35, 37, 39, 40, 41a: Bultmann, 288f.; vs. 32, 35, 37a, 39a, 40a, b, 41a, 40c, 41b: Linnemann, 24–32; vs. 32 (part), 33b, 34, 35a, 36–37, 38b, 40b, 41 (part), 42: Schenke, 461–540; cf. also W. Mohn*); 2. combination of two parallel sources (A: vs. 32, 35, 40–41; B: 33–34, 36–38: K. G. Kuhn*: cf. E. Hirsch, as reported by Linnemann, *Studien*, 14–17); 3. Marcan creation on basis of isolated fragments of tradition (Dibelius, 212–214; W. H. Kelber*). Moreover, we have a separate tradition about the incident in Heb. 5:7f. The disentangling of this problem is beyond our province here. Linnemann, *Studien*, 34–40, has shown that Luke could be dependent simply upon Mk., with considerable editorial freedom; her case is stronger than that of Lescow, who argues that Luke was editing Mark's source 'B' (Kuhn's analysis). On her view, Luke has considerably abbreviated Mk., removing the threefold pattern which governs it and the repetition of Jesus' prayer, and making the reference to the disciples more general; in this way the human fear of Jesus and the weakness of the disciples are played down. But we have already seen that the latter motif is present in the narrative, and the former is not completely absent. The reasoning, therefore, is not compelling; and if a simpler narrative lies behind Mk., the possibility that Luke has been influenced by a variant form of this tradition cannot be ruled out; while this is a less tidy solution than Linnemann's, it may well do more justice to the complexity of the situation as regards the development of tradition in the early church (cf. Dodd, 65f.; K. G. Kuhn*, 272; *pace* Linnemann, 18 n. 20). Although the original form of the tradition is obscure, the tradition of Jesus' prayer is no doubt historical (cf. Schweizer, *Markus*, 178f.; R. S. Barbour*, 234f.).

See L. Brun, 'Engel und Blutschweiss Lc. 22, 43–44', ZNW 32, 1933, 265–276; Dibelius, *Botschaft*, I, 258–271; K. G. Kuhn, 'Jesus in Gethsemane', Ev.T 12, 1952–53, 260–285; T. Lescow, 'Jesus in Gethsemane bei Lukas und im Hebräerbrief', ZNW 58, 1967, 215–239; R. S. Barbour, 'Gethsemane in the Passion Tradition', NTS 16, 1969–70, 231–251; Linnemann, *Studien*, 11–40; Schenke, 461–540; Taylor, *Passion*, 68–72; W. H. Kelber, 'Mark 14:32–42: Gethsemane', ZNW 63, 1972, 166–187; W. Mohn, 'Gethsemane (Mk. 14:32–42)', ZNW 64, 1973, 194–208; A. Feuillet, 'Le récit lucanien de l'agonie de Gethsémani (Le. xxii, 39–46)', NTS 22, 1975–76, 399–417.

(39) The present verse corresponds to Mk. 14:26, 32; Luke has no equivalent to the shepherd-saying in Mk. 14:27f., and he has already included the prediction of Peter's denial in the supper scene, so that Jesus is represented as moving directly from the upper room to the place of prayer. He makes no mention of the singing (diff. Mk. ὑμνήσαντες) which concluded the meal. The use of the third person sing., diff. Mk. (plural), is perhaps meant to emphasise the initiative of Jesus, certainly to place him at the centre of the stage as he goes out and makes the brief journey to the Mount of Olives. κατὰ τὸ ἔθος is Lucan (1:9; 2:42) and gives an allusion to 21:37; for the same tradition cf. Jn. 18:2. The note explains how Judas knew where Jesus was likely to be (Conzelmann,

74). In the light of what follows the implication may be that Jesus regularly prayed here, and there may possibly be the thought that a mountain is an appropriate place for prayer (Ott, 84), but since it was only 140 ft higher than Jerusalem, the idea of a lofty place of solitude is not present. Hence it is unlikely that Luke has a different idea of the topography from Mk., especially since Mark too mentions the Mount of Olives as the scene. The omission of the name Γεθσημανί (Mk. 14:32; Mt. 26:36**) may therefore be due simply to a dislike of place-names in Aramaic which would be meaningless to Luke's readers. Only after the action of Jesus has been described are the disciples (possibly add αὐτοῦ with Γ Δ* pm; TR; Diglot; but the external evidence is weak) mentioned.

(40) For ἐπί as used here cf. 23:44; 24:22; Acts 21:35; τόπος is the place where Jesus and the disciples normally gathered ('their encampment', Leaney, 272); cf. 23:33; the phrase sounds like a fragment from a wider context. Luke has no mention of Jesus telling the rest of the disciples to stay and pray while he and his three companions went on further. Instead Jesus addresses all the disciples with the same words as are used at the conclusion of the scene (22:46 par. Mk. 14:38). Thus the theme of the pericope is made clear at the outset (cf. 14:7; 18:1, 9; 19:1; Linnemann, Studien, 37). The use of the infinitive after προσεύχομαι (diff. 22:46, with subjunctive) is unusual; Loisy suggested that Luke's source included με. The thought of πειρασμός links with 22:28-38, and indicates that temptations are now at hand; the absence of the article forbids a reference to the great, eschatological temptation. The effect of including the command is to make the disciples as a whole more culpable than in Mk. (where the command to stay awake is addressed only to three of them). The implication is that Jesus himself also faces temptation.

(41) But Luke omits the whole of Jesus' conversation with the three in which he expresses his agonised state of mind (Mk. 14:33-34), and proceeds to give an equivalent to Mk. 14:35. Jesus withdraws a short distance from the disciples. ἀποσπάω, originally 'to tear away', is used in the passive to mean 'to withdraw' (Acts 20:34 (active); 21:1; cf. Mt. 26:51**). The word is Lucan, but Luke has otherwise no aversion to Mk. προέρχομαι (cf. 1:17; 22:47; Acts 12:10). ὡσεί is Lucan (3:23; et al.); βολή** is 'throw', and the phrase resembles Gn. 21:16; cf. Thucydides 5:65:2; Jos. Ant. 20:213 (AG 144 cite T. Gad 1:3, but the phrase is absent from de Jonge's text). The phrase is more definite than Mk. μικρόν and may be an interpretation of the latter (cf. 22:59). For θεὶς τὰ γόνατα cf. Acts 7:60; 9:40; 20:36; 21:5; cf. Mk. 15:19 and also Rom. 11:4; 14:11; Eph. 3:14; Phil. 2:10. The phrase is Lucan, and the unusual attitude for prayer (instead of standing; cf. SB II, 259-262) stresses the urgency and humility of Jesus; but the thought is already present in Mk. where Jesus is said to fall on the ground.

(42) Where Mark has the prayer of Jesus twice, once in indirect and once in direct speech, Luke has one simple statement in direct

speech, which is largely parallel to Mk. 14:36. For Mark's Aramaic phrase ἀββά with its Greek equivalent, Luke has πάτερ (cf. Mt. πάτερ μου; Jn. 12:27); cf. 10:21; et al. Mark's references to what is possible for God are replaced by an appeal to the will of God; the thought is thus more personal, but the basic motif is already present in Mk. 14:36b; for the use of the phrase in Jewish prayers see SB I, 607. But it is possible that it should be construed differently. Although all editions have the reading παρένεγκε (imperative, par. Mk.), there is strong evidence for reading the infinitive, whether παρενέγκαι, א K L f13 al, or παρενεγκεῖν (A W Γ Δ pm; TR). This is undoubtedly the harder reading, giving either omission of the apodosis with aposiopesis ('If you are willing to remove this cup from me (well and good) '; cf. 19:42; Acts 23:9; cf. BD 482), or with εἰ introducing a direct question ('Are you willing to remove this cup from me?' cf. 13:23; 22:49; Zahn, 688; Klostermann, 215; Grundmann, 411f.) τοῦτο τὸ ποτήριον (for the order, diff. Mk., cf. 22:20) is a metaphor for the impending suffering of Jesus (cf. especially Is. 51:22; Mk. 10:38). It refers especially to the infliction of punishment associated with the wrath of God (Pss. 11:6; 75:8; Is. 51:17; Je. 25:15, 17, 28; La. 4:21; Ezk. 23:31–33; Hab. 2:16). L. Goppelt, TDNT VI, 149–153, rightly finds this OT background in the concept as used here, and emphasises that the thought is not simply of fate but of judgment; Luke's use of πλήν, par. Mt., avoids the awkward double use of ἀλλά in Mk. and heightens the contrast. Instead of Mark's personal construction, Luke has the impersonal τὸ θέλημα ... γινέσθω (cf. Acts 21:14; Mt. 6:10 (diff. Lk.); 26:42; Jn. 5:30; 6:38). The coincidence with Mt. 6:10 and especially 26:42 is interesting (cf. also Dodd, 363f.), and suggests the possible influence of an oral tradition; it is a pointer to the possibility that Luke was indebted to another source than Mk. at this point. The effect of the saying is that Jesus, facing the temptation to avoid the path of suffering appointed by God, nevertheless accepts the will of God despite his own desire that it might be otherwise. He does not seek to disobey the will of God, but longs that God's will might be different. But even this is to be regarded as temptation, and it is overcome by Jesus.

(43) Vs. 43 and 44 are omitted by p⁷⁵ א* A B T W f13 579 al f syˢ sa boᵖᵗ Mcion Clem Orig; WH; (Synopsis); (UBS); J. Weiss, 514; Wellhausen, 127; Easton, 330; Plummer, 544; K. Aland, NTS 12, 1965–66, 199, 203; Metzger, 177. Some MSS (Cᵐᵍ f13 pc) insert the verses at Mt. 26:39/40. The textual evidence for omission is strong; the authorities that include the verses are 'a frequent Western combination' (WH, App. 66, cf. 64–67), and those that exclude them are old and diverse. Omission in so many different branches of the tradition is hardly due to accident. Nevertheless, it is hard to believe that the pericope is pure invention, and those who reject the verses from the text argue that they have been drawn from some floating tradition which had not found its way into the Synoptic tradition. On the other hand, it can be argued

that the verses might have been excised for doctrinal reasons (as Epiphanius testifies; cf. Streeter, 137f.); further, the language is compatible with Lucan authorship (Klostermann, 217; L. Brun*), and their thought likewise fits in with Luke's point of view. Hence the verses, which are read by ℵ* D L X ΓΔ Θ Ψ f1 565 700 *pm* lat sy ᶜ ᵖ bo ᵖᵗ Justin Iren; TR; *Diglot*, are accepted by Zahn, 688; Lagrange, 561–563; Schlatter, 433; Dibelius, 202; Id., *Botschaft* I, 258–271; K. G. Kuhn*, 268; T. Lescow*, 217; Grundmann, 410; Linnemann, *Studien*, 38; A. Feuillet*, 397f. On the whole, the internal evidence inclines us to accept the verses as original, but with very considerable hesitation.

For ὤφθη ... ἄγγελος cf. 1:11. The addition ἀπ' οὐρανοῦ is unusual (cf. Gal. 1:8). ἐνισχύω is 'to strengthen' (Acts 9:19**, intransitive). Klostermann, 217 and Creed, 273, note that the appearance of the angel before the agony of Jesus is unexpected: the reverse order would seem more probable. It is possible that two separate motifs are present (cf. L. Brun*, 273), but more probably the strengthening is regarded as necessary after the fresh acceptance of the way of suffering in v. 42 (Grundmann, 412), or the angel appears to strengthen Jesus as the full implications of his prayer are realised in an even deeper contest with Satan (L. Brun*, ibid.). For the thought of angelic help cf. 1 Ki. 19:5f.; Mk. 1:13; Mt. 4:11; but closer parallels can be seen in Dn. 10:17f. and the thought of divine help in Is. 41:9f.; 42:6. The thought may, however, be of the provision of a divine answer to prayer (cf. Jn. 12:27f.; Acts 6:15; 7:56; Brun, 269–272). Grundmann, 412, cites Gn. R. 44, where Michael comes to help the three men in the fiery furnace. The motif of answered prayer is found in a different form in Heb. 5:7.

(44) The effect of the angelic help is that Jesus is enabled to pray more earnestly (ἐκτενέστερον**, comparative of ἐκτενῶς, 'eagerly, fervently' (Acts 12:5; 1 Pet. 1:22**), from ἐκτενής, literally, 'strained' (1 Pet. 4:8**); cf. the noun, Acts 26:7**). Temptation is overcome by more intense prayer (Ott, 97). Jesus is in a state of ἀγωνία**, 'agony, anxiety'. This may mean 'fear' (2 Mac. 3:14, 16; 15:19; so Plummer, 510, following F. Field), but E. Stauffer, TDNT I, 140, interprets these passages to refer not to fear of death but to concern for victory in face of the approaching battle. Having committed himself to the battle, Jesus now sets his face firmly towards it. The agony of soul finds physical expression in sweat (ἱδρώς**) which appears like drops (θρόμβος**) of blood falling on the ground. This metaphor has been variously explained: 1. It is simply a rhetorical expression like our 'tears of blood'. 2. The sweat was *falling* like drops of blood (Zahn, 691; Grundmann, 412). 3. The sweat was the colour of blood (cf. Jos. et Asen. 4:11; Apollon. Rhod. 4:1282f.; Aristotle, H.A. 3:19; Theophrastus, De Sudore 11f.). Plummer, 510f. cites cases of blood exuding through the pores of the skin; J. Weiss, 514, regards the description as legendary; and L. Brun sees it theologically as an anticipation of Jesus' baptism by blood. The ancient parallels support view 3., but view 2. fits in better with Lucan style (3:22); the stress is on the falling, rather than the colour, and the implication is that the sweat was like the shedding of blood.

(45) V. 45 could link with v. 42 or v. 44. It is just possible that ἀναστάς is symbolical of the resurrection, as the prayer was symbolical of the death of Jesus (Danker, 227; cf. Mk. 9:27 diff. Lk.), and then the return of Jesus to the sleeping disciples could be interpreted as a warning of what might happen at the parousia (cf. Mk. 13:36f.), but this is improbable. The language is close to Mk. 14:37, but the order κοιμωμένους αὐτούς is inverted as compared with Mk. (the Marcan order is found in A W Γ Δ Θ f1 pm; TR; Diglot), and Luke uses κοιμάομαι*, 'to sleep' (Acts 7:60; 12:6; 13:36), diff. Mk. καθεύδω (8:52; 22:46*), possibly for variety. Luke's version lacks the threefold return of Jesus to the sleeping disciples, so that the emphasis is much more on the prayer of Jesus than the failure of the disciples. This omission and the fact that Luke attributes their sleep to 'grief' (λύπη*; for the use of ἀπό cf. 19:3; 24:41) have been thought to be attempts to exonerate the disciples, as compared with the Marcan picture. The thought of sleep as a result of grief has also been thought to be psychologically unlikely (Ps. 6:6; La. 1:2; Danker, 227). For the motif, however, see Jn. 16:6, 20–22; Mk. 14:19. Grief is psychologically comprehensible in the situation of leave-taking; whether it would lead to sleep is more debatable, but the NEB translation ('worn out by grief') points in this direction. Luke may be based on tradition here.

(46) The final comments of Jesus are addressed to all the disciples (cf. Mk. 14:38, but v. 37 is addressed solely to Peter); they are commanded to get up and pray, as in v. 40; the thought of keeping awake (Mk. γρηγορέω) is dropped; contrast 12:37; Acts 20:31 (does Luke prefer to use it metaphorically?). On this note the narrative closes abruptly; the πειρασμός, i.e. 'testing' or 'trial', follows immediately with the arrest of Jesus. The rest of Mark's account, which is repetitious and not without difficulty, is omitted.

ii. The Arrest of Jesus 22:47–53

Jesus has not finished speaking to the disciples before the arrival of the arrest party takes place. It is Judas who takes the lead and proceeds to greet Jesus with a kiss: Jesus rebukes him for using the sign of friendship as a means of betrayal. The disciples, promptly falling into temptation, ask whether they should resist the party, and do not wait for permission. One of them attacks the high priest's servant, only to be rebuked by Jesus who heals the wound. It is the responsible leaders of the temple and people who have come to arrest Jesus, and now Jesus turns to them, and rebukes them for treating him like a brigand; he had taught peacably in the temple, and could have been arrested there without a commotion; but, says Jesus, this is the hour for them to act according to their sinful nature, captives to the power of darkness.

The differences between this narrative and that of Mark are conspicuous. The action of Judas is emphasised and the crowd falls initially into the background. It becomes clear only when Jesus addresses Judas that the kiss is meant as a means of betrayal, Mark's explanation being omitted. In Mk. the actual arrest precedes the retaliation by the disciples, but in Lk. (and Jn.) the order is reversed. The healing of the wounded ear is new. Then at the end it emerges that the arresting party is not merely sent by the authorities but actually includes them; Jesus' final remark to them is peculiar to Lk. There is no mention of the flight of the disciples. Several of these points are also found in Jn. 18:1–12.

Many commentators hold that Luke has used Mk. as his sole source with considerable redaction (Creed, 272; Finegan, *Überlieferung*, 20f.). On this view, it is Luke who has reformulated the scene in order to stress the position of Judas and to portray Jesus as the resolute martyr, who is in full command of what happens and who follows his appointed way. Luke thus presupposes the facts, and he explains and completes them (Lagrange, 563). But this view requires that Luke has invented various details for which no convincing explanation can be given; and if John is not dependent on Lk., some of these details are independently attested. It is, therefore, more probable that Luke has made use of another source which incorporates details omitted by Mark, and that he has woven together Marcan and non-Marcan material at this point (Rengstorf, 243f.; Dodd, 66f., Grundmann, 413; Taylor, *Passion*, 72–76). This view has been considerably elaborated by Rehkopf, 31–82, but some of his argumentation is unconvincing and does not strengthen his case. Despite this fact, it seems probable that some non-Marcan source material has been used.

The question of sources is the more difficult to solve since there is great uncertainty about the character of the material at Mark's disposal. While Linnemann, *Studien*, 41–69, claims that Mark has brought together three originally independent pieces of tradition (Mk. 14:43, 48, 49b; Mk. 14:44–46; and Mk. 14:47, 50–52), G. Schneider* has elaborated the view of Taylor, 557, that the original narrative was Mk. 14:43–46 to which various 'appendices' have been added. Whatever be the process by which the narrative developed, it is clear that Luke was dependent on a developed form of it which has preserved features lost in Mk. The historicity is hard to assess. Many critics would regard the healing of the servant's ear as legendary, and even the attack on him as an accretion meant to show the disciples as prepared to defend Jesus (but, in the view of the Evangelists, misunderstanding the situation); the conversational elements are also regarded as additions. Opinions may differ on these points, but it is hard to deny a historical core to the story. There is good reason to believe that it formed part of a pre-Marcan tradition of the passion, the existence of which has not been disproved by Linnemann's discussion (*Studien*, 54–68).

See Bultmann, 289f.; Finegan, *Überlieferung*, 20f.; Dibelius, *Botschaft* I, 272–277;

Rehkopf, 31–82; Linnemann, *Studien*, 41–69; Taylor, *Passion*, 72–76; G. Schneider, 'Die Verhaftung Jesu', ZNW 63, 1972, 188–209.

(47) The story is joined as closely as possible to the preceding one by means of asyndeton (diff. Mk. καὶ εὐθύς; cf. 8:49 par. Mk. 5:35; Acts 10:44). ἔτι αὐτοῦ λαλοῦντος is found in Mk. here and 5:35 (Lk. 8:49); cf. Lk. 22:60; Acts 10:44. As a result of Luke's omission of Mk. 14:38b–42, the phrase, which in Mk. emphasises the fulfilment of Jesus' prophecy (Mk. 14:42), here stresses the element of πειρασμός in the new scene. ἰδού is a natural addition (par. Mt.) to indicate the commencement of the action. Luke brings forward mention of the ὄχλος which accompanied Judas and drops the description of them; in this way the narrative is focused on the figure of Judas. The description of Judas as 'one of the Twelve' (par. Mk.) is not surprising; it may reflect an original form of the story in which this was the first mention of him, but in the context of the Gospels it serves to underline the enormity of the betrayal. But the introductory phrase ὁ λεγόμενος is unusual. To translate 'the so-called' (Klostermann, 214; Rengstorf, 243; Schmid, 240) or 'the man called' (RSV; *et al.*) gives an odd phrase. Rehkopf, 37f., thinks that it derives from a source in which Judas had not previously been mentioned. For this possibility cf. Mk. 15:7 (but see Taylor, 581, for the suggestion that originally it introduced a by-name here). J. Weiss, 514, took it to mean 'the aforementioned' (i.e. in 22:3), which would give the best Lucan sense, but is not attested elsewhere. Is the phrase possibly contemptuous, 'the fellow called'? For προέρχομαι, cf. 1:17 note; here it means 'to lead' or 'to go before'. Rehkopf, 38–40, adopts the former meaning, and explains the following accusative (instead of the expected genitive) as a Latinism (*antecedebat eos*); but his claim that the use of the imperfect rules out the latter meaning is not convincing, and the latter translation in fact gives the better sense in the context; Judas is not the leader, but the man who goes on ahead and shows the others the way to Jesus. Whereas Mark relates that Judas, having approached Jesus, addressed him as Rabbi and kissed him, Luke simply says that he drew near to Jesus (ἐγγίζω, diff. Mk. προσέρχομαι, is Lucan) in order to kiss him; for φιλέω, 'to kiss', cf. Mk. 14:44; Mt. 26:48 (diff. Mk. καταφιλέω, which is Lucan, 7:38 note); detailed background is given in G. Stählin, TDNT IX, 114–146. For the misuse of the kiss cf. Gn. 27:46f.; 2 Sa. 15:5; Pr. 7:13; 27:6; Sir. 29:5, and especially 2 Sa. 20:9. It is strange that Luke prefers the simple form of the verb to Mark's compound (Rehkopf, 42), since both forms have the same meaning (G. Stählin, TDNT IX, 119 n. 42). It is difficult to decide whether there is a change of meaning. Many scholars hold that in Lk. Judas does not actually carry out his intention to kiss Jesus (since Jesus' statement interrupts him; B. Weiss, 648; J. Weiss, 210, 514; Dibelius, 203; Taylor, *Behind*, 47; Klostermann, 217; Finegan, *Überlieferung*, 20; Conzelmann, 76; Stuhlmueller, 159). It would be wiser to say that in Lk. the question is left open (Rengstorf, 243), and that Luke often leaves the reader's

imagination to draw obvious conclusions. It becomes obvious from Jesus' reply that the kiss was a means of betraying Jesus, but Luke does not offer Mark's explanation that it was a means of identifying Jesus in the dark to the police. But this remains the most likely interpretation of the act, and Rehkopf's attempt (48–50) to explain it as a last, sudden act of reverence for Jesus falls foul of v. 48.

(48) Mark has no reaction by Jesus at this point, but Matthew and Luke supply the lack in different ways. Matthew's enigmatic phrase (ἑταῖρε, ἐφ' ὅ πάρει) may possibly have a force similar to Lk. 22:48 (F. Rehkopf, "Ἑταῖρε, ἐφ' ὅ πάρει (Mt. 26, 50)', ZNW 52, 1961, 109–115; see further G. Stählin, TDNT IX, 140 n. 241), but is quite independent of it; its difficulty suggests that it is not a Matthaean creation. In Luke the mention of Ἰησοῦς (without article, p⁷⁵ ℵ B; with article, rell; TR; Diglot), which is unnecessary after v. 47, helps to stress the contrast between Jesus and Judas, who is addressed in the vocative (cf. 1:13, 30; 7:40; 10:41; 19:5; 22:34 for this stylistic feature). The position of φιλήματι (7:45*) is emphatic and stresses the enormity of using a kiss in such a hypocritical manner (Danker, 227). The self-reference of Jesus as the Son of man has roused critical suspicion. Tödt, 152; Higgins, 80f.; and Linnemann, Studien, 40, argue that the saying is Luke's substitute for Mk. 14:41, and is 'a dramatized form of the theme "the Son of man is betrayed"' (Higgins). Rehkopf, 56, argues that the use is pre-Lucan, and C. Colpe, TDNT VIII, 446f., holds that it was changed from an original με (as in 22:22) in the pre-Lucan tradition. A verdict on the saying depends on whether Luke is thought to be creating on the basis of Mk. 14:41 or is following a source. Here, if anywhere, 'Son of man' could be originally a surrogate for 'me', understood in a titular sense in the tradition; Higgins' objection to the saying as a saying of Jesus thus falls to the ground. Further, the saying is integral to the narrative, and does not simply repeat 22:21 (Colpe). It is probably not based on Mk.

(49) The opening of the verse is Lucan in style (cf. 8:34, 47; 23:47; et al.). Luke does not mention the arrest of Jesus at this point, so that the intervention of the disciples precedes the actual arrest. Mark's order gives the impression that the account of the intervention is an addition to the narrative, and does not really fix the order of the events. Luke's order binds the scene together more effectively and is more likely to be historical. In Mk. the intervention is ascribed to οἱ παρεστηκότες, a vague phrase perhaps meant to hide the identity of the disciples as men prepared to take up arms. Luke's phrase, οἱ περὶ αὐτόν, is also vague. Rehkopf, 57f., suggests that it reflects the existence of a passion narrative that began with the story of the arrest, but this is doubtful. The use of the future participle ἐσόμενον is Lucan (Acts 8:27; 20:22; 24:11, 17). For εἰ in a direct question cf. 22:42 note; it is hardly pre-Lucan (pace Rehkopf, 59). πατάσσω, 'to strike' (22:50 par. Mt. 26:51; Lk. 22:64 par. Mt. 26:68; Rev. 9:5**), is a more appropriate word for attacking with a sword than Mk. παίω. The future indicative in a

deliberative question refers to an action definitely expected to take place: Jesus is not being asked for permission! (Rehkopf, 60; cf. BD 366²). The reference to the sword echoes 22:38, but it is not necessary to assume that the saying has been constructed in order to make the allusion. The instrumental use of ἐν may be a pointer to the use of a source (contrast 21:24; Acts 12:2).

(50) The description of the attack is very close to Mk. 14:47 and raises the question of dependence, but there are sufficient differences to suggest the influence of a variant tradition. εἷς τις has been taken to mean 'someone whose name I could tell you' (cf. Sophocles, Oed. Tyr. 118; Lagrange, cited by Taylor, 559f.). The word order τοῦ ἀρχιερέως τὸν δοῦλον (ℵ B L 69 pc; inverted in rell; TR; Diglot) differs from Mk. and is hard to attribute to Luke (Rehkopf, 68f.). It may well reflect an original motif that such a wound rendered a person unfit for priestly service (Jos. Ant. 14:366), and that an attack on the servant indirectly insulted the master (2 Sa. 10:4f.; Mk. 12:1ff.; D. Daube, 'Three Notes having to do with Johanan ben Zaccai', JTS ns 11, 1960, 53–62 ('III. Slitting the High Priest's Ear', 59–62); cf. Lohmeyer, 322 n. 5). But armed resistance is perhaps the only motif (F. Horst, TDNT V, 558). Luke uses οὖς rather than Mark's ὠτίον but see v. 51). He adds the detail that it was the right ear (par. Jn. 18:10); cf. 6:6 and contrast 6:25 diff. Mt. 5:39. The motif of the superiority of the right side (cf. W. Grundmann, TDNT II, 37f.) is hardly relevant; the description is either a legendary accretion or a historical detail of interest to a doctor.

(51) Again Jesus responds to the situation (for the formula cf. 1:60; et al.; Mk. 14:48). The saying is probably addressed to the disciples. ἐάω (4:41*) can mean 'to let go, leave alone'; and ἕως τούτου means 'up to this point'. 1. This gives the sense: 'Leave alone; thus far (and no further)'; i.e. 'Stop; go only as far as this and no further' (TNT note; cf. 'Leave off; that will do', JB; cf. AG 212, 336; Rehkopf, 62; similarly RSV; TEV; NIV). 2. Others supply αὐτούς as the implied object: 'Let them (sc. the police) have their way' (NEB; Barclay; i.e. 'let them go even as far as arresting me'). Similarly, Creed, 274: 'Let events take their course – even to my arrest'. 3. An older view (Alford, 644; cf. Stuhlmueller, 159) regards the words as addressed to the police: 'Permit me, thus far (i.e. to touch the ear of the wounded man) '. The second view is perhaps to be preferred. The vocabulary is Lucan, and such brief statements are frequent in Luke's special material (cf. 22:38; Rehkopf, 62f.). ὠτίον is 'the outer ear'; contrast 22:50; it is used for variety; αὐτοῦ is added by A Γ Δ f13 pm; TR; Diglot. The detail of the healing is peculiar to Lk. By healing the man Jesus shows that he does not rely on the sword, and that his movement is not based on force (Grundmann, 414). But the fact that the healing can be accounted for in this way does not necessarily imply that it is legendary.

(52) In Mk. the audience for Jesus' final comment is vague (αὐτοῖς), and Luke correctly interprets it as addressed to the arresting

party. The inclusion of Ἰησοῦς as subject (p⁷⁵ ℵ A B T Θ 0171 pc; with the article, L W Γ Δ f13 pl; TR; Diglot) is redundant, and it is omitted by D f1 b e i l syˢᶜ; but it gives emphasis to the following important statement (Metzger, 177 – 'a slight break' between the action and the statement). The anarthrous use may be pre-Lucan (cf. 22:48 note). Since he has not described the party earlier, Luke now has to do so, and the language betrays his hand. Whereas in Mk. the party has been sent by the authorities, here it includes some of them. Moreover, in Mk. the three parties forming the sanhedrin are mentioned, but here there is a mixture of temple authorities and lay members of the sanhedrin. In addition to the ἀρχιερεῖς, i.e. the leading priests who had official duties in connection with the temple (Jeremias, Jerusalem, 160–181), there is mention of στρατηγοὶ τοῦ ἱεροῦ. This is an unusual phrase; τοῦ ἱεροῦ is omitted by syˢ and τοῦ λαοῦ (for ναοῦ?) is substituted by D. But it also occurs in 22:4 (see note) and refers to the temple police. There is nothing improbable about the composition of the party; it would not be the last time that high officials had accompanied the police to arrest their enemies. Jesus' words to them follow Mk. closely. He reproaches them for coming out to arrest him (Mk. συλλαβεῖν με, omitted by Luke) with swords and clubs (ξύλον, Mk. 14:43, 48; literally 'wood') as if he were a brigand (λῃστής, 10:30).

(53) The authorities had not taken the opportunity to arrest Jesus peaceably when he was teaching in the temple. καθ' ἡμέραν may imply a ministry of some length. Luke has substituted an illogical genitive absolute for Mark's parataxis, and has μετά, diff. Mk. πρός, for an expression of place. The use of the temple courts as a place for teaching appears to have been common; Luke omits διδάσκων, diff. Mk., perhaps to get a neater sentence. He dislikes κρατέω (cf. 20:19 diff. Mk.) and substitutes ἐξετείνατε τὰς χεῖρας (cf. Je. 6:12 and frequently in LXX). The final part of the saying is peculiar to Lk. The present time is the appointed hour for Jesus' enemies to act, in accordance with God's plan; the saying could be based on Mk. 14:41, but the change of thought from 'the hour' to 'your hour' speaks against this. The second part of the clause is added loosely. This is the hour in which the power (ἐξουσία, 4:6; cf. 23:7) of darkness (cf. 1:79) is revealed and exercises its force. The light shed by Jesus has failed to dispel it (Danker, 228). For the terminology cf. Acts 26:18; it could be Lucan, but it is too widely attested in the early church for this to be certain, and it could equally well have been used by Jesus.

iii. Peter's Denial of Jesus 22:54–62

In Mk. the arrest of Jesus is followed by a night-time trial of Jesus, the mocking of Jesus and the denial by Peter (Mk. 14:53–65); since Luke has recorded a morning trial in place of Mark's night-time trial, he has necessarily placed the accounts of the denial and the mockery before *his* trial scene. The result is that we are given a further example of the πειρασμός in which the disciples were placed (22:46), which is at the same time an example of the power of darkness (22:53). The story of Peter stands over against that of Jesus, demonstrating the correctness of Jesus' prediction (22:31–34), the continuing concern of Jesus for Peter (22:61), and the weakness of the disciple in contrast to the steadfastness of the Master.

The structure of the scene is formally the same as in Mk., with three separate denials by Peter. But the detailed content is remarkably different. In Lk. all three acts of denial take place in the courtyard around the fire, while in Mk. Jesus goes outside into the entry after the first denial. In Mk. the actors are a servant girl (twice) and a man, in Lk. a servant girl and two men. In Mk. the accusations are directed to Peter, to the bystanders and to Peter, respectively; but in Lk. to the bystanders, to Peter, and to the bystanders. The wording of the accusations and replies differs, and there is no mention of the first cockcrow in Lk. For the details see the chart in Brown, *John*, II, 838f. The effect of the changes is variously estimated by scholars. It is common to see in them an attempt to present Peter in a better light than in Mk. He does not curse and swear in Lk., and he does not retreat from the courtyard when challenged. The force of his replies is also said to be weaker (Linnemann, *Studien*, 100; Schneider, 73–96). But while this motif may be present to some extent, it by no means fully explains the changes in Lk. According to Dietrich, 145–157, the Lucan narrative is more forensic in character, various witnesses in turn making an accusation against Peter, first a woman (whose testimony is *ipso facto* suspect) and then two men (whose testimonies confirm each other). The scene reaches its climax in the confrontation of the denier by the One who has been denied. Thus the roles of Satan as accuser and Jesus as the defender of Peter (22:31f.) are depicted in the actual narrative.

The question now is whether the differences in the narrative are to be explained as the result purely of Lucan redaction of Mk. (Finegan, *Überlieferung*, 23f.; Linnemann, *Studien*, 97–101; Taylor, *Passion*, 77f.; Schneider, 73–96). Some scholars would allow that oral traditions may have exercised some influence on Luke's redaction (Taylor, Schneider). Others consider that Luke has used another source alongside Mk. (Bultmann, 290 (but see Erg. 40); Schlatter, 140, 436f.; Rengstorf, 245–248; Grundmann, 415f.; Klein, 53–55; Catchpole, 160–174; Dietrich does not discuss the question). The question is discussed at length by Schneider and Catchpole, whose views on the non-Marcan origin of much of 22:63–71 are similar, but who come to opposite conclusions on this particular pericope. Schneider's case is based mainly on detailed examination of the wording, and shows that much can be regarded as redaction of Mk. Catchpole concentrates more on the structure as a whole, and is able to draw attention to a number of points where Schneider is not wholly convincing (cf. Catchpole, 272–278, for discussion of Schneider). The evidence is finely balanced, but perhaps tips slightly in favour of Catchpole's position; this is the more probable if we are right in thinking that Luke's special source contained a prediction of the denial.

The historicity of the denial story has been strongly attacked. The existence of two separate accounts of it (three, if John's narrative is independent) can be regarded as casting doubt on the precise course of the underlying events or as confirming the basic historicity of the denial. But the three accounts are sufficiently close to one another to make it probable that one basic tradition has developed in different ways. The objections to historicity are: 1. doubt as to whether the story formed part of the passion narrative; 2. the 'legendary' nature of the story as a story about Peter rather than Jesus (cf. Dibelius, 184, 215–218); 3. the schematic nature of the story with its threefold structure and the improbability of Peter remaining in the scene of danger for so long; 4. the possibility of explaining the story as a concretizing of the flight of all the disciples (Linnemann, *Studien*, 70–108) or as a reflection of Peter's changing position in the early church (Klein, 49–98). None of these objections is convincing. 1. Dodd, 84 n. 1, rightly observes that the narrative could have been circulated both as a part of the passion story (from which setting it derives much of its force) and as an independent piece of Christian edification. 2. Characterization of a story as a 'legend' in no way determines whether or not it is historical. 3. The possibility of repeated accusations against Peter is perfectly natural, even if some schematisation has inevitably crept in to the telling of the story. It has been suspected that originally there was only one denial and that Mark has (wrongly) added together two different traditions, telling of one and the same denial, but this is pure hypothesis. 4. Attempts to explain the story as a reflection of other events fail to convince. Their proponents have failed to show how such a discreditable story could have been invented about Peter (cf. Schweizer, 189f.; Brown, *John*, II, 836–842). It is altogether more probable that the story has a historical basis, although it may not be easy to work out its character in detail.

See Bultmann, 290; Dibelius, 215–218; Finegan, *Überlieferung*, 23f.; Klein, 49–98 (originally as 'Die Verleugnung des Petrus, ZTK 58, 1961, 285–328); Linnemann, *Studien*, 70–108 (originally as 'Die Verleugnung des Petrus', ZTK 63, 1966, 1–32); Schneider, *passim*; Catchpole, 160–174; M. Wilcox, 'The Denial-Sequence in Mark xiv. 26–31, 66–72', NTS 17, 1970–71, 426–436; Dietrich, 139–157; Taylor, *Passion*, 77f.; R. Pesch, 'Die Verleugnung des Petrus', in Gnilka, *Neues Testament*, 42–62.

(54) The account of Jesus' arrest and movement from the garden to the house of the high priest forms the background for the story of Peter. Jesus is arrested (συλλαμβάνω, Mk. 14:48; Lk. 1:24; *et al.*) only after he has, as it were, given permission (Schneider, 63, 73f.). The combination ἤγαγον καὶ εἰσήγαγον is awkward, but not unprecedented in Lk. (Rehkopf, 41 n. 4); for Mk. ἀπάγω cf. 22:66. The detail about the house of the high priest (τὴν οἰκίαν; τὸν οἶκον, A D W Γ Δ Θ f13 *pm*; TR;

Diglot) could be based on Mk. 14:54. Nothing further is said about what happened to Jesus at this point; the interest of the narrative is centred on Peter. In Mk. a gathering of the members of the sanhedrin is described, then comes a brief mention of Peter's presence, followed by details of the night-time meeting of the sanhedrin, after which Peter's denial is recorded separately. In Jn. 18:13–27 there is a brief note about an examination of Jesus by Annas before being sent to Caiaphas, and interwoven with this is the account of Peter's denial. Catchpole, 169–172, argues strongly that for Lk. the high priest in question was Annas, so that Luke reflects independently the Johannine tradition (similarly, Lagrange, 568; Rengstorf, 246f.). Otherwise, the mention of Jesus going to his house lacks motivation other than to provide a place for Jesus to spend the night and a scenario for the denial; this is unlikely. All the Gospels record how Peter followed Jesus; the implication is that the other disciples did not do so (but see Jn. 18:15f.). The use of the imperfect ἠκολούθει (par. Mt., Jn.; diff. Mk., aorist) can be understood as conative or iterative, to stress how Peter tried to keep close to Jesus (Schneider, 49f. – as redaction of Mk.); Catchpole, 163, is unconvincing in his attempt to deny that the use of the imperfect fits in with Lucan style. The verse as a whole could be derived from Mk., but could equally well come from a non-Marcan source.

(55) The scene is set by reference to the kindling of a fire (cf. Jn. 18:18) in the middle of the courtyard which was a typical feature of a big, Hellenistic house. περιάπτω**, 'to kindle', is perhaps used to convey the idea of a fire sufficiently large for several people to sit all round it (cf. LS: 'to light a fire all round'; Grundmann, 416). Luke uses πῦρ as the appropriate word; in v. 56 he uses φῶς, par. Mk., where the light of the fire is significant (cf. 1 Mac. 12:29). συγκαθίζω is 'to sit together' (Eph. 2:6**). The scene thus being set, Luke describes how Peter joins the circle already seated round the fire (Schneider, 77); hence he has ἐκάθητο, diff. Mk. ἦν συγκαθήμενος (in Jn. 18:18 Peter *stands*). The repetition of Peter's name may be simply for emphasis, or could indicate use of a source (perhaps different from that (Mk.?) used in v. 54). The use of μέσος with the genitive is found here only in Lk., although μέσος is Lucan. Luke fails to identify the people round the fire (diff. Mk. μετὰ τῶν ὑπηρετῶν), an omission which Schneider, 65, 77f., fails to explain convincingly in terms of redaction of Mk. Omission of the reference to Peter warming himself (par. Mt.; diff. Mk., Jn.) may be due to a desire to avoid suggesting that Peter entered the courtyard merely to keep warm (cf. Mt. ἰδεῖν τὸ τέλος).

(56) The first actor in the drama is a servant girl (the noun with τις (diff. Mk. εἷς) appended is Lucan). The phrase καθήμενον πρὸς τὸ φῶς (which is separated from its antecedent) is regarded by Catchpole, 161f., as an addition to Luke's non-Marcan material from Mk. 14:54. But it is unlikely to be an addition since it is necessary after ἰδοῦσα and gives the picture of the girl getting an indistinct glimpse of Peter and then looking

more closely (ἀτενίζω, 4:20; *et al.*; diff. Mk. ἐμβλέπω) to be sure of her facts before making her accusation (as in Mk.: Schneider, 80). The accusation is couched in the third person (diff. Mk.), and has σὺν αὐτῷ diff. Mk. μετὰ τοῦ Ναζαρηνοῦ τοῦ Ἰησοῦ. Schneider's attempt (80) to explain the change of person as due to the creation of a climax with the use of σύ in the second accusation collapses in face of the resumption of the third person in the third accusation. No plausible explanation of the change has been suggested, unless we accept Dietrich's suggestion (144f.) that the woman is accusing Peter before the bystanders; or is it more likely that in popular story-telling a general accusation would precede a particular accusation directed to Peter himself? It is hard to attribute the change to Luke himself. In the same way no convincing reason for Luke's alteration of 'the Nazarene' is forthcoming.

(57) Peter's response is one of denial. ἀρνέομαι can mean 'to refuse to recognise' or 'to abandon, deny solidarity with' (Ellis, 260); the former meaning is primary, but the ambiguity allows the term to be applied to cases of apostasy in the church (cf. 12:9; further, H. Schlier, TDNT I, 469–471). The wording of Peter's reply differs from that in Mk. 14:68, but is close to that in Mk. 14:71 where it has climactic effect. He denies acquaintance with Jesus (cf. 22:34). This wording may be reminiscent of the Jewish ban-formula, 'I have never known you' (SB I, 469; cf. H. Merkel, in Bammel, 69; Catchpole, 273). A different Jewish form of asseveration appears in Mk. 14:68. Lucan redaction seems unlikely. The accuser is finally addressed as γύναι (cf. the vocatives in 22:58, 60 diff. Mk.); cf. 13:12; Jn. 2:4; and, for the position of the vocative, Lk. 5:8; Acts 2:37; 26:7; BD 474⁶. The usage in Acts weakens the likelihood that this is a pre-Lucan usage (claimed by Rehkopf, 98; Catchpole, 173), but the weight of evidence for vocative usage in Luke's special material certainly allows for this possibility here. Dietrich, 145f., thinks that the use of the vocatives emphasises the identity of the accusers as female and male.

(58) In Mk. Peter now departs to the προαύλιον; in place of this geographical 'gap' in the narrative Luke has a time-gap, μετὰ βραχύ (probably Lucan; for βραχύς, 'short', cf. Acts 5:34; 27:28; Jn. 6:7; Heb. 2:7, 9; 13:22**). Peter thus remains in the one place (par. Jn. 18:25). He does not retreat; rather he stays where he can see Jesus and where Jesus can see him (Schneider, 82). This detail can thus be explained as Lucan redaction of Mk. Whereas in Mk. the maid again accuses Peter, addressing herself to the bystanders, here in Lk. it is another person (a man) who addresses Peter directly (cf. Mk. 14:70). Schneider, 83f., thinks that Luke avoids the humiliation of Peter being accused twice by a woman, and suggests that the second appearance of the woman in Mk. may be due to his combining two traditions. Since the Lucan tradition is reinforced by Jn., it may be that the traditions should be combined: the woman's comments led the others to take up her accusation. While ἕτερος is a favourite word of Luke, Catchpole, 173, makes the point that

its redactional use is normally to convey the idea of other-ness/distinctness found in the source. The use of φημί (frequent in Acts) may be Lucan (see Schürmann, *Abschiedsrede*, 27f.). For καὶ σύ cf. Mk. 14:67; the force of the καί here and in v. 56 is not clear. ἐξ αὐτῶν must presumably refer to the disciples of Jesus (cf. Jn. 18:25). Luke avoids ἀρνέομαι (diff. Mk., Mt., Jn.) and simply records Peter's reply, οὐκ εἰμί (par. Jn.; omitted in Mk.).

(59) As in Mk. there is a time-gap before the third dialogue, but where Mark is vague (μετὰ μικρόν), Luke has a definite interval of about an hour; the vocabulary is Lucan (διΐστημι, 'to go away' 24:51; Acts 27:28**; cf. Acts 5:7). Schneider, 86, follows Lagrange in suggesting that in this way Luke is filling out the time between the arrest and cockcrow. The accusation is made by the bystanders in Mk. (par. Mt.), and by a servant, identified as the kinsman of the servant wounded in the arrest, in Jn. ἄλλος is appropriate to describe another person belonging to the same group as the one previously named. This man is sure of his ground, despite Peter's earlier denials, and so the narrative reaches its climax in his firm statement (διϊσχυρίζομαι, Acts 12:15; 15:2 D**) that Peter is certainly one of the group, since he is a Galilean.

ἐπ' ἀληθείας (4:25; 20:21) replaces Mk. ἀληθῶς, a word which Luke reserves as an equivalent for ἀμήν (except Acts 12:11). The ac-cusation is in the third person, diff. Mk., Mt., Jn., a change for which no redactional motive can be seen. μετά is equivalent to σύν in v. 56 and may refer to Peter being present in the garden at the arrest (cf. Jn. 18:26); it is unlikely to be redactional. καὶ γὰρ Γαλιλαῖός ἐστιν agrees with Mk., and does not fit too neatly into the accusation (note the change of tense); Catchpole, 162f., argues that it is a Marcan insertion into non-Marcan material.

(60) In Mk. the third denial reaches a climax in Peter's cursing and swearing. Luke's omission of this detail can be seen as an attempt to sof-ten the harshness of Mark's picture. He has Peter say, 'I don't know what you mean', rather than 'I don't know the man you're talking about'. It seems unlikely that this wording is Lucan. It is similar to that in Mk. 14:67, and there is no reason why Luke should have removed it to the end of the narrative. If it reflects a Jewish formula (cf. v. 57 note; Sheb. 8:3, 6, in SB II, 51), it may well represent pre-Lucan tradition. Or is Peter questioning the suggestion that because he is a Galilean (which he could not very well deny) he must therefore be an associate of Jesus – or perhaps even a revolutionary? In the latter case could καὶ (σύ) (v. 58) refer to the other revolutionaries in custody at the time? All four Gospels record how immediately (παραχρῆμα, diff. Mk. εὐθύς) the cock crowed; Luke has only one cockcrow, diff. Mk. (14:30, 68, 72, despite the textual uncertainty in some of these verses); here he and the other Evangelists may be influenced by a different tradition from Mk. The addition ἔτι λαλοῦντος αὐτοῦ is Lucan and stresses the literal fulfilment of Jesus' prophecy.

(61) The first part of the verse is peculiar to Luke with its description of how the Lord turned and looked at Peter. The detail is regarded as a Lucan invention by many scholars (Bultmann, 290; Dibelius, 112; Leaney, 275; Klein, 54; Schneider, 91f.), but as pre-Lucan by Catchpole, 168f. It is possible that Jesus was being taken from the house of Annas to the next stage in his trial (Rengstorf, 248) or that he too was being guarded in the courtyard (Grundmann, 417; Catchpole, 168, argues that v. 56 is more meaningful if Jesus (σὺν αὐτῷ) is present). στραφείς is found at 7:9; et al., always in Luke's special material; it may, however, be Lucan. The use of ὁ κύριος derives from Luke's special source material, but on occasion can be redactional; Luke, however, never inserts it in a Marcan context. For ἐμβλέπω cf. Mk. 14:67; here it signifies a reproachful look (also found by Schneider, 92f., at 20:17, but this is doubtful; cf. also Acts 22:11). The evidence is insufficient to demonstrate Lucan creation. Dietrich's comparison (155f.) with 5:8 is too weak to suggest that this passage has been formed on the analogy of the other. The second part of the verse is also commonly regarded as being Lucan redaction, based on Mk., but there are some indications that this solution is oversimple. Luke's use of ὑπομιμνῄσκομαι*, 'to remember', diff. Mk. ἀναμιμνῄσκομαι, may reflect his liking for ὑπο- compounds. The reading ῥήματος (p[69] p[75] ℵ B L T 0124 0153 al) may be an assimilation to Mk. and Mt.; and λόγου (rell; TR; Synopsis; Diglot) is perhaps to be preferred. On the basis of the latter reading. Schneider, 93f., claims that Luke has altered Mk. ῥῆμα to λόγος under the influence of his liking for the phrase ὁ λόγος τοῦ κυρίου, but in fact this phrase is used for the gospel message and not for individual sayings of Jesus (in Acts 20:35 the plural form is used); it is the less likely that Luke would have altered Mark's ῥῆμα here (Catchpole, 165f.). Luke omits δίς, diff. Mk., with reference to the cock crowing; the introduction of σήμερον may be regarded as a substitute for this (cf. 22:34 par. Mk. 14:30), but Catchpole, 164f., holds that Luke avoids Jewish time notes an⟨d⟩ that his alteration of the word-order here cannot be explained reda⟨c⟩tionally, since he normally repeats earlier statements with precision.

(62) The textual status of this verse is uncertain. It agrees ⟨v⟩erbally with Mt. 26:75, diff. Mk., and is omitted by 0171[vid] a b e ff[2] i l* r[1], Diglot; NEB; and many commentators (cf. Schneider, 95f.). The language of the verse is Matthaean, but with so short a sentence a sure verdict cannot be based on this. The problem is whether the verse has been accidentally omitted from a few MSS (including only one Greek MS; Metzger, 178); or wrongly added to all the rest. It would have been natural for scribes to add a suitable ending to a narrative which finished with v. 61, less natural for it to be omitted accidentally (possibly, however, by homoioarcton with the next verse). If it is retained, we have a particularly strong link with Mt. (where the words are textually secure) in a passage which otherwise shows no strong links (cf. Schneider, 46–60). If the verse is omitted, Luke agrees with Jn. in finishing the story with the

cock-crow. On the whole internal evidence favours omission, while the weight of external evidence strongly supports inclusion.

iv. The Mockery of Jesus 22:63-65

During the night Jesus was subjected not only to the denial of Peter but also to the mockery of the people who had arrested him; they treated him roughly, insulted him, and tried to make him show his prophetic powers by guessing who hit him while he was blindfolded. The mockery *takes place* in Lk. before the morning trial, whereas in Mk. it is *recorded* after the night-trial and before Peter's denial. Nothing as regards its source can be deduced from the Lucan order which leaves it at the same point of time as in Mk. But the contents strongly suggest that Luke is drawing on another source. The opening is badly linked to the preceding incident (at the end of which Luke is probably following Mk.); the details of the action are rather different (especially if the shorter text of Mk. (Streeter, 325-327) is followed), and Mark's allusions to the suffering Servant have disappeared. Hence the view that Luke is here dependent on a non-Marcan source is strongly based (Plummer, 517; Bultmann, 293; Rengstorf, 246f. (by implication); Grundmann, 417f.; Taylor, *Passion*, 79f.; Schneider, 96–104; Catchpole, 174–183). This source offers a more primitive version of the incident than Mk. (Catchpole). There is no reason to doubt its historicity; Dibelius' suggestion (193) that it was invented on the basis of Is. 50:6 comes to grief on the lack of reference to that verse in the Lucan account; it is more probable that the story of the incident was embellished from the OT than vice versa.

See Bultmann, 293; W. C. van Unnik, 'Jesu Verhöhnung vor dem Synedrium (Mc 14, 65 par)', ZNW 29, 1930, 310f.; Taylor, *Passion*, 79f.; Schneider, 96–104; Catchpole, 174–183.

(63) In its present context the object ($a\dot{v}\tau \acute{o}v$) of this verse should be Peter (cf. 22:61, 62), but clearly Jesus is meant. Often it is taken for granted in Gospel narratives that Jesus is the principal actor, but here it seems likely that two different sources have been joined, although there is no agreement as to the cause of the difficulty; vs. 55–61 (62) or vs. 63–65 may be an insertion into the present context; if Luke has concluded the denial story with material from Mk., this may account for the inconcinnity (Schneider, 97f.; cf. 21:21 for a similar instance). The mockery is ascribed to the men who had arrested Jesus; $\sigma v v \acute{e} \chi \omega$ (4:38; *et al.*) here means 'to hold in custody' (AG s.v.) and is probably Lucan. It is historically more likely that the mockery was done by the guards or servants than by members of the sanhedrin (as may be intended in Mk. 14:65), and it could be claimed that Luke has made a historical correction to Mk. here; on the other hand, there is a good case that historically the mockery preceded the sanhedrin hearing, and this favours the view that Luke is not redacting Mk. here. For $\dot{e} \mu \pi a \acute{\iota} \zeta \omega$ cf. 14:29; 18:32; 23:11, 36; Mk. 10:34; 15:20, 31; Luke appears elsewhere to take the word from tradition, and here it replaces Mk. $\dot{e} \mu \pi \tau \acute{v} \omega$ (used by Lk. 18:32

par. Mk. 10:34) which carries an allusion to Is. 50:6. δέρω (12:47f.; 20:10f.) replaces Mk. κολαφίζω (cf. Is. 50:6 for the sense). The imperfect tense is retained throughout the section, perhaps to suggest what was going on during Peter's denial (Manson, 251; Schneider, 97).

(64) περικαλύπτω is 'to cover all round, blindfold' (Mk. 14:65, *si vera lectio*; cf. Heb. 9:4**); Mark adds τὸ πρόσωπον, which is not necessary for the sense (although some MSS add it in Lk.). The guards then proceeded (ἐπηρώτων, imperfect) to ask Jesus to exercise his gift of clairvoyance as a prophet (προφητεύω) and declare which of them had struck him (παίω, Mt. 26:68; Mk. 14:47 par. Jn. 18:10; Rev. 9:5**). For this meaning of προφητεύω cf. W. C. van Unnik*. The relation to Mk. and Mt. is not clear. The generally accepted text of Mk. gives the same impression of the incident as Lk. (with the omission of the question, 'Who struck you?', added in some MSS). But the reference to blindfolding is omitted in Mk. by D a f sy^s bo^pt, and is absent from Mt. This leaves a picture of Jesus being told to exercise the powers of a prophet by giving an oracle (cf. Dibelius, 193 n. 1; Streeter, 325–327; Taylor, 571). Mark and Luke would then each offer a separate, self-consistent picture. On this theory, however, there is the difficulty of explaining how Matthew offers the same picture as Lk. since there is no MS authority for omitting 'Who struck you?' in Mt. It is unlikely that Luke is dependent on Mt., and it would be necessary to assume that Matthew, who shows other non-Marcan features in his passion narrative, is indebted ultimately to the same tradition as appears in Lk.

(65) The narrative closes with a statement that the guards also said many other things against Jesus. For the phrase see 3:18; 8:3; Acts 15:35; cf. 2:40; it appears to be Lucan (*contra* Catchpole, 183, who implies that here and in 3:18 Luke is following his source). βλασφημέω (12:10; 23:39) can be used of speaking against Jesus and the apostles (Acts 13:45; 18:6): the word represents a Christian interpretation of the mockery, seeing in it blasphemy against God and his appointed messengers. εἰς has the sense 'against', and is used with βλασφημέω in 12:10; Mk. 3:29. Catchpole, 182f., regards the verse as possibly a pre-Lucan comment on the mockery, which misunderstands it in that the hostility in vs. 63f. is physical, not verbal. But this criticism fails to recognise that implicit in the command to Jesus to act the prophet is the insinuation that he is not really a prophet. The verse is probably Lucan.

v. Jesus before the Sanhedrin 22:66–71

The different Gospel accounts of the Jewish examinations of Jesus vary so much among themselves as to make it extremely difficult to know precisely what happened. According to Luke, Jesus was first taken to the house of the high priest, whom we have identified above as Annas (22:54; cf. Jn. 18:13f., 19–23). Then at daybreak, after Peter's denial and the mockery, Jesus is taken to the sanhedrin where he is briefly examined as to what role he claims to fulfil. He refuses to answer directly whether he is the Messiah, but prophesies the exaltation of the Son of man to the right hand of God. When he is then asked if he is the Son of God, he makes a guarded affirmative statement. This is sufficient to satisfy his inquisitors, and thereafter they take him before Pilate.

It is clear that Luke intends to describe a meeting of the sanhedrin; it takes place at daybreak, and it includes an informal enquiry regarding Jesus, nothing being said about the summoning of witnesses or the giving of a verdict. There is no detail about this examination in Jn., but there is a brief reference to Jesus being taken before Caiaphas (who would in fact have presided over a meeting of the sanhedrin), and the two incidents can be identified. But in Mk. we hear of a meeting of the sanhedrin, apparently at night, at which a judicial enquiry is instituted, witnesses are heard, and Jesus himself is examined in a manner very similar to that in Lk.; his words are denounced as blasphemous, and the audience decide that he deserves to die; then, as soon as it is morning, they come to a decision and send Jesus to Pilate. The historical difficulties surrounding an official meeting of the sanhedrin by night are well known, and do not need to be rehearsed here. Historical probability favours the view that a decision was taken in the morning rather than by night. Linnemann, *Studien*, 109 n. 1, correctly notes that Mark's account of the 'trial' itself contains no time-reference; the references to night-time are redactional. In fact the appearance of a night-time meeting in Mk. results from the juxtaposition of the trial with Peter's denial (which certainly took place by night) and from the fact that business began extremely early in the morning. It is, therefore, probable that Mark and Luke are reporting the same incident from different points of view, namely an enquiry by the sanhedrin which took place at dawn: cf. a similar difference of expression at 4:42 par. Mk. 1:35 (cf. Blinzler, 214 n. 94). Whether Luke's time note (22:66) is derived from Mk. 15:1 or not, the evidence suggests that his account of the trial is based on a separate tradition which is more primitive than that in Mk. and shows connections with Jn. 10:24, 33, 36.

It may well be, however, that Luke has omitted elements taken either from Mk. (or from parallel passages in his special source) which he considered it inappropriate to include at this point; thus allusion to Jesus' destroying the temple is reserved for Acts 6:14. It has been claimed that Luke's account represents a rewriting of Mk. to bring out his own christological conceptions – e.g. to bring out the equivalence of the various christological titles and to replace the thought of the parousia by that of the exaltation of the Son of man (Conzelmann, 77); to express a two-level christology and so make an existential demand on the reader (Flender, 44–46); to show that the christological titles are complementary to one another (rather than identical; Tödt, 101–103). But Catchpole, 193–200, argues that the christology is not Lucan; the identification of Messiah and Son of God is not made, and the language shows Semitic colour, so that the thought is in fact more primitive than in Mk. To achieve this understanding Catchpole has to argue that the Son of man saying (22:69) is a Lucan addition to his source, based on Mk. 14:62 (157–159), and expressing Luke's view of the parousia. The alternative view is that Lk. 22:69 represents a more primitive form of the saying, but the evidence is very evenly balanced.

The view that Luke is following a special tradition here for at least part of the scene is developed by Schneider, 105–132; Catchpole, 183–203; cf. Taylor, *Passion*, 80–84, and earlier, J. Weiss, 516; Schlatter, 140, 436–438; Rengstorf, 245–250; Grundmann, 418f.; Ellis, 260f. For the contrary view see Creed, 274; Finegan, *Überlieferung*, 24f.; Blinzler, 170–173, 210–215. P. Winter* regards vs. 66b–71 as a later interpolation. For the theory that Luke's timing of the session of the sanhedrin is to be preferred, see Benoit, *Passion*, 79f., 99; *contra* Blinzler, 210–216. In reply to the contention of Winter that Jesus was not tried and condemned by the sanhedrin, see Blinzler, *passim*; Catchpole, *passim*. The historical problems surrounding the trial of Jesus are too great to be discussed adequately here; J. Blinzler, however, has demonstrated the essential reliability of the Gospel accounts.

See Bultmann, 292f.; Finegan, *Überlieferung*, 24f.; P. Winter, 'Luke XXII. 66b–71', ST 9, 1956, 112–115; Sherwin-White, 24–47; Blinzler, *passim*; Benoit, *Passion*, 93–114; Schneider, *passim*; G. Schneider, 'Gab es eine vorsynoptische Szene "Jesus vor dem Synedrium"?' Nov.T 12, 1970, 22–39; Catchpole, *passim*; Taylor, *Passion*, 80–84; Winter, *passim*; P. W. Walaskay, 'The Trial and Death of Jesus in the Gospel of Luke', JBL 94, 1975, 81–93.

(66) Luke dates the meeting of the sanhedrin ὡς ἐγένετο ἡμέρα; the phraseology is Lucan (cf. 4:42; 6:13; Acts 12:18; 23:12; 27:39), and may reflect Mk. 15:1 or be drawn from a separate tradition; the evidence is insufficient to settle the issue (cf. Catchpole, 186–190). Mark's time-note refers to the members of the sanhedrin reaching a decision, while Luke is thinking of the beginning of a meeting. It is possible that Mark has conflated the preliminary examination before Annas with the examination before the sanhedrin. If Luke is following Mk., however, his change of vocabulary (συνάγω (3:17; *et al.*) diff. Mk. συνέρχομαι) is inexplicable; this is especially the case with the description of those who came together. τὸ πρεσβυτήριον could mean 'the elders', as a constituent part of the sanhedrin, but it is more likely that it means the sanhedrin itself ('the assembly of the elders', RSV), and is followed in apposition by the names of two of the constituent groups (cf. Acts 22:5; G. Bornkamm, TDNT VI, 654); on this view, the elders are omitted from the list of groups, although Luke clearly knows that there are three groups (9:22; 20:1; Acts 4:5, 23; 6:12; *et al.*). The addition τοῦ λαοῦ gives a link with Mt. 27:1. The conjunction τε is omitted by Γ Δ *al*; TR; (*Diglot*); and replaced by καί before ἀρχιερεῖς in D. ἀπάγω is a regular term to use of prisoners on trial; cf. Mk. 14:53 diff. Lk. 22:54. συνέδριον can mean 'council' (Blinzler, 166–170), or, more probably, 'council chamber' (AG; E. Lohse, TDNT VII, 870 n. 73; Winter, 28 n. 4); on the

location (which was, in any case, not in the high priest's residence, unless a very informal gathering is in mind), cf. SB I, 997–1001; Winter, 27–29; Blinzler, 166–170.

(67) Luke omits details of the calling of witnesses and the evidence regarding Jesus' statements on the temple, diff. Mk. 14:56–61, and moves straight to the questions about Jesus' role. In Mk. the question is put by the high priest (Mk. 14:61) as the chairman of the assembly; here (cf. Mk. 14:55) the questions are put by the sanhedrin as a body. The connection (λέγοντες, qualifying the unstated subject of ἀπήγαγον, Klostermann, 220) is difficult; further Luke is unlikely to have changed Mark's definite subject to a vague one (Catchpole, 193f.); and hence it is probable that Luke here reflects a non-Marcan source. Jesus is asked first whether he is the Christ; εἰ may be conditional or interrogative, probably the former (Jn. 10:24; cf. BD 372¹; Schneider, 56), but the line between the two senses is fluid. For εἰπὸν ἡμῖν, diff. Mk., cf. Mt. 26:63, ἡμῖν εἴπῃς εἰ...; the similarity in wording between Lk., Mt. and Jn. 10:24 strongly suggests the existence of a non-Marcan tradition. The title of Messiah plays an important part in the passion narrative (23:2, 35, 39; 24:26, 46; cf. the use of 'the king of the Jews', 23:3); for earlier use in the Gospel see 2:11, 26; 3:15; 4:41; 9:20; 20:41. Since Jesus was clearly sent to Pilate as a messianic pretender (this is implied by the inscription over the cross), it is highly probable that the question of messiahship came up at the Jewish investigation; although Jesus himself had avoided the title, it is very likely that his conduct and teaching had led to popular suspicion that this was the role which he claimed. In Mk. the question is completed by the addition in apposition of 'the Son of God'. Since it is unlikely that the equation of Messiah and Son of God was made by Jews at this time, it is probable that Mark.has conflated the two distinct questions found in Lk. Jesus replies to the question by a refusal to say anything directly; the form of his answer resembles Je. 45:15 LXX: ἐὰν ἀναγγείλω σοι, οὐχὶ θανάτῳ με θανατώσεις, καὶ ἐὰν συμβουλεύσω σοι, οὐ μὴ ἀκούσῃς μου, but the content is quite different (cf. 20:5f., par. Mk. 11:31f.). The language is not Lucan, and the content is reminiscent of Jn. 3:12; 10:25f., so that use of a source is probable (Schneider, 114–116). Luke is not fond of ἐάν, and does not use οὐ μή of his own accord; nor does he use πιστεύω freely in the Gospel. Jesus has a different view of messiahship from the sanhedrin, and therefore, even if he were to say 'Yes' to their question, they would not accept what he said (cf. W. Grundmann, TDNT IX, 532f. and n. 274).

(68) If the meaning of the first part of Jesus' answer is clear enough, the second part is obscure. The whole verse is omitted by a Mcion; the opening δέ is replaced by καί in A W Γ Δ Θ f1 f13 pm; TR; Diglot. Jesus says that if he asks the sanhedrin a question, they will not answer. Schneider, 117, draws attention to the parallel with 20:1–8, and even argues that Matthew and Luke have used a non-Marcan tradition here (alongside Mk.) which may have formed part of a passion

narrative; Catchpole, 276–278, has shown the weakness of this view. Nevertheless, it remains possible that what Jesus has in mind here is the earlier refusal of the Jewish leaders to enter into dialogue with him and take up an honest position. They are thinking on a different level from Jesus, like Pilate in Jn. 18:33–38. After ἀποκριθῆτε (p⁷⁵ ℵ B L T bo), a few witnesses add μοι (Θ f1 sa) and many add μοι ἢ ἀπολύσητε (A D W Γ Δ Θ) f13 pl lat (sy); TR; Diglot. The longer text is regarded as possible by Creed, 278; Schneider, 118; see the discussion by J. Duplacy, 'Une variante méconnue du texte reçu: "... ΜΟΙ Η ΑΠΟΛΥΣΗΤΕ" (Lc. 22, 68)', in Blinzler, Aufsätze, 42–52. It could have been abbreviated to avoid the impression that Jesus wished to be set free. But it is illogical (why should release follow asking a question?), and its omission, if original, cannot be explained by homoioteleuton in Θ f1 (Metzger, 178).

(69) As in 9:20–22, a discussion about the Messiah is followed by a statement from Jesus about the Son of man. In Mk. the statement is that the members of the sanhedrin will see (cf. possibly Zc. 12:10) the Son of man sitting on the right hand of God (Ps. 110:1) and coming with the clouds of heaven (Dn. 7:13). Luke's version of the saying omits the reference to Dn. 7:13, and understands the exaltation of the Son of man to be about to take place (ἀπὸ τοῦ νῦν; cf. Mt. ἀπ' ἄρτι). The reference to seeing the Son of man is omitted and replaced by a periphrastic future ἔσται ... καθήμενος. The Marcan circumlocution for God, ἡ δύναμις, is clarified by the addition of τοῦ θεοῦ. The saying is generally regarded as being due to redaction of Mk. (Bultmann, 292; Grässer, 176 n. 3; Conzelmann, 107; see especially Catchpole, 157–159, 193; Grundmann, 420 n. 8; Tödt, 101–103; Higgins, 96); it is ascribed to a pre-Lucan tradition by E. Bammel ('Erwägungen zur Eschatologie Jesu', TU 88, 1964, 3–32, especially 24); C. Colpe, TDNT VIII, 435f. In favour of the former view are the facts that the saying interrupts the connection between vs. 67f. and 70 and that its form can be explained as Lucan redaction to avoid the unfulfilled prophecy of the sanhedrin seeing the Son of man and to stress the present exaltation of the Son of man (it is Stephen who sees the exalted Son of man; Acts 7:56). On this view, the question of the Son of man did not play any part in the Lucan tradition of the trial. But this view is not free from difficulty. The reference to the Son of man can be seen as an allusion to the heavenly court before which those who refuse to confess Jesus (v. 68) will have to stand; his role is the same as that implied in 12:8f., namely as counsel for the prosecution. Thus the saying can be tied to what precedes. A further point is the link between Lk. and Mt. in the introduction of ἀπὸ τοῦ νῦν/ἀπ' ἄρτι (cf. 22:18 with Mt. 26:29); it is hard to explain this similarity other than in terms of a common, non-Marcan tradition.

(70) With Catchpole, 274–278, this verse is to be attributed to Luke's source rather than to Lucan redaction of Mk. (Schneider, 122–126). For πάντες cf. Mk. 14:64. The connection made by οὖν is not clear. Catchpole, 197, regards it as a simple connective, rather than as a

logical connective (for this weak use he cites 3:7, 18; 7:31; 14:34; 20:17, 29, 44; 21:7). The sanhedrin goes on to ask Jesus whether he claims to be the Son of God. It could be that in the present form of the narrative Jesus is regarded as claiming to be the Son of man who sits alongside God, and the sanhedrin asks whether this implies that he is the Son of God. For Luke sitting on the right hand of God is tantamount to divine Sonship (cf. E. Schweizer, TDNT VIII, 381). It is unlikely that divine Sonship is regarded simply as a metaphorical attribute of the Messiah. In any case Jesus replies with ὑμεῖς λέγετε ὅτι ἐγώ εἰμι, a form of words similar to Mt. 26:64 σὺ εἶπας, diff. Mk. ἐγώ εἰμι (cf., however, Mk. 15:2; the variant σὺ εἶπας ὅτι ἐγώ εἰμι, in Mk. 14:62 Θ f13 565 700 pc arm Or, is probably secondary). The form of expression is not a direct affirmation; but it is certainly not a denial, and is best regarded as a grudging admission with the suggestion that the speaker would put it otherwise or that the questioners fail to understand exactly what they are asking; see BD 441³; D. Catchpole, 'The Answer of Jesus to Caiaphas (Matt. xxvi. 64)', NTS 17, 1970–71, 213–226; Vermes, 148f. Jesus refuses a direct affirmation of what men of discernment ought to be able to see (and believe) for themselves. For Catchpole, this is the decisive point in the trial, and is to be regarded as historical; the sanhedrin suspected that Jesus made claims to be the Son of God in an unusual sense and now had them confirmed, and this constituted the basis (or part of the basis) for the charge of blasphemy made in Mk. (Catchpole, 141–148).

(71) The scene closes with words reminiscent of Mk. The speakers remain the sanhedrin generally, diff. Mk. There is no further need of evidence; Luke has μαρτυρία, diff. Mk. μάρτυρες, since he has not brought any witnesses into play; the word means 'evidence'. Schneider, 129f., argues that Luke's omission of the witnesses is simply due to his following a different account of the trial. The final clause explains that Jesus' answer is taken as affirmative, and he stands self-condemned; for ἀπὸ τοῦ στόματος cf. 4:22; 11:54; 19:22. The political charge will be used to incriminate Jesus before Pilate; the theological claim drops into the background (but see Jn. 19:7).

vi. Jesus before Pilate 23:1–5

As soon as possible in the morning Jesus is taken before Pilate, who conveniently happens to be in Jerusalem (instead of the seat of Roman government, Caesarea) on account of the Passover festival. The Roman working day began extremely early, but if the Jewish proceedings took place very early, there is no need to suppose (with Sherwin-White, 45) that Luke has made it impossible for Pilate to be consulted at his normal working hours. With the defendant goes a list of charges against him, peculiar to Luke, which provide the basis for Pilate's interrogation of Jesus; the political danger caused by Jesus is strongly emphasised. We are not told on what grounds Pilate judged that Jesus was innocent; a more detailed examination, such as is described in Jn. 18:33–38, must be presupposed. When the Jews press their charges and mention Galilee as the scene of Jesus' activity, Pilate sees his cue.

V. 3 agrees closely with Mk. 15:2 and is clearly based on it; this makes the non-Marcan character of the surrounding narrative all the plainer and strongly suggests that Luke has used another source for his account of the proceedings before Pilate, although he has edited it in his own style. If Luke were drawing purely on Mk., it would be inexplicable why he had left this one verse unedited. The proceedings in Lk. are more logical; the account of Pilate's interrogation is preceded by a note of the charges against Jesus. There is a link between v.4 and Jn. 18:38 which confirms this view. See Taylor, *Passion*, 86f.; Grundmann, 421; *contra* Bultmann, 294; Finegan, *Überlieferung*, 27.

The scene stresses the innocence of Jesus, as attested by a Roman governor; the political charges against Jesus and his followers are empty. It is arguable that this stress on the political charges against Jesus, which turn out to be false, is due to Luke himself who has deliberately created the reference to 20:20f. in order that the reader may see for himself the falsity of the Jews' statement (cf. Conzelmann, 78). On this view, Luke would be simply elaborating Mk. But while Lucan editing is plainly visible, it appears probable that he was using other traditions or another source alongside Mk.

See Bultmann, 294; Finegan, *Überlieferung*, 27; Bailey, 64–77; Sherwin-White, 24–47; Blinzler, 245–283; Taylor, *Passion*, 86f.; Winter, *passim*.

(1) This verse corresponds to Mk. 15:1b, but the wording is entirely different and shows strong signs of Lucan redaction, so that it is impossible to tell whether Luke was following Mk. or another source. Luke omits reference to Jesus being bound, diff. Mk. ἀναστάς is Lucan (1:39; *et al.*); for ἅπαν τὸ πλῆθος cf. 8:37; 19:37; Acts 25:24; and for the use of πλῆθος to refer to the membership of the sanhedrin cf. Acts 23:7 (G. Delling, TDNT VI, 279). ἄγω is also used by Jn. 18:28, diff. Mk. ἀπήνεγκαν καὶ παρέδωκαν; it is not clear why Luke should have changed the wording here if he is following Mk. For ἄγω of being brought before legal authorities cf. 12:58; 21:12; Acts 9:21; 16:19; 25:12. On Pilate see 3:1; 13:1; Blinzler, 260–273; Winter, 70–89.

(2) Only Luke relates clearly the charges brought against Jesus. For ἤρξαντο (plural ad sensum) cf. 19:17. κατηγορέω (6:7) is used in Mk. 15:3f. The emphatic τοῦτον is probably derogatory, 'this fellow'. For διαστρέφω cf. 9:41 (par. Mt. 17:17); Acts 13:8, 10; 20:30; Phil. 2:15**, here with the meaning 'to mislead, pervert'; Jews can describe themselves as an ἔθνος (7:5); charges that Jesus was a sorcerer and deceiver of the people are found in Jewish tradition (SB II, 262f.). The second charge, forbidding the paying of taxes (φόρος, 20:22; Rom. 13:6f.**) to Caesar, stands in open contradiction to 20:20f., and indicates to the reader the falsity of the accusations. The third charge presumably rests on Jesus' equivocal answer before the sanhedrin.

χριστός is explained for gentile ears by βασιλεύς in apposition, 'Christ, a king'; the alternative translation, 'an anointed king' (F. C. Burkitt, *The Gospel History and its Transmission*, Edinburgh, 1911, 139) is less likely. After the first accusation the addition καὶ καταλύοντα τὸν νόμον καὶ τοὺς προφήτας is attested by it Mcion (cf. Mt. 5:17). Another Marcionite addition καὶ ἀποστρέφοντα τὰς γυναῖκας καὶ τὰ τέκνα is found after the second charge (so *Synopsis*; but see Metzger, 178f.), and this is found in an expanded form in c e. Neither addition has any claim to authenticity.

(3) Pilate's examination is confined to the single question: 'Are you the king of the Jews?', to which Jesus replies, 'The statement is yours.' The verse is based on Mk. with slight alterations par. Mt. (But one alteration disappears if we read ἐπηρώτησεν with A D L W Γ Δ Θ f1 f13 pm; TR; *Diglot*.) It is not clear whether the statement is to be regarded as a denial or whether Pilate simply refuses to take it seriously; probably the latter is to be understood. But the train of thought is not crystal clear, and it looks as though Luke has omitted something at this point, preferring to use Mark's wording.

(4) Having interrogated Jesus, presumably more fully than Luke recounts, Pilate reports his findings to the high priests (regarded as the instigators of the accusation) and the crowds; the latter appear suddenly from nowhere, but their presence is presupposed in all the Gospel accounts. Pilate finds no 'cause' or 'guilt' (αἴτιον, as noun; cf. 23:14, 22; Acts 19:40;** diff. Jn. 18:38; 19:4, 6 αἰτία, which Luke uses in Acts 13:28; *et al.*). The affirmation is repeated in 23:14, 22 for emphasis, and also appears three times in Jn. 18:38; 19:4, 6, a feature that suggests use of a common tradition. There is nothing corresponding in Mk. (except for Pilate's question in Mk. 15:14). It might be suspected of representing a Lucan emphasis, but its attestation in Jn. speaks against this (*pace* Bailey, 69–72), and it is probable that from an early stage the church stressed the point.

(5) In the development of the scene this verse corresponds to Mk. 15:3, where the dialogue with Jesus is followed by accusations from the Jews. οἱ δέ will refer primarily to the chief priests. ἐπισχύω, 'to grow strong, insist', occurs here only. ἀνασείω, 'to shake, stir up, incite', is used in Mk. 15:11** of the *chief priests* stirring up the crowds: has Luke with subtle irony used Mark's word? The word repeats the idea expressed in διαστρέφω, 23:2; cf. ἀποστρέφω, 23:14; Dodd, 117 n. 1, suggests that these words convey the sense of *hēsît*, used in Sanh. 43b to express the charge against Jesus, and that they contain a reminiscence of the actual language of the accusation. The rest of the phraseology appears to be Lucan. For καθ' ὅλης τῆς Ἰουδαίας cf. Acts 9:31; 10:37; and for ἄρχομαι ἀπό cf. 24:27, 47; Acts 1:22; 8:35; 10:37; Mt. 20:8; Jn. 8:9; 1. Pet. 4:17. The phrase is appended in an odd manner, and appears to be quasi-adverbial; it is Semitic, but is probably a Lucanism (Wilcox, 148–150; cf. Black, 299). In its context the whole phrase expresses how

Jesus' influence has spread the length of Judaea, and at the same time it provides Pilate with his cue for sending Jesus to Herod Antipas.

vii. Jesus before Herod 23:6–12

Pilate availed himself of the fact that Jesus came from Galilee to send him to Herod Antipas, who was also conveniently present in Jerusalem at Passover time, so that he might offer an opinion on him; it is unlikely that Pilate was transferring the case from his own court. The procedure served to satisfy the curiosity of Herod who was already keen to see Jesus (cf. 9:9, which prepares for this scene), but to such a person, merely desirous of seeing some miraculous happenings, Jesus had nothing to show or to say. There was nothing that Herod could regard as evidence against Jesus, which would substantiate the accusations made by the Jewish leaders (cf. 23:15). So he satisfied his disappointed feelings by indulging in horseplay at the expense of Jesus, and then sent him back to Herod. If the event did nothing else, it at least made two rogues (as Christians regarded them) into allies. From the Christian point of view, the incident served to provide a second official witness to the innocence of Jesus (cf. Dt. 19:15; Grundmann, 424). At the same time, it could be regarded as a fulfilment of the prophecy in Ps. 2:1f., according to which the kings and rulers of the world plotted together against the Lord's anointed (Acts 4:25–28).

The fact that the story is unknown to the other Evangelists has not unnaturally led to the suspicion that it is a Lucan creation and, in any case, unhistorical. Thus it has been argued that it reflects the motif found in Acts 4:25–28 where Ps. 2 is seen to be fulfilled in the case of Jesus (Dibelius*; Bultmann, 294; Klostermann, 221; Dodd, 117f.). Further arguments against the historicity of the story are assembled by Creed, 280, who claims that it is unlikely that Pilate would have sent a prisoner within his own jurisdiction to Herod; that there is a discrepancy between 23:10 and 15 as to whether the Jewish leaders went to Herod; and that the mockery by Herod's soldiers is reminiscent of that by Pilate's men in Mk. 15:16f. (which Luke omits). These arguments are joined together by Finegan, *Überlieferung*, 27–29, in an attempt to show that Luke created the incident.

The historicity of the incident has been defended by A. W. Verrall* and Hoehner*. It is noted that Pilate was not transferring an unwelcome prisoner, but probably seeking the advice of an expert in Jewish affairs (cf. how Festus consulted Herod Agrippa II in the case of Paul; Klostermann, 223; Grundmann, 424). It is not at all clear that 23:15 excludes the possibility of the Jewish leaders having gone to Herod, and in any case it is probable that a small group of them would have gone to Herod in order that their case might not be lost by default (Easton, *ad loc.*). The mockery is the kind of event that could easily have happened more than once, and there is considerable difference in detail from Mk. 15:16f. Finally, in view of the fact that Herod and Pilate both pronounced Jesus innocent, it is doubtful whether Ps. 2:1f. could have given rise to the incident; the accents in Lk. 23 and Acts 4 are somewhat different (cf. Hoehner, 228–230), and the Psalm is too vague to have been the basis of the story (Benoit, *Passion*, 144–146). The language of the section is markedly Lucan (Taylor, *Passion*, 87), and Taylor concludes that there is little evidence to suggest the use of a source. But Luke appears to have had special knowledge of Herod's court (cf. 8:3 note), and the origin of the story is hard to explain on any other hypothesis than that it reflects a historical episode told in the Lucan manner (cf. Blinzler, 284–293; Sherwin-White, 28–32).

See A. W. Verrall, 'Christ before Herod', JTS 10, 1908–09, 321–353; Dibelius, *Botschaft* I, 278–292 (originally as 'Herodes und Pilatus', ZNW 16, 1915, 113–126); Bultmann, 294; Sherwin-White, 28–32; Benoit, *Passion*, 144f.; Blinzler, 284–300; Hoehner, 224–250.

(6) Luke again links the incident with what precedes by ἀκούσας (p⁷⁵ ℵ B *pc*; other MSS add (τήν, D sa) Γαλιλαίαν (A W Γ Δ Θ f1 f13 *pl*; TR; *Diglot*), probably by way of explanation). For εἰ cf. 6:7; *et al.* ὁ ἄνθρωπος is no doubt derogatory (cf. Jn. 19:5). Jesus was regarded as a Galilean because of his upbringing there, and the fact that it was the main scene of his ministry.

(7) ἐπιγνούς suggests that Pilate came to realise a fact that could be useful to him in his present extremity. If Jesus was a Galilean, then he was under the political jurisdiction (ἐξουσία, 4:6) of Herod Antipas. So he seized the opportunity to send Jesus to him. ἀναπέμπω can be used in a technical sense (cf. Latin *remitto*), 'to send to a higher authority' (Acts 25:21). But Herod was not a higher authority, and the same verb is used of Herod returning Jesus to Pilate in v. 11; the usage is, therefore, non-technical. The procedure itself probably does not reflect the later custom of trying a person in his own province rather than in the province where the crime was committed (cf. Sherwin-White, 28–31), and it is more likely that Pilate wanted a Jewish opinion on the matter (cf. 23:15 – 'not even Herod'), or simply to find a way out of a difficulty that he could not solve. Whether he acted in order to achieve a reconciliation with Herod cannot be determined. The presence of Herod in Jerusalem at this time, sc. during the Passover, is likely enough (cf. Acts 12:4, 19); and he would probably have stayed in the Hasmonaean palace just west of the temple (cf. Jos. Bel. 2:344; Hoehner, 239 n. 3; Benoit, *Passion*, 144).

(8) Luke portrays Herod's feeling on seeing Jesus as great satisfaction (λίαν*, 'greatly' – not taken over by Lk. from Mk. 1:35; 6:51; 9:3; 16:2). He had been anxious to see him for a long time (for χρόνοι ἱκανοί cf. 20:9), as 9:9 indicates; ἰδεῖν may have the sense 'to learn to know, get to know' (AG s.v.). The rumours flying around Galilee had reached his ears (πολλά is added after ἀκούειν by A W Γ Δ f13 *pm*; TR; *Diglot*), and Herod continued to hope that he might see an example of the miracles of which he had heard (for σημεῖον cf. 11:16, 29; and for the use of γίνομαι

cf. Acts 2:43; 4:16, 22, 30; 5:12; 8:13; 14:3; the phraseology is thus Lucan).

(9) So Herod conducted a lengthy interrogation of Jesus; note the use of the imperfect (contrast v. 6). But Jesus made no reply to him, a motif also found in Mk. 14:61 par. Mt. 26:63; Mk. 15:4f. par. Mt. 27:12, 14; Jn. 19:9. The motif has been thought to reflect Is. 53:7 (J. Jeremias, TDNT V, 713). It is not, however, historical invention based on the prophecy, since, as Hooker, 87–89, has demonstrated, Jesus is consistently presented in all the Gospels as one who 'is prepared to answer an honest question but ignores partisan assertions'. Probably the Evangelists saw in Jesus' silence a fulfilment of Is. 53:7. Grundmann, 425, cites the Mithras Liturgy 6:42 to show that to Hellenists silence was a symbol of God, but it is less likely that this thought is present here. F. C. Burkitt, *Evangelion da Mepharreshe*, Cambridge, 1904, II, 303, drew attention to the additions '*quasi non audiens*' in c and 'as if he were not there' in sy^c (cf. Plummer, 522).

(10) Vs. 10–12 are omitted by sy^s, followed by Wellhausen, 129f., who thus avoided the apparent contradiction with v. 15; less drastically, J. Weiss, 519, omitted v. 10 for the same reason. But the language is Lucan, the verses are necessary for the sense, and the external evidence for omission is wretched (cf. Creed, 282). The present verse is parallel to Mk. 15:3 (but vs. 8f. are parallel to Mk. 15:4, thus giving an alteration in order); the language, however, is Lucan. For the use of the pluperfect εἱστήκα cf. 23:35, 49; Acts 9:7; Rev. 7:11; Mt. 12:46; 13:2. The mention of the scribes is surprising (diff. Mk. 15:3; Mt. 27:12), but in 22:66 they appear along with the high priests as the main actors against Jesus. εὐτόνως, 'powerfully, vehemently', reappears in Acts 18:28**. The purpose of the verse is to show that both Herod's own interrogation of Jesus and the accusations brought against him did not lead Herod to condemn Jesus, but merely to despise him and mock him; the charges were not to be taken seriously. The verse has thus a definite purpose in the scene, and is not parenthetical or superfluous.

(11) Herod's decision, then, was that Jesus was fit only for contempt; for ἐξουθενέω cf. 18:9; Acts 4:11 and see Jesus' prophecy in Mk. 9:12. καὶ ὁ Ἡρῴδης is read by p⁷⁵ ℵ L T X f13 *al* a d; (UBS); *Diglot*; καὶ ὁ is omitted by W *pc*; and καί is omitted by A B D Γ Δ Θ f1 *pm* lat; TR. See Metzger, 179, who observes that the difficulty of understanding the force of καί could be an argument in favour of its originality. στράτευμα, 'army, detachment' (Acts 23:10, 27; Rev. 19:19), is used in the plural to mean 'troops' (Mt. 22:7; Rev. 9:16**); only a small group of men, probably the tetrarch's bodyguard, is meant (cf. O. Bauernfeind, TDNT VII, 709 n. 34; Hoehner, 241 n. 4). The use of ἐμπαίζω is reminiscent of the prophecy in 18:32; cf. 22:63; 23:36; Mk. 15:20. Part of the mockery consists in dressing up Jesus (for περιβάλλω cf. 12:27; the object αὐτόν is added in most MSS; TR; *Diglot* (αὐτῷ in R S Γ 69 *pc*), but omitted by p⁷⁵ ℵ B *pc*). ἐσθής is 'clothing' (24:4; Acts 1:10 (on

which see AG s.v.; BD 47⁴); 10:30; 12:21; Jas. 2:2f.**). λαμπρός is 'bright, shining, radiant', and is used of the clothing of a wealthy man (Jas. 2:2f.) or of an angel (Acts 10:30); it describes the bright garments of linen worn by heavenly beings in Rev. 15:6; 19:8. The colour is not mentioned, but this has not prevented considerable debate on the matter. Many commentators think that a white mantle is meant: cf. *candidus* (a); *albus* (f vg) as the sign of a candidate for office (with doubt, A. Oepke, TDNT IV, 17; Grundmann, 425) or as the garb of a king (Jos. Ant. 8:186). Others prefer purple, as in Mk. 15:17; Jn. 19:2 at the mocking by Pilate's soldiers (Klostermann, 223; Creed, 282, suggests that Luke deliberately avoided a reference to Jesus aping the imperial purple). There is no way of deciding (cf. Blinzler, 290 n. 18). It may be assumed that the garment was indeed put upon Jesus and not upon Herod himself (*contra* Bornhäuser, *Death*, 143f.). The merit of this suggestion is that it explains why the detail about the robe follows the mockery (contrast Mk. 15:17–20); but in fact περιβαλών is simply epexegetic of the preceding participles. The whole scene is recorded with the minimum of detail, and it is hardly likely that Luke has abbreviated the more colourful description in Mk. 15:17–20.

(12) Having failed to come to any decision, Herod sent back Jesus to Pilate. The incident served to bring them together as friends after an earlier period of enmity. For ἐν αὐτῇ τῇ ἡμέρᾳ cf. 2:58 note. προϋπάρχω, 'to exist before', takes a participle, and is Lucan (Acts 8:9**; BD 414⁴). For ἔχθρα, 'enmity', cf. Rom. 8:7; Gal. 5:20; Eph. 2:15f.; Jas. 4:4**. αὐτούς is used as an equivalent to ἀλλήλους (BD 287); it is tantamount to ἑαυτούς (read by A W Γ Δ Θ f1 f13 *pl*; TR; *Diglot*); editors are uncertain whether to print it with a rough or smooth breathing (but the latter prevails in recent discussions (cf. Metzger, 615f.). The cause of the enmity is not known; J. Blinzler (article cited at 13:1–9 note) thinks that Pilate's conduct reported in 13:1 could have alienated Herod (cf. Hoehner, 175f., who also thinks that the episode of the gilded shields (Philo, Leg. 299–305), which was the object of an appeal to Tiberius by four sons of Herod the Great, is relevant, ibid., 176–183). It is unlikely that the motif of reconciliation arose from Ps. 2:2 (so Grundmann, 425), and hence it may well be historical.

viii. Jesus sentenced to die 23:13–25

The final trial scene falls into three parts. The first (vs. 13–16) is in effect the conclusion to the examination by Herod. Pilate again calls together the Jews and their leaders to inform them officially of Herod's verdict, which confirms his own belief that Jesus is innocent of their charges, and proposes to let Jesus off with no more than a scourging. In the second part (vs. (17) 18–23) the Jews are the main actors, repeating their demands for the execution of Jesus and asking that, if Pilate is going to show mercy to anybody, it should be to Barabbas. For the first time the word 'crucify' appears. Pilate's protestations that Jesus is innocent fall on deaf ears. In the third part of the scene (vs. 24f.) Pilate bows to the wishes of the Jews and delivers sentence. The total impression made by the scene is of the condemnation of an innocent man, thrown into stronger relief by the acquittal of a guilty man. It is the will of the Jews which prevails, Pilate weakly complying with their desire.

The literary origin of the scene is difficult to assess. Vs. 13–16 are closely linked with the preceding scene and could be regarded as its conclusion. If so, the whole of vs. 6–16 could be an insertion into a Marcan context. But the position is not quite so simple. Only v. 15 refers to Herod, and v. 14 contains the second of Pilate's three protestations of Jesus' innocence. If v. 17 is not part of Luke's text, the mention of Barabbas in v. 18 is unmotivated, and it is hard to regard this section as being a remodelling of Mk. (cf. Rengstorf, 256) although vs. 20–22 are close to Mk. in substance. On the whole it seems more likely that Luke is following a parallel source and conflating it with Mk.; as a result traces of his editing are frequent. Rengstorf, 257, and Grundmann, 426f., support this conclusion by drawing attention to various contacts with Jn. which may reflect the use of a common tradition (but see Bailey, 64–77, for the view that John is here dependent on Lk.).

See Rengstorf, 256f.; Bailey, 64–77; Blinzler, 201–256; Winter, 131–143; Taylor, *Passion*, 88f.

(13) After the return of Jesus Pilate calls together ($\sigma\upsilon\gamma\kappa\alpha\lambda\acute{\epsilon}\omega$, 9:1; *et al.*) the Jews in order that he may deliver his verdict; it is the reassembling of a meeting after a brief adjournment. The mention of 'the rulers' ($\check{\alpha}\rho\chi\omega\nu$, 8:41; cf. especially 23:35; 24:20; Acts 3:17; 4:5, 8, 26; 13:27) alongside the high priests is odd, and presumably the phrase means in effect 'the other Jewish leaders' (cf. 24:20). The people are here associated with their leaders. Since elsewhere in Lk. the people are regarded as friendly to Jesus or at least neutral, their presence here is strange. Luke may be following the tradition in Mk. 15:8–15 that the crowds demanded the release of Barabbas and the condemnation of Jesus. G. Rau, 'Das Volk in der lukanischen Passionsgeschichte', ZNW 56, 1965, 41–51, adopts the view (suggested by P. Winter) that $\tau o\tilde{\upsilon}$ $\lambda\alpha o\tilde{\upsilon}$ should be read for $\kappa\alpha\grave{\iota}$ $\tau\grave{o}\nu$ $\lambda\alpha\acute{o}\nu$, but this suggestion entirely lacks textual support, and is opposed by the presentation in 23:4. 18. More plausibly Grundmann, 425, suggests that the $\lambda\alpha\acute{o}\varsigma$ are here as witnesses to Pilate's statement of Jesus' innocence.

(14) Pilate's statement is designed to take the heat out of the situation; $\pi\rho o\sigma\phi\acute{\epsilon}\rho\omega$, used of a person, is perhaps meant to be derogatory; the same may be true of $\acute{o}$ $\check{\alpha}\nu\theta\rho\omega\pi o\varsigma$ $o\tilde{\upsilon}\tau o\varsigma$ (cf. 14:30) but 23:14b and 47 are against this view, and the usage may reflect legal terminology. $\acute{\omega}\varsigma$ is 'on the pretext that' (16:1; cf. BD 425³). On $\grave{\alpha}\pi o\sigma\tau\rho\acute{\epsilon}\phi\omega$, 'to turn away, mislead' (23:2 v.l.; Acts 3:26; 20:30 v.l.), see 23:2, 5 notes; the basic element in the charge, that of causing a public disturbance and possible revolt, is repeated. But public examination has shown the emptiness of

the charges. For ἀνακρίνω*, 'to question, examine', see Acts 4:9; 12:19; et al. For οὐθέν (p⁷⁵ ℵ B 0124 pc; cf. 22:35) οὐδέν is read by rell; TR; Diglot, probably by assimilation to v. 15. For the language cf. Acts 23:9; 26:31f., which suggests that standard legal phraseology is being employed. For αἴτιον cf. 23:4; ὧν is abbreviated from τούτων ὧν.

(15) To Pilate's own opinion can be added that of Herod also: the force of οὐδέ may be 'not even Herod – whose opinion as a Jewish ruler is weightier than mine'. The text is confused at this point, the best attested wording being ἀνέπεμψεν γὰρ αὐτὸν πρὸς ἡμᾶς (ὑμᾶς f13) (p⁷⁵ ℵ B K L Θ aur f sa bo), with the force: Herod has sent him back to us without finding him guilty. Other authorities have ἀνέπεμψα γὰρ ὑμᾶς πρὸς αὐτόν (A D W Γ Δ f1 pm lat; TR) or ἀνέπεμψα γὰρ αὐτὸν πρὸς αὐτόν (274 syᶜ ˢ ᵖ arm geo; Wellhausen, 131f.; Easton 344). These readings are clarifications, perhaps designed to avoid a possible contradiction with v. 10, where the Jews accompany Jesus to Herod. See Metzger, 179. The καὶ ἰδού construction is repeated from v. 14; for the rest of the verse cf. Acts 25:11, 25. αὐτῷ is dative of the agent, a Classical Greek construction with the perfect passive (MH II, 459; cf. BD 191).

(16) Having established that Jesus is innocent, Pilate proposes to let him go, but at the same time to appease the Jews and to punish Jesus for his nuisance-value by submitting him to a scourging (παιδεύω; similarly in 23:22; elsewhere, 'to bring up, educate', Acts 7:22; 22:3; 'to chasten', 1 Cor. 11:32; et al. For the usage here cf. 1 Ki. 12:11, 14; 2 Ch. 10:11, 14; it arises from the fact that the education of children was understood to include whipping as well as instruction, G. Bertram, TDNT V, 621). The word may indicate a less severe punishment than φραγελλόω, which is used in Mk. 15:15 of the scourging which was a preliminary to crucifixion; here an alternative to crucifixion is in mind (cf. John 19:1; Sherwin-White, 27f., adduces Acts 16:22–28; 22:24). A linguistic reminiscence of Is. 53:5 (Stuhlmueller, 161) is not very likely.

(17) This verse is omitted by p⁷⁵ A B L T pc a sa boᵖᵗ and most modern editions of the text; it is included at this point by all other authorities (but with variant wording in Θ Ψ al) except D d syᶜ ˢ eth which include the variant found in Θ at the end of v. 19. The verse is accepted by Diglot, and is defended by Kilpatrick, 195, as having been omitted by homoeoarcton with v. 18. The use of ἀνάγκην εἶχεν could be regarded as Lucan on the basis of 14:18, and Black, 228, thinks ἀνάγκη represents a Hebrew legal term, the 'law' of the feast; but this is a sufficiently common phrase (1 Cor. 7:37; Heb. 7:27; Jude 3) to make this a weak argument. The external evidence for omission is strong, and the text reads more smoothly if it is omitted, although admittedly the crowd's motivation in asking for the release of Barabbas then becomes unclear. The verse is probably a scribal addition, based on Mt. 27:15 and Mk. 15:6 (see Metzger, 179f.). The omission of the verse makes derivation of Luke's account direct from Mk. the less likely.

(18) The response of the Jews to Pilate's suggestion of releasing Jesus is uproar; Luke omits Mark's note that the crowd were instigated by the high priests and leaves it unclear who is responsible for the shouts. ἀνέκραγον is a second aorist form (Classical) found only here (BD 75); for the verb cf. 4:33; 8:28*. αἴρω, 'to take away', has here the sense 'to do away with, to kill', as in Jn. 19:15; cf. Acts 21:36; 2:22, of Paul; there may be a reminiscence for Luke of Is. 53:8 (quoted in Acts 8:33) – so Wilcox, 67f., but he overlooks the usage in Jn. 19:15 when he suggests that the terminology has been drawn by Luke from the LXX. For Βαραββᾶς, literally 'son of the father', see Mk. 15:7, 11, 15. The request for his release is no doubt to be understood in the light of Mark's explanation (Mk. 15:6; cf. Mt. 27:15; Jn. 18:39) that it was customary for a prisoner to be given an amnesty at the feast of the Passover. Such an act would fall within the general competence of a Roman governor and there is good reason to suppose that it was practised in Palestine (Blinzler, 317–320, following C. B. Chavel, 'The Releasing of a Prisoner on the Eve of Passover in Ancient Jerusalem', JBL 60, 1941, 273–278; see, however, Jeremias, *Words*, 73; Winter's argument from silence (132–134) is not a convincing objection). Since, however, Jesus' release should have followed automatically after the declaration of his innocence, it is hard to see why the granting of such an amnesty should have come into the picture, since the latter was a remission of a guilty person from his deserved penalty. Presumably Pilate was trying to appease the Jews, who claimed that Jesus was guilty, by trying to get them to apply this act of mercy to a prisoner who deserved release in any case. Luke's narrative presupposes that the Jews understood Pilate's intention to release Jesus (v. 16) in terms of such an amnesty; on this assumption, they asked that the amnesty be given to Barabbas instead.

(19) Luke now describes (belatedly, compared with Mk. 15:7) who Barabbas was. For ὅστις, cf. Mk. 15:7. στάσις is 'uprising, riot, revolt' (23:25; Acts 19:40; Mk. 15:7). There is no other record of this particular riot in Jerusalem, which would have been too trivial to merit mention in the history books. Luke alone states that it took place ἐν τῇ πόλει. βάλλω is often used of imprisonment (23:25; Jn. 3:24; Mt. 5:25; Acts 16:23, 24, 37; Rev. 2:10). ἐν is used for εἰς.

(20) Pilate's further appeal to the people corresponds to Mk. 15:12. Luke again stresses his desire (θέλων...; cf. 10:29; 23:8) to release Jesus, and gives the impression that he tells the people what he intends to do, rather than asks their advice. But his wishes and intentions are thwarted.

(21) For ἐπιφωνέω, cf. 21:34; 12:22; Acts 22:24**. Here the sense is 'to cry out against (*not* again)'; the imperfect expresses duration. For the doubling of σταύρου cf. Jn. 19:6; the use of the present imperative is peculiar to Luke at this point, and is odd if he is following Mk. or Jn.

(22) The narrative reaches its climax as Luke emphasises the third attempt of Pilate to establish the innocence of Jesus. He follows the

wording of Mark with the rhetorical question, 'What evil has he done?' and then repeats the declaration in v. 15 (slightly altered in wording) and the intention expressed in v. 16. The innocence of Jesus could not be more firmly underlined.

(23) It is, therefore, the will of the Jews, not of Pilate, which leads to the sentence. They go on pressing (ἐπίκειμαι; cf. 5:1) their demand at the top of their voices (4:33) that Jesus be crucified, and their cries win the day. For κατισχύω cf. 21:36; Mt. 16:18. After αὐτῶν (p⁷⁵ ℵ B lat sa boᵖᵗ) καὶ τῶν ἀρχιερέων is added by rell; TR; Diglot; this may be a copyist's addition to make clear who was responsible for the sentence on Jesus (Metzger, 180). The verse as a whole has undergone Lucan editing, perhaps in order to give the sense of climax.

(24) Pilate comes to his decision; ἐπικρίνω**, 'to decide, determine', is used here only (reflecting Luke's liking for ἐπι- compounds). He agrees that the request of the Jews should be granted (αἴτημα, Phil. 4:6; 1 Jn. 5:15**). Luke avoids Mark's statement that he gave in to the crowds by doing them a favour.

(25) Thus he released Barabbas (the indirect object αὐτοῖς is read by K M f1 f13 al lat; Diglot), despite the fact that he was lying in prison (βεβλημένος, perfect; contrast the aorist participle, 23:19, for his initial commitment to prison) because of rioting and murder; but as for Jesus (note the careful contrast, diff. Mk.) he handed him over to their will. For the use of παραδίδωμι (Mk. 15:15) cf. Is. 53:6, 12. In Mk. the indirect object of παρέδωκεν is apparently the soldiers who carry out the crucifixion. In Lk. αὐτῶν appears to refer rather to the Jews (cf. Winter, 79), so that it is made clear that it is by their will, not Pilate's, that Jesus is crucified. The formulation is probably Lucan, and it is not clear how far he may be reflecting a source other than Mk.

c. The Crucifixion of Jesus (23:26–49)

Luke's account of the death of Jesus is similar in general structure to that in Mk., but it has a distinctive content. In the preliminary section (vs. 26–31) the customary mourning of the women of Jerusalem for a victim on his way to execution is the occasion for a final prophecy by Jesus regarding the fate of Jerusalem. The details of the execution (vs. 32–38) appear in a different order from that in Mk. with greater stress being laid on the two other victims alongside Jesus; the crowds no longer mock Jesus; and the description of the inscription over the cross is almost an after-thought. There is a new conversation between Jesus and the two criminals (vs. 39–43) which culminates in Jesus' promise of a place in paradise to one of them. Finally (vs. 44–49), the account of Jesus' end accentuates his final prayer of trust in God, the centurion's belief in his innocence, the sorrow of the people (who do not share in the mocking) and the witness of his own followers.

In this version of the story we may see an accent on the way in which Jesus died as a martyr, innocent of the charges against him, trusting to the end in God, and assured of his own place in paradise. The whole scene vindicates the claim that he is the Messiah of God.

Lucan theology is thus expressed in the story, but, as we have seen earlier, it is probable that it reflects the use of non-Marcan source material rather than that it is his entirely his own composition.

i. The Way to the Cross 23:26–31

Luke passes over the mockery of Jesus by Pilate's soldiers (Mk. 15:16–20), since he has already recorded a similar incident in respect of Herod's soldiers; it may be the case that he wished to exonerate the Romans of such conduct. He is thus able to proceed straight from the sentence to the crucifixion. It can be argued that Luke leaves it unclear who actually carries out the sentence (v. 26 has an indefinite subject), but since crucifixion was known to be a Roman punishment, carried out by soldiers, it is unlikely that Luke's readers would have been left in uncertainty. Luke includes the incident of Simon of Cyrene (from Mk.) who may have been seen by him as a picture of the ideal disciple; it is less likely that a deliberate contrast is intended with the weeping women (but so Ellis, 266). These latter are warned by Jesus that they have better cause to weep for themselves than for his fate. For the time will come when they will wish that they had never had children and will long for the mountains to cover them and hide them from the grim fate that is in store for them. For if this is how the innocent suffer, what will be the fate of guilty Jerusalem?

The passage falls into the pattern of warnings to Jerusalem found earlier in the Gospel (11:49–51; 13:1–5, 34f.; 19:41–44; 21:20–24). Finegan, *Überlieferung*, holds that Luke composed the section using 21:23 and Ho. 10:8 as a basis. Although the vocabulary shows Lucan editing, there are also pre-Lucan features (Taylor, *Passion*, 89f.). Bultmann, 37, 121f., holds that vs. 29–31 are a Christian prophecy put on the lips of Jesus, with v. 28 constructed as an introduction; the prophecy is old and shows signs of composition in Aramaic. The whole section thus forms a biographical apophthegm. W. Käser* argues that vs. 27f., 31 form the original unit, to which vs. 29–30 have been added as an explanation of the enigmatic saying, apparently by Luke; Luke uses the novel blessing form to express yet again the woe ahead for Jerusalem (cf. 21:23), and makes use of a motif from Is. 54:1, so that the saying contrasts the fleshly Israel (the daughters of Jerusalem) with the spiritual Israel (the apparently unfruitful women; cf. Gal. 4:27). This interpretation of the text reads back into it the later Christian interpretation found in 2 Clem. 2:1–3; Justin Apol. 1:53; which is probably based on Gal. 4:27, and is too allusive to be convincing. Nor is it necessary to separate vs. 29f. off from the rest of the section; Käser's main argument is that the sort of reflection offered in vs. 29f. is less primitive than the simple unreflected statement in v. 28, and that v. 28 is complete in itself, but this is quite unconvincing.

See Bultmann, 37f., 121f.; Finegan, *Überlieferung*, 30f.; Manson, *Sayings*, 342f.; W. Käser, 'Exegetische und theologische Erwägungen zur Seligpreisung der Kinderlosen, Lc 23:29b', ZNW 54, 1963, 240–254; Taylor, *Passion*, 89f.; Schenk, 86–93.

(26) ὡς has the sense 'while', rather than 'when' (12:58; 24:32). Luke uses ἀπάγω par. Mt. diff. Mk. The subject is undefined, and could logically be the Jews (αὐτῶν, v. 25); but the later reference to the soldiers makes the identity of the actors clear (Lagrange, 584), and Luke alters subjects without clear pointers sufficiently often (e.g. 23:32/33) to make it probable that he meant the soldiers here. The inconcinnity may have arisen as a result of his omission of the mockery by the soldiers. Luke's choice of ἐπιλαμβάνομαι (9:47; *et al.*), diff. Mk. ἀγγαρεύω, has also been thought to be part of an attempt to disguise the activity of the Romans who alone had power to impress men for service in this way; but more probably it reflects Luke's dislike of a foreign word. ἐπιλαμβάνομαι normally takes the genitive, and this case is read in many MSS (so BD 170²) instead of the accusative which might (perhaps less plausibly) be regarded as due to scribal assimilation to Mk. The order Σίμωνά τινα (diff. Mk.) is Lucan (Rehkopf 84 n.). Luke preserves the detail that Simon was from Cyrene (Κυρηναῖος), possibly because he knows of Cyrenians in the early history of the church (Acts 6:9; 11:20; 13:1), but he omits Mark's details about his family connections which would have meant nothing to his readers. The fact that Simon was coming into Jerusalem from the country conveys no information regarding what day of the week it was. It was the normal custom for condemned men to carry their own cross (Plutarch, De Ser. Num. Vind. 554a, cited by Creed, 285). It must therefore be assumed that Jesus was breaking down under the weight, so that the soldiers found it necessary to force Simon to aid him. For ἐπιτίθημι in this sense cf. Gn. 22:6. φέρειν is epexegetic. For ὄπισθεν cf. 8:44. An allusion to Jesus' saying about disciples bearing the cross (9:23, 14:27), of which Simon provides a literal example, is probably present, but it is remarkable that Luke has altered the wording from αἴρω (9:23 par. Mk. 8:34; so Mk. 15:20) to φέρω, and uses ὄπισθεν diff. ὀπίσω (9:23; 14:27). Nothing more than literary variation may be at work.

(27) Jesus (αὐτῷ, but Rehkopf, 84 n. 3, observes that grammatically Simon could be meant) was followed by a large crowd of the people (6:17) who here appear in the role of sympathisers rather than mockers. This is demonstrated by the action of the women among them (καὶ γυναικῶν is 'including women') who (αἵ; αἳ καί is read by C³ W Γ Δ Θ f1 f13 *pm*; TR; *Diglot*) bewailed (8:52) and lamented (7:32 par Mt. 11:17; Jn. 16:20**) him. The presence of crowds at an execution out of curiosity was natural (Lucian, Mort. Pereg. 34; Ps.-Quintilian, Declam. 274; cf. Klostermann, 227), and the presence of mourning women was

likewise commonplace (Bultmann, 37 n. 3; SB II, 263f.). The latter action was one of religious merit (SB IV:1, 582–590), and is inherently probable historically (Benoit, *Passion*, 167).

(28) Jesus' attention was arrested by the women and he turned (στραφείς; 7:9; *et al.*) to address them. Before Ἰησοῦς the article is read by A C D W Θ f1 f13 *pm*; TR; *Diglot*. The women are not his own followers from Galilee, but local women who turned out to witness executions and provide opiates for the condemned men (Sanh. 43a; SB I, 1037), and so they are addressed as Jerusalemites, literally 'daughters of Jerusalem' (cf. Is. 3:16; Ct. 1:5; also 2 Sa. 1:24; Zc. 9:9). Jesus' words probably have the force, 'Do not weep so much for me as for yourselves and your children' (cf. 10:20 note for this idiom, which is Semitic; Stuhlmueller, 161). The thought is of the fate of both the women and above all their children, the fighting men who would especially suffer in time of war. The motif has several parallels in Greek and Hellenistic thought. Creed cites Sophocles, Philoct., 339f., but closer is Seneca, Agamemnon, 659–61 ('*cohibete lacrimas, omne quas tempus petet, Troades, et ipsae vestra lamentabili lugete gemitu funera*', quoted by Grundmann, 429).

(29) The reason why the women should reserve their tears for another occasion is given. A period of time is coming (cf. 5:35; *et al.* for this phrase) when people will reflect that it would be better not to have had children than to see their sufferings. The saying has the form of a blessing, which W. Käser*, 245, thinks is Luke's way of avoiding repetition of the 'woe' form in 21:23; it is more likely that the phraseology comes from the same type of thinking. Käser also finds reflection of Is. 54:1, but if so the meaning is considerably changed. Barrenness was normally counted a reproach (cf. 1:25; for στεῖρα cf. 1:7, 36; Gal. 4:27). Here it is the ground for a blessing, not because it will be taken away (Is. 54:1), but because of the dreadful situation ahead in which normal values will be reversed. The thought is emphasised by repetition in the manner of 11:27; τρέφω (4:16) here means 'to nurse, nourish'. For the thought cf. Euripides, Androm. 395; Seneca, Controv. 2:5:2; Apuleius, Apoll. 85; Ovid, Metam. 13:464).

(30) A second saying follows, parallel in construction to v. 29, in which the terrible situation ahead is further outlined. For τότε ἄρξονται cf. 13:26. This saying is based on Ho. 10:8 LXX (ἐροῦσιν τοῖς ὄρεσιν, Καλύψατε ἡμᾶς, καὶ τοῖς βουνοῖς, Πέσατε ἐφ' ἡμᾶς; so B; but A interchanges καλύψατε and πέσατε ἐφ', as in Lk. and Rev. 6:16; Holtz, 27–29, concludes that Luke used an LXX text similar to A). For the vocabulary cf. 3:5 (LXX). πέσετε is attested by p⁷⁵ ℵ* A B D Γ Θ *pm*; TR, but the first aorist ending -ατε is read by *rell*; *Synopsis*; *Diglot*; in support of the former reading see MH II, 209. For the thought see Homer, Il. 17:416; Virgil, Aen. 12:892f. Most commentators interpret the saying as a wish for an earthquake or similar convulsion to put people out of their misery (cf. Rev. 9:6; W. Foerster, TDNT V, 483 n. 96),

but it could also be a desire simply to be hidden from the impending catastrophe, as in Rev. 6:15f.

(31) This saying is not a continuation of the cry of the women, but Jesus' comment justifying the point which he has just made. The future outlook is bleak because, if this is what men (possibly God, Zerwick, 2) do to a green tree (ὑγρός**, 'moist, pliant', hence 'green'; ξυλόν, 22:52*, 'tree, wood'; cf. Schlatter, 449), what will happen to a dry one? γένηται is deliberate subjunctive with a future or potential meaning (BD 366[1]; MH III, 99). The use of ἐν is Semitic (cf. b[e]; BD 157[1]). The article τῷ is read before ὑγρῷ by TR; UBS; *Diglot*; its omission in B C 0124 pc; *Synopsis*, is probably accidental. The thought is based on the fact that green wood does not burn as easily as dry. If God has not spared the innocent Jesus, how much more severe will be the fate of guilty Jerusalem (J. Schneider, TDNT V, 38; Schenk, 93, however, finds a contrast between the fate of the women who at least sympathise with Jesus and that of the guilty Jewish people). Cf. Ezk. 20:47; Pr. 11:31; 1 Pet. 4:17f. and especially the Jewish proverbial usage of the idea: R. Jose ben Joezer on his way to be crucified said to his mocking nephew: 'If this (crucifixion) happens to those who offend him (God), what of those who do his will!' and: 'If this happens to those who do his will, what of those who offend him?' (150 BC; cited SB II, 263f.; cf. Manson, *Sayings*, 343). K. G. Kuhn comments (TDNT V, 38 n. 7): 'It may be seen plainly that the Gospel depiction of the conduct and saying of Jesus on his last journey corresponds in every point to what, on the basis of Rabb. accounts, we should expect in such a situation of pious Jews aware of God's requirement. This is a strong point in favour of the historical fidelity of Luke.'

ii. The Crucifixion 23:32-38

The whole account of the death of Jesus forms one continuous narrative, so that it is difficult to divide it into sub-sections. Thus the reference to the two criminals could be regarded as forming the end of the previous section, since it deals with the way to the cross (so *Synopsis*), but it is so closely connected with the present section that it can equally well be reckoned part of it; it is a bridge passage. Similarly, the words of the criminal in v. 39 form the first part of the section dealing with the two criminals, but at the same time they form part of the series of mocking statements addressed to Jesus. Grundmann, 431, divides the narrative as a whole into four parts, each with a threefold structure (vs. 33f., 35-43, 44-46, 47-49).

The present section relates how Jesus is crucified along with the two criminals. He pronounces a word of forgiveness upon his executioners (v. 34a, *si vera lectio*). They for their part are occupied in sharing out his garments. While the crowd stand and watch, he is mocked in turn by the rulers, by the soldiers and by the action of Pilate in placing the inscription on the cross, 'The king of the Jews'. But there is dramatic irony in the mockery, and the scene works to a climax in asserting the kingship of Jesus.

The section as a whole shows contacts with Mk. (cf. v. 34b, 38), but in general the order of events is considerably different from Mk. and there is a notable difference in content (see Taylor, *Passion*, 91–99). The differences are such as to make even Creed, 284., concede the possibility of use of another source alongside Mk., although he notes that several of the differences could be explained in terms of Lucan redaction. It is perhaps the scale of the alterations which most strongly suggests use of a non-Marcan source. Taylor notes that in the four places where Mk. is most clearly echoed, the verses in question do occur in Marcan order and give the impression of being insertions into an existing framework. On the other hand, the narrative can be explained simply as a redaction of Mk. (Schenk, 93–102). Luke has then rewritten the scene in order to draw the picture of the martyr being mocked by one group of people after another. Here, as throughout the crucifixion narrative, decision between these two alternatives is difficult, but on the whole it is more probable that Luke's differences from Mk. have some basis in tradition.

See Bultmann, 294f.; D. Daube, ' "For they know not what they do". Luke 23, 34', TU 79, 1961, 58–70; Taylor, *Passion*, 91–99; Dauer, 222–226; Schenk, 93–102.

(32) Luke alone includes the two criminals at the outset of the narrative, the other Gospels not mentioning them until after the actual crucifixion of Jesus (Mk. 15:27; Jn. 19:18). Since Luke will develop the story of the two criminals in vs. 39–43, it may be that he has deliberately given notice of his intentions (Lagrange, 586f.) or wishes to recall 22:37. But since he does not avoid a double mention of them (vs. 33; cf. Mk. 15:27), it is possible that a non-Marcan source is responsible for their inclusion at this point. The language is Lucan (δὲ καί; 2:4; *et al.*; ἕτερος, 3:18; *et al.* (cf. Jn. 19:18 ἄλλος); ἀναιρέω, 22:2; Acts frequently). κακοῦργος is 'criminal, evil-doer'; 23:33, 39; 2 Tim. 2:9**; diff. Mk. λῃστής (Lk. 10:30; *et al.*). There is no obvious reason for the change from λῃστής (other than use of a source), unless Luke is trying to avoid all association of Jesus with revolutionaries (but 23:19 is against this view). The order of words ἕτεροι κακοῦργοι δύο (p⁷⁵ א B), 'two other criminals', could suggest that Jesus is also a criminal, and most other MSS invert the order to give 'two others, criminals', while a few MSS omit ἕτεροι for the same reason. In some MSS the criminals are named (Metzger, 180).

(33) Both Luke and Matthew avoid Mark's use of φέρω with respect to the soldiers taking Jesus to crucifixion and use ἔρχομαι. The designation of the location as a τόπος is common to all four Gospels and sounds like a stereotyped form of words. Luke names the place (καλέω, 1:36; *et al.*, diff. Mk. μεθερμηνεύω; Mt., Jn. λέγω) as Κρανίον*, diff. Mk. κρανίου τόπος, where κρανίου is an epexegetic genitive (AG s.v.). κρανίον, 'skull', occurs only in this connection in the NT. All the other Gospels give its Semitic name, Golgotha, in addition; Grundmann, 432,

cites the opinion of Hirsch that some places may have had two names in Jerusalem, as in bi-lingual communities today. Before the actual act of crucifixion Mark (and Matthew) state that Jesus was offered drugged wine, which he refused. The detail is omitted by Luke and John, who may have regarded the action of the soldiers (Lk. 23:36; Jn. 19:28–30) as a doublet (cf. H. W. Heidland, TDNT V, 288f.). But it is surprising that Luke has not retained a feature which would have underlined the martyr spirit of Jesus, and therefore it is more probable that it was missing from his non-Marcan source. Since ἐκεῖ is slightly redundant and is not a characteristic of Luke (he adds it to his sources demonstrably only at 21:2), it may confirm that a source is being used (cf. Jn. 19:18, ὅπου). Luke again brings forward mention of the two criminals, who do not appear in Mk. until after the details about Jesus' clothes, the time of the incident and the superscription on the cross; here Luke agrees in order with Jn. 19:18, but the ordering is more logical than in Mk. and could be due to independent editing. Luke uses better Greek than Mark here (ὃν μέν ... ὃν δέ ..., diff. Mk. ἕνα ... καὶ ἕνα ...). Luke has ἐξ ἀριστερῶν, 'on the left' (Mk. 10:37; 2 Cor. 6:7; Mt. 6:3**), diff. Mk. and Mt. ἐξ εὐωνύμων (Mk. 10:40; Acts 21:3); the phrases are synonymous and there is no obvious reason for a change by Luke.

(34) The textual status of v. 34a is very uncertain. It relates a prayer by Jesus in which he addresses God as Father (πάτερ, 10:21; 11:2; 22:42; 23:46) and asks him to forgive 'them' (the executioners, possibly all who are involved in his crucifixion), on the grounds of their ignorance; their sin is unwitting – a motif familiar in Luke (Acts 3:17; 13:27; cf. 7:60) and in Jewish and pagan thought (Philo, Flacc. 7; SB II, 264; Ovid, Her. 20:187; cf. also Eus. 2:23:16 for an echo of this text). The saying is omitted by p75 ℵa vid B D* W Θ 0124 1241 579 pc a sys sa bopt Cyril; RV mg; RSV mg; NEB mg; J. Weiss, 520; Klostermann, 226; Easton, 348; Creed, 286f.; Schenk, 96–99; it is bracketed by WH and UBS which both regard the verse as embodying ancient tradition (possibly of dominical origin) but not coming from the pen of Luke (WH App. 67–69; Metzger, 180; cf. J. Jeremias, TDNT V, 713 n. 455). It is accepted as Lucan by Lagrange, 587f.; Dibelius 203 n. 2; Benoit, Passion, 123; Ellis, 267f. Against its genuineness it can be argued: 1. the combination of early MS evidence against its inclusion is particularly impressive, and leads to the supposition that it is a western interpolation into the text. On the other hand, we have already seen cases in Lk. where internal and external considerations stand in opposition, and the balance of favour may lie with the internal evidence. 2. If the saying is a genuine part of Luke, it is impossible to account for its wilful excision. It reflects too well how Christians regarded the attitude of Jesus. However, Epp, 45, claims (following J. R. Harris; Streeter, 138f., and A. Harnack) that omission as a result of anti-Judaic polemic is quite possible, since anti-Judaic influences can be seen in the text of Acts. Schlatter, 446, argues that the saying could have been thought to conflict with the sentiments

expressed in vs. 28–31. Again, scribes could have thought that the events of AD 66–70 showed that a prayer attributed to Jesus had not been answered. Excision does not seem impossible. 3. The saying could have been modelled on Acts 7:60 (cf. Eusebius, HE 2:23:16; Ott, 96). It is, however, more likely that Acts 7:60 was modelled on this saying, so that Stephen is seen to follow the pattern of Jesus in his martyr death. 4. The saying breaks the connection between 23:33 and 34b. It could, however, be argued that v. 34b is deliberately placed to emphasise the callousness of the executioners. On the other hand, it can be claimed: 5. The saying is not based on any OT prophecy, except possibly Is. 53:12, and is unlikely to be a Christian invention. Stauffer, 112, comments that the idea of intercession for transgressors is absent from 1QIs ᵃ 53:12, which he takes to be the text current in the first century. But this is a questionable assumption, since several forms of text were probably current, and does not strengthen the argument. 6. The motif of forgiveness for sins of ignorance, and the thought of Jesus giving a last chance to the Jews fits in with Lucan thought. Instead of confessing his own sins, Jesus prays with respect to the sins of his executioners (Grundmann, 433; Ellis, 267f.). But this motif also appears as a scribal insertion in 6:5 D (Schenk, 98). 7. Sayings by Jesus are found in each main section of the Lucan crucifixion narrative (23:28–31, 43, 46); the lack of such a saying at this point would disturb the pattern. 8. The language is Lucan. The balance of the evidence thus favours acceptance of the saying as Lucan, although the weight of the textual evidence against the saying precludes any assurance in opting for this verdict.

The second part of the verse describes how the executioners proceeded, according to custom (Blinzler, 368f.), to divide out the clothes of Jesus among themselves by casting lots for them. The verse, which is based on Ps. 21:19 LXX, is drawn from Mk., a fact which may explain the abrupt change of subject from v. 34a. Luke has διαμεριζόμενοι ... ἔβαλον, diff. Mk. διαμερίζονται ... βάλλοντες; for putting the main idea in the participle in this way cf. 7:8 note; 13:28. Luke also omits the explanatory addition ἐπ' αὐτὰ τίς τί ἄρῃ found in Mk. The incident might be regarded as having been created out of the scriptural 'proof' (Bultmann, 294f.), were it not that a historically attested custom is reflected (so rightly Dibelius, 188).

(35) Luke passes over the time note given by Mark (15:25) at this point without apparent reason (since he retains Mark's timetable later), and he reserves mention of the superscription on the cross (Mk. 15:26) till further on; he has already mentioned the two criminals (Mk. 15:27). He now reaches the next section of his narrative in which the attitudes of the bystanders are described. Instead of a description of the mockery by the passers-by (Mk. 15:29f.) he records simply that the people stood (εἱστήκα, 23:10) watching. The use of θεωρέω may reflect Ps. 21:8a LXX (Mark uses v. 8b): πάντες οἱ θεωροῦντές με ἐξεμυκτήρισάν με. At first sight it appears as though Luke is absolving the people from mock-

ing Jesus, in line with a tendency noted elsewhere in the Gospel (cf. 23:13 note): their attitude is 'respectful' (Creed, 287, – although he notes the Psalm allusion) and 'curious' (Grundmann, 433). Jesus' death is witnessed by the Jewish people as such. But the use of δὲ καί in v. 35b (cf. the v.1. σὺν αὐτοῖς A W Γ Δ Θ f13 *pm*; TR; *Diglot*) and the possible allusion to Ps. 21:8 LXX suggest that the people are not excluded from mocking Jesus, even if Luke plays this fact down.

But in any case the Jewish rulers certainly join in the mockery. Luke refers to them as ἄρχοντες (cf. 23:13); for ἐκμυκτηρίζω cf. 16:14**; Ps. 21:8a LXX. This part of the verse is Lucan, but the words of the rulers are probably based on Mk. 15:31f. σῴζω refers to the healing work of Jesus ('to save and succour in mortal stress', W. Foerster, TDNT VII, 989), and the clause is equivalent to a condition. The use of the third person imperative here is peculiar to Lk.: it reflects a conflation of Mk. 15:30 and 31 (the parallel with M. Tannaim 3:23 (Smith, 138) is purely verbal). Both Luke and Matthew clarify Mark's next statement into a conditional clause, in order to avoid giving the impression that the Jewish rulers accepted that Jesus was the Messiah. For the thought cf. Ps. 22:7 (21:9), but the saying has been reworded to deal with the special case of one who claims to be the Messiah. It is not clear whether τοῦ θεοῦ should be taken with ὁ χριστός or ὁ ἐκλεκτός, an uncertainty reflected in the MSS (τοῦ θεοῦ ὁ ἐκλεκτός (א^c B (D) L W f1 *al*); ὁ τοῦ θεοῦ ἐκλεκτός (A C³ Γ Δ Θ *pm*; TR); ὁ ἐκλεκτὸς τοῦ θεοῦ (C* ff²); ὁ τοῦ θεοῦ ὁ ἐκλεκτός (א*); ὁ υἱὸς τοῦ θεοῦ ὁ ἐκλεκτός (p⁷⁵ (0124) f13 *al* Eus)). See Dietrich, 96f., who cites 18:7; Jn. 1:34 v.1.; Rom. 8:33; Col. 3:12; Tit. 1:1; 1 Pet. 2:4 in favour of a connection with ὁ ἐκλεκτός; but see 2:26 and 9:20 for a connection with ὁ χριστός. Probably it goes grammatically with the former and in sense with both nouns. For Jesus as the chosen one of God cf. 9:35; Jn. 1:34 v.1.; 1 Pet. 2:4; Is. 42:1; 1 En. 39:6; 40:5; 45:3f.; G. Schrenk, TDNT IV, 189, notes that the concept appears to be used of Jesus as the One who is chosen by God in view of his suffering. The hope that God will rescue the righteous from suffering and even death (Wis. 2:18) is fulfilled in a way other than the Jews expect. The usage is probably Lucan, but it may possibly be from a pre-Lucan tradition (so J. Jeremias, TDNT V, 689).

(36) The second stage in the mockery is attributed to the soldiers. This motif does not appear to be present in the other Gospels, and may be based on Mark's account of how someone (presumably a soldier, since he had a spear) offered sour wine to Jesus. Luke could then have repeated the words of the first mockery to complete the incident. But, in view of the superscription, mockery in terms of it could easily have been carried out by the soldiers, and Luke's version may rest on a non-Marcan source. For ἐμπαίζω, cf. 14:29; *et al.*; Mk. 15:31 (of the rulers); instead of the aorist (p⁷⁵ א B L 0124 1241) most MSS; TR; *Diglot* have the imperfect, which may be original. προσέρχομαι is often added by Luke (7:14; *et al.*). ὄξος (p⁷⁵ א A B C* L Ψ 579 *pc*: καὶ ὄξος *rell*; TR;

Diglot) is 'sour wine, vinegar' (Mk. 15:36; Mt. 27:48; Jn. 19:29, 30**)
which was drunk by soldiers and ordinary people (SB II, 264). The act
could be understood as one of kindness to a thirsty, dying man, which
Luke has misunderstood as mockery, perhaps as the offering of a cheap
drink to the *king* of the Jews (H. W. Heidland, TDNT V, 288f. – the latter part of this suggestion is far-fetched). But Lindars, 100, draws attention to Ps. 69:21 LXX (see also 1QH 4:11: 'When they were thirsty,
they made them drink vinegar'; Ellis, 268), in the light of which the act
could be understood as hostile.

(37) The mockery attributed to the soldiers replaces the allusion to
Elijah's coming in Mk. 15:36. The soldiers address Jesus with words
based on the superscription and put in the second person (Mk. 15:30). If
Jesus is the king of the Jews (diff. Mk. 15:32, Ἰσραήλ, which is less appropriate on the lips of gentiles), let him save himself.

(38) A climax to the mockery (cf. the use of δὲ καί yet again) is
provided by the superscription (ἐπιγραφή; 20:24; cf. Suetonius, Calig.
32; Eusebius, HE 5:1 for the custom) placed over Jesus. The wording is
as in Mk. ὁ βασιλεὺς τῶν Ἰουδαίων, with the addition of a contemptuous οὗτος (cf. Mt. οὗτός ἐστιν; Creed, 287). Many MSS add a
reference to the three languages used, but the wording, omitted by p[75] ℵ[c]
B C* L a sy[sc] sa bo[pt], and recorded in a variety of forms, is probably
based on Jn. 19:20 and is secondary. The verse may have been based on
Mk. (Taylor, *Passion*, 93), in which case the reference to the mockery by
the criminal (v. 39) may originally have been the third in the series.

iii. The Two Criminals 23:39–43

This incident, which is peculiar to Lk., is regarded by Ellis, 267, as con-
stituting the core of Luke's crucifixion narrative. Whereas in Mk. we are
told only of the mockery, by the two criminals alongside Jesus, in Lk.
only one indulges in mockery in words similar to those already used by
the soldiers (but calling upon Jesus to save them as well as himself). His
companion suggests that he is lacking in fear of God; since he deserves
his fate (unlike Jesus) he should not rail at Jesus but accept his own
punishment. But if there is no hope of being saved from death, at least
there may be salvation after death, and the second criminal asks Jesus to
show favour to him when he is king. He is offered more than he asks for.
If his thoughts are fixed on entry to the kingdom of God at the end of the
world, Jesus promises him salvation here and now, the certainty of being
in paradise with him that very day. Jesus' kingly power is to be operative
for salvation forthwith.

The story contrasts the two attitudes which lead to condemnation
and salvation, although it is improbable that they are meant to mirror
the attitudes of Jews and pagans respectively to Jesus (Benoit, *Passion*,
179). The new understanding of death brought about by Jesus is
revealed: for his people it leads straight into the presence of Jesus. The

second thief perhaps typifies the Christian attitude of acceptance of law-fully imposed punishment, and at the same time is yet another witness to Jesus' innocence. Jesus himself is revealed as Saviour, even while dying, for the outcast and criminal who turns to him in faith.

Bultmann, 306f., and Dibelius, 204, are followed by many com-mentators in the view that this is a legend created by Luke himself in the interests of his own theology. Thus Easton, 350f., states that it has little historical basis and displays didactic motives (cf. Klostermann, 225). On the other hand, J. Weiss, 521, Rengstorf, 261f., and Creed, 285, hold (with varying degrees of certainty) that the story has been drawn from Luke's source material. Creed notes the similarities with the stories of the penitent harlot and Zacchaeus and the parable of the Pharisee and the tax collector, but allows that in these stories the Evangelist's own theological sympathies are apparent. The narrative is manifestly written in Luke's own style; however, it betrays sufficient Palestinian features to suggest that Luke was not creating out of nothing. But 'how much is to be set down to his own account it seems impossible to say' (Creed).

See Bultmann, 306f.; Taylor, *Passion*, 95; Schenk, 102–109.

(39) The verse is parallel to Mk. 15:32b but has no linguistic con-tacts with it. For εἷς δέ cf. 17:15; 24:18. κρεμάννυμι, 'to hang', is used of crucifixion in Acts 5:30; 10:39; Gal. 3:13 (LXX); for other uses see Mt. 18:6; 22:40; Acts 28:4**; cf. the use of ἐκκρέμομαι 19:48**; see G. Ber-tram, TDNT III, 915–921. Luke uses βλασφημέω, diff. Mk. ὀνειδίζω; cf. 12:10; 22:65; Mk. 15:29. To mock Jesus by refusing to take his powers seriously is to blaspheme against him; the use of the verb represents a Christian verdict in the light of who Jesus really is (H. W. Beyer, TDNT I, 623). The use of the imperfect is required, since the first speaker is in-terrupted by the second. Rengstorf, 261f., notes that conversation among victims undergoing execution is attested in Jewish sources. The participle λέγων is omitted by B D L e 1; *Synopsis*, and D e also omit (presumably accidentally) the following saying. οὐχί usually expects the answer 'Yes', but the question is equivalent to a condition; the context makes it clear that the criminal does not seriously believe that Jesus is the Messiah. Rengstorf, 262, suggests that if he was a person of Zealot outlook, he could not have accepted as Messiah one who made no moves towards political revolution, and would therefore reserve only scorn for him.

(40) But the second man, who also may have held Zealot views, is of a different mind, and rebukes his companion (ἐπιτιμάω; 4:35; *et al.*; ἐπιτιμῶν αὐτῷ ἔφη is read by p⁷⁵ ℵ B C* L X *pc*; other MSS have ἐπετίμα αὐτὸν λέγων; so TR; *Diglot*; cf. 15:17 note and Kilpatrick, 204.). He accuses him of not fearing God, i.e. not fearing God's judg-ment, a thing which he ought to do since he stands under the same situa-tion of condemnation as Jesus. οὐδέ compares the first criminal with the other mockers of Jesus, and has the force: do not even you (who of all

men should know better) fear God? To mock Jesus in the present situation is to fail to fear God. For fearing God cf. 1:50; 18:2; Acts 10:2, 22, 35; 13:16, 26. For κρίμα cf. 20:47.

(41) The criminal acknowledges that he and his companion are suffering their punishment justly (δικαίως*), since they are receiving things (i.e. a penalty) fitting their deeds (ἀπολαμβάνω is characteristic of Luke's special source). The attitude expressed is one that reconciles a man to God: to accept one's punishment as justified is an expression of penitence (Bornhäuser, *Death*, 159f.; E. Lohse, *Märtyrer und Gottesknecht*, Göttingen, 1955, 38 n.). But the criminal does not in the end rest his hope of acceptance with God on the atoning power of his own death. He appeals to Jesus, to whose innocence he offers a further testimony: he has done nothing wrong, literally 'out of place' (ἄτοπος, Acts 25:5; 28:6**). This last statement may be Lucan in wording, but the Jewish sentiment expressed in the first part makes it unlikely that the whole saying is due to Luke.

(42) καὶ ἔλεγεν has the sense, 'and he went on to say'. The verb is necessary in view of the change of person addressed. Jesus is addressed directly (p⁷⁵ ℵ B C L; other MSS have the more reverent κύριε); Rehkopf, 98f., claims that the usage is pre-Lucan (cf. 17:13; Acts 7:59), an estimate which depends on one's judgment on Acts 7:59. μιμνῄσκομαι has the sense 'to remember for good' ('be graciously mindful of me', J. Jeremias, TDNT V, 770; cf. 1:54; *et al.*). Similar phrases are found on some contemporary gravestones (Ellis, 268). ἔρχομαι has the sense 'to come *again*' in accordance with Semitic idiom (J. Jeremias, ibid.). εἰς τὴν βασιλείαν is read by p⁷⁵ B L it vg Or Hil; UBS; *Synopsis*; *Diglot*; and ἐν τῇ βασιλείᾳ is read by ℵ A C W *IΔ* Θ f1 f13 *pl* sy sa bo; TR; Lagrange, 591. Metzger, 181, notes that the UBS reading is more consonant with Lucan theology, although it could be considered a scribal correction. It presumably refers to the entry of Jesus upon his kingly rule, which for Luke would begin at his ascension and exaltation. But the alternative reading reflects a Semitism, bᵉmalkûṭāk, with the meaning 'as king' (Dalman, 133), so that the whole phrase means 'when you come again as king'; this was misunderstood by taking βασιλεία in a spatial sense, and led to the substitution of εἰς for ἐν (J. Jeremias, ibid.; cf. *Words*, 249 n. 2). On this view (which is to be preferred), the reference is to the parousia of Jesus as the Son of man as a future event associated with the raising of the dead. The criminal thus regards Jesus as more than a martyr; he implicitly confesses his faith that Jesus is the Messiah or Son of man.

(43) Jesus' reply (for minor textual additions, see Metzger, 181f.) is a solemn ἀμήν – saying (4:24; *et al.*), in which he pledges to the man that he will enjoy fellowship with him that same day in paradise. παράδεισος, a Persian word meaning 'garden, park', was used in the LXX for the garden of Eden (Gn. 2:8; *et al.*) and in secular contexts. It then became a type of the future bliss for God's people in Is. 51:3, and

received a technical sense in T. Levi 18:10f. The future paradise was identified with the garden of Eden, thus leading to the view that it existed in between the creation and the final age in hidden form. It came to be regarded as the intermediate resting place for the souls of the righteous dead (J. Jeremias, TDNT V, 765–773; cf. SB IV:2, 1118–1165). It is used as a symbol for heaven and its bliss in 2 Cor. 12:4; Rev. 2:7. In the present passage it represents the state of bliss which Jesus promises to the criminal directly after death. The use of σήμερον thus presents no problem; it refers to the day of crucifixion as the day of entry into paradise. Nevertheless, it is significant that Jesus can use the term σήμερον which signifies that the era of salvation has become a reality and echoes the usage in 2:11; 4:21; 5:26 (diff. Mk.); 19:11. The difficulty with this view is its apparent conflict with teaching elsewhere which suggests that Jesus 'descended' to Hades (Acts 2:31; Mt. 12:40; Rom. 10:7) or with the view that Jesus attained to heaven only after the resurrection (and ascension); these difficulties are more imaginary than real. Ellis, 268f. (cf. NTS 12, 1965–66, 35–40), notes the difficulties caused by supposing a body/soul distinction here and suggests that the corporate inclusion of believers in the body of Christ lies behind the thought here; this is unnecessarily subtle. A similar hope of entry into the world to come after a martyr death is expressed by a converted 'philosopher' in S. Dt. 32:4 307 (133a) (SB II, 264). The philosopher was converted by R. Hanina ben Teradion of whom it is further related that when he was being burned to death as a martyr (c. AD 135) the executioner asked if he would bring him to the life of the world to come if he cut short his torments for him; the rabbi agreed to this, and the executioner jumped into the fire with him; then came a heavenly voice which said 'R. Hanina ben Teradion and the executioner are destined for life in the world to come' (AZ 18a; SB I, 223). Grundmann, 434f., observes that the Rabbi had the right to make his statement on the basis of the power of the keys held by the scribes (Mt. 23:13), but Jesus acts as the Messiah who has the kingly right to open the doors of paradise to those who come into fellowship with him. The criminal's petition expresses the hope that he will attain to life at the parousia; Jesus' reply assures him of immediate entry into paradise.

iv. The Death of Jesus 23:44–49

As Jesus hangs dying on the cross, two portents take place, a darkness over the whole land and the splitting of the curtain in the temple. The former can be seen as a symbol of divine displeasure at the rejection of Jesus by men; in Mk. it appears to be expressive of the sense of distance from God felt by Jesus, but this motif is absent from Lk. as a result of his omission of Mk. 15:34. The latter is not interpreted, but may symbolise the beginning of the divine judgment upon the temple prophesied by Jesus, whereas in Mk., coming after the death of Jesus, it may symbolise the new way into the presence of God opened up by Jesus. (This meaning may possibly also be present in Lk.; Ellis, 270.)

The portents are followed by a loud cry in which Jesus utters a prayer of trust in God, such as was used before sleep by pious Jews, and then breathes his last. The peacefulness of his dying stands in contrast to the preceding apocalyptic signs.

The effect of his death is to elicit a recognition by the centurion in charge of the execution that he was an innocent man – this being the final witness to his undeserved suffering. The scene comes to a conclusion with the departure of the crowds who lament his death; whether they feel penitent about it is disputable. The only thing left to record is the presence of Jesus' friends – standing at a distance and witnessing the scene. They include the women from Galilee who will play a vital part in the next stage of the story.

Throughout this part of the narrative Luke follows Mk., but with some rearrangement, some omissions and a certain amount of change in wording. The cry of desolation and the reference to Elijah coming to help Jesus are omitted. The tearing of the temple curtain is brought forward to link up with the other portent. The closing words of Jesus are peculiar to Lk., and the saying of the centurion is altered. The description of the departure of the crowds is new. All of this can plausibly be explained as due to Lucan editing, and the case for a separate passion narrative used by him is at its weakest here (*pace* Taylor, *Passion*, 95f.).

See Bultmann, 295f.; G. D. Kilpatrick, 'A Theme of the Lucan Passion Story and Luke 23:47', JTS 43, 1942, 34–36; G. R. Driver, 'Two Problems in the New Testament', JTS ns 16, 1965, 327–337, especially 331–337; Taylor, *Passion*, 95f.; Schenk, 109–119; J. F. A. Sawyer, 'Why is a Solar Eclipse Mentioned in the Passion Narrative (Luke xxiii, 44–5)?' JTS ns 23, 1972, 124–128.

(44) Although Luke is following Mk. here, it is curious that he has dropped Mark's genitive absolute in favour of paratactic expression in his own style (cf. Mk. 15:25; Schenk, 109). Grundmann, 435, cites the possibility (raised by Hirsch) that vs. 44b–45 are a Marcan insertion, so that in Luke's source the sixth hour was that of Jesus' death (in contrast to Mk. where Jesus does not die until after the ninth hour, and also in contrast to Jn., where the crucifixion is not till after the sixth hour). This does not seem very likely. The use of ἤδη is puzzling. Does it simply mean 'now', or has it the sense of 'already' (which is found in its other occurrences in Lk. and Acts)? In the latter case, it may be Luke's way of indicating that a lengthy period of time has already passed. Darkness (σκότος; cf. 22:53) covers the whole area for three hours; γῆ need not refer to more than the locality. For this motif cf. Je. 15:9; 8:9; Mk. 13:24; and the pagan parallels in Virgil, Geor. 1:463ff.; Diogenes L. 4:64; Plutarch, Pelop. 295A.; see also SB I, 1040–1042; H. Conzelmann, TDNT VII, 439.

(45) The reason for the darkness is explained by Luke as the sun ceasing to shine. τοῦ ἡλίου ἐκλιπόντος is read by 𝔭⁷⁵* ℵ C* L 0124 579

pc; the present participle ἐκλείποντος is read by p⁷⁵ᶜ B 597 *al*; and καὶ ἐσκοτίσθη (ἐσκοτίσθη δέ D) ὁ ἥλιος by A D W Γ Δ Θ f1 f13 *pl* lat sy Mcion; TR. The former reading could be understood to mean an eclipse of the sun (so Creed, 288, J. F. A. Sawyer* thinks that Luke was using symbolical language, inspired by the eclipse of 24th Nov, AD 29); but an actual eclipse is impossible at the Passover season of full moon, and knowledge of this fact may have led to the easing of the text in the alternative reading (WH App. 69–71). Plummer, 545, cites the view of E. C. Selwyn and J. W. Burgon that the genitive phrase is a corruption of a marginal note, τοῦ Ἠλείου ἐκλείποντος, referring to the omission of the Elijah passage (Mk. 15:34–36) from Lk. But these attempts to avoid an apparent astronomical blunder by Luke are unnecessary. As WH observe, and G. R. Driver* elaborates, the phrase means merely that the sun failed to give its light (cf. Job 31:26; Is. 60:20; Sir. 22:11), a phenomenon which could have been caused locally by a *hamsîn* or sirocco wind. What remains uncertain is why Luke thought it necessary to introduce this comment; perhaps it is to stress the fulfilment of Joel 2:31 (cf. Acts 2:20), but this is not altogether satisfactory since there is no evidence that Luke looked for any fulfilment of the remainder of that verse.

The second part of the verse links another sign with the darkening of the sun (instead of ἐσχίσθη δέ the variant καὶ ἐσχίσθη is found in A W Γ Δ Θ f13 *pm* sy; TR; *Diglot*). The passive ἐσχίσθη may refer to an act by God (Rengstorf, 263), but this is rather subtle. καταπέτασμα is 'veil, curtain' (Mk. 15:38; Mt. 27:51; Heb. 6:19; 9:3; 10:20**). In the LXX it refers to the curtain separating the holy place from the holy of holies in the tabernacle (Ex. 26:31ff.; Lv. 21:23; 24:3; Philo, Mos. 2:86, 101; Jos. Ant. 8:75). It is also used for the curtain at the entry to the holy place (Ex. 26:37; 38:18; Nu. 3:26). Most commentators think that the former is meant (so AG; SB I 1043–1045), but others prefer the latter (Klostermann, 227; Lohmeyer, 347; G. R. Driver, art. cit.). Lohmeyer rightly observes that a reference to something generally visible is required; and Driver suggests that the same sirocco wind which caused the darkness could have split the outer curtain of the holy place. μέσον can be taken as a predicative adjective with adverbial force ('down the middle'; cf. 22:55; Acts 1:18; Jn. 1:26; *et al.*). The event is a forewarning of the destruction of the temple; cf. the similar Jewish references to such portents forty years before the fall of Jerusalem (SB I, 1045f.), but the portents are dated by Josephus in AD 66.

(46) Luke records only one cry by Jesus towards the end of his suffering, whereas Mark has two (15:34, 37). Only Luke uses φωνέω here (8:8; *et al.*; cf. Mk. 15:35), diff. Mk. βοάω, which Luke does not use of Jesus. For φωνῇ μεγάλῃ with φωνέω cf. Acts 16:28; Mk. 1:26; Rev. 14:18; the phrase is Lucan. A loud cry is unusual from a man nearly dead by crucifixion, but is not perhaps completely impossible (Blinzler, 372f.). The wording of Jesus' cry is peculiar to Lk. Jesus addresses God

as Πάτερ (10:21 note) and uses the words of Ps. 30: 6 LXX: εἰς χεῖράς σου παραθήσομαι τὸ πνεῦμά μου. The slight verbal change in the tense of the verb accommodates the quotation to the occasion. For the thought cf. Acts 7:59; 1 Pet. 4:19. For a similar dying sentiment Grundmann, 435, cites Seneca, Heracles Octaeus 1707f., 1729f. The quotation was used as part of an evening prayer (SB II, 269; cf. J. Jeremias, 'Das Gebetsleben Jesu', ZNW 25, 1926, 123–140, especially 126 n. 3); the use of this prayer fits the evening of life as it does evening before sleep, sleep being regarded as the threshold of death (Rengstorf, 264). Stauffer, 117, suggests that the time was in fact that of the evening prayer (the ninth hour). But the prayer is found only in Luke, and the case that it is inauthentic is assembled by Lindars, 93–95, who notes that the Psalm was known and used by the early church (Mt. 26:3f.; Acts 7:59; 1 Pet. 4:19), and that Luke, following Mk., is here offering a substitute for Ps. 21:1 LXX which he has omitted; he has drawn from the devotional life of the early church and added Jesus' usual address to God at the beginning of the prayer. This is a plausible case, but it remains possible that the early church usage of the Psalm arose from Jesus' use. τοῦτο δὲ εἰπών is used as a connective (καὶ τοῦτο . . . K M P Π al; Diglot; καὶ ταῦτα . . ., A C³ Γ Δ al; TR, are weakly attested variants). ἐκπνέω, 'to breathe one's last' (sc. βίον or ψυχήν), is used only of the death of Jesus (Mk. 15:37, 39**). The swift and sudden death is unusual but perfectly possible.

(47) The effect of what has happened (τὸ γενόμενον, diff. Mk. ὅτι οὕτως ἐξέπνευσεν; cf. Mt. τὸν σεισμὸν καὶ τὰ γινόμενα) moves the centurion in charge; Luke has ἑκατοντάρχης (7:2, 6) diff. Mk. κεντυρίων (a Latinism). Luke omits any description of him (contrast Mk.): his readers would take for granted the presence of such an officer at the execution. Luke describes his reaction as one of glorifying God (cf. 2:20; et al.); this is a favourite Lucan reaction to a revelation of divine power and mercy, and the estimate of Jesus which follows can be regarded as praise to God for the way in which Jesus died. In the death of Jesus the centurion sees the sacrifice of a martyr who has perished innocently, For this use of δίκαιος cf. Klostermann, 226; AG s.v.; and especially G. D. Kilpatrick* who cites Pr. 6:7; Joel 4:19; Jon. 1:14; cf. Mt. 23:35; 27:19; Jas. 5:6; 1 Pet. 3:18. Thus a Lucan theme in the passion story reaches its final statement. Luke's description alters Mark's form of the statement in which the centurion confesses that Jesus is the Son of God. It may well be that Luke's stress on innocence is sufficient to motivate this alteration, but some scholars argue that Luke is unlikely to have weakened Mark's statement (Lagrange, 593). Luke uses ὄντως ('really, truly'; 24:34) diff. Mk. ἀληθῶς (a word which he reserves for use as a substitute for ἀμήν on the lips of Jesus).

(48) After the centurion's reaction we have that of the crowds. It is noteworthy that they are not described as the λαός (cf. 23:4). συμπαραγίνομαι** is 'to come together', and θεωρία** is 'spectacle, sight'. There is an awkward repetition of the root in θεωρήσαντες

(θεωροῦντες, W Γ Δ Θ f1 *pm*; TR; *Diglot*; scribes were prone to alter present into aorist participles, but the attestation here is weak). The crowds express their feelings by beating their breasts (18:13) as they begin to depart (ὑπέστρεφον, imperfect). Their act has been understood as a sign of repentance for their part in sentencing Jesus to death (Grundmann, 435f.). One or two MSS and the Gospel of Peter 25 make their act into one of pity for themselves as they recognise the fate that lies ahead of them for their sins (see Metzger, 182); this is not quite the same thing as repentance. It is more likely that the action is a simple expression of grief at the death of a victim of execution, perhaps grief at his undeserved death; to read repentance into it is unjustified. The action may be seen as fulfilment of Zc. 12:10–14, but there is no linguistic evidence that Luke recognised it. The verse is peculiar to Luke, however, and may be his own editorial comment (Dodd, 137), but if so, it is difficult to see the purpose of it.

(49) Luke closes his account of the crucifixion with a reference to Jesus' friends standing (εἱστήκει; cf. Jn. 19:25; diff. Mk. εἰμί; cf. ἔστησαν Ps. 37:12 LXX) at a distance. For γνωστός see 2:44; elsewhere Luke uses it only in the neuter. Instead of αὐτῷ (p⁷⁵ A B L 0124 33 *pc*) most MSS have αὐτοῦ; so TR; *Diglot*. The reference is to Jesus' friends rather than his relatives, and is meant to include such of his disciples as were there (cf. Jn. 19:26) and to prepare for the role of Joseph (Lagrange, 594). For ἀπὸ μακρόθεν cf. Mk. 15:40, but the whole phrase is reminiscent of Ps. 37:12 LXX. A second subject is loosely added, namely the women (i.e. 'including the women') who had accompanied him from Galilee. αἱ is added in p⁷⁵ B *pc*; was it lost in the other MSS by homoioteleuton? For συνακολουθέω cf. Mk. 5:37; 14:51**; AG give the meaning 'to be a disciple', but Luke's stress is on their accompanying Jesus from Galilee (cf. 23:55). Luke has not retained Mark's wording ἠκολούθουν ... συναναβᾶσαι (although he uses the latter word in Acts 13:31**). He omits the names of the women, possibly because he has already given them in 8:2f. The verse has contacts with Jn. 19:25f. and differences of wording from Mk. which suggest that traces of a non-Marcan source lie behind it. Rengstorf's suggestion, 265, that Luke depicts the disciples (whom he does not name as such) as having broken off their relationship with Jesus, over-interprets the verse.

d. The Resurrection of Jesus (23:50 – 24:53)

In all the Gospels except Mk. (which is probably incomplete) the death of Jesus is followed by accounts of his burial, the discovery of the empty tomb, appearances of Jesus to his disciples, and a closing scene. This structure is varied by other items. Matthew includes some apologetic details, and John's account is complicated by the existence of the 'appendix' to his Gospel in ch. 21. The basic pattern appears most clearly in

Lk., although it would seem that it has been achieved as a result of some schematisation in both the time and the place of the resurrection appeaances. Thus all the appearances in Lk. take place in or around Jerusalem and on Easter Sunday, although Acts 1 makes it certain that Luke knew of a longer period of appearances. If Jerusalem is the place of Jesus' death, it is also the place of his victory and the beginning of the church, but Luke stresses that those involved in this victory came from Galilee. (Galilee as a place plays little part in the Gospel as a whole; Lagrange, 598.)

Luke's narrative is largely based on material peculiar to himself, but for the burial and empty tomb stories he is indebted to Mk.; some of his other material shows important contacts with Johannine tradition and it is probable that a common strand of tradition is reflected (Dodd, 137–151; but for the possibility of Johannine dependence on Lk. see Bailey, 85–102).

See K. Lake, *The Historical Evidence for the Resurrection of Jesus Christ*, London, 1907; L. Brun, *Die Auferstehung Jesu in der urchristlichen Überlieferung*, Oslo/Giessen, 1925; P. Gardner-Smith, *The Narratives of the Resurrection*, London, 1926; Bultmann, 308–316; Finegan, *Überlieferung*, 85–111; P. Schubert, 'The Structure and Significance of Luke 24', in W. Eltester (ed.), *Neutestamentliche Studien für Rudolf Bultmann*, Berlin, 1954, 165–186; Grass; H. von Campenhausen, *Tradition and Life in the Church*, London, 1968, 42–89 (originally as *Der Ablauf der Osterereignisse und das leere Grab*, Heidelberg, 1958); C. F. Evans, *Resurrection and the New Testament*, London, 1970, 92–115; W. Marxsen, *The Resurrection of Jesus of Nazareth*, London, 1970 (originally as *Die Auferstehung Jesu von Nazareth*, Gütersloh, 1968); U. Wilckens, *Auferstehung*, Stuttgart, 1970; E. L. Bode, *The First Easter Morning*, Rome, 1970; R. H. Fuller, *The Formation of the Resurrection Narratives*, London, 1972; Taylor, *Passion*, 99–115; I. H. Marshall, 'The Resurrection of Jesus in Luke', Tyn.B 24, 1973, 55–98; B. Rigaux, *Dieu l'a ressuscité*, Gembloux, 1973; X. Léon-Dufour, *Resurrection and the Message of Easter*, London, 1974 (originally as *Résurrection de Jésus et message pascal*, Paris, 1971).

i. The Burial of Jesus 23:50–56a

Luke's account of the burial of Jesus follows lines familiar from Mk., and does not differ in any important particular. The burial is carried out by a godly councillor, Joseph from Arimathaea, who obtains the body of Jesus from Pilate, prepares it reverently for burial, and places it in an unused tomb. This event took place on the day of preparation, and the Galilean women were able to see where the tomb was and make preparations for further anointing of the body.

The narrative is plain and straightforward, and has no important nuances absent from Mk. It is simplest to explain it as resting on Mark's account (Finegan, *Überlieferung*, 34f.; Grass, 32–35). Taylor, *Passion*, 99–101, accepts this verdict on vs. 50–54, but claims (101–103) that vs. 55–56a rest on non-Marcan material, having links with Jn.; Grundmann, 436, goes further in arguing that vs. 50, 51a, 53b and 54–56 come from Luke's special source. Grundmann's view is unacceptable, but there is some evidence that suggests that Taylor may be right, and that Luke may have used a source which prepared for the story of the resurrection appearances by reference to the women concerned.

The general historicity of the account is dependent upon our estimate of Mark's narrative, and there is no good reason to doubt this: see Taylor, 599; Schweizer, *Markus*, 209f.; Blinzler, 385–415.

See Bultmann, 296f.; Finegan, *Überlieferung*, 34f.; Grass, 32–35; Blinzler, 385–415; Taylor, *Passion*, 99–103; I. Broer, *Die Urgemeinde und das Grab Jesu*, München, 1972; R. Pesch, 'Der Schluss der vormarkinischen Passionsgeschichte und des Markusevangeliums: Mk. 15, 42–16, 8', in Sabbe, 365–409.

(50) Luke omits Mark's time-note at the beginning of the narrative and transfers it rather awkwardly to follow the actual burial in v. 54; cf. its position in Jn. 19:42. This change may reflect use of a different source in vs. 54f., since it is difficult to see any other good reason for the change. The opening of the narrative is rewritten in Lucan style; cf. 1:36 note and 19:2 for the pattern followed here. The note that Joseph came ἀπὸ 'Αριμαθαίας is transferred to the next verse. He is described as a βουλευτής (Mk. 15:43**), i.e. a member of the sanhedrin; the view that he belonged to some other official body is unlikely in the absence of any further qualification (Blinzler 392 n. 39). ὑπάρχω is Lucan (7:25; *et al.*); after it καί is read by p⁷⁵ ℵ (C) L X 0124 33 1241 *pc*; (UBS); *Diglot*, perhaps to improve a stylistically poor sentence. The phrase ἀγαθὸς καὶ δίκαιος replaces Mk. εὐσχήμων, probably in the light of Mark's further comment that Joseph was awaiting the kingdom of God. εὐσχήμων can mean both 'noble (i.e. upper-class), wealthy' and 'noble (of upright and good character)'; for the former cf. Acts 13:50; 17:12 and for the latter Rom. 13:13; 1 Cor. 7:35; 14:40; 1 Thes. 4:12. Creed, 291, cites Phrynichus, 309, on the ambiguity in the word and suggests that Luke has taken the wrong alternative out of Mk. (similarly, H. Greeven, TDNT II, 770–772). But Luke is not interested in Joseph's wealth, but in his piety, and he is probably not even trying to interpret Mark's word but to make a different point. For his own phraseology cf. 2:25; Acts 10:22; 11:24.

(51) The first point made about Joseph in v. 50, his being a member of the sanhedrin, is followed up in the light of the second point by an express declaration that he did not share the verdict of his fellow-members on Jesus. The verse is a parenthetical comment (cf. 2:25; 8:41; Acts 17:24; 18:25). συγκατατίθημι is 'to put down the same vote as', i.e. 'to agree with, consent to' (elsewhere in the NT only in Acts 4:18 v.l.; 15:12 v.l.). βουλή (7:30*) here has the sense 'resolution, decision'; cf. Acts 5:38; 27:12, 42; the echo of Ps. 1:1 (Klostermann, 230) is accidental. πρᾶξις, 'act, deed' (Acts 19:18), can convey the sense of an evil deed (Rom. 8:13; Col. 3:9) or be neutral (Mt. 16:27; Rom. 12:4; cf. C. Maurer, TDNT VI, 642–644). The antecedent of αὐτῶν is assumed to be obvious (cf. 4:15; BD 282³). 'Αριμαθαία is mentioned only here and in the parallels. The site is generally identified with Ramathaim-zophim (1 Sa. 1:1), mod. Rentis, 20 miles NW of Jerusalem. For Luke's addition, πόλις

τῶν Ἰουδαίων, to help non-Jewish readers, cf. 4:31; 8:26. In the second part of the verse, Luke uses Mark's description of Joseph to fill out the earlier mention of him as a good and just man. He was awaiting (προσδέχομαι; cf. 2:25, 38) the kingdom of God, a phrase which joins him with the pious Israelites described in the birth narratives and suggests that he was a disciple of Jesus (Jn. 19:38; Mt. 27:57).

(52) Anxious to preserve the body of Jesus from the dishonour of a common grave, he went to Pilate (προσέρχομαι, par. Mt., diff. Mk. εἰσέρχομαι; cf. 8:24, 44; 20:27; Streeter, 323, tries to explain the agreement away) and requested the body of Jesus. Luke and Matthew both omit reference to his boldness in so doing and to Pilate's surprise that Jesus was already dead, but this is probably coincidental.

(53) Joseph then took the body of Jesus down from the cross (καθαιρέω (1:52) par. Mk.; αὐτό is added in A Δ pm; TR; Diglot; the MSS are confused at this point). He wrapped it in a linen cloth. ἐντυλίσσω, 'to wrap, fold up', is used in Mt. 27:59 (cf. Jn. 20:7), diff. Mk. ἐνειλέω (which is more colloquial); Streeter's suggestion (324) that ἐνείλησεν (f13) be read here to avoid the agreement with Mt. is weak. For σινδών, 'linen cloth', cf. Mk. 14:15f.; 15:46; Mt. 27:59**; both Luke and Matthew omit Mk. ἀγοράσας. There is no mention of Joseph anointing the body, and Easton, 353f., suggests that this gave the women their desire to repair the omission. But John 19:39f. attests that Joseph did anoint the body, and it is improbable in eastern conditions that the women would have come afterwards to perform rites on a body that had not already had some kind of anointing to preserve it (Ellis, 270f.; cf. Jos. Ant. 17:199; Bel. 1:673, but these references do not attest a second anointing). The body was then placed (τίθημι, par. Mt., diff. Mk. κατατίθημι) in a tomb (μνῆμα, par. Mk.; cf. 8:27); λαξευτός** means 'hewn in rock'; Wellhausen's claim (136) that it means 'made with hewn stones' is rebutted by Dt. 4:49 LXX (cf. Creed, 291f.; on the word see also BD 2). The further comment that nobody had yet been buried in the tomb (which would have had space for several burials) is also found in Jn. 19:41 and implied in Mt. καινός. Like John, Luke makes no mention of the closing of the tomb with a stone (diff. Mk., Mt.; see, however, the scribal additions noted in Metzger, 182f.). For the method of Jewish burial, see especially Finegan 166–168, 181–219. This verse has a number of contacts with Mt. and Jn. against Mk. which might suggest use of a non-Marcan source, although it is clear that Luke is basically following Mk.; there may have been some influence from oral tradition, or Luke may have been influenced by a brief non-Marcan account of the burial (so Taylor).

(54) Luke closes the account of the burial with a time note, which is probably meant to prepare for what follows and to explain the action of the women. He clarifies for non-Jewish readers by the use of ἡμέρα, and thus has to put παρασκευή in the genitive. The latter word, 'preparation', can mean 'day of preparation' (Mk. 15:42; 27:63; Jn.

19:14, 31, 42**). It refers to the day of the Jewish week immediately preceding the Sabbath (i.e. Thursday evening to Friday evening; in Jn. 19:14 it is usually taken to mean the day of preparation for the Passover, but might mean the Friday in Passover week; cf. Jos. Ant. 16:163; M. Poly. 7:1; Did. 8:1). Here Friday must be meant, as the next clause makes clear. ἐπιφώσκω is 'to shine forth, dawn' (Mt. 28:1**). In G. Peter 2:5 (based on Lk.) it is used of the approach of the Sabbath at sunset; but in 9:34, 35, it is used of dawn. Black, 136–138, thinks the phrase may reflect a Semitic phrase referring to the 'breaking of day' at sunset; JB finds a reference to the lighting of lamps at sunset on Friday (so earlier J. Lightfoot; cf. Lagrange, 596), while others think that the appearance of the evening star is meant (Rengstorf, 266; Grundmann, 437; E. Lohse, TDNT VII, 20 n. 159), and this is the most likely view. A reference to dawn on Saturday morning (G. R. Driver* (23:44–49 note), 327–331) is improbable.

(55) The account concludes with a note that the women who had come with Jesus (συνέρχομαι, 5:15; et al.; αὐτῷ is strangely separated from the verb in p⁷⁵ ℵ B L, but the transposition in rell; TR; Diglot is surely secondary) followed (κατακολουθέω, Acts 16:17**) Joseph to the tomb. They were able to see (θεάομαι, diff. Mk. θεωρέω) the tomb (μνημεῖον, synonymous with μνῆμα) and to note how (ὡς, diff. Mk. ποῦ, 'where') Jesus had been placed (ἐτέθη, diff, Mk. τέθειται, is grammatically better). The possibility that they later visited the wrong tomb is implicitly ruled out. Luke does not name the women at this point, diff. Mk. 15:47 (cf. Mk. 15:40; 16:1), and indeed does not do so until 24:10 where the names are added rather as a second thought. It is a moot point whether he is following a source which omitted the names at this point or himself decided to omit them in view of the redundancy and appearance of confusion in Mark's lists; the latter view is perhaps more likely.

(56a) After seeing the tomb the women returned (ὑποστρέφω is Lucan) to the city and prepared perfumes (ἄρωμα, usually plural, 'spices, aromatic oils', 24:1; Mk. 16:1; Jn. 19:40**) and ointments (μύρον, 7:37; cf. Ct. 1:3f.) to anoint the body of Jesus. This action is described as if it took place before the Sabbath, but in Mk. 16;1 it clearly follows the Sabbath. It has been suggested that Luke misunderstood Mark to be referring to a purchase of perfumes after the Sabbath ended at midnight and wrote a more plausible version of the story, but this is not very likely. The detail may reflect use of a different source from Mk. (Grundmann, 436). In any case it should be noted that Luke does not explicitly say when the perfumes were bought. We should take v. 56a as the conclusion of the burial story, and v. 56b as the beginning of a new section (UBS; RV) in which Luke refers back to the burial story without reflecting on the apparent contradiction with Mk. which has resulted; cf. Geldenhuys, 620 (but his other suggestion of two separate purchases of perfumes is harmonistic desperation).

ii. The Empty Tomb 23:56b – 24:12

Early on the first day of the week a group of women made their way to the tomb of Jesus with perfumes, found that the stone protecting the entrance had been removed, and went in, only to discover that his body was not there. Two angels appeared to them and assured them that Jesus had risen in accordance with the earlier prophecies that he had made in Galilee. The women then left the tomb and went to tell the eleven disciples and the other companions of Jesus what had happened, but were met by disbelief. Only Peter went to the tomb to confirm their story, found the grave clothes of Jesus lying there, and was filled with mystification.

The general outline of this story is close to that in Mk. 16:1–8. There are considerable traces of Lucan style and thought, and the details of the story differ from those in Mk. The women's purpose of anointing Jesus almost disappears. The women discover that the body of Jesus has gone before they see the angel(s); in Mk. it is not explicitly stated that they saw that the body had gone. Thus the emptiness of the tomb is stressed in Lk. Mark's one angel has become two (cf. Jn. 20:12), and they appear *after* the women have entered the tomb. The message of the angels is different from that in Mk., only the words, 'He is not here, but has risen', being common to both, and the prophecy that the disciples will see him in Galilee has disappeared in favour of a report of what Jesus said in Galilee about his passion and resurrection. While Mark emphasises the silence of the women after the incident, Luke narrates how they told their story. Since, however, Mk. is no longer available for comparison after this point, it is impossible to say with certainty how far Luke is editing his source material. Thus the disbelief of the apostles and the story of Peter's visit to the tomb may well have figured in Luke's source. But the names of the women, given at a late stage in the story by Luke, differ from those in Mk.

There are one or two contacts with Mt., which need reflect nothing more than common editing of Mk., and other contacts with Jn. (the two angels and especially the story of how Peter and the beloved disciple went to the tomb) which suggest use of common traditions. It is possible that Luke has drawn his story from Mk. with editorial modifications (Bultmann, 311; Finegan, *Überlieferung*, 86–87; Grass, 35) or with small additions from other sources (Rengstorf, 267), or that he has drawn his story from a special source with additions from Mk. (Grundmann, 439; Ellis, 272; Taylor, *Passion*, 106–109). Decision between these possibilities is not easy. See I. H. Marshall*, 65–75, for the conclusion that Luke has supplemented Mk. with isolated additions from oral sources. I am now less certain about this verdict, and would leave open the possibility that Luke was following an alternative source, closely similar to Mk. Owing to the strong degree of Lucan editing and the manifest use of Mk., it is difficult to prove that any other continuous source was employed, but the presence of non-Marcan material before and after this story strengthens the case for it here also.

The historical basis of the tradition is also much debated, but there are no compelling arguments against the view that certain women found the tomb of Jesus to be empty early on the first day of the week. The doubling of the angel in Lk. and Jn., and the variety of statements attributed to him (them) may indicate that the angelic message is a literary device to bring out the significance of the discovery, which the different Evangelists felt free to develop in different (and characteristic) ways; on the other hand, the possibility of angelic manifestations is not to be dismissed out of hand (cf. Cranfield, 465f.), even if the nature of the sources make it difficult to establish exactly what happened.

See (in addition to works cited in 23:50 – 24:53 note), A. R. C. Leaney, 'The Resurrection Narratives in Luke (xxiv. 12–53) ', NTS 2, 1955–56, 110–114; L. Schenke, *Auferstehungsverkündigung und leeres Grab*, Stuttgart, 1968; K. P. G. Curtis, 'Luke xxiv. 12 and John xx. 3–10', JTS ns 22, 1971, 512–515; R. Pesch (23:50–56 note).

(56b) Luke's account expands the brief note that the Sabbath was over into a positive statement that the women rested (ἡσυχάζω, 1 Thes. 4:11; in the sense 'to remain silent', 14:4; Acts 11:18; 21:14; 22:2 v.1.**) during the Sabbath in accordance with the commandment (ἐντολή, 1:6; *et al.*) found in Ex. 20:10; Dt. 5:14. As in the birth stories the leading actors who receive the fulfilment of God's promises are portrayed as loyal, pious Jews, so here the women are presented in the same light. Godet, II, 343, claimed that this was the last Sabbath of the old order, scrupulously kept by the followers of Jesus before the new celebration of the first day of the week took its place; this thought may have been in Luke's mind, but hardly in the minds of the women. The actions necessary for the burial of Jesus would not have broken the Jewish Sabbath law in any case (Shab. 23:5; Jeremias, *Words*, 74–79).

(1) Then comes the contrast (note the μέν ... δέ construction) on the first day of the week (ἡ μία τῶν σαββάτων; Mk. 16:2; Mt. 28:1; Jn. 20:1). The same phrase is used in all four Gospels, even down to the use of μία (cardinal number for ordinal; the usage is found in Greek (MH I, 95f., 237; II, 174, 439) but is on occasion due to Semitic influence (so clearly Jos. Ant. 1:29; Black, 124; BD 247¹). But it was no doubt a stereotyped usage for Sunday (Acts 20:7; 1 Cor. 16:2; Jn. 20:19). ὄρθρος (a masc. noun) is 'dawn, early morning' (Jn. 8:2; Acts 5:21**); cf. Luke's use of ὀρθρινός, 24:22** which suggests that the noun is Lucan. βαθύς, 'deep' (Acts 20:9; Jn. 4:11; 1 Pet. 3:4; Rev. 2:24), is used in the genitive (the form is not adverbial; cf. BD 46³; AG s.v.), and refers (as in Classical usage) to first dawn; Rengstorf, 268, suggests 'while it was still dark' (cf. Jn. 20:1; the same time is indicated in Mt. 28:1, as interpreted by G. R. Driver* (23:44–49 note), 327–331). In Mk. 16:1, however, the phrase 'very early' (λίαν πρωΐ) is qualified by 'when the sun had risen', i.e. just after dawn. The contradiction with Lk. and Jn. is

trivial; it suggests that possibly two varying traditions of the story were extant, or that there is some corruption in the text of Mk. The women arrived at the tomb (ἐπὶ τὸ μνῆμα, par. Mk.) and brought the spices which they had prepared. Note how the relative clause is almost an attribute of the antecedent. ἑτοιμάζω refers back to 23:56a, and appears to place the preparation of the perfumes before the sabbath, diff. Mk. 16:1. At the end of the verse many MSS add καί τινες σὺν αὐταῖς (so TR; Diglot; there is a further addition based on Mk. 16:3 in D 0124 c sa); the shorter text (p⁷⁵ ℵ B C* L 33 pc lat boᵖᵗ) is to be preferred, the addition apparently being based on v. 10.

(2) Luke omits the questioning of the women on the way to the tomb about who would take away the stone (par. Jn. 20:1; diff. Mk.); the verse could be an addition in Mark's narrative, designed to prepare the way for the discovery of the open tomb. Luke's narrative introduces the stone on the assumption that his readers were familiar with Jewish modes of burial – a possible sign of pre-Lucan tradition. ἀποκυλίω is 'to roll away' (Mk. 16:3, omitted by Luke; Mt. 28:2**), diff. Mk. 16:4, ἀνακυλίω**. There is no mention of the size of the stone. The discovery is the first hint of the resurrection (Grundmann, 440).

(3) It is followed quickly by the second hint. There is a neat balance between 'they found the stone' and 'but they did not find the body'. For εἰσελθοῦσαι δέ there is the variant καὶ εἰσελθοῦσαι (A C³ W Γ Θ pm; TR; Diglot) which may be assimilation to Mk. Wellhausen, 136, omitted the phrase on the grounds that so many women could not have got into the tomb together. But there need have been no more than about half a dozen of them, and entry would not have been impossible. The body of Jesus was not there (24:6; Mk. 16:6). The discovery is brought forward for emphasis. There is some discrepancy between the narratives as to who entered the tomb and when, and there is no satisfactory means of ironing it out. For Luke the body is that of the Lord Jesus, τοῦ κυρίου Ἰησοῦ. The whole phrase is omitted by D a b d e ff²l r¹ Eus ⸓, and τοῦ Ἰησοῦ is read by 579 pc sy boᵖᵗ. The whole phrase is bracketed in BFBS and omitted by Diglot; κυρίου was bracketed by UBS (first edition). This is one of a series of passages where words or phrases are absent from representatives of the western text (22:19b–20; 24:3, 6, 12, 36, 40, 51, 52; Mt. 27:49). Earlier critical opinion rejected these phrases as early interpolations into the text (WH II, 175–177; App. ad loc.). Recent scholarship, recognising the early origins of the Alexandrian type of text, has come to the contrary opinion (Jeremias, Words, 145–152; K. Aland, 'Neue Neutestamentliche Papyri II', NTS 12, 1965–66, 193–210; Metzger, 191–193). Each case must be considered on its merits with attention to the theological tendencies of the Evangelists and the scribes. In the present case, the external evidence for omission is weak; the phrase is one used of the risen Jesus in Acts 1:21; 4:33; 8:16 (cf. Jn. 20:2); and the omission may be due to assimilation to 24:23 (cf. Mt. 27:58; Mk. 15:43; Metzger, 183). The phrase declares the new

status of the risen Jesus; he is the Lord (cf. I. de la Potterie, in Descamps, 123).

(4) The story continues in typical Lucan style (cf. 1:8; *et al.*; 5:1; *et al.*) with reference to the perplexity (ἀπορέω; Mk. 6:20; Acts 25:20; cf. ἀπορία, 21:25**) of the women. Apparently while they are still in the tomb (but an unsignalled change of scene is possible), two men in shining raiment appear to them (cf. Acts 1:10 for a close parallel). The description is of angels. ἐφίστημι (2:9; *et al.*; cf. Acts 12:7) can be used of the appearance of supernatural visitors. ἐσθής (23:11) can be used of the clothing of an angel (Acts 10:30; cf. ἔσθησις, Acts 1:10**), and ἀστράπτω (17:24**) indicates the shining appearance of heavenly garments (cf. ἐξαστράπτω of the transfiguration appearance (9:29) and ἀστραπή with reference to the angel's face (Mt. 28:3)). The parallel figure in Mk. 16:5 is a νεανίσκος, a word used elsewhere by Luke in its literal sense; he uses ἀνήρ of angels (Acts 1:10; 10:30; cf. Lk. 9:30 of heavenly visitors). The two angels parallel the two visitors at the transfiguration and the two angels at the ascension (Acts 1:10), and are paralleled in Jn. 20:12; cf. G. Peter 36 and (simple plural) Mk. 16:4 k. The doubling of the figure may be meant to provide two witnesses to the important fact about to be described; an attempt to provide a parallel with the transfiguration (Stuhlmueller, 162) is unlikely. But the number may be traditional (Lagrange, 599, notes that they *both* speak), and is not necessarily due to Luke himself, especially in view of Jn. 20:12 (cf. Lohfink, 198).

(5) Mark's simple ἐξεθαμβήθησαν (signifying amazement) is replaced by a fuller description of the fear felt by the women (cf. Mk. 16:8; Mt. 28:5). For ἔμφοβος, 'afraid, startled', cf. 24:37; Acts 10:4; 24:25; Rev. 11:13**; the phraseology is Lucan. The women bow (κλίνω, 9:12; *et al.*) their heads (the singular form τὸ πρόσωπον is found in A C[3] W Γ (Δ) f13 *pm* lat; TR; *Diglot*, and is defended by Alford, 660; it corresponds to Semitic style (Mt. 17:6) and should be accepted). The action expresses fear or perhaps avoidance of the bright light (cf. Acts 9:4). The angels then address them. Luke omits the conventional, 'Do not be afraid/amazed', and goes straight to the point. The women are reproached for seeking (Jn. 20:15) the living one among the dead. For ζάω in this sense cf. 15:32; 24:23; Acts 1:3; 9:41; 25:19; Mk. 16:11; and also Rom. 14:9; 2 Cor. 13:4; Gal. 2:20; Heb. 7:25; 1 Pet. 3:18; Rev. 1:18; Bartsch, 22, suggests, probably rightly, that the language of the angels has been shaped by the kerygma. There is a parallel to the whole phrase in Ex. R 5 (71c) (SB II, 269) which may suggest that a proverbial phrase is here being given a new meaning (Rengstorf, 268). The change from Mark's statement to a question is probably due to Luke.

(6) The opening statement is omitted by D it, and some MSS show minor variations in wording; it is omitted by *Diglot*; NEB; and bracketed by BFBS. Kilpatrick, 193, claims that it is an assimilation to Mt. 28:6 (similarly, Tasker, 424), but this argument ignores the ἀλλά,

and the phrase should be retained (Metzger, 183f.). The inversion of order from Mk. gives a better climax. The presence of the body of Jesus in the tomb is incompatible with the fact of his resurrection. The women should not have been surprised by this for what had occurred was simply fulfilment of prophecy – in this case not OT prophecy (as in 24:25f., 44, 46) but Jesus' own prophecy (Harvey, 297) of what was to happen to him. The women should have remembered what Jesus said while he was still with them in Galilee. For μιμνήσκομαι cf. 24:8; 1:54; et al. The phrase ὡς ἐλάλησεν is parallel to Mt. 28:6 (καθὼς εἶπεν) and probably based on Mk. 16:7b where it refers to Jesus' promise to see the disciples in Galilee. The women are assumed to have been with the disciples when Jesus made his prophecy, or to have heard from the disciples. But whereas Mark refers forward to a meeting in Galilee, Luke looks back to what Jesus said in Galilee. This alteration fits in with Luke's restriction of the resurrection appearances to Jerusalem and his insistence (based on Mk.) that it was people from Galilee who heard Jesus there and then bore witness to the resurrection (Acts 1:22; 10:37–41). The alteration is thus due to Luke himself (Lagrange, 600).

(7) The statement of Jesus' prophecy about himself can be regarded either as being drawn from tradition in view of some apparent Semitisms (M. Black, 'The "Son of Man" Passion Sayings in the Gospel Tradition', ZNW 60, 1969, 1–8) or as a Lucan summary based on the sayings in Mk. 14:41; 16:6. The evidence rather favours the latter view. The use of τὸν υἱὸν τοῦ ἀνθρώπου as an anticipatory accusative before the noun clause of which it is the logical subject can be explained as hyperbaton due to Aramaic influence (Black, 53), but the appearance of the same construction in 9:31; Acts 13:32f. (cf. Mk. 7:2) suggests that it is a Lucanism (cf. BD 476[3]). The combination of δεῖ and παραδοθῆναι is not found in any of the earlier predictions (Mk. 8:31; 9:31; 10:33f.). For εἰς χεῖρας ἀνθρώπων ἁμαρτωλῶν cf. 9:43 par. Mk. 9:31; less close is Mk. 14:41 which uses εἰς τὰς χεῖρας τῶν ἁμαρτωλῶν. It is significant that Luke made no use earlier of Mk. 14:41, so that the present verse may be regarded as his equivalent for it. σταυρόω occurs in Mt. 20:19 (diff. Lk. 18:33) and Mk. 16:6; it is the natural word to use in the light of the event, and is not a sign of late formulation (pace Tödt, 152). For τῇ τρίτῃ ἡμέρᾳ cf. 18:33; 24:46. The saying thus contains elements drawn from a variety of earlier sayings; with the exception of δεῖ (which may be Lucan) it fits into the pattern of Mk. 9:31a; 14:41c in which the Son of man is delivered into the hands of men (note the paronomasia; 9:44 note). Behind the saying may lie the tradition attested in these verses rather than direct influence from Mk. itself; cf. J. Roloff, 'Anfänge der soteriologischen Deutung des Todes Jesu (Mk. x.45 und Lk. xxii.27)', NTS 19, 1972–73, 38–64, especially 39; cf. C. Colpe, TDNT VIII, 458 (but Colpe's argument that Luke does not use 'Son of man' independently is not valid here, if Luke is in fact giving an equivalent for Mk. 14:41). In any case, the angelic message reproduces the general content

of what Jesus had said earlier, and the message loses its force if Jesus had not spoken in such terms of his resurrection; see 9:22 note.

(8) The women's 'recognition memory' was aroused (cf. Acts 11:16 for the motif which may be Lucan). The scene comes to a rather abrupt end, and we are not told whether the women believed that Jesus was risen, or what happened to the angels or anything else. The women figure very much as messengers to the disciples.

(9) They therefore departed from the tomb (ἀπὸ τοῦ μνημείου omitted by D it arm, probably accidentally; Metzger, 184), and announced (ἀπαγγέλλω par. Mt.) these things (ταῦτα πάντα, p⁷⁵ A B G L W f1 f13; TR; inverted by rell; Diglot; but the order in the text is Lucan) to the Eleven (24:33; Acts 1:26; 2:14; Mt. 28:16; Mk. 16:14**) and the rest of Jesus' companions (cf. 24:22f.). Mark states that the women told nobody; but since the other Gospels state the contrary (Mt. 28:8; Jn. 20:17), it may be presumed that the lost ending of Mark agreed with them.

(10) Only towards the end of the narrative does Luke include the names of the women involved; for a similar procedure see Acts 1:13 which suggests that the positioning may be due to Luke himself. On the other hand, the list of names may be drawn from a source in view of its contents, although Taylor, *Passion*, 108, regards v. 10a as an insertion by Luke from Mk. The syntax of the verse is obscure, and the obscurity is compounded by the textual uncertainty. The following possibilities arise: 1. 'Now (the women) were Mary . . .; and the other women with them told . . .' (RV). 2. 'Now (the women) were Mary . . .; the other women with them also told . . .' (JB; cf. NEB; TNT; TEV; Lagrange, 401). 3. With asyndeton: 'Now (the women) were Mary . . . and the other women with them; they told . . .' (B. Weiss, as reported in *Synopsis*); 4. With anacolouthon: 'Now (the women) were Mary . . . and the other women with them told . . .' 5. Omitting ἦσαν δέ (A D W syˢᶜ) to avoid the anacolouthon (but at the cost of asyndeton at the beginning of the verse): 'Mary . . . and the other women with them told . . .' 6. Inserting αἵ (אᶜ Θ al; TR; Diglot): 'Now (the women) were Mary . . . and the other women with them who told . . .' (RSV; NIV; similarly 157 inserts καί). The textual changes are clearly secondary simplifications. Translation 4. gives the required sense (as does translation 3.); translations 1. and 2. lay the stress on the other women who confirm the message of the three named ones (Lagrange, 601). Either there is some primitive corruption in the text (rectified in אᶜ Θ al), or else Luke has failed to revise his text correctly, as is the case not infrequently in Acts. Mary Magdalene figures in all the lists of women at the tomb (Mk. 16:1; cf. 15:40, 47; Jn. 20:1, 18; cf. 19:25); cf. 8:2. The order of words ἡ Μαγδαληνὴ Μαρία is unparalleled, although it is a perfectly regular form (Jos. Bel. 2:520), and suggests use of a source other than Mk. Ἰωάννα appears elsewhere only in 8:3** as one of Jesus' companions in Galilee. The third woman is Μαρία ἡ Ἰακώβου, which in the absence of further

definition would presumably mean 'Mary the wife of James' (cf. BD 162). In Mk. 15:40, however, we hear of Mary the mother of James and Joses; in Mk. 15:47 we have Mary the (?) of Joses, and in 16:1 Mary the (?) of James. If the same woman is meant throughout in Mk. then we should supply 'mother' in each case. It is possible that the same interpretation of ἡ 'Ιακώβου should be given in the present verse, although in the absence of other guidance it would be more natural to think that the wife of James was meant. It is unlikely, however, that Luke would misunderstand Mk. 16:1 if he had also read Mk. 15:40, 47, and we should probably interpret here in the light of Mk. (as do all the translations). For αἱ λοιπαί cf. 23:49. The imperfect ἔλεγον perhaps indicates that they tried repeatedly to get their story across to the apostles (i.e. the Eleven; cf. 6:13), or that they spoke one by one (Lagrange, 601).

(11) To the apostles, however, what they said seemed (ἐφάνησαν, plural, with neuter plural subject) like nonsense (λῆρος**), and they were unwilling to believe them (cf. 24:41; Mt. 28:17; Mk. 16:11, 14; Jn. 20:25, 27 for this motif). Since the motif is a widespread one, it is not necessarily Lucan, although the verse is clearly Lucan in style. Luke says nothing about any of the women having seen Jesus (Mt. 28:9f.; Mk. 16:9–11; Jn. 20:11–18) before telling the apostles their story, and betrays no knowledge of this detail. He may have preferred to tell the story of the appearance of Jesus to the disciples on the way to Emmaus.

(12) But before he does so, he has one qualification to make of the disbelief recorded in v. 11 – assuming, that is, that v. 12 is a genuine part of the text. It is omitted by D a b d e l r¹ sy^pal (mss) Mcion Diat Eus⸓; WH (see WH App. 71); *Synopsis*; *Diglot*; RSV t; NEB t; see Easton, 257; Kilpatrick, 193; H. von Campenhausen*; K.P.G. Curtis*. The verse is defended by Lagrange, 601f.; Jeremias, *Words*, 149–151; A. R. C. Leaney*; K. Aland, NTS 12, 1965–66, 205f.; Grundmann, 439f.; Ellis, 272f.; Danker, 247; Morris, 335f. The external evidence for omission is not decisive. The passage has been regarded as an interpolation, based on Jn. 20:3–10 (cf. Mt. 27:49, an interpolation based on Jn. 19:34; Metzger, 71), but the evidence suggests that Luke has the tradition in an earlier form, and v. 24 appears to be a cross-reference to the present verse. The style is Lucan; Curtis's suggestion that a later redactor imitated Luke's style is not convincing. The same author's suggestion that the vocabulary is Johannine is also unconvincing. The difficulty of explaining why the verse was omitted still remains, however. Grundmann, 440, suggests that it was left out because it did not relate a proper appearance to Peter. Indeed, the verse might have been thought to stand in contradiction to v. 34.

For ἀναστάς, cf. 1:39; *et al.*; K. P. G. Curtis*, notes that elsewhere in Lk.-Acts it follows the subject, but this is not a very strong point. Peter alone is mentioned, whereas in Jn. 20:3 he is accompanied by the beloved disciple; the presence of more than one person is implied by v. 24, and suggests that Luke has deliberately omitted reference to the

common meal of fellowship fails to accept satisfactorily for various features of the story. (Betz's reinterpretation of this point in existential terms need not concern us here.) The main purpose of the story is rather to guarantee the fact of the resurrection (cf. Acts 1:3) by emphasising 1. that it is the expected fulfilment of the OT (as it was of the word of Jesus, 24:6f.), and 2. that the risen Lord appeared to witnesses and was recognised to be Jesus. The story demonstrates the reality of the resurrection and the identity of the Risen One with Jesus; the application to the presence of Jesus in the worship of the church is secondary. But if this is the case, the story falls into the same pattern as the other appearance stories and may be presumed to have come out of the same tradition.

But if the story has a basis in tradition, does it have any claims to historicity? In the nature of the case, it is impossible to provide proof of its historicity, but at least it may be claimed that the objections raised to its historicity are weak. To categorise the *form* of the story as 'legend' is in no way to prove its fictional character, since a form-critical verdict of this kind cannot affect historicity. A characterisation of the *contents* of the story as legendary rests on a prior rejection of the possibility of the resurrection. The fact that parallels to features of the story can be cited from pagan legends does not alter this verdict; in reality none of the alleged parallels is sufficiently forceful to suggest that motifs from folklore have played a vital part in the development of the story. (The parallel in Philostratus, Vita Apoll. 8:11f. (30f.), may even be dependent on the NT; cf. A. A. T. Ehrhardt, 195–201.) The most puzzling feature is perhaps the initial blindness of the disciples, but this is more theological than legendary in character, and it has parallels in some of the other resurrection appearance narratives; the motif that the risen Jesus looked 'different' is widespread.

As for the other historical difficulties, the story does not conflict with the fact that the first appearance was to Peter since it makes no claim to be an account of the original appearance of Jesus. It remains a mystery why Luke has not recounted the story of the appearance of Jesus to Peter, but this mystery affects all the Gospels. Nor does the fact that according to other traditions Jesus appeared to his disciples in Galilee rule out the possibility of appearances in Jerusalem. If the appearances 'were real and objective, there is no reason why they should have been confined to any one locality, and if they were the merest hallucination, there is still less cause for thinking that it was peculiar to any one circle of disciples' (K. Lake*, 211f.).

These considerations suggest that we are justified in regarding this story as having a basis in tradition, and that this tradition can have a historical basis. The hand of Luke in the formation of the narrative cannot be denied, but he was by no means creating his story *de novo*.

See the bibliography for 23:50 – 24:53, especially K. Lake; P. Schubert; R. H. Fuller, 103–113; I. H. Marshall, 78–91; and also J. Dupont, 'Les pèlerins d'Emmaüs', *Miscellanea*

Biblica, Monserrat, 1953, 349–374 (as reported in NTA 2, 1957, no. 58); C. F. D. Moule, 'The Post-Resurrection Appearances in the Light of Festival Pilgrimages', NTS 4, 1957–58, 58–61; A. A. T. Ehrhardt, 'The Disciples of Emmaus', NTS 10, 1963–64, 182–201; Bouwman, 13–15; H.-D. Betz, 'Ursprung und Wesen christlichen Glaubens nach der Emmauslegende (Lk. 24:13–32)', ZTK 66, 1969, 7–21 (also as 'The Origin and Nature of Christian Faith according to the Emmaus Legend', *Interpretation* 23, 1969, 32–46); J. Carmignac, 'Les apparitions de Jésus ressuscité et le calendrier biblico-qumranien', RQ 7:4 (28), 1971, 483–504; J. Wanke, *Die Emmauserzählung*, Leipzig, 1973.

(13) Luke's story is about two of the disciples of Jesus mentioned in vs. 9, 11, and it takes place on the same day as the discovery of the empty tomb. Ellis's claim, 276, that Luke's time references identify this as the 'eighth day', the beginning of a new creation (cf. 9:28; Barn. 15:8f.; Justin, Dial. 138) is a doubtful attempt to explain Lk. in the light of later Christian thought and has no real basis in the text. ἦσαν πορευόμενοι is placed before ἐν αὐτῇ τῇ ἡμέρᾳ (on which see note) by most authorities (so TR; *Diglot*), except p⁷⁵ (ℵ) B which preserve the slightly more awkward and therefore original order. The disciples were possibly returning home after the celebration of the festival (cf. SB II, 147f.; Jeremias, *Words*, 72 n. 2; see further C. F. D. Moule*; J. Carmignac*). Their destination was a village not far from Jerusalem (Lohfink, 207f., 264f., argues that the point of the geographical note is to emphasise that the appearance of Jesus took place in the vicinity of Jerusalem.) The distance is measured in terms of the στάδιον, i.e. 600 Greek feet (equivalent to 625 Roman feet; or 607 English feet; or 192 metres; cf. AG s.v.; the noun can have a neuter or masculine plural (BD 49³); cf. Mt. 14:24; Jn. 6:19; 11:18; Rev. 14:20; 21:16; also meaning 'stadium, arena', 1 Cor. 9:24**). 60 stades is thus roughly 7 miles. Instead of ἑξήκοντα some MSS have ἑκατὸν ἑξήκοντα (ℵ K* N Θ Π 079 ᵛⁱᵈ 1079* syᵖᵃˡ arm Eus Hier), i.e. about 18½ miles; this reading is due to an attempt to find a reference to Amwas (mod. Nicopolis), 20 miles from Jerusalem on the road to Joppa (cf. Lagrange, 617–622; Metzger, 184f.). The similarity in spelling quickly led to the identification of this well-known site with the mere village mentioned here (1 Mac. 3:40, 57; 4:3; cf. 9:50; Jos. Ant. 12:306f.; Bel. 1:222 and frequently); so Eusebius and Jerome, and in modern times SB II, 269–271; Dalman, *Sites*, 226–232; Abel, II, 314–316; Bouwman, 13; Finegan, 177–180; J. Wanke*, 37–42. If so, either Luke got the distance wrong, or the variant reading is a correct emendation of a primitive textual corruption. The obvious difficulty is the great distance from Jerusalem, but Abel asserts that this is no problem to those familiar with the capabilities of Palestinian people. Other identifications, more in accord with a seven-mile radius from Jerusalem, have been suggested. Of these the favourite is El-Qubeibeh, a village seven miles NW of Jerusalem where Crusaders found a fort (1099) called Castellum Emmaus, and where recent archaeology has found a village of first-century date (so Zahn, 716–720; Plummer, 551f.; Rengstorf, 271; Geldenhuys, 636). The difficulty here is the lack of firm evidence for the name of the site in the first century.

Also, the Hebrew word means 'spring', and there are no springs at this site (cf. Rengstorf). Third, Josephus mentions a military colony of Vespasian 30 stadia W of Jerusalem at 'Αμμαοῦς (Bel. 7:217). This site has been identified with modern Kaloniye (i.e. Latin *colonia*) some four miles W. of Jerusalem or with Mozah (a village just north of Kaloniye; modern Kh. Beit Mizza; cf. SB II, 271, for rabbinic evidence suggesting that the old village became a Roman camp). This site is accepted by Schürer, *History*, 512 n. 142; Wellhausen, 138; J. Weiss, 523; K. Lake*, 99f.; Harvey, 297 n.; Benoit, *Passion*, 271–274. The difficulty here is that the distance is half that given by Luke; Benoit suggests that Luke has mistakenly given the distance for the journey there and back. It must be admitted, therefore, that in both of the two possible identifications the distance given by the present text of Luke is wrong. On the whole Amwas has more to be said for it, since later on the point of the story is the return of the disciples to Jerusalem despite an apparently lengthy journey; but certainty is impossible.

(14) During the journey the disciples were conversing (ὁμιλέω, 24:15; Acts 20:11; 24:26**) about all (περὶ πάντων, 3:19; *et al.*, is comparatively frequent in Lk.-Acts) these things which had happened (συμβαίνω; Acts 3:10; 20:19; 21:35; rest of NT 4x**).

(15) During their conversation and discussion (συζητέω, 22:23 – but here in a weak sense) Jesus himself (αὐτὸς Ἰησοῦς, as 20:42; but αὐτὸς ὁ Ἰησοῦς is read by D W Γ Δ Θ f1 f13 *pm*; TR; *Diglot*) drew near and began to walk along the road with them (συνπορεύομαι 7:11; *et al.*). He was evidently in human form, as would be appropriate for a supernatural being appearing on earth; there is no necessary discrepancy with Paul's insistence on the spiritual character of the resurrection body.

(16) The disciples, however, did not recognise that it was Jesus. Their eyes were 'prevented' (κρατέω, 8:54) so that they could not recognise him (ἐπιγινώσκω, 24:31). For this motif cf. 9:45; 18:34. An action by God (cf. the use of the passive) rather than Satan is no doubt meant. The story depends on this element of dramatic concealment. The lack of recognition is more due to a spiritual blindness by the disciples than to something unusual about the appearance of Jesus (for the latter see Mk. 16:12). Its purpose is to enable the disciples to be prepared for the revelation of the risen Jesus by a fresh understanding of the prophecies of his resurrection; it may also be meant to show that one can know the presence of the risen Jesus without being able to see him, and thus to give help to Christians living in the era after the cessation of the resurrection appearances. It would, however, be difficult for later people to believe that their experience was related to the unseen, risen Jesus, if there were not evidence, such as this story provides, that Jesus really rose from the dead.

(17) The stranger is pictured as hearing something of their conversation as he catches up with them on the road and this give him his opportunity to intervene. For οἱ λόγοι οὗτοι cf. 24:44; Acts 5:5, 24.

ἀντιβάλλω** is 'to put, place against' (2 Mac. 11:13), here 'to exchange'; πρὸς ἀλλήλους is Lucan. Hence the question means, 'What is the subject of your discussion?' (AG 73). At the question they stopped in their tracks (ἐστάθησαν; but perhaps the verb translates an Aramaic auxiliary verb with the following adjective – 'and they were downcast'; cf. Wilcox, 125). The verb is omitted by D Or; and ἐστέ is read by Aᶜ W Γ Δ Θ f1 f13 pl lat (sy); TR; thus making it part of the preceding question. For σκυθρωπός, 'with a sad, gloomy, or sullen look', cf. Mt. 6:16**.

(18) One of the two travellers replies; the article is prefixed before εἷς by A W Γ Δ pm; TR; Diglot). For ὀνόματι cf. 1:5. Κλεοπᾶς** is an abbreviated form of Κλεόπατρος (cf. Ἀντίπας and Ἀντίπατρος), and was probably used as an equivalent to the Semitic form Κλωπᾶς; the latter name occurs as the husband of a Mary who was present at the crucifixion (Jn. 19:25) and also as the name of a brother of Joseph (Hegesippus, cited by Eusebius, HE 3:11, 32; 4:22). If these persons are identified (Grundmann, 443; contra Klostermann, 235) we have an account of a resurrection appearance to the father of Simeon, the later head of the church in Jerusalem. In any case, it is likely that the person was known to Luke's readers, and the naming of the one traveller rather than both rather suggests that a well-known person is in mind; it is unlikely that the detail is legendary. Luke's failure to name the other traveller has naturally led to speculation regarding his or her identity. Cleopas' wife or son has been suggested (cf. Metzger, 185; Bornhäuser, Death, 221f.); of these the former is the more likely, since the son (if he was the later bishop of Jerusalem) would surely have been named. Benoit, Passion, 275, favours Philip the deacon as the source of this story and other early incidents in Acts situated W of Jerusalem; this is an intriguing conjecture, but beyond proof. To the two travellers the third man is another festival pilgrim returning home; παροικέω will then have its usual meaning 'to inhabit as a stranger' (Heb. 11:9** – 'to migrate to'), and the force of the question is 'Are you alone so much of a stranger in Jerusalem that you do not know what everybody there is talking about?' (cf. Klostermann, 235; Creed, 295); there are close parallels in Cicero, Pro Milone 12 (33); Pro Rab. Perd. 10 (28). The evidence for inserting ἐν before Ἰερουσαλήμ (Λ 69 al; TR; Diglot) is too weak to be taken seriously.

(19) To the stranger's 'What things (ποῖος, 5:19; et al.)?' the travellers reply with an account of the things that had happened in respect of Jesus the Nazarene. The τὰ περί . . . formula is Lucan (2:39; et al.; especially Acts 18:25; 28:31). Ναζαρηνοῦ is read by p⁷⁵ ℵ B L 0124 pc lat Or; the variant reading Ναζωραίου (rell; TR; Diglot) is probably a scribal correction to the more usual form (Metzger, 185); cf. 4:34* par. Mk. The use of the unusual word suggests that Luke is here following tradition; in a report to a stranger it is used to identify Jesus more closely by his home town. ἐγένετο has the force 'he showed himself to be' (Creed, 296). The use of the redundant ἀνήρ is Lucan, and is perhaps

respectful (cf. Acts 1:16; 2:29, 37; 7:2). Before knowledge of his resurrection the highest description that can be applied to Jesus is that of prophet (4:24 note; Acts 3;22; 7:37; cf. Bartsch, 24). Nevertheless, he was a mighty prophet both in word and action; cf. the description of Moses in Acts 7:22; the combination of 'word and deed' is frequent (Rom. 15:18; 2 Cor. 10:11; Col. 3:17; 2 Thes. 2:17; 1 Jn. 3:18). ἐναντίον τοῦ θεοῦ suggests that he was approved by God (1:6) as well as by men.

(20) The use of a clause to continue a phrase (τὰ περί ... ὅπως τε ...) is paralleled in 24:35 (τὰ ἐν τῇ ὁδῷ καὶ ὡς ...); ὅπως is here used to introduce an indirect question. The use of τε as a conjunction is strange; BD 443¹ prefer the reading ὅπως τοῦτον (cf. ὡς τοῦτον, D), and *Diglot* brackets τε without any MS authority. For παραδίδωμι cf. 9:44; 24:7; here it is used of the action of the high priests and rulers (23:13; cf. Acts 13:27) in handing Jesus over to death (for κρίμα cf. 20:47; 23:40) and crucifying him (23:21; 24:7; Acts 2:36; 4:10). Note how the Jews themselves are said to carry out the crucifixion here, although παρέδωκαν contains a hint of Jesus being handed over to the Romans.

(21) If the people thought of Jesus merely as a mighty prophet – and let him suffer the fate of a prophet – the disciples (ἡμεῖς δέ) had held a different opinion. Their hope (cf. Acts 28:20) was that Jesus would crown his prophetic work by redeeming the people, i.e. by setting them free from their enemies and inaugurating the kingdom of God (cf. 1:68; 2:38; 21:28; and (for the verb λυτρόομαι) Tit. 2:14; 1 Pet. 1:18**; F. Büchsel, TDNT IV, 349–351). The disciples naturally think in terms of the redemption of God's own people, Israel (cf. Acts 28:20). But their hopes had been dashed by his death. Nevertheless (ἀλλά γε καί; BD 439²; cf. Phil. 3:8; γε is Lucan, 5:36; *et al.*) in addition to all these things (σὺν πᾶσιν τούτοις; on the text see Jeremias, *Words*, 151; for the phrase cf. 16:26; Jos. Ant. 17:171; BD 221), it was now the third day since his death, and nothing further had happened. The phraseology is strange. ἄγει is generally thought to be used impersonally ('it is spending the third day ...'; Moule, 27), but BD 129 suggests 'He is now spending the third day' (similarly AG 14, citing Barn. 15:9). ταύτην must be separated from τρίτην ... ἡμέραν since the article is missing (1:36; 2:2; Jn. 2:11; 4:54; Achilles Tacitus 7:11:2, cited by AG 602; cf. BD 292): 'This is the third day that he has spent since ...' σήμερον is added unnecessarily by A (D) W Γ Δ Θ f13 *pm*; TR; *Diglot*. For ἀφ' οὗ cf. 13:7 note; ταῦτα is the death of Jesus, and refers back to τὰ γενόμενα, 24:18. The reference to the third day appears to reflect the Jewish belief that by the fourth day the soul had left the body (Jn. 11:39), or possibly a dim memory that Jesus had spoken enigmatically of something happening on the third day. From a literary point of view it prepares the way for the coming miracle (Creed, 296).

(22) What the disciples have said remains valid despite what has been reported concerning the body of Jesus; neither the empty tomb nor

the story of an angelic message provide conclusive support that Jesus is alive, but simply heighten the tragedy. Wellhausen, 139, thought that vs. 22–24 were an interpolation, but v. 21 suggests that more is to follow, and the rebuke in vs. 25f. makes better sense after the present verses (cf. Klostermann, 236). ἐξίστημι is 'to change, displace', hence 'to confuse, amaze, astound' (intransitive: 2:47; 8:56*; transitive, Acts 8:9, 11). γενόμεναι is loosely attached. ὀρθρινός** is 'early in the morning' (cf. 24:1).

(23) After failing to find the body of Jesus the women returned from the tomb with a story that they had seen also (i.e. in addition to the empty tomb) a vision (ὀπτασία, 1:22) of angels who declared that Jesus was alive. (The present tense is retained in the indirect speech, and implies the continuing validity of the message.)

(24) This verse has also been regarded as an interpolation, in view of its allusion to the suspect v. 12 (J. Weiss, 523f.), but it should be retained. More than one disciple (cf. Jn. 20:3–10, diff. Lk. 24:12) went to the tomb to check up on the story and found things just as the women had said, but him (αὐτὸν δέ, emphatic) they did not see. The content of these verses is modelled on that of 24:1–12 and is Lucan in character, but can well be based on an actual conversation; the characterisation of the disciples' estimate of Jesus is certainly realistic.

(25) The stranger's reply is introduced by ὦ, an exclamation which implies strong emotion (9:41 par. Mk. 9:19; Acts 13:10; Gal. 3:1; weak use in Acts 1:1; 18:14; 27:21; Zerwick, 35). ἀνόητος* is 'unintelligent, foolish' (Gal. 3:1, 3); βραδύς is 'slow' (Jas. 1:19**). The use of τοῦ with the infinitive is Lucan (1:73; et al.). πιστεύειν ἐπί may be a Semitism (Wilcox, 85f.; cf. Acts 9:42; 11:17; 16:31; 22:19), but due to Luke himself. For λαλέω used of prophecy cf. 1:55, 70; Acts 3:21, 24; et al., and for the thought cf. 18:31. Acceptance of what the prophets said should have led the disciples to believe the reports of the women at the tomb; one may believe in the resurrection on the evidence of others, although this does not mean that the Lord withholds personal evidence from those who need it.

(26) The stranger now states the basic pattern of experience for the Messiah in a way which implies that the disciples should have been aware of it already; for οὐχί cf. 24:32, and for ἔδει cf. 24:7. For πάσχω in christological formulae cf. 9:22; 24:46; Acts 3:18; 17:3; 26:23. But it is not clear whether pre-Christian Judaism expected the Messiah (2:26; et al.; 24:46) to suffer; cf. SB II, 273–299; J. Jeremias, TDNT V, 677–700; H. H. Rowley, 'The Suffering Servant and the Davidic Messiah', Oudtestamentische Studien 8, 1950, 100–136; M. Rese, 'Überprüfung einiger Thesen von J. Jeremias zum Thema des Gottesknechts im Judentum', ZTK 60, 1963, 21–41. At best the expectation can hardly have been a widespread one, but the evidence is hard to assess since there is good reason to suppose that anti-Christian polemic has led to suppression of some of the evidence. But it is clear that here

the stranger is taking up the earlier passion predictions by Jesus, and applying what was said then about the Son of man to the Messiah. δόξα is the glory of the exalted Messiah/Son of man (cf. 9:26; 21:27; Phil. 2:5–11; 1 Tim. 3:16; 1 Pet. 1:11, 18f., 21; Hahn, 217). The passage of the Messiah to glory by way of suffering is a Lucan theme, but is by no means peculiarly Lucan, appearing as it does in the passion predictions in Mk. No significance should be attached to the omission of the resurrection and the period of the appearances in the present statement, as if the Messiah were regarded as passing straight from the cross to his heavenly glory (but cf. J. Weiss, 524).

(27) The rest of what Jesus said is given in summary form. He proceeded through the OT beginning with (ἀρξάμενος ἀπό, 14:18; 23:5; et al.) the books of Moses and the prophets (Luke likes to use 'all' in such contexts; cf. ἐν πάσαις ταῖς γραφαῖς). The clause may be construed in two ways: 1. It may mean that the speaker started from the law and the prophets in finding things written about himself. 2. More probably it means that he searched in all the Scriptures, but starting from (i.e. principally from) the law and the prophets. If we adopt this latter view, then ἐν πάσαις ταῖς γραφαῖς will refer to the books of the OT generally (24:32, 45; Acts 17:2, 11; 18:24, 28; A. Oepke, TDNT I, 752). The view that the phrase refers purely to the third part of the OT canon, the 'writings' (Grundmann, 446; cf. 24:44) is difficult syntactically. διερμηνεύω* is 'to translate, explain, interpret' (Acts 9:36*); the aorist is read by p⁷⁵ ℵᶜ B L al; most other authorities (followed by TR; Diglot) have the imperfect which is more appropriate for an extended discourse. The verb signifies that the speaker chose out those passages which might be regarded as 'messianic' and then proceeded to show how they should be understood, so that they could now 'speak' to the disciples.

(28) So the journey passed, and they approached (or arrived at – ἐγγίζω could have either force) the village to which (οὗ, 4:16; et al.; of place whither, 10:1) they were journeying. The stranger made as if to proceed further; προσποιέομαι** can mean 'to pretend', but this is too strong here, since, although on one level of understanding he intends to stay with them, he is merely giving them the opportunity to invite him in, and will not force his presence on them. The imperfect is again read by W Γ Δ Θ f13 pm; TR; Diglot, but the external evidence is weak, although the reading can be justified internally. For πορρώτερον** cf. the simple form in 14:32*.

(29) By early afternoon the main part of the day is regarded as over, and hence the insistence of the two disciples (παραβιάζομαι, 'to use force', hence 'to urge strongly', Acts 16:15**) that the stranger should break his journey rings true (Harvey, 298; cf. Bornhäuser, Death, 219, who thinks, however, that it is merely a question of sharing a meal with the disciples before the stranger goes further). For the motif cf. Gn. 24:55; Jdg. 19:9; Tob. 10:8; Acts 16:15; Lk. 19:5; Jn. 1:38; Jos. et As. 42, 50; it is not surprising that it is widespread. For ἑσπέρα, 'evening', cf.

Acts 4:3; 28:23**, and for κλίνω cf. 9:12; it is noteworthy that Luke, who often abbreviates Mark's double time-expressions, here has one of his own. Grundmann, 447, compares the use of εἰσέρχομαι here with that in Rev. 3:20; it is a happy coincidence of language.

(30) Bultmann, 316, comments that the early church associated the resurrection appearances with meals (24:41–43; ? Acts 1:4; 10:41; Jn. 21:12f.; cf. Mk. 16:14), since it expected Jesus to 'appear' at the Lord's Supper. The connection between the two types of event is rightly observed, but the wrong inference has been drawn; it was because Jesus had appeared at meal times that the church expected his presence at the Lord's Supper. The meal is generally taken to be the evening meal, but Bornhäuser, *Death*, 219f., has made out a case for the midday meal which was a simpler affair. In either case unleavened bread would figure in the meal. No subject is supplied for the clause, and none is needed; it is supplied naturally from the αὐτόν, and the reader expects a reference to the stranger. He takes the bread (9:16; 22:19; cf. 24:43; Acts 27:35), says the blessing (9:16; Mk. 14:22; diff. Lk. 22:19) and breaks it (22:19; Mt. 14:19; 15:36; 26:26; Mk. 8:6, 19; 14:22; Acts 2:46; 20:7, 11; 27:35; 1 Cor. 10:16; 11:24**) before distributing it (ἐπιδίδωμι, 4:17; 11:11f.; 24:42). The actual eating is not mentioned (Lagrange, 608f.).

(31) The language of the previous verse points irresistibly to the action of Jesus at the last supper (and at the feeding of the multitudes), and serves to identify the stranger to the disciples; their eyes are opened (διανοίγω, 2:23; *et al.*; cf. 24:32, 45) by God to see the significance of the action and thus to recognise Jesus (contrast 24:16). But his appearance is short-lived. He becomes invisible (ἄφαντος**) once he has been recognised; cf. Euripides, Or. 1496; Hel. 605f.; Virgil, Aen. 9:657; 2 Mac. 3:34 for the motif. It is as a supernatural visitor that the risen Jesus is portrayed.

(32) The effect of the recognition of Jesus was to make the disciples realise that at the earlier point when Jesus had been opening up the meaning (διανοίγω, cf. Acts 17:3) of the Scriptures to them on the road they had experienced an unusual elation. Their hearts (the use of the 'distributive singular' is a common idiom; Col. 3:16; BD 410) had been burning within them. For καίω in this sense cf. Pss. 38:4 (39:3); 73:21 (72:21) v.l.; Je. 20:9; T. Naph. 7:4 (cf. Cicero, Brutus, 80). The meaning, however, is obscure, and this has led to textual variants – κεκαλυμμένη, D; see Metzger, 185f., for details). Torrey suggested confusion of Aramaic *yaqqir*, 'heavy', with *daqqir*, 'burning'; Black, 254f., notes that the Old Syriac has *yaqqir* and links this with *optusum* (an old Latin reading); he suggests that the Syriac has preserved the true Aramaic tradition of what the disciples were reported to have said from an extra-canonical source. On this view the disciples are referring back to Jesus' description of them in v. 25. But that verse refers to how the disciples felt *before* Jesus spoke to them, and the text should not be emended without good reason. Elsewhere 'to burn' expresses an

uncontrollable longing to speak or pray, usually in a situation of distress; something more than mere elation or ardour (P. Grenfell I, 1:1:9) is expressed. Barclay translates 'strangely warmed', an allusion to John Wesley's conversion experience as he heard the gospel being expounded in the words of Martin Luther. The reality of the risen Jesus was already making itself known to the disciples as he spoke to them, struggling to put itself into conscious form, and only being recognised for what it was after the visual revelation of Jesus. The story may then be suggesting that in the light of the disciples' experience later believers may be able to recognise their inward warmth of heart as springing from the presence of the risen Lord. The words ἐν ἡμῖν are omitted by p⁷⁵ B D d geo Or and bracketed by UBS; they probably appeared redundant to scribes (cf. Metzger, 186). Before the conjunction ὡς, καί is added by A W Γ Δ Θ f1 f13 pm; TR; Diglot.

(33) The news could naturally not be kept to themselves; there were others in Jerusalem who did not know whether Jesus had risen. So they arose and returned; αὐτῇ τῇ ὥρᾳ (cf. 24:13) means 'just at that time' (2:38 note). Back in Jerusalem they found the Eleven (24:9) gathered together (ἀθροίζω*; cf. ἐπαθροίζομαι, 11:29**) with their companions, οἱ σὺν αὐτοῖς (cf. 5:9; et al.; cf. 24:9f.).

(34) According to the majority text, the two disciples found the Eleven declaring that the Lord had risen and appeared to Simon. This affirmation has been thought to be difficult in view of 24:1–11, 22–24 and of 24:37, 41 (cf. Mk. 16:13f.). The former passages create no real problem, since the implication is that something fresh has happened since the departure of the two disciples earlier in the day. As for the latter passages, it may seem strange that the disciples should be afraid and disbelieving if they knew that Jesus was risen; but psychologically it is perfectly understandable that a supernatural appearance should cause consternation even when people are half-expecting it. Moreover, the effect of v. 12 is to prepare the reader for Peter to have some further experience. Mk. 16:13f. is a telescoping of the whole narrative, Lk. 24:13–43, and should not be played off against v. 34 in particular; it is clear that there was some division of opinion over the reality of the resurrection. Nevertheless, some scholars (e.g. K. Lake*, 102) have been inclined to accept the reading λέγοντες (D Or; the Latin and Syriac are ambiguous) which would make the two disciples the speakers. But the reading of D is no more than a transcriptional error (Metzger, 186), and the meaning of the variant is difficult. Since the two do not know that Jesus has appeared to Simon Peter, they can hardly be referring to him. Another Simon may be meant (cf. the identification of one of the two as Cleopas and the other as his son), but this is a strange kind of self-identification. Dietrich, 158–163, thinks it odd that Peter is referred to in the third person when he is present, and suggests that an independent tradition has been incorporated here. But the premiss is weak. It is more relevant to observe (with Dietrich) that the language is confessional

(ὄντως, 23:47), but in the confessional text in 1 Cor. 15:5 it is striking that Κῆφας is used and not Σίμων. The real problem lies not in the wording of the present verse, which fits its context neatly, but in the fact that Luke can record the appearance to Peter only indirectly. In this respect, however, he is no different from the other NT writers, none of whom seems to have known the story for reasons which cannot now be discovered. Note how the risen Jesus is referred to as ὁ κύριος; cf. v. 3. ὄντως appears at the end of the clause in most MSS (except p⁷⁵ ℵ B D L Ψ 1 579 pc lat), a position which Kilpatrick, 198, regards as corresponding to Semitic word order and therefore original.

(35) The report of the two disciples accordingly confirms the story of the appearance to Peter. ἐξηγέομαι, 'to explain, interpret, tell, report, describe', is Lucan (Acts 10:8; 15:12, 14; 21:19; Jn. 1:18**). It singles out the two facts of the appearance of Jesus on the road and his conversation and the way in which the stranger was identified as Jesus by the breaking of the bread (κλάσις, Acts 2:42); for the combination of a noun phrase and a clause cf. 24:19f. In the reading of Scripture and at the breaking of bread the risen Lord will continue to be present, though unseen.

iv. The Appearance to the Disciples 24:36–43

If the previous story has given the impression that the spiritual presence of Jesus is what ultimately matters, Luke redresses the balance in this narrative in which the physical reality of the risen Jesus is heavily emphasised. The story follows on without a break from that of the two disciples. In the space of three verses (34–36) three separate appearances of Jesus are listed, the third of which is now related. Again Jesus appears suddenly (cf. Jn. 19:19) to the consternation of the disciples who think that they must be seeing a ghost. But the risen Jesus removes their doubts and fears by showing, first, that it is indeed he who is present, and, second, that he is no spirit but has flesh and bones. When some continue to disbelieve, he provides further confirmation by eating food in their presence.

The narrative is not concerned to refute docetism in the proper sense of that term, since it is concerned with the nature of the risen Jesus and not with the nature of the earthly Jesus. Its point is to stress the identity of the risen One with Jesus and to emphasise the physical reality of his resurrection body. This leads to an apparent contradiction with Paul's dictum that 'flesh and blood shall not inherit the kingdom of God' and his insistence on the spiritual nature of the resurrection body, but the conflict is apparent rather than real. Paul is concerned with the nature of the body in the new life after the resurrection of the dead in the kingdom of God, while Luke is concerned with the appropriate form of manifestation of the risen Jesus in earthly conditions, and his narrative makes it plain that although Jesus has flesh and bones he is able to appear and vanish in a way that is not possible for ordinary men. Both writers agree that resurrection is concerned with the body and not with a bodiless soul or spirit.

It is generally agreed that the story was not created by Luke. The links with Jn. 20:19–23 are so close that it cannot be doubted that the same tradition is reflected in both Gospels (*pace* Bailey, 92–95). Although it has been claimed that Luke has embellished the tradition in the interests of an anti-docetic emphasis (Finegan, *Überlieferung*, 91; Taylor, *Passion*, 112–114; Roloff, *Kerygma*, 255), the stress on the bodily reality of the risen Jesus is also found in Jn. and is not therefore a Lucan invention. Bultmann, 310, thinks that Luke has used an existing legend about an appearance of Jesus in Galilee (cf. the similar motifs in Mt. 28:16–20). There is, however, no evidence in the narrative itself to support this judgment. Danker, 252, draws attention to a number of parallels with Mk. 6:45–52 (omitted by Luke earlier) and suggests that Luke is deliberately using motifs from that story here; but the parallels are individually weak and may arise more from the common epiphany motif in both stories than from conscious transfer by Luke.

See Bailey, 92–95; Taylor, *Passion*, 112–114; K. P. G. Curtis, 'Linguistic Support for Three Western Readings in Luke 24', Exp.T 83, 1971–72, 344f.

(36) The link with the preceding narrative, ταῦτα δὲ αὐτῶν λαλούντων, may well be Lucan (cf. Acts 4:1); it joins together the two stories very tightly, to show how the truth of the earlier reports of the appearances of Jesus to individuals are now confirmed by his appearance to a larger group. The same pattern of appearance to an individual followed by appearance to a group is found in the other Gospels (Mt. 28:9f., 16–20; Jn. 20:11–18, 19–23). The appearance is dated on Easter Sunday, as in Jn. 20:19; the feature is traditional and is not due to Luke's desire to secure unity of time and place for the resurrection stories. For ἔστη ἐν μέσῳ αὐτῶν, cf. Jn. 20:19, but the wording has been edited by Luke (cf. 2:46; *et al.*). The words καὶ λέγει αὐτοῖς, εἰρήνη ὑμῖν are found in all MSS except D it; they are omitted by most editors (including *Synopsis*; *Diglot*; cf. Kilpatrick, 193; Tasker, 424) and bracketed by WH as an insertion from Jn. 20:19 (cf. Dodd, 145 n.; Grundmann, 450f.). Some MSS add: ἐγώ εἰμι, μὴ φοβεῖσθε (G (W 579) *pc* aur c f vg sy^p bo^pt), a gloss that may be based on Jn. 6:20. But the parallel with Jn. 20:19 may well be based on common tradition, and the wording is accepted by UBS; Jeremias, *Words*, 151; K. Aland, NTS 12, 1965–66, 206–208; Metzger, 186f. The use of the historic present stems from the tradition, and need not be explained as evidence of a gloss from Jn. (*contra* K. P. G. Curtis*). The greeting εἰρήνη ὑμῖν may be 'an old essential part of the report about the Christophany before the disciples' (J. Jeremias); the promise of peace associated with the coming of Jesus now reaches its fulfilment (2:14; cf. 7:50; Acts 10:36), and the conventional greeting is transformed.

(37) But the greeting is swallowed up in the panic of the disciples (πτοέω, 21:9**). In their fear (ἔμφοβος, 24:5*) they imagined that they were seeing a ghost; for πνεῦμα in this sense cf. 24:39; Acts 23:8f. The reading φάντασμα (D Mcion; cf. Mk. 6:49) is regarded as the harder text by Grundmann, 451), but the external evidence is strongly against it (cf. Metzger, 187).

(38) Rhetorically Jesus asks 'why' (τί for διὰ τί) or 'in respect of what' (Lagrange, 612) they are alarmed (ταράσσω, cf. 1:12 in a similar context of fear of the supernatural) and have questionings (διαλογισμός, 2:35; et al.) in their hearts (i.e. minds) about the reality of his resurrection; for ἀναβαίνω in this metaphorical sense cf. Acts 7:23; 1 Cor. 2:9.

(39) The disciples need have no doubts; all that they have to do is to look at Jesus for the marks of identification. Let them examine his hands and his feet. Why these should be recognisable features is not clear from Lk., but Jn. 20:25–27 indicates that they retained the marks of the nails used in the crucifixion. Strictly speaking, the nails would have been through the wrists, but 'hands' can be used in a broad sense. ὅτι ἐγώ εἰμι αὐτός is added loosely; the force is: '(and you will see) that it is I myself'. Let them even touch him (ψηλαφάω, Acts 17:27; 1 Jn. 1:1; Heb. 12:18**; Ignatius, Smyr. 3:2) and they will see (that it really is Jesus) because a spirit does not have flesh and bones. For ὀστέον, 'bone', cf. Mt. 23:37; Jn. 19:36; Heb. 11:22**); bones were regarded as essential for a resurrected body (Grundmann, 451).

(40) The invitation to touch Jesus is followed in most MSS by a description of how he showed the disciples (ἔδειξεν, par. Jn.; many MSS have ἐπέδειξεν A W Γ Δ Θ f13 pm; TR) his hands and feet. The verse is omitted by D it sy^{sc} Mcion; followed by Synopsis; Diglot; WH bracket it as a 'western non-interpolation'; cf. Dodd, 145 n.; Tasker, 424, Kilpatrick, 193. As in v. 36 and other cases, the question is whether the verse has been added by a scribe from Jn. or reflects a pre-Johannine tradition. The wording is slightly different, notably the substitution of τοὺς πόδας for τὴν πλευράν, and the possible use of ἐπιδείκνυμι (which could be Lucan; cf. 17:14; Acts 9:39; 18:28; rest of NT, 4x**). Jeremias, Words, 151, suggests that it may have been omitted by oversight, or to avoid an apparent contradiction with Jn. 20:17; it may have seemed redundant after v. 39 (K. Aland, NTS 12, 1965–66, 206f.; Metzger, 187). On the whole, the evidence favours retention. Luke thus indicates that the necessary confirmation of Jesus' identity and bodily appearance was provided.

(41) Even this demonstration was not absolutely convincing. For ἔτι with genitive absolute cf. 8:49; et al., and for ἀπιστέω cf. 24:11. Luke attributes the disbelief of the disciples to joy: it was too good to be true. For the use of ἀπό in this sense cf. 22:45 and especially Acts 12:14. The motif of joy is shared with Jn. 20:20 and is pre-Lucan, but Luke has used the motif in his own way. It is thoroughly credible from a psychological point of view (contra Grass, 41): cf. Livy 39:49:5, 'vix sibimet

ipsi prae necopinato gaudio credentes' (cited by Plummer, 560). The addition of καὶ θαυμαζόντων may indicate the growth of faith in the marvel that was before their eyes. Final proof was provided by Jesus' question whether they had anything eatable (βρώσιμος**) available (ἐνθάδε, 'here', Acts, 5x; Jn., 2x**, is Lucan).

(42) The disciples gave him a piece of cooked (ὀπτός**) fish; so p[75] ℵ A B D L W *pc* e sy[s] sa bo[pt] Clem Orig; but later MSS add καὶ ἀπὸ μελισσίου κηρίον (κηρίου), probably under the influence of later liturgical practice, since honey was sometimes used in the Lord's Supper and at baptism (Metzger, 187f.). The mention of fish has been thought to suggest an originally Galilean locale for the story (Creed, 299; Klostermann, 241), but the evidence that fish was readily available in Jerusalem is indisputable (cf. Ne. 3:3; 13:16; Jeremias, *Jerusalem*, 20; for the use of salted fish, which could be readily transported, see SB I, 683f.).

(43) The fact that Jesus ate in the presence of the disciples is treated as a proof that he is no ghost; for eating by supernatural visitors cf. Gn. 18:8; 19:3; Tob. 6:6; and contrast Jdg. 13:16; Tob. 12:9; Homer, Il. 5:341. A few MSS add καὶ τὰ ἐπίλοιπα ἔδωκεν αὐτοῖς (K 13 *al* (c) sy[c] bo[pt]; with varying wording, *pc* aur vg). A eucharistic motif may have been originally present in the narrative, but it has not survived in Lk. He has used the well-attested tradition of Jesus' eating with his disciples after the resurrection (Jn. 21:13; Acts 1:4; 10:41) to stress the reality of his presence with them, and he has not developed allusions to the feeding of the multitude or the Last Supper.

v. The Command to Mission 24:44–49

All of the Gospels (except Mk. in its present form) record the final instructions of Jesus to his disciples, and in each case the wording reflects to a considerable extent the style of the Evangelist. Thus in the present section the risen Jesus reminds his disciples of what he had said to them during his earthly ministry. The Scriptures relating to his destiny had to be fulfilled, and the disciples as a body had to be given the key to understanding the 'messianic' prophecies in the Scriptures, just as had been the case with the two disciples on the way to Emmaus. But now a new element enters. If the accent so far has been on what the Scriptures prophesied concerning the Messiah, now there is a switch to the prophecy of the preaching of the gospel to all nations, starting from Jerusalem. The disciples are implicitly called to undertake this task. For they have seen the ministry of Jesus and can act as witnesses; they will receive the promised power of God to equip them for their task if they continue to wait in the city for God to fulfil his promise.

The links of this material with Mt. 28:16–20 and Jn. 20:21–23 are obvious. Luke shares with Mt. the commission to go to the nations and the promise of divine power. He shares with Jn. the promise of the Spirit and the reference to forgiveness of sins. It cannot be doubted, therefore, that common traditions underlie these accounts, the basic nucleus being that Jesus commanded his disciples to spread the good news widely and offer forgiveness of sins and that he promised them divine power for their task. Taylor, *Passion*, 114, is right in concluding that while 'these are ideas congenial to Luke, in presenting them he is only underlining beliefs present in the primitive tradition'; this verdict is better founded than theories which essentially regard the section as a Lucan composition (Bultmann, 310; Finegan, *Überlieferung*, 91.). But to work out the exact content of this basic nucleus and to determine how far it goes back to actual sayings of the risen Lord is perhaps impossible. That there are historical difficulties about a command to mission by the risen Lord is obvious enough; it has often been noted that the slowness of the church to engage in world mission implies that it was not aware of such a command. But it may well be that this tardiness has been exaggerated, and that the instructions of Jesus were misunderstood (not for the first time). It remains more probable that the kerygma of the early church reflects the teaching of Jesus than that it has been read back onto his lips.

See Bultmann, 310; Finegan, *Überlieferung*, 91; Taylor, *Passion*, 112–114.

(44) The teaching given by Jesus follows on directly from the recognition scene and also leads on directly to the departure scene. The whole series is thus placed on Easter Sunday evening, although in Acts 1 Luke puts the departure forty days after the resurrection. Unless Luke altered his chronology between the composition of the Gospel and the Acts (which is improbable in view of the unified character of Lk.-Acts), he has consciously telescoped his story at some point. A break at the end of the present scene is probable. Klostermann, 239f., suggests that the same is true at the beginning in view of the lateness of the hour, which would have precluded a lengthy discourse by Jesus. Whether or not this consideration was in Luke's mind, it is probable that he is here summarising what Jesus said to his disciples over the period of the resurrection appearances. The force of the opening words is not clear: 1. Most translations give: 'This is what I told you while I was still with you, when I said that all that is written concerning me ... must be fulfilled' (TNT). On this view the ὅτι clause is epexegetic of οὗτοι οἱ λόγοι. 2. Creed, 300, suggests: 'These events (my death and resurrection) explain the words which I spoke, namely that all that is written concerning me ... must be fulfilled' (cf. NEB; JB; possibly RSV). On this view, which goes back to Grotius and Wellhausen (cf. Klostermann, 241), the ὅτι clause is the object of ἐλάλησα, and οὗτοι (for ταῦτα) has been attracted to the gender of the predicate οἱ λόγοι μου. The former of these two interpretations is the more natural, since with the latter οὗτοι has no obvious antecedent. In either case the risen Jesus is referring back to what he said to the disciples while he was still with them. ἔτι ὢν σὺν ὑμῖν draws a distinction between the earthly life of Jesus and his present state in which he is no longer with them; yet in a sense he is still with them, and the words sound slightly odd. The phrase is best seen as Luke's way (ἔτι,

1:15 and frequently) of expressing the difference between the period of Jesus' earthly life and that of his absence from the disciples. The reference backwards is to his statements in 9:22, 44; 17:25; 18:31f.; 22:37; which were made with reference to what the Son of man must undergo. The fulfilment of Scripture is a divine necessity. For πληρόω in this sense cf. 4:21; Acts 1:16; 3:18; 13:27; Mk. 14:49; Mt. 1:22; et al. For γεγραμμένος cf. 4:17; 18:31; 20:17; 21:22; 22:37; Acts 13:29; 24:14. Here only in the NT are the Psalms (ψαλμός, 20:42; Acts 1:20; 13:33) named alongside the law of Moses (2:22) and the prophets. It is debatable whether the reference is simply to the Psalms themselves as a primary source of messianic texts (Creed, 300f.) or to the 'Writings', i.e. the third division of the OT canon here named after its principal component. For the latter view cf. Philo, Cont. 25 (ὕμνος); the three-fold division of the OT was in existence by this date (Sir. Pr.).

(45) Explanation of the OT in terms of its fulfilment in Jesus can be regarded as an 'opening' (διανοίγω, 2:23; et al.) of either the Scriptures (24:32; Acts 17:3) or of the minds of the readers; νοῦς is found here only in the Gospels (cf. Acts 16:14; cf. 2 Mac. 1:4 for καρδία in the same sense; see J. Behm; TDNT IV, 951–960). Until this time the disciples' minds had been unable to perceive the prophetic meaning of the OT, i.e. to see that certain prophecies were about the Messiah and were fulfilled in Jesus.

(46) The things which Jesus saw to be prophesied in the Scriptures are now listed. The force of οὕτως is uncertain: 1. Most translations make it refer forwards to the content of what has been written: 'This is what Scripture says: the Messiah must suffer . . .' (TNT); cf. 19:31; Acts 7:6. 2. It may refer backwards to v. 24.: 'Thus (i.e. because the Scriptures about me must be fulfilled), it is written that the Messiah must suffer . . .' (cf. JB). 3. οὕτως could mean 'likewise', adding a new statement to v. 44. 4. Klostermann, 242, takes οὕτως with παθεῖν: 'It has been written that the Messiah must suffer in this way (i.e. as it has actually happened)'. But the word order is against this interpretation. View 2. is perhaps the best in context, although view 1. is supported by Lucan usage elsewhere. (The expression may have caused difficulty to scribes. οὕτως ἔδει is read by 72 pc (sy ͬ), and the conflation οὕτως γέγραπται καὶ οὕτως ἔδει is read by A C² W Γ Δ Θ f1 f13 pl aur f q vg sy ᵖ sa ᵖᵗ; TR; Diglot.) The formula παθεῖν τὸν Χριστόν is repeated from 24:26 (cf. Acts 17:3), and ἀναστῆναι . . . τῇ τρίτῃ ἡμέρα is repeated from 24:7 (cf. 18:33; Acts 10:41; 17:3). But what was said earlier about the Son of man is now predicated of the Messiah. Thereby the identification of the Son of man in Jesus' teaching with the Messiah in the church's teaching is established.

(47) The scriptural necessity of the passion and resurrection of Jesus has been established. But now a new feature is added: the mission of the church is also traced to scriptural prophecy, the interpretation of which is given by the risen Lord. This motif disappears if we accept

Wellhausen's suggestion (140f.) that κηρυχθῆναι be taken as the equivalent of a Hebrew infinitive in a jussive sense, so that it expresses an independent command to the disciples. Creed, 301, notes that this interpretation would require the reading ἐπὶ τῷ ὀνόματί μου, and that in any case 'it is good Lucan doctrine that the proclamation of repentance to all nations is foretold in prophecy'; cf. Acts 10:43; 13:47; and especially 26:23. For μετάνοια cf. 3:3; et al. ἐπὶ τῷ ὀνόματι αὐτοῦ means 'on the basis of the name of Jesus' (H. Bietenhard, TDNT V, 278; for the phrase see idem, 271). For the preaching of repentance see 3:3; Acts 13:24; 20:21. The phrase is tantamount to 'to give an opportunity of repentance' (Acts 5:31). Such repentance leads to forgiveness of sins (reading εἰς, with p75 ℵ B syh sa bo; the variant καί, accepted by Klostermann, 242, finds support in Acts 5:31; 20:21. See further Metzger, 188). The second εἰς phrase follows slightly awkwardly; for this use with κηρύσσω see 4:44; (cf. Mk. 1:39); Mk. 14:9; 1 Thes. 2:9; it may be Semitic (BD 207[1]; Black, 299). Preaching to the gentiles (ἔθνος, 2:32; et al.) is foretold in Mk. 13:10 (to which Luke has no parallel; cf. Wilson, 47); cf. Acts 2:5; 10:35; 15:17; 17:26; Mk. 16:15; Mt. 28:19; Rom. 1:13; 4:17f.; 15:11; 16:26; et al. The OT basis for the thought is probably to be found in Is. 49:6 (quoted in Acts 13:47); cf. 42:6; Joel 2:1; Wis. 3:14 (Wilson, 48 n.); see also Rom. 9:24f.; 10:12f., 20; 15:9–12. The Pauline use of the idea shows that it is not a late development by Luke. Luke may also have found scriptural backing for the thought of beginning from Jerusalem in Is. 2:2f. par. Mi. 4:1f. This phrase is generally taken with the preceding clause; it is loosely added and has adverbial force (BD 137[3]); WH mg and B. Weiss (see Synopsis) took it with the following verse. In both cases the syntax is harsh, and suggests that Luke had not wholly mastered and revised his material. The difficulty led to textual emendation by scribes. ἀρξάμενοι, ℵ B C* L 33 pc sa bo, is the lectio difficilior; other authorities have ἀρξάμενον (p75 A C3 W Γ Δ* f1 f13 pm it sysp – i.e. accusative absolute); ἀρξαμένων (D Δc lat – i.e. sc. ὑμῶν) and ἀρξάμενος (Θ Ψ al). For the expression cf. 24:27 note; here the force is 'beginning with' (BD 419[3]), and the implication is that the Christian mission was to commence in Jerusalem and possibly with the Jews themselves.

(48) But the Scripture can be fulfilled only if those who are equipped to attest the saving facts are sent out to proclaim the message in the power of the Spirit. Here, therefore, Jesus appoints them as his witnesses (μάρτυς, 11:48; Acts 1:8 and frequently), since they have been able to see his death and can testify to his resurrection (cf. Acts 1:22, where companionship with Jesus throughout his ministry is an added qualification). Thus the Gospel and Acts are linked together.

(49) Finally comes Jesus' promise. The textual status of ἰδού is uncertain, the longer text being attested by A B C (W) Γ Δ Θ f1 f13 pl f q; (UBS); Diglot; Synopsis; καὶ ἐγώ is read by p75 D and κἀγώ by ℵ L 33 579 (with lat sysp sa bo also supporting the omission of ἰδού). There is no

obvious reason why ἰδού, if original, should have been omitted, but it has good attestation; decision is impossible (cf. Metzger, 188f.). ἐξαποστέλλω is a futuristic present. ἐπαγγελία, 'promise' (Acts 1:4; et al.), is often linked with the Holy Spirit (Acts 1:4; 2:33; Gal. 3:14; Eph. 1:13), and it is surprising that there is no actual mention of the Spirit here. The wording implies both promise and fulfilment (J. Schniewind and G. Friedrich, TDNT II, 581f.). Whether the Father's promise was made by Jesus or in the OT (or both) is not clear; in Acts 1:4f. there is a further reference to the promise 'which you heard from me', but it is hard to decide whether that is meant as a repetition of the present verse or as a reference back to it. If the former interpretation is correct, Luke is thinking of earlier promises made by Jesus (cf. 12:12 par. Mt. 10:20; Jn. 14:16f.; et al.). The OT background is to be found in Joel 2:28f.; cf. Is. 32:15; 44:3; Ezk. 39:29. For ὁ πατήρ μου cf. 11:13; Acts 1:4; Mt. 10:20. ἐφ' ὑμᾶς is used of the coming of the Spirit in Acts 1:8; 2:3, 17f.; et al. The disciples are to remain (for καθίζω in this sense cf. Acts 18:11; 1 Ch. 19:5; 2 Esd. 21:1f.) in Jerusalem until (ἕως οὗ, 13:21) they are clothed (ἐνδύομαι, used metaphorically, Rom. 13:12, 14; cf. SB II, 301) with power (δύναμις, 1:17; et al; see especially Acts 1:8) from on high; for ἐξ ὕψους cf. 1:78 and Is. 32:15 (France, 96f.); δύναμιν is placed before ἐξ ὕψους in A C² D W ΓΔ Θ f1 f13 pm; TR; Diglot.

vi. The Departure of Jesus 24:50–53

Having given his farewell instructions to the disciples, Jesus led them out of Jerusalem to Bethany. Here he prayed that the blessing of God would rest upon them, and then departed from them. Luke relates with the utmost brevity that he was carried up into heaven. Despite his departure the disciples were filled with joy as they returned to Jerusalem where they spent their time praising God in the temple.

This account of the departure of Jesus is peculiar to Lk., but has something of a parallel in the closing scene in Mt. (where, however, no departure of Jesus is actually recorded). It anticipates the fuller description of the ascension of Jesus found in Acts 1:1–11. It is improbable that the present account is of a different event from the ascension recorded in Acts (pace Ellis, 280). Although there is some textual confusion in both accounts, it is probable that both accounts referred to the ascension, and that Acts 1:2 refers back to the present scene, before we are given the fuller, parallel account in Acts 1:4–11. In this way Luke makes the departure of Jesus the climax of the Gospel and the commencement of the Acts. P. A. van Stempvoort* has noted the doxological motif which characterises the present account with its stress on Jesus' priestly action in blessing the disciples and on their praise to God in the temple.

There are some differences between the two accounts, but none that precludes common authorship. The present account is brief and lacking in the circumstantial detail found in the second. Although it has been argued that Luke later received fuller information, which he incorporated in Acts (Benoit, *Exégèse*, I, 399), it is more probable that he reserved the fuller account for Acts, and was content to give a summary of it, with a particular slant, in the Gospel. If so, answers to the questions of the sources and historicity of the present scene are dependent upon the investigation of Acts 1:1–11. The whole conception has been traced by Lohfink to the mind of Luke who had no basis in tradition for this concrete scene in which many of his own theological ideas are given expression (cf. Wilson, 96–107). Nowhere else in the NT is a visible ascension of Jesus recorded. But this verdict is open to considerable criticism, and it is more likely that Luke's account had some kind of traditional basis (F. Hahn*, cf. Benoit, *Exégèse*, I, 363–411).

With the ascension the Gospel reaches its climax. What began in the temple concludes in the temple with praise to God, and the path of Jesus now reaches its goal. The programme has been established for the second volume of Luke's work in which the church will obey the command of the risen Jesus to take the gospel to all the nations.

See Bultmann, 310f.; Benoit, *Exégèse* I, 363–411 (originally as 'L'ascension', RB 56, 1949, 161–203); C. F. D. Moule, 'The Ascension', Exp.T 68, 1956–57, 205–209; P. A. van Stempvoort, 'The Interpretation of the Ascension in Luke and Acts', NTS 5, 1958–59, 30–42; Wilson, 96–107 (originally as 'The Ascension: A Critique and an Interpretation', ZNW 59, 1968, 269–281); Franklin, 29–41 (cf. E. Franklin, 'The Ascension and the Eschatology of Luke-Acts', SJT 23, 1970, 191–200); Lohfink; F. Hahn, 'Die Himmelfahrt Jesu; Ein Gespräch mit Gerhard Lohfink', Bib. 55, 1974, 418–426.

(50) ἐξάγω, 'to lead out' is Lucan (Acts, 8x; rest of NT, 3x); Lohfink, 163f., notes that the word was used in the LXX for the Exodus in which God led Israel out, and thinks that this may have influenced Luke's use of the word. He traces the idea of the risen Jesus walking with the disciples to the influence of the Emmaus story, but he has overlooked the similar motif in Jn. 21:20 (indirect, and therefore the more significant). ἕως with a preposition of place is Lucan (Acts 17:14; 21:5; 26:11; cf. Gn. 38:1; Ezk. 48:1) and means 'right to the neighbourhood of' (Lohfink, 166f.). It is preceded by ἔξω in A C³D W Γ Δ Θ f13 *pl*; TR; *Diglot*; (UBS), which may have appeared redundant to scribes (it is omitted by p⁷⁵ ℵ B C* L 1 33 157 *pc* a e sy^{s p}). For Βηθανία see 19:29. In Acts 1:12, however, the disciples return from the Mount of Olives after the ascension. There is no obvious reason for the alteration. The two places were regarded as close together (19:29 par. Mk. 11:1), Bethany lying on the E slope of the mountain. Lohfink, 202–207, argues that this was the only site outside Jerusalem known to Luke, and therefore the inevitable choice for a private revelation of Jesus to his disciples, but he admits that the detail could have come to Luke from tradition. The centre of interest is the way in which Jesus raised his hands (cf. 1 Tim. 2:8; Lv. 9:22) and blessed the disciples (εὐλογέω, 1:42; *et al.*). The picture is reminiscent of the priestly blessing in Sir. 50:20f., which is accompanied by the raising of the priest's hands and the worship and

praise of the people. Lohfink, 167–169, holds that Luke has modelled his scene on this solemn conclusion to Sir.; cf. also 2 En. 56:1; 57:2; 64:4 for Enoch's blessing before his translation. The idea of Jesus as a priest does not seem to play any role in Lk. Lohfink also suggests that Luke has omitted the blessing of the children in Mk. 10:16 in order to reserve the motif for use here, but this is a precarious argument, especially since a different action (laying on of hands) is described there. Luke's motif may, however, correspond with the 'insufflation' in Jn. 20:22; this may suggest that some such element was present in the tradition and that Luke has expressed it in his own way.

(51) After Jesus has blessed the disciples (for the construction cf. 1:8), he departs from them (διΐστημι is Lucan, 22:59; Acts 27:28**). Lohfink, 170f., notes that Luke often describes the departure of super-natural visitors (1:38; 2:15; 9:33; 24:31; Acts 10:7; 12:10), and that this is a common motif in such stories (Gn. 17:22; 35:13; Jdg. 6:21; 13:20; Tob. 12:20f.; 2 Mac. 3:34; et al.). Contrast, for example, John who does not record the ends of the resurrection appearances. The narrative goes on to describe the manner of Jesus' departure: he was led up (ἀναφέρω, Mk. 9:2; par. Mt. 17:1; elsewhere used of offering sacrifices) into heaven; the imperfect suggests a gradual departure, as in Acts 1:9f. The whole phrase is omitted by א* D it (sy^s) geo^1 Aug$^{1/3}$; Synopsis; Diglot, as a western non-interpolation (WH App. 73). But it is almost certain that the words should be retained. The textual evidence for omission is weak. Acts 1:2 recapitulates what has been described in the Gospel, including the ascension of Jesus. Mk. 16:18f. probably reflects the long text of Lk. The choice of ἀναφέρω is unusual, and un-likely to be due to a copyist at a time when ἀναλαμβάνω had become the established term for the ascension. The literary structure of the passage (three sets of coordinate clauses) requires the clause. Moreover, it is easy to understand the clause being omitted to harmonise with the 40 days tradition in Acts or to avoid the presence of two successive accounts of the same event in Lk.-Acts, or possibly by homoioarcton with the repeated καί. See Jeremias, Words, 151 (with bibliography); K. Aland, NTS 12, 1965–66, 208f.; Metzger, 189f. The alternative theory is to suppose that additions to the text were made when Lk. and Acts were separated from each other in the church's canon (Creed, 301f.; cf. Tasker, 424), but this is much less probable in view of the above argu-ments. For the concept of ascension see Lohfink, 32–79. The motif was especially associated with Romulus, Heracles and Apollonius of Tyana. Jewish examples of men being caught up to heaven are Enoch, Elijah, Ezra, Baruch and Moses; references to the Messiah being caught up do not appear to be significant. The NT tradition that Jesus is at the right hand of God presupposes his 'ascension', but it is not described elsewhere as a visible event. Luke, however, lays little stress on the ac-tual ascent at this point. His concern is with the disciples and their relationship to Jesus.

(52) For the first time Luke refers to worship being offered to Jesus (προσκυνέω, 4:7, 8; Mk. 5:6; 15:19; Mt. frequently, especially 28:9, 17). He appears to have deliberately avoided the word until this point, conscious that recognition of the divinity of Jesus by men did not precede the resurrection. The motif of an ascent leading to recognition of the divinity of the person involved is found in Hellenism (Sophocles, Oed. Col. 1654; Plutarch, Rom. 27:8f; Lucian, De Morte Per. 39; see also Jdg. 13:20; Sir. 50:20–22, where the people bow in worship to receive the priestly blessing). Lohfink, 171–174, accordingly derives the motif from Hellenistic influence upon Luke. It may well have seemed to be the appropriate reaction to him. This is to assume that the words προσκυνήσαντες αὐτόν should be accepted as part of the text; they are omitted by D it sy^s; *Synopsis*; and bracketed by WH; but this omission hangs with the earlier omission in v. 51 (cf. Metzger, 190) and requires no further discussion. The departure of Jesus is followed by the return of the disciples to Jerusalem with great rejoicing (cf. 2:10); here again a Lucan motif is discernible (Lohfink, 174–176, draws attention to a similar motif in the story of Romulus; Plutarch, Romulus, 27.7f.). The birth of Jesus and his ascension are occasions for joy.

(53) The Gospel closes with a scene in the temple, as it began with one. For the disciples worshipping there cf. Acts 2:46; 3:1; 5:42. The description of them being there continually (διὰ παντός (sc. χρόνου); Mt. 18:10; Mk. 5:5; Acts 2:25; 10:2; 24:16; *et al.*) is obviously not to be taken with strict literalness, and therefore need not conflict with the description in Acts 1:12–14 of prayer in the upper room. Their time was spent in praising God. εὐλογοῦντες is read by p^75 ℵ B C* L pc; αἰνοῦντες by D it; and αἰνοῦντες καὶ εὐλογοῦντες by A C^2 W Γ Δ Θ f1 f13 pl lat sy^p; TR. The third reading is generally agreed to be conflate, and εὐλογοῦντες is to be preferred (Metzger, 190f.). Luke is likely to have used εὐλογέω, since it was already in his mind and since he prefers it to αἰνέω; scribes may have thought that εὐλογέω should not be used in two different senses in adjacent verses. The addition of ἀμήν in many MSS is due to liturgical usage; it is omitted by p^75 ℵ C* D L W 1 33 pc it sa bo^pt (Metzger, 191). The verse supplies a fitting end to the Gospel with praise addressed to God: is Luke suggesting to his readers that this is the appropriate response for them to his story?

INDEX OF AUTHORS

INDEX OF SUBJECTS

SELECT INDEX OF GREEK WORDS
AND PHRASES